HITLER

1889–1936: HUBRIS

HITLER

1889–1936: HUBRIS

Ian Kershaw

W. W. Norton & Company

NEW YORK • LONDON

Copyright © 1998 by Ian Kershaw
First American edition 1999

All rights reserved
Printed in the United States of America

Excerpts from *Mein Kampf* by Adolf Hitler. Copyright © 1939, 1943 by Houghton
Mifflin Company. Reprinted by permission of Houghton Mifflin Company.
All rights reserved.

For information about permission to reproduce selections from this book, write to
Permissions, W. W. Norton & Company, Inc., 500 Fifth Avenue, New York, NY 10110.

Library of Congress Cataloging-in-Publication Data
Kershaw, Ian.
Hitler, 1889–1936 : hubris / Ian Kershaw. —1st American ed.
p.   cm.
Includes bibliographical references and index.
ISBN 0-393-04671-0
1. Hitler, Adolf, 1889–1945. 2. Hitler, Adolf, 1889–1945—Childhood and youth.
3. Germany—Politics and government—1918–1933. 4. Heads of state—Germany—
Biography. 5. Germany—Politics and government—1933–1945. 6. Antisemitism—
Austria. 7. Antisemitism—Germany. I. Title.
DD247.H5K462   1999
943.086'092—dc21
[B]   98-29569
CIP

W. W. Norton & Company, Inc., 500 Fifth Avenue, New York, N.Y. 10110

http://www.wwnorton.com

W. W. Norton & Company Ltd., 10 Coptic Street, London CW1A 1PU

2 3 4 5 6 7 8 9 0

CONTENTS

LIST OF ILLUSTRATIONS

Every effort has been made to contact all copyright holders. The publishers will be glad to make good in future editions any errors or omissions brought to their attention. (Photographic acknowledgements are given in brackets.)

PREFACE

I had never thought, until a few years ago, that I would write a biography of Hitler. For one thing, a number of biographies of the Dictator which I rated highly already existed. I had read as a student, with endless fascination, Alan Bullock's early masterpiece. And on its appearance in 1973 I immediately devoured Joachim Fest's new biography, admiring as all did its stylistic brilliance. It was only with initial reluctance, and due sense of modesty in the light of the achievements of Bullock and Fest, that I allowed myself in 1989 to be persuaded to undertake the present work.

Another reason for hesitation was that biography had never figured in my intellectual plans as something I might want to write. If anything, I was somewhat critically disposed towards the genre. From the early part of my scholarly career onwards, first as a medievalist, I had been much more drawn to social history than to a focus on high politics, let alone a focus on any individual. These tendencies were enhanced when I encountered the prevalent trends – strongly anti-biographical – in German historiography in the 1970s. When changing course at that time to undertake research on the Third Reich, it was the behaviour and attitudes of ordinary Germans in that extraordinary era that excited my attention, not Hitler and his entourage. My early works, arising from my involvement in the pioneering 'Bavaria Project' and profiting from the enormous stimulation offered by a brilliant mentor, Martin Broszat, pursued those interests by exploring popular opinion and political dissent under Nazi rule, and by examining Hitler's image among the population. The latter work certainly exposed me to the historiographical debates raging in Germany in the 1970s about Hitler. But as a non-German, primarily interested in the reception of Hitler's image and the reasons for his popularity rather than Hitler himself, in his actions and role, I remained essentially an outsider to the debates.

This I felt to be less so after participating, as little more than a novice at the scene, in an important conference at Cumberland Lodge near London in 1979, attended by most of the German 'big guns' writing on the Third Reich, and revealing in graphic and startling force the chasmic divisions of interpretation among leading historians on Hitler's role in the Nazi system of rule. Experiencing the conference was a spur to immersing myself much further in the differing approaches in German historiography, prompting the publication of a survey in which my sympathies for the 'structuralist' approaches to Nazi rule, looking beyond and away from biographical preoccupation with the Nazi Dictator, were evident.

There is no little irony, therefore, in my eventually arriving at the writing of a biography of Hitler in that I come to it, so to say, from the 'wrong' direction. However, the growing preoccupation with the structures of Nazi rule and with the gulf in the divides on Hitler's own position within that system (if 'system' it can be called) pushed me inexorably to increased reflection on the man who was the indispensable fulcrum and inspiration of what took place, Hitler himself. It drove me, too, to considering whether the striking polarization of approaches could not be overcome and integrated by a biography of Hitler written by a 'structuralist' historian – coming to biography with a critical eye, looking instinctively, perhaps, in the first instance to downplay rather than to exaggerate the part played by the individual, however powerful, in complex historical processes.

What follows is a work which reflects, through the medium of a biography of Hitler, such an attempt to bind together the personal with the impersonal elements in the shaping of some of the most vitally important passages in the whole of human history. What has continued in the writing of the book to interest me more than the strange character of the man who held Germany's fate in his hands between 1933 and 1945 is the question of how Hitler was possible: not just how this initially most unlikely pretender to high state office could gain power; but how he was able to extend that power until it became absolute, until field marshals were prepared to obey without question the orders of a former corporal, until highly skilled 'professionals' and clever minds in all walks of life were ready to pay uncritical obeisance to an autodidact whose only indisputable talent was one for stirring up the base emotions of the masses. If the answer to that question cannot be presumed in the first instance to lie in those attributes, such as they were, of Hitler's personality, then it follows that the answer must be sought chiefly in German society – in the social and political motivations which went into the making of Hitler. To search out those motivations and to fuse them with Hitler's personal contribution to the attainment and expansion of his power to the point where he could determine the fate of millions is the aim of the study.

If I have found one concept more than any other which has helped me find a way to bind together the otherwise contradictory approaches through biography and the writing of social history, it is Max Weber's notion of 'charismatic leadership' – a notion which looks to explanations of this extraordinary form of political domination primarily in the perceivers of 'charisma', that is, in the society rather than, in the first instance, in the personality of the object of their adulation.

An attempt to undertake a new biography of Hitler, bold though it may be, found further encouragement (as well, it must be admitted, as some discouragement or even dismay) through the massive outpouring of first-rate scholarly research on practically all aspects of the Third Reich since the major biographies of Fest – even more so of Bullock – were written. It is surprising, in retrospect, for instance, how little anti-Jewish policy and the genesis of the 'Final Solution' figured in such earlier biographies. The difficulties of pinning down Hitler's own, often shadowy, involvement in the 'twisted road to Auschwitz' is, of course, among the reasons for this. But the major advances made in research on this area make it both necessary and possible now to redress the balance – something which Marlis Steinert's most recent major biography had already begun to do.

Not only the extent of the secondary literature, but the availability of primary sources on Hitler makes the time for a new biography opportune. The superb multi-volume edition of Hitler's speeches and writings between the refoundation of the Nazi Party in 1925 and his appointment as Reich Chancellor in 1933 is one major addition to scholarship. This now makes it possible, in tandem with the equally excellent edition of his speeches and writings down to 1924, to survey the development of Hitler's ideas, as he publicly expressed them, for the entire period before he took power. A second indispensable source which can now be used for the first time in full in a biography of Hitler is the diary of the Propaganda Minister Joseph Goebbels, only recently discovered in its entirety, surviving on glass plates (an early form of photocopy) in formerly inaccessible state archives in Moscow. For all the caution which must naturally be attached to Goebbels's regularly reported remarks by Hitler in a text which the Propaganda Minister, intent on later publication, wrote for ultimate self-glorification and for securing his place in history high in the Nazi pantheon of heroes, the immediacy as well as the frequency of the comments makes them a vitally important source of insight into Hitler's thinking and actions. One alleged source, used for decades as an authentic guide to Hitler's thoughts and plans, prominently deployed by both Bullock and Fest, has, however, fallen by the wayside. I have on no single occasion cited Hermann Rauschning's *Hitler Speaks*, a work now regarded to have so little authenticity that it is best to disregard it altogether. Other sources, too, particularly memoirs but even the 'table-talk' monologues of the last months (the so-called '*Bunkergespräche*'), of which no original German text has ever been brought to light, have to be treated with due caution. The combination of Hitler's innate secretiveness, the emptiness of his personal relations, his unbureaucratic style, the extremes of adulation and hatred which he stirred up, and the apologetics as well as distortions built into post-war memoirs and gossipy anecdotes of those in his entourage, mean that, for all the surviving mountains of paper spewed out by the governmental apparatus of the Third Reich, the sources for reconstructing the life of the German Dictator are in many respects extraordinarily limited – far more so than in the case, say, of his main adversaries, Churchill and even Stalin.

Hitler and Nazism amount, unsurprisingly, to a lasting trauma for German society and of course, though in very different ways, for the regime's millions of victims. But the legacy of Hitler belongs to all of us. Part of that legacy is the continuing duty to seek understanding of how Hitler was possible. Only through history can we learn for the future. And no part of history is more important in that respect than the era dominated by Adolf Hitler.

Ian Kershaw
Sheffield/Manchester, April 1998

ACKNOWLEDGEMENTS

The greatest pleasure at the completion of a book is to thank publicly those who have contributed directly or indirectly, in a major or minor way, to its creation. In a work on this scale my debts of gratitude are naturally extensive.

I am grateful, first of all, for the expert assistance in dealing with my inquiries and requests of the Directors and staff of several record repositories and libraries which have allowed me access to their archives and supplied me with unpublished material. These include, in Germany, the Archiv der Sozialen Demokratie, Bonn; the different departments of the Bayerisches Hauptstaatsarchiv; the Bayerische Staatsbibliothek; the Berlin Document Center (where I was helped, quite especially, by the former Director, Dr David Marwell); the Bundesarchiv Koblenz; the Forschungsstelle für die Geschichte des Nationalsozialismus in Hamburg; the former Institut für Marxismus-Leninismus, Zentrales Parteiarchiv, in East Berlin (GDR); the Niedersächisches Staatsarchiv, Oldenburg; the Staatsarchiv München; and the former Zentrales Staatsarchiv, Potsdam (GDR); in Great Britain, the BBC Archives; the Borthwick Institute (York), notably its Director, Professor David Smith, for access to the Halifax papers; the Public Record Offices in London and Belfast; the University of Birmingham Library (for use of the Chamberlain papers); and the excellent Wiener Library, London (whose Director, Professor David Cesarani, and librarians and staff I would particularly like to thank); in the USA, the Hoover Institution, Stanford, California (where I was helped especially by Myriam Beck and Christoph Schlichting); the Library of Congress, Washington; the National Archives, Washington; and Princeton University Library; in Austria, the Archiv der Stadt Linz; the Oberösterreichisches Landesarchiv (where I was especially grateful to Dr Gerhard Marckhgott); and the Wiener Stadt- und Landesarchiv; and in Russia the former Sonderarchiv (Special Archive), now the Centre for Historical and Documentary Collections, Moscow.

I am also grateful to the editors and publishers of those works from which I have cited extracts, and for the owners of the copyright of the photographs reproduced in the book for permission to publish them.

The major debt of gratitude owed to the Director, Professor Horst Möller, and all the staff of the incomparable Institut für Zeitgeschichte in Munich will come as no surprise to anyone who has undertaken research on the Nazi era. I have always been made extremely welcome in the Institut since first working there in the mid-1970s. Like so many others engaged in research on twentieth-century German history, I have benefited enormously both from its outstanding library and archival holdings and from the expertise of its researchers, archivists, and librarians. In particular, I would wish to single out Norbert Frei (recently moved to the Ruhr-Universität, Bochum), a good personal friend over many years, alongside Elke Fröhlich, Hermann Graml, Lothar Gruchmann (who made available to me parts of the new edition of Hitler's trial material in advance of publication), Klaus-Dietmar Henke (now Dresden), Hermann Weiß (who gave generous help with a number of archival queries), and Hans Woller. I am also extremely grateful for the kindness shown on many occasions by Georg Maisinger, the business manager of the Institut. Not least, I would like to thank the staff of the Institut's archive and library for all their assistance in dealing so patiently and efficiently with all of my many requests.

Essential time for reflection, reading, and writing was provided by a stay in 1989–90 at the marvellous Wissenschaftskolleg in Berlin. Preliminary work for this biography was undertaken at the time, and I was able to profit from interchanges with scholars of widely varying disciplines. I am grateful to the Rector, Wolf Lepenies, and his staff, all the Fellows, and not least to the librarians for complying with my innumerable requests. A good part of the writing was undertaken during a spell in 1994–5 away from my regular duties, thanks to support from a Leverhulme–British Academy Senior Scholarship and from the University of Sheffield. The Alexander von Humboldt-Stiftung continued the generous support of my work which began in 1976–7 with the funding for a month in the summer of 1997 spent checking references in Munich. My son, David, kindly took a week's holiday from his work to help me for part of this time.

I have enjoyed great (and exceedingly patient) support from my publishers in Britain, Germany, and the USA while this book has been in preparation. At Penguin, Ravi Mirchandani (who commissioned the book in what seems an age ago) and Simon Winder (who adopted it and has skilfully overseen all stages of its completion) have been pillars of strength. Their encouragement has been of great importance to me. I would also like to express my thanks to Thomas Weber for his work in drawing up the bibliography, to Diana LeCore for compiling the index, and, quite especially, to Annie Lee for her excellent copy-editing. At Norton, Donald Lamm's meticulous and constructive suggestions for amending or improving points of the text were invariably perceptive, and I greatly appreciated his insights. At Deutsche Verlags-Anstalt I have benefited from the expertise of Ulrich Volz and Michael Neher, while Jörg W. Rademacher (who translated the bulk of the text) and Jürgen Peter Krause, assisted by Cristoforo Schweeger, performed heroics in the speed of their accomplished translation. And at Deutscher Taschenbuch-Verlag, Margit Ketterle and Andrea Wörle have taken the keenest interest in the project since its inception and have been unfailing in their good advice.

Many friends and colleagues have helped enormously (at times unwittingly) over the years, through discussions or correspondence, through encouragement, and through their own published work, to shape my thinking on the Nazi era. I hope that a collective expression of my most sincere thanks will not appear like a diminution of my great indebtedness to each of them.

My warmest thanks are also owing to Gerald Fleming, Brigitte Hamann, Ronald Hayman, Robert Mallett, Meir Michaelis, Stig Hornshøh-Møller, Fritz Redlich, Gitta Sereny, Michael Wildt, and Peter Witte, all of whom were generous in supplying me with documentary material, giving me insight into their work prior to publication, and engaging in extensive discussion or correspondence on some issues of interpretation. Eberhard Jäckel has kindly allowed me to exploit his great expertise on Hitler on a number of occasions. I am grateful, too to Richard Evans for suggesting in the first place that I should undertake the biography, and to Niall Ferguson for inspiration with the subtitles of the two volumes. I would also like to thank Neil Bermel (Department of Russian and Slavonic Studies, University of Sheffield) for translating for me an article on Hitler published in Czech.

To Jeremy Noakes my debt is of a very special order. His exemplary regional study of Lower Saxony was one of the works, in the early 1970s, which inspired me to consider undertaking research on Nazi Germany. Since that time, he has remained a good friend as well as an outstanding scholar of modern German history. The documentary collection he has put together over many years (Jeremy Noakes and Geoffrey Pridham (eds.), *Nazism 1919–1945: A Documentary Reader*, 4 vols., Exeter, 1983–98) is a gathering of primary sources in English (with superb commentary) on the Nazi regime which surpasses in range and quality any German collection. A good number of the sources referred to in the chapters which follow, which I have cited wherever possible from a specific German location, will be found in the collection. This applies to one document quite especially, quoted in Chapter 13, which was first published in English translation in the second volume of Jeremy's collection. This somewhat obscure document, citing a speech by a Nazi functionary which spoke of 'Working towards the Führer along the lines he would wish', immediately attracted my attention by its strikingly simple insight into how a dictatorship operated. Having adopted the idea, I developed it to inform my overall approach to Hitler. But I owe it to Jeremy's collection that I was alerted to the document in the first place. I am also grateful to him for casting his expert eye over the entire typescript.

Two German scholars had the most profound influence on my work, and I would like to express my especial gratitude to them here. I had the privilege of working for a time with the late Martin Broszat, Director of the Institut für Zeitgeschichte, and profited immensely both from his expertise and from his inspiration. Working in Munich in the late 1970s under his guidance was a formative experience for me. A second crucial influence has been that of Hans Mommsen, formerly of the Ruhr-Universität Bochum, with whom over many years now I have enjoyed good friendship as well as continued scholarly dialogue. When I first told Hans that I had decided to write a biography of Hitler, his immediate response was: 'I wouldn't, if I were you.' I fear the biographical approach to Hitler is not one he will ever find fruitful. But even where our interpretations of Hitler differ, I hope he will detect unmistakable traces of his own influence on my approach. My admiration for his own scholarly achievement goes hand in hand with my most sincere thanks.

Some friends have contributed more than they perhaps realize. This applies especially to the late William Carr, and to Dick Geary, as it does to Joe Bergin, John Breuilly, Joe Harrison, Bob Moore, Frank O'Gorman, and Mike Rose. Not least, it applies to Traude Spät.

The support I have received from the University of Sheffield, especially from my colleagues in the Department of History, which I have felt privileged to be part of over the past few years, has been of great importance to me. Above all, I would like to thank Beverley Eaton for her quite exceptional help and encouragement during the entire period that I have been writing this book, and even before that arduous task began.

Finally, as always, I would like to thank my family for all they have done to make this work possible. Only Betty, David, and Stephen know the full extent of my debt of gratitude.

I. K.
April 1998

REFLECTING ON HITLER

'Charismatic rule has long been neglected and ridiculed, but apparently it has deep roots and becomes a powerful stimulus once the proper psychological and social conditions are set. The Leader's charismatic power is not a mere phantasm – none can doubt that millions believe in it.'

Franz Neumann, 1942

Has this been Hitler's century? Certainly, no other individual has stamped a more profound imprint on it than Adolf Hitler. Other dictators – most notably Mussolini, Stalin, and Mao – have engaged in wars of conquest, held subjugated peoples in thrall, presided over the perpetration of im-measurable inhumanity and left their indelible mark on the character of the twentieth century. But the rule of none of them has seared people's consciousness beyond their own countries, the world over, like the rule of Adolf Hitler has done. In an 'age of extremes',[1] there have also been political leaders who have symbolized the positive values of the century, have epitomized belief in humanity, hope for the future. Roosevelt, Churchill, Kennedy, and in more recent times Mandela would be high up a list of such figures. But Hitler's mark on the century has been deeper than that of each of them.

Hitler's dictatorship, far more than that of Stalin or Mao, has the quality of a paradigm for the twentieth century. In extreme and intense fashion it reflected, among other things, the total claim of the modern state, unforeseen levels of state repression and violence, previously unparalleled manipulation of the media to control and mobilize the masses, unprecedented cynicism in international relations, the acute dangers of ultra-nationalism, and the immensely destructive power of ideologies of racial superiority and ultimate consequences of racism, alongside the perverted usage of modern technology and 'social engineering'. Above all, it lit a warning beacon that still burns brightly: it showed how a modern, advanced, cultured society can so rapidly sink into barbarity, culminating in ideological war, conquest of scarcely imaginable brutality and rapaciousness, and genocide such as the world had never previously witnessed. Hitler's dictatorship amounted to the collapse of modern civilization – a form of nuclear blow-out within modern society. It showed what we are capable of.

Important questions still remain open. What in that catastrophic process was peculiar to Germany? What was peculiar to the epoch? What was part of a more general European malaise? Was what happened a product and a feature of modern civilization itself? Is its potential still perhaps lying dormant, or even as the century closes partly resurgent?

The twelve years of Hitler's rule permanently changed Germany, Europe, and the world. He is one of the few individuals of whom it can be said with absolute certainty: without him, the course of history would have been different.[2] Hitler's immediate legacy, the Cold War – a Germany split by a Wall, a Europe split by an Iron Curtain, a world split between hostile superpowers armed with weapons able to blow up the planet – ended only a decade ago. The deeper legacy – the moral trauma he bequeathed to posterity – has still not passed.

The century which, in a sense, his name has dominated has gained much of its character by war and genocide – Hitler's hallmarks. As the century comes to a close, it seems, therefore, a matter of some importance to reassess, as carefully as is feasible and on the basis of the latest scholarship, the forces which made Hitler possible and shaped the barbarity for which his name remains the symbol and the warning. What happened under Hitler took place – in fact, could only have taken place – in the society of a modern, cultured, technologically advanced, and highly bureaucratic country. Within only a few years of Hitler becoming head of government, this sophisticated country in the heart of Europe was working towards what turned out to be an apocalyptic genocidal war that left Germany and Europe not just riven by an Iron Curtain and physically in ruins, but morally shattered. That still needs explaining. The combination of a leadership committed to an ideological mission of national regeneration and racial purification; a society with sufficient belief in its Leader to work towards the goals he appeared to strive for; and a skilled bureaucratic administration capable of planning and implementing policy, however inhumane, and keen to do so, offers a starting-point. How and why this society could be galvanized by Hitler requires, even so, detailed examination.

It would be convenient to look no further, for the cause of Germany's and Europe's calamity, than the person of Adolf Hitler himself, ruler of Germany from 1933 to 1945, whose philosophies of breathtaking inhumanity had been publicly advertised almost eight years before he became Reich Chancellor. But, for all Hitler's prime moral responsibility for what took place under his authoritarian regime, a personalized explanation would be a gross short-circuiting of the truth. Hitler could be said to provide a classic illustration of Karl Marx's dictum that 'men *do* make their own history, but . . . under given and imposed conditions'.[3] How far 'given and imposed conditions', impersonal developments beyond the control of any individual, however powerful, shaped Germany's destiny; how much can be put down to contingency, even historical accident; what can be attributed to the actions and motivations of the extraordinary man ruling Germany at the time: all need investigation. All form part of the following inquiry. Simple answers are not possible.

A biography of Hitler is not the only approach that could be attempted.[4] But it has potential – as well as pitfalls – as the following chapters hope to demonstrate. A feasible inbuilt danger in any biographical approach is that it demands a level of empathy with the subject which can easily slide over into sympathy, perhaps even hidden or partial admiration. The pages which follow must stand witness to the avoidance of this risk. Perhaps, in fact, it is even the case that comprehensive repulsion more than the possibility of sympathy poses the greater drawback to insight.[5]

Biography also runs the natural risk of over-personalizing complex historical developments, over-emphasizing the role of the individual in shaping and determining events, ignoring or playing down the social and political context in which those actions took place.[6] Avoiding this pitfall has been the very challenge of undertaking this biography at all. It has been the spur to attempting a new approach to Hitler.

It is a risky venture. There is, after all, no shortage of literature on Hitler and the Third Reich, much of it of high quality. An outstanding survey written a decade and a half ago covered more than 1,500 titles.[7] A more recent attempt to draw the balance of interpretations mentioned 120,000 pieces of work on Hitler.[8] Remarkably, even so, there are only a handful of full, serious, scholarly biographies of the Nazi leader. Interpretations, as is to be expected, vary widely.[9]

Since he first entered the limelight in the 1920s, Hitler has been viewed in many different and varied fashions, often directly contrasting with each other. He has been seen, for example, as no more than 'an opportunist entirely without principle', 'barren of all ideas save one – the further extension of his own power and that of the nation with which he had identified himself', preoccupied solely with 'domination, dressed up as the doctrine of race', and consisting of nothing but 'vindictive destructiveness'.[10] In complete contrast, he has been portrayed as fanatically driving on a pre-planned and pre-ordained ideological programme.[11] There have been attempts to see him as a type of political con-man, hypnotizing and bewitching the German people, leading them astray and into disorder, or to 'demonize' him – turning him into a mystical, inexplicable figure of Germany's destiny. No less a figure than Albert Speer, Hitler's architect, then Armaments Minister, for much of the Third Reich as close to the Dictator as anyone, described him soon after the end of the war as a 'demonic figure', 'one of those inexplicable historical phenomena which emerge at rare intervals among mankind', whose 'person determined the fate of the nation'.[12] Such a view runs the risk of mystifying what happened in Germany between 1933 and 1945, reducing the cause of Germany's and Europe's catastrophe to the arbitrary whim of a demonic personality. The genesis of the calamity finds no explanation outside the actions of an extraordinary individual. Complex developments become no more than an expression of Hitler's will.

An absolutely contrary view – tenable only so long as it was part of a state ideology and consequently evaporating as soon as the Soviet bloc which had sustained it collapsed – rejected out of hand any significant role of personality, relegating Hitler to no more than the status of an agent of capitalism, a cypher for the interests of big business and its leaders who controlled him and pulled the strings of their marionette.[13]

Some accounts of Hitler have scarcely recognized any problem at all of understanding, or have promptly ruled one out.[14] Ridiculing Hitler has been one approach. Describing him simply as a 'lunatic' or 'raving maniac' obviates the need for an explanation – though it of course leaves open the key question: why a complex society would be prepared to follow someone who was mentally deranged, a 'pathological' case, into the abyss.[15]

Far more sophisticated approaches have clashed on the extent to which Hitler was actually 'master in the Third Reich', or could even be described as 'a weak dictator'.[16] Did he in fact exercise total, unrestricted, and sole power?[17] Or did his regime rest on a hydra-like 'polycracy' of power-structures with Hitler, on account of his undeniable popularity and the cult that surrounded him, as its indispensable fulcrum but little else – remaining no more than the propagandist he had in essence always been, exploiting opportunities as they came along, though without programme, plan, or design?[18]

Differing views about Hitler have never been purely a matter of arcane academic debate. They have wider currency than that – and more far-reaching implications. When Hitler was put forward as a sort of reverse copy of Lenin and Stalin, a leader whose paranoid fear of Bolshevik terror, of class genocide, motivated him to perpetrate race genocide, the implications were plain. Hitler was wicked, no doubt, but less wicked than Stalin. His was the copy, Stalin's the original. The underlying cause of Nazi race genocide was Soviet class genocide.[19] It also mattered when the spotlight was turned away from the crimes against humanity for which Hitler bears ultimate responsibility and on to his ruminations on the transformation of German society. This Hitler was interested in social mobility, better housing for workers, modernizing industry, erecting a welfare system, sweeping away the reactionary privileges of the past; in sum, building a better, more up-to-date, less class-ridden, German society, however brutal the methods. This Hitler was, despite his demonization of Jews and gamble for world power against mighty odds, 'a politician whose thinking and actions were far more rational than up to now thought'.[20] From such a perspective, Hitler could be seen as wicked, but with good intentions for German society – or at least intentions which could be viewed in a positive light.[21]

Such revised interpretations were not meant to be apologetic. The comparison of Nazi and Stalinist crimes against humanity was intended, however distorted the approach, to shed light on the terrible ferocity of ideological conflict in inter-war Europe and the motive forces of the German genocide. The depiction of Hitler as a social-revolutionary was attempting to explain, perhaps in somewhat misconceived fashion, why he found such wide appeal in Germany in a time of social crisis. But it is not hard to see that both approaches contain, however unwittingly, the potential for a possible rehabilitation of Hitler which could begin to see him, despite the crimes against humanity associated with his name, as nevertheless a great leader of the twentieth century, one who, had he died before the war, would have had a high place in the pantheon of German heroes.[22]

The question of 'historical greatness' was usually implicit in the writing of conventional biography – particularly so in the German tradition.[23] The figure of Hitler, whose personal attributes – distinguished from his political aura and impact – were scarcely noble, elevating or enriching, posed self-evident problems for such a tradition.[24] A way round it was to imply that Hitler possessed a form of 'negative greatness'; that, while he lacked the nobility of character and other attributes taken to pertain to 'greatness' in historical figures, his impact on history was undeniably immense, even if catastrophic.[25] Yet 'negative greatness' can also be taken to have tragic connotations – mighty endeavour and astounding achievements vitiated; national grandeur turned into national catastrophe.

It seems better to avoid altogether the issue of 'greatness' (other than seeking to understand why so many contemporaries saw 'greatness' in Hitler). It is a red herring: misconstrued, pointless, irrelevant, and potentially apologetic. Misconstrued because, as 'great men' theories cannot escape doing, it personalizes the historical process in extreme fashion. Pointless because the whole notion of historical greatness is in the last resort futile. Based on a subjective set of moral and even aesthetic judgements, it is a philosophical-ethical concept which leads nowhere. Irrelevant because, whether we were to answer the question of Hitler's alleged 'greatness' in the affirmative or the negative, it would in itself explain nothing whatsoever about the terrible history of the Third Reich. And potentially apologetic, because even to pose the question cannot conceal a certain admiration for Hitler, however grudging and whatever his faults; and because to look for greatness in Hitler bears the almost automatic corollary of reducing in effect those who directly promoted his rule, those agencies which sustained it, and the German people themselves who gave it so much backing, to the role of mere supernumeraries to the 'great man'.

Rather than the issue of 'historical greatness', we need to turn our attention to another question, one of far greater importance. How do we explain how someone with so few intellectual gifts and social attributes, someone no more than an empty vessel outside his political life, unapproachable and impenetrable even for those in his close company, incapable it seems of genuine friendship, without the background that bred high office, without even any experience of government before becoming Reich Chancellor, could nevertheless have such an immense historical impact, could make the entire world hold its breath?

Perhaps the question is, in part at least, falsely posed. For one thing, Hitler was certainly not unintelligent, and possessed a sharp mind which could draw on his formidably retentive memory. He was able to impress not only, as might be expected, his sycophantic entourage but also cool, critical, seasoned statesmen and diplomats with his rapid grasp of issues. His rhetorical talent was, of course, recognized even by his political enemies.

And he is certainly not alone among twentieth-century state leaders in combining what we might see as deficiencies of character and shallowness of intellectual development with notable political skill and effectiveness. It is as well to avoid the trap, which most of his contemporaries fell into, of grossly underestimating his abilities.

Moreover, others beside Hitler have climbed from humble backgrounds to high office. Napoleon was the first to achieve it in modern times, though he did rise through the key institution of the army (in which Hitler gained no higher rank than corporal) and through unusual prowess and achievements in military command. He was also far more intellectually talented with more diverse personal skills than Hitler. In the twentieth century, the possibilities for rank outsiders to the social and political élite to rise to the pinnacle of state power have expanded. Even so, such instances are still few, and tend to occur in periods of political turmoil from among the leaders of revolutionary movements (as with Stalin, Mao, or Castro) rather than in stable democracies.

If his rise from utter anonymity is not entirely unique, the problem posed by Hitler remains. One reason why Hitler has proved 'a riddle wrapped in a mystery inside an enigma' (to quote Winston Churchill, though in a quite different context),[26] is the emptiness of the private person. He was, as has frequently been said, tantamount to an 'unperson'.[27] There is, perhaps, an element of condescension in this judgement, a readiness to look down on the vulgar, uneducated upstart lacking a rounded personality, the outsider with half-baked opinions on everything under the sun, the uncultured self-appointed adjudicator on culture. Partly, too, the black hole which represents the private individual derives from the fact that Hitler was highly secretive – not least about his personal life, his background, and his family. The secrecy and detachment were features of his character, applying also to his political behaviour; they were also politically important, components of the aura of 'heroic' leadership he had consciously allowed to be built up, intensifying the mystery about himself. Even so, when all qualifications are made, it remains the case that outside politics Hitler's life was largely a void. Napoleon, Bismarck, Churchill, Kennedy: all were figures of substance outside their public lives. Plutarch's remark: 'When destiny raises a base character by acts of great importance, it reveals his lack of substance', has been applied to Stalin.[28] It is tempting to invoke it once more in the case of Hitler.

A biography of an 'unperson', one who has as good as no personal life or history outside that of the political events in which he is involved, imposes, naturally, its own limitations. But the drawbacks only exist as long as it is presumed that the private life is decisive for the public life. Such a presumption would be a mistake. There was no 'private life' for Hitler. Of course, he could enjoy his escapist films, his daily walk to the Tea-House at the Berghof, his time in his alpine idyll far from government ministries in Berlin. But these were empty routines. There was no retreat to a sphere outside the political, to a deeper existence which conditioned his public reflexes. It was not that his 'private life' became part of his public persona. On the contrary: so secretive did it remain that the German people only learned of the existence of Eva Braun once the Third Reich had crumbled into ashes. Rather, Hitler 'privatized' the public sphere.[29] 'Private' and 'public' merged completely and became inseparable. Hitler's entire being came to be subsumed within the role he played to perfection: the role of 'Führer'.

The task of the biographer at this point becomes clearer. It is a task which has to focus not upon the personality of Hitler, but squarely and directly upon *the character of his power – the power of the Führer*.

That power derived only in part from Hitler himself. In greater measure, it was a social product – a creation of social expectations and motivations vested in Hitler by his followers. This does not mean that Hitler's own actions, in the context of his expanding power, were not of the utmost importance at key moments. But the impact of his power has largely to be seen not in any specific attributes of 'personality', but in his role as Führer – a role made possible only through the underestimation, mistakes, weakness, and collaboration of others. To explain his power, therefore, we must look in the first instance to others, not to Hitler himself.

Hitler's power was of an extraordinary kind. He did not base his claim to power (except in a most formal sense) on his position as a party leader, or on any functional position. He derived it from what he saw as his historic mission to save Germany. His power, in other words, was 'charismatic', not institutional. It depended upon the readiness of others to see 'heroic' qualities in him.[30] And they did see those qualities – perhaps even before he himself came to believe in them.

As one of the most brilliant contemporary analysts of the Nazi phenomenon, Franz Neumann, noted: 'Charismatic rule has long been neglected and ridiculed, but apparently it has deep roots and becomes a powerful stimulus once the proper psychological and social conditions are set. The Leader's charismatic power is not a mere phantasm – none can doubt that millions believe in it.'[31] Hitler's own contribution to the expansion of this power and to its consequences should not be underrated. A brief counter-factual reflection underlines the point. Is it likely, we might ask, that a terroristic police state such as that which developed under Himmler and the SS would have been erected without Hitler as head of government? Would Germany under a different leader, even an authoritarian one, have been engaged by the end of the 1930s in *general* European war? And would under a different head of state discrimination against Jews (which would almost certainly have taken place) have culminated in out-and-out genocide? The answer to each of these questions would surely be 'no'; or, at the very least, 'highly unlikely'. Whatever the external circumstances and impersonal determinants, Hitler was not interchangeable.

The highly personalized power which Hitler exercised conditioned even shrewd and intelligent individuals – churchmen, intellectuals, foreign diplomats, distinguished visitors – to be impressed by him. They would not for the most part have been captivated by the same sentiments expressed to a raucous crowd in a Munich beerhall. But with the authority of the Reich Chancellorship behind him, backed by adoring crowds, surrounded by the trappings of power, enveloped by the aura of great leadership trumpeted by propaganda, it was scarcely surprising that others beyond the completely naive and gullible could find him impressive. Power was also the reason why his underlings – subordinate Nazi leaders, his personal retinue, provincial party bosses – hung on his every word, before, when that power was at an end in April 1945, fleeing like the proverbial rats from the sinking ship. The mystique of power surely explains, too, why so many women (especially those much younger than he was) saw him, the Hitler whose person seems to us the antithesis of sexuality, as a sex-symbol, several attempting suicide on his behalf.

A history of Hitler has to be, therefore, a history of his power – how he came to get it, what its character was, how he exercised it, why he was allowed to expand it to break all institutional barriers, why resistance to that power was so feeble. But these are questions to be directed at German society, not just at Hitler.

There is no necessity to play down the contribution to Hitler's gaining and exercise of power that derived from the ingrained features of his character. Single-mindedness, inflexibility, ruthlessness in discarding all hindrances, cynical adroitness, the all-or-nothing gambler's instinct for the highest stakes: each of these helped shape the nature of his power. These features of character came together in one overriding element in Hitler's inner drive: his boundless egomania. Power was Hitler's aphrodisiac. For one as narcissistic as he was, it offered purpose out of purposeless early years, compensation for all the deeply-felt setbacks of the first half of his life – rejection as an artist, social bankruptcy taking him to a Viennese doss-house, the falling apart of his world in the defeat and revolution of 1918. Power was all-consuming for him. As one perceptive observer commented in 1940, even before the triumph over France: 'Hitler is the potential suicide *par excellence*. He owns no ties outside his own "ego" . . . He is in the privileged position of one who loves nothing and no one but himself . . . So he can dare all to preserve or magnify his power . . . which alone stands between him and speedy death.'[32] The thirst for personalized power of such magnitude embraced an insatiable appetite for territorial conquest amounting to an almighty gamble – against extremely heavy odds – for a monopoly of power on the European continent and, later, world power. The relentless quest for ever greater expansion of power could contemplate no diminution, no confinement, no restriction. It was, moreover, dependent upon the continuance of what were taken to be 'great achievements'. Lacking any capacity for limitation, the progressive megalomania inevitably contained the seeds of self-destruction for the regime Hitler led. The match with his own inbuilt suicidal tendencies was perfect.

All-consuming though power was for Hitler, it was not a matter of power for its own sake, devoid of content or meaning. Hitler was not just a propagandist, a manipulator, a mobilizer. He was all those. But he was also an ideologue of unshakeable convictions – the most radical of the radicals as exponent of an internally coherent (however repellent to us) 'world-view', acquiring its thrust and potency from its combination of a very few basic ideas – integrated by the notion of human history as the history of racial struggle. His 'world-view' gave him a rounded explanation of the ills of Germany and of the world, and how to remedy them. He held to his 'world-view' unwaveringly from the early 1920s down to his death in the bunker. It amounted to a utopian vision of national redemption, not a set of middle-range policies. But it was not only capable of incorporating within it all the different strands of Nazi philosophy; combined with Hitler's rhetorical skills, it also meant that he soon became practically unchallengeable on any point of Party doctrine.

Hitler's ideological goals, his actions, and his personal input into the shaping of events need, then, to be accorded the most serious attention. But they explain far from everything. We need to examine the dictatorship as well as the Dictator;[33] and beyond the structures of rule, the social impulses which underpinned the dictatorship, gave it its dynamic, provided it with its underlying consensus. What Hitler did not do, did not instigate, but which was nevertheless set in train by the initiatives of others is as vital as the actions of the Dictator himself in understanding the fateful 'cumulative radicalisation' of the regime.[34]

A new biography of Hitler requires, then, a new approach: one which attempts to integrate the actions of the Dictator into the political structures and social forces which conditioned his acquisition and exercise of power, and its extraordinary impact. An approach which looks to the expectations and motivations of German society (in all its complexity) more than to Hitler's personality in explaining the Dictator's immense impact offers the potential to explore the expansion of his power through the internal dynamics of the regime he headed and the forces he unleashed. The approach is encapsulated in the maxim enunciated by a Nazi functionary in 1934 – providing in a sense a leitmotiv for the work as a whole and the title for Chapter 13 – that it was the duty of each person in the Third Reich 'to work towards the Führer along the lines he would wish' without awaiting instruction from above.[35] This maxim, put into practice, was one of the driving-forces of the Third Reich, translating Hitler's loosely-framed ideological goals into reality through initiatives focused on working towards the fulfilment of the Dictator's visionary aims. Hitler's authority was, of course, decisive. But the initiatives which he sanctioned derived more often than not from others.

Hitler was no tyrant imposed on Germany. Though he never attained majority support in free elections, he was legally appointed to power as Reich Chancellor just like his predecessors had been, and became between 1933 and 1940 arguably the most popular head of state in the world. Understanding this demands reconciling the apparently irreconcilable: the personalized method of biography and the contrasting approaches to the history of society (including the structures of political domination).[36] Hitler's impact can only be grasped through the era which created him (and was destroyed by him). A convincing study of Hitler must be, therefore, at the same time in a certain sense a history of the Nazi era.[37] Though biography is, of course, not the only approach which could be taken to attain such an end – if attainable at all, that is – there is something to be said for directly focusing on the figure of Hitler – the person who indisputably played the central, often decisive role in the 'running amok' of the Third Reich.[38]

No attempt to produce a comprehensive understanding of the phenomenon of Nazism without doing justice to 'the Hitler factor' can hope to succeed.[38] But such an interpretation must not only take full account of Hitler's ideological goals, his actions, and his personal input into the shaping of events; it must at the same time locate these within the social forces and political structures which permitted, shaped, and promoted the growth of a system that came increasingly to hinge on personalized, absolute power – with the disastrous effects that flowed from it.

The Nazi assault on the roots of civilization has been a defining feature of the twentieth century. Hitler was the epicentre of that assault. But he was its chief exponent, not its prime cause.

I

FANTASY AND FAILURE

'When the postmaster asked him one day what he wanted to do for a living and whether he wouldn't like to join the post-office, he replied that it was his intention to become a great artist.'

A neighbour of the Hitler family in Urfahr

'I was so convinced that I would be successful that when I received my rejection, it struck me as a bolt from the blue.'

Hitler, on failing his entry examination to study
at the Academy of Fine Arts in Vienna

I

The first of many strokes of good fortune for Adolf Hitler took place thirteen years before he was born. In 1876, the man who was to become his father changed his name from Alois Schicklgruber to Alois Hitler. Adolf can be believed when he said that nothing his father had done had pleased him so much as to drop the coarsely rustic name of Schicklgruber.[1] Certainly, 'Heil Schicklgruber' would have sounded an unlikely salutation to a national hero.

The Schicklgrubers had for generations been a peasant family, smallholders in the Waldviertel, a picturesque but poor, hilly and (as the name suggests) woody area in the most north-westerly part of Lower Austria, bordering on Bohemia, whose inhabitants had something of a reputation for being dour, hard-nosed, and unwelcoming.[2] Hitler's father, Alois, had been born there on 7 June 1837, in the village of Strones, as the illegitimate child of Maria Anna Schicklgruber, then forty-two years old and daughter of a poor smallholder, Johann Schicklgruber, and baptized (as Aloys Schicklgruber) in nearby Döllersheim the same day. The baptismal register left a blank in the space allocated to the baby's father.[3] The name of Hitler's paternal grandfather was not disclosed and, despite much speculation, has remained unknown ever since.

Five years later, Maria Anna married Johann Georg Hiedler, a fifty-year-old miller's journeyman from Spital, some fifteen miles away. Hiedler's aimless and meandering lifestyle had brought him to Strones, where he had for some time dwelt in the same house as Maria Anna and her father.[4] The marriage lasted five years. Maria Anna died in 1847, and Hiedler's hand-to-mouth existence was ended by a stroke a decade later.

No later than the time of his mother's death, and perhaps earlier, the

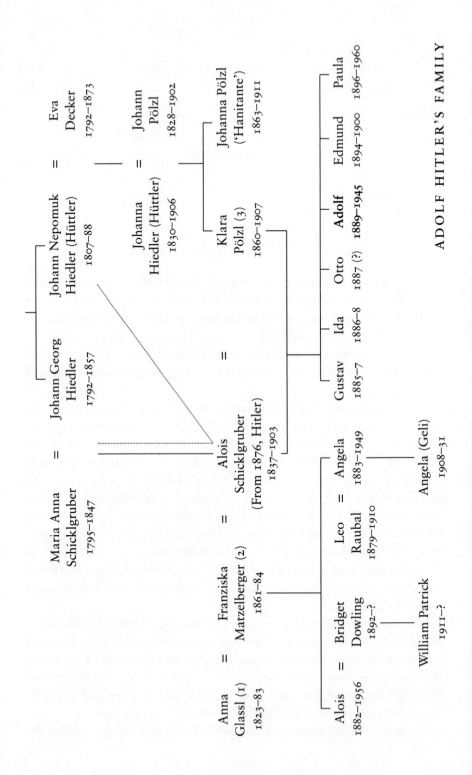

Maria Anna
Schicklgruber
1795–1847

=

Johann Georg
Hiedler
1792–1857

Johann Nepomuk
Hiedler (Hüttler)
1807–88

=

Eva
Decker
1792–1873

Johanna
Hiedler (Hüttler)
1830–1906

=

Johann
Pölzl
1828–1902

Alois
Schicklgruber
(From 1876, Hitler)
1837–1903

Johanna Pölzl
('Hanitante')
1863–1911

Klara
Pölzl (3)
1860–1907

=

Anna
Glassl (1)
1823–83

Franziska
Matzelberger (2)
1861–84

=

Alois
1882–1956

=

Bridget
Dowling
1892–?

Leo
Raubal
1879–1910

=

Angela
1883–1949

Gustav
1885–7

Ida
1886–8

Otto
1887 (?)

Adolf
1889–1945

Edmund
1894–1900

Paula
1896–1960

William Patrick
1911–?

Angela (Geli)
1908–31

ADOLF HITLER'S FAMILY

youngster Alois was taken by Johann Georg's brother, Johann Nepomuk Hiedler, fifteen years his junior, to live on Nepomuk's middling-sized farm in Spital.[5] The reasons for Nepomuk's effective adoption of young Alois are unclear. But to all appearances the boy was provided with a modest but good home. After going to elementary school, Alois took up an apprenticeship with a local cobbler, and already at the age of thirteen, like many country lads, made his way to Vienna to continue his training in leatherwork.

Hitler's father was the first social climber in his family. In 1855, by the time he was eighteen, Alois had gained employment at a modest grade with the Austrian ministry of finance.[6] For a young man of his background and limited education, his advancement in the years to come was impressive. After training, and passing the necessary examination, he attained low-ranking supervisory status in 1861 and a position in the customs service in 1864, becoming a customs officer in 1870 before moving the following year to Braunau am Inn, and attaining the post of customs inspector there in 1875.[7]

A year later came the change of name. This had nothing to do with any social stigma attached to Alois's illegitimacy. Though castigated by the Catholic Church, illegitimacy was scarcely an unusual feature of Austrian country life.[8] Alois did not attempt to conceal his illegitimacy, even after 1876. It is unclear whether the impulse for the change of name came from Alois himself, or from his uncle (and effective stepfather) Nepomuk, who, deprived of male heirs, seems to have made a legacy to Alois dependent upon the adoption of his own name.[9] The legalization protocol of a notary in Weitra on 6 June 1876, signed by three witnesses, recorded Alois as the son of Georg *Hitler* – the name is already entered here in this form, not as 'Hiedler'.[10] Then the following day the legitimation of Alois, thirty-nine years after he had been born, was completed when the parish priest of Döllersheim altered the birth register to strike out the name 'Schicklgruber', replacing 'out of wedlock' by 'within wedlock', and entering in the hitherto empty box for the father's name 'Georg Hitler'.[11] This was the Johann Georg Hiedler who had married Alois's mother as long ago as 1842, had been dead for nineteen years, but had, according to the three witnesses of the legitimizing ceremony (all of whom had family connections) and according to Alois himself, acknowledged his paternity.[12] The priest's entry notes also the testimony of the witnesses that Alois's father had requested the entry of his name in the baptismal register.[13]

The change of name – an event at the time of significance only for the history of a peasant family in provincial Austria – has attracted unceasing speculation purely because it is inextricably bound up with the identity of the grandfather of Adolf Hitler. Only three possibilities need consideration. And of these, the first two amount to little more than whether there was an undisclosed minor scandal within the Hiedler family, while the third possibility, which would historically have been of some importance, can, in the light of the evidence, be discounted.

The first possibility is that the father of Alois was indeed the person named in the amended baptismal register, and officially accepted in the Third Reich as Hitler's grandfather: Johann Georg Hiedler. But if he was indeed the father, why did Hiedler make no attempt during his lifetime – even at the time of his marriage – to legitimize the birth of his son? Poverty is unlikely to have been the reason. Though it was rumoured that after their marriage, Johann Georg and Maria Anna were so poor that they had to sleep in a cattle-trough for a bed, it has been established that Maria Anna was less impoverished than once thought.[14] And if this was the case, then the normal reason given for the 'adoption' by Nepomuk – an act of humanity, rescuing Alois from the dire poverty in which his parents lived – disappears. Why, then, was Maria Anna, who clearly did not disclose the father's name at the baptism, prepared to be separated from her only son? Why was Alois not brought up by his apparent father, but instead in the home of his father's brother? And why was the legitimation – accompanied by some minor irregularities (no legal acknowledgement of paternity in the absence of the father), possibly amounting to a little charade by Alois, Nepomuk and the three witnesses, all closely connected with or related to Nepomuk, to deceive the notary and parish priest – delayed until 1876?[15] That a legacy from Nepomuk to Alois was involved seems likely. But why would this have necessitated the change of name? That Nepomuk, with only female offspring, was preoccupied with the continuation of the family name through Alois, who at the time had a fifty-year-old wife, seems an unlikely, or at least insufficient, motive.

The answers to these questions are lost in the mists of time, and would in any case scarcely be of historical importance. But if there are question marks over Johann Georg's paternity, who else might the father have been? The other obvious candidate is Nepomuk himself. He 'adopted', cared for, and brought up Alois. And he was perhaps the moving spirit beyond the name change – three years after his wife, Eva Maria, had died. The name change seems to have been connected with making Alois a legatee of his will. At Nepomuk's death in 1888, his expectant heirs were told, to their surprise, that there was nothing to inherit. But only six months later Alois Hitler, up to then without any notable amounts of money to play with, purchased a substantial house and adjoining property not far from Spital, costing between 4,000 and 5,000 Gulden.[16] It seems conceivable, then, that Nepomuk, not Johann Georg, was the actual father of Alois, that Johann Georg had rejected Alois, the son of his brother, at the time of his marriage to Maria Anna, but that the family scandal had been kept quiet, and that a change of name had not been possible as long as Nepomuk's wife had lived.[17]

However, there is no proof and, even after his wife's death, Nepomuk, if he was himself the actual father, was keen to avoid public admission of the fact. Some significance has been read into Adolf Hitler's comment at the beginning of *Mein Kampf* that his father had been the son of a 'poor, small cottager' (which was not a description of Johann Georg, a miller's journeyman).[18] But Hitler was frequently inaccurate or careless with detail in the autobiographical parts of *Mein Kampf*, and it would be a mistake to read too much into his brief and vague reference to his grandfather (who, if it referred to Nepomuk, was in any case rather more than a 'poor cottager'). It has also been claimed that the form of name chosen by Alois in 1876 – 'Hitler' – was a deliberate reflection of 'Hüttler' (Nepomuk's name) rather than Hiedler (that of Johann Georg). But this would be to interpret too much from the adoption of one form of a name which remained fluid and fluctuating before the late nineteenth century. The names 'Hiedler', 'Hietler', 'Hüttler', 'Hütler', and 'Hitler' – the name meant 'smallholder' – occur interchangeably in documents of the early and mid-nineteenth century and were phonetically scarcely distinguishable.[19] Nepomuk himself was baptized 'Hiedler' and married as 'Hüttler'.[20] Alois, the social climber, may have preferred the less rustic form of 'Hitler'. But 'Hitler' may have been no more than the particular form chosen by the notary in Weitra at the legalization, and copied by the parish priest of Döllersheim the next day.[21] Whatever the reason for the selection of the form of name, Alois seemed well satisfied with it. He thereafter never deviated in his usage of the name, and from the final authorization in January 1877 always signed himself 'Alois Hitler'. His son was equally pleased with the more distinctive form 'Hitler'.[22]

The third possibility is that Adolf Hitler's grandfather was Jewish. Rumours to that effect circulated in Munich cafés in the early 1920s, and were fostered by sensationalist journalism of the foreign press during the 1930s. It was suggested that the name 'Hüttler' was Jewish, 'revealed' that he could be traced to a Jewish family called Hitler in Bucharest, and even claimed that his father had been sired by Baron Rothschild, in whose house in Vienna his grandmother had allegedly spent some time as a servant.[23] But the most serious speculation about Hitler's supposed Jewish background has occurred since the Second World War, and is directly traceable to the memoirs of the leading Nazi lawyer and Governor General of Poland, Hans Frank, dictated in his Nuremberg cell while awaiting the hangman.

Frank claimed that he had been called in by Hitler towards the end of 1930 and shown a letter from his nephew William Patrick Hitler (the son of his half-brother Alois, who had been briefly married to an Irish woman) threatening, in connection with the press stories circulating about Hitler's background, to expose the fact that Hitler had Jewish blood flowing in his veins. Allegedly commissioned by Hitler to look into his family history, Frank reportedly discovered that Maria Anna Schicklgruber had given birth to her child while serving as a cook in the home of a Jewish family called Frankenberger in Graz. Not only that: Frankenberger senior had reputedly paid regular instalments to support the child on behalf of his son, around nineteen years old at the birth, until the child's fourteenth birthday. Letters were allegedly exchanged for years between Maria Anna Schicklgruber and the Frankenbergers. According to Frank, Hitler declared that he knew, from what his father and grandmother had said, that his grandfather was not the Jew from Graz, but because his grandmother and her subsequent husband were so poor they had conned the Jew into believing he was the father and into paying for the boy's support.[24]

Frank's story gained wide circulation in the 1950s.[25] But it simply does not stand up. There was no Jewish family called Frankenberger in Graz during the 1830s. In fact, there were no Jews at all in the whole of Styria at the time, since Jews were not permitted in that part of Austria until the 1860s. A family named Frankenreiter did live there, but was not Jewish. There is no evidence that Maria Anna was ever in Graz, let alone was employed by the butcher Leopold Frankenreiter. No correspondence between Maria Anna and a family called Frankenberg or Frankenreiter has ever turned up. The son of Leopold Frankenreiter and alleged father of the baby (according to Frank's story and accepting that he had merely confused names) for whom Frankenreiter was seemingly prepared to pay child support for thirteen years was ten years old at the time of Alois's birth. The Frankenreiter family had moreover hit upon such hard times that payment of any support to Maria Anna Schicklgruber would have been inconceivable.[26] Equally lacking in credibility is Frank's comment that Hitler had learnt from his grandmother that there was no truth in the Graz story: his grandmother had been dead for over forty years at the time of Hitler's birth. And whether in fact Hitler received a blackmail letter from his nephew in 1930 is also doubtful. If such was the case, then Patrick – who repeatedly made a nuisance of himself by scrounging from his famous uncle – was lucky to survive the next few years which he spent for the most part in Germany, and to be able to leave the country for good in December 1938.[27] His 'revelations', when they came in a Paris journal in August 1939, contained nothing about the Graz story.[28] Nor did a number of different Gestapo inquiries into Hitler's family background in the 1930s and 1940s contain any reference to the alleged Graz background.[29] Indeed they discovered no new skeletons in the cupboard. Hans Frank's memoirs, dictated at a time when he was waiting for the hangman and plainly undergoing a psychological crisis,[30] are full of inaccuracies and have to be used with caution. With regard to the story of Hitler's alleged Jewish grandfather, they are valueless. Hitler's grandfather, whoever he was, was not a Jew from Graz.[31]

The only serious contenders for the paternity of Hitler's father remain, therefore, Johann Georg Hiedler and Johann Nepomuk Hiedler (or Hüttler). The official version always declared Johann Georg to be Adolf's grandfather. The evidence is insufficient to know. And perhaps Adolf did not know, though there is no firm reason to believe that he doubted that it was Johann Georg Hiedler.[32] In any case, as regards Adolf the only significance is that, were Nepomuk his grandfather, the family descent would have been even more incestuous than if his grandfather had been Johann Georg: for Nepomuk was also the grandfather of Adolf's mother.[33]

Klara Pölzl, who was to become Adolf Hitler's mother, was the eldest of only three surviving children out of eleven – the other two were Johanna and Theresia – from the marriage of Nepomuk's eldest daughter, Johanna Hüttler, with Johann Baptist Pölzl, also a smallholder in Spital. Klara herself grew up on the adjacent farm to that of her grandfather Nepomuk. Klara's mother, Johanna, and her aunt Walburga had in fact been brought up with Alois Schicklgruber in Nepomuk's house.[34] Officially, after the change of name and legitimation in 1876, Alois Hitler and Klara Pölzl were second cousins. In 1876, aged sixteen, Klara Pölzl left the family farm in Spital and moved to Braunau am Inn to join the household of Alois Hitler as a maid.[35]

By this time, Alois was a well-respected customs official in Braunau. His personal affairs were, however, less well regulated than his career. He would eventually marry three times, first to a woman much older than himself, then to women young enough to be his daughters. A pre-marital liaison and his last two marriages would give him nine children, four of whom were to die in infancy. It was a private life of above average turbulence – at least for a provincial customs officer.[36] He had already fathered an illegitimate child in the 1860s.[37] In 1873 he married Anna Glassl, then aged fifty. It is unlikely to have been a love-match. The marriage to a woman fourteen years older than himself had almost certainly a material motive, since Anna was relatively well off, and in addition had connections within the civil service.[38] Within a short time, if not from the outset, Anna became ill. Her illness cannot have been helped by knowledge of the affair Alois was conducting by the later 1870s with Franziska (Fanni) Matzelberger, a young maid at the Gasthaus Streif, where the Hitlers lived. By 1880 Anna had finally had enough, and was granted a legal separation.[39]

Alois now lived openly with Fanni, one of whose first acts was to insist that Klara Pölzl, a year older than she was and evidently regarded as a potential rival for Alois's favours, should leave the Hitler household. In 1882 Fanni gave birth to a son, baptized Alois Matzelberger but legitimized as soon as Anna Hitler's death in 1883 cleared the way for the marriage, six weeks later, between Alois and Franziska. A second child, Angela, was born less than two months after the wedding. But in 1884 Fanni developed tuberculosis, and she died in August that year aged only twenty-three.[40]

During her illness, Fanni had been moved to the fresh air of the countryside outside Braunau. For someone to look after his two young children, Alois turned straight away to Klara Pölzl, and brought her back to Braunau. While Fanni was dying, Klara became pregnant. Since they were officially second cousins, a marriage between Alois and Klara needed the dispensation of the Church. After a wait of four months, in which Klara's condition became all the more evident, the dispensation finally arrived from Rome in late 1884, and the couple were married on 7 January 1885. The wedding ceremony took place at six o'clock in the morning. Soon after a perfunctory celebration, Alois was back at his work at the customs post.[41]

The first of the children of Alois's third marriage, Gustav, was born in May 1885, to be followed in September the following year by a second child, Ida, and, with scarcely a respite, by another son, Otto, who died only days after his birth. Further tragedy for Klara came soon afterwards, as both Gustav and Ida contracted diphtheria and died within weeks of each other in December 1887 and January 1888.[42] By the summer of 1888 Klara was pregnant again. At half-past six in the evening on 20 April 1889, an overcast and chilly Easter Saturday,[43] she gave birth in her home in the 'Gasthof zum Pommer', Vorstadt Nr. 219, to her fourth child, the first to survive infancy: this was Adolf.[44]

In the very first sentences of *Mein Kampf*, Adolf was to emphasize – what became a Nazi stock-in-trade – how providential it was that he had been born in Braunau am Inn, on the border of the two countries he saw it as his life's task to unite.[45] He remembered, however, little or nothing of Braunau, since in 1892 his father was promoted to the position of Higher Collector of Customs – the highest rank open to an official with only an elementary school education behind him – and the family moved to Passau, in Bavaria, before he was three years old and was based for a time on the German side of the border.[46] It was one of numerous changes of address which the young Hitler was to experience.

The historical record of Adolf's early years is very sparse. His own account in *Mein Kampf* is inaccurate in detail and coloured in interpretation. Post-war recollections of family and acquaintances have to be treated with care, and are at times as dubious as the attempts during the Third Reich itself to glorify the childhood of the future Führer. For the formative period so important to psychologists and 'psycho-historians', the fact has to be faced that there is little to go on which is not retrospective guesswork.[47]

In material terms, the Hitler family led a comfortable middle-class exist-ence. In addition to Alois, Klara, the two children of Alois's second marriage, Alois Jr (before he left home in 1896) and Angela, Adolf, and his younger brother Edmund (born in 1894, but died in 1900) and sister Paula (born in 1896), the household also ran to a cook and maid, Rosalia Schichtl. In addition, there was Adolf's aunt Johanna, one of his mother's younger sisters, a bad-tempered, hunchbacked woman who was, however, fond of Adolf and a good help for Klara around the house. After his inheritance and property purchase in 1889, Alois was a man of moderate means. His income was a solid one – rather more than that of an elementary school headmaster.[48]

Family life was, however, less than harmonious and happy.[49] Alois was an archetypal provincial civil servant – pompous, status-proud, strict, humourless, frugal, pedantically punctual, and devoted to duty. He was regarded with respect by the local community. But both at work and at home, he had a bad temper which could flare up quite unpredictably. He smoked like a chimney, and enjoyed a few drinks after work and a discussion around the beer table more than going back home. He took little interest in bringing up his family, and was happier outside rather than inside the family home.[50] His passion was bee-keeping. His daily half-hour walk to and from his bees from his Passau work-post before visiting the inn on his way back doubtless marked a peaceful respite from a boisterous household of young children. His aim of owning a plot of land where he could keep his beehives was realized in 1889 when the legacy from Nepomuk helped him to buy a property near his birthplace at Spital in the Waldviertel.

Though he sold this three years later, he went on to buy two further plots.[51] At home, Alois was an authoritarian, overbearing, domineering husband and a stern, distant, masterful, and often irritable father. For long after their marriage, Klara could not get out of the habit of calling him 'Uncle'.[52] And even after his death, she kept a rack of his pipes in the kitchen and would point to them on occasion when he was referred to, as if to invoke his authority.[53]

What affection the young children missed in their father was more than recompensed by their mother. According to the description given much later by her Jewish doctor, Eduard Bloch, after his own forced emigration from Nazi Germany, Klara Hitler was 'a simple, modest, kindly woman. She was tall, had brownish hair which she kept neatly plaited, and a long, oval face with beautifully expressive grey-blue eyes.'[54] In personality, she was submissive, retiring, quiet, a pious churchgoer, taken up in the running of the household, and above all absorbed in the care of her children and stepchildren. The deaths within weeks of each other of her first three children in infancy in 1887–8, and the subsequent death of her fifth child, Edmund, under the age of six in 1900, must have been hammer blows for her.[55] Her sorrows can only have been compounded by living with an irascible, unfeeling, overbearing husband. It is scarcely surprising that she made an impression of a saddened, careworn woman. Nor is it any wonder that she bestowed a smothering, protective love and devotion on her two surviving children, Adolf and Paula.[56] Klara was in turn held in love and affection by her children and stepchildren, by Adolf quite especially. 'Outwardly, his love for his mother was his most striking feature,' Dr Bloch later wrote. 'While he was not a "mother's boy" in the usual sense,' he added, 'I have never witnessed a closer attachment.'[57] In one of the few signs of human affection recorded in *Mein Kampf*, Adolf wrote 'I had honoured my father, but loved my mother.'[58] He carried her picture with him down to the last days in the bunker. Her portrait stood in his rooms in Munich, Berlin, and at the Obersalzberg (his alpine residence near Berchtesgaden).[59] His mother may well, in fact, have been the only person he genuinely loved in his entire life.

Adolf's early years were spent, then, under the smothering protectiveness of an over-anxious mother in a household dominated by the threatening presence of a disciplinarian father, against whose wrath the submissive Klara was helpless to protect her offspring. Adolf's younger sister, Paula, spoke after the war of her mother as 'a very soft and tender person, the compensatory element between the almost too harsh father and the very lively children who were perhaps somewhat difficult to train. If there were ever quarrel[s] or differences of opinion between my parents,' she continued, 'it was always on account of the children. It was especially my brother Adolf who challenged my father to extreme harshness and who got his sound thrashing every day . . . How often on the other hand did my mother caress him and try to obtain with her kindness what the father could not succeed [in obtaining] with harshness!'[60] Hitler himself, during his late-night fireside monologues in the 1940s, often recounted that his father had sudden bursts of temper and would then immediately hit out. He did not love his father, he said, but instead feared him all the more. His poor beloved mother, he used to remark, to whom he was so attached, lived in constant concern about the beatings he had to take, sometimes waiting outside the door as he was thrashed.[61]

Quite possibly, Alois's violence was also turned against his wife. A passage in *Mein Kampf*, in which Hitler ostensibly describes the conditions in a workers' family where the children have to witness drunken beatings of their mother by their father, may well have drawn in part on his own childhood experiences.[62] What the legacy of all this was for the way Adolf's character developed must remain a matter for speculation.[63] That its impact was profound is hard to doubt.

Beneath the surface, the later Hitler was unquestionably being formed. Speculation though it must remain, it takes little to imagine that his later patronizing contempt for the submissiveness of women, the thirst for dominance (and imagery of the Leader as stern, authoritarian father-figure), the inability to form deep personal relationships, the corresponding cold brutality towards humankind, and – not least – the capacity for hatred so profound that it must have reflected an immeasurable undercurrent of self-hatred concealed in the extreme narcissism that was its counterpoint must surely have had roots in the subliminal influences of the young Adolf's family circumstances. But assumptions have to remain guesswork. The outer traces of Adolf's early life, so far as they can be reconstructed, bear no hint of what would emerge. Attempts to find in the youngster 'the warped person within the murderous dictator' have proved unpersuasive.[64] If we exclude our knowledge of what was to come, his family circumstances invoke for the most part sympathy for the child exposed to them.[65]

I I

The childhood years were also punctuated by the instability caused by several changes of home. Alois's promotion in 1892 brought the move to Passau. Klara remained there with the children, now including the new baby Edmund, when her husband was assigned to Linz in April 1894. The separation from the family, interrupted only by brief visits, lasted a year. With his mother taken up by the new baby, and his stepsister and stepbrother Angela and Alois Jr busy with their schooling, Adolf had for a time the run of the house. He showed in these months the first signs of tantrums if he did not get his way.[66] He would remark much later that even as a boy he was used to having the last word.[67] But for the most part, he was free to play cowboys and Indians or war games to his heart's content.

In February 1895, Alois had bought a small farm in the hamlet of Hafeld, part of the community of Fischlham, near Lambach, some thirty miles away from Linz, and two months later the family joined him there. It was at the tiny primary school at Fischlham that Adolf began his schooling on 1 May 1895, and for the next two years he made good headway, attaining high marks for his schoolwork and behaviour.[68] Outside school, Adolf continued to have fun with his friends in outdoor games. At home, however, the tensions increased once Alois took retirement in June 1895 after forty years in the service of the Austrian state in order to devote himself to his bee-keeping. Alois was now present in the home more than ever before; the farm was too much for him and also a financial liability, the children – now with the further addition of baby Paula – trying his nerves. When Alois Jr left home at this time, incurring the wrath of his father, Adolf became, apart from baby Edmund, the only boy in the household and more directly exposed to his father's irritability.[69]

In 1897, Alois sold the Hafeld property and the family moved to temporary accommodation in the tiny market town of Lambach, moving house within Lambach again in early 1898. Adolf's schooling, now in Lambach, continued to produce good reports from his teachers, though he later claimed that he was already becoming 'rather hard to handle'.[70] At this time Adolf also went to the nearby monastery at Lambach for singing lessons – probably at the prompting of his father, who enjoyed choral singing. According to his later testimony, he was intoxicated by the ecclesiastical splendour and looked up to the abbot as the highest and most desirable ideal.[71]

Alois Hitler had always been a restless soul. The Hitlers had moved house several times within Braunau during the lengthy stay there, and had subsequently been uprooted on a number of occasions. In November 1898, a final move for Alois took place when he bought a house with a small plot of attached land in Leonding, a village on the outskirts of Linz. From now on, the family settled in the Linz area, and Adolf – down to his days in the bunker in 1945 – looked upon Linz as his home town.[72] Linz reminded him of the happy, carefree days of his youth.[73] It held associations with his mother. And it was the most 'German' town of the Austrian Empire. It evidently symbolized for him the provincial small-town Germanic idyll – the image he would throughout his life set against the city he would soon come to know, and detest: Vienna. In the 1940s he would speak repeatedly of making Linz the cultural counterweight to Vienna, and the most beautiful city on the Danube. He would pour vast sums into the town's reconstruction. With the Red Army at his portals, he was still poring over the model constructed by his architect, Hermann Giesler, of the city of his youth, where he had intended to spend his last days and lie buried.[74]

Adolf was now in his third elementary school. He seems to have established himself rapidly with a new set of schoolmates, and became 'a little ring-leader'[75] in the game of cops and robbers which the village boys played in the woods and fields around their homes.[76] War games were a particular favourite.[77] Adolf himself was thrilled by an illustrated history of the Franco-Prussian war, which he had come across at home.[78] And once the Boer War broke out, the games revolved around the heroic exploits of the Boers, whom the village boys fervently supported.[79] About this same time, Adolf became gripped by the adventure stories of Karl May, whose popular tales of the Wild West and Indian wars (though May had never been to America) enthralled thousands of youngsters. Most of these youngsters graduated from the Karl May adventures and the childhood fantasies they fostered as they grew up. For Adolf, however, the fascination with Karl May never faded.[80] As Reich Chancellor he still read the May stories, recommending them, too, to his generals, whom he accused of lacking imagination.[81]

Adolf later referred to 'this happy time', when 'school work was ridicu-lously easy, leaving me so much free time that the sun saw more of me than my room', when 'meadows and woods were then the battleground on which the ever-present "antagonisms"' – the growing conflict with his father – 'came to a head'.[82]

In 1900, however, the carefree days were drawing to a close. And just around the time when important decisions had to be made about Adolf's future, and the secondary education path he should follow, the Hitler family was once more plunged into distress with the death, through measles, of Adolf's little brother Edmund on 2 February 1900.[83] With Alois's elder son, Alois Jr, already spiting his father and living away from home, any careerist ambitions for his offspring now rested upon Adolf. They were to lead to tension between father and son in the remaining years of Alois's life.

Adolf began his secondary schooling on 17 September 1900. His father had opted for the *Realschule* rather than the *Gymnasium*, that is, for a school which attached less weight to the traditional classical and humanistic studies but was still seen as a preparation for higher education, with an emphasis upon more 'modern' subjects, including science and technical studies.[84] According to Adolf, his father was influenced by the aptitude his son already showed for drawing, together with a disdain for the impracticality of humanistic studies deriving from his own hard way to career advancement.[85] It was not the typical route for a would-be civil servant – the career which Alois had in mind for his son. But, then, Alois himself had made a good career in the service of the Austrian state with hardly any formal education at all to speak of.

The transition to secondary school was a hard one for young Adolf. He had to trek every day from his home in Leonding to school in Linz, a journey of over an hour each way, leaving him little or no time for developing out-of-school friendships. While he was still a big fish in a little pond among the village boys in Leonding, his classmates in his new school took no special notice of him. He had no close friends at school; nor did he seek any. And the attention he had received from his village teacher was now replaced by the more impersonal treatment of a number of teachers responsible for individual subjects. The minimum effort with which Adolf had mastered the demands of the primary school now no longer sufficed.[86] His school work, which had been so good in primary school, suffered from the outset. And his behaviour betrayed clear signs of immaturity.[87]

In his first year in his secondary school, 1900–1901, Adolf was recorded as 'unsatisfactory' in mathematics and natural history, ensuring that he had to repeat the year. His diligence was noted as 'variable'. There was some improvement during the repeated year, presumably following a wigging at home, but it was not sustained, and Adolf's school record, down to the time he left in autumn 1905, hovered between poor and mediocre.

In a letter to Hitler's defence counsel on 12 December 1923, following the failed putsch attempt in Munich, his former class teacher, Dr Eduard Huemer, recalled Adolf as a thin, pale youth commuting between Linz and Leonding, a boy not making full use of his talent, lacking in application, and unable to accommodate himself to school discipline. He characterized him as stubborn, high-handed, dogmatic, and hot-tempered. Strictures from his teachers were received with a scarcely concealed insolence. With his classmates he was domineering, and a leading figure in the sort of immature pranks which Huemer attributed to too great an addiction to Karl May's Indian stories together with a tendency to waste time furthered by the daily trip from Leonding and back.[88]

Whether in fact Hitler was a leading light among his schoolmates, as Huemer suggested, is doubtful. Other teachers and classmates claimed Hitler had not stood out at school in any particular fashion, either negatively or positively.[89]

There can be little doubting, however, that Hitler's attitude towards his school and teachers (with one exception) was scathingly negative. He left school 'with an elemental hatred' towards it, and later mocked and derided his schooling and teachers.[90] Only his history teacher, Dr Leonard Pötsch, was singled out for praise in *Mein Kampf* for firing Hitler's interest through vivid narratives and tales of heroism from the German past, stirring in him the strongly emotional German-nationalist, anti-Habsburg feelings (which were in any case widely prevalent in his school, as in Linz generally).[91]

The problems of adjustment that Adolf encountered in the *Realschule* in Linz were compounded by the deterioration in relations with his father and the running sore of the disputes over the boy's future career. Hitler's own account in *Mein Kampf* heroicizes his own defiance of his father's attempts to turn him into a civil servant and blames his poor performance in school upon this intentional rejection of his father's wishes.[92] This was an over-simplification. But there seems no doubt that his early years at the Linz school had a backcloth of conflict at home with his father. Even in the 1940s, Hitler recounted how he had been taken, when he was thirteen years old, into the Linz customs office to encourage him to take an interest in a civil service career, not realizing that it would only fill him with horror, hatred, and lasting disgust for the life of a civil servant.[93] For Alois, the virtues of a civil service career could not be gainsaid. But all his attempts to enthuse his son met with adamant rejection. 'I yawned and grew sick to my stomach at the thought of sitting in an office, deprived of my liberty; ceasing to be master of my own time,' wrote Adolf in *Mein Kampf*.[94]

The more Adolf resisted the idea, the more authoritarian and insistent his father became. Equally stubborn, when asked what he envisaged for his future, Adolf claimed he replied that he wanted to be an artist – a vision which for the dour Austrian civil servant Alois was quite unthinkable.

'Artist, no, never as long as I live!', Hitler has him saying.[95] Whether the young Adolf, allegedly at the age of twelve, so plainly stipulated he wanted to be an artist may be doubted. But that there was a conflict with his father arising from his unwillingness to follow a career in the civil service, and that his father found fault with his son's indolent and purposeless existence, in which drawing appeared to be his main interest, seems certain.[96] Alois had worked his way up through industry, diligence, and effort from humble origins to a position of dignity and respect in the state service. His son, from a more privileged background, saw fit to do no more than dawdle away his time drawing and dreaming, would not apply himself in school, had no career path in view, and scorned the type of career which had meant everything to his father. The dispute amounted, therefore, to more than a rejection of a civil service career. It was a rejection of everything his father had stood for; and with that, a rejection of his father himself.

There was an added dimension to the conflict between father and son. The almost homogeneously German population of the provincial town of Linz, numbering around 60,000, was strongly German nationalist, but politically divided in its expression of nationalist feelings. Hitler's father's nationalist sentiment was of the kind which vehemently supported the continued dominance of German interests within the Austrian state (especially at the time in the later 1890s when they seemed threatened by concessions made to the Czechs). He would have no truck, however, with the pan-German nationalism of the Schönerer variety – the ideas of the movement that had emerged in the 1870s, led by Georg Ritter von Schönerer – which rejected the Austrian state and lauded the virtues of Wilhelmine Germany. Adolf, on the other hand, was plainly drawn in his Linz school – a hotbed of German nationalism – to the symbols and incantations of the shriller Schönerer-style pan-German nationalism which, whatever its limited general appeal in Linz, found ready backers for its emotional appeal among the youth.[97] Adolf was not actively involved in any way with the Schönerer movement. But it is almost certain that the opinionated and disputatious son further riled his father through his pan-German ridiculing and deriding of the very state to which his father had devoted his life.[98]

Adolf's adolescence, as he commented in *Mein Kampf*, was 'very painful'.[99] With the move to the secondary school in Linz, and the start of the rumbling conflict with his father, an important formative phase in his character development had begun. The happy, playful youngster of the primary school days had grown into an idle, resentful, rebellious, sullen, stubborn, and purposeless teenager.

When, on 3 January 1903, his father collapsed and died over his usual morning glass of wine in the Gasthaus Wiesinger,[100] the conflict of will over Adolf's future was over. Alois had left his family in comfortable circumstances.[101] And whatever emotional adjustments were needed for his widow, Klara, it is unlikely that Adolf, now the only 'man about the house', grieved over his father.[102] With his father's death, much of the parental pressure was removed. His mother did her best to persuade Adolf to comply with his father's wishes. But she shied away from conflict and, however concerned she was about his future, was far too ready to give in to Adolf's whims.[103] In any case, his continued poor school performance in itself ruled out any realistic expectation that he would be qualified for a career in the civil service.

In 1902–3 – the year in which his father died – Adolf's school report again registered a failure in mathematics and he had to pass a re-sit examination before being allowed into a higher class. His application was once more recorded as 'variable', and remained so in 1903–4, when he was registered as 'unsatisfactory' in French. He was granted a pass in the re-sit examination, but only on condition that he leave the *Realschule* in Linz. At this failure, Adolf was removed to the *Realschule* in Steyr, some fifty miles away, where he had to take up lodgings because the school was too far from his home.[104] He recalled much later how sick at heart he was at being sent away to school, and how he detested Steyr to that very day.[105]

Adolf's performance at Steyr showed no initial improvement.[106] In his school report for the first semester in 1904–5 he gained good marks for physical education and drawing. His 'moral conduct' was satisfactory, his diligence 'variable', and he received mediocre results in religious instruction, geography and history (which he later claimed to have been his best subjects),[107] and chemistry, a marginally better grade in physics, but failures in the optional course in stenography and two obligatory subjects, German language and mathematics.[108] These failures, had they been continued in the second half of the school year, would have condemned him to yet another repeated year.[109] By September 1905, according to the report for the second semester, he had evidently applied himself better and was able to improve his grades and effort in most subjects, now passing mathematics and German, though failing in geometry, which meant a re-sit before being allowed to pass the final-year examination in the lower *Realschule*. On 16 September, Adolf returned to Steyr, and passed the re-sit in geometry. With this qualification, he was now eligible for consideration for entry to the higher *Realschule*, or to a technical school.[110] Whether he would have been admitted with his mediocre school record of the previous five years is doubtful.[111] But in any case Adolf by this time had no more stomach for schooling. He used illness – feigned, or most likely genuine but exaggerated[112] – to persuade his mother that he was not fit to continue school and in autumn 1905, at the age of sixteen, gladly put his schooling behind him for good with no clear future career path mapped out.[113]

The time between leaving school in autumn 1905 and his mother's death at the end of 1907 is passed over almost completely in *Mein Kampf*. From the vagueness of the account, it could be presumed that Klara's death followed two, not four, years after that of her husband, and that Adolf's time was spent in careful preparation for attendance at the Viennese Academy of Art, before orphanage and poverty meant that he had to fend for himself.[114] Reality was somewhat different.

In these two years, Adolf lived a life of parasitic idleness – funded, provided for, looked after, and cosseted by a doting mother, with his own room in the comfortable flat in the Humboldtstraße in Linz, which the family had moved into in June 1905. His mother, his aunt Johanna and his little sister Paula were there to look after all his needs, to wash, clean and cook for him. His mother even bought him a grand piano, on which he had lessons for four months between October 1906 and January 1907.[115] He spent his time during the days drawing, painting, reading, or writing 'poetry'; the evenings were for going to the theatre or opera; and the whole time he daydreamed and fantasized about his future as a great artist. He stayed up late into the night and slept long into the mornings. He had no clear aim in view.[116] The indolent lifestyle, the grandiosity of fantasy, the lack of discipline for systematic work – all features of the later Hitler – can be seen in these two years in Linz. It was little wonder that Hitler came to refer to this period as 'the happiest days which seemed to me almost like a beautiful dream'.[117]

A description of Adolf's carefree life in Linz between 1905 and 1907 is provided by the one friend he had at that time, August Kubizek, the son of a Linz upholsterer with dreams of his own about becoming a great musician. Kubizek's post-war memoirs need to be treated with care, both in factual detail and in interpretation. They are a lengthened and embellished version of recollections he had originally been commissioned by the Nazi Party to compile.[118] Even retrospectively, the admiration in which Kubizek continued to hold his former friend coloured his judgement. But more than that, Kubizek plainly invented a great deal, built some passages around Hitler's own account in *Mein Kampf,* and deployed some near plagiarism to amplify his own limited memory.[119] However, for all their weaknesses, his recollections have been shown to be a more credible source on Hitler's youth than was once thought, in particular where they touch upon experiences related to Kubizek's own interests in music and theatre.[120] There can be no doubt that, whatever their deficiencies, they do contain important reflections of the young Hitler's personality, showing features in embryo which were to be all too prominent in later years.

August Kubizek – 'Gustl' – was some nine months older than Adolf. They met by chance in autumn 1905 (not 1904, as Kubizek claimed)[121] at the opera in Linz. Adolf had for some years been a fanatical admirer of Wagner,[122] and his love of opera, especially the works of the 'master of Bayreuth', was shared by Kubizek. Gustl was highly impressionable; Adolf out for someone to impress. Gustl was compliant, weak-willed, subordinate; Adolf was superior, determining, dominant. Gustl felt strongly about little or nothing; Adolf had strong feelings about everything. 'He had to speak,' recalled Kubizek, 'and needed someone to listen to him.'[123] For his part, Gustl, from his artisanal background, having attended a lower school than the young Hitler, and feeling himself therefore both socially and educationally inferior, was filled with admiration at Adolf's power of expression. Whether Adolf was haranguing him about the deficiencies of civil servants, schoolteachers, local taxation, social welfare lotteries, opera performances, or Linz public buildings, Gustl was gripped as never before.[124] Not just what his friend had to say, but how he said it, was what he found attractive.[125] Gustl, in self-depiction a quiet, dreamy youth, had found an ideal foil in the opinionated, cocksure, 'know-all' Hitler. It was a perfect partnership.

In the evenings they would go off, dressed in their fineries, to the theatre or the opera, the pale and weedy young Hitler, sporting the beginnings of a thin moustache, looking distinctly foppish in his black coat and dark hat, the image completed by a black cane with an ivory handle.[126] After the performance Adolf would invariably hold forth, heatedly critical of the production, or effusively rapturous. Even though Kubizek was musically more gifted and knowledgeable than Hitler, he remained the passive and submissive partner in the 'discussions'.

Hitler's passion for Wagner knew no bounds.[127] A performance could affect him almost like a religious experience, plunging him into deep and mystical fantasies.[128] Wagner amounted for him to the supreme artistic genius, the model to be emulated.[129] Adolf was carried away by Wagner's powerful musical dramas, his evocation of a heroic, distant, and sublimely mystical Germanic past. *Lohengrin*, the saga of the mysterious knight of the grail, epitome of the Teutonic hero, sent from the castle of Monsalvat by his father Parzival to rescue the wrongly condemned pure maiden, Elsa, but ultimately betrayed by her, had been his first Wagner opera, and remained his favourite.[130]

Even more than music, the theme, when Adolf and Gustl were together, was great art and architecture. More precisely, it was Adolf as the future great artistic genius. The young, dandified Hitler scorned the notion of working to earn one's daily bread.[131] He enraptured the impressionable Kubizek with his visions of himself as a great artist, and Kubizek himself as a foremost musician. While Kubizek toiled in his father's workshop, Adolf filled his time with drawing and dreaming. He would then meet Gustl after work, and, as the friends wandered through Linz in the evenings, would lecture him on the need to tear down, remodel, and replace the central public buildings, showing his friend countless sketches of his rebuilding plans.[132]

The make-believe world also included Adolf's infatuation with a girl who did not even know of his existence. Stefanie, an elegant young lady in Linz to be seen promenading through the town on the arm of her mother, and occasionally greeted by an admirer among the young officers, was for Hitler an ideal to be admired from a distance, not approached in person, a fantasy figure who would be waiting for the great artist when the right moment for their marriage arrived, after which they would live in the magnificent villa that he would design for her.[133]

Another glimpse into the fantasy world is afforded by Adolf's plans for the future when, around 1906, the friends bought a lottery ticket together. Adolf was so certain they would win first prize that he designed an elaborate vision of their future residence. The two young men would live an artistic existence, tended by a middle-aged lady who could meet their artistic requirements – neither Stefanie nor any other woman of their own age figured in this vision – and would go off to Bayreuth and Vienna and make other visits of cultural value. So certain was Adolf that they would win, that his fury at the state lottery knew no bounds when nothing came of their little flutter.[134]

In spring 1906, Adolf persuaded his mother to fund him on a first trip to Vienna, allegedly to study the picture gallery in the Court Museum, more likely to fulfil a growing ambition to visit the cultural sites of the Imperial capital. For two weeks, perhaps longer, he wandered through Vienna as a tourist taking in the city's many attractions. With whom he stayed is unknown.[135] The four postcards he sent his friend Gustl and his comments in *Mein Kampf* show how captivated he was by the grandeur of the buildings and the layout of the Ringstraße. Otherwise, he seems to have spent his time in the theatre and marvelling at the Court Opera, where Gustav Mahler's productions of Wagner's *Tristan* and *The Flying Dutchman* left those of provincial Linz in the shade.[136] Nothing had changed on his return home. But the sojourn in Vienna furthered the idea, probably already growing in his mind, that he would develop his artistic career at the Viennese Academy of Fine Arts.[137]

By the summer of 1907, this idea had taken more concrete shape. Adolf was now aged eighteen but had still never earned a day's income and was continuing his drone's life without career prospects. Despite the advice of relatives that it was about time he found a job, he had persuaded his mother to let him return to Vienna, this time with the intention of entering the Academy.[138] Whatever her reservations, the prospect of systematic study at the Academy in Vienna must have seemed to her an improvement on his aimless existence in Linz. And she did not need to worry about her son's material welfare. Adolf's 'Hanitante' – Aunt Johanna – had come up with a loan of 924 Kronen to fund her nephew's artistic studies. It gave him something like a year's salary for a young lawyer or teacher.[139]

By this stage, his mother was seriously ill with breast cancer. She had already been operated on in January, and in the spring and early summer was frequently treated by the Jewish family doctor, Dr Bloch.[140] Frau Klara – now in the new family home at Urfahr, a suburb of Linz – must have been seriously worried not only about the mounting medical costs, but about her eleven-year-old daughter Paula, still at home and looked after by Aunt Johanna, and about her darling boy Adolf, still without a clear future. Adolf, described by Dr Bloch as a tall, sallow, frail-looking boy who 'lived within himself', was certainly worried about his mother. He settled the bill of 100 Kronen for her twenty-day stay in hospital at the start of the year.[141] He wept when Dr Bloch had to tell him and his sister the bad news that their mother had little chance of surviving her cancer.[142] He tended her during her illness and was anguished at the intense pain she suffered.[143] He had, it seems, to take responsibility for whatever decisions had to be made about her care.[144] Despite his mother's deteriorating condition, however, Adolf went ahead with his plans to move to Vienna. He left for the capital in early September 1907, in time to take the entrance examination for the Academy of Fine Arts.

Admission to the examination itself was decided on the basis of an entry test resting on assessment of pieces of work presented by the candidates.

Adolf had, he later wrote, left home 'armed with a thick pile of drawings'.[145] He was one of 113 candidates and was allowed to proceed to the examination itself. Thirty-three candidates were excluded following this initial test.[146] At the beginning of October, he sat the two tough three-hour examinations in which the candidates had to produce drawings on specified themes. Only twenty-eight candidates succeeded. Hitler was not among them. 'Test drawing unsatisfactory. Few heads,' was the verdict.[147]

It apparently never occurred to the supremely self-confident Adolf that he might fail the entrance examination for the Academy. He had been, he wrote in *Mein Kampf*, 'convinced that it would be child's play to pass the examination . . . I was so convinced that I would be successful that when I received my rejection, it struck me as a bolt from the blue.'[148] He sought an explanation, and was told by the Rector of the Academy that there was no doubt about his unsuitability for the school of painting, but that his talents plainly lay in architecture. Hitler left the interview, as he put it, 'for the first time in my young life at odds with myself'. After a few days pondering his fate, he concluded, so he wrote, that the Rector's judgement was right, and 'that I should some day become an architect' – not that he then or later did anything to remedy the educational deficiencies which provided a major obstacle to studying for a career in architecture.[149] In reality, Adolf probably did not bounce back anything like so quickly as his own story suggests, and the fact that he reapplied the following year for admission to the painting school casts some doubt on the version of a lightning recognition that his future was as an architect. At any rate, the rejection by the Academy was such a body blow to his pride that he kept it a secret. He avoided telling either his friend Gustl, or his mother, of his failure.[150]

Meanwhile, Klara Hitler lay dying. The sharp deterioration in her condition brought Adolf back from Vienna to be told by Dr Bloch, towards the end of October, that his mother's condition was hopeless.[151] Deeply affected by the news, Adolf was more than dutiful. Both his sister, Paula, and Dr Bloch later testified to his devoted and 'indefatigable' care for his dying mother.[152] But despite Dr Bloch's close medical attention, Klara's health worsened rapidly during the autumn. On 21 December 1907, aged forty-seven, she passed away quietly.[153] Though he had witnessed many deathbed scenes, recalled Dr Bloch, 'I have never seen anyone so prostrate with grief as Adolf Hitler.'[154] His mother's death was 'a dreadful blow', Hitler wrote in *Mein Kampf*, 'particularly for me'.[155] He felt alone and bereft at her passing.[156] He had lost the one person for whom he had ever felt close affection and warmth.

'Poverty and hard reality,' Hitler later claimed, 'now compelled me to take a quick decision. What little my father had left had been largely exhausted by my mother's grave illness; the orphan's pension to which I was entitled was not enough for me even to live on, and so I was faced with the problem of somehow making my own living.'[157] When after her death he returned to Vienna for the third time, he continued, now to stay for some years, his old defiance and determination had come back to him, and his goal was now clear: 'I wanted to become an architect and obstacles do not exist to be surrendered to, but only to be broken.' He claimed he set out to overcome the obstacles, inspired by the example of his own father's rise through his own efforts from poverty to the position of a government official.[158]

In reality, his mother's careful housekeeping – aided by not insignificant contributions from her sister Johanna – had left more than sufficient to pay for the considerable medical costs, as well as a relatively expensive funeral.[159] Nor was Adolf left nearly penniless. There was no question of immediately having to earn his own living. Certainly, the monthly orphan's pension of 25 Kronen which he and his younger sister Paula – now brought up by their half-sister Angela and her husband Leo Raubal – received could scarcely provide for his upkeep in inflation-ridden Austria. And apart from interest, Adolf and Paula could not touch the inheritance from their father until their twenty-fourth year. But what his mother had left – perhaps in the region of 2,000 Kronen once the funeral expenses had been covered – was divided between the two orphaned minors. Adolf's share, together with his orphan's pension, was enough to provide for his upkeep in Vienna for a year without work.[160] And on top of that, he still had the residue of his aunt's generous loan. He scarcely had the financial security which has sometimes been attributed to him.[161] But, all in all, his financial position was, during this time, substantially better than that of most genuine students in Vienna.[162]

Moreover, Adolf was in less of a hurry to leave Linz than he implies in *Mein Kampf*. Though his sister almost forty years later stated that he moved to Vienna within a few days of their mother's death, Adolf was still recorded as in Urfahr in mid-January and mid-February 1908.[163] Unless, as seems unlikely, he made brief visits to Vienna between these dates, it looks as if he stayed in Urfahr for at least seven weeks after the death of his mother.[164] The family household account-book indicates that the break with Linz was not made before May.[165]

When he did return to Vienna, in February 1908, it was not to pursue with all vigour the necessary course of action to become an architect, but

BLANDING LIBRARY
REHOBOTH MA 02769

to slide back into the life of indolence, idleness, and self-indulgence which he had followed before his mother's death. He even now worked on Kubizek's parents until they reluctantly agreed to let August leave his work in the family upholstery business to join him in Vienna in order to study music.[166]

His failure to enter the Academy and his mother's death, both occurring within less than four months in late 1907, amounted to a crushing double blow for the young Hitler. He had been abruptly jolted from his dream of an effortless path to the fame of a great artist; and the sole person upon whom he depended emotionally had been lost to him at almost the same time. His artistic fantasy remained. Any alternative – such as settling down to a steady job in Linz – was plainly an abhorrent thought. A neighbour in Urfahr, the widow of the local postmaster, later recalled: 'When the postmaster asked him one day what he wanted to do for a living and whether he wouldn't like to join the post office, he replied that it was his intention to become a great artist. When he was reminded that he lacked the necessary funding and personal connections, he replied tersely: "Makart and Rubens worked themselves up from poor backgrounds." '[167] How he might emulate them was entirely unclear. His only hope rested upon retaking the entrance examination for the Academy the following year. He must have known his chances were not high. But he did nothing to enhance them. Meanwhile, he had to get by in Vienna.

Despite the drastic alteration in his prospects and circumstances, Adolf's lifestyle – the drifting existence in an egoistic fantasy-world – remained unchanged. But the move from the cosy provincialism of Linz to the political and social melting-pot of Vienna nevertheless marked a crucial transition. The experiences in the Austrian capital were to leave an indelible mark on the young Hitler and to shape decisively the formation of his prejudices and phobias.

2

DROP-OUT

'Wherever I went, I now saw Jews, and the more I saw, the more sharply they set themselves apart in my eyes from the rest of humanity.'

Hitler, in *Mein Kampf*

'In those days Hitler was by no means a Jew hater. He became one afterward.' Reinhold Hanisch, a friend of Hitler in 1909–10

'I owe it to that period that I grew hard.' Hitler was referring to the years he spent in Vienna between February 1908 and May 1913, when he left the Austrian capital for Munich and the beginning of a new life in Germany. The 'mother's darling' had lost his 'soft downy bed' and the carefree existence he had enjoyed in Linz. Instead of 'the hollowness of comfortable life', he was now thrown into 'a world of misery and poverty', with 'Dame Care' as his new mother. Even as he dictated *Mein Kampf*, during his internment in Landsberg in 1924, Vienna aroused in Hitler only 'dismal thoughts' of 'the saddest period' of his life.

But the Vienna years, Hitler stressed, were crucial to the formation of his character and his political philosophy. 'In this period my eyes were opened to two menaces of which I had previously scarcely known the names . . . : Marxism and Jewry.' The social and political naïvety with which he arrived in the city was during this time replaced, he claimed, by the 'world-view' that formed the 'granite foundation' of his political struggle.[1] His own account of these years, spread over two chapters of *Mein Kampf*,[2] describes graphically how deprivation, dire poverty, life among the dregs of society, and avid study brought him political understanding and the decisive shaping of his 'world-view'. 'Vienna was and remained for me,' wrote Hitler more than a decade after he had left the city, 'the hardest, though most thorough, school of my life.'[3]

Hitler was writing, as always in his public statements, for effect. By 1924 the failed putsch, fiasco though it was, and the subsequent trial that he had turned into a propaganda triumph had brought him celebrity on the extreme nationalist Right. But the Nazi Party was by then banned, and the *völkisch* movement hopelessly divided. Hitler was seeking in *Mein Kampf* to establish sole and undisputed claim to leadership of the *völkisch* Right. The heroic image of a genius whose unique personality and 'world-view' had been forged through the triumph of willpower over adversity was the basis of that claim. It was largely myth. National leaders who emerged from the traditional ruling classes and background – a Bismarck, say, or a Churchill – left few mysteries in their early development. But the very contrast between Hitler's early anonymity – culminating in his disappearance into the black hole of Vienna's doss-houses – and his later elevation to almost demi-god status invited both myth and counter-myth.

The autobiographical parts of Hitler's tract were not, then, written with an eye to their factual correctness, but only to their political purpose. But an accurate reconstruction of Hitler's period in Vienna is far from easy.[4] Much, apart from the evidence of Mein Kampf itself, has to rest upon the testimony – in varying degrees questionable – of four individuals: August Kubizek, Reinhold Hanisch, Karl Honisch (despite the similarity in name not to be confused with Hanisch), and a further passing acquaintance who remains anonymous. Each knew Hitler for only brief periods during his stay in Vienna.[5] A fifth alleged eye-witness account, that of Josef Greiner, like the others compiled many years after the events it purported to describe, has been used by most historians writing on this part of Hitler's life, but is, in fact, largely if not wholly a fabrication – so thoroughly flawed and discredited that it has to be discounted.[6] Many details, some of them significant, of Hitler's Vienna years remain unclear. Not least, how and when Hitler's 'world-view' came to be formed is far less evident than his own account suggests. Yet, whatever the uncertainties, there can be no doubting that the Vienna 'schooling' did indeed stamp its lasting imprint on his development.

I

The city where Hitler was to live for five years was an extraordinary place. More than any other European metropolis, Vienna epitomized tensions – social, cultural, political – that signalled the turn of an era, the death of the nineteenth-century world.[7] They were to mould the young Hitler.[8]

Vienna in the first years of the twentieth century was a city of contradictions. The capital radiated imperial grandeur, dazzling opulence and splendour, cultural excitement, and intellectual fervour. But behind its resplendent royal palaces, imposing civic buildings, elegant cafés, spacious parks and splendid boulevards, behind its pomp and glitter, lay some of the direst poverty and human misery in Europe. It oozed bourgeois solidity and respectability, self-righteousness, moral rectitude, refined manners, and proper etiquette. But beneath the surface, vice, prostitution, and criminality were rampant. It offered the very limits of the avant-garde, the pinnacle of innovation and modernism, outshining even Paris and Berlin in the brilliance of its cultural and intellectual life. But both cultural traditionalism and popular philistinism fiercely resisted the new art, antagonized by those with whose artistic and intellectual achievements – Klimt and the Sezession, Schnitzler, Hofmannsthal, Mahler, Schönberg, Otto Wagner, Freud – the city is indelibly linked. The long reign of Franz Joseph on the Habsburg throne implied the stability of an ancient empire. But in reality it was an empire wracked by modern nationalist and ethnic conflict, ill at ease with itself, struggling to cope with new social and political forces pulling it apart, decaying. Fear and anxiety were in the air. Germans felt their culture, way of life, living-standards, and status under threat. The liberal bourgeoisie felt pessimistic about the future, menaced by the new forces of mass politics and democracy; small traders and craftsmen resented department stores, large outlets, and modern mass-production; the rise of organized labour reminded them too of Marx's prophecy that they were doomed to slide into the proletariat. The mood of disintegration and decay, anxiety and impotence, the sense that the old order was passing, the climate of a society in crisis, was unmistakable.[9]

It was easy to transfer the impotent anger and fear into race hatred – above all into hatred of Jews, the 'supra-national people of the multi-national state'.[10] The uncrowned king of Vienna, its mayor Karl Lueger, whom Hitler greatly admired, and Vienna's gutter press that supported him, which Hitler read with relish, were adept at it.[11] No major city apart from Berlin had grown as fast as Vienna in the second half of the nineteenth century. Its population had increased two-and-a-half-fold between 1860 and 1900 – four times the growth of Paris or London.[12] Of the 1,674,957 residents of Vienna in 1900, fewer than one in two had been born there.[13] Many had poured into it from the eastern parts of the massive empire of over 50 million, with its ethnic mix of Germans, Czechs, Slovaks, Poles, Ruthenians, Slovenes, Serbs, Croats, Italians, Rumanians and Hungarians. Among them was a sizeable minority of Jews. Vienna's Jewish population was larger than that of any German city at the time. In mid-century, there had been only a little over 6,000 Jews in Vienna, some 2 per cent of the population. By 1910 this had risen to 175,318 Jews, or 8.6 per cent of the population.[14] As in Germany, Jews had historically had a strong presence – far greater than their numbers in the population – in the professions, academic life, the mass media, the arts, and in business and finance.[15] And as in Germany, Jews had striven to be assimilated to liberal society and German culture.[16] Different to German cities, however, was the stratum of poor Jews, similar to that in a good number of east European towns and cities. Many were Galician, or were descendants of families that had originally fled from the pogroms in Russia. Among these poorer sectors of the Jewish community, accepted by none, hated by many, doctrines of Marxism and Zionism (whose founder, Theodor Herzl, had grown up in Vienna) held some appeal.[17] Conveniently, therefore, Jews could be blamed both as capitalist exploiters and as social revolutionaries. The poorer Jews lived in the old city, and especially in the run-down districts in the north of Vienna. In Leopoldstadt, the site of the old ghetto, a third of the down-at-heel population was Jewish, mainly small traders and pedlars, often dressed in the traditional caftan and black hat. In adjacent Brigittenau, the depressing district where Hitler would spend his last three years in Vienna, some 17 per cent of the inhabitants were Jews.[18] This was the setting in which Hitler would be fully subjected to race hatred. Repelled by the 'conglomeration of races' in the capital, he later wrote: 'to me the giant city seemed the embodiment of racial desecration (*Blutschande*)'.[19]

On the Habsburg throne he had occupied for more than fifty years, Kaiser Franz Joseph signified unchangeability in a changing world. His court at the Hofburg, or in summer at the Schönbrunn Palace, retained all the gilt and glitter, the pomp and circumstance, of past centuries. Power in the vast and sprawling multi-ethnic empire stretching from the Carpathians to the Adriatic was still in the hands of ministers, all from traditional noble families, directly appointed by the Kaiser. But beneath the façade, the edifice was crumbling. New social and political pressures were undermining the foundations.

The empire was increasingly beset by its mounting internal contradictions. The granting, in the complex constitutional arrangement of 1867, following the defeat in the 'German brothers' war' the previous year, of near autonomy to Magyar national leaders in the Hungarian half of the Dual Monarchy had stirred nationalist feelings throughout the empire. Slavs became increasingly resentful of the continued domination of the Magyars and, in the Austrian 'half' of the empire, of the German-speaking minority – only around a third of the population even there.[20] The Austrian Germans, enjoying disproportionate prosperity, position, and power, responded by ever shriller defence of their advantage. Attempted concessions made to national demands, as in the proposed Badeni reforms of 1897 which sought to grant the Czech language equality with German in Bohemia and Moravia, massively exacerbated the tensions.[21] By the beginning of the new century, these tensions were reflected in bitter forms of mass politics, superseding the liberal factionalism of the bourgeois notables and threatening to tear apart the fragile balance of the empire and the semblance of Imperial unity personalized in the Emperor and King. Any dignity of parliament (where Germans after the introduction of universal male suffrage in 1907 were no longer the strongest national group)[22] had collapsed in the face of the vituperation and threatening rhetoric of nationalist fanatics.[23] Sessions could be chaotic – a heady mixture of nationalist and class politics frequently reducing them to a shambolic farce. A bill in February 1909, again aiming to put the Czech language on an equal footing to German in Bohemia, had, for instance, to be abandoned and the parliamentary session suspended when a cacophony of noise from rattles, bells, children's trumpets, horns, and banging desk-lids rendered debate impossible, leading to fisticuffs amid chaotic scenes while rival sets of deputies chimed in with competing anthems.[24] Laws could only be passed by horse-trading between the numerous interests and factions represented. The unseemly spectacle of squabbling deputies trading multilingual insults, and even swapping blows, was capable of alienating any observer.[25] It certainly filled the young pan-German supporter Adolf Hitler with the lasting contempt and revulsion for parliamentarism that poured out when he wrote of his Vienna experience more than a decade and a half later.[26]

Most responsible for introducing the raucous aggression of nationalist agitation into parliament was Georg Ritter von Schönerer. Born in Vienna in 1842 to wealthy parents, Schönerer became a modernizing and benevolent landlord in the Waldviertel, the poor region on the borders of Bohemia where Hitler's own forebears had their smallholdings. He was deeply affected by Austria's defeat at the hands of Prussia in 1866 at the battle of Königgrätz. Shame at Austria's exclusion from the German Federation, adulation of Bismarck, and, eventually, agitation aimed at the reuniting of Austria with the German Reich followed. He had first come to prominence in the 1870s as the voice of German small farmers and radicalized artisans, castigating the rapaciousness of big business and liberal laissez-faire economics.[27] His programme came to embrace an early brand of 'national socialism' – above all else radical German nationalism (meaning the primacy and superiority of all things German), social reform, anti-liberal popular democracy, and racial antisemitism. 'The strongest and most thoroughly consistent anti-Semite that Austria produced'[28] – before Hitler, that is – Schönerer's antisemitism was the cement of his anti-liberal, anti-socialist, anti-Catholic, and anti-Habsburg ideology. Hitler had imbibed the Schönerer creed in nationalist

Linz. The 'Heil' greeting, the title of 'Führer' (bestowed by Schönerer on himself and used by his followers), and the intolerance towards any semblance of democratic decision-making in his movement were among the lasting elements of the Schönerer legacy which Hitler carried over to the later Nazi Party.[29]

By the time Hitler came to Vienna, popular support for the ageing Schönerer had dwindled and fragmented. Schönerer had, in any case, never advocated a mass party, believing that, as always in the course of history, any breakthrough would come from a loyal elite.[30] His appeal had always been primarily located in student circles and among the nationalist middle classes.[31] Schönerer's programme, of which Hitler later wrote so approvingly, had, however, if anything hardened and become more radical and implacable in its demands for integral connection with Germany, in its boundless adoration of Kaiser Wilhelm and his German Reich, its 'away-from-Rome' church policy, and its attacks on the Habsburg polyglot state, all laced together with ferocious racial antisemitism.[32] Though he thought Schönerer's political philosophy correct, Hitler would later criticize his readiness to participate in sterile parliamentarism, his mistake in antagonizing the Catholic Church, and above all his neglect of the masses.[33] This was where Hitler was prepared to learn from his second Austrian political hero, Karl Lueger, the Viennese 'tribune of the people'.

The rise of Lueger's Christian Social Party made a deep impression on Hitler.[34] Starting as a Schönerer supporter, he came increasingly to admire Lueger. The main reason lay in the presentation of politics. Where Schönerer neglected the masses, Lueger, as Hitler approvingly recognized, gained his support by 'winning over the classes whose existence was threatened', the small- and lower-middle classes and artisans.[35] With a heady brew of populist rhetoric and accomplished rabble-rousing, Lueger soldered together an appeal to Catholic piety and the economic self-interest of the German-speaking lower-middle classes who felt threatened by the forces of international capitalism, Marxist Social Democracy, and Slav nationalism. Like Schönerer, the vehicle used to whip up the support of the disparate targets of his agitation was antisemitism, sharply on the rise among artisanal groups suffering economic downturns and only too ready to vent their resentment both on Jewish financiers and on the growing number of Galician back-street hawkers and pedlars. Back in the 1880s, he had supported Schönerer's bill to block Jewish immigration into Vienna.[36] But unlike Schönerer's, Lueger's antisemitism was more functional and pragmatic than ideological: 'I say who a Jew is' ('*Wer a Jud ist, bestimm i!*'), was a phrase commonly attributed to him.[37] It was more political and economic – the coating for an attack on liberalism and capitalism – than it was doctrinally racial.[38]

But it was nasty all the same. In a speech in 1890, he had quoted with no dissent a remark made by one of Vienna's wildest antisemites, that the 'Jewish problem' would be solved, and a service to the world achieved, if all Jews were placed on a large ship to be sunk on the high seas.[39] By the time Emperor Franz Joseph was compelled to retreat from his earlier refusal and to appoint 'handsome Karl' to be Lord Mayor of Vienna in 1897, the overt antisemitism had been sublimated into a programme of social reform, municipal renewal, populist democracy, and loyalty to the Habsburg monarchy all welded together by popular Catholicism.[40] But it remained vitriolic – in sentiment little different from the poison Hitler would later spread in the beerhalls of Munich. In a speech in 1899, to thunderous applause, Lueger spoke, for instance, of Jews exercising a 'terrorism, worse than which cannot be imagined' over the masses through the control of capital and the press. It was a matter for him, he continued, 'of liberating the Christian people from the domination of Jewry'.[41] On another occasion, he declared wolves, leopards, and tigers to be more human than the Jews – 'these beasts of prey in human form'.[42] When taken to task for stirring up hatred of the Jews through his agitation, he retorted that antisemitism would 'perish when the last Jew perished'.[43] Accused of saying that it was a matter of indifference to him whether Jews were hanged or shot, he provided the correction: 'Beheaded! is what I said.'[44]

When Hitler came to live in Vienna, it was Lueger's city. Two years later, on Lueger's death, Hitler was among the mourning thousands who watched his funeral cortège pass by.[45] Lueger's pro-Habsburg, Catholic programme held little appeal for him. And in his later appraisal of Lueger, he criticized the shallowness and artificiality of the antisemitism on which his Christian Social Party had been built.[46] But what he took from the Viennese mayor was Lueger's command of the masses, the moulding of a movement 'to attain his purposes', his use of propaganda to influence 'the psychological instincts' of the broad mass of his supporters.[47] That is what endured.

Following in the wake of liberalism's demise and forming the third new current of Viennese mass politics besides nationalism and Christian Socialism was Social Democracy. Here, too, Hitler's Vienna years were to leave lasting impressions. His fear of organized labour dated back to this time.

The Social Democrats had won no seats in the 1891 elections, three years after the foundation of the Social Democratic Workers' Party.[48] But in the year that Hitler moved to Vienna, 1907, they won eighty-seven out of 516

Reichsrat seats in the first election held under universal male suffrage.[49] It was nowhere near a controlling representation. But a third of the votes cast in Lueger's own domain of Vienna, and 41 per cent of all votes in Bohemia, was by any reckoning impressive.[50] The party, led by Viktor Adler, from a wealthy Prague Jewish family, was committed to a Marxist programme that it saw, somewhat along the lines of Bernstein revisionism, coming to fruition through evolution within the existing framework of the Austro-Hungarian multinational state.[51] Internationalism (though in fact there was a growing schism between German and Czech Social Democrats),[52] equality of individuals and peoples, universal, equal, and direct suffrage, fundamental labour and union rights, separation of church and state, and a people's army were what the Social Democrats stood for.[53] It was little wonder that the young Hitler, avid supporter of Schönerer's pan-Germanism, hated the Social Democrats with every fibre of his body. But what did impress him was their organization and activism.[54] In autumn 1905, just before Hitler went to Vienna, it had been Social Democratic agitation that had influenced Franz Joseph to agree, in the wake of the concessions made by the Tsar following the Russian revolution that year, to universal male suffrage.[55] The demonstration of approaching a quarter of a million workers in red armbands that followed in Vienna in late November took four hours to march past the Parliament building.[56] A similar spectacle some years later was to leave a lasting impression on Hitler, as he stood for nearly two hours, gazing at 'the endless columns of a mass demonstration of Viennese workers that took place one day as they marched past four abreast', 'watching with bated breath the gigantic human dragon slowly winding by'. It struck him as 'a menacing army', and his reaction, as he made his way home, was one of 'oppressed anxiety'. But from Social Democracy, he said later, he also learnt the value of intimidation and intolerance, that 'the psyche of the great masses is not receptive to anything that is half-hearted and weak'.[57]

Such lessons were all in the future when Hitler made his way back to Vienna in early 1908. Politics were not in his mind then, or in the months that followed.

II

The eighteen-year-old Adolf Hitler left Linz for Vienna in February 1908. He kept up the connection with the family home at least until May.[58] In August, probably in the hope of shoring up his dwindling funds, he visited his relatives in the Waldviertel.[59] But after the death of his mother, his family held few attractions for him. Letters home soon dried up.[60] The only relative of real interest was his Aunt Johanna, now back in the Waldviertel, whose life-savings had already provided him with financial support.[61] After her death in 1911, the links with his family faded and were not revived for many years.[62]

Following his mother's death, his guardian, Josef Mayrhofer, a simple man of peasant stock and mayor of Leonding, tried once more to persuade him to take up the apprenticeship as a baker that he had found for him. Adolf was contemptuous.[63] Equally vain was a last attempt by Aunt Johanna to get him to follow in his father's footsteps and join the civil service.[64] Once family matters following his mother's death had been settled, and the Raubals had agreed to look after his sister, Paula, Adolf went to see his guardian, in January 1908, and simply told him he was going back to Vienna. Mayrhofer later recounted that it was pointless trying to dissuade him: he was as stubborn as his father had been.[65] The decision to move to Vienna had, in fact, already been taken the previous summer. Anticipating that he would be studying at the Academy of Fine Arts, he had in late September or the beginning of October rented a small room on the second floor of a house in Stumpergasse 31, near the Westbahnhof in Vienna, owned by a Czech woman, Frau Zakreys.[66] This is where he returned, some time between 14 and 17 February 1908, to pick up where he had left off before his mother's death.

He was not long alone. We can recall that he had persuaded August Kubizek's parents to let their son join him in Vienna to carry out his studies to become a musician. Kubizek's father had been most reluctant to let his son go off with someone he regarded as no more than a failure at school and who thought himself above learning a proper trade.[67] But Adolf had prevailed. On 18 February he sent a postcard to his friend, urging him to come as quickly as possible. 'Dear Friend,' he wrote, 'am anxiously expecting news of your arrival. Write soon so that I can prepare everything for your festive welcome. The whole of Vienna is awaiting you.' A postscript added: 'Beg you again, come soon.'[68] Four days later, Gustl's tearful parents bade him goodbye, and he left to join his friend in Vienna. Adolf met a tired Kubizek at the station that evening, took him back to Stumpergasse to stay the first night, but, typically, insisted on immediately showing him all the sights of Vienna. How could someone come to Vienna and go to bed without first seeing the Court Opera House? So Gustl was dragged off to view the opera building, St Stephen's cathedral (which could scarcely be seen through the mist), and the lovely church of St Maria am Gestade. It was after midnight when they returned to Stumpergasse, and later still when an exhausted Kubizek fell asleep with Hitler still haranguing him about the grandeur of Vienna.[69]

The next few months were to be a repeat, on a grander scale, of the lifestyle of the two youths in Linz.[70] An early search for lodgings for Gustl was rapidly given up, and Frau Zakreys was persuaded to swap her larger room and move into the cramped little room that Hitler had occupied.[71] Adolf and his friend now occupied the same room, paying double the rent (10 Kronen each) that Hitler had paid for his earlier room.[72] Within the next few days, Kubizek learnt that he had passed the entrance examination and been accepted for study at the Vienna Conservatoire. He rented a grand piano which took up most of the available space in the room, just allowing Hitler the three paces to do his usual stomping backwards and forwards.[73] Apart from the piano, the room was furnished with simple necessities: two beds, a commode, a wardrobe, a washstand, a table, and two chairs.[74]

Kubizek settled down into a regular pattern of music study. What Hitler was up to was less clear to his friend. He stayed in bed in the mornings, was missing when Kubizek came back from the Conservatoire at lunchtimes, hung around the grounds of Schönbrunn Palace on fine afternoons, pored over books, fantasized over grandiose architectural and writing plans, and spent a good deal of time drawing until late into the night. Gustl's puzzlement about how his friend could combine so much leisure time with studying at the Academy of Fine Arts was ended only after some considerable time. A show of irritation about Kubizek practising his piano scales led to a full-scale row between the two friends about study timetables and ended in Hitler shouting that 'the whole Academy ought to be blown up', exploding with rage about the 'old-fashioned, fossilized civil servants, bureaucrats, devoid of understanding, stupid lumps of officials' who ran it. He then admitted that 'they rejected me, they threw me out, they turned me down'.[75] When Gustl asked him what, then, he was going to do, Hitler rounded on him: 'What now, what now? . . . Are you starting too: what now?'[76] The truth was, Hitler had no idea where he was going or what he would do. He was drifting aimlessly.

Kubizek had plainly touched a raw nerve. Adolf had for mercenary reasons not told his family about his failure to enter the Academy. Otherwise, his guardian would probably have denied him the 25 Kronen a month he received as his share of the orphan's pension.[77] And he would have come under even more pressure to find a job. But why did he deceive his friend?

For a teenager to fail to pass an extremely tough entrance examination is in itself neither unusual nor shameful. But Adolf could evidently not bear to tell his friend, to whom he had always claimed to be so superior in all matters of artistic judgement, and whose own studies at the Conservatoire had started so promisingly, of his rejection. The blow to his self-esteem had been profound. And the bitterness showed. According to Kubizek, he would fly off the handle at the slightest thing.[78] His loss of self-confidence could flare up in an instant into boundless anger and violent denunciation of all who he thought were persecuting him. 'Choking with his catalogue of hates, he would pour his fury over everything, against mankind in general who did not understand him, who did not appreciate him and by whom he was persecuted and cheated.'[79] On another occasion, railing against the lack of 'understanding for true artistry' at the Academy, he spoke of traps laid – Kubizek claimed to remember his exact words – 'for the sole purpose of ruining his career'.[80] 'Altogether, in these early days in Vienna,' commented Kubizek, 'I had the impression that Adolf had become unbalanced.'[81] The tirades of hate directed at everything and everybody were those of an outsized ego desperately wanting acceptance and unable to come to terms with his personal insignificance, with failure and mediocrity.

Adolf had still not given up hope of entering the Academy. But, typically, he took no steps to ensure that his chances would be better a second time round. Just before he left Linz, he had been given an introduction, arranged by the owner of the block of flats in Urfahr where the Hitlers lived, to Professor Alfred Roller, brilliant stage designer at the Court Opera and a prominent member of the Viennese cultural scene, who offered to talk to Hitler when he came to Vienna.[82] Hitler made no use of the recommendation.[83] That alone suggests there is nothing in the suggestion that Adolf, through Roller's help, took art lessons under the guidance of a sculptor by the name of Panholzer.[84] Systematic preparation and hard work were as foreign to the young Hitler as they would be to the later dictator. Instead, his time was largely spent in dilettante fashion, as it had been in Linz, devising grandiose schemes shared only with the willing Kubizek – fantasy plans that usually arose from sudden whims and bright ideas and were dropped almost as soon as they had begun.[85]

One idea was to write a play. Kubizek was astonished when Adolf showed him a few hastily written sides describing the Wagnerian-style scene for a drama he intended to write, set in the Bavarian Alps at the time of the arrival of Christianity.[86] The project was taken no further. It was the same with a number of other supposed dramas, each derived from Germanic

mythology, all with an eye particular to the massive scale of the production
– dwarfing even the most pretentious Wagnerian settings. The more down-to-
earth Kubizek pointed out that it would be impossible to finance such
productions, but Hitler contemptuously dismissed suggestions for more
modest ventures.[87]

The Wagnerian model was even more evident in the idea Hitler had of
writing an opera. A chance remark by Kubizek that he had heard in one of
his music lectures that Wagner's writings included a brief sketch for a
musical drama of *Wieland the Smith* led to Hitler immediately looking up
the saga in a book he had on *Gods and Heroes*, then starting to write the
same night. The following day, sitting at the piano, Hitler told Kubizek he
was going to turn *Wieland* into an opera. He would compose the music and
Kubizek would write it down. For days, despite difficulties which the patient
Kubizek raised along with hesitant remarks on Adolf's limited musical
expertise, he was engrossed in the work, eating, drinking, and sleeping little.
But after a while he 'spoke less and less of it, and in the end did not mention
it at all'.[88]

Other utopian schemes included, according to Kubizek, plans to solve
Vienna's housing problems and design new houses for workers, the creation
of a new popular drink to replace alcohol, a travelling orchestra to take
culture into the provinces, and – as always – the grandiose cultural rebuilding
of Linz.[89] Kubizek unquestionably embellished Hitler's social conscience, as
in the story of Adolf returning from spending three nights wandering the
streets of Vienna studying the housing problem,[90] and his far-sightedness,
as in plans for social and cultural reform in his imagined 'ideal state'.[91] But
the description of a Hitler opinionated on all subjects, gripped by sudden
and temporary enthusiasm for wholly unrealistic ideas, and fantasizing
wildly ambitious pipe-dreams that dissolved as quickly as they were formulated, rings true. And always there was the obsession with the monumental,
the grandiose, the spectacular. The avant-garde Jugendstil architecture of
Otto Wagner passed Hitler by, as did the modern art of the Sezession and
its major star Gustav Klimt.[92] He showed not the slightest interest in this
cultural revolution which had gripped end-of-the-century Vienna.[93] His
architectural and artistic tastes were traditional and anti-modernist, firmly
anchored in the neo-classicism and realism of the nineteenth century. And
buildings for him were primarily for representation. The sketches he was
constantly making were invariably of grandiose buildings. The magnificent
Ringstraße, begun towards the end of the 1850s, with its majestic buildings
– the neo-baroque Hofburg, the classical-style Parliament and Rathaus, the

imposing museums, opera, and Burgtheater (which he specially admired) – enthralled him from the first time he saw them.[94] He regaled Kubizek for hours on their architectural history and design, fascinated – as was the later master of propaganda – by the visual impact on the individual of buildings representing power and grandeur.[95]

Kubizek, naïve and impressionable as ever, did not cease to be astonished by Hitler's knowledge of detail on the subjects he pontificated about, quite especially on architectural matters.[96] He describes Hitler as constantly immersed in his studies. He could not imagine his friend without books, he stated: 'books were his world'.[97] Hitler had arrived in Vienna, wrote Kubizek, with four cases mainly full of books.[98] He had been a member of three libraries in Linz, and was now a regular user of the Hof Library in Vienna.[99] There were always, he added, piles of books in the room in Stumpergasse.[100] However, only one title – *Legends of Gods and Heroes: the Treasures of Germanic Mythology* – stuck in Kubizek's memory.[101] Soon after the war, when asked about Hitler's reading, he could recall only that Adolf had two books in the room for several weeks, and owned a travel guide as well.[102] Kubizek's later claim that Hitler had read an impressive list of classics – including Goethe, Schiller, Dante, Herder, Ibsen, Schopenhauer, and Nietzsche – has to be treated with a large pinch of salt.[103] Whatever Hitler read during his Vienna years – and apart from a number of newspapers mentioned in *Mein Kampf*,[104] we cannot be sure what that was – it was probably far less elevated than the works of such literary luminaries. However, there is no reason to doubt that Hitler did read extensively in his Vienna period, as he himself later claimed.[105] After the end of the Third Reich, in fact, Hitler's sister Paula recalled him writing to recommend books to her (and sending her a copy of *Don Quichote*) during the first months he was in Vienna in 1908, before communications with his family faded.[106] But like everything else he undertook at this time, his reading was unsystematic. And the factual knowledge that he committed to his formidable memory was used only to confirm already existing opinions.

Hitler explained his style of reading in *Mein Kampf*:

I know people who 'read' enormously, book for book, letter for letter, yet whom I would not describe as 'well-read'. True, they possess a mass of 'knowledge', but their brain is unable to organize and register the material they have taken in. They lack the art of sifting what is valuable for them in a book from that which is without value . . . For reading is no end in itself, but a means to an end . . . A man who possesses the art of correct reading will, in studying any book, magazine, or pamphlet, instinctively and immediately perceive everything which in his opinion is worth permanently remembering, either because it is suited to his purpose or generally worth knowing. Once the knowledge he has achieved in this fashion is correctly coordinated within the somehow existing picture of this or that subject created by the imagination, it will function either as a corrective or a complement, thus enhancing either the correctness or the clarity of the picture . . . Only this kind of reading has meaning and purpose . . . Since my earliest youth I have endeavoured to read in the correct way, and in this endeavour I have been most happily supported by my memory and intelligence. Viewed in this light, my Vienna period was especially fertile and valuable.[107]

Apart from architecture, Hitler's main passion, as it had been in Linz, was music. Particular favourites, certainly in later years, were Beethoven, Bruckner (an especial favourite), Liszt and Brahms. He greatly enjoyed, too, the operettas of Johann Strauß and Franz Lehár.[108] Wagner was, of course, the *non plus ultra*. Adolf and Gustl were at the opera most nights, paying their 2 Kronen to gain the standing place that they had often queued for hours to obtain. They saw operas by Mozart, Beethoven, and the Italian masters Donizetti, Rossini, and Bellini as well as the main works of Verdi and Puccini. But for Hitler only German music counted. He could not join in the enthusiasm for Verdi or Puccini operas, playing to packed houses in Vienna. When he heard a street organ-grinder intoning 'La donna è mobile', he said to Kubizek: 'There you have your Verdi.' To his friend's protest that any composer might have his work debased in such a way, he replied: 'Can you imagine Lohengrin's grail narration on a barrel organ?'[109] Adolf's passion for Wagner, as in Linz, knew no bounds. Now he and his friend were able to see all Wagner's operas performed at one of the best opera houses in Europe.[110] In the short time they were together, Kubizek reckoned they saw *Lohengrin* – which remained Hitler's favourite – ten times.[111] 'For him,' remarked Kubizek, 'a second-rate Wagner was a hundred times better than a first-class Verdi.' Kubizek was of a different mind; but to no avail. Adolf would not rest until his friend agreed to forget about going to see Verdi at the Court Opera and accompany him to a Wagner performance at the less highbrow Popular Opera House. 'When it was a matter of a Wagner performance, Adolf would stand no contradiction.'[112]

Hitler was, of course, only one of the thousands of Wagner fanatics who flocked to the Hofoper in Vienna around the turn of the century to hear the works of the Bayreuth master. To the younger generation especially, Wagner was 'the vindicator of the heart against the head, the *Volk* against the mass, the revolt of the young and vital against the old and ossified'.[113] The Wagner cult was at its height around this time. Easily the most popular composer of the era, his operas were played at the Court Opera alone on no fewer than 426 evenings during Hitler's time in Vienna.[114] Many attending the performances, including Kubizek himself, were far more skilled than Hitler, with his self-taught, amateurish, opinionated approach, in understanding and interpreting Wagner's music. But for Hitler, Wagner was more than the music alone. 'Listening to Wagner,' commented Kubizek, 'meant to him, not a simple visit to the theatre, but the opportunity of being transported into that extraordinary state which Wagner's music produced in him, that trance, that escape into a mystical dream-world . . .'[115] 'When I hear Wagner,' Hitler himself much later recounted, 'it seems to me that I hear rhythms of a bygone world.'[116] It was a world of Germanic myth, of great drama and wondrous spectacle, of gods and heroes, of titanic struggle and redemption, of victory and of death. It was a world where the heroes were outsiders who challenged the old order, like Rienzi, Tannhäuser, Stolzing, and Siegfried; or chaste saviours like Lohengrin and Parsifal.[117] Betrayal, sacrifice, redemption and heroic death were Wagnerian themes which would also preoccupy Hitler down to the *Götterdämmerung* of his regime in 1945. And it was a world created with grandiose vision by an artist of genius, an outsider and revolutionary, all-or-nothing refuser of compromise, challenger of the existing order, dismissive of the need to bow to the bourgeois ethic of working for a living,[118] surmounting rejection and persecution, overcoming adversity to attain greatness. It was little wonder that the fantasist and drop-out, the rejected and unrecognized artistic genius in the dingy room in the Stumpergasse, could find his idol in the master of Bayreuth.[119] Hitler, the nonentity, the mediocrity, the failure, wanted to live like a Wagnerian hero. He wanted to become himself a new Wagner – the philosopher-king, the genius, the supreme artist. In Hitler's mounting identity crisis following his rejection at the Academy of Arts,[120] Wagner was for Hitler the artistic giant he had dreamed of becoming but knew he could never emulate, the incarnation of the triumph of aesthetics and the supremacy of art.[121]

III

The strange coexistence of the young Hitler and Kubizek continued into midsummer 1908. During those months, almost the only other person, apart from his friend, with whom Hitler had regular contact was his landlady,

Frau Zakreys. Nor did Kubizek and Hitler have any joint acquaintances. Adolf regarded his friendship with Gustl as exclusive, allowing him no other friendships.[122] When Gustl brought a young woman, one of a small number of his music pupils, back to his room, Hitler, thinking she was a girlfriend, was beside himself with rage. Kubizek's explanation that it was simply a matter of coaching a pupil in musical harmony merely provoked a tirade about the pointlessness of women studying.[123] In Kubizek's view, Hitler was outrightly misogynist.[124] He pointed out Hitler's satisfaction that women were not permitted in the promenade stalls of the opera.[125] Apart from his distant admiration for Stefanie in Linz, Kubizek knew of Hitler having no relations with any woman during the years of their acquaintance in both Linz and Vienna.[126] This would not alter during his remaining years in the Austrian capital. None of the accounts of Hitler's time in the Men's Home gives a hint of any women in his life. When his circle of acquaintances got round to discussing women – and, doubtless, their own former girlfriends and sexual experiences – the best Hitler could come up with was a veiled reference to Stefanie, who had been his 'first love' – though 'she never knew it, because he never told her'. The impression left with Reinhold Hanisch was that 'Hitler had very little respect for the female sex, but very austere ideas about relations between men and women. He often said that, if men only wanted to, they could adopt a strictly moral way of living.'[127] This was entirely in line with the moral code preached by the Schönerer pan-Germans. Celibacy until the twenty-fifth year, the code advocated, was healthy, advantageous to strength of will, and the basis of physical or mental high achievement. The cultivation of corresponding dietary habits was advised. Eating meat and drinking alcohol – seen as stimulants to sexual activity – were to be avoided. And upholding the strength and purity of the Germanic race meant keeping free of the moral decadence and danger of infection which accompanied consorting with prostitutes, who should be left to clients of 'inferior' races.[128] Here was ideological justification enough for Hitler's chaste lifestyle and prudish morals. But, in any case, certainly in the time in Vienna after he parted company with Kubizek, Hitler was no 'catch' for women.[129]

It can be said with near certainty, then, that by the time he left Vienna at the age of twenty-four Hitler had had no sexual experience. In a city in which sexual favours were so widely on offer to young men as the Vienna of that day, who were widely expected to visit prostitutes while publicly upholding a strict moral codex, this was in all likelihood unusual.[130] Probably, he was frightened of women – certainly of their sexuality. Hanisch recalled

Hitler telling him of a brief encounter with a milkmaid while he was still at school, ending abruptly when she made advances and he ran away, knocking over a churn of milk in his haste.[131] Hitler later described his own ideal woman as 'a cute, cuddly, naïve little thing – tender, sweet, and stupid'.[132] His assertion that a woman 'would rather bow to a strong man than dominate a weakling'[133] may well have been a compensatory projection of his own sexual complexes.

Kubizek was adamant that Hitler was sexually normal (though on the basis of his own account it is difficult to see how he was in a position to judge).[134] This was also the view of doctors who at a much later date thoroughly examined him.[135] Biologically, it may well have been so.[136] Claims that sexual deviance arising from the absence of a testicle were the root of Hitler's personality disorder rest on a combination of psychological speculation and dubious evidence provided by the Russian autopsy after the capture of the burnt remains of his body in Berlin.[137] And stories about his Vienna time such as that of his alleged obsession with an attempted rape of a model engaged to a half-Jew, and his resort to prostitutes, derive from a single source with no credence and can be regarded as baseless.[138] However, Kubizek's account, together with the language Hitler himself used in *Mein Kampf*, does point at the least to an acutely disturbed and repressed sexual development.

Hitler's prudishness, shored up by Schönerian principles, was to a degree merely in line with middle-class outward standards of morality in the Vienna of his time. These standards had been challenged by the openly erotic art of Klimt and literature of Schnitzler.[139] But the solid bourgeois puritanism prevailed – at least as a thin veneer covering the seamier side of a city teeming with vice and prostitution.[140] Where decency demanded that women were scarcely allowed even to show an ankle, Hitler's embarrassment – and the rapidity with which he fled with his friend – when a prospective landlady during the search for a room for Kubizek let her silk dressing-gown fall open to reveal that she was wearing nothing but a pair of knickers was understandable.[141] But his prudishness went far beyond this. It amounted, according to Kubizek's account, to a deep disgust and repugnance at sexual activity.[142] Hitler avoided contact with women, meeting with cold indifference during visits to the opera alleged attempts by young women, probably seeing him as something of an oddity, to flirt with or tease him.[143] He was repelled by homosexuality.[144] He refrained from masturbation.[145] Prostitution horrified, but fascinated, him. He associated it with venereal disease, which petrified him.[146] Following a visit to the theatre one evening to see

Frank Wedekind's play *Frühlingserwachen* (*Spring Awakening*), which dealt with sexual problems of youth, Hitler suddenly took Kubizek's arm and led him into Spittelberggasse to see at first hand the red-light district, or 'sink of iniquity' as Hitler called it. Adolf took his friend not once, but twice, along the row of lit windows behind which scantily clad women advertised their wares and touted for custom. His voyeurism was then cloaked in middle-class self-righteousness by the lecture he proceeded to give Kubizek on the evils of prostitution.[147] Later, in *Mein Kampf*, he was to link the Jews – echoing a commonplace current among antisemites of his Vienna years – with prostitution.[148] But if this association was present in his mind in 1908, Kubizek did not record it.

Though seemingly repelled by sex, Hitler was at the same time plainly fascinated by it.[149] He discussed sexual matters quite often in lengthy talks late at night with Gustl, regaling him, wrote Kubizek, on the need for sexual purity to protect what he grandly called the 'flame of life'; explaining to his naïve friend, following a brief encounter with a businessman who invited them to a meal, about homosexuality; and ranting about prostitution and moral decadence.[150] Hitler's disturbed sexuality, his recoiling from physical contact,[151] his fear of women, his inability to forge genuine friendship and emptiness in human relations, presumably had their roots in childhood experiences of a troubled family life.[152] Attempts to explain them will inevitably remain speculative. Later rumours of Hitler's sexual perversions are similarly based on dubious evidence. Conjecture – and there has been much of it – that sexual repression later gave way to sordid sado-masochistic practices rests, whatever the suspicions, on little more than a combination of rumour, hearsay, surmise, and innuendo, often spiced up by Hitler's political enemies.[153] And even if the alleged repulsive perversions really were his private proclivities, how exactly they would help explain the rapid descent of the complex and sophisticated German state into gross inhumanity after 1933 is not readily self-evident.

Hitler was to describe his life in Vienna as one of hardship and misery, hunger and poverty.[154] This was notably economical with the truth as regards the months he spent in Stumpergasse in 1908 (though it was accurate enough as a portrayal of his condition in the autumn and winter of 1909–10). Even more misleading was his comment in *Mein Kampf* that 'the orphan's pension to which I was entitled was not enough for me even to live on, and so I was faced with the problem of somehow making my own living'.[155] As we have noted, the loan from his aunt, his share of his mother's legacy, and his monthly orphan's pension certainly gave him sufficient to live comfortably

– perhaps even equivalent to the income of a young teacher – over a year or so at least.[156] And his appearance, when he put on his fineries for an evening at the opera, was anything but that of a down-and-out. When Kubizek first saw him on their reunion at the Westbahnhof in February 1908, young Adolf was wearing a dark, good-quality overcoat, and dark hat. He was carrying the walking-stick with the ivory handle that he had had in Linz, and 'appeared almost elegant'.[157] As for working, in those first months of 1908, as we have noted, Hitler certainly did nothing whatsoever about making his own living, or taking any steps to ensure that he was on the right track to do so.

If he had a reasonable income during his time with Kubizek, Hitler nevertheless scarcely led a life of wild extravagance. His living conditions were unenviable. The sixth district of Vienna, close to the Westbahnhof, where Stumpergasse was situated, was an unattractive part of the city, with its dismal, unlit streets and scruffy tenement blocks overhung with smoke and soot surrounding dark inner courtyards. Kubizek himself was appalled at some of the accommodation on view when he was looking for a room the day after he had arrived in Vienna.[158] And the lodging he and Adolf came to share was a miserable room that stank constantly of paraffin, with crumbling plaster peeling off dank walls, and bug-ridden beds and furniture.[159] The lifestyle was frugal. Little was spent on eating and drinking. Adolf was not a vegetarian at that time, but his main daily fare usually consisted only of bread and butter, puddings made from oatmeal flour (*Mehlspeisen*), and often in the afternoons a piece of poppy- or nut-cake. Sometimes he went without food altogether. When Gustl's mother sent a food parcel every fortnight, it was like a feast.[160] Adolf drank milk as a rule, or sometimes fruit-juice, but no alcohol.[161] Nor did he smoke.[162] The one luxury was the opera. How much he spent on the almost daily visits to an opera or a concert can only be guessed. But at 2 Kronen for a standing place[163] – it infuriated Hitler that young officers more interested in the social occasion than the music had to pay only 10 Heller, a twentieth of the sum[164] – regular attendance over some months would certainly begin to eat away at whatever savings he had.[165] Hitler himself remarked, over three decades later: 'I was so poor, during the Viennese period of my life, that I had to restrict myself to only the very best performances. This explains that already at that time I had heard *Tristan* thirty or forty times, and always from the best companies.'[166] By the summer of 1908, he must have made big inroads into the money he had inherited. But he presumably still had some of his savings left, as well as the orphan's pension that Kubizek presumed was his only income,[167] which would allow him to last out for a further year.[168]

Though Kubizek was unaware of it, by summer the time he was spending with his friend in Vienna was drawing to a close. By early July 1908, Gustl had passed his examinations at the Conservatoire and term had ended. He was going back to Linz to stay with his parents until autumn. He arranged to send Frau Zakreys the rent every month to guarantee retention of the room, and Adolf, again saying how little he was looking forward to remaining alone in the room, accompanied him to the Westbahnhof to see him off.[169] They were not to meet again until the Anschluß in 1938.[170] Adolf did send Gustl a number of postcards during the summer, one from the Waldviertel, where he had gone without enthusiasm to spend some time with his family.[171] It was to be the last time he would see his relatives for many years.[172] Nothing suggested to Kubizek that he would not be rejoining his friend in the autumn. But when he left the train at the Westbahnhof on his return in November, Hitler was nowhere to be seen. Some time in the late summer or autumn, he had moved out of Stumpergasse. Frau Zakreys told Kubizek that he had left his lodgings without giving any forwarding address.[173] By 18 November he was registered with the police as a 'student' living at new lodgings in room 16 of Felberstraße 22, close by the Westbahnhof, and a more airy room – presumably costing more – than that he had occupied in Stumpergasse.[174]

What had caused the sudden and unannounced break with Kubizek? The most likely explanation is Hitler's second rejection – this time he was not even permitted to take the examination – by the Academy of Fine Arts in October 1908.[175] He had probably not told Kubizek he was applying again. Presumably he had spent the entire year in the knowledge that he had a second chance and in the expectation that he would not fail this time. Now his hopes of an artistic career lay totally in ruins. He could not now face his friend again as a confirmed failure.[176]

Kubizek's recollections, for all their flaws, paint a portrait of the young Hitler whose character traits are recognizable with hindsight in the later party leader and dictator.[177] The indolence in lifestyle but accompanied by manic enthusiasm and energy sucked into his fantasies, the dilettantism, the lack of reality and a sense of proportion, the opinionated autodidactism, the egocentrism, the quirky intolerance, the sudden rise to anger and the outbursts of rage, the diatribes of venom poured out on everyone and everything blocking the rise of the great artist – all these can be seen in the nineteen-year-old Hitler portrayed by Kubizek. Failure in Vienna had turned Hitler into an angry and frustrated young man increasingly at odds with the world around him. But he was not yet the Hitler who comes clearly into view after 1919, and whose political ideas were fully outlined in *Mein Kampf*.

Kubizek had had time to read *Mein Kampf* by the time he wrote his own account of Hitler's political development – something which in any case was of less interest to him than matters cultural and artistic. His passages are in places heavily redolent of Hitler's own tale of his 'political awakening' in Vienna. They are not, therefore, reliable and often not credible – scarcely so when he claims Hitler was a pacifist, an opponent of war at this stage.[178] However, there is no reason to doubt Hitler's growing political awareness. His bitter contempt for the multi-language parliament (which Kubizek visited with him),[179] his strident German nationalism, his intense detestation of the multinational Habsburg state, his revulsion at 'the ethnic babel on the streets of Vienna',[180] and 'the foreign mixture of peoples which had begun to corrode this old site of German culture'[181] – all these were little more than an accentuation, a personalized radicalization, of what he had first imbibed in Linz.[182] Hitler fully described them in *Mein Kampf*.[183] The first months of the Viennese experience doubtless already deepened and sharpened these views. However, even by Hitler's own account it took two years in Vienna for his attitude towards the Jews to crystallize.[184] Kubizek's assertion that Hitler attained his 'world-view' during the time they were together in Vienna is an exaggeration.[185] Hitler's rounded 'world-view' was still not formed. The pathological hatred of the Jews that was its cornerstone had still to emerge.

IV

There are no witnesses to Hitler's activity during the nine months that he stayed in Felberstraße.[186] A young woman called Marie Rinke later claimed to recall speaking to him occasionally in the tenement block where he lived, and that his quiet manner had made a good impression on her, setting him apart from other young men.[187] Otherwise, this phase of Hitler's life in Vienna remains obscure. It has often been presumed, nevertheless, that it was in precisely these months that he became an obsessive racial antisemite.[188]

Close to where Hitler lived in Felberstraße was a kiosk selling tobacco and newspapers. Whatever newspapers and periodicals he bought beyond those that he devoured so avidly in cafés, it was probably from this kiosk. Which exactly he read of the many cheap and trashy magazines in circulation at the time is uncertain. One of them was very likely a racist periodical called *Ostara*.[189] The magazine, which first appeared in 1905, was the product of the extraordinary and warped imagination of an eccentric former Cistercian monk, who came to be known as Jörg Lanz von Liebenfels (though his real name was plain Adolf Lanz).[190] He later founded his own order, the 'New Templar Order' (replete with a full panoply of mystical signs and symbols, including the swastika), in a ruined castle, Burg Werfenstein, on a romantic stretch of the Danube between Linz and Vienna.

Lanz followed in the ideological footsteps of Guido von List – the 'von' was added to denote his membership of the 'Aryan ruling class' – whose prolific writings had established his credentials as the guru of the cultist believers in the superiority of the Aryan-German race, destined for mastery of the world. List had helped popularize the swastika, the sign of the sun found among ancient Hindu symbols which he took as the sign of the 'Unconquerable', the Germanic Hero, the 'Strong One from Above'.[191] That Hitler was acquainted with List's ideas is certain.[192] Lanz – also an enthusiastic supporter of Schönerer[193] – even managed the near-impossible and took List's zany notions a stage further.

Lanz and his followers were obsessed by homoerotic notions of a mani-chean struggle between the heroic and creative 'blond' race and a race of predatory dark 'beast-men' who preyed on the 'blond' women with animal lust and bestial instincts that were corrupting and destroying mankind and its culture. Lanz's recipe, laid down in *Ostara*, for overcoming the evils of the modern world and restoring the domination of the 'blond race' was racial purity and racial struggle, involving the slavery and forced sterilization or even extermination of the inferior races, the crushing of socialism, democracy and feminism which were seen as the vehicles of their corrupting influence, and the complete subordination of Aryan women to their hus-bands.[194] It amounted to a creed of 'blue-eyed blondes of all nations, unite'.[195] There are indeed elements in common between the bizarre fantasies of Lanz and his band of woman-hating, racist crackpots and the programme of racial selection which the SS were to put into practice during the Second World War. Whether Lanz's ideas had direct influence on Himmler's SS is, however, questionable. Unsustainable is Lanz's claim to a unique place in history as the man 'who gave Hitler his ideas'.[196]

It is usually taken for granted that Hitler read *Ostara* and was at least to some extent influenced by it.[197] Writing in *Mein Kampf* of his 'conversion' to antisemitism, Hitler recounted – no date is given – that he started to read on the subject and:

for a few hellers I bought the first anti-Semitic pamphlets of my life. Unfortunately, they all proceeded from the supposition that in principle the reader knew or even understood the Jewish question to a certain degree. Besides, the tone for the most part was such that doubts again arose in me, due in part to the dull and amazingly unscientific arguments favouring the thesis.

I relapsed for weeks at a time, once even for months.

The whole thing seemed to me so monstrous, the accusations so boundless, that, tormented by the fear of doing injustice, I again became anxious and uncertain.[198]

Hitler mentions no pamphlet by name in this passage, suggesting that he read several, not just a single one. And whether *Ostara* would have compelled him to focus his attentions so acutely on the 'Jewish Question' might be doubted. *Ostara* was, in fact, far more centred upon racist theory than it was upon antisemitism, which figured only in a subordinate role.[199] The main evidence that Hitler was acquainted with *Ostara* comes from a post-war interview in which Lanz claimed to have remembered Hitler, during the time he lived in Felberstraße in 1909, paying him a visit and asking him for back-copies of the magazine. Since Hitler looked so run-down, Lanz went on, he let him have the copies for nothing, and gave him 2 Kronen for his journey home.[200] How Lanz knew that this young man had been Hitler, when it was to be well over ten years before the latter would become a local celebrity even in Munich, he was never asked in the interview more than forty years after the purported meeting.[201] Another witness to Hitler's reading of *Ostara* in post-war interviews was Josef Greiner, the author of some fabricated 'recollections' of Hitler in his Vienna years. Greiner did not mention *Ostara* in his book, but, when later questioned about it in the mid-1950s, 'remembered' that Hitler had a large pile of *Ostara* magazines while he was living in the Men's Home from 1910 to 1913, and had vehemently supported Lanz's racial theories in heated discussions with an ex-Catholic priest called Grill (who does not figure in his book at all).[202] A third witness, a former Nazi functionary called Elsa Schmidt-Falks, could only remember that she had heard Hitler mention Lanz in the context of homosexuality, and *Ostara* in connection with the banning of Lanz's works (though there is in fact no evidence of a ban).[203]

Most likely, Hitler did read *Ostara* along with other racist pulp which was prominent on Vienna newspaper stands. But we cannot be certain.[204] Nor, if he did read it, can we be sure what he believed. His first known statements on antisemitism immediately following the First World War betray no traces of Lanz's obscure racial doctrine.[205] He was later frequently scornful of *völkisch* sects and the extremes of Germanic cultism.[206] As far as can be seen, if we discount Elsa Schmidt-Falk's doubtful testimony, he never mentioned Lanz by name. For the Nazi regime, the bizarre Austrian racist eccentric, far from being held up to praise, was to be accused of 'falsifying racial thought through secret doctrine'.[207]

When Hitler, his savings almost exhausted, was forced to leave Felberstraße in mid-August 1909 to move for a very short time to shabbier accommodation in nearby Sechshauserstraße 58, it was certainly not as a devotee of Lanz von Liebenfels.[208] Nor, anti-Jewish though he undoubtedly already was as a Schönerer supporter, is it likely that he had yet found the key to the ills of the world in a doctrine of racial antisemitism.

Hitler stayed in Sechshauserstraße for less than a month. And when he left, on 16 September 1909, it was without filling in the required police registration form, without leaving a forwarding address, and probably without paying his rent.[209] During the next months, Hitler did learn the meaning of poverty. His later recollection that autumn 1909 had been 'an endlessly bitter time' was not an exaggeration.[210] All his savings had now vanished. He must have left some address with his guardian for his orphan's pension of 25 Kronen to be sent to Vienna each month. But that was not enough to keep body and soul together.[211] During the wet and cold autumn of 1909 he lived rough, sleeping in the open, as long as the weather held, probably in cheap lodgings when conditions forced him indoors.[212] Reinhold Hanisch, who came to know Hitler soon afterwards, told of him sleeping in a cheap café on Kaiserstraße.[213] He was later said to have stayed for a while in November at Simon-Denk-Gasse 11, but this is unlikely. It is doubtful that by this date he had the money to pay for regular lodgings; the address lay well away from his usual haunts in the south of the city, in a fairly middle-class district; and no official registration of Hitler living there has survived.[214]

Hitler had now reached rock-bottom. Some time in the weeks before Christmas 1909, thin and bedraggled, in filthy, lice-ridden clothes, his feet sore from walking around, Hitler joined the human flotsam and jetsam finding their way to the large, recently established doss-house for the homeless (*Asyl für Obdachlose*) in Meidling, not far from Schönbrunn Palace.[215] The social decline of the petty-bourgeois so fearful of joining the proletariat was complete.[216] The twenty-year-old would-be artistic genius had joined the tramps, winos, and down-and-outs in society's basement.

It was at this time that he met Reinhold Hanisch, whose testimony, doubtful though it is in places, is all that casts light on the next phase of

Hitler's time in Vienna.[217] Hanisch, living under the assumed name of 'Fritz
Walter', came originally from the Sudetenland and had a police record for
a number of petty misdemeanours. He was a self-styled draughtsman, but
in reality had drifted through various temporary jobs as a domestic servant
and casual labourer before tramping his way across Germany from Berlin
to Vienna.[218] He encountered a miserable-looking Hitler, down at heel in a
shabby blue check suit, tired, hungry, and with sore feet, in the hostel
dormitory one late autumn night, shared some bread with him and told
tales of Berlin to the young enthusiast for all things German.[219] The hostel
was a night-shelter offering short-term accommodation only. A bath or
shower, disinfection of clothes, soup and bread, and a bed in the dormitory
were provided. But during the day the inmates were turned out to fend for
themselves. Hitler, looking in a sorry state and in depressed mood, went in
the mornings along with other destitutes to a nearby convent in Gumpendor-
ferstraße where the nuns doled out soup. The time was otherwise spent
visiting public warming-rooms, or trying to earn a bit of money. Hanisch
took him off to shovel snow, but without an overcoat Hitler was in no
condition to stick at it for long.[220] He offered to carry bags for passengers
at the Westbahnhof, but his appearance probably did not win him many
customers.[221] Whether he did any other manual labour during the years he
spent in Vienna is doubtful. While his savings had lasted, he had not been
prepared to entertain the prospect of working.[222] At the time he was in most
need of money, he was physically not up to it.[223] Later, even Hanisch, his
'business associate', lost his temper over Hitler's idleness while eking out a
living by selling paintings.[224] The story he told in *Mein Kampf* about learning
about trade unionism and Marxism the hard way through his maltreatment
while working on a building site is almost certainly fictional.[225] Hanisch, at
any rate, never heard the story at the time from Hitler, and later did
not believe it.[226] The 'legend' probably drew on the general anti-socialist
propaganda in the Vienna of Hitler's day.[227]

Hanisch had meanwhile thought of a better idea than manual labouring.
Hitler had told him of his background, and was persuaded by Hanisch to
ask his family for some money, probably under the pretext that he needed
it for his studies. Within a short time he received the princely sum of 50
Kronen, almost certainly from his Aunt Johanna.[228] With that he could buy
himself an overcoat from the government pawn-shop.[229] With this long coat
and his greasy trilby, shoes looking like those of a nomad, hair over his
collar, and dark fuzz on his chin, Hitler's appearance even provoked his
fellow vagrants to remark on it. They nicknamed him 'Ohm Paul Krüger',

after the Boer leader.[230] But the gift from his aunt meant that better times were on the way. He was now able to acquire the materials needed to begin the little business venture that Hanisch had dreamed up. On hearing from Hitler that he could paint – Hitler actually told him he had been at the Academy – Hanisch suggested he should paint scenes of Vienna which he would then peddle for him, and they would share the proceeds. Whether this partnership began already in the doss-house, or only after Hitler had moved, on 9 February 1910, to the more salubrious surrounds of the Men's Home in the north of the city, is unclear from Hanisch's garbled account. What is certain is that with his aunt's gift, the move to Meldemannstraße, and his new business arrangement with Hanisch, Hitler was now over the worst.[231]

The Men's Home was a big step up from the Meidling hostel. The 500 or so residents were not down-and-out vagrants, but, for the most part, a mixed bunch of individuals, some – clerks and even former academics and pensioned officers – just down on their luck, others simply passing through, looking for work or in temporary employment, all without a family home to go to. Unlike the hostel, the Men's Home, built a few years earlier, funded by private donations (some from wealthy Jewish families), offered a modicum of privacy, and for an overnight price of only 50 Heller. Residents had their own cubicles, which had to be vacated during the day but could be retained on a more or less indefinite basis. There was a canteen where meals and alcohol-free drinks could be obtained, and a kitchen where they could prepare their own food; there were washrooms and lockers for private possessions; in the basement were baths, along with a cobbler's, a tailor's, and a hairdresser's, a laundry, and cleaning facilities; there was a small library on the ground floor, and on the first floor lounges and a reading-room where newpapers were available. Most of the residents were out during the day, but a group of around fifteen to twenty, mainly from lower-middle-class backgrounds and seen as the 'intelligentsia', usually gathered in a smaller room, known as the 'work-room' or 'writing-room', to undertake odd jobs – painting advertisements, writing out addresses and the like.[232] This is where Hanisch and Hitler set up operations.

Hanisch's role was to hawk Hitler's mainly postcard-size paintings around pubs. He also found a market with frame-makers and upholsterers who could make use of cheap illustrations. Most of the dealers with whom he had a good, regular trade were Jewish. Hitler's view, according to Hanisch, was that Jews were better businessmen and more reliable customers than 'Christian' dealers.[233] More remarkably, in the light of later events and his own claims about the importance of the Vienna period for the development of his antisemitism, his closest partner (apart from Hanisch) in his little art-production business, Josef Neumann, was also a Jew – and one with whom Hitler was, it seems, on friendly terms.[234]

Hitler invariably copied his pictures from others, sometimes following visits to museums or galleries to find suitable subjects. He was lazy and had to be chivvied by Hanisch, who could offload the pictures faster than Hitler painted them. The usual rate of production was about one picture a day, and Hanisch reckoned to sell it for around 5 Kronen, split between him and Hitler. In this fashion, they managed to make a modest living.[235]

Politics was a frequent topic of conversation in the reading-room of the Men's Home, and the atmosphere easily became heated, with tempers flaring. Hitler took full part.[236] His violent attacks on the Social Democrats caused trouble with some of the inmates.[237] He was known for his admiration for Schönerer and Karl Hermann Wolf (founder and leader of the German Radical Party, with its main base in the 'Sudetenland').[238] He also waxed lyrical about the achievements of Lueger.[239] When he was not holding forth on politics, Hitler was lecturing his comrades – keen to listen or not – on the wonders of Wagner's music and the brilliance of Gottfried Semper's designs of Vienna's monumental buildings.[240]

Whether politics or art, the chance to involve himself in the reading-room 'debates' was more than sufficient to distract Hitler from working.[241] By summer, Hanisch had become more and more irritated with Hitler's failure to keep up with orders.[242] Hitler claimed he could not simply paint to order, but had to be in the right mood. Hanisch accused him of only painting when he needed to keep the wolf from the door.[243] Following a windfall from the sale of one of his paintings, Hitler even disappeared from the Men's Home for a few days in June with Neumann. According to Hanisch, Hitler and Neumann spent their time sight-seeing in Vienna and looking around museums.[244] More likely they had other 'business' plans, which, then, quickly fell through, possibly including a quick visit to the Waldviertel to try to squeeze a bit more money out of Aunt Johanna.[245] Hitler and his cronies in the Men's Home were at this time prepared to entertain any dotty scheme – a miracle hair-restorer was one such idea – that would bring in a bit of money.[246] Whatever the reason for his temporary absence, after five days, his money spent, Hitler returned to the Men's Home and the partnership with Hanisch. Relations now, however, became increasingly strained and the bad feeling eventually exploded over a picture Hitler had painted, larger than usual in size, of the parliament building. Through an intermediary –

another Jewish dealer in his group in the Men's Home by the name of Siegfried Löffner – Hitler accused Hanisch of cheating him by withholding 50 Kronen he allegedly received for the picture, together with a further 9 Kronen for a watercolour. The matter was brought to the attention of the police, and Hanisch was sentenced to a few days in jail – but for using the false name of Fritz Walter. Hitler never received what he felt was owing to him for the picture.[247]

With Hanisch's disappearance, Hitler's life recedes into near obscurity for two years or so. When he next comes into view, in 1912–13, he is still in residence in the Men's Home, now a well-established member of the community, and a central figure among his own group – the 'intelligentsia' who occupied the writing-room.[248] He was by now well over the depths of degradation he experienced in 1909 in the doss-house, even if continuing to drift aimlessly.[249] He could earn a modest income from the sale of his pictures of the Karlskirche and other scenes of 'Old Vienna'.[250] His outgoings were low, since he lived so frugally.[251] His living costs in the Men's Home were extremely modest: he ate cheaply, did not drink, smoked a cigarette only rarely, and had as his only luxury the occasional purchase of a standing place at the theatre or opera (about which he would then regale the writing-room 'intellectuals' for hours).[252] Descriptions of his appearance at this time are contradictory. A fellow resident in the Men's Home in 1912 later described Hitler at the time as shabbily dressed and unkempt, wearing a long greyish coat, worn at the sleeves, and battered old hat, trousers full of holes, and shoes stuffed with paper. He still had shoulder-length hair and a ragged beard.[253] This is compatible with the description given by Hanisch which, though not precisely dated, appears from the context to refer to 1909–10.[254] On the other hand, according to Jacob Altenberg, one of his Jewish art dealers, in the later phase at least in the Men's Home Hitler was clean-shaven, took care to keep his hair cut, and wore clothes which, though old and worn, were kept neat.[255] Given what Kubizek wrote about Hitler's fussiness about personal hygiene when they were together in 1908, and what was later little short of a cleanliness fetish, Altenberg's testimony rings truer than that of the anonymous acquaintance for the final period in Meldemannstraße.

But, whatever his appearance, Hitler was scarcely enjoying the lifestyle of a man who had come by a substantial windfall – what would have amounted to a king's ransom for someone living in a men's hostel. Yet this is what was long believed. It was suggested – though based on guesswork, not genuine evidence – that towards the end of 1910 Hitler had become the recipient of a sizeable sum, perhaps as much as 3,800 Kronen, which represented the life-savings of his Aunt Johanna.[256] Post-war inquiries indicated that this was the amount withdrawn from her savings account by Johanna on 1 December 1910, some four months before she died, leaving no will.[257] The suspicion was that the large sum had gone to Adolf. This feeling was enhanced by the fact that his half-sister Angela, still looking after his sister Paula, soon afterwards, in 1911, staked a claim to the whole of the orphan's pension, still at that time divided equally between the two children. Adolf who, 'on account of his training as an artist had received substantial sums from his aunt, Johanna Pölzl', conceded that he was in a position to maintain himself, and was forced to concede the 25 Kronen a month which he up to then received from his guardian.[258] But, as we have already noted, the household account-book of the Hitler family makes plain that Adolf, alongside smaller gifts from 'Hanitante', received from her a loan – amounting in reality to a gift – of 924 Kronen, probably in 1907 and providing him with the material basis of his first, relatively comfortable, year in Vienna.[259] Whatever became of Aunt Johanna's money in December 1910, there is not the slightest indication that it went to Hitler. And the loss of the 25 Kronen a month orphan's pension would have amounted to a serious dent in his income.[260]

Though his life had stabilized while he had been in the Men's Home, during the time he had been trafficking in paintings, Hitler seems to have remained unsettled. He was still, as has been rightly said, 'more threatened by than threatening to the social order' in which he lived.[261] He was disdainful about the quality of his own 'dilettante' paintings, as he described them, and felt he still needed to learn how to paint. He seems, indeed, for a time in 1910 to have entertained yet a further attempt to enter the Academy in Vienna, but nothing came of it, and his bitterness and anger about his rejection remained unabated.[262]

Karl Honisch – keen to distance himself from his near-namesake Hanisch, of whom he had heard nothing good – knew Hitler in 1913. His account, written in the 1930s for the NSDAP-Hauptarchiv, was consciously intended to portray Hitler in the best light possible, but for all that paints a plausible picture of him towards the end of his stay in the Men's Home. Honisch described Hitler at the time as slight in build, poorly nourished, with hollow cheeks, dark hair flopping in his face, and wearing shabby clothes. Hitler was rarely absent from the Home and sat each day in the same corner of the writing-room near the window, drawing and painting on a long oak-table. This was known as his place, and any newcomer venturing to take it was rapidly reminded by the other inmates that 'this place is taken. Herr Hitler sits there.'[263] Among the writing-room regulars, Hitler was seen as a somewhat unusual, artistic type. He himself wrote later: 'I believe that those who knew me in those days took me for an eccentric.'[264] But, other than his painting skills, no one imagined he had any special talents. Though well regarded, he had a way, noted Honisch, of keeping his distance from the others and 'not letting anyone come too close'. He could be withdrawn, sunk in a book or his own thoughts. But he was known to have a quick temper. This could flare up at any time, particularly in the frequent political debates that took place. Hitler's strong views on politics were plain to all. He would often sit quietly when a discussion started up, putting in the odd word here or there but otherwise carrying on with his drawing. But if he took exception to something said, he would jump up from his place, hurling his brush or pencil on the table, and heatedly and forcefully make himself felt before, on occasion, breaking off in mid-flow and with a wave of resignation at the incomprehension of his comrades, taking up his drawing again. Two subjects above all roused his aggression: the Jesuits and the 'Reds' – at whose hands it was well known that he had suffered unpleasant experiences.[265] No mention was made of tirades against the Jews.

The criticism of the 'Jesuits' suggests that some embers of his former enthusiasm for Schönerer's vehement anti-Catholicism were still warm, though the Schönerer movement had by this time effectively collapsed.[266] His hatred for the Social Democrats was also long established by now. His own version in *Mein Kampf* of the emergence of this hatred tells the story – as we have already suggested, almost certainly fictional – of the victimization and personal threats he allegedly experienced, on account of his rejection of their political views and refusal to join a trade union, at the hands of Social Democrat workers when he was employed for a short time on a building site.[267] If Hitler had suffered physical maltreatment, perhaps while living rough or later in the Men's Home, through making no secret of the evidently strong aversion he already felt towards Social Democracy, it might have been expected that he would have spoken about it to his cronies. Yet none of those who later recounted anecdotes of Hitler at the time refers to it – with the exception of Josef Greiner, whose account is a plain fabrication, no more than an elaborated and embellished variant of the *Mein Kampf* story.[268]

There is, in fact, no need to look beyond the strength of Hitler's pan-German nationalism as an explanation of his detestation of the internationalism of the Social Democrats. The radical nationalist propaganda of Franz Stein's pan-German 'working-class movement', with its repeated shrill attacks on 'social democratic bestialities' and 'red terror', and its boundless agitation against Czech workers, was the type of 'socialism' soaked up by Hitler.[269] A more underlying source of the hatred most likely lay in Hitler's pronounced sense of social and cultural superiority towards the working class that Social Democracy represented.[270] 'I do not know what horrified me most at that time,' he later wrote of his contact with those of the 'lower classes': 'the economic misery of my companions, their moral and ethical coarseness, or the low level of their intellectual development'.[271] In a further telling passage in *Mein Kampf*, Hitler wrote:

The environment of my youth consisted of petty-bourgeois circles, hence of a world having very little relation to the purely manual worker . . . The cleft between this class . . . and the manual worker is often deeper than we imagine. The reason for this hostility . . . lies in the fear of a social group, which has but recently raised itself above the level of the manual worker, that it will sink back into the old despised class, or at least become identified with it. To this, in many cases, we must add the repugnant memory of the cultural poverty of this lower class, the frequent vulgarity of its social intercourse; the petty bourgeois' own position in society, however insignificant it may be, makes any contact with this outgrown stage of life and culture intolerable.[272]

Though Hitler's account of his first encounter with Social Democrats is almost certainly in the main apocryphal, status-consciousness runs through it, not least in his comment that at that time 'my clothing was still more or less in order, my speech cultivated, and my manner reserved'.[273] As we noted, Hitler's appearance and lifestyle while with Kubizek were anything other than proletarian.[274] Later, in the Men's Home, his status as an 'artist' in the 'intellectual' group that frequented the writing-room preserved his distance from the manual workers in the Home. Given such status-consciousness, the level of degradation he must have felt in 1909–10 when the threat of social decline into the proletariat for a time became dire reality can be readily imagined. But far from eliciting any solidarity with the ideals of the working-class movement, this merely sharpened his antagonism towards it. Not social and political theories, but survival, struggle, and 'every man for himself' marked the philosophy of the doss-house.[275]

Hitler went on in *Mein Kampf* to stress the hard struggle for existence of the 'upstart', who had risen 'by his own efforts from his previous position in life to a higher one', that 'kills all pity' and destroys 'feeling for the misery of those who have remained behind'.[276] This puts into context his professed interest in 'the social question' while he was in Vienna. His ingrained sense of superiority meant that, far from arousing sympathy for the destitute and the disadvantaged, the 'social question' for him amounted to a search for scapegoats to explain his own social decline and degradation. 'By drawing me within its sphere of suffering', the 'social question', he wrote, 'did not seem to invite me to "study", but to experience it in my own skin'.[277]

Similarly, Hitler's views on Social Democracy were shaped by personal experience. Hitler not only hated Social Democracy; he feared it. We noted earlier his anxiety at watching 'the gigantic human dragon' of marching workers through the streets of Vienna.[278] The threat he sensed in Social Democracy left its lasting mark in an 'understanding of the importance of physical terror'.[279] Hitler's 'gut feeling' – truly a visceral hatred – that arose from his status-consciousness and first-hand experience of Social Democracy was 'confirmed' by voracious but one-sided reading. Whether he read any serious theoretical works may be doubted. His understanding of Marxism was probably for the most part picked up in Social Democratic literature, such as the *Arbeiterzeitung* which he read, and in anti-Marxist articles in the nationalist and bourgeois press.[280] By the end of his Vienna period, it is unlikely that Hitler's detestation of Social Democracy, firmly established though it was, had gone much beyond that which had been current in Schönerer pan-German nationalism – apart from the additional radicality deriving from his own bitter first-hand experiences of the misery and degradation that enhanced his utter rejection of international socialism as a solution. That his hatred of Social Democracy had already by this date, as Hitler claimed in *Mein Kampf*, married with a racial theory of antisemitism to give him a distinctive 'world-view' that remained thereafter unchanged, can be discounted.

V

Why and when did Hitler become the fixated, pathological antisemite known from the writing of his first political tracts in 1919 down to the writing of his testament in the Berlin bunker in 1945? Since his paranoid hatred was to shape policies that culminated in the killing of millions of Jews, this is self-evidently an important question. The answer is, however, less clear than we should like. In truth, we do not know for certain why, nor even when, Hitler turned into a manic and obsessive antisemite.

Hitler's own version is laid out in some well-known and striking passages in *Mein Kampf*. According to this, he had not been an antisemite in Linz.

On coming to Vienna, he had at first been alienated by the antisemitic press there. But the obsequiousness of the mainstream press in its treatment of the Habsburg court and its vilification of the German Kaiser gradually led him to the 'more decent' and 'more appetizing' line taken in the antisemitic paper the *Deutsches Volksblatt*. Growing admiration for Karl Lueger – 'the greatest German mayor of all times' – helped to change his attitude towards the Jews – 'my greatest transformation of all' – and within two years (or in another account a single year) the transformation was complete.[281] Hitler highlights, however, a single episode which opened his eyes to the 'Jewish Question'.

Once, as I was strolling through the Inner City, I suddenly encountered an apparition in a black caftan and black hair locks. Is this a Jew? was my first thought.

For, to be sure, they had not looked like that in Linz. I observed the man furtively and cautiously, but the longer I stared at this foreign face, scrutinizing feature for feature, the more my first question assumed a new form:

Is this a German?[282]

Following this encounter, Hitler continued, he started to buy antisemitic pamphlets. He was now able to see that Jews 'were not Germans of a special religion, but a people in themselves'. Vienna now appeared in a different light. 'Wherever I went, I began to see Jews, and the more I saw, the more sharply they became distinguished in my eyes from the rest of humanity.'[283]

Now, to stay with his own account, his revulsion rapidly grew. The language Hitler uses in these pages of *Mein Kampf* betrays a morbid fear of uncleanliness, dirt, and disease – all of which he associated with Jews.[284] He also quickly formed his newly-found hatred into a conspiracy theory. He now linked the Jews with every evil he perceived: the liberal press, cultural life, prostitution, and – most significant of all – identified them as the leading force in Social Democracy. At this, 'the scales dropped from my eyes'.[285] Everything connected with Social Democracy – party leaders, Reichsrat deputies, trade union secretaries, and the Marxist press that he devoured with loathing – now seemed to him to be Jewish.[286] But this 'recognition', he wrote, gave him great satisfaction. His already existent hatred of Social Democracy, that party's anti-nationalism, now fell into place: its leadership was 'almost exclusively in the hands of a foreign people'. 'Only now,' Hitler remarked, 'did I become thoroughly acquainted with the seducer of our people.'[287] He had linked Marxism and Jewry through what he called 'the Jewish doctrine of Marxism'.[288]

It is a graphic account. But it is not corroborated by the other sources that cast light on Hitler's time in Vienna. Indeed, in some respects it is directly at variance with them. It is generally accepted that, for all the problems with the autobiographical parts of *Mein Kampf*, Hitler was indeed converted to manic racial antisemitism while in Vienna. But the available evidence, beyond Hitler's own words, offers little to confirm that view. Interpretation rests ultimately on the balance of probabilities.

Kubizek claimed Hitler was already an antisemite before leaving Linz. In contrast to Hitler's assertion that his father had 'cosmopolitan views' and would have regarded antisemitism as 'cultural backwardness', Kubizek stated that Alois's regular drinking cronies in Leonding were Schönerer supporters and that he himself was certainly therefore anti-Jewish. He pointed also to the openly antisemitic teachers Hitler encountered in the *Realschule*. He allegedly recalled, too, that Adolf had said to him one day, as they passed the small synagogue: 'That doesn't belong in Linz.' For Kubizek, Vienna had made Hitler's antisemitism more radical. But it had not created it. In his opinion, Hitler had gone to Vienna 'already as a pronounced antisemite'.[289] Kubizek went on to recount one or two episodes of Hitler's aversion to Jews during the time they were together in Vienna.[290] He claimed an encounter with a Galician Jew was the caftan story of *Mein Kampf*. But this, and a purported visit to a synagogue in which Hitler took Kubizek along to witness a Jewish wedding, have the appearance of an outright fabrication.[291] Palpably false is Kubizek's assertion that Hitler joined the Antisemitenbund (Antisemitic League) during the months in 1908 that the friends were together in Vienna. There was no such organization in Austria-Hungary before 1918.[292]

In fact, Kubizek is generally unconvincing in the passages devoted to the early manifestations of Hitler's antisemitism. These are among the least trustworthy sections of his account – partly drawing on *Mein Kampf*, partly inventing episodes which were not present in the original draft version of his recollections, and in places demonstrably incorrect. Kubizek was keen to distance himself in his post-war memoirs from the radical views of his friend on the 'Jewish Question'.[293] It suited him to emphasize that Hitler had from Linz days hated the Jews. His suggestion that Hitler's father (whom he had not known) had been a pronounced antisemite is probably incorrect. As we have seen, Alois Hitler's own more moderate form of pan-Germanism had differed from that of the Schönerer movement in its continued allegiance to the Emperor of Austria and accorded with the line adopted by the dominant party in Upper Austria, the Deutsche Volkspartei (German People's Party), which admitted Jews to membership.[294] The vehemently antisemitic as well as radical German nationalist Schönerer movement certainly had a strong following in and around Linz, and no doubt included some at least of Hitler's teachers among its supporters. But antisemitism seems to have been relatively unimportant in his school compared with the antagonism towards the Czechs.[295] Hitler's own later recollection was probably in this respect not inaccurate, when he told Albert Speer that he had become aware of the 'nationalities problem' – by which he meant vehement hostility towards the Czechs at school – but the 'danger of Jewry' had only been made plain to him in Vienna.[296]

The young Hitler, himself taken while still in Linz by Schönerer's ideas, could scarcely have missed the emphatic racial antisemitism which was so integral to them.[297] But for the Schönerer supporters in the Linz of Hitler's day, antisemitism appears to have been a subdominant theme in the cacophony of anti-Czech clamour and trumpeted Germanomania. It certainly did not prevent Hitler's warm expressions of gratitude in postcards and the present of one of his watercolours to Dr Bloch, the Jewish physician who had treated his mother in her last illness.[298] The deep, visceral hatred of his later antisemitism was of a different order altogether. That was certainly not present in his Linz years.

There is no evidence that Hitler was distinctively antisemitic by the time he parted company with Kubizek in the summer of 1908. Hitler himself claimed that he became an antisemite within two years of arriving in Vienna.[299] Could, then, the transformation be placed in the year he spent, mainly in Felberstraße, between leaving Kubizek and becoming a vagrant? The testimony of Lanz von Liebenfels would fit this chronology.[300] But we have seen that this is of highly doubtful value. Hitler's descent into abject poverty in autumn 1909 might seem an obvious time to search for a scapegoat and find it in the figure of the Jew. But he had the opportunity less then than at any other time in Vienna to 'read up' on the subject, as he claimed in *Mein Kampf*.[301]

Not only that: Reinhold Hanisch, his close companion over the following months, was adamant that Hitler 'in those days was by no means a Jew hater. He became one afterwards.'[302] Hanisch emphasized Hitler's Jewish friends and contacts in the Men's Home to demonstrate the point. A one-eyed locksmith called Robinsohn spared Hitler some small change to help him out financially from time to time. (The man's name was actually Simon Robinson, traceable in the Men's Home in 1912–13.[303]) Josef Neumann, as we have seen, became, as Hanisch put it, 'a real friend' to Hitler. He was said to have 'liked Hitler very much' and to have been 'of course highly esteemed' by him. A postcard salesman, Siegfried Löffner (misnamed Loeffler by Hanisch), was also 'one of Hitler's circle of acquaintances', and, as we remarked, took sides with him in the acrimonious conflict with Hanisch in 1910.[304] Hitler preferred, as we have seen, to sell his pictures to Jewish dealers, and one of them, Jacob Altenberg, subsequently spoke well of the business relationship they had conducted.[305] Hanisch's testimony finds confirmation in the later comment of the anonymous resident of the Men's Home in the spring of 1912, that 'Hitler got along exceptionally well with Jews, and said at one time that they were a clever people who stick together better than the Germans do.'[306]

The three years that Hitler spent in the Men's Home certainly gave him every opportunity to pore over antisemitic newpapers, pamphlets, and cheap literature. But, leaving aside the fact that the chronology no longer matches Hitler's own assertion of a transformation within two years of arriving in Vienna, Karl Honisch, as we have seen, makes a point of emphasizing Hitler's strong views on 'Jesuits' and the 'Reds', vehemently expressed in his numerous interventions in the debates in the writing-room, though makes no mention at all of any hatred of Jews. Hitler certainly joined in talk about the Jews in the Men's Home. But his standpoint was, according to Hanisch's account, by no means negative. Hanisch has Hitler admiring the Jews for their resistance to persecution, praising Heine's poetry and the music of Mendelssohn and Offenbach, expressing the view that the Jews were the first civilized nation in that they had abandoned polytheism for belief in one God, blaming Christians more than Jews for usury, and dismissing the stock-in-trade antisemitic charge of Jewish ritual murder as nonsense.[307] Only Josef Greiner, of those who claimed to have witnessed Hitler at first hand in the Men's Home, speaks of him as a fanatical Jew-hater in that period.[308] But, as we have noted, Greiner's testimony is worthless.

There is, therefore, no reliable contemporary confirmation of Hitler's paranoid antisemitism during the Vienna period. If Hanisch is to be believed, in fact, Hitler was not antisemitic at all at this time. Beyond that, Hitler's close comrades during the First World War also recalled that he voiced no notable antisemitic views.[309] The question arises, then, whether Hitler had not invented his Viennese 'conversion' to antisemitism in *Mein Kampf*; whether, in fact, his pathological hatred of the Jews did not emerge only in the wake of the lost war, in 1918–19.[310]

Why might Hitler fabricate the claim that he had become an ideological antisemite in Vienna? And, equally, why might a 'conversion' at the end of the war be regarded as something to be concealed by a story of an earlier transformation? The answer lies in the image Hitler was establishing for himself in the early 1920s, and particularly following the failed putsch and his trial. This demanded the self-portrait painted in *Mein Kampf*, of the nobody who struggled from the first against adversity, and, rejected by the academic 'establishment', taught himself through painstaking study, coming – above all through his own bitter experiences – to unique insights about society and politics that enabled him without assistance to formulate at the age of around twenty a rounded 'world-view'. This unchanged 'world-view', he was saying in 1924, provided him with the claim to leadership of the national movement, and indeed with the claim to be Germany's coming 'great leader'.[311] Perhaps by then Hitler had even convinced himself that all the pieces of the ideological jigsaw had indeed fallen into place during his Vienna years. In any case, by the early 1920s no one was in a position to gainsay the story. An admission that he had become an ideological antisemite only at the end of the war, as he lay blinded from mustard gas in a hospital in Pasewalk and heard of Germany's defeat and the revolution, would certainly have sounded less heroic, and would also have smacked of hysteria.

However, it is difficult to believe that Hitler of all people, given the intensity of his hatred for the Jews between 1919 and the end of his life, had remained unaffected by the poisonous antisemitic atmosphere of the Vienna he knew – one of the most virulently anti-Jewish cities in Europe. It was a city where, at the turn of the century, radical antisemites advocated punishing sexual relations between Jews and non-Jews as sodomy, and placing Jews under surveillance around Easter to prevent ritual child-murder.[312] Schönerer, the racial antisemite, had notably helped to stir up the hatred. Lueger, as we noted, was able to exploit the widespread and vicious antisemitism to build up his Christian Social Party and consolidate his hold on power in Vienna. Hitler greatly admired both. Once more, it would have been strange had he of all people admired them but been unaffected by such an essential stock-in-trade of their message as their antisemitism. Certainly, he learnt from Lueger the gains to be made from popularizing hatred against the Jews.[313] The explicitly antisemitic newspaper Hitler read, and singled out for praise, the *Deutsches Volksblatt*, selling around 55,000 copies a day at the time, described Jews as agents of decomposition and corruption, and repeatedly linked them with sexual scandal, perversion, and prostitution.[314] Leaving aside the probably contrived incident of the caftan-Jew, Hitler's description of his gradual exposure through the antisemitic gutter press to deep anti-Jewish prejudice and its impact upon him while in Vienna has an authentic ring about it.[315]

Probably no single encounter produced his loathing for Jews. Given his relations with his parents, there may have been some connection with an unresolved Oedipal complex, though this is no more than guesswork.[316] Hitler's linkage of Jews and prostitution has prompted speculation that sexual fantasies, obsessions, or perversions provide the key.[317] Again, there is no reliable evidence. The sexual connotations were no more than Hitler could have picked up from the *Deutsches Volksblatt*. Another explanation would be a simpler one. At the time that Hitler soaked up Viennese antisemitism, he had recently experienced bereavement, failure, rejection, isolation, and increasing penury. The gulf between his self-image as a frustrated great artist or architect, and the reality of his life as a drop-out, needed an explanation. The Viennese antisemitic gutter press, it could be surmised, helped him to find that explanation.[318]

But if Hitler's antisemitism was indeed formed in Vienna, why did it remain unnoticed by those around him? The answer might well be banal: in that hotbed of rabid antisemitism, anti-Jewish sentiment was so commonplace that it could go practically unnoticed. The argument from silence is, therefore, not conclusive. However, there is still the evidence from Hanisch and Anonymous about Hitler's friendship with Jews to contend with. This seems to stand in flat contradiction to Hitler's own lurid account of his conversion to antisemitism in Vienna. One remark by Hanisch, however, suggests that Hitler had indeed already developed racist notions about the Jews. When one of their group asked why Jews remained strangers in the nation 'Hitler answered that it was because they were a different race.' He added, according to Hanisch, that 'Jews had a different smell.' Hitler was said also to have frequently remarked 'that descendants of Jews are very radical and have terroristic inclinations'. And when he and Neumann discussed Zionism, Hitler said that any money of Jews leaving Austria would obviously be confiscated 'as it was not Jewish but Austrian'.[319] If Hanisch is to be believed, then, Hitler was advancing views reflecting racial antisemitism at the same time that he was closely associated with a number of Jews in the Men's Home. Could it have been that this very proximity, the dependence of the would-be great artist on Jews to off-load his little street paintings, at precisely the same time that he was reading and digesting the antisemitic bile poured out by Vienna's gutter press, served only to underline and deepen the bitter enmities taking shape in his mind?[320] Would the outsized ego of the unrecognized genius reduced to *this* not have translated his self-disgust into inwardly fermenting race-hatred when the plainly antisemitic Hanisch remarked to him that 'he must be of Jewish blood, since such a large beard rarely grows on a Christian chin' and 'he had big feet, as a desert wanderer must have'?[321] Whether Hitler was on terms of real friendship with the Jews around him in the Men's Home, as Hanisch states, might be doubted. Throughout his life Hitler made remarkably few genuine friendships. And throughout his life, despite the torrents of words that poured from his mouth as a politician, he was adept at camouflaging his true feelings even to those in his immediate company. He was also a clever manipulator of those around him. His relations with the Jews in the Men's Home were clearly, at least in part, self-serving. Robinson helped him out with money. Neumann, too, paid off small debts for him.[322] Löffner was Hitler's go-between with the dealers.[323] Whatever his true feelings, in his contacts with Jewish dealers and traders, Hitler was simply being pragmatic: as long as they could sell his paintings for him, he could swallow his abstract dislike of Jews.[324]

Though it has frequently been claimed, largely based on Hanisch's evidence and on the lack of reference to his antisemitic views in the paltry sources available, that Hitler was not a racial antisemite during his stay in Vienna, the balance of probabilities surely suggests a different interpretation? It seems more likely that Hitler, as he later claimed, indeed came to hate Jews during his time in Vienna. But, probably, at this time it was still little more than a rationalization of his personal circumstances rather than a thought-out 'world-view'. It was a personalized hatred – blaming the Jews for all the ills that befell him in a city that he associated with personal misery. But any expression of this hatred that he had internalized did not stand out to those around him where antisemitic vitriol was so normal. And, paradoxically, as long as he *needed* Jews to help him earn what classed as a living, he kept quiet about his true views and perhaps even on occasion, as Hanisch indicates, insincerely made remarks which could be taken, if mistakenly, as complimentary to Jewish culture. Only later, if this line of argument is followed, did he rationalize his visceral hatred into the fully-fledged 'world-view', with antisemitism as its core, that congealed in the early 1920s. The formation of the ideological antisemite had to wait until a further crucial phase in Hitler's development, ranging from the end of the war to his political awakening in Munich in 1919.

VI

That was all still in the future. In spring 1913, after three years in the Men's Home, Hitler was still drifting, vegetating – not any longer down and out, it is true, and with responsibility to no one but himself, but without any career prospects. He gave the impression that he had still not given up all hope of studying art, however, and told the writing-room regulars in the Men's Home that he intended to go to Munich to enter the Art Academy.[325] He had long said 'he would go to Munich like a shot', eulogizing about the 'great picture galleries' in the Bavarian capital.[326] He had a good reason for postponing any plans to leave for Munich. His share of his father's inheritance became due only on his twenty-fourth birthday, on 20 April 1913. More than anything else, it might be surmised, the wait for this money was what kept Hitler so long in the city he detested.[327] On 16 May 1913 the District Court in Linz confirmed that he should receive the sizeable sum, with interest added to the original 652 Kronen, of 819 Kronen 98 Heller, and that this would be sent by post to the 'artist' (Kunstmaler) Adolf Hitler in Meldemannstraße, Vienna.[328] With this long-awaited and much-welcome prize in his possession, he needed to delay his departure for Munich no further.

He had another reason for deciding the time was ripe to leave Vienna. In autumn 1909 he had failed to register for military service, which he would have been due to serve the following spring, after his twenty-first birthday.[329] Even if found unfit, he would still have been eligible in 1911 and 1912 to undertake military service for a state he detested so fervently.[330] Having avoided the authorities for three years, he presumably felt it safe to cross the border to Germany following his twenty-fourth birthday in 1913. He was mistaken. The Austrian authorities had not overlooked him. They were on his trail, and his avoidance of military service was to cause him difficulties and embarrassment the following year.[331] The attempt to put any possible snoopers off the scent in later years is why, once he had become well known, Hitler persistently dated his departure from Vienna to 1912, not 1913.[332]

On 24 May 1913, Hitler, carrying a light, black suitcase containing all his possessions, in a better set of clothes than the shabby suit he had been used to wearing, and accompanied by a young, short-sighted, unemployed shop-assistant, Rudolf Häusler, four years his junior, whom he had known for little over three months in the Men's Home, left the co-residents from the writing-room who had escorted them a short distance, and set off for Munich.[333]

The Vienna years were over. They had indelibly marked Hitler's personality and the 'basic stock of personal views' he held.[334] But these 'personal opinions' had not yet coagulated into a fully-fledged ideology, or 'world-view'. For that to happen, an even harder school than Vienna had to be experienced: war and defeat. And only the unique circumstances produced by that war and defeat enabled an Austrian drop-out to find appeal in a different land, among the people of his adopted country.

3

ELATION AND EMBITTERMENT

'Overpowered by stormy enthusiasm, I fell down on my knees and thanked Heaven from an overflowing heart for granting me the good fortune of being permitted to live at this time . . . There now began the greatest and most unforgettable time of my earthly existence.'

'And so it had all been in vain . . . Did all this happen only so that a gang of wretched criminals could lay hands on the fatherland? . . . In these nights hatred grew in me, hatred for those responsible for this deed.'

Hitler in *Mein Kampf*, on his feelings at
the beginning and end of the First World War

I

The First World War made Hitler possible. Without the experience of war, the humiliation of defeat, and the upheaval of revolution the failed artist and social drop-out would not have discovered what to do with his life by entering politics and finding his métier as a propagandist and beerhall demagogue. And without the trauma of war, defeat and revolution, without the political radicalization of German society that this trauma brought about, the demagogue would have been without an audience for his raucous, hate-filled message. The legacy of the lost war provided the conditions in which the paths of Hitler and the German people began to cross. Without the war, a Hitler on the Chancellor's seat that had been occupied by Bismarck would have been unthinkable.

Hitler, it was once commonplace to presume (at least outside Germany itself), was the logical consequence of deep-seated flaws in the German national character, the culmination of a malformed history, misshapen through a propensity for authoritarianism, militarism and racism. There was never much to be said for such a crude misreading of the past. To be taken far more seriously was the view that the failure of liberalism following the Revolution of 1848, when pressure for sweeping constitutional reform eventually collapsed in disarray, had left the forces of authoritarianism, represented above all by the pre-industrial military-landholding caste, with unshaken dominance and prepared to use any methods, however unscrupulous, to defend their position of power against the pressures for democratization. Hitler's triumph was accordingly traced back to the legacy of Bismarck's 'revolution from above' – political transformation through war and Unification that left social bases of power intact – producing continuities that linked the Second Reich with the Third, straddling the ill-fated Weimar experiment of a democracy without democrats. The explanation of Hitler was located in a society whose path to modernity had been peculiar, a 'faulted nation'[1] whose institutions, structures, power-relations and mentalities had remained pre-modern, at odds with the swift encroachment of the modern world, the rapidity of competing (and menacing) modern economic, cultural, and political forces.[2]

Much of this seems plausible, even persuasive. But as it stands the argument is too neat, too self-contained, ultimately too simple to be compelling. For it has become much clearer that Germany's social and economic development in the late nineteenth century were far more similar to those of Britain and France – the countries with which it has so often been contrasted – than was once thought. Its problems, by and large, were those of a modern, highly developed, culturally advanced, industrial society. Certainly, Germany encountered tensions in coping with rapid economic and social change. Some were profound. But few were peculiar to Germany, though they did often find acute expression there.

The constitutional framework of the German Reich did, on the other hand, differ sharply in key respects from that of Britain and France, whose diversely structured but relatively flexible parliamentary democracies offered better potential to cope with the social and political demands arising from rapid economic change. In Germany, the growth of party-political pluralism, which found its representation in the Reichstag, had not been translated into parliamentary democracy. Powerful vested interests – big landholders (most of them belonging to the aristocracy), the officer corps of the army, the upper echelons of the state bureaucracy, even most of the Reichstag parties – continued to block this. The Reich Chancellor remained the appointee of the Kaiser, who could make or break him whatever the respective strength of Reichstag parties. The government itself stood above the Reichstag, independent (at least in theory) of party politics. Whole tracts of policy, especially on foreign and military matters, lay outside parliamentary control. Power was jealously guarded, in the face of mounting pressure for radical change, by the beleaguered forces of the old order. Some of these, increasingly fearful of revolution, were prepared even to contemplate war as a way of holding on to their power and fending off the threat of socialism.

It is, perhaps, less obvious than was once thought that the very real constitutional and political problems faced by Germany on the eve of the First World War would have been insurmountable without the massive gamble of a war aimed at saving the old order. The prospect, without war, of a gradualist conversion into a constitutional monarchy and parliamentary democracy was not completely illusory.[3] But a betting man would probably not have wagered too much on this as the likely outcome. It is hard to see how a gradual change to parliamentarism – something ultimately conceded by Germany's rulers only when the war had been given up as lost – could have come about when the constitution was so inflexible and the resistance to democratization among powerful groups so entrenched. The rigidly authoritarian political system was ill-equipped to introduce the fundamental reform of its own structures.[4]

In short, Germany in the years before the calamity of 1914–18 was in some – though only some – ways more 'normal' than was once thought. The Second Reich was not the Third Reich waiting to happen. At the same time, even features common to much of Europe had a flavour or colouring shaped by the particular political culture and social fabric of the German nation-state. While it took the catastrophe of a first world war to produce conditions in which a Hitler was even thinkable, a specifically German political culture that had emerged in the Wilhelmine era (or at any rate strains of it which, however, had before 1914 by no means been dominant) provided the soil in which the seeds of the ideas that National Socialism would later harvest could germinate and then sprout rapidly. Even here, the developments were often shaded rather than clear-cut.[5] It would be a mistake to present selectively a catalogue of extremist opinions and attitudes as if they were representative of a whole society. But just as it is a distortion to read into German history an inexorable pattern of development culminating in Hitler, so it would be misleading to imply that Hitler was a bolt from a clear blue sky, that nothing in Germany's development had prepared the ground for the catastrophe of Nazism; and dangerous to presume that a single individual had so hypnotized the nation that he had driven its otherwise healthy progress off the rails.[6]

It was more than anything else the ways in which nationalism had developed in late nineteenth-century Germany that provided the set of ideas that, if often in distorted – even perverted – form, offered the potential for Nazism's post-war appeal. In particular, the years between 1909 and 1914 saw a strengthening and regrouping of the radical Right that formed a bridge spanning the war to the post-war political world.[7] Crucial to the character of German nationalism was the pervasive sense, present already long before the war, of incomplete unity, of persistent, even widening division and conflict within the nation. What, in the changed conditions after the war, Hitler was able most signally to exploit was the belief that pluralism was somehow unnatural or unhealthy in a society, that it was a sign of weakness, and that internal division and disharmony could be suppressed and eliminated, to be replaced by the unity of a national community. The desire for national unity to supplant internal dissension and overcome division was a hallmark of all shadings of nationalist feeling in Imperial Germany. The very superficiality of the unity that Bismarck had constitutionally forged in 1871 and superimposed upon a highly fragmented society – divided by religion, class, and region – encouraged the deliberate 'nationalisation of the masses',[8] not least through the manufacture of a sense of nationhood which was exclusivist, ringed off against those who did not 'belong' to it. Leading historian Heinrich von Treitschke, a prominent spokesman of a sharpened, aggressive national consciousness, an integral nationalism excluding 'enemies of the Reich', was one of many well-known intellectuals who helped inordinately to strengthen such ideas among the educated bourgeoisie.[9] 'The Jews are our misfortune' was among the influential sentiments to which Treitschke lent his weighty name.[10] Poles and Jews, Catholics, and especially Social Democrats were all targeted 'outsiders' under Bismarck. But the discrimination and repression backfired. The *Kulturkampf* – Bismarck's attack on Catholic education, institutions and clergy in Germany during the 1870s – substantially strengthened Catholicism, while the twelve years of the Socialist Law, which imposed bans on socialist associations, meetings and publications, produced a greatly enlarged Social Democratic Party committed to a Marxist programme. By the eve of the First World War, following the 1912 Reichstag election, the SPD was easily the largest party in the Reichstag, provoking alarm and deepening hatred in the upper and middle classes. By this time, the largest socialist movement in Europe, whose Marxist programme sought the demolition of the existing state, stood opposed by a highly aggressive integral nationalism aiming to destroy Marxist socialism.

That the German nation-state arose from the unification of a number of individual states further encouraged a sense of nationhood which had gained definition from culture and language rather than attaching itself to and emerging from the institutions of a pre-existing unitary state as in the case of England or France. This promoted an ethnic definition of nationhood which could easily slide over (though it by no means always did so) into forms of racism, especially when, as was the case in Germany as elsewhere in Europe, nationalism blended into imperialism and was directed aggressively outwards as well as defensively inwards, voicing shrill demands for a colonial 'place in the sun'.

All nationalisms need their myths. In this case, a powerful one was the

'Reich myth'.[11] The very name of the new nation-state, 'German Reich', evoked for many the mystical claim to reinstate the first Reich of Frederick Barbarossa – sleeping, according to the saga, in his holy mountain beneath the Kyffhäuser in Thuringia until the rebirth of his medieval Reich. The new aesthetics of nationalism called for the continuity to be symbolized in the gigantic monument to Kaiser Wilhelm I, mainly funded by veterans' associations, erected on the Kyffhäuser in 1896.[12] The 'Reich myth' linked national unity and the ending of division to heroic deeds and individual greatness, interpreting previous German history as the prelude to the ultimate attainment of national unity. Schoolbooks glorified the exploits of a pantheon of national heroes, filled with warriors reaching back to the legendary Hermann the Cherusker, the name attached to Arminius, the Germanic leader who inflicted a crushing defeat on three Roman legions in 9 AD. His colossal monument in the Teutoburger Wald, and that of Germania on the Niederwald Monument near Rüdesheim on the Rhine, which so impressed Hitler when he saw it for the first time in 1914, *en route* for the battlefields of Flanders,[13] gave granite expression to the 'Reich myth'. And once the foundation of the German Reich itself passed from current politics into history, and its architect's contentious career had been peremptorily ended by the new Kaiser, Bismarck himself became the focal point of a cult which eulogized him as the greatest hero of all, statesman and warrior combined. Hundreds of 'Bismarck Towers', initiated by student bodies and erected the length and breadth of the country, represented the national hero as the intended symbol of nation, state and people.[14] And the more, after Bismarck's departure, the Reichstag – initially, together with the monarchy, the embodiment of national unity – came to be seen as the barometer of national division, a house of squabbling politicians and competing parties, the more there appeared to be the need for a new Bismarck, a new national hero.

A claim to such a role was initially advanced by no less than the Kaiser himself. The caesaristic tendencies, increasingly a feature of German nationalism towards the end of the nineteenth century, were deliberately furthered after 1890 by the promotion of a Hohenzollern cult, focused on the new and ambitious Kaiser, Wilhelm II, and intended to represent in his person 'the two images of the governing statesman and the sleeping Hero-Kaiser'.[15] The new Kaiser, it was implied, would lead Germany to external greatness and eliminate divisions within. Increasingly shrill voices on the nationalist Right demanded nothing less. However, the gap between words and deeds was too great. Disappointment and disillusionment in the Kaiser both helped promote the Bismarck cult and led to increasingly vociferous nationalist opposition, its most radical voices demanding the extension of German power and greatness through expansion and conquest of inferior peoples.

The assertiveness of German nationalism at the turn of the century was in no small measure aggression born of fear – not just the traditional antagonism towards the French and the growing rivalry with Great Britain, but also the presumed threat seen in the Slavic east, and, internally, the perceived looming menace of Social Democracy, and culturally pessimistic worries about national degeneration and decline.

In a climate shaped by an often irrational fear of enemies, within and without, who allegedly threatened the future of the nation, it is not surprising that alongside extreme anti-Marxism, racial ideologies – not just antisemitism, but social Darwinism and eugenics – should increasingly gain currency. None was confined to Germany, of course. Social Darwinism was influential in Britain; the classic lands of racial antisemitism around the turn of the century were Austria-Hungary and France; the region of the most vicious physical persecution of Jews, Russia.[16] But in the German context the racial ideas of the populist radical Right, taken over in good part by conservatives, acquired a level of backing that necessarily posed a substantial threat to individuals and minorities.[17] The supremacy of the nation over the individual, the stress on order and authority, opposition to internationalism and equality, became increasingly pronounced features of German national feeling.[18] With them grew demands for 'racial consciousness', and antagonism towards the tiny Jewish minority, overwhelmingly seeking assimilation, increased.[19]

Jews could be described, as they were in a widely-read text of the 1890s, as 'poison for us and will have to be treated as such', and, in increasingly common bacteriological language, as a 'pest and a cholera'.[20] Such extreme views were by no means representative. Most Jews in Imperial Germany could feel reasonably sanguine about the future, could regard antisemitism as a throwback to a more primitive era that was on the way out.[21] But they underestimated both the pernicious ways in which modern racial antisemitism differed from archaic forms of persecution of Jews, however vicious, in its uncompromising emphasis upon biological distinctiveness, its links with assertive nationalism, and the ways it could be taken over and exploited in new types of political mass movements. And they were too ready to overlook the appeal of racist classics like Houston Stewart Chamberlain's *Grundlagen des 19. Jahrhunderts* (*Foundations of the 19th Century*), a bestseller since its appearance in 1900, and Theodor Fritsch's popularizing 'catechism for antisemites', his *Handbuch der Judenfrage* (*Handbook of the Jewish Question*), which went through twenty-five editions within seven years of publication in 1887.[22] While purely antisemitic parties proved too narrowly focused and were in decline in the late Imperial era, racial antisemitism had by then been increasingly taken over by parties, associations, pressure-groups, student unions and interest organizations, and intermingled with the rest of the package of anti-Marxist, imperialist, militaristic, radical nationalism.

The eugenics movement, originating in England and finding followers in Scandinavia and America, but gaining new levels of support in Germany, fomented the fears, bordering on paranoia, of racial degeneration resulting from a declining birthrate among the better social groups and a rise in the proportion of 'inferiors' within the population. There was also growing resentment at the cost of supporting those seen as a burden on society – the 'worthless lives' of antisocials, the handicapped, 'inferiors', and especially the mentally sick whose alleged uninhibited sexual drive was regarded as a further stimulus to racial degeneration. It was in this context that the idea of sterilizing certain categories of 'degenerates' – an idea already described by one doctor in 1889 as 'a sacred duty of the state' – found growing support in medical circles.[23]

Above all, national assertiveness derived from the sense of greatness attained through conquest and based on cultural superiority – the feeling that Germany was a great and expanding power, and that a great power needed and deserved an empire. Germany had been late on the act in the imperialist carve-up in Africa. The bits and pieces of territory it had acquired in the 1880s could by no means match its pretensions, least of all satisfy the growing clamour on the Right that the rapid growth of population had left Germany a 'people without space'.[24] The demand for colonial and commercial empire built into the slogan of '*Weltpolitik*' was in essence little different to the claims of British and French imperialists. But alongside '*Weltpolitik*' grew ideas of territorial expansion into eastern Europe at the expense of Slav '*Untermenschen*' – ideas voiced ever more shrilly by some of the most important nationalist pressure-groups and increasingly entering the ideology of the German Conservative Party.[25] These pressure-groups, crucial to the dissemination of nationalist, imperialist, and racist ideas of all varieties, offered new possibilities of propaganda, agitation, and extra-parliamentary opposition. The largest, the Navy League, founded in 1898 to push for the building of a large battle fleet, had over a million members and associates by 1914.[26] The propaganda output – newpapers, pamphlets, even films – of such organizations was massive.[27] While the Navy

League could be said to have been mainstream in its nationalist message, the Eastern Marches Association (Ostmarkenverein) and, especially, the Pan-German League were, if smaller, more radical and more racist. The former advocated harsh measures of legal discrimination in a racial struggle against the Poles in the Prussian border provinces.[28] The Pan-Germans, influential beyond their numbers and with a high leaven of teachers and academics in their ranks, were the most radical of all in their ideology built up of *völkisch* nationalism and racist imperialism, embedded in a Manichaean 'world-view' of a struggle between good and evil – ideas which anticipated a good part of the Nazi 'world-view' – and an organization, though small, that formed a link to the huge Fatherland Party of 1917 and the post-war radical Right.[29] The leader of the Pan-German League, Heinrich Claß, writing in 1912 under the pseudonym of Daniel Frymann, advocated in his polemical tract, *Wenn ich der Kaiser wär* (*If I Were the Kaiser*), franchise restrictions, press censorship, repressive laws against socialism, and anti-Jewish legislation as the basis of national renewal.[30] Not least, given the widespread profound disappointment in the Kaiser, he demanded 'a strong able leader', whom 'all who have remained unseduced by the teachings of ungerman democracy yearn for ... because they know that greatness can only be brought about through the concentration of individual forces, which again can only be achieved by the subordination to a leader'.[31] By the time the war began, Claß's book had gone through five editions – an indication that the ideas of the 'new Right', though still a minority, were falling increasingly on fertile ground in the years before Germany became enveloped in the European conflagration.[32] This shift on the nationalist Right already before the war is important for an understanding of the radicalization that took place during the war itself, and the links with the rapid spread of *völkisch* politics immediately thereafter.[33]

On the eve of the First World War, Germany was certainly a state with some unattractive features – among them those of the unbalanced character sitting on the Imperial throne.[34] But nothing in its development predetermined the path to the Third Reich. What happened under Hitler was not presaged in Imperial Germany. It is unimaginable without the experience of the First World War and what followed it.

II

Looking back just over a decade later, Hitler spoke of the fifteen months he spent in Munich before the war as 'the happiest and by far the most contented' of his life.[35] The fanatical German nationalist exulted in his arrival in 'a *German* city', which he contrasted with the 'Babylon of races' that, for him, had been Vienna.[36] He gave a number of reasons why he had left Vienna: bitter enmity towards the Habsburg empire for pro-Slav policies that were disadvantaging the German population; growing hatred for the 'foreign mixture of peoples' who were 'corroding' German culture in Vienna; the conviction that Austria-Hungary was living on borrowed time, and that its end could not come soon enough; and the intensified longing to go to Germany, to where his 'childhood secret desires and secret love' had drawn him.[37] The last sentiments were plainly romanticized. Otherwise, the feelings were genuine enough. And of his determination not to fight for the Habsburg state there can be no doubt. This is what Hitler meant when he said he left Austria 'primarily for political reasons'.[38] But the implication that he had left as a form of political protest was disingenuous and deliberately misleading. As we have already noted, the prime and immediate reason he crossed the border into Germany was very tangible: the Linz authorities were hot on his trail for evasion of military service.

The city to which Hitler became 'more attached ... than to any other spot of earth in this world'[39] was, in the years before the First World War, alongside Paris, Vienna, and Berlin, one of Europe's most vibrant cultural capitals, a hotbed of creativity and artistic innovation. Schwabing, the pulsating centre of Munich's artistic and bohemian life, drew artists, painters, and writers from all over Germany, and from other parts of Europe as well. They turned Schwabing's cafés, pubs, and cabarets into experimental hothouses of 'the modern'. 'In no city in Germany did old and new clash so forcefully as in Munich,' commented Lovis Corinth, one celebrated artist who experienced the atmosphere there at the turn of the century.[40] The theme of decline and renewal, the casting off of the sterile, decaying order, contempt for bourgeois convention, for the old, the stale, the traditional, the search for new expression and aesthetic values, the evocation of feeling over reason, the glorification of youth and exuberance, linked many of the disparate strands of Munich's modernist cultural scene. The Stefan George circle; the scourge of bourgeois morality, playwright and cabaret balladist Franz Wedekind; the great lyric poet Rainer Maria Rilke; and the Mann brothers – Thomas, famous since the publication in 1901 of his epic novel of bourgeois decline, *Buddenbrooks*, and whose vignette of bourgeois decay, *Der Tod in Venedig* (*Death in Venice*) had been published the year that Hitler arrived, and his elder, more politically radical brother Heinrich – were but some among the galaxy of literary luminaries in pre-war Munich. In painting, too, the challenge of 'the modern' characterized the era. Around the very time that Hitler was in Munich, Wassily Kandinsky, Franz Marc, Paul Klee, Alexej von Jawlensky, Gabriele Münter, and August Macke were leading lights in the group Der Blaue Reiter, revolutionizing artistic composition in brilliant and exciting new forms of expressionist painting. The visual arts would never be the same again.

It was not for political reasons, but as a 'metropolis of German art' that Munich attracted the drop-out, failed artist, and street-scene painter Adolf Hitler.[41] Once again, as a few years earlier, he made his way to an epicentre of the modernist cultural revolution. But in Munich as in Vienna, the avant-garde passed him by. His cultural taste remained locked in the nineteenth century, closed to modern art forms, hostile to the works of all those for whom Munich before the First World War is renowned. What impressed him, as they had done in Vienna, were the imposing representative buildings, the neo-classical façades, the wide boulevards, the great galleries of works of the old masters, the architecture of grandeur and power. It was the city of the Wittelsbachs, not the city of artistic innovation, that appealed to Hitler.[42] He rhapsodized about the Pinakothek, a 'most marvellous achievement' attributable to one man alone: 'what Munich owes to Ludwig I is unimaginable'.[43] The Glyptothek and Propyläen on the Königsplatz (later the scene of the Nazi commemoration each year of the 'heroes of the Movement' who had been killed in the putsch fiasco of 1923), the Wittelsbach Residenz and the expansive Ludwigstraße flanked by its monumental façades were other constructions of that era that stirred the impressionistic Hitler.[44] He later saw similarities in the representative buildings of nineteenth-century Munich to those of Berlin in the time of Frederick the Great; in both cases they had been erected cheaply, since funding was so limited.[45] His own plans for a gigantic rebuilding of Munich after a second war were not intended to encounter similar difficulties: the massive bill would have been paid by the conquered peoples of Europe.[46]

Hitler wrote that he came to Munich in the hope of some day making a name for himself as an architect.[47] He described himself on arrival as an 'architectural painter'.[48] In the letter he wrote to the Linz authorities in 1914, defending himself against charges of evading military service, he stated that he was forced to earn his living as a self-employed artist (*Kunstmaler*) in order to fund his training as an architectural painter (*Architekturmaler*).[49] In the biographical sketch he wrote in 1921, he stated that he went to Munich as an 'architecture-designer and architecture-painter'.[50] At his trial three years later, in February 1924, he implied that he had already completed his training as an 'architecture-designer' (*Architekturzeichner*) by the time he came to Munich, but wanted to train to be a master builder.[51] Many years later he claimed his intention was to undertake practical training in Germany; that on coming to Munich he had hoped to study for three years before joining the major Munich construction firm Heilmann and Littmann as a designer and then showing, by entering the first architectural competition to design an important building, just what he could do.[52] None of these varying and conflicting accounts was true. There is no evidence that Hitler took any practical steps during his time in Munich to improve his poor and dwindling career prospects. He was drifting no less aimlessly than he had done in Vienna.

After arriving in Munich on 25 May 1913, a bright spring Sunday, Hitler followed up an advertisement for a small room rented by the family of the tailor Joseph Popp on the third floor of 34 Schleißheimerstraße, in a poorish district to the north of the city, on the edge of Schwabing and not far from the big barracks area.[53] His travelling companion, Rudolf Häusler, shared the cramped room with him until mid-February 1914. Apparently, Hitler's habit of reading late at night by the light of a petroleum lamp prevented Häusler from sleeping, and so irritated him that he eventually moved out, returning after a few days to take the room adjacent to Hitler's, where he stayed until May 1914.[54] According to his landlady, Frau Popp, Hitler quickly set himself up with the equipment to begin painting.[55] As he had done in Vienna, he developed a routine where he could complete a picture every two or three days, usually copied from postcards of well-known tourist scenes in Munich – including the Theatinerkirche, the Asamkirche, the Hofbräuhaus, the Alter Hof, the Münzhof, the Altes Rathaus, the Sendlinger Tor, the Residenz, the Propyläen – then set out to find customers in bars, cafés, and beerhalls.[56] His accurate but uninspired, rather soulless water-colours were, as Hitler himself later admitted when he was German Chancellor and they were selling for massively inflated prices, of very ordinary quality.[57] But they were certainly no worse than similar products touted about the beerhalls, often the work of genuine art students seeking to pay their way. Once he had found his feet, Hitler had no difficulty finding buyers. He was able to make a modest living from his painting and exist about as comfortably as he had done in his last years in Vienna. When the Linz authorities caught up with him in 1914, he acknowledged that his income – though irregular and fluctuating – could be put at around 1,200 Marks a year, and told his court photographer Heinrich Hoffmann at a much later date that he could get by on around 80 Marks a month for living costs at that time.[58]

As in Vienna, Hitler was polite but distant, self-contained, withdrawn, and apparently without friends (other than, in the first months, Häusler). Frau Popp could not recall Hitler having a single visitor in the entire two years of his tenancy.[59] He lived simply and frugally, preparing his paintings during the day and reading at night.[60] According to Hitler's own account, 'the study of the political events of the day', especially foreign policy, preoccupied him during his time in Munich.[61] He also claimed to have immersed himself again in the theoretical literature of Marxism and to have examined thoroughly once more the relation of Marxism to the Jews.[62] There is no obvious reason to doubt his landlady's witness to the books he brought back with him from the Bayerische Staatsbibliothek, not far away in Ludwigstraße.[63] In all the millions of recorded words of Hitler, however, there is nothing to indicate that he ever pored over the theoretical writings of Marxism, that he had studied Marx, or Engels, or Lenin (who had been in Munich not long before him), or Trotsky (his contemporary in Vienna). Reading for Hitler, in Munich as in Vienna, was not for enlightenment or learning, but to confirm prejudice.

Most of it was probably done in cafés, where Hitler could continue his habit of devouring the newspapers available to customers. All of human kind and the whole gamut of views on politics and society, God and the universe, were represented at this time in Munich's cafés, pubs, and beerhalls. In well-known venues like Café Stephanie in Amalienstraße, left-wing intellectuals – some of whom would several years later be involved in the revolutionary upheavals – and Schwabing's artists and writers voiced their biting social and political critique, designing innumerable variants of the coming utopia. Hitler's scene was less high-flying. His milieu was that of the beer-table philosophers and corner-café improvers of the world, the cranks and half-educated know-alls. This is where he kept abreast of political developments, and where, at the slightest provocation, he could flare up and treat anyone in proximity to his fiercely held views on whatever preoccupied him at the time.[64] Café and beerhall 'discussions' were the nearest Hitler came in his Munich period to political involvement. His statement in *Mein Kampf* that 'in the years 1913 and 1914, I, for the first time in various circles which today in part faithfully support the National Socialist movement, expressed the conviction that the question of the future of the German nation was the question of destroying Marxism' elevates coffee-house confrontation into the philosophy of the political prophet.[65]

Hitler's captive audiences in the cafés and beerhalls were for most part the closest he came to human contact in his months in Munich, and presumably offered some sort of outlet for his pent-up prejudice and emotions. It is likely, as an Austrian who despised the Habsburg monarchy and had arrived starry-eyed in Germany, that, as his account in *Mein Kampf* suggests, he was much exercised by the approving views on the German-Austrian alliance that he was hearing in Bavaria and could neither comprehend nor tolerate.[66] But most of his 'reflections' on foreign policy in the chapter dealing with his time in Munich plainly postdate his pre-war stay in the city, and present his position in 1924. Contrary to his own depiction of the Munich months as a time of further preparation for what fate would eventually bring him, it was in reality an empty, lonely, and futile period for him. He was in love with Munich; but Munich was not in love with him. He did not belong in the avant-garde café culture of Schwabing and the 'smart set' of Munich's artists and literati; he was not in tune with 'white-blue' Bavarian provincialism, the dominance of political Catholicism, and the strength of anti-Prussian feeling that ran from the ruddy-faced vegetable sellers on the Viktualienmarkt to the sophisticated lampooners of the Kaiser in the satirical magazine *Simplicissimus*; he was left to his own form of the Munich *Bohème* – loitering in cafés, browsing in newspapers and periodicals, and waiting for the chance to harangue those around him on the error of their political ways. As regards his own future, he had no more idea where he was going than he had done during his years in the Vienna Men's Home.

He very nearly ended up in an Austrian prison. Already in August 1913 the Linz police had started inquiries about Hitler's whereabouts because of his failure to register for military service. Evasion of military service was punishable by a hefty fine. And leaving Austria to avoid it was treated as desertion and carried a jail sentence. By way of his relatives in Linz, the Viennese police, and the Men's Home in Meldemannstraße, the trail eventually led to Munich, where the police were able to inform their Linz counterparts that Hitler had been registered since 26 May 1913 as living with the Popps at 34 Schleißheimerstraße.[67] Hitler was shaken to the core when an officer of the Munich criminal police turned up on Frau Popp's doorstep on the afternoon of Sunday, 18 January 1914 with a summons for him to appear two days later in Linz under pain of fine and imprisonment to register for military service, and promptly took him under arrest prior to handing him over to the Austrian authorities.[68] The Munich police had for some reason delayed delivery of the summons for several days before the Sunday, leaving Hitler as a consequence extremely short notice to comply with its demand to be in Linz by the Tuesday. That, together with Hitler's run-down appearance, lack of ready money, apologetic demeanour, and somewhat pathetic explanation, influenced the Austrian consulate in Munich to look with some sympathy on his position. Hitler's request by telegram on Monday, 19 January to delay the summons to the subsequent mustering in Linz on 5 February was rejected by the Linz magistracy. But the telegram from Linz arrived in Munich only much later that day, after the consulate was closed. The consulate handled it the following morning with customary bureaucratic sluggishness so that Hitler received it only at 9a.m. on Wednesday, 21 January, the day after he had been due to appear in Linz. Luck was again on Hitler's side. But he was left in no doubt about the seriousness of the situation. In some agitation, he now wrote a three-and-a-half-page letter humbly accepting his fault in failing to register in autumn 1909, at a very bitter time for him, when he had hit rock-bottom, but claiming he had done so retrospectively in February 1910, and heard nothing thereafter even though he had been registered throughout with the police in Vienna.[69] He impressed the consular officials, who thought him 'worthy of consideration', and the Linz magistracy now granted him permission to appear, as he had requested, on 5 February, in Salzburg instead of Linz. No fine or imprisonment was imposed; his travel expenses were paid by the consulate. And, in the event, on duly attending at Salzburg he was found to be too weak to undertake military service.[70] Hitler had escaped with shock and embarrassment, but little else, from the difficulties he had created for himself. He still had to cope at a later date with the capital his political enemies would draw from the affair.[71] And his frantic efforts to recover the files immediately after the Anschluß were doomed to failure: before the Gestapo could get its hands on them, they had already been removed into safe keeping, from which they could be retrieved for publication in the 1950s.[72]

Hitler returned to his mundane life as a small-time artist; but not for long. The storm-clouds were gathering over Europe. Hitler described, in a rare and apposite lyrical passage of *Mein Kampf*, an atmosphere that 'lay on the chests of men like a heavy nightmare, sultry as feverish tropic heat'. He spoke of 'constant anxiety' and 'the sense of approaching catastrophe' turning into a longing for action, for the cleansing and freshness that the storm brings.[73] His first reaction on hearing, on Sunday, 28 June 1914, the sensational news of the assassination in Sarajevo of the heir to the Austrian throne, Archduke Franz Ferdinand, and his wife was to fear that it had been perpetrated by German students. Given Franz Ferdinand's support for pro-Slav policies, this was a not unreasonable assumption, and a more likely eventuality than his murder at the hands of Serbian nationalists. Hitler's relief at the identity of the perpetrators mingled with his sense 'that a stone had been set rolling whose course could no longer be arrested', that 'at last war would be inevitable'.[74] By the beginning of August, the countries of Europe, as Lloyd George put it, had indeed 'slithered over the brink into the boiling cauldron'.[75] The continent was at war.

III

For Hitler, the war was a godsend. Since his failure in the Art Academy in 1907, he had vegetated, resigned to the fact that he would not become a great artist, now cherishing a pipe-dream that he would somehow become a notable architect – though with no plans for or realistic hope of fulfilling this ambition. Seven years after that failure, the 'nobody of Vienna',[76] now in Munich, remained a drop-out and nonentity, futilely angry at a world which had rejected him. He was still without any career prospects, without qualifications or any expectation of gaining them, without any capacity for forging close and lasting friendships, and without real hope of coming to terms with himself – or with a society he despised for his own failure. The war offered him his way out. At the age of twenty-five, it gave him for the first time in his life a cause, a commitment, comradeship, an external discipline, a sort of regular employment, a sense of well-being, and – more than that – a sense of belonging. His regiment became home for him. When he was wounded in 1916 his first words to his superior officer were: 'It's not so bad, Herr Oberleutnant, eh? I can stay with you, stay with the regiment.'[77] Later in the war, the prospect of leaving the regiment may well have influenced his wish not to be considered for promotion.[78] And at the end of the war, he had good practical reasons for staying in the army as long as possible: the army had by then been his 'career' for four years, and he had no other job to go back to or look forward to. For the first time in his life – certainly the first time since the carefree childhood days as a mummy's boy in Upper Austria – Hitler felt truly at ease with himself in the war. He referred later to the war years as 'the greatest and most unforgettable time of my earthly existence'.[79] Later still, in the midst of a second war that he himself had done more than any other single person to unleash on Germany, Europe, and the world, he reminisced incessantly – and always in glowing terms – about his experiences in the First World War. His years in the army were 'the one time', he commented on one occasion, 'when I had no worries'. Food, clothing, and accommodation were all provided.[80] He had been, he said, 'passionately glad to be a soldier'.[81] The war and its aftermath made Hitler. After Vienna, it was the second formative period in decisively shaping his personality.

Germany, like other countries in Europe, had been gripped by war fever in the wake of Franz Ferdinand's assassination. On the very evening of the assassination, a riotous crowd in Munich had smashed up the well-known Café Fahrig in the city centre because the band entertaining the customers had refused to play Germany's stirringly patriotic unofficial anthem, 'Die Wacht am Rhein'.[82] A few weeks later, an angry mob in the same part of the city set upon two women overheard speaking French who, faces bleeding and with torn clothes, had to be rescued by the police.[83] The 'spirit of 1914' was more varied in expression than often presumed, and, despite such outrages, in general probably more defensive than outrightly aggressive in tone.[84] But no sector of society was immune from the heady atmosphere of patriotic fervour. Even Social Democrat internationalists and left-wing liberals could not escape it, though their defensive patriotism, weak though it was as a bulwark against belligerent chauvinism, was markedly different from the aggression and bellicosity of nationalist circles, where war-euphoria was unrestrained. Among middle-class youth, and especially in student groups, enthusiasm for war was often linked to an optimism that it would bring final release from the shackles of a decadent and sterile bourgeois order. 'We want to glorify war, the only cure for the world,' the Italian Futurist Manifesto had proclaimed only a few years earlier.[85] The sentiment struck a chord with many – though certainly not all – of the younger generation across Europe in July and August 1914. Among Germany's leaders, as among ruling groups elsewhere in Europe, there was a feeling that armed conflict was necessary and salutary as a liberation from the prolonged tension and repeated crises of previous years.[86] Strangest of all for subsequent generations to grasp, there was, most prominent among intellectuals, a sense of war as an almost religious experience, as redemption and renewal, as a welling up of sublime national unity to overcome discord and disharmony, as the creative force of a national community. 'What we are now, with deepest emotion, experiencing,' ran the florid outpouring of a leading journal on social policy:

is a resurrection, a rebirth of the nation. Suddenly shocked out of the troubles and pleasures of everyday life, Germany stands united in the strength of moral duty, ready for the highest sacrifice. The Kaiser, today truly a People's Kaiser, proclaimed: 'I know no parties any longer, I know only Germans' . . . And the Reichstag, unanimous and united, a true herald of the nation, swore by its deeds to go with the Kaiser 'through thick and thin, through suffering and death'. These first days of August are undying, incomparable days of glory. Whatever had arisen over four decades of peace by way of strife and discord of parties, confessions, classes, and races has been totally consumed by the breath of flame of national fervour.[87]

Many prepared to fight with a heavy heart and from a sense of duty.[88] Others could hardly wait for action. Hitler was among the tens of thousands in Munich in the thrall of emotional delirium, passionately enthused by the prospect of war. As for so many others, his elation would later turn to deep embitterment. With Hitler, the emotional pendulum set moving by the onset of war swung more violently than for most. 'Overpowered by stormy enthusiasm,' he wrote, 'I fell down on my knees and thanked Heaven from an overflowing heart for granting me the good fortune of being permitted to live at this time.'[89] That on this occasion his words were true cannot be doubted. Years later, noticing a photograph taken by Heinrich Hoffmann (who was to become his court photographer) of the huge patriotic demonstration in front of the Feldherrnhalle on Munich's Odeonsplatz on 2 August 1914, the day after the German declaration of war on Russia, Hitler pointed out that he had been among the emotional crowd that day, carried away with nationalist fervour, hoarse with singing 'Die Wacht am Rhein' and 'Deutschland über alles'. Hoffmann immediately set to work on enlargements, and discovered the face of the twenty-five-year-old Hitler in the centre of the photograph, gripped and enraptured by the war hysteria. The subsequent mass reproduction of the photograph helped contribute to the establishment of the Führer myth – and to Hoffmann's immense profits.[90]

It was doubtless under the impact of the same elation swaying tens of thousands of young men in Munich and many other cities in Europe during those days to rush to join up that, according to his own account, on 3 August, the day following the mass demonstration at the Feldherrnhalle, Hitler submitted his request – a personal petition to King Ludwig III of Bavaria – to serve as an Austrian in the Bavarian army. The granting of his request by the cabinet office, he went on, arrived, to his unbounded joy, the very next day.[91] Though this version has been accepted in most accounts, it is scarcely credible. In the confusion of those days, it would have required truly remarkable bureaucratic efficiency for Hitler's request to have been approved overnight. In any case, not the cabinet office but the war ministry was alone empowered to accept foreigners (including Austrians) as volunteers.[92] In reality, Hitler owed his service in the Bavarian army not to bureaucratic efficiency, but to bureaucratic oversight.[93] Detailed inquiries carried out by the Bavarian authorities in 1924 were unable to clarify precisely how, instead of being returned to Austria in August 1914 as should have happened, he came to serve in the Bavarian army. It was presumed that he was among the flood of volunteers who rushed to their nearest place of recruitment in the first days of August, leading, the report added, to not unnatural inconsistencies and breaches of the strict letter of the law. 'In all probability,' commented the report, 'the question of Hitler's nationality (*Staatsangehörigkeit*) was never even raised.' Hitler, it was concluded, almost certainly entered the Bavarian army by error.[94]

Probably, as Hitler wrote in a brief autobiographical sketch in 1921, he volunteered on 5 August 1914 for service in the First Bavarian Infantry Regiment. Like many others in these first chaotic days, he was initially sent away again since there was no immediate use for him.[95] On 16 August he was summoned to report at Recruiting Depot VI in Munich for kitting out by the Second Reserve Battalion of the Second Infantry Regiment. By the beginning of September he had been assigned to the newly formed Bavarian Reserve Infantry Regiment 16 (known from the name of its first commander as the 'List Regiment'), largely comprising raw recruits. Together with his fellow soldiers, he then underwent a period of training and drilling in Munich followed by exercises at Lechfeld near Augsburg that lasted until 20 October.[96] On that day, Hitler dropped a note to the Popps, telling them his unit was about to leave for the front, probably Belgium, how much he was looking forward to it, and that he hoped they would get to England.[97] In the early hours of the next morning, the troop train carrying Hitler left for the battlefields of Flanders.[98]

On 29 October, within six days of arriving in Lille, Hitler's battalion had its baptism of fire on the Menin Road near Ypres. In letters from the front to Joseph Popp and to a Munich acquaintance, Ernst Hepp, Hitler wrote that after four days of fighting, the List Regiment's fighting force had been reduced from 3,600 to 611 men.[99] The initial losses have indeed been estimated at around 70 per cent, partly even incurred through 'friendly fire' as Württemberg and Saxon regiments mistook the Bavarians, in the gloom, for English soldiers.[100] Colonel List himself was among the fallen. Hitler's initial idealism, he said later, gave way on seeing the thousands killed and injured, to the realization 'that life is a constant horrible struggle'.[101]

On 3 November 1914 (with effect from 1 November), Hitler was promoted to corporal. It was his last promotion of the war, though he could certainly have been expected to advance further, as least as far as non-commissioned officer (*Unteroffizier*). Later in the war, he was in fact nominated for promotion by Max Amann, then a staff sergeant, subsequently Hitler's press baron, and the regimental staff considered making him *Unteroffizier*.[102] Fritz Wiedemann, the regimental adjutant who in the 1930s became for a time one of the Führer's adjutants, testified after the end of the Third Reich that Hitler's superiors had thought him lacking in leadership qualities.[103] However, both Amann and Wiedemann made clear that Hitler, probably because he would have been then transferred from the regimental staff, actually refused to be considered for promotion.[104]

Hitler had been assigned on 9 November to the regimental staff as an orderly (*Ordonnanz*) – one of a group of eight to ten dispatch runners (*Meldegänger*) whose task was to carry orders, on foot or sometimes by bicycle, from the regimental command post to the battalion and company leaders at the front, three kilometres away.[105] Strikingly, in his *Mein Kampf* account, Hitler omitted to mention that he was a dispatch runner, implying that he actually spent the war in the trenches.[106] But the attempts of his political enemies in the early 1930s to belittle the dangers involved in the duties of the dispatch runner and decry Hitler's war service, accusing him of shirking and cowardice, were misplaced.[107] When, as was not uncommon, the front was relatively quiet, there were certainly times when the dispatch runners could laze around at staff headquarters, where conditions were greatly better than in the trenches. It was in such conditions at regimental headquarters in Fournes, near Fromelles in the Ypres region of Flanders, where Hitler spent nearly half of his wartime service, that he could find the time to paint pictures and read (if his own account can be believed) the works of Schopenhauer that he claimed he carried around with him.[108] Even so, the dangers faced by the dispatch runners during battles, carrying messages to the front through the firing line, were real enough. The losses among dispatch runners were relatively high.[109] If at all possible, two runners would be sent with a message to ensure that it would get through if one happened to be killed.[110] Three of the eight runners attached to the regimental staff were killed and another one wounded in a confrontation with French troops on 15 November. Hitler himself – not for the only time in his life – had luck on his side two days later when a French shell exploded in the regimental forward command post minutes after he had gone out, leaving almost the entire staff there dead or wounded.[111] Among the seriously wounded was the regimental commander, Oberstleutnant Philipp Engelhardt, who had been about to propose Hitler for the Iron Cross for his part, assisted by a colleague, in protecting the commander's life under fire a few days earlier.[112] On 2 December, Hitler was finally presented with the Iron Cross, Second Class, one of four dispatch runners among the sixty men from his regiment to receive the honour.[113] It was, he said, 'the happiest day of my life'.[114]

From all indications, Hitler was a committed, rather than simply conscientious and dutiful, soldier, and did not lack physical courage. His superiors held him in high regard. His immediate comrades, mainly the group of dispatch runners, respected him and, it seems, even quite liked him, though he could also plainly irritate as well as puzzle them.[115] His lack of a sense of fun made him an easy target for good-natured ribbing. 'What about looking around for a Mamsell?' suggested a telephonist one day. 'I'd die of shame looking for sex with a French girl,' interjected Hitler, to a burst of laughter from the others. 'Look at the monk,' one said. Hitler's retort was: 'Have you no German sense of honour left at all?'[116] Though his quirkiness singled him out from the rest of his group, Hitler's relations with his immediate comrades were generally good. Most of them later became members of the NSDAP, and, when, as usually happened, they reminded Reich Chancellor Hitler of the time that they had been his comrades in arms, he made sure they were catered for with cash donations and positions as minor functionaries.[117] For all that they got on well with him, they thought 'Adi', as they called him, was distinctly odd. They referred to him as 'the artist' and were struck by the fact that he received no mail or parcels (even at Christmas) after about mid-1915, never spoke of family or friends, neither smoked nor drank, showed no interest in visits to brothels, and used to sit for hours in a corner of the dug-out, brooding or reading.[118] Photographs of him during the war show a thin, gaunt face dominated by a thick, dark, bushy moustache. He was usually on the edge of his group, expressionless where others were smiling.[119] One of his closest comrades, Balthasar Brandmayer, a stonemason from Bruckmühl in the Bad Aibling district of Upper Bavaria, later described his first impressions of Hitler at the end of May 1915: almost skeletal in appearance, dark eyes hooded in a sallow complexion, untrimmed moustache, sitting in a corner buried in a newspaper, occasionally taking a sip of tea, seldom joining in the banter of the group.[120] He seemed an oddity, shaking his head disapprovingly at silly, light-hearted remarks, not even joining in the usual soldiers' moans, gripes, and jibes.[121] 'Haven't you ever loved a girl?' Brandmayer asked Hitler. 'Look, Brandmoiri,' was the straight-faced reply, 'I've never had time for anything like that, and I'll never get round to it.'[122] His only real affection seems to have been for his dog, Foxl, a white terrier that had strayed across from enemy lines. Hitler taught it tricks, revelling in how attached it was to him and how glad it was to see him when he returned from duty. He was distraught late in the war when his unit had to move on and Foxl could not be found. 'The swine who took him from me doesn't know what he did to me,' was his comment many years later.[123] He felt as strongly about none of the thousands of humans he saw slaughtered about him. The emptiness and coldness that Hitler showed throughout his life in his dealings with human beings were absent in the feeling he had for his dog. In the Führer Headquarters during the Second World War, his alsatian, Blondi, would again offer him the nearest thing he could find to friendship.[124] But with his dogs, as with every human being he came into contact with, any relationship was based upon subordination to his mastery. 'I liked [Foxl] so much,' he recalled; 'he only obeyed me.'[125]

About the war itself, Hitler was utterly fanatical. No humanitarian feelings could be allowed to interfere with the ruthless prosecution of German interests. He vehemently disapproved of the spontaneous gestures of friendship at Christmas 1914, when German and British troops met in no man's land, shaking hands and singing carols together. 'There should be no question of something like that during war,' he protested.[126] His comrades knew that they could always provoke Hitler with defeatist comments, real or contrived. All they had to do was to claim the war would be lost and Hitler would go off at the deep end. 'For us the war can't be lost' were invariably his last words.[127] The lengthy letter he sent on 5 February 1915 to his Munich acquaintance, Assessor Ernst Hepp, concluded with an insight (written in typical Hitler prose-style) into his view of the war redolent of the prejudices that had been consuming him since his Vienna days:

I think so often of Munich, and each of us has only one wish, that it may soon come to the final reckoning with the gang, to the showdown (*Daraufgehen*), cost what it will, and that those of us who have the fortune to see their homeland again will find it purer and cleansed of alien influence (*Fremdländerei*), that through the sacrifices and suffering that so many hundred thousand of us make daily, that through the stream of blood that flows here day for day against an international world of enemies, not only will Germany's external enemies be smashed, but that our inner internationalism will also be broken. That would be worth more to me than all territorial gains. As far as Austria is concerned, things will happen as I always said.[128]

Hitler evidently carried such deep-seated sentiments throughout the war. But this political outburst, tagged on to a long description of military events and wartime conditions, was unusual. He appears to have spoken little to his comrades on political matters.[129] Perhaps the fact that his comrades thought him peculiar hindered him from giving voice to his strong opinions. 'I was a soldier then, and I didn't want to talk about politics,' he himself stated; though in direct contradiction he added that he often expressed his views on Social Democracy to his closer comrades.[130] During his interrogation in Nuremberg in 1947, Max Amann was adamant that Hitler had not harangued his comrades on politics during the war.[131] He appears, too, to have scarcely mentioned the Jews. Several former comrades claimed after 1945 that Hitler had at most made a few off-hand though commonplace comments about the Jews in those years, but that they had no inkling then of the unbounded hatred that was so visible after 1918.[132] Balthasar Brandmayer recalled on the other hand in his reminiscences, first published in 1932, that during the war he had 'often not understood Adolf Hitler when he called the Jew the wire-puller behind all misfortune'.[133] According to Brandmayer, Hitler became more politically involved in the latter years of the war and made no secret of his feelings on what he saw as the Social Democrat instigators of growing unrest in Germany.[134] Such comments, like all sources that postdate Hitler's rise to prominence and, as in this case, glorify the prescience of the future leader, have to be treated with caution. But it is difficult to dismiss them out of hand. It indeed does seem very likely, as his own account in *Mein Kampf* claims, that Hitler's political prejudices sharpened in the latter part of the war, during and after his first period of leave in Germany in 1916.[135]

Between March 1915 and September 1916, the List Regiment fought in the trenches near Fromelles, defending a two-kilometre stretch of the stalemated front. Heavy battles with the British were fought in May 1915 and July 1916, but in one and a half years the front barely moved a few metres.[136] On 27 September 1916, two months after heavy fighting in the second battle of Fromelles, when a British offensive was staved off with difficulty, the regiment moved southwards from Flanders and by 2 October was engaged on the Somme.[137] Within days, Hitler was wounded in the left thigh when a shell exploded in the dispatch runners' dug-out, killing and wounding several of them.[138] After treatment in a field hospital, he spent almost two months, from 9 October until 1 December 1916, in the Red Cross hospital at Beelitz, near Berlin. He had not been in Germany for two years. He soon noticed how different the mood was from the heady days of August 1914. He was appalled to hear men in the hospital bragging about their malingering or how they had managed to inflict minor injuries on themselves to make sure they could escape from the front. He encountered much the same low morale and widespread discontent in Berlin during the period of his recuperation. It was his first time in the city, and allowed him to pay a visit to the Nationalgalerie. But Munich shocked him most of all. He scarcely recognized the city: 'Anger, discontent, cursing, wherever you went!' Morale was poor; people were dispirited; conditions were miserable; and, as was traditional in Bavaria, the blame was placed on the Prussians. Hitler himself, according to his own account written about eight years later, recognized in all this only the work of the Jews. He was struck too, so he said, by the number of Jews in clerical positions – 'nearly every clerk was a Jew and nearly every Jew was a clerk' – compared with how few of them were serving at the front.[139] (In fact, this was a base calumny: there was as good as no difference between the proportion of Jews and non-Jews in the German army, relative to their numbers in the total population, and many served – some in the List Regiment – with great distinction.[140]) There is no reason to presume, as has sometimes been the case, that this account of his anti-Jewish feelings in 1916 was a backwards projection of feelings that in reality only existed from 1918–19 onwards.[141] Though, as we have noted, Hitler did not stand out for his antisemitism in the recollections of some of his former wartime comrades, two of them, Brandmayer and Westen-kirchner, did refer to his negative comments about the Jews.[142] And Hitler would have been voicing sentiments that were increasingly to be heard in the streets of Munich as anti-Jewish prejudice became more widespread and more ferocious in the second half of the war.[143]

Hitler wanted to get back to the front as soon as possible, and above all to rejoin his old regiment.[144] He eventually returned to it on 5 March 1917 in its new position a few miles to the north of Vimy.[145] In the summer it was back to the same ground near Ypres that the regiment had fought over almost three years earlier, to counter the major Flanders offensive launched by the British in mid-July 1917.[146] Battered by the heavy fighting, the regiment was relieved at the beginning of August and transported to Alsace. At the end of September, Hitler took normal leave for the first time. He had no wish to go back to Munich, which had dispirited him so much, and went to Berlin instead, to stay with the parents of one of his comrades.[147] His postcards to friends in the regiment spoke of how much he enjoyed his eighteen-day leave, and how thrilled he was by Berlin and its museums.[148] In mid-October, he returned to his regiment, which had just moved from Alsace to Champagne. Bitter fighting in April 1918 brought huge losses, and during the last two weeks of July the regiment was involved in the second battle of the Marne.[149] It was the last major German offensive of the war. By early August, when it collapsed in the face of a tenacious Allied counter-offensive, German losses in the previous four months of savage combat had amounted to around 800,000 men. The failure of the offensive marked the point where, with reserves depleted and morale plummeting, Germany's military leadership was compelled to recognize that the war was lost.

On 4 August 1918, Hitler received the Iron Cross, First Class – a rare achievement for a corporal – from the regimental commander, Major von Tubeuf. By a stroke of irony, he had a Jewish officer, Leutnant Hugo Gutmann, to thank for the nomination.[150] The story was later to be found in all school books that the Führer had received the EK I for single-handedly capturing fifteen French soldiers.[151] The truth, as usual, was somewhat more prosaic. From the available evidence, including the recommendation of the List Regiment's Deputy Commander Freiherr von Godin on 31 July 1918, the award was made – as it was also to a fellow dispatch runner – for bravery shown in delivering an important dispatch, following a breakdown in telephone communications, from command headquarters to the front through heavy fire. Gutmann, from what he subsequently said, had promised both dispatch runners the EK I if they succeeded in delivering the message. But since the action was, though certainly courageous, not strikingly exceptional, it was only after several weeks of his belabouring the divisional commander that permission for the award was granted.[152]

By mid-August 1918, the List Regiment had moved to Cambrai to help combat a British offensive near Bapaume, and a month later was back in action once more in the vicinity of Wytschaete and Messines, where Hitler had received his EK II almost four years earlier. This time Hitler was away from the battlefields. In late August he had been sent for a week to Nuremberg for telephone communications training, and on 10 September he began his second period of eighteen days' leave, again in Berlin.[153] Immediately on his return, at the end of September, his unit was put under pressure from British assaults near Comines. Gas was now in extensive use in offensives, and protection against it was minimal and primitive. The List Regiment, like others, suffered badly. On the night of 13–14 October, Hitler himself fell victim to mustard gas on the heights south of Wervick, part of the southern front near Ypres.[154] He and several comrades, retreating from their dug-out during a gas attack, were partially blinded by the gas and found their way to safety only by clinging on to each other and following a comrade who was slightly less badly afflicted.[155] After initial treatment in Flanders, Hitler was transported on 21 October 1918 to the military hospital in Pasewalk, near Stettin, in Pomerania.

The war was over for him. And, little though he knew it, the Army High Command was already manoeuvring to extricate itself from blame for a war it accepted was lost and a peace which would soon have to be negotiated.[156] It was in Pasewalk, recovering from his temporary blindness, that Hitler was to learn the shattering news of defeat and revolution – what he called 'the greatest villainy of the century'.[157]

IV

In reality, of course, there had been no treachery, no stab-in-the-back. This was a pure invention of the Right, a legend the Nazis would use as a central element of their propaganda armoury. Unrest at home was a consequence, not a cause, of military failure. Germany had been militarily defeated and was close to the end of its tether – though nothing had prepared people for capitulation. In fact, triumphalist propaganda was still coming from the High Command in late October 1918. The army was by then exhausted, and in the previous four months had suffered heavier losses than at any time during the war.[158] In addition, illness took its toll. Around 1.75 million German soldiers had fallen victim to an influenza epidemic between March and July, and around 750,000 were wounded in the same period. It was little wonder that the medical service could not cope, that discipline sagged drastically, and that desertions and 'shirking' – deliberately ducking duty (estimated at close on a million men in the last months of the war) – rose dramatically.[159] At home, the mood was one of mounting protest – embittered, angry, and increasingly rebellious. The revolution was not fabricated by Bolshevik sympathizers and unpatriotic troublemakers, but grew out of the profound disillusionment and rising unrest, which had set in even as early as 1915 and from 1916 onwards had flowed into what finally became a torrent of disaffection. The society which had seemingly entered the war in total patriotic unity ended it completely riven – and traumatized by the experience.

Over 13 million Germans, just below a fifth of the population, served in the army during the war, over 10.5 million of them in the field. Around 2 million were killed; almost 5 million were wounded. A third of those killed had wives; almost all had families and friends.[160] Such losses could not be experienced without leaving the most searing mark on mentalities. But experiences of the war, and the impact of such experiences, were in reality far from uniform. Certainly, death, injury, and on the 'home front' hunger, were omnipresent. Certainly, too, for those at the fighting front, the fatalism of existence in the trenches, the dangers and suffering, the anxieties and fears, the immensity of the losses – human and material – in the man-made wasteland of industrialized warfare, the interdependence for survival of the wholly male trench 'community', were inescapable impressions.

But the experience that left Hitler as an arch-glorifier of war converted the expressionist playwright and writer Ernst Toller into a pacifist and left-wing revolutionary. Where, for Hitler, the defeat was betrayal, for Toller the betrayal was the war itself. 'The war itself had turned me into an opponent of war,' he wrote; 'I felt that the land I loved had been betrayed and sold. It was for us to overthrow these betrayers.'[161] Experience of the war divided far more than it united: the front line against the 'shirkers' in the rear; men against officers; the front against the 'home front'; above all, annexationists, imperialists, ardent believers in the war effort against those who detested it, disparaged it, and condemned it. The 'national community' which intellectuals saw forged in the trenches was largely a myth. Even the trench cameraderie, the 'community of fate' of a 'front generation', was in some measure a later literary mythologization.[162] When the soldiers returned to the turmoil of a homeland in the throes of a revolution, it was not to form a unified 'front generation' pitting the 'classless community' of the trenches against a divided society changed out of all recognition, a militaristic, disillusioned mass ready-made to enter the Freikorps, and from there the SA. Certainly, Hitler was later able to play upon such sentiments. But twice as many men entered the anti-war Reich Association of War Disabled, War Veterans, and War Dependants as joined the Freikorps.[163] The soldiers took back with them divided experiences of the front that were to fuel the enormous divisions and tensions of post-war German society.

Aside from worrying about loved ones at the front, those at home had to cope as best they could with massively worsening material conditions, leading often to extreme hardship. Women, drafted into industry, driving trams, running farms, increasingly found a main occupation in queuing for food. Most Germans, certainly those living in towns and cities, knew what

Without the Reichswehr's 'discovery' of his talent for nationalist agitation, Hitler had every prospect of returning to the margins of society – an embittered war veteran with little chance of personal advancement. Without his self-discovery that he could 'speak', he would not have been able to contemplate the possibility of making a living from politics. But without the extraordinary political climate of post-war Germany, and, quite especially, the unique conditions in Bavaria, Hitler would have found himself in any case without an audience, his 'talent' pointless and unrecognized, his tirades of hate without echo, the backing from those close to the avenues of power, on whom he depended, unforthcoming.

When he joined the infant German Workers' Party in September 1919, he was still, as he himself put it, among the 'nameless' – a nobody.[1] Within three years, he was being showered with letters of adulation, spoken of on in nationalist circles as Germany's Mussolini, even compared with Napoleon.[2] And little more than four years later, he had attained national, not just regional, notoriety as a leader of an attempt to take over the power of the state by force. He had of course failed miserably in this – and his political 'career' looked to be (and ought to have been) at an end. But he was now a 'somebody'. The first part of Hitler's astonishing rise from anonymity to prominence dates from these years in Munich – the years of his political apprenticeship.

It is natural to presume that such a swift rise even to provincial celebrity status must have been the result of some extraordinary personal qualities. Without doubt, Hitler *did* possess abilities and traits of character that contributed towards making him a political force to be reckoned with. To ignore them or disparage them totally would be to make the same mistakes of underestimation made by his political enemies, who ridiculed him and regarded him as a mere cipher for the interests of others. But Hitler's personality and his talents, such as they were, alone do not explain the adulation already being lavished on him by growing numbers in the *völkisch* camp by 1922. The origins of a leadership cult reflected mentalities and expectations prevalent in some sectors of German society at the time, more than they did special qualities of Hitler. Nor would his abilities as a mob-orator, which were most of what he had to offer at the time, in themselves have been sufficient to have lifted him to a position where he could, even if for a mere few hours – in retrospect, hours of pure melodrama, even farce – head a challenge to the might of the German state. To come this far, he needed influential patrons.

Without the changed conditions, the product of a lost war, revolution, and a pervasive sense of national humiliation, Hitler would have remained a nobody. His main ability by far, as he came to realize during the course of 1919, was that in the prevailing circumstances he could inspire an audience which shared his basic political feelings, by the way he spoke, by the force of his rhetoric, by the very power of his prejudice, by the conviction he conveyed that there *was* a way out of Germany's plight, and that *only* the way he outlined was the road to national rebirth. Another time, another place, and the message would have been ineffective, absurd even. As it was, indeed, in the early 1920s the great majority of the citizens of Munich, let alone of a wider population to whom Hitler was, if at all, only known as a provincial Bavarian hot-head and rabble-rouser, could not be captivated by it. Nevertheless, at this time and in this place, Hitler's message did capture exactly the uncontainable sense of anger, fear, frustration, resentment, and pent-up aggression of the raucous gatherings in the Munich beerhalls. The compulsive manner of his speaking derived in turn much of its power of persuasion from the strength of conviction that combined with appealingly simple diagnoses of and recipes to Germany's problems.

Above all, what came naturally to Hitler was to stoke up the hatred of others by pouring out to them the hatred that was so deeply embedded in himself. Even so, this had never before had the effect it was to have now, in the changed post-war conditions. What, in the Men's Home in Vienna, in the Munich cafés, and in the regimental field headquarters, had been at best tolerated as an eccentricity now turned out to be Hitler's major asset. This in itself suggests that what had changed above all was the milieu and context in which Hitler operated; that we should look in the first instance less to his own personality than to the motives and actions of those who came to be Hitler's supporters, admirers, and devotees – and not least his powerful backers – to explain his first breakthrough on the political scene. For what becomes clear – without falling into the mistake of presuming that he was no more than the puppet of the 'ruling classes' – is that Hitler would have remained a political nonentity without the patronage and support he obtained from influential circles in Bavaria. During this period, Hitler was seldom, if ever, master of his own destiny. The key decisions – to take over the party leadership in 1921, to engage in the putsch adventure in 1923 – were not carefully conceived actions, but desperate forward moves to save face – behaviour characteristic of Hitler to the end.

It was as a propagandist, not as an ideologue with a unique or special set of political ideas, that Hitler made his mark in these early years. There was nothing new, different, original, or distinctive about the ideas he was peddling in the Munich beerhalls. They were common currency among the various *völkisch* groups and sects and had already been advanced in all their essentials by the pre-war Pan-Germans. What Hitler did was to advertise unoriginal ideas in an original way. Others could say the same thing but make no impact at all. It was less *what* he said than *how* he said it that counted. As it was to be throughout his 'career', presentation was what mattered. He consciously learnt how to make an impression through his speaking. He learnt how to devise effective propaganda and to maximize the impact of targeting specific scapegoats. He learnt, in other words, that he was able to mobilize the masses. For him this was from the outset *the* route to the attainment of political goals. The ability to convince himself that his way and no other could succeed was the platform for the conviction that he conveyed to others. Conversely, the response of the beerhall crowds – later the mass rallies – gave him the certainty, the self-assurance, the sense of security, which at this time he otherwise lacked. According to Heinrich Hoffmann, when asked to give a short speech at Hermann Esser's wedding party in the early 1920s, he refused. 'I must have a crowd when I speak,' he explained. 'In a small intimate circle I never know what to say. I should only disappoint you all, and that is a thing I should hate to do. As a speaker either at a family gathering or a funeral, I'm no use at all.'[3] Hitler's frequently demonstrated diffidence and unease in dealings with individuals contrasted diametrically with his self-confident mastery in exploiting the emotions of his listeners in the theatrical setting of a major speech. He needed the orgasmic excitement which only the ecstatic masses could give him. The satisfaction gained from the rapturous response and wild applause of cheering crowds must have offered compensation for the emptiness of his personal relations. More than that, it was a sign that he was a success, after three decades in which – apart from the pride he took in his war record – he had no achievements of note to set against his outsized ego.

Simplicity and repetition were two key ingredients in his speaking armoury. These revolved around the unvarying essential driving-points of his message: the nationalization of the masses, the reversal of the great 'betrayal' of 1918, the destruction of Germany's internal enemies (above all the 'removal' of the Jews), and material and psychological rebuilding as the prerequisite for external struggle and the attainment of a position of world power.[4] This conception of the path to Germany's 'salvation' and rebirth was already partially devised, at least in embryo, by the date of his letter to Gemlich in September 1919.[5] Important strands remained, however, to be added. The central notion of the quest for 'living-space' in eastern Europe was, for instance, not fully incorporated until the middle of the decade. It was only in the two years or so following the putsch débâcle, therefore, that his ideas finally came together to form the characteristic fully-fledged *Weltanschauung* that thereafter remained unaltered.

But all this is to run ahead of the crucial developments which shaped the first passage of Hitler's political 'career' as the beerhall agitator of an insignificant Munich racist party and the circumstances under which he came to lead that party.

I

The equation of National Socialism with Hitler, the frequently heard claim that it is no more than Hitlerism, always was a quite misleading oversimplification.[6] That Hitler was indispensable to the rise to and exercise of power of National Socialism is, of course, undeniable. But the phenomenon itself existed before Hitler was heard of, and would have continued to exist if Hitler had remained a 'nobody of Vienna'.[7] Much of the pot-pourri of ideas that went to make up Nazi ideology – an amalgam of prejudices, phobias, and utopian social expectations rather than a coherent set of intellectual propositions – was to be found in different forms and intensities before the First World War, and later in the programmes and manifestos of fascist parties of many European countries. Integral nationalism, anti-Marxist 'national' socialism, social Darwinism, racism, biological antisemitism, eugenics, elitism intermingled in varying strengths to provide a heady brew of irrationalism attractive to some cultural pessimists among the intelligentsia and bourgeoisie of European societies undergoing rapid social, economic, and political change in the late nineteenth century. There was nothing especially Teutonic about them, though, naturally, as we noted in an earlier chapter, some of the ideas took on a particular form and developed a specific intonation in Germany and German-speaking Austria.

Ideas of a 'national', or 'German', socialism, in contrast to the international socialism of Marxism, were nothing new in Germany in 1919, though the war had given such notions a strong boost. The liberal pastor Friedrich Naumann had founded a 'National-Social Association' in the 1890s with a view to weaning industrial workers from class-struggle and integrating them as the pillars of the new nation-state. The attempt had failed dismally by 1903, and the notion of a 'German' socialism came to be wholly associated with the extreme anti-liberal politics of the antisemitic and *völkisch* movement. The appeal here was mainly to the lower-middle classes – traders, craftsmen, small farmers, lower civil servants – and rooted in a combination of antisemitism, extreme nationalism, and vehement anti-capitalism (usually interpreted as 'Jewish' capitalism).[8] Similar tendencies in Austria, during the time of Hitler's youth, were to be found, as we noted in an earlier chapter, in the Schönerer movement. We noted, too, that conflicts between Czech and German workers in Bohemia had already led by 1904 to the establishment of a German Workers' Party at Trautenau in what came to be known as the Sudetenland, combining *völkisch* nationalism and anti-Marxist, anti-capitalist socialism.[9] Hitler acknowledged the foundation, twenty years earlier, of this Austrian National Socialist Party, at his trial after the Putsch, though disclaimed any connection with his own movement.[10] Certainly, there is no hint that he showed any interest in it or even acknowledged its existence during his time in Austria. The similarity of name continued after the war, when the Trautenau party became the German National Socialist Workers' Party (DNSAP, Deutsche Nationalsozialistische Arbeiterpartei). There were contacts with Hitler's movement in the early 1920s, but by 1923 the supremacy of the latter was established and in 1926 Hitler became acknowledged as the sole leader of both the Austrian and German branches of the re-established NSDAP.[11]

The *völkisch* variant of nationalism remained a minority taste before the First World War, though gaining influential backing through the Pan-Germans, through the dissemination of popular racist works such as those of Theodor Fritsch and Houston Stewart Chamberlain, and through the popularizing of exclusivist and aggressive ethnic nationalism in countless schools and youth organizations. The central strands of *völkisch* ideology were extreme nationalism, racial antisemitism, and mystical notions of a uniquely German social order, with roots in the Teutonic past, resting on order, harmony, and hierarchy.[12] Most significant was the linkage of a

romanticized view of Germanic culture (seen as superior but heavily threatened by inferior but powerful forces, particularly Slavs and Jews), with a
social Darwinian emphasis upon struggle for survival, imperialist notions
of the need for expansion to the Slavic east in order to safeguard national
survival, and the necessity of bringing about racial purity and a new élite
by eradicating the perceived arch-enemy of Germandom, the spirit of Jewry.

We have already seen how conditions in the last two years of the war
were conducive to the rapid spread of antisemitism and *völkisch* nationalism,
of which it was an integral part. The massive political upheaval and disarray
that followed defeat and revolution gave even greater sustenance to the
ideas of extreme nationalism. These ideas were represented in a variety of
forms by a myriad of different political groups and movements. But of
importance, in the changed circumstances, was that *völkisch* nationalism,
in all its extremes, could now blend into more mainstream nationalist forces
to offer a frontal ideological rejection of democracy and the Weimar state.
The foundations of a rounded anti-democratic ideology, an antithesis to
Weimar, were established not in the primitive beer-table discussions of
völkisch 'thinkers' and 'philosophers', but by neo-conservative writers,
publicists and intellectuals such as Wilhelm Stapel, Max Hildebert Boehm,
Moeller van den Bruck, Othmar Spann, and Edgar Jung. Ideas of an organic
Volk, resting on purity of blood and race, forming a national community
(*Volksgemeinschaft*) that transcended each individual within it, producing
a true 'national' socialism which was anti-liberal as it was anti-capitalist
and anti-bourgeois, binding each individual at the same time to service to
that community through subordination to leaders of notable ability, wisdom,
and substance, formed central elements of this ideology.[13]

The anti-capitalist and anti-bourgeois ideas of this ensemble naturally
did not endear themselves to the conservative nationalists in the German
National People's Party, the DNVP, the mainstream nationalist party which
had arisen from the ashes of the old German Conservative Party.[14] And the
neo-conservatives generally thought the Nazis were vulgar and primitive.
Even so, defeat, revolution, and the establishment of democracy had fostered
a climate in which a counter-revolutionary set of ideas could gain wide
currency, blending in part both into older forms of conservative nationalism
and into the newer, popularized and vulgarized brands of *völkisch* nationalism. The 'national disgrace' felt throughout Germany at the humiliating
terms imposed by the victorious Allies and reflected in the Versailles Treaty
signed on 28 June 1919, with its confiscation of territory and, even more
so, its 'guilt clause', enhanced the creation of a mood in which such ideas

were certain of a hearing. The first Reichstag election in June the following year, in its calamitous losses for the parties supportive of the new democracy, revealed, as is often said, that Weimar was now 'a Republic without republicans' – a notable exaggeration, but expressive of the state's low esteem in the eyes of a majority of its citizens (including many of its most powerful).[15] The potential was thus provided for extreme nationalism to move from the fringes of politics towards the centre ground.

The crowds that began to flock in 1919 and 1920 to Hitler's speeches were not motivated by refined theories. For them, simple slogans, kindling the fires of anger, resentment, and hatred, were what worked. But what they were offered in the Munich beerhalls was nevertheless a vulgarized version of ideas which were in far wider circulation. Hitler acknowledged in *Mein Kampf* that there was no essential distinction between the ideas of the *völkisch* movement and those of National Socialism.[16] He had little interest in clarifying or systematizing these ideas. Of course, he had his own obsessions – a few basic notions which never left him after 1919, became formed into a rounded 'world-view' in the mid-1920s, and provided the driving-force of his 'mission' to 'rescue' Germany. But ideas held no interest for Hitler as abstractions. They were important to him only as tools of mobilization.

When Hitler joined the German Workers' Party, it was one of some seventy-three *völkisch* groups in Germany, most of them founded since the end of the war.[17] In Munich alone there were at least fifteen in 1920.[18] Like the DAP, most of these were small, insignificant organizations. An exception, however, and an important bridge to the early following of the Nazi Party, was the German Nationalist Protection and Defiance Federation (Deutschvölkischer Schutz- und Trutz-Bund), founded at the beginning of 1919 on an initiative of the Pan-German League to amalgamate a number of smaller *völkisch* associations into an organization capable of winning the masses to the antisemitic movement.[19] Though its headquarters were located in Hamburg, where *völkisch* ideas were already widespread in the white-collar workers' union, the Deutschnationaler Handlungsgehilfenverband, it found significant resonance in the heated antisemitic climate in Munich. Its propaganda output was formidable. In 1920 alone it distributed 7.6 million pamphlets, 4.7 million handbills, and 7.8 million stickers.[20] As the symbol of the *völkisch* struggle it chose the swastika. Some of its early membership had drained into it from the short-lived Fatherland Party. Within a year it had expanded from 30,000 to 100,000 members and went on to more than double this to over 200,000 members in the three years of its existence. Prominent among them were former soldiers angered at their treatment after a war allegedly lost through a 'stab-in-the-back', artisans feeling their status under threat from the proletariat, teachers attracted to pan-German ideology, and students resentful at their own altered prospects and insulted by national humiliation.[21] Many of its members later found their way into the NSDAP.[22] The fact that the Schutz- und Trutzbund was a purely agitatory organization, not allied to any political party, and had no clear political aims hampered its effectiveness. But its rapid expansion was an indication of the growing potential for *völkisch* ideas – and particularly for the mobilizing force of antisemitism – if they could be 'marketed' effectively.

Within the *völkisch* pool of ideas, the notion of a specifically *German* or *national* socialism, tied in with an onslaught on 'Jewish' capitalism, had gained ground in the last phase of the war, and spawned both Drexler's German Workers' Party and what was soon to become its arch-rival, the German-Socialist Party (Deutschsozialistische Partei).[23] The latter's founder, Alfred Brunner, a Düsseldorf engineer, had been involved in *völkisch* politics since 1904. Radical land and finance reform featured in a programme that had many close affinities with the Nazi Party Programme of 1920. By the end of 1919 the DSP had sizeable branches in Düsseldorf, Kiel, Frankfurt am Main, Dresden, Nuremberg, and Munich. Other branches were set up elsewhere, including Berlin, during 1920. By the middle of the year, the party had thirty-five branches and approaching 2,000 members. The organizational spread eventually proved a weakness compared with the regional concentration of the Nazi Party. And attempts to merge the DSP with the Nazi Party in 1920 and 1921 were to form the backcloth to the bitter conflict in the party in summer 1921 that culminated in Hitler taking over the leadership.

Already during the war, Munich had been a major centre of anti-government nationalist agitation by the Pan-Germans, who found a valuable outlet for their propaganda in the publishing house of Julius F. Lehmann – a prominent Munich member of the Fatherland Party – otherwise renowned for the publication of texts on medicine.[24] Lehmann was also a member of the Thule Society, a *völkisch* club of a few hundred well-heeled members, run like a masonic lodge, that had been founded in Munich at the turn of the year 1917–18 out of the pre-war Germanen-Orden, set up in Leipzig in 1912 to bring together a variety of minor antisemitic groups and organizations.[25] Its membership list, including alongside Lehmann the 'economics expert' Gottfried Feder, the publicist Dietrich Eckart, the journalist and co-founder of the DAP Karl Harrer, and the young nationalists Hans Frank, Rudolf Heß, and Alfred Rosenberg, reads like a *Who's Who* of early Nazi sympathizers and leading figures in Munich. The colourful and rich head of the Thule Society, Rudolf Freiherr von Sebottendorff – a cosmopolitan adventurer and a self-styled aristocrat who was actually the son of a train-driver and had made his fortune through shady deals in Turkey and an opportune marriage to a rich heiress – ensured that meetings could be held in Munich's best hotel, the 'Vier Jahreszeiten', and provided the *völkisch* movement in Munich with its own newspaper, the *Münchener Beobachter* (renamed in August 1919 as the *Völkischer Beobachter*, and eventually bought by the Nazis in December 1920). It was from the Thule Society that the initiative arose towards the end of the war to try to influence the working class in Munich. Karl Harrer was commissioned to attempt this, and made contact with a railway workshop locksmith, Anton Drexler. Having been found unfit for military service, Drexler had in 1917 temporarily found an expression of his nationalist and racist sentiments in the Fatherland Party. Then, in March 1918, he had founded a 'Workers' Committee for a Good Peace' in an effort to stir enthusiasm for the war effort among Munich's working class. He combined his extreme nationalism with an anti-capitalism demanding draconian action against profiteers and speculators. Harrer, a sports-reporter on the right-wing *Münchner-Augsburger Abendzeitung*, persuaded Drexler and a few others to set up a 'Political Workers' Circle' (Politischer Arbeiterzirkel). The 'Circle', a group of usually three to seven members, met periodically for about a year from November 1918 onwards to discuss nationalist and racist themes – such as the Jews as Germany's enemy, or responsibility for the war and defeat – usually introduced by Harrer.[26] Whereas Harrer preferred the semi-secretive *völkisch* 'club', Drexler thought discussing recipes for Germany's salvation in such a tiny group had scant value, and wanted to found a political party. He proposed in December the setting up of a 'German Workers' Party' which would be 'free of Jews (*judenrein*)'.[27] The idea was well received, and, on 5 January 1919, at a small gathering – mainly contacts from the railway yards – in the Fürstenfelder Hof in Munich, the German Workers' Party was formed. Drexler was elected chairman of the Munich branch (the only one that existed), while Harrer was given the honorary title of 'Reich Chairman'.[28] Only in the more favourable climate after the crushing of the Räterepublik was the infant party able to stage its first public meetings. Attendance was sparse. Ten members were present on 17 May, thirty-eight when Dietrich Eckart spoke in August, and forty-one on 12 September. This was the occasion on which Hitler attended for the first time.[29]

II

Hitler's part in the early development of the German Workers' Party (subsequently the NSDAP) is obscured more than it is clarified by his own tendentious account in *Mein Kampf*. As usual, this is characterized less by pure invention than by selective memory and distortion of facts. And, as throughout his book, Hitler's version of events is aimed, more than all else, at elevating his own role as it denigrates, plays down, or simply ignores that of all others involved. It amounts, as always in Hitler's own account, to the story of a political genius going his way in the face of adversity, a heroic triumph of the will. The story was the core of the 'party legend' which in later years Hitler never tired of retelling at inordinate length as the preface to his major speeches. It was that of the political genius who joined a tiny body with grandiose ideas but no hope of realizing them, raising it single-handedly to a force of the first magnitude which would come to rescue Germany from its plight.

Hitler wrote contemptuously of the organization he had joined. The state of the party was depressing in the extreme. The committee constituted practically the whole membership. Though it attacked parliamentary rule, its own matters were decided, after 'interminable argument', by majority vote. It met in the dingy back rooms of Munich pubs. It had no permanent headquarters. In fact, it had no membership forms, no printed matter, not even a rubber stamp. Invitations to party meetings were handwritten or produced on a typewriter. The same few people turned up.[30] Eventually, a move to mimeographed notices brought a modest rise in numbers attending, and funds were raised to allow a newspaper advertisement in the *Münchener Beobachter* for a meeting on 16 October 1919 which attracted 111 people to the Hofbräukeller, the large drinking saloon attached to one of Munich's big breweries, situated in Wienerstraße to the east of the city centre (and not to be confused with the better-known Hofbräuhaus, located in the city centre itself). The main speaker was a Munich professor, but Hitler – according to his own account – then spoke for the first time in public (apart from to captive audiences in the Lechfeld Camp), for half an hour instead of his scheduled twenty minutes. He electrified his audience and prompted a collection of 300 Marks for the party coffers. He brought some of his army contacts into the movement, breathing much-needed new life into it. The party leaders, Harrer and Drexler, were in his view uninspiring: they were neither good speakers, nor had they served in the war. Hitler and the party leadership were at odds about future strategy. On the basis of his initial success, Hitler insisted on more frequent and larger meetings. He got his way, and these took place in the Eberlbräukeller and the 'Gasthaus Zum Deutschen Reich', on Dachauerstraße near the barracks area, with Hitler speaking to bigger audiences and with great success.[31] By the seventh meeting, a few weeks later, the attendance had swollen to over 400 people. Hitler's star was now in the ascendant within the party. Early in 1920, his account went on, he urged the staging of the first great mass meeting. Again there were major differences of opinion within the party leadership, doubters arguing that it was premature and would be a disastrous failure. The cautious Harrer, the party's first chairman, resigned because of his disagreement with Hitler, and was replaced by Drexler. Again, Hitler prevailed. The mass meeting was organized for 24 February 1920 in the Festsaal of the Hofbräu-haus in the centre of Munich. The big, noisy hall on the first floor – above the even rougher and rowdier 'Schwemme' down below – had, like all the city's numerous big drinking establishments, rows of tables stacked with the stone beermugs and benches groaning under the weight of thick-set men in Bavarian short leather trousers while hefty waitresses bustled between the tables delivering foaming litres of beer. When it was not hired out, as it frequently was, for large political meetings, the beer-swilling crowds would sway merrily to drinking songs played by a Bavarian brass band. At political meetings, heavy drinking, prompting verbal interjections and sometimes brawls, was commonplace. Moving to such a venue – a far bigger hall than the infant party had so far used – was risky, courting the embarrassment of a small turn-out.

A good deal of effort was put into designing striking red posters and leaflets advertising the meeting. The party's programme, to be announced at the meeting, was also printed and distributed. The publicity worked. The huge hall was packed when Hitler arrived at quarter past seven that evening. Still according to his own account, after a first speaker, whose name he does not mention, had spoken, Hitler – chairing the meeting in the absence of Drexler, who had apparently suffered some sort of nervous collapse – took the floor. Clashes between his supporters and those trying to heckle the speaker took place, but Hitler continued speaking, to mounting applause, and expounded the programme, swaying his audience to rapturous and unanimous acclamation of its twenty-five points.[32] Finally, declares Hitler in his *Mein Kampf* version, 'there stood before me a hall full of people united by a new conviction, a new faith, a new will'. The German hero was setting out on his quest: 'A fire was kindled from whose flame one day the sword must come which would regain freedom for the Germanic Siegfried and life for the German nation ... Thus slowly the hall emptied. The movement took its course.'[33]

The story has been aptly described as 'a heroic legend in half-naturalistic style, young Siegfried warbling his wood-notes wild in Munich beer halls'.[34] The legend was framed to portray the beginnings of the Führer figure, Germany's coming great leader and saviour, as it had emerged by the writing of the first volume of *Mein Kampf* in 1924. Towering over the weak and vacillating early leaders of the party, certain of himself and of the coming to fruition of his mighty vision, proven successful in his methods, his greatness – so his account was designed to illustrate – was apparent even in these first months after joining the movement. There could be no doubt about his claim to supremacy in the *völkisch* movement against all pretenders.

After dealing with subsequent successes in building up the party's following, Hitler returned to the early party history in a later passage in *Mein Kampf* when, surprisingly briefly and remarkably vaguely, he described his takeover of the party leadership in mid-1921. His terse summary simply indicates that after intrigues against him and 'the attempt of a group of *völkisch* lunatics', supported by the party chairman (Drexler), to obtain the leadership of the party had collapsed, a general membership meeting unanimously gave him leadership over the whole movement. His reorganiz-ation of the movement on 1 August 1921 swept away the old, ineffectual quasi-parliamentary way of running party matters by committee and internal democracy, and substituted for it the leadership principle as the organiz-ational basis of the party. His own absolute supremacy was thereby assured.[35]

Here, it seems, embodied in the description in *Mein Kampf*, is the realiz-ation of Hitler's ambition for dictatorial power in the movement – sub-sequently in the German state – which could be witnessed in his early conflicts with Harrer and Drexler, and his rejection of the initial inner-party democratic style. The weakness of lesser mortals, their inability to see the light, the certainty with which he went his own way, and the need to follow a supreme leader who alone could ensure ultimate triumph – these, from the outset, are the dominant themes. The beginning of his claim to leadership can thus be located in the earliest phase of his activity within the party. In turn, this suggests that the self-awareness of political genius was present from the beginning.

Little wonder that, on the basis of this story, the enigma of Hitler is profound. The 'nobody of Vienna', the corporal who is not even promoted to sergeant, now appears with a full-blown political philosophy, a strategy for success, and a burning will to lead his party, and sees himself as Germany's coming great leader. However puzzling and extraordinary, the underlying thrust of Hitler's self-depiction has found a surprising degree of acceptance.[36] But, though not inaccurate in all respects, it requires substantial modification and qualification.

III

The break with Karl Harrer soon came. It was not, however, an early indicator of Hitler's relentless striving for dictatorial power in the movement. Nor was it simply a matter of whether the party should be a mass movement or a type of closed *völkisch* debating society.[37] A number of *völkisch* organizations at the time faced the same problem, and attempted to combine an appeal to a mass audience with regular meetings of an exclusive 'inner circle'. Harrer tended strongly towards the latter, represented by the 'Workers' Circle', which he himself controlled, in contrast to the party's 'Working Committee', where he was simply an ordinary member. But Harrer found himself increasingly isolated. Drexler was as keen as Hitler to take the party's message to the masses. He later claimed that he, and not Hitler, had proposed announcing the party's programme at a mass meeting in the Hofbräuhausfestsaal, and that Hitler had initially been sceptical about the prospects of filling the hall.[38] As long as Harrer directed the party through his control of the 'Workers' Circle', the question of the more viable propaganda strategy would remain unresolved. It was necessary, therefore, to enhance the role of the Committee, which Drexler and Hitler did in draft regulations that they drew up in December, giving it complete authority and ruling out any 'superior or side government, whether as a circle or lodge'.[39] The draft regulations – bearing Hitler's clear imprint – determined that the Committee's members and its chairman should be elected in an open meeting. Their unity, it went on, would be ensured through strict adherence to the programme of the party (which Hitler and Drexler were already preparing). The new regulations were plainly directed against Harrer. But they were not devised as a stepping-stone on the way to Hitler's supreme power in the party. Evidently, he had no notion of dictatorial party rule at the time. He was ready to accept the corporate leadership of an elected committee. Decisions to stage mass meetings in the next months were, it seems, those of the Committee as a whole, approved by a majority of its members, not Hitler's alone, though, once Harrer had departed and in view of Hitler's increasing success in drawing the crowds to listen to his speeches, it is hard to believe that there was any dissension. Harrer alone, it appears, opposed the staging of an ambitious mass meeting in early 1920, and accepted the consequences of his defeat by resigning. Personal animosity also played a role. Harrer, remarkably, thought little of Hitler as a speaker. Hitler was in turn contemptuous of Harrer.[40]

The party's first mass meeting was initially planned to take place in the Bürgerbräukeller (another large beerhall, on Rosenheimerstraße, just over the river Isar about half a mile south-east of the city centre) in January 1920, but had to be postponed because of a general ban on public meetings at the time.[41] It was rescheduled for the Hofbräuhaus on 24 February. The fear that the meeting would be broken up through planned disturbances by political opponents, anxious to disrupt the first big meeting of a party calling itself a 'workers' party', was probably exaggerated at this early stage in the party's development. Large antisemitic meetings were nothing new in Munich at the time. Disturbances had to be reckoned with. A high-point of the antisemitic wave of agitation that had begun in Munich in summer 1919 had already taken place: a huge meeting of the Schutz- und Trutzbund on 7 January 1920, attended by 7,000 people, had provoked scenes of uproar.[42] Corporal Hitler, who made a brief contribution to the 'discussion', cannot fail to have been impressed by the resonance of antisemitic agitation – or by the mark on public opinion in Munich made by such a piece of political theatre.[43] The main worry of Hitler, as of Drexler, was not that there would be disruption, but that the attendance would be embarrassingly small. This was why, since Drexler recognized that neither he nor Hitler had any public profile, he approached Dr Johannes Dingfelder, not even a party member but well known in Munich *völkisch* circles, to deliver the main speech, on 'What We Are Needing' (*Was uns not tut*). Hitler's name was not even mentioned in any of the publicity. Nor was there any hint that the party's programme would be proclaimed at the meeting.[44]

The twenty-five points of this programme – which would in the course of time be declared 'unalterable' and be in practice largely ignored – had been worked out and drafted over the previous weeks by Drexler and Hitler. Discussion was already under way in mid-November 1919; Drexler had a draft ready a month later, and produced a further draft by 9 February, before the final version was produced in time for the Hofbräuhaus meeting.[45] The content had much in common with the programme of the DSP.[46] Its points – among them, demands for a Greater Germany, land and colonies, discrimination against Jews and denial of citizenship to them, breaking 'interest slavery', confiscation of war profits, land reform, protection of the middle class, persecution of profiteers, and tight regulation of the press – contained little or nothing that was original or novel on the *völkisch* Right.[47] Religious neutrality was included in the attempt to avoid alienating a large church-going population in Bavaria. 'Common good before individual good' was an unobjectionable banality. The demand for 'a strong central power' in the Reich, and 'the unconditional authority' of a 'central parliament', though clearly implying authoritarian, not pluralistic, government, gives no indication that Hitler envisaged himself at this stage as the head of a personalized regime. There are some striking omissions. Neither Marxism nor Bolshevism is mentioned. The entire question of agriculture is passed over, apart from the brief reference to land reform. The authorship of the programme cannot fully be clarified.[48] Probably, the individual points derived from several sources among the party's leading figures. The attack on 'interest slavery' obviously drew on Gottfried Feder's pet theme. Profit-sharing was a favourite idea of Drexler. The forceful style, in comparison with the more wordy DSP programme, sounds like Hitler's.[49] As he later asserted, he certainly worked on it.[50] But probably the main author was Drexler himself. Certainly, Drexler himself claimed this in the private letter he wrote to Hitler (though did not send) in January 1940. In this letter, he stated that 'following all the basic points already written down by me, Adolf Hitler composed *with* me – and with no one else – the 25 theses of National Socialism, in long nights in the workers' canteen at Burghausenerstraße 6'.[51]

Despite worries about the attendance at the party's first big meeting, some 2,000 people (perhaps a fifth of them socialist opponents) were crammed into the Festsaal of the Hofbräuhaus on 24 February when Hitler, as chairman, opened the meeting.[52] Dingfelder's speech was unremarkable. Certainly, it was un-Hitler like in style and tone. The word 'Jew' was never mentioned. He blamed Germany's fate on the decline of morality and religion, and the rise of selfish, material values. His recipe for recovery was 'order, work, and dutiful sacrifice for the salvation of the Fatherland'. The speech was well received and uninterrupted.[53] The atmosphere suddenly livened when Hitler came to speak. His tone was harsher, more aggressive, less academic, than Dingfelder's. The language he used was expressive, direct, coarse, earthy – that used and understood by most of his audience – his sentences short and punchy. He heaped insults on target-figures like the leading Centre Party politician and Reich Finance Minister Matthias Erzberger (who had signed the Armistice in 1918 and strongly advocated acceptance of the detested Versailles Treaty the following summer) or the

Munich capitalist Isidor Bach, sure of the enthusiastic applause of his audience. Verbal assaults on the Jews brought new cheers from the audience, while shrill attacks on profiteers produced cries of 'Flog them! Hang them!' When he came to read out the party programme, there was much applause for the individual points. But there were interruptions, too, from left-wing opponents, who had already been getting restless, and the police reporter of the meeting spoke of scenes of 'great tumult so that I often thought it would come to brawling at any minute'. Hitler announced, to storms of applause, what would remain the party's slogan: 'Our motto is only struggle. We will go our way unshakably to our goal.' The end of Hitler's speech, in which he read out a protest at an alleged decision to provide 40,000 hundredweight of flour for the Jewish community, again erupted into uproar following further opposition heckling, with people standing on tables and chairs yelling at each other. In the subsequent 'discussion', four others spoke briefly, two of them opponents. Remarks from the last speaker that a dictatorship from the Right would be met with a dictatorship from the Left were the signal for a further uproar, such that Hitler's words closing the meeting were drowned. Around 100 Independent Socialists and Communists poured out of the Hofbräuhaus on to the streets cheering for the International and the Räterepublik and booing the war-heroes Hindenburg and Luden-dorff, and the German Nationalists.[54] The meeting had not exactly produced the 'hall full of people united by a new conviction, a new faith, a new will' that Hitler was later to describe.[55]

Nor would anyone reading Munich newspapers in the days following the meeting have gained the impression that it was a landmark heralding the arrival of a new, dynamic party and a new political hero. The press's reaction was muted, to say the least. The newspapers concentrated in their brief reports on Dingfelder's speech and paid little attention to Hitler.[56] Even the *Völkischer Beobachter*, not yet under party control but sympathetic, was surprisingly low-key. It reported the meeting in a single column in an inside page four days later. Most of the report dealt with Dingfelder's speech. Hitler's contribution was summarized in a single sentence: 'Herr Hitler (DAP) presented some striking political points (*entwickelte einige treffende politische Bilder*) which evoked spirited applause, but also roused the numer-ous already prejudiced opponents present to contradiction; and he gave a survey of the party's programme, which in its basic features comes close to that of the Deutschsozialistische Partei.'[57]

Despite this initial modest impact, it was already apparent that Hitler meetings meant political fireworks. Even in the hothouse of Munich politics, the big meetings of the National Socialist German Workers' Party (NSDAP), as the movement henceforth called itself, were something different.[58] Hitler wanted above all else to make his party noticed. In this he rapidly succeeded. 'It makes no difference whatever whether they laugh at us or revile us,' he later wrote, 'whether they represent us as clowns or criminals; the main thing is that they mention us, that they concern themselves with us again and again . . .'[59] He observed the dull, lifeless meetings of bourgeois parties, the deadening effect of speeches read out like academic lectures by dignified, elderly gentlemen. Nazi meetings, he recorded with pride, were, by contrast, *not* peaceful. He learnt from the organization of meetings by the Left, how they were orchestrated, the value of intimidation of opponents, techniques of disruption, and how to deal with disturbances. The NSDAP's meetings aimed to attract confrontation, and as a result to make the party noticed. Posters were drafted in vivid red to provoke the Left to attend.[60] In mid-1920 Hitler personally designed the party's banner with the swastika in a white circle on a red background devised to make as striking a visual impact as possible.[61] The result was that meetings were packed long before the start, and the numbers of opponents present guaranteed that the atmosphere was potentially explosive.[62] To combat trouble, a 'hall protection' squad (Saalschutz) was fully organized by mid-1920, became the 'Gymnastic and Sports Section' in August 1921, and eventually developed into the 'Storm Section' (Sturmabteilung, or SA).[63]

Only Hitler could bring in the crowds for the NSDAP. To this extent, his self-centred account in *Mein Kampf* was perfectly correct. It was a month after feeling provoked into joining in the discussion at the DAP meeting on 12 September 1919 before his first 'performance' as a party speaker in the Hofbräukeller on 16 October 1919.[64] The memory of his success, as we have seen, lasted with him. In *Mein Kampf* he used the almost identical phrase with which he had already described his 'self-discovery' in the Lechfeld Camp: 'What before I had simply felt within me, without in any way knowing it, was now proved by reality: I could speak!'[65] Though plainly stylized, as the double rendition of this phrase demonstrates, there can be no doubting the self-confidence that flowed through Hitler as a result of the confirmation, for the first time before a non-captive audience, that the way he spoke could stir his audience.

In the company of an individual, Hitler's egocentric manner could be totally off-putting. An acquaintance at the time, contemptuous of Hitler's activity as a Reichswehr spy, but forced to suffer an involuntary lecture on the future mission of German artists, could eventually stand no more of the peroration: 'Tell me, have they shit in your brain and forgotten to flush it?' he asked, leaving Hitler speechless.[66] But in front of a beerhall audience Hitler's style was electrifying.

While in his Nuremberg cell awaiting the hangman, Hans Frank, the ex-Governor General of Poland, recalled the moment, in January 1920, while he was still only nineteen years old (though already committed to the *völkisch* cause), that he had first heard Hitler speak. The large room was bursting at the seams. Middle-class citizens rubbed shoulders with workers, soldiers, and students. Whether old or young, the state of the nation weighed heavily on people. Germany's plight polarized opinions, but left few unmoved or disinterested. Most political meetings were packed. But, to Frank – young, idealistic, fervently anti-Marxist and nationalistic – speakers were generally disappointing, had little to offer. Hitler, in stark contrast, set him alight.

The man with whom Hans Frank's fate would be bound for the next quarter of a century was dressed in a shabby blue suit, his tie loosely fastened. He spoke clearly, in impassioned but not shrill tones, his blue eyes flashing, occasionally pushing back his hair with his right hand. Frank's most immediate feeling was how sincere Hitler was, how the words came from the heart and were not just a rhetorical device. 'He was at that time simply the grandiose popular speaker without precedent – and, for me, incomparable,' wrote Frank.

I was strongly impressed straight away. It was totally different from what was otherwise to be heard in meetings. His method was completely clear and simple. He took the overwhelmingly dominant topic of the day, the Versailles Diktat, and posed the question of all questions: What now German people? What's the true situation? What alone is now possible? He spoke for over two-and-a-half hours, often interrupted by frenetic torrents of applause – and one could have listened to him for much, much longer. Everything came from the heart, and he struck a chord with all of us . . . He uttered what was in the consciousness of all those present and linked general experiences to clear understanding and the common wishes of those who were suffering and hoping for a programme. In the matter itself he was certainly not original . . . but he was the one called to act as spokesman of the people . . . He concealed nothing . . . of the horror, the distress, the despair facing Germany. But not only that. He showed a way, the only way left to all ruined peoples in history, that of the grim new beginning from the most profound depths through courage, faith, readiness for action, hard work, and devotion to a great, shining, common goal . . . He placed before the protection of the Almighty in the most serious and solemn exhortation the salvation of the honour of the German soldier and worker as his life-task . . . When he finished, the applause would not die down . . . From this evening onwards, though not a party member, I was convinced that if one man could do it, Hitler alone would be capable of mastering Germany's fate.[67]

Whatever the pathos of these comments, they testify to Hitler's instinctive ability, singling him out from other speakers relaying a similar message, to speak in the language of his listeners, and to stir them through the passion and – however strange it might now sound to us – the apparent sincerity of his idealism.

Rising attendances, as he noted in *Mein Kampf*, followed in the next weeks, between his first appearance as main speaker – on one of his favourite topics, 'Brest-Litovsk and Versailles?' – in the Eberlbräukeller in November 1919, and the big Hofbräuhaus meeting in February 1920. This was merely a prelude to Hitler's growing success and mounting reputation as the party's star speaker. By the end of 1920 he had addressed over thirty mass meetings – mostly of between 800 and 2,500 persons – and spoken at many smaller internal party gatherings.[68] In early February 1921 he would speak at the biggest meeting so far – over 6,000 people in the Circus Krone, which could accommodate the biggest indoor crowds in Munich, near the Marsfeld just to the west of the city centre.[69] Until mid-1921 he spoke mainly in Munich, where the propaganda and organization of the meetings would ensure a satisfactory turn-out, and where the right atmosphere was guaranteed. But, not counting the speeches made during a fortnight's visit to Austria in early October, he held ten speeches outside the city in 1920, including one in Rosenheim where the first local group of the party outside Munich had just been founded. It was largely owing to Hitler's public profile that the party membership increased sharply from 190 in January 1920 to 2,000 by the end of the year and 3,300 by August 1921.[70] He was rapidly making himself indispensable to the movement.

IV

Hitler spoke from rough notes – mainly a series of jotted headings with key words underlined.[71] As a rule, a speech would last around two hours or more.[72] In the Festsaal of the Hofbräuhaus he used a beer table on one of the long sides of the hall as his platform in order to be in the middle of the crowd – a novel technique for a speaker which helped create what Hitler regarded as a special mood in that hall.[73] The themes of his speeches varied little: the contrast of Germany's strength in a glorious past with its current weakness and national humiliation – a sick state in the hands of traitors and cowards who had betrayed the Fatherland to its powerful enemies; the reasons for the collapse in a lost war unleashed by these enemies, and behind them, the Jews; betrayal and revolution brought about by criminals and Jews;[74] English and French intentions of destroying Germany, as shown in the Treaty of Versailles – the 'Peace of shame', the instrument of Germany's slavery; the exploitation of ordinary Germans by Jewish racketeers and profiteers; a cheating and corrupt government and party system presiding over economic misery, social division, political conflict, and ethical collapse; the only way to recovery contained in the points of the party's programme – ruthless showdown with internal enemies and build-up of national consciousness and unity, leading to renewed strength and eventual restored greatness.[75] The combination of traditional Bavarian dislike of the Prussians and the experience of the Räterepublik in Munich meant that Hitler's repeated onslaught on the 'Marxist' government in Berlin was certain to meet with an enthusiastic response among the still small minority of the local population drawn to his meetings.

While Hitler basically appealed to negative feelings – anger, resentment, hatred – there was also a 'positive' element in the proposed remedy to the proclaimed ills. However platitudinous, the appeal to restoration of liberty through national unity, the need to work together of 'workers of the brain and hand' (Zusammenarbeiten des Geistes- und Handarbeiters),[76] the social harmony of a 'national community', and the protection of the 'little man' through the crushing of his exploiters, were, to go from the applause they invariably produced, undeniably attractive propositions to Hitler's audiences.[77] And Hitler's own passion and fervour successfully conveyed the message – to those already predisposed to it – that no other way was possible; that Germany's revival would and could be brought about; and that it lay in the power of ordinary Germans to make it happen through their own struggle, sacrifice, and will.[78] The effect was more that of a religious revivalist meeting than a normal political gathering.[79]

What Hitler was saying had long belonged to the standard repertoire of nationalist and völkisch speakers. It was as good as indistinguishable from what the Pan-Germans had been preaching for years. And though Hitler was invariably up-to-date in finding easy targets in the daily politics of the crisis-ridden Republic, his main themes were tediously repetitive. Some, in fact, often taken for granted to be part of Hitler's allegedly unchanging ideology were missing altogether at this stage. There was, for example, not a single mention of the need for 'living-space' (*Lebensraum*) in eastern Europe.[80] Britain and France were the foreign-policy targets at this time. Indeed, Hitler jotted among the notes of one of his speeches, in August 1920, 'brotherhood towards the east' (*Verbrüderung nach Osten*).[81] Nor did he clamour for a dictatorship. Such a demand occurs in only one speech in 1920, on 27 April, in which Hitler declared that Germany needed 'a dictator who is a genius' if it were to rise up again.[82] There was no implication that he himself was that person.[83] Surprisingly, too, his first outright public assault on Marxism did not occur before his speech at Rosenheim on 21 July 1920 (though he had spoken on a number of occasions before this of the catastrophic effects of Bolshevism in Russia, for which he blamed the Jews).[84] And, remarkably, even race theory – where Hitler drew heavily for his ideas from well-known antisemitic tracts such as those of Houston Stewart Chamberlain, Adolf Wahrmund, and, especially, the arch-popularizer Theodor Fritsch (one of whose emphases was the alleged sexual abuse of women by Jews) – was explicitly treated in only one speech by Hitler during 1920.[85]

This scarcely meant, however, that Hitler neglected to attack the Jews. On the contrary: the all-devouring manic obsession with the Jews to which all else is subordinated – not observable before 1919, never absent thereafter – courses through almost every Hitler speech at this time. Behind all evil that had befallen or was threatening Germany stood the figure of the Jew.[86] In speech after speech he lashed the Jews in the most vicious and barbaric language imaginable.

Genuine socialism, declared Hitler, meant to be an antisemite.[87] Germans should be ready to enter into a pact with the devil to eradicate the evil of Jewry.[88] But, as in his letter to Gemlich the previous autumn, he did not see emotional antisemitism as the answer.[89] He demanded internment in concentration camps to prevent 'Jewish undermining of our people',[90] hanging for racketeers,[91] but ultimately, as the only solution – similar to the Gemlich letter – the 'removal of the Jews from our people'.[92] The implication, as in his explicit demands with regard to *Ostjuden*,[93] was their expulsion from Germany. This was undoubtedly how it was understood. But, as with some pre-war antisemites, the language itself was both terrible and implicitly genocidal in its biological similes.[94] 'You don't talk about what to do with parasites (*Trichinen*) and bacilli. Parasites and bacilli are also not reared. They are as quickly and fully as possible destroyed (*vernichtet*).' This was not Hitler. It was Paul de Lagarde, leading oriental scholar and specialist in semitic languages, in 1887, writing of how, in his view, Jews should be treated.[95] The atmosphere had become immeasurably more menacing towards the Jews when Hitler deployed similar terminology over thirty years later. 'Don't think that you can combat racial tuberculosis,' he declared in August 1920, 'without seeing to it that the people is freed from the causative organ of racial tuberculosis. The impact of Jewry will never pass away, and the poisoning of the people will not end, as long as the causal agent, the Jew, is not removed from our midst.'[96]

His audiences loved it. More than anything else, these attacks evoked torrents of applause and cheering.[97] His technique – beginning slowly, plenty of sarcasm, personalized attacks on named targets, then a gradual crescendo to a climax – whipped his audiences into a frenzy.[98] His speech in the Festsaal of the Hofbräuhaus on 13 August 1920 on 'Why Are We Antisemites?' – his only speech that year *solely* relating to the Jews and probably intended as a basic statement on the topic – was interrupted fifty-eight times during its two hours' duration by ever wilder cheering from the 2,000 strong audience.[99] To go from a report on another Hitler speech a few weeks later, the audience would have been mainly drawn from white-collar workers, the lower-middle class, and better-off workers, with around a quarter women.[100]

At first, Hitler's antisemitic tirades were invariably linked to anti-capitalism and attacks on 'Jewish' war profiteers and racketeers, whom he blamed for exploiting the German people and causing the loss of the war and the German war dead. He later claimed, in a horrific passage of *Mein Kampf*, that a million German lives lost at the front would have been saved if 'twelve to fifteen thousand of these Hebrew corrupters of the people had been held under poison gas'.[101] The influence of Gottfried Feder can be seen in the distinction Hitler drew between essentially healthy 'industrial capital' and the real evil of 'Jewish finance capital'.[102]

There was no link with Marxism or Bolshevism at this stage. Contrary to what is sometimes claimed, Hitler's antisemitism was not prompted by his anti-Bolshevism; it long predated it.[103] There was no mention of Bolshevism in the Gemlich letter of September 1919, where the 'Jewish Question' is related to the rapacious nature of finance capital.[104] Hitler spoke in April and again in June 1920 of Russia being destroyed by the Jews, but it was only in his Rosenheim speech on 21 July that he explicitly married the images of Marxism, Bolshevism, and the Soviet system in Russia to the brutality of Jewish rule, for which he saw Social Democracy preparing the ground in Germany.[105] Hitler admitted in August 1920 that he knew little of the real situation in Russia.[106] But – perhaps influenced above all by Alfred Rosenberg, who came from the Baltic and experienced the Russian Revolution at first hand,[107] but probably also soaking up images of the horror of the Russian civil war which were filtering through to the German press[108] – he plainly became preoccupied with Bolshevik Russia in the second half of the year.[109] The dissemination of the *Protocols of the Elders of Zion* – the forgery about Jewish world domination, widely read and believed in antisemitic circles at the time – probably also helped to focus Hitler's attention on Russia.[110] These images appear to have provided the catalyst to the merger of antisemitism and anti-Marxism in his 'world-view' – an identity which, once forged, never disappeared.

V

Hitler's speeches put him on the political map in Munich. But he was still very much a local taste. And however much noise he made, his party was still insignificant compared with the established socialist and Catholic parties. Moreover, though it is going too far to see him as no more than the tool of powerful vested interests 'behind the scenes', without influential backers and the 'connections' they could provide his talents as a mob-agitator would not have got him very far.

Though Hitler had already signalled his intention of making a living as a political speaker, he was, in fact, until 31 March 1920 still drawing pay from the army. His first patron, Captain Mayr, continued to take a close interest in him and, if his later account can be believed, provided limited funding towards the staging of the mass meetings.[111] At this time, Hitler was still serving both the party and the army. In January and February 1920, Mayr had 'Herr Hittler' lecturing on 'Versailles' and 'Political Parties and their Significance' in the company of distinguished Munich historians Karl Alexander von Müller and Paul Joachimsen to Reichswehr soldiers under-taking 'citizenship education courses'.[112] In March, during the Kapp Putsch, when a short-lived armed coup had attempted to overthrow the government, forcing it to flee from the Reich capital, he sent him with Dietrich Eckart to Berlin to instruct Wolfgang Kapp on the situation in Bavaria. They arrived too late. The Right's first attempt to take over the state had already collapsed. But Mayr was undeterred. He retained both his contact with Kapp and his interest in Hitler. He still had hopes, so he told Kapp six months later, that the NSDAP – which he thought of as his own creation – would become the 'organization of national radicalism', the advance-guard of a future, more successful, putsch.[113] He wrote to Kapp, now exiled in Sweden:

The national workers' party must provide the basis for the strong assault-force (*Stoßtrupp*) that we are hoping for. The programme is still somewhat clumsy and also perhaps incomplete. We'll have to supplement it. Only one thing is certain: that under this banner we've already won a good number of supporters. Since July of last year I've been looking . . . to strengthen the movement . . . I've set up very capable young people. A Herr Hitler, for example, has become a motive force, a popular speaker (*Volksredner*) of the first rank. In the Munich branch we have over 2,000 members, compared with under 100 in summer 1919.[114]

Early in 1920, before Hitler had left the Reichswehr, Mayr had taken him along to meetings of the 'Iron Fist' club for radical nationalist officers, founded by Captain Ernst Röhm. Hitler had been introduced to Röhm by Mayr, probably the previous autumn.[115] Interested in a variety of nationalist parties, particularly with a view to winning the workers to the nationalist cause, Röhm had attended the first meeting of the DAP addressed by Hitler on 16 October 1919 and had joined the party shortly afterwards. Now Hitler came into far closer contact with Röhm, who rapidly came to replace Mayr as the key link with the Reichswehr. Röhm had been responsible for arming the volunteers and 'civil defence' (Einwohnerwehr) units in Bavaria and had in the meantime become an important player in paramilitary politics, with excellent connections in the army, the 'patriotic associations', and throughout the *völkisch* Right. He was, in fact, at this time, along with his fellow officers on the Right, far more interested in the massive Einwohnerwehren, with a membership of over quarter of a million men, than he was in the tiny NSDAP. Even so, he provided the key contact between the NSDAP and the far larger 'patriotic associations' and offered avenues to funding which the constantly hard-up party desperately needed.[116] His connections proved invaluable – increasingly so from 1921 onwards, when his interest in Hitler's party grew.

Another important patron at this time was the *völkisch* poet and publicist Dietrich Eckart.[117] More than twenty years older than Hitler, Eckart, who had initially made his name with a translation of *Peer Gynt*, had not been notably successful before the war as a poet and critic. Possibly this stimulated his intense antisemitism. He became politically active in December 1918 with the publication of his antisemitic weekly *Auf gut deutsch* (*In Plain German*), which also featured contributions from Gottfried Feder and the young emigré from the Baltic, Alfred Rosenberg. He spoke at DAP meetings in the summer of 1919, before Hitler joined,[118] and evidently came to regard the party's new recruit as his own protégé. Hitler himself was flattered by the attention paid to him by a figure of Eckart's reputation in *völkisch* circles. In the early years, relations between the two were good, even close. But for Hitler, as ever, it was Eckart's usefulness that counted. As Hitler's self-importance grew, his need for Eckart declined and by 1923, the year of Eckart's death, the two had become estranged.[119]

At first, however, there could be no doubt of Eckart's value to Hitler and the NSDAP. Through his well-heeled connections, Eckart afforded the beerhall demagogue an entrée into Munich 'society', opening for him the door to the salons of wealthy and influential members of the city's bourgeoisie. And through his financial support, and that of his contacts, he was able to offer vital assistance to the financially struggling small party. Since membership fees did not remotely cover outgoings, the party was dependent upon help from outside. It came in part from the owners of Munich firms and businesses, including the publisher Lehmann. Some aid continued to come from the Reichswehr. Mayr's office paid for the 3,000 brochures, attacking the detested Versailles Treaty (seen not just on the extreme Right as cripplingly punitive and humiliating for Germany), which Lehmann had published for the party in June 1920.[120] But Eckart's role was crucial. He arranged, for example, the funding from his friend, the Augsburg chemist and factory-owner Dr Gottfried Grandel, who also backed the periodical *Auf gut deutsch*, for the plane that took him and Hitler to Berlin at the time of the Kapp Putsch. Grandel later served as a guarantor for the funds used to purchase the *Völkischer Beobachter* and turn it into the party's own newspaper in December 1920.[121]

The party leadership had been looking to buy the near-bankrupt *Beobachter* since the summer to provide the wider publicity that was needed. But it was only in mid-December, when rival bidders for the newspaper emerged, that Hitler moved. Together with Hermann Esser and the deputy party-chairman Oskar Körner, he turned up in an agitated state at Drexler's flat at two o'clock in the morning on 17 December claiming the *Beobachter* was 'in danger', that it was about to fall into Bavarian separatists' hands. Drexler's mother was wakened up to make coffee, and around the kitchen table it was decided that Drexler would first thing the next morning call on Eckart to persuade him to encourage his wealthy contacts to provide the financial backing to acquire the newspaper. Hitler, meanwhile, would seek out Dr Grandel in Augsburg. Six hours later, Drexler was drumming an irritable Eckart out of bed, disgruntled at being awakened so early. They were soon on their way to see General von Epp. Eckart convinced the latter how vital it was to gain possession of the *Beobachter* and stood guarantor with his house and property for the 60,000 Marks which Epp provided from the funds of the Reichswehr. Other sources yielded a further 30,000 Marks, and Drexler himself, earning 35 Marks a week, took over the remaining debts of 113,000 Marks before, that afternoon, becoming the legal owner of the *Völkischer Beobachter*.[122] Thanks to Eckart, the Reichswehr, and in no small measure to Drexler himself, Hitler now had his newspaper. His thanks to Eckart were suitably fulsome.[123]

VI

To the Munich public, by 1921, Hitler *was* the NSDAP. He was its voice, its representative figure, its embodiment. Asked to name the party's chairman, perhaps even politically informed citizens might have guessed wrongly. But Hitler did not want the chairmanship. Drexler offered it him on a number of occasions. But Hitler refused.[124] Drexler wrote to Feder in spring 1921, stating 'that each revolutionary movement must have a dictatorial head, and therefore I also think our Hitler is the most suitable for our movement, without wanting to be pushed into the background myself'.[125] But for Hitler, the party chairmanship meant organizational responsibility. He had – this was to remain the case during the rise to power, and when he headed the German state – neither aptitude nor ability for organizational matters. Organization he could leave to others; propaganda – mobilization of the masses – was what he was good at, and what he wanted to do. For that, and that alone, he would take responsibility. Propaganda, for Hitler, was the highest form of political activity. He had learnt at first from the Social Democrats as well as from the antisemites of the Schutz- und Trutzbund. He probably also learnt from Gustave Le Bon's tract on crowd psychology – though most likely at second hand.[126] But most of all he learnt from his own experience of the power of the spoken word, given the right political climate, the right crisis atmosphere, and a public ready to trust in political faith more than reasoned argument. In Hitler's own conception, propaganda was the key to the nationalization of the masses, without which there could be no national salvation. It was not that propaganda and ideology (*Weltanschauung*) were distinctive entities for him. They were inseparable, and reinforced each other. An idea for Hitler was useless unless it mobilized. The self-confidence he gained from the rapturous reception of his speeches assured him that his diagnosis of Germany's ills and the way to national redemption was right – the only one possible. This in turn gave him the self-conviction that conveyed itself to those in his immediate entourage as well as those listening to his speeches in the beerhalls. To see himself as 'drummer' of the national cause was, therefore, for Hitler a high calling. It was why, before the middle of 1921, he preferred to be free for this role, and not to be bogged down in the organizational work which he associated with the chairmanship of the party.[127]

The outrage felt throughout Germany at the punitive sum of 226 thousand million Gold Marks to be paid in reparations, imposed by the Paris Conference at the end of January 1921, ensured there would be no let-up in agitation.[128] This was the background for the biggest meeting that the NSDAP had until then staged, on 3 February in the Circus Krone. Hitler risked going ahead with the meeting at only one day's notice, and without the usual advance publicity. In a rush, the huge hall was booked and two lorries hired to drive round the city throwing out leaflets.[129] This was another technique borrowed from the 'Marxists', and the first time the Nazis had used it. Despite worries until the last minute that the hall would be half-empty and the meeting would prove a propaganda débâcle, more than 6,000 turned up to hear Hitler, speaking on 'Future or Ruin' (*Zukunft oder Untergang*), denounce the 'slavery' imposed on Germans by the Allied reparations, and castigate the weakness of the government for accepting them.[130] 'The known leader of the antisemites, Hitler' had less success three days later when, as third speaker at a mass rally of 20,000 members of the 'patriotic associations' in Odeonsplatz, he made no impact with his 'party-political tendencies'.[131]

Hitler wrote that after the Circus Krone success he increased the NSDAP's propaganda activity in Munich still further.[132] And indeed the propaganda output was impressive. Hitler spoke at twenty-eight major meetings in Munich and twelve elsewhere (nearly all still in Bavaria), apart from several contributions to 'discussions', and seven addresses to the newly-formed SA in the latter part of the year. Between January and June 1921 he also wrote thirty-nine articles for the *Völkischer Beobachter*, and from September onwards contributed a number of pieces to the party's internal information leaflets (*Mitteilungsblätter*).[133] Of course, he had the time in which to devote himself solely to propaganda. Unlike the other members of the party leadership, he had no other occupation or interest.

Politics consumed practically his entire existence. When he was not giving speeches, or preparing them, he spent time reading. As always, much of this was the newspapers – giving him regular ammunition for his scourge of Weimar politicians. He had books – a lot of them popular editions – on history, geography, Germanic myths, and, especially, war (including Clausewitz) on the shelves of his shabby, sparsely furnished room at 41 Thierschstraße, down by the Isar.[134] But what, exactly, he read is impossible to know. His lifestyle scarcely lent itself to lengthy periods of systematic reading. He claimed, however, to have read up on his hero Frederick the Great, and pounced on the work of his rival in the *völkisch* camp, Otto Dickel, a 320-page treatise on *Die Auferstehung des Abendlandes* (*The Resurrection of the Western World*), a mystical tract attempting to turn Spengler's pessimism on its head, immediately on its appearance in 1921 in order to be able to castigate it.[135]

Otherwise, as it had been since the Vienna days, much of his time was spent lounging around cafés in Munich. According to his photographer Heinrich Hoffmann, he specially liked the Café Heck in Galerienstraße, his favourite. In a quiet corner of the long, narrow room of this coffee-house, frequented by Munich's solid middle class, he could sit at his reserved table, his back to the wall, holding court among the new-found cronies that he had attracted to the NSDAP.[136] Among those coming to form an inner circle of Hitler's associates were the young student Rudolf Heß, the Baltic-Germans Alfred Rosenberg (who had worked on Eckart's periodical since 1919) and Max Erwin von Scheubner-Richter (an engineer with excellent contacts to wealthy Russian emigrés).[137] Certainly by the time Putzi Hanfstaengl, the cultured half-American who became his Foreign Press Chief, came to know him, late in 1922, Hitler had a table booked every Monday evening at the old-fashioned Café Neumaier on the edge of the Viktualienmarkt.[138] His regular accompaniment formed a motley crew – mostly lower-middle class, some unsavoury characters among them. Christian Weber, former pub bouncer and horse-dealer, who, like Hitler, invariably carried a dog-whip and relished the brawls with Communists, was one. Another was Hermann Esser, formerly Mayr's press agent, himself an excellent agitator, and an even better gutter journalist. Max Amann, another roughneck, Hitler's former sergeant who became overlord of the Nazi press empire, was also usually there, as were Ulrich Graf, Hitler's personal bodyguard, and, frequently, the 'philosophers' of the party, Gottfried Feder and Dietrich Eckart. In the long room, with its rows of benches and tables, often occupied by elderly couples, Hitler's entourage would discuss politics, or listen to his monologues on art and architecture, while eating the snacks they had brought with them and drinking their litres of beer or cups of coffee.[139] At the end of the evening, Weber, Amann, Graf, and Lieutenant Klintzsch, a veteran of the Ehrhardt-Brigade who had taken part in the Kapp Putsch, would act as a bodyguard, escorting Hitler – wearing the long black overcoat and trilby that 'gave him the appearance of a conspirator' – back to his apartment in Thierschstraße.[140]

Hitler scarcely cut the figure of a mainstream politician. Not surprisingly, the Bavarian establishment regarded him largely with contempt. But they could not ignore him. The old-fashioned monarchist head of the Bavarian government at the time, Minister President Gustav Ritter von Kahr, who had assumed office on 16 March 1920 following the Kapp Putsch and aimed to turn Bavaria into a 'cell of order' representing true national values, thought Hitler was a propagandist and nothing more. This was a not unjustifiable assessment at the time. But Kahr was keen to gather 'national forces' in Bavaria in protest at the 'fulfilment policy' of Reich Chancellor Wirth. And he felt certain that he could make use of Hitler, that he could control the 'impetuous Austrian'.[141] On 14 May 1921 he invited a delegation from the NSDAP, led by Hitler, to discuss the political situation with him. It was the first meeting of the two men whose identical aim of destroying the new Weimar democracy was to link them, if fleetingly, in the ill-fated putsch of November 1923 – a chequered association that would end with Kahr's murder in the 'Night of the Long Knives' at the end of June 1934. Whatever Kahr's disdain for Hitler, his invitation to a meeting in May 1921 amounted to recognition that the latter was now a factor in Bavarian politics, proof that he and his movement had to be taken seriously.

Rudolf Heß, still studying at Munich under the geopolitician Professor Karl Haushofer, introverted and idealistic, and already besotted with Hitler, was part of the delegation. Three days later, unsolicited and unprompted by Hitler, he wrote a lengthy letter to Kahr, describing Hitler's early life and eulogizing about his political aims, ideals, and skills. Hitler, he wrote, was 'an unusually decent, sincere character, full of kind-heartedness, religious, a good Catholic', with only one aim: 'the welfare of his country'. Heß went on to laud Hitler's self-sacrifice in this cause, how he received not a penny from the movement itself but made his living purely from the fees he received for other speeches he occasionally made.[142]

This was the official line that Hitler himself had put out the previous September in the *Völkischer Beobachter*. It was quite disingenuous. On no more than a handful of occasions did he speak at nationalist meetings other than those of the NSDAP.[143] The fees from these alone would certainly not have been enough to keep body and soul together. Rumours about his income and lifestyle were avidly taken up on the Left. Even on the *völkisch* Right there were remarks about him being chauffeured around Munich in a big car, and his enemies in the party raised questions about his personal financial irregularities and the amount of time the 'king of Munich' spent in an expensive lifestyle cavorting with women – even women smoking cigarettes.[144] In fact, Hitler was distinctly touchy about his financial affairs. He repeated in court in December 1921 in a libel case against the socialist *Münchener Post* that he had sought no fees from the party for sixty-five speeches delivered in Munich.[145] But he accepted that he was 'supported in a modest way' by party members and 'occasionally' provided with meals by them.[146] One of those who looked after him was the first 'Hitler-Mutti', Frau Carola Hofmann, the elderly widow of a headmaster, who plied Hitler with endless supplies of cakes and turned her house at Solln on the outskirts of Munich for a while into a sort of unofficial party headquarters.[147] A little later the Reichsbahn official Theodor Lauböck – founder of the Rosenheim branch of the NSDAP, but subsequently trans-ferred to Munich – and his wife saw to Hitler's well-being, and could also be called upon to put up important guests of the party.[148] In reality, the miserable accommodation Hitler rented in Thierschstraße, and the shabby clothes he wore, belied the fact that even at this date he was not short of well-to-do party supporters. With the growth of the party and his own expanding reputation in 1922–3, he was able to gain new and wealthy patrons in Munich high society.

VII

The party was, however, perpetually short of money. It was on a fund-raising mission in June 1921 to Berlin by Hitler, to try (in the company of the man with the contacts, Dietrich Eckart) to find backing for the ailing *Völkischer Beobachter*, that the crisis which culminated in Hitler's takeover of the party leadership unfolded.[149]

The background was shaped by moves to merge the NSDAP with the DSP. To go from the party programmes, despite some differences of accent, the two *völkisch* parties had more in common than separated them. And the DSP had a following in north Germany, which the Nazi Party, still scarcely more than a small local party, lacked. In itself, therefore, there was certainly an argument for joining forces. Talks about a possible merger had begun the previous August in a gathering in Salzburg, attended by Hitler, of national socialist parties from Germany, Austria, Czechoslovakia and Poland.[150] A number of overtures followed from the DSP leaders between then and April 1921. At a meeting in Zeitz in Thuringia at the end of March, Drexler – presumably delegated by the NSDAP, but plainly in the teeth of Hitler's disapproval – even agreed to tentative proposals for a merger and – anathema to Hitler – a move of the party headquarters to Berlin.[151] Hitler responded with fury to Drexler's concessions, threatened to resign from the party, and succeeded 'amid unbelievable anger' in reversing the agreement reached at Zeitz.[152] Eventually, at a meeting in Munich in mid-April, amidst great rancour and with Hitler in a towering rage, negotiations with the DSP collapsed. The DSP was in no doubt that Hitler, the 'fanatical would-be big shot', whose successes had gone to his head, was solely responsible for the NSDAP's obstructionism. Hitler, dismissive of notions of a specific political programme to be implemented, interested only in agitation and mobilization, had set his face rigidly from the outset against any possible merger. To Hitler, the similarities in programme were irrelevant. He objected to the way the DSP had rushed to set up numerous branches without solid foundations, so that the party was 'everywhere and nowhere', and to its readiness to resort to parliamentary tactics.[153] But the real reason was a different one. Any merger was bound to threaten his supremacy in the small but tightly-knit NSDAP. That he was so fearful of losing his dominance is a further pointer probably to Hitler's personal as well as to his political insecurity.

Of importance for the crisis in the party that was to erupt three months later was the fact that, although he had succeeded in torpedoing the merger, Hitler had encountered significant opposition from within his own movement on the part of those who were by no means convinced that a strategy based on no more than a constant barrage of agitation would ultimately prove successful. It was not simply, as has often been claimed, a matter of the old party leadership against the Hitler clique, thrusting for power. There were genuine differences about political strategy. Four or five members of the committee were sceptical about Hitler's approach, and favoured more traditional *völkisch* methods. Gottfried Feder, no less, complained bitterly to Drexler about Hitler's crude style of propaganda and criticized the chairman's conciliatory attitude towards him. But Drexler replied by defending both Hitler and his approach.[154] Personal factors also played a part. Hitler knew he was the only star the party had, and was not reticent in exploiting the power this gave him. But, as the July crisis was to show, there were those on the party's committee who bitterly resented his special position and the way he was using this to veto all suggestions on the future of the party that did not meet with his approval.

Hitler's actions were not, as they have again often been seen, part of a preconceived scheme to take over the party leadership. As we have already noted, Hitler had several months earlier turned down the offer to become a member of a small 'action committee', and even the chairmanship of the party. In spring 1921, he made no attempt to initiate a takeover of the party leadership, though the conditions for such a move were by no means unfavourable. Instead of a calculated, rational strategy to secure his position, his response was highly emotional, prima-donna-like. But behind the bluster, he betrayed signs of uncertainty, hesitancy, and inconsistency. The hypersensitivity to personal criticism, the inability to engage in rational argument and, instead, rapid resort to extraordinary outbursts of uncontrolled temper, his extreme aversion to any institutional anchoring: these features of an unbalanced personality repeatedly manifested themselves to the end of his days. At this time, they indicated that, far from taking clear, decisive steps to shape events as he wanted them to develop – which an organized move to take over the leadership would have allowed – he was largely reacting to developments outside his own control.[155] This was to be the case, too, in the July crisis.

Though the merger with the DSP had been fended off for the time being, an even bigger threat, from Hitler's point of view, arose while he was away in Berlin. Dr Otto Dickel, who had founded in March 1921 in Augsburg another *völkisch* organization, the Deutsche Werkgemeinschaft, had made something of a stir on the *völkisch* scene with his book *Die Auferstehung des Abendlandes* (*The Resurrection of the Western World*). Dickel's mystic *völkisch* philosophizing was not Hitler's style, and, not surprisingly, met with the latter's contempt and angry dismissal.[156] But some of Dickel's ideas – building up a classless community through national renewal, combating 'Jewish domination' through the struggle against 'interest slavery' – bore undeniable similarities to those of both the NSDAP and the DSP. And Dickel, no less than Hitler, had the conviction of a missionary and, moreover, was also a dynamic and popular public speaker. Following the appearance of his book, which was lauded in the *Völkischer Beobachter*, he was invited to Munich, and – with Hitler absent in Berlin – proved a major success before a packed audience in one of Hitler's usual haunts, the Festsaal of the Hofbräuhaus. Other speeches were planned for Dickel. The NSDAP's leadership was delighted to find in him a second 'outstanding speaker with a popular touch' (*volkstümlichen und ausgezeichneten Redner*).[157]

1. Adolf Hitler (*top row, centre*) in his Leonding school photo, 1899

2. Klara Hitler, the mother of Adolf

3. Alois Hitler, Adolf's father

4. Karl Lueger, Oberbürgermeister of Vienna, admired by Hitler for his antisemitic agitation

5. August Kubizek, Hitler's boyhood friend in Linz and Vienna

6. The crowd in Odeonsplatz, Munich, greeting the proclamation of war,
2 August 1914. Hitler circled.

7. Hitler (*right*) with fellow dispatch messengers Ernst Schmidt and
Anton Bachmann and his dog 'Foxl' at Fournes, April 1915
8. German soldiers in a trench on the Western Front during a lull
in the fighting

9. Armed members of the KPD from the Neuhausen district of Munich
during a 'Red Army' parade in the city, 22 April 1919
10. Counterrevolutionary Freikorps troops entering Munich, beginning of
May 1919

11. Anton Drexler, founder in 1919 of the DAP (German Workers' Party)
12. Ernst Röhm, the 'machine-gun king', whose access to weapons and contacts in the Bavarian army were important to Hitler in the early 1920s

13. Hitler's DAP membership card, contradicting his claim
to be the seventh member of the party

14. Hitler speaking on the Marsfeld in Munich at the first Party Rally of
the NSDAP, 27 January 1923

15. 'Hitler speaks!' NSDAP mass meeting, Cirkus Krone, Munich, 1923

16. Paramilitary organizations during the church service at the 'German Day' in Nuremberg, 2 September 1923

17. Alfred Rosenberg, Hitler, and Friedrich Weber during the march-past of the SA and other paramilitary groups to mark the laying of the war memorial foundation stone, Munich, 4 November 1923

18. The putsch: armed SA men (*centre*, holding the old Reich flag, Heinrich Himmler) manning a barricade outside the War Ministry in Ludwigstraße, Munich, 9 November 1923

19. The putsch: armed putschists from the area around Munich, 9 November 1923

20. Defendants at the trial of the putschists: *left to right*, Heinz Pernet, Friedrich Weber, Wilhelm Frick, Hermann Kriebel, Erich Ludendorff, Adolf Hitler, Wilhelm Brückner, Ernst Röhm, Robert Wagner

21. Hitler posing for a photograph, hurriedly taken by Hoffman because of the cold, at the gate to the town of Landsberg am Lech, immediately after his release from imprisonment

22. Hitler in Landsberg, postcard, 1924

23. The image: Hitler in Bavarian costume (rejected), 1925/6
24. The image: Hitler in a raincoat (accepted), 1925/6

25. The image: Hitler with his alsatian, Prinz, 1925
(rejected, from a broken plate)

26. The Party Rally, Weimar, 3–4 July 1926: Hitler, standing in a car in light-coloured raincoat, taking the march-past of the SA, whose banner carries the slogan: 'Death to Marxism'. Immediately to Hitler's right is Wilhelm Frick and, beneath him, facing the camera, Julius Streicher

27. The Party Rally, Nuremberg, 21 August 1927: *left to right*, Julius Streicher, Georg Hallermann, Franz von Pfeffer, Rudolf Heß, Adolf Hitler, Ulrich Graf

Hitler, meanwhile, was still in Berlin. He failed to turn up at a meeting with a DSP representative on 1 July for further merger talks, and did not return to Bavaria until ten days later. He had evidently by then got wind of the alarming news that a delegation of the NSDAP's leaders was due to have talks there with Dickel and representatives of the Augsburg and Nuremberg branches of the Deutsche Werkgemeinschaft. He appeared before the NSDAP delegates themselves arrived, beside himself with rage, threatening the Augsburg and Nuremberg representatives that he would see that a merger was stopped. But when his own people eventually turned up, his uncontrolled fury subsided into sulky silence. Three hours of suggestions from Dickel for the formation of a loose confederation of the different groups and recommendations for improvements to the NSDAP's programme prompted numerous outbursts from Hitler before, being able to stand it no longer, he stormed out of the meeting.[158]

If Hitler hoped his tantrums would convince his colleagues to drop the negotiations, he was mistaken. They were embarrassed by his behaviour and impressed by what Dickel had to offer. Even Dietrich Eckart thought Hitler had behaved badly. It was accepted that the party programme needed amending, and that Hitler 'as a simple man', was not up to doing this. They agreed to take back Dickel's proposals to Munich and put them to the full party committee.[159]

Hitler resigned from the party in anger and disgust on 11 July. In a letter to the committee three days later, he justified his move on the grounds that the representatives in Augsburg had violated the party statutes and acted against the wishes of the members in handing over the movement to a man whose ideas were incompatible with those of the NSDAP. 'I will and can not be any longer a member of such a movement,' he declared.[160] Hitler had resigned 'for ever' from the party's committee in December 1920.[161] As we have noted, he threatened resignation yet again following the Zeitz conference in late March 1921. The histrionics of the prima donna were part and parcel of Hitler's make-up – and would remain so. It would always be the same: he only knew all-or-nothing arguments; there was nothing in between, no possibility of reaching a compromise. Always from a maximalist position, with no other way out, he would go for broke. And if he could not get his way he would throw a temper-tantrum and threaten to quit. In power, in years to come, he would sometimes deliberately orchestrate an outburst of rage as a bullying tactic. But usually his tantrums were a sign of frustration, even desperation, not strength. It was to be the case in a number of future crises. And it was so on this occasion. The resignation was not a carefully planned manoeuvre to use his position as the party's star performer to blackmail the committee into submission. It was an expression of fury and frustration at not getting his own way. His threat of resignation had worked before, after the Zeitz conference. Now he was risking his only trump card again. Defeat would have meant the party's amalgamation in Dickel's planned 'Western League' (Abendländischer Bund) and left Hitler with only the option – which he seems to have contemplated – of setting up a new party and beginning again.[162] There were those who would have been glad, whatever his uses as an agitator, to have been rid of such a troublesome and egocentric entity. And the spread of the party that the merger with Dickel's organization presented offered more than a little compensation.

But the loss of its sole star performer would have been a major, perhaps fatal, blow to the NSDAP. His departure would have split the party. In the end, this was the decisive consideration. Dietrich Eckart was asked to intervene, and on 13 May Drexler sought the conditions under which Hitler would agree to rejoin the party. It was full capitulation from the party leadership. Hitler's conditions all stemmed from the recent turmoil in the party. His key demands – to be accepted by an extraordinary members' meeting – were 'the post of chairman with dictatorial power'; the party headquarters to be fixed once and for all as Munich; the party programme to be regarded as inviolate; and the end of all merger attempts.[163] All the demands centred upon securing Hitler's position in the party against any future challenges. A day later the party committee expressed its readiness in recognition of his 'immense knowledge', his services for the movement, and his 'unusual talent as a speaker' to give him 'dictatorial powers'. It welcomed his willingness, having turned down Drexler's offers in the past, now to take over the party chairmanship. Hitler rejoined the party, as member no.3680, on 26 July.[164]

Even now the conflict was not fully at an end. While Hitler and Drexler publicly demonstrated their unity at a members' meeting on 26 July,[165] Hitler's opponents in the leadership had his henchman Hermann Esser expelled from the party and prepared placards denouncing Hitler, and had printed 3,000 copies of an anonymous pamphlet attacking him in the most denigratory terms as the agent of sinister forces intent on damaging the party.[166] But Hitler, who had shown once more to great effect how irreplaceable he was as a speaker in a meeting, packed to the last seat, in Circus Krone on 20 July, was now in the driving seat.[167] Now there was no hesitancy. This was Hitler triumphant. To tumultuous applause from the 554 paid-up members attending the extraordinary members' meeting in the Festsaal of the Hofbräuhaus on 29 July, he defended himself and Esser and rounded on his opponents. He boasted that he had never sought party office, and had turned down the chairmanship on several occasions. But this time he was prepared to accept. The new party constitution, which Hitler had been forced to draft hurriedly, confirmed on three separate occasions the sole responsibility of the First Chairman for the party's actions (subject only to the membership meeting). There was only one vote against accepting the new dictatorial powers over the party granted to Hitler. His chairmanship was unanimously accepted.[168]

The reform of the party statutes was necessary, stated the *Völkischer Beobachter*, in order to prevent any future attempt to dissipate the energies of the party through majority decisions.[169] It was the first step on transforming the NSDAP into a new-style party, a 'Führer party'. The move had come about not through careful planning, but through Hitler's reaction to events which were running out of his control. Rudolf Heß's subsequent assault on Hitler's opponents in the *Völkischer Beobachter* contained the early seeds of the later heroization of Hitler, but also revealed the initial base on which it rested. 'Are you truly blind,' wrote Heß, 'to the fact that this man is the leader personality who alone is able to carry through the struggle? Do you think that without him the masses would pile into the Circus Krone?'[170]

6

THE 'DRUMMER'

'I am nothing but a drummer and rallier.'

Hitler, to Arthur Moeller van den Bruck, 1922

'Our task is to give the dictator, when he comes, a people ready for him!'

Hitler, in a speech on 4 May 1923

'Not from modesty did I want at that time to be the drummer. That is the highest there is. The rest is unimportant.'

Hitler, at his trial, 27 March 1924

When Hitler assumed the leadership of his party in July 1921, he was still no more than a beerhall agitator – a local celebrity, to be sure, but otherwise scarcely known. The takeover of the party leadership itself followed internal squabbles – of little moment to the outside world – within the intrinsically fractious *völkisch* movement. The NSDAP certainly made a great deal of noise, and had made its presence felt on the Munich political scene. But it was hardly yet a significant force. Without the extraordinary conditions in Bavaria – the self-proclaimed 'cell of order' – and without the backcloth nationwide of political instability, economic crisis, and social polarization, everything suggests it would have remained insignificant. As it was, while *völkisch* parties struggled to make much of a mark in most German states, including Prussia – by far the largest state – the NSDAP could become by 1923 a key player in the upsurge of nationalist opposition in Bavaria to Weimar democracy. And from a local beerhall agitator, the party's leader emerged between 1921 and 1923 as the 'drummer' of the nationalist Right. That would be his role down to the ill-fated attempt in November 1923 to take over the state by force – the notorious 'Beerhall Putsch'. Only in the light of those dramatic events and their aftermath would a crucial transformation in his self-image be sealed.

Hitler was content in the early 1920s to be the 'drummer' – whipping up the masses for the 'national movement'. He saw himself at this time not, as portrayed in *Mein Kampf*, as Germany's future leader in waiting, the political messiah whose turn would arise once the nation recognized his unique greatness. Rather, he was paving the way for the great leader whose day might not dawn for many years to come. 'I am nothing more than a drummer and rallier (*Trommler und Sammler*),' he told Arthur Moeller van den Bruck in 1922.[1] Some months earlier, he had reputedly stated in an interview in May 1921 with the chief editor of the Pan-German newspaper *Deutsche*

Zeitung that he was not the leader and statesman who would 'save the Fatherland that was sinking into chaos', but only 'the agitator who understood how to rally (*sammeln*) the masses'. Nor, he allegedly went on, was he 'the architect who clearly pictured in his own eyes the plan and design of the new building and with calm sureness and creativity was able to lay one stone on the other. He needed the greater one behind him, on whose command he could lean.'[2]

To be the 'drummer' meant everything to Hitler at this time. It was the 'vocation' that replaced his dreams of becoming a great artist or architect. It was his main task, practically his sole concern. Not only did it allow full expression to his one real talent. It was also in his eyes the greatest and most important role he could play. For politics to Hitler – and so it would in all essence remain – *was* propaganda: ceaseless mass mobilization for a cause to be followed blindly, not the 'art of the possible'.

I

Hitler owed his rise to at least regional prominence on the nationalist Right in Bavaria not simply to his unparalleled ability as a mob-orator at mass meetings in Munich. As before, this was his chief asset. But linked to this, and of crucial importance, was the fact that he was the head of a movement which, in contrast to the earliest phase of the party's existence, now came to develop its own substantial paramilitary force and to enter the maelstrom of Bavarian paramilitary politics.

Acceptance of a high level of political violence was a hallmark of the political culture of Germany between the wars. The brutalization of society engendered by war and near-civil war together with the upheaval and turmoil of the revolution prepared the ground for a readiness to tolerate violence paradoxically seen to be serving the interests of a return to order and normality. It was a mentality which not only contributed to the rise of National Socialism, but also to the moral indifference to violence that was so widespread during the Third Reich itself.[3] The exponents of the extreme political violence were for the most part the counter-revolutionary private armies – the Freikorps, the Volunteer Associations, the Citizens' Defence Forces – which sprang up in Germany after the war and were actively supported and deployed by state authorities. Gustav Noske had begun the use of non-state forces in the service of the state in the brutal suppression of the Spartacus Rising in January 1919. The Freikorps participated, as we have already noted, in the smashing of the Räterepublik in Munich four months later. A plethora of paramilitary organizations emerged across the political spectrum, but most prominently on the counter-revolutionary Right. It was above all in the peculiar conditions of post-revolutionary Bavaria that the private armies, with the toleration and often active support of the Bavarian authorities, could fully flourish.

The massive Citizens' Defence Force (Einwohnerwehr) – comprising up to 400,000 men with 2½ million weapons – that was established in Bavaria immediately after the crushing of the Räterepublik was the product of a mentality obsessed by the need for protection against a presumed threat from the Left and ready, as the popularity of the counter-revolutionary violence in spring 1919 showed, to resort to any measures to ensure that protection.[4] The Einwohnerwehr, and a number of other, similar, organizations that emerged alongside it, represented 'white-blue' Bavarian traditionalism and, as the name suggested, was in essence defensively orientated. But more sinister paramilitary organizations found a welcome refuge in the Bavarian 'cell of order' after the collapse of the Kapp Putsch in 1920. The vehemently anti-socialist, counter-revolutionary regime of Minister President Gustav Ritter von Kahr turned Bavaria into a haven for right-wing extremists from all over Germany, including many under order of arrest elsewhere in the country. From a new protected base in Munich, for example, Captain Hermann Ehrhardt, a veteran of orchestrated anti-socialist violence in the Freikorps, including the suppression of the Räterepublik, and a leader of the Kapp Putsch, was able to use his Organisation Consul to build up a network of groups throughout the whole of the German Reich and carry out many of the political murders – there were 354 in all perpetrated by the Right between 1919 and 1922 – that stained the early years of the troubled new democracy.[5] And Kahr's strident line of Bavarian frontal opposition to the central government of the Reich – feeding the traditional hatred of Berlin that had been acutely shored up during the war, and the resentments at the diminished powers of Bavaria in the Reich constitution – had the effect of linking 'white-blue' particularist feeling with 'black-white-red' nationalist antagonism towards 'red' Berlin. The theologian Ernst Troeltsch commented in September 1921:

Since Reich policy stood, and must stand, strongly under the influence of socialism, this has continued to be identified with the hated Berlin and with Jewry, thus directing the torrents of particularism and antisemitism on to the mills of anti-socialism . . . In addition there is then the strong force of monarchism, the bitterness of former members of the military, the collaboration of Prussian emigrants, and the very understandable disaffection of idealist patriots. All this is knotted together into the idea of allocating Bavaria the mission of saving the Reich from socialism, and seeing it as the cell of order and starting-point of reconstruction.[6]

By spring 1921 Kahr was no longer able to prevent the dissolution of the Bavarian Einwohnerwehr after holding out for a year against the Reich's insistence (under Allied pressure) on confiscation of weapons and dismantling of civilian defence units.[7] The resulting fury towards Berlin prompted further radicalization. And out of the dissolved Einwohnerwehr arose a bewildering array of new or already existing but now strengthened 'patriotic associations' competing with each other in their activism and radicalism. The largest – and intended to be the successor to the Einwohnerwehr, though in reality a coalition of numerous fractions which would eventually split – was the Bund Bayern und Reich, a 'white-blue' Bavarian loyalist organization, combining strong monarchist and Christian traditionalist strains with vehement anti-Marxism and antisemitism, operating under the slogan 'First the Homeland, then the World!'[8] It was run by the Regensburg public health inspector Dr Otto Pittinger, formerly prominent in the district leadership of the civil defence units in the Upper Palatinate province of Bavaria. Since Pittinger had difficulty in exercising authority over his organization, smaller but more radical associations moved in to fill the vacuum and expand their influence. Among them were the Bund Oberland, which had emerged from Epp's Freikorps Oberland, had been involved in the ending of the 'Councils Republic', and had further cut its teeth in the campaign against the Poles in Upper Silesia in 1921; the Reichsflagge, previously with a following mainly confined to Franconia but now, under the direction of Ernst Röhm (head of the Munich branch), expanding into southern Bavaria; the Vaterländische Vereine Münchens (VVM, Patriotic Associations of Munich), the successor to the Einwohnerwehr in the Bavarian capital; and a variety of organizations and sub-organizations, most prominent of them the Wiking-Bund, headed by Captain Ehrhardt.[9] It was Ehrhardt, alongside Ernst Röhm, who was to play a leading role in establishing the NSDAP's own paramilitary organization, which was to emerge from 1921 onwards into a significant feature of the Nazi Movement and an important factor in paramilitary politics in Bavaria.[10]

The beginnings of the SA, as we have noted, reach back to the start of 1920, when the DAP set out to stage bigger meetings in the Munich beerhalls and, as was the practice in other parties, needed a squad of bouncers – a 'hall protection' (Saalschutz) to deal with any disturbances.[11] This was turned in November 1920 into the party's 'Gym and Sport Section' (Turn- und Sportabteilung). Following Hitler's 'seizure of power' within the party in July 1921, it was reshaped and given a pivotal role, responsible according to the new party statutes for the 'bodily training of the male youth in the movement'.[12] Hitler regarded its quasi-military structure as valuable in establishing his claim to leadership throughout the movement. However, the SA (Sturmabteilung, 'Storm Section') – as it became known from October 1921 onwards[13] – was not, as has been claimed, 'his personal creation', solely a product of his will, or designed as an instrument of his personal power.[14] The key figures in transforming the party's hall protection squad into a paramilitary organization were Ernst Röhm and, initially, Captain Ehrhardt.

Röhm was, more even than Hitler, typical of the 'front generation'. As a junior officer, he shared the dangers, anxieties, and privations of the troops in the trenches – shared, too, the prejudice and mounting anger levelled at those in staff headquarters behind the lines, at the military bureaucracy, at 'incapable' politicians, and at those seen as shirkers, idlers and profiteers at home. Against these highly negative images, he heroicized the 'front community', the solidarity of the men in the trenches, leadership resting on deeds rather than status, and the blind obedience that this demanded. What he wanted was a new 'warrior' élite whose actions and achievements had proved their right to rule. Though a monarchist, there was for Röhm to be no return to pre-war bourgeois society. His ideal was the community of fighting men. As for so many who joined the Freikorps and their successor paramilitary organizations, this ideal combined male fantasy with the cult of violence.[15] Like so many, Röhm had gone to war in 1914 in wild enthusiasm, suffered serious facial injury within weeks when shell fragments tore away part of his nose, permanently disfiguring him, had returned to lead his company, but had been forced out of service at the front after being again badly injured at Verdun. His subsequent duties in the Bavarian War Ministry, and as the supply officer of a division, sharpened his political antennae and gave him experience in organizational matters. The trauma of defeat and revolution drove him into counter-revolutionary activity – including service in the Freikorps Epp during its participation in the crushing of the Räterepub- lik. After brief membership of the DNVP, he joined the tiny DAP soon after Hitler, in autumn 1919, and, as he himself claimed, was probably responsible for others from the Reichswehr entering the party.[16] Röhm's interest continued, however, to be dictated by military and paramilitary, rather than party, politics. He showed no exclusive interest in the NSDAP before the SA became a significant element in paramilitary politics.

But Röhm's value to the party in engineering its paramilitary connections is hard to overrate. His access both to leading figures on the paramilitary scene and, especially, to weaponry was crucial. His position in control of weapon supplies for the Brigade Epp (the successor to the Freikorps unit, now integrated into the Reichswehr) gave him responsibility for providing the Einwohnerwehr with weapons. The semi-secrecy involved in concealing the extent of weaponry from Allied control – not difficult since there was no occupying army to carry out inspections – also gave Röhm a great deal of scope to build up a large stockpile of mainly small arms in 1920-21. After the dissolution of the Einwohnerwehr, and the official confiscation of weaponry, various paramilitary organizations entrusted him with their weapon supplies. Presiding over such an arsenal, deciding when and if weapons should be handed out, the 'machine-gun king' (*Maschinen-gewehrkönig*), as he became known, was thus in a pivotal position with regard to the demands of all paramilitary organizations. And, through the protection he gained from Epp, Kahr, and the Munich political police, he enjoyed influence beyond his rank on the politics of the nationalist Right.[17]

It was in all probability Röhm who arranged the agreement reached between Hitler and Ehrhardt in August 1921 which brought former members of Ehrhardt's naval brigade, seasoned campaigners in paramilitary activity, most of them just returned from the action in Upper Silesia, into the party's 'Sport Section'. This was placed under the leadership of the Ehrhardt veteran Leutnant Klintzsch (later suspected of having a hand in 1922 in the murder of Walter Rathenau – the Reich Foreign Minister, of Jewish background and, as main author of the 'fulfilment policy' towards the Versailles Treaty, a detested figure on the extreme Right),[18] who was given the task of building up a fighting unit and provided by Ehrhardt with the funding to do this. During the first months, this was mainly a matter of sport (especially boxing), marching, exercises, and occasional sharpshooter practice. The members – there were around 300 by November 1921, all under the age of twenty-four and mainly from Munich's lower-middle class – combined this paramilitary training with political activism. They took the 'friend–foe' mentality of the front into what they saw as practically a civil war at home, preparing for violent combat with the political enemy, evoking the spirit of aggressive camaraderie and blind commitment to the leader.[19] From the beginning, the dual role of paramilitary organization (initially linked to Ehrhardt) and party shock troops under Hitler's leadership contained the seeds of the tension that was to accompany the SA down to 1934.[20] The interest of Röhm and Ehrhardt lay on the paramilitary side.[21] Hitler tried to integrate the SA fully into the party, though organizationally it retained considerable independence before 1924.[22] The build-up of the SA was steady, not spectacular, before the second half of 1922. It was after that date, in conditions of rapidly mounting crisis in Bavaria and in the Reich, that the SA's numbers swelled, making it a force to be reckoned with on the nationalist Right.[23]

II

Hitler, meanwhile, now undisputed leader of his party, carried on his ceaseless agitation much as before, able to exploit the continued tension between Bavaria and the Reich. The murder of Reich Finance Minister Matthias Erzberger on 26 August 1921 – an indication of the near-anarchism that still prevailed in Germany – and Kahr's refusal to accept the validity for Bavaria of the state of emergency declared by Reich President Friedrich Ebert, kept things on the boil.[24] Material discontent played its own part. Prices were already rising sharply as the currency depreciated. Foodstuffs were almost eight times more expensive in 1921 as they had been at the end of the war. By the next year they would be over 130 times dearer. And that was before the currency lost all its value in the hyperinflation of 1923.[25]

Hitler's provocation of his political enemies and of the authorities to gain publicity was stepped up. In mid-September he led the planned violent disruption by his followers of a meeting in the Löwenbräukeller, to be addressed by one of his arch-enemies at the time, the separatist leader of the Bayernbund, Otto Ballerstedt. Hitler's arrival in the packed hall was the signal for his supporters, many of them young thugs from the 'Sport Section' who had taken up seats around the platform early in the evening, to storm the podium, screaming 'Hitler' continually in chorus, and prevent Ballerstedt from speaking. Someone had the idea of switching off the lights to prevent a brawl. But this only made the disturbance worse. When the lights went on again, Ballerstedt and another member of his party were physically attacked and injured before the police could arrive.[26] Even then, it seems, the police had to ask Hitler's help in calling his men to order. He was by this time happy enough to do so. The aim had been met. 'Ballerstedt won't speak any more today,' he declared.[27]

The matter did not, however, end there. Ballerstedt pressed charges against

Hitler, who was sentenced in January 1922 to three months' imprisonment for breach of the peace – two months suspended against future good behaviour (though conveniently forgotten about when the good behaviour did not materialize). Even his powerful friends could not prevent him serving the other month of his sentence. Between 24 June and 27 July 1922 he took up residence in Stadelheim prison in Munich.[28]

Apart from this short interlude, Hitler did not let up with his agitation. Brushes with the police were commonplace. The police noted some thirty bans on publications, placards, and other Nazi publicity in 1921.[29] Even while awaiting trial in the Ballerstedt case, Hitler was warned by the police – in connection with Nazi disruption of an SPD meeting on 16 October and subsequent disturbances – that he could expect his expulsion from Bavaria if things carried on in the same way.[30] It was not to be the last time that expulsion was posed as a vain threat. Hitler simply commented that he could not be held responsible for the disturbances and promised to do what he could to prevent any in future.[31] Within little over a week, on 4 November 1921, he was the centre of further riotous scenes, this time at a meeting he himself was addressing in the Hofbräuhaus. As a full-scale brawl broke out, Hitler continued speaking amid a hail of beermugs that his opponents – socialists, but perhaps also including some veteran beerhall brawlers, spoiling for a fight – had been quietly storing beneath their tables as ammunition. He later idealized the scene in *Mein Kampf* as the 'baptism of fire' of his SA men, greatly outnumbered but triumphant over their socialist enemies.[32] For Hitler, these violent clashes with his opponents were the lifeblood of his movement. They were above all good for publicity.

Hitler was still dissatisfied with the coverage – even of a negative kind – he received in the press.[33] Nevertheless, the actions of the NSDAP and its leader ensured that they remained in the public eye. Nor could the party any longer be ignored in the Bavarian Landtag. Following Kahr's resignation as Minister President in September 1921 – the consequence of his intransigence in the conflict with the Reich – the unpopularity and weaker stance towards Berlin of his successor, Hugo Graf Lerchenfeld-Koefering, an arch-conservative, from a non-party Catholic, aristocratic, and diplomatic background, provided an easy target for undiminished Nazi agitation throughout the first half of 1922.[34] This was no time for young Germans to spend studying philosophy and sitting behind a desk full of books, proclaimed Dietrich Eckart: it was a question now of 'into the stormtroops who must rescue Germany'. Open attacks on opponents became the order of the day. Rubber truncheons and knuckle-dusters were the main weapons, but pistols and even, on occasion, home-made bombs and grenades were also used in the campaign of violence.[35] Hitler kept up unabated his torrent of abuse directed at both the Reich and Bavarian governments. Reich President Ebert was booed, whistled at, insulted, and spat upon by Nazi demonstrators when he visited Munich in summer 1922.[36] Hitler poured scorn on Minister President von Lerchenfeld – a man with the brain of a sheep, he ranted, totally out of touch with reality and the will of the people, who clamoured for genuine, born leaders.[37] While his leading supporters hinted darkly at dire consequences if the Bavarian government expelled him from Germany, Hitler made propaganda capital out of the threat of expulsion by pointing to his war record, when he had fought as a German for his country while others had done no more than stay at home and preach politics.[38]

On 16 August 1922, Hitler spoke alongside other leaders of the nationalist associations at a huge protest rally of the Vereinigte Vaterländische Verbände Bayerns (United Patriotic Associations of Bavaria) on the Königsplatz in Munich. The rally, held under the slogan 'For Germany – Against Berlin', directed at 'the approaching Jewish Bolshevism under the protection of the Republic',[39] was the first time that the SA had appeared in public as a paramilitary formation under its own banners. Its numbers – no more than 800 or so men about this time – were, however, dwarfed by the 30,000 armed men of Pittinger's Bund Bayern und Reich, and by the large, well-armed formations of Bund Oberland and the Reichsflagge.[40] Talk of a putsch against Lerchenfeld in favour of the restoration of Kahr was in the air. There were rumours that this would take place at a further mass protest rally against Lerchenfeld, planned for 25 August. Indeed there *was* a plot, involving Pittinger and Röhm, which became known to the police, but a ban on the rally and the prevention of the armed bands of the nationalist associations from other parts of Bavaria travelling to Munich left only a few thousand National Socialists assembled on the Karolinenplatz. Eventually, around 5,000 made their way to a meeting in the Kindlkeller, one of the big Munich beerhalls where Hitler occasionally held speeches. Feelings were running high. There were rumours that a putsch was about to happen. But nothing materialized. A thousand Communists assembled outside, and violence threatened. The police acted against the Communists, but did no more against the Nazis than appeal to Hitler to calm things down. Hitler told his men that it was the duty of every single one of them 'to become an agitator in order to bring the mass of the people on to the street' against the government.[41] But at the request of the police he called them to order. They obeyed, quietly dispersing.[42] Hitler was said to be furious at the way the day had fizzled out into such an anticlimax. Next time he would act – alone if necessary, he stated.[43] The danger of a Hitler Putsch was not lost on the authorities. The Württemberg ambassador in Munich reported to Stuttgart, following discussions in the Bavarian foreign ministry on 31 August: 'The National Socialists especially were gaining enormous support and were capable of anything. . . The leader Hitler must be quite a fascinating personality. So it's not impossible that they will try a putsch here before long, using the mounting inflation as an excuse.'[44]

Hitler's most notable propaganda success in 1922 was his party's partici- pation in the so-called 'German Day' (*Deutscher Tag*) in Coburg on 14–15 October. Coburg, on the Thuringian border in the north of Upper Franconia and part of Bavaria for only two years, was virgin territory for the Nazis. Hitler had been invited to take part in the German Day with a small delegation by the organizational committee of the Schutz- und Trutzbund. He saw it as an opportunity not to be missed. He scraped together what funds the NSDAP had to hire a special train – in itself a novel propaganda stunt – to take 800 stormtroopers to Coburg. In Hitler's compartment were the hard-core of his entourage – Amann, Esser, Eckart, Christian Weber, Graf and Rosenberg. On arrival on the Saturday afternoon, the Nazis were greeted at the station with shouts of 'Heil' by a sizeable gathering of nationalists and with a torrent of abuse from 200–300 socialist workers and trade unionists who had assembled at the same spot. The SA men were instructed by Hitler to ignore explicit police orders, banning a formation march with unfurled banners and musical accompaniment, and marched with hoisted swastika flags through the town. Workers lining the streets insulted them and spat at them. Nazis in turn leapt out of the ranks beating their tormentors with sticks and rubber truncheons. A furious battle with the socialists ensued. After ten minutes of mayhem, in which they had police support, the stormtroopers triumphantly claimed the streets of Coburg as theirs. The local authorities blamed the workers of Coburg for provoking the violence, but, with some contradiction, acknowledged that the other nationalists would have caused no problems and 'that the German Day would have passed by completely peacefully if the Hitler people (*Hitlerleute*) had not come to Coburg'.[45] For Hitler, the propaganda victory was what counted. The German Day in Coburg went down in the party's annals. The NSDAP had made its mark in northern Bavaria.

It was Hitler's second major success in Franconia within a few days. On 8 October, Julius Streicher, head of the sizeable Nuremberg branch of the Deutsche Werkgemeinschaft, had written to Hitler offering to take his sizeable following, together with his newspaper the *Deutscher Volkswille*, into the NSDAP.[46] In the wake of the Coburg triumph, the transfer took place on 20 October. Streicher, a short, squat, shaven-headed bully, born in 1885 in the Augsburg area, for a time a primary schoolteacher as his father had been, and, like Hitler, a war veteran decorated with the Iron Cross, First Class, was utterly possessed by demonic images of Jews. Shortly after the war he had been one of the founding members of the Deutschsozialistische Partei (German-Socialist Party), as antisemitic as the NSDAP and, as we noted in the previous chapter, with a similar programme. His newspaper *Der Stürmer*, established in 1923 and becoming notorious for its obscene caricatures of evil-looking Jews seducing pure German maidens and ritual-murder allegations, would – despite Hitler's personal approving comments, and view that 'the Jew' was far worse than Streicher's 'idealized' picture – for a while be banned even in the Third Reich.[47] Streicher was eventually tried at Nuremberg, and hanged. Now, back in 1922, in a step of vital importance for the development of the NSDAP in Franconia, in the northern regions of Bavaria, he subordinated himself personally to Hitler.[48] The arch-rival DSP was now fatally weakened in Franconia. The Nazi Party practically doubled its membership. From around 2,000 members about the beginning of 1921 and 6,000 a year later, the party was overnight some 20,000 strong.[49] More than that: the Franconian countryside – piously Protestant, fervently nationalist, and stridently antisemitic – was to provide the NSDAP with a stronghold far greater than was offered by its home city of Munich in the Catholic south of Bavaria, and a symbolic capital in Nuremberg – later designated the 'city of the Reich Party Rallies'. It was little wonder that Hitler was keen to express his gratitude to Streicher publicly in *Mein Kampf*.[50]

Even so, it was striking that, away from his Munich citadel, Hitler's power was still limited. He showed himself quite incapable of exercising his authority on the internecine strife that dominated the Nuremberg branch of the NSDAP over the coming year. Neither arbitrary decree from Munich nor even Hitler's personal intervention could impose a solution on the bitter power-struggle erupting in the early months of 1923 between Streicher and his rival in Nuremberg, Walther Kellerbauer, nine years older, a former naval officer, good publicist and speaker, editor of a party newspaper, the *Deutscher Volkswille* (German Will of the People), and with his own pretensions to running the branch. After months of bitter wrangling, Streicher proved victorious. This was despite Kellerbauer, someone Hitler was not keen to alienate, for a time being able to call upon the party leader's support.[51] Hitler was the undisputed propaganda champion of the party. But away from his Munich base, his writ still did not always run.

This was in itself ample reason for the interest which his Munich following began to show in building up the leadership cult around Hitler. A significant boost to the aura of a man of destiny attaching itself to Hitler came from outside Germany. On 28 October 1922, Mussolini's Blackshirts had marched on Rome and seized power. At least that was the myth that was propagated. In reality, around 20,000 badly-armed, ill-equipped and hungry Fascists, approaching Rome from four directions, had halted around twenty miles from the city, some of them leaving for home in streaming rain. There was, in fact, no 'March on Rome', which the Italian army could in any case easily have crushed if necessary. On 29 October, King Victor Emmanuel III simply invited Mussolini to form a government. When the Fascist Leader arrived in Rome the following day he was wearing a black shirt, black trousers, and a bowler hat.[52]

Mussolini's so-called 'March on Rome' on 28 October 1922 – fictitious though it was in the Fascist legend of a heroic 'seizure of power' – nevertheless deeply stirred the Nazi Party. It suggested the model of a dynamic and heroic nationalist leader marching to the salvation of his strife-torn country. The Duce provided an image to be copied. Less than a week after the *coup d'état* in Italy, on 3 November 1922, Hermann Esser proclaimed to a packed Festsaal in the Hofbräuhaus: 'Germany's Mussolini is called Adolf Hitler.'[53] It marked the symbolic moment when Hitler's followers invented the Führer cult.

III

Notions of 'heroic' leadership had been part of the political culture of the nationalist Right in the years before the First World War. The Bismarck cult, exaggerated hopes invested in the Kaiser and then dashed, grandiose images of Imperial grandeur and military glory contrasting starkly with counter-images of weak and puny party-politicians squabbling in the Reichstag, helped, as we have seen, to advance the idea of national salvation. A rebirth of the nation was promised through the subordination to a 'great leader' who would invoke the values of a 'heroic' (and mythical) past. The nationalist associations, most prominently the Pan-German League, popularized and disseminated such notions. The Protestant 'educated' middle classes were affected more than most by them. Germanic myths and romantic imagery in the bourgeois youth movement provided a base for their cultivation among the younger generation. Even so, such ideas hardly occupied a central position in German political culture before 1914.

However, war and revolution gave new substance to images of 'heroic' leadership. The subsequent idealization of the 'community of fate' in the trenches, and the 'great deeds' and heroism of 'true' leadership in the struggle for national survival – undermined, according to the legend, from within – provided a mass of new potential adherents on the counter-revolutionary Right to the idea of a coming 'great leader'. Images of leadership varied. Ernst Röhm, whose background we have briefly glimpsed, stands proxy for thousands in his idolization of the leadership of the military 'man of action'. For the neo-conservative Right, the shock of the Revolution and the dominance of the detested Social Democrats, contempt for the 'party system' and parliamentary government, and Germany's international humiliation and weakness meant an evocation of Bismarck in the yearning for a great 'statesman'. Literary figures were among the most expressive advocates of 'heroic' leadership. The author Ernst Jünger saw 'the great politician of the future' as a 'modern man of power' in the 'machine era' – 'a man of outstanding intelligence', perhaps emerging from a party, but standing 'above parties and divisions', whose natural instinct and will would select the right path and overcome all obstacles.[54] The Bonn writer Ernst Bertram linked his vision of a coming Leader, in a poem composed in 1922, with notions of 'renewal' arising from the banks of the Rhine and staving off the threat from Asia.[55] Within the Protestant Church, there were those who looked to the coming Leader to bring about spiritual renewal and moral revival. The fall of the monarchy and collapse of 'God-given' authority, the secularization of society, and the perceived 'crisis of faith' in German Protestantism all contributed to a readiness to look to a new form of leadership which could reinvoke 'true' Christian values. The shadings of the various leadership images came together in the tract of the nationalist publicist Wilhelm Stapel, a former liberal turned *völkisch* enthusiast, member of the Hamburg group of neo-conservatives associated with the ideas of Moeller van den Bruck, who depicted the 'true statesman' as 'at one and the same time ruler, warrior, and priest'.[56] It amounted to a secularized belief in salvation, wrapped up in pseudo-religious language.

Whatever the particular emphasis, the conservative and *völkisch* Right juxtaposed the negative view of a 'leaderless democracy' with a concept of a true leader as a man of destiny, born not elected to leadership, not bound by conventional rules and laws, 'hard, straightforward, and ruthless', but embodying the will of God in his actions. 'God give us leaders and help us to true following,' ran one text.[57] Devotion, loyalty, obedience, and duty were the corresponding values demanded of the followers.

The spread of fascist and militaristic ideas in post-war Europe meant that 'heroic leadership' images were 'in the air' and by no means confined to Germany. The emergence of the Duce cult in Italy provides an obvious parallel. But the German images naturally had their own flavour, drawing on the particular elements of the political culture of the nationalist Right. And the crisis-ridden nature of the Weimar state, detested by so many powerful groups in society and unable to win the popularity and support of the masses, guaranteed that such ideas, which in a more stable environment might have been regarded with derision and confined to the lunatic fringe of politics, were never short of a hearing. Ideas put into circulation by neo-conservative publicists, writers, and intellectuals were, in more vulgarized form, taken up in paramilitary formations and in the varied groupings of the bourgeois youth movement. The model of Mussolini's triumph in Italy now offered the opening for such ideas to be incorporated into the vision of national revival preached by the National Socialists.

The Führer cult was not yet the pivot of the party's ideology and organization. But the beginnings of a conscious public profiling of Hitler's leadership qualities by his entourage, with strong hints in his own speeches, dates back to the period following Mussolini's 'March on Rome'.[58] Hitler was beginning to attract fawning excesses of adulation – even stretching to grotesque comparisons with Napoleon – from admirers on the nationalist Right. The ground for the later rapid spread of the Führer cult was already well fertilized.[59]

There had been no trace of a leadership cult in the first years of the Nazi Party. The word 'leader' ('*Führer*') had no special meaning attached to it. Every political party or organization had a leader – or more than one. The NSDAP was no different. Drexler was referred to as the party's 'Führer', as was Hitler; or sometimes both in practically the same breath.[60] Once Hitler had taken over the party leadership in July 1921, the term 'our leader' ('*unser Führer*') became gradually more common.[61] But its meaning was still interchangeable with the purely functional 'chairman of the NSDAP'. There was nothing 'heroic' about it. Nor had Hitler endeavoured to build up a personality cult around himself. But Mussolini's triumph evidently made a deep impression on him. It gave him a role-model. Referring to Mussolini, less than a month after the 'March on Rome', Hitler reportedly stated: 'So will it be with us. We only have to have the courage to act.

Without struggle, no victory!'[62] However, the reshaping of his self-image also reflected how his supporters were beginning to see their leader. His followers portrayed him, in fact, as Germany's 'heroic' leader before he came to see himself in that light. Not that he did anything to discourage the new way he was being portrayed from autumn 1922 onwards. It was in December 1922 that the *Völkischer Beobachter* for the first time appeared to claim that Hitler was a special kind of leader – indeed *the* Leader for whom Germany was waiting. Followers of Hitler leaving a parade in Munich were said 'to have found something which millions are yearning for, a leader'.[63] By Hitler's thirty-fourth birthday, on 20 April 1923, when the new head of the SA, Hermann Göring – thirty years old, Bavarian born but from the time of his military training in Berlin a self-styled Prussian, handsome (at this time), wildly egocentric, well connected and power-hungry, bringing the glamour of the World-War-decorated flying ace as well as important links to the aristocracy to the Nazi Movement – labelled him the 'beloved leader of the German freedom-movement', the personality cult was unmistakable.[64] Political opponents scorned it.[65] That it was not without its mark on Hitler himself is plain. Eckart told Hanfstaengl, while on holiday with Hitler near Berchtesgaden in the Bavarian Alps bordering on Austria in May 1923, that Hitler had 'megalomania halfway between a Messiah complex and Neroism', after he had allegedly compared the way he would deal with Berlin with Christ throwing money-changers out of the temple.[66] Similar signs can be read into the letter no less a figure than Gottfried Feder addressed to his party leader on 10 August 1923, strongly criticizing his lifestyle, his 'anarchy in the allocation of time', and not least the way Hitler was now placing himself above the party. 'We gladly yield first place to you. But we have no understanding for tyrannical tendencies,' Feder witheringly concluded.[67]

During 1923 there are indications in Hitler's speeches that his self-perception was changing. He was now much more preoccupied than he had been in earlier years with leadership, and the qualities needed in the coming Leader of Germany. At no time before his imprisonment in Landsberg did he unambiguously claim those qualities for himself. But a number of passages in his speeches hint that the edges of what distinguished the 'drummer' from the 'Leader' might be starting to blur.

In November 1922, Hitler spoke of obedience to the leader as the first duty. According to the police report of his speech in Munich's Bürgerbräukeller, however, he went on to speak in the plural of 'leaders' who were elected and could, if found wanting, be rejected.[68] A few days later, he emphasized that only the leader was answerable to the masses, that commissions and committees were a hindrance to a movement.[69] Such comments were no different from views expressed by Hitler at the time that he took over the party leadership. But before 1923 he had rarely spoken of a dictatorship in Germany, and then in somewhat veiled terms which did not necessarily imply the rule of a single individual.[70] By 1923, in the wake of Mussolini's success, with mounting crisis in the Reich, and with adulation being heaped on him by his own supporters, Hitler looked increasingly to 'a strong man who would rescue Germany'.[71] He continued to speak in the plural, however, of the need for leaders – of a non-parliamentary kind – who would rule if necessary against the will of the majority in the interests of the nation.[72] 'The people don't want ministers any longer, but leaders,' he proclaimed.[73] On 4 May 1923, in a speech castigating the parliamentary system as the 'downfall and end of the German nation',[74] Hitler gave the clearest hint to date of how he saw his own role. With reference to Frederick the Great and Bismarck, 'giants' whose deeds contrasted with those of the Reichstag, 'Germany's grave-digger', he declared: 'What can save Germany is the dictatorship of the national will and national determination. The question arises: is the suitable personality to hand? Our task is not to look for such a person. He is a gift from heaven, or is not there. Our task is to create the sword that this person will need when he is there. Our task is to give the dictator, when he comes, a people ready for him!'[75]

By July he was saying that only the value of personality, not majority decisions of parliament, could save Germany: 'as Leader of the National Socialist Party I see my task in accepting the responsibility'.[76] His call for a dictatorship met with great applause.[77] As his remarks show, he saw himself still as the 'drummer'.[78] But there was an element of ambiguity. In an interview with the British *Daily Mail* on 2 October 1923, Hitler was reported as saying: 'If a German Mussolini is given to Germany . . . people would fall down on their knees and worship him more than Mussolini has ever been worshipped.'[79] If he was seeing himself – as his followers were seeing him – as the 'German Mussolini', then he was apparently beginning to associate the greatness of national leadership with his own person.[80] In Nuremberg, asking whether Kahr deserved support, he denied the Bavarian ruler any claim to true leadership. He located 'greatness' solely in heroic qualities of the individual, and found these in 'three of our greatest Germans': Martin Luther, Frederick the Great and Richard Wagner. All three were 'pioneers' (*Wegbereiter*) in the national cause and thereby 'heroes of their people'. Kahr was 'decent', and a capable administrator. But these were things to be taken for granted.[81] Kahr thought only in Bavarian defensive terms, and was incapable of leading from Munich the struggle for national liberation.[82] 'A freedom-fighter must have the right instinct, he must have will and nothing more than will.'[83] The juxtaposition of heroic leadership, its denial to Kahr, and the qualities required of the 'freedom-fighter' again suggest that Hitler was beginning to stake a claim for himself to the position of supreme (and heroic) national leader. The ambiguity remained. He saw his own aim as that of the 'pioneer', the one 'paving the way for the great German freedom-movement'.[84] On the one hand, this still suggested the 'drummer'.[85] On the other, he had already just linked the path-breaking pioneer with the great national heroes of the past. At any rate, he felt by this time, so he said, 'the call to Germany's salvation within him', and others detected 'outright Napoleonic and messianic allures' in what he said.[86]

The lack of clarity in Hitler's comments about the future leadership was, in part, presumably tactical. There was nothing to be gained by alienating possible support through a premature conflict about who would later be supreme leader. As Hitler had stated in October, the leadership question could be left unanswered until 'the weapon is created which the leader must possess'. Only then would the time be ripe to 'pray to our Lord God that he give us the right leader'.[87] But it was predominantly a reflection of Hitler's concept of politics as essentially agitation, propaganda, and 'struggle'.[88] Organizational forms remained of little concern to him as long as his own freedom of action was not constrained by them. The crucial issue was the leadership of the 'political struggle'. But it is hard to imagine that Hitler's self-confidence in this field and his ingrained refusal to compromise would not subsequently have meant his demand for total, unconstrained leadership of the 'national movement'. At any rate, Hitler's comments on leadership in the crisis-ridden year of 1923 seem to indicate that his self-image was in a process of change. He still saw himself as the 'drummer', the highest calling there was in his eyes. But it would not take much, following his triumph in the trial after the failed putsch, to convert that self-image into the presumption that he was the 'heroic leader' himself.

IV

That was all in the future. Around the beginning of 1923, few, if any, outside the ranks of his most fervent devotees thought seriously of Hitler as Germany's coming 'great leader'. But his rise to star status on Munich's political scene – alongside the Hofbräuhaus, the city's only notable curiosity, as one newspaper put it[89] – meant that individuals from quite outside his normal social circles began to take a keen interest in him.

Two were converts to the party who were able to open up useful new contacts for Hitler. Kurt Lüdecke, a well-connected former gambler, play-boy, and commercial adventurer, a widely-travelled 'man of the world', was 'looking for a leader and a cause' when he first heard Hitler speak at the rally of the 'Patriotic Associations' in Munich in August 1922.[90] Lüdecke was enthralled. 'My critical faculty was swept away,' he later wrote. 'He was holding the masses, and me with them, under a hypnotic spell by the sheer force of his conviction . . . His appeal to German manhood was like a call to arms, the gospel he preached a sacred truth. He seemed another Luther . . . I experienced an exaltation that could be likened only to religious conversion . . . I had found myself, my leader, and my cause.'[91] According to his own account, Lüdecke used his connections to promote Hitler's standing with General Ludendorff, a war-hero since repulsing the Russian advance into East Prussia in 1914, in effect Germany's dictator during the last two war years, and now the outstanding figure on the radical Right, whose name alone was sufficient to open further doors to Hitler. He also sang Hitler's praises to the former Munich chief of police, already an important Nazi sympathizer and protector, Ernst Pöhner.[92] Abroad Lüdecke was able to establish contacts just before the 'March on Rome' with Musso-lini (who at that time had never heard of Hitler), and in 1923 with Gömbös and other leading figures in Hungary.[93] His foreign bank accounts, and sizeable donations he was able to acquire abroad, proved valuable to the party during the hyperinflation of 1923.[94] He also fitted out and accommodated at his own cost an entire stormtrooper company. Even so, many of Lüdecke's well-placed contacts were impatient at his constant proselytizing for the NSDAP, and quietly dropped him. And within the party, he was unable to overcome dislike and distrust. He was even denounced to the police by Max Amann as a French spy and jailed under false pretences for two months.[95] By the end of 1923, Lüdecke had used up almost his entire income on behalf of the party.[96]

An even more useful convert was Ernst 'Putzi' Hanfstaengl, a six-foot-four-inch-tall, cultured part-American – his mother, a Sedgwick-Heine, was a descendant of two generals who had fought in the Civil War – from an upper-middle-class art-dealer family, Harvard graduate, partner in an art-print publishing firm, and extremely well-connected in Munich *salon* society. Like Lüdecke, his first experience of Hitler was hearing him speak.[97]

Hanfstaengl was greatly impressed by Hitler's power to sway the masses. 'Far beyond his electrifying rhetoric,' he later wrote, 'this man seemed to possess the uncanny gift of coupling the gnostic yearning of the era for a strong leader-figure with his own missionary claim and to suggest in this merging that every conceivable hope and expectation was capable of fulfilment – an astonishing spectacle of suggestive influence of the mass psyche.'[98] Hanfstaengl was plainly fascinated by the subaltern, petty-bourgeois Hitler in his shabby blue suit, looking part-way between an NCO and a clerk, with awkward mannerisms, but possessing such power as a speaker when addressing a mass audience.[99] Hanfstaengl remained in part contemptuous of Hitler – not least of his half-baked cliché-ridden judgements on art and culture (where Hanfstaengl was truly at home and Hitler merely an opinionated know-all).[100] On Hitler's first visit to the Hanfstaengl home, 'his awkward use of knife and fork betrayed his background,' wrote (somewhat snobbishly) his host.[101] At the same time, Putzi was plainly captivated by this 'virtuoso on the keyboard of the mass psyche'.[102] He was appalled at catching Hitler sugaring a vintage wine he had offered him. But, added Hanfstaengl, 'he could have peppered it, for each naïve act increased my belief in his homespun sincerity'.[103]

Soon, Hitler was a regular guest at Hanfstaengl's home, where he regularly gorged himself on cream-cakes, paying court to Hanfstaengl's attractive wife, Helena, in his quaint Viennese style.[104] She took Hitler's attentions in her stride. 'Believe me, he's an absolute neuter, not a man,' she told her husband.[105] Putzi himself believed, for what it was worth, that Hitler was sexually impotent, gaining substitute gratification from his intercourse with the 'feminine' masses.[106] Hitler was taken by Putzi's skills as a pianist, especially his ability to play Wagner. He would accompany Putzi by whistling the tune, marching up and down swinging his arms like the conductor of an orchestra, relaxing visibly in the process.[107] He plainly liked Hanfstaengl – his wife even more so. But the criterion, as always, was usefulness. And above all Hanfstaengl was useful. He became a type of 'social secretary',[108] providing openings to circles far different from the petty-bourgeois roughnecks in Hitler's entourage who gathered each Monday in the Café Neumaier.[109]

Hanfstaengl introduced Hitler to Frau Elsa Bruckmann, the wife of the publisher Hugo Bruckmann, a Pan-German sympathizer and antisemite who had published the works of Houston Stewart Chamberlain. Hitler's ingratiating manners and social naïvety brought out the mother instinct in her.[110] Whether it was the wish to afford him some protection against his enemies that persuaded her to make him a present of one of the dog-whips he invariably carried around is not clear. (Oddly, his other dog-whip – the first he possessed – had been given to him by a rival patroness, Frau Helene Bechstein, while a third heavy whip, made from hippopotamus hide, which he later carried, was given to him by Frau Büchner, the landlady of the Platterhof, the hotel where he stayed on the Obersalzberg.[111]) Everyone who was someone in Munich would be invited at some stage to the soirées of Frau Bruckmann, by birth a Rumanian princess, so that Hitler was brought into contact here with industrialists, members of the army and aristocracy, and academics.[112] In his gangster hat and trenchcoat over his dinner jacket, touting a pistol and carrying as usual his dog-whip, he cut a bizarre figure in the *salons* of Munich's upper-crust. But his very eccentricity of dress and exaggerated mannerisms – the affected excessive politeness of one aware of his social inferiority – saw him lionized by condescending hosts and fellow-guests. His social awkwardness and uncertainty, often covered by either silence or tendency to monologues, but at the same time the consciousness of his public success that one could read in his face, made him an oddity, affording him curiosity value among the patronizing cultured and well-to-do pillars of the establishment.[113] 'Weak but wanting to be hard, half-educated wishing to be an all-rounder (*universell*), a Bohemian who had to be a soldier if he wanted to impress true soldiers. A man mistrustful towards himself and what he was capable of (*seine Möglichkeiten*), and so full of inferiority-complex towards all who were anything or were on the way to outflank him ... He was never a gentleman, even later in evening dress,' was how one contemporary, the Freikorps leader Gerhard Roßbach, described Hitler around this time.[114]

Hitler was also a guest from time to time of the publisher Lehmann, for long a party sympathizer. And the wife of piano manufacturer Bechstein – to whom he had been introduced by Eckart – was another to 'mother' Hitler, as well as lending the party her jewellery as surety against 60,000 Swiss Francs which Hitler was able to borrow from a Berlin coffee merchant in September 1923. The Bechsteins, who usually wintered in Bavaria, used to invite Hitler to their suite in the 'Bayerischer Hof', or to their country residence near Berchtesgaden. Through the Bechsteins, Hitler was introduced to the Wagner circle at Bayreuth.[115] He was transfixed at the first visit, in October 1923, to the shrine of his ultimate hero at Haus Wahnfried, where he tiptoed around the former possessions of Richard Wagner in the music-room and library 'as though he were viewing relics in a cathedral'. The Wagners had mixed views of their unusual guest, who had turned up looking 'rather common' in his traditional Bavarian outfit of lederhosen, thick woollen socks, red and blue checked shirt and ill-fitting short blue jacket. Winifred, the English-born wife of Wagner's son Siegfried, thought he was 'destined to be the saviour of Germany'. Siegfried himself saw Hitler as 'a fraud and an upstart'.[116]

The rapid growth in the party during the latter part of 1922 and especially in 1923 that had made it a political force in Munich, its closer connections with the 'patriotic associations', and the wider social contacts which now arose meant that funding flowed more readily to the NSDAP than had been the case in its first years. Now, as would be the case later, the party's finances relied heavily upon members' subscriptions together with entrance-fees and collections at meetings.[117] The more came to meetings, the more were recruited as members, the more income came to the party, to permit yet more meetings to be held. Propaganda financed propaganda.[118]

But even now, the party's heavy outgoings were difficult to meet, and funding was not easy to drum up in conditions of rip-roaring inflation. A fund-raising trip that Hitler made to Berlin in April 1922 proved disappointing in its yield.[119] Party finances were still in many respects a hand-to-mouth operation.[120] Hitler was constantly seeking to tap party friends and supporters for donations. But any payment in Marks, however large, was immediately devalued through the galloping currency depreciation.[121] There was a premium, therefore, on donations made in hard foreign currency. Lüdecke and Hanfstaengl, as already noted, were useful in this regard. Hanfstaengl also financed with an interest-free loan of 1,000 dollars – a fortune in inflation-ridden Germany – the purchase of two rotary presses that enabled the *Völkischer Beobachter* to appear in larger, American-style format.[122] Rumours, some far wide of the mark, about the party's finances were repeatedly aired by opponents in the press. Even so, official inquiries in 1923 revealed considerable sums raised from an increasing array of benefactors.

One important go-between was Max Erwin von Scheubner-Richter, born in Riga, linguistically able, with diplomatic service in Turkey during the war, and later imprisoned for a time by Communists on his return to the Baltic. After the war he had participated in the Kapp Putsch, then, like so many counter-revolutionaries, made his way to Munich, where he joined the NSDAP in autumn 1920.[123] A significant, if shadowy, figure in the early Nazi Party, he used his excellent connections with Russian emigrés, such as Princess Alexandra, wife of the Russian heir to the throne Prince Kyrill, to acquire funds directed at Ludendorff and, through him, deflected in part to the NSDAP. Other members of the aristocracy, including Frau Gertrud von Seidlitz, who used monies from foreign stocks and shares, also contributed to Nazi funds.[124] Hitler was almost certainly a co-beneficiary (though probably in a minor way) of the generous gift of 100,000 Gold Marks made by Fritz Thyssen, heir to the family's Ruhr steelworks, to Ludendorff, but Germany's leading industrialists, apart from Ernst von Borsig, head of the Berlin locomotive and machine-building firm, showed little direct interest in the Nazis at this time.[125] Police inquiries which remained inconclusive suggested that Borsig and car-manufacturers Daimler were among other firms contributing to the party.[126] Some Bavarian industrialists and businessmen, too, were persuaded by Hitler to make donations to the movement.[127]

Valuable funds were also obtained abroad. Anti-Marxism and the hopes in a strong Germany as a bulwark against Bolshevism often provided motive enough for such donations. The *Völkischer Beobachter*'s new offices were financed with Czech Kronen.[128] An important link with Swiss funds was Dr Emil Gansser, a Berlin chemist and long-standing Nazi supporter, who engineered a gift of 33,000 Swiss Francs from right-wing Swiss benefactors.[129] Further Swiss donations followed a visit from Hitler himself to Zürich in the summer of 1923.[130] And from right-wing circles in the arch-enemy France, 90,000 Gold Marks were passed to Captain Karl Mayr, Hitler's first patron, and from him to the 'patriotic associations'. It can be presumed that the NSDAP was among the beneficiaries. In addition to monetary donations, Röhm saw to it that the SA, along with other paramilitary organizations, was well provided with equipment and weapons from his secret arsenal.[131] Whatever the financial support, without Röhm's supplies an armed putsch would scarcely have been possible.

In November 1922, rumours were already circulating that Hitler was planning a putsch.[132] By January 1923, in the explosive climate following the French march into the Ruhr, the rumours in Munich of a Hitler putsch were even stronger.[133] The crisis, without which Hitler would have been nothing, was deepening by the day. In its wake, the Nazi movement was expanding rapidly. Some 35,000 were to join between February and November 1923, giving a strength of around 55,000 on the eve of the putsch. Recruits came from all sections of society. Around a third were workers, a tenth or more came from the upper-middle and professional classes, but more than half belonged to the crafts, commercial, white-collar, and farming lower-middle class.[134] Most had joined the party out of protest, anger, and bitterness as the economic and political crisis mounted. The same was true of the thousands flocking into the SA. Hitler had won their support by promising them action. The sacrifices of the war would be avenged. The revolution would be overturned.[135] He could not hold them at fever-pitch indefinitely without unleashing such action. The tendency to 'go for broke' was not simply a character-trait of Hitler; it was built into the nature of his leadership, his political aims, and the party he led. But Hitler was not in control of events as they unfolded in 1923. Nor was he, before 8 November, the leading player in the drama. Without the readiness of powerful figures and organizations to contemplate a putsch against Berlin, Hitler would have had no stage on which to act so disastrously. His own role, his actions – and reactions – have to be seen in that light.

V

Hitler's incessant barrage of anti-government propaganda was nearly undermined by an event that invoked national unity in January 1923: the French occupation of the Ruhr. On this occasion at least, the Reich government seemed to be acting firmly – and acting with mass popular support.

The request by the government of Reich Chancellor Wilhelm Cuno for a moratorium for two years on reparations payments in money had been turned down by the allied heads of government meeting in Paris at the end of December. Germany had fallen behind in its reparations payments in wood – it owed 200,000 metres of telegraph poles and had delivered only 65,000 metres – and coal deliveries to the tune of 24 million Gold Marks. Compared with payments made of 1,480 million Gold Marks it was a trivial amount. But 135,000 metres of missing telegraph poles sufficed for French and Belgian troops on 11 January to march into the Ruhr district to ensure coal deliveries. Germany was gripped by an elemental wave of national fury that crossed all social and political divides. A 'national unity front' stretching from Social Democrats to German Nationals was founded.[136] The unity – invoking the 'Burgfrieden' (civil truce) of 1914, when in the wake of war fever class conflict and internal disputes had temporarily given way to a sense of national accord – had little chance of lasting. But it was an immediate expression of the depth of feeling in the country. On 13 January the Reich government declared a campaign of 'passive resistance' against the Ruhr occupation. 14 January was to be a day of mourning throughout Germany. The gunning-down by French soldiers – possibly provoked by German nationalists – of workers in the Krupp factory at Essen on 31 March, leaving thirteen dead and forty-one wounded, was the worst of numerous confrontations that wildly inflamed an already overheated situation.[137] The policy of 'passive resistance' was, therefore, certain of widespread public support. For radical nationalists, it did not, however, go nearly far enough. Disbanded Freikorps groups were reinstated again, with the clandestine help of the Reichswehr. Acts of sabotage were carried out in the occupied zone, again supported by the army.[138] The extent and vehemence of the opposition to the Ruhr occupation posed, nevertheless, a problem for the National Socialists. The popular protest threatened to take the wind out of their sails. Attacks on a Berlin government engaged in protest at the Ruhr occupation were not guaranteed to have mass appeal.[139] Undeterred, Hitler saw advantage to be gained from the French occupation.[140] As usual, he went on a propaganda offensive.

On the very day of the French march into the Ruhr he spoke in a packed Circus Krone. 'Down with the November Criminals' was the title of his speech. It was not the first time he had used the term 'November Criminals' to describe the Social Democrat revolutionaries of 1918. But from now on, the slogan was seldom far from his lips.[141] It showed the line he would take towards the Ruhr occupation. The real enemy was within. 'The German rebirth is externally only possible when the criminals are faced with their responsibility and delivered to their just fate,' he declared.[142] Marxism, democracy, parliamentarism, internationalism, and, of course, behind it all the power of the Jews, were held by Hitler to blame for the national defencelessness that allowed the French to treat Germany like a colony.[143] Hitler poured scorn on the newly proclaimed 'national unity'. He announced that any party members involved in active resistance to the occupation would be expelled.[144] His own supporters were temporarily taken aback. But the tactic worked.

The propaganda offensive was stepped up with preparations for the NSDAP's first 'Reich Party Rally', scheduled to take place in Munich on 27–9 January. It brought confrontation with the Bavarian government, so frightened about rumours of a putsch that on 26 January it declared a state of emergency in Munich, but so weak that it lacked the power to carry through its intended ban on the rally.[145] Hitler was beside himself with rage when told the rally was prohibited. For him, as usual, there could be no retreat. He promised to go ahead despite the ban, and threatened disturbances of the peace and possibly bloodshed. He was prepared, he declared, somewhat melodramatically, to stand in the front row when the shots were fired.[146] It needed Röhm to calm him down and put forward a more constructive approach. The Reichswehr once more came to Hitler's aid. Röhm persuaded Epp to prevail upon the commander of the 7th Reichswehr Division, stationed in Bavaria, General Otto Hermann von Lossow, to come down on Hitler's side. Röhm was ordered to bring Hitler to an audience with Lossow. Hitler guaranteed the peaceful conduct of the rally, and promised on his 'word of honour' that no putsch would be attempted. Hitler and Röhm then hastened to Kahr, at the time Government President of Upper Bavaria, who also offered his support, as did the Police President Eduard Nortz. Hitler was given permission to go ahead with the twelve mass meetings – all of which he addressed on the same evening – that had been arranged as well as the theatrical display of the dedication of SA standards on the Marsfeld, a big parade-ground close to the centre of Munich, on 28 January in front of 6,000 uniformed stormtroopers.[147] Had the party had fewer friends in high places, and had the government held firm, it would, as Ernst Röhm recognized, have been a heavy blow to Hitler's prestige.[148] As it was, thanks to the Bavarian authorities, he could celebrate another propaganda triumph.

At the meetings during the rally, Hitler could once more appear self-confident, certain of success, to the masses of his supporters. The whole rally had been devised in the form of a ritual homage-paying to the 'leader of the German freedom-movement'.[149] The leadership cult, consciously devised to sustain maximum cohesion within the party, was taking off. According to a newspaper report, Hitler was greeted 'like a saviour' when he entered the Festsaal of the Hofbräuhaus during one of his twelve speeches in the evening of 27 January.[150] In the feverish atmosphere in the Löwenbräukeller the same evening, he was given a similar hero's welcome as he entered the hall, deliberately late, shielded by his bodyguard, arm outstretched in the salute – probably borrowed from the Italian Fascists (and by them from Imperial Rome) – which would become standard in the Movement by 1926.[151] It was an unrecognizable Hitler, noted Karl Alexander von Müller, to the diffident individual he had encountered in private gatherings.[152]

Hitler's near-exclusive concentration on propaganda was not Röhm's approach, while the latter's emphasis on the paramilitary posed a latent threat to Hitler's authority.[153] At the beginning of February, directly after breaking with Pittinger, Röhm founded a 'Working Community of the Patriotic Fighting Associations' (Arbeitsgemeinschaft der Vaterländischen Kampfverbände) comprising, alongside the SA, the Bund Oberland, Reichsflagge, Wikingbund, and Kampfverband Niederbayern.[154] The direct military control was in the hands of retired Oberstleutnant Hermann Kriebel, previously a chief of staff in the Bavarian Einwohnerwehr and Organisation Escherich (or Orgesch).[155] The formations were trained by the Bavarian Reichswehr – not for incorporation in any defence against further inroads by the French and Belgians (the threat of which was by this time plainly receding), but evidently for the eventuality of conflict with Berlin.[156] Once subsumed in this umbrella organization, the SA was far from the biggest paramilitary grouping and there was little to distinguish it from the other bodies.[157] In a purely military organization, it had only a subordinate role.[158] The conversion of the SA to a paramilitary organization now not directly or solely under his own control was not to Hitler's liking. But there was nothing he could do about it.[159] However, Hitler was pushed by Röhm into the foreground of the political leadership of the 'Working Community'. He it was who was asked by Röhm to define the political aims of the 'Working Community'.[160] He was now moving in high circles indeed. In early 1923 he was brought into contact by Röhm with no less than the Chief of the Army Command (*Chef der Heeresleitung*) of the Reichswehr, General Hans von Seeckt (who remained, however, distinctly unimpressed by the Munich demagogue, and unprepared to commit himself to the demands for radical action in the Ruhr conflict for which Hitler was pressing).[161] Röhm also insisted to the new Bavarian Commander, Lossow, that Hitler's movement, with its aim of winning over the workers to the national cause, offered the best potential for building a 'patriotic fighting front' to upturn the November Revolution.[162]

Connected with all the strands of nationalist paramilitary politics, if openly directing none, was the figure of General Ludendorff, regarded generally as the symbolic leader of the radical nationalist Right. The former war-hero had returned to Germany from his Swedish exile in February 1919, taking up residence in Munich. His radical *völkisch* nationalism, detestation of the new Republic, and prominent advocacy of the 'stab-in-the-back' legend, had already taken him effortlessly into the slipstream of the Pan-Germans, brought him fringe participation in the Kapp Putsch, and now led to his close involvement with the counter-revolutionary extreme Right, for whom his reputation and standing were a notable asset. The hotbed of Munich's *völkisch* and paramilitary politics provided the setting within which, remarkably, the famous Quartermaster-General, virtual dictator of Germany and chief driving-force of the war effort between 1916 and 1918, could come into close contact and direct collaboration with the former army corporal, Adolf Hitler. Even more remarkable was the rapidity with which, in the new world of rabble-rousing politics to which General Ludendorff was ill-attuned, the ex-corporal would come to eclipse the one-time military commander as the leading spokesman of the radical Right.

Hitler had been first brought to Ludendorff's attention by Rudolf Heß in May 1921, since when the general's name had opened up a number of doors for him.[163] At a meeting in Berlin on 26 February Ludendorff now brought the leaders of the north German paramilitary organizations together with Hitler and Röhm's spokesman for his 'Working Community', Captain Heiß, leader of the Reichsflagge. Ludendorff, thinking a strike against the French imminent, demanded support for Seeckt and the Cuno government. Despite his public stance, Hitler did not demur. Only one group, the Jungdeutscher Orden, rejected the suggestion to place the paramilitary organizations at the behest of the Reichswehr for training.[164] Hitler came away nevertheless sorely disappointed from his four-hour meeting with a non-committal Seeckt in March, and at an audience with the Bavarian head of the Reichswehr, Lossow, angrily rejected the conclusion drawn by the latter that Bavaria should then go its own way and consider separation from the Reich.[165] Nevertheless, the military training of the SA by the Reichswehr which Hitler had agreed with Lossow in January proceeded. The SA, along with other paramilitary bands, handed its weapons over to the army in preparation for mobilization against the French.[166]

The paramilitary politics of spring 1923, in the wake of the French occupation of the Ruhr, were confused and riddled with conflict and intrigue. But, largely through Röhm's manoeuvrings, Hitler, the beerhall agitator, had been brought into the arena of top-level discussions with the highest military as well as paramilitary leadership, not just in Bavaria, but in the Reich. He was now a player for big stakes. But he could not control the moves of other, more powerful, players with their own agendas. His constant agitation could mobilize support for a time. But it could not be held at fever-pitch indefinitely. It demanded action. Hitler's impatience, his 'all-or-nothing' stance, was not simply a matter of temperament. He described the military training of the SA in spring 1923 as possessing solely the 'motive of absolute attack' against the French. 'This was one of the factors that finally forced a decision. For it was not possible to keep on restraining people whose heads were exclusively filled in the barracks night after night, morning after morning, with the idea of war. They asked, "When's it going to happen, when are we finally going to fight and chuck that lot (die Bande) out?" The people could not be held back week in and week out, and that was one of the reasons for what we later brought about (unseres späteren Auswirkens) and at the same time one of the reasons why this necessarily had at some time to make itself felt (*sich auswirken mußten*).'[167]

The direct result was the next major confrontation with the Bavarian government on May Day 1923 – and this time a serious loss of face for Hitler. The trade union programme for a parade of the socialists through the streets of Munich on 1 May, which had been approved by the police, was seen by the nationalist Right as an outright provocation. In Munich, May Day was not only for the Left the symbolic day of socialism. It was for the Right the commemoration of the 'liberation' of the city from the detested Räterepublik (Councils Republic), the short-lived Soviet-style takeover in Munich in April 1919. Serious trouble could, therefore, be expected if Left and Right clashed. And such a clash seemed very likely. The climate was already tense. There had been a serious shooting incident in one district of Munich between Communists and National Socialists on 26 April, leaving four wounded.[168] In addition, the Social Democrats had again tried to have the stormtroops banned, though their proposal, put to the Bavarian Landtag on 24–5 April, had been duly defeated. But above all, the radical Right were spoiling for a fight. As Georg Escherich, the former Einwohnerwehr leader, noted, 'The right Radicals in Munich are looking eagerly for every opportunity for "deeds".'[169]

Activists, as Hitler later acknowledged, could not be kept in a state of tension indefinitely without some release. He proposed a national demonstration on May Day, and an armed attack on the 'Reds'.[170] Increasingly alarmed by the prospect of serious disturbances, the Munich police revoked its permission for the Left's street-parade, and now confined permission only to the holding of a limited demonstration on the spacious Theresienwiese near the city centre. Rumours of a putsch from the Left, almost certainly set into circulation by the Right, served as a pretext for a 'defence' by the paramilitary bodies.[171] They demanded 'their' weapons back from safe keeping under the control of the Reichswehr. But on the afternoon of 30 April, at a meeting with paramilitary leaders, Lossow, concerned about the danger of a putsch from the *Right*, refused to hand over the armaments. Hitler, in a blind rage, accused Lossow of breach of trust.[172] But there was nothing to be done. Hitler had been overconfident. And this time, for once, the state authorities had remained firm. All that could be salvaged was a gathering the following morning of around 2,000 men from the paramilitary formations – about 1,300 from the National Socialists – on the Oberwiesenfeld in the barracks area north of the city, well away from the May Day demonstration and firmly ringed by a cordon of police. Tame exercises carried out with arms distributed from Röhm's arsenal were no substitute for the planned assault on the Left. After standing around for much of the time since dawn holding their rifles and facing the police, the men handed back their arms around two o'clock and dispersed. Many had left already. There were one or two skirmishes reported in the city. In the most serious, a group of workers on their way home from the left-wing demonstration were set upon and beaten up by SA men leaving the Oberwiesenfeld. The police did not intervene.[173] Compared with the bloodshed that might have taken place, it was of minor significance. The May Day rally on the Theresien-wiese, with its 25,000 participants, had ended without incident around midday.

Most of those taking part had already left to attend the May Day celebra-tions in the Hirschgarten, a large beer-garden two or three miles to the west of the city centre, that afternoon. Attended by an estimated 30,000 socialists, these passed without incident.[174] Hitler made virtue out of necessity at a packed meeting that evening in the Circus Krone. He announced to huge applause that the day had been a special one in bringing about an alliance of National Socialists with Bund Oberland, Bund Blücher, Reichsflagge, and Wikingbund. Otherwise he had to resort to his usual attacks on Jews, socialists and the International, appealing, according to a police report, to the basest instincts of the masses in such an antisemitic tirade – denouncing the Jews as 'racial tuberculosis' – that it prompted a 'pogrom mood'.[175] That was Hitler's way of rebounding from a setback. It fooled few people outside Nazi fanatics. Most recognized the events of May Day to have been a severe embarrassment for Hitler and his followers. The Württemberg ambassador reported the frequently expressed view that Hitler's star was now on the wane.[176]

The Bavarian Minister President, Eugen von Knilling, had commented in April that 'the enemy stands Left, but the danger [stands] on the Right'.[177] The remark typified the hopeless attempt by the BVP-led government to steer a middling course in the crisis. Its weak and vacillating stance was, as Knilling's comment suggests, based upon the need to head off the menace of a right-wing putsch, but at the same time on a rooted fear of the Left – even of the moderate Majority Social Democrats. The May Day affair ought to have shown the government that firm and resolute action could defeat Hitler. But by this time, the Bavarian government had long since ruled out any potential for working together with the democratic forces on the Left. It was permanently at loggerheads with the Reich government. And it had no effective control over its own army leaders, who were playing their own game. It was little wonder in this context that it was buffeted in all directions. Incapable of tackling the problem of the radical Right because both will and power were ultimately lacking to do so, it allowed the Hitler movement the space to recover from the temporary setback of 1 May.[178]

But above all, the lesson of 1 May was that Hitler was powerless without the support of the Reichswehr. In January, when the Party Rally had been initially banned, then allowed to go ahead, Lossow's permission had given Hitler the chance to escape the blow to his prestige. Now, on 1 May, Lossow's refusal had prevented Hitler's planned propaganda triumph. Deprived of his lifeblood – regular outlets for his propaganda – the main base of Hitler's effectiveness would have been undermined. But the Bavarian Reichswehr was to remain largely an independent variable in the equation of Bavarian politics in the latter part of 1923. And the part accommodating, part vacillating attitude of the Bavarian authorities to the radical Right, driven by fierce anti-socialism linked to its antagonism towards Berlin, ensured that the momentum of Hitler's movement was not seriously checked by the May Day events.[179] Hitler could, in fact, have been taken out of circulation altogether for up to two years, had charges of breach of the peace, arising from the May Day incidents, been pressed. But the Bavarian Justice Minister Franz Gürtner saw to it that the inquiries never came to formal charges – after Hitler had threatened to reveal details of Reichswehr complicity in the training and arming of the paramilitaries in preparation for a war against France – and the matter was quietly dropped.[180]

For his part, Hitler continued unabated his relentless agitation against the 'November criminals' during the summer of 1923. The fierce animosity towards Berlin, now as before providing a bond between the otherwise competing sections of the Right, ensured that his message of hatred and revenge towards internal as well as external enemies would not be short of an audience.[181] He alone remained able to fill the cavernous Circus Krone. Between May and the beginning of August he addressed five overfilled meetings there, and also spoke at another ten party meetings elsewhere in Bavaria.[182] Relations with the Bavarian authorities, for all their tolerance towards the NSDAP, remained tense. Unlike the leaders of some of the paramilitary organizations, Hitler refused to let the SA serve as auxiliary police. That would have been to compromise his freedom of action towards the Bavarian state.[183] At the Deutsches Turnfest (Rally of German Gymnastic Organizations) in Munich on 14 July, it came to violent clashes between the SA and the police as the Nazi formations, leaving the meeting at the Circus Krone, disobeyed police orders prohibiting the display of party banners.[184] Such confrontations – and rumours started by Nazi leaders themselves of alleged assassination threats against Hitler[185] – certainly served their purpose of keeping the NSDAP and its leader in the public eye. But Hitler was aware that agitation without action could not be sustained indefinitely. Outside observers were of the same opinion. 'A party so attuned to activism to which so many adventurers belong, must lose appeal if it does not come to action within a certain time,' reported the Württemberg ambassador in Munich on 30 August 1923.[186] But Hitler could not act alone. He needed most of all the support of the Reichswehr. But he also needed the cooperation of the other paramilitary organizations. And in the realm of paramilitary politics, he was not a free agent. Certainly, new members continued to pour into the SA during the summer.[187] But after the embarrassment of 1 May, Hitler was for some time less prominent, even retreating at the end of May for a while to stay with Dietrich Eckart in a small hotel at Berchtesgaden.[188] Among the members of the various branches of the 'patriotic associations', Ludendorff, not Hitler, was regarded as the symbol of the 'national struggle'. Hitler was in this forum only one of a number of spokesmen. In the case of disagreement, he too had to bow to Ludendorff's superiority.[189]

The former World War hero took centre stage at the *Deutscher Tag* (German Day) in Nuremberg on 1–2 September 1923, a massive rally – the police reckoned 100,000 were present – of nationalist paramilitary forces and veterans' associations scheduled to coincide with the anniversary of the German victory over France at the battle of Sedan in 1870.[190] Along with the Reichsflagge, the National Socialists were particularly well represented.[191] The enormous propaganda spectacular enabled Hitler, the most effective of the speakers, to repair the damage his reputation had suffered in May. At the two-hour march-past of the formations, he stood together with General Ludendorff, Prinz Ludwig Ferdinand of Bavaria, and the military head of the 'patriotic associations', Oberstleutnant Kriebel, on the podium.[192]

What came out of the rally was the uniting of the NSDAP, the Bund Oberland, and the Reichsflagge in the newly formed Deutscher Kampfbund (German Combat League). While Kriebel took over the military leadership, Hitler's man Scheubner-Richter was made business manager.[193] Three weeks later, thanks to Röhm's machinations, Hitler was given, with the agreement of the heads of the other paramilitary organizations, the 'political leadership' of the Kampfbund.[194]

What this meant in practice was not altogether clear. Hitler was no dictator in the umbrella organization. And so far as there were specific notions about a future dictator in the 'coming Germany', that position was envisaged as Ludendorff's.[195] For Hitler, 'political leadership' seems to have indicated the subordination of paramilitary politics to the building of a revolutionary mass movement through nationalist propaganda and agitation. But for the leaders of the formations, the 'primacy of the soldier' – the professionals like Röhm and Kriebel – was what still counted. Hitler was seen as a type of 'political instructor'.[196] He could whip up the feelings of the masses like no one else. But beyond that he had no clear idea of the mechanics of attaining power. Cooler heads were needed for that. As an 'Action Programme' of the Kampfbund drawn up by Scheubner-Richter on 24 September made plain, the 'national revolution' in Bavaria had to follow, not precede, the winning over of the army and police, the forces that sustained the power of the state. Scheubner-Richter concluded that it was necessary to take over the police in a formally legal fashion by placing Kampfbund leaders in charge of the Bavarian Ministry of the Interior and the Munich police.[197] Hitler, like his partners in the Kampfbund, knew that an attempt at a putsch in the teeth of opposition from the forces of the military and police in Bavaria stood little chance of success.[198] But for the time being his approach, as ever, was to go on a frontal propaganda offensive against the Bavarian government. His position within the Kampfbund now ensured that the pressure to act – even without a clear strategy for the practical steps needed to gain control of the state – would not relent.

VI

Crisis was Hitler's oxygen. He needed it to survive. And the deteriorating conditions in Germany (with their distinctive flavour in Bavaria) as summer turned to autumn, and the currency collapsed totally under the impact of the 'passive resistance' policy, guaranteed an increasing appeal for Hitler's brand of agitation. By the time he took over the political leadership of the Kampfbund, Germany's searing crisis was heading for its denouement.

By 13 August, when the leader of the DVP Gustav Stresemann – former ardent monarchist and wartime annexationist turned pragmatic Republican – replaced Cuno as Reich Chancellor, taking over the Foreign Ministry at the same time – it was obvious that passive resistance by the shaky Republic had to be ended. It was an inevitable capitulation to the French. The country was bankrupt, its currency ruined. Inflation had gone into a dizzy tailspin. Where there had been 4.20 Marks to the dollar on the eve of the First World

War, there were 17,972 Marks in January 1923, 4,620,455 Marks in August, 98,860,000 Marks in September, 25,260,280,000 in October, and a barely credible 4,200,000 million Marks by 15 November. By mid-September, a kilo of butter was costing 168 million Marks. For Nazi Party members, buying the *Völkischer Beobachter* on the day of the putsch cost 5,000 million Marks.[199]

Speculators and profiteers thrived. But the material consequences of the hyper-inflation for ordinary people were devastating, the psychological effects incalculable. Savings of a lifetime were wiped out within hours. Insurance policies were not worth the paper they were written on. Those with pensions and fixed incomes saw their only source of support dissolve into worthlessness. Workers were initially less badly hit. Employers, eager to prevent social unrest, agreed with trade unions to index wages to living costs. Even so, it was little wonder that the massive discontent brought sharp political radicalization on the Left as well as on the Right. Communist-inspired strikes rocked the country in the summer. The entry of the Social Democrats into the Stresemann 'grand coalition' had a temporary calming effect on the working class, which remained despite the radicalization for the most part loyal to the SPD. But for nationalists, not least in Bavaria, this was seen as another provocation. On the Left, overestimating their strength and potential, the Communists planned revolutionary uprisings in Thuringia and Saxony after they had quite legally entered the governments of these states. In Hamburg, where the local party was thirsting for action and keen to become the centre of the German revolution, a short-lived rising – manifesting itself mainly in attacks on police stations – did actually take place between 23 and 26 October. It ended bloodily: twenty-four Communists and seventeen policemen were left its victims.[200] In central Germany, the Reich government moved swiftly. By the end of October, any danger of Communist insurgency had been suppressed by the Reichswehr, sent in by the Reich government with an alacrity not shown against the extreme Right.[201] The Thuringian government yielded; the Communist ministers withdrew from government. In Saxony, where the state government refused to disband the paramilitary units that had been set up, a show of force was needed. Twenty-three persons were left dead and thirty-one injured in one Saxon town when troops opened fire on demonstrators. There was shooting in a number of other towns. The elected government was deposed, allegedly at gunpoint.[202] The proclaimed threat from the Left had fizzled out at the first show of government force. The failure of the KPD's planned 'German October' did not, however, prevent the extreme Right, especially in Bavaria, continuing to use the 'red threat' in Middle Germany as a pretext for schemes to march on Berlin.

Bavaria's immediate response to the ending of passive resistance on 26 September was to proclaim a state of emergency and make Gustav Ritter von Kahr General State Commissar with near-dictatorial powers. Knilling hoped to take the wind out of Hitler's sails by putting the so-called Bavarian strong man Kahr in charge.[203] The reaction of the NSDAP indicated that the party felt Kahr's appointment to have been in reality a blow to its hopes of seizing power.[204] The Reich responded with the declaration of a general state of emergency and the granting of emergency powers to the Reichswehr. One of Kahr's first acts was to ban – amid renewed putsch rumours – the fourteen meetings which the NSDAP had planned for the evening of 27 September. Hitler was in a frenzy of rage.[205] He felt bypassed by the manoeuvre to bring in Kahr, and certain that the head of the Bavarian state was not the man to lead a national revolution. Alongside attacks on the Reich government for betraying the national resistance – a contrary, though more popular, line to that he had taken earlier in the year towards the policy of passive resistance – Hitler now turned his fire on Kahr.[206]

The weeks following Kahr's appointment were filled with plot, intrigue, and tension which mounted to fever-pitch. The mood of the people, according to police reports, was one of expectancy. Conditions were appalling in Bavaria, as in the rest of the country. 'Unemployment and hunger stand like threatening ghosts at many doors,' ran a report from Swabia in the second half of August.[207] A report from Franconia indicated the level of distress there: black bread cost 1,000 million Marks a pound; unemployment was rapidly rising; industry had no orders; large numbers of people were unable to feed themselves; the government could not even pay its own employees.[208] It was reported from Upper Bavaria that the mood was comparable with that of November 1918 and April 1919.[209] Growing hatred of foreigners, profiteers and those in government was noted in the same region.[210] The Munich police registered a worsening mood by September, looking for an outlet in some sort of action. Political meetings were, however, not well attended because of the high entry charges and the price of beer. Only the Nazis could continue to fill the beerhalls.[211] As rumours of a forthcoming putsch continued to circulate, there was a feeling that something would have to happen soon.[212]

Hitler was under pressure to act. The leader of the Munich SA regiment, Wilhelm Brückner, told him: 'The day is coming when I can no longer hold my people. If nothing happens now the men will sneak away.'[213]

Scheubner-Richter said much the same: 'In order to keep the men together, one must finally undertake something. Otherwise the people will become Left radicals.'[214] Hitler himself used almost the identical argument with head of the Landespolizei Colonel Hans Ritter von Seißer at the beginning of November: 'Economic pressures drive our people so that we must either act or our followers will swing to the Communists.'[215] He argued in similar fashion retrospectively, days after the putsch's failure, during his first interrogation in Landsberg: 'The Kampfbund people had pressed. They could not have been held back any longer. They had been given prospect of action for so long, and been trained for so long, that finally they had wanted to see something really tangible . . . There was also no more money. People had become discontented. There would have been the danger of the Kampfbund falling apart.'[216] Hitler's instincts were in any case to force the issue as soon as possible. The favourable circumstances of the comprehensive state crisis could not last indefinitely. He was determined not to be outflanked by Kahr. And his own prestige would wane if nothing was attempted and enthusiasm dissipated, or if the movement were faced down again as it had been on 1 May.

However, the cards were not in his hands. Kahr and the two other members of the triumvirate which was effectively ruling Bavaria (State Police chief Seißer and Reichswehr commander Lossow) had their own agenda, which differed in significant detail from that of the Kampfbund leadership. In extensive negotiations with north German contacts throughout October, the triumvirate was looking to install a nationalist dictatorship in Berlin based on a directorate, with or without Kahr as a member but certainly without the inclusion of Ludendorff or Hitler, and resting on the support of the Reichswehr. The Kampfbund leadership, on the other hand, wanted a directorate in Munich, centring on Ludendorff and Hitler, certainly without Kahr, which would take Berlin by force. And while Lossow took it for granted that any move against the Berlin government would be carried out by the military, the Kampfbund presumed that it would be a paramilitary operation with Reichswehr backing. If need be, declared the Kampfbund military leader, Oberstleutnant Kriebel, the Kampfbund would even resist any attempts by the Bavarian government to use armed force against the 'patriotic associations'. Hitler did his best to win over Lossow and Seißer, subjecting the latter on 24 October to a four-hour lecture on his aims. Neither was persuaded to throw in his lot with the Kampfbund, though the position of Lossow – with chief responsibility for order in Bavaria – was ambiguous and wavering.[217]

At a meeting he called of paramilitary leaders on 24 October, Lossow spoke – presumably with Mussolini's 'March on Rome' in mind – in favour of a march on Berlin and the proclamation of a national dictatorship.[218] But actually, both he and Seißer temporized – offering token and conditional support to the Kampfbund, though in reality reserving their position.[219] By the end of October, the stand-off between the triumvirate and the Kampfbund was much as it had been at the beginning of the month.[220] But the atmosphere was even more fevered. The Bavarian authorities regarded the dangers of a putsch by Hitler as particularly great, and feared that disillusioned supporters of Kahr would swing over to him, that he would take over the government in Munich, and would immediately set out on his march on Berlin.[221] The authorities were not over-reacting. There were indications that the Kampfbund intended to act on 4 November, the day when Munich's war memorial would be dedicated before civic and military dignitaries.[222] However, if such plans were seriously envisaged, they were rapidly called off.[223]

At the beginning of November, Seißer was sent to Berlin to conduct negotiations on behalf of the triumvirate with a number of important contacts, most vitally with Seeckt. The Reichswehr chief made plain at the meeting on 3 November that he would not move against the legal government in Berlin.[224] With that, any plans of the triumvirate were effectively scuppered. At a crucial meeting in Munich three days later with the heads of the 'patriotic associations', including Kriebel of the Kampfbund, Kahr warned the 'patriotic associations' – by which he meant the Kampfbund – against independent action. Any attempt to impose a national government in Berlin had to be unified and follow prepared plans. Lossow stated he would go along with a rightist dictatorship if the chances of success were 51 per cent, but would have no truck with an ill-devised putsch. Seißer also underlined his support for Kahr and his readiness to put down a putsch by force.[225] It was plain that the triumvirate was not prepared to act against Berlin.

Lossow later claimed he told Hitler to wait two to three weeks until the other defence district commanders could be won over. Then the coup would be undertaken.[226] But Hitler was now faced with the thread slipping through his fingers. He was not prepared to wait any longer and risk losing the initiative. On the evening of 6 November, in direct response to the meeting addressed by Kahr (which he had not attended), Hitler met Kriebel (military head of the Kampfbund) and Dr Friedrich Weber (head of Bund Oberland), to discuss an attempt to persuade Kahr to reverse the opposition to the Kampfbund which he had shown since the beginning of November. Weber was commissioned to ask Ludendorff to arrange a meeting between Hitler and Kahr. But on 7 November, Kahr refused to meet Hitler either the following day, or after the meeting on 8 November in the Bürgerbräukeller which the General State Commissar would address.[227] It was plain, now as before, that a putsch would only be successful with the support of police and army. But whatever the outcome of the intended deliberations with Kahr, Hitler was determined to delay no longer.

At another meeting on the evening of 6 November with Scheubner-Richter, Theodor von der Pfordten (a member of the supreme court in Bavaria and shadowy figure in pre-putsch Nazi circles), and probably other advisers (though this is not certain), he decided to act – in the hope more than the certainty of forcing the triumvirate to support the coup.[228] The decision to strike was confirmed the next day, 7 November, at a meeting of Kampfbund leaders. Ludendorff later denied being present at the meeting, but apart from the Kampfbund leadership attending the meeting – Hitler, Weber, Kriebel, Scheubner-Richter and Göring – he was the only person fully initiated into what was to happen.[229] The number of people in the know was to be kept, at Hitler's insistence, to an absolute minimum. Plans were laid down for the action. Priority was given to the seizure of communications and takeover of police stations and town halls in the major cities of Bavaria. Communist, socialist, and trade union leaders were to be arrested.[230] Kriebel argued for the night of 10–11 November. Members of the government would be arrested in their beds, and the triumvirate forced to take up the offices foreseen for them in the national government.[231] The others rejected the suggestion because, it seems, of the difficulty of ensuring the arrest of all members of the government. Instead, after a good deal of discussion, Hitler's alternative plan was adopted. It was decided that the strike would be carried out on the following day, 8 November, when all the prominent figures in Munich would be assembled in the Bürgerbräukeller to hear an address from Kahr on the fifth anniversary of the November Revolution, fiercely denouncing Marxism. The meeting, arranged at short notice, was seen by the Kampfbund leadership as a threat, all the more so in the light of Kahr's refusal to meet Hitler before it took place. At the very least the meeting was seen as an attempt to strengthen Kahr's position and weaken the power of the Kampfbund. Whether they believed that Kahr intended to seal the breach with the nationalists by proclaiming the restoration of the Bavarian monarchy is uncertain. They were probably more concerned about the possibility of Kahr instigating the 'action' against Berlin without the Kampfbund's involvement – all the more since Hitler was aware of Lossow's comment on 24 October, that the 'march on Berlin' to erect a national dictatorship would take place at the latest within fourteen days.[232] At any rate, Hitler felt his hand forced by Kahr's meeting. If the Kampfbund were to lead the 'national revolution', there was nothing for it but to act on its own initiative immediately.[233] Much later, Hitler stated: 'Our opponents intended to proclaim a Bavarian revolution around the 12th of November ... I took the decision to strike four days earlier.'[234]

Late on the evening of 7 November, Hitler discussed the plans with his SA leaders, telling his bodyguard, Ulrich Graf, as he left the meeting, 'tomorrow at 8 o'clock it's happening'.[235] He returned to his apartment in Thierschstraße around 1a.m. Some eleven hours later, wearing his long trenchcoat and carrying his dog-whip, he was in excited mood in Rosenberg's office, looking for Göring. Hanfstaengl was there with Rosenberg, discussing the next edition of the *Völkischer Beobachter*. Hitler told them 'the moment for action has arrived', swore them to secrecy, and ordered them to be at his side that evening in the Bürgerbräukeller. They were to bring pistols.[236] Heß had been told earlier that morning what was planned. Pöhner, too, had been put in the picture.[237] Other Hitler intimates such as Hoffmann were left in the dark.[238] Drexler, the NSDAP's founder and honorary chairman, was actually on his way to Freising in the early evening of 8 November (where he thought he was appearing on the same speakers' platform as Hitler), when he bumped into Amann and Esser and was told that he did not need bother going to Freising; the meeting had been cancelled.[239]

Kahr had been reading out his prepared speech to the 3,000 or so packed into the Bürgerbräukeller for around half an hour when, around 8.30p.m., there was a disturbance at the entrance. Kahr broke off his speech. A body of men in steel helmets appeared. Hitler's stormtroopers had arrived. A heavy machine-gun was pushed into the hall.[240] People were standing on their seats trying to see what was happening as Hitler advanced through the hall, accompanied by two armed bodyguards, their pistols pointing at the ceiling. Hitler stood on a chair but, unable to make himself heard in the tumult, took out his Browning pistol and fired a shot through the ceiling.[241] He then announced that the national revolution had broken out, and that the hall was surrounded by 600 armed men. If there was trouble, he said, he would bring a machine-gun into the gallery.[242] The Bavarian government was deposed; a provisional Reich government would be formed. It was by this time around 8.45p.m. Hitler requested – though it was really an order – Kahr, Lossow, and Seißer to accompany him into the adjoining room. He guaranteed their safety. After some hesitation, they complied.[243] There was bedlam in the hall, but eventually Göring managed to make himself heard. He said the action was directed neither at Kahr nor at the army and police. People should stay calm and remain in their places. 'You've got your beer,' he added.[244] This quietened things somewhat, but most were still critical of what they were comparing with the theatricals that might happen in Latin American countries.

In the adjoining room, Hitler announced, waving his pistol about, that no one would leave without his permission. He declared the formation of a new Reich government, headed by himself. Ludendorff was to be in charge of the national army, Lossow would be Reichswehr Minister, Seißer Police Minister, Kahr himself would be head of state (*Landesverweser*), and Pöhner Minister President with dictatorial powers in Bavaria. He apologized for having to force the pace, but it had to be done: he had had to enable the triumvirate to act. If things went wrong, he had four bullets in his pistol – three for his collaborators, the last for himself.[245]

Hitler returned to the hall after about ten minutes amid renewed tumult. He repeated Göring's assurances that the action was not directed at the police and Reichswehr, but 'solely at the Berlin Jew government and the November criminals of 1918'. He put forward his proposals for the new governments in Berlin and Munich, now mentioning Ludendorff as 'leader, and chief with dictatorial power, of the German national army'.[246] He told the crowded hall that matters were taking longer than he had earlier predicted. 'Outside are Kahr, Lossow, and Seißer,' he declared. 'They are struggling hard to reach a decision. May I say to them that you will stand behind them?' As the crowd bellowed back its approval, Hitler, with his pronounced sense of the theatrical, announced in emotional terms: 'I can say this to you: Either the German revolution begins tonight or we will all be dead by dawn!'[247] By the time he had finished his short address – a 'rhetorical masterpiece' in the opinion of Karl Alexander von Müller, an eye-witness – the mood in the hall had swung completely in his favour.[248]

About an hour had passed since Hitler's initial entry into the hall before he and Ludendorff (who had meanwhile arrived, dressed in full uniform of the Imperial Army), together with the Bavarian ruling triumvirate, returned to the podium. Kahr, calm, face like a mask, spoke first, announcing to tumultuous applause that he had agreed to serve Bavaria as regent for the monarchy.[249] Hitler, with a euphoric expression resembling childlike delight, declared that he would direct the policy of the new Reich government, and warmly clasped Kahr's hand. Ludendorff, deadly earnest, spoke next, mentioning his surprise at the whole business. Lossow, wearing a somewhat impenetrable expression, and Seißer, the most agitated of the group, were pressed by Hitler into speaking. Pöhner finally promised cooperation with Kahr. Hitler shook hands once more with the whole ensemble.[250] He was the undoubted star of the show. It appeared to be his night.

From this point, however, things went badly wrong. The hurried improvisation of the planning, the hectic rush to prepare at only a day's notice, that had followed Hitler's impatient insistence that the putsch should be advanced to the evening of the Bürgerbräukeller meeting, now took its toll, determining the shambolic course of the night's events. Before the hall was cleared, those members of the government present in the Bürgerbräukeller tamely surrendered to arrest when Heß read out a list of names given to him by Hitler. News of a successful coup was relayed to the meeting at the Löwenbräukeller on the other side of the city centre, where Kampfbund troops were being addressed by Esser and Röhm. There was delirium in the hall. But outside, things were running less smoothly. Röhm did manage to take over the Reichswehr headquarters, though amazingly failed to take over the telephone switchboard, allowing Lossow to order the transport to Munich of loyalist troops in nearby towns and cities. Frick and Pöhner were also initially successful in taking control at police headquarters. Elsewhere, the situation was deteriorating rapidly. In a night of chaos, the putschists failed dismally, largely owing to their own disorganization, to take control of barracks and government buildings.[251] The early and partial successes were for the most part rapidly overturned. Neither the army nor the state police joined forces with the putschists.

Back at the Bürgerbräukeller, Hitler, too, was making his first mistake of the evening. Hearing reports of difficulties the putschists were encountering at the Engineers' Barracks, he decided to go there himself in what proved a vain attempt to intervene. Ludendorff was left in charge at the Bürgerbräukeller and, believing the word of officers and gentlemen, promptly let Kahr, Lossow, and Seißer depart. They were then free to renege on the promises extracted from them under duress by Hitler.[252]

A visitor to Munich staying in a city centre hotel that night recalled disturbances into the small hours as bands of young men in high spirits marched through the streets, convinced that the Bavarian revolution had been successful.[253] Placards were put up proclaiming Hitler as Reich Chancellor – the first time this designation had been attached to him.[254] Surprisingly, and a reflection of the haphazard and chaotic organization of the putsch, Hitler delayed putting out this proclamation of the 'national dictatorship' until 9 November.[255] Some time before midnight, he placed Julius Streicher, the Jew-baiting head of the NSDAP in Franconia, in charge of the party's organization and propaganda – presumably because he was expecting his hands to be more than full if developments went according to plan.[256] The reality was that by midnight, even if the putschist leaders had not by then fully realized it themselves, the ill-fated attempt to take control of the state had failed.

By late evening, Kahr, Lossow and Seißer were in positions to ensure the state authorities that they repudiated the putsch. All German radio stations were informed of this by Lossow at 2.55a.m.[257] By the early hours, it was becoming clear to the putschists themselves that the triumvirate and – far more importantly – the Reichswehr and state police opposed the coup.[258] At 5a.m. Hitler was still giving assurances that he was determined to fight and die for the cause – a sign that by this time at the latest he, too, had lost confidence in the success of the putsch.[259] Shortly before, on the way back to the Bürgerbräukeller from the Wehrkreiskommando, he had in fact already told Ulrich Graf that 'it's looking very serious for us'.[260] From what he later said, it was on returning to find that Ludendorff had let Kahr, Lossow, and Seißer go that he had immediately had the feeling that the cause was lost.[261] The mood in the beerhall itself was dispirited. The pall of stale tobacco smoke hung over the hundreds who listlessly lounged around the tables or stretched out wearily on chairs they had dragged together.[262] The mountains of bread rolls and gallons of beer which contributed in good measure to the bill of 11,347,000 Marks eventually sent to the Nazi Party for the evening's entertainment had by now largely been consumed.[263] And still there were no orders. No one knew what was happening.

The putschist leaders were themselves by this time unclear what to do next. They sat around arguing, while the government forces regrouped. There was no fall-back position. Hitler was as clueless as the others. He was far from in control of the situation. Clutching wildly at straws, he even contemplated driving to Berchtesgaden to win over Prinz Rupprecht, known to be hostile to the putschists.[264] Kriebel argued for armed resistance, organized from Rosenheim. Ludendorff said he was not prepared to see the affair end in the slush of a country road. Hitler, too, favoured armed resistance, but had few practical suggestions to offer, and was cut short in mid-peroration by Ludendorff. For hours, the putschist troops in the city received no orders from their leaders.[265] As the bitterly cold morning dawned, depressed troops began to drift off from the Bürgerbräukeller.[266] Around 8a.m. Hitler sent some of his SA men to seize bundles of 50-billion Mark notes direct from the printing press to keep his troops paid.[267] It was more or less the only practical action taken as the putsch started rapidly to crumble.

Only during the course of the morning did Hitler and Ludendorff come up with the idea of a demonstration march through the city. Ludendorff appararently made the initial suggestion.[268] The aim was predictably confused and unclear. 'In Munich, Nuremberg, Bayreuth, an immeasurable jubilation, an enormous enthusiasm would have broken out in the German Reich,' Hitler later remarked. 'And when the first division of the German national army had left the last square metre of Bavarian soil and stepped for the first time on to Thuringian land, we would have experienced the jubilation of the people there. People would have had to recognize that the German misery has an end, that redemption could only come about through a rising.'[269] It amounted to a vague hope that the march would stir popular enthusiasm for the putsch, and that the army, faced with the fervour of the mobilized masses and the prospect of firing on the war-hero Ludendorff, would change its mind.[270] The gathering acclaim of the masses and the support of the army would then pave the way for a triumphant march on Berlin.[271] Such was the wild illusion – gesture politics born out of pessimism, depression, and despair. Reality did not take long to assert itself.

Around noon, the column of around 2,000 men – many of them, including Hitler, armed – set out from the Bürgerbräukeller. Pistols at the ready, they confronted a small police cordon on the Ludwigsbrücke and under threat swept it aside, headed through Isartor and up the Tal to Marienplatz, in the centre of the city, and decided then to march to the War Ministry. They gained encouragement from throngs of shouting and waving supporters on the pavements. Some thought they were witnessing the arrival of the new government.[272] The putschists could not help but note, however, that many of the posters proclaiming the national revolution had already been ripped down or papered over with new directions from the ruling triumvirate. Earlier in the morning some bystanders had already started to make fun of the putsch. 'Has your mummy given you permission to play with such dangerous things here on the street?' one worker had asked, as Hans Frank's unit had taken up position with machine-guns not far from the Bürgerbräukeller.[273] The participants on the march knew the cause was lost. One of them remarked that it was like a funeral procession.[274]

At the top of the Residenzstraße, as it approaches Odeonsplatz, the marchers, accompanied by the occasional 'Heil' from the crowd and trying to keep up their spirits by singing the 'Sturm-Lied' (Storming Song) composed by Dietrich Eckart, encountered the second, and larger, police cordon. 'Here they come. Heil Hitler!' a bystander cried out.[275] Then shots rang out. Who fired the first shot was never fully clarified, but the evidence points to it being one of the putschists.[276] A furious gun-battle lasting almost half a minute followed. When the firing ceased, fourteen putschists and four policemen lay dead.[277]

The dead included one of the putsch architects, Erwin von Scheubner-Richter, who had been in the front line of the putsch leaders, linking arms with Hitler, just behind the standard-bearers. Had the bullet which killed Scheubner-Richter been a foot to the right, history would have taken a different course. As it was, Hitler either took instant evasive action, or was wrenched to the ground by Scheubner-Richter.[278] In any event, he dislocated his left shoulder.[279] Göring was among those injured, shot in the leg. He and a number of other leading putschists were able to escape over the Austrian border.[280] Some, including Streicher, Frick, Pöhner, Amann and Röhm, were immediately arrested. Ludendorff, who had emerged from the shoot-out totally unscathed, gave himself up and was released on his officer's word.[281]

Hitler himself was attended to by Dr Walter Schultze, chief of the Munich SA medical corps, pushed into his car, stationed nearby, and driven at speed from the scene of the action. He ended up at Hanfstaengl's home in Uffing, near the Staffelsee, south of Munich, where the police, on the evening of 11 November, found and arrested him.[282] While at Hanfstaengl's – Putzi himself had taken flight to Austria – he composed the first of his 'political testaments', placing the party chairmanship in Rosenberg's hands, with Amann as his deputy.[283] Hitler, according to Hanfstaengl's later account, based on his wife's testimony, was desolate on arrival in Uffing.[284] But later stories that he had to be restrained from suicide have no firm backing.[285] He was depressed but calm, dressed in a white nightgown, his injured left arm in a sling, when the police arrived to escort him to prison in the old fortress at Landsberg am Lech, a picturesque little town some forty miles west of Munich. Thirty-nine guards were on hand to greet him in his new place of residence. Graf Arco, the killer of Kurt Eisner, the Bavarian premier murdered in February 1919, was evicted from his spacious Cell no.7 to make room for the new, high-ranking prisoner.[286]

In Munich and other parts of Bavaria, the putsch fizzled out as rapidly as it had started. With the sympathies of a good part of the population in Munich behind the putschists, there were initial demonstrations there and elsewhere against the 'treachery' of Kahr.[287] But the adventure was over. Hitler was finished. At least, he should have been. The American consular representative in Munich, Robert Murphy, presumed Hitler would serve his sentence then be deported from Germany.[288] The author Stefan Zweig

later remarked: 'In this year 1923, the swastikas and stormtroops disappeared, and the name of Adolf Hitler fell back almost into oblivion.
Nobody thought of him any longer as a possible in terms of power.'[289]

VII

Like the high-point of a dangerous fever, the crisis had passed, then rapidly
subsided. The following months brought currency stabilization with the
introduction of the Rentenmark, regulation of the reparations issue through
the Dawes Plan (named after the American banker Charles G. Dawes, head
of the committee which established in 1924 a provisional framework for
the phased repayment of reparations, commencing at a low level and linked
to foreign loans for Germany), and the beginning of the political stabilization
that marked the end of the post-war turbulence and was to last until the
new economic shock-waves of the late 1920s. With Hitler in jail, the NSDAP
banned, and the *völkisch* movement split into its component factions, the
threat from the extreme Right lost its immediate potency.

Sympathies with the radical Right by no means disappeared. With 33 per
cent of the votes in Munich, the Völkischer Block (the largest grouping in
the now fractured *völkisch* movement) was the strongest party in the city
at the Landtag elections on 6 April 1924, gaining more votes than both the
Socialists and Communists put together.[290] At the Reichstag election on 4
May, the result was little different. The Völkischer Block won 28.5 per cent
of the vote in Munich, 17 per cent overall in the electoral region of Upper
Bavaria and Swabia, and 20.8 per cent in Franconia.[291] But the bubble had
burst. As Germany recovered and the Right remained in disarray, voters
deserted the *völkisch* movement. By the second Reichstag elections of 1924,
a fortnight before Hitler's release from Landsberg, the vote for the Völkischer
Block had dwindled to residual limits of 7.5 per cent in Franconia, 4.8 per
cent in Upper Bavaria/Swabia, and 3.0 per cent in Lower Bavaria (compared
with 10.2 per cent there seven months earlier).[292]

Bavaria, for all its continuing ingrained oddities, was no longer the boiling
cauldron of radical Right insurgency it had been between 1920 and 1923.
The paramilitary organizations had had their teeth drawn in the confrontation with the legal forces of the state. Without the support of the army,
they were shown to be little more than a paper tiger. In the aftermath of
the putsch, the Kampfbund organizations were dissolved, and the 'patriotic
associations' in general had their weaponry confiscated, a ban imposed

on their military exercises, and their activities greatly curtailed.[293] The triumvirate installed by the Bavarian government as a force on the Right to contain the wilder and even more extreme nationalist paramilitaries lost power and credibility through the putsch. Kahr, Lossow, and Seißer were all ousted by early 1924.[294] With the General State Commissariat terminated, conventional cabinet government under a new Minister President, Dr Heinrich Held – the leading figure in the Catholic establishment party in Bavaria, the BVP – and with it a degree of calm, returned to Bavarian politics.

Even now, however, the forces which had given Hitler his entrée into politics and enabled him to develop into a key factor on the Bavarian Right contrived to save him when his 'career' ought to have been over. The 'Hitler-Putsch' was, as we have seen, by no means merely Hitler's putsch. Hitler had provided the frenetic pressure for action without delay – a reflection of his 'all-or-nothing' temperament, but also of the need to prevent the dynamism of his movement ebbing away. The half-baked planning, dilettante improvisation, lack of care for detail all bore the imprint of Hitler's characteristic impulse to act without clear thought for the consequences, and without a fall-back position. But Hitler's influence on the undertaking of the putsch would not have been possible had the idea of a strike against Berlin not been kept alive within the Bavarian government and army leadership as well as among the different and competing factions of the paramilitary formations for months before the actual events of November 1923. Without the dogmatic anti-Berlin stance of the ruling groups in Bavaria, where shrill anti-democratic, anti-socialist, and anti-Prussian feeling combined to bracket together otherwise antagonistic forces to the general aim of counter-revolution, Hitler's all-or-nothing gamble in the Bürgerbräukeller could never have occurred. The Bavarian Reichswehr had colluded massively in the training and preparation of the forces which had tried to take over the state. And important personages had been implicated in the putsch attempt. Whatever their subsequent defence of their actions, the hands of Kahr, Lossow, and Seißer were dirty, while the war-hero General Ludendorff had been the spiritual figurehead of the entire enterprise. There was every reason, therefore, in the trial of the putsch leaders held in Munich between 26 February and 27 March 1924 – the sentences were read out four days later, on 1 April – to let the spotlight fall completely on Hitler.[295] He was only too glad to play the role assigned to him.

Hitler's first reaction to his indictment had been very different to his later triumphalist performance in the Munich court. He had initially refused to say anything, and announced that he was going on hunger-strike. At this time, he plainly saw everything as lost. According to the prison psychologist – though speaking many years after the event – Hitler stated: 'I've had enough. I'm finished. If I had a revolver, I would take it.'[296] Drexler later claimed that he himself had dissuaded Hitler from his intention to commit suicide.[297]

By the time the trial opened, Hitler's stance had changed diametrically. He was allowed to turn the court-room into a stage for his own propaganda, accepting full responsibility for what had happened, not merely justifying but glorifying his role in attempting to overthrow the Weimar state. This was in no small measure owing to his threats to expose the complicity in treasonable activity of Kahr, Lossow, and Seißer – and in particular the role of the Bavarian Reichswehr.

The way Hitler would exploit his trial could scarcely have come as a surprise to the Bavarian authorities. It was signalled as early as two days after his arrest, during his interrogation by Hans Ehard, a brilliant lawyer who, after 1945, became Minister President of Bavaria. At first, Hitler had refused all comment on the putsch attempt. Ehard had said that his silence might prolong his internment and that of his fellow-prisoners. Hitler had replied that there was more at stake for him than for the others. 'It was a matter for him of justifying before history his action and his mission (*sein Tun und seine Sendung*); what the court's position would be was a matter of indifference to him. He denied the court any right to pass judgement on him.' He then issued a veiled threat. He would save his best trump cards to play in the court-room. And he would call numerous witnesses, summoning them only during the trial to prevent prior notification.

Ehard rapidly gave up the idea of taking an official statement. The typewriter that had been brought in was taken away. In five hours of patient questioning and listening to lengthy political speeches in reply, the subtle lawyer gradually prompted Hitler to open up to a degree, even if remaining cautious and reserved. When he spoke, Hitler added – acknowledging his major strength – he would find the right words, whereas he could not do so by writing it down. His responses to Ehard gave plain clues to the way he would behave before the court.

He denied that he had committed high treason, since 'the crime of November 1918' had not been expunged and the constitution based on this 'crime' could have no validity. But if the constitution *were* taken to have legal force, then acts such as the deposition of the Bavarian government of Hoffmann in 1920 or the creation in 1923 of the General State Commissariat of Kahr with near dictatorial powers ought also to be considered high treason. Ultimately, however, there was a natural right of a people, higher than the formal right of a constitution, to self-defence against the wishes of an incapable parliament.

Hitler now turned to the role played by Kahr, Lossow and Seißer in the putsch, and hinted strongly at damaging revelations. The triumvirate had, he claimed, willingly cooperated in 'his' high treason. He would prove that they had not been feigning consent in the Bürgerbräukeller, but had had the full intention of implementing the agreement reached, and had only broken the agreement through persuasion and, in part, compulsion once they had left the beerhall. He had foreseen the possibility of this, which is why he had given the order that they should not be permitted to leave. Ludendorff's trust in an officer's word, during his own temporary absence from the Bürgerbräukeller, had then seen them released – something he himself would never have allowed. This had dismayed him on his return to the beerhall, and he had in that moment had the feeling that the cause was lost. But the triumvirate had not only gone along with his action on the evening of 8 November. What they had agreed with him that evening had been prepared together with him for months. They had discussed at length the 'march to Berlin', down to points of fine detail. There was full agreement. They and he had wanted and worked for identical aims. 'Hitler offers the prospect,' noted Ehard, 'of opening up the entire question of the "secret mobilization"' – the support and training of the paramilitary forces by the Bavarian Reichswehr in preparation for the planned *coup d'état*.[298]

This was a telling point. The ruling forces in Bavaria did what they could to limit potential damage. The first priority was to make sure that the trial was held under Bavarian jurisdiction. In strict legality, the trial ought not to have taken place in Munich at all, but at the Reich Court in Leipzig. Hitler even initially favoured this, since he thought the Bavarian court would be biased in favour of the triumvirate. 'In Leipzig,' he told Ehard, 'various gentlemen would enter the court-room perhaps still as witnesses, but would certainly leave it as prisoners. In Munich that will naturally not happen.'[299] However, the Reich government gave way to pressure from the Bavarian government. The trial was set for the People's Court in Munich.[300] And Hitler's early apprehension turned out to be entirely misconceived.

Kahr had hoped to avoid any trial, or at least have no more than a perfunctory one where the indicted would plead guilty but claim mitigating grounds of patriotism. Since some at least of the putschists would not agree, this course of action had to be dropped. But it seems highly probable that the accused were offered leniency for such a proposal even to have been considered.[301] Hitler had, at any rate, become confident about the outcome. He still held a trump card in his hand. When Hanfstaengl visited him in his cell in the courthouse, during the trial, he showed no fear of the verdict. 'What can they do to me?' he asked. 'I only need to come out with a bit more, especially about Lossow, and there's the big scandal. Those in the know are well aware of that.'[302] This, and the attitude of the presiding judge and his fellow judges, explains Hitler's self-confident appearance at the trial.

Among those indicted alongside Hitler were Ludendorff, Pöhner, Frick, Weber (of Bund Oberland), Röhm and Kriebel. But the indictment itself was emphatic that 'Hitler was the soul of the entire enterprise'.[303] Judge Neithardt, the president of the court, had reputedly stated before the trial that Ludendorff – 'still the only plus' that Germany possessed – would be acquitted. The judge replaced a damaging record of Ludendoff's first interrogation by one which indicated his ignorance about the putsch preparations.[304] Hitler, meanwhile, was given the freedom of the court-room. One journalist attending the trial described it as a 'political carnival'. He compared the deference shown to the defendants with the brusque way those arraigned for their actions in the Räterepublik had been handled. He heard one of the judges, after Hitler's first speech, remark: 'What a tremendous chap, this Hitler!' Hitler was allowed to appear in his suit, not prison garb, sporting his Iron Cross, First Class. Ludendorff, not held in prison, arrived in a luxury limousine.[305] Dr Weber, though under arrest, was allowed to take a Sunday afternoon walk round Munich. The extraordinary bias of the presiding judge was later most severely criticized both in Berlin and by the Bavarian government, irritated at the way attacks on the Reichswehr and state police had been allowed without contradiction. Judge Neithardt was informed in no uncertain terms during the trial of the 'embarrassing impression' left by allowing Hitler to speak for four hours. His only response was that it was impossible to interrupt his torrent of words. Hitler was also allowed the freedom to interrogate witnesses – above all Kahr, Lossow, and Seißer – at length, frequently deviating into politically loaded statements.[306]

When the verdicts were read out, on 1 April 1924, Ludendorff was duly acquitted – which he took as an insult. Hitler, along with Weber, Kriebel and Pöhner, was sentenced to a mere five years' imprisonment for high treason (less the four months and two weeks he had already been in custody), and a fine of 200 Gold Marks (or a further twenty days' imprisonment). The others indicted received even milder sentences.[307] The lay judges, as Hitler later hinted, had only been prepared to accept a verdict of 'guilty' on condition that he received the mildest sentence, with the prospect of early release.[308] The court explained why it rejected the deportation of Hitler under the terms of the 'Protection of the Republic Act': 'Hitler is a German-Austrian. He considers himself to be a German. In the opinion of the court, the meaning and intention of the terms of section 9, para II of the Law for the Protection of the Republic cannot apply to a man who thinks and feels as German as Hitler, who voluntarily served for four and a half years in the German army at war, who attained high military honours through outstanding bravery in the face of the enemy, was wounded, suffered other damage to his health, and was released from the military into the control of the District Command Munich I.'[309]

Even on the conservative Right in Bavaria, the conduct of the trial and sentences prompted amazement and disgust.[310] In legal terms, the sentence was nothing short of scandalous. No mention was made in the verdict of the four policemen shot by the putschists; the robbery of 14,605 billion paper Marks (the equivalent of around 28,000 Gold Marks) was entirely played down; the destruction of the offices of the SPD newspaper *Münchener Post* and the taking of a number of Social Democratic city councillors as hostages were not blamed on Hitler; and no word was made of the text of a new constitution, found in the pocket of the dead putschist von der Pfordten.[311] Nor did the judge's reasons for the sentence make any reference to the fact that Hitler was still technically within the probationary period for good behaviour imposed on him in the sentence for breach of the peace in January 1922. Legally, he was not eligible for any further probation.[312]

The judge in that first Hitler trial was the same person as the judge presiding over his trial for high treason in 1924: the nationalist sympathizer Georg Neithardt.[313]

Hitler returned to Landsberg to begin his light sentence in conditions more akin to those of a hotel than a penitentiary. The windows of his large, comfortably furnished room on the first floor afforded an expansive view over the attractive countryside. Dressed in lederhosen, he could relax with a newspaper in an easy wickerchair, his back to a laurel wreath provided by admirers, or sit at a large desk sifting through the mounds of correspondence he received. He was treated with great respect by his jailers, some of whom secretly greeted him with 'Heil Hitler', and accorded every possible privilege. Gifts, flowers, letters of support, encomiums of praise, all poured in. He received more visitors than he could cope with – over 500 of them before he eventually felt compelled to restrict access. Around forty fellow-prisoners, some of them volunteer internees, able to enjoy almost all the comforts of normal daily life, fawned on him.[314] He read of the demonstration on 23 April, to celebrate his thirty-fifth birthday three days earlier, of 3,000 National Socialists, former front soldiers, and supporters of the *völkisch* movement in the Bürgerbräukeller 'in honour of the man who had lit the present flame of liberation and *völkisch* consciousness in the German people'.[315] Under the impact of the star-status that the trial had brought him, and the Führer cult that his supporters had begun to form around him, he began to reflect on his political ideas, his 'mission', his 'restart' in politics once his short sentence was over, and pondered the lessons to be learnt from the putsch.

The débâcle at the Bürgerbräukeller and its denouement next day at the Feldherrnhalle taught Hitler once and for all that an attempt to seize power in the face of opposition from the armed forces was doomed. He felt justified in his belief that propaganda and mass mobilization, not paramilitary putschism, would open the path to the 'national revolution'. Consequently, he distanced himself from Röhm's attempts to revitalize in new guise the Kampfbund and to build a type of people's militia.[316] Ultimately, the different approaches, as well as power-ambitions, of Hitler and Röhm would lead to the murderous split in 1934. It would be going too far, however, to presume that Hitler had renounced the idea of a takeover of the state by force in favour of the 'legal path'. Certainly, he subsequently had to profess a commitment to legality in order to involve himself in politics again. And later, electoral success appeared in any case to offer the best strategy to win power. But the putschist approach was never given up. It continued, as the lingering problems with the SA would indicate, to coexist alongside the proclaimed 'legal' way. But, Hitler was adamant, on any future occasion it could only be with, not against, the Reichswehr.

Hitler's experience was to lead to the last, and not least, of the lessons he would draw from his 'apprenticeship years': that to be the 'drummer' was not enough; and that to be more than that meant he needed not only complete mastery in his own movement but, above all, greater freedom from external dependencies, from competing groupings on the Right, from paramilitary organizations he could not fully control, from the bourgeois politicians and army figures who had smoothed his political rise, used him, then dropped him when it suited them.[317]

The ambivalence about his intended role after the 'national revolution' was still present in his comments during his trial. He insisted that he saw Ludendorff as the 'military leader of the coming Germany' and 'leader of the coming great showdown'. But he claimed that he himself was 'the political leader of this young Germany'. The precise division of labour had, he said, not been determined.[318] In his closing address to the court, Hitler returned to the leadership question – though still in somewhat vague and indeterminate fashion. He referred to Lossow's remarks to the court that during discussions in spring 1923 he had thought Hitler had merely wanted 'as propagandist and awakener (*Weckrufer*) to arouse the people'. 'How petty do small men think,' went on Hitler. He did not see the attainment of a ministerial post as worthy of a great man. What he wanted, he said, was to be the destroyer of Marxism. *That* was his task. 'Not from modesty did I want at that time to be the drummer. That is the highest there is (*das Höchste*). The rest is unimportant (*eine Kleinigkeit*).'[319] When it came to it, he had demanded two things: that he should be given the leadership of the political struggle; and that the organizational leadership should go to 'the hero . . . who in the eyes of the entire young Germany is called to it'. Hitler hinted – though did not state explicitly – that this was to have been Ludendorff.[320] On the other hand, in his address to Kampfbund leaders a fortnight before the putsch, he had seemed to envisage Ludendorff as no more than the reorganizer of the future national army.[321] Then again, the proclamation put up during the putsch itself over Hitler's name as Reich Chancellor appeared to indicate that the headship of government was the position he foresaw for himself, sharing dictatorial power with Ludendorff as head of state (*Reichsverweser*, or regent).[322]

Whatever the ambivalence, real or simply tactical, still present in Hitler's remarks at the trial, it soon gave way to clarity about his self-image. For in Landsberg the realization dawned on Hitler: he was not the 'drummer' after all; he was the predestined Leader himself.

7

EMERGENCE OF THE LEADER

'The secret of this personality resides in the fact that in it the deepest of what lies dormant in the soul of the German people has taken shape in full living features . . . That has appeared in Adolf Hitler: the living incarnation of the nation's yearning.'

Georg Schott, *Das Volksbuch vom Hitler*, 1924

'The combination of theoretician, organizer, and leader in one person is the rarest thing that can be found on this earth; this combination makes the great man.'

Hitler, in *Mein Kampf*

The year that ought to have seen the spectre of Hitler banished for good brought instead – though this could scarcely be clearly seen at the time – the genesis of his later absolute pre-eminence in the *völkisch* movement and his ascendancy to supreme leadership. In retrospect, the year 1924 can be seen as the time when, like a phoenix arising from the ashes, Hitler could begin his emergence from the ruins of the broken and fragmented *völkisch* movement to become eventually the absolute leader with total mastery over a reformed, organizationally far stronger, and internally more cohesive Nazi Party. The months of his imprisonment saw his rivals for the leadership on the radical *völkisch* Right attempt, and fail, to assert their dominance. Without him, any semblance of unity collapsed. As the Reichstag elections of December 1924 just before his release showed, the *völkisch* Right had by then been all but obliterated as a serious factor in German politics.

Within some fractions of the splintered *völkisch* movement, however, Hitler became almost deified after his trial in the spring. Admiration for him in *völkisch* circles stretched, indeed, far beyond the effusions of the hard-core fanatics. But it was such effusions that were ceaselessly at work on Hitler's egomania, which, as the trial itself had demonstrated, had only temporarily been dented by the putsch failure. The fan-mail that teemed daily into Landsberg; the fawning disciples who hung on his every word; the sycophancy of his guards; the non-stop flow of admiring visitors: such adulation could not fail to affect someone with self-belief transcending all normal bounds, someone already looking for 'historical greatness' and by no means averse to hearing from his adoring following that he possessed it.

The public projection of greatness on to Hitler at this time by his followers and admirers met with no more unconstrained expression than in Georg Schott's *Das Volksbuch vom Hitler*, published in 1924. Schott's eulogy included sub-headings such as: 'The Prophetic Person', 'The Genius', 'The Religious Person', 'The Humble One', 'The Loyal One', 'The Man of Will', 'The Political Leader', 'The Educator', 'The Awakener', and 'The Liberator'. In a dense text full of literary and religious allusions, Hitler was turned into nothing short of a demi-god. 'There are words,' wrote Schott, 'which a person does not draw from within himself, which a god gave him to declare. To these words belongs this confession of Adolf Hitler . . . "I am the political leader of the young Germany".' Just as mystically, Schott rhapsodized in equally pseudo-religious terminology about the person of Hitler: 'The secret of this personality resides in the fact that in it the deepest of what lies dormant in the soul of the German people has taken shape in full living features . . . That has appeared in Adolf Hitler: the living incarnation of the nation's yearning.'[1]

As his movement was dissolving into the myriad of rival factions that offered apparent proof of his indispensability, the enforced idleness in Landsberg and his inability to direct events outside led Hitler to the writing of *Mein Kampf* and the 'rationalization' and partial modification of his political ideas. The process of writing the first volume of his book cemented and rounded off his 'world-view'. It also reinforced his unbounded, narcissistic self-belief. It gave him absolute conviction in his own near-messianic qualities and mission, the feeling of certainty that he was destined to become the 'Great Leader' the nation awaited, who would expunge the 'criminal betrayal' of 1918, restore Germany's might and power, and create a reborn 'Germanic State of the German nation'.[2] By the time he left Landsberg, the transition – in his own mind, as in that of his followers – from 'drummer' to 'leader' was complete.

The fragmentation of the *völkisch* movement in Hitler's absence, the extraordinary adulation he received from those who already saw greatness in him, and the recognition in himself of 'great' leadership were closely interlinked. By the date of his release from Landsberg, on 20 December 1924, the basis for his later incontestable position as Leader had been laid.

I

Nothing could have demonstrated more plainly how indispensable Hitler was to the *völkisch* Right than the thirteen months of his imprisonment, the 'leaderless time' of the movement. With Hitler removed from the scene and, from June 1924, withdrawing from all involvement in politics to concentrate on the writing of *Mein Kampf*, the *völkisch* movement descended into squabbling factionalism and internecine strife. By courtesy of Bavarian justice, Hitler had been allowed to use the court-room to portray himself as the hero of the Right for his role in the putsch. Competing individuals and groups felt compelled to assert Hitler's authority and backing for their actions. But in Hitler's absence, this was insufficient in itself to ensure success.[3] Moreover, Hitler was often inconsistent, contradictory, or unclear in his views on developments. His claim to a leadership position could not be ignored, and was not disputed. Any claim to an exclusive leadership position was, however, upheld only by a minority in the *völkisch* movement. And as long as Hitler was in no position directly to influence developments, the narrow core of his fervent devotees was largely marginalized even within the broad *völkisch* Right, often at war with each other, and split on tactics, strategy, and ideology. By the time of his release in December 1924, the Reichstag elections of that month had reflected the catastrophic decline of support for the *völkisch* movement, which had come to form little more than a group of disunited nationalist and racist sects on the extreme fringe of the political spectrum.

Just before his arrest on 11 November 1923, Hitler had placed Alfred Rosenberg, editor of the *Völkischer Beobachter*, in charge of the banned party during his absence, to be supported by Esser, Streicher, and Amann.[4] Like a number of leading Nazis (including Heß, Scheubner-Richter, and Hitler himself), Rosenberg's origins did not lie within the boundaries of the German Reich. Born into a well-off bourgeois family in Reval (now Tallinn), Estonia, the introverted self-styled party 'philosopher', dogmatic but dull, arrogant and cold, one of the least charismatic and least popular of Nazi leaders, united other party bigwigs only in their intense dislike of him.[5] Distinctly lacking in leadership qualities, he was scarcely an obvious choice, and was as surprised as others were by Hitler's nomination.[6] Possibly, as is usually surmised, it was precisely Rosenberg's lack of leadership ability that commended itself to Hitler.[7] Certainly, a less likely rival to Hitler could scarcely be imagined. But this would presume that Hitler, in the traumatic aftermath of the failed putsch, was capable of lucid, machiavellian planning, that he anticipated what would happen and actually wanted and expected his movement to fall apart in his absence.[8] A more likely explanation is that he made a hasty and ill-conceived decision, under pressure and in a depressed frame of mind, to entrust the party's affairs to a member of his Munich coterie whose loyalty was beyond question. Rosenberg was, in fact, one of the few leading figures in the Movement still available.[9] Scheubner-Richter was dead. Others had scattered in the post-putsch turmoil, or had been arrested. Even – though Hitler could scarcely have known this – the three trusted lieutenants he had designated to support Rosenberg were temporarily out of action. Esser had fled to Austria, Amann was in jail, and Streicher was preoccupied with matters in Nuremberg. Rosenberg was probably no more than a hastily chosen least bad option.

Whatever the reasoning, Rosenberg soon found that his writ did not run: simply calling on Hitler's authority did not help. One immediate sign was the insistence of the acting head of the now illegal SA, Major Walter Buch, that the organization of the Storm Section, while retaining its loyalty to Hitler, would not be subjected to the party's leadership and would keep out of party-political conflict.[10] This was the direct opposite of Hitler's instructions, that the SA would be subordinated to the party.[11] Rosenberg also found in any case that there was no party organization to speak of. The haphazard way in which the party had developed before the putsch had left it unprepared for illegality. Close coordination even of groups in southern Bavaria was now impossible. Rosenberg devised the code-name 'Rolf Eidhalt' – 'Keep the Oath' – as an anagram of 'Adolf Hitler', and used it in letters passed on by courier.[12] Camouflage organizations – hiking clubs and the like – were established. Local party groups were sent copies of postcards carrying a picture of Hitler which, they were told, had to be sold in millions 'as a symbol of our Leader', since 'the name of Adolf Hitler must always be kept alive for the German people'.[13] Successor newspapers to the banned *Völkischer Beobachter* attempted to keep the flame alight among Nazi followers. Hitler himself contributed articles and drawings to one clandestine production smuggled out of Landsberg.[14] Whatever the difficulties of communication at first, any cloak-and-dagger activity was soon shown to be unnecessary. The authorities proved willing to permit the creation of obvious successor organizations to the banned NSDAP.[15]

On 1 January 1924, Rosenberg founded the Großdeutsche Volksgemeinschaft (GVG, 'Greater German National Community'), intended to serve, during the NSDAP's ban, as its successor organization.[16] By the summer, Rosenberg had been ousted and the GVG had fallen under the control of Hermann Esser (returned in May from his exile in Austria) and Julius Streicher.[17] But the coarse personalities, insulting behaviour and clumsy methods of Esser and Streicher merely succeeded in alienating many Hitler followers. Far from all Hitler loyalists, in any case, had joined the GVG. Gregor Strasser, for example, a Landshut apothecary who was to emerge in the post-putsch era as the leading figure in the party after Hitler, joined the Deutschvölkische Freiheitspartei (DVFP), a rival *völkisch* organization headed by Albrecht Graefe, formerly a member of the conservative DNVP, with its stronghold in Mecklenburg and its headquarters in Berlin.

Graefe and two other dissidents from the DNVP, Reinhold Wulle and Wilhelm Henning, all members of the Reichstag with good connections to former officers and businessmen, had formed the DVFP in Berlin in the late autumn of 1922, wanting a more radical *völkisch* line than that offered by the DNVP. Hitler had been forced to a temporary agreement with Graefe in March 1923, allowing the DVFP dominance in northern Germany, with the south retained for the NSDAP. A further agreement, reaffirming that of March and recommending close cooperation between the two parties, had been signed by Hermann Esser on 24 October 1923. It was subsequently claimed by Rosenberg and others that Esser had acted without Hitler's knowledge, and that the latter had not disowned the pact only to save Esser's face. But since Hitler had agreed to the March arrangement, and since it is scarcely probable that Esser could or would have taken such a step without his approval, this is unlikely.[18]

The agreement had not caused any conflict before the putsch, and, in fact, Graefe had taken part in the march to the Feldherrnhalle on 9 November. But conflict was not long deferred once Hitler was in prison. The DVFP had been less affected by proscription than had the NSDAP. In contrast to the disarray within the Hitler Movement, Graefe and the other DVFP leaders were still at liberty to control a party organization left largely in place. And though the DVFP leaders lauded Hitler's actions in the putsch in an attempt to win over his supporters, they were actually keen to take advantage of the situation and to establish their own supremacy. That the DVFP leaders advocated electoral participation by the *völkisch* movement added to the growing conflict. A move towards a parliamentary strategy alienated many Nazis, and was vehemently opposed by NSDAP diehards in northern Germany. Their spokesman, Ludolf Haase, the leader of the Göttingen branch, was increasingly critical of Rosenberg's authority, and above all keen to keep the north German NSDAP from the clutches of Graefe. Rosenberg's position was still further undermined when a draft agreement with Graefe, allowing for unified party organization and combined leadership, which the acting Nazi leader had turned down at a secret meeting in Salzburg at the end of January, was then accepted after all, at Ludendorff's insistence, on 24 February. This was with Hitler's express permission (though stipulation that the agreement should last for only six months). It was a further sign of how little clear and unequivocal guidance those left trying to run a party banned and in disarray were given by their imprisoned leader. Immediately after this, on the day before the trial of the putschists began, Ludendorff publicly recommended support for Graefe as his representative in north Germany, thereby lending his prestige to the DVFP and at the same time tacitly claiming leadership of the *völkisch* movement.[19]

Those *völkisch* groups that were prepared, however reluctantly, to enter parliament in order to be in a position one day to destroy it, decided to enter into electoral alliances to allow them to contest the series of regional (Landtag) elections that began in February, and the Reichstag election – the first of two that year – on 4 May 1924. Hitler was opposed to this strategy. As Rudolf Heß, on Hitler's behalf, was still explaining over a year later: 'Herr H. was against participating in the elections from the first moment onwards, and said this clearly and plainly to a number of gentlemen, including His Excellency L[udendorff]. He was convinced that the Movement was not mature enough, that we also had to stay true to our principle of anti-parliamentarism, and that money was only squandered pointlessly.'[20] Hitler's opposition made no difference. The decision to participate went ahead. It seemed to be borne out by the results. In the February Landtag elections in Mecklenburg-Schwerin, Graefe's stronghold, the DVFP won thirteen out of sixty-four seats. And on 6 April in the Bavarian Landtag elections, the Völkischer Block, as the electoral alliance called itself there, won 17 per cent of the vote.[21]

Even after these results, Hitler was still letting it be known that he opposed the activities of the Völkischer Block in the forthcoming Reichstag elections. Yet at the very same time he allowed his name to go over an electoral proclamation of the Block. And soon after the election, he told Kurt Lüdecke that policy would have to change, and that 'we shall have to hold our noses and enter the Reichstag against the Catholic and Marxist deputies'.[22] How he viewed this was made plain a year or so later by Rudolf Heß, replying for Hitler to a letter from a party member: 'Herr Hitler is of the view that, after parliament was entered against his will, participation in parliament has to be seen as one of many methods of combating the present system, including parliamentarism. But participation should not be "positive cooperation", as was unfortunately carried out by the *völkisch* parliamentarists with very little success, but only be through the fiercest opposition and obstruction, through constant criticism of the existing system in parliament. Parliament, or better still parliamentarism, should be taken to absurdity in parliament.'[23]

The Reichstag election results had, it seems, helped persuade Hitler that the parliamentary tactic, pragmatically and purposefully deployed, promised to pay dividends. The *völkisch* vote, bolstered by the publicity and outcome of the Hitler trial, had stood up well, with a result of 6.5 per cent and thirty-two seats in the Reichstag.[24] The results in Graefe's territory of Mecklenburg (20.8 per cent) and Bavaria (16 per cent) were particularly good.[25] That only ten of the *völkisch* Reichstag members were from the NSDAP and twenty-two from the DVFP gave some indication, however, of the relative weakness of the remnants of the Hitler Movement at the time.[26]

In the first of two visits he paid to Landsberg in May, Ludendorff, whose contacts in north Germany were extensive despite his continued residence near Munich, seized the moment to try to persuade Hitler to agree to a merger of the NSDAP and DVFP fractions in the Reichstag, and in the second meeting even to full unity of the two parties. Hitler equivocated. He agreed in principle, but stipulated preconditions that needed to be discussed with Graefe. One of these, it transpired, was that the headquarters of the movement would be based in Munich.[27] The meeting with Graefe did not take place, however, before the Reichstag deputies of the two parties came together in Berlin on 24 May and agreed to merge for parliamentary purposes under the name of the National Socialist Freedom Party (Nationalsozial-istische Freiheitspartei, NSFP). Ludendorff compromised Hitler's position by announcing in a press release that the latter supported the creation of a single, unified party. Hitler was in difficulties because, though he had always insisted on a separate and unique identity for the NSDAP, there was the danger, following the electoral success of the Völkischer Block, that such an uncompromising stance would seem less than compelling to his supporters. Moreover, the DVFP was the stronger of the two parties, as the election had shown, and Ludendorff was now generally regarded as the leading figure in the *völkisch* movement.[28]

Hitler's weakness, reflected in his habit of telling people what they wanted to hear, was revealed in a hastily arranged visit to Landsberg by a four-man north German Nazi delegation, led by Haase, at the end of May. Hitler insisted that the agreement with the DVFP of 24 February had been presented to him as a *fait accompli*, that he had opposed electoral participation but had been unable to prevent it, and that unity with the DVFP went no further than the combining of the Reichstag fractions.[29] Ludendorff immediately cast doubt on Hitler's sincerity in a published statement on 11 June flatly contradicting such a version, and stressing Hitler's acceptance of the need for a merger.[30] However, the result of the visit by Haase's delegation was the establishment on 3 June 1924 in Hamburg by the north German Hitler loyalists of a 'Directorate' under the leadership of Dr Adalbert Volck, a lawyer based in Lüneburg whose embracing of the *völkisch* movement was strongly coloured by his Baltic origins.[31] The Directorate totally rejected any notion of a merger with the DVFP which, it felt, would lead to it being sucked into 'parliamentarism' and becoming a party like others. Consequently, the Directorate aimed to be a tightly knit, centrally controlled organization, loyal to Hitler and holding to his principles until he could be released to take up the reins again.[32]

Even so, some north German Nazis were, not surprisingly, confused and uncertain about Hitler's position regarding any merger. In a letter of 14 June, Haase sought confirmation that Hitler rejected a merger of the two parties. Replying two days later, Hitler denied that he had fundamentally rejected a merger, though he had stipulated preconditions for such a step. He acknowledged the opposition among many Nazi loyalists to a merger with the DVFP, which, he also pointed out, had made plain its rejection of some of the old guard of the party. Under the circumstances, he went on, he could no longer intervene or accept responsibility. He had decided, therefore, to withdraw from politics until he could properly lead again. He refused henceforth to allow his name to be used in support of any political position, and asked for no further political letters to be sent to him.[33] A week later, Hermann Fobke, a young Nazi from the Göttingen area, imprisoned with Hitler in Landsberg and acting as his general factotum and go-between with the north German faction, tried to assuage Haase by assuring him of Hitler's support for the opposition of the north German National Socialists to the DVFP. 'All in all,' Fobke summed up, 'H[itler] thinks things have gone so hopelessly off the rails that he is in no doubt that he will have to begin completely afresh when he is free. But in such a case, he is very optimistic and of the view that he will have firm control again within a few days.' Fobke could not resist, however, pointing out his own disappointment at Hitler's indifference to the 'cries of distress' of the north German NSDAP.[34]

Hitler announced his decision to withdraw from politics in the press on 7 July. He requested no further visits to Landsberg by his supporters, a request he felt compelled to repeat a month later. The press announcement gave as his reasons the impossibility of accepting practical responsibility for developments while he was in Landsberg, 'general overwork', and the need to concentrate on the writing of his book (the first volume of *Mein Kampf*).[35] A not insignificant additional factor, as the opposition press emphasized, was Hitler's anxiety to do nothing to jeopardize his chances of parole, which could be granted from 1 October.[36] The occasion for his decision was Ludendorff's press statement on 11 June which had embarrassed and angered Hitler by claiming, despite the latter's caution and equivocation, that he openly supported the merger of the two parties.[37] Fobke told Haase on 23 June that the decision to withdraw from politics had been 'born out of the anger over this statement'.[38] However, the dominant reason was doubtless the one he had given Haase: his impotence at controlling developments from within Landsberg. The Ludendorff press release had simply been the last indication of this impotence. His withdrawal was not a machiavellian strategy to exacerbate the split that was already taking place, increase confusion, and thereby bolster his image as a symbol of unity.[39] This was the outcome, not the cause. In June 1924, the outcome could not be clearly foreseen. Hitler acted from weakness, not strength. He was being pressed from all sides to take a stance on the growing schism. His equivocation frustrated his supporters. But any clear stance would have alienated one side or the other. His decision not to decide was characteristic. 'Hitler habitually rationalizes his choices,' commented Lüdecke. 'He was prepared to risk everything rather than delegate a portion of his personal authority while he remained confined.'[40]

Hitler's frustration was also increased by his inability, despite his outright disapproval, to curtail Röhm's determination to build up a nationwide paramilitary organization called the Frontbann. This was intended to absorb and unify other existing paramilitary leagues of the völkisch movement, including the SA and the other banned units of the former Kampfbund, and to be placed under the military leadership of Ludendorff. Hitler was allergic to the inevitable loss of control over the SA which would certainly follow and concerned to avoid his own dependence, as before the putsch, on leaders of paramilitary organizations. Above all, he was anxious that what might be seen as his renewed involvement in paramilitary politics would hinder his chances of early parole and encourage moves to deport him back to Austria. Unable to deter Röhm – already freed on 1 April, bound over on probation, his derisory fifteen-month prison sentence for his part in the putsch set aside on condition of good behaviour – Hitler ended their last meeting before he left Landsberg, on 17 June, by telling him that, having laid down the leadership of the National Socialist Movement, he wished to hear no more about the Frontbann. Röhm nevertheless simply ignored Hitler and pressed on with his plans, looking to Ludendorff for patronage and protection.[41]

Following Hitler's press statement about his withdrawal from all political involvement, Ludendorff and Graefe moved quickly, with their own press release two days later, to claim the leadership of the *völkisch* movement 'until the liberated hero of Munich can again step into their circle as the third leader'. Hitler, they stated, had asked them to take over the leadership in his place. At the same time, Rosenberg had resigned his position, and Gregor Strasser had been brought into the Reich Leadership (*Reichs-führerschaft*) of the NSFP along with Ludendorff and Graefe for the duration of Hitler's internment. A conference planned to take place in Weimar in mid-August would bring unity in the *völkisch* movement, they added.[42] This horrified the northern Nazis. The Directorate sought clarification from Fobke. They were told that Hitler had given up his leadership only during his imprisonment, had delegated his powers to no one, and had had no part in the appointment of Strasser to the Reich Leadership, though this step had met with his approval.[43] The Directorate's leader, Volck, once more, on 18 July, made plain where the northern National Socialists stood on questions of a merger: 'Our programme consists of two words: "Adolf Hitler".'[44] But a meeting of eighty NSDAP representatives from across Germany at Weimar on 20 July, gathered to discuss the merger issue (which would explicitly arise in the conference in the same town the following month) and the question of a parliamentary strategy, and with Ludendorff as guest of honour, ended in acrimony, recrimination, disorder, and greater division than ever.[45]

Volck immediately compiled a highly critical report of events, which he sent to Landsberg.[46] Hitler's reply, through his intermediary Fobke, offered some encouragement to the northern group. He said they were 'on the right track'. He strongly criticized Ludendorff, who, he commented, should concentrate solely on the military side of the movement. He was also critical of Esser and Streicher. However, he refused adamantly to deviate from his position of neutrality towards the various rival factions. At the same time he regarded the merger issue as finished, and played down the significance of the conflict. He had scant sensitivity for the north German National Socialists in their 'despairing struggle'. He knew what he had to do on release, and the rebuilding of the movement could only start from Bavaria.[47] Volck was unenthusiastic about Hitler's response which, he thought, showed little understanding for the NSDAP's position in the north. It was the first sign of Volck's growing criticism of Hitler. 'When leaders in the first place think they can judge everything alone and better,' he commented, 'we won't get any farther.'[48]

The much-vaunted conference in Weimar on 15–17 August, intended to cement the organizational merger of the NSDAP and DVFP, produced only the most superficial unity in a newly proclaimed National Socialist Freedom Movement (Nationalsozialistische Freiheitsbewegung, NSFB). A high-point of the conference was a greetings telegram from 'your leader Adolf Hitler' that was read out to ecstatic applause and threatened to upstage Ludendorff (though he had in fact solicited it in the first place). Unity without Hitler's leadership could not be attained, was the implication of the conference. But Hitler's leadership – of the kind he would demand – was, it became increasingly apparent, incompatible with the expectations of Ludendorff and Graefe of a type of leadership triumvirate.[49]

Once more the embattled northern group of fundamentalists, worried by Hitler's greetings telegram to the conference, turned to him for clear, unambiguous guidance. Once more he disappointed them. Fobke's reply tried to reassure his northern comrades that Hitler did not accept that the two parties had completely merged, nor that the movement had become 'parliamentarized'. But he accepted the need for compromise, and for parliamentary action. Hitler, through Fobke, expressed once more his wish to refrain from any statement of opinion. He ended by emphasizing that his priority on release (which he fully expected to be on 1 October) would be to restore order in Bavaria. He simply exhorted the northern Directorate to hold out until then. The north Germans were distinctly unimpressed.[50]

By the end of the summer, the fragmentation of the NSDAP, and of the *völkisch* movement in general, was, despite all the talk of merger and unity, advancing rather than receding. The crudely insulting, overbearing, and bullying style of Streicher and Esser stirred deep rancour even within the GVG, caused great antagonism with the Völkischer Block (whose leader in Bavaria, Gregor Strasser, was also of course a member of the Reich Leadership of the NSFB), and totally alienated the northern National Socialists. They in turn rejected the Reich Leadership of the NSFB, which for its part refused to accept that the Directorate had any authority.[51] Only Hitler's position was emerging significantly strengthened by the inner-party warfare.

As summer dragged into autumn, then winter approached, the rifts in the *völkisch* movement widened still further. Hitler assured the northern loyalist faction in mid-September that on release he would seek a clean break and summon all those in leading positions to a meeting. The only question at issue would be: who should lead the movement? Or rather: who stood behind Hitler as sole leader? 'H[itler] does not recognize a Reich Leadership,'

Fobke's letter stated, 'and will never be part of such a soldiers' council construction.' So there was no question of him joining Ludendorff and Graefe in a combined Reich Leadership. But he refused to make a public statement to that effect. The frustration and impatience of his northern supporters mounted. His failure to gain the release on parole from 1 October that his supporters had been anticipating further complicated the situation. From the NSFB's point of view, unity without Hitler, and in the face of his continued refusal to commit himself publicly to a unified organization, was impossible.[52] In Bavaria, the *völkisch* feud surrounding the figures of Esser and Streicher widened into open breach. On 26 October, the Völkischer Block decided to join the NSFB to create a united organization to fight the coming elections. With this, it accepted the NSFB's Reich Leadership. Gregor Strasser, the spokesman of the Völkischer Block, hoped that the Großdeutsche Volksgemeinschaft would also soon join the NSFB, but at the same time openly condemned its leaders, Esser and Streicher. Esser's reply in a letter to all GVG affiliations, a bitter attack on the leaders of the Völkischer Block, with a side-swipe at Ludendorff for his support of the Block's position, reaffirmed the Munich loyalist position: 'the only man who has a right to exclude someone who has fought for years for his place in the Movement of National Socialists is solely and singly Adolf Hitler'.[53] But Esser's bravado, and the brash attacks of Streicher, supported by the Thuringian National Socialist Artur Dinter, could not conceal the sharp decline of the GVG.[54]

The Reichstag elections that took place on 7 December demonstrated just how marginal this perpetual squabbling in the *völkisch* movement was to the overall shaping of German politics. The NSFB won only 3 per cent of the vote. It had lost over a million votes compared with the *völkisch* showing in the May election. Its Reichstag representation fell from thirty-two to fourteen seats, only four of whom were National Socialists. It was a disastrous result. But it pleased Hitler.[55] In his absence, *völkisch* politics had collapsed, but his own claims to leadership had, in the process, been strengthened. The election result also had the advantage of encouraging the Bavarian government to regard the danger from the extreme Right as past. There was now, it seemed, no need for undue concern about Hitler's release from Landsberg, for which his supporters had been clamouring since October.[56]

II

The hopes of Hitler and his supporters for his early parole on 1 October, once the stipulated six months since his sentence had elapsed, had depended on attestation of his good conduct while in prison, and on his intentions after release.[57] In a report on 15 September, the governor of Landsberg prison, Oberregierungsrat Otto Leybold – along with most of the warders warmly sympathetic to Hitler – painted a eulogistic picture of his prize inmate:

Hitler shows himself to be a man of order, of discipline, not only with regard to his own person, but also towards his fellow internees. He is contented, modest, and accommodating. He makes no demands, is quiet, and reasonable, serious and without any abusiveness, scrupulously concerned to obey the confinements of the sentence. He is a man without personal vanity, is content with the catering of the institution, does not smoke or drink, and, despite all comradeliness, knows how to command a certain authority with his fellow inmates . . . He is not drawn to the female sex. He meets women with whom he comes into contact on visits here with great politeness without becoming engaged with them in serious political discussions. He is always polite and never insulting towards the officials of the institution. Hitler, who at the beginning had a great number of visitors, has kept for some months, as is well known, as far as possible from political visits, and writes only few letters, mainly notes of thanks. He occupies himself every day for many hours with the draft of his book, which should appear in the next weeks and will contain his autobiography, thoughts on the bourgeoisie, Jewry and Marxism, German revolution and Bolshevism, on the National Socialist Movement and the prehistory of the 8th of November 1923 . . . During the ten months of his remand and sentence he has without doubt become more mature and quiet than he had been. He will not return to liberty with threats and thoughts of revenge against those in public office who oppose him and frustrated his plans in November 1923. He will be no agitator against the government, no enemy of other parties with a nationalist leaning. He emphasizes how convinced he is that a state cannot exist without firm internal order and firm government.[58]

This paean of praise convinced neither the Munich police nor the state prosecutor's office, both of which provided clear and compelling reasons for rejecting Hitler's early release.

The report of the Deputy Police President of Munich, Oberregierungsrat Friedrich Tenner, of 23 September 1923, warned in the strongest terms against parole. The Deputy Police President recalled the assessment the Police Direction had earlier made, in a report of 8 May 1924: given Hitler's temperament and the energy with which he pursued his goals, that report had stated, it could be taken for granted that he would not give up his aim after release from prison and 'would constitute a constant danger for the internal and external security of the state'. Events since then had confirmed that assessment. The Deputy Police President drew attention to the statements of Hitler, Kriebel and Weber at their trial that they would continue in the same vein after release. And he referred to documents found on 16 September in the offices of the Frontbann which, it was claimed, proved the involvement of the internees in the reformation of the dissolved paramilitary bodies.[59] There could in these circumstances be no question of parole, the report went on, but should the court grant it, against all expectations, then it would be crucial to deport Hitler 'as the soul of the entire *völkisch* movement' and so remove the imminent danger for the Bavarian state. The report described prophetically what could be expected after Hitler's release: 'Hitler's influence on all those of a *völkisch* mind – he is today more than ever the soul of the whole movement – will not only stop the regressive development of the *völkisch* movement, but will unite the currently fragmented parts and lead great masses of those supporters of his idea who have already fallen off and are still detached back to the NSDAP.' Meetings, demonstrations, public outrages, and a 'ruthless struggle with the government' would be the outcome.[60]

The state prosecutor for the judicial district of Munich I, Ludwig Stenglein, who had served as the chief prosecutor in the Hitler trial, also emphatically underlined, in a letter of 23 September, how little Hitler's intentions had changed during his imprisonment, that it could be presumed he would take up where he had left off, and what a danger for public order Hitler's release would constitute. Implicitly hinting how scandalous the trial had been, he also stressed the serious criminal nature of Hitler's behaviour before and during the putsch. Not only had the attempted putsch endangered the Bavarian state and the German Reich. It had resulted in considerable loss of life, a major robbery of banknotes, and premeditated armed conflict with the police. The prosecutor pointed out that Hitler's conviction in 1922 for breach of the peace had earned him a month's jail sentence with two months suspended sentence, on probation, until 1 March 1926 (something which ought to have been, but was not, mentioned at his trial). He sought the withdrawal of the probation. The evidence connecting Hitler with the plans to reconstitute the banned paramilitary organizations showed, the prosecutor alleged, what he and his fellow internees Kriebel and Weber had in mind after such a release. It also demonstrated, through the misuse of their privileges in Landsberg (in smuggling out letters by way of visitors who had been allowed to see them in private), their *lack* of good conduct during their internment. There could be no grounds, he concluded, for an early release and he recommended rejection of parole.[61]

The court simply set aside the state prosecutor's arguments and on 25 September approved the parole. It took the view that considering the persons concerned and the motives for their actions the serving of a relatively light sentence would be sufficient punishment. It regarded the by-passing of the censor in smuggling out a few letters of insignificant content as a minor consideration, which did not affect the excellent conduct of the internees, attested by the declaration of the prison governor.[62] There was no proof, it stated, of connections between Hitler and Kriebel and the Frontbann. In this, the court was presumably influenced by the public declarations by Röhm and others, dissociating Hitler from the Frontbann.[63] Nor were there any grounds, the court stated, to accept the state prosecution's request for a revocation of the existing probationary period being served by Hitler (from his sentence of 1922).[64]

Undeterred, State Prosecutor Stenglein worked over the weekend to prepare a further appeal against parole for Hitler, Kriebel and Weber, to be sent to the Bavarian Supreme Court. This was delivered on Monday, 29 September. It repeated the charges of poor conduct (through at least nine cases of smuggled letters), strong suspicion of participation in further illegal organizations (through involvement with the Frontbann), and the security risk that would present itself for the state on their release.[65] With this appeal, there was no possibility that Hitler could be released, as he and his supporters had pressed for, on 1 October.[66]

However, the matter was pending, the court would soon have to decide on the parole, and the prospects of preventing Hitler's early release were not great. Even if parole were not immediately forthcoming, the chances were that it would be granted before much longer, not least given the unrelenting pressure from Hitler's supporters.[67] With this in mind, a representative of the Bavarian government visited Vienna at the beginning of October to try to secure the deportation of Hitler to Austria, which it wanted to achieve immediately if he were released on parole.[68] In response to a Bavarian inquiry as early as 26 March 1924 the authorities in Upper Austria had, in fact, recognized Hitler's Austrian citizenship on 20 April and been prepared to accept his deportation over the border at Passau.[69] A report by the Munich

Police Direction on 8 May then recommended his deportation in the interest of Bavarian state security.[70] But no steps were taken then, or at any other time before late September. Presumably, the matter had simply been deferred as non-urgent. By September, when a sense of urgency was certainly present, the Bavarian cabinet was divided on Hitler's deportation.[71] In any case, by then the Passau border authorities were reporting that they had received orders from Vienna not to accept Hitler.[72] The directive had been sent on the instructions of no less authority than that of the Federal Chancellor, Ignaz Seipel, himself.[73] Subsequent Bavarian attempts to use legal arguments – in themselves persuasive – to pressurize the Austrian government to take back Hitler were to no avail. Seipel simply refused to take him, remaining adamant that Hitler's service in the German army incurred loss of Austrian citizenship. It was legally not a sound argument. But it sufficed.[74] Despite Hitler's fears, nothing more came of the attempt to deport him.[75] Following his release from Landsberg, Hitler inquired in March 1925 how he could relinquish his Austrian citizenship. He was told to put in a formal request, which he then did on the grounds of his war service in the German army and desire to acquire German citizenship. On 30 April 1925, he received the anxiously awaited authorization that his Austrian citizenship was terminated.[76] This removal of any fear of deportation at a future date cost him the grand sum of 7.50 Austrian Schillings.[77] It would be seven years before he acquired German citizenship. Until then, he would remain stateless.

Meanwhile, on 6 October, the Bavarian Supreme Court gave its judgement, rejecting the state prosecutor's plea opposing Hitler's parole. The court took the view that the strong suspicion against Hitler, Kriebel and Weber for involvement with banned paramilitary organizations had still to be proved. The decision on parole hinged on this evidence, and could only be taken when it was available. The judgement paved the way for the eventual order of 19 December which would grant Hitler's release. The state prosecution office had still not given up. It made a last attempt to prevent Hitler's release in a carefully argued appeal of 5 December. Even if the evidence assembled might not suffice for a court conviction, it claimed, it *did* suffice to demonstrate the 'strong suspicion' that Hitler and Kriebel, whatever their protestations to the contrary, were guilty of actions in the same context as those for which they had been sentenced, and that they were unlikely to be of good conduct after release. The Bavarian Supreme Court then requested, on 12 December, a report from the Governor of Landsberg on the conduct of Hitler and Kriebel since his earlier report of 15 September. Reading the signals, Leybold replied within two days with another glowing account of

Hitler's character and behaviour in the prison. 'He is in his conduct during his sentence,' Leybold concluded, 'quite especially worthy of parole.'[78] With this new documentation of Hitler's good conduct, the Bavarian Supreme Court, on 19 December, finally rejected the state prosecution's case against early release, and ordered his parole – the clamour for which had not ceased in the *völkisch* press since October.[79] That the December elections were out of the way, and appeared to show National Socialism in steep decline, doubtless helped. But only political bias explains the determination of the Bavarian judiciary to insist upon Hitler's early release, despite the well-reasoned opposition of the Munich police and the state prosecutor's office.

State Prosecutor Stenglein, who had himself done what he could to hinder Hitler's parole, now passed on the court order to Landsberg by telegram.[80] The Governor, his voice faltering, gave his prisoner the news. Hitler assured him there would be no demonstrations outside the prison and asked to be collected by Adolf Müller, proprietor of a Munich publishing firm and the party's printer. Müller drove the next morning to Landsberg in his Daimler-Benz together with the photographer Heinrich Hoffmann.[81] On 20 December, at 12.15p.m., Hitler was released. A calculation in the files of the state prosecution office noted that he had three years, 333 days, twenty-one hours, fifty minutes of his short sentence still to serve.[82] History would have taken a different course had he been made to serve it.

The prison staff, all sympathetic to Hitler, gathered to bid their famous prisoner an emotional farewell. He paused for photographs by the gates of the old fortress town, hurrying Hoffmann because of the cold, then was gone. Within two hours he was back at his Munich apartment in Thierschstraße, greeted by friends with garlands of flowers, and nearly knocked over by his dog, Wolf.[83] Hitler said later that he did not know what to do with his first evening of freedom.[84] Politically, he continued at first to remain publicly non-committal. He needed to take stock of the situation in view of the months of internecine warfare in the *völkisch* movement. More important, it was necessary in order to establish with the Bavarian authorities the conditions for his re-entry into politics and to ensure that the ban on the NSDAP was lifted. Now that he was released, serious preparation for his party's new start could begin.

III

'Landsberg', Hitler told Hans Frank, was his 'university paid for by the state'. He read, he said, everything he could get hold of: Nietzsche, Houston Stewart Chamberlain, Ranke, Treitschke, Marx, Bismarck's *Gedanken und Erinnerungen* (*Thoughts and Memories*), and the war memoirs of German and allied generals and statesmen.[85] Other than dealing with visitors and answering correspondence – neither of which preoccupied him much once he had withdrawn from public involvement in politics in the summer – the long days of enforced idleness in Landsberg were ideal for reading and reflection.[86] But Hitler's reading and reflection were anything but academic. Doubtless he did read much. However, as we noted in an earlier chapter, he made clear in *Mein Kampf* that reading, for him, had purely an instrumental purpose.[87] He read not for knowledge or enlightenment, but for confirmation of his own preconceptions. He found what he was looking for. As he told Hans Frank – the party's legal expert who would eventually become Governor General in occupied Poland – through the reading he did in Landsberg, 'I recognized the correctness of my views.'[88]

Sitting in his cell in Nuremberg many years later, Frank adjudged the year 1924 to have been one of the most decisive turning-points in Hitler's life.[89] This was an exaggeration. Landsberg was not so much a turning-point as a period in which Hitler inwardly consolidated and rationalized for himself the world-view he had been developing since 1919 and, in some significant ways, modifying in the year or so before the putsch. As the Nazi Movement fell apart in his absence, and with time on his hands, away from the hurly-burly of active politics, Hitler could scarcely avoid ruminating on past mistakes. And, expecting his release within months, he was even more strongly compelled to look to the way forward for himself and his broken movement. During this time, he revised in certain respects his views on how to attain power. In so doing, his perception of himself changed. He came to think of his own role in a different way. In the wake of the triumph of his trial, he began to see himself, as his followers had started to portray him from the end of 1922 onwards, as Germany's saviour. In the light of the putsch, one might have expected his self-belief to be crushed once and for all. On the contrary: it was elevated beyond measure. His almost mystical faith in himself as walking with destiny, with a 'mission' to rescue Germany, dates from this time.

At the same time, there was an important adjustment to another aspect of his world-view. Ideas which had been taking shape in his mind since late 1922, if not earlier, on the direction of future foreign policy were now elaborated into the notion of a quest for 'living-space', to be gained at the expense of Russia. Blended into his obsessive antisemitism, aimed at the destruction of 'Jewish Bolshevism', the concept of a war for 'living-space' – an idea which Hitler would repeatedly emphasize in the following years – rounded off his 'world-view'. Thereafter, there would be tactical adjustments, but no further alteration of substance. Landsberg was no 'Jordan conversion' for Hitler.[90] In the main, it was a matter of adding new emphases to the few basic *idées fixes* already formed, at least in embryo, or clearly taking shape in the years before the putsch.[91]

The modifications in Hitler's world-view that had already been taking shape in the year before the putsch are clearly evident in *Mein Kampf*. Hitler's book offered nothing new. But it was the plainest and most expansive statement of his world-view that he had presented. He acknowledged that without his stay in Landsberg the book which after 1933 (though not before) would sell in its millions would never have been written.[92] Its genesis is not altogether clear. If Otto Strasser – admittedly a biased and often unreliable source – is to believed, it was his brother, Gregor, who, during the short time he spent in Landsberg, had the 'machiavellian idea' of suggesting to Hitler that he write his 'memoirs' in order to relieve the burden on the other inmates of having to listen to endless monologues from 'the man on the first floor'. Hitler was taken with the idea, began work on it straight away, and the prisoners on the ground floor were left in peace to return to playing cards, eating and drinking.[93] At least, they thought they would be left in peace. If the story has any substance to it, they must have been sorely disappointed when Hitler took to reading out each day the sections he had written to a literally captive audience.[94] More likely, if more prosaic than Otto Strasser's colourful explanation, is that the suggestion to Hitler to write his autobiography came from Max Amann, persuading him to cash in on the publicity stirred up by his trial.[95] Amann was expecting revelations about the background to the putsch.[96] Instead, he and many disappointed readers found largely a repetition of what Hitler had said in countless speeches, interspersed with superficial and triumphalist accounts of parts of his own life story.[97]

Hitler was already at work on what would become the first volume when Haase and the north German delegation visited him on 26–7 May 1924. He called his book at that time by the scarcely catchy title: 'Four and a Half Years of Struggle against Lies, Stupidity, and Cowardice'.[98] The eventual pithy title seems to have been suggested by Max Amann.[99] The book was dictated by Hitler to chauffeur and general dogsbody Emil Maurice, then, from July onwards, to Rudolf Heß (both of whom were also serving sentences for their part in the putsch).[100] The first volume, which appeared on 18 July 1925, was largely autobiographical – though, as we have noted, with many distortions and inaccuracies. It ended with Hitler's triumph at the announcement of the party programme in the Hofbräuhaus on 24 February 1920. The second volume, which Hitler wrote only after his release, and which was published on 11 December 1926, dealt more extensively with his ideas on the nature of the *völkisch* state, questions of ideology, propaganda and organization, concluding with chapters on foreign policy.

Badly written and rambling as the published version of *Mein Kampf* was, it was a considerable improvement on what Hitler had initially produced, thanks to editorial interventions from a number of people. 'A veritable chaos of banalities, schoolboy reminiscences, subjective judgements, and personal hatred' was how Otto Strasser described the draft.[101] Amann, the party printer Müller, Heß, and Hanfstaengl (whose brother turned down flat the prospect of *Mein Kampf* appearing in the family publishing house) all had a hand in altering and revising the text.[102] The music critic of the *Völkischer Beobachter*, Stolzing-Cerny, together with a former Hieronymite, Father Bernard Stempfle, one-time editor-in-chief of the *Miesbacher Anzeiger*, a provincial Bavarian newspaper that sympathized with the Nazi Movement, played the main role in re-couching whole sections into a style still inimitably Hitlerian, often barely readable, but nonetheless more literate than the original.[103] Even then, there were many later alterations before the volume appeared in print.[104] Hitler himself, according to Hans Frank, accepted that it was badly written, and described it as no more than a collection of leading articles for the *Völkischer Beobachter*.[105]

Before Hitler came to power, *Mein Kampf*, brought out in the party's own publishing house, the Franz Eher-Verlag, run by Max Amann, was scarcely the runaway bestseller he had apparently expected it to be. Its turgid content, dreadful style, and relatively high price of 12 Reich Marks a volume evidently deterred many potential readers.[106] By 1929, the first volume had sold around 23,000 copies, the second only 13,000. Sales increased sharply following the NSDAP's electoral successes after 1930, and reached 80,000 in 1932. From 1933, they rose stratospherically. One and a half million copies were sold that year. Even the blind could read it – should they have wished to do so – once a braille version had been published in 1936. And from that year, a copy of the people's edition of both volumes bound together was given to each happy couple on their wedding day. Some

10 million copies were sold by 1945, not counting the millions sold abroad, where *Mein Kampf* was translated into sixteen languages.[107] How many people actually read it is unknown.[108] For Hitler, it was of little importance. Having from the early 1920s described himself in official documents as a 'writer', he could well afford in 1933 to refuse his Reich Chancellor's salary (in contrast, he pointed out, to his predecessors): *Mein Kampf* had made him a very rich man.[109]

No policy outline was offered in *Mein Kampf*. But the book did provide, however garbled the presentation, an uncompromising statement of Hitler's political principles, his 'world-view', his sense of his own 'mission', his 'vision' of society, and his long-term aims. Not least, it established the basis of the Führer myth. For in *Mein Kampf*, Hitler portrayed himself as uniquely qualified to lead Germany from its existing misery to greatness.

Mein Kampf gives an important insight into his thinking in the mid-1920s.[110] By then, he had developed a philosophy that afforded him a complete interpretation of history, of the ills of the world, and how to overcome them. Tersely summarized, it boiled down to a simplistic, Manichaean view of history as racial struggle, in which the highest racial entity, the Aryan, was being undermined and destroyed by the lowest, the parasitic Jew.[111] 'The racial question,' he wrote, 'gives the key not only to world history but to all human culture.'[112] The culmination of this process was taken to be the brutal rule of the Jews through Bolshevism in Russia, where the 'blood Jew' had, 'partly amid inhuman torture killed or let starve to death around 30 million people in truly satanic savagery in order to secure the rule over a great people of a bunch of Jewish *literati* and stock-market bandits'.[113] The 'mission' of the Nazi Movement was, therefore, clear: to destroy 'Jewish Bolshevism'. At the same time – a leap of logic that moved conveniently into a justification for outright imperialist conquest – this would provide the German people with the 'living-space' needed for the 'master race' to sustain itself.[114] He held rigidly to these basic tenets for the rest of his life. Nothing of substance changed in later years. The very inflexibility and quasi-messianic commitment to an 'idea', a set of beliefs that were unalterable, simple, internally consistent and comprehensive, gave Hitler the strength of will and sense of knowing his own destiny that left its mark on all those who came into contact with him. Hitler's authority in his entourage derived in no small measure from the certainty in his own convictions that he could so forcefully express. Everything could be couched in terms of black and white, victory or total destruction. There were no alternatives. And, like all ideologues and 'conviction politicians', the self-reinforcing components of his 'world-view' meant that he was always in a position to deride or dismiss out of hand any 'rational' arguments of opponents. Once head of state, Hitler's personalized 'world-view' would serve as 'guidelines for action' for policy-makers in all areas of the Third Reich.[115]

Hitler's book was not a prescriptive programme in the sense of a short-term political manifesto. But many contemporaries made a mistake in treating *Mein Kampf* with ridicule and not taking the ideas Hitler expressed there extremely seriously. However base and repellent they were, they amounted to a set of clearly established and rigidly upheld political principles.[116] Hitler never saw any reason to alter the content of what he had written.[117] Their internal coherence (given the irrational premises) allows them to be described as an ideology (or, in Hitler's own terminology, a 'world-view').[118] Hitler's 'world-view' in *Mein Kampf* can now be more clearly seen than used to be possible in the context of his ideas as they unfolded between his entry into politics and the writing of his 'Second Book' in 1928.

On Hitler's central, overriding and all-embracing obsession, the 'removal of the Jews', *Mein Kampf* added nothing to the ideas he had already formulated by 1919–20. Extreme though the language of *Mein Kampf* was, it was no different to that which Hitler had been proclaiming for years. Nor, for that matter, did the inherently genocidal terminology substantially vary from that of other writers and speakers on the *völkisch* Right, extending, as we have already seen, well back beyond the First World War.[119] His bacterial imagery implied that Jews should be treated in the way germs were dealt with: by extermination. Already in August 1920, Hitler had spoken of combating 'racial tuberculosis' through removal of the 'causal agent, the Jew'.[120] And there could be little doubt whom Hitler had in mind when, four years later in *Mein Kampf*, he wrote: 'The nationalization of our masses will succeed only when, aside from all the positive struggle for the soul of our people, their international poisoners are exterminated.'[121] The notion of poisoning the poisoners ran through another, notorious, passage of *Mein Kampf*, already cited in Chapter 5, in which Hitler suggested that if 12–15,000 'Hebrew corrupters of the people' had been held under poison gas at the start of the First World War, then 'the sacrifice of millions at the front would not have been in vain'.[122] These terrible passages are not the beginning of a one-way track to the 'Final Solution'. The road there was 'twisted', not straight.[123] But however little he had thought out the practical implications of what he was saying, its inherent genocidal thrust is undeniable. However indistinctly, the connection between destruction of the Jews, war, and national salvation had been forged in Hitler's mind.

As we saw in Chapter 5, the initial anti-capitalist colouring of Hitler's antisemitism had given way by mid-1920 to the connection in his thinking of the Jews with the evils of Soviet Bolshevism. It was not that Hitler substituted the image of the Jews behind Marxism for that of the Jews behind capitalism. Both coexisted in his fixated loathing. It was a hatred so profound that it could only have been based on deep fear. This was of a figure in his imagination so powerful that it was the force behind both international finance capital and Soviet Communism. It was the image of a 'Jewish world conspiracy' that was almost unconquerable – even for National Socialism.

Once the link with Bolshevism was made, Hitler had established his central and lasting vision of a titanic battle for supremacy, a racial struggle against a foe of ruthless brutality. What he visualized, he had stated in June 1922, was a fight to the death between two competing ideologies, the idealistic and the materialistic. The mission of the German people was to destroy Bolshevism, and with it 'our mortal enemy: the Jew'.[124] By October the same year he was writing of a life and death struggle of two opposed 'world-views', incapable of existing alongside one another. Defeat in this great showdown would seal Germany's destruction. The struggle would leave only victors and the annihilated. It meant a war of extermination. 'A victory of the Marxist idea signifies the complete extermination of the opponents,' he remarked. 'The Bolshevization of Germany . . . means the complete annihilation of the entire Christian-western culture.' Correspondingly, the aim of National Socialism could be simply defined: 'Annihilation and extermination of the Marxist *Weltanschauung*.'[125]

By now Marxism and the Jew were synonymous in Hitler's mind. At the end of his trial, on 27 March 1924, he had told the court that what he wanted to be was the breaker of Marxism.[126] The Nazi Movement knew only *one* enemy, he had emphasized the following month – the mortal enemy of the whole of mankind: Marxism.[127] There was no mention of the Jews. Some newspapers picked up the change of emphasis and claimed Hitler had altered his position on the 'Jewish Question'. There were Nazi followers who were also puzzled. One, visiting him in Landsberg at the end of July, asked Hitler whether he had changed his views about Jewry. He received a characteristic reply. Indeed his position on the struggle against Jewry had altered, Hitler remarked. He had realized while at work on *Mein Kampf* that he had up to then been too mild. In future, only the toughest measures could be deployed if success were to be attained. The 'Jewish Question', he declared, was an existential matter for all peoples, not just the German people, 'for Juda is the world plague'.[128] The logic of the position was that only the complete eradication of the international power of Jewry would suffice.

Hitler's obsession with the 'Jewish Question' was inextricably interwoven with his notions of foreign policy. Once his antisemitism had, by the middle of 1920, fused with anti-Bolshevism into the image of 'Jewish Bolshevism', it was inevitable that his thinking on foreign policy would be affected. However, not only ideological influences, but questions of pure power politics shaped Hitler's changing position. In their concentration on France as the arch-enemy, hostility to Britain, recovery of colonies, and the restoration of Germany's borders of 1914, Hitler's early views on foreign policy were conventionally pan-German.[129] They were no different from those of many nationalist hot-heads. In fact, in essence (if not in the extreme way they were advanced) they accorded with a revisionism that enjoyed wide popular backing. Nor, in his emphasis on military might to overthrow Versailles and defeat France, however unrealistic it sounded in the early 1920s, did he differ from many others on the Pan-German and *völkisch* Right. Already in 1920, before he had heard of Fascism, he was contemplating the value of an alliance with Italy. He was determined even then that the question of South Tyrol – the predominantly German-speaking part of the former Austrian province of Tyrol lying beyond the Brenner, ceded to Italy in 1919, and since then subjected to a programme of 'Italianization' – would not stand in the way of such an alliance.[130] By late 1922, an alliance with Britain, whose world empire he admired, was in his mind. This idea had sharpened in 1923 when the disagreements of the British and French over the Ruhr occupation became clear.[131]

The presumed rule of the Jews in Russia stood, on the other hand, as Hitler had pointed out as early as July 1920, firmly in the way of any alliance with Russia. Even so, at this time Hitler shared the view of many on the *völkisch* Right that a distinction could be drawn between 'national' Russians – where the Germanic influence was strong – and the 'bolshevization' of Russia brought about by the Jews.[132] Hitler's approach to Russia was partly shaped by Rosenberg, the early NSDAP's leading 'expert' on eastern questions, whose Baltic origins fed a ferocious antipathy towards Bolshevism. It was, most likely, reinforced by Scheubner-Richter, another prolific writer on eastern policy in the infant party, with extremely strong connections to Russian exiles. Dietrich Eckart, too, who was already in early 1919 writing of the identity of Jewry and Bolshevism, probably also exerted some influence.[133]

Russia was coming already before the putsch to loom larger in Hitler's thoughts on foreign policy. He had somewhat vaguely mentioned the 'land question', comparing Germany unfavourably with Russia in its relation of population to the land at its disposal, as early as December 1919.[134] He already hinted in a speech on 31 May 1921, through praise of the Brest-Litovsk Treaty of 1918 (which had ended Russian participation in the war) for giving Germany the additional land it needed to sustain its people, at an expansion of German 'living-space' at the expense of Russia.[135] On 21 October 1921 he was still speaking, somewhat cryptically, of an expansion with Russia against England opening up 'an unlimited possibility of expansion towards the east'.[136] Such remarks indicated that at this time, Hitler still shared – even if vaguely expressed – the Pan-German view on eastern expansion. This amounted broadly to the notion that eastern expansion could be carried out through collaboration with a non-Bolshevik Russia, whose own territorial demands would be settled also through looking eastwards, towards Asia, leaving the former Russian border areas in the west to Germany. It would have amounted, essentially, to something like a resurrection of the Brest-Litovsk arrangement, while Russia would have been left to find compensation in the lands on its own eastern borders.[137]

By early 1922, these views had shifted. By now, Hitler had abandoned any idea of collaboration with Russia. He saw no prospect of Russia looking only eastwards. Extension of Bolshevism to Germany would prove an irresistible urge.[138] The logic of the changed position was evident. Only through the destruction of Bolshevism could Germany be saved. And at the same time, this – through expansion into Russia itself – would bring the territory which Germany needed. During the course of 1922 – perhaps reinforced towards the end of the year by contact with the arch-expansionist, Ludendorff – the changed approach to future policy towards Russia was consolidated.[139] By December 1922, Hitler was explaining in private to Eduard Scharrer, co-owner of the *Münchner Neueste Nachrichten* and favourably disposed towards the Nazi Party, the outline of the foreign alliance ideas which he was to elaborate in *Mein Kampf*. He ruled out the colonial rivalry with Britain that had caused conflict before the First World War. He told Scharrer:

Germany would have to adapt herself to a purely continental policy, avoiding harm to English interest. The destruction of Russia with the help of England would have to be attempted. Russia would give Germany sufficient land for German settlers and a wide field of activity for German industry. Then England would not interrupt us in our reckoning with France.[140]

In the light of his comments to Scharrer, it can scarcely be claimed that Hitler developed an entirely new concept of foreign policy while in Landsberg, one based on the idea of war against Russia to acquire *Lebensraum*. And what he wrote in *Mein Kampf* on Germany's need for land being satisfied at the expense of Russia had indeed already been anticipated in an essay he wrote in spring 1924, which was published in April that year.[141] There was no 'transformation' of Hitler's 'vision of the world' in Landsberg.[142] What he came to write in Landsberg was the result of the gradual gestation of his ideas, rather than a flash of intuition, set of new insights, or overnight conversion to a different approach.

The imperialist and geopolitical ideas that went to make up the idea of *Lebensraum* were, in fact, common currency on the imperialist and *völkisch* Right in Weimar Germany. As we noted in an earlier chapter, the idea of *Lebensraum* had been a prominent strand of German imperialist ideology since the 1890s. It had been strongly represented in the Pan-German League under Heinrich Claß, supported by the press controlled by founder-member of the League, director of Krupp's and media tycoon Alfred Hugenberg.[143] For Pan-Germans, *Lebensraum* could both justify territorial conquest by evoking the colonizing of Slav lands by Teutonic knights in the Middle Ages and, emotively, conjure up notions of uniting in the Reich what came to be described as *Volksdeutsche* (ethnic Germans) scattered throughout eastern Europe. For the most part these constituted fairly small minorities, as in the parts of Poland (outside the towns) which Prussia had ruled before 1918. But in a number of areas – Danzig, for example, parts of the Baltic, or the area of Czechoslovakia later known as the Sudetenland – the German-speaking population was sizeable, and often vociferously nationalist. The idea of *Lebensraum* symbolized, then, for Pan-Germans the historic conquest of the East while at the same time, in emphasizing German alleged over-population, cloaking real, modern, power-political imperialist ambitions. It existed alongside, rather than blending with, the mainstream imperialist concentration on overseas trading colonies, encapsulated in the slogan of *Weltpolitik*.[144] In the Weimar era it came to be popularized by Hans Grimm's best-selling novel *Volk ohne Raum* (*People without Space*), published in 1926.[145]

Hitler could scarcely have avoided the imperialist and geopolitical writings in circulation on 'living-space'. Among them, whether read at first hand or in bowdlerized form, it seems highly likely that Haushofer's were one significant source for his notion of *Lebensraum*.[146] Through Rudolf Heß, Hitler already knew Karl Haushofer, the leading exponent of 'geopolitics', by 1922 at the latest.[147] Haushofer's influence was probably greater than the Munich professor was later prepared to acknowledge.[148] If he was not acquainted with them before, Hitler certainly had time on his hands while in prison to read his works, as well as those of Friedrich Ratzel, the other foremost geopolitics theorist. Whether he did so or not cannot be proved. But it seems at the very least likely that the broad lines of their arguments were made known to him by Haushofer's former pupil, Rudolf Heß.[149]

At any rate, by the time of the Scharrer discussion at the end of 1922, Hitler's thinking on Russia and the 'living-space' question was essentially in place. And by spring 1924, his views were effectively fully formed. What Landsberg and the writing of *Mein Kampf* did was to provide elaboration. Beyond that, it showed that Hitler had by then firmly established the link between the destruction of the Jews and a war against Russia to acquire *Lebensraum*.[150]

Already in the first volume of *Mein Kampf*, the choice – which Hitler had still rhetorically left open in his article of April 1924 – of a land-policy directed against Russia, with Britain's support, or a world trading policy upheld by sea-power directed against Britain with Russia's support, was emphatically determined.[151] By the second volume, mainly written in 1925 (and published at the end of the following year), the enemy in the short term was still seen as France. But in the baldest language, the long-term goal was now stated to be the attaining of 'living-space' at the expense of Russia.

The right to possess soil can become a duty if without extension of its soil a great nation seems doomed to destruction [wrote Hitler] . . . Germany will either be a world power or there will be no Germany. And for world power she needs that magnitude which will give her the position she needs in the present period, and life to her citizens.

And so we National Socialists consciously draw a line beneath the foreign policy tendency of our pre-War period. We take up where we broke off six hundred years ago. We stop the endless German movement to the south and west, and turn our gaze towards the land in the east. At long last we break off the colonial and commercial policy of the pre-War period and shift to the soil policy of the future.

If we speak of soil in Europe today, we can primarily have in mind only Russia and her vassal border states . . . For centuries Russia drew nourishment from [the] Germanic nucleus of its upper leading strata. Today it can be regarded as almost totally exterminated and extinguished. It has been replaced by the Jew . . . He himself is no element of organization, but a ferment of decomposition. The giant empire in the east is ripe for collapse. And the end of Jewish rule in Russia will also be the end of Russia as a state . . .

The mission of the National Socialist Movement was to prepare the German people for this task. 'We have been chosen by Fate,' wrote Hitler, 'as witnesses of a catastrophe which will be the mightiest confirmation of the soundness of the *völkisch* theory.'[152]

With this passage, the two key components of Hitler's personalized 'world-view' – destruction of the Jews and acquisition of 'living-space' – came together. War against Russia would, through its annihilation of 'Jewish Bolshevism', at the same time deliver Germany its salvation by providing new 'living-space'. Crude, simplistic, barbaric: but this invocation of the most brutal tenets of late nineteenth-century imperialism, racism and anti-semitism, transposed into eastern Europe in the twentieth century, was a heady brew for those ready to consume it.

Hitler himself repeatedly returned to the 'living-space' notion, which became a dominant theme of his writings and speeches in the following years. His foreign policy ideas were to be more clearly laid out, but in no significant way altered, in his 'Second Book', written in 1928 (though left unpublished in Hitler's own lifetime).[153] Once established, the quest for *Lebensraum* – and with it the destruction of 'Jewish Bolshevism' – would remain a keystone of Hitler's ideology. One element remained to complete the 'world-view': the leader of genius who would accomplish this quest. In Landsberg, Hitler found the answer.

IV

Many years later, Hitler regarded 'the self-confidence, optimism, and belief that simply could not be shaken by anything more' as deriving from his time in Landsberg.[154] Hitler's self-perception did indeed alter while he was in prison. Even at his trial, as we have seen, he had been proud to be the 'drummer' of the national cause. Anything else was a triviality, he had declared.[155] In Landsberg this changed – though, as we have noted, the change had already been under way during the year preceding the putsch.

Hitler was preoccupied from the beginning of his sentence with the question of his own future and that of his party after his release. Since he expected his release within six months, the question was an urgent one. For Hitler, there was no turning back. His political 'career', which had developed into his political 'mission', left him nowhere to go but forwards. He could not return to anonymity, even had he wanted to do so. A conventional 'bourgeois' lifestyle was out of the question. Any retreat, after the acclaim he had won on the nationalist Right at his trial, would have confirmed the impression of his opponents that he was a figure of farce, and would have exposed him to ridicule. And as he pondered over the failed putsch, transforming it in his mind into the martyrs' triumph that would come to have its central place in Nazi mythology, he had no trouble in assigning the blame to the mistakes, weakness, and lack of resolve of all the leading figures to whom he was at the time bound.[156] They had betrayed him, and the national cause: this was his conclusion. More than that: the triumph at his trial; the torrents of adulation ever-present in the *völkisch* press or pouring unabated from letters sent to Landsberg; and not least the collapse of the *völkisch* movement in his absence into derisory sectarian squabbling, and the growing conflict with Ludendorff and the other *völkisch* leaders; all these contributed towards giving him an elevated sense of his own importance and of his unique historic 'mission'. The idea, embryonically forming in 1923, took firm hold in the strange atmosphere of Landsberg. Surrounded by sycophants and devotees, foremost among them the fawning Heß, Hitler now became certain: he himself was Germany's coming 'great leader'.

Such a notion in its full implications was unimaginable before his triumph at the trial and the acclaim that followed. The 'heroic' leadership he now claimed for himself was an invention of his followers before he saw himself in that role. But the role fitted the temperament of one whose personal failures in early life had found an exaggerated wish-fulfilment in unbound admiration for heroic figures, above all the artist-hero Wagner.[157] Whether an extraordinary depth of self-loathing is a necessary precondition for such an abnormal elevation of self-esteem into that of the heroic saviour of the nation is a matter best left to psychologists. But whatever the deep-seated reasons, for such a narcissistic egomaniac as Hitler, the hero-worship which others directed towards him, combined with his own inability to find fault or error in himself, now produced a 'heroic'-leadership self-image of monumental proportions. No one in mainstream German political life, outside the tiny and fractured *völkisch* movement, was aware of or would have taken seriously the change in Hitler's self-perception. At the time it was of no consequence. But for Hitler's demands on the *völkisch* movement, and for his own self-justification, it was a vital development.[158]

In *Mein Kampf*, Hitler pictured himself as a rare genius who combined the qualities of the 'programmatist' and the 'politician'. The 'programmatist' of a movement was the theoretician who did not concern himself with practical realities, but with 'eternal truth', as the great religious leaders had done. The 'greatness' of the 'politician' lay in the successful practical implementation of the 'idea' advanced by the 'programmatist'. 'Over long periods of humanity,' he wrote, 'it can once happen that the politician is wedded to the programmatist.' His work did not concern short-term demands that any petty bourgeois could grasp, but looked to the future, with 'aims which only the fewest grasp'. Among the 'great men' in history, Hitler singled out at this point Luther, Frederick the Great, and Wagner.[159] Seldom was it the case, in his view, that 'a great theoretician' was also 'a great leader'. The latter was far more frequently an 'agitator': 'For leading means: being able to move masses.' He concluded: 'the combination of theoretician, organizer, and leader in one person is the rarest thing that can be found on this earth; this combination makes the great man.'[160] Unmistakably, Hitler meant himself.

The 'idea' he stood for was not a matter of short-term objectives. It was a 'mission', a 'vision' of long-term future goals, and of his own part in the accomplishment of them. Certainly, these goals – national salvation through 'removal' of the Jews and acquisition of 'living-space' in the east – did not amount to short-term practical policy guidelines. But, incorporated into the notion of the 'heroic' leader, they did amount to a dynamic 'world-view'. This 'world-view' gave Hitler his unremitting drive. He spoke repeatedly of his 'mission'. He saw the hand of 'Providence' in his work. He regarded his fight against the Jew as 'the work of the Lord'.[161] He saw his life's work as a crusade. The invasion of the Soviet Union, when it was launched many years later, was for him – and not just for him – the culmination of this crusade. It would be a serious error to underestimate the ideological driving-force of Hitler's few central ideas. He was no mere propagandist or 'unprincipled opportunist'.[162] He was indeed both a masterly propagandist *and* an ideologue. There was no contradiction between the two.

Hitler's conviction of his own uniqueness conveyed itself to some, if not all, of those imprisoned alongside him in Landsberg. It was only in Landsberg, wrote Rudolf Heß, that he fully grasped the 'mighty significance' of Hitler's personality.[163] Some of the inmates, like Heß, would, on release, be instrumental in transmitting the 'heroic' image of Hitler within the party. Hermann Fobke, Hitler's liaison with the north German faction and an internee in Landsberg along with around two dozen other young members of Hitler's bodyguard, gave an indication of the impression Hitler was making on him in one of his letters to the Göttingen leader of the National Socialists, Ludolf Haase:

It is my rock solid conviction that Hitler will not move one iota from his National Socialist thinking . . . And if it nonetheless sometimes looks as if that is the case, then it is only for the sake of more important goals. For he combines in himself the programmatist and the politician. He knows his goal, but also sees the ways to accomplish it. My stay here has strengthened what I still doubted in Göttingen: the faith in Hitler's political instinct.[164]

When he left Landsberg, to try to rebuild a crippled movement, Hitler's leadership claims were, therefore, not only externally enhanced within the *völkisch* movement, but had been inwardly transformed and consolidated into a new perception of himself and awareness of his role. His sense of realism had by no means altogether disappeared beneath his messianic claims. He had no concrete notion of how his aims might be achieved. He still imagined that his goals might be brought to fruition only in the distant future.[165] Since it consisted of only a few basic, but unchangeable tenets, his 'world-view' was compatible with short-term tactical adjustments. And it had the advantage of accommodating and reconciling a variety of otherwise conflicting positions on particular issues and fine points of ideology adopted by subordinate Nazi leaders. Within the framework of his basic 'world-view', Hitler himself was flexible, even indifferent, towards ideological issues which could obsess his followers. Opponents at the time, and many later commentators, frequently underestimated the dynamism of Nazi ideology because of its diffuseness, and because of the cynicism of Nazi propaganda.[166] Ideology was often regarded as no more than a cloak for power-ambitions and tyranny.[167] This was to misinterpret the driving-force of Hitler's own basic ideas, few and crude as they were. And it is to misunderstand the ways those basic ideas came to function within the Nazi Party then, after 1933, within the Nazi state. What mattered for Hitler was indeed the road to power. He was prepared to sacrifice most principles for that. But some – and those were for him the ones that counted – were not only unchangeable. They formed the essence of what he understood by power itself. Opportunism was always itself ultimately shaped by the core ideas that determined his notion of power.

Following his months in Landsberg, Hitler's self-belief was now such that, unlike the pre-putsch era, he could regard himself as the *exclusive* exponent of the 'idea' of National Socialism and the sole leader of the *völkisch* movement, destined to show Germany the path to its national salvation. The task facing him on release would be to convince others of that.

8

MASTERY OVER THE MOVEMENT

'Duke and liegeman! In this ancient German . . . relationship of leader to companions, lies the essence of the structure of the NSDAP.'

Gregor Strasser, 1927

'I subordinate myself without further ado to Herr Adolf Hitler. Why? He has proved that he can lead; on the basis of his view and his will, he has created a party out of the united national socialist idea, and leads it. He and the party are one, and offer the unity that is the unconditional premiss of success.'   Ernst Graf zu Reventlow,
a former critic of Hitler, 1927

Between the refoundation of the NSDAP in February 1925 and the beginnings of the new political and economic turmoil that was to usher in the shattering impact of the world economic crisis, the Nazi Movement was no more than a fringe irritant in German politics. Its leader, Hitler, faced with the rebuilding of his party from scratch after it had fractured into warring factions during his imprisonment in 1924, and banned from speaking in public in most of Germany until 1927 (in the biggest state of all, Prussia, until 1928), was confined to the political wilderness. A confidential report by the Reich Minister of the Interior in 1927, pointing out that the NSDAP 'was not advancing', realistically described the party as 'a numerically insignificant . . . radical-revolutionary splinter group incapable of exerting any noticeable influence on the great mass of the population and the course of political events'.[1]

In the conditions of economic recovery and apparent consolidation that prevailed in the four years following the currency stabilization the major props of Nazi success before 1923 were removed. A semblance of 'normality' came over the Weimar Republic. These were Weimar's 'golden years'. With Stresemann at the helm, the Locarno Treaty of 1925 (recognizing the western borders of the Reich as determined in the Versailles Treaty) and Germany's entry into the League of Nations the following year brought the country back into the international fold. At home, despite nationalist opposition, the Dawes Plan took much of the heat out of the reparations issue by regulating and substantially easing the rate of German repayment. It would be five years before the issue became sensitive again, when a further attempt – the Young Plan – in 1929 to establish terms for clearing the reparations burden stirred a new wave of nationalist agitation. Meanwhile, despite governmental instability, the new Republic seemed to be settling down. Beneath the four changes of administration between 1925 and 1927, there was a good deal of continuity in government coalitions.[2] In the economy, after a sharp but short-lived recession in 1926, industrial production for the first time came to surpass the pre-war level. Real wages did the same. The welfare state made impressive progress. Health provision was far superior to the pre-war period. Public spending on housing increased massively. By the later 1920s, over 300,000 new houses a year were being built – a level to be reached in only two years during the Third Reich. Industrial disturbances fell. So did crime levels. The first glimmers of a mass-consumer society were visible. More people had radios, telephones, even cars.[3] Shopping was increasingly carried out in big department stores. In all this, Germany in the mid-1920s followed patterns recognizable in much of Europe. America was the model, though Germany lagged far behind. These years also marked the high-point of Weimar culture, of *neue Sachlichkeit* (New Objectivity) and the thriving of an extraordinary cultural avant-garde. The modernist architectural experiments of the Bauhaus, the Expressionist painting of leading artists such as Paul Klee and Wassily Kandinsky, the biting social commentaries in the pictures of Otto Dix and caricatures of Georg Grosz, the bold new musical forms attained by Arnold Schönberg and Paul Hindemith, the cynical genius of Bertolt Brecht's plays: all became synonymous with Germany's cultural pre-eminence in the 1920s.[4] Mass entertainment also flourished. Sporting events drew increasing numbers of spectators. Boxing, football, and motor-sports were especially popular.[5] Cinemas and dance-halls sprouted up on urban street-corners. The Charleston, shimmy and jitterbug were the rage. Young people in big cities were more likely to be attracted to hot jazz than to *Heimatlieder*.[6] In the countryside, life continued at a more leisurely pace. 'Apart from a few cases of fire, there are no notable disturbances of public safety to report,' began the sleepy half-monthly dispatch of the Government President of Upper Bavaria in February 1928.[7] Five years earlier, his reports had been dominated by the activities of Hitler and his Movement. It was as if a storm had burst in 1923. The calm that followed held out little hope of future success for the Nazi Party.

The *völkisch* Right's residual support had dwindled to around 3 per cent of the population by late 1924. In the 1928 Reichstag election this fell still further: the NSDAP (campaigning in a Reichstag election for the first time under its own name) gained a mere 2.6 per cent of the vote. Over 97 per cent of the electorate did not want Hitler. Under the present-day constitution of the Federal Republic, the Nazis' percentage of the vote would have gained them no seats at all. Even under the Weimar electoral system, only twelve

Nazis took their seats among the 491 deputies returned to the Reichstag.[8] Growing unrest in farming communities and agitation surrounding the Young Plan helped the NSDAP to improve on this disastrous performance in regional elections in 1929. Even so, without the Depression and the calamitous effect upon Germany from the end of that year, the Nazi Party may well have broken up and faded into oblivion, remembered essentially as a passing phenomenon of the post-war upheaval. Hitler himself would have been recalled as a one-time firebrand who burnt his fingers in an absurd putsch attempt and never again became a force in German politics.

As long as the German economy offered prospects of recovery and future prosperity, the fragile political fabric of the new democracy did not collapse. Without such a collapse, and as long as the anti-democratic élites with a leverage on power – particularly the army leadership, but also the big landowners, many of the captains of industry, and the top echelon of the civil service – retained their detached loyalty to the Republic, there was little or nothing that Hitler and his party could do to gain a foothold in the mainstream of politics, let alone to stake a claim to power. However, it is as well not to be dismissive of the importance of these 'wilderness years' between 1924 and 1929 in laying the platform for the later triumphant rise of Hitler and the Nazi Party. During this period, Hitler became incontestably established as the leader of the radical Right. In the process, the NSDAP was transformed into a 'leader party' of a unique kind, with the character it was to retain, and later to impart to the German state. Hitler by this time was no conventional party chairman, nor even a leader among others, *primus inter pares*. He was now 'the Leader'. Between 1925 and 1929, at first with some difficulty, he had established outright and complete mastery over his movement.

By 1929, the organization of the party, which had been built up to accompany its nationwide expansion (however thinly spread at first), bore little comparison with the hand-to-mouth administration of the pre-putsch party, and placed it in a far stronger position to exploit the new crises that descended on Germany from the autumn of that year. The activist cadres had also grown in strength. Despite its miserable showing at the polls, the party's own figures of 100,000 members in October 1928 were almost twice as high as the membership rolls on the eve of the putsch.[9] Though the voters were still few in number, the activist core of mainly dedicated fanatics was relatively large.[10] Finally, though the factionalism inherent in radical rightist movements still simmered just below the surface, not infrequently breaking through into open conflict, the NSDAP was a far more cohesive force by

1929 than it had been before the putsch. And by then, its rivals on the extreme Right had disappeared, lost all significance, or been absorbed into the Nazi Movement.

These developments were strongly influenced by Hitler's changed leadership position. As we have noted, Hitler was before the putsch only one of the leaders of the Right, and, with the main emphasis in 1923 on paramilitary politics, heavily dependent upon forces outside his own movement. Despite the beginnings of the leadership cult which some of his followers attached to him, he was still regarded at that time as merely one exponent – however important – of National Socialism (with its myriad forms of emphasis and interpretation). By 1929, his dominance in the movement was absolute, the 'idea' now as good as inseparable from the Leader. The Hitler cult had caught hold among the party faithful in ways scarcely imaginable before 1923, and was now well on the way to elevating the Leader above the party. For some leading figures in the party, the cult was encouraged, or at least tolerated, because it served successfully as the focus of growing support. Above all, it was accepted because it was a crucial adhesive, alone capable of holding together the party which otherwise, as 1924 had shown, was likely to splinter into feuding factions. But for opponents and for supporters alike, National Socialism came in these years to mean exclusively 'the Hitler Movement'. The platform was created for the subsequent rapid spread of the Leader cult, once the breakthrough of popular support had been attained in 1930, and for the later near deification of Hitler in the Third Reich itself.

Hitler's own contribution to the transformation of the NSDAP in these years should not be exaggerated. What is remarkable, indeed, is not how much, but how little, Hitler personally had to do to bring about the restructuring of the NSDAP in these years so that it was in a position to challenge for power once circumstances again began to favour it.

In essence, Hitler's crude scheme of the path to national redemption and rebirth remained as it had been since his entry into politics: mobilization of the masses, takeover of the state, destruction of internal enemies, preparation for external conquest.[11] His ideological 'vision' was, at this stage at least, of importance mainly in further 'rationalizing' to himself the prejudices and phobias he had long carried with him, and in conveying a compelling image of a political 'visionary' to his followers. His sole recipe, as always, was to work for the 'nationalization' of the masses through ceaseless propaganda and agitation, and to wait for events to turn in his favour. The certainty that they would do so – the certainty of the fanatic – impressed those drawn to his message. It helped to shape the aura around Hitler, the 'messianic', 'visionary' image. However, the growth of the Führer cult – though Hitler did nothing to prevent it, other than prohibiting its most tasteless excesses – was brought about by his followers. And the important restructuring of the party's organization was largely the work of Gregor Strasser. Hitler's indispensability to the *völkisch* Right had been demonstrated when it disintegrated during his time in Landsberg. No other leader could rally it and hold it together as he could. And no speaker could draw the crowds like he could. Beyond that, his main contribution to the inner strengthening of the NSDAP in this period amounted to an uncompromising stance – even in adversity – towards all potential threats to his authority, and the utilization of his unique leadership position to bypass or override all ideological conflicts in the single-minded pursuit of power.

Despite the modest growth (from a low base) in party support in 1929, neither Hitler nor any other leading Nazi had any inkling about the speed with which the political breakthrough was to follow. But once the breakthrough came, the party was, following the changes since its refoundation in 1925, in a position to exploit the new conditions it had been powerless to produce.

I

Hitler spent Christmas Eve 1924 with the Hanfstaengls in their splendid new villa in Munich's Herzogpark. He had put on weight during his time in prison, and looked a little flabby. His blue suit was flecked with dandruff on the collar and shoulders. Four-year-old Egon Hanfstaengl was glad to see his 'Uncle Dolf' again.[12] Within two minutes, Hitler was asking to hear Isolde's 'Liebestod' on Hanfstaengl's elegant Blüthner grand piano. Wagner's music, as Hanfstaengl had often noticed, could transform Hitler's mood. His initial nervousness and tension disappeared. He became relaxed and cheerful. He admired the new house, then suddenly stopped in mid-sentence, glanced over his shoulder, and explained that he had not lost his habit from prison of imagining he was being observed through the peephole. It was, as Hanfstaengl realized, a pathetic piece of play-acting. Putzi had seen Hitler in Landsberg, relaxed and comfortable; and there had been no peephole in his room. He noticed that Hitler had a good appetite during the meal of turkey followed by his favourite Viennese sweet pastries, but that he scarcely touched the wine. Hitler subsequently explained that he had begun on leaving Landsberg to cut out meat and alcohol in order to lose weight.[13] He had convinced himself that meat and alcohol were harmful for him, and, 'in his fanatical way,' went on Hanfstaengl, 'finally made a dogma out of it and from then on only took vegetarian meals and alcohol-free drinks.'[14] After the meal, Hitler treated the family to his war-memories, marching up and down the room, imitating the sounds of different sorts of artillery fire at the battle of the Somme. Late in the evening, a well-connected artist, Wilhelm Funk, dropped in at the Hanfstaengls. He had known Hitler for quite some time, and now ventured his views on how the party could be built up again. Hitler replied in a familiar, and revealing, tone. For one who had 'come up from the bottom', he said, 'without name, special position, or connection', it was less a matter of programmes than hard endeavour until the public was ready to see 'a nameless one' as identical with a political line. Hitler thought he had now reached that position, and that the putsch had been of value to the movement: 'I'm no longer an unknown, and that provides us with the best basis for a new start.'[15]

The new start was Hitler's priority. The immediate aim was to have the ban on the NSDAP lifted. His first political act was to call on his old ally Pöhner, the former Munich Police President. Through a well-placed intermediary, Theodor Freiherr von Cramer-Klett, a meeting with the Bavarian Minister President Heinrich Held was arranged for 4 January. Pöhner was also influential in persuading Gürtner, the Bavarian Minister of Justice (whom Hitler was to make Reich Minister of Justice in 1933), to have the other Nazis detained in Landsberg released, among them Rudolf Heß.[16]

The meeting with Minister President Held on 4 January, only a fortnight after Hitler's release and the first of three meetings between the two, went well. No one else was present. Hitler was prepared to act humbly. It was his 'journey to Canossa'. He agreed to respect the authority of the state without condition, and to support it in the struggle against Communism. He distanced himself sharply from Ludendorff's attacks on the Catholic Church, a necessary step since the General's vociferous anti-clericalism – scarcely a winning formula in Bavaria – had recently become notably strident, and linked to an all too public row (involving a court case for libel, which Ludendorff lost) with Rupprecht, the Crown Prince of Bavaria.[17] Behind the public façade of continued reverence for the figurehead of the *völkisch* movement, Hitler's willingness during his meeting with the Bavarian premier to dissociate himself from Ludendorff was not only shrewd, but also a sign of his increasing estrangement from the General, which would rapidly accelerate into complete alienation by 1927.

Not least, Hitler promised Held – an easy promise to make in the circumstances – that he would not again attempt a putsch.[18] Held told Hitler in the most forthright terms that times had changed. He would not tolerate any return to the sort of circumstances that had prevailed before the putsch. Nor would the constitutional government treat the 'revolutionaries of yesterday' as an equal partner.[19] But Hitler got what he wanted. With Gürtner's backing, the way was now paved for the removal of the ban on the NSDAP and the *Völkischer Beobachter* on 16 February.[20] By that time, Hitler's relations with his rivals in the NSFB had been clarified.

A meeting of the NSFB in Berlin on 17 January marked the effective end of the attempt to create a unified *völkisch* movement. Reinhold Wulle, one of the original DVFP founders, sought to undermine Hitler's authority, especially among the strong north German contingent present. He accused Hitler of being worn-out through his imprisonment and of giving in to the international power of the Catholic Church. Wulle reckoned this to be a bigger threat than 'the Jewish danger'. The point carried some weight among *völkisch* leaders in the Protestant North. He also suggested that under Hitler's weakened leadership Bavarian particularism would come to dominate. It would be South against North. Playing to his audience, Wulle emphasized his own Prussian orientation. Clever politicians were needed in the present conditions. Hitler was not one of them. Henning, another co-founder of the DVFP, was even plainer. Hitler was 'perhaps the drummer, but no politician'. Another vehement critic claimed that Hitler wanted to be 'pope' of the movement, to which he had contributed nothing, and accused him of breaking his word of honour. Graefe reinforced the accusation. He said he passed no judgement on Hitler. The facts spoke for themselves. The alleged breach of trust was seen as Hitler's refusal to answer a letter by Graefe earlier in January, effectively posing him an ultimatum to break his links with the Streicher and Esser faction, or the DVFP would go its own way. The accusations produced a tumult. The National Socialists present were outraged. The meeting ended with the swapping of insults and all hopes of unity in the *völkisch* movement dead.[21]

A glimpse of National Socialist thinking at the meeting can be gleaned from the comments of Walther von Corswant-Cuntzow, later Gauleiter of Pomerania. 'Rather,' he said, 'that the *one* leader in whom one has most trust fails, than this hither and thither of the many from whom everybody wants something different. I now believe in the godly grace of Hitler, whom I have personally never seen, and believe that God will enlighten him now to find the correct way out of this chaos.'[22] The patent inability to reach any basis of unity in the *völkisch* movement over the previous year made increasing numbers now susceptible to such sentiments.

But not everyone in the *völkisch* movement felt the same way. Some still stated openly that Ludendorff was the leader they wanted.[23] There was said to be a rising anti-Hitler mood in one of the Munich branches of the NSFB after the Nazi leader had brusquely refused to meet a deputation from the branch for even a few minutes and had stated that its written submission had gone, like all others he received, unread into the waste-paper basket.[24]

Hitler himself was concerned only with the removal of the ban on his party in Bavaria, which he knew was imminent. He was prepared to undertake nothing which would jeopardize it. He let the north German National Socialists know, however, that he had no intention of entering into any pact with Graefe's Freedom Party, and that a statement refounding the party throughout the Reich would be made once the ban was lifted. He insisted that his hands were free. He had entered into no political arrangements, and had promised Held only that he would not undertake a putsch. As regards his relationship with Ludendorff, he commented, referring to the position he had adopted during the days of the pre-putsch Kampfbund and subsequently at his trial, he had viewed the General only as the military leader, with himself as the political leader. The only breach of faith towards Ludendorff, he added, had come from those who had dragged his name through the 'swamp of the parliament', devaluing it in the process. He wanted 'only true National Socialists' in leadership positions after the refoundation. Far from being worn down by his imprisonment, he was more flexible than ever. But his line was unchanged: the fight above all against Marxism.[25] Its positive expression was the 'nationalization of German workers'. As for his attitude towards the heavily criticized leaders of the GVG – Streicher, Esser and Dinter – Hitler had a characteristic reply. All that mattered for him, he stated, was what those concerned had achieved. Streicher had built a following of more than 60,000 supporters in Nuremberg – more than the Reich Leadership of the NSFB had in the remainder of Bavaria. He could not offend these supporters for the sake of any personal antipathy.[26]

By mid-February, events were moving Hitler's way. On 12 February, Ludendorff dissolved the Reich Leadership of the NSFB.[27] Shortly afterwards, just before the lifting of the ban on the party, Hitler announced his decision to refound the NSDAP. A flood of declarations of loyalty to Hitler now poured in. At a meeting at Hamm in Westphalia on 22 February, Gauleiter of the former NSFB from Westphalia, the Rhineland, Hanover and Pomerania, together with over 100 district leaders from the northern provinces of Germany, attested anew their 'unshakeable loyalty and adherence

(*Gefolgschaft*) to their leader Adolf Hitler'.[28] The refounded NSI
not, unlike its pre-putsch predecessor, be largely confined to Ba

On 26 February, the *Völkischer Beobachter* appeared for th
since the putsch. Hitler's leading article 'On the Renewal of Our Movement'
placed the emphasis on avoiding recriminations for the divisions in the
völkisch movement and, learning from past mistakes, on looking towards
the future. There was to be no place in the movement for religious disputes
– a necessary disclaimer in mainly Catholic Bavaria, and a criticism of the
völkisch movement which had accused Hitler of making concessions to
Catholicism.[30] He refused to accept any external conditions limiting his
own leadership, proclaimed the aims of the movement as unchanged, and
demanded internal unity. His 'Call to Former Members' in the same edition
struck the same tone. Where party members rejoined, said Hitler, he would
not ask about the past, and would concern himself only that past disunity
should not repeat itself. He demanded unity, loyalty, and obedience.[31] He
made no concessions. What was on offer was a 'pax Hitleriana'.[32] The
newspaper also carried the new regulations for the reformed NSDAP,
based on the statutes of July 1921. Leadership and unity were once more
the keynotes. All splits were to be avoided in the struggle against 'the most
terrible enemy of the German people ... Jewry and Marxism'.[33] The SA
was to return to the role of party support troop and training ground for
young activists that it had occupied before becoming incorporated in the
Bavarian paramilitary scene in February 1923. (This was to prove, within
weeks, the breaking-point with Ernst Röhm, who, unable to persuade Hitler
to agree to retaining the SA as a conventional paramilitary organization,
withdrew from political life and departed for Bolivia.)[34] Entry into the
refounded party could only come about by taking out new membership.
There could be no renewal or continuation of former membership. This
had both symbolic value, and also accorded with the stipulation of centralized
control of membership from Munich.[35] Retention of his Munich power-base
was vital to Hitler. When Lüdecke suggested moving the headquarters to
Thuringia – strategically well situated in central Germany, associated with
Luther and the cultural traditions of Weimar, in a Protestant area which
did not have to reckon with the opposition of the Catholic establishment,
as in Bavaria, and, not least, a region with an existing strong base of *völkisch*
sympathizers – Hitler conceded that there was something to be said for the
idea. 'But I can't leave Munich,' he immediately added. 'I'm at home here;
I mean something here; there are many here who are devoted to me, to me
alone, and to nobody else. That's important.'[36]

At eight o'clock on the evening of 27 February 1925, Hitler, with his usual sense of theatre, made his re-entry to the Munich political scene where he had left it sixteen months earlier: at the Bürgerbräukeller. The meeting had originally been envisaged for the 24th. But that was Fasching-Tuesday.[37] So the Friday was settled upon. Just as before the putsch, red placards advertising the speech had been plastered around Munich for days. People began to take up their seats in the early afternoon. Three hours before the scheduled start, the huge beerhall was packed. Over 3,000 were jammed inside, 2,000 more turned away, and police cordons set up to block off the surrounding area.[38] Some prominent faces were missing. Rosenberg was one. He was irritated at being excluded from Hitler's inner circle in the weeks since his return from Landsberg.[39] He told Lüdecke: 'I won't take part in that comedy . . . I know the sort of brother-kissing Hitler intends to call for.'[40] Ludendorff, Strasser and Röhm were also absent.[41] Hitler wanted the first party-leader, Drexler, to chair the meeting. But Drexler insisted that Hermann Esser be evicted from the party.[42] Hitler would accept no conditions. And for him, Esser had 'more political sense in his fingertips than the whole bunch of his accusers in their buttocks'.[43] So one of Hitler's most trusted Munich followers, his business-manager Max Amann, opened the meeting.

Hitler spoke for almost two hours.[44] The first three-quarters of his speech offered his standard account of Germany's plight since 1918, the Jews as the cause of it, the weakness of bourgeois parties, and the aims of Marxism (which, he stated, could only be combated by a doctrine of higher truth but 'similar brutality of execution'). Hitler was frank about the need to focus all energy on one goal, on attacking a single enemy to avoid fragmentation and disunity. 'The art of all great popular leaders,' he proclaimed, 'consisted at all times in concentrating the attention of the masses on a single enemy.' From the context, it was plain that he meant the Jews. Only in the last quarter of the speech did Hitler arrive at his real theme of the evening. No one should expect him, he said, to take sides in the bitter dispute still raging in the *völkisch* movement. He saw in each party comrade only the supporter of the common idea, he declared, to lasting applause. His task as leader was not to explore what had happened in the past, but to bring together those pulling apart. At last he came to the climacteric. The dispute was at an end. Those prepared to join should sink their differences. For nine months, others had had time to 'look after' the interests of the party, he pointed out with sarcasm. To great and lasting applause, he added: 'Gentlemen, let the representation of the interests of the movement from now on be my concern!' His leadership had, however, to be accepted unconditionally. 'I am not prepared to allow conditions as long as I carry personally the responsibility,' he concluded. 'And I now carry again the complete responsibility for everything that takes place in this movement.' After a year, he would hold himself to account.[45] There were tumultuous cheers and cries of 'Heil'. Everyone stood for the singing of 'Deutschland über alles'.[46]

Then came the finale. It was a piece of pure theatre. But it had symbolic meaning, not lost on those present. Arch-enemies over the past year and more – Hermann Esser, Julius Streicher, Artur Dinter from the GVG, Rudolf Buttmann, Gottfried Feder, Wilhelm Frick from the 'parliamentary' Völkischer Block – mounted the platform and, among emotional scenes, with many standing on chairs and tables and the crowd pressing forward from the back of the hall, shook hands, forgave each other, and swore undying loyalty to the leader.[47] It was like medieval vassals swearing fealty to their overlord. Others followed. Whatever the hypocrisy, the public show of unity, it was plain, could only have been attained under Hitler as leader. He could with some justice claim to have restored the 'homogeneity' of the party.[48] In the following years, it would become more and more apparent: Hitler, and the 'idea' increasingly embodied in his leadership, constituted the sole, indispensable force of integration in a movement that retained the potential to tear itself apart. Hitler's position as supreme leader standing over the party owed much to the recognition of this fact.

Outside loyalist circles, the immediate response to Hitler's speech on the *völkisch* Right was often one of disappointment. This was mainly because of the way Hitler was plainly distancing himself from Ludendorff, still seen by many as the leader of the *völkisch* movement. In his proclamation of 26 February, Hitler had referred merely in bland terms to the General as 'the most loyal and selfless friend' of the National Socialist Movement. In his speech, he had not mentioned Ludendorff at all. Only in the scenes that followed, as calls of 'Heil' to the General were heard in the hall, had he spoken – diplomatically, but vaguely – of belonging to him 'in heart' even though he had not referred to his name.[49] Ludendorff's supporters saw Hitler's treatment of him as a calculated insult. Ludendorff's standing remained a potential problem.[50] But as so often, luck came to Hitler's aid.

On 28 February 1925, the day after the refoundation of the NSDAP, the first Reich President of the Weimar Republic, the Social Democrat Friedrich Ebert, died at the age of fifty-four from the effects of an appendicitis operation. The Right had so persistently tried to defame him for his participation in the munitions strike of January 1918 – when the SPD leadership had become involved in the unrest (demanding democratization and peace without annexations) that spread from the Berlin armaments factories, bringing a million workers out on strike, temporarily threatening war production, and later fostering the 'stab-in-the-back' legend – that he had been forced to defend himself in 170 libel cases.[51] Such was the feeling against Ebert, and such was the level of anti-socialism in conservative Catholic as well as in nationalist circles, that the Archbishop of Munich and Freising, Cardinal Faulhaber, who had notoriously on one occasion dubbed the 1918 Revolution 'high treason', refused to have the church bells rung in his diocese in honour of the dead President.[52] The NSDAP had no expectation of having any significant influence on the election of Ebert's successor. Hitler openly as good as admitted this. He told a party meeting that it was immaterial who became Reich President. Whoever it was would be 'only a man who is in reality no "man" at all'.[53] But against the arguments of some of his advisers, Hitler insisted on putting forward Ludendorff as the National Socialist candidate, and persuaded the General to stand.[54] He regarded the General as no more than a token candidate, without a chance of winning.[55] Why Ludendorff agreed to stand is less easy to understand than why Hitler wanted the candidacy of a rival of whom he was by now in private extremely scathing.[56] It seems that Hitler persuaded the General that the conservative candidate of the Right, Karl Jarres, had to be stopped, and, flattering Ludendorff's prestige, inveigled him into standing. 'Hitler knows perfectly well that although he has a great following in Bavaria he can count on very few votes in North Germany and East of Berlin,' the General told his dismayed wife, who immediately foresaw the likely consequences to which the arrogant former warlord was blind. 'In particular, the East Prussians and Silesians have been bound to me by gratitude and devotion ever since the war,' he went on, his mind made up. They, in fact, showed their gratitude and devotion by almost completely ignoring him in the poll.[57] Probably Ludendorff reckoned, too, with the backing of his *völkisch* friends. But when the DVFB decided – in order not to split the right-wing vote – to put their support behind Jarres, the General's fate was effectively sealed.[58] What had seemed to some in Hitler's entourage a risky strategy was, in fact, no great risk at all, and was more or less guaranteed to damage Ludendorff. That this was the intention was scarcely concealed, even by some leading Nazis.[59]

For Ludendorff, the election on 29 March was a catastrophe. He polled only 286,000 votes, 1.1 per cent of the votes cast. This was 600,000 fewer than the *völkisch* Right had gained at the Reichstag election in December 1924, itself a disastrous result.[60] Hitler was anything but distressed at the outcome. 'That's all right,' he told Hermann Esser, 'now we've finally finished him.'[61] The election winner in the run-off on 26 April was another war-hero, Field Marshal Hindenburg. Weimar democracy was now in the hands of one of the pillars of the old order. Not only did the national-conservative Right vote for him. Had the BVP and the KPD supported the Centre Party's candidate Wilhelm Marx, instead of the BVP perversely supporting the candidate of the reactionary Right and Communists sticking with Ernst Thälmann, Hindenburg would have lost. The price would be paid heavily in 1933.

Ludendorff never recovered from his defeat. Hitler's great rival for the leadership of the *völkisch* Right no longer posed a challenge. He was rapidly on his way into the political wilderness. Influenced by Mathilde von Kemnitz, who in 1926 would become his second wife, he had since around 1924 become increasingly susceptible to a persecution complex bound up with conspiracy theories, which included freemasons, Jews, Marxists, and also Jesuits. His increasing eccentricity – bolstered by Mathilde's even greater zaniness – now took him increasingly to the fringes of the radical Right, itself scarcely renowned for its cool rationality. The curious sect he and Mathilde founded in 1925, the Tannenbergbund, published a wealth of literature which was so hair-brained in its persecution paranoia that even Nazi ideologues rejected it. Not only was Ludendorff no longer of any use to Hitler; he was outrightly counter-productive. By 1927, Hitler was openly attacking his former ally – and accusing him of freemasonry (an accusation which was never countered).[62]

The *völkisch* movement itself, in 1924 numerically stronger and geographi-cally more widespread than the NSDAP and its successor organizations, was not only weakened and divided, but had now effectively lost its figure-head.[63] At first, especially in southern Germany, there were difficulties where local party leaders refused to accede to Hitler's demand that they break their ties with *völkisch* associations and subordinate themselves totally to his leadership. But increasingly they went over to Hitler.[64] Most realized the way the wind was blowing. Without Hitler, they had no future. For his part, Hitler was particularly assiduous during the coming months in visiting local party branches in Bavaria. The ban on speaking at public meetings which the Bavarian authorities had imposed on him on 9 March (followed in subsequent months by a similar ban in most other states, including Prussia) gave him more time for speaking in closed party meetings.[65] The handshake with individual members, invariably a part of such meetings, symbolically cemented the bonds between himself and the local membership.

A sturdy platform of support for Hitler's leadership was thus laid in Bavaria. In the north, the path was less even.

II

On 11 March, two days after the speaking ban had been imposed, Hitler commissioned Gregor Strasser to organize the party in north Germany.[66] Strasser, a Landshut apothecary, a big, bluff Bavarian, in the pre-putsch days SA chief in Lower Bavaria, a diabetic who mixed it with the roughest in beerhall brawls but relaxed by reading Homer in the original, was probably the most able of the leading Nazis. Above all he was a superb organizer. It was largely Gregor Strasser's work, building on the contacts he had established while in the Reich Leadership of the NSFB, that resulted in the rapid construction of the NSDAP's organization in north Germany.[67] Most of the local branches in the north had to be created from scratch. By the end of 1925, these branches numbered 262, compared with only seventy-one on the eve of the putsch.[68] While Hitler spent much of the summer of 1925 in the mountains near Berchtesgaden, working on the second volume of his book, and taking time out to enjoy the Bayreuth Festival, bothering little about the party outside Bavaria, Strasser was unceasing in his efforts in the north. His own views on a 'national socialism' had been formed in the trenches. He was more idealistic, less purely instrumentalist, than Hitler in his aim to win over the working class. And, though of course strongly antisemitic, he thought little of the obsessive, near-exclusive emphasis on Jew-baiting that characterized Hitler and his entourage in the Munich party. In fact, dating from the period of the rancorous split in 1924, he could barely tolerate the leading lights in the Bavarian NSDAP, Esser and Streicher. Even if he expressed them somewhat differently, however, he shared Hitler's basic aims. And though he never succumbed to Hitler-worship, he recognized Hitler's indispensability to the movement, and remained a Hitler loyalist.[69]

Strasser's views, and his approach, fitted well into the way the party had developed in north Germany, far away from the Bavarian heartlands. A central issue there was the intense detestation, deriving from the deep clashes of the 'leaderless time' of 1924, of the three individuals they saw as dominating affairs in Bavaria – Esser, Streicher and Amann. The rejection of these figures had been practically the sole area of agreement between the Directorate and the NSFB leaders in 1924. It was to remain a point of tension between the north German NSDAP and the Munich headquarters throughout 1925.[70] This went hand in hand with the refusal to be dictated to by the Munich headquarters, where the party secretary, Philip Bouhler, was attempting to impose centralized control over party membership, and with it Munich's complete authority over the whole movement.[71] A further integrally related factor was the concern over Hitler's continuing inaction while the crisis in the NSDAP deepened. It was his passivity, in the eyes of the northern party leaders, that allowed the Esser clique its dominance and kept him far too much under the unsavoury influence of the former GVG leaders. His support for them remained a source of intense disappointment and bitterness.[72] Hitler had also disappointed in his neglect of the north, despite his promises, since the refoundation. Beyond this, there were continuing disagreements about electoral participation. The Göttingen party leadership, especially, remained wholly hostile to parliamentary tactics, which, it felt, would result in the 'movement' being turned into a mere 'party', like others.[73] Not least, there were different accents on policy and different emphases on the National Socialist 'idea'. Some of the north German leaders, like Strasser, advocated a more 'socialist' emphasis. This aimed at maximum appeal to workers in the big industrial regions. The different social structure demanded a different type of appeal than that favoured in Bavaria.

But it was not just a matter of cynical propaganda. Some of the leading activists in the north, like the young Joseph Goebbels in the Elberfeld area of the Ruhr, were attracted by the ideas of 'national Bolshevism'.[74] Possessed of a sharp mind and biting wit, the future Propaganda Minister, among the most intelligent of the leading figures in the Nazi Movement, had joined the NSDAP at the end of 1924. Brought up in a Catholic family of moderate means, from Rheydt, a small industrial town in the Rhineland, his deformed right foot exposed him from childhood days to jibes, taunts, and lasting feelings of physical inadequacy. That his early pretensions as a writer met with little recognition further fostered his resentment. 'Why does fate deny to me what it gives to others?' he asked himself in an entry in March 1925 in the diary he would keep till the end of his days in the Berlin bunker twenty years later, adding, self-piteously, Jesus's words on the Cross – 'My God, my God, why hast Thou forsaken me?'[75] His inferiority complex produced driving ambition and the need to demonstrate achievement through mental agility in a movement which derided both physical weakness and 'intellectuals'. Not least, it produced ideological fanaticism.

Goebbels showed his own ideological preferences at that time in an exchange in mid-September 1925 with the head of the Pomeranian Gau,

Theodor Vahlen, a professor at Greifswald University and owner of a small printing-house in the town, whose incompetence alongside the animosity he attracted from the future Propaganda Leader led to his replacement as Gauleiter by 1927.[76] 'National and socialist! What goes first, and what comes afterwards? With us in the west, there can be no doubt. First socialist redemption, then comes national liberation like a whirlwind. Professor Vahlen takes a different view. First nationalize the workers. But the question is, how?' Goebbels had gained a false impression of Hitler's position. 'Hitler stands between both opinions,' he wrote. 'But he is on the way to coming over to us completely.'[77] Goebbels and some other northern leaders thought of themselves as revolutionaries, with more in common with the Communists than with the hated bourgeoisie. There were some sympathies for Russia. And there was talk of a party trade union.[78]

Finally, there was the attitude towards Hitler and towards the party's programme. The north German Directorate had been fanatically pro-Hitler during the time of his imprisonment. But it had been disappointed at his equivocal stance towards the NSFB, and the issue of elections. And its leaders, Adalbert Volck and then Ludolf Haase, had shied away from the way a personality cult was being built around Hitler, and its implications for the party. All the north German leaders accepted Hitler's position, and his right to head the party. They recognized him as the 'hero of Munich' for his part in the putsch, and for his stance at the trial. His standing and reputation needed no emphasis, and faults were attributed to those around him – especially Esser and Streicher.[79] But many of the north German party faithful did not know Hitler personally, had not even met him.[80] Their relationship to him was, therefore, quite different than that of Bavarian party members, especially those in Munich. Hitler was their leader; that was not in question. But Hitler, too, in their eyes, was bound to the 'idea'. Moreover, the 1920 Programme that outlined the 'idea' in terms of the aims of the party was itself in their view deficient and in need of reform.[81]

By late summer 1925, the northern leaders, differing among themselves in matters of interpretation and emphasis on points of the programme, aims, and meaning of National Socialism, were at least agreed that the party was undergoing a crisis. This was reflected in declining membership and stagnation. It was associated by them, above all, with the state of the party in Munich.[82] Hitler himself was totally taken up with work on *Mein Kampf* and, they felt, prepared to do nothing. In the circumstances, this amounted to support for Esser. Hitler defended Esser and his clique on the grounds that their usefulness was the decisive factor, ignoring how limited this 'usefulness' was if it meant the opposition of the party in the rest of the Reich.

It was to create a counter to the 'Esser dictatorship' that Gregor Strasser, described by Fobke as 'the honest, extraordinarily diligent, if not genial, collaborator of Hitler', summoned a meeting of northern party leaders to Hagen in Westphalia on 10 September 1925. Strasser himself had to drop out at the last minute because of the serious illness of his mother.[83] As a result, the discussions did not go entirely according to plan. But most of the northern and western party leaders were present. In Strasser's absence, the intention (which had not been revealed to most of those attending) of forming a block to combat 'the harmful Munich direction' could not be fulfilled. Divisions were quickly revealed. When the issue of Esser was raised, there was resistance to anything that smacked of a 'palace revolution'. A unanimous rejection of participation in elections, recorded and sent on to Hitler, simply papered over other serious divisions. Beyond that, all that could be achieved was the establishment, under Strasser's leadership, of a loose organization of northern party districts, mainly for arranging the exchange of speakers.[84]

This 'Working Community (*Arbeitsgemeinschaft*) of the North and West German Gaue of the NSDAP' (AG), and its publicity organ, the *National-sozialistische Briefe* (National Socialist Letters), edited by Goebbels, were not in any way intended as a challenge to Hitler.[85] His approval was explicitly acknowledged in the Community's statutes, and its members committed themselves to work 'in comradely spirit of the idea of National Socialism under their leader Adolf Hitler'.[86] Hitler recommended the publications of the Community to party members. The members of the Community opposed Hitler's entourage, not Hitler himself. And here, too, there were compromises in practice – even stretching to relations with Esser and Streicher.[87] There was, therefore, no hint of a secession.

Even so, despite its internal divisions, the Community did come to pose a threat to Hitler's authority. The clashes over the Esser clique, and over electoral participation, were not in themselves critical. Of far greater significance was the fact that Gregor Strasser and Goebbels, especially, looked to the Community as an opportunity to reshape the party's programme. Ultimately, Strasser hoped to replace the Programme of 1920.[88] In November, Strasser took the first steps in composing the Community's own draft programme. It advocated a racially integrated German nation at the heart of a central European customs union, the basis of a united states of Europe. Internally, it proposed a corporate state. In the economy, it looked to tying peasants to their landholdings, and public control of the means of production while protecting private property.[89]

Not only was the draft vague, incoherent, and contradictory. It could only be divisive. So it proved even before the Community's meeting in Hanover on 24 January 1926 to consider it.[90] The meeting resolved to consider the suggestions sent in by various members in a commission run by Gregor Strasser.[91] But this bland resolution did not reflect a heated, acrimonious debate, at which uncomplimentary comments were made about Gottfried Feder, the party's economics 'expert' whose ideas had made a strong impression on Hitler while the latter was undergoing his ideological training course for the Reichswehr in the summer of 1919. The Community's draft programme had not been sent to either Feder or Hitler. When he obtained a copy, Feder, the self-styled 'father' of the original party programme – though his influence had probably extended no further than the inclusion of his obsessive demand for the 'breaking of interest slavery' – was furious. He turned up unannounced at Hanover and did not hide his anger at the direction of the intended changes.[92] Feeling aggrieved and insulted, he made notes of what was said, plainly with a view to reporting them in Munich.[93] Some of the Gauleiter – the party's regional bosses, in charge of the thirty or so sizeable districts (*Gaue*) into which the Reich was divided – present did not shy away from direct criticism of Hitler's leadership qualities – though they realized they could not do without him.[94] The meeting had previously also decided unanimously to support the plebiscite (to take place in June) for the expropriation of the German princes without compensation – an initiative of the Left, and at the time a significant and divisive public issue.[95]

Hitler had previously been unconcerned about the Working Community. But Feder now prompted him into action. Hitler plainly recognized the danger signals. He summoned about sixty party leaders to a meeting on 14 February 1926 at Bamberg, in Upper Franconia.[96] There was no agenda. Hitler, it was stated, simply wanted to discuss some 'important questions'. The local branch in Bamberg, large and loyalist, had been well cultivated by Hitler and Streicher during 1925. The northern leaders, though several of the most prominent among them were present, were both outnumbered and could not but be impressed by the show of support for Hitler which had been orchestrated in the town.[97] On the journey to Bamberg, Feder had once more taken the opportunity to underline to Hitler the threat to his authority.[98]

Hitler spoke for two hours.[99] He addressed in the main the issue of foreign policy and future alliances. His position was wholly opposed to that of the Working Community. Alliances were never ideal, he said, but always 'purely a matter of political business'. Britain and Italy, both distancing themselves from Germany's arch-enemy France, offered the best potential. Any thought of an alliance with Russia could be ruled out. It would mean 'the immediate political bolshevization of Germany', and with it 'national suicide'. Germany's future could be secured solely by acquiring land, by eastern coloniz- ation as in the Middle Ages, by a colonial policy not overseas but in Europe. On the question of the expropriation of the princes, Hitler again ruled out the position of the Working Community. 'For us there are today no princes, only Germans,' he declared. 'We stand on the basis of the law, and will not give a Jewish system of exploitation a legal pretext for the complete plundering of our people.' Such a rhetorical slant could not conceal the outright rejection of the views of the northern leaders. Finally, Hitler repeated his insistence that religious problems had no part to play in the National Socialist Movement.[100]

Goebbels was appalled.

I feel devastated. What sort of Hitler? A reactionary? Amazingly clumsy and uncertain. Russian question: completely by the way. Italy and England natural allies. Terrible! Our task is the smashing of Bolshevism. Bolshevism is a Jewish creation! We must be Russia's heir! 180 Millions! Expropriation of the princes! Law is law. Also for the princes. Don't shake the question of private property! (sic!)[101] Dreadful! Programme is sufficient! Content with it. Feder nods. Ley nods.[102] Streicher nods. Esser nods. I'm sick at heart when I see you in such company!!! Short discussion. Strasser speaks. Hesitant, trembling, clumsy, the good, honest Strasser. God, how poor a match we are for those swine down there! . . . Probably one of the greatest disappointments of my life. I no longer believe fully in Hitler. That's the terrible thing: my inner support has been taken away.[103]

The potential threat from the Working Community had evaporated. Hitler had reasserted his authority. Despite some initial signs of defiance, the fate of the Community had been sealed at Bamberg. Gregor Strasser promised Hitler to collect all copies of the draft programme he had distrib- uted, and wrote to members of the Community on 5 March asking for them to be returned.[104] The Community now petered out into non-existence. On 1 July 1926, Hitler signed a directive stating that 'since the NSDAP rep- resents a large working community, there is no justification for smaller working communities as a combination of individual *Gaue*'.[105] By that time, Strasser's Working Community of northern and western Gauleiter was finished. With it went the last obstacle to the complete establishment of Hitler's supreme mastery over the party.

Hitler was shrewd enough to be generous after his Bamberg triumph. He voiced no objection to the creation in March of a greatly enlarged Gau in the Ruhr under the combined leadership of the Working Community members Goebbels, Karl Kaufmann (an energetic activist in his mid-twenties, later Gauleiter of Hamburg, who had cut his teeth through organizing sabotage in the French-occupied Ruhr), and Franz Pfeffer von Salomon (Gauleiter of Westphalia, a former army officer who had subsequently joined the Freikorps, participated in the Kapp Putsch, and been active in opposition to the French in the Ruhr).[106] He paid Gregor Strasser, recovering from a car accident, a surprise visit at his Landshut home. Following discussions with Strasser, he excluded Esser from the Reich Leadership of the NSDAP in April.[107] And by September, Strasser had himself been called to the Reich Leadership as Propaganda Leader of the party, while Franz Pfeffer von Salomon was appointed head of the SA.[108] Most important of all, the impressionable Goebbels was openly courted by Hitler and completely won over.

To bring about what has often been called Goebbels's 'Damascus' in fact took little doing.[109] Goebbels had idolized Hitler from the beginning. 'Who is this man? Half plebian, half God! Actually Christ, or only John [the Baptist]?' he had written in his diary in October 1925 on finishing reading the first volume of *Mein Kampf*.[110] 'This man has everything to be a king. The born tribune of the people. The coming dictator,' he added a few weeks later. 'How I love him.'[111] Like others in the Working Community, he had wanted only to liberate Hitler from the clutches of the Esser clique.[112] Bamberg was a bitter blow. But his belief in Hitler was dented, not destroyed. It needed only a sign from Hitler to restore it. And the sign was not long in coming.

In mid-March Goebbels made his peace with Streicher after a long talk in Nuremberg.[113] At the end of the month he received a letter from Hitler inviting him to speak in Munich on 8 April.[114] Hitler's car was there to meet him at the station in Munich to take him to his hotel. 'What a noble reception,' noted Goebbels in his diary.[115] Hitler's car was again provided the next day to take Goebbels to visit Lake Starnberg, a few miles outside Munich. In the evening after Goebbels's speech in the Bürgerbräukeller, in which he evidently retreated from his more radical version of socialism, Hitler embraced him, tears in his eyes. His north German colleagues, Kaufmann and Pfeffer, were less impressed. Disappointed at his sudden reversal of the opposition to Munich he had up to then so vehemently advocated, they told Goebbels his speech was 'rubbish'.[116] The next morning Goebbels was taken to party headquarters. He, Kaufmann, and Pfeffer were summoned to Hitler's room. There they were subjected to a dressing-down for their parts in the Working Community and Gau Ruhr. But Hitler promptly offered to wipe the slate clean. 'At the end unity follows,' wrote Goebbels. 'Hitler is great. He gives us all a warm handshake.' In the afternoon Hitler spent three hours going over the same ground he had covered at Bamberg. Then, Goebbels had been sorely disappointed. Now, he thought it was 'brilliant'. 'I love him ... He has thought through everything,' Goebbels continued. 'He's a man, taking it all round. Such a sparkling mind can be my leader. I bow to the greater one, the political genius.'[117] Goebbels's conversion was complete. A few days later, he met Hitler again, this time in Stuttgart. 'I believe he has taken me to his heart like no one else,' he wrote. 'Adolf Hitler, I love you because you are both great and simple at the same time. What one calls a genius.'[118] Towards the end of the year, Hitler appointed Goebbels as Gauleiter of Berlin – a key position if the party were to advance in the capital.[119] Goebbels was Hitler's man. He would remain so, adoring and subservient alike to the man he said he loved 'like a father', down to the last days in the bunker.[120]

The Bamberg meeting had been a milestone in the development of the NSDAP. The Working Community had neither wanted nor attempted a rebellion against Hitler's leadership. But once Strasser had composed his draft programme, a clash was inevitable. Was the party to be subordinated to a programme, or to its leader? The Bamberg meeting decided what National Socialism was to mean. It was not to mean a party torn, as the *völkisch* movement had been in 1924, over points of dogma. The Twenty-Five-Point Programme of 1920 was therefore regarded as sufficient. 'It stays as it is,' Hitler was reported as saying. 'The New Testament is also full of contradictions, but that hasn't prevented the spread of Christianity.'[121] Its symbolic significance, not any practical feasibility, was what mattered. Any more precise policy statement would not merely have produced continuing inner dissension. It would have bound Hitler himself to the programme, subordinated him to abstract tenets of doctrine that were open to dispute and alteration. As it was, his position as leader *over* the movement was now inviolable.

At Bamberg, too, an important ideological issue – the anti-Russian thrust of foreign policy – had been reaffirmed. The alternative approach of the northern group had been rejected. The 'idea' and the Leader were coming to be inseparable. But the 'idea' amounted to a set of distant goals, a mission for the future. The only way to it was through the attainment of power. For that, maximum flexibility was needed. No ideological or organizational disputes should in future be allowed to divert from the path. Fanatical willpower, converted into organized mass force, was what was required. That demanded freedom of action for the leader; and total obedience from the following. What emerged in the aftermath of Bamberg was, therefore, the growth of a new type of political organization: one subjected to the will of the Leader, who stood over and above the party, the embodiment in his own person of the 'idea' of National Socialism.[122]

By the time of the General Members' Meeting on 22 May, attended by 657 party members,[123] Hitler's leadership had emerged inordinately strengthened. He frankly admitted that he attributed no value to the meeting, which had been called simply to meet the legal requirements of a public association. The forthcoming Party Rally in Weimar – the opportunity for a visual display of the new-found unity – was what counted in his eyes.[124] Following his 'report' on the party's activities since its refoundation, Hitler was unanimously 're-elected' as party chairman.[125] The party administration remained in the hands of those close to Hitler.[126] A few amendments were made to the party statutes. Altered five times since 1920, these were now couched in their finalized form. They assured Hitler of the control of the party machine. The appointment of his most important subordinates, the Gauleiter, was in his hands. In effect, the statutes reflected the leader party which the NSDAP had become.[127] In the light of the conflict with the Working Community over a new programme, not least significant was the reaffirmation of the Twenty-Five Points of 24 February 1920. 'This Programme is immutable,' the statutes unambiguously declared.[128]

A few weeks later, the Party Rally held at Weimar – where Hitler was permitted to speak in public – on 3–4 July 1926 provided the intended show of unity behind the leader. The rally was intended as 'a great display of the youthful strength of our movement'. What was expected was 'an image of disciplined force ... visible proof of the regained inner health of the movement'. The events of 1924 were held up as a warning. All potential for discord was to be avoided. Matters of substance were referred to special commissions. Discussion was to be kept to a minimum. The chairman of each commission was to be held personally responsible for any resolutions, which were then subject to Hitler's own veto.[129] Otherwise, the rally consisted of speeches, ritual, and marching. An estimated 7–8,000, including 3,600 stormtroopers and 116 SS men, attended.[130] It was the first time that the Schutzstaffel (SS, Protection Squad), founded in April 1925 and arising initially out of Hitler's personal bodyguard, the Stoßtrupp Adolf Hitler (Adolf Hitler Assault Squad), had been on public display.[131] Also on display for the first time, and handed to the SS as a sign of Hitler's approbation of his new élite organization, was the 'Blood Flag' of 1923, which had led the procession to the Feldherrnhalle. Every stormtrooper present swore a personal oath of loyalty to Hitler.[132] The party leader received a rapturous reception from delegates after his speech.[133] 'Deep and mystical. Almost like a gospel . . . I thank fate, that it gave us this man,' wrote Goebbels.[134]

The Nazi Party was still far smaller than it had been at the time of the putsch.[135] In the overall framework of national politics, it was wholly insignificant. To outside observers, its prospects seemed bleak. But internally, the crisis period was over. Though small, the party was better organized as well as geographically more widespread than the pre-putsch party had been. Its image of unity and strength was beginning to persuade other *völkisch* organizations to throw in their lot with the NSDAP.[136] Above all, it was turning into a new type of political organization – a Leader Party. Hitler had established the basis of his mastery over the movement. In the next years, while still in the political wilderness, that mastery would become complete.

III

Few people saw Hitler on a regular basis in these years. Only his substitute family – the trusted and devotedly loyal group of Munich cronies who formed his coterie of bodyguards, chauffeurs, and secretaries – were in constant touch with him. Some, like Julius Schaub (his general factotum) and Rudolf Heß (his secretary), had served in Landsberg with Hitler for their part in the putsch. This 'houseguard' escorted him, protected him, shielded him from the increasing numbers wanting an audience. Getting to see Hitler was difficult.[137] Those running party business in Munich often had to wait for days before they could sort out some matter with him. For leading figures in the movement, too, he could prove inaccessible for weeks at a time.[138] Even on public occasions he was largely unapproachable. Before a speech, he would remain closeted in his room. Only once the hall was reported as full would he set out. Afterwards, when away from Munich, he would immediately return to his hotel. Journalists might be permitted to see him for a few minutes, if an interview had been prearranged. But scarcely anyone else was allowed an audience.[139]

Hitler's pronounced sense of 'mission', his heroic self-image of 'greatness', the necessity of upholding the aura increasingly attached to him by his supporters, and the olympian detachment from the intrigues and in-fighting of his subordinates demanded a high degree of isolation.[140] Beyond this, the distance he deliberately placed between himself and even high-ranking members of his movement was calculated to emphasize the sense of awe and admiration in those admitted to his presence, or encountering him at a theatrically staged mass meeting or rally. At the same time, it enhanced the enigmatic in him. Even those who knew him found it hard to dissect and understand his personality.[141] Hitler was happy to encourage the sense of mystery and fascination.

He was above all a consummate actor. This certainly applied to the stage-managed occasions – the delayed entry to the packed hall, the careful construction of his speeches, the choice of colourful phrases, the gestures and body-language.[142] Here, his natural rhetorical talent was harnessed to well-honed performing skills. A pause at the beginning to allow the tension to mount; a low-key, even hesitant, start; undulations and variations of diction, not melodious certainly, but vivid and highly expressive; almost staccato bursts of sentences, followed by well-timed *rallentando* to expose the emphasis of a key point; theatrical use of the hands as the speech rose in crescendo; sarcastic wit aimed at opponents: all were devices carefully nurtured to maximize effect. As in the meticulous attention to detail in the preparations for the party rallies at Weimar in 1926 and Nuremberg in 1927 and 1929, Hitler was preoccupied with impact and impression. His clothing was also selected to match the occasion: the light-brown uniform with swastika armband, belt, attached diagonal strap crossing over the right shoulder, and knee-high leather boots when among the faithful at big party meetings and rallies; dark suit, white shirt, and tie, when appropriate to conveying a less martial, more 'respectable', appearance to a wider audience.

But the acting was not confined to such occasions. Those who came into contact with Hitler, while retaining a critical distance from him, were convinced that he was acting much of the time. He could play the parts as required. 'He was a kindly conversationalist, kissing the hands of ladies, a friendly uncle giving chocolate to children, a simple man of the people shaking the calloused hands of peasants and workers.'[143] He could be the model of friendliness in public to someone he was privately castigating and deriding. The play-acting and hypocrisy did not mean that he was solely a cynical manipulator, that he did not believe in the central tenets of his 'world-view'. This fervent belief, coupled with the strength of his domineering personality, carried conviction among those drawn to his message. But for one perceptive and critical observer, the one-time Gauleiter of Hamburg, Albert Krebs, Hitler's ability to sway the masses rested essentially on a 'very conscious art' of manipulation – cool calculation, 'without inner sympathy and truthfulness'.[144] Krebs summed up: 'The art of the mask and dissimulation should not be forgotten. It made it so difficult to grasp the core of Hitler's being.'[145]

The irresistible fascination that many – not a few of them cultured, educated, and intelligent – found in his extraordinary personality-traits doubtless owed much to his ability to play parts.[146] As many attested, he could be charming – particularly to women – and was often witty and amusing. Much of the time it was show, put on for effect. The same could be true of his rages and outbursts of apparently uncontrollable anger, which were in reality often contrived. The firm handshake and 'manly' eye-to-eye contact which Hitler cultivated on occasions when he had to meet ordinary party members was, for the awestruck lowly activist, a moment never to be forgotten. For Hitler, it was merely acting; it meant no more than the reinforcement of the personality cult, the cement of the movement, the bonding force between Leader and followers. In reality, Hitler showed remarkably little human interest in his followers.[147] Even one of his leading supporters accused him of 'contempt for mankind' (*Menschenverachtung*) in 1928.[148] His egocentrism was of monumental proportions. The propaganda image of 'fatherliness' concealed inner emptiness. Other individuals were of interest to him only in so far as they were useful.

Hitler's 'coffee-house tirades, his restlessness, his resentments against possible rivals in the party leadership, his distaste for systematic work, his paranoid oubursts of hatred' were seen by Putzi Hanfstaengl as a sign of sexual deficiency.[149] This was no more than guesswork. But Hitler's relations with women were indeed odd in some ways. Why this was so can only be surmised. Yet here, too, he was often acting out a role. On one occasion, he took advantage of Putzi Hanfstaengl's brief absence from the room to fall on his knees in front of Helene Hanfstaengl, describing himself as her slave and bemoaning the fate that had led him to her too late. When Helene told him of the incident, Putzi put it down to Hitler's need to play the role of the languishing troubadour from time to time.[150]

In physical appearance, Hitler was little changed from the time before the putsch. Away from the speaker's podium he looked anything but impressive.[151] His face had hardened.[152] But, as he told Hanfstaengl would be the case, he soon lost the weight he had put on in Landsberg once he started speaking again.[153] Hitler reckoned he lost up to five pounds in weight through perspiration during a big speech. To counter this, his aides insisted on twenty bottles of mineral water being provided at the side of the lectern.[154] Has dress sense was anything but stylish. He still often favoured his plain blue suit.[155] His trilby, light-coloured raincoat, leather leggings and riding-whip gave him – especially when arriving with his bodyguards in the big black six-seater Mercedes convertible he had bought in early 1925 – the appearance of an eccentric gangster.[156] For relaxation, he preferred to wear traditional Bavarian lederhosen.[157] But even when he was in prison, he hated to be seen without a tie.[158] During the heat of the summer, he would never be seen in a bathing costume. Whereas Mussolini revelled in virile images of himself as a sportsman or athlete, Hitler had a deep aversion to being seen other than fully clothed.[159] More than petty-bourgeois proprieties, or prudishness, image was the vital consideration. Anything potentially embarrassing, or inviting ridicule was to be avoided at all costs.

As they had done before the putsch, the Bruckmanns helped him to establish useful contacts in 'better' social circles. He had to adjust to a different type of audience from that in the beerhalls – more critical, less amenable to crude sloganizing and emotion.[160] But in essence, little or nothing had changed. Hitler was at ease only when dominating the conversation. His monologues were a cover for his half-baked knowledge. There was no doubting that he had a quick mind and a biting and destructive wit. He formed instant – often damning – judgements on individuals. And the combination of a domineering presence, resort to factual detail (often distorted), for which he had an exceptional memory, and utter conviction (brooking no alterative argument) based on ideological certitude was impressive to those already half-persuaded of his extraordinary qualities. But those with knowledge and critical distance could often quickly see behind his crude arguments.[161] His arrogance was breathtaking. 'What could I learn that's new?' he asked Hanfstaengl, on being encouraged to learn a foreign language and travel abroad.[162]

Shortly after the Weimar Party Rally, in mid-July 1926, Hitler left Munich with his entourage for a holiday on the Obersalzberg.[163] He stayed in a secluded and beautiful spot situated high in the mountains on the Austrian border above Berchtesgaden, flanked by the Untersberg (where legend had it that Barbarossa lay sleeping), the Kneifelspitze, and the highest of them, the Watzmann. The scenery was breathtaking. Its monumental grandeur had first captivated Hitler when, under the pseudonym of 'Herr Wolf', he had visited Dietrich Eckart there in the winter of 1922–3. The Büchners, owners of the Pension Moritz where he stayed, were early supporters of the Movement. He liked them, and could enjoy in this mountain retreat a level of seclusion which he could never expect in Munich. He had, he later recalled, gone there when he needed peace and quiet to dictate parts of the second volume of *Mein Kampf*.[164] Whenever he could, he returned to the Obersalzberg. Then he learnt that an alpine house there, Haus Wachenfeld, belonging to the widow of a north German businessman, was available to let. The widow, whose maiden name had been Wachenfeld, was a party member. He was offered a favourable price of 100 Marks a month. Soon, he was in a position to buy it. That the widow was in financial difficulties at the time helped.[165] Hitler had his summer retreat. He could look down from his 'magic mountain' and see himself bestriding the world.[166] In the Third Reich, at massive cost to the state, Haus Wachenfeld would be turned into the massive complex known as the Berghof, a palace befitting a modern dictator, and a second seat of government for those ministers who each year had to set up residence nearby if they had a hope of contacting the head of state and expediting government business.[167] Before that, on renting Haus Wachenfeld back in 1928, Hitler had – rather surprisingly since they had never been close – telephoned his half-sister Angela Raubal in Vienna and asked her to keep house for him. She agreed, and soon brought her daughter, a lively and attractive twenty-year-old, also named Angela, though known to all as Geli, to stay with her.[168] Three years later, Geli was to be found dead in Hitler's flat in Munich.

By 1926 the Büchners had sold Pension Moritz and were gone. Hitler detested the new owner, a Saxon named Dressel, and moved – the Bechsteins had asked him to join them – to the Marineheim. He did not enjoy the stuffy atmosphere there, and moved down the mountain to Berchtesgaden itself and the Deutsches Haus, a hotel where he spent his time in summer 1926 finishing the second volume of *Mein Kampf* and relaxing with his cronies.[169] Rudolf Heß, Emil Maurice (Hitler's chauffeur), and Heinrich Hoffmann were among them. Gregor Strasser and Bernhard Rust, the Gauleiter of Hanover-North (later to become Reich Minister of Education) were also there. Goebbels, already on holiday himself in Berchtesgaden, joined them for drives through the mountains, and down to the Königssee for boat-rides. As usual, they were subjected at length to 'the chief's' monologues – on 'the social question', 'racial questions', the meaning of political revolution, how to gain control of the state, the architectural shape of the future, the nature of a new German constitution. Goebbels was ecstatic. 'He is a genius,' he gushed. 'The natural, creative instrument of a divine fate . . . Out of deep distress a star is shining! I feel completely bound to him. The last doubt in me has disappeared.'[170]

During a further stay at the Deutsches Haus in Berchtesgaden in early autumn 1926, Hitler came into contact with Maria Reiter. Her friends called her Mimi. For Hitler she was Mimi, Mimilein, Mizzi, Mizzerl – whichever diminutive occurred to him. He also called her 'my dear child'. He was thirty-seven years of age; she was sixteen. Like his father, he preferred women much younger than himself – girls he could dominate, who would be obedient playthings but not get in the way. The two women with whom he would become most intimately associated, Geli Raubal (nineteen years younger than he was) and Eva Braun (twenty-three years younger), fitted the same model – until, that is, Geli became rebellious and wanted a level of freedom which Hitler was unwilling to permit. But these relationships were still to come when Hitler encountered Mimi Reiter.

A fortnight or so before she met Hitler, Mimi's mother had died of cancer. During her mother's illness, her father, a founder member of the Berchtesgaden branch of the SPD, had brought Mimi home from a boarding-school run by nuns in the Catholic pilgrimage centre, Altötting, to help run the family clothes shop on the ground-floor of the Deutsches Haus, where Hitler was staying. She had already heard that the famous Adolf Hitler had taken rooms in the hotel when he introduced himself one day when she was sitting on a bench in the nearby Kurpark, together with her sister Anni, playing with their alsatian dog, Marco. Soon, he was flirting with her. She and Anni were invited to a meeting he addressed in the hotel.[171] 'Wolf', as he asked her to call him, using his own favourite nickname, took her for trips in his Mercedes, driven by the discreet Maurice. Hitler was evidently taken with the attractive, blonde young girl, charming in her naïve, youthful way, flirtatious, hanging on his every word. He flattered her, and played with her affections. She may have been emotionally disturbed, so soon after her mother's death. At any rate, a sense of being courted by one enveloped in such an aura of power and fame must also have played its part. She found him an imposing figure. His manner of dress – complete with knee-length boots and whip – impressed her. Hitler demonstrated his domination by thrashing his own dog, an Alsatian called Prinz, when it misbehaved by fighting Mimi's dog. She was in awe of him, and plainly became completely infatuated. According to her own account, long after the war, on one trip into the countryside near Berchtesgaden, Hitler took her to a remote forest glade, stood her against a tree, admired her from a distance, calling her his 'woodland spirit', then kissed her passionately. He intimated his undying love. Soon afterwards, he was gone – back to real life: politics, meetings, speeches, the regular whirl of activities in Munich. He gave her a leather-bound copy of *Mein Kampf* for Christmas; she gave him two sofa-cushions that she had embroidered. It was not enough. She dreamt of marriage. Nothing was further from his thoughts. Still following her own story, she attempted to hang herself in despair the following year but was found by her brother-in-law and rescued in time. She also told of visits to Hitler's flat in Munich, on one occasion, in 1931, staying overnight, being held tightly by her lover, and letting 'everything happen to me'. At this precise time, however, another woman – Geli Raubal – was the centre of Hitler's attention. Whether Mimi's story is located in the earlier part of 1931, when Geli was residing in Hitler's apartment, or towards the end of the year, when the scandal of Geli's death was reverberating through Munich, it is stretching belief to accept that she slept with Hitler in his flat at that time. This alone prompts suspicion that much of Mimi's later story was an elaboration of part-fantasized memories of a lovestruck young girl who, through two marriages, never lost a devotion to Hitler which saw her make frequent visits to his mother's grave in Leonding.[172]

She wrote him a number of fond letters. His own letters to her (whose authenticity has not been called into question) were affectionate, though in a fatherly, patronizing fashion. 'My dear, good child,' began his reply on 8 February 1927 to a letter from her, thanking her belatedly for her present – presumably the cushions,

I was truly happy to receive this sign of your tender friendship to me. I have nothing in my apartment whose possession gives me more pleasure. I am given a constant reminder of your cheeky head and your eyes ... As regards what is causing you personal pain, you can believe me that I sympathize with you. But you should not let your little head droop in sadness and must only see and believe: even if fathers sometimes don't understand their children any longer because they have got older not only in years but in feelings, they mean only well for them. As happy as your love makes me, I ask you most ardently to listen to your father. And now, my dear treasure (*Goldstück*), receive warmest greetings from your Wolf, who is always thinking of you.[173]

For Mimi, Germany's great leader had fallen in love with her in the late summer of 1926. For Hitler, Mimi – a child holding the allure of a lover – had been an attractive temporary distraction.

While dictating the last chapters of *Mein Kampf* during his stay on the Obersalzberg, Hitler had, as we have seen, consolidated his thinking on foreign policy, notably the acquisition of territory in the east. This idea, especially, was to dominate his speeches and writings of the mid-1920s. However, he was skilful in tailoring his speeches to his audience, as he showed in an important speech he delivered a few months earlier. Hopes of gaining financial support and of winning influential backing for his party had made him keen to accept the invitation of the prestigious Hamburger Nationalklub to address its members in the elegant Hotel Atlantic on 28 February 1926. It was not his usual audience. Here, he faced a socially exclusive club whose 400–450 members were drawn from Hamburg's upper bourgeoisie – many of them high-ranking officers, civil servants, lawyers, and businessmen.[174] His tone was different to that he used in the Munich beerhalls. In his two-hour speech, he made not a single mention of the Jews. He was well aware that the primitive antisemitic rantings that roused the masses in the Circus Krone would be counter-productive in this audience. Instead, the emphasis was placed entirely on the need to eliminate Marxism as the prerequisite of Germany's recovery. By 'Marxism', Hitler did not merely mean the German Communist Party, which had attained only 9 per cent of the vote at the last Reichstag election, in December 1924, and by this time had a substantially smaller membership than in 1923.[175] Beyond the KPD, the term served to invoke the bogy of Soviet Communism, brought into power by a Revolution less than a decade earlier, and followed by a civil war whose atrocities had been emblazoned across a myriad of right-wing publications. 'Marxism' had even wider application. Hitler was also subsuming under this rubric all brands of socialism other than the 'national' variety he preached, and using it in particular to attack the SPD and trade unionism. In fact, to the chagrin of some of its followers, the SPD – still Germany's largest political party – had moved in practice far from its theoretical Marxist roots, and was wedded to upholding the liberal democracy it had been instrumental in calling into being in 1918–19. No 'Marxist' apocalypse threatened from that quarter. But Hitler's rhetoric had, of course, long branded those responsible for the Revolution and the Republic which followed it 'the November criminals'. 'Marxism' was, therefore, also convenient shorthand to denigrate Weimar democracy. As a rhetorical device, therefore, 'Marxism' served a multiplicity of purposes. And to his well-heeled bourgeois audience in Hamburg, anti-Marxist to the core, his verbal assault on the Left was music to the ears.

Hitler reduced it to a simple formula: if the Marxist 'world-view' was not 'eradicated' (*ausgerottet*), Germany would never rise again. The task of the National Socialist Movement was straightforward: 'the smashing and annihilation of the Marxist *Weltanschauung*'.[176] Terror must be met with terror. The bourgeoisie itself was incapable of defeating the threat of Bolshevism. It needed a mass movement as intolerant as that of the Marxists themselves to do it. Winning the masses rested on two premisses. The first was to recognize their social concerns. But in case his audience thought this was back-door Marxism, Hitler was quick to reassure them: social legislation demanded 'the promotion of the welfare of the individual in a framework that guaranteed retention of an independent economy'. 'We are all workers,' he stated. 'The aim is no longer to get higher wages, but increase production, because that is to the advantage of each individual.' His audience was unlikely to disagree with such sentiments. The second premiss was to offer the masses 'a programme that is unalterable, a political faith that is unshakeable'. The usual party programmes, manifestos, and philosophies of bourgeois parties would not win them over. Hitler's contempt for the masses was plain. 'The broad mass is feminine,' he stated, 'one-sided in its attitude; it knows only the hard "either-or".' It wanted only a single view-point upheld – but then with all available means, and, he added, now mixing his genders and pointing to what is normally taken to be a more masculine characteristic, 'does not shrink from using force'.[177] What the mass had to feel was its own strength.[178] Among a crowd of 200,000 in Berlin's Lustgarten, the individual felt no more than 'a small worm', subject to mass-suggestion, aware only of those around him being prepared to fight for an ideal.[179] 'The broad masses are blind and stupid and don't know what they are doing,' he claimed.[180] They were 'primitive in attitude'. For them, 'understanding' offered only a 'shaky platform'. 'What is stable is emotion: hatred.'[181] The more Hitler preached intolerance, force, and hatred, as the solution to Germany's problems, the more his audience liked it. He was interrupted on numerous occasions during these passages with cheers and shouts of 'bravo'. At the end there was a lengthy ovation, and cries of 'Heil'.[182]

National revival through terroristic anti-Marxism built on the cynical manipulation and indoctrination of the masses: that was the sum total of Hitler's message to the upper-crust of the Hamburg bourgeoisie. Nationalism and anti-Marxism were scarcely peculiarities of the Nazis alone. Nor did they amount in themselves to much of an ideology. What distinguished Hitler's approach to his Hamburg audience was not the ideas themselves, but the impression of fanatical will, utter ruthlessness, and the creation of a nationalist movement resting on the support of the masses. And it was plain from the enthusiastic response that selective terror deployed against 'Marxists' would meet with little or no opposition from the élite of Germany's most liberal city.

Back among his 'own sort', little or nothing had changed. The tone was very different to that adopted in Hamburg. In closed party meetings or, after the speaking ban had been lifted in early 1927, once more in Munich beerhalls and the Circus Krone, the attacks on the Jews were as vicious and unconstrained as ever. In speech after speech, as before the putsch, he launched brutal assaults against the Jews, bizarrely depicted both as the wire-pullers of finance capital and as poisoning the people with subversive Marxist doctrine.[183] Explicit attacks on the Jews occurred more frequently and extensively in 1925 and 1926 than in the subsequent two years. Antisemitism seemed now rather more ritualist or mechanistic. The main stress had moved to anti-Marxism.[184] But only the presentation of his ideas had been modified to some extent; their meaning had not. His pathological hatred of Jews was unchanged. 'The Jew is and remains the world enemy,' he once more asserted in an article in the *Völkischer Beobachter* in February 1927, 'and his weapon, Marxism, a plague of mankind.'[185]

Between 1926 and 1928, Hitler became more preoccupied with the 'question of [living]-space' (*Raumfrage*) and 'land policy' (*Bodenpolitik*).[186] Though, as we have seen, the idea of an eastern 'land policy' at the expense of Russia had been present in Hitler's mind at the latest by the end of 1922, he had mentioned it in his public statements – written or spoken – only on a handful of occasions before the end of 1926. He referred in a speech on 16 December 1925 to the 'acquisition of land and soil' as the best solution to Germany's economic problems and alluded to the colonization of the east 'by the sword' in the Middle Ages.[187] He remarked on the need for a colonial policy in eastern Europe at Bamberg in February 1926.[188] And he returned to the theme as a central element of his speech at the Weimar Party Rally on 4 July 1926.[189] The completion of *Mein Kampf*, which ends with the question of eastern colonization, must have further focused his mind on the issue.[190] Once he was allowed to speak in public again in spring 1927, the question of 'living-space' became frequently, then from the summer onwards, obsessively emphasized in all his major addresses. Speech after speech highlights in more or less the same language ideas that became embodied in the 'Second Book', dictated during the summer of 1928. Other economic options are mentioned only to be dismissed. The lack of space (*Raumnot*) for Germany's population could by overcome only by attaining power, then by force. The 'eastern colonization' of the Middle Ages was praised. Conquest 'by the sword' was the only method. Russia was seldom explicitly mentioned. But the meaning was unmistakable.

The social-Darwinist, racist reading of history offered the justification.

'Politics is nothing more than the struggle of a people for its existence.' 'It is an iron principle,' he declared: 'the weaker one falls so that the strong one gains life.'[191] Three values determined a people's fate: 'blood-' or 'race-value', the 'value of personality', and the 'sense of struggle' (*Kampfsinn*) or 'self-preservation drive' (*Selbsterhaltungstrieb*). These values, embodied in the 'Aryan race', were threatened by the three 'vices' – democracy, pacifism, and internationalism – that comprised the work of 'Jewish Marxism'.

The theme of personality and leadership, little emphasized before 1923, was a central thread of Hitler's speeches and writings in the mid- and later 1920s. The people, he said, formed a pyramid. At its apex was 'the genius, the great man'.[192] Following the chaos in the *völkisch* movement during the 'leaderless time', it was scarcely surprising that there was heavy emphasis in 1925 and 1926 on the leader as the focus of unity. In his refoundation speech on 27 February 1925, Hitler had stressed his task as leader as 'bringing together again those who are going different ways'.[193] The art of being leader lay in assembling the 'stones of the mosaic'.[194] The leader was the 'central point' or 'preserver' of the 'idea'.[195] This demanded, Hitler repeatedly underlined, blind obedience and loyalty from the followers.[196] The cult of the leader was thus built up as the integrating mechanism of the movement. With his own supremacy firmly established by mid-1926, Hitler never lost an opportunity to highlight the 'value of personality' and 'individual greatness' as the guiding force in Germany's struggle and coming rebirth. He avoided specific reference to his own claims to 'heroic' status. This was unnecessary. It could be left to the growing number of converts to the Hitler cult, and to the orchestrated outpourings of propaganda. For Hitler himself, the 'Führer myth' was both a propaganda weapon *and* a central tenet of belief. His own 'greatness' could be implicitly but unmistakably underscored by repeated references to Bismarck, Frederick the Great and Luther, along with allusions to Mussolini. Speaking of Bismarck (if without mentioning his name) in May 1926, he commented: 'It was necessary to transmit the national idea to the mass of the people.' 'A giant had to fulfil this task.' The sustained applause showed that the meaning was not lost on his audience.[197]

Goebbels had been thrilled on more than one occasion in 1926 by Hitler's exposition of the 'social question'. 'Always new and compelling', was how Goebbels described his ideas.[198] In reality, Hitler's 'social idea' was simplistic, diffuse, and manipulative. It amounted to little more than what he had told his bourgeois audience in Hamburg: winning the workers to nationalism, destroying Marxism, and overcoming the division between nationalism and socialism through the creation of a nebulous 'national community'

(*Volksgemeinschaft*) based on racial purity and the concept of struggle. The fusion of nationalism and socialism would do away with the class antagonism between a nationalist bourgeoisie and Marxist proletariat (both of which had failed in their political goals). This would be replaced by a 'community of struggle' where nationalism and socialism would be united, where 'brain' and 'fist' were reconciled, and where – denuded of Marxist influence – the building of a new spirit for the great future struggle of the people could be undertaken. Such ideas were neither new, nor original. And, ultimately, they rested not on any modern form of socialism, but on the crudest and most brutal version of nineteenth-century imperialist and social Darwinistic notions.[199] Social welfare in the trumpeted 'national community' did not exist for its own sake, but to prepare for external struggle, for conquest 'by the sword'.

Hitler repeatedly stated that he was uninterested in day-to-day issues. What he offered, over and over again, was the same vision of a long-term goal, to be striven after with missionary zeal and total commitment. Political struggle, eventual attainment of power, destruction of the enemy, and build-up of the nation's might were stepping-stones to the goal. But how it was to be then attained was left open. Hitler himself had no concrete notion. He just had the certainty of the fanatical 'conviction politician' that it *would* be attained. Clarity was never aimed at. The acquisition of 'living-space' through conquest implied at some distant future date aggression against Russia. But it had no more precise meaning than that. Hitler's own firm belief in it need not be doubted. But, even for many of his followers, in the world of the mid-1920s, with Germany engaged diplomatically with the Soviet Union following the Rapallo Treaty of 1922 as well as improving relations with the western powers through the 1925 Treaty of Locarno then membership of the League of Nations, this must have seemed little more than sloganizing or a pipe-dream.

Even on the 'Jewish Question', the wild tirades, vicious as they were, offered no concrete policies. 'Getting rid of the Jews' (*Entfernung der Juden*) could only reasonably be taken to mean the expulsion of all Jews from Germany, as when Hitler called for chasing 'that pack of Jews . . . from our Fatherland . . . with an iron broom'.[200] But even this aim seemed less than clear when Hitler stated – to tumultuous applause from the stalwarts of the Movement gathered in Munich's Hofbräuhaus on 24 February 1928 to celebrate the eighth anniversary of the launch of the Party Programme – that 'the Jew' would have to be shown 'that we're the bosses here; if he behaves well, he can stay – if not, then out with him'.[201]

In the 'Jewish Question', the 'question of [living]-space', and the 'social question', Hitler suggested a vision of a distant utopia. He did not chart the path to it. But no other Nazi leader or *völkisch* politician could match the internal unity, simplicity, and all-encompassing character of this 'vision'. His sense of conviction – he spoke frequently of his 'mission', 'faith', and of the 'idea' – combined with an unrivalled talent for mobilization through reduction to simple 'black–white' choices, was where the ideologue and the propagandist came together.

The interdependence of the various strands of Hitler's pernicious 'world-view' is most plainly evident in his 'Second Book' (an updated statement of his views on foreign policy, left, in the event, unpublished), dictated hurriedly to Max Amann during a stay on the Obersalzberg in the summer of 1928.[202] Hitler felt prompted to produce the book by the heated debates at the time about policy towards South Tyrol. Under Mussolini, Fascist policies of Italianization of the largely German-speaking area had stirred strong anti-Italian feeling in nationalist circles in Austria and Germany, particularly in Bavaria. Hitler's readiness to renounce German claims on South Tyrol in the interest of an alliance with Italy had seen him attacked by German nationalists as well as being accused by socialists of taking bribes from Mussolini.[203] Hitler had dealt with the South Tyrol issue in *Mein Kampf*, and published the relevant sections from the second volume as a separate pamphlet in February 1926.[204] When the issue flared up again in 1928, Hitler was driven to outline his position at length.[205] Probably financial considerations – Amann may well have advised against having the 'Second Book' compete against the second volume of *Mein Kampf*, with its dis-appointing and diminishing sales – dissuaded Hitler from publishing the book.[206] But in addition, as the South Tyrol question lost its urgency, new issues like the Young Plan arose, and Hitler had neither time nor inclination to revise the text, it may have been felt that its publication would have offered political hostages to fortune.[207]

If occasioned by the South Tyrol question, the 'Second Book' went far beyond it, ranging more expansively than *Mein Kampf* had done over Hitler's broad ideas on foreign policy and 'territorial issues' (*Raumfragen*), linking them, as always, with his racial interpretation of history and, in the final pages, with the need to destroy what he saw as the threat of 'Jewish domination'.[208] But the 'Second Book' offered nothing new.[209] As we have seen, the essence of Hitler's 'world-view' was fully developed by the time he completed the second volume of *Mein Kampf* in 1926, existent in embryonic form, in fact, since late 1922. The ideas dominating the 'Second Book' –

including the issue of South Tyrol and his interest in the growing economic power of the United States of America – were repeatedly advanced in Hitler's speeches and writings from 1927 onwards. Several passages from these speeches recur almost verbatim at key points in the 'Second Book'.

Long before the dictation of the 'Second Book', then, Hitler was a fixated ideologue.[210] His own inner certainty of the 'truths' about history as racial struggle, and Germany's future mission to obtain 'living-space' and, at the same time, eradicate the power of the Jews for ever, were of immense importance as a personal driving-force. Their significance in attracting support for National Socialism can, however, easily be exaggerated. The growth of the NSDAP to a mass party had little directly to do with the arcanum of Hitler's personalized 'world-view'. More complex processes have to be taken into account.

IV

At the end of January 1927, Saxony became the first large German state to lift the speaking ban on Hitler. On 5 March, the Bavarian authorities finally conceded to the pressure to allow Hitler to speak again. One of the conditions was that his first public speech in the state should not be held in Munich.[211] Consequently, when, on 6 March, he spoke publicly in Bavaria for the first time in two years, it took place well away from Munich, at Vilsbiburg in the backwaters of Lower Bavaria. Many of the 1,000-strong audience, only two-thirds filling the hall, were party members and SA men who had been brought from outside to ensure the occasion was a success.[212]

But three days later, he was back in Munich – in the Circus Krone again, for the first time since 1923. Everything was done to make it a theatrical success. The huge hall was nearly full to its 7,000 capacity by the time Hitler, in a brown raincoat, preceded by marching SA men, accompanied by his retinue, took the rostrum to the sound of fanfares. Most of the audience were from the lower-middle classes, though some were plainly well-to-do, their wives in fur coats. A good number were young, many of them dressed in windjammers. The crowd went wild at Hitler's entrance, standing on chairs and benches, waving, shouting 'Heil', stamping their feet. Around 200 stormtroopers in serried ranks with banners filed past Hitler greeting him with the fascist salute. Hitler returned the greeting with outstretched arm. The speech met with the usual euphoric applause. The audience regarded Hitler's comments as 'gospel', even though what he said could have been nothing new to them. The police reporter was less impressed. He thought the speech long-winded in structure, repetitive, with dull passages and illogical arguments full of crude comparisons and cheap allusions. Nor was Hitler's performance as a speaker, studded with theatrical and exaggerated gestures, to his liking. He was only surprised that Hitler had been so highly praised, if his speeches had been similar in 1923. The applause, in his eyes, was directed not at what Hitler had to say, but at the person of the speaker.'[213]

Some of the dullness of Hitler's speech was because he was unduly anxious to avoid any comments likely to land him in further trouble with the authorities. The report of the speech in the *Völkischer Beobachter* was surprisingly short.[214] The shorthand writer who had taken it down had lost her notes.[215]

For his next big speech in Munich at the end of the month, the Circus Krone was only between a half and three-quarters full.[216] Another week later, on 6 April, only 1,500 were present, in a hall that accommodated almost five times that many.[217] Hitler's magic was no longer working, even in Munich. Outside Munich, his return to the public arena caused little of a stir. 'In Ingolstadt, earlier a party bastion, Hitler's renewal of his speaking activity was scarcely noted by the population, not even by most of the former supporters,' it was reported.[218] Other reports from the Bavarian provinces indicated little interest in the NSDAP, for all its vigorous propaganda. Party meetings were often badly attended. In January 1928, the Munich police reported that 'the advances of the National Socialist Movement repeatedly claimed by Hitler are not true, especially in Bavaria. In reality, interest in the movement both in the countryside and in Munich is strongly in decline. Branch meetings attended by 3–400 people in 1926 now have an attendance of at most 60–80 members.'[219] Even the Party Rally, held for the first time at Nuremberg, on 19–21 August 1927, despite careful orchestration for maximum propaganda effect, failed to raise the expected level of support or interest.[220]

Most other German states followed the examples of Saxony and Bavaria in lifting the ban on Hitler speaking in public. Only Prussia, the largest state, and Anhalt held out until autumn 1928.[221] The authorities, it seemed with justification, could believe that the Nazi menace had passed. Hitler no longer appeared a threat.

Though outwardly making little or no headway in the more settled political climate of the mid-1920s, as Germany's new democracy at last showed signs of stability, significant developments were taking place within the NSDAP. Eventually, these would help to place the party in a stronger position to exploit the new economic crisis that was to hit Germany in autumn 1929.

Most importantly, the NSDAP had become a self-conscious 'leader-movement', focused ideologically and organizationally on the Hitler cult. In retrospect, the 'leaderless time' of 1924, and Hitler's obstinacy – born out of weakness – in refusing to take sides in the internecine strife of the *völkisch* movement, had been enormously advantageous. The defeat at Bamberg of those looking to programmatic changes was, as we have seen, at the same time the victory of those loyalists prepared to look no further than Hitler as the embodiment of the 'idea'. For these, the programme detached from the leader had no meaning. And, as 1924 had proven, without Hitler there could be no unity, and hence no movement.

This point alone was sufficient to persuade even those, like Gregor Strasser, who retained their critical distance from Hitler that the Führer cult had to be built up in order to hold the party together. An outward sign of the unity invested in the person of the Leader was the 'German greeting' of 'Heil Hitler' with outstretched arm, the fascist-style salute increasingly used since 1923 and compulsory within the Movement since 1926.[222] The 'Heil Hitler' greeting, Strasser wrote in January 1927, was not only a symbol of personal dependence on the Leader, but contained in itself the pledge of loyalty. The 'great secret' of the movement was the combination of 'the inner devotion to the idea of National Socialism, a glowing faith in the victorious strength of this doctrine of liberation, of redemption' with 'a deep love of the person of our Leader, who is the shining duke of the new freedom fighters'. 'Duke and liegeman!' he continued. 'In this ancient German, . . . both aristocratic and democratic, relationship of leader to companions, lies the essence of the structure of the NSDAP. . . Friends, raise your right arm and cry out with me proudly, eager for the struggle, and loyal to death "Heil Hitler".'[223]

For Rudolf Heß, for years a submissive, fawning Hitler-devotee, the leader-cult was a matter of deep belief, even psychological necessity, not just functional value.[224] In a letter to Walter Hewel, later to be one of Ribbentrop's right-hand men in the Foreign Ministry, Heß reminded him of the 'leadership principle' that Hitler had already outlined while they were all in Landsberg: 'unconditional authority downwards, and responsibility upwards'. He called it 'Germanic democracy'.[225] He underlined the importance of the image of discipline, unity, and strength.[226] He ended by comparing 'the great popular leader' with 'the great founder of a religion'. His task was not to weigh up pros and cons like an academic; not to allow freedom to reach alternative judgements. 'He must communicate to his listeners an apodictic faith. Only then can the mass of followers be led where they should be led. They will then also follow the leader if setbacks are encountered; but only then, if they have communicated to them unconditional belief in the absolute rightness . . . in the mission of the Führer and . : . of their own people.'[227]

Hitler idolatry was deliberately fostered by the party leadership. In a booklet published in 1926, Goebbels – well on the way, as we have seen, to becoming that very year a worshipper of Hitler – used mystical language redolent of German romanticism and the ideology of the pre-Nazi Youth Movement, to describe his Leader as 'the fulfilment of a mysterious longing', bringing faith in deepest despair, 'a meteor before our astonished eyes', working 'a miracle of enlightenment and belief in a world of scepticism and despair'.[228] But such sentiments, whatever their propaganda intent, obviously struck a rich vein among the rank-and-file membership. A war veteran dated his Führer worship to Hitler's speeches during his trial in 1924. 'From that time on I had no thought for anyone but Hitler. His behaviour moved me to give him my whole faith, without reserve.'[229] One party member who heard Hitler speak in Bonn in 1926 thought he evoked 'the feelings of every good German. The German soul spoke to German manhood in his words. From that day on I could never violate my allegiance to Hitler. I saw his unlimited faith in his people and the desire to set them free.'[230] A Russian refugee, a former aristocrat, also heard Hitler speak in 1926, in Mecklenburg. The content of the speech evidently left no mark on him. But by the end he was crying with emotion: 'a liberating scream of the purest enthusiasm discharged the unbearable tension as the auditorium rocked with applause'.[231]

The longing for authority and subaltern mentality was widespread in those who found appeal in the early Nazi movement. Romantics, neo-conservatives, those fixated on mythical glories of the past, despairing and resentful of the present, dreaming of a heroic future, could all find hope in a coming 'great leader', a national redeemer. Whether such individuals looked subconsciously to a monarch, a military commander, a statesman, a priest, or simply a father-figure, their naïve feelings about the need for authority, bringing with it, they imagined, the yearned-for national unity, were hugely magnified by the evident divisions in Weimar politics and society, which could only too easily be exploited by the nationalist Right. The 'search for the strong man' was commonplace in inter-war Europe as part of the assault on democracy. It is not surprising that it was at its most vehement in the two democracies – Italy and Germany – that experienced the deepest crises of pluralist politics.

The establishment of the Führer cult was decisive for the development of the Nazi Movement. Without it, as 1924 had shown, it would have been torn apart by factionalism. With it, the still precarious unity could be preserved by calling on loyalty to Hitler as a prime duty. Among the party leadership, feelings had to be subordinated to the overriding need for unity. When there was criticism of Hitler, and Ludendorff was advanced as 'the greater man' in a dispute in the Hanover party in April 1927, Karl Dincklage, the Deputy Gauleiter and an important party speaker, wrote: 'We in Gau Hanover retain our loyal following to Hitler. It's quite immaterial whether we think Ludendorff or Hitler is the greater. That's left to each one of us to decide.'[232] And when a serious conflict dividing allegiances in the faction-ridden Berlin party arose in June that year, the loyalty-card was played once more. The bitter dispute was occasioned by the competition between Goebbels's new Berlin newspaper *Der Angriff* (The Attack), and the struggling *Berliner Arbeiter-Zeitung* (Berlin Workers' Newspaper), edited by Gregor Strasser. It rapidly degenerated into the trading of personal insults between the two former allies, gratefully exploited by the Nazis' political enemies. The row dragged on until the winter. It was ended when Hitler brought both rivals to Munich to offer to a packed Hofbräuhaus their public demonstration of unity 'bolstered by the common belief in a lofty, holy mission and by the feeling of loyalty binding them to the common idea and also to the common leader in the person of Adolf Hitler'. Party members were told that 'the authority of the idea and the authority of the Leader' had 'become one in the person of Adolf Hitler'.[233]

Within the movement, the SA had always been the most difficult element to control – and so it would continually prove down to 1934. But here, too, Hitler was successfully able to diffuse trouble by invoking loyalty to his own person. In May 1927, he made an impassioned speech to the Munich stormtroopers, demoralized and rebellious towards the SA leader Franz von Pfeffer. At the end of his speech, he resorted to his usual ploy. He stepped down from the rostrum, shook hands with each SA-man, and gained their renewed pledge of personal loyalty to him.[234]

Clashes over strategy, factional disputes, personal rivalries – all were endemic in the NSDAP. The interminable conflicts and animosities, normally personal or tactical rather than ideological, almost invariably stopped short of any attack on Hitler. He intervened as little as possible. In fact, the rivalry and competition simply showed him, according to his own concept of social-Darwinist struggle, who among his competing underlings was the stronger.[235] Nor did Hitler make any effort to reconcile ideological nuances within the party, unless they threatened to become counter-productive by deviating the single-minded drive for power through mass mobilization into sectarian squabbling. The Führer cult was accepted because it offered all parties the only remedy to this. Personal loyalty to Hitler, whether genuine or forced, was the price of unity. In some cases, Nazi leaders were wholly convinced of Hitler's greatness and 'mission'. In others, their own ambitions could only be upheld by lip-service to the supreme Leader. Either way, the result was that Hitler's mastery over the Movement increased to the position where it was well-nigh unchallengeable. And either way, the transmission belt within the party faithful had been manufactured for the subsequent extension of the Führer cult to wider sectors of the German electorate. The Leader cult was indispensable to the party. And the subsummation of the 'idea' in Hitler's own person was necessary, if party energy was not to be dissipated in harmful factional divides. By avoiding doctrinal dispute, as he had done in 1924, and focusing all energies on the one goal of obtaining power, Hitler could – sometimes with difficulty – hold the party together. Along the way, the Führer cult had developed its own momentum. Though he fully recognized its propaganda value, Hitler himself was on occasion forced to intervene to prevent absurdities of excess, which only brought merciless lampooning from his political enemies.[236]

Hitler's supremacy now paid dividends in its impact on his former rivals. In February 1927, Graf Reventlow, one of the most prominent members of the DVFP, whose social revolutionary position had brought him into increasing conflict with the more conservative German nationalist leadership around Graefe and Wulle, joined the NSDAP. He was accompanied by Wilhelm Kube and Christian Mergenthaler, the leading figures in the DVFP in Brandenburg and Württemberg respectively. Another Reichstag deputy, Franz Stöhr, also deserted the DVFP in favour of the NSDAP. Hitler and Goebbels travelled to Stuttgart to welcome Mergenthaler personally into the party, amid festive scenes. As one who had earlier crossed swords with Hitler, Reventlow's justification for joining the NSDAP was significant:

I have gone over to the National Socialist German Workers' Party without so-called leadership claims and without reservations. I subordinate myself without further ado to Herr Adolf Hitler. Why? He has proved that he can lead; on the basis of his view and his will, he has created a party out of the united national socialist idea, and leads it. He and the party are one, and offer the unity that is the unconditional premiss of success. The previous two years have shown that the National Socialist German Workers' Party is on the right road, that it is on the march, that it possesses unbroken and unbreakable social-revolutionary energy.[237]

It amounted to the seal of approval on the leadership principle, and the merging of the 'idea' and organization in Hitler's person.

The process was still not complete by the end of 1927. However, the Nuremberg Party Rally in August 1927 depicted Hitler's mastery over the Movement more emphatically than had the Weimar rally a year earlier. Hitler could afford to be relaxed about conflicting programmatic statements put forward by the arch-ideologues Feder and Rosenberg. Even Artur Dinter, who a few weeks later was to be removed from his post as Gauleiter of Thuringia and then the following year expelled from the party altogether, was allowed to speak, and received a favourable notice in the *Völkischer Beobachter*. What passed for 'discussion' at Nuremberg fell within the broad contours of the Nazi 'actionist' programme: anti-liberal, anti-Marxist, emotionally anti-capitalist and 'national' socialist, not least antisemitic. As long as doctrinaire 'theorists' did nothing to hinder this broad appeal of the party, and nothing to challenge Hitler's leadership position, they were left a good deal of room for manoeuvre.[238]

In the case of Dinter, however, the strength of Hitler's position became plain. Though once a powerful supporter of Hitler, Dinter's religious obsessions – he insisted upon National Socialism being a religious reformation through purification of blood and race – incurred increasing unpopularity within the Movement, especially in Thuringia, his own Gau. Hitler felt compelled, therefore, to remove him as Gauleiter in September 1927. Dinter, as fanatically obsessive as Hitler, persisted. The religious neutrality which Hitler could not afford to endanger was placed in jeopardy by Dinter's high profile and publicity.[239] When, finally, Dinter challenged Hitler himself, accusing him of being a tool of the Catholic Church, and advocating a senate to advise the Leader, he had gone too far. Amid booing, his proposal was unanimously rejected by the General Members' Meeting in September 1928. Even then, it was typical of Hitler that he was reluctant to expel Dinter, knowing the adverse publicity the expulsion would bring. Dinter refused, however, to accept Hitler's exclusive authority, and publicly attacked him and the party programme. His expulsion, in early October 1928, was then inevitable.[240] Strikingly, Gregor Strasser secured a written statement signed by at least eighteen Gauleiter expressing unanimity with Hitler's decision. 'In this situation,' Strasser's letter to the Gauleiter ran, 'there must be a clear expression to the public, opponents, and especially our own party comrades, that every attempt to establish even the smallest difference of opinion in this question of principle [the mixing of religious issues with the political programme of the movement] between Adolf Hitler and his fellow workers is an impossibility.'[241] No less revealing was Hitler's self-description in a letter he wrote to Dinter the previous July. 'As leader of the National Socialist Movement and as a person who possesses the blind faith of someday belonging to those who make history,' Hitler wrote, 'I have [as a politician] the boldness to claim for myself in this sphere the same infallibility that you reserve for yourself in your [religious] reformationist area.' He put the time at his disposal to attain power and shape Germany's fate, at least as regards the 'racial problem', at most at twenty years.[242]

With the build-up of the Führer cult, Hitler's image was at least as important as his practical contribution to the modest growth of the party in the 'wilderness years'.[243] Of course, a Hitler-speech remained a major event for a local party branch. And Hitler retained the ability in his mass meetings to win over initially sceptical audiences.[244] But whatever limited success the NSDAP enjoyed before the Depression cannot simply – or even mainly – be attributed to Hitler. As an agitator, Hitler was distinctly less directly prominent than he had been before the putsch. The speaking-ban was, of course, a major hindrance in 1925 and 1926. He spoke at only thirty-one meetings in 1925 and thirty-two in 1926, mainly internal party affairs, a good number of them in Bavaria. In 1927, his speeches increased in number to fifty-six, more than half of them within Bavaria. Most of his sixty-six speeches in 1928 took place in the first five months, up to the Reichstag election. More than two-thirds of them were held in Bavaria. During the whole of 1929, as the NSDAP began to gain ground in regional elections, he gave only twenty-nine speeches, all but eight in Bavaria.[245]

One limitation on Hitler's availability as a speaker in these years was posed by his frequent trips to try to establish important contacts and drum up funding for a party with chronic financial problems.[246] Not surprisingly, for a party in the political doldrums, his efforts met with little success. Though (not to the liking of the 'social-revolutionaries' in the NSDAP) he courted Ruhr industrialists and businessmen in a number of speeches in 1926 and 1927, which went down well, they showed little interest in a party that seemed to be going nowhere.[247] The Bechsteins and Bruckmanns, long-standing patrons, continued to give generously.[248] But the aged Emil Kirdorf, whom Frau Bruckmann had brought into personal contact with Hitler, was almost alone among leading Ruhr industrialists in sympathizing with Hitler to the extent of joining the NSDAP, and in making a sizeable donation of 100,000 Marks that went a long way towards overcoming the party's immediate financial plight.[249] As would remain the case, the party was heavily dependent for its income on the contributions of ordinary members. So the stagnation, or at best slow growth, in party membership meant continued headaches for the party treasurer.[250]

As earlier, Hitler paid little attention to administration and organization. Party bosses were resigned to his lengthy absences and inaccessibility on even important concerns.[251] He left financial matters to his trusted business manager, Max Amann, and the party treasurer, Franz Xaver Schwarz.[252] Behind the scenes in Munich, Hitler could rely in the party's secretariat upon the indefatigable and subservient Philipp Bouhler, the retiring but inwardly ambitious individual who was later to play a central role in the emergence of the 'euthanasia action'.[253] Above all, it was Gregor Strasser, as Propaganda Leader between September 1926 and the end of 1927 (during which time he streamlined and coordinated propaganda activities throughout the Reich) and especially after he was made Organizational Leader on 2 January 1928, who built up, from the faction-ridden and incoherently structured movement, the nationwide organization that from 1929 onwards was in a position to exploit the new crisis conditions.[254] Hitler's part in this development was minimal, though placing Strasser in charge of organizational matters was one of his more inspired appointments.

Hitler's instinct, as ever, was for propaganda, not organization. His 'feel', when it came to matters of mobilizing the masses, seldom let him down. As director of party propaganda, Gregor Strasser had been given a great deal of scope – Hitler's usual style – to shape the character and pattern of agitation. Following his own leanings, Strasser had made a strong push to win over, especially, the urban proletariat. Even to outside observers, it was plain by autumn 1927 that this strategy was not paying worthwhile dividends, and was at the same time in danger of alienating the lower-middle-class support of the NSDAP.[255] Reports came in from Schleswig-Holstein, Thuringia, Mecklenburg, Pomerania, and other areas indicating that growing unrest in rural areas offered promising terrain for the NSDAP.[256] Hitler was evidently well-informed. And at a meeting of Gau leaders on 27 November 1927 in the 'Hotel Elefant' in Weimar, he announced a change of course. He made plain that significant gains could not be expected at the coming election from 'the Marxists'. Small shopkeepers, threatened by department stores, and white-collar workers, many of them already antisemites were singled out as better targets.[257] In December 1927, Hitler addressed for the first time a rally of several thousand peasants from Lower Saxony and Schleswig-Holstein.[258] In the New Year, he himself took over the position of party Propaganda Leader. His deputy, Heinrich Himmler, undertook the routine tasks. The future overlord of the SS empire was at this time still in his twenties, a well-educated and intelligent former agricultural student who had briefly worked for a fertilizer firm and reared chickens. With his short-back-and-sides haircut, small moustache, round glasses, and unathletic build, he resembled a small-town bank clerk or pedantic schoolmaster. Whatever appearances might have suggested, he had, however, few peers in ideological fanaticism and, as time would prove, cold ruthlessness. The young nationalist idealist, already imagining dire conspiracies involving 'the red International', Jews, Jesuits and freemasons ranged against Germany, had joined the NSDAP in the summer of 1923, influenced by the man whose murder he would orchestrate eleven years later, Ernst Röhm. It was at Röhm's side that, on 8 November that year, the night of the putsch, he had carried the banner at the head of the Reichskriegsflagge unit engaged in attempting to storm the Bavarian War Ministry. From the time of the party's refoundation, he had been active, initially as secretary to Gregor Strasser, then, from 1926, as Deputy Gauleiter of Upper Bavaria-Swabia, and Deputy Reich Propaganda Leader. In the latter capacity in the later 1920s – he was also Deputy Reichsführer-SS from 1927 before being appointed to lead the SS two years later – he proved both efficient and imaginative – apparently coming up with the idea of blanket propaganda coverage of a specific area during a brief period of time, something that became a Nazi hallmark.[259]

But significantly, and in contrast to his normal habits, Hitler intervened directly in drafting texts and in shaping central propaganda.[260] In April 1928, he 'corrected' the interpretation of Point 17 of the Party's 'unalterable' 1920 Programme: 'expropriation without compensation' meant, for a party based on the principle of private property, merely the creation of legal means to take over land not administered in the public good; that is, Jewish land-speculation companies.[261]

The shift in propaganda emphasis was less dramatic than the transformation of a failed 'urban plan' into a 'rural-nationalist plan'.[262] But it did amount to a further move away from a 'programmatic' stance directed primarily at winning workers from Marxism to a broader 'catch-all' approach to mobilization. It was a pragmatic readjustment, recognizing the possibility of a widened appeal to a variety of social groups not previously addressed in any systematic way in party propaganda. The suggestion to move in this direction came, as we have noted, initially from several Gauleiter, recognizing the potential support in their own non-urban regions. Hitler's positive response to their suggestions accorded with his own opportunistic approach to mobilization. Unlike some in the party, wedded to a type of 'social-revolutionary' emotive anti-capitalism, which social groups were attracted to Nazism was for him a matter of indifference. The important thing was that they *were* won over. Hitler's aim was to gain power. Any weapon to that end was useful. But it did mean that the NSDAP became even more of a loose coalition of competing interest-groups. Only the *absence* of a clear programme and a set of utopian, distant goals built into the image of the Leader could hold them together – for a time.

V

Few Germans had Hitler on their mind in Weimar's 'golden years' of the mid-1920s. The internal developments within his party were of neither interest nor concern to the overwhelming majority of people. Little attention was paid to the former Munich troublemaker who now seemed no more than a fringe irritant on the political scene. Those who did take notice of Hitler were often dismissive or condescending, or both. Not untypical was the comment of Germany's leading liberal daily, the *Frankfurter Zeitung*, casting as usual from time to time merely a contemptuous eye in the direction of the National Socialists. 'Hitler has no thoughts, no responsible reflection, but nonetheless an idea. He has a demon in him,' ran an article in the newspaper on 26 January 1928. 'It is a matter of a manic idea of atavistic origin that pushes aside complicated reality and replaces it with a primitive fighting unit . . . Naturally, Hitler is a dangerous fool . . . But if one asks how the son of a petty Upper Austrian customs officer arrives at his craze, then one can only say one thing: he has taken war ideology perfectly literally and interpreted it in almost as primitive a way that one might be living in the era of the *Völkerwanderung*' – the period of Barbarian invasions at the end of the Roman Empire.[263]

The results of the Reichstag election on 20 May 1928 appeared to confirm the correctness of those commentators who for years had been preaching the end of Hitler and his Movement.[264] The electorate showed relatively little interest in the campaign – a reflection of the more settled conditions.[265] As many as thirty-two parties put up lists, many representing specific interest-groups. Hitler would later make great play of this to parody the workings of pluralist democracy.[266] The clear winners were the parties of the Left. Both the SPD and KPD made significant gains. The most serious losses were suffered by the German Nationalists (DNVP). Small parties and splinter-groups won, cumulatively, almost twice as many votes (13.9 per cent) as they had done in December 1924.[267] With its miserable return of 2.6 per cent, the NSDAP won only twelve seats. Electorally, it had lost ground, compared with the Völkischer Block in December 1924.[268] In the cities, with a handful of exceptions, the results were disastrous. Despite Goebbels's efforts to take the fight to the 'red' districts in Berlin, the Nazis won only 1.57 per cent of the vote in the capital city. In 'red' Wedding, typical of working-class districts of the inner city, the NSDAP's 1,742 votes paled against the 163,429 votes cast for the parties of the Left. But there were some rays of light. The returns from some rural areas, as anticipated, held out hope for the future. The best results, apart from the traditional Franconian heartlands and parts of Upper Bavaria, were mainly to be found in the north German countryside, afflicted by the deepening agricultural depression.[269] In Weser-Ems, for example, assisted by the propaganda razzmatazz of the tub-thumping, virulently antisemitic unfrocked pastor Ludwig Münchmeyer, a convert from the DVFB, the vote for the NSDAP was twice the national average.[270] Even in eastern Germany, where support remained very low, the loss of confidence in the dominant DNVP gave some grounds for optimism.[271] Finally, there was at least the consolation that the twelve Nazis who entered the Reichstag now had immunity from legal action for their venomous attacks on opponents and – if anything even more important – daily allowances and free rail passes for first-class travel on the Reichsbahn to ease pressure on party finances.[272] Among the new deputies were Gregor Strasser, Frick, Feder, Goebbels, Ritter von Epp – the former Freikorps leader, a new, much-trumpeted convert from the BVP – and Hermann Göring, recently returned to the fold after his absence since the putsch. 'We are going into the Reichstag . . . like the wolf into the sheepflock,' Goebbels told his readers in the *Angriff*.[273]

There was understandable disappointment and dejection within the party. But the public response was one of resilience.[274] Lessons were to be learnt. It was as obvious to Gregor Strasser as to other party leaders that the concentration on the industrial working class had not paid dividends. Richer potential lay in the countryside.[275] The need for a readjustment of party propaganda and organization was plain. Hitler reinforced the message at the Leaders' Meeting in Munich between 31 August and 2 September – replacing the Party Rally which lack of funds, following the election campaign, did not permit in 1928.[276] He announced a thorough reorganization of the Gau structure, according to Gregor Strasser's plan.[277] Under Strasser's organizational leadership, greater attention was paid to the countyside, and first steps were taken in constructing a panoply of affiliated sub-organizations that became extremely important in tapping the specific interests of middle-class groups.[278]

Hitler's own reaction to the election disaster was characteristic. On election night itself, in a packed meeting in the Bürgerbräukeller, flanked by Epp and the recently returned Röhm, he rejoiced first in the dismal showing of rival parties. The first conclusion from the election, he stated, was that there was now only a single *völkisch* movement: the NSDAP. He emphasized the fact that in Munich, the party had gained some 7,000 votes compared with December 1924. The poor results in almost every other city were not mentioned. As a second consequence, he underlined the large increase in the 'Marxist' vote, after three years of government by the Bavarian People's Party and the German Nationals. He contrasted this with the fall in the vote for the Left in Munich in 1924. Finally, he added a defiant third conclusion: 'The election campaign is fought. The struggle continues! . . . For us there is no rest, no break. We carry on working . . .'[279] In fact, Hitler left within days for a holiday in his mountain retreat, to recuperate and dictate his 'Second Book'.[280] He was forced to authorize a statement on 27 June to editors of the National Socialist press, reaffirming his commitment to the legal path to power, after the poor election result had led some to the conclusion that the party would again seek power through violent action.[281] Otherwise, he remained out of the public eye until early July.[282]

The election results confirmed to many observers that the Hitler Movement was finished.[283] The Prussian government also thought so. At the end of September it lifted the ban preventing Hitler speaking at public meetings.[284] On 16 November, he spoke for the first time in the Sportpalast in Berlin. The gigantic hall was packed to capacity by the time he arrived, accompanied by fanfares and banner-waving SA men. The atmosphere bore little resemblance to a conventional political meeting. His speech on 'The Struggle that Will Sometime Break the Chains' was repeatedly interrupted by storms of applause.[285] There was nothing new in the speech. Presentation, not content, was what counted. As always, the appeal was solely to the emotions. The Revolution, pacifism, internationalism, democracy were all inevitably castigated. Economic recovery could only be brought about through national freedom. And 'the premiss of freedom is power'. For this, heroic leaders were needed. Hitler did not explicitly refer to the 'Jewish Question'. But he soon turned to his central obsession of 'racial defilement'. The 'bastardization' of culture, morals and blood was undermining the value of the

individual. But 'a people that resists the bastardization of its spirit and blood
can be saved. The German people has its specific value and cannot be set
on an equal level to 70 million negroes . . . Negro music is dominant, but
if we put a Beethoven symphony alongside a shimmy, victory is clear . . .
From our strong faith the strength will come to deploy self-help against this
bastardization. That is the aim that the NSDAP has set itself: to lift the
terms nationalism and socialism out of their previous meaning. To be
national can only mean to be behind your people, and to be socialist can
only be to stand up for the right of your people, also externally.'[286]

With this vaguest of definitions, he was keeping open the appeal to all
sections of society. Class divisions could only be overcome by national unity.
The NSDAP stood above classes. It was 'not purely nationalist or socialist,
bourgeois or proletarian' but stood for all 'who honestly want to construct
the national community, put aside class-pride and conceit in order to fight
together'. As a result, he went on, 'the party is a movement which can call
itself with pride a workers' party because there is no one in it who is not
toiling and working for the existence of the people'. The NSDAP was
engaged in a 'gigantic struggle against internationalism'. It did not rest on
'votes' and the 'error' of democracy, but on the 'authority of the leader'.[287]
This was the way to overcoming Marxism and attaining the land and soil
that would remove Germany's slavery. He ended by pouring scorn on the
speaking-ban that had succeeded in filling 'the biggest hall in the Reich',
and with an appeal to God to bless Germany's struggle. The crowd went
delirious. Critical observers could remain uncomprehending at a mélange
of half-truths, distortions, over-simplifications, and vague, pseudo-religious
redemptionist promises.[288] But the 16,000 people jammed into the Sportpalast
had not turned up to listen to an intellectual discourse. They had heard
what they had come to hear.

By the time Hitler spoke in the Sportpalast, the first dark clouds were
already gathering over Germany's economy. The mounting crisis in agriculture was leading to widespread indebtedness, bankruptcies, forced sales of
land, and enormous bitterness in the farming community. In the biggest
industrial belt, Ruhr industrialists refused to accept an arbitration award
and locked out the whole work-force of the iron and steel industry, leaving
230,000 workers without jobs or wages for weeks.[289] Meanwhile, unemployment was sharply on the rise, reaching almost 3 million by January 1929,
an increase of a million over the previous year.[290] Politically, too, there
were growing difficulties. The 'grand coalition' under the SPD Chancellor
Hermann Müller was shaky from the outset. A split, and serious loss of

face for the SPD, occurred over the decision to build a battle cruiser (a policy opposed by the Social Democrats before the election). The Ruhr iron dispute further opened the rifts in the government and exposed it to its critics on Left and Right. It was the first shot of the concerted attempt by the conservative Right to roll back the social advances made in the Weimar welfare state. The ensuing conflict over social policy would ultimately lead to the demise of the Müller government. And by the end of the year, the reparations issue began to loom again. It would become acute in 1929.

Remarkably, as intelligent an analyst as the sociologist Joseph Schumpeter could still, in autumn 1928, look with unclouded optimism at 'the growing stability of our social relations'.[291] More percipient was the Reich foreign minister Gustav Stresemann, who warned in November 1928 of the dire consequences for Germany should America withdraw its short-term credits, on which the economy had rested in the previous years.[292]

In reality, the 'golden years' of Weimar had been less 'golden' than they had seemed. Germany had been throughout a society profoundly divided. The brief interlude of relative stability had done nothing to diminish the depth of the class and confessional fissures.[293] Social grievances remained acute. Relatively high levels of unemployment – over 2 million were out of work in 1926 – radicalized many workers, a good number of them young.[294] Small shopkeepers and producers felt threatened and angered by department stores and consumer cooperatives. Along with many craftsmen, feeling their traditional status and livelihood undermined by modern mass-production, and white-collar workers keen to keep their distance from blue-collar wage-earners, they had no affection for Weimar democracy, even in its best years. Farmers, as already mentioned, were up in arms at the collapse of agricultural prices.

Culturally, the divisions were equally acute. Weimar avant-garde art forms repelled far more people than they attracted. Cultural conservativism and philistinism were, as ever, closely allied. Popular culture was equally decried. Goebbels's attacks on 'asphalt culture' would later find an echo, not just among hard-core Nazis, but among a solid reactionary bourgeoisie, alienated by the 'Americanization' of big-city popular culture in the 1920s.

The sharply divided social milieus and 'sub-cultures' were reflected in a highly unstable political landscape. The 1928 election had only at the most superficial glance been a success for democracy. The increased KPD vote marked a shift away from democracy on the Left. The liberal parties of the centre and centre-right had lost an alarming proportion of their support since 1919. Their disintegration and fragmentation reflected disillusionment with democracy and a rightward shift of voters, even before the Nazis made a significant electoral mark.[295] On the nationalist Right, the loss of support by the DNVP was only at first sight a comfort to democrats. Many of the party's erstwhile supporters had drifted still further to the Right, into a variety of interest and protest parties that would ultimately be swept into the NSDAP.[296] Above all, Weimar democracy was unable, even in its 'golden years', to win a firm enough base of support to counter those powerful sectors of society that opposed its very existence. Its problem of legitimacy remained acute. Renewed economic crisis would evidently pose an immense threat.

And here, as Stresemann had emphasized, stability was far less assured than the outward glitter of the 'golden twenties' suggested. The German economy depended upon American short-term loans. Its own productivity and investment lagged, profitability was declining as wages were rising, public finances were coming increasingly under strain, and a heavily subsidized agricultural sector was lurching into deep crisis, following a collapse of world food-prices, at least two years before the Wall Street Crash.[297]

In the worsening conditions of the winter of 1928–9, the NSDAP began to attract increasing support. By the end of 1928, the number of membership cards distributed had reached 108,717.[298] Social groups that had scarcely been reached before could now be tapped. In November 1928, Hitler received a rapturous reception from 2,500 students at Munich University.[299] Before he spoke, the meeting had been addressed by the recently appointed Reich Leader of the Nazi Students' Federation, the twenty-one-year-old Baldur von Schirach. The future Hitler Youth leader came from a highly cultured bourgeois family, based in Weimar – Germany's literary capital – where his father had been a highly regarded director of the Court Theatre. Unusually for a leading Nazi, he spoke excellent English; his American mother, with imperfect command of the language of her adopted country, had spoken only English to him in his childhood, so that at the age of six he spoke, so he later said, not a word of German. The end of the war had brought tragedy for the Schirachs: Baldur's father lost his job; his brother, Karl, committed suicide, despairing at the block on his officer's career as a consequence of the Versailles Treaty and attributing his decision to kill himself to 'Germany's misfortune'. In Weimar, a town conscious of past glories but by now infested with *völkisch* nationalist and antisemitic clamour, Baldur had found his way – helped by his mentor, later Deputy Gauleiter in Thuringia, Hans Severus Ziegler – into a paramilitary youth organization and was an admirer of Ludendorff before for the first time hearing Hitler speak, at the time of the elections for Reich President in March 1925. So thrilled was he at the experience that he ran home and wrote a poem about Hitler which was published, bringing him a signed photograph from his hero. He devoured the first volume of *Mein Kampf* in a single evening, and joined the party at the beginning of May. He was Hitler's man – and would see to it that the Führer cult would flourish in the infant Nazi youth organization and in the Students' League. By late 1928, Schirach could gain credit for a big increase in the Nazi vote in student union elections – up to 32 per cent in Erlangen, and 20 per cent in Greifswald and Würzburg. The success secured him Hitler's support, paving the way for him to take over the leadership of the Hitler Youth in 1931.[300]

The student union elections gave Hitler an encouraging sign of gathering Nazi strength. But it was above all in the countryside, among the radicalized peasants, that the Nazis began to make particularly rapid advances. In Schleswig-Holstein, bomb attacks on government offices gave the clearest indication of the mood in the farming community. In January 1929, rad-icalized peasants in the region founded the Landvolk, an inchoate but violent protest movement that rapidly became prey to Nazi inroads. Two months later, following an NSDAP meeting in the village of Wöhrden, a fight between SA men and KPD supporters led to two stormtroopers being killed and a number of others injured. Local reactions showed graphically the potential for Nazi gains in the disaffected countryside. There was an immedi-ate upsurge in Nazi support in the locality. Old peasant women now wore the party badge on their work-smocks. From conversations with them, ran the police report, it was clear that they had no idea of the aims of the party. But they were certain that the government was incapable and the authorities were squandering taxpayers' money. They were convinced 'that only the National Socialists could be the saviours from this alleged misery'. Farmers spoke of a Nazi victory through parliament taking too long. A civil war was what was needed. The mood was 'extraordinarily embittered' and the population were open to all forms of violent action. Using the incident as a propaganda opportunity, Hitler attended the funeral of the dead SA men, and visited those wounded. This made a deep impression on the local inhabitants. He and the other leading Nazis were applauded as 'liberators of the people'.[301]

As the 'crisis before the crisis' – economic and political – deepened, Hitler kept up his propaganda offensive.[302] In the first half of 1929 he wrote ten articles for the party press and held sixteen major speeches before large, rapturous audiences. Four were in Saxony, during the run-up to the state elections there on 12 May. Outright attacks on the Jews did not figure in the speeches.[303] The emphasis was on the bankruptcy at home and abroad of the Weimar system, the exploitation of international finance and the suffering of 'small people', the catastrophic economic consequences of democratic rule, the social divisions that party politics caused and replicated, and above all the need to restore German strength and unity and gain the land to secure its future. 'The key to the world market has the shape of the sword,' he declared.[304] The only salvation from decline was through power: 'The entire system must be altered. Therefore the great task is to restore to people their belief in leadership (*Führerglauben*),' he concluded.[305]

Hitler's speeches were part of a well-organized propaganda campaign, providing saturation coverage of Saxony before the election. It was planned by Himmler, but under Hitler's own supervision.[306] The growing numerical strength of the party, and the improvements made in its organization and structure, now allowed more extensive coverage. This in turn helped to create an image of dynamism, drive and energy. Local activism, and the winning of influential figures in a community, usually held the key to Nazi progress.[307] Hitler had to be used sparingly – for best effect, as well as to avoid too punishing a schedule.[308] A Hitler speech was a major bonus for any party branch. But in the changing conditions from 1929 onwards, the NSDAP was chalking up successes in places where people had never seen Hitler.[309]

The NSDAP won 5 per cent of the vote in the Saxon election.[310] The following month, the party gained 4 per cent in the Mecklenburg elections – double what it had achieved the previous year in the Reichstag election. Its two elected members held a pivotal position in a Landtag evenly balanced between Left and Right.[311] Towards the end of June, Coburg, in northern Bavaria, became the first town in Germany to elect a Nazi-run town council.[312] By October, the NSDAP's share of the popular vote had reached 7 per cent in the Baden state elections.[313] This was still before the Wall Street Crash ushered in the great Depression.

The revival of the reparations issue provided further grist to the mill of Nazi agitation. The results of the deliberations of the committee of experts, which had been working since January 1929 under the chairmanship of Owen D. Young, an American banker and head of the General Electric Company, to regulate the payment of reparations, were eventually signed on 7 June. Compared with the Dawes Plan, the settlement was relatively favourable to Germany. Repayments were to be kept low for three years, and would overall be some 17 per cent less than under the Dawes Plan.[314] But it would take fifty-nine years before the reparations would finally be paid off. The Allies' quid pro quo was the offer to withdraw from the Rhineland by 30 June, five years earlier than stipulated under the Versailles Treaty. Stresemann was therefore ready to accept.[315] The nationalist Right were outraged. Alfred Hugenberg, former Krupp director, leader of the DNVP and press baron, controlling the nationalist press and with a big stake in the UFA film company, formed in July a 'Reich Committee for the German People's Petition' to organize a campaign to force the government to reject the Young Plan. He persuaded Hitler to join.[316] Franz Seldte and Theodor Duesterberg from the Stahlhelm, Heinrich Claß from the Pan-German League, and the industrial magnate Fritz Thyssen were all members of the committee.[317] Hitler's presence in this company of capitalist tycoons and reactionaries was not to the liking of the national revolutionary wing of the NSDAP, headed by Otto Strasser.[318] But, ever the opportunist, Hitler recognized the chances the campaign offered. The draft 'Law against the Enslavement of the German People' drawn up by the Committee in September, rejecting the Young Plan and the 'war guilt lie', marginally gained the necessary support to stage a plebiscite. But when the plebiscite eventually took place, on 22 December 1929, only 5.8 million – 13.8 per cent of the electorate – voted for it.[319] The campaign had proved a failure – but not for Hitler. He and his party had benefited from massive exposure freely afforded him in the Hugenberg press.[320] And he had been recognized as an equal partner by those in high places, with good contacts to sources of funding and influence.

Some of Hitler's new-found bedfellows had been honoured guests at the Party Rally that took place in Nuremberg from 1 to 4 August 1929. The deputy leader of the Stahlhelm, Theodor Duesterberg, and Count von der Golz, head of the Vereinigte Völkische Verbände (United Racist-Ethnic Associations) graced the Rally with their presence.[321] The Ruhr industrialist and benefactor of the party Emil Kirdorf had also accepted an invitation. Winifred Wagner, the Lady of Bayreuth, was also an honoured guest.[322] Thirty-five special trains brought 25,000 SA and SS men and 1,300 members of the Hitler Youth to Nuremberg. Police estimated an attendance of around 30–40,000 in all. It was a far bigger and more grandiose spectacle than the previous rally, two years earlier, had been. It reflected a new confidence and optimism in a party whose membership had grown by this time to some 130,000.[323] And compared with two years earlier, Hitler's dominance was even more complete. Working sessions simply rubber-stamped policy determined from above. Hitler showed little interest in them. His only concern, as always, was with the propaganda display of the Rally.[324]

He had reason to feel satisfied with the way his movement had developed over the four years since its refoundation. The party was now almost three times as large as it had been at the time of the putsch, and growing fast. It was spread throughout the country, and making headway in areas which had never been strongholds. It was now far more tightly organized and structured. There was much less room for dissension. Rivals in the *völkisch* movement had been amalgamated or had faded into insignificance. Not least, Hitler's own mastery was complete. His own recipe for success was unchanged: hammer home the same message, exploit any opportunity for agitation, and hope for external circumstances to favour the party. But although great strides forward had been made since 1925, and though the party was registering modest electoral gains at state elections and acquiring a good deal of publicity, no realist could have reckoned much to its chances of winning power. For that, Hitler's only hope was a massive and comprehensive crisis of the state.

He had no notion just how quickly events would turn to the party's advantage. But on 3 October, Gustav Stresemann, the only statesman of real standing in Germany, who had done most to sustain the shaky Müller government, died following a stroke. Three weeks later, on 24 October 1929, the largest stock-market in the world, in Wall Street, New York, crashed. The crisis Hitler needed was about to envelop Germany.

9

BREAKTHROUGH

'I had lost all I possessed through adverse economic conditions. And so, early in 1930, I joined the National Socialist Party.'

An unskilled labourer,
newly won over to the Hitler Movement

'How many look to him in touching faith as the helper, saviour, the redeemer from overgreat distress. To him, who rescues the Prussian prince, the scholar, the clergyman, the peasant, the worker, the unemployed.'

Luise Solmitz, a schoolteacher,
on hearing Hitler speak in Hamburg, April 1932

The terrible burden of the breakdown threatened to bring all economic life to a standstill. Thousands of factories closed their doors. Hunger was the daily companion of the German working man. Added to this was the artificial whip of scarcity, wielded by the Jews, which sent working men scurrying from their homes to beg for food from the farmers ... The government carried its measures against the public so far that many an honest working man had to resort to theft to obtain food ... Burglaries, too, became daily occurrences, and the police had their hands full protecting the citizens' property. All fellow citizens, with the exception of the Communists, yearned for better times. As for me, like many another, I had lost all I possessed through adverse economic conditions. And so, early in 1930, I joined the National Socialist Party.[1]

This was one individual's story of how he became a Nazi. Another recounted:

When we consider that on the one hand the policies of the Red government, particularly the inflation and taxes, deprived me of all means of livelihood, while on the other hand we soldiers of the front were being ruled by a gang of exploiters ready to stoop to any means to seize the starvation wages of our suffering, duped comrades, it will become clear why a number of us welcomed the activities of patriotic groups, particularly those of the Hitler movement. The combination of patriotic aims along with social reform led many an old soldier and idealist under the banner of the National Socialist Workers' Party.[2]

These two new recruits were won over to the NSDAP as the economic crisis began to grip Germany. Neither the first, an unskilled labourer in his early thirties, nor the second, a small trader of around the same age who had been forced to sell up his bakery in 1926 for a low price (which he blamed on Jewish creditors) and eke out a living thereafter as a pedlar, were exact fits for the abstract sociological model of a typical Nazi supporter.[3]

But their short accounts offer a glimpse of the type of psychology and motivation that were beginning to drive thousands – predominantly male, and for the most part young – to join the Hitler Movement as the storm-clouds gathered over Germany in 1930. In each case the personal bitterness and loss of self-esteem found a simple explanation in policies of the 'Red' government and a ready scapegoat in the Jews. The sense of betrayal and exploitation was acute. And it was not just a feeling that a change of government was needed. Among those drawn in increasing numbers from a wide variety of motives to the NSDAP in 1930 there was a common feeling of elemental, visceral hatred for the Weimar state itself, for the 'system' as it was so often called. Hatred, as Hitler had recognized, was among the most powerful of emotions. That was what he consciously appealed to. That is what drove so many of his followers. But there was idealism, too – misplaced, certainly, but idealism none the less: hopes of a new society, of a 'national community' that would transcend all existing social divides. There would, recruits to the Nazi Party believed, be no return to the class-ridden, hierarchical society of the past, resting on status, privilege, and the wealth of the few at the expense of the many. The new society would be fair without destroying talent, flair, ability, initiative, creativity in the way they saw threatened by the social egalitarianism preached by the Marxists. It would be one in which achievement, not status, would gain recognition, where the high-and-mighty would be deprived of their seeming God-given rights to lord it over the humble and lowly, where sweeping social reform would ensure that those who deserved it would gain their just rewards, where the 'little man' would no longer be exploited by big capital or threatened by organized labour, where Marxist internationalism would be crushed and replaced by loyal devotion to the German people. Discrimi-natory feelings were built into the idealism. Those who did not belong in the 'national community' – 'shirkers', 'spongers', 'parasites', and, of course, those deemed not to be German at all, notably Jews – would be ruthlessly suppressed. But for true 'comrades of the people' (*Volksgenossen*) – the term the Nazis invented to replace 'citizen' (*Bürger*) for those who *did* belong – the new society would be a genuine 'community', where the rights of the individual were subordinated to the common good of the whole, and where duty preceded any rights. Only on this basis could the German nation become strong again, recover its pride, cast aside the shackles unfairly imposed on it by its enemies in the Versailles Treaty. But only through complete destruction of the hated, divisive democratic system could the 'national community' be accomplished at all.

In this crude but powerful imagery that attracted many who found their way to the NSDAP, nationalism and socialism were not seen as opposites; they went together, were part of the same utopian dream of a reborn nation, strong and united. Many who, as the crisis set in during 1930, came to vote for the NSDAP or even to join the party had never encountered Hitler personally and were often becoming interested in him for the first time. Usually, they were already predisposed to the Nazi message. Its ideology did not in itself distinguish the Nazi Party from its rivals on the Right. Nationalism and anti-Marxism were, in different shadings, common currency in all but the parties of the Left. Antisemitism was far from the preserve of the NSDAP. What set Hitler's movement apart was above all its image of activism, dynamism, élan, youthfulness, vigour. To many, it marked the future, 'the new Germany', born out of a complete break with the present, but resting on the true values – as they saw it – of the Teutonic past. Hitler encapsulated their hopes of a ruthless showdown with their enemies and exploiters, and embodied their dreams of a reborn Germany. 'Any true German,' declared another new member around this time, 'in his soul longed for a German saviour, and sought to raise his eyes in trust and confidence to a truly great leader.'[4]

Economic crises frequently unseat governments. It is much rarer for them to destroy *systems* of government. Even the extreme severity of the Depression of the early 1930s was compatible in some countries with the survival of democracy – where democracy was already firmly anchored, and not undermined by a lost war. The terrible privations that accompanied mass unemployment and economic collapse in the USA and Britain brought turbulence but no serious challenge to the democratic state. Democracy could emerge intact, perhaps strengthened. Even France, where democracy had a much more flimsy base, survived with some scares. But in Germany, the 'system' itself, the very nature of the state, was at stake from the beginning of the crisis. Hitler and his party were the beneficiaries of this systemic crisis of the Weimar state. They were not its primary cause. Even in its 'golden' years, Weimar democracy had never won the hearts and minds of large numbers of Germans. And even in those years, powerful sectors of society – business, the army, big landowners, leading civil servants in charge of government administration, academics, many intellectuals and opinion-leaders – had tolerated rather than actively supported the Republic. Not a few among the power élites were awaiting the opportunity to discard the democracy they detested so much. Now, as the crisis started to unfold, such groups began to show their true colours at the same time as the masses began to desert the Republic in droves. In Britain and America, the élites backed the existing, and long-established, democratic system, deeply embedded constitutionally, because it continued to serve their interests. In Germany, where the roots of democracy were far more shallow, they looked to change a system which, they felt, less and less upheld their interests, and to move to authoritarian rule. (For most of them this did not mean, at the time, Nazi rule.) In Britain and America the masses were, despite misery and discontent, faced with little alternative to the existing, well-established political parties. Nor, with few exceptions, did they look for any. In Germany, 'political space' was opened up for the Nazi breakthrough by the prior fragmentation of support for the parties of the centre and Right.[5] In Germany, therefore, the economic crisis ushered in from the beginning a fundamental crisis of the state. The battleground was, from the outset, the state itself. That was what Hitler wanted.

I

The Nazi leadership did not immediately recognize the significance of the American stock-market crash in October 1929. The *Völkischer Beobachter* did not even mention Wall Street's 'Black Friday'.[6] But Germany was soon reverberating under its shock-waves. Its dependence upon American short-term loans ensured that the impact would be extraordinarily severe. Industrial output, prices, and wages began the steep drop that would reach its calamitous low-point in 1932.[7] The agricultural crisis that had already been radicalizing Germany's farmers in 1928 and 1929 was sharply intensified. By January 1930, the labour exchanges recorded 3,218,000 unemployed – some 14 per cent of the 'working-age' population. The true figure, taking in those on short-time, has been estimated as over 4½ million.[8]

The protest of ordinary people who took the view that democracy had failed them, that 'the system' should be swept away, became shriller on both Left and Right. Nazi advances in regional elections reflected the growing radicalization of the mood of the electorate. The Young Plan plebiscite had given the party much-needed publicity in the widely read Hugenberg press. Its value, said Hitler, was that it had provided 'the occasion for a propaganda wave the like of which had never been seen in Germany before'.[9] It had allowed the NSDAP to project itself as the most radical voice of the Right, a protest-movement *par excellence* that had never been tarnished with any involvement in Weimar government. In the Baden state elections on 27

October 1929, the NSDAP won 7 per cent of the vote. In the Lübeck city elections a fortnight or so later, the percentage was 8.1. Even in the Berlin council elections on 17 November, the party almost quadrupled its vote of 1928, though its 5.8 per cent was still marginal, compared with over 50 per cent that went to the two left-wing parties. Most significantly of all, in the Thuringian state elections held on 8 December, the NSDAP trebled its vote of 1928 and broke the 10 per cent barrier for the first time, recording 11.3 per cent of the votes cast. The Nazi votes were won mainly at the expense of the DVP, the DNVP, and the Landbund. In many of the small towns and villages of the Thüringer Wald, where the craftsmen producing toys and Christmas-tree decorations had been hard hit by the onset of the Depression, the Nazis were able to increase their vote five-fold. The six seats (from fifty-three) that the NSDAP won in the Landtag left the construction of a Thuringian anti-Marxist coalition government in the hands of the Nazis.[10] Should the Nazi Party exploit the situation by agreeing to enter government for the first time but run the risk of courting unpopularity through its participation in an increasingly discredited system? Hitler decided the NSDAP had to enter government. Had he refused, he said, it would have come to new elections and voters could have turned away from the NSDAP.[11] What happened gives an indication of the way at this time the 'seizure of power' in the Reich itself was envisaged.[12]

Hitler demanded the two posts he saw as most important in the Thuringian government: the Ministry of the Interior, controlling the civil service and police; and the Ministry of Education, overseeing culture as well as policy for school and university. 'He who controls both these ministries and ruthlessly and persistently exploits his power in them can achieve extraordinary things,' wrote Hitler.[13] When his nominee for both ministries, Wilhelm Frick, was rejected – the DVP claimed it could not work with a man who (for his part in the Beerhall Putsch) had been convicted of high treason – Hitler went himself to Weimar and imposed an ultimatum. If within three days Frick were not accepted, the NSDAP would bring about new elections. Industrialists from the region, lobbied by Hitler, put heavy pressure on the DVP – the party of big business – and Hitler's demands were finally accepted. Frick was given the task of purging the civil service, police, and teachers of revolutionary, Marxist, and democratic tendencies and bringing education in line with National Socialist ideas. A first step would be to appoint Dr Hans Günther, a race-theory 'expert', to a new chair of Racial Questions and Racial Knowledge (*Rassenfragen und Rassenkunde*) at the University of Jena.[14]

The first Nazi experiment in government was anything but successful. Frick's attempts to reconstruct educational and cultural policy on a basis of ideological racism were not well received, and moves to nazify the police and civil service were blocked by the Reich Ministry of the Interior. After only a year, Frick was removed from office following a vote of no-confidence supported by the NSDAP's coalition partners.[15] The strategy – to prove so fateful in 1933 – of including Nazis in government in the expectation that they would prove incompetent and lose support was, on the basis of the Thuringian experiment, by no means absurd.

In his letter of 2 February 1930 to an overseas party supporter outlining the developments that led to participation in the Thuringian government, Hitler pointed to the rapid advances the party was making in gaining support. By the time he was writing, party membership officially numbered 200,000 (though the actual figures were somewhat lower).[16] The Nazis were starting to make their presence felt in places where they had been scarcely noticed earlier.

In Northeim, a small town in Lower Saxony, divided along class lines but otherwise a fairly balanced and economically by no means deprived community, the NSDAP had been wholly insignificant before 1929. In the 1928 elections, the party had won only 2.3 per cent of the vote; the SPD's share was almost 45 per cent.[17] But local activists began to revitalize the party the following year. They peppered the town with propaganda in early 1930. Despite the fact that the town was at first relatively unaffected by the looming Depression, its middle class and the farmers in the adjacent countryside already felt aggrieved by levels of taxation, problems of credit, and economic competition. They blamed the government, which they saw as in the hands of Marxists. Nazi propaganda, making full play of well-chosen speakers, started to make inroads. Though attendance was still small, the image of the party was one of unparalleled vitality, drive, and youthful vigour. 'There was a feeling of restless energy about the Nazis,' was one housewife's comment. 'You constantly saw the swastika painted on the sidewalks or found them littered by pamphlets put out by the Nazis. I was drawn by the feeling of strength about the party, even though there was much in it which was highly questionable.'[18] Image was crucial to the spread of Nazi success. The NSDAP was known predominantly in Northeim as a vehemently anti-Marxist – that is, anti-SPD – party, and one that was avidly nationalist and militarist. The NSDAP had no special purchase on such 'ideas'. Image counted for more. That was what distinguished them from rival parties with a not dissimilar message and ideology. Manipulation of nationalist and religious symbols helped to win middle-class support. Important, too, was the example set by well-respected figures in the town. That the popular and well-regarded local bookseller in Northeim, a local worthy, pillar of the Protestant Church in the town, was a member of the party made others take note. 'If he's in it, it must be all right,' was what they said.[19] Antisemitism was relatively unimportant as a drawing-card. It did not deter the townspeople from supporting the NSDAP. But it was seldom the prime reason for doing so.[20] Few, if any, of the local inhabitants had seen Hitler in person by the time they started to find the NSDAP attractive. Again it was image – what Hitler was said to stand for, as relayed in innumerable propaganda meetings – that was important.

What was happening in Northeim was happening in countless other towns and villages the length and breadth of Germany. Since the Young Campaign the previous autumn, rejecting the plan for long-term repayment of reparations, the NSDAP had been building up to around a hundred propaganda meetings a day.[21] This would reach a crescendo during the Reichstag election campaign later in the summer. Many of the speakers were now of good quality, hand-picked, well-trained, centrally controlled but able to latch on to and exploit local issues as well as putting across the unchanging basic message of Nazi agitation. The National Socialists were increasingly forcing themselves on to the front pages of newspapers, forming more and more the talking-point around the *Stammtisch*. They began to penetrate the network of clubs and associations (*Vereine*) that were the social framework of so many provincial communities. Where local leaders, enjoying respectability and influence, were won over, further converts often rapidly followed.[22] In the relatively homogeneous villages in Schleswig-Holstein, where feelings about the Weimar 'system' were, as we have seen, running high on account of the agrarian crisis, the push from one or two farmers' leaders could result in a local landslide to the NSDAP.[23] Other non-Marxist parties seemed, in the gathering crisis, to be increasingly weak, ineffectual and discredited, or to relate, like the Zentrum (the Catholic party), to only one particular sector of the population. Their disarray could only enhance the appeal of a large, expanding, dynamic and *national* party, seen more and more to offer the best chance of combating the Left, and increasingly regarded as the only party capable of representing the interests of each section of society in a united 'national community'. And as increasing numbers joined the party, paid their entry fees to the growing number of Nazi meetings, or threw their Marks into the collection boxes, so the funds grew that enabled still further propaganda activity to unfold.[24] The tireless activism was, then, already showing signs of success even in the early months of 1930. The extraordinary breakthrough of the September Reichstag election did not come out of thin air.

Encouraged by his party's advances, Hitler felt bold enough, in the private letter he wrote in early February 1930, to 'prophesy' that the Nazi Movement would get to power within two and a half to three years.[25] This was typical Hitler bravado. He saw the tide turning in his favour. But his conviction of an inexorable path to triumph was simple 'gut feeling', not based on rational calculation. As NSDAP leaders recognized, agitation had so far been based on little more than negative propaganda: attacking the Weimar Republic.[26] The party's programme, in Gregor Strasser's eyes, was purely ideological, not constructive. Its creators, he claimed, had no idea how they would implement it, given the chance. The party was committed to a fight for power without knowing what to do with it once attained.[27] Planning for the future had only just begun in the party, and remained vague and ill-thought-out.[28] Hitler himself was little interested in such notions. He remained fixated on propaganda and mobilization. Everything was targeted on the fight for power.[29] But how to get power remained unclear. No cogent strategy was developed.

Electoral gains were extremely important. But they did not translate directly into power. At the Reich level, elections were not due until 1932. At provincial level, the Thuringian elections had opened up a new possible avenue of gaining power through infiltrating state government. But Nazi participation in the Thuringian government was soon to prove that this route was unlikely to yield positive results, and guaranteed to bring a fall in support for the NSDAP. Even with the deepening Depression and every prospect of increasing National Socialist electoral gains, the road to power was blocked. Only crass errors by the country's rulers could open up a path. And only a blatant disregard by Germany's power élites for safeguarding democracy – in fact, the hope that economic crisis could be used as a vehicle to bring about democracy's demise and replace it by a form of authoritarianism – could induce such errors. Precisely this is what happened in March 1930.

II

The fall of the Social Democrat Chancellor Hermann Müller and his replacement by Heinrich Brüning of the Zentrum was the first unnecessary step on the suicidal road of the Weimar Republic. Without the self-destructiveness of the democratic state, without the wish to undermine democracy of those who were meant to uphold it, Hitler, whatever his talents as an agitator, could not have come close to power.

The Müller administration eventually came to grief, on 27 March 1930, over the question of whether employer contributions to unemployment insurance should be raised, as from 30 June 1930, from 3.5 to 4 per cent of the gross wage.[30] The issue had polarized the ill-matched coalition partners, the SPD and DVP, since the previous autumn. If the will had been there, a compromise would have been found. But by the end of 1929, in the context of the increasing economic difficulties of the Republic, the DVP had – in company with the other 'bourgeois' parties – moved sharply to the right. Stresemann's death had removed a strong force for pragmatism and common sense. Now, the DVP, with its close links with big business and anxious about the demands on employers' social contributions in the context of rapidly rising unemployment, launched a general attack on the Weimar welfare-state. For the DVP, and for other 'bourgeois' parties of the Right, this was more or less synonymous with an attack on the Weimar 'party state' itself. The SPD was for its part increasingly intransigent. It was unwilling to allow Müller any room for compromise on the unemployment insurance issue.[31]

Even with the stalemate between the coalition partners, the fall of government could have been avoided. Reich President Hindenburg could have used his powers to enable Müller to resolve the issue of unemployment contributions by presidential decree. Ebert had supported Stresemann with this device during the 1923 crisis. Hindenburg was to extend it to each of Müller's successors – completely undermining parliamentary government in the process. But in early 1930 use of Article 48 was denied to Müller.[32] With no way out of the government crisis, the Chancellor tendered his resignation on 27 March. It marked the beginning of the end for the Weimar Republic.

The fall of Müller had in fact been planned long beforehand. The Reich President had spoken to the former leader and chairman of the DNVP's parliamentary delegation Graf Westarp as early as March 1929 about the necessity of ruling without the Social Democrats. The following August, Major-General Kurt von Schleicher, protégé of Defence Minster Groener and head of the newly created Ministerial Bureau (*Ministeramt*) in the Defence Ministry, already with the ear of the Reich President, let Heinrich Brüning – a cautious, conscientious but somewhat desiccated figure, aloof and ascetic, on the right of the Zentrum and the party's expert on finance policy – know of Hindenburg's readiness to use Article 48 to 'send the Reichstag home for a while' and rule by emergency decree.[33] In December, Brüning, by now parliamentary leader of the Zentrum, learnt that Hindenburg was determined to oust Müller as soon as the Young Plan had been accepted. Brüning himself was earmarked to take over as Chancellor, backed where necessary by the President's powers under Article 48 of the Weimar Constitution. Soundings were taken in January about the willingness of the DNVP to support such an administration. A 'government crisis on account of financial reform' was expected in February or March, it was said in confidence. The Reich President was anxious not to miss the chance of creating an 'anti-parliamentary and anti-Marxist' government and afraid of being forced to retain a Social Democrat administration.[34]

Brüning was appointed Chancellor on 30 March 1930. His problems soon became apparent. Under the Weimar Constitution, even making full use of emergency decrees, he could not completely dispense with the support of the Reichstag. Should presidential decrees under Article 48 fail to gain the necessary majority, the President could dissolve the Reichstag. But new elections had then to be held within sixty days. By June, Brüning was running into serious difficulties in his attempts to reduce public spending through emergency decrees. On 16 July, his wide-ranging finance bill – aimed at reforming state finances through a stringent deflationary policy of cuts in public expenditure and higher taxes – was rejected by the Reichstag. Brüning had made no serious effort to explore all possibilities of securing a Reichstag majority. He now resorted to emergency decree to make the bill law – the first time this had happened for a bill rejected by the Reichstag, and a step of doubtful legality. When an SPD motion, supported by the NSDAP, to withdraw the decree was passed by the Reichstag, Brüning sought and received, on 18 July 1930, the Reich President's dissolution of parliament.[35] The temptation to seek a dissolution rather than undergo wearisome negotiations to arrive at a Reichstag majority had proved irresistible. New elections were set for 14 September. For democracy's prospects in Germany, they were a catastrophe. They were to bring the Hitler Movement's electoral breakthrough.

The decision to dissolve the Reichstag was one of breathtaking irresponsibility. Brüning evidently took a sizeable vote for the Nazis on board in his calculations.[36] After all, the NSDAP had won 14.4 per cent of the vote only a few weeks earlier in the Saxon regional election.[37] But in his determination to override parliamentary government by a more authoritarian system run by presidential decree, Brüning had greatly underestimated the extent of anger and frustration in the country, grossly miscalculating the effect of the deep alienation and dangerous levels of popular protest. The Nazis could hardly believe their luck. Under the direction of their newly appointed propaganda chief, Joseph Goebbels, they prepared feverishly for a summer of unprecedented agitation.[38]

III

In the meantime, internal conflict within the NSDAP only demonstrated the extent to which Hitler now dominated the Movement, how far it had become, over the previous five years, a 'leader party'. The dispute, when it came to a head, crystallized once more around the issue of whether there could be any separation of the 'idea' from the Leader.

Otto Strasser, Gregor's younger brother, had continued to use the publications of the Kampfverlag, the Berlin publishing house which he controlled, as a vehicle for his own version of National Socialism.[39] This was a vague and heady brew of radical mystical nationalism, strident anti-capitalism, social reformism, and anti-Westernism. Rejection of bourgeois society produced admiration for the radical anti-capitalism of the Bolsheviks. Otto shared his doctrinaire national-revolutionary ideas with a group of theorists who used the Kampfverlag as the outlet for their views. As long as such notions neither harmed the party nor impinged on his own position, Hitler took little notice of them. He was even aware, without taking any action, that Otto Strasser had talked of founding a new party. By early 1930, however, the quasi-independent line of Otto Strasser had grown shriller as Hitler had sought since the previous year to exploit closer association with the bourgeois Right. A showdown came closer when the Kampfverlag continued to support striking metal-workers in Saxony in April 1930, despite Hitler's ban, under pressure from industrialists, on any backing of the strike by the party.[40]

Goebbels had by this time for weeks been venting his own spleen to Hitler about the Strasser brothers, whose newspapers were in rivalry to his own *Angriff*.[41] Hitler promised to support Goebbels. 'He can't stand the Strassers and passes the hardest judgement on this salon socialism,' wrote the Berlin party boss.[42] But Hitler did nothing.[43] His hesitancy and reluctance to act frustrated and annoyed Goebbels. Already angered in February at Hitler's refusal to attend the funeral of Horst Wessel – a Berlin SA leader, shot in his apartment by Communists after his landlady had complained to them that he was refusing to pay his rent, and converted by Goebbels into a martyr for the movement, savagely murdered by its political enemies – he threatened to resign as Gauleiter of Berlin if Hitler did not act against the Strassers.[44] But he thought Hitler, as usual, would not intervene.[45] 'Munich, incl. Chief, has lost all credit with me,' he bitterly noted in mid-March. 'I don't believe anything from them any longer. Hitler has – for whatever reasons, they don't matter – broken his word to me five times. That's bitter to realize, and I inwardly draw my conclusions. Hitler keeps to himself (*verbirgt sich*), he takes no decisions, he doesn't lead any more but lets things happen.'[46]

Hitler was stirred into action in early April by the publication in the Strasser press, against his orders, of his decision to break with Hugenberg and leave the Reich Committee against the Young Plan. 'Hitler is in a stinking rage,' noted Goebbels.[47] 'He is ready to act against this *literati* tendency, since he is himself threatened by it,' he added.[48] In a two-hour speech to a meeting in Munich on 27 April, to which all top party leaders had been expressly summoned, Hitler tore into the Kampfverlag and its 'salon bolsheviks'.[49] At the end of the meeting, he announced Goebbels's appointment as Propaganda Leader of the party. The Berlin Gauleiter was triumphant. 'Hitler leads again, thank God,' he wrote.[50] But still Hitler was reluctant to bring matters to a head.

After further inaction, he travelled to Berlin on 21 May and invited Otto Strasser to his hotel for lengthy discussions. Hitler preferred even then to avoid a breach. His tactic was to remove the problem of the Kampfverlag – which remained in serious financial difficulties – by buying it out.[51] He even offered to make Otto Strasser his press chief.[52] But Strasser was obdurate. Hitler turned from blandishments to threats. He wanted an immediate decision. Otherwise he would take steps within days to have the Kampfverlag banned.[53] Undeterred, Strasser moved the discussion on to ideological issues. According to his published account – the only one that exists, though it rings true and was not denied by Hitler – the key points were leadership and socialism.[54] 'A Leader must serve the Idea. To this alone can we devote ourselves entirely, since it is eternal whereas the Leader passes and can make mistakes,' claimed Strasser. 'What you are saying is outrageous nonsense (*ein unerhörter Unsinn*),' retorted Hitler. 'That's the most revolting democracy that we want nothing more to do with. For us, the Leader is the Idea, and each party member has to obey only the Leader.'[55] Strasser accused Hitler of trying to destroy the Kampfverlag because he wanted 'to strangle' the 'social revolution' through a strategy of legality and collaboration with the bourgeois Right. Hitler angrily denounced Strasser's socialism as 'nothing but Marxism'. The mass of the working class, he went on, wanted only bread and circuses, and would never understand the meaning of an ideal. 'There is only one possible kind of revolution, and it is not economic or political or social, but racial,' he avowed.[56] Pushed on his attitude towards big business, Hitler made plain that there could be no question for him of socialization or worker control. The only priority was for a strong state to ensure that production was carried out in the national interest.[57]

The meeting broke up. Hitler's mood was black. 'An intellectual white Jew, totally incapable of organization, a Marxist of the purest ilk', was his withering assessment of Otto Strasser. 'Hitler is full of rage,' added Goebbels, somewhat superfluously.[58] Gregor Strasser noted a few weeks later that after this discussion it was impossible for his brother to remain in the party.[59] But Hitler still took no action. And, though he promised Goebbels that he would deal with Otto Strasser after the Saxony elections,[60] he did nothing until late June. When he did finally act, it was following pressure from Göring and Walter Buch as well as Goebbels, and only after Otto Strasser had effectively left him little choice by publicizing his account of their discussions in Berlin in May.[61] On the eve of the Saxony election, Hitler again promised Goebbels he would purge the Strasser faction.[62] But three days later, on 25 June, following a telephone conversation with Hitler, the party's propaganda boss felt: 'Chief wants me to throw out the little ones, but doesn't touch the big-shots. That's so typically Hitler. In Plauen high on his horse, today he pulls back again . . . He makes promises, and doesn't keep them.'[63] By 28 June, Goebbels was even more critical. Hitler 'backs away from the decision. So everything is turned upside down again. I'm certain he won't come on Monday [to Berlin] to save himself from having to make decisions. That's the old Hitler. The waverer! For ever putting things off!'[64] As Goebbels predicted, Hitler – taken up with coalition negotiations in Saxony – cancelled his planned speech to the Berlin Gau meeting on 3 July.[65] The propaganda chief was not consoled by a message from Göring that Walter Buch would read out a letter written by Hitler attacking the Strasser clique.[66] However, when he saw the letter, its aggressive tone pleased him. It gave Goebbels backing for the 'ruthless purge' of the Berlin party.[67] Strasser and twenty-five supporters had, in fact, already anticipated their expulsion, and publicly announced on 4 July that 'the socialists are leaving the NSDAP'.[68] The rebels had in effect purged themselves. 'The whole thing ends in a great declaration of loyalty to the Movement, Hitler, and me,' wrote Goebbels.[69] 'Berlin is in order . . . The air is cleared,' he added shortly afterwards.[70] 'The entire revolt of the *literati* reveals itself to be a storm in a teacup. Otto Strasser has lost completely.'[71] Goebbels's confidence in Hitler was still not completely restored. 'Hitler acts from anxiety,' he noted in his diary on 16 July 1930. 'He is not in the least free in his decisions any longer.'[72]

Within two days, little of this seemed to matter any longer. Brüning declared the Reichstag dissolved. Goebbels was thrown headlong into the preparations for the election campaign. He was shown the lavish offices being built for him in the newly purchased 'Brown House' headquarters in Munich, provided with a flat in the city, and given massive financial backing for his propaganda department.[73] 'Hitler listens to me completely. It's good like that,' he commented.[74] Disappointments of the early summer forgotten, he was Hitler's man again.

Goebbels's account, one-sided though it was, of the crisis provoked by Otto Strasser is revealing for its repeated criticism of Hitler's indecision. Tactics – the proximity of the Saxon elections, the wait for the most opportune moment when Strasser would provide the occasion to strike at him – obviously played their part in Hitler's dilatory behaviour. Hitler plainly wanted to wait until the elections in Saxony, where Strasser had some support, before acting against him.[75] And it was only after Strasser had effectively decided to force the break by publishing his version of the discussion with Hitler that the latter felt compelled to intervene. But Goebbels plainly recognized the trait in Hitler's character that other Nazi leaders were also well aware of: his instinctive tendency to put off tough decisions and his chronic wavering in a crisis. Not visible to outsiders, this trait would be apparent in so many of the major crises during the Third Reich itself. If it was a weakness, however, it was a strange one. There was never any suggestion that Hitler might be bypassed or ignored, that anyone but he could make a key decision. And, once he finally decided to act, Hitler did so, as on this occasion, with ruthlessness. Such dilatoriness followed by boldness was a feature of Hitler as party leader, then later as dictator.

The Strasser crisis showed, above all, the strength of Hitler's position. Otto Strasser had not, in fact, been a popular member of the party. And his influence was less extensive than it had seemed. Once outside the NSDAP, he lost all significance. No major leader followed him; there were no repercussions; the rebellion fizzled out overnight.[76] Gregor Strasser broke completely with his brother.[77] He dissociated himself from Otto's views and described his continued agitation against the party as 'total lunacy' (*heller Wahnsinn*).[78] Otto's 'Union of Revolutionary National Socialists', subsequently the 'Black Front', emerged as no more than a tiny oppositional right-wing sect.[79] With the elimination of the Strasser clique, any lingering ideological dispute in the party was over. Things had changed drastically since 1925 and the days of the 'Working Community'. Now it was clear: Leader and Idea were one and the same.

IV

During the summer of 1930, the election campaign built up to fever pitch. The campaign was centrally organized by Goebbels, under broad guidelines laid down by Hitler. A wide array of different techniques was available to local party branches. Lists were circulated of over a hundred Reich speakers with expertise capable of appealing to different interest groups – farmers, civil servants, workers, and so on. The overriding theme was an attack on the disintegration of German political life into a 'heap of special interests' (*Haufen von Interessenten*).[80]

Two years earlier, the press had largely ignored the NSDAP. Now, the Brownshirts forced themselves on to the front pages.[81] It was impossible to ignore them. The high level of agitation – spiced with street violence – put them on the political map in a big way. Their political opponents provided confirmation of the maxim that all publicity is good publicity. In the Ruhr, one of the toughest areas for the NSDAP, given the strength of support for the Socialists, Communists and Zentrum, a hostile Dortmund newspaper did not let up in its fierce attacks on the Nazis. But it had to acknowledge the dynamism of the party's propaganda. 'Here one can only accord the strongest recognition to the organization, activity, and will to power which inspires the National Socialists,' the newspaper commented. 'For years, the flag-bearers of the party have not avoided going into the most outlying villages and casting their slogans to the masses in at least a hundred meetings a day in Germany.'[82] The energy and drive of the National Socialist agitation were truly astonishing. No fewer than 1,000 meetings saturated Upper and Middle Franconia during the campaign.[83] The authorities in the area expected big Nazi gains, noting the attractiveness of their agitation rooted in disaffection at the 'inability of parliaments to regulate the finances' and corresponding sympathy for a 'fundamental alteration of the state of political affairs'.[84] In Germany as a whole, as many as 34,000 meetings were planned for the last four weeks of the campaign.[85] No other party remotely matched the scale of the NSDAP's effort.

Hitler himself gave twenty big speeches in the six weeks running up to polling-day.[86] The attendances were massive. At least 16,000 came to listen to him in the Sportpalast in Berlin on 10 September.[87] Two days later, in Breslau, as many as 20–25,000 thronged into the Jahrhunderthalle, while a further 5–6,000 were forced to listen to the speech on loudspeakers outside.[88] In the early 1920s, Hitler's speeches had been dominated by vicious attacks on the Jews. In the later 1920s, the question of 'living-space' became the central theme. In the election campaign of 1930, Hitler seldom spoke explicitly of the Jews. The crude tirades of the early 1920s were missing altogether. 'Living-space' figured more prominently, posed against the alternative international competition for markets. But it was not omnipresent as it had been in 1927–8. The key theme now was the collapse of Germany under parliamentary democracy and party government into a divided people with separate and conflicting interests, which only the NSDAP could overcome by creating a new unity of the nation, transcending class, estate and profession. Where the Weimar parties represented only specific interest groups, asserted Hitler, the National Socialist Movement alone stood for the nation as a whole.[89] In speech after speech, Hitler hammered this message home. Again and again he pilloried the Weimar system, not now crudely and simply as the regime of the 'November criminals', but for its failed promises on tax reductions, financial management and employment. All parties were blamed. They were all part of the same party system that had ruined Germany. All had had their part in the policies that had led from Versailles through the reparations terms agreed under the Dawes Plan to their settlement under the Young Plan. Lack of leadership had led to the misery felt by all sections of society. Democracy, pacifism, and internationalism had produced powerlessness and weakness – a great nation brought to its knees. It was time to clear out the rot.[90]

But his speeches were not simply negative, not just an attack on the existing system. He presented a vision, a utopia, an ideal: national liberation through strength and unity. He did not propose alternative policies, built into specific election promises. He offered 'a programme, a gigantic new programme behind which must stand not the new government, but a new German people that has ceased to be a mixture of classes, professions, estates'. It would be, he declared, with his usual stress on stark alternatives (and, as it turned out, prophetically) 'a community of a people which, beyond all differences, will rescue the common strength of the nation, or will take it to ruin'.[91] Only a 'high ideal' could overcome the social divisions, he stated.[92] It was to be found, he claimed, in National Socialism, which placed the nation, the people as a whole, above any individual sector of society. In place of the decayed, the old, a new Reich had to be built on racial values, selection of the best on the basis of achievement, strength, will, struggle, freeing the genius of the individual personality, and re-establishing Germany's power and strength as a nation.[93] Only National Socialism could bring this about. The NSDAP was not about day-to-day policies like other parties. It could not tread the path of other parties. 'What we promise,' Hitler proclaimed to storms of frenetic cheers from his massive audience in the Sportpalast on 10 September, 'is not material improvement for the individual estate (*Stand*), but increase in the strength of the nation, because only this indicates the way to power and with it to the liberation of the *entire* people.'[94] It was not a conventional political programme. It was a political crusade. It was not about a change of government. It was a message of national redemption. In a climate of deepening economic gloom and social misery, anxiety, and division, amid perceptions of the failure and ineptitude of seemingly puny parliamentary politicians, the appeal was a powerful one.

'This idea has no idea and no principle, and will therefore be unable to live,' pronounced Carl von Ossietzky, pacifist and outspoken defender of democracy, in the *Weltbühne*, the radical journal he edited, shortly before the election. 'No National Socialist is in a position to define the "socialism" of his party ... So nothing remains but the rather peculiar dogma of the calling of Adolf Hitler to save the German nation,' he continued. 'The belief in the personality called to leadership is the only thing at all that has developed into a sort of theory of National Socialism. But that is mysticism, and with mysticism it's possible to pull the wool over people's eyes for a while, but you can't fill their stomachs with it.'[95] As an intellectual analysis of Nazi ideology, this showed notable insight. But politically, the judgement was less astute. Ossietzky joined the army of those premature in their obituaries of National Socialism, grossly underestimating the missionary appeal, emotive force, and potential for mobilization of Hitler's message of national salvation, to be attained through the strength of social unity and solidarity.

The message appealed not least to the idealism of a younger generation, not old enough to have fought in the war, but not too young to have experienced at first hand little but crisis, conflict, and national decline. Many from this generation, born between about 1900 and 1910, coming from middle-class families, no longer rooted in the monarchical tradition of the pre-war years, outrightly rejecting socialism and Communism, but alienated by the political, economic, social, and ideological strife of the Weimar era, were on the search for something new.[96] Laden with all the emotive baggage that belonged to the German notions of '*Volk*' (ethnic people) and '*Gemein-schaft*' (community), the aim of a 'national community' which would overcome class divisions seemed a highly positive one.[97] That the notion of 'national community' gained its definition by those it excluded from it, and that social harmony was to be established through racial purity and homogeneity, was taken for granted if not explicitly lauded. It would become clear, once the Third Reich was established, that discriminatory policies directed at those groups to be excluded were easier to bring about than was the reality of a harmonious 'national community'.

In the absence of opinion surveys, the motivating factors behind support of the NSDAP cannot be established with precision. But an indication – even if the sample cannot be regarded as a representative one – is provided by the life stories of 581 ordinary members of the NSDAP, collected in 1934, most of whom joined before Hitler gained power and a majority even by 1930.[98] In almost a third of the cases, the social solidarity of the 'national community' was the most dominant ideological theme. A further third were prompted mainly by nationalist, revanchist, super-patriotic, and German-romantic notions. In only about an eighth of the cases was antisemitism the prime ideological concern (though two-thirds of the biographies revealed some form of dislike of Jews). Almost a fifth were motivated by the Hitler cult alone. From a different angle, ranked by chief object of hostility, two-thirds of the party members were predominantly anti-Marxists, while over a half of the respondents looked forward to a 'nation reborn' and free of 'the system'.[99] The figures are no more than suggestive. But they are sufficient to show again that the appeal of Hitler and his Movement was not based on any distinctive doctrine.[100] It was a pastiche of different ideas drawn from the ideological baggage mainly of pan-Germanism and neo-conservatism, blended with an amalgam of varying phobias, resentments, and prejudice. All were represented, in some form, by other political parties and movements. But none of these had National Socialism's image of strength and dynamism, the missionary drive of the national crusade. And Hitler was simply better than anyone else at tapping the rich vein of raw anger, barely concealed in the 1920s and now opened up by the perceived failure of democracy amid mounting crisis. In addition, and something contemporaries could easily overlook in their scornful dismissal of the poverty of Nazism's intellectual offerings, the Hitler Movement alone on the Right offered an idealistic vision of a new society in a reborn Germany. This, it is clear, was the leading attraction for many.

Though the NSDAP claimed to be above sectional interest, it was, in fact, as the crisis gripped ever more tightly, better than any other party in tapping a whole panoply of mainly middle-class interest-groups through the sub-organizations it built up. From the 'Agrarian Apparatus' set up under R. Walther Darré, the party's 'Blood and Soil' (*Blut und Boden*) theorist, in August 1930, through organizations to cope with the special interests of workers, civil servants, lawyers, doctors, pharmacists, teachers, university lecturers, students, women, youth, small traders, even coal dealers, the party erected – mainly from 1930 onwards – a framework of affiliations that enabled it at one and the same time to speak to those specific interests but claim best to represent them by incorporating them in an appeal to the overriding interest of the nation.[101] In this sense, the NSDAP came to function increasingly as a 'super-interest-party'. The rhetoric of the 'national community' and the Führer cult stood for a rebirth for Germany in which *all* the various interests would have a new deal. As the economic and political situation deteriorated, the rationality of voting for a small and weak interest party rather than a massive and strong *national* party – upholding interests but transcending them – was less and less compelling. A vote for the Nazis could easily seem like common sense. In this way, the NSDAP started to penetrate and destroy the support of interest-parties such as the Bayerischer Bauernbund (Bavarian Peasants' League) and seriously to erode the hold of the traditional parties such as the DNVP in rural areas.[102] This process was only in its early stages in summer 1930. But it would make rapid advances following the Nazi triumph of 14 September 1930.

V

What happened on that day was a political earthquake. In the most remarkable result in German parliamentary history, the NSDAP advanced at one stroke from the twelve seats and mere 2.6 per cent of the vote gained in the 1928 Reichstag election, to 107 seats and 18.3 per cent, making it the second largest party in the Reichstag. Almost 6½ million Germans now voted for Hitler's party – eight times as many as two years earlier.[103] The Nazi bandwagon was rolling.

The party leadership had expected big gains. The run of successes in the regional elections, the last of them the 14.4 per cent won in Saxony as recently as June, pointed to that conclusion.[104] Goebbels had reckoned in April with about forty seats when it looked as if there would be a dissolution of the Reichstag at that time.[105] A week before polling-day in September he expected 'a massive success' (*einen Riesenerfolg*).[106] Hitler later claimed he had thought 100 seats were possible.[107] In reality, as Goebbels admitted, the size of the victory took all in the party by surprise. No one had expected 107 seats.[108] Hitler was beside himself with joy.[109]

The political landscape had dramatically changed overnight. Alongside the Nazis, the Communists had increased their support, now to 13.1 per cent of the vote. Though still the largest party, the SPD had lost ground as, marginally, did the Zentrum. But the biggest losers were the bourgeois parties of the centre and Right. The DNVP had dropped in successive elections since 1924 from 20.5 to only 7.0 per cent, the DVP from 10.1 to 4.7 per cent.[110] The Nazis were the main profiteers. One in three former DNVP voters, it has been estimated, now turned to the NSDAP, as did one in four former supporters of the liberal parties. Smaller, but still significant gains, were made from all other parties. These included the SPD, KPD, and Zentrum/BVP, though the working-class milieus dominated by the parties of the Left and, above all, the Catholic sub-culture remained, as they would continue to be, relatively unyielding terrain for the NSDAP.[111] The increased turn-out – up from 75.6 to 82 per cent – also benefited the Nazis, though less so than has often been presumed.[112]

The landslide was greatest in the Protestant countryside of northern and eastern Germany. With the exception of rural parts of Franconia, piously Protestant, the largely Catholic Bavarian electoral districts now for the first time lagged behind the national average. The same was true of most Catholic regions. In big cities and industrial areas – though there were some notable exceptions, such as Breslau and Chemnitz-Zwickau – the Nazi gains, though still spectacular, were also below average. But in Schleswig-Holstein, the NSDAP vote had rocketed from 4 per cent in 1928 to 27 per cent. East Prussia, Pomerania, Hanover, and Mecklenburg were among the other regions where Nazi support was now over 20 per cent.[113] At least three-quarters of Nazi voters were Protestants (or, at any rate, non-Catholics).[114] Significantly more men than women voted Nazi (though this was to alter between 1930 and 1933).[115] At least two-fifths of Nazi support came from the middle classes. But a quarter was drawn from the working class (though the unemployed were more likely to vote for Thälmann's party, the KPD, than Hitler's).[116] The middle classes were indeed over-represented among Nazi voters. But the NSDAP was no mere middle-class party, as used to be thought.[117] Though not in equal proportions, the Hitler Movement could reasonably claim to have won support from all sections of society. No other party throughout the Weimar Republic could claim the same.

The social structure of the party's membership points to the same conclusion.[118] A massive influx of members followed the September election. The party recruited, if not evenly, from all sections of society. The membership was overwhelmingly male, and only the KPD was as youthful in its membership profile. The Protestant middle classes were, as among voters, over-represented. But there was also a sizeable working-class presence, even more pronounced in the SA and the Hitler Youth than in the party itself.[119] At the same time, the political breakthrough meant that 'respectable' local citizens now felt ready to join the party.[120] Teachers, civil servants, even some Protestant pastors were among the 'respectable' groups altering the party's social standing in the provinces. In Franconia, for example, the NSDAP already had the appearance by 1930 of a 'civil service party'.[121] The penetration by the party of the social networks of provincial towns and villages now began to intensify notably.[122]

There are times – they mark the danger point for a political system – when politicians can no longer communicate, when they stop understanding the language of the people they are supposed to be representing. The politicians of Weimar's parties were well on the way to reaching that point in 1930. Hitler had the advantage of being undamaged by participation in unpopular government, and of unwavering radicalism in his hostility to the Republic. He could speak in language more and more Germans understood – the language of bitter protest at a discredited system, the language of national renewal and rebirth. Those not firmly anchored in an alternative political ideology, social milieu, or denominational sub-culture found such language increasingly intoxicating.

The results of what the *Frankfurter Zeitung* called the 'bitterness election' – seeing the electorate partly motivated by the desire to upturn the current political system, but largely stirred by protest at economic misery – were a sensation.[123] The immediate reaction in some quarters was fear of a bloody takeover of power by the National Socialists.[124] Herbert Blank, one of Otto Strasser's associates, spoke of a 'suitcase-packing mood' in Berlin editorial offices, and of stock-market shares being packed into a descending paternoster-lift.[125] The hysteria soon calmed. But democracy had certainly been dealt a heavy blow. The Nazis had moved at one fell swoop from the fringe of the political scene, outside the power-equation, to its heart. Before the election, commented Blank sardonically, the word 'Nazis' had immediately prompted thoughts of the madhouse. But no longer.[126] Brüning could now cope with the Reichstag only through the 'toleration' of the SPD, which saw him as the lesser evil.[127] The Social Democrats entered their policy of 'toleration' with heavy hearts but a deep sense of responsibility. As their leading theoretician, Rudolf Hilferding, put it, support for a government that had moved so far to the right amounted to a sacrifice comprehensible only 'as necessary defence of democracy in a parliament with an anti-parliamentary majority'.[128] As for Hitler, whether he was seen in a positive or a negative sense – and there was little about him that left people neutral or indifferent – his name was now on everyone's lips. He was a factor to be reckoned with. He could no longer be ignored.

But he could still be grossly underrated. The anarchist revolutionary writer Erich Mühsam, a veteran of the Munich Räterepublik, saw Hitler's victory as a 'true blessing' for the working class. All that was needed was to give the Nazis some ministerial responsibility, and their true reactionary colours would alienate workers more rapidly than the Social Democrats in power had done. The real danger, in Mühsam's crass misjudgement, was the leadership of the DNVP, especially Hugenberg, 'the true leader of the fascist movement in Germany'.[129] Another writer with similar revolutionary credentials, Ernst Toller, was an exception on the Left in regarding the danger as acute. In an article in the *Weltbühne* entitled 'Reich Chancellor Hitler', he signalled that 'the clock shows one minute to twelve'.[130] Among 'bourgeois' writers, Thomas Mann provided a thoughtful analysis of the dangers following the Nazi landslide in his 'German Address' (*Deutsche Ansprache*), a lecture in Berlin on 17 October that was much interrupted by Nazi hecklers.[131] But his cultural pessimism, his dismay at the collapse of the humanistic and idealistic values of the nineteenth century into the wild and raw, crude and primitive, emotions of mass society, led him also to a simplistic assessment of the NSDAP's breakthrough. National Socialism offered, for him, merely 'politics in the grotesque style with salvation-army attractions (*Allüren*), mass fits, showground-stall bell-ringing, hallelujah, and dervish-like repetition of monotonous slogans till everyone is foaming at the mouth'.[132]

After the September elections, not just Germany but the world outside had to take notice of Hitler. He was now sought after for interviews by the foreign press.[133] One newspaper he was more than ready to talk to was the British conservative organ the *Daily Mail*, whose owner, Lord Rothermere, had publicly greeted the election result as 'the rebirth of Germany as a nation' and welcomed the prospect of the National Socialists taking power as a bulwark against Bolshevism.[134] Hitler's interviewer, Rothay Reynolds, was won over. 'Hitler spoke with great simplicity and with great earnestness. There was not a trace in his manner of those arts which political leaders are apt to employ when they wish to impress. I was conscious that I was talking to a man whose power lies not, as many still think, in his eloquence and in his ability to hold the attention of the mob, but in his conviction. He is not a robust-looking man. He is slight in figure, and last night, after an exhausting day in the law-courts – where he stood for over two hours while giving evidence – followed by a conference, he looked exhausted and his face was dead white. But the moment he spoke I realized that there was in him a burning spirit that could triumph over bodily weariness. He speaks very rapidly, and in his voice there is a nervous energy that makes one feel the intense conviction behind his words.'[135]

Hitler's 'exhausting day in the law-courts' had, in fact, been another well-exploited propaganda opportunity to allay suspicions of a putsch and to emphasize his commitment to a legal takeover of power. Hitler had throughout 1930, and especially during the election campaign, repeatedly stressed that he would win power legally.[136] In the immediate aftermath of his electoral triumph, the trial of three young Reichswehr officers from a regiment stationed in Ulm, whose Nazi sympathies saw them accused of 'Preparing to Commit High Treason' (*Vorbereitung zum Hochverrat*) through working towards a military putsch with the NSDAP and breaching regulations banning members of the Reichswehr from activities aimed at altering the constitution, gave Hitler the chance, now with the eyes of the world's press on him, of underlining his party's commitment to legality. The trial of the officers, Hanns Ludin, Richard Scheringer, and Hans Friedrich Wendt, began on 23 September. On the first day, Wendt's defence counsel, Hans Frank, was given permission to summon Hitler as a witness. Two days later, huge crowds demonstrated outside the court building in favour of Hitler as the leader of the Reichstag's second largest party went into the witness-box to face the red-robed judges of the highest court in the land.[137]

Once more he was allowed to use a court of law for propaganda purposes. The judge even warned him on one occasion, as he heatedly denied any intention of undermining the Reichswehr, to avoid turning his testimony into a propaganda speech. It was to little avail. Hitler emphasized that his movement would take power by legal means and that the Reichswehr – again becoming 'a great German people's army' – would be 'the basis for the German future'.[138] He declared that he had never wanted to pursue his ideals by illegal measures. He used the exclusion of Otto Strasser to dissociate himself from those in the movement who 'played with the term "revolution"'. But he assured the presiding judge: 'If our movement is victorious in its legal struggle, then there will be a German State Court and November 1918 will find its atonement, and heads will roll.'[139] This brought cheers and cries of 'bravo' from onlookers in the courtroom – and an immediate admonishment from the court president, reminding them that they were 'neither in the theatre nor in a political meeting'.[140] He expected, Hitler continued, that the NSDAP would win a majority following two or three further elections. 'Then it must come to a National Socialist rising (*Erhebung*), and we will shape the state as we want to have it.'[141] When asked how he envisaged the erection of the Third Reich, Hitler replied: 'The National Socialist Movement will seek to attain its aim in this state by constitutional means. The constitution shows us only the methods, not the goal. In this constitutional way, we will try to gain decisive majorities in the legislative bodies in order, in the moment this is successful, to pour the state into the mould that matches our ideas.' He repeated that this would only be done constitutionally.[142] He was finally sworn in on oath to the truth of his testimony.[143] Goebbels told Scheringer, one of the defendants, that Hitler's oath was 'a brilliant move'. 'Now we are strictly legal,' he is said to have exclaimed.[144] The propaganda boss was delighted at the 'fabulous' press reportage.[145] Hitler's newly appointed Foreign Press Chief, Putzi Hanfstaengl, saw to it that there was wide coverage of the trial abroad. He also placed three articles by Hitler on the aims of the movement in the Hearst press, the powerful American media concern, at a handsome fee of 1,000 Marks for each. Hitler said it was what he needed to be able now to stay at the Kaiserhof Hotel – plush, well situated near the heart of government, and his headquarters in the capital until 1933 – when he went to Berlin.[146]

What Hitler said in the Leipzig Reichswehr trial – which ended on 4 October in eighteen-month custodial sentences on each of the three Reichswehr officers and the cashiering from the army of Ludin and Scheringer – was nothing new. As we have noted, he had been anxious for months to emphasize his 'legal' path to power. But the massive publicity surrounding the trial ensured that his declaration now made maximum impact. As Hans Frank later commented, the avowal of legality dispelled the fears of many that Hitler intended a violent takeover.[147] The belief that Hitler had broken with his revolutionary past helped to win him further support in 'respectable' circles.[148]

There were those who encouraged Brüning after the election to take the NSDAP into a coalition government, arguing that government responsibility would put the Nazis to the test and limit their agitation. Brüning rejected such a notion out of hand, though he did not rule out cooperation at some future date should the party hold by the principle of legality. After deflecting

Hitler's request for an audience immediately after the election, Brüning did arrange to see him – as he did the leaders of the other parties – in early October.[149] The Chancellor was hoping to reach an arrangement whereby Hitler would engage in 'loyal opposition' and moderate his clamour for an immediate end to reparations payments while delicate negotiations for an international loan of $125,000,000, seen as indispensable to prevent economic collapse, were under way. Their meeting on 5 October, which took place to avoid publicity in the apartment of Reich Minister Treviranus, established, however, that there was no prospect of cooperation. A chasm separated them. After Brüning's careful statement of the government's foreign policy – a delicate strategy aimed at acquiring a breathing-space leading to the ultimate removal of reparations – Hitler responded with an hour-long monologue. He simply ignored the issues Brüning had raised. Evidently, he did not understand the intricacies of the financial strategy that the Chancellor had outlined. Instead, starting so hesitantly that Brüning and Treviranus initially felt a little sorry for him and made remarks to encourage him, he was soon in full stride. Regular march-pasts of a singing SA troop, clearly prearranged though the meeting was meant to be a secret one, seemed to spur Hitler on. He was soon haranguing the four persons present – Frick and Gregor Strasser were there as well as Brüning and Treviranus – as if he were addressing a mass rally. Brüning was struck by the number of times Hitler used the word 'annihilate' (*vernichten*). He was going to 'annihilate' the KPD, the SPD, 'the Reaction', France as Germany's arch-enemy, and Russia as the home of Bolshevism. It was plain to the Chancellor, so Brüning later remarked, that Hitler's basic principle would always be: 'First power, then politics.'[150]

There was a telling aftermath. Despite giving his word to Brüning that the discussion of government strategy on foreign policy was absolutely confidential, Hitler immediately dictated a resumé of what had been said, and his Foreign Press Chief Hanfstaengl leaked it to the American Ambassador.[151]

Brüning clearly saw Hitler as a fanatic – unsophisticated, but dangerous. Though they parted amicably enough, Hitler formed a deep loathing towards Brüning, taking on manic proportions and permeating the whole party. According to Albert Krebs, it stemmed from his strong inferiority complex towards the Chancellor during their meeting.[152]

Hitler was left to continue his relentless, unbridled opposition to a system whose symbolic hate-figure was now Chancellor Brüning. Continuing the agitation was, in any case, what Hitler, like Goebbels, preferred.[153] That was his instinct. 'Don't write "victory" on your banners any longer,' Hitler had told his supporters immediately after the election. 'Write the word in its place that suits us better: "struggle!"'[154] In any case, it was the only option available. As one contemporary put it, the Nazis followed the maxim: '"After a victory, fasten on the helmet more tightly" . . . Following the election victory they arranged 70,000 meetings. Again an "avalanche" passed through the Reich . . . Town after town, village after village is stormed.'[155] The election victory made this continued high level of agitation possible. The new interest in the party meant a vast influx of new members bringing new funds that could be used for the organization of still further propaganda and new activists to carry it out.[156] Success bred success. But the structure of the party's support was changing in some ways. Many of the recent converts were not the fanatics of the early years, prepared to sacrifice everything for their beliefs. Their support was in some ways conditional, dependent upon success.[157] Many left the party as quickly as they had joined. The turnover in membership was considerable.[158] They could not be held together by specific policies – which would immediately have alienated part of the heterogeneous following – but only by common denominator slogans: 'national community', national rebirth, 'power, glory, and prosperity'.[159] Above all, the prospect of victory now presented itself as a real one. Everything had to be subordinated to this single goal. The massive but shallow, organizationally somewhat ramshackle, protest movement – a loose amalgam of different interests bonded by the politics of utopia – could be sustained only by the NSDAP coming to power within a relatively short time, probably something like the space of two or three years. This was to create mounting pressure on Hitler. All he could do for the present was what he had always done best: step up the agitation still further.

VI

Behind the public persona, the private individual was difficult to locate. Politics had increasingly consumed Hitler since 1919. There was an extraordinary gulf between his political effectiveness, the magnetism not just felt by ecstatic crowds in mass rallies but by those who were frequently in his company, and the emptiness of what was left of an existence outside politics. Those who knew Hitler personally around this time found him an enigma. 'In my recollection, there is no rounded image of Hitler's personality,' reflected Putzi Hanfstaengl many years later. 'Rather, there are a number of images and shapes, all called Adolf Hitler and which *were* all Adolf

Hitler, that can only with difficulty be brought together in overall relation to each other. He could be charming and then a little later utter opinions that hinted at a horrifying abyss. He could develop grand ideas and be primitive to the point of banality. He could fill millions with the conviction that only his will and strength of character guaranteed victory. And at the same time, even as Chancellor, he could remain a bohemian whose unreliability drove his colleagues to despair.'[160]

For Franz Pfeffer von Salomon, the head of the SA until his dismissal in August 1930, Hitler combined the qualities of common soldier and artist. 'A trooper with gypsy blood' was, given Nazi racial thinking, Pfeffer's reported extraordinary characterization. He thought Hitler had something like a sixth sense in politics, 'a supernatural talent'. But he wondered whether he was at bottom *only* a type of Freikorps leader, a revolutionary who might have difficulty in becoming a statesman after the movement had taken power.[161] Pfeffer took Hitler to be a genius, something the world might experience only once in a thousand years. But the human side of Hitler, in his view, was deficient. Pfeffer, torn between adulation and criticism, saw him as a split personality, full of personal inhibitions in conflict with the 'genius' inside him, arising from his upbringing and education, and consuming him.[162] Gregor Strasser, retaining his own critical distance from the fully-blown Führer cult, was nevertheless also, Otto Wagener recounted, prepared to see 'genius' of a kind in Hitler.[163] 'Whatever there is about him that is unpleasant,' Otto Erbersdobler, Gauleiter of Lower Bavaria, later recalled Gregor Strasser saying, 'the man has a prophetic talent for reading great political problems correctly and doing the right thing at the opportune moment despite apparently insuperable difficulties.'[164] Such unusual talent as Strasser was ready to grant Hitler lay, however, as he saw it, in instinct rather than in any ability to systematize ideas.[165]

Otto Wagener, who had been made SA Chief of Staff in 1929, was among those totally entranced by Hitler. His captivation by this 'rare personality'[166] had still not deserted him many years later when he compiled his memoirs in British captivity. But he, too, was unsure what to make of Hitler. After hearing him one day in such a towering rage – it was a row with Pfeffer about the relations between the SA and SS – that his voice reverberated through the entire party headquarters, Wagener thought there was something in him resembling 'an Asiatic will for destruction' (a term still betraying after the war Wagener's entrenchment in Nazi racial stereotypes). 'Not genius, but hatred; not overriding greatness, but rage born of an inferiority complex; not Germanic heroism, but the Hun's thirst for revenge' was how, many years later, using Nazi-style parlance in describing Hitler's alleged descent from the Huns, he summarized his impressions.[167] In his incomprehension – a mixture of sycophantic admiration and awestruck fear – Wagener was reduced to seeing in Hitler's character something 'foreign' (*fremdartig*) and 'diabolical'. Hitler remained for him altogether a puzzle.[168]

Even for leading figures in the Nazi movement such as Pfeffer and Wagener, Hitler was a remote figure. He had moved in 1929 from his shabby flat in Thierschstraße to a luxury apartment in Prinzregentenplatz in Munich's fashionable Bogenhausen.[169] It matched the change from the beerhall rabble-rouser to politician cavorting with the conservative establishment. He seldom had guests, or entertained. When he did, the atmosphere was always stiff and formal.[170] Obsessives rarely make good or interesting company, except in the eyes of those who share the obsession or those in awe of or dependent upon such an unbalanced personality. Hitler preferred, as he always had done, the usual afternoon round in Café Heck, where cronies and admirers would listen – fawningly, attentively, or with concealed boredom – to his monologues on the party's early history for the umpteenth time, or tales of the war, 'his inexhaustible favourite theme'.[171]

Only with very few people was he on the familiar 'Du' terms. He would address most Nazi leaders by their surname alone. 'Mein Führer' had not yet fully established itself, as it would do after 1933, as their normal mode of address to him. For those in his entourage he was known simply as 'the boss' (*der Chef*). Some, like Hanfstaengl or 'court' photographer Heinrich Hoffmann, insisted on a simple 'Herr Hitler'.[172] The remoteness of his personality was complemented by the need to avoid the familiarity which could have brought with it contempt for his position as supreme Leader. The aura around him dared not be sullied in any way. Along with the remoteness went distrust. Important matters were discussed only with small – and changing – groups or individuals. That way, Hitler remained in full control, never bound by any advice of formal bodies, never needing to adjudicate on disagreements between his paladins. With his fixed views and dominant personality, he was able, as Gregor Strasser pointed out, to overwhelm any individual in his presence, even those initially sceptical.[173] This in turn strengthened his self-confidence, his feeling of infallibility.[174] In contrast, he felt uncomfortable with those who posed awkward questions or counter-arguments. Since his 'intuition' – by which, between the lines, Strasser meant his ideological dogmatism coupled with tactical flexibility and opportunism – could not in itself be combated by logical argument, the party's organizational leader went on, Hitler invariably dismissed any objections as coming from small-minded know-alls. But he registered who the critics were. Sooner or later, they would fall from grace.[175]

Some of the most important matters he discussed, if at all, only with those in his close circle – the group of adjutants, chauffeurs, and long-standing cronies such as Julius Schaub (his general factotum), Heinrich Hoffmann (his photographer) and Sepp Dietrich (later head of his SS bodyguard).[176] Distrust – and vanity – went hand in hand with his type of leadership, in Gregor Strasser's view. The danger, he pointed out with reference to the dismissal of Pfeffer, was the self-selection of what Hitler wanted to hear and the negative reaction towards the bearer of bad tidings. There was something other-worldly about Hitler, thought Strasser; a lack of knowledge of human beings, and with it a lack of sound judgement of them. Hitler lived without any bonds to another human being, Strasser went on. 'He doesn't smoke, he doesn't drink, he eats almost nothing but greenstuff, he doesn't touch any woman! How are we supposed to understand him to put him across to other people?'[177]

Hitler contributed as good as nothing to the running and organization of the massively expanded Nazi Movement. His 'work-style' (if it could be called such) was unchanged from the days when the NSDAP was a tiny, insignificant *völkisch* sect. He was incapable of systematic work and took no interest in it.[178] He was as chaotic and dilettante as ever. He had found the role where he could fully indulge the unordered, indisciplined, and indolent lifestyle that had never altered since his pampered youth in Linz and drop-out years in Vienna. He had a huge 'work-room' (*Arbeitszimmer*) in the new 'Brown House' – a building of tasteless grandiosity that he was singularly proud of. Pictures of Frederick the Great and a heroic scene of the List Regiment's first battle in Flanders in 1914 adorned the walls. A monumental bust of Mussolini stood beside the outsized furniture. Smoking was forbidden.[179] To call it Hitler's 'work-room' was a nice euphemism. Hitler rarely did any work there. Hanfstaengl, who had his own room in the building, had few memories of Hitler's room since he had seen the party leader there so seldom. Even the big painting of Frederick the Great, noted the former foreign press chief, could not motivate Hitler to follow the example of the Prussian king in diligent attention to duty. He had no regular working hours. Appointments were there to be broken. Hanfstaengl had often to chase through Munich looking for the party leader to make sure he kept appointments with journalists. He could invariably find him at four o'clock in the afternoon, surrounded by his admirers, holding forth in the Café Heck.[180] Party workers at headquarters were no more favoured. They could never find a fixed time to see Hitler, even about extremely important business. If they managed, clutching their files, to catch him when he entered the Brown House, he would as often as not be called to the telephone and then apologize that he had to leave immediately and would be back the next day. Should they manage to have their business attended to, it was normally dispatched with little attention to detail. Hitler would in his usual manner turn the point at issue into a matter on which, pacing up and down the room, he would pontificate for an hour in a lengthy monologue.[181] Often he would completely ignore something brought to his attention, deviating at a tangent into some current whim. 'If Hitler gets a cue to something he is interested in – but that's something different every day,' Pfeffer is reported to have told Wagener in 1930, 'then he takes over the conversation and the point of the discussion is shelved.'[182] On matters he did not understand, or where a decision was awkward, he simply avoided discussion.[183]

This extraordinary way of operating was certainly built into Hitler's personality. Masterful and domineering, but uncertain and hesitant; unwilling to take decisions, yet then prepared to take decisions bolder than anyone else could contemplate; and refusal, once made, to take back any decision: these are part of the puzzle of Hitler's strange personality. If the domineering traits were signs of a deep inner uncertainty, the overbearing features the reflection of an underlying inferiority complex, then the hidden personality disorder must have been one of monumental proportions.[184] To ascribe the problem to such a cause redescribes it rather than explains it. In any case, Hitler's peculiar leadership style was more than just a matter of personality, or instinctive social-Darwinist inclination to let the winner emerge after a process of struggle. It reflected too the unceasing necessity to protect his position as leader. Acting out the leader's role could never be halted. The famous handshake and steely blue eyes were part of the act. Even leading figures in the party never ceased to be impressed with the apparent sincerity and bond of loyalty and comradeship that they thought accompanied Hitler's unusually long handshake and unblinking stare into their eyes.[185] They were too in awe of Hitler to realize what an elementary theatrical trick it was. The greater became the nimbus of the infallible leader, the less the 'human' Hitler, capable of mistakes and misjudgements, could be allowed on view. The 'person' Hitler was disappearing more and more into the 'role' of the almighty and omniscient Leader.

Very occasionally, the mask slipped. Albert Krebs related a scene from early 1932 that reminded him of a French comedy. From the corridor of the elegant Hotel Atlantik in Hamburg he could hear Hitler plaintively shouting:

'My soup, [I want] my soup.' Krebs found him minutes later hunched over a round table in his room, slurping his vegetable soup, looking anything other than a hero of the people. He appeared tired and depressed. He ignored the copy of his speech the previous night that Krebs had brought him, and to the Gauleiter's astonishment asked him instead what he thought of a vegetarian diet. Fully in character, Hitler launched, not waiting for an answer, into a lengthy discourse on vegetarianism. It struck Krebs as a cranky outburst, aimed at overpowering, not persuading, the listener. But what imprinted the scene on Krebs's memory was how Hitler revealed himself as an acute hypochondriac to one to whom he had presented himself up to then 'only as the political leader, never as a human being (*Mensch*)'. Krebs did not presume that Hitler was suddenly regarding him as a confidant. He took it rather as a sign of the party leader's 'inner instability'. It was an unexpected show of human weakness which, Krebs plausibly speculated, was overcompensated by an unquenchable thirst for power and resort to violence. According to Krebs, Hitler explained that a variety of worrying symptoms – outbreaks of sweating, nervous tension, trembling of muscles, and stomach cramps – had persuaded him to become a vegetarian.[186] He took the stomach cramps to be the beginnings of cancer, leaving him only a few years to complete 'the gigantic tasks' he had set himself. 'I must come to power before long . . . I must, I must,' Krebs has him shouting. But with this, he gained control of himself again. His body-language showed he was over his temporary depression. His attendants were suddenly called, orders were given out, telephone calls booked, meetings arranged. 'The human being Hitler had been transformed back into the "Leader".'[187] The mask was in place again.

Hitler's style of leadership functioned precisely because of the readiness of all his subordinates to accept his unique standing in the party, and their belief that such eccentricities of behaviour had simply to be taken on board in someone they saw as a political genius. 'He always needs people who can translate his ideologies into reality so that they can be implemented,' Pfeffer is reported as stating.[188] Hitler's way was, in fact, not to hand out streams of orders to shape important political decisions. Where possible, he avoided decisions. Rather, he laid out – often in his diffuse and opinionated fashion – his ideas at length and repeatedly. These provided the general guidelines and direction for policy-making. Others had to interpret from his comments how they thought he wanted them to act and 'work towards' his distant objectives. 'If they could all work in this way,' Hitler was reported as stating from time to time, 'if they could all strive with firm, conscious tenacity towards a common, distant goal, then the ultimate goal must one day be achieved. That mistakes will be made is human. It is a pity. But that will be overcome if a common goal is constantly adopted as a guideline.'[189] This instinctive way of operating, embedded in Hitler's social-Darwinist approach, not only unleashed ferocious competition among those in the party – later in the state – trying to reach the 'correct' interpretation of Hitler's intentions. It also meant that Hitler, the unchallenged fount of ideological orthodoxy by this time, could always side with those who had come out on top in the relentless struggle going on below him, with those who had best proven that they were following the 'right guidelines'. And since only Hitler could determine this, his power position was massively enhanced.

Inaccessibility, sporadic and impulsive interventions, unpredictability, lack of a regular working pattern, administrative disinterest, and ready resort to long-winded monologues instead of attention to detail were all hallmarks of Hitler's style as party leader. They were compatible – at least in the short term – with a 'leader party' whose exclusive middle-range goal was getting power. After 1933, the same features would become hallmarks of Hitler's style as dictator with supreme power over the German state. They would be incompatible with the bureaucratic regulation of a sophisti-cated state apparatus and would become a guarantee of escalating govern-mental disorder.

VII

At the beginning of 1931, a familiar, scarred face not seen for some time returned to the scene. Ernst Röhm, recalled by Hitler from his self-imposed exile as a military adviser to the Bolivian army, was back. He took up his appointment as new Chief of Staff of the SA on 5 January.[190]

The case of Otto Strasser had not been the only crisis that the party leadership had had to deal with during 1930. More serious, potentially, had been the crisis within the SA. It had been simmering for some time before it exploded in the summer of 1930, during the election campaign. In reality, the crisis merely brought to a head – not for the last time – the structural conflict built into the NSDAP between the party's organization and that of the SA. This had its origins, as we have noted, in the years before the putsch. The insistence after 1925 that the SA was the party's 'auxiliary troop' (Hilfstruppe), not a paramilitary formation, had never succeeded fully in quelling the separate *esprit de corps* which existed among the stormtroopers. The contempt of these 'party soldiers' for the 'civilians' in the Gau offices was a constant.[191] Regular reminders that they were subordinate to the party organization were not always easily swallowed by stormtroopers, who felt that *they* were the ones who went where the going was toughest, who suffered the casualties from the street warfare with Communists and Socialists.

Matters had come to a head in 1930 over the question of the placing of three SA leaders on the list of Reichstag candidates. This was, however, the occasion rather than the underlying cause. It was coupled with the financial disadvantages that the SA felt through its lack of autonomy and dependence on Gau offices and the demands for an immediate improvement. After Walter Stennes, the SA leader in the eastern regions of Germany and impatient like many of his men at the strategy of attempting to gain power by legal – and slow – means, had travelled to Munich in August to confront Hitler, but gained no audience, his subordinates in Berlin resigned their positions and refused to carry out any propaganda or protection duties for the party. A flashpoint arose when SA men assigned to protect a big Goebbels meeting in the Sportpalast on 30 August were ordered by Stennes to appear at a parade elsewhere in Berlin. Shortly afterwards, a meeting of Berlin SA leaders ended in stormtroopers forcing their way into party headquarters – overcoming the resistance of SS men (whose organization was actually still subordinate to the SA) and seriously vandalizing the building.[192] Goebbels was shocked at the extent of the demolition. Hitler rushed to Berlin. Goebbels told him that a settlement was urgently needed. Otherwise the rebellion, already spreading throughout the land, would result in a catastrophe.[193] Hitler, after speaking first to some groups of the aggrieved SA men, had two meetings during the night with Stennes, without apparent success. But the next day, 1 September, he appealed to a rapidly assembled mass meeting of around 2,000 Berlin stormtroopers. Pfeffer, the supreme SA leader, had resigned three days earlier. Hitler now announced – a move received with great jubilation – that he himself was taking over the supreme leadership of the SA and SS. He outlined the achievements of the SA in the growth of the movement. He ended, his voice almost hysterical, with an appeal for loyalty. In a piece of theatre reminiscent of the party refoundation meeting in 1925, the eighty-year-old war-hero General Litzmann was brought out to offer an oath of loyalty to Hitler on behalf of all SA men. Loyalty had not been without its price. Stennes read out Hitler's order providing for substantial financial improvements for the SA deriving from increased party dues.[194] The immediate crisis was over.

A memorandum from the Deputy to the Supreme Leader in South Germany, Obergruppenführer August Schneidhuber, dated 19 September 1930, did not exempt Hitler from blame for the rebellious feeling among stormtroopers. The SA had gained little recognition for an election victory which it could claim as its own, he wrote. The Berlin events had shown that Hitler had not had sufficient contact with his SA, Schneidhuber continued. Things had been brewing for some considerable time. The demand for recognition by Hitler of the achievements of the SA had been growing: 'The Führer unfortunately did not hear the warning voices.'[195]

The day-to-day running of the SA was temporarily taken over by Otto Wagener, a businessman recruited the previous year by Pfeffer, a former Freikorps comrade, as his chief of staff. Wagener had used his business contacts to persuade a cigarette firm to produce 'Sturm' cigarettes for SA men – a 'sponsorship' deal benefiting both the firm and the SA coffers. Stormtroopers were strongly encouraged to smoke only these cigarettes. A cut from the profit went to the SA – though after Pfeffer's resignation, the Reich Party Treasurer made sure that control over the funds was exercised by the party itself, not by the SA.[196] In October 1930, Wagener passed down guidelines from Hitler indicating 'special tasks' for the SA in the 'struggle for power', and offering the expectation that after a takeover of power it would become the 'reservoir . . . for a future German national army'.[197] The claim within the SA leadership for a high degree of autonomy from the party leadership was, however, undiminished. The scope for continued conflict was still there.

This was the situation awaiting the return of Röhm, not as supreme head but as chief of staff, which was announced by Hitler to assembled SA leaders in Munich on 30 November 1930. Röhm's high standing from the pre-putsch era, together with his lack of involvement in any of the recent intrigues, made his appointment a sensible one. However, his notorious homosexuality was soon used by those SA subordinates who resented his leadership to try to undermine the position of the new chief of staff. Hitler was forced as early as 3 February 1931 to reject attacks on 'things that are purely in the private sphere', and to stress that the SA was not a 'moral establishment' but 'a band of rough fighters'.[198]

Röhm's moral standards were not the real point at issue. Hitler's action the previous summer had defused the immediate crisis. But it was papering over the cracks. The tension remained. Neither the precise role nor degree of autonomy of the SA had been fully clarified. Given the character of the Nazi Movement and the way the SA had emerged within it, the structural problem was insoluble. And the putschist strain, always present in the SA, was resurfacing. Since his demands for Reichstag seats had been brusquely rejected, it could hardly be surprising that Stennes rebounded to an anti-parliamentary strategy. But his advocacy of taking power by force, advanced in articles in the Berlin party newspaper *Der Angriff*, was increasingly alarming to the Nazi leadership. Such noises flatly contradicted, and directly placed in question, the commitment to legality that Hitler had made, most publicly and on oath, following the Reichswehr trial in Leipzig the previous September, and had stressed on numerous occasions since then.[199] Hitler was forced in February to fire a shot across the bows to Stennes in an article in the *Völkischer Beobachter*, denouncing the 'lie' that the National Socialists were planning a violent coup, saying he understood the needs and feeling of anger of the SA and SS, but warning against 'provocateurs' in the movement's own ranks who were delivering to the government the legitimation for 'persecuting' the party.[200] In a speech to SA men in Munich on 7 March, Hitler stated: 'I am accused of being too cowardly to fight illegally. I am certainly not too cowardly for that. I am only too cowardly to lead the SA to face machine-gun fire. We need the SA for more important things, namely for the construction of the Third Reich. We'll keep to the constitution and will still come to our goal. The constitution prescribes the right to come to power. What means we use is our concern.'[201] The spectre of a ban on the party loomed very much larger with the promulgation of an emergency decree on 28 March, giving the Brüning government wide-ranging powers to combat political 'excesses'.[202] 'The party, above all the SA, seems to be facing a ban,' wrote Goebbels in his diary.[203] Hitler ordered the strictest compliance with the emergency decree by all members of the party, SA and SS.[204] But Stennes was not prepared to yield. 'It is the most serious crisis the party has had to go through,' commented Goebbels.[205]

It was high time to take action. Goebbels was summoned to a meeting with Hitler and other party leaders in Weimar and told on arrival that Stennes had been deposed as SA leader in eastern Germany. No sooner had Goebbels received the news than the telephone rang from Berlin to tell him that the SA had occupied the party headquarters and the offices of the *Angriff*. Despite putting a brave face on it to his immediate entourage, Hitler was shocked. The Berlin SA leadership published on 2 April a frontal attack on his 'ungerman (*undeutsche*) and boundless party despotism and the irresponsible demagogy'.[206] Hitler's immediate reply was to renew his bestowal of plenipotentiary powers on Goebbels to undertake with whatever ruthlessness necessary the purge of all 'subversive elements' from the Berlin party. 'Whatever you need to do in fulfilling [this task],' wrote Hitler, 'I will back you.'[207]

Hitler and Goebbels worked hard to ensure declarations of loyalty from all the Gaue. Stennes, increasingly revolutionary in tone, succeeded in winning support from parts of the SA in Berlin, Schleswig-Holstein, Silesia and Pomerania. But his success was short-lived. A full-scale rebellion did not occur. Ironically, the Berlin police – the butt of so many vicious attacks by Goebbels in the *Angriff* – now helped the party win back control over its headquarters and over the newspaper's offices.[208] On 4 April, Hitler published in the *Völkischer Beobachter* a lengthy and cleverly constructed denunciation of Stennes and an emotional appeal to the loyalty of SA men.[209] He stressed his own unique role in creating and building up the movement 'as its founder and as its leader'.[210] He poured scorn on Stennes's contribution, compared with the sacrifices he himself and others had made for the movement. He accused Stennes of systematically undermining the loyalty of the SA men to him through attempting to separate the 'idea' from the 'person' – the same distinction he had rejected in the case of Otto Strasser the previous May. Hitler labelled anyone trying to lead the movement 'into an open war against the state' as 'either a fool or a criminal'.[211] Having marched himself in 1923, he had to recognize that any further attempt would be 'madness'. He declared his intention 'to eradicate this conspiracy against National Socialism root and branch' and demanded SA men choose between 'Police Sergeant (ret.) Stennes or the founder of the National Socialist Movement and the Supreme Leader of your SA Adolf Hitler'.[212]

Even before he wrote, the revolt was crumbling. Support for Stennes evaporated. About 500 SA men in north and eastern Germany were purged.[213] The rest came back into line. Göring was empowered to re-establish control in Stennes's area.[214] Berlin was excluded from his remit. Jealously guarding his position, Goebbels had discovered that Göring had tried to exploit the situation to take over some of his own powers in Berlin. 'I'll never forget that of Göring,' he wrote. 'One could despair of mankind. It's a heap of frozen shit.'[215] He was placated when Hitler publicly called upon all Berlin SA men to show loyalty to his 'friend' Goebbels.[216]

The crisis was over. The SA had been put back on the leash. It would be kept there with difficulty until the 'seizure of power'. Then, the pent-up violence would only be fully released in the first months of 1933. With great energy and no little organizational skill Röhm now took the restructuring of the SA in hand. By the end of 1931 its numbers had trebled from 88,000 in January to 260,000 in December.[217] With such a rapid increase, a more tightly-knit organization was necessary. The SA's image was also changing in some ways. Outside the big cities, the SA were not always archetypal street fighters and 'political hooligans'.[218] 'Marxists' were often scarce on the ground in rural areas. The SA's role looked correspondingly different. Farmers' sons and lads from other 'upstanding' local families, attracted by the success of the Nazi Movement and often encouraged by friends, now often joined the SA instead of (or as well as) shooting or sporting clubs. Much of their party 'work' was often little more than pageantry and parading. In some places, the 'pious' SA marched in uniform each Sunday to church.[219] It was far from disreputable to belong to such an organization.

Under Röhm's hand, nevertheless, the SA was returning to its character as a paramilitary formation – and now a much more formidable one than it had been in the early 1920s. Röhm had behaved with exemplary loyalty to Hitler during the Stennes crisis. But his own emphasis on the 'primacy of the soldier', and his ambitions, suppressed as they were in 1931, for the transformation of the SA into a popular militia, bore the seeds of conflict still to come. It prefigured the course of events which would reach their denouement only in June 1934.

VIII

Not only political, but personal crisis beset Hitler in 1931. On moving in 1929 into his spacious new apartment in Prinzregentenplatz, his niece, Geli Raubal, who had been living with her mother in Haus Wachenfeld on the Obersalzberg, had come to join him. During the following two years she was frequently seen in public with Hitler. Rumours already abounded about the nature of her relations with 'Uncle Alf', as she called him. On the morning of 19 September 1931, aged twenty-three, she was found dead in Hitler's flat, shot with his pistol.

Hitler's relations with women, as we have already remarked, were in some respects abnormal. He liked the company of women, especially pretty ones, best of all young ones. He flattered them, sometimes flirted with them, called them – in his patronizing Viennese petty-bourgeois manner – 'my little princess', or 'my little countess'.[220] Occasionally, if the stories are to be believed, he made a clumsy attempt at some physical contact, as in the case of Helena Hanfstaengl and Henriette Hoffmann, the daughter of his photographer, who was to marry Baldur von Schirach (from 30 October 1931 the Reich Youth Leader of the NSDAP).[221] His name was linked at various times with women from as diverse backgrounds as Jenny Haug, the sister of his chauffeur in the early years, and Winifred Wagner, the Bayreuth maestro's daughter-in-law.[222] But, whatever the basis of the rumours – often malicious, exaggerated, or invented – none of his liaisons, it seems, had been more than superficial. No deep feelings were ever stirred. Women were for Hitler an object, an adornment in a 'men's world'. Whether in the Men's Home in Vienna, the regiment during the war, the Munich barracks until his discharge, and his regular gatherings of party cronies in Café Neumaier or Café Heck in the 1920s, Hitler's environment had always been overwhelmingly male. 'Very occasionally a woman would be admitted to our intimate circle,' recalled Heinrich Hoffmann, 'but she never was allowed to become the centre of it, and had to remain seen but not heard . . . She could, occasionally, take a small part in the conversation, but never was she allowed to hold forth or to contradict Hitler.'[223] Beginning with the semi-mythical Stefanie in Linz, Hitler's relations with women had usually been at a distance, a matter of affectation, not emotion. The brief flirtation with Mimi Reiter had not broken the mould. Fond of Mimi though he had been, the loving devotion of the besotted sixteen-year-old remained unrequited. Nor was his long-standing relationship with Eva Braun, one of Hoffmann's employees whom he had first met in autumn 1929, an exception. 'To him,' remarked Hoffmann, 'she was just an attractive little thing, in whom, in spite of her inconsequential and feather-brained outlook – or perhaps just because of it – he found the type of relaxation and repose he sought . . . But never, in voice, look or gesture, did he ever behave in a way that suggested any deeper interest in her.'[224]

It was different with Geli. Whatever the exact nature of the relationship – and all accounts are based heavily upon guesswork and hearsay – it seems certain that Hitler, for the first and only time in his life (if we leave his mother out of consideration), became emotionally dependent on a woman. Whether his involvement with Geli was explicitly sexual cannot be known beyond doubt.[225] Some have hinted darkly at the incestuous relationships in Hitler's ancestry – presumably along the lines that he was keeping incest in the family.[226] But lurid stories of alleged deviant sexual practices put about by Otto Strasser ought to be viewed as the fanciful anti-Hitler propaganda of an outright political enemy.[227] Other tales, also to be treated with scepticism, circulated of a compromising letter and of pornographic drawings by Hitler that had to be bought off a blackmailer by the Party Treasurer Schwarz.[228] But whether actively sexual or not, Hitler's behaviour towards Geli has all the traits of a strong, latent at least, sexual dependence. This manifested itself in such extreme shows of jealousy and domineering possessiveness that a crisis in the relationship was inevitable.

Geli, broad-featured, with dark-brown, wavy hair, was no stunning beauty but nonetheless, all accounts agree, a vivacious, extrovert, attractive young woman. She livened up the gatherings in Café Heck. Hitler allowed her, something he permitted no one else, to become the centre of attraction. He took her everywhere with him – to the theatre, concerts, the opera, the cinema, restaurants, for drives in the countryside, picnics, even shopping for clothes.[229] He sang her praises, showed her off. Geli was in Munich ostensibly to study at the university. But little studying was done. Hitler paid for singing lessons for her. But she was clearly never going to make an operatic heroine. She was bored by her lessons.[230] She was more interested in having a good time. Flighty and flirtatious, she had no shortage of male admirers and was not backward in encouraging them. When Hitler found out about Geli's liaison with Emil Maurice, his bodyguard and chauffeur, there was such a scene that Maurice feared Hitler was going to shoot him.[231] He was soon forced out of Hitler's employment. Geli was sent to cool her ardour under the watchful eye of Frau Bruckmann.[232] Hitler's jealous possessiveness took on pathological proportions. If she went out without him, Geli was chaperoned, and had to be home early.[233] Everything she did was monitored and controlled. She was effectively a prisoner. She resented it bitterly. 'My uncle is a monster,' she is reported as saying. 'No one can imagine what he demands of me.'[234]

By mid-September 1931 she had had enough. She planned to return to Vienna. It was later rumoured that she had a new boyfriend there, even that he was a Jewish artist whose child she was expecting.[235] Geli's mother, Angela Raubal, told American interrogators after the war that her daughter had wanted to marry a violinist from Linz, but that she and her half-brother, Adolf, had forbidden her to see the man.[236] At any rate it seems certain that Geli was desperate to get away from her uncle's clutches. Whether he had been physically maltreating her is again impossible to ascertain. It was said that her nose was broken and there were other indications of physical violence, when her body was found.[237] Once more the evidence is too flimsy to be certain, and the story was one put out by Hitler's political enemies.[238] The police doctor who examined the body, and two women who laid out the corpse, found no wounds or bleeding on the face.[239] But that Hitler was at the very least subjecting his niece to intense psychological pressure cannot be doubted. According to the version put out a few days later by the Socialist *Münchener Post* – vehemently denied in a public statement by Hitler –

during a heated argument on Friday, 18 September he refused to let her go to Vienna.[240] Later that day, Hitler and his entourage departed for Nuremberg.[241] He had already left his hotel the next morning when he was urgently recalled to be told the news that Geli had been found dead in his apartment, shot with his revolver. He immediately raced back to Munich – in such a rush that his car was stopped by the police for speeding about half-way between Nuremberg and Munich.[242]

Hitler's political enemies had a field day.[243] There were no holds barred on the newspaper reports. Stories of violent rows and physical mistreatment mingled with sexual innuendo and even the allegation that Hitler had either killed Geli himself or had had her murdered to prevent scandal.[244] Hitler himself was not in Munich when his niece died. And it is not easy to see the reasoning for a commissioned murder to prevent a scandal being carried out in his own flat.[245] As it was, the scandal was enormous. The party's own line that the killing had been an accident, which had occurred when Geli was playing with Hitler's gun, also lacked all conviction.[246] The truth will never be known. But suicide – possibly intended as a *cri de coeur* that went wrong – driven by the need to escape from the vice of her uncle's clammy possessiveness and – perhaps violent – jealousy, seems the most likely explanation.

Hitler appears to have been near-hysterical, then fallen into an intense depression. Those close to him had never seen him in such a state. He seemed to be on the verge of a nervous breakdown. He spoke of giving up politics and finishing it all. There were fears that he might be suicidal. Hans Frank's account implies that his despair at the scandal and press campaign against him outweighed any personal grief during these days. He took refuge in the house of his publisher, Adolf Müller, on the shores of the Tegernsee. Frank used legal means to block the press attacks. And once he had visited Geli's grave in Vienna's sprawling Central Cemetery, a few days after the funeral, Hitler was suddenly able to snap out of his depression.[247] All at once, the crisis was over.

At his first speech a few days later, in Hamburg, he received an even more rapturous reception than usual.[248] According to one person who was there, he looked 'very strained (*angegriffen*)' but spoke well.[249] He was back in business. More than ever, the orgiastic frenzy he worked himself up into during his big public addresses, and the reponse he encountered in what he saw as the 'feminine mass', provided a substitute for the emptiness and lack of emotional bonds in his private life.

Some who saw Hitler at close quarters were convinced that Geli could have exerted a restraining influence upon him.[250] It is a highly dubious theory. His emotional involvement with Geli, whatever its precise nature, was – everything points to this – more intense than any other human relationship he had before or after. There was something both obsessive and cloyingly sentimental about the way her rooms in the Prinzregentenplatz apartment and in Haus Wachenfeld were turned into shrines.[251] In a personal sense, Geli was indeed irreplaceable (though Hitler soon enough had Eva Braun in tow). But it was a purely selfish dependency on Hitler's part. Geli had been allowed to have no existence of her own. Hitler's own extreme dependency insisted that she should be totally dependent upon him. In human terms, it was a self-destructive relationship. Politically, apart from the short-lived scandal, it was of no significance. It is difficult to imagine Geli turning Hitler away from his deeper, less personal, obsession with power. Nor was his embittered thirst for vengeance and destruction altered by her death. History would have been no different had Geli Raubal survived.

IX

Little over a week after Geli's death, the city elections in the relatively unresponsive territory of Hamburg gave the Nazis 26.2 per cent of the vote, ahead of the Communists and only fractionally behind the SPD.[252] With as high a vote as 37.2 per cent in rural Oldenburg the previous May, the NSDAP had become for the first time the largest party in a state parliament.[253] In the last state elections of the year, in Hessen on 15 November, this feat was repeated in a remarkable poll that gave the Nazis, with 37.1 per cent, a higher proportion of the vote than the Communists and Socialists put together, and twenty-seven seats in a Landtag where they had previously been unrepresented.[254] The electoral landslide showed no signs of abating. With the Brüning government under siege, ruling by emergency decree, its policies – calculated to demonstrate Germany's inability to pay reparations – sending the economy plummeting to disaster in a catastrophic downward spiral of cascading production levels and soaring levels of unemployment and social misery, more and more voters were cursing the wretched Republic. By the time of the calamitous bank crash in July, when two of Germany's major banks, the Darmstädter and the Dresdner, collapsed, those voters looking to the survival and recovery of democracy were in a dwindling minority. But what sort of authoritarian solution might follow the liquidation of the Weimar Republic was still anything but clear. Germany's power élites were no more united on this issue than were the mass of the population.

With the levels of popular support the Nazis now enjoyed, no potential right-wing solution could afford to leave them out of the equation. In July, Hugenberg, the leader of the DNVP, and Franz Seldte, the head of the huge veterans' organization, the Stahlhelm, had renewed their alliance with Hitler – resurrecting the former grouping to fight the Young Plan – in the 'National Opposition'. Hugenberg assuaged the criticisms of Reich President Hindenburg, who thought the Nazis not only vulgar but dangerous socialists, by assuring him that he was 'politically educating' them towards the national cause to prevent them slipping into Socialism or Communism. Hitler's line was, as ever, pragmatic. The publicity and contacts won through allying with Hugenberg were valuable. But he made sure he kept his distance. At the highly publicized rally of Nationalist Opposition forces at Bad Harzburg on 11 October, resulting in the creation of the 'Harzburg Front' and a manifesto (which he thought worthless) demanding new Reichstag elections and the suspension of emergency legislation, Hitler stood for the march-past of the SA then demonstratively left before the Stahlhelm could begin, having left them waiting for twenty-five minutes. He also refused to attend the joint lunch of the nationalist leaders. He could not suppress his repulsion at such meals, he wrote – deflecting the criticism of his behaviour into a further advertisement for his image as a leader who shared the privations of his followers – 'when thousands of my supporters undertake service only at very great personal sacrifice and in part with hungry stomachs'.[255] A week later, to underline the NSDAP's independent strength, he took the salute at a march-past of 104,000 SA and SS men in Braunschweig, the largest Nazi paramilitary demonstration to date.[256]

Among those taking part at Bad Harzburg, and whose presence there made a stir, was the former President of the Reichsbank Hjalmar Schacht, now turned political adventurer. Some other figures – though not prominent ones – from the world of business were also there.[257] Schacht – a freemason, and founding member of the pro-Republican DDP – was an unlikely fellow-traveller of Nazism. But he had moved strongly to the Right after resigning the presidency of the Reichsbank in March 1930 in protest at the ways of implementing the Young Plan, and had publicly expressed admiration for vitality of the NSDAP in December 1930.[258] Göring, with whom he was on good terms, arranged for Schacht to come to dinner and meet Hitler on 5 January 1931. The dinner was also attended by another Nazi sympathizer from big business, Fritz Thyssen, the chairman of the supervisory board of the United Steel Works.[259] Hitler arrived, wearing party uniform, only after the meal was over. As usual, he dominated the 'conversation', contributing, thought Schacht, some 95 per cent of what was said.[260] Even so, Schacht, intelligent and with sharply critical acumen, was impressed:

His skill in exposition was most striking. Everything he said he demonstrated as incontrovertible truth; nevertheless his ideas were not unreasonable and were entirely free from any propagandist pathos. He spoke with moderation and was obviously anxious to avoid anything that might shock us in our capacity as representatives of a more traditional society . . . The thing that impressed me most about this man was his absolute conviction of the rightness of his outlook and his determination to translate this outlook into practical action. Even at this first meeting it was obvious to me that Hitler's power of propaganda would have a tremendous pull with the German population if we did not succeed in overcoming the economic crisis and weaning the masses from radicalism. Hitler was obsessed by his own words, a thorough fanatic with the most powerful effect on his audience; a born agitator in spite of a hoarse, sometimes broken and not infrequently croaking voice.[261]

Schacht tried at the time to persuade Brüning to include the NSDAP in a coalition, presuming the responsibilities of government would have tamed it. Thyssen, attracted by the corporatist ideas in the NSDAP's programme, had similarly advocated working with the Nazis to the Chancellor.[262] Neither Schacht nor Thyssen was, however, representative of the leaders of big business.

During the 1920s, big business had, not surprisingly, shown little interest in the NSDAP, a fringe party in the doldrums without, it seemed, any prospect of power or influence. The election result of 1930 had compelled the business community to take note of Hitler's party. A series of meetings were arranged at which Hitler explained his aims to prominent businessmen. At the end of September 1930 he put his views to the former Chancellor and current head of the Hamburg-America shipping line, Wilhelm Cuno, who was rumoured to be contemplating running for Reich President with NSDAP support when Hindenburg's term of office expired in 1932.[263] Cuno was impressed with Hitler, who advanced a 'moderate' economic programme upholding capitalist enterprise and even claiming that there would be no violent persecution of Jews under Nazi rule.[264] Hitler also spoke again at the Hamburger Nationalklub, a meeting arranged by Cuno, and to a group of Ruhr industrialists at the home of Emil Kirdorf, the aged Ruhr coal magnate and long-standing Nazi sympathizer, near Mülheim.[265] Further meetings with a number of business leaders, arranged by Walther Funk, the former editor of the financial newspaper the *Berliner Börsen-Zeitung*, followed early in 1931 in Hitler's suite at the Kaiserhof Hotel, at which considerable funding was reportedly pledged in the event of an attempted left-wing coup.[266] The reassurances given by Hitler at such meetings, as well as by Göring (who had good links to top businessmen), were, however, not able to dispel the worries of most business leaders that the NSDAP was a socialist party with radical anti-capitalist aims. Hitler was seen by many of them as a 'moderate'.[267] But whatever favourable impression Hitler himself was able to make, it was insufficient to remove the 'socialist' image of his party in the eyes of many businessmen. The NSDAP's support of the Berlin metalworkers' strike in autumn 1930, and the participation of the Nazis' surrogate trade union, the Nationalsozialistische Betriebszellenorganisation (NSBO, National Socialist Factory Cell Organization), in four strikes the following year, alongside the continued anti-capitalist rhetoric of some party spokesmen, seemed active proof of its 'dangerous' tendencies.[268]

Despite growing disillusionment with the Brüning administration, most 'captains of industry' retained their healthy scepticism about the Hitler Movement during 1931. There were exceptions, such as Thyssen, but in general it was the owners of smaller and medium-sized concerns who found the NSDAP an increasingly attractive proposition.[269] The story put about in the memoirs of the later press chief Otto Dietrich of Hitler ceaselessly touring Germany in his big Mercedes in the second half of 1931, cultivating big business leaders and breaking down their resistance to the NSDAP, was no more than part of the myth that Hitler had won power by conquering the hearts and minds of every section of the German people.[270] No more solidly founded was the view of the Left at the time that the Nazi Movement was the creature of big business and sustained by its funding. Most leaders and executives of big business were shrewd enough to spread their funding round as a form of political insurance, once the Nazi breakthrough had taken place. But most of it still went to the Nazis' political opponents on the conservative Right.[271] The leaders of big business were no friends of democracy. But nor, for the most part, did they want to see the Nazis running the country.

This remained the case throughout most of 1932, a year dominated by election campaigns in which the Weimar state disintegrated into all-embracing crisis. Hitler's much publicized address on 27 January 1932 to a gathering of some 650 members of the Düsseldorf Industry Club in the grand ballroom of Düsseldorf's Park Hotel did nothing, despite the later claims of Nazi propaganda, to alter the sceptical stance of big business.[272] The response to his speech was mixed. But many were disappointed that he had nothing new to say, avoiding all detailed economic issues by taking refuge in his well-trodden political panacea for all ills.[273] And there were indications that workers in the party were not altogether happy at their leader fraternizing with industrial leaders. Intensified anti-capitalist rhetoric, which Hitler was powerless to quell, worried the business community as much as ever.[274] During the presidential campaigns of spring 1932, most business leaders stayed firmly behind Hindenburg, and did not favour Hitler. And during the Reichstag campaigns of summer and autumn, the business community overwhelmingly supported the parties that backed the cabinet of Franz von Papen – from a Westphalian aristocratic family, married to the daughter of a Saarland industrialist, well connected to industrial leaders, landowners, and Reichswehr officers – a somewhat lightweight, dilettante politician, but one who epitomized the ingrained conservatism, reactionary tendencies, and desire for a return to 'traditional' authoritarianism of the German upper class.[275] He was the establishment figure; Hitler the outsider and, in some respects, unknown quantity. Papen, not Hitler, was, not surprisingly then, the favourite of big business. Only in autumn 1932, when Papen was ousted by Kurt von Schleicher, the general at the heart of most political intrigues, maker and breaker of governments, did the attitude of most leading figures in business, worried by the new Chancellor's approach to the economy and opening to the trade unions, undergo a significant change.[276]

The NSDAP's funding continued before the 'seizure of power' to come overwhelmingly from the dues of its own members and the entrance fees to party meetings.[277] Such financing as came from fellow-travellers in big business accrued more to the benefit of individual Nazi leaders than the party as a whole. Göring, needing a vast income to cater for his outsized appetite for high living and material luxury, quite especially benefited from such largesse. Thyssen in particular gave him generous subsidies, which Göring – given to greeting visitors to his splendidly adorned Berlin apartment dressed in a red toga and pointed slippers, looking like a sultan in a harem – found no difficulty in spending on a lavish lifestyle.[278] Walther Funk, one of Hitler's links to leading industrialists, also used his contacts to line his own pockets. Gregor Strasser, too, was a recipient.[279] Corruption at all levels was endemic.

It would be surprising if none of such donations had reached Hitler. Indeed, Göring is alleged to have said that he passed on to Hitler some of the funding he received from Ruhr industrialists.[280] Hitler had from the earliest years of his 'career', as we have seen, been supported by generous donations from benefactors.[281] But by the early 1930s he was less dependent on financial support from private patrons, even if his celebrity status now unquestionably brought him many unsolicited donations. His sources of income have remained largely in the dark. They were kept highly secret, and totally detached from party finances. Schwarz, the party treasurer, had no insight into Hitler's own funds. But his taxable income alone – and much was doubtless left undeclared – trebled in 1930 to 48,472 Marks as sales of *Mein Kampf* soared following his election triumph. That alone was more than Funk had earned from a year's salary as editor of a Berlin daily. Though for image purposes he repeatedly emphasized that he drew no salary from the party, nor any fee for the speeches he delivered on its behalf, he received hidden fees in the form of lavish 'expenses' calculated on the size of the takings at his meetings. In addition, he was paid handsomely for the articles he contributed to the *Völkischer Beobachter* and, between 1928 and 1931, to the *Illustrierter Beobachter*. And with the foreign press now clamouring for interviews, another door to a lucrative source of income opened. Partly subsidized, if indirectly, by the party, partly drawing substantial royalties from his stated occupation as a 'writer', and partly benefiting from unsolicited donations from admirers, Hitler's sources of income were more than adequate to cover the costs of an affluent lifestyle. His proclaimed modest demands in matters of food and clothes – a constant element of his image as a humble man of the people – fell within a context of chauffeur-driven Mercedes, luxury hotels, grand residences, and a personal livery of body-guards and attendants.[282]

X

During 1932, the terminal nature of Weimar's ailing democracy became unmistakable. A prelude to the drama to follow had its setting in the presidential election in the spring.

Reich President Hindenburg's seven-year term of office was due to expire on 5 May 1932. In the prevailing conditions of economic depression and political turmoil, the prospect of a bitterly contested election for the presi-dency was hardly enticing. But the chances of the parties agreeing on a single candidate were zero. Moves, initially prompted by Papen, had already therefore been afoot since the previous autumn to have the eighty-four-year-old war-hero Paul von Hindenburg und Beneckendorff confirmed by the Reichstag for a further period in office, without the need for a divisive election. But a constitutional change would be required to achieve this, necessitating a two-thirds majority in the Reichstag. This could only be obtained if the National Socialists and DNVP were prepared to support it.[283] Hitler was summoned early in January 1932 to a meeting in Berlin with the Reich Defence and acting Interior Minister Wilhelm Groener and Hindenburg's State Secretary Otto Meissner, where the proposition was put to him. Hitler did not commit himself immediately. But the Nazi leadership recognized that such a move could only strengthen Brüning's position. The Chancellor's tactics had put them on the spot. 'The chessmatch for power begins,' noted Goebbels.[284]

A week later, Hitler notified the Chancellor of his party's rejection of the proposal – on 'constitutional, foreign-political, domestic, and moral grounds'.[285] A rancorous public exchange with Brüning followed.[286] How genuine Hitler's constitutional scruples were became clear in his offer to support Hindenburg's candidacy if the Reich President dismissed Brüning and announced new Reichstag and Prussian elections, following which the newly elected Reichstag – which Hitler was confident of controlling – would extend his period of office.[287]

Hindenburg's refusal, expected though it was, left Hitler in a quandary. In the event of presidential elections, he could scarcely refrain from standing. Not to stand would be incomprehensible, and a massive disappointment to his millions of supporters. They might start to turn away from a leader who shied away from the challenge. On the other hand, a personal contest between the corporal and the field-marshal, between the upstart political adventurer and the revered hero of Tannenberg, widely regarded as the symbol of national values above the fray of party politics, could hardly be expected to result in a victory for Hitler. Faced with his dilemma, Hitler dithered for more than a month before deciding to run for president. Goebbels was almost in despair at the indecision, as party morale wavered and Hitler preoccupied himself with grandiose schemes for rebuilding Berlin.[288] At last, on 22 February, Goebbels was given permission to announce Hitler's candidacy during his speech at a big rally in the Sportpalast that evening. 'Thank God' was the propaganda chief's reaction. The cheering following the announcement lasted for ten minutes. Goebbels's barely concealed criticism of Hitler's leadership in the past weeks was immediately dispelled. 'He is and remains our Leader,' he reminded himself. And a few days later, he added that the Führer was 'again on top of the situation'.[289]

A technicality had to be cleared up: Hitler was still not a German citizen. Previous ideas of attaining citizenship for him, in Bavaria in 1929 and Thuringia the following year, had foundered. He remained 'stateless'. Rapid steps were now taken to appoint Hitler to the post of *Regierungsrat* (government councillor) in the Office of State Culture and Measurement (*Landeskultur- und Vermessungsamt*) in Braunschweig and as a state representative in Berlin. Through his nomination as a civil servant, Hitler acquired German citizenship. On 26 February 1932, he swore his oath as a civil servant to the German state he was determined to destroy.[290]

Just how far the political centre of gravity had shifted to the Right was shown by the perverse alignments in the presidential election campaign. Hindenburg was dependent for support on the Socialists and Catholics, who had formed his main opposition seven years earlier, and made strange and unwelcome bedfellows for the staunchly Protestant and arch-conservative doyen of the military caste. The bourgeois Right, headed by Hugenberg, refused Hindenburg their support. Showing how fragile the professed unity of the Harzburg Front had been, they also denied it to Hitler. But their largely unknown nominee, the deputy leader of the Stahlhelm, Theodor Duesterberg, was hardly a serious candidate.[291] On the Left, the Communists nominated their leader, Ernst Thälmann, sure of support only from his own camp. It was plain from the outset, therefore, that the main contenders were Hindenburg and Hitler. Equally plain was the Nazi message: a vote for Hitler was a vote for change; under Hindenburg, things would stay as they were. 'Old man ... you must step aside,' proclaimed Hitler at a rally attended by an estimated 25,000 in the Berlin Sportpalast on 27 February.[292]

The Nazi propaganda machine went into top gear. The country was engulfed during the first of five major campaigns that year with a veritable flood of Nazi meetings, parades, and rallies, accompanied by the usual pageantry and razzmatazz. Hitler himself, his indecision resolved, poured all his energies as usual into his speaking tourneys, travelling the length and breadth of Germany, and addressing huge crowds in twelve cities during the eleven-day campaign. In Breslau he arrived four hours late, in Stuttgart two hours behind schedule. The crowds still waited. The *Völkischer Beobachter* claimed – though certainly with some exaggeration – that he spoke in all to around half a million people.[293]

Expectations were built up. 'Everywhere there's a victory mood,' wrote Goebbels on election day, 13 March. But he added, cautiously: 'I'm somewhat sceptical.' He shared the bitter disappointment and depression of Hitler's supporters when the results were announced.[294] The 30 per cent won by Hitler was more or less in line with expectations, though lower than the NSDAP's showing in the Oldenburg and Hessen state elections the previous year. But Thälmann, with only 13 per cent, had done less well than anticipated, Duesterberg had gained under 7 per cent, and the SPD's supporters, whatever their distaste for the President, had evidently stuck by Hindenburg, whose vote had, therefore, held up well. With over 49 per cent of almost 38 million votes cast, the Reich President ended up a mere 170,000 votes short of the absolute majority.[295] There had to be a second round.

This time Nazi propaganda had a new gimmick. Hitler took to the skies in a hired plane, American-style, in his first 'Germany Flight' (*Deutschlandflug*), embellished with the slogan of 'the Führer over Germany'. Flying from city to city in a truncated campaign squeezed into less than a week to accommodate an Easter truce in politicking, Hitler was able to hold twenty major speeches in different venues before huge audiences, totalling close to a million persons.[296] It was a remarkable electioneering performance, the like of which had never before been seen in Germany. This time there was no disappointment in the Nazi camp. Hindenburg, with 53 per cent, was re-elected. But while Thälmann had slumped to only 10 per cent, Hitler had increased his support to 37 per cent. He had done much more than merely save face. Well over 13 million, 2 million more than in the first round, had voted for him.[297] The Führer cult, the manufactured commodity of Nazi propaganda and once the property of a tiny collection of fanatics, was now on the way to being sold to a third of the German population.

Quite literally while the votes were being counted, Goebbels was laying the preparations for the next battle: the series of state elections on 24 April in Prussia, Bavaria, Württemberg and Anhalt, and the city elections in Hamburg.[298] All in all, this amounted to about four-fifths of the country.[299] Without a break, the frenetic campaigning continued. In his second 'Germany Flight' between 16 and 24 April, Hitler – this time taking his campaign not just to the cities but deep into the provinces – gave twenty-five big speeches.[300] In small towns in provincial backwaters, the impact was enormous. Nothing had been seen like it before. At Miesbach, in Upper Bavaria, the local press described Hitler's speech as 'an unprecedented sensation'. Thousands had waited for hours in pouring rain for it.[301] Elsewhere it was 'Führer weather'. 'The April sun shone as in summer, turning everything into a picture of happiest expectation,' wrote Luise Solmitz, a Hamburg schoolteacher, about the atmosphere in which Hitler addressed over 120,000 people crowded on to the speedway track at Lokstedt in the Hamburg district on 23 April.

The streams of people arriving by foot and unloading from trains seemed endless. Most had a lengthy wait to see their hero. Frau Solmitz herself was there two and a half hours before Hitler was due to speak. But the massive crowd was well-behaved, controlled only by stewards with the police keeping in the background. Most of those attending were already attracted to the Nazi cause. 'No one said "Hitler", always just "the Führer",' recorded Frau Solmitz. '"The Führer says", "the Führer" wants, and what he said and wanted, that seemed good and proper.' Her description continued:

The hours passed, the sun shone, the expectation mounted . . . It got to 3 o'clock. 'The Führer's coming!' A thrill goes through the masses. Around the platform hands could be seen raised in the Hitler greeting . . . There stood Hitler in a simple black coat, looking expectantly over the crowd. A forest of swastika banners rustled upwards. The jubilation of the moment gave vent to a rousing cry of 'Heil'. Then Hitler spoke. Main idea: out of the parties a people (*Volk*) will emerge, the German people. He castigated the 'system' . . . For the rest, he refrained from personal attacks and also unspecific and specific promises. His voice was hoarse from speaking so much in previous days. When the speech was over, there were roars of jubilation and applause. Hitler saluted, gave his thanks, the 'Germany Anthem' sounded over the track. Hitler was helped into his coat. Then he went. How many look to him in touching faith as the helper, saviour, the redeemer from overgreat distress. To him, who rescues the Prussian prince, the scholar, the clergyman, the peasant, the worker, the unemployed out of the party into the people.[302]

The results were closely in line with the votes won by Hitler in the run-off presidential election. Leader and party were largely indistinguishable in the eyes of the voters. In the giant state of Prussia, embracing two-thirds of Reich territory, the NSDAP's vote of 36.3 per cent made it easily the largest party, now far ahead of the SPD which had been the dominant party since 1919. Since the previous election, in 1928, the Nazis had held six seats in the Prussian Landtag. Now they had 162 seats. In Bavaria, with 32.5 per cent, they came to within 0.1 per cent of the ruling BVP. In Württemberg, they rose from 1.8 per cent in 1928, to 26.4 per cent. In Hamburg, they attained 31.2 per cent. And in Anhalt, with 40.9 per cent, they could nominate the first Nazi Minister President of a German state.[303]

'It's a fantastic victory that we've attained,' noted Goebbels, with justification. But he added: 'We must come to power in the foreseeable future. Otherwise we'll win ourselves to death in elections.'[304] Mobilizing the masses was in itself going to be insufficient, Goebbels was recognizing. Despite the immense gains over the previous three years, there were signs that the limits of mobilization were being reached. The way ahead was still anything but clear. But another door was about to open.

XI

The state election campaign had been fought in the wake of a ban on the SA and SS. Chancellor Brüning and Interior and Defence Minister Groener, under pressure from the state authorities, had persuaded Hindenburg three days after the President's re-election to dissolve 'all military-like (*militärähn-liche*) organizations' of the NSDAP.[305] The dissolution was directly occasioned by the Prussian police's discovery, following a tip-off to Reich Minister of the Interior Groener, in raids on Nazi Party offices, shortly after the first round of the presidential election, of material indicating the SA's readiness for a takeover of power by force following an electoral victory by Hitler.[306] Despite Hitler's repeated declarations that he would come to power by legal means, the concern of the authorities about the putschist intentions within the party, particularly within the SA, had persisted. The sensational discovery the previous autumn of the 'Boxheimer Documents' – named after the place in Hessen, the Boxheimer Hof, where they were found – outlining Nazi plans for taking power by force, had strongly underlined the justification for such concern. Actually, the 'Boxheimer Documents' had amounted to a half-baked concoction of measures to be taken in the event of a Nazi takeover of state power following the smashing of a Communist attempted putsch, devised on his own initiative by the ambitious head of the party's legal section in Gau Hessen, Werner Best.[307] At the time, an embarrassed Hitler, whose claim to have known nothing of the incriminating material was in fact correct, had satisfied Groener with a renewed declaration of his legal intentions.[308] But there had been distinct signs during the presidential election campaigns that the SA – now close to 400,000 strong – was straining at the leash.[309] Talk of a putsch attempt by the Left in the event of a Hitler victory was in the air.[310] The SA had been placed on nationwide alarm. But instead of action, the stormtroopers had sat depressed in their quarters after Hitler's defeat.[311] Goebbels noted the impatience of the SA again on 2 April, commenting that a premature strike with force could destroy Nazi hopes at one fell swoop.[312] News of the impending ban leaked to the Nazi leadership two days before it was imposed.[313] Some preparations could therefore be made to retain the SA as distinct units within the party organization by simply reclassing the stormtroopers now as ordinary party members.[314] And since the Left also had its paramilitary organizations which did not fall under the Groener dissolution order, the authorities had delivered the Nazis a further effective propaganda weapon, which Hitler was quick to exploit.[315]

More importantly, the SA ban opened up the machinations that were to undermine the position not only of Groener, but of Brüning too, and to move the Reich government sharply to the Right. The key figure was to be General von Schleicher, head of the Ministerial Office, the army's political bureau, in the Reichswehr Ministry, and seen up to now as Groener's protégé. Schleicher's aim was an authoritarian regime, resting on the Reichswehr, with support from the National Socialists. The idea was to 'tame' Hitler, and incorporate the 'valuable elements' from his Movement into what would have been essentially a military dictatorship with populist backing.[316] Schleicher opposed the ban on the SA, therefore, which he wanted as a feeder organization for an expanded Reichswehr, once the reparations issue was out of the way. In secret talks with Schleicher on 28 April, Hitler had learnt that the Reichswehr leadership no longer supported Brüning.[317] He followed this on 7 May with what Goebbels described as 'a decisive discussion with General Schleicher', attended by some of Hindenburg's immediate entourage. 'Brüning is to go in the next days,' he added. 'The Reich President will withdraw his confidence. The plan is to install a presidential cabinet. The Reichstag will be dissolved; all coercive laws will be dropped. We will be given freedom of action, and will then deliver a masterpiece of propaganda.'[318] Removal of the SA ban and new elections were, then, Hitler's price for supporting a new right-wing cabinet.[319] With the emphasis on elections, it is clear that Hitler thought, as always, essentially of little more than coming to power by winning over the masses.

Brüning was able to survive longer than the conspirators had imagined. But his days were plainly numbered. In the meantime, the orchestrated campaign by the Nazis to pressurize Groener into resignation proved successful. After rowdy scenes in the Reichstag during his speech on 10 May, and after being told by Schleicher that he had lost the confidence of the Reichswehr, Groener announced his resignation on 12 May.[320] It was seen as the beginning of the end for Brüning. Hitler was 'extraordinarily content'.[321] The next day, Goebbels noted: 'We get message from General Schleicher: the crisis continues according to plan.'[322]

The last straw for Brüning was Hindenburg's displeasure, influenced by lobbying from fellow estate-owners in eastern Germany, at a planned emergency decree to break up bankrupt estates to create smallholder settlements. This was, however, only a contributory factor to Brüning's downfall.

His deflationary policies that had precipitated the steepest economic collapse outside war witnessed in a modern industrial society had served their purpose. The end of reparations was now in sight, and would effectively be brought about at the Lausanne Conference only a few weeks later. With that, the move to the Right that Hindenburg favoured and Schleicher had worked for could now be actively implemented. On 29 May, Hindenburg brusquely sought Brüning's resignation. The following day, in the briefest of audiences, it was submitted.[323]

'The system is collapsing,' wrote Goebbels. Hitler saw the Reich President that afternoon. The meeting went well, he told his propaganda chief in the evening: 'The SA ban will be dropped. Uniforms are to be allowed again. The Reichstag will be dissolved. That's the most important of all. v. Papen is foreseen as Chancellor. But that is not so interesting. Voting, voting! Out to the people. We're all very happy.'[324]

XII

The new Chancellor, Franz von Papen, an urbane and well-connected member of the Catholic nobility, a former diplomat and arch-conservative formerly on the right of the Zentrum, had been sounded out by Schleicher some days before Brüning's fall. Schleicher had not only cleared the ground with Hindenburg for Papen's appointment, but had also drawn up a list of cabinet ministers and discussed the matter with some of them even before Papen agreed to serve.[325] With his 'cabinet of barons' independent of parties, Papen made no pretence at parliamentary government. With no prospect of finding a majority in the Reichstag, he was dependent solely upon presidential emergency decrees – and the toleration of the NSDAP. Just over a week after coming into office, he met Hitler for the first time. 'I found him curiously unimpressive,' wrote Papen after the war.

I could detect no inner quality which might explain his extraordinary hold on the masses. He was wearing a dark blue suit and seemed the complete *petit-bourgeois*. He had an unhealthy complexion, and with his little moustache and curious hair style had an indefinable bohemian quality. His demeanour was modest and polite, and although I had heard much about the magnetic quality of his eyes, I do not remember being impressed by them ... As he talked about his party's aims I was struck by the fanatical insistence with which he presented his arguments. I realized that the fate of my Government would depend to a large extent on the willingness of this man and his followers to back me up, and that this would be the most difficult problem with which I should have to deal. He made it clear that he would not be content for long with a subordinate role and intended in due course to demand plenary powers for himself. 'I regard your Cabinet only as a temporary solution, and will continue my efforts to make my party the strongest in the country. The Chancellorship will then devolve on me,' he said.[326]

Five days earlier, as prearranged, the Reich President had dissolved the Reichstag, setting new elections for the latest possible date, 31 July 1932. Hitler now had his chance to try to win power by the ballot-box. State elections in Oldenburg at the end of May and in Mecklenburg-Schwerin on 5 June brought the NSDAP respectively 48.4 and 49.0 per cent of the vote.[327] On 19 June in Hessen the Nazis increased their proportion of the vote there to 44 per cent.[328] An absolute majority in the Reichstag election did not seem out of the question.

The second part of Schleicher's deal with Hitler, the lifting of the ban on the SA and SS, eventually took place, after some delay, on 16 June.[329] It was already by then being openly flouted.[330] It ushered in a summer of political violence throughout Germany such as had never been seen before. The latent civil war that had existed throughout the Weimar Republic was threatening to become an actual civil war. Armed clashes and street-fighting between the SA and the Communists were daily occurrences. Nazi violence, it might be thought, ought to have put off the 'respectable' bourgeois following it was increasingly attracting.[331] But since such Nazi supporters saw the threat as lying on the Left, the anti-Communist thuggery purporting to serve the interests of the nation alienated remarkably few voters.

The level of violence was frightening. In the second half of June, after the lifting of the SA ban, there were seventeen politically motivated murders. During July, there were a further eighty-six killings, mainly Nazis and Communists. The numbers of those seriously injured rose into the hundreds. Four were killed and thirty-four injured in a single clash on 10 July in Ohlau in Silesia. In the worst incident, the Altona 'Blood Sunday' of 17 July, seventeen people were killed and sixty-four injured as shooting broke out during an SA parade seen as a direct provocation by the town's Communists.[332]

The Papen government immediately took up plans it had temporarily postponed to depose the Prussian government, still headed by the Social Democrat Otto Braun with another Socialist, Carl Severing, as Interior

Minister, and placed the largest state in Germany in the hands of a Reich Commissar. On 20 July, representatives of the Prussian government were told that they were deposed, and that Papen was now acting as Reich Commissar for Prussia. The biggest and most important state, and the vital bulwark of Social Democracy, capitulated without resistance. Militant opposition would almost certainly have been futile. A general strike, of the kind that had broken the back of the Kapp Putsch in 1920, was unthinkable with 6 million unemployed. There were fears, too, that an attempt at a general strike would provoke a military dictatorship. But the passivity of the main defender of the Republic in the face of such a blatant breach of the constitution was desperately demoralizing for the SPD's supporters. And it showed Hitler he had little to fear from that quarter. Papen's destruction of the Prussian bastion without a blow being struck in anger was undertaken by conservatives, not Nazis. But it set the model for the takeover of power in the states more than six months before Hitler became Chancellor.[333]

Meanwhile, Hitler's party had entered upon its fourth election campaign within four months. Goebbels had claimed in mid-April that shortage of money was hindering propaganda.[334] There was little sign of either money or energy being spared, however, as the propaganda machine was cranked up once more. Nazi toleration of the Papen government counted for little once the campaign was under way. But the main aim was to destroy the remnants of voting for the bourgeois splinter parties and attempt to make inroads into the Zentrum's support.[335] There was a good deal of parading and pageantry.[336] A novel touch was the use of film propaganda and production of 50,000 gramophone records of an 'Appeal to the Nation' by Hitler.[337] There was awareness that boredom with the constant electioneering was setting in.[338] Hitler began a speaking marathon in fifty-three towns and cities during his third 'Germany Flight'.[339] The monotony for his entourage was scarcely bearable. He arrived, gave his speech, had his bags packed, and left for the next venue. His attendants, commented Hanfstaengl, were like boxing seconds who had to keep their man fit between rounds – in Hitler's case, speaking bouts.[340] His theme was unchanged: the parties of the November Revolution had presided over the untold ruin of every aspect of German life; his own party was the only one that could rescue the German people from its misery.[341]

When the results were declared on 31 July, the Nazis could record another victory – of sorts. They had increased their share of the vote to 37.4 per cent. This made them, with 230 seats, easily the largest party in the

Reichstag.[342] The Socialists had lost votes, compared with 1930; the KPD and Zentrum had made slight gains; the collapse of the bourgeois parties of the centre and right had advanced still further.

The victory for the Nazis was, however, only a pyrrhic one. Compared with the Reichstag election results of 1930, let alone 1928, their advance was indeed astonishing. But from a more short-term perspective the outcome of the July election could even be regarded as disappointing. They had scarcely improved on the support they had won in the second presidential election and in the April state elections. Goebbels gave a sober assessment of the position: 'We have won a tiny bit . . . Result: now we must come to power and exterminate (*ausrotten*) Marxism. One way or another! Something must happen. The time for opposition is over. Now deeds! Hitler is of the same opinion. Now events have to sort themselves out and then decisions have to be taken. We won't get to an absolute majority this way.'[343]

On 2 August, Hitler was still uncertain what to do. He talked over the possibilities of action with Goebbels while recuperating from the election campaign by the Tegernsee. A coalition with the Zentrum was one option briefly considered but discarded. No conclusions were reached. It was decided to wait and see how things developed. Music, films, relaxation, and a visit to *Tristan und Isolde* in Munich filled the space.[344] Within two days, while at Berchtesgaden, Hitler had decided how to play his hand. He arranged a meeting with Schleicher in Berlin to put his demands: the Chancellorship for himself, Interior Ministry for Frick, Air Ministry for Göring, Labour Ministry for Strasser, and a Ministry for the People's Education (*Volkserziehung*) for Goebbels. He was confident that 'the barons would give way'. But he left a question mark over the response of 'the old man', Hindenburg.[345]

The secret negotiations with Reichswehr Minister Schleicher, at Fürstenberg, fifty miles north of Berlin, lasted for several hours on 6 August. When Hitler reported back to other Nazi leaders gathered at Berchtesgaden, he was confident. 'Within a week the matter will burst open,' thought Goebbels. 'Chief will become Reich Chancellor and Prussian Minister President, Strasser Reich and Prussian Interior, Goebbels Prussian and Reich Education, Darré Agriculture in both, Frick state secretary in the Reich Chancellery, Göring Air Ministry. Justice [Ministry] stays with us. Warmbold Economy. Crosigk [i.e. Schwerin von Krosigk] Finance. Schacht Reichsbank. A cabinet of men. If the Reichstag rejects the enabling act, it will be sent packing (*nach Hause geschickt*). Hindenburg wants to die with a national cabinet.

We will never give up power again. They'll have to carry us out as corpses . . . I still can't believe it. At the gates of power.'[346]

The deal with Schleicher appeared to offer Hitler all he wanted. It was not total power. But there was little left wanting so far as internal power and control over domestic politics was concerned. From Schleicher's point of view, the concession of a Hitler Chancellorship was a significant one. But the Reichswehr Minister presumably reckoned that as long as the army remained under his own control, Hitler could be kept in check, and would provide the popular basis for an authoritarian regime in which he himself would continue to be the *eminence grise*.[347] The prospect of a civil war, into which the Reichswehr might be drawn, would recede sharply. And the teeth of the Nazis would be drawn by the inevitable compromises they would have to make in the face of the realities of political responsibility. Such was the thinking behind all variants of a 'taming strategy' which would unfold over the following months.

Schleicher later claimed he had put Hitler's demands to the Reich President on the latter's estate in Neudeck in East Prussia. Influential though he was with Hindenburg, Schleicher had been firmly rebuffed. The Reich President informed Schleicher in no uncertain terms, according to the Reichswehr Minister's account, that it was 'his "irrevocable" will' not to appoint Hitler to the Chancellorship.[348] Just after Hindenburg had returned from Neudeck to Berlin on 10 August, Papen had also raised with him the possibility of a Hitler Chancellorship, heading a 'brown-black' majority government of NSDAP and Zentrum.[349] It was at this meeting that Hindenburg made his contemptuous remark, frequently cited, that it would be a fine thing indeed were he to make the 'Bohemian corporal' Reich Chancellor.[350]

In the dark about these developments, Hitler and Goebbels talked over the 'problems of the seizure of power'. Goebbels was rapturous about the 'historic task' facing him in the 'national education of the German people'.[351] Nazi supporters scented triumph. The whole party expected power, it was reported by telephone from Berlin. The leader of the Berlin SA, Graf Helldorf, was unfolding his own big plans for the takeover of power. Stormtroopers were leaving work in expectation of what was about to happen. Party functionaries were in readiness for 'the great hour'. 'If things go badly, there'll be a dreadful backlash,' commented Goebbels.[352]

The Papen cabinet was divided on whether Hitler should be given power. Finance Minister Krosigk thought the best way to avoid civil war was to turn the poacher into a gamekeeper. The Minister of the Interior, Freiherr von Gayl, vehemently opposed any such idea. Supported by Foreign Minister

Neurath, he proposed retention of the existing government, acknowledging that this would require a breach of the constitution. The Reichstag should be dissolved, but no date set for fresh elections, and a new, restricted franchise imposed. Justice Minister Gürtner hedged his bets. To continue the current cabinet without new elections would indeed be unconstitutional. He voiced no disapproval of the inclusion in government of the National Socialists – whose idea of the state, he pointed out, rested on their 'instinct for retaliation' (*Vergeltungsinstinkt*) against Jews and Marxists – but feared the notion was illusory unless they were to be offered leadership of the government. Other cabinet ministers favoured a continuation of the current administration. Papen and Schleicher wanted to keep their options open.[353] While Gayl was publicly announcing – ironically, in a speech on 'Constitution Day', 11 August – his wish to replace the Weimar Constitution by an authoritarian system where government was not dependent upon the Reichstag, the armed SA were demonstratively taking up positions of apparent readiness for action around the government quarter of Berlin. 'Makes the gentlemen very nervous,' wrote Goebbels. 'That's the point of the exercise.'[354]

On 11 August, Hitler held a last conference with party leaders at Prien on the Chiemsee, the biggest of the Bavarian lakes, eighty or so miles east of Munich, close to the Austrian border. He was by now aware of the growing opposition in the corridors of power to his Chancellorship. There was still the possibility of threatening a coalition with the Zentrum. But Hitler was adamant that nothing less than the Chancellorship would do. After resting in his flat in Munich, he travelled next day to Berlin by car to avoid all publicity. Röhm had meetings with Schleicher and Papen that day, 12 August, but his soundings about a Hitler Chancellorship were inconclusive. Hitler arrived in darkness at Goebbels's house in Caputh, on the outskirts of Berlin, in the late evening. He was told that matters were still unresolved after Röhm's meetings. It was now 'either-or', he insisted. But if it had been as simple as that, he would not have spent what was left of the evening pacing up and down, pondering how much hinged on the decision of the Reich President. It was clear to Goebbels what was at stake. Unless Hitler were to be given extensive power, meaning the Chancellorship, he would have to refuse office. In that case, 'a mighty depression in the movement and in the electorate would be the consequence'. He added: 'And we have only this one iron in the fire.'[355]

The following morning, 13 August, accompanied by Röhm, Hitler met Schleicher, followed shortly afterwards, this time together with Frick, by a meeting with Chancellor Papen. He was informed by both that Hindenburg was not prepared to appoint him Chancellor. 'I soon realized that I was dealing with a very different man from the one I had met two months earlier,' von Papen recalled. 'The modest air of deference had gone, and I was faced by a demanding politician who had just won a resounding electoral success.' Papen suggested Hitler join the government as Vice-Chancellor. The alternative of continued opposition, he argued (convinced that support for the NSDAP had peaked), would surely mean that his party's campaign would start to flag. Whereas, in the event of Hitler's fruitful cooperation and 'once the President had got to know him better', so Papen later wrote, he would be prepared to resign the Chancellorship in the Nazi leader's favour. Hitler rejected point-blank the notion of the head of such a large movement playing second fiddle, and was if anything even more dismissive of the idea that he might consider staying in opposition but allowing one of his associates to take up the post of Vice-Chancellor. Papen advised him at the end of the meeting, at times heated, that the decision was the Reich President's, but he would have to inform Hindenburg that the discussions had led to no positive outcome.[356]

Hitler and his entourage, gathered in Goebbels's house on the Reichs-kanzlerplatz, had by now, not surprisingly, become pessimistic. They could do nothing but wait. When State Secretary Planck rang from the Reich Chancellery around three o'clock, he was asked whether there was any point in Hitler seeing the Reich President, since the decision had evidently been taken. He was told that Hindenburg wanted first to speak to him. Perhaps there was still a chance.[357] Hundreds were gathered in Wilhelmstraße as Hitler arrived at the Presidential Palace for his audience, set for 4.15p.m. Hindenburg was correct, but cool. According to the notes made by Hindenburg's State Secretary, Otto Meissner, Hitler was asked whether he was prepared to serve in Papen's government. His cooperation would be welcome, the President stated. Hitler declared that, for the reasons he had given to the Chancellor in full that morning, there was no question of his involvement in the existing government. Given the significance of his movement, he must demand the leadership of the government and 'the leadership of the state to its full extent (*die Staatsführung in vollem Umfange*) for himself and his party'. The Reich President firmly refused. He could not answer, he said, before God, his conscience and the Fatherland if he handed over the entire power of the government to a single party, and one which was so intolerant towards those with different views. He was also worried about unrest at home and the likely impact abroad. When Hitler repeated that for him every other solution was ruled out, Hindenburg advised him then to conduct his opposition in a gentlemanly (*ritterlich*) fashion, and that all acts of terror would be treated with utmost severity. In a gesture of pathos more than political reality, he shook Hitler's hand as 'old comrades'. The meeting had lasted a mere twenty minutes. Hitler had controlled himself. But outside, in the corridor, he threatened to explode. Events would inexorably lead to the conclusion he had put forward and to the fall of the President, he declared. The government would be put in an extremely difficult position, the opposition would be fierce, and he would accept no responsibility for the consequences.[358] According to the Nazis' own version, the brief, heated exchange outside the President's room ended with an airy gesture by Reich Chancellor Papen dismissing the importance of the Reichstag and remarking to the Nazi delegation: 'If you had been prepared to enter the government, you would in any case have been within three weeks where you wanted to be today.'[359]

'The notion of the Führer as Vice-Chancellor of a bourgeois cabinet is too grotesque to be taken seriously,' recorded Goebbels after Hitler had returned within half an hour empty-handed.[360] But his embellished account in the published version of his diaries hid the deep dismay within the movement.[361]

Hitler was aware that he had suffered a major political defeat. It was his greatest setback since the failure of the putsch, nine years earlier.[362] The strategy he had followed all those years, that mobilizing the masses – his natural instinct, and what he did best – would suffice to gain power, had proved a failure. He had taken his party into a cul-de-sac. The breakthrough had been made. The NSDAP's rise to the portals of power had been meteoric. He had just won a crushing election victory. But he had been flatly rejected as Reich Chancellor by the one person whose assent, under the Weimar Constitution, was indispensable: Reich President Hindenburg. The 'all-or-nothing' gamble had left Hitler with nothing. With a tired, depressed, desperately disappointed, and fractious party, the prospect of continued opposition was not an enticing one. But it was all that was left. Even given new elections, the chances were that it would prove difficult to hold on to the level of support already mobilized.

The thirteenth of August 1932 ought to have been a defining moment in Hitler's bid for power. After that, it should never have come to a 30th of January 1933. Without allies in high places, able eventually to persuade the Reich President to change his mind, Hitler would never – even as head of a huge movement, and with over 13 million supporters in the country –

have been able to come to power. That power was refused Hitler after he had won a victory, and handed to him after he had suffered a defeat (in the ensuing Reichstag election in November), was not attributable to any 'triumph of the will'.

10

LEVERED INTO POWER

'We've hired him.'   Franz von Papen, end of January 1933

'We're boxing Hitler in.'   Alfred Hugenberg, end of January 1933

'I solemnly prophesy that this accursed man will cast our Reich into the abyss and bring our nation to inconceivable misery. Future generations will damn you in your grave for what you have done.'
Ludendorff to Reich President Hindenburg,
end of January 1933

During the autumn of 1932, the state crisis of the Weimar Republic deepened. No resolution was in sight. In the first months of the winter of 1932–3, it entered its climacteric phase. During this phase, leverage over power passed increasingly into the hands of a small number of individuals – most notably Papen, Schleicher and Hindenburg. Behind them stood powerful lobbies – big business, estate-owners, and not least the army. But these élite groups did not form a solid or united 'ruling class'. Nor did they act in unison. In fact, they were divided among themselves both in terms of their economic interests and their preferred political strategies.[1] All wanted an end to the 'party system' of democratic politics and the breaking of 'Marxism' (including the SPD) and trade unionism, together with the reversion to some form of authoritarianism. Beyond that, there was little agreement on any patent solution to the crisis. There was for a while among different sections of the élite, and particularly articulated by the Papen cabinet and its supporters, the illusion that the masses could be excluded indefinitely from any involvement in the shaping of power. In the short term, this was indeed no illusion. The German people had by this time no direct influence on the shape of the government. The attempt to emasculate the Reichstag and dispense with party rule had begun under Brüning as a way of coping with crisis. Under Papen, it became the key principle of government. But the mobilized masses could not simply be wished away. Nor were they the creation of or the tools of the élites. And on the Right, they were controlled almost wholly by Hitler.

The dilemma for all non-Nazis looking for an authoritarian solution was how to bring one about without Hitler. For Hitler, the problem was how, having mobilized the masses, to get to power if those holding power continued to refuse to give it to him. This was the impasse of autumn 1932. In the breaking of the stalemate, the actions of individuals played the vital part. Hitler could not be ignored. He had built up a mass movement of great size. It had put him in a position where he could effectively block any political options which did not give him what he wanted. But his movement, on its own, was insufficiently strong to give him power. He needed help in high places. It came precisely at the time that he might otherwise have been witnessing the beginnings of the break-up of his movement and the onset of his own political demise.

The greater the multidimensional crisis of the Weimar state became, and the tighter the straitjacket on alternative political strategies gripped, the more extensive was the scope for maverick personal 'initiatives' on the non-Nazi national-conservative Right. Hitler's eventual triumph arose from such 'initiatives' which turned out to be grave political miscalculations. But it can scarcely be seen as a 'works accident'. For such miscalculations were themselves the product of long-standing predispositions on the conservative Right.[2] Hindenburg himself and those able to influence him were so intent on finding a rightist solution that they dismissed any consideration of looking to a parliamentary way out. And the different forms of 'taming strategy', aimed at incorporating the National Socialists in government, which all around Hindenburg advocated at one time or another and in one form or another, reflected an underestimation of and contempt for Hitler corresponding to an ingrained over-confidence in the ability of the 'natural' governing classes to control the upstarts.

Hitler's own actions were of only secondary importance in bringing him to power. They consisted exclusively, apart from sustained agitation, of holding out for the highest stakes – the Chancellorship in a presidential cabinet – and of refusing all compromise attempts to involve him otherwise in government. The policy worked in the end. But this was as a consequence of the actions of others more than of Hitler himself.

I

Hitler took the events of 13 August 'as a personal defeat'.[3] His anger and humiliation were intensified by the government's deliberately brusque communiqué – instigated by Schleicher – on the meeting, which had briefly emphasized Hindenburg's rebuff of Hitler's demand for total power. Hitler's pedantically correct, piqued rejoinder could only claim that he had not demanded 'total' power.[4] At the time, his anger was chiefly directed at Papen.[5] Sent to intercede with Hitler, by then staying at Obersalzberg, a few days later, Joachim von Ribbentrop – the vain and humourless future Reich Foreign Minister, on his upward career path not least through his marriage to the heiress of Germany's biggest Sekt manufacturers, Henkel, and a recent recruit to the NSDAP – found him 'full of resentment towards Herr von Papen and the entire cabinet in Berlin'.[6] But if the events of January 1933 were to redeem Papen, Schleicher would emerge as the central target of Nazi aggression for his role in the months between August 1932 and January 1933.[7] 'The decision was right. Adolf Hitler could not have been given power,' was the General's reported response to Hindenburg's decision on 13 August.[8] Schleicher's manoevrings behind the scenes, particularly his 'betrayal' in August which had led to Hitler's humiliation, were not forgotten. He would pay for them with his life.[9]

As usual, Hitler had the capacity to channel disappointment and depression into outright aggression. And, whatever hesitation he showed before making a decision, once made, he never doubted that he had been right, that no other course of action had been possible. So it was after 13 August 1932. 'We'll have to see how things go,' Hitler murmured to himself *en route* to Munich to address party leaders on 15 August.[10] He also took the opportunity publicly to state his side of the case in a friendly interview with the *Rheinisch-Westfälische Zeitung* – a newspaper closely associated with Ruhr big business, and with Hitler's press chief Otto Dietrich – on 16 August. Open opposition to the hated Papen government was now proclaimed. The shadow-boxing of the summer was over. To head off any possible recurrence of a ban, and cool the temperature among the disappointed stormtroopers, the SA was sent on leave for two weeks.[11] 'The question,' he declared in an interview for the Associated Press, 'is not whether I shall march on Berlin but rather who will have to march out of Berlin. My Storm Troops are the best disciplined body and will not attempt an illegal march. Why should I march on Berlin when I am here already?'[12]

Within days, Hitler had an opportunity to turn attention away from the débâcle of his audience with Hindenburg. On 10 August, a group of SA men had murdered an unemployed labourer and Communist sympathizer in the Silesian village of Potempa.[13] The murder was carried out with extraordinary savagery, and in front of the victim's mother and brother. As so often, personal and political motives intermingled. Horrifically brutal though the killing was, it is an indication of how far public order had collapsed that the event was in itself little more than a routine act of terror in the awful summer of 1932, symptomatic of the climate of violence in near civil war conditions. No one took particular notice of it at first. Given a list of three dozen acts of political violence recorded in a single day and night around the time, the Potempa incident did not stand out. However, the murder had been committed an hour and a half after the Papen government's emergency decree to combat terrorism, prescribing the death penalty for premeditated political murder and setting up special courts to provide swift justice for cases arising under the decree, had come into effect. The trial took place at Beuthen in a tense atmosphere and amid great publicity between 19 and 22 August and ended with the pronouncement of the death penalty on five of the accused. To inflame feelings in the Nazi camp still further, two Reichsbanner men were given relatively light sentences on the very same day for killing two SA men during disturbances in Ohlau in July. These murders had not been premeditated, and had taken place before Papen's emergency decree. But such differences naturally did not weigh among Hitler's supporters. The Potempa murderers were portrayed as martyrs. The local SA leader, Heines, threatened an uprising if the death sentences were to be carried out. His rabble-rousing tirade incited the crowd to break the windows of Jewish-owned shops in Beuthen and attack the offices of the local SPD newspaper. In this heated atmosphere, Göring praised the condemned men and sent money to their families. Röhm was sent to visit them in jail. On 22 August, Hitler himself sent the telegram that caused a sensation. 'My comrades!' he wrote, 'in view of this most monstrous verdict in blood (*Bluturteil*), I feel tied to you in unbounded loyalty. Your freedom is from this moment on a question of our honour. The struggle against a government under which this was possible is our duty!'[14] The head of Germany's largest political party was publicly expressing solidarity with convicted murderers. It was a scandal Hitler had to take on board.[15] Not to have sympathized with the Potempa murderers would have risked alienating his SA in a particularly sensitive area, Silesia, and at a time when it was vitally important to keep the restless stormtroopers on the leash.

The next day, Hitler put out a proclamation castigating the Papen cabinet, and taking the opportunity to turn the events of 13 August on their head by claiming his own refusal to participate in a government capable of such sentences. 'Those of you who possess a feel for the struggle for the honour and freedom of the nation will understand why I refused to enter this bourgeois government,' he declared. 'With this deed, our attitude towards this national cabinet is prescribed once and for all.'[16]

In the event, Papen, acting in his capacity as Reich Commissar in Prussia, backed down and had the death sentences for the Potempa murderers commuted into life imprisonment – a decision which Papen himself acknowledged was political rather than legal.[17] The murderers were freed under a Nazi amnesty as early as March 1933.[18]

The Potempa affair had cast glaring light, at precisely the juncture where the power-brokers were still examining ways and means of incorporating Hitler in government, on Nazi attitudes towards the law. Hitler had, in fact, welcomed Papen's emergency decrees of 9 August, seeing them as directed at 'the murderous banditry' of Marxists.[19] But the decrees would have looked different under a National Socialist government, announced the *Völkischer Beobachter*. They would have brought the immediate arrest and sentencing of all Communist and Social Democrat party functionaries, the 'concentrated smoking out' (*konzentrierte Ausräucherung*) of the 'murder areas' (*Mordviertel*), and 'the internment of those under suspicion and intellectual inciters in concentration camps'.[20] After the sentencing of the Potempa murderers, Alfred Rosenberg added in the same official party organ that the Beuthen judgement showed that 'according to bourgeois justice, one Polish Communist has the same weighting as five Germans, front soldiers'. That was why National Socialism had to look at matters ideologically. In such a philosophy, 'one soul does not equal another, one person not another'. For National Socialism, he went on, 'there is no "law as such". Rather, its goal is the strong German person, its belief is the protection of this German. And all law and social life, politics and economics, have to fall into line with this aim.'[21] Such unmistakable indications of what a Hitler government would mean for the rule of law in Germany posed no deterrent to those who still thought the only way out of the crisis was somehow to involve the Nazis in the responsibility of public office.

Hitler's rejection of anything less than the office of Chancellor had not only created difficulties for the NSDAP. The problems for the government were now acute. Schleicher had now given up the idea of a Hitler Chancellorship as long as Hindenburg remained Reich President.[22] Papen, himself resolutely opposed, took Hindenburg's continued opposition for granted. Only two possibilities, neither attractive, appeared to remain. The first was a 'black-brown' – taken from the colour associated with each party – coalition of Zentrum and National Socialists. Feelers were put out from the Zentrum about such a possibility following the events of 13 August. It never stood much chance of emerging as a solution. Gregor Strasser was keen to proceed, but could do nothing without Hitler's backing – and the tension between the two was beginning to come into the open.[23] The Zentrum continued to insist that the NSDAP concede the Chancellorship, but a

Hitler Chancellorship had meanwhile become a 'question of honour'.[24] Brüning also refused to yield the offices, including the posts of Minister President and Minister of the Interior in Prussia, which Hitler demanded for his party.[25] Hitler, for his part, was unwilling now, as he was to be following the November elections when the possibility was once more raised, to head a government dependent upon Reichstag majorities for support.[26] In any case, the thought of a reversion to parliamentary government was anathema to Hindenburg and his advisers.[27]

The second alternative was to persevere with a 'cabinet of struggle' (*Kampfkabinett*) without any hope of support in the Reichstag, where the Nazis and Communists together prevailed over a 'negative majority'. This implied going ahead with plans, first advanced by Interior Minister Gayl earlier in the month, for dissolving the Reichstag and postponing new elections in order to provide time to undertake a far-reaching reduction in the powers of the Reichstag through restricted franchise and a two-chamber system with a non-elected first chamber.[28] The intention was to end 'party rule' once and for all. Necessary for such a drastic step were the support of the Reich President and the backing of the army to combat the expected opposition from the Left and possibly also from National Socialists. This solution for a dissolution of the Reichstag and postponement – in breach of the constitution – of elections beyond the sixty-day limit prescribed was put to Hindenburg by Papen at a meeting in Neudeck on 30 August. Schleicher and Gayl were also present. Hindenburg gave Papen the dissolution order without ado, and also agreed to the unconstitutional postponement of new elections on the grounds of a national state of emergency. Some leading constitutional lawyers – most prominent among them Carl Schmitt, the renowned constitutional theorist who in 1933 would place himself at the service of the Third Reich – were ready with their legal arguments to back the introduction of an authoritarian state through such a device.[29]

Probably, if he wanted to risk such a solution, Papen should have had the new Reichstag dissolved at its very first sitting on 30 August. By the second sitting, on 12 September, the initiative had been lost.[30] As it was, Papen stayed away from the opening session, and the Reichstag merely heard on 30 August an attack on capitalism and advocacy of a Soviet Germany from the oldest member of the Reichstag, Clara Zetkin, given the right of speaking in the opening formalities, followed by the election on the votes of the NSDAP, BVP and Zentrum of Hermann Göring as Reichstag President.[31] Göring lost no time in emphasizing that, as his election showed, there was a working majority in the Reichstag and no case for pronouncement by the government of a state of emergency. A joint statement by the NSDAP and Zentrum on 1 September, indicating that negotiations had begun between the two parties, had the same aim of deflecting a possible declaration of a state of emergency.[32] It was from the Nazi side no more than a tactical device.[33] The Nazi leadership were, however, prepared for a dissolution of the Reichstag. 'If the opposite side breaks the constitution,' wrote Goebbels, 'then all compulsion to legality stops for us; then come tax strikes, sabotage, and uprising.'[34] At a meeting of Nazi leaders on 8 September, Hitler emphasized that new elections were inevitable – the sooner, the better. He rejected out of hand a suggestion by Gregor Strasser, of whom he was becoming increasingly suspicious, to accept a cabinet led by Schleicher. Hitler as Reich Chancellor – but of a presidential cabinet, not dependent on coalition partners – remained the sole aim.[35]

The Reichstag met for its second – and last – sitting on 12 September. The only item on the list of the day's agenda was a government declaration on the financial situation, announcing details of a programme aimed at economic recovery. A debate was expected to last for several days. However, the Communist Deputy Ernst Torgler proposed an alteration to the order of proceedings.[36] He sought first to put a proposal of his party to repeal the emergency decrees of 4 and 5 September (which had made deep incisions in the system of tariff wage-bargaining), and to couple this with a vote of no-confidence in the government. No one expected much of such a proposal. The amendment to the order of proceedings would have fallen had there been a single objection. The Nazis expected the DNVP deputies to object. Astonishingly, not one did so. In the confusion that followed, Frick obtained an adjournment of half an hour to seek Hitler's decision on how to proceed. Papen, completely taken aback, had to send a messenger to the Reich Chancellery during the adjournment to pick up the dissolution order, signed by Hindenburg on 30 August, which he had not even bothered to bring into the chamber with him.

Meanwhile, the Zentrum tried to persuade the National Socialists to reject the Communist proposals. But at a brief meeting with his chief henchmen, Hitler decided that the opportunity to embarrass the government could not be missed: the Nazi deputies should immediately support the Communist vote of no confidence, thus pre-empting Papen's dissolution order which no one doubted he would now put forward.[37] When the Reichstag reassembled, Papen appeared with the red dispatch box which traditionally contained the orders of dissolution under his arm. Amid chaotic scenes, the Reichstag President Göring announced straight away that he would proceed with the vote on the Communist proposal. At this, Papen tried to speak. Göring ignored him, looking intentionally away from the Chancellor to the left side of the chamber. Papen's State Secretary Planck pointed out to Göring that the Chancellor wished to exercise his right to speak. Göring retorted simply that the vote had begun. After again trying vainly to speak, Papen marched over to the Reichstag President's platform and slapped the dissolution order down on Göring's table. Followed by his cabinet, he then walked out of the chamber to howls of derision. Göring blithely pushed the dissolution order to one side, and read out the result of the division. The government was defeated by 512 votes to 42, with five abstentions and one invalid ballot paper. Only the DVNP and DVP had supported the government. All the major parties, including the Zentrum, had supported the Communist proposal. There had never been a parliamentary defeat like it. It was received with wild cheering and applause in the Reichstag.

Göring now read out Papen's dissolution order, which he declared invalid since the government had already fallen through a vote of no-confidence. This was technically incorrect. Göring was subsequently compelled to concede that the Reichstag had indeed been formally dissolved by the presentation of Papen's order. The no-confidence motion was, therefore, without legal standing. But this was of purely procedural significance. The government remained, as a consequence, in office. The reality was, however, that it had been rejected by more than four-fifths of the people's representatives. Papen had been shown in the most humiliating way possible to be a Chancellor almost devoid of public support.[38] Hitler was beside himself with joy.[39] The cynical Nazi tactics had meanwhile given a foretaste of how they would behave in power, given the opportunity.[40]

New elections – the fifth of the year – loomed. Papen still had in his possession Hindenburg's approval to postpone the election beyond the sixty days allowed by the constitution. But after the fiasco of 12 September, the cabinet decided two days later that now was not the time to proceed with that experiment.[41] New elections were set for 6 November. The Nazi leadership was aware of the difficulties. The bourgeois press was now completely hostile. The NSDAP could make little use of broadcasting.[42] The public were weary of elections. Even leading party speakers found it difficult to sustain top form. Not least, noted Goebbels, previous campaigns had drained all available funds. The party's coffers were empty. Funding was difficult to come by. Getting through the 'financial calamity' was not going to be easy, thought the Propaganda Leader, who had his organization moved from Munich to Berlin for the duration of the campaign.[43]

Hitler himself seemed in confident mood on his way from Berlin to Munich shortly after the extraordinary events in the Reichstag.[44] Whatever the doubts in the party, he was also able to convey optimism to the propagandists assembled in Munich on 6 October, when he laid down the guidelines for the campaign: 'I look forward to the struggle with absolute confidence,' he said. 'The battle can begin. In four weeks we will emerge from it as the victor.'[45]

A few days earlier, on 2 October, he had attended the 'Reich Youth Rally' staged by the Hitler Youth in Potsdam. He had, according to Lüdecke's account, been reluctant to go. But Schirach persuaded him not to miss such an inviting propaganda opportunity just before the election. Lüdecke was part of the accompaniment of sundry adjutants and bodyguards that formed the northward-bound cavalcade. Hitler wanted to hear about America, where Lüdecke had spent the previous few years in a variety of insignificant jobs and small-time business ventures. He was glad to discover Lüdecke's interest in the Karl May cowboy and Indian stories which he had devoured as a boy. He said he could still read them and get a thrill out of them. The bodyguards had to be on alert as roadworks in Saxony forced the cars to slow down to overtake a procession of lorries carrying Communists waving red flags. But nothing more than insults were hurled at Hitler and his entourage. The danger passed. By the time they were approaching Potsdam, they were slowed down again – but this time by the crowds of Hitler Youth on their way to the rally.[46]

An estimated 110,000 boys and girls from all over Germany, and also from Austria, Bohemia, Danzig, and Memel, had come to Potsdam – twice the number expected. Many had been on the road for days. Those who could not be accommodated had to sleep in the open, though it was already chilly in early October. Hitler was greeted with wild enthusiasm on entering the stadium, a blaze of torches, where the rally was held. 'Tens of thousands of boys and girls stood in formation on the field,' recalled Lüdecke. 'When Hitler stood alone at the front of the platform, a fantastic cry went up into the night, a sound of matchless jubilation. Then he raised his arms and dead silence fell. He burst into a flaming address which lasted scarcely fifteen minutes. Again he was the old Hitler, spontaneous, fiery, full of appeal.'[47] As always when at the centre of a propaganda spectacular, he was himself gripped by the atmosphere, by the thrill of the performance. He could appear tireless, sleeping little, conveying the impression to those around him of concern for the well-being of his young supporters, then standing with outstretched arm for seven hours while the Hitler Youth paraded past him.

In the evening he dined with the Kaiser's fourth son and party member Prince August Wilhelm – Auwi as he was known – whom he addressed courteously, even deferentially, then went back to Goebbels's house. Only when finally 'off-stage', slumped in his train compartment at the beginning of the journey back to Munich, could the image be put to one side as he sagged with tiredness. 'Leave him alone,' his adjutant Brückner told Hoffmann and Lüdecke. 'The man's played out.'[48]

Electioneering reinvigorated him. And in the fifth long campaign of the year, he set out yet again to do what he did best: make speeches. Once more, his indispensability as the chief propaganda focus of the movement meant he had to embark upon a punishing schedule of speeches and rallies. During his fourth 'Germany Flight' between 11 October and 5 November he gave no fewer than fifty speeches, again sometimes three a day, on one occasion four.[49] He briefly interrupted his campaign when he heard of Eva Braun's apparent attempted suicide by shooting late on 1 November.[50] Despairing of the man she had fallen in love with but scarcely saw, and who was so taken up with his political activities that he was hardly acknowledging her existence, Eva had shot herself – allegedly aiming at the heart – with her father's pistol. She had not, however, been too injured to telephone immediately for a doctor. She was immediately taken to hospital, where Hitler visited her bearing a large bouquet of flowers – and some doubts about whether the suicide attempt had been a genuine one.[51] If he momentarily feared another scandal like the one involving Geli Raubal the previous summer, he gave no indication of it. Without delay, he was back on the campaign trail, speaking on the evening of 2 November at a big rally in the Berlin Sportpalast.[52]

Hitler's attack now focused squarely on Papen and 'the Reaction'. The vast support for his own movement was contrasted with the 'small circle of reactionaries' keeping the Papen government, lacking all popular backing, in office.[53] 'There the head of a government which depends on a small circle of reactionaries, a government on which the German people with 512 to 42 votes has given its devastating verdict; here a leader of his own strength, rooted in the people, who has worked and struggled to gain trust,' was how Nazi propaganda depicted the contest.[54] Hitler emphasized how little ministerial titles meant to him. 'He preferred to be the leader of his party.' Nor did he need a ministerial salary, since he had his own income as a writer. Papen, with his property worth 5 million Marks, Hitler went on, still drew his Chancellor's salary. He, on the other hand, had no intention of claiming one: 'decisive for him was working for the people'.[55] Hitler declared that it was plain to see why he had not entered the 'cabinet of the barons' on 13 August. He was prepared, he said, to take responsibility – full responsibility – but not to take it where it was evident that he would be deprived of influence. 'My opponents deceive themselves above all,' he railed, 'about my enormous determination. I've chosen my path and will follow it to its end.'[56]

The Nazi press inevitably portrayed Hitler's campaign as a victory march. 'The Führer begins his new struggle for Germany,' proclaimed the *Völkischer Beobachter* on 13 October. It followed with 'The Führer's Victory Parade through Bavaria's Gaue' two days later. 'Grandiose Progress of the Hitler Days,' ran the banner headline of the *Coburger National-Zeitung* on 17 October. 'Huge participation from the entire Reich . . . Coburg, the Hitler town, mirrors symbolically the emergence and struggle of the German freedom movement.' 'Where once Marxism ruled, the people now stands by Hitler,' professed the party's main organ again, after its leader had spoken in Schweinfurt in Lower Franconia.[57] 'Fourteen Years Ago War-Blind in Hospital – Now the Leader of Millions. Adolf Hitler in the Pomeranian Town of Pasewalk, the starting-point of his struggle for the German soul,' ran another headline towards the end of the month.[58] But not even all Nazi followers read the party press. And the main bourgeois papers, with their far larger circulation, were unremittingly hostile. The triumphalist headlines in the *Völkischer Beobachter* in any case merely disguised worries within the movement that the party's support was falling off, that morale among the often fickle members was low, that the SA were unwilling in many places to take part in propaganda work, and that the NSDAP was heading for a serious electoral setback.[59] Grossly inflated attendances at Hitler rallies provided in the party press – in rural areas especially thousands were brought in from outside the area to swell the numbers – hid the plain signs of disillusionment and electoral fatigue. Hitler acknowledged that the party was likely to lose votes, perhaps a large number, but characteristically, if not logically, still thought the election would be 'a great psychological success'.[60] Even Hitler was now unable to fill the halls as he previously had done. For his speech in Nuremberg on 13 October, the Festhalle in Luitpoldhain was only half full.[61] While a Hitler speech might have made a difference to the election result in some places, observers were already predicting in October that his campaign tour would do little to prevent the expected drop in Nazi support.[62] The day before the election, Goebbels, too, was anticipating a defeat.[63]

When the votes were counted, Nazi fears were realized. In the last election before Hitler came to power (and the last fully free election in the Weimar Republic) the NSDAP had lost 2 million voters. In a reduced turn-out – the lowest (at 80.6 per cent) since 1928 – its percentage of the poll had fallen from 37.4 in July to 33.1, its Reichstag seats reduced from 230 to 196. The SPD and Zentrum had also lost ground slightly. The winners were the Communists, who had increased their vote to 16.9 per cent (now little more than 3 per cent behind the SPD), and the DNVP, which had risen to 8.9 per cent.[64] The DNVP's gains had been largely in winning back former supporters who had drifted to the NSDAP. The lower turn-out was the other main factor that worked to the disadvantage of Hitler's party, as earlier Nazi voters stayed at home.[65] Not only had the party failed, as before, to make serious inroads into the big left-wing and Catholic voting blocks; it had this time lost voters – it seems to all other parties, but predominantly to the DNVP.[66] The middle classes were beginning to desert the Nazis.

Goebbels consoled himself that the results were less bad than pessimists had predicted. But he accepted they were a blow.[67] The regional and local propaganda offices of the party provided their own analysis of what had gone wrong. Lack of funding had been a major handicap in mounting a good campaign.[68] But there were less superficial reasons. An important one was Hitler's refusal to enter the cabinet in August. This had provoked division within the party membership and among the electorate, it was reported. People had expressed reluctance to vote again for Hitler, after he had rejected the opportunity of joining the government and remained as distant from power as ever.[69] Party members in some parts were quoted as saying that they had had enough of 'a party whose leader does not know what he wants and has no programme'.[70] Some Protestant support had also been alienated by Hitler's negotiations with the Zentrum in August.[71]

Beyond these reasons, the pronounced socialist image of the NSDAP that had come across strongly during the campaign – inevitably, since the main target had been Papen's reactionary conservatism – had plainly alienated middle-class support.[72] The attacks of the Nazis had seemed to many little different from the class-warfare of the Communists. The similarity of 'red' and 'brown' varieties of 'Bolshevism' appeared proven by the NSDAP's support for the Communist-inspired strike of Berlin transport workers during the days immediately preceding the election.[73] The transport strike had illustrated the party's cleft stick in the autumn campaign. Now that the DNVP, the main bourgeois conservative party, was its open enemy, the NSDAP could no longer square the electoral circle and avoid alienating one or other side of its heterogeneous 'catch-all' following.[74] Goebbels acknowledged that the party had been faced with no choice other than to support the Berlin workers. Otherwise, its support from the working-class population would have been seriously shaken. 'We are in a by no means envious position,' he wrote. 'Many bourgeois circles are frightened off by our participation in the strike. But that's not decisive. These circles can later be very easily won back. But if we'd have once lost the workers, they'd have been lost for ever.'[75] Hitler, with whom he was in constant telephone contact, had fully approved of Goebbels's action in supporting the strike. The loss of 'a few ten-thousand votes' in 'a more or less pointless election' was of no consequence 'in the active, revolutionary struggle', the propaganda boss commented.[76]

Many shocked rural voters – a mainstay of party support since 1928 – indeed stayed away from the polls as a result of the Nazi support for the strike.[77] In the middle class it was little different. Luise Solmitz, the Hamburg ex-schoolteacher so thrilled by Hitler earlier in the year, now voted – disappointed, and without enthusiasm – for the DNVP. She saw the Berlin transport strike as evidence that Hitler was arm in arm with Marxism. An acquaintance said he had twice voted for Hitler, but not again. Another thought Hitler far on the Left.[78] 'Above all his approval of the Berlin transport strike; yes, his demand to take part in it, has cost him at the last moment thousands of voters,' Frau Solmitz summed up, the day after the election. Hitler had lost, in her eyes, his claim to stand selflessly for the national interest. 'For him, it's not a matter of Germany, but of power,' she noted. 'Why has Hitler deserted us after showing us a future that we could welcome. Hitler awake!'[79]

II

The November election had changed nothing in the political stalemate – except, perhaps, to make the situation even worse. The parties supporting the government, the DNVP and DVP, had only just over 10 per cent of the population behind them. And with the drop in the vote of both the NSDAP and the Zentrum, a coalition between the two parties, such as had been discussed in August, would in itself not suffice to produce an absolute majority in the Reichstag.[80] The only majority, now as before, was a negative one. Hitler was undeterred by the election setback. He told party leaders in Munich to continue the struggle without any relenting. 'Papen has to go. There are to be no compromises,' is how Goebbels recalled the gist of

Hitler's comments.[81] In the light of his humiliating experience on 13 August – the memory of being out-manoeuvred rankled greatly with him – the Nazi leader insisted on replying in writing, which he did on 16 November, flatly rejecting the Chancellor's formal entreaty to enter discussions with a view to working with the government. Papen's request indeed marked no advance for Hitler on the position of 13 August.[82] Equally vain were the continued hopes of the Zentrum and its sister Catholic party, the BVP, that Hitler might be persuaded to enter a coalition – also with the smaller parties – to provide a working majority. The BVP leader, Fritz Schäffer, told Papen he was even prepared to operate under Hitler as Chancellor in such a coalition.[83] Three days later, the same party leader was telling Reich President Hindenburg that he was well disposed towards Hitler in person; the danger lay in those around him, who would have to be controlled through strong counterweights in the government.[84] The misreading and underestimation of Hitler was not confined to mavericks on the nationalist Right. It extended, too, into the leadership of political Catholicism.

Now, as before, Hitler had no interest in power at the behest of other parties in a majority government dependent on the Reichstag. By mid-November, Papen's attempts to find any basis of support for his government had failed. On 17 November, mourned by few, his entire cabinet resigned. It was now left to Hindenburg himself to try to negotiate a path out of the state crisis. Meanwhile, the cabinet would continue to conduct the daily business of governmental administration.[85]

On 19 November, the day that Hindenburg received Hitler as part of his meetings with the heads of the political parties, the Reich President was handed a petition carrying twenty signatures from businessmen demanding the appointment of Hitler as Chancellor.[86] It did not mark proof, as was once thought, of extensive big business support for Hitler, and its machinations to get him into power. The idea was, in fact, that of Wilhelm Keppler, emerging as Hitler's link with a group of pro-Nazi businessmen, and put into operation in conjunction with Himmler, who served as the liaison to the Brown House. Keppler and Schacht began with a list of around three dozen possible signatories. But they found it an uphill task. Eight of the 'Keppler Circle', headed by Schacht and the Cologne banker Kurt von Schroeder, signed the petition. The results with industrialists were disappointing. A single prominent industrialist, Fritz Thyssen, signed. But he had for long made no secret of his sympathies for the National Socialists. The acting President of the Reichslandbund (Reich Agrarian League), the Nazi-infiltrated lobby of big landowners, was another signatory. The rest were middle-ranking businessmen and landholders. It was misleadingly claimed that leading industrialists Paul Reusch, Fritz Springorum and Albert Vögler sympathized, but had withheld their names from the actual petition. Big business on the whole still placed its hopes in Papen, though the petition was an indication that the business community did not speak with a single voice. The agricultural lobby, in particular, was the one to watch.[87]

In any case, the petition had no bearing on Hindenburg's negotiations with Hitler. The Reich President remained, as the exchanges of mid-November were to show, utterly distrustful of the Nazi leader. Hitler, for his part, was privately contemptuous of Hindenburg.[88] But he had no way of attaining power without the President's backing.

At his meeting with Hitler on 19 November, Hindenburg repeated, as in August, that he wanted to see him and his movement participating in government. The President expressed the hope that Hitler would take soundings with other parties with a view to forming a government with a parliamentary majority. This was calling Hitler's bluff. Hindenburg knew that it would prove impossible, given the certain opposition of the DNVP.[89] The outcome would have been the exposure of Hitler's failure, and a weakening of his position. Hitler saw through the tactic straight away.

In what Goebbels called a 'chessmatch for power',[90] Hitler replied that he had no intention of involving himself in negotiations with other parties before he had been entrusted by the Reich President, in whose hands the decision lay, with constructing a government. In such an eventuality, he was confident of finding a basis which would provide his government with an enabling act, approved by the Reichstag. He alone was in the position to obtain such a mandate from the Reichstag. The difficulties would be thereby solved.[91]

He repeated to Hindenburg in writing two days later his 'single request', that he be given the authority accorded to those before him.[92] This was precisely what Hindenburg adamantly refused to concede. He remained unwilling to make Hitler the head of a presidential cabinet. He left the door open, however, to the possibility of a cabinet with a working majority, led by Hitler, and stipulated his conditions for accepting such a cabinet: establishment of an economic programme, no return to the dualism of Prussia and the Reich, no limiting of Article 48, and approval of a list of ministers in which he, the President, would nominate the foreign and defence ministers.[93] Hitler replied, seeking clarification of the conditions, but still pressing for appointment as Chancellor of a presidential cabinet.[94] Hindenburg's state secretary, Otto Meissner, reiterated the distinction the

President drew between a presidential cabinet, depending on Article 48, standing above parties, and requiring the leadership of a man 'with the special trust of the Reich President', and a parliamentary government resting on a Reichstag majority and following the aims of one or more political parties. Correspondingly, Meissner pointed out, 'a party leader, all the more the leader of a party demanding the exclusivity of his movement, cannot be leader of a presidential cabinet'. He left open the possibility that, as in the case of Brüning, a Hitler-led parliamentary government could evolve into a presidential cabinet. But, it was made clear, only the leadership of a parliamentary majority cabinet was currently on offer to Hitler.[95] Hindenburg's preference remained, plainly, for a presidential cabinet, if possible run by Papen, his favourite, including Hitler in a subordinate role, or at least tolerated by his party. But a presidential cabinet under Hitler's leadership, as in August, was ruled out. Hitler immediately wrote back to Meissner. Goebbels called his letter 'a masterpiece of political strategy'.[96] Hitler pointed to the recent judgement of the constitutional court (*Staatsgerichtshof*) about the powers of the Reich Commissar in Prussia which emphasized that Article 48 was intended to be used only in specific cases and for a limited period of time, not as a general method of government. Where parliamentary procedures hindered government in an emergency situation, the constitutional way, wrote Hitler, was through the deployment of an enabling act, approved by parliament, over a fixed period of time. Only his party had the prospect of obtaining such backing. He also rejected as unconstitutional – since they fell within the powers of the appointed head of government – the conditions imposed by the Reich President. Instead, he proposed his own terms for accepting the Chancellorship. He would put forward a political programme within forty-eight hours. On approval by the President, he would proffer a list of ministers. He would propose in advance Schleicher, known as the President's 'personal *confidant*', as Defence Minister, and Neurath as Foreign Minister. Finally, and the key point, the President would grant him 'those plenipotentiary powers which in such critical and difficult times have never been denied also to parliamentary Reich Chancellors'.[97] By this, Hitler implied the dissolution of the Reichstag and the prescribing of new elections, in the hope of winning the majority he needed to obtain an enabling act without depending on other parties.[98] Once more, Hitler was not kept waiting for an answer.

The Reich President's unyielding views were communicated to him on 24 November, effectively repeating the sentiments Hindenburg had expressed in August: 'that a presidential cabinet led by you would develop necessarily into a party dictatorship with all its consequences for an extraordinary accentuation of the conflicts in the German people'. For that, said the President, he could answer neither before his oath nor to his own conscience.[99] It was his second outright rejection of Hitler within little over three months. It seemed final. Hitler, for his part, remained adamant that he would do nothing to assist the current presidential cabinet.[100] On 30 November he rejected as pointless a further invitation to discussions with Hindenburg.[101] The deadlock continued.

Schleicher had been gradually distancing himself from Papen. He was imperceptibly shifting his role from *eminence grise* behind the scenes to main part. He had helped draft Meissner's letters to Hitler. And with Hindenburg's approval, he had met Hitler on 23 November. Less to the President's liking, he took soundings about whether Hitler might support a Schleicher cabinet. Hitler was unbending.[102] On 1 December Schleicher sent his right-hand man, Lieutenant-Colonel Eugen Ott, to Weimar to hold talks with Hitler. On the surface, this was to make a last attempt to persuade him to participate in government. The hidden agenda was, however, exactly the opposite. Certain of Hitler's response, Schleicher wanted to demonstrate to Hindenburg – and probably to Gregor Strasser – that the Nazi leader had to be left out of the equation. Beyond that, he had hopes of incorporating Gregor Strasser – backed by at least parts of the NSDAP – in his cabinet.[103] Hitler did not disappoint Schleicher. Ott was subjected to a three-hour monologue, denouncing the prospect of a Schleicher cabinet. Knowing word would get back to the army leadership, Hitler also expressed concern at the Reichswehr being dragged into domestic politics.[104] Meanwhile, Schleicher was making sure that lines were kept open to Gregor Strasser, who had played no part in the flurry of correspondence between Hitler and Hindenburg's office, and was thought to be ready 'to step personally into the breach' if nothing came of the discussions with Hitler.[105]

Schleicher threw this possibility into the ring during discussions between himself, Papen, and Hindenburg on the evening of 1 December. Strasser and one or two of his supporters would be offered places in the government. About sixty Nazi Reichstag deputies could be won over. Schleicher was confident of gaining the support of the trade unions, the SPD, and the bourgeois parties for a package of economic reforms and work creation. This, he claimed, would obviate the need for the upturning of the constitution, which Papen had again proposed. Hindenburg nevertheless sided with Papen, and asked him to form a government and resume office – something which had been his intention all along. Behind the scenes, however, Schleicher had been warning members of Papen's cabinet that if there were to be no change of government, and the proposed breaking of the constitution in a state of emergency were to take place, there would be civil war and the army would not be able to cope. This was reinforced at a cabinet meeting the following morning, 2 December, at which Lieutenant-Colonel Ott was brought in to report on a 'war games' exercise which the Reichswehr had conducted, demonstrating that they could not defend the borders and withstand the breakdown of internal order which would follow from strikes and disruption. The army was almost certainly too pessimistic in its judgement. But the message made its mark on the cabinet, and on the President. Hindenburg was afraid of possible civil war. Reluctantly, he let Papen, his favourite, go and appointed Schleicher as Reich Chancellor.[106]

III

In the wake of Schleicher's overtures to Gregor Strasser, Hitler's movement entered upon its greatest crisis since the refoundation of 1925. The affair surrounding the exclusion of Gregor's brother, Otto, in 1930 and the Stennes uprising a year later had occurred with the party riding the crest of a wave. Hitler's authority, as we have seen, was such that it could sweep away the revolts with ease. In the case of Gregor Strasser, it was different. Gregor was no fringe character. His contribution to the growth of the NSDAP had been second only to that of Hitler himself. The organization of the party, in particular, had been largely his work. His reputation inside the party – though he had made powerful enemies, not least his one-time acolyte Goebbels – was high. He was generally seen as Hitler's right-hand man.[107] Some outside the party also regarded him with admiration. Oswald Spengler, for instance, author of the best-selling *Der Untergang des Abendlandes* (*The Decline of the West*), held Hitler in contempt. 'A dreamer (*Phantast*), a numbskull (*Hohlkopf*) . . . a man without idea, without strength of purpose, in a word: stupid', was how he described him. But he liked Strasser, who had 'a sense of reality'.[108] Strasser's resignation of all his party offices on 8 December 1932 naturally, therefore, caused a sensation. Moreover, it hit a party already rocked by falling support and shaky morale. The decline in voter support had again been vividly demonstrated in the first days of December as the results of the Thuringian local elections showed a devastating drop of around 40 per cent since the high-point of the July Reichstag election.[109] Internal reports were commenting with alarm on the numbers leaving the party. Subscriptions to the party press were being cancelled. Unrest within the SA was scarcely containable in some areas. And the party was massively in debt after a year of non-stop electioneering.[110] All in all, the Strasser affair struck a party undergoing a full-scale crisis of confidence. If power were not attained soon, the chances that the party might fall apart altogether could not be discounted.

Bombshell though it was when news broke of Gregor Strasser's resignation of his party offices, trouble had been brewing for some considerable time. Despite his image in the 1920s as a radical spokesman for the NSDAP's populist versions of socialism and anti-capitalism, Strasser had by the early 1930s come to be seen by many in influential positions as something of a 'moderate' in the Nazi Movement.[111] His work in restructuring the party's organization had made him more pragmatic about extending National Socialism's appeal. He had not only masterminded the turn to cultivate the middle classes and peasantry, but had also coordinated the links with other right-wing organizations in the anti-Young Plan campaign.[112] In 1930 he had publicly broken with his brother Otto, whose brand of socialism had led to his secession from the NSDAP. By 1932, he had built up good contacts with some leading Ruhr industrialists, and benefited from their financial subventions.[113] By the autumn of 1932, as Hitler – once seen by sections of business as a 'moderate' – was viewed as an intransigent obstacle to a conservative-dominated right-wing government, Strasser came to be seen as a more responsible and constructive politician who could bring Nazi mass support behind a conservative cabinet.[114] Indeed, by this time Strasser, increasingly influenced by the neo-conservative ideas of Hans Zehrer's *Tat* group, was advocating notions of a broad front on the Right.[115] Now as before, though there were variations of emphasis, Strasser's differences with Hitler were not primarily ideological. Strasser was an out-and-out racist; he did not shy away from violence; his 'social ideas' were hardly less vague than Hitler's own; his economic ideas, eclectic and contradictory, were more utopian than, but still compatible with, Hitler's cruder and more brutal notions;[116] his foreign policy ambitions were no less extensive than Hitler's; and he was ruthless and single-minded in the drive for power. But tactically, there were fundamental differences. And after 13 August, as Hitler's political inflexibility threatened increasingly to block the road to power forever, these differences came more and more to the surface. Strasser, never a complete convert to the Führer myth, continued to take the view that the party which now showed plain signs of potential disintegration was not solely Hitler's creation.[117] In contrast to Hitler's 'all-or-nothing' stance, Strasser thought the NSDAP ought to be prepared to join coalitions, explore all possible alliances, and if necessary enter government even without the offer of the Chancellorship.[118] Immediately following the 13 August setback, Strasser was exhorted by Reventlow and some other supporters to stand out against Hitler; otherwise, they argued, the party leader's hard-line strategy would have catastrophic consequences for the movement.[119]

Through members of the 'Tat Circle', Strasser had been introduced to General Schleicher in the summer of 1932. Schleicher was particularly interested in the possibility that Gregor Strasser could help bring the trade unions behind a 'national' – that is, authoritarian – government. This was something which the 'Tat Circle' had favoured. Unlike Hitler, whose dislike of trade unions had never wavered, Strasser was openly conciliatory towards the unions. Given his growing contacts with union leaders interested in a broad coalition to head off the dangers they saw on the far Right and far Left, the prospects of winning their support for a Schleicher cabinet that had Strasser in the government and offered an expansive work-creation programme could not be lightly dismissed.[120]

During the autumn, the rift between Hitler and Strasser widened. Already in September, Hitler distanced himself from Strasser's economic ideas by dissolving the Political Economy Section (Wirtschaftspolitische Abteilung), which had been run by Otto Wagener, and banning further distribution of the Economic Emergency Programme (Wirtschaftliches Sofortprogramm), both of which Strasser had inspired. Then in October, Hitler had refused to endorse a speech Strasser made to the NSBO which contained pro-unionist sentiments. After the November election, Strasser lost his place in Hitler's inner circle.[121] Privately, he was contemptuous of those he thought decisively influencing Hitler. Göring he thought 'a brutal egoist'; Goebbels was 'from the bottom up devious'; and Röhm simply 'a swine'. Things looked black, he told Hans Frank.[122]

Goebbels, his old enemy since the inner-party conflicts of the mid-twenties, in particular, had repeatedly castigated the 'Strasser clique', and had wasted no opportunity to poison Hitler against the Organization Leader. On 31 August, Goebbels had noted in his diary: 'For the first time [Hitler] speaks openly about the doings of the Strasser clique in the party. Here, too, he has kept his eyes open; and if he has said nothing, then that's not because he had seen nothing.'[123] Four days later, he added: 'I spoke for a long time with the Führer. He distrusts Strasser very strongly.'[124] Already in early September, Hitler had rejected out of hand Strasser's suggestion that the way forward would be to support a Schleicher cabinet. Around the same time, Strasser was the only Nazi leader advising against holding out for Hitler's appointment to the Chancellorship.[125] Goebbels wrote, towards the end of September: 'It would be a blessing if he [Strasser] would carry out his secret sabotage work in the open so that the Führer could act against him.'[126] Given the political sensitivities of the autumn, a public split in the party leadership was scarcely opportune. But by the first week of December, matters could rest no longer.

At a meeting held in secret in Berlin on 3 December, Schleicher offered Strasser the posts of Vice-Chancellor and Minister President in Prussia.[127] The English journalist Sefton Delmer apparently passed on news to Hanfstaengl that the two had met. Hitler gave no outward indication of his feelings when he heard of the meeting.[128] That it had produced the offer of the Vice-Chancellorship to the second man in the party, who had not turned it down, only became clear to Hitler and other leading figures in the party, it seems, when they gathered for discussions in the Kaiserhof two days later. At this meeting, Hitler and Strasser became involved in heated exchanges. According to Goebbels, Strasser pleaded in vain for toleration of the Schleicher cabinet. But those present again approved of Hitler's flat rejection of any compromise whatsoever.[129]

Strasser's choices were now to back Hitler, to rebel against him in the hope of winning over some of the party, or to do what by 8 December he had made up his mind to do: resign his offices and withdraw from an active role in politics. After the meeting on 5 December, Strasser must have realized that the chances of leading a palace revolution against Hitler were minimal. His best support lay among the Nazi Reichstag members. But here, too, he controlled nothing amounting to a firmly organized faction. Pride, as well as his principled objections, prevented him from backing down and accepting Hitler's all-or-bust strategy. He was left, therefore, with only the third possibility. Perhaps disappointed at the lack of open support from his party friends, he withdrew to his room in Berlin's Hotel Exzelsior and wrote out his letter resigning his party offices.[130]

On the morning of 8 December, he summoned those Regional Inspectors (Landesinspekteure) of the party – the senior Gauleiter – who happened to be in Berlin to his office in the Reichstag. Six were present besides Reich Inspector Robert Ley – Goebbels, not surprisingly, was missing – when Strasser addressed them. According to the post-war account of one of them, Hinrich Lohse, Strasser told them he had written the Führer a letter, resigning his party offices. He did not criticize Hitler's programme, but rather his lack of any clear policy towards attaining power since the meeting with

Hindenburg in August. Hitler was clear, he said, about one thing only: he wanted to become Reich Chancellor. But just wanting the post was not going to overcome the opposition he had encountered. And meanwhile the party was under great strain and exposed to potential disintegration. Strasser said he was prepared to go along with either the legal or the illegal – that is, putschist – way to power. But what he was not prepared to do was simply wait for Hitler to be made Reich Chancellor and see the party fall apart before that happened. Hitler, in his view, should have accepted the Vice-Chancellorship in August, and used that position as a bargaining counter to build up further power. On a personal note, Strasser expressed his pique at being excluded from top-level deliberations, and had no wish to play second fiddle to Göring, Goebbels, Röhm, and others. Now at the end of his tether, he was resigning his offices and leaving to recuperate.[131]

Strasser's letter was delivered to Hitler in the Kaiserhof at midday on 8 December.[132] It amounted to a feeble justification of Strasser's position, couched in terms of wounded pride, and not touching on the fundamentals that separated him from Hitler. It had the ring of defeat in the very way it was formulated.[133] Hitler had been forewarned by Gauleiter Bernhard Rust, who had attended the meeting called by Strasser, to expect the letter. He had immediately summoned the same group of party Inspectors whom Strasser had addressed to the Kaiserhof for a meeting at noon.[134] The group, in dejected mood, were left standing in Hitler's apartment while, in an agitated state, he provided a point-by-point counter to Strasser's reasons for his resignation, as summarized by Robert Ley from the earlier meeting. Entering the Papen cabinet, he said, would have given the initiative to the party's enemies. He would soon have been forced, through fundamental disagreement with Papen's policies, into resignation. The effect on public opinion would have been the apparent demonstration of his incapacity for government – that which his enemies had always claimed. The electorate would have turned their backs on him. The movement would have collapsed. The illegal route was even more dangerous. It would simply have meant – the lessons of 1923 plainly recalled – standing 'the prime of the nation's manhood' (das beste Mannestum der Nation) in front of the machine-guns of the police and army. As for overlooking Strasser, Hitler disingenuously claimed he entered into discussions with whomsoever was necessary for a particular purpose, distributed tasks according to specific circumstances, and – according to availability – was open to all. He shifted the blame back on Gregor Strasser for avoiding him.

His address went on for the best part of two hours. Towards the end, the well-worn tactic was deployed once more: he made a personal appeal to loyalty. According to Lohse's account, he became 'quieter and more human, more friendly and appealing in his comments'. He had found

that comradely tone which those assembled knew and which completely convinced them. Now he was their friend, their comrade, their leader who had visibly for each one again freed the way out of the completely muddled situation which Strasser had presented, convincing them emotionally and intellectually. As he spoke, Strasser sank with his dark prophecy ever more into a shadowy distance, although those present in consideration and under the impact of what he had said had come with considerable reservations . . . Increasingly persuasive to his audience and inexorably drawing them under his spell, he [Hitler] triumphed and proved to his wavering, but upright and indispensable fighters in this toughest test of the movement, that he was the master and Strasser the journeyman . . . So he had remained the outright victor also in this last and most serious attack, directed at the substance of the movement from within its own ranks . . . The old bond with him was again sealed by those present with a handshake.[135]

The mood that evening at Goebbels's house, where Hitler returned, was nevertheless still sombre. There was real concern that the movement would fall apart. If that were to happen, announced Hitler, 'I'll finish things in three minutes.'[136] Dramatic gestures soon gave way to concerted moves to counter the possible ramifications of the 'treachery'. Goebbels was summoned the same night at 2a.m. to a meeting in the Kaiserhof, where he found Röhm and Himmler already with Hitler. Hitler, still stunned by Strasser's action, spent the time pacing the floor of his hotel-room. The meeting lasted until dawn. The main outcome was the decision to dismantle the organizational framework that Strasser had erected, and which had given him his power-base in the party.[137] In time-honoured fashion, as he had taken over the SA leadership following the Stennes affair, Hitler himself now formally took over the leadership of the political organization, with Robert Ley as his chief of staff.[138] A new Political Central Commission was set up, under Rudolf Heß, and the two Reich Inspectorates created by Strasser were abolished.[139] A number of known Strasser supporters were removed from their posts.[140] And a major campaign was begun, eliciting countless declarations of loyalty to Hitler from all parts of Germany – also from Strasser sympathizers.[141] Strasser was rapidly turned into the movement's arch-traitor. Hitler began the appeals to loyalty the very next day, 9 December, when he addressed the Gauleiter, Regional Inspectors, and Reichstag deputies. According to the report in the *Völkischer*

Beobachter, every single person present felt the need to offer a personal show of loyalty by shaking hands with the Führer.[142] 'Strasser is isolated. Dead man!' noted Goebbels triumphantly.[143] Soon afterwards, Hitler set off on a speaking tour, addressing party members and functionaries at seven meetings in nine days.[144] Again and again the personal appeal was successful. No secession followed Strasser's resignation. The crisis was past.

Following the shock announcement of his resignation, Gregor Strasser had immediately left for holiday in Italy. His resignation and departure sounded the death-knell for Schleicher's political hopes. Belated discussions in early January between a dispirited Strasser and a Chancellor whose star was evidently on the wane were a mere empty postscript to the December drama.[145] On 16 January, following the revival of the party's fortunes (after a massive propaganda input) the previous day in the state elections of the dwarf-state Lippe-Detmold, Hitler delivered a three-hour verbal assault on Strasser to his assembled Gauleiter at a meeting in Weimar.[146] 'His shares are no longer sought after. A short performance on the stage of significance. Now he sinks again into the void from which he came,' was Goebbels's – stylistically embellished – dismissal of Gregor Strasser in his diary entry.[147] Strasser now retired fully from all political activity and from public view. He was not excluded from the party. In fact, early in 1934 he applied for, and was granted, the NSDAP's badge of honour, awarded to him as party member No.9, dating from the refoundation of the party on 25 February 1925.[148] Neither this nor a plaintive letter he wrote to Rudolf Heß on 18 June 1934 emphasizing his lengthy service and continuing loyalty to the party could save his skin.[149] Hitler was unforgiving to those he felt had betrayed him. His final reckoning with Gregor Strasser came on 30 June 1934, when the former second man in the party was murdered in what came to be known as 'the Night of the Long Knives'.

Had Gregor Strasser succeeded in splitting the party, bringing one part of it behind the Schleicher government, and joining the cabinet himself, the chances are that a Hitler takeover of power would never have occurred. History would have taken a different course. But in fact Strasser never even seriously attempted to create a party rebellion.[150] He turned his protest into a personal one by the nature of his resignation. As a consequence, it was all the easier to isolate him as Hitler and Goebbels orchestrated their recovery. And since his resignation, and the way it was carried out, fully undermined Schleicher's plans and left the Chancellor increasingly exposed, it paradoxically cleared the path, which had appeared – also to Strasser – blocked, to a Hitler Chancellorship.[151]

Ultimately, the Strasser affair – the most serious of the inner-party crises since 1925 – revealed once again most graphically just how strong Hitler's hold over the party had become, how much the NSDAP had become a 'leader party'. The implications of this for the character of the party on the eve of its becoming the state party of the Third Reich were illustrated in Hitler's guidelines for the organization of the party after Strasser's departure. Hitler's memorandum of 15 December 1932 'on the inner reasons for the instructions to produce a heightened fighting power (*Schlagkraft*) of the Movement' demonstrates plainly the key differences between his conception of the party and that of Strasser.[152]

'The basis of the political organization is loyalty. In it is revealed as the most noble expression of emotion (*Gefühlsausdruck*) the recognition of the necessity of obedience as the premiss for the construction of every human community. Loyalty in obedience can never be replaced by formal technical measures and institutions, of whatever sort. The aim of the political organization is the enabling of the widest possible dissemination of the knowledge seen as necessary for the maintenance of the life of the nation as well as the will that serves it. The final aim is thereby the mobilization (*Erfassung*) of the nation for this idea. The victory of the National Socialist idea is the goal of our struggle, the organization of our party a means to attaining this goal.' Such ethereal language emphasizes how remote Hitler's conception of the party was from any notion of a bureaucratic organization. Ideal, though in practice impossible, he went on, would be to do without organization altogether. As it was, organization should be kept to a minimum since 'a world-view (*Weltanschauung*) needs for its dissemination not civil servants but fanatical apostles'. In preparing for the time when it would be able to permeate the state with this world-view, it was important to remember that the state too offered no end in itself, but was merely 'an institution that had to serve the maintenance and continuation of the life of a people'. The 'supreme and most sublime mission' of the party was, therefore, to provide for the expansion of the 'idea'. To do this, it had continually to return to its 'greatest and first task: propaganda'. Leaders were not to be imposed from above, because of their administrative competence, but to emerge from below, through their talents and achievements on behalf of the movement's struggle. There would be inevitable difficulties in working together between individual leaders of different temperament and ability. But this must be taken on board. The key issue was 'that the essentials of unconditional party discipline should not be affected by this'. The party was engaged in 'the hardest ideological struggle'. Hence, Hitler underlined once more, 'all its institutions have somehow to serve the propaganda of ideas'.[153]

For Hitler, the organization of the party, his memorandum makes clear, had no meaning in itself. It was there solely to serve the ends of propaganda, as a means to obtaining power.[154] Propaganda and mobilization remained for Hitler the purpose of the party. Where Strasser had worked, conventionally enough, towards a bureaucratic structuring of the party, mirroring in essence the administrative framework of the state, Hitler intentionally destroyed any inherent bureaucratic rationality in favour of an instrument devoted solely to propaganda, to upholding the 'idea' of National Socialism as embodied in the Leader. The intrinsic contradiction between 'leadership of people' (*Menschenführung*) and 'administration' (*Verwaltung*), which would be laid bare during the Third Reich, was, his memorandum plainly shows, inherent to Hitler's conception of the party and approach to power. The untrammelled personalized form of power that he represented could not dispense with bureaucratic organization, but was nevertheless inimical to it. As long as the party existed only to attain power, the contradiction could be sustained. In government, it was a recipe for chaos.

IV

The mass of the German people had no part in, or knowledge of, the intrigues of high politics in the second half of 1932. They were by now largely powerless to affect the political dramas which would determine their future. As autumn turned to winter, they were entering upon the fourth year of deepening misery in the apparently unending Depression.

Statistics provide only an abstract glimmer of the human suffering. Industrial production had fallen by 42 per cent since 1929. The stocks and shares index had dropped by more than two-thirds. In the hard-hit agrarian sector, which had felt crisis long before the general Depression had caught hold, compulsory farm-sales had more than doubled. Falling demand, prices, and income had brought mounting indebtedness.[155] Above all, the dark shadow of mass unemployment on an unprecedented scale hung over the country. The Employment Offices recorded 5,772,984 persons without work at the end of 1932; in January 1933 the figure was 6,013,612. Taking into account short-time workers and hidden unemployment, it was reckoned that the real total already in October 1932 had reached 8,754,000.[156] This meant that close on half of the work-force was either fully or partially unemployed.[157] Towns offered free meals at soup kitchens, cheap or free warm baths for the unemployed, and warming-houses where they could shelter in winter.[158]

The politically radicalized among the unemployed had fed mainly the ranks of the KPD – *par excellence* the party of the young, unemployed males – the overwhelming proportion of whose 320–360,000 members by late 1932 had no work.[159] Not a few also found their way to the Nazi stormtroopers.[160] Both the Communists and the Nazis offered an organizational framework of support, forms of political activism, and the vision of a better society to the young unemployed.[161] But alongside the unemployed who became radicalized, a great number were simply resigned and apathetic, imagining that all governments had failed and none was capable of mastering the problems which had brought about their fate. A few days before Hitler's appointment to the Chancellorship, in conditions of freezing cold, the people of the small town of Ettlingen in Baden could not engender the slightest interest in an SA parade. There had been no shortage of demonstrations, they said. 'If only we had as much bread and work.'[162]

Nor could a younger generation whose 'working lives' had been entirely without work find much enthusiasm for a self-professed working-class party, the SPD, which had – however necessary it had objectively been – kept Brüning in office and voted Hindenburg back into power. Not a few would shrug their shoulders several years later and say that at least Hitler had brought them work, which the working-class parties before 1933 had failed to do. It was abbreviated logic. But it was how many felt.

Mass unemployment split and atomized the working class not just at the party-political and ideological level, but at its social roots.[163] For those still fortunate enough to have work, self-confidence was eaten away by fear of losing their jobs, by the loss of the power of the unions, exposure to employer aggressiveness, and – so far as they were sympathizers of the Social Democrats – by the SPD's perceived failure to look after working-class interests. The disorientation and disillusionment of so many former SPD supporters after 1933, however little they were won over by the Nazi regime, stemmed from what they saw as its unmitigated failure in the crisis of the state of which it was the main pillar.

In the countryside, too, there was a widespread feeling of hopelessness.[164] Apathy sprang from the sense that there was no sign of improvement, whoever was in government. The mood of deep resignation had spread in areas of bedrock Nazi support in autumn 1932 after Hitler had turned down the chance of entering government and the NSDAP's promises were no nearer to realization.[165] From one district of Franconia, where the NSDAP had built up a high level of support, it was reported in the first days of

January 1933 that 'the mood of the rural population is calm but extraordinarily depressed on account of the continued fall in prices of all agricultural products. A certain despondency has taken over. One gains the impression that many of those who had previously put their hopes in Hitler have become sceptical and have lost hope in any improvement.' The sentiments, the report claimed, were general ones, not confined to that district.[166]

The disconsolate mood intermingled with enormous bitterness and political radicalization. From Lower Bavaria in January 1933 it was reported that 'all attacks on the government find a lively echo among the peasants; the more caustic the language, the more pleasant it sounds in their ears'.[167] The anger was further fired up by news that 'Eastern Aid' (*Osthilfe*), intended for restoring agricultural prosperity on impoverished properties in eastern Germany, was lining the pockets of big landowners and being used for luxury expenditure.[168] Bitterness towards all Weimar governments and parties, each of which was seen to have failed the people, was a hallmark of popular feeling in the countryside as it was in the towns. 'No one wants to know anything of a parliamentary government, since all large parties had failed' was the reported mood in one Bavarian region in December 1932 – a feeling certainly not confined to that part of the country. The Nazi Party was not excluded from such criticism. 'The party leaders are blamed for being led in their decisions less by considerations of people and Fatherland than by those of the party and themselves. It is especially held against the NSDAP that it has recently shunned responsibility and does not follow its wide-ranging promises with action.' No expectations were placed in Hitler in this region. 'Apart from National Socialists,' the report went on, at this point reflecting the weighting of a heavily Catholic region, 'more or less all the remaining sections of society are negatively disposed towards a Hitler dictatorship.' It concluded: 'Under the impact of economic distress and the disunity of the other parties, the KPD is flourishing.'[169] At the same time, the despair was such that *any* political leader outside the ranks of the dreaded Marxists who could bring about economic improvement was guaranteed – at least in the short term – to attract support. This was to Hitler's advantage once he became Chancellor. The feeling that Hitler should at least be given the chance to see what he could do coexisted with initial scepticism.[170]

For other social groups, too, the expectations placed in Hitler's movement and the motivations that underpinned their subsequent support or antipathy were strongly influenced by experiences in the Depression years. The way society and government had fallen apart in those years brought to the boil the welling resentment at the democratic system and sense of national humiliation that had been simmering throughout the Weimar era. The depth of anger towards those held responsible was one side of the response. The desire for social harmony and unity – to be imposed by the elimination of those seen to threaten it – was the other, and intrinsically related, side.[171]

The report from one locality in Franconia in December 1932 brought out how sectionalized grievances combined to create generalized disaffection. Businessmen were complaining about poor turnover, ran the report, farmers about low produce prices, teachers and civil servants about their salaries, workers about unemployment, the unemployed about levels of support, and war-cripples and war-widows about drops in their pensions. All in all, there was 'general discontent, the best preparation (*Wegbereiter*) for Communism'.[172]

Middle-class disaffection was, naturally enough, fragmented along the lines of sectional interest. The outlook remained bleak. But despite some drop in confidence in Hitler in autumn 1932 from groups which had been a backbone of his support, no political alternatives were on offer on the Right which appeared capable of creating the conditions of national renewal and imposed social harmony needed for economic recovery. For businessmen, craftsmen and small-scale producers, the Nazis held out the prospect of salvation from the economic threat posed by department stores, consumer associations, mail-order firms and mass-production. Authoritarian rule was far from an unattractive proposition. Part of its illusion was an implied return to the 'good old days' before the First World War and protection of the 'little man' from the incursions of the modern, interventionist state.[173] Civil servants, smarting under Brüning's salary cuts, had their own illusions of a state which would restore their own traditional status – and financial position. Teachers and lawyers also looked to renewed authority once the shackles of democratic 'interference' had been removed, and to enhanced status. Doctors, too, like lawyers a social group traditionally sympathetic to the nationalist Right, had their resentment at diminished career prospects, falling earnings, and a 'leftist' imposed funding system greatly amplified during the Depression years.[174] Many looked to a new, authoritarian regime for rescue.

For young people, the Depression years had both in material and in psychological terms been appallingly damaging. Hopes and ideals had been blighted almost before they could take shape. By the end of 1932, four consecutive cohorts of pupils had left school to miserable prospects. Those lucky enough to find work had done so in deteriorating conditions, and were usually dismissed at the end of their apprenticeships. The youth welfare system was close to collapse. Growing suicide and youth criminality rates told their own tale. Those from more well-to-do backgrounds faced greatly diminished chances of launching a career in the professions to match their ambitions. Above average support for the Nazis among university students was one indication of middle-class youth's alienation from the Weimar Republic. In fact, the attractiveness of extremist parties of Right and Left – the NSDAP and the KPD – to young people is an indication of their different forms of alienation from Weimar democracy and their readiness to resort to political radicalism. In many respects, it was a generational revolt against a system and a society that had failed them. Militant parties capable of playing to utopian expectations could fill the void produced by the alienation. Young Germans in late 1932 were still split largely along party-political lines which themselves reflected in the main class and religious divisions. The socialist, Catholic, and – taken together – the collectivity of bourgeois youth organizations still dwarfed the Hitler Youth. But the overlap of ideals and ideology with the bourgeois youth organizations, especially, offered a rich potential for expansion to the Nazi youth leader, Baldur von Schirach, should his party start to recover from its setbacks of autumn 1932, and should his Leader manage to get to power soon.[175]

The disaffection in German society did not, it seems, divide on gender lines. The Depression heightened the discrimination against women in the jobs market that had existed throughout the Weimar Republic. Traditional prejudice that a woman's role should be confined to 'children, kitchen, and church' was strongly reinforced. The witchhunt against 'double-earners' – where both husband and wife worked and the woman was regarded as unnecessarily occupying a 'man's job' – was an indication of growing intolerance.[176] Nazi propaganda had no difficulty in playing on such intolerance, both before and after 1933. But anti-feminism was by no means confined to Hitler's Movement. Despite its 'macho' image, the NSDAP's views on the role of women were essentially shared by all conservative and denominational parties. Women's political behaviour in the Depression was little influenced by anti-feminism or, conversely, by pro-feminist issues. Women voted, it appears, much like men did, and presumably for the same reasons. They voted in disproportionately large numbers for the conservative and Christian parties, which were anti-feminist. They voted in smaller numbers than men for the radical parties of both Left and Right. The party with the most pronounced emancipatory stance regarding women, the KPD, was the least successful of all in attracting women's votes, and was as male-dominated a party as was the NSDAP. Despite all the talk of Hitler's mesmerizing attraction for women, the elderly, statesmanlike Hindenburg, not the dynamic Nazi leader, had been their choice in the presidential elections earlier in 1932. But by the November Reichstag election, the gap between female and male voting support for the NSDAP had narrowed almost to vanishing-point. Women were just about as likely as men to find the prospect of a Hitler dictatorship an attractive one. The mentalities which Nazism could build upon and exploit crossed the gender divide.

Despite the disappointment in Hitler and decline in support for the NSDAP in the autumn of 1932, such mentalities, which would benefit the Nazi regime once Hitler had taken power, were kept alive and given sustenance by the bruising years of the Depression. Though two-thirds of the people had not voted for Hitler, many were less than root-and-branch opposed to all that Nazism stood for, and could fairly easily be brought in the coming months to find *some* things in the Third Reich that they might approve of. The loathing and deep fear of Communism that ran through some four-fifths of society was one important common denominator. Faced with a stark choice between National Socialism and Communism – which was how Hitler was increasingly able to portray it after his takeover of power – most middle-class and well-to-do Germans, and even a considerable leaven of the working class, preferred the Nazis. The Communists were revolutionaries, they would take away private property, impose a class dictatorship, and rule in the interests of Moscow. The National Socialists were vulgar and distasteful, but they stood for German interests, they would uphold German values, and they would *not* take away private property. Crudely put, this reflected a widespread train of thought, not least in the middle classes.

Fear, bitterness, and radicalization were part of a climate of political violence. These tensions of the Depression years had made political violence an everyday occurrence, even in the sleepiest of places.[177] People became used to it. If it was targeted at the 'Reds' they often approved of it – even 'respectable' sections of society which decried the breakdown of 'order' in public life. Paradoxically, the party responsible for much of the mayhem, the NSDAP, could benefit by portraying itself – enhanced by the image of serried ranks of marching stormtroopers – as the only party capable of ending the violence by imposing order in the national interest. The acceptance of a level of outright violence in public life, which had been there at the birth and in the early years of the Weimar Republic and again become pronounced in the Depression years, helped to pave the way for the readiness to accept Nazi terror in the aftermath of the 'seizure of power'.[178]

Along with this went a vindictiveness that the deprivations and tensions of the Depression years had promoted. Someone had to be blamed for the misery. Scapegoats were needed. Enemies were targeted. Political enemies were lined up for scores to be settled. Personal and political enmities often went hand in hand. If the anonymity of the big city could offer some protection, that was not the case in small towns and in villages. Here there was no hiding-place. Once the power of the state could be used to support violence, not contain it, there would be no shortage of those volunteering to participate in the bloodletting. For countless others, the social and political conflicts of the Depression years stored up personal grudges that would be paid back after 1933 through denunciation for real or fictional political 'offences'.

As regards scapegoats, the Jews were an easy target. Nazi diabolization of Jews enabled them to be portrayed as both the representatives of rapacious big capital and of pernicious and brutal Bolshevism. Most Germans did not go along with such crude images. Nor were they likely to become involved in, or approve of, physical violence directed at individual Jews and their property. But dislike of Jews extended far beyond Nazi sympathizers. No political party, pressure-group, or trade union, and neither main Christian denomination, made the defence of the Jewish minority an issue. And, when times were hard, it was simple enough to stir envy and resentment against a tiny minority of the population – 0.76 per cent in 1933 belonged to the Jewish faith – by stressing how they dominated out of all proportion to their numbers sections of business, the arts, and the professions.[179] It was no coincidence, for instance, that one of the most viciously antisemitic Nazi sub-organizations was the Fighting League of the Commercial Middle Class (Kampfbund des gewerblichen Mittelstandes), where small traders campaigned against department stores that they claimed to be largely in Jewish hands. Most people during the Depression years, as we have already commented, did not vote for the NSDAP, or even join the party, primarily *because* of its antisemitism. But the widespread latent antisemitism in Weimar Germany – the feeling that Jews were somehow different, 'un-German', and a harmful influence – did not provide any deterrent to people offering their enthusiastic support to Hitler's movement in full cognizance of its hatred of Jews. And since that hatred *was* central to the ethos of a Movement which was massively expanding its membership in the early 1930s – by the end of 1932 its membership numbers had reached 1,414,975[180] – more and more people were becoming exposed, once in the Movement, to the full brutality and viciousness of Nazi antisemitism. The same applied to the SA, by this time numbering around 400,000 stormtroopers.[181] Even many of the young thugs who had been attracted to it in increasing numbers were not outrightly antisemitic before they joined.[182] But once members, they were part of an organization whose 'Fighting Song' contained the lines: 'When Jews' blood spurts from the knife, good times are once more here.'[183]

The half-a-million-strong Jewish community – the vast majority patriotic, liberal-minded Germans, anxious to be assimilated into, not separated from, their fellow countrymen – was divided in its reactions to the upsurge of antisemitism. The main Jewish organization, the Centralverein – the 'Central Association of German Citizens of Jewish Faith' – took the danger very seriously, and put up a sturdy defence of Nazi inroads into civil rights.[184] Others were more complacent – a feeling they often combined with a sense of helplessness. They thought the danger would blow over. Few had direct experience of racist attacks – something Jews themselves associated with Russia, Poland or Rumania, not with Germany. It was possible to accept some discrimination, avoid threatening situations, and generally keep out of trouble.[185] It was still possible to feel 'at home' in Germany.[186] It was still possible on the very last day of 1932, as Lion Feuchtwanger's fictional characters in *Geschwister Oppermann* did, to joke about whether 'the Führer' would end up as a market salesman or an insurance agent.[187]

Three years of crippling Depression had left Germany a more intolerant society. A sign that the humane principles on which the Republic had been based were being whittled away during the Depression, as German society lurched towards the Right, was the reintroduction of the death penalty in the early 1930s. A few years earlier it had seemed close to abolition. The Nazis were to make it the pivot of their proclaimed restoration of 'order'.[188] Another indicator of a changing climate in which liberal values were being rapidly eroded was the radicalization of medical views on eugenics and 'racial hygiene'. The costs of keeping mental patients in asylums at a time of drastic cuts in public expenditure brought increased pressure for legislation to introduce the voluntary sterilization of those with hereditary defects. Growing support for such measures among doctors, psychiatrists, lawyers, and civil servants led to draft proposals, supported by the German Doctors' Association, for a Reich Sterilization Law. Württemberg and Prussian Chambers of Doctors underlined their backing for such legislation in November and December 1932.[189] Hitler's party, with a third of the voters behind it, went further and advocated *compulsory* sterilization of the hereditarily sick. In 1933, the Nazis wasted little time after coming to power in introducing notorious legislation to this effect. But the ground had been prepared by the 'experts' before Hitler took office.

At the end of 1932, images of Hitler continued to reflect, as they always had done, the main ideological divides and sub-cultures of German society.[190] For the Socialist and Communist Left – with only minor differences between them in this regard – Hitler was portrayed as the hireling of big capitalism, the front-man for imperialists, the political strike-force of the enemies of the working class. Such views were to persist after 1933 in the left-wing underground resistance organizations, the underestimation of Hitler they contained hindering clear perceptions of the ideological dynamism of Nazism. For Catholics – the other sub-culture which Nazism found greatest difficulty in penetrating, before and after 1933 – Hitler was above all seen as the head of a 'godless', anti-Christian movement. In Protestant church-going circles, impressions of Hitler varied. Some looked to the dangers of a neo-heathen movement which had roused the base instincts of the masses. Others saw the potential, at a time when church attendance was dwindling and moral and religious values were allegedly being undermined, of Hitler's 'national renewal' bringing in its wake ethical and religious revival. On the nationalist-conservative Right, the relatively sympathetic treatment of Hitler at the time of the Young Plan Campaign had given way to hostility. Hitler was portrayed for the most part as intransigent and irresponsible, a wild and vulgar demagogue, not a statesman, an obstacle to political recovery, the head of an extremist movement with menacing socialistic tendencies. Against these negative images had to be set the adulation of the third of the population that, despite the setbacks of summer and autumn, still saw in Hitler the only hope for Germany's future. More than 13.5 million had voted for Hitler in the July election. They were all potential or real devotees of the Führer cult. Despite the losses in November, it still amounted to a huge reservoir of support, its focal point personalized in the extraordinary Leader of the NSDAP. And if Hitler could once get to power, and achieve some success, then there was the distinct chance that the strands of an ideological consensus rooted in strident anti-Marxism, hostility to party politics and pluralist democracy, and yearning for a restoration of national pride under authoritarian leadership, might come together to widen the basis of his support. The key would be whether he could shed the divisive image of a party leader, and appear to stand above party, for the nation. In January 1933, two-thirds of the German population were still dismissive of such a notion.

V

The events of January 1933 amounted to an extraordinary political drama. It was a drama that unfolded largely out of sight of the German people.

A fortnight after Schleicher had taken over from him as Reich Chancellor, Franz von Papen had been guest of honour at a dinner at the Berlin Herren-klub. Among the 300 or so guests listening to his speech on 16 December, justifying his own record in government, criticizing the Schleicher cabinet, and indicating that he thought the NSDAP should be included in government, was the Cologne banker Baron Kurt von Schröder. A few weeks earlier, Schröder had been a signatory to the petition to Hindenburg to make Hitler Chancellor. For months before that he had been a Nazi sympathizer, and was a member of the 'Keppler Circle' – the group of economic advisers that Wilhelm Keppler, a one-time small businessman, had set up on Hitler's behalf. Already in November – though nothing came of it at the time – Keppler had told Schröder that Papen might be prepared to intercede with Hindenburg in favour of a Hitler Chancellorship. Now, after Papen's Herrenklub speech, interested by what the former Chancellor had had to say, Schröder met him for a few minutes late in the evening to discuss the political situation. The two had known each other for some time. And since Schröder also knew Hitler, he was the ideal intermediary at a time that relations between the Nazi leader and the former Chancellor were still icy. Out of the discussion came the suggestion, probably from Schröder though it is impossible to be sure, of a meeting between Hitler and Papen. Just before the end of December, Schröder rang Papen to ask whether he were free for a meeting during the next few days. The meeting was fixed to take place at Schröder's house in Cologne on 4 January 1933. Since Papen was travelling to Berlin from his home in the Saar that day, intending to stop off at his mother's house in Düsseldorf, and since Hitler would be in the vicinity *en route* to begin the election campaign in Lippe-Detmold that evening, the venue was chosen because of its mutual convenience, though Keppler had, in fact, already suggested Schröder's house to Hitler as a meeting-place following the banker's discussion with Papen on 16 December.[191]

In his own post-war account of the meeting, Schröder indicated that he had already taken soundings among figures from the business community about collaboration in government between Papen and Hitler, and found them favourably disposed. Fear of Bolshevism, the hope that National

Socialism in power would provide a stable political climate for economic recovery, and removal of constraints on business autonomy were what they wanted. They hoped that 'a strong leader' would come to power and form a government that would remain for a long time in office.[192] Schröder's soundings had, in fact, extended no further than the Keppler Circle – the limited number of businessmen whose sympathies for Hitler had not been in doubt. He had not consulted leading industrialists, either individually or through the main industrialists' organization, the Reichsverband der deutschen Industrie (Reich Association of German Industry). The view, long taken for granted, that Schröder was acting as an agent of big business is without substance. Schröder did not know the leading figures in the business world, and they, for their part, had no idea of his attempts to bring Papen and Hitler together.[193] Big business was, in fact, divided in its opinion of the Schleicher government. Its early fears of the 'Red General', regarded by business leaders as a crypto-socialist, had not materialized. Relations with National Socialism were in the meantime poor.[194] For major figures in industry, Papen was still their man. His return to the Chancellor's seat, with Hitler in a subordinate role to bring the NSDAP behind the government, remained their favoured scenario.[195] As January progressed, it would prove to be the big landowners, through their lobbying organization the Reichslandbund (Reich Agrarian League), rather than the 'captains of industry', who emerged as the mortal enemies of the Schleicher cabinet and the leading proponents of an elevation of Hitler to the Chancellorship.[196]

Papen later disingenuously claimed that his aim was to try to persuade Hitler to join the Schleicher government.[197] His actual aim was to take first soundings about the prospects of collaborating with Hitler in a new cabinet. Papen, whatever his later altruistic claims, was smarting from his ousting by Schleicher. Hitler knew that if anyone could unlock the door to Hindenburg's approval, it was Papen.[198]

Papen arrived around midday at Schröder's house. The meeting was meant to be secret, but word of it had leaked out. As he stepped out of his taxi, Papen was photographed. The following day, the *Tägliche Rundschau*, the *Tat* Circle's newspaper, reported that the meeting revolved around considerations of bringing about a Hitler government through using Papen's good offices with the Reich President. Papen and Hitler were both forced to deny that anything was discussed beyond 'the possibility of a great national political unity front'.[199] Papen found Hitler – who had entered through the back door – together with Hess, Himmler and Keppler, waiting for him. Hitler, Papen and Schröder adjourned to another room, while the

others waited. Schröder took no part in the discussions.[200] Hitler began
aggressively, with an attack on Papen's treatment of him on 13 August and
a denunciation of the sentences on the Potempa murderers. When he calmed
down, talk revolved around the format for a new government. Hitler
reportedly spoke of involvement of Papen's supporters in a cabinet under
his leadership, as long as they were prepared to accept the removal of
Social Democrats, Communists and Jews from 'leading positions', and the
'restoration of order in public life'.[201] But for the first time, in the course of
the discussions, Hitler seems to have hinted that he might accept less than
the Chancellorship – at least for a while. A few days later he told Goebbels
that Papen was keen to bring Schleicher down, and had the ear of the
President: 'Arrangement with us prepared. Either the Chancellorship or
power ministries. Defence and Interior. That's still to be heard about.'[202]
Probably, Papen had reminded him – if he needed reminding – that Hindenburg's objections to him becoming Chancellor would still be difficult to
overcome. Most likely, the question of who was to lead the new government
was left open at the meeting. Papen spoke loosely of some sort of duumvirate,
and left open the possibility of ministerial posts, even if Hitler himself did
not feel ready to take office, for some of his colleagues. After about two
hours, discussions ended for lunch with an agreement to deal with further
issues at a subsequent meeting, in Berlin or elsewhere. Papen evidently felt
progress had been made. A few days later, reporting on the meeting to
industrialists, he gave the impression that Hitler was prepared to play the
role of a 'junior partner' in a cabinet dominated by conservatives.[203] In
discussion with Chancellor Schleicher on 9 January, Papen inferred that the
Nazi leader would be satisfied with the Defence and Interior Ministries.
The implication was that the talks with Hitler had been about incorporating
him in a Schleicher cabinet, not toppling it. And in a private audience with
the Reich President the same day, Papen informed Hindenburg that Hitler
had lessened his demands and would be prepared to take part in a coalition
government with parties of the Right. The unspoken assumption was that
Papen would lead such a government. The Reich President told Papen to
keep in touch with the Nazi leader.[204]

A second meeting between Hitler and Papen soon followed. It took place
this time in the study of Ribbentrop's house in Dahlem, a plush residential
suburb of Berlin, on the night of 10–11 January. Nothing came of it, since
Papen told Hitler that Hindenburg still opposed his appointment to the
Chancellorship. Hitler angrily broke off further talks until after the Lippe
election.[205]

Elections in the mini-state of Lippe-Detmold, with its 173,000 inhabitants,[206] would at other times scarcely have been a first priority for Hitler and his party. But now they were a chance to prove the NSDAP was again on the forward march after its losses the previous November and after the Strasser crisis. Despite the poor state of the party's finances, no effort was spared towards obtaining a good result in Lippe.[207] For close on a fortnight before the election, on 15 January, Lippe was saturated with Nazi propaganda. All the Nazi big guns were fired. Göring, Goebbels, Frick, and Prince Auwi spoke.[208] Hitler himself gave seventeen speeches in eleven days.[209] It paid off. The NSDAP won almost 6,000 more votes compared with the November result, and increased its share of the poll from 34.7 to 39.5 per cent. The Nazis presumably won back most of the voters they had lost to the DNVP, whose support now dropped by over 3,000. The Communists also lost over 3,000 votes, while the SPD gained over 4,000. In reality, the Nazi success was less impressive than portrayed. Their support in the region still lagged by some 3,000 votes behind the result the party had obtained in the July Reichstag election.[210] This was naturally overlooked. The optical impression was what counted. The bandwagon seemed to be rolling again.[211]

Hitler's position was strengthened, however, less by the Lippe result than by Schleicher's increasing isolation. Not only had his lingering hopes of Gregor Strasser and gaining support from the Nazi ranks practically evaporated by mid-January.[212] The Reichslandbund had by then declared open warfare on his government because of its unwillingness to impose high import levies on agricultural produce. Schleicher was powerless to do anything about such opposition, which had backing not only within the DNVP but also within the NSDAP. Accommodation with the big agrarians would axiomatically have meant opposition both from both sides of industry, bosses and unions, together with consumers. Hugenberg's offers to bring the DNVP behind Schleicher if he were to be given the combined ministries of Economics and Food were therefore bound to fall on deaf ears. Correspondingly, by 21 January, the DNVP had also declared its outright opposition to the Chancellor. Shrill accusations, along with those of the agrarians, of the government's 'Bolshevism' in the countryside because of its schemes to divide up bankrupt eastern estates to make smallholdings for the unemployed were a reminder of the lobbying which had helped bring down Brüning. Schleicher's position was also weakened by the Osthilfe (Eastern Aid) scandal which broke in mid-January. The agrarian lobby was incensed that the government had not hushed up the affair. Since some of Hindenburg's close friends and fellow landowners were implicated, the ire directed at Schleicher could be transmitted directly through the Reich President. And when, in the wake of the scandal, it was revealed that the President's own property at Neudeck, presented to him by German business five years earlier, had been registered in his son's name to avoid death-duties, Schleicher was held responsible by Hindenburg for allowing his name to be dragged through the mud.[213]

At a cabinet meeting on 16 January, the day after the Lippe result had been announced, Schleicher had again raised the issue which had occupied Papen in the autumn: whether to seek a dissolution of the Reichstag and postponement of new elections; in other words, to risk a breach of the constitution. In contrast to Papen's last cabinet meeting, no minister opposed such a move. Schleicher remained optimistic that, over a period of time, he could broaden the support for his government, and thought, following the line that Papen had fed him, that Hitler had now given up pretensions to the Chancellorship and had the more modest aim of the Defence Ministry, which Hindenburg would certainly refuse him.[214] Schleicher's strategy for a breach of the constitution was in effect no different from that, which he himself had rejected, put forward by Papen. It required the support of the Reich President. At the beginning of December, Schleicher had persuaded Hindenburg that a breach of the constitution and declaration of a state of emergency would risk a civil war, and that the Reichswehr would not be able to withstand the civil unrest. He now faced the difficult task of persuading the President that what he had prophesied would happen in December would not happen in January – even though conditions were little different. His prospects were not good.

Serving as the go-between, Ribbentrop had arranged another meeting between Hitler and Papen on 18 January.[215] Accompanied by Röhm and Himmler, Hitler – encouraged by the Lippe success and by Schleicher's mounting difficulties – now hardened his position from the earlier meetings in the month and expressly demanded the Chancellorship. When Papen demurred, claiming his influence with Hindenburg was not sufficient to bring this about, Hitler, in his usual way, told the former Chancellor he saw no point in further talks. Ribbentrop then suggested that it might be worth talking to Hindenburg's son, Oskar. The following day, Ribbentrop took his suggestion further with Papen. The result was a meeting, arranged for late on the Sunday evening, 22 January, at Ribbentrop's house, at which Oskar von Hindenburg and the Reich President's State Secretary Otto Meissner agreed to be present. Frick accompanied Hitler. Göring joined them later.[216] Hitler had not felt well the previous day. Goebbels put it down to his sleeping and eating too little.[217] Perhaps he was still unwell, or perhaps his meeting later that evening with Oskar von Hindenburg was on his mind, when he delivered a below-par speech to party functionaries in the Sportpalast in Berlin on 22 January.[218] But when he arrived at Ribbentrop's at ten o'clock, he was determined to make an impression on Hindenburg junior. The main part of the meeting consisted of a two-hour discussion between Hitler and the President's son. Hitler also spoke with Papen, who told him that the President had not changed his mind about making him Chancellor, but recognized that the situation had changed and that it was necessary to incorporate the National Socialists in this or a new government. Hitler was unyielding. He made it plain that Nazi cooperation could only come under his Chancellorship. The official communiqué following the ill-fated meeting on 13 August still rankled with him. He was adamant that he had not sought total power then, and had no objection to extensive representation of bourgeois politicians in his cabinet, as long as they were not serving as representatives of political parties.[219] Apart from the Chancellorship for himself, he insisted only upon the Reich Ministry of the Interior for Frick and a further cabinet post for Göring. These claims were more modest – and were recognized as being such – than those he had put forward to Schleicher the previous August.[220] Papen demanded the post of Vice-Chancellor for himself.[221] On that basis, he now agreed to press for Hitler to become Chancellor – a notable breakthrough – but promised to withdraw if there was any sign that he did not have Hitler's confidence.[222] Oskar von Hindenburg commented to Meissner on the way back from Dahlem that he had been impressed by what Hitler had had to say.[223] Hitler was less complimentary about the President's son. 'Young Oskar', he told Goebbels, cut 'a rare image of stupidity'.[224]

The following day, Chancellor Schleicher, by now aware of the threat to his position, informed the Reich President that a vote of no-confidence in the government could be expected at the delayed recall of the Reichstag on 31 January. He requested an order of dissolution and postponement of new elections. Hindenburg agreed to consider a dissolution, but rejected the breach of Article 25 of the Weimar Constitution.[225] What he had been prepared to grant Papen five months earlier, he now refused Schleicher. But since Schleicher himself had argued against the wisdom of such a drastic step as recently as the beginning of December, he could scarcely criticize the President for continuing to follow the advice he had given at that time, rather than the reverse advice he was now offering.

At the same time, Hindenburg had left himself with little room for

ADOLF HITLER

Mögen Jahrtausende vergehen, so wird man nie von Heldentum
reden dürfen, ohne des deutschen Heeres des Weltkrieges zu
gedenken.

28. (*previous page*) Hitler in SA uniform (rejected), 1928/9

29. (*left*) Hitler in rhetorical pose. Postcard from August 1927. The caption reads: 'In the passing of thousands of years, heroism will never be spoken of without remembering the German army of the world war'

30. Hitler speaking to the NSDAP leadership, Munich, 30 August 1928. *Left to right*: Alfred Rosenberg, Walter Buch, Franz Xaver Schwarz, Hitler, Gregor Strasser, Heinrich Himmler. Sitting by the door, hands clasped, is Julius Streicher: to his left is Robert Ley

31. Geli Raubal and Hitler, *c.* 1930

32. Eva Braun in Heinrich Hoffmann's studio, early 1930s

33. (*facing page*) Reich President Paul von Hindenburg

34. (*facing page*) Reich Chancellor Heinrich Brüning (*left*) with Benito Mussolini, Rome, August 1931

35. Reich Chancellor Franz von Papen (*front, right*), with State Secretary Dr Otto Meissner, at the annual celebration of the Reich Constitution, 11 August 1932. Behind von Papen is Reich Minister of the Interior Wilhelm Freiherr von Gayl, who, that very day, put forward proposals to make Weimar's liberal constitution distinctly more authoritarian

36. Gregor Strasser and Joseph Goebbels watching the SA parade past Hitler, Braunschweig, 18 October 1931

37. Ernst Thälmann, leader of the KPD, at a rally of the 'Red Front' during the growing crisis of Weimar democracy, *c.* 1930

38. Nazi election poster, 1932, directed against the SPD and the Jews. The slogan reads: 'Marxism is the Guardian Angel of Capitalism. Vote National Socialist, List 1'

39. Candidate placards for the presidential election, Berlin, April 1932

40. Discussion at Neudeck, the home of Reich President Paul von Hindenburg, 1932. *Left to right*: Reich Chancellor Franz von Papen, State Secretary Otto Meissner (back to camera), Reich Minister of the Interior Wilhelm von Gayl, Hindenburg, and Reichswehr Minister Kurt von Schleicher

41. Reich Chancellor Kurt von Schleicher speaking in the Berlin Sportpalast, 15 January 1933

42. A photo taken of Hitler in the Kaiserhof Hotel, Berlin, in January 1933, just before his appointment as Chancellor, to test how he looked in evening dress

43. The 'Day of Potsdam', 21 March 1933: a deferential Hitler bows to Reich President von Hindenburg

44. SA violence against Communists in Chemnitz, March 1933

45. The boycott of Jewish doctors, April 1933. The stickers read:
'Take note: Jew. Visiting Forbidden'

46. An elderly Jew being taken into custody by police in Berlin, 1934

47. Hindenburg and Hitler on their way to the rally in Berlin's Lustgarten on the 'Day of National Labour', 1 May 1933. The following day, the trades union movement was destroyed

48. Hitler with Ernst Röhm at a parade of the SA in summer 1933, as problems with the SA began to emerge

Was
der König eroberte,
der Fürst formte,
der Feldmarschall verteidigte,
rettete und einigte der Soldat.

Hans vom Norden
Nachdruck verboten

DER FÜHRER ALS TIERFREUND

49. The Führer cult: a postcard, designed by Hans von Norden in 1933,
showing Hitler in a direct line from Frederick the Great, Otto von Bismarck,
and Paul von Hindenburg. The caption reads: 'What the King conquered, the
Prince shaped, the Field Marshal defended, the Soldier saved and united'

50. The Führer cult: 'The Führer as animal-lover', postcard, 1934

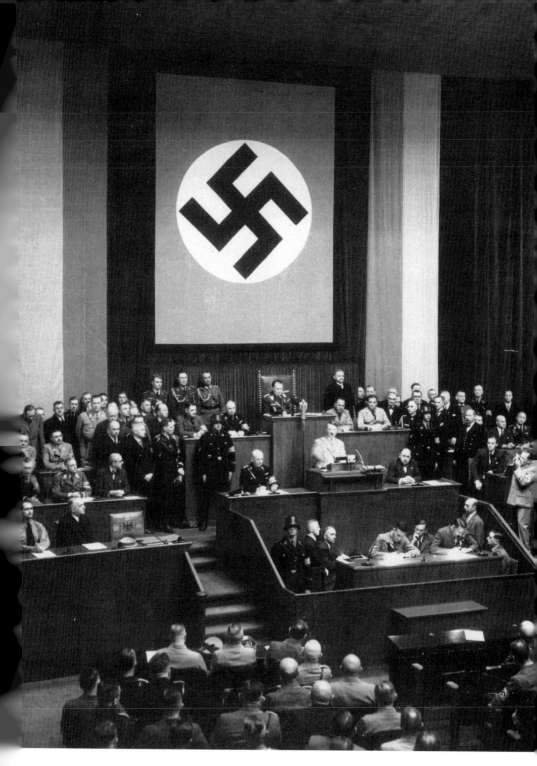

51. Hitler justifying the 'Röhm purge' to the Reichstag, 13 July 1934

52. Hitler, Professor Leonhard Gall, and architect Albert Speer inspecting the half-built 'House of German Art' in Munich. Undated cigarette-card, *c.* 1935

53. Hitler with young Bavarians. Behind him (*right*) in Bavarian costume, Hitler-Youth leader Baldur von Schirach. Undated photograph

54. The Mercedes-Benz showroom at Lenbachplatz, Munich, April 1935
55. Hitler during a visit to the Ruhr in 1935, accompanied (*left to right*) by his general factotum Julius Schaub, and the leading industrialists Albert Vögler, Fritz Thyssen, and Ernst Borbet, all important executives of the United Steel Works

Hitler in seinen Bergen

56. 'Hitler in his Mountains': cover of a Heinrich Hoffmann publication of
1935, featuring 88 photographs of the Führer in picturesque settings

57. The swearing-in of new recruits at the Feldherrnhalle in Odeonsplatz,
Munich, on the anniversary of the putsch, 7 November 1935

58. German troops entering the demilitarized Rhineland across the
Hohenzollern Bridge in Cologne, 7 March 1936

manoeuvre. He had once more rejected the idea of a Hitler Chancellorship.[226] That left only the return to a Papen cabinet – Hindenburg's favoured outcome, but scarcely likely to resolve the crisis, and regarded with scepticism even by Papen himself. As rumours hared round Berlin, the prospect of a reversion to Papen's 'cabinet of struggle', with a major role for Hugenberg, and a declaration of a state of emergency was, remarkable though it now seems, seen as more worrying than a cabinet led by Hitler.[227] Fears of such an eventuality were sharply intensified after Schleicher, on 28 January, having been refused the dissolution order by the Reich President, submitted his own resignation and that of his entire cabinet.[228] Within hours, Hindenburg asked Papen to try to work towards a solution within the framework of the Constitution and with the backing of the Reichstag.[229] According to Papen's own account, he was asked by the President to take soundings about the possibilities of a Hitler cabinet.[230] Papen told Ribbentrop that Hitler must be contacted without delay. A turning-point had been reached. After his talk with Hindenburg, he now thought a Hitler Chancellorship a possibility.[231]

By this time, Papen had come round to full acceptance of a government led by Hitler. The only question in his mind was to ensure that Hitler was firmly contained by 'reliable' and 'responsible' conservatives. On 27 January, the day before Schleicher's resignation, Hitler had been practically incapable of rational deliberation. He told his advisers he had no more to say to Hindenburg. And he broke off discussions with Hugenberg in great anger when the DNVP leader rejected his demands to install a National Socialist as Prussian Minister of the Interior in a new cabinet and – a point of great importance to Hitler – for new Reichstag elections.[232] Hitler was beside himself with anger and frustration. He had to be calmed down by Göring and Ribbentrop, and dissuaded from leaving Berlin immediately for Munich. 'I have never seen Hitler in such a state,' commented Ribbentrop. 'I proposed to him and Göring that I should see Papen alone that evening' – Hitler had declined to meet him – 'and explain the whole situation to him. In the evening I saw Papen and convinced him eventually that the only thing that made sense was Hitler's Chancellorship, and that he must do what he can to bring this about. Papen declared that the matter of Hugenberg was of secondary importance, and that he was now absolutely in favour of Hitler becoming Chancellor; this was the decisive change in Papen's attitude . . . This recognition by Papen is, I believe, the turning-point.'[233]

Following the resignation of the Schleicher cabinet on 28 January, Papen had meetings with Hugenberg and Hitler.[234] Hugenberg agreed that a Hitler cabinet was the only way forward, but stressed the importance of limiting his power. He demanded for himself the Reich and Prussian Ministries of Economics as the price of the DNVP's support. Hitler, unsurprisingly, refused – as he had done since August – to entertain the notion of a government dependent on a parliamentary majority, and held out for the headship of a presidential cabinet with the same rights that had been granted to Papen and Schleicher. He reiterated his readiness to include those from previous cabinets whom the President favoured, as long as he could be Chancellor and Commissioner for Prussia, and could place members of his own party in the Ministries of the Interior in the Reich and Prussia.[235] The demands for extensive powers in Prussia caused problems. Ribbentrop and Göring tried to persuade Hitler to settle for less. Eventually, 'with a bad grace', as Papen put it, he accepted that the powers of Reich Commissar for Prussia would remain with Papen, in his capacity as Vice-Chancellor.[236]

Meanwhile, Papen had taken soundings by telephone from several former cabinet members, conservatives held in esteem by Hindenburg. All replied that they would be prepared to work in a Hitler cabinet, with Papen as Vice-Chancellor, but not in a Papen–Hugenberg 'cabinet of struggle'. This impressed Hindenburg, when Papen reported to him late on the night of 28 January. He was also gratified by the 'moderation' of Hitler's demands. For the first time, the Reich President was now amenable to a Hitler cabinet.[237] The deadlock was broken.

Hindenburg and Papen discussed the composition of the cabinet. The President was glad that the trusted Neurath would remain at the Foreign Ministry. He wanted someone equally sound at the Defence Ministry, following Schleicher's departure. His own suggestion was General von Blomberg, the army commander in East Prussia and currently technical adviser of the German delegation to the Disarmament Conference in Geneva. Hindenburg thought him extremely reliable and 'completely apolitical'. The following morning he was ordered back to Berlin.[238]

Papen continued his power-brokerage on the morning of 29 January in discussions with Hitler and Göring. The composition of the cabinet was agreed. All posts but two (other than the Chancellorship) were to be occupied by conservatives, not Nazis. Neurath (Foreign Minister), Schwerin von Krosigk (Finance), and Eltz-Rübenach (Post and Transport Ministry) had been members of the Schleicher cabinet. The occupancy of the Justice Ministry was left open for the time being. Frick was nominated by Hitler as Reich Minister of the Interior. Compensation for the concession made over the position of Reich Commissar of Prussia was the acceptance by

Papen that Göring would serve nominally as his deputy in the Prussian Ministry of the Interior.[239] This key appointment effectively gave the Nazis control over the police in the giant state of Prussia, embracing two-thirds of the territory of the Reich. There was no place as yet for Goebbels in a propaganda ministry, part of Nazi expectations the previous summer. But Hitler assured Goebbels that his ministry was waiting for him. It was simply a matter of necessary tactics for a temporary solution. Apart from all else, Hitler needed Goebbels for the election campaign he was insisting must follow his appointment as Chancellor.[240]

Papen had talks the same day with Hugenberg and with the Stahlhelm leaders, Seldte and Duesterberg. Hugenberg still objected to the Nazi demands for new elections, from which his own party had nothing to gain. But, tempted by the offer of the powerful Economics Ministry, which he had long coveted, he tentatively offered his cooperation.[241] The previous November, Hugenberg had told Hindenburg he thought Hitler untrustworthy. 'His entire way of dealing with political matters makes it extraordinarily difficult to give him the political leadership,' was Hugenberg's judgement at the time. He would have very great reservations about such a step, he added.[242] Now, his own power ambitions removed such reservations. When, in late January, the deputy Stahlhelm leader Theodor Duesterberg warned him of the consequences of entrusting the Chancellorship to someone as dishonest as Hitler, Hugenberg waved the objections aside. Nothing could happen. Hindenburg would remain Reich President and supreme commander of the armed forces; Papen would be Vice-Chancellor; he himself would have control of the entire economic sphere, including agriculture; Seldte (the Stahlhelm leader) would be in charge of the Labour Ministry. 'We're boxing Hitler in,' concluded Hugenberg. Duesterberg replied darkly that Hugenberg would find himself one night fleeing through ministerial gardens in his underpants to avoid arrest.[243]

Some of Papen's conservative friends also expressed their deep concern at the prospect of a Hitler cabinet. Papen told them there was no alternative within the framework of the Constitution.[244] To one who warned him that he was placing himself in Hitler's hands, Papen replied: 'You are mistaken. We've hired him.'[245]

A last problem still had to be resolved. Hitler insisted at his meeting with Papen on new elections to be followed by an enabling act. For Hitler, this was crucial. An enabling act was vital to be able to rule without dependency on either the Reichstag or on presidential backing for emergency decrees. But the current composition of the Reichstag offered no hope of passing an enabling act. Papen reported back, via Ribbentrop, that Hindenburg was not in favour of new elections. Hitler told Ribbentrop to inform the President that there would be no further elections after these. By the afternoon of 29 January, Papen was able to tell Göring and Ribbentrop that all was clear. 'Everything perfect,' Göring reported back to the Kaiserhof.[246] Hitler was expected by the Reich President at eleven o'clock the next morning to be sworn in as Chancellor.[247]

In the evening there was another scare. Werner von Alvensleben, one of Schleicher's go-betweens, turned up at Goebbels's house with rumours that Hindenburg was, after all, going to install a Papen minority cabinet. That was something the Reichswehr would not accept. Oskar von Hindenburg would be arrested the next day. The President himself, no longer seen as fit for office, had been taken off to his estate at Neudeck. Hitler and Göring, in the adjacent room, were immediately informed. Göring wasted no time in letting Meissner and Papen know what was afoot. Goebbels was sceptical. But the Nazi leadership took the rumours seriously enough to put the SA on alert in Berlin.[248] The President's entourage also acted. The next morning, Oskar von Hindenburg was sent to the Anhalter Bahnhof to intercept Blomberg, on his arrival from Geneva, before he could be whisked away to army headquarters by the adjutant of General von Hammerstein, the army chief of staff, also waiting on the station platform. Blomberg was taken directly to the President, informed of the alleged putsch plans, and sworn in as new Defence Minister – itself a technical breach of the Constitution, since ministers could only be sworn in on the recommendation of the head of government. Blomberg was told by Hindenburg that it was his duty to reverse Schleicher's course, and keep the Reichswehr out of politics.[249]

Quarter of an hour before the time of its appointment with the Reich President, at eleven o'clock on Monday, 30 January 1933, there was still dissension in the ranks of the members of the new cabinet who were wending their way through the ministerial gardens to the Reich Chancellery – Hindenburg's residence while the Reich President's Palace was under repair. Hitler was still unhappy at the restriction on his powers through the blockage on his appointment as Reich Commissar for Prussia. He insisted again on new elections. Hugenberg was opposed. Hitler and Hugenberg were still locked in heated argument even as they waited in Meissner's room to meet the President. There was a chance that the cabinet might collapse before it had even been sworn in. Hitler promised that the composition of the cabinet would remain unaltered by the results of the election. Hugenberg remained unimpressed. The time for the appointment arrived. But the arguing continued. Meissner warned that the President could not be kept waiting much longer. Papen interceded to ask Hugenberg to respect the word of a German man. A last concession wrung out of Hitler by Papen was worthless: that he would consult the Zentrum and BVP without delay about broadening the support for the government. Just before the new cabinet entered the Reich President's chambers, it was finally agreed that they would seek the dissolution order that Hitler so badly wanted.[250]

At last, by now shortly after noon, the members of the Hitler cabinet trooped into the Reich President's rooms. Hindenburg, piqued at being kept waiting, gave a brief welcoming address, expressing satisfaction that the nationalist Right had finally come together.[251] Papen then made the formal introductions. Hindenburg nodded his approval as Hitler solemnly swore to carry out his obligations without party interests and for the good of the whole nation. He again approvingly acknowledged the sentiments expressed by the new Reich Chancellor who, unexpectedly, made a short speech emphasizing his efforts to uphold the Constitution, respect the rights of the President, and, after the next election, to return to normal parliamentary rule. Hitler and his ministers awaited a reply from the Reich President. It came, but in only a single sentence: 'And now, gentlemen, forwards with God.'[252]

VI

'Hitler is Reich Chancellor. Just like a fairy-tale,' noted Goebbels.[253] Indeed, the extraordinary had happened. What few beyond the ranks of Nazi fanatics had thought possible less than a year earlier had become reality. Against all odds, Hitler's aggressive obstinacy – born out of lack of alternatives – had paid off. What he had been unable to achieve himself, his 'friends' in high places had achieved for him. The 'nobody of Vienna', 'unknown soldier', beerhall demagogue, head of what was for years no more than a party on the lunatic fringe of politics, a man with no credentials for running a sophisticated state-machine, practically his sole qualification the ability to muster the support of the nationalist masses whose base instincts he showed an unusual talent for rousing, had now been placed in charge of government of one of the leading states in Europe. His intentions had scarcely been kept secret over the years. Whatever the avowals of following a legal path to power, heads would roll, he had said. Marxism would be eradicated, he had said. Jews would be 'removed', he had said. Germany would rebuild the strength of its armed forces, destroy the shackles of Versailles, conquer 'by the sword' the land it needed for its 'living-space', he had said. A few took him at his word, and thought he was dangerous. But far, far more, from Right to Left of the political spectrum – conservatives, liberals, socialists, communists – underrated his intentions and unscrupulous power instincts at the same time as they scorned his abilities.[254] The Left's underestimation was at least not responsible for getting him into power. Socialists, communists, trade unions were all little more than by-standers, their scope for influencing events emasculated since 1930. It was the blindness of the conservative Right to the dangers which had been so evident, arising from their determination to eliminate democracy and destroy socialism and the consequent governmental stalemate they had allowed to develop, that delivered the power of a nation-state containing all the pent-up aggression of a wounded giant into the hands of the dangerous leader of a political gangster-mob.

There was no inevitability about Hitler's accession to power. Had Hindenburg been prepared to grant to Schleicher the dissolution that he had so readily allowed Papen, and to prorogue the Reichstag for a period beyond the constitutional sixty days, a Hitler Chancellorship might have been avoided. With the corner turning of the economic Depression, and with the Nazi Movement facing potential break-up if power were not soon attained, the future – even if under an authoritarian government – would have been very different. Even as the cabinet argued outside Hindenburg's door at eleven o'clock on 30 January, keeping the President waiting, there was a possibility that a Hitler Chancellorship might not materialize. Hitler's rise from humble beginnings to 'seize' power by 'triumph of the will' was the stuff of Nazi legend. In fact, political miscalculation by those with regular access to the corridors of power rather than any actions on the part of the Nazi leader played a larger role in placing him in the Chancellor's seat.

His path ought to have been blocked long before the final drama of January 1933. The most glaring opportunity was missed through the failure to impose a hefty jail sentence after the putsch fiasco of 1923 – and to compound this disastrous omission by releasing him on parole within a matter of months and allowing him a fresh start. But those miscalculations, as well as those during the Depression years that opened up the possibility, then the reality, of a Hitler Chancellorship, were not random acts. They were the miscalculations of a political class determined to inflict what injury it could on (or at least make only the faintest attempts to defend) the new, detested, or at best merely tolerated democratic Republic. The anxiety to destroy democracy rather than the keenness to bring the Nazis to power was what triggered the complex developments that led to Hitler's Chancellorship.

Democracy was surrendered without a fight. This was most notably the case in the collapse of the grand coalition in 1930. It was again the case – however vain the opposition might have proved – in the lack of resistance to the Papen coup against Prussia in July 1932. Both events revealed the flimsiness of democracy's base. This was not least because powerful groups had never reconciled themselves to democracy, and were by this time actively seeking to bring it down. During the Depression, democracy was less surrendered than deliberately undermined by élite groups serving their own ends. These were no pre-industrial leftovers, but – however reactionary their political aims – modern lobbies working to further their vested interests in an authoritarian system.[255] In the final drama, the agrarians and the army were more influential than big business in engineering Hitler's takeover.[256] But big business, also, politically myopic and self-serving, had significantly contributed to the undermining of democracy which was the necessary prelude to Hitler's success.

The masses, too, had played their part in democracy's downfall. Never had circumstances been less propitious for the establishment of successful democracy than they were in Germany after the First World War. Already by 1920, the parties most supportive of democracy held only a minority of the vote. Democracy narrowly survived its early travails, though great swathes of the electorate opposed it root and branch. Who is to say that, had not the great Depression blown it completely off course, democracy might not have settled down and consolidated itself? But democracy was in a far from healthy state when the Depression struck Germany. And in the course of the Depression, the masses deserted democracy in their droves. By 1932, the only supporters of democracy were the weakened Social Democrats (and even many of these were by this time lukewarm), some sections of the Zentrum (which had itself moved sharply to the Right), and a handful of liberals. The Republic was dead. Still open was what sort of authoritarian system would replace it.

Hitler did not represent a classic 'Bonapartist' solution. There was no 'class equilibrium' in 1932.[257] The working class was cowed and broken by Depression, its organizations enfeebled and powerless. But the ruling groups did not have the mass support to maximize their ascendancy and destroy once and for all the power of organized labour. Hitler was brought in to do the job for them. That he might do more than this, that he might outlast all predictions and expand his own power immensely and at their own expense, either did not occur to them, or was regarded as an exceedingly unlikely outcome. The underestimation of Hitler and his movement by the power-brokers remains a leitmotiv of the intrigues that placed him in the Chancellor's office.

The mentalities which conditioned the behaviour both of the élites and of the masses, and which made Hitler's rise possible, were products of strands of German political culture that were plainly recognizable in the twenty years of so before the First World War.[258] Analogous trends can be seen elsewhere, most notably in Italy. But the parallels do not amount to close similarity, let alone identity. Most of the elements of political culture that fed into Nazism were peculiarly German. And the consciousness – especially among intellectuals – of Germany's distinctiveness, even cultural superiority, as a nation was something which Hitler's chauvinistic and bowdlerized version of this could build upon.[259] Even so, Hitler was no inexorable product of a German 'special path', no logical culmination of long-term trends in specifically German culture and ideology.[260]

Nor was he a mere 'accident' in the course of German history. Without the unique conditions in which he came to prominence, Hitler would have been nothing. It is hard to imagine him bestriding the stage of history at any other time. His style, his brand of rhetoric, would, deprived of such conditions, have been without appeal. The impact on the German people of war, revolution, and national humiliation, and the acute fear of Bolshevism in wide sections of the population, gave Hitler his platform. He exploited the conditions brilliantly. More than any other politician of his era, he was the spokesman for the unusually intense fears, resentments, and prejudices of ordinary people not attracted by the parties of the Left or anchored in the parties of political Catholicism. And more than any other politician of his era, he offered such people the prospect of a new and better society – though one seeming to rest on 'true' German values with which they could identify. The vision of the future went hand in hand with the denunciation of the past in Hitler's appeal. The total collapse of confidence in a state system resting on discredited party politics and bureaucratic administration had led over a third of the population to place its trust and its hopes in the politics of national redemption. The personality cult carefully nurtured around Hitler turned him into the embodiment of such hopes.[261]

Whatever the future held, for those who could not share the delirium of the SA hordes marching through the Brandenburg Gate in celebration on the evening of 30 January 1933, it was at best uncertain. 'A leap into the dark' was how one Catholic newspaper described Hitler's appointment to the Chancellorship.[262]

And there were those, not just on the defeated Left, who foresaw disaster. 'You have delivered up our holy German Fatherland to one of the greatest demagogues of all time,' wrote Ludendorff – who had experience of what he was writing about – to his former wartime colleague Hindenburg. 'I solemnly prophesy that this accursed man will cast our Reich into the abyss and bring our nation to inconceivable misery. Future generations will damn you in your grave for what you have done.'[263]

II

THE MAKING OF THE DICTATOR

'It can't be denied: he has grown. Out of the demagogue and party leader, the fanatic and agitator, the true statesman ... seems to be developing.'   Diary entry of the writer Erich Ebermayer,
for 21 March 1933

'What the old parliament and parties did not accomplish in sixty years, your statesmanlike foresight has achieved in six months.'
Letter to Hitler from
Cardinal Michael von Faulhaber, 24 July 1933

'In nine months, the genius of your leadership and the ideals which you have newly placed before us have succeeded in creating, from a people inwardly torn apart and without hope, a united Reich.'
Franz von Papen, 14 November 1933,
speaking on behalf of the members of the Reich Government

Hitler is Reich Chancellor! And what a cabinet!!! One such as we did not dare to dream of in July. Hitler, Hugenberg, Seldte, Papen!!! A large part of my German hopes are attached to each. National Socialist drive, German National reason, the non-political Stahlhelm, and – not forgotten by us – Papen. It is so unimaginably wonderful . . . What an achievement by Hindenburg![1]

This was the ecstatic response of Hamburg schoolteacher Luise Solmitz to the dramatic news of Hitler's appointment to the Chancellorship on 30 January 1933. Like so many who had found their way to Hitler from middle-class, national-conservative backgrounds, she had wavered the previous autumn when she thought he was slipping under the influence of radical socialist tendencies in the party. Now that Hitler was in office, but surrounded by her trusted champions of the conservative Right, heading a government of 'national concentration', her joy was unbounded. The national renewal she longed for could now begin. Many, outside the ranks of diehard Nazi followers, their hopes and ideals invested in the Hitler cabinet, felt the same way.

But millions did not. Fear, anxiety, alarm, implacable hostility, illusory optimism at the regime's early demise, and bold defiance intermingled with apathy, scepticism, condescension towards the presumed inability of the new Chancellor and his Nazi colleagues in the cabinet – and indifference.

Reactions varied according to political views and personal disposition. 'What will this government do?' asked Julius Leber, SPD Reichstag deputy, before, his immunity ignored, being taken into custody the very night after Hitler's accession to power after being beaten up by a group of Nazi thugs. 'We know their aims. Nobody knows what their next measures will be. The dangers are enormous. But the firmness of German workers is unshakeable. We don't fear these men. We are determined to take up the struggle.'[2]

Alongside such misplaced hopes in the strength and unity of the labour movement went the crass misapprehension of Hitler as no more than the stooge of the 'real' wielders of power, the forces of big capital, as represented by their friends in the cabinet. Leber's fellow SPD-deputy Kurt Schumacher's assessment was: 'The cabinet is called after Adolf Hitler. But the cabinet is really Alfred Hugenberg's. Adolf Hitler may speak; Alfred Hugenberg will act. With the construction of this government, the last veil has fallen. National Socialism has openly showed itself as that which we always took it for, the high-capitalist nationalist party of the Right. National Capitalism is the true firm!'[3] The lurid rhetoric of the Communist proclamation of 30 January was closer to the mark: 'Shameless wage robbery and boundless terror of the brown murderous plague smash the last pitiful rights of the working class. Unrestrained course towards imperialist war. All this lies directly ahead.'[4]

The leadership of the Zentrum concentrated on seeking assurances that unconstitutional measures would be avoided.[5] The Catholic hierarchy remained reserved, its disquiet about Hitler and the anti-Christian tendencies of his movement unchanged.[6] Influenced by years of warnings from their clergy, the Catholic population were apprehensive and uncertain. Among many Protestant church-goers there was, according to the later recollections of one pastor, a great optimism that national renewal would bring with it inner, moral revitalization: 'It is as if the wing of a great turn of fate is fluttering above us. There was to be a new start.'[7] The Land Bishop of Württemberg, Theophil Wurm, soon to run into conflict with the new rulers, also recalled how the Protestant Church welcomed the Hitler Chancellorship since the National Socialists had resolutely fought Marxist 'anti-Church agitation', and now offered new hope for the future and the expectation of a 'favourable impact on the entire people'.[8] One of the leading Protestant theologians, Karl Barth, later dismissed from his Chair at Bonn University for his hostility to the 'German Christians' (the nazified wing of the Protestant Church), took a different view, airly dismissing any major significance in Hitler's appointment. 'I don't think that this will signify the start of great new things in any direction at all,' he wrote to his mother on 1 February 1933.[9]

Many ordinary people, after what they had gone through in the Depression, were simply apathetic at the news that Hitler was Chancellor. According to the British Ambassador in Berlin, Horace Rumbold, people throughout the country 'took the news phlegmatically'.[10] Those in provincial Germany who were not Nazi fanatics or committed opponents often shrugged their shoulders and carried on with life, doubtful that yet another change of government would bring any improvement. Some thought that Hitler would not even be as long in office as Schleicher, and that his popularity would slump as soon as disillusionment set in on account of the emptiness of Nazi promises.[11] But perceptive critics of Hitler were able to see that, now he enjoyed the prestige of the Chancellorship, he could swiftly break down much of the scepticism and win great support by successfully tackling mass unemployment – something which none of his predecessors had come close to achieving. 'The Hitler cabinet will be aware that nothing could bring it so much trust as success here,' noted a hostile journalist on 31 January 1933. Should it indeed succeed, 'then no German will deny the new cabinet the thanks which it should be its first endeavour to earn,' he concluded.[12]

For the Nazis themselves, of course, 30 January 1933 was the day they had dreamed about, the triumph they had fought for, the opening of the portals to the brave new world – and the start of what many hoped would be opportunities for prosperity, advancement, and power. Wildly cheering crowds accompanied Hitler on his way back to the Kaiserhof after his appointment with Hindenburg. 'Now we've got there,' Hitler declared, carried away with the euphoria around him, as he stepped out of the lift on the first floor of the Kaiserhof to be greeted, alongside Goebbels and other Nazi leaders, by waiters and chambermaids, all anxious to shake his hand.[13] By seven o'clock that evening Goebbels had improvised a torchlight procession of marching SA and SS men through the centre of Berlin that lasted beyond midnight.[14] He wasted no time in exploiting the newly available facilities of state radio to provide a stirring commentary.[15] Goebbels claimed a million men had taken part. The Nazi press halved the number. The British Ambassador estimated a maximum figure of some 50,000. His military attaché thought there were around 15,000.[16] Whatever the numbers, the spectacle was an unforgettable one – exhilarating and intoxicating for Nazi followers, menacing for those at home and abroad who feared the consequences of Hitler in power.[17] One fifteen-year-old girl was mesmerized by what she saw. For Melita Maschmann, the marching columns gave 'magical splendour' to the idea of the 'national community' which had fascinated her. Afterwards, she could scarcely wait to join the BDM (Bund deutscher Mädel, the German Girls' League, the female section of the Hitler Youth organization).[18] Her idealism was shared by many, particularly among the young, who saw the dawn of a new era symbolized in the spectacular torchlight procession through the centre of Berlin.

The seemingly endless parade was watched from his window in the Wilhelmstraße by Reich President Hindenburg. Berliners later joked that the President liked torchlight processions because he was allowed to stay up late when they took place.[19] There were respectful shouts when the procession passed him by.[20] But when the marchers came to the window a little farther on, where Hitler was standing, the respect gave way to wild acclaim.[21] For Papen, a few feet behind Hitler, it symbolized the transition 'from a moribund regime to the new revolutionary forces'.[22]

The day of Hitler's appointment to the Chancellorship became immediately stylized in Nazi mythology as the 'day of the national uprising'.[23] Hitler even contemplated – so, at least, he claimed later – changing the calendar (as the French revolutionaries had done) to mark the beginning of a 'new world order'.[24] At the same time he – and other Nazi spokesmen generally followed suit – avoided the term 'seizure of power', with its putschist connotations, and preferred the more descriptive 'takeover of power' to underline the formal legality of his accession to the highest office of government.[25] Power had indeed not been 'seized'. It had been handed to Hitler, who had been appointed Chancellor by the Reich President in the same manner as had his immediate predecessors. Even so, the orchestrated ovations, which put Hitler himself and other party bosses into a state of ecstasy,[26] signalled that this was no ordinary transfer of power. And almost overnight, those who had misunderstood or misinterpreted the momentous nature of the day's events would realize how wrong they had been. After 30 January 1933, Germany would never be the same again.

That historic day was an end and a beginning. It denoted the expiry of the unlamented Weimar Republic and the culminating point of the comprehensive state crisis that had brought its demise. At the same time Hitler's appointment as Chancellor marked the beginning of the process which was to lead into the abyss of war and genocide, and bring about Germany's own destruction as a nation-state. It signified the start of that astonishingly swift jettisoning of constraints on inhumane behaviour whose path ended in Auschwitz, Treblinka, Sobibor, Majdanek, and the other death camps whose names are synonymous with the horror of Nazism.

As earlier chapters have tried to show, what made Hitler's triumph possible were important strands of continuity in German political culture stretching back beyond the First World War – chauvinistic nationalism, imperialism, racism, anti-Marxism, glorification of war, the placing of order above freedom, caesaristic attractions of strong authority are some of them – as well as the specific and more short-term consequences of the multi-layered crises that afflicted Weimar democracy from the start.[27] But if such continuities helped 'make Hitler possible', and if his triumph can at least partially be explained by his unique capacity in 1933 to bind together for a time all the strands of continuity with 'old Germany',[28] the following twelve years would see these elements of continuity exploited, warped and distorted out of all recognition by the ever intensifying radicalism of the regime, then ultimately broken in the maelstrom of defeat and destruction in 1945 that Hitler's rule had produced.

The rapidity of the transformation that swept over Germany between Hitler's takeover of power on 30 January 1933 and its crucial consolidation and extension at the beginning of August 1934, after Reich President Hindenburg's death and following close on the major crisis of the 'Röhm affair', was astounding for contemporaries and is scarcely less astonishing in retrospect. It was brought about by a combination of pseudo-legal measures, terror, manipulation – and willing collaboration. Within a month, civil liberties – as protected under the Weimar Constitution – had been extinguished. Within two months, with most active political opponents either imprisoned or fleeing the country, the Reichstag surrendered its powers, giving Hitler control of the legislature. Within four months the once powerful trade unions were dissolved. In less than six months, all opposition parties had been suppressed or gone into voluntary liquidation, leaving the NSDAP as the only remaining party. In January 1934, the sovereignty of the Länder – already in reality smashed the previous March – was formally abolished. Then, in the summer, the growing threat from within Hitler's own movement was ruthlessly eliminated in the 'Night of the Long Knives' on 30 June 1934.

By this time, almost all organizations, institutions, professional and representative bodies, clubs, and societies had long since rushed to align themselves with the new regime. 'Tainted' remnants of pluralism and democracy were rapidly removed, nazified structures and mentalities adopted. This process of 'coordination' (*Gleichschaltung*) was for the most part undertaken voluntarily and with alacrity.

The Christian churches were exceptions to the process. Attempts to 'coordinate' the divided Protestant Church caused great conflict and had eventually to be abandoned. No attempt was even made to alter the organizational framework of the Catholic Church. The lasting tension and frequent clashes between the churches – especially the Catholic Church – and the regime in the following years were rooted in alternative sources of loyalty which the Christian denominations continued to command. But the political compromises which each of them made with the new rulers in the first months nevertheless pushed them on to the defensive, forcing them to become largely reactive and inward-looking.

The army, too, remained 'uncoordinated', its officer corps still largely national-conservative, not Nazi. Without the army's backing, Hitler could not rule. But however contemptuous many of the reactionary and conservative officers, often from aristocratic backgrounds, were of the upstart former corporal now running the government, his offer of 'everything for the armed forces', and his readiness to eradicate those forces in his own movement that threatened the army's position, won him their support. The oath of allegiance which the army swore to Hitler personally at the death of the Reich President and war-hero Field Marshal Hindenburg on 2 August 1934 symbolically marked its full acceptance of the new order. With this act, Hitler's dictatorship was firmly established.

The speed of the transformation, and the readiness of the army and other traditionally powerful groups to put themselves at the service of the new regime, derived in no small measure from the conditions in which Hitler took power. The weakness of the established élites of the 'old order' had eventually led to Hitler's appointment to the Chancellorship. The traditional power-groups had helped undermine and destroy the democracy they so detested. But they had been incapable of imposing the type of counter-revolution they had wanted. Hitler had needed them in order to gain power. But they had needed Hitler, too, to provide mass support for their intended counter-revolution. This was the basis of the 'entente' that put Hitler in the Chancellor's seat.

The balance of power in the 'entente' between Hitler and his conservative partners was nevertheless tilted from the outset towards the new Chancellor. In particular, the anxiety of the army to avoid civil strife and to attain domestic peace as a prerequisite of remilitarization assured its cooperation and willingness to support Hitler's brutal deployment of the power of the state. For only Hitler, and the huge – if potentially unstable – mass movement he headed, could ensure control of the streets and bring about the 'destruction of Marxism', the basis of the desired counter-revolution. Yet precisely this dependence on Hitler and eagerness to back the most ruthless measures adopted in the early weeks and months of the new regime guaranteed that the weakness of the traditional élite groups would become laid bare in the years to come as the intended counter-revolution gave way to the attempted Nazi racial revolution in Europe and opened the path to world conflagration and genocide.[29]

Remarkable in the seismic upheavals of 1933–4 was not how much, but how little, the new Chancellor needed to do to bring about the extension and consolidation of his power. Hitler's dictatorship was made as much by others as by himself. As the 'representative figure' of the 'national renewal', Hitler could for the most part function as activator and enabler of the forces he had unleashed, authorizing and legitimating actions taken by others now rushing to implement what they took to be his wishes. 'Working towards the Führer' functioned as the underlying maxim of the regime from the outset.

Hitler was, in fact, in no position to act as an outright dictator when he came to office on 30 January 1933. As long as Hindenburg lived, there was a potential rival source of loyalty – not least for the army. But by summer 1934, when he combined the headship of state with the leadership of government, his power had effectively shed formal constraints on its usage. And, by then, the personality cult built around Hitler had reached new levels of idolatry and made millions of new converts as the 'people's chancellor' – as propaganda had styled him – came to be seen as a national, not merely party, leader. Disdain and detestation for a parliamentary system generally perceived to have failed miserably had resulted in willingness to entrust monopoly control over the state to a leader claiming a unique sense of mission and invested by his mass following with heroic, almost messianic, qualities. Conventional forms of government were, as a consequence, increasingly exposed to the arbitrary inroads of personalized power. It was a recipe for disaster.

I

There were few hints of this at the beginning. Aware that his position was by no means secure, and not wanting to alienate his coalition partners in the government of 'national concentration', Hitler was at first cautious in cabinet meetings, open to suggestions, ready to take advice – not least in complex matters of finance and economic policy – and not dismissive of opposing viewpoints. This only started to change in April and May.[30] In the early weeks, Finance Minister Schwerin von Krosigk, who had met Hitler for the first time when the cabinet was sworn in, was not alone in finding him 'polite and calm' in the conduct of government business, well-briefed, backed by a good memory, and able to 'grasp the essentials of a problem', concisely sum up lengthy deliberations, and put a new construction on an issue.[31]

Hitler's cabinet met for the first time at five o'clock on 30 January 1933. The Reich Chancellor began by pointing out that millions greeted with joy the cabinet now formed under his leadership, and asked his colleagues for their support. The cabinet then discussed the political situation. Hitler commented that postponing the recall of the Reichstag – due to meet on 31 January after a two-month break – would not be possible without the Zentrum's support. A Reichstag majority could be achieved by banning the KPD, but this would prove impracticable and might provoke a general strike. He was anxious to avoid any involvement of the Reichswehr in suppressing such a strike – a comment favourably received by Defence Minister Blomberg. The best hope, Hitler went on, was to have the Reichstag dissolved and win a majority for the government in new elections. Only Hugenberg – as unwilling as Hitler to have to rely on the Zentrum, but also aware that new elections would be likely to favour the NSDAP – spoke out expressly in favour of banning the KPD in order to pave the way for an Enabling Act. He doubted that a general strike would take place. He was appeased when Hitler vouched for the fact that the cabinet would remain unchanged after the election. Papen favoured proposing an Enabling Act immediately and reconsidering the position once it had been rejected by the Reichstag. Other ministers, anticipating no promises of support from the Zentrum, preferred new elections to the threat of a general strike. The meeting was adjourned without firm decisions.[32] But Hitler had already outflanked Hugenberg, and won support for what he wanted: the earliest possible dissolution of the Reichstag and new elections.

Hitler was keen to prevent any dependence upon the Zentrum. The meeting with Zentrum representatives Prälat Ludwig Kaas (the party leader) and Dr Ludwig Perlitius (who headed the party's Reichstag fraction) the following morning was predictably fruitless.[33] The Zentrum would only consider a postponement of the Reichstag for two months, not the twelve months which Hitler – knowing full well what the answer would be – had requested. Hitler was in effect asking for the Zentrum's full backing, without guarantees.[34] All that he offered in return – and there were valid doubts as to the seriousness of his offer – was the possibility of including a Zentrum member in the cabinet as Minister of Justice, something to which Hugenberg had strenuously objected.[35] The lack of serious intent behind Hitler's approach to the negotiations was shown by how quickly he took the opportunity to break them off. The written questions which the Zentrum then submitted on the future conduct of the new government he simply left unanswered.[36] Hitler reported back to the cabinet already that day, 31

January, that further negotiations with the Zentrum were pointless. New elections were now unavoidable. But Hitler's dealings with the Zentrum had sounded alarm bells among the conservatives that he might indeed rule with the backing of the Zentrum after the election, remove the German Nationalists and Stahlhelm from the cabinet, and thereby free himself from his dependence on Papen and Hugenberg.[37] Once more, therefore, it was a conservative, not a Nazi, who sounded most radical. Papen sought, and was promptly given, an assurance 'that the coming election to the Reichstag would be the last one and a return to the parliamentary system would be avoided for ever'.[38]

That evening, Hindenburg was persuaded to grant Hitler that which he had refused Schleicher only four days earlier: the dissolution of the Reichstag. Hitler had argued, backed by Papen and Meissner, that the people must be given the opportunity to confirm its support for the new government. Though it could attain a majority in the Reichstag as it stood, new elections would produce a larger majority, which in turn would allow a general Enabling Act to be passed, giving a platform for measures to bring about a recovery.[39] The dissolution scarcely conformed to the spirit of the constitution. Elections were turned into a consequence, not a cause, of the formation of a government. The Reichstag had not even been given the opportunity of demonstrating its confidence (or lack of it) in the new government. A decision which was properly parliament's had been placed directly before the people. In its tendency, it was already a step towards acclamation by plebiscite.[40]

Hitler's opening gambit stretched no further than new elections, to be followed by an Enabling Act.[41] His conservative partners, as keen as he was to end parliamentarism and eliminate the Marxist parties, had played into his hands. On the morning of 1 February he told the cabinet of Hindenburg's agreement to dissolve the Reichstag. The elections were set for 5 March. The Reich Chancellor himself provided the government's slogan: 'Attack on Marxism.' Göring immediately stated that it was necessary, in view of the rising number of 'acts of terror' by the Communists, to promulgate without delay the decree prepared under the Papen administration at the time of the Berlin transport strike, providing for restrictions on press freedom and introduction of 'protective custody'.[42] Slightly amended, Papen's draft decree was to come into force on 4 February as the 'Decree for the Protection of the German People', and serve during the election campaign as an important weapon used to ban opposition newspapers and meetings.[43]

At the second cabinet meeting on 1 February, at seven o'clock that evening, Hitler read out the draft of a proclamation to the German people to be broadcast three hours later.[44] Papen had contributed some passages upholding conservative values on Christianity and the family.[45] But the language of the draft plainly bore Hitler's hallmark. Later that evening, with his cabinet standing behind him in his room in the Reich Chancellery, wearing a dark blue suit with a black and white tie, sweating profusely from nervousness, and speaking – unusually – in a dull monotone, Hitler addressed the German people for the first time on the radio.[46] The 'Appeal of the Reich Government to the German People' that he read out was full of rhetoric but vacuous in content – the first propaganda shot in the election campaign rather than a stated programme of political measures. Since the 'days of treachery' fourteen years earlier, 'the Almighty has withdrawn his blessing from our people,' he began. National collapse had opened the way for 'the Communist method of madness finally to poison and undermine the inwardly shaken and uprooted people'. Nothing had been spared the pernicious Communist influence, which had afflicted the family, all notions of honour and loyalty, people and Fatherland, culture and economy down to the basis of morality and belief. 'Fourteen years of Marxism have ruined Germany. One year of Bolshevism would annihilate Germany,' Hitler continued. Reich President Hindenburg had entrusted the national government with the 'mission' of rescuing Germany. The inheritance was a terrible one, the task more difficult than any in memory facing German statesmen. National unity, resting on the protection of Christianity 'as the basis of our entire morality' and the family 'as the germ of our body of nation and state', would be restored. 'Spiritual, political, and cultural nihilism' challenging this aim would be mercilessly attacked to prevent Germany sinking into Communist anarchism. Hitler then announced – it smacked of Soviet methods to Papen[47] – two 'big four-year plans' to tackle 'the great work of the reorganization of the economy'. 'Within four years,' he proclaimed, 'the German peasant must be saved from impoverishment. Within four years unemployment must be finally overcome.' No hints were given as to how this would be achieved, other than on the basis of restored financial stability (it was wholly misleadingly asserted), and through the introduction of labour service and a settlement policy for farmers, neither of which ideas were novel. In foreign policy, the aspirations of the new government were no more precise. The government saw its 'highest mission' in upholding 'the rights of existence (*Lebensrechte*) and thereby the reattainment of the freedom of our people'. Full of pathos, Hitler appealed on behalf of the government to the people to overcome class divisions, and to sign alongside the government an act of reconciliation to permit Germany's resurgence. 'The parties of Marxism and those who went along with them had fourteen years to see what they could do. The result is a heap of ruins. Now, German people, give us four years and then judge and sentence us,' he declared. He ended, as he often concluded major speeches, in pseudo-religious terms, with an appeal to the Almighty to bless the work of the government.[48] With that, the election campaign had begun. It was to be a different campaign to the earlier ones, with the government – already enjoying wide backing – clearly separating itself from all that had preceded it in the Weimar Republic.

Towards the end of his proclamation, Hitler had posed for the first time as a man of peace, stating, despite love of the army as the bearer of arms and symbol of Germany's great past, how happy the government would be 'if through a restriction of its armaments the world should make an increase of our own weapons never again necessary'.[49] His tone when invited by Blomberg to address military leaders gathered in the home of the head of the army (Chef der Heeresleitung) General Kurt Freiherr von Hammerstein-Equord on the evening of 3 February was entirely different.[50]

The atmosphere was cool, the attitude of many of the officers reserved, when Hitler began his lengthy speech. The overall political aim, he stated, was to regain political power. Everything was to be directed towards this end. Internally, there had to be a complete reversal of the current circumstances, no tolerance of opposition. 'Those unwilling to be converted must be crushed. Extermination of Marxism root and branch.' Youth, and the population in general, had to come to see that struggle alone was the salvation. Everything had to be subordinated to this idea. Training of youth and strengthening of the will to fight should be advanced with all means possible. Firmest authoritarian leadership and 'removal of the damaging cancer of democracy' were the bases of the internal recovery. Hitler then turned to foreign and economic policy. The struggle at the Disarmament Conference in Geneva against Versailles and for Germany's equality was pointless, he said, if the people were not indoctrinated with the will to fight. In the economic sphere, he ruled out increasing exports as a solution on the grounds that world capacity was limited. Settlement policy was the only way to save the peasantry and incorporate many of the jobless. But this would take time, and in any case was not an adequate solution 'since the living-space for the German people is too small'.

Hitler turned to the area of greatest interest to his audience. What he said could not fail to find appeal. The build-up of the armed forces was the most important premiss to the central aim of regaining political power. General conscription had to be brought back. But before that, the state leadership had to see to it that all traces of pacifism, Marxism, and Bolshevism were eradicated from those eligible for military service. The armed forces – the most important institution in the state – must be kept out of politics and above party. The internal struggle was not its concern, and could be left to the organizations of the Nazi movement. Preparations for the build-up of the armed forces had to take place without delay. This period was the most dangerous, and Hitler held out the possibility of a preventive strike from France, probably together with its allies in the east. 'How should political power, once won, be used?' he asked. It was still too early to say. Perhaps the attainment of new export possibilities should be the goal, he hinted. But since earlier in the speech he had already dismissed the notion of increasing exports as the solution to Germany's problems, this could not be taken by his audience as a favoured suggestion. 'Perhaps – and probably better – conquest of new living-space in the east and its ruthless Germanization' was his alternative.[51] The officers present could have been left in no doubt that this was Hitler's preference.

Hitler had not put forward a plan for war to his generals. Nor had he outlined a stage-by-stage programme for the acquisition of 'living-space'. In broad terms, he had restated the fixed ideas he had held to since the mid-1920s at the latest. A war for 'living-space' in the east was certainly implicit in what he was saying. But few had taken his earlier utterances and writings as a serious statement of intent. And few of the generals now regarded 'living-space' as more than a loose metaphor for expansionism – of which they did not disapprove.

Hitler's sole aim at Hammerstein's had been to woo the officers and ensure army support. He largely succeeded. The military leaders' reaction to the speech was mixed. General Ludwig Beck later claimed he had immediately forgotten its content – an indication, if true, that he was unconcerned by what Hitler had to say. Others, such as Werner von Fritsch, Friedrich Fromm, and Eugen Ott, were apparently worried initially by what they heard. Erich Freiherr von dem Bussche-Ippenburg thought Hitler spoke nonsense for an hour, before coming on to the matters concerning the army. Generalleutnant Wilhelm Ritter von Leeb commented acidly that a businessman with a good product did not need to shout about it like a market seller. But there was no opposition to what Hitler had said. And many of those present, as Admiral Erich Raeder later commented, found Hitler's speech 'extraordinarily satisfying'.[52] This was hardly surprising. However disdainful they were of the vulgar and loudmouthed social upstart, the prospect he held out of restoring the power of the army as the basis for expansionism and German dominance accorded with aims laid down by the army leadership even in what they had seen as the dark days of 'fulfilment policy' in the mid-1920s.[53] And Hitler's promises to remove the army from internal politics, place it above party, and to build up the armed forces as the pillar of a militarized nation were music to the ears of the generals – according completely with what Blomberg had told Group- and Army District Commanders earlier in the day.[54] Hitler was, in effect, protecting the army from any possible involvement in a civil war – a danger taken most seriously in late 1932.[55] From the point of view of the army leadership, rearmament and rebuilding the armed forces (predicated on removal of the shackles of Versailles) as the vehicle for restoring Germany's great-power status through expansion (accepting the risk of war) had remained unbroken aims throughout the 1920s and had been restated with new urgency towards the end of the decade. They went hand in hand with the axiom that the officer caste (which was in reality now greatly altered – less 'feudal', more professionally 'modern', youthful, and bourgeois)[56] would regain the status and power in the state that it had traditionally wielded before the Revolution, but which had been threatened and partially undermined by 'Marxism' and democracy. Whatever the generals' scepticism about Hitler, the mass support he commanded offered the prospect of these aims now being fulfilled. While their aims were not identical, it meant that there was a significant overlap in what Hitler and the army leadership wanted. The 'pact' of 1933 was founded on this 'partial identity'.[57]

The strong man in Blomberg's ministry, his Chief of the Ministerial Office, Colonel Walther von Reichenau – bright, ambitious, 'progressive' in his contempt for class-ridden aristocratic and bourgeois conservatism, and long a National Socialist sympathizer – was sure of how the army should react to what Hitler offered. 'Into the new state and uphold there the position due to us,' he is reported to have stated.[58] Never before had the armed forces been 'so identical with the state', he went on, indicating the clear aim, if not the full reality of the position, at the very beginning of the Third Reich.[59] The real meaning of keeping the army out of politics was also made plain by Reichenau, when – in the midst of Göring's unleashed police terror against the Left in Prussia – he remarked at a meeting of army commanders: 'It has to be recognized that we are in a revolution. What is rotten in the state has to go, and that can only happen through terror. The party will ruthlessly proceed against Marxism. Task of the armed forces: stand at ease. No support if those persecuted seek refuge with the troops.'[60] Some of those present were concerned at what they heard. But the message got through, and was passed on. Only one of the officers there protested, and lost his command as a consequence.[61] Though not for the most part as actively sympathetic towards National Socialism as was Reichenau, the leaders of the army which had blocked by force Hitler's attempt to seize power in 1923 had now, within days of his appointment as Chancellor, placed the most powerful institution in the state at his disposal.

Hitler, for his part, lost no time in making plain to the cabinet that military spending was to be given absolute priority. During a discussion in cabinet on 8 February on the financial implications of building a dam in Upper Silesia, he intervened to tell his cabinet colleagues that 'the next five years must be devoted to the restoration of the defence capacity (*Wiederwehrhaftmachung*) of the German people'. Every state-funded work-creation scheme had to be judged with regard to their necessity for this end. 'This idea must always and everywhere be placed in the foreground.'[62]

At a meeting the next day of the Committee for Work Creation to deal with the expenditure envisaged of the 500 million RM available under the revamped Immediate Programme for Work Creation, which Reichskommissar Gereke had prepared for the Schleicher administration, Blomberg expressed his readiness to accept for rearmament purposes the 50 million RM assigned to him by the Finance Minister, while the newly created Reich Commissary for Air Travel was allocated 42.3 million RM in 1933 (out of 127 million RM over a three-year period). Hitler could not contain his impatience. He referred to his comments of the previous day on the absolute priority for rearmaments and the need to assess all public spending on the Immediate Programme in that light. 'For Germany's rearmament,' the Reich Chancellor continued, according to the minutes of the meeting,

billions (*Milliardenbeträge*) are necessary. The sum of 127 million RM for aviation purposes was the minimum that one could consider at all. Germany's future depended exclusively and solely on rebuilding the armed forces. All other expenditure had to be subordinated to the task of rearmament. He could only be satisfied with the petty funds requested by the Defence Ministry on the grounds that the tempo of rearmament could not be more sharply accelerated during the coming year. At any rate he took the view that in any future clash between demands of the armed forces and demands for other purposes the interest of the armed forces had, whatever the circumstances, to take precedence. The provision of funds from the Immediate Programme had also to be decided on this understanding. He viewed the combating of unemployment through the provision of public orders as the most suitable means of aid. The 500-Million Programme was the greatest of its kind and specially suited to be placed at the service of the interests of rearmament. It best allowed the camouflage of works for improving the defence of the country. It was necessary to place special weight on this camouflage in the immediate future since he was convinced that the period between the theoretical recognition of equal military rights of Germany and the re-attainment of a certain level of armament would be the most difficult and most dangerous one. Only when Germany had rearmed to such a level that it was capable of alliance with another power, if need be also against France, would the main difficulties of rearmament have been overcome.[63]

These early meetings, within days of Hitler becoming Chancellor, were crucial in determining the primacy of rearmament. They were also typical of the way Hitler operated, and of the way his power was exercised. Keen though Blomberg and the Reichswehr leadership were to profit from the radically different approach of the new Chancellor to armaments spending, there were practical limitations – financial, organizational, and not least those of international restrictions while the disarmament talks continued – preventing the early stages of rearmament being pushed through as rapidly as Hitler wanted. But where Blomberg was content at first to work for expansion within the realms of the possible, Hitler thought in different – initially quite unrealistic – dimensions. He offered no concrete measures. But his dogmatic assertion of absolute primacy for rearmament, opposed or contradicted by not a single minister, set new ground-rules for action. It changed the concept of the Gereke-Programme for work creation entirely, turning it into a framework for rearmament. It provided, whatever the early practical limits on the scope of rearmament, immediate opportunities for new planning and rebuilding within the armed forces. It prompted by the beginning of April the 'Second Armaments Programme', with funding provided outside the state budget and placed in the hands of the army itself. With Hjalmar Schacht succeeding Hans Luther in March as President of the Reichsbank, Hitler found the person he needed to mastermind the secret and unlimited funding of rearmament. Where the Reichswehr budget had on average been 700–800 million RM a year, Schacht, through the device of Mefo-Bills – a disguised discounting of government bills by the Reichsbank – was soon able to guarantee to the Reichswehr the fantastic sum of 35 billion RM over an eight-year period.[64]

Given this backing, after a sluggish start, the rearmament programme took off stratospherically in 1934. The result, as Schacht later acknowledged, was an inevitable collision between armaments and consumer spending, which would eventually lead to major economic difficulties.[65] These were to surface in the first substantial economic impasse of 1935-6 that culminated in the Four-Year Plan. But since that Plan underlined and reaffirmed the absolute primacy of rearmament, the problem could only deepen in the remaining peacetime years and not be resolved outside war. The ruination of state finances was implicit in the decision – taken on political and ideological grounds at the very outset of Hitler's Chancellorship – to make unlimited funding available for rearmament, whatever the consequences for the economy. Though war was not actually planned in February 1933, the rearmament policy then adopted tilted the economy in a direction which could only be remedied either by a re-entry into the international economy or by conquest and domination attained through the gamble of war. Hitler had never made a secret of which option he would prefer.

The decision to give absolute priority to rearmament was the basis of the pact, resting on mutual benefit, between Hitler and the army which, though frequently troubled, was a key foundation of the Third Reich. Hitler established the parameters in February 1933. But these were no more than the expression of the entente he had entered into with Blomberg on becoming Chancellor.[66] The new policy was possible because Hitler had bound himself to the interests of the most powerful institution in the land. The army leaders, for their part, had their interests served because they had bound themselves, in their eyes, to a political front-man who could nationalize the masses and restore the army to its rightful power-position in the state. What they had not reckoned with was that within five years the traditional power-élite of the officers corps would be transformed into a mere functional élite, serving a political master who was taking it into uncharted territory.[67]

II

In the first weeks of his Chancellorship, Hitler took steps to bring not just the 'big battalions' of the army leadership behind the new regime, but also the major organizations of economic leaders. Landholders needed little persuasion. Their main organization, the Reich Agrarian League (Reichslandbund) – dominated by East Elbian estate-owners – had been strongly pro-Nazi before Hitler became Chancellor. Hitler left agrarian policy in its initial stage to his German National Coalition partner Hugenberg. Early measures taken in February to defend indebted farm property against creditors and to protect agricultural produce by imposing higher import duties and provide support for grain prices ensured that the agrarians were not disappointed.[68] With Hugenberg at the Economics Ministry, their interests seemed certain to be well looked after.

Tensions between agrarians and industrialists over the vexed issue of protection of agriculture had existed since the 1890s. The new favouritism shown to agriculture seemed destined to sour relations with big business. The initial scepticism, hesitancy, and misgivings of most business leaders immediately following Hitler's accession to the Chancellorship were not dispelled overnight. There was still considerable disquiet in the business community when Gustav Krupp von Bohlen und Halbach, head of the mighty Krupp iron and steel concern and chairman of the Reich Association of German Industry, and other leading industrialists received invitations to a meeting at Göring's official residence on 20 February, at which Hitler would outline his economic policy.[69] Krupp, up to then critical of Hitler, went to the meeting prepared, as he had done at meetings with previous Chancellors, to speak up for industry. In particular, he intended to stress the need for export-led growth and to underline the damaging consequences of protectionism in favour of agriculture. In the event, he could make neither point. The businessmen were kept waiting by Göring, and had to wait even longer till Hitler appeared. They were then treated to a classic Hitler monologue. In a speech lasting an hour and a half, he barely touched on economic matters, except in the most general sense. He assuaged his business audience, as he had done on earlier occasions, by upholding private property and individual enterprise, and by denying rumours of planned radical experimentation in the economy. The rest was largely a restatement of his views on the subordination of the economy to politics, the need to eradicate Marxism, restore inner strength and unity, and thus be in a position to face external enemies. The coming election marked a final chance to reject Communism by the ballot-box. If that did not happen, force – he darkly hinted – would be used. It was a fight to the death between the nation and Communism, a struggle that would decide Germany's fate for the next century.[70] When Hitler had finished, Krupp felt in no position to deliver his prepared speech. He merely improvised a few words of thanks and added some general remarks about a strong state serving the well-being of the country.[71] At this point, Hitler left.

The hidden agenda of the meeting became clear once Göring started speaking. He repeated Hitler's assurances that economic experiments need not be feared, and that the balance of power would not be altered by the coming election – to be the last for perhaps a hundred years. But the election, he claimed, was nonetheless crucial. And those not in the forefront of the

political battle had a responsibility to make financial sacrifices.[72] Once
Göring, too, had left, Schacht bade those present to visit the cash-till.
Three million marks were pledged, and within weeks delivered.[73] With this
donation, big business was helping consolidate Hitler's rule. But the offering
was less one of enthusiastic backing than of political extortion.[74]

Despite their financial support, industrialists continued at first to look
with a wary eye at the new regime. Some drew satisfaction from Hitler's
vague expression of support for export trade and commitment to currency
stability in his speech on 23 March, and the Reich Association correspondingly voiced its support for the new government. But its members were
already realizing that their position was also not left untouched by the
changes sweeping over Germany. In early April, Krupp capitulated to Nazi
pressure to replace the Reich Association by a new, nazified body. He also
agreed to the dismissal of Jewish employees, and the removal of all Jewish
businessmen from representative positions in commerce and industry. The
following month, the once-mighty Association dissolved itself and was
replaced by the nazified Reich Estate of German Industry (Reichsstand
der Deutschen Industrie). Alongside such pressure, business recovery, high
profits, secure private property (apart from that of Jewish businessmen),
the crushing of Marxism, and the subduing of labour saw big business
increasingly content to adjust to full collaboration with the new regime,
whatever the irksome bureaucratic controls imposed on it.[75]

Hitler's style, as the industrialists experienced on 20 February, was certainly different to that of his predecessors in the Chancellor's office. His
views on the economy were also unconventional. He was wholly ignorant
of any formal understanding of the principles of economics. For him, as he
stated to the industrialists, economics was of secondary importance, entirely
subordinated to politics. His crude social-Darwinism dictated his approach
to the economy, as it did his entire political 'world-view'. Since struggle
among nations would be decisive for future survival, Germany's economy
had to be subordinated to the preparation, then carrying out, of this struggle.
That meant that liberal ideas of economic competition had to be replaced
by the subjection of the economy to the dictates of the national interest.
Similarly, any 'socialist' ideas in the Nazi programme had to follow the
same dictates. Hitler was never a socialist. But although he upheld private
property, individual entrepreneurship, and economic competition, and disapproved of trade unions and workers' interference in the freedom of owners
and managers to run their concerns, the state, not the market, would
determine the shape of economic development. Capitalism was, therefore,

left in place. But in operation it was turned into an adjunct of the state. There is little point in inventing terms to describe such an economic 'system'. Neither 'state capitalism', nor a 'third way' between capitalism and socialism suffices. Certainly, Hitler entertained notions of a prosperous German society, in which old class privileges had disappeared, exploiting the benefits of modern technology and a higher standard of living. But he thought essentially in terms of race, not class, of conquest, not economic modernization. Everything was consistently predicated on war to establish dominion. The new society in Germany would come about through struggle, its high standard of living on the backs of the slavery of conquered peoples. It was an imperialist concept from the nineteenth century adapted to the technological potential of the twentieth.[76]

Lacking, as he did, a grasp of even the rudiments of economic theory, Hitler can scarcely be regarded as an economic innovator.[77] The extraordinary economic recovery that rapidly formed an essential component of the Führer myth was not of Hitler's making. He showed no initial interest in the work-creation plans eagerly developed by civil servants in the Labour Ministry. With Schacht (at this stage) sceptical, Hugenberg opposed, Seldte taking little initiative, and industry hostile, Hitler did nothing to further the work-creation schemes before the end of May. By then, they had been taken up by the State Secretary in the Finance Ministry, Fritz Reinhardt, and put forward as a programme for action. Even at this stage, Hitler remained hesitant, and had to be convinced that the programme would not lead to renewed inflation. Wilhelm Lautenbach, a senior civil servant in the Economics Ministry whose own full-scale programme had had no chance of implementation under Brüning in 1931, persuaded him that, though he was the most powerful man in Germany, even he could not produce inflation in the prevailing economic circumstances.[78] Finally, on 31 May, Hitler summoned ministers and economic experts to the Reich Chancellery, and heard that all but Hugenberg were in favour of the Reinhardt Programme. The following day, the 'Law for Reduction of Unemployment' was announced. Within a month or so, Schacht's early scepticism had turned into enthusiasm. Through the device of exchange-bills underwritten by the government (an idea earlier developed under Papen by Lautenbach, and the forerunner of the Mefo-Bills, soon to be introduced as a way of funding the early stages of rearmament), Schacht now conjured up the necessary short-term credits.[79] The rest was largely the work of bankers, civil servants, planners and industrialists.[80] As we have noted, Hitler saw the work-creation programme (which simply extended the earlier schemes devised under Papen and Schleicher) merely in the context of rearmament plans. Otherwise, his main interest was in its propaganda value. And, indeed, as public works schemes initially, then increasingly rearmament, began to pull Germany out of recession and wipe away mass unemployment more quickly than any forecasters had dared speculate, Hitler garnered the full propaganda benefit.[81]

But indirectly Hitler did make a significant contribution to the economic recovery by reconstituting the political framework for business activity and by the image of national renewal that he represented. The ruthless assault on 'Marxism' and reordering of industrial relations which he presided over, the work-creation programme that he eventually backed, and the total priority for rearmament laid down at the outset, helped to shape a climate in which economic recovery – already starting as he took office as Chancellor – could gather pace. And in one area, at least, he provided a direct stimulus to recovery in a key branch of industry: motor-car manufacturing.

Hitler's propaganda instinct, not his economic know-how, led him towards an initiative that both assisted the recovery of the economy (which was beginning to take place anyway) and caught the public imagination. On 11 February, a few days before his meeting with the industrialists, Hitler had sought out the opportunity to deliver – instead of Reich President Hindenburg, who was unwell – the opening address at the International Automobile and Motor-Cycle Exhibition on the Kaiserdamm in Berlin. That the German Chancellor should make the speech was itself a novelty: this alone caused a stir. The assembled leaders of the car industry were delighted. They were even more delighted when they heard Hitler elevate car manufacture to the position of the most important industry of the future and promise a programme including gradual tax relief for the industry and the implementation of a 'generous plan for road-building'. If living-standards had previously been weighed against kilometres of railway track, they would in future be measured against kilometres of roads; these were 'great tasks which also belong to the construction programme of the German economy', Hitler declared.[82] The speech was later stylized by Nazi propaganda as 'the turning-point in the history of German motorization'.[83] It marked the beginning of the 'Autobahn-builder' part of the Führer myth.

Hitler had, in fact, offered no specific programme for the car industry; merely the prospect of one.[84] The ideas for tax relief for the industry had, not surprisingly, come from the car manufacturers themselves.[85] The tax reductions actually implemented in spring 1933 did not represent a preconceived Nazi motorization programme, but were part of a wider framework of measures to stimulate the economy.[86] What road-building plans were in

Hitler's mind were not made clear in his speech. In all likelihood they were those that the Munich road-engineer Fritz Todt had outlined in a brief memorandum composed in December 1932, and sent shortly afterwards to Hitler, arguing for the construction of 5–6,000 kilometres of motorway to be built within the framework of 'a National Socialist construction programme'.[87] It was conceived on a scale that could not rely on private companies, but had to have state planning and control. Moreover, Todt envisaged his scheme needing up to 600,000 unemployed workers – some 10 per cent of the total number of unemployed – and thus contributing to the combating of unemployment. Todt himself was, in fact, no outright innovator in his motorization schemes. Autostradas were already being built in Fascist Italy. And Todt was taking up and greatly expanding ideas for a north–south Autobahn of 881 kilometres advanced in the 1920s by the clumsily entitled 'Association for the Preparation of the Motorway (*Autostraße*) Hansestädte–Frankfurt–Basel' (HAFRABA for short).[88] But Hitler was impressed – not least at the grandiosity of Todt's scheme, and its implications for reducing unemployment. It made good propaganda in the election campaign.

Even so, the significance of Hitler's speech on 11 February should not be underrated. It sent positive signals to car manufacturers. They were struck by the new Chancellor, whose long-standing fascination for the motor-car and his memory for detail of construction-types and -figures meant he sounded not only sympathetic but knowledgeable to the car bosses.[89] The *Völkischer Beobachter*, exploiting the propaganda potential of Hitler's speech, immediately opened up to its readers the prospect of car-ownership. Not a social élite with its Rolls-Royces, but the mass of the people with their people's car (*Volksauto*), was the alluring prospect.[90] It was an idea – a car for everyman, at a price of no more than 1,000 Reich Marks – that Hitler, with his eye on propaganda more than the automobile market, was already advancing early in 1933.[91]

In the weeks following his speech, there were already notable signs that the car industry was picking up. More than twice as many four-wheeled vehicles were produced in the second quarter of 1933 compared with the same period in the previous year.[92] The removal of car licence tax for vehicles registered after 31 March gave the industry a further boost. The beginnings of recovery for the automobile industry had spin-off effects for factories producing component parts, and for the metal industry.[93] The recovery was not part of a well-conceived programme on Hitler's part. Nor can it be wholly, or even mainly, attributed to his speech. Much of it would have happened anyway, once the slump had begun to give way to cyclical recovery.[94] It remains the case, however, that the car manufacturers were still gloomy about their prospects before Hitler spoke.

Hitler, whatever importance he had attached to the propaganda effect of his speech, had given the right signals to the industry. Car manufacturers and others with a vested interest lost no time in interpreting the signals to their own advantage – and to the advantage of the regime. Unsolicited, the business manager of HAFRABA provided Hitler already in March with detailed plans for a stretch of motorway in the Main-Neckar valley. Hitler took up the plan 'with great enthusiasm', called it 'a gigantic idea' which would open up a 'new epoch' and declared his readiness to ensure its implementation.[95] After the 'gigantic progamme' of road-building he announced on 1 May had met substantial obstacles in the Transport Ministry (backed by the German Railways, the Reichsbahn), which argued that the ordinary road network should first be improved and indicated principled doubts about the virtues of a motorway programme, Hitler insisted that the 'Enterprise Reich Motorways' (Unternehmen Reichsautobahnen) be carried through. This was eventually placed at the end of June in the hands of Fritz Todt as General Inspector for German Roadways (Generalinspektor für das deutsche Straßenwesen). Further objections to Todt's new powers raised by Interior Minister Frick and Transport Minister Eltz-Rübenach were swept aside by Hitler. By the end of November, Todt had been given wide-ranging powers, answering only to Hitler himself in the road-construction programme, and was provided by Reichsbank President Schacht with extensive funding credit.[96]

In the stimulus to the car trade and the building of the motorways – areas which, inspired by the American model, had great popular appeal and appeared to symbolize both the leap forward into an exciting, technological modern era and the 'new Germany', now standing on its own feet again – Hitler had made a decisive contribution.[97]

III

By the time Hitler addressed the leaders of the automobile industry on 11 February, the Reichstag election campaign was under way. Hitler had opened it the previous evening with his first speech in the Sportpalast since becoming Chancellor. The enormous hall was packed to the rafters. With the mass media now at his disposal, the speech was carried live on radio to the whole country. Under great banners attacking Marxism, Goebbels set the scene in graphic detail for radio listeners, numbering, he claimed, as many as 20 million. Skilfully, he built up the expectations of the massive radio audience:

I ask you to let your fantasy take hold [the Propaganda Minister told his listeners]. Imagine: this enormous building, down below a huge stalls arena, flanked with side aisles, the circle, the upper circle – all *one* mass of people! You can't recognize individuals, you see only (shouts and choruses of voices rise up) people, people, people – a mass of people. You can hear how out of the masses the cries 'Germany arise!' ring out, how shouts resound of 'Heil' to the Leader of the Movement . . . to the Reich Chancellor Adolf Hitler. The SA leader – Standartenführer Voß – now gives the signal for the entry of the flags and standards. Down there, from the end of the Sportpalast, the four Berlin standards are moved, followed by the hundreds of Berlin party banners. (The German anthem sounds out and is sung.) . . . Amid the tones of the German anthem the flags are borne through the wide hall. The entire mass is rapturously singing the German anthem . . . The Sportpalast offers a wonderful, imposing picture of the mass demonstration. The people stand and wait and sing with raised hands. You see only people, people, people. All around the galleries are decked with swastika flags. The mood intensifies, the expectancy is full of tension . . . Any moment the Reich Chancellor can arrive . . .

Then Hitler came. 'A crescendo of shouts of "Heil" and rapturous cheering' could be heard over Goebbels's broadcast. 'You can hear it,' the Propaganda Minister exulted. 'The Führer has arrived!'[98]

Hitler began quietly, almost hesitantly. For fourteen years the Weimar parties had ruined Germany. Rebuilding the country had to begin from the bottom. He promised a government that would not lie to and swindle the people as Weimar governments had done. Rebuilding could only be done by the people itself, by its own efforts, by its will, without any help from outside. Not class theories but 'eternal laws' would be the basis of the recovery: the struggle to sustain the German people's existence was the goal. And only strength would bring world peace. He raised the tempo. Parties of class division would be destroyed. 'Never, never will I depart from the task of eradicating from Germany Marxism and its accompaniments,' he declared. '*One* must be the victor here: either Marxism or the German people. And Germany will be victorious.' National unity, resting on the German peasant and the German worker – restored to the national community – would be the basis of the future society. The value of personality, the creative strength of the individual, would be upheld. All manifestations of a parliamentary democratic system would be combated. The end of corruption in public life would go hand in hand with a 'restoration of German honour'. Not least, young people would have instilled in them the great traditions of the German past. It was, he declared, 'a programme of national revival (*Wiedererhebung*) in all areas of life, intolerant towards anyone who sins against the nation, brother and friend to anyone willing to fight alongside for the resurrection of his people, of our nation'. Hitler reached the rhetorical climax of his speech. 'German people, give us four years, then judge and sentence us. German people, give us four years, and I swear that as we and I entered into this office, I will then be willing to go.' The pathos of his finale included an adaptation of the ending of the 'Our Father' (in its Protestant form). 'I can't free myself from belief in my people, can't get away from the conviction that this nation will once again arise, can't distance myself from the love of this, my people, and hold as firm as a rock to the conviction that some time the hour will come when the millions who today hate us will stand behind us and with us will welcome what has been created together, struggled for under difficulty, attained at cost: the new German Reich of greatness and honour and strength and glory and justice. Amen.'[99]

'A fantastic speech', Goebbels called it. 'Wholly against Marxism. At the end great pathos. "Amen". That has force and strikes home.'[100] It was indeed a powerful piece of rhetoric. But it was little more than that. The 'programme' offered nothing concrete – other than the showdown with Marxism. National 'resurrection' to be brought about through will, strength, and unity was what it amounted to. Jews were not mentioned. For all nationalists – not just for Nazis – the sentiments Hitler expressed could not fail to find appeal. 'Exactly the right mixture for his listeners: brutality, threats, display of strength, then again humility before the often cited "Almighty". The masses in the Sportpalast go into a frenzy,' commented one of the 20 million or so radio listeners, a cultured member of the Leipzig bourgeoisie, unsympathetic to the Nazis. 'The man grows visibly through the task which has fallen on him,' he remarked.[101] For another listening to his speech over the radio, the Hamburg middle-class nationalist, not Nazi, Luise Solmitz, Hitler's castigation of 'the dirt of these dreadful fourteen years' was 'what we felt'. 'Not a speaker, but leader of genius' was how she described him.[102]

The accompaniment to the campaign (during which Hitler once more was tireless in his propaganda efforts, speaking to huge audiences in numerous cities) was a wave of unparalleled state-sponsored terror and repression against political opponents in states under Nazi control. Above all, this was the case in the huge state of Prussia, which had already come under Reich control in the Papen takeover of 20 July 1932. The orchestrator here was the commissary Prussian Minister of the Interior Hermann Göring. Under his aegis, heads of the Prussian police and administration were 'cleansed' (following the first purges after the Papen coup) of the remainder of those who might prove obstacles in the new wind of change that was blowing. Göring provided their successors with verbal instructions in unmistakably blunt language as to what he expected of police and administration during the election campaign. And in a written decree of 17 February, he ordered the police to work together with the 'national associations' of SA, SS, and Stahlhelm, support 'national propaganda with all their strength', and combat the actions of 'organizations hostile to the state' with all the force at their disposal, 'where necessary making ruthless use of firearms'. He added that policemen using firearms would, whatever the consequences, be backed by him; those failing in their duty out of a 'false sense of consideration' had, on the contrary, to expect disciplinary action.[103] Unsurprisingly in such a climate, the violence unleashed by Nazi terror bands against their opponents and against Jewish victims was uncontrolled. This was especially the case once the SA, SS, and Stahlhelm had been brought in on 22 February as 'auxiliary police' on the pretext of an alleged increase in 'left-radical' violence. Intimidation was massive. Communists were particularly savagely repressed. Individuals were brutally beaten, tortured, seriously wounded, or killed, with total impunity. Communist meetings and demonstrations were banned, in Prussia and in other states under Nazi control, as were their newspapers. Bans, too, on organs of the SPD and restrictions on reporting imposed on other newspapers effectively muzzled the press, even when the bans were successfully challenged in the courts as illegal, and the newspapers reinstated.[104]

During this first orgy of state violence, Hitler played the moderate. His acting ability was undiminished. He gave the cabinet the impression that radical elements in the movement were disobeying his orders but that he would bring them under control, and asked for patience to allow him to discipline the sections of the party that had got out of hand. 'We all agreed that there was no reason to doubt Hitler's intentions, and hoped that experience in the Cabinet would have a beneficial effect on him,' recalled Papen.[105] When the Zentrum – which Hitler knew he might still need on his side – protested to Hindenburg and Papen at 'the unbelievable conditions', Hitler put out a party proclamation denouncing 'provocatory elements' who had broken up Zentrum meetings, and ordering 'extreme discipline'. All the energies of the campaign had to be directed against Marxism, he added.[106]

In actual fact, the violence directed at the Zentrum had been in no small measure attributable to Hitler's own tirade against the head of the Zentrum-run state government of Württemberg a week earlier, a speech whose radio transmission – to Hitler's fury – had been abruptly ended when unknown persons severed the radio cable.[107]

Hitler had no need to involve himself in the violence of February 1933. Its deployment could be left safely to Göring, and to leading Nazis in other states. In any case, it needed only the green light to Nazi thugs, sure now of the protection of the state, to unleash their pent-up aggression against those well known to them as long-standing enemies in their neighbourhoods and work-places. The terror-wave in Prussia in February was the first sign that state-imposed constraints on inhumanity were now suddenly lifted. It was an early indicator of the 'breach of civilization' that would give the Third Reich its historical character.

But it was not that the brutality and violence damaged Hitler's reputation in the population. Many who had been initially sceptical or critical were beginning, during February, to think that Hitler was 'the right man', and should be given a chance.[108] A slight upturn in the economy helped. But the fervent anti-Marxism of much of the population was more important. The long-standing hatred of Socialism and Communism – both bracketed together as 'Marxism' – was played upon by Nazi propaganda and turned into outright anti-Communist paranoia. Pumped up by the Nazis, fear of a Communist rising was in the air. The closer the election came, the shriller grew the hysteria. The full-scale assault on the Left was, therefore, sure of massive popular support. One characteristic report from a Catholic area, where 'Marxists' were seen as the enemies of religion, order and the nation, lauded the strong-arm tactics in Prussia, and gave direct credit for them to Hitler himself. 'Hitler's clearing up nicely in Prussia. He's throwing the parasites and spongers on the people straight out on their ear. He should follow it up in Bavaria, too, especially in Munich, and carry out a similar purge . . . If Hitler carries on the work as he has done so far, he'll have the trust of the great proportion of the German people at the coming Reichstag election.'[109]

The violence and intimidation would probably have continued in much the same vein until the election on 5 March. Nothing suggests the Nazi leadership had anything more spectacular in mind.[110] But on 27 February, Marinus van der Lubbe set fire to the Reichstag.

Marinus van der Lubbe came from a Dutch working-class family, and had formerly belonged to the Communist Party youth organization in

Holland. He had eventually broken with the Communist Party in 1931. He arrived in Berlin on 18 February 1933. He was twenty-four years old, intelligent, a solitary individual, unconnected with any political groups, but possessed of a strong sense of injustice at the misery of the working class at the hands of the capitalist system. In particular, he was determined to make a lone and spectacular act of defiant protest at the 'Government of National Concentration' in order to galvanize the working class into struggle against their repression. Three attempts at arson on 25 February in different buildings in Berlin failed.[111] Two days later he succeeded in his protest – though the consequences were scarcely those he had envisaged.[112]

On the evening of 27 February, Putzi Hanfstaengl should have been dining at Goebbels's house, along with Hitler. But, suffering from a heavy cold and high temperature, he had taken to his bed in a room in Göring's official residence, where he was temporarily accommodated, in the immediate vicinity of the Reichstag building. In mid-evening he was awakened by the cries of the housekeeper: the Reichstag was on fire. He shot out of bed, looked out of the window, saw the building in flames, and immediately rushed to ring up Goebbels, saying, breathlessly, that he urgently had to speak to Hitler. When Goebbels asked what it was about, and whether he could pass on a message, Hanfstaengl said: 'Tell him the Reichstag is burning.' 'Is that meant to be a joke?' was Goebbels's reply.[113] Goebbels thought it was 'a mad fantasy report' and refused at first to tell Hitler. But his inquiries revealed that the report was true. At that, Hitler and Goebbels raced through Berlin, to find Göring already on the scene and 'in full flow' (ganz groß in Fahrt). Papen soon joined them. The Nazi leaders were all convinced that the fire was a signal for a Communist uprising – a 'last attempt', as Goebbels put it, 'through fire and terror to sow confusion in order in the general panic to grasp power for themselves'.[114] Fears that the Communists would not remain passive, that they would undertake some major show of force before the election, had been rife among the Nazi leadership – and among non-Nazi members of the national government. A police raid on the KPD's central offices in Karl-Liebknecht-Haus on 24 February had intensified the anxieties. Though they actually found nothing of note, the police claimed to have found vast amounts of treasonable material, including leaflets summoning the population to armed revolt. Göring added to this with a statement to the press. The police discoveries showed that Germany was about to be cast into the chaos of Bolshevism, he alleged. Assassinations of political leaders, attacks on public buildings, and the murder of wives and families of public figures were among the horrors he evoked. No evidence was ever made public.[115] The fears – genuine and fabricated – were in some ways a direct continuation of the anxieties about a Communist-led general strike that had been the basis of the Reichswehr's 'war-games' scenario which had brought down the Papen government at the beginning of December 1932. They were also fuelled by Hitler's lasting phobia about November 1918. The anti-Communist hysteria of late February 1933 gave such fears an altogether sharper edge.[116] The panic reaction of the Nazi leadership to the Reichstag fire, and the rapidity with which the draconian measures against the Communists were improvised, derived directly from those fears.

The first members of the police to interrogate van der Lubbe, who had been immediately apprehended and had straight away confessed, proclaiming his 'protest', had no doubt that he had set fire to the building alone, that no one else was implicated.[117] But Göring, whose first reactions to learning of the fire appear to have been concern for the precious tapestries in the building, took little convincing from officials on the spot that the fire must have been the product of a Communist plot.[118] Hitler, who arrived towards 10.30p.m., an hour or so after Göring, was rapidly persuaded to draw the same conclusion. Göring told him that the fire was unquestionably the work of the Communists. One arsonist had already been arrested and several Communist deputies had been in the building only minutes before the blaze.[119] It was the beginning of the Communist uprising, claimed Göring. Not a moment must be lost.[120] Hitler told Papen: 'This is a God-given signal, Herr Vice-Chancellor! If this fire, as I believe, is the work of the Communists, then we must crush out this murderous pest with an iron fist!'[121] When Rudolf Diels, later to become the first head of the Prussian Gestapo, tried to tell Hitler about the interrogation of van der Lubbe, he found the Reich Chancellor in a near-hysterical state. Diels tried to say that the fire was the work of a 'madman' (einen Verrückten). But Hitler brusquely interrupted, shouting that it had been planned long in advance. The Communist deputies were to be hanged that very night, he raged. Nor was any mercy to be shown to the Social Democrats or Reichsbanner.[122] Hitler's furious tirades, intent on terroristic revenge against the Communists, dominated a hastily convened consultation, involving Göring, Goebbels and Frick, in Göring's official residence. Good actor though he was, Hitler was not feigning. Nor was he sufficiently in control of himself to give clear orders.[123] It was Göring who emitted a frenzied stream of confused directions to Diels, ordering a full-scale police alert, unsparing use of firearms, and mass arrests of Communists and Socialists. Diels thought the whole atmosphere resembled that of a madhouse.[124]

Hitler then went to an improvised meeting around 11.15p.m. in the Prussian Ministry of the Interior, dealing mainly with security implications for Prussia, and from there accompanied Goebbels to the Berlin offices of the *Völkischer Beobachter*, where an inflammatory editorial was rapidly prepared and a new front page of the party newspaper made up.[125]

At the meeting in the Prussian Ministry of the Interior, it was the German National State Secretary Ludwig Grauert, firmly convinced himself that the Communists had set the Reichstag alight, who proposed an emergency decree for the State of Prussia aimed at arson and acts of terror.[126] By the following morning, however, Reich Minister of the Interior Wilhelm Frick had come up with the draft of a decree 'For the Protection of People and State' which extended the emergency measures to the whole of the Reich – something attributed by Blomberg to Hitler's presence of mind – and gave the Reich government (in the initial draft it was the Reich Minister of the Interior) powers of intervention in the Länder. Frick could use as his basis draft schemes for a state of emergency prepared at the time of the Papen coup against Prussia the previous July and the 'war-games' of Colonel Ott in December.[127] But a crucial difference was that under Frick's draft decree emergency executive power was placed not in the hands of the Reichswehr, but given to the Reich Minister of the Interior (later altered to the Reich Government). A military state of emergency would have limited Hitler's power. It might also have jeopardized the holding of the elections on which the Chancellor was relying. As it was, with one move, the improvised emergency decree had decisively strengthened Hitler's hand. The road to dictatorship was now wide open.[128]

The emergency decree 'For the Protection of People and State' was the last item dealt with by the cabinet at its meeting on the morning of 28 February.[129] With one brief paragraph, the personal liberties enshrined in the Weimar Constitution – including freedom of speech, of association and of the press, and privacy of postal and telephone communications – were suspended indefinitely. With another brief paragraph, the autonomy of the Länder was overridden by the right of the Reich government to intervene to restore order.[130] This right would be made ample use of in the immediate aftermath of the election to ensure Nazi control throughout all the German states. The hastily constructed emergency decree amounted to the charter of the Third Reich.

By the time of the cabinet meeting, Hitler's near-hysterical mood of the previous evening had given way to colder ruthlessness. The 'psychologically correct moment for the showdown' with the KPD had arrived. It was pointless to wait longer, he told the cabinet. The struggle against the Communists should not be dependent on 'juristical considerations'.[131] There was no likelihood that this would be the case. The rounding up of Communist deputies and functionaries had already been set in train by Göring during the night in raids carried out with massive brutality.[132] Communists were the main targets. But Social Democrats, trade unionists, and left-wing intellectuals such as Carl Ossietzky were also among those dragged into improvised prisons, often in the cellars of SA or SS local headquarters, and savagely beaten, tortured, and in some cases murdered.[133] By April, the number taken into 'protective custody' in Prussia alone was some 25,000.[134]

The violence and repression were widely popular. The 'emergency decree' that took away all personal liberties and established the platform for dictatorship was warmly welcomed. A provincial newspaper from the alpine outreaches of Bavaria – though long sympathetic towards the Nazis almost certainly reflecting feelings extending beyond the immediate support for the NSDAP – declared that the 'Emergency Decree' had 'finally got to the centre of the German disease, the ulcer which had for years poisoned and infected the German blood, Bolshevism, the deadly enemy of Germany . . . This Emergency Decree will find no opponent despite the quite draconian measures which it threatens. Against murderers, arsonists, and poisoners there can only be the most rigorous defence, against terror the reckoning through the death penalty. The fanatics who would like to make a robbers' cave out of Germany must be rendered harmless.' The whole of western culture, resting on Christianity, was at stake, the leading article concluded. 'And for this reason we welcome the recent Emergency Decree.'[135] The tone directly reflected Göring's account of the supposed findings in the Karl-Liebknecht-Haus.[136]

From the other end of the country, the Hamburg former schoolteacher Luise Solmitz also swallowed Göring's story in its entirety: 'They wanted to send armed gangs into the villages to murder and and start fires. Meanwhile, the terror was to take over the large cities stripped of their police. Poison, boiling water, all tools from the most refined to the most primitive, were to be used as weapons. It sounds like a robbers' tale – if it were not Russia that had experienced asiatic methods and orgies of torture that a Germanic mind, even if sick, cannot imagine, and if healthy cannot believe.'[137]

Luise Solmitz, like her friends and neighbours, was persuaded to cast her vote for Hitler. 'Now it's important to support what he's doing with every means,' an acquaintance who had up to then not supported the

NSDAP told her.[138] 'The entire thoughts and feelings of most Germans are dominated by Hitler,' Frau Solmitz commented. 'His fame rises to the stars, he is the saviour of a wicked, sad German world.'[139]

On 4 March, Hitler made a final, impassioned plea to the electorate in a speech broadcast from Königsberg. At the end, he stated with great pathos that the Reich President, the liberator of East Prussia, and he, the ordinary soldier who had done his duty on the western front, had joined hands. As the speech ended, the sounds of the 'Niederländisches Dankgebet', the 'chorale of Leuthen' associated with Frederick the Great's victory over the Austrians in 1757, blended with the bells of Königsberg Cathedral. Goebbels had left nothing out in the suggested uniting of the old and the new Germany. Loudspeakers stationed in the streets allowed those marching in the torch-light processions all over Germany on the 'Day of the Awakening Nation' to listen to their Leader.[140]

When the results were declared the next day, the Nazis had won 43.9 per cent of the vote, giving them 288 out of 647 seats in the new Reichstag. Their nationalist coalition partners had gained 8.0 per cent. Despite the draconian terror, the KPD had still managed an astonishing 12.3 per cent, and the SPD 18.3 per cent – together the parties of the Left, even now, gaining almost a third of all votes cast. The Zentrum received only a marginally smaller proportion of the vote (11.2 per cent) than it had done the previous November. Support for the remaining parties had dwindled almost to nothing.[141] Goebbels claimed the result as a 'glorious triumph'.[142] It was rather less than that. Substantial gains had been certain. They had undoubtedly been assisted by a late surge following the Reichstag fire. Hitler had hoped for an absolute majority for the NSDAP. As it was, the absolute majority narrowly attained by the government coalition left him dependent on his conservative allies. He would now not be rid of them at least as long as Hindenburg lived, he was reported as saying on hearing the results.[143] Still, even allowing for the climate of intense repression against the Left, 43.9 per cent of the vote was not easy to attain under the Weimar electoral system. The NSDAP had profited above all from the support of previous non-voters in a record turn-out of 88.8 per cent.[144] And though the heaviest support continued to come from Protestant parts of the country, sizeable gains had this time also been made in Catholic areas which the NSDAP had earlier found difficult to penetrate. In Lower Bavaria, for instance, the Nazi vote rose from 18.5 per cent in November 1932 to 39.2 per cent; in Cologne-Aachen from 17.4 to 30.1 per cent.[145] Not least: leaving aside the Left, not all those who voted for parties other than the NSDAP were opposed to everything that Hitler stood for. Once Hitler, the pluralist system liquidated, was able to transform his public image from party to national leader, a potentially far larger reservoir of support than that given to him in March 1933 would be at his disposal.

IV

The election of 5 March was the trigger to the real 'seizure of power' that took place over the following days in those Länder not already under Nazi control. Hitler needed to do little. Party activists needed no encouragement to undertake the 'spontaneous' actions that inordinately strengthened his power as Reich Chancellor.[146]

The pattern was in each case similar: pressure on the non-Nazi state governments to place a National Socialist in charge of the police; threatening demonstrations from marching SA and SS troops in the big cities; the symbolic raising of the swastika banner on town halls; the capitulation with scarcely any resistance of the elected governments; the imposition of a Reich Commissar under the pretext of restoring order. The 'coordination' process began in Hamburg even before the election had taken place. In Bremen, Lübeck, Schaumburg-Lippe, Hessen, Baden, Württemberg, Saxony, and finally Bavaria – the largest state after Prussia – the process was repeated. Between 5 and 9 March these states, too, were brought in line with the Reich government. In Bavaria, in particular, long-standing acolytes of Hitler were appointed as commissary government ministers: Adolf Wagner in charge of the Ministry of the Interior, Hans Frank as Justice Minister, Hans Schemm as Education Minister. Even more significant were the appointments of Ernst Röhm as State Commissar without Portfolio, Heinrich Himmler as commander of the Munich police, and Reinhard Heydrich – the tall, blond head of the Party's Security Service (Sicherheitsdienst, SD), a cashiered naval officer, still under thirty, in the early stages of his meteoric rise to command over the security police in the SS empire – as head of the Bavarian Political Police. The weakening of Prussia through the Papen coup and the effective Nazi takeover there in February provided the platform and model for the extension of control to the other Länder. These now passed more or less completely into Nazi hands, with little regard for their German Nationalist partners. Despite the semblance of legality, the usurpation of the powers of the Länder by the Reich was a plain breach of the Constitution. Force and pressure by the Nazi organizations themselves – political blackmail

– had been solely responsible for creating the 'unrest' that had prompted the alleged restoration of 'order'. The terms of the emergency decree of 28 February provided no justification since there was plainly no need for defence from any 'communist acts of violence endangering the state'. The only such acts were those of the Nazis themselves.[147]

In the triumphalist atmosphere following the election, the open violence of rampant bands of Nazi thugs prompted protests from high quarters to the Reich President as well as to Hitler himself.[148] Hitler responded in characteristic vein with an aggressive defence of his SA men in response to Papen's complaints about affronts to foreign diplomats, prompted by an incident where a mob (including SA and SS men) had behaved threateningly towards the wives of prominent diplomats, beating up one of their chauffeurs, and tearing the flag from the car of the Rumanian ambassador. He had the impression, he said, that the bourgeoisie had been rescued too early. Had they experienced six weeks of Bolshevism, then they would have 'learnt the difference between the red revolution and our uprising. I once graphically saw this difference in Bavaria and have never forgotten it. And I will not let myself be taken away by anyone at all from the mission that I repeatedly announced before the election: the annihilation and eradication of Marxism.'[149] Even so, the violence was becoming counter-productive. On 10 March, directly referring to harassment of foreigners but blaming it on Communist provocateurs, Hitler proclaimed that from this day on, the national government controlled executive power in the whole of Germany, and that the future course of the 'national uprising' would be 'directed from above, according to plan'. All molesting of individuals, obstruction of automobiles, and disturbances to business life had to stop as a matter of principle.[150] He repeated the sentiments in a radio address two days later.[151] The exhortations had little effect.

The levels of terror and repression experienced in February in Prussia had by then wracked the rest of the country. Conditions in Bavaria, wrote the former peasant leader Dr Georg Heim to Hindenburg, were worse than 'under the terror regime of the Communists'.[152] Under the aegis of Himmler and Heydrich, the scale of arrests in Bavaria was proportionately even greater than it had been in Prussia. Around 10,000 Communists and Socialists were arrested in March and April. By June, the numbers in 'protective custody' – most of them workers – had doubled.[153] A good number of those arrested were the victims of denunciations by neighbours or workmates. So great was the wave of denunciations following the Malicious Practices Act of 21 March 1933 that even the police criticized it.[154] Just outside the town of Dachau, about twelve miles from Munich, the first concentration camp was set up in a former powder-mill on 22 March.

There was no secret about the camp's existence. Himmler had even held a press conference two days earlier to announce it. It began with 200 prisoners. Its capacity was given as 5,000. It was intended, stated Himmler, to hold the Communist and, if necessary, Reichsbanner and Marxist (i.e. Social Democrat) functionaries. Its establishment was announced in the newspapers.[155] It was meant to serve as a deterrent, and did so. Its dreaded name soon became a byword for the largely unspoken horrifying events known or presumed to take place within its walls. 'Keep quiet or you'll end up in Dachau' was soon to join common parlance. But apart from the political enemies and racial targets of the Nazis, few were disconcerted at the foundation of the camp, and others like it. The middle-class townsfolk of Dachau, watching the column of their Communist fellow-citizens from the town being marched to the nearby camp as political prisoners, thought them troublemakers, revolutionaries, 'a class apart', simply not part of their world.[156]

The day after Himmler had announced the creation of Dachau concentration camp, the regime showed its other face. If keen to keep at one remove from the shows of terror, Hitler was again in his element at the centre of another propaganda spectacular. This was the 'Day of Potsdam', a further masterly concoction of the newly appointed Reich Minister of People's Enlightenment and Propaganda, Joseph Goebbels. In complete detachment from the sordid bestialities in the brutal showdown with the Left, National Socialism here put on its best clothes, and proclaimed its union with Prussian conservatism. The 'comedy of Potsdam', as the French ambassador called it, captured the imagination of the German public, diverted attention from the unseemly events of the previous weeks, and, not least, helped further to cement the alliance of the army and the new regime.[157]

The decision to have the opening ceremony of the new Reichstag in Potsdam was taken at a meeting between the Reich President and Hitler, Papen, Frick, Blomberg and Göring on 7 March. The broad contours of the ceremonials were agreed at this meeting. The opening was originally scheduled for the week between 3 and 8 April.[158] The date was then changed to 21 March – the start of a new spring, and the date on which the first Reichstag had met after Bismarck's foundation of the Reich.[159] The 'great plan' for a symbolic festive opening of the Reichstag was worked out in meticulous detail by Goebbels five days before the event.[160] The 'Day of Potsdam' was to represent the start of the new Reich, building upon the glories of the old. It was also to denote the forging of the links between the new Germany and the traditions of Prussia. The Garnisonkirche (garrison church) in Potsdam, where the main ceremony was to take place, had been founded by the Hohenzollern kings of Prussia in the early eighteenth century. Household guards had dedicated themselves there to service to God and the King. Frederick Wilhelm I, the 'Soldier King', and his son Frederick the Great were buried in the crypt. The church symbolized the bonds between the Prussian military monarchy, the power of the state, and the Protestant religion.

On 21 March 1933, Reich President Hindenburg, in the uniform of a Prussian field-marshal and raising his baton to the empty throne of the exiled Kaiser, represented those bonds: throne, altar, and the military tradition in Prussia's glory. He was the link between the past and the present. Hitler marked the present and the future. Dressed not in party uniform but in a dark morning-suit, he played the part of the humble servant, bowing deeply before the revered and elderly Reich President and offering him his hand.[161] National renewal through unity was the theme of Hitler's address. Only with one phrase did he mention those who formed no part of that unity: they were to be rendered 'unharmful'. Hindenburg was elevated to the protector of the 'new uprising of our people'. He it was who had 'entrusted on 30 January the leadership of the Reich to this young Germany'.[162] 'It can't be denied,' wrote one non-Nazi observer, impressed by the 'moderation' of Hitler's speech, 'he has grown. Out of the demagogue and party leader, the fanatic and agitator, the true statesman seems – for his opponents surprisingly enough – to be developing.'[163] The blending of Prussian tradition and the National Socialist regime was underlined at the end of the ceremony by the laying of wreaths on the tombs of the Prussian kings, while the 'Niederländisches Dankgebet' rang through the church and outside a twenty-one gun salute sounded.[164] Afterwards, Hindenburg took the salute at a parade, lasting several hours, of the army and the 'national associations' of SA, SS, and Stahlhelm. Hitler stood modestly with his ministers several rows behind the military guests of honour.[165]

Two days later, it was a different Hitler, brown-shirted again and imperious, who entered the Kroll Opera House in Berlin, where Reichstag meetings were now to be held, to the jubilant cheers of serried ranks of uniformed Nazi deputies to propose the Enabling Act that he had wanted since the previous November. The atmosphere for their opponents, particularly the SPD deputies, was menacing. A giant swastika dominated the chamber. Armed men from the SA, SS, and Stahlhelm guarded all exits and surrounded the building. They were giving a hint to opposition deputies of what would be the outcome were the Enabling Act not to find the necessary level of support. In the absence of the eighty-one Communist deputies who had been arrested or taken flight, the Nazis were now in a majority in the Reichstag. But to pass the Enabling Act a two-thirds majority was necessary.[166]

Already on 7 March, Hitler – now visibly more self-confident among the conservative ministers – had told the cabinet that he expected to gain the two-thirds majority for an Enabling Act since the Communist deputies were in custody and would not be attending.[167] Just over a week later, on 15 March, he informed his ministers that the political situation had now been clarified. 'The national revolution had taken place without great shocks.' It was now necessary, he cynically continued, 'to divert the entire activity of the people on to the purely political plane (*auf das rein Politische abzulenken*) because economic decisions had still to be awaited'. Hitler then came to the Enabling Act. Its passage with a two-thirds majority would in his opinion not meet with any difficulties. Frick explained that the Zentrum was not ill-disposed towards the idea of an Enabling Act, but merely sought an audience first with the Chancellor. Frick advocated – making no bones about the intention behind the act – an act so widely framed that subsequent deviations from the Reich Constitution would be possible. He suggested a three-line draft, though in the event that scarcely sufficed and the final version was substantially longer. To ensure the two-thirds majority, Frick had worked out that if the Communist deputies were simply deducted from the total membership of the Reichstag, only 378, not 432, votes would be needed. Göring added that, if necessary, some Social Democrats could be ejected from the chamber. That is how little the Nazis' 'legal revolution' had to do with legality. But the conservatives present raised no objections. Nor did they to Meissner's acknowledgement that the Reich President's involvement in the passage of acts under the Enabling Act would not be necessary.[168] By 20 March, Hitler could confidently report to the cabinet that, following his discussions, the Zentrum had seen the necessity of the Enabling Act. Their request for a small committee to oversee the measures taken under the Act should be accepted. There would then be no reason to doubt the Zentrum's support. 'The acceptance of the Enabling Act also by the Zentrum would signify a strengthening of prestige with regard to foreign countries,' Hitler commented, aware as always of the propaganda implications.[169] Frick then introduced the draft of the bill, which was eventually accepted by the cabinet. The Reich Minister of the Interior also proposed a blatant manipulation of the Reichstag's procedures to make certain of the two-thirds majority. Deputies absent without excuse should now be counted as present.[170] There would, therefore, be no problem about a quorum. Absenteeism as a form of protest abstention was ruled out. Again the conservatives raised no objections.[171]

The way was clear. On the afternoon of 23 March 1933, Hitler addressed the Reichstag. The programme he outlined in his tactically clever two-and-a-half-hour speech, once he had finished painting the grim picture of the conditions he had inherited, was framed in the broadest of terms. He promised 'far-reaching moral renewal' supported by the whole sphere of education, the media and the arts. The national government saw in both Christian denominations, he declared, 'the most important factors for upholding our nationhood'. Their rights would not be touched: words of a German Chancellor intended to weigh, and weighing, with the Zentrum deputies. Judges would have to show some 'elasticity of judgement' for the good of society – an attack on liberal legal principles that earned warm applause. Business, too, would be made to serve the people, not the interests of capital. Experiments with the currency would be avoided. The salvation of the peasantry and *Mittelstand* and removal of unemployment, at first through work-creation schemes and labour service, were the main economic aims. The army was held up for praise. But Hitler said the government had no intention of increasing its size and weaponry if the rest of the world would undertake a radical disarmament. Germany wanted no more than similar rights and freedom. At the end of his speech, Hitler made what appeared to be important concessions. The existence of neither the Reichstag nor the Reichsrat was threatened, he stated. The position and rights of the Reich President remained untouched. The Länder would not be abolished. The rights of the Churches would not be reduced and their relations with the state not altered.[172]

All the promises were soon to be broken. But for the time being they served their purpose. They appeared to give the binding declarations safeguarding the position of the Catholic Church which the Zentrum had demanded in its discussions with Hitler. Even so, the Zentrum deputies, meeting before the vote was taken, were divided. There was talk of civil war, of a resort to force, if the Enabling Act were not granted. Once more, Hitler's implicit blackmailing tactic had worked. The party leader, Prälat Kaas, argued that 'the Fatherland is in the greatest danger. We dare not fail.' Eventually, with the greatest reservations and evincing their feelings of responsibility for the nation, other leading figures, such as Heinrich

Brüning (the former Chancellor) and Joseph Ersing (one of the party's most prominent trade unionists), and the rest of the Zentrum deputies supported him.[173]

It was shortly after six o'clock when the Reichstag resumed its business. The SPD leader, Otto Wels, spoke courageously, given the menacing atmosphere. Though most of his speech was low-key, he ended movingly, upholding the principles of humanity, justice, freedom, and socialism held dear by Social Democrats.[174] Hitler had made notes as Wels spoke. He now returned to the rostrum, to storms of applause from NSDAP deputies, to make the most savage of replies, every sentence cheered to the rafters. Departing now from the relative moderation of his earlier prepared speech, Hitler showed more of his true colours. A sense of law was alone not enough; possession of power was decisive. There had been no need to put the current bill before the Reichstag: 'we appeal in this hour to the German Reichstag to grant us that which we could have taken anyway'. He would not fall into the error of simply irritating opponents instead of either destroying them or making amends with them. He would offer his hand to those who differed from him but were committed to Germany. But this did not apply to the Social Democrats. They should not misunderstand him. He did not recognize the dictates of the International. The mentality of the Social Democrats was quite incapable of grasping the intentions behind the Enabling Act. He did not even want them to vote for the bill. 'Germany will become free, but not through you,' he concluded to wild cheering.[175] After Kaas for the Zentrum, without any guarantees beyond the verbal assurances Hitler had given in his speech, had declared his party's readiness to support the bill, and other party leaders had followed suit, the vote was taken.[176] With 441 votes to the ninety-four votes of the Social Democrats, the Reichstag, as a democratic body, voted itself out of existence.

The 'Act for the Removal of Distress from People and Reich' – the Enabling Act – went into effect the next day.[177] Hitler's bullying tactics had worked – for neither the first nor the last time. Power was now in the hands of the National Socialists. It was the beginning of the end for political parties other than the NSDAP. The Zentrum's role had been particularly ignominious. Fearing open terror and repression, it had given in to Hitler's tactics of pseudo-legality. In so doing, it had helped in the removal of almost all constitutional constraints on his power. He needed in future to rely neither on the Reichstag, nor on the Reich President. Hitler was still far from wielding absolute power. But vital steps towards consolidating his dictatorship now followed in quick succession.

V

During the spring and summer of 1933, Germany fell into line behind its new rulers. Hardly any spheres of organized activity, political or social, were left untouched by the process of *Gleichschaltung* – the 'coordination' of institutions and organizations now brought under Nazi control. Pressure from below, from Nazi activists, played a major role in forcing the pace of the 'coordination'. But many organizations showed themselves only too willing to anticipate the process and to 'coordinate' themselves in accordance with the expectations of the new era. By the autumn, the Nazi dictatorship – and Hitler's own power at its head – had been enormously strengthened. What is striking is not how much, but how little, Hitler needed to do to bring this about. Beyond indications that his instinct for the realities of power and the manipulative potential of propaganda were as finely tuned as ever, Hitler took remarkably few initiatives.

One initiative that did come from Hitler was, however, the creation of Reich Governors (*Reichsstatthalter*) to uphold the 'lines of policy laid down by the Reich Chancellor' in the Länder.[178] Referring to them at first as 'State Presidents', Hitler pressed for their instalment in the Länder at a cabinet meeting on 29 March.[179] With their hastily contrived establishment in the 'Second Law for the Coordination of the Länder with the Reich' of 7 April 1933, the sovereignty of the individual states was decisively undermined.[180] All indications are that Hitler was anxious, with the establishment of the Reich Governors, to have trusted representatives in the Länder who could counter any danger that the grass-roots 'party revolution' might run out of control, ultimately even possibly threatening his own position. The position in Bavaria, where the SA and SS had their headquarters and where radicals had effected an actual 'seizure of power' in the days since the March election, was especially sensitive. The improvised creation of the Reich Governors was brought about with Bavaria, in particular, in mind, to head off the possibility of a party revolution against Berlin. The former Freikorps 'hero' of the crushing of the Räterepublik, Ritter von Epp, was already appointed as Reich Governor on 10 April. A further ten Reich Governors were installed less hurriedly, during May and June, in the remaining Länder, apart from Prussia, and were drawn from the senior and most powerful Gauleiter. Their dependence on Hitler was no less great than his on them. They could be relied upon, therefore, to serve the Reich government in blocking the revolution from below when it was becoming counter-productive.[181] Their creation hardly, however, provided a guarantee of coherent government administration in the regions. Superimposed on existing structures, and uneasily straddling the divisions of party and state, the Reich Governors soon became unclear themselves about their precise function. This was all the less clear once the abolition of the autonomy of the Länder in January 1934 had in theory removed the very need for Reich representatives.[182] Typically, however, once created, the position of Reich Governor was not abolished. 'Elbow-power', as usual, was what counted. Each of the 'viceroys' of the Reich should make out of his position what he could, was Hitler's characteristic definition of their role.[183] In cases of dispute of Reich Governors with Reich Ministers in 'questions of special political significance', Hitler reserved to himself the final decision. 'Such a ruling corresponds in the view of the Reich Chancellor to his position as leader,' Frick was told.[184]

In Prussia, Hitler reserved the position of Reich Governor for himself. This effectively removed any purpose in retaining Papen as Reich Commissioner for Prussia.[185] Possibly Hitler was contemplating reuniting the position of head of government in Prussia with that of Reich Chancellor, as had been the position under Bismarck. If so, he reckoned without Göring's own power ambitions. Since Papen's coup the previous July, there had been no Minister President in Prussia. Göring had expected the position to become his following the Prussian Landtag elections on 5 March. But Hitler had not appointed him. Göring therefore engineered the placing on the agenda of the newly-elected Prussian Landtag, meeting on 8 April, the election of the Minister President. Though he had only the previous day taken over the rights of Reich Governor in Prussia himself, Hitler now had to bow to the *fait accompli*. On 11 April, Göring was appointed Prussian Minister President (retaining his powers as Prussian Minister of the Interior), and on 25 April the rights of Reich Governor in Prussia were transferred to him. The 'Second Coordination Law' had indirectly but effectively led to the consolidation of Göring's extensive power-base in Prussia, built initially on his control over the police in the most important of the German states. It was little wonder that Göring responded with publicly effusive statements of loyalty to Hitler, whom he served as his 'most loyal paladin'.[186] The episode reveals the haste and confusion behind the entire improvised 'coordination' of the Länder. But at the price of strengthening the hand of Göring in Prussia, and the most thrusting Gauleiter elsewhere, Hitler's own power had also been notably reinforced across the Länder.

During the spring and summer of 1933, Hitler stood between countervailing forces. The dilemma would not be resolved until the 'Night of the

Long Knives'. On the one hand, the pressures, dammed up for so long and with such difficulty before Hitler's takeover of power, had burst loose after the March elections. Hitler not only sympathized with the radical assault from below on opponents, Jews, and anyone else getting in the way of the Nazi revolution; he needed the radicals to push through the upturning of the established political order and to intimidate those obstructing to fall in line. On the other hand, as the creation of the Reich Governors had shown, he was aware of the dangers to his own position if the radical upheaval got out of hand. And he was sensitive to the fact that the traditional national-conservative bastions of power, not least sceptics about National Socialism in the army and important sectors of business, while having no objections to violence as long as it was directed at Communists and Socialists, would look differently upon it as soon as their own vested interests were threatened. Hitler had no choice, therefore, but to steer an uncomfortable course between a party revolution which he could by no means fully control and the support of the army and business which he could by no means do without. Out of these inherently contradictory forces, the showdown with the SA would ultimately emerge. In the meantime, however, there were clear signs of what would become a lasting trait of the Third Reich: pressure from party radicals, encouraged and sanctioned at least in part by Hitler, resulting in the state bureaucracy reflecting the radicalism in legislation and the police channelling it into executive measures. The process of 'cumulative radicalization' was recognizable from the earliest weeks of the regime.[187]

Hitler's call for discipline on 10 March had itself been half-hearted, encouraging the immediate breaking of resistance to orders of the state leadership wherever encountered and exhorting his followers not to lose sight for a second of the task of the 'annihilation of Marxism'.[188] The order, perhaps not surprisingly, had been widely ignored, as had subsequent attempts by Göring and Frick to ban 'individual actions' (Einzelaktionen) and impose harsh sentences on 'excesses' (Übergriffe) by party members.[189]

Apart from the all-out assault on the Left in the first weeks of Nazi rule, many of the 'individual actions' had been outrages perpetrated by Nazi radicals against Jews. Since antisemitism had been the 'ideological cement' of the National Socialist Movement from the beginning, offering at one and the same time a vehicle for actionism and substitute for revolutionary leanings threatening the fabric of society, this was scarcely surprising. The takeover of power by the arch-antisemite Hitler had at one fell swoop removed constraints on violence towards Jews. Without any orders from above, and without any coordination, assaults on Jewish businesses and the beating-up of Jews by Nazi thugs became commonplace. As one of many such incidents, the *Frankfurter Zeitung* reported on 12 March how a Jewish theatre director in Breslau had been hustled into a car in broad daylight by five SA men before having his clothes removed and being beaten by rubber truncheons and thrashed with a dog-whip. He later suffered a nervous breakdown.[190] A Jewish eye-witness in the same city recounted groups of six to eight SA men, carrying coshes and revolvers, breaking into the houses of wealthy Jews, and extorting large sums of money from them. They even interrupted court proceedings to throw Jewish lawyers and judges out on to the streets, beating them up as they did so.[191] Some Jews suffered an even worse fate. The German correspondent of the *Manchester Guardian* described on 16 March how four men with guns had broken into the house of a Jewish businessman and money-lender in Straubing (Lower Bavaria), who had won a libel suit two years earlier against a Bavarian Landtag deputy, dragged him out of bed, forced him into a car, and driven him away. He was later found shot dead.[192] Countless such atrocities took place in the weeks following Hitler's assumption to power.

Many were carried out by members of the so-called Fighting League of the Commercial Middle Class (Kampfbund des gewerblichen Mittelstandes), in which violent antisemitism went hand in hand with equally violent opposition to department stores (many of them Jewish owned).[193] The extent of the anti-Jewish violence prompted Jewish intellectuals and financiers abroad, especially in the USA, to undertake attempts to mobilize public feeling against Germany and to organize a boycott against German goods – a real threat, given the weakness of the German economy. Beginning in mid-March, the boycott gathered pace and was extended to numerous European countries. The reaction in Germany, led by the Kampfbund des gewerblichen Mittelstandes, was predictably aggressive. A 'counter-boycott' of Jewish shops and departmental stores throughout Germany was demanded. The call was taken up by leading antisemites in the party, at their forefront and in his element the Franconian Gauleiter and pathological antisemite Julius Streicher. They argued that the Jews could serve as 'hostages' to force a halt to the international boycott.[194]

Hitler's instincts favoured the party radicals. But he was also under pressure to act. On the 'Jewish Question', on which he had preached so loudly and so often, he could scarcely now, once in power, back down in the face of the demands of the activists without serious loss of face within the party. When, on 26 March, it was reported through diplomatic contacts that the American Jewish Congress was planning to call the next day for a

THE MAKING OF THE DICTATOR

world-wide boycott of German goods, Hitler was forced into action.[195] As usual, when pushed into a corner Hitler had no half-measures. Goebbels was summoned to the Obersalzberg. 'In the loneliness of the mountains,' he wrote, the Führer had reached the conclusion that the authors, or at least beneficiaries, of the 'foreign agitation' – Germany's Jews – had to be tackled. 'We must therefore move to a widely framed boycott of all Jewish businesses in Germany.'[196] Streicher was put in charge of a committee of thirteen party functionaries who were to organize the boycott. The party's proclamation of 28 March, prompted by the Reich Chancellor himself and bearing his imprint, called for action committees to carry out a boycott of Jewish businesses, goods, doctors and lawyers, even in the smallest village of the Reich.[197] The boycott was to be of indefinite duration. Goebbels was left to undertake the propaganda preparations. Behind the entire operation stood pressure from the Kampfbund des gewerblichen Mittelstandes.[198]

Led by Schacht and Foreign Minister Neurath, counter-pressures began to be placed on Hitler to halt an action which was likely to have disastrous effects on the German economy and on its standing abroad. Hitler at first refused to consider any retreat. Even doubts about the boycott which the Reich President was said to have expressed met only the response from Hitler that 'he had to carry out the boycott and was no longer in a position to hold up history'.[199] But by 31 March, Neurath was able to report to the cabinet that the British, French, and American governments had declared their opposition to the boycott of German goods in their country. He hoped the boycott in Germany might be called off.[200] It was asking too much of Hitler to back down completely. The activists were by now fired up. Abandonment of the boycott would have brought not only loss of face for Hitler, but the probability that any order cancelling the 'action' would have been widely ignored.[201] However, Hitler did indicate that he was now ready to postpone the start of the German boycott from 1 to 4 April in the event of satisfactory declarations opposing the boycott of German goods by the British and American governments. Otherwise, the German boycott would commence on 1 April, but would then be halted until 4 April.[202] A flurry of diplomatic activity resulted in the western governments and, placed under pressure, Jewish lobby groups distancing themselves from the boycott of German goods. Hitler's demands had largely been met. But by now Hitler had changed his mind, and was again insisting on the German boycott being carried out. Further pressure from Schacht resulted in the boycott being confined to a single day – but under the propaganda fiction that it would be restarted the following Wednesday, 5 April, if the 'horror agitation' abroad against Germany had not ceased altogether.[203] There was no intention of that. In fact, already on the afternoon of the boycott day, 1 April, Streicher announced that it would not be resumed the following Wednesday.[204]

The boycott itself was less than the success that Nazi propaganda claimed.[205] Many Jewish shops had closed for the day anyway. In some places, the SA men posted outside 'Jewish' department stores holding placards warning against buying in Jewish shops were largely ignored by customers. People behaved in a variety of fashions. There was almost a holiday mood in some busy shopping streets, as crowds gathered to see what was happening. Groups of people discussed the pros and cons of the boycott. Not a few were opposed to it, saying they would again patronize their favourite stores. Others shrugged their shoulders. 'I think the entire thing is mad, but I'm not bothering myself about it,' was one, perhaps not untypical, view heard from a non-Jew on the day.[206] Even the SA men seemed at times rather half-hearted about it in some places. In others, however, the boycott was simply a cover for plundering and violence.[207] For the Jewish victims, the day was traumatic – the clearest indication that this was a Germany in which they could no longer feel 'at home', in which routine discrimination had been replaced by state-sponsored persecution.[208]

Reactions in the foreign press to the boycott were almost universally condemnatory. A damage-limitation exercise had to be carried out by the new Reichsbank President Schacht immediately after the boycott to assure foreign bankers of Germany's intentions in economic policy.[209] But within Germany – something which would repeat itself in years to come – the dynamic of anti-Jewish pressure from party activists, sanctioned by Hitler and the Nazi leadership, was now taken up by the state bureaucracy and channelled into discriminatory legislation. The exclusion of Jews from state service and from the professions had been aims of Nazi activists before 1933. Now, the possibility of pressing for the implementation of such aims had opened up. Suggestions for anti-Jewish discriminatory measures came from various quarters. Preparations for overhauling civil service rights were given a new anti-Jewish twist at the end of March, possibly (though this is not certain) on Hitler's intervention. On the basis of the notorious 'Aryan Paragraph' – there was no definition of a Jew – in the hastily drafted 'Law for the Restoration of the Professional Civil Service' of 7 April Jews as well as political opponents were dismissed from the civil service. An exception was made, on Hindenburg's intervention, only for Jews who had served at the front. The three further pieces of anti-Jewish legislation passed in April – discriminating against the admission of Jews to the legal profession, excluding Jewish doctors from treating patients covered by the national insurance scheme, and limiting the number of Jewish schoolchildren permitted in schools – were all hurriedly improvised to meet not simply pressure from below but *de facto* measures which were already being implemented in various parts of the country. The legislation against Jews entering the legal profession followed steps already undertaken by the Prussian and Bavarian Justice Ministers, Hans Kerrl and Hans Frank, adopted by the Reich Justice Ministry, and passed on for Hitler's approval. That against doctors was pushed forward by Reich Labour Minister Franz Seldte after Hitler had in fact indicated that there was no immediate necessity for legal regulation of the 'doctor question'. The restrictions on numbers of places for Jewish schoolchildren represented an attempt by Reich Interior Minister Frick to give some legislative unity to the quite varied position which had arisen through arbitrary discriminatory measures being imposed even within different parts of the same state. Hitler's role was largely confined to giving his sanction to the legalization of measures already often illegally introduced by party activists with vested interests in the discrimination running alongside whatever ideological motivation they possessed. These had shown themselves on occasion unprepared to recognize the Reich Chancellor's tactical readiness to accept for the time being less than the most radical discriminatory measures.[210]

The seismic shift in the political scene which had taken place in the month or so following the Reichstag fire had left the Jews fully exposed to Nazi violence, discrimination, and intimidation. It had also totally undermined the position of Hitler's political opponents. Following the ruthless demolition of the KPD, which was never formally banned, the main blocks of potential resistance were those of the SPD and Free Trade Unions, political Catholicism (focused on the Zentrum), and the conservatives (still with their majority in the cabinet). In May and June, each of the blocks was eliminated. Intimidation certainly played its part. But there was now little fight left in oppositional parties. The readiness to compromise soon became a readiness to capitulate.

Already in March, Theodor Leipart, the chairman of the trade union confederation, the ADGB, had tried to blow with the wind, distancing the unions from the SPD and offering a declaration of loyalty to the new regime.[211] By then, there had been frequent incidents in which union functionaries had been beaten up by squads of SA or NSBO men, and union offices ransacked. But, keen above all to protect the organization, and tempted by the prospect held out of a single, unified trade union for all sectors of the working class, the ADGB was ready to cooperate with the still relatively insignificant NSBO to have 'Marxist' functionaries thrown off works councils.[212] The planning of the destruction of the unions was undertaken by the NSBO boss Reinhold Muchow and, increasingly, by Robert Ley, the NSDAP's Organization Leader. Hitler was initially hesitant, until the idea was proposed of coupling it with a propaganda coup.[213] Along the lines of the 'Day of Potsdam', Goebbels prepared another huge spectacular for 1 May, when the National Socialists usurped the traditional celebration of the International and turned it into the 'Day of National Labour'. The ADGB took a full part in the rallies and parades. Over 10 million people altogether turned out – though for many a factory work-force attendance was scarcely voluntary. Hitler spoke, as on so many occasions, to the half million assembled on the Tempelhofer Feld in Berlin, the wide expanse of open land adjacent to the aerodrome, of the need to leave the divisions of class struggle behind and come together in a united national community.[214] Many who were far from sympathetic to National Socialism were moved by the occasion.[215]

The following day, the razzmatazz over, SA and NSBO squads occupied the offices and bank branches of the Social Democratic trade union movement, confiscated its funds, and arrested its functionaries. Within an hour, the 'action' was finished. The largest democratic trade union movement in the world had been destroyed. In a matter of days, its members had been incorporated into the massive German Labour Front (Deutsche Arbeitsfront, DAF), founded on 10 May under Robert Ley's leadership.[216] By the autumn, the DAF had itself been emasculated as a trade union – even a Nazi one – and been turned into little more than a gigantic propaganda machine to organize the activities of the German work-force in the interests of the regime. Behind the propaganda, by then, the reordering of relations in the work-place was firmly under the direction of the bureaucracy of the Reich Labour Ministry. Workers now faced the reality of harsher, more aggressive industrial management, backed by the power of the state.[217]

The once-mighty Social Democratic Party of Germany, the largest labour movement that Europe had known, was also at an end. It had been forced during the last years of Weimar into one unholy compromise after another in its attempts to uphold its legalistic traditions while at the same time hoping to fend off the worst. When the worst came, it was ill-equipped. The Depression years and internal demoralization had taken their toll. Otto Wels's speech on 23 March had shown courage. But it was far too little, and far too late. Support was haemorrhaging away. During March and

April, the SPD's paramilitary arm, the huge Reichsbanner, was forced into dissolution. Party branches were closing down. Activists were under arrest, or had fled abroad. Some already began preparations for illegality. Optimists – there still were a few – expected the fascist hurricane quickly to blow itself out. The party had survived Bismarck's repression in the 1880s. It would survive this. Most party members were more pessimistic, realizing it was high time to keep their heads below the parapet. Alongside the fear, there was wide disillusionment with Social Democracy. The flight into exile of many party leaders – necessary safety measure that it was – enhanced a sense of desertion. The SPD was by now a rudderless ship. Divisions in the party leadership over the decision – taken under duress – to back Hitler's 'peace speech' on 17 May, in which the Reich Chancellor renounced war as the solution to Europe's problems and demanded disarmament of the western powers,[218] led now to Otto Wels and other party leaders leaving for Prague, where a party headquarters in exile had already been established. The first publication in Prague of the exiled party's weekly, *Neuer Vorwärts*, on 18 June was the pretext four days later for all party activities within the Reich to be banned, its parliamentary representation abolished, its assets confiscated.[219]

The remaining parties now rapidly caved in, falling domino-style. The Staatspartei (formerly the DDP), which had entered into an electoral alliance with the SPD the previous March, dissolved itself on 28 June, followed a day later by the dissolution of the DVP. The Nazis' conservative coalition partner, the DNVP – renamed in May the German National Front (Deutschnationale Front, DNF) – also capitulated on 27 June. It had been losing members to the NSDAP at an increasing rate; its grass-roots organizations had been subjected to repression and intimidation; the Stahl-helm – many of whose members supported the DNVP – had been placed under Hitler's leadership in late April and was taken into the SA in June; and the party's leader, Hugenberg, had become wholly isolated in cabinet, even from his conservative colleagues. Hugenberg's resignation from the cabinet (which many had initially thought he would dominate), on 26 June, was inevitable after embarrassing the German government through his behaviour at the World Economic Conference in London earlier in the month. Without consulting Hitler, the cabinet, or Foreign Minister Neurath, Hugenberg had sent a memorandum to the Economic Committee of the Conference rejecting free trade, demanding the return of German colonies and land for settlement in the east. His departure from the cabinet signified the end for his party.[220] Far from functioning as the 'real' leader of

Germany, as many had imagined he would do, and far from ensuring with his conservative colleagues in the cabinet that Hitler would be 'boxed in', Hugenberg had rapidly become yesterday's man. Few regretted it. Playing with fire, Hugenberg, along with his party, the DNVP, had been consumed by it.

The Catholic parties held out a little longer. But their position was undermined by the negotiations, led by Papen, for a Reich Concordat with the Holy See, in which the Vatican accepted a ban on the political activities of the clergy in Germany. This meant in effect that, in the attempt to defend the position of the Catholic Church in Germany, political Catholicism had been sacrificed. By that stage, in any case, the Zentrum had been losing its members at an alarming rate, many of them anxious to accommodate themselves to the new times. Its leader, Prälat Kaas, had already left Germany in April, and had taken a leading part in the Concordat discussions. Moreover the Catholic hierarchy, naïvely over-impressed by Hitler's promises to uphold the position of the Church in his speech before the 'Enabling Act', had produced a rapid volte-face on 28 March, calling for loyal support of the new regime.[221] Thereafter, the Catholic bishops had taken over from the Zentrum leaders as the main spokesmen for the Church in dealings with the regime, and were more concerned to preserve the Church's institutions, organizations and schools than to sustain the weakened position of the Catholic political parties. Intimidation and pressure did the rest. The arrest of 2,000 functionaries in late June by Himmler's Bavarian Political Police concentrated minds and brought the swift reading of the last rites for the BVP on 4 July. A day later, the Zentrum, the last remaining political party outside the NSDAP, dissolved itself.[222] Little over a week later, the 'Law against the New Construction of Parties' left the NSDAP as the only legal political party in Germany.[223]

VI

What was happening at the centre of politics was happening also at the grass-roots – not just in political life, but in every organizational form of social activity. Intimidation of those posing any obstacle and opportunism of those now seeking the first opportunity to jump on the bandwagon proved an irresistible combination. In countless small towns and villages, Nazis took over local government.[224] Mayors and councillors who had belonged to the 'Marxist' parties were, of course, rapidly hounded out. With representatives from the bourgeois and Catholic parties there was often greater continuity in practice. Cases where a previous incumbent of the Bürgermeister's office was forcibly removed stood alongside instances where long-standing and respected local worthies, earlier members of one of the Catholic or bourgeois parties, turned coat and continued in office.[225] Teachers and civil servants were particularly prominent in the rush to join the Nazis. So swollen did the NSDAP's membership rolls become with the mass influx of those anxious to cast in their lot with the new regime – the 'March Fallen' (*Märzgefallene*) as the 'Old Fighters' cynically dubbed them – that on 1 May a bar was imposed on further entrants. Two and a half million Germans had by now joined the party, 1.6 million of them since Hitler had become Chancellor.[226]

'Coordination' – meaning nazification – extended deep into the social fabric of every town and village. Few corners of the rich panoply of clubs and societies that formed the social network of every town in the country were left untouched. 'Coordination (*Gleichschaltung*): The Veterans' Association was coordinated on 6.8.33, on 7.8.33 the Singing Association in Theisenort. With the Shooting Club in Theisenort this was not necessary, since the board and committee are up to 80 per cent party members,' ran an 'activity report' from a tiny community of 675 souls in Upper Franconia.[227] A few months earlier, members of the 'Small Garden Association' in Hanover were told that 'also in the area of small gardens the true national community now has to emerge in accordance with the will of the government of the national uprising'.[228] Business and professional associations, sports clubs, choral societies, shooting clubs, patriotic associations, and most other forms of organized activity were taken under – or more frequently hastened to place themselves under – National Socialist control in the first months of the Third Reich.[229] 'There was no more social life; you couldn't even have a bowling club' that was not 'coordinated', was how one inhabitant of Northeim in Lower Saxony remembered it.[230]

Beyond the former clubs and societies associated with the left-wing parties, which had been dissolved, smashed, or forcibly taken over, there was a good deal of quite voluntary 'adjustment' to the new circumstances. Opportunism intermingled with genuine idealism.

Much the same applied also to the broad cultural sphere. Goebbels took up with great energy and enthusiasm his task of ensuring that the press, radio, film production, theatre, music, the visual arts, literature, and all other forms of cultural activity were reorganized in line with Hitler's promise in March.[231] The aim, he had said in his first speech as Propaganda Minister, was 'to work on people until they have capitulated to us', 'to unite the nation behind the ideal of the national revolution' and to bring about a complete 'mobilization of Spirit'.[232]

The reordering of German cultural life along Nazi lines was far-reaching indeed. But the most striking feature of the 'coordination' of culture was the alacrity and eagerness with which intellectuals, writers, artists, performers and publicists actively collaborated in moves which not only impoverished and straitjacketed German culture for the next twelve years, but banned and outlawed some of its most glittering exponents – fellow intellectuals, writers, artists, performers and publicists.

There were many illusions – in most cases rapidly to be shattered – and a good deal of misplaced idealism. But idealism often blended with careerism. Prominent actors like Gustav Gründgens, Werner Krauß or Emil Jannings felt flattered by the new regime's favours – and put themselves at its disposal.[233] The world-famous composer Richard Strauß, the leading conductor Wilhelm Furtwängler, fêted by the regime, and the rising star conductor Herbert von Karajan continued to bestow distinction on German achievements in music; but the music of Arnold Schönberg or Kurt Weill was no longer acceptable, its composers forced into exile, as were leading conductors Bruno Walter and Otto Klemperer, along with hundreds of other, mainly Jewish, musicians.[234] The writer Gerhart Hauptmann had been honoured by the Weimar Republic on the occasion of his sixtieth birthday in 1922. But he hastened to ingratiate himself with the new regime in 1933, openly giving the Nazi salute and joining in the singing of the 'Horst-Wessel-Lied' at public gatherings.[235] The brilliant essayist and poet Gottfried Benn, who had belonged to the Expressionist generation, also openly proclaimed his allegiance to National Socialism. High expectations, illusions and idealism played their part. 'I declare myself quite personally to be in favour of the new state, because it is my people that lays out its path here . . . My mental and economic existence, my language, my life, my human contacts, the entire sum of my brain I owe in the first instance to this people,' he emotively explained.[236] In a radio address in April 1933, Benn equated the intellectual freedom of Weimar (Geistesfreiheit) with 'freedom to subvert' (Zersetzungsfreiheit) and saw the marching columns of the 'brown battalions' as the dawn of a new cultural era.[237] He was impressed by Nazi notions of 'eugenics' and 'racial hygiene'. But he was also delighted to be elevated to the Prussian Academy of Arts, and played an active role in its 'coordination', showing himself willing to cast aside his fellow-writers who were no longer comfortable bedfellows.[238]

The example set by such 'glitterati' was followed by lesser lights, falling under the spell of the 'national rebirth' – and with careers to gain or lose. The 'Oath of Loyalty of German Poets to the People's Chancellor Adolf Hitler' in spring 1933 was a characteristic expression of eager and enthusiastic 'self-coordination' (*Selbstgleichschaltung*).[239]

It was no different among the intellectual leaders in universities. The most eminent philosopher, Martin Heidegger, and the best-known constitutional lawyer, Carl Schmitt, placed themselves behind the regime. Heidegger spoke in his inaugural lecture as Rector of Freiburg University on 27 May 1933 of German students 'on the march', leaving behind negative academic freedom, and placing themselves in the service of the *völkisch* state. He also helped to instigate a manifesto of German professors declaring their allegiance to 'Adolf Hitler and the National Socialist State', which had brought about not simply a change of government, but 'the entire upturning of our German existence (*Dasein*)'.[240] Lesser-known academics were probably more representative than Heidegger. But the tune was much the same. In a lecture on 3 May, the Germanist Ernst Bertram spoke of the 'uprising against rationality (*ratio*) inimical to life (*lebensfeindlich*), destructive enlightenment, alien political dogmatism, every form of the "ideas of 1789", all anti-germanic tendencies and excessive foreign influences (*Überfremdungen*)'. Failure of the 'struggle' against such tendencies, he went on, would lead to 'the end of the white world, chaos, or a planet of termites'.[241] The Berlin professor Julius Petersen declared, several months later, that 'tomorrow had become today', that the 'end-of-the-world mood (*Weltuntergangsstimmung*) had been transformed into awakening (*Aufbruch*). The final goal moves into the vision of the present . . . The new Reich is planted. The Leader, yearned for and prophesied, has appeared.'[242]

Intellectuals were no exceptions in the rush to join the NSDAP after January 1933. But there were relatively few arch-Nazis among their ranks. For the most part, they were national-conservatives, steeped in the intellectual traditions of the 'educated bourgeoisie' (*Bildungsbürgertum*) formed in the Wilhelmine era. Widespread detestation for the Revolution of 1918 and for the 'un-German' form of parliamentary democracy imported from the West made them open to the allure of a new start in 1933, blind or oblivious to the intellectual castration of their own profession, to the persecution of those from within their ranks who were politically or racially unacceptable to the new masters. Even one so contemptuous of the Nazis as Thomas Mann admitted to some initial uncertainties about the new regime, and hinted at approval of the anti-Jewish legislation of April 1933. His antipathy towards Hitler and the boycott against the Jews on 1 April is plain.[243] But on 9 April, he confided to his diary: '. . . For all that, might not something deeply significant and revolutionary be taking place in Germany? The Jews . . . It is no calamity after all that . . . the domination of the legal system by Jews has been ended.'[244]

The hopes long cherished of the coming great leader eradicated the critical faculties of many intellectuals, blinding them to the magnitude of the assault on freedom of thought as well as action that they often welcomed. 'Since this leader, from wherever he comes, can only be national, his way will be the right one because it will be the way of the nation,' the influential editor of the neo-conservative *Tat* journal had written in October 1931. 'In this moment an order of things which liberalism has sought to portray to us as dismal servitude (*dumpfe Knechtschaft*) will be to us freedom, since it *is* order, has meaning and provides an answer to questions which liberalism cannot answer: why, to what end, for what reason?'[245]

Many of the neo-conservative intellectuals whose ideas had helped pave the way for the Third Reich were soon to be massively disillusioned. Hitler turned out for them in practice to be not the mystic leader they had longed for in their dreams. But they had helped prepare the ground for the Führer cult that was taken up in its myriad forms by so many others. And their way of thinking – rejection of 'ideas of 1789' and the rationality and relativism of liberal thought in favour of a deliberate plunge into conscious irrationalism, the search for meaning not in individuality but in the 'national community', the sense of liberation through a 'national awakening' – was the platform on which so much of the German intellectual élite bound itself to the anti-intellectualism and primitive populism of Hitler's Third Reich.[246]

Hardly a protest was raised at the purges of university professors under the new civil service law in April 1933 as many of Germany's most distinguished academics were dismissed and forced into exile. The Prussian Academy of Arts had by then already undertaken its own 'cleansing', demanding loyalty to the regime from all choosing to remain within its hallowed membership. Thomas Mann and Alfred Döblin were among those refusing to do so.[247] Lists were drawn up and published of scholars and writers whose works were to be struck from those acceptable in the new order. Einstein, Freud, Brecht, Döblin, Remarque, Ossietzky, Tucholsky, Hofmannsthal, Kästner and Zuckmayer were among those whose writings were outlawed as decadent or materialistic, as representative of 'moral decline' or 'cultural Bolshevism'.

The symbolic moment of capitulation of German intellectuals to the 'new spirit' of 1933 came with the burning on 10 May of the books of authors unacceptable to the regime.[248] 'Here sinks the intellectual basis of the November Revolution to the ground,' proclaimed Goebbels at the spectacular scene at the Opernplatz in Berlin, as 20,000 books of poets and philosophers, writers and scholars, were cast into the flames of the vast auto-da-fé.[249] But the 'Action against the Ungerman Spirit' – the burning of books which took place at all Germany's universities that night of shame – had not been initiated by Goebbels. It had been prompted by the leadership of the German Students' Association (Deutsche Studentenschaft) in an attempt to outflank the rival National Socialist German Student Federation (NSDStB). Not just Nazi student organizations had taken part. Others on the nationalist Right had also been involved. Local authorities and police had voluntarily assisted in clearing out the books to be burned from public libraries. University faculties and senates had hardly raised a protest of note at the 'Action'. Their members, with few exceptions, attended the bonfires.[250] The poet Heinrich Heine, whose works were among those consumed by the flames, had written: 'Where books are burnt, in the end people are also burnt.'[251]

VII

Scarcely any of the transformation of Germany during the spring and summer of 1933 had followed direct orders from the Reich Chancellery. Hitler had rarely been personally involved. But he was the main beneficiary. During these months popular adulation of the new Chancellor had reached untold levels. The Führer cult was established, not now just within the party, but throughout state and society, as the very basis of the new Germany. Hitler's standing and power, at home and increasingly abroad, were thereby immeasurably boosted.

Already in spring 1933, the personality cult surrounding Hitler was burgeoning, and developing extraordinary manifestations. 'Poems' – usually unctuous doggerel verse, sometimes with a pseudo-religious tone – were composed in his honour. 'Hitler-Oaks' and 'Hitler-Lindens', trees whose ancient pagan symbolism gave them special significance to *völkisch* nationalists and Nordic cultists, were planted in towns and villages all over Germany.[252] Towns and cities rushed to confer honorary citizenship on the new Chancellor. Streets and squares were named after him. Hitler let it be known that he had nothing against this, except in the case of the traditional names of long-standing historic streets or squares. He refused, accordingly, to allow the 700-year-old Marktplatz in Strausberg to be renamed. On the other hand, he had agreed to the renaming of the historic Hauptmarkt in Nuremberg as Adolf Hitler-Platz before deciding that old and historic names could not be altered. A request from the Organization Leader of the Deutsch-Völkische Freiheitsbewegung (German Ethnic Freedom Movement) in Franconia to revert to the original name of 'Hauptmarkt' did not, therefore, meet with his approval. In one case, an entire village – Sutzken in East Prussia – sought, and was given permission, to rename itself after the hero, and became 'Hitlershöhe', while in Upper Silesia, near Oppeln, a lake was renamed 'Hitlersee'. But the mayor of Bad Godesberg was not allowed to advertise the elegant Rhineland resort as the 'favourite place to stay of the Reich Chancellor Adolf Hitler'. Nor were canny traders, seeking to use the Hitler cult for their own ends, successful in their attempts to name a café or a rose after the Chancellor.[253] Even so, commercial exploitation of the Führer cult created an entire industry of kitsch – pictures, busts, reliefs, postcards, figurines, penknives, badges, illuminated buttons, zinc plates – until its tastelessness forced Goebbels in May 1933 to ban the use of Hitler's image on commercial products.[254]

The levels of hero-worship had never been witnessed before in Germany. Not even the Bismarck cult in the last years of the founder of the Reich had come remotely near matching it. Hitler's forty-fourth birthday on 20 April 1933 saw an extraordinary outpouring of adulation as the entire country glutted itself with festivities in honour of the 'Leader of the New Germany'.[255] However well orchestrated the propaganda, it was able to tap popular sentiments and quasi-religious levels of devotion that could not simply be manufactured. Hitler was on the way to becoming no longer the party leader, but the symbol of national unity.

And it became more and more difficult for bystanders who were less than fanatical worshippers of the new god to avoid at least an outward sign of acquiescence in the boundless adoration. The most banal expression of acquiescence, the 'Heil Hitler' greeting, now rapidly spread. For civil servants, it was made compulsory a day before Hitler's party was established as the only one permissible in Germany. Those unable to raise the right arm through physical disability were ordered to raise their left arm.[256] The 'German Greeting' – 'Heil Hitler!' – was the outward sign that the country had been turned into a 'Führer state'.[257]

By the summer, the sense that recovery was under way, the new impressions of activity, energy, dynamism after years of Depression and hopelessness, the feeling that the government was doing something to tackle the problems and restore national pride all accrued directly to Hitler's benefit. 'Since the man has taken history into his hands, things work ... At last things are happening,' was how one provincial newspaper put it.[258] The Obersalzberg, when Hitler took up residence in his house there during the summer, became 'a sort of pilgrimage place'. Such were the crowds of admirers trying to glimpse the Reich Chancellor that Himmler, as Commander of the Bavarian Political Police, had to lay down special traffic restrictions for the Berchtesgaden area and to warn against the use of field-glasses by those trying to observe 'every movement of the people's Chancellor'.[259]

What of the man at the centre of this astonishing idolization? Putzi Hanfstaengl, by now head of the Foreign Press Section of the Propaganda Ministry, though not part of the 'inner circle', still saw Hitler at that time frequently and at close quarters. He later commented how difficult it was to gain access to Hitler, even at this early period of his Chancellorship. Hitler had taken his long-standing Bavarian entourage – the 'Chauffeureska' as Hanfstaengl called it – into the Reich Chancellery with him. His adjutants and chauffeurs, Brückner, Schaub, Schreck (successor to Emil Maurice, sacked in 1931 as chauffeur after his flirtation with Geli Raubal), and his court photographer Heinrich Hoffmann were omnipresent, often hindering contact, frequently interfering in a conversation with some form of distraction, invariably listening, later backing Hitler's own impressions and prejudices. Even Foreign Minister Neurath and Reichsbank President Schacht found it difficult to gain Hitler's attention for more than a minute or two without some intervention from one or other member of the 'Chauffeureska'. Only Göring and Himmler, according to Hanfstaengl, could invariably reckon with a brief private audience on request with Hitler. Goebbels, at least, should be added to Hanfstaengl's short list. Hitler's unpredictability and lack of any form of routine did not help. As had always been the case, he tended to be late in bed – often after relaxing by watching a film (one of his favourites was *King Kong*) in his private cinema. Sometimes he scarcely appeared during the mornings, except to hear reports from Hans Heinrich Lammers, the head of the Reich Chancellery, and to look over the press with Goebbels's right-hand man in the Propaganda Ministry, Walther Funk. The high-point of the day was lunch. The chef in the Reich Chancellery, who had been brought from the Brown House in Munich, had a difficult time in preparing a meal ordered for one o'clock but often served as much as two hours later, when Hitler finally appeared. Otto Dietrich, the press chief, took to eating in any case beforehand in the Kaiserhof, turning up at 1.30p.m. prepared for all eventualities. Hitler's table guests changed daily but were invariably trusty party comrades. Even during the first months, conservative ministers were seldom present. Given the company, it was obvious that Hitler would seldom, if ever, find himself contradicted. Any sort of remark, however, could prompt a lengthy tirade – usually resembling his earlier propaganda attacks on political opponents or recollections of battles fought and won.

Plainly, in such circumstances, it would have been impossible for Hitler to have avoided the effects of the fawning sycophancy which surrounded him daily, sifting the type of information that reached him, and cocooning him from the outside world. His sense of reality was by this very process distorted. His contact with those who saw things in a fundamentally different light was restricted in the main to stage-managed interviews with dignitaries, diplomats or foreign journalists. The German people were little more than a faceless, adoring mass, his only direct relationship to them in now relatively infrequent speeches and radio addresses. But the popular adulation he received was like a drug to him. His own self-confidence was already soaring. Casual disparaging comments about Bismarck indicated that he now plainly saw the founder of the Reich as his inferior.[260] What would turn into a fatal sense of infallibility was more than embryonically present.[261]

How much of the adulation of Hitler that spread so rapidly throughout society in 1933 was genuine, how much contrived or opportunistic, is impossible to know. The result was in any case much the same. The near-deification of Hitler gave the Chancellor a status that left all other cabinet ministers and all other party bosses in the shade. Possibilities of questioning, let alone opposing, measures which Hitler was known to favour were becoming as good as non-existent. Already in April, Goebbels could note that the authority of the Führer was now fully established in the cabinet.[262] Hitler's authority now opened doors to radical action previously closed, lifted constraints, and removed barriers on measures that before 30 January 1933 had seemed barely conceivable. Without direct transmission of orders, initiatives imagined to be in tune with Hitler's aims could be undertaken – and have good chances of success.

One such case was the 'sterilization law' – the 'Law for the Prevention of Hereditarily Diseased Offspring' (Gesetz zur Verhütung erbkranken Nachwuchses) – approved by the cabinet on 14 July 1933.[263] As we have noted in earlier chapters, medical opinion had become strongly influenced by prevailing notions of 'eugenics' long before Hitler came to power. However, recommendations, including proposals for a draft Reich Sterilization Law presented to the Prussian government in July 1932, had never gone beyond the voluntary sterilization of those with hereditary illnesses. But now, within months of Hitler becoming Chancellor, the newly appointed special commissioner for medical affairs within the Prussian government, Dr Leonardo Conti – an arch-Nazi – placed a previous outsider in the medical profession, Dr Arthur Gütt, in an influential post in the medical department of the Reich Ministry of the Interior. Gütt, already a Nazi district leader in 1923 and author of 'race-policy guidelines' on 'the sterilization of ill and inferior persons', which he had sent to Hitler the following year, surrounded himself with a committee of 'experts' on population and race questions.[264] By early July he and his committee had come up with the draft prepared in the Prussian Health Office the previous year, but now vitally amended to establish as its keystone the *compulsory* sterilization of those suffering from a wide array of hereditary illness, physical or mental (stretching to chronic alcoholism). Hitler had nothing directly to do with the preparation of the law (which was portrayed as having benefits for the immediate family as well as for society in general). But it was prepared in the knowledge that it accorded with his expressed sentiments. And when it came before the cabinet, it did meet with his outright approval in the face of the objections of Vice-Chancellor Papen, concerned about Catholic feeling regarding the law. Papen's plea for sterilization only with the willing consent of the person concerned was simply brushed aside by the Chancellor. 'All measures were justified which served the upholding of nationhood (*Volkstum*),' was his terse response. Not only, he remarked, were the envisaged measures small-scale, but – he added, with bizarre logic – they were 'also morally incontestable if acknowledged that hereditarily ill people reproduced themselves in considerable quantity (*in erheblichem Maße*) while in contrast millions of healthy children remained unborn'.[265]

Though from a Nazi point of view a modest beginning in racial engineering, the consequences of the law were far from minor: some 400,000 victims would be compulsorily sterilized under the provisions of the act before the end of the Third Reich.[266]

If Papen was hinting at the cabinet meeting that the Catholic Church might cause difficulties over the sterilization law, he knew better than anyone that this was unlikely to be the case. Less than a week before, he had initialled on behalf of the Reich Government the Reich Concordat with the Vatican which he himself had done so much to bring about.[267] The Concordat would be signed among great pomp and circumstance in Rome on 20 July.[268] Despite the continuing molestation of Catholic clergy and other outrages committed by Nazi radicals against the Church and its organizations, the Vatican had been keen to reach agreement with the new government. Even

serious continued harassment once the Concordat had been signed did not
deter the Vatican from agreeing to its ratification on 10 September.[269] Hitler
himself had laid great store on a Concordat from the beginning of his
Chancellorship, primarily with a view to eliminating any role for 'political
Catholicism' in Germany. As we have already seen, this aim was achieved
with the dissolution of the Zentrum and BVP in early July. If Papen's
account is to be trusted, Hitler overrode objections among party radicals
to a rapprochement with the Church, emphasizing the need for 'an atmosphere of harmony in religious matters'.[270] He was also directly involved in
formulating the German terms which Papen negotiated, and, with other
ministers, in vetting the draft treaty.[271] At the very same cabinet meeting at
which the sterilization law was approved, he underlined the triumph which
the Concordat marked for his regime. He rejected any debate on the detail
of the treaty, emphasizing that it was necessary to keep in mind only its
great success. It 'gave Germany a chance' and 'created a sphere of trust
which in the pressing struggle against international Jewry would be of
especial significance', he went on. Any defects in the treaty could be improved
at a later date when the foreign-policy situation was better. Only a short time
earlier, he remarked, he would not have thought it possible 'that the Church
would be ready to commit the bishops to this state. That this had happened,
was without doubt an unreserved recognition of the present regime.'[272]

Indeed, it was an unqualified triumph for Hitler. The German episcopacy,
which had changed course abruptly in its attitude towards the regime
immediately after the passing of the Enabling Act, and had reinforced its
positive stance – despite reservations about the anti-Catholic actions of the
party – in a pastoral letter read out in most dioceses in early June 1933, now
poured out effusive statements of thanks and congratulations to Hitler.[273]
Cardinal Faulhaber, the Catholic leader of Bavaria and long a thorn in
the side of the National Socialists in Munich, congratulated Hitler in a
handwritten letter: 'What the old parliament and parties did not accomplish
in sixty years, your statesmanlike foresight has achieved in six months.' He
ended his letter: 'May God preserve the Reich Chancellor for our people.'[274]

Surprisingly, the Protestant Church turned out to be less easy to handle
in the first months of Hitler's Chancellorship. Hitler invariably assessed
institutions, as he did individuals and social groups, in power-terms. And
in contrast to his respect for the power of the unified international organization of the Catholic Church, and the strength of its hold over a third of
the German population, he was little more than contemptuous of the German
Evangelical Church. Though nominally supported by some two-thirds of

the population, it was divided into twenty-eight separate regional Churches, with different doctrinal emphases. Theological and ideological rifts, opened up by the disarray within the Church following the 1918 Revolution, were wider than ever by 1933.

Perhaps Hitler's scant regard led him to underestimate the minefield of intermingled religion and politics that he entered when he brought his influence to bear in support of attempts to create a unified Reich Church. His own interest, as always in such matters, was purely opportunistic. He was initially forced to intervene partly because of the actions of Nazi radicals in Mecklenburg-Schwerin, who tried to take over Church affairs by the state in the province.[275] Partly, too, the very divisions of the Church meant that the widespread desire for renewal and unification needed Hitler's authority behind it if a centralized Church were to be brought about. From Hitler's point of view, a national Church was of interest purely from the point of view of control and manipulation. Hitler's choice – on whose advice is unclear – as prospective Reich Bishop fell on Ludwig Müller, a fifty-year-old former naval chaplain and head of the 'German Christians' in East Prussia, with no obvious qualifications for the position except a high regard for his own importance and an ardent admiration for the Reich Chancellor and his Movement. Hitler told Müller he wanted speedy unification, without any trouble, and ending with a Church accepting Nazi leadership.

Müller turned out, however, to be a disastrous choice. At the election of the Reich Bishop on 26 May by leaders of the Evangelical Church, he gained the support of the nazified German Christian wing but was rejected by all other sides. Friedrich von Bodelschwingh, director of the welfare centre in Bethel, Westphalia, and a strong upholder of the autonomy of the Church, was elected by fifty-two votes to eighteen instead of Hitler's candidate.[276] Hitler refused to meet Bodelschwingh, and expressed his extreme displeasure at the outcome. In the heated aftermath, the leaders of the Prussian Church (Altpreußische Union) resigned, and a heavy-handed takeover by the Prussian government – bringing the removal of Church administrators and forcing Bodelschwingh's resignation as Reich Bishop-elect – resulted in direct intervention by Hindenburg, pressure from Hitler to have the state commissioners in Prussia removed, and announcement of Church elections to fill a range of vacancies of Church administrators. If occupied by the 'right' persons, these would, it was assumed, then provide the necessary backing for the restructuring of the Evangelical Church. Nazi propaganda supported the German Christians. Hitler himself publicly backed Müller and on the day before the election broadcast his support for the forces within the Church behind the new policies of the state.[277]

The German Christians swept to a convincing victory on 23 July. But it turned out to be a pyrrhic one. By September, Martin Niemöller, the pastor of Dahlem, a well-to-do suburb of Berlin, had received some 2,000 replies to his circular inviting pastors to join him in setting up a 'Pastors' Emergency League', upholding the traditional allegiance to the Holy Scripture and Confessions of the Reformation.[278] It was the beginning of what would eventually turn into the 'Confessing Church', which would develop for some pastors into the vehicle for opposition not just to the Church policy of the state, but to the state itself.

Ludwig Müller was finally elected Reich Bishop on 27 September. But by then, Nazi support for the German Christians – Müller's chief prop of support – was already on the wane. Hitler was by now keen to distance himself from the German Christians, whose activities were increasingly seen as counter-productive, and to detach himself from the internal Church conflict. A German Christian rally, attended by 20,000 people, in the Sportpalast in Berlin in mid-November caused such scandal following an outrageous speech attacking the Old Testament and the theology of the 'Rabbi Paul', and preaching the need for depictions of a more 'heroic' Jesus, that Hitler felt compelled to complete his dissociation from Church matters. The '*Gleichschaltung*' experiment had proved a failure. It was time to abandon it. Hitler promptly lost whatever interest he had had in the Protestant Church.[279] He would in future on more than one occasion again be forced to intervene. But the Church conflict was for him no more than an irritation.

VIII

By autumn 1933, the discord in the Protestant Church was in any case a mere side-show in Hitler's eyes. Of immeasurably greater moment was Germany's international position. In a dramatic move on 14 October, Hitler took Germany out of the disarmament talks at Geneva, and out of the League of Nations. Overnight, international relations were set on a new footing. The Stresemann era of foreign policy was definitively at an end. The 'diplomatic revolution' in Europe had begun.[280]

Hitler had played only a limited role in foreign policy during the first months of the Third Reich. The new, ambitious revisionist course – aimed at reversion to the borders of 1914, re-acquisition of former colonies (and winning of some new ones), incorporation of Austria, and German dominance in eastern and south-eastern Europe – was worked out by foreign ministry professionals and put forward to the cabinet as early as March 1933.[281] By the end of April, Germany's delegate to the Geneva disarmament talks, Rudolf Nadolny, was already speaking in private about intentions of building a large army of 600,000 men. If Britain and France were to agree to only a far smaller army of 300,000 while minimally reducing their own armed forces, or if they agreed to disarm substantially but refused to allow any German rearmament, Nadolny held out the prospect of Germany walking out of the disarmament negotiations, and perhaps of the League of Nations itself.[282] Meanwhile, the new, hawkish Reichswehr Minister, Blomberg, was impatient to break with Geneva without delay, and to proceed unilaterally to as rapid a rearmament programme as possible. Hitler's own line at this time was a far more cautious one. He entertained real fears of intervention – the prospect he had held out to the military in his speech of 3 February – while German defences were so weak.[283]

The talks at Geneva remained deadlocked. A variety of plans were advanced by the British, French and Italians offering Germany some concessions beyond the provisions of Versailles, but retaining clear supremacy in armaments for the western powers. None had any prospect of acceptance in Germany, though Hitler was prepared to follow a tactically more moderate line than that pressed by Neurath and Blomberg. In contrast to the army's impatience for immediate – but unobtainable – equality of armaments, Hitler, the shrewder tactician, was prepared to play the waiting game.[284] At this point, he could only hope that the evident differences between Britain and France on the disarmament question would play into his hands. Eventually, they would do so. Though both major western powers were anxious at the prospect of a rearming Germany, worried by some of the aggressive tones coming from Berlin, and concerned at the Nazi wave of terror activity in Austria, there were significant divisions between them. These meant there was no real prospect of the military intervention that Hitler so feared.[285] Britain was prepared to make greater concessions to Germany. The hope was that through minor concessions, German rearmament could effectively be retarded. But the British felt tugged along by the French hard line, while fearing that it would force Germany out of the League of Nations.[286]

It was, however, Britain that took the lead, on 28 April, supported by France, in presenting Germany with only the minimal concession of the right to a 200,000-man army, but demanding a ban on all paramilitary organizations. Blomberg and Neurath responded angrily in public. Hitler, worried about the threat of sanctions by the western powers, and Polish sabre-rattling in the east, bowed to superior might.[287] He told the cabinet that the question of rearmament would not be solved around the conference table. A new method was needed. There was no possibility at the present time of rearmament 'by normal methods'. The unity of the German people in the disarmament question had to be shown 'to the world'. He picked up a suggestion put to cabinet by Foreign Minister Neurath of a speech to the Reichstag, which would then find acclamation as government policy. He repeated that the greatest caution was needed about rearmament. The cabinet meeting ended with Blomberg and Neurath arguing for Germany withdrawing from participation in negotiations in Geneva.[288] Hitler ignored them. His cautious approach persuaded him to take advice in the preparation of his speech from his old adversary Heinrich Brüning, who underlined the dangers of intervention by France and Poland, with Britain and the USA agreeing to do nothing.[289] Hitler promised Brüning – of course, the promises meant nothing to him – that he would afterwards discuss with the former Chancellor ways of altering the restrictions on personal liberties introduced after the Reichstag fire. Brüning, to whom Hitler offered a position in the government,[290] said he was ready to persuade his colleagues in the Zentrum, and even the SPD deputies, to support the government declaration.[291]

This they did. 'Even Stresemann could not have delivered a milder peace speech,' later commented the SPD deputy Wilhelm Hoegner, an antagonist of Hitler for over a decade, who voted in favour of the resolution proposed by the Chancellor.[292] Indeed, Hitler had seemed to speak, in his address to the Reichstag on 17 May, in the diction of a statesman interested in securing the peace and well-being of his own country, and of the whole of Europe. 'We respect the national rights also of other peoples,' he stated, and 'wish from the innermost heart to live with them in peace and friendship'. With an eye on Pilsudski's Poland, he even rejected expressly 'the concept of germanization'.[293] His demands for equal treatment for Germany in the question of disarmament could sound nothing but justified to German ears, and outside Germany, too. He made a virtue out of emphasizing German weakness in armaments in contrast to French intransigence when superiority was so immense. Germany was prepared to renounce weapons of aggression, if other countries would do the same, he declared. Any attempt to force a disarmament settlement on Germany could only be dictated by the intention of driving the country from the disarmament negotiations, he claimed. 'As a continually defamed people, it would be hard for us to stay within the League of Nations,' ran his scarcely veiled threat.[294] It was a clever piece of rhetoric. Whatever their political persuasion, it was difficult for patriotic members of the Reichstag to vote against such sentiments. And abroad, Hitler sounded the voice of reason, putting his adversaries in the western democracies on a propaganda defensive. Everywhere, Hitler had gained popularity and prestige.

The stalemated Geneva talks were postponed until June, then until October. During this period there were no concrete plans for Germany to break with the League of Nations. Blomberg continued to make hawkish noises, clamouring for Germany to pull out of the talks and undertake the full rearmament of the Reichswehr with heavy defensive weaponry. One of his right-hand men, Colonel Karl-Heinrich von Stülpnagel, told the French attaché in early September that Germany would leave the rearmament conference in the near future. But even later that month, neither Hitler nor his Foreign Minister Neurath were reckoning with an early withdrawal.[295] As late as 4 October, Hitler appears to have been thinking of further negotiations.[296] But on that very day news arrived of a more unyielding British stance on German rearmament, toughened to back the French, and taking no account of demands for equality. That afternoon, Blomberg sought an audience with Hitler in the Reich Chancellery. Neurath later acknowledged that he, too, had advised Hitler at the end of September that there was nothing more to be gained in Geneva.[297] By the time State Secretary Bernhard Wilhelm von Bülow, nephew of Wilhelm II's favourite Chancellor, from the Foreign Ministry, also supportive of the move, saw Hitler, the decision to withdraw from the disarmament talks and break with the League of Nations had been made. Bülow was left to work out the details.[298] Hitler recognized that the time was now ripe to leave the League in circumstances which looked as if Germany was the wronged party. The propaganda advantage, especially at home where he could be certain of massive popular support, was too good a chance to miss. Once the decision was taken – only two ministers, Neurath and Blomberg, and seven people in all were fully informed – any moves that might provoke compromise or concessions from the western powers were avoided.[299]

The cabinet was finally informed on 13 October. With a sure eye as always on the propaganda value of plebiscitary acclaim, Hitler told his ministers that Germany's position would be strengthened by the dissolution of the Reichstag, the setting of new elections, and 'requiring the German people to identify with the peace policy of the Reich government through a plebiscite. With these measures we deprive the world of the possibility of accusing Germany of an aggressive policy. This procedure also provides the

possibility of capturing the attention of the world in an entirely new way.'
No minister dissented.[300]

The following day, the Geneva Conference received official notification
of the German withdrawal.[301] The consequences were far-reaching. The
disarmament talks now lost their meaning. The League of Nations, which
Japan had already left earlier in the year, was fatally weakened. The
inaction of the western powers persuaded Pilsudski to commission the Polish
ambassador to Berlin to explore the possibilities of coming to a diplomatic
arrangement with Germany. The resulting ten-year non-aggression pact
between Poland and Germany, eventually signed on 26 January 1934, pushed
through by Hitler against the traditional anti-Polish thrust of the Foreign
Ministry, was a serious blow to France's alliance system in eastern Europe
and freed Germany from encirclement.[302] All this had followed directly or
indirectly from Hitler's decision to take Germany out of the League of
Nations. In that decision, the timing and propaganda exploitation were
vintage Hitler. But, as we have noted, Blomberg, especially, and Neurath
had been pressing for withdrawal long before Hitler became convinced that
the moment had arrived for Germany to gain maximum advantage. Hitler
had not least been able to benefit from the shaky basis of European diplomacy
at the outset of his Chancellorship. The world economic crisis had undermined the 'fulfilment policy' on which Stresemann's strategy, and the basis
of European security, had been built. The European diplomatic order was,
therefore, already no more stable than a house of cards when Hitler took
up office. The German withdrawal from the League of Nations was the first
card to be removed from the house. The others would soon come tumbling
down.

On the evening of 14 October, in an astutely constructed broadcast sure
of a positive resonance among the millions of listeners throughout the
country, Hitler announced the dissolution of the Reichstag.[303] New elections,
set for 12 November, now provided the opportunity to have a purely
National Socialist Reichstag, free of the remnants of the dissolved parties.
Even though only one party was contesting the elections, Hitler flew once
more throughout Germany holding election addresses.[304] On one occasion,
when the plane's compass had failed, he assisted his pilot, Hans Baur, to
locate his bearings through recognizing a hall in the town of Wismar where
he had once spoken. Baur eventually landed in nearby Travemünde with
scarcely any fuel left.[305] The propaganda campaign directed its energies
almost entirely to accomplishing a show of loyalty to Hitler personally –
now regularly referred to even in the still existent non-Nazi press as simply

'the Führer'.[306] Hitler's name did not appear in the loaded question posed on the plebiscite ballot-sheet: 'Do you, German man, and you, German woman, approve this policy of your Reich government, and are you ready to declare it to be the expression of your own view and your own will, and solemnly to give it your allegiance?'[307] It was, however, obvious that 'Reich government' and 'Hitler' were by now synonymous.

Electoral manipulation was still not as refined as it was to become in the 1936 and 1938 plebiscites. But it was far from absent. Various forms of chicanery were commonplace. Secrecy at the ballot-box was far from guaranteed.[308] And pressure to conform was obvious.[309] Even so, the official result – 95.1 per cent in the plebiscite, 92.1 per cent in the 'Reichstag election' – marked a genuine triumph for Hitler.[310] Abroad as well as at home, even allowing for manipulation and lack of freedom, it had to be concluded that the vast majority of the German people backed him. In a matter of national importance, in which even those who had rigorously opposed the NSDAP overwhelmingly favoured the stance taken towards the League of Nations, Hitler had won genuine acclaim. His stature as a *national* leader above party interest was massively enhanced.

The obsequious language used by Vice-Chancellor Papen at the first cabinet meeting after the plebiscite confirmed the total dominance Hitler had attained during his first months in office. Papen spoke of the 'unique, most overwhelming profession of support (*Bekenntnisses*) that a nation has ever given to its leader'. 'In nine months,' he continued, 'the genius of your leadership and the ideals which you have newly placed before us have succeeded in creating, from a people inwardly torn apart and without hope, a united Reich.' He went on to portray Hitler as Germany's 'unknown soldier' who had won over his people. 'Probably never in the history of nations has such a measure of fervent trust been shown to a statesman. The German people has thereby let known that it has grasped the meaning of the changing times and is determined to follow the Leader on his path.' The members of cabinet rose from their seats to salute their Chancellor. Hitler replied that the tasks ahead would be easier on the basis of the support that he now enjoyed.[311]

Hitler's conquest of Germany was still, however, incomplete. Behind the euphoria of the plebiscite result, a long-standing problem was now threatening to endanger the regime itself: the problem of the SA.

12

SECURING TOTAL POWER

'I gave the order to shoot those most guilty of this treason, and I further gave the order to burn out down to the raw flesh the ulcers of our internal well-poisoning . . .'

Hitler, addressing the Reichstag on 13 July 1934

'The Reich Chancellor kept his word when he nipped in the bud Röhm's attempt to incorporate the SA in the Reichswehr. We love him because he has shown himself a true soldier.'

Walther von Reichenau, part of guidelines for political instruction of the troops, 28 August 1934

The making of the dictator was still incomplete at the end of 1933. Despite an astonishing transformation of the political scene which, at a speed few if any could have foreseen, had inordinately strengthened Hitler's position, two notable obstacles remained, blocking his route to untrammelled power in the state. The obstacles were closely bound up with each other.

Hitler's unruly party army, the SA, had outlived its purpose. That had been to win power. Everything had been predicated on the attainment of that single goal. What would follow the winning of power, what would be the purpose and function of the SA in the new state, what benefits would flow for ordinary stormtroopers, had never been clarified. Now, months after the 'seizure of power', the SA's 'politics of hooliganism'[1] were a force for disruption in the state. And particularly in the military ambitions of its leader, Ernst Röhm, the SA was an increasingly destabilizing factor, above all in relations with the Reichswehr. But its elimination, or disempowering, was no simple matter. It was a huge organization, far bigger than the party itself. It contained many of the most ardent 'old fighters' (in a literal sense) in the Movement. And it had been the backbone of the violent activism which had forced the pace of the Nazi revolution since Hitler had become Chancellor. Röhm's ambitions, as we have seen in earlier chapters, had never been identical with those of Hitler. A large paramilitary organization that had never accepted its subordination to the political wing of the party had caused tensions, and occasional rebellion, since the 1920s. But, whatever the crises, Hitler had always managed to retain the SA's loyalty. To challenge the SA's leadership risked losing that loyalty. It could not be done easily or approached lightly. Faced with the dilemma of what to do about the SA, Hitler for months did little to resolve the tensions which continued to build. Characteristically, he acted finally when there was no longer a choice – but then with utter ruthlessness.

The problem of the SA was inextricably bound up with the other threat to the consolidation of Hitler's power. Reich President Hindenburg was old and frail. The issue of the succession would loom within the foreseeable future. Hindenburg, the symbol of 'old' Germany, and 'old' Prussia, was the figurehead behind which stood still powerful forces with somewhat ambivalent loyalties towards the new state. Most important among them was the army, of which as Head of State Hindenburg was supreme commander. The Reichswehr leadership was intensely and increasingly alarmed by the military pretensions of the SA. Failure on Hitler's part to solve the problem of the SA could conceivably lead to army leaders favouring an alternative as Head of State on Hindenburg's death – perhaps resulting in a restoration of the monarchy, and a *de facto* military dictatorship. Such a development would have met with favour among sections, not just of the military old guard, but of some national-conservative groups, which had favoured an authoritarian, anti-democratic form of state but had become appalled by the Hitler regime. The office of the Vice-Chancellor, Papen, gradually emerged as the focal point of hopes of blunting the edge of the Nazi revolution. Since Papen continued to enjoy the favour of the Reich President, such 'reactionaries', though small in number, could not be discounted in power-political terms. And since at the same time there were growing worries among business leaders about serious and mounting economic problems, the threat to the consolidation of Hitler's power – and with that of the regime itself – was a real one.

Hitler did not act before he was compelled to do so. The pressure from the Reichswehr leadership and the machinations of Göring, Himmler and Heydrich played decisive roles in bringing matters to a head in summer 1934. Then, within a matter of five weeks, the destruction of the SA leadership in the Night of the Long Knives (accompanied by the murder of leading figures in the 'reaction') and the rapid takeover by Hitler of the headship of state on Hindenburg's death (under a law agreed by the cabinet while he was still alive) amounted to a decisive phase in the securing of total power.

I

Ernst Röhm's SA had been the spearhead of the Nazi revolution in the first months of 1933. The explosion of elemental violence had needed no commands from above. The SA had long been kept on a leash, told to wait for the day of reckoning. Now it could scarcely be contained. Orgies of hate-filled revenge against political enemies and horrifically brutal assaults on Jews were daily occurrences. A large proportion of the estimated 100,000 persons taken into custody in these turbulent months were held in makeshift SA prisons and camps. Some hundred of these were set up in the Berlin area alone. Many victims were bestially tortured. The minimal figure of some 500–600 murdered in what the Nazis themselves proclaimed as a bloodless and legal revolution can largely be placed on the account of the SA.[2] The first Gestapo chief, Rudolf Diels, described after the war the conditions in one of the SA's Berlin prisons: 'The "interrogations" had begun and ended with a beating. A dozen fellows had laid into their victims at intervals of some hours with iron bars, rubber coshes, and whips. Smashed teeth and broken bones bore witness to the tortures. As we entered, these living skeletons with festering wounds lay in rows on the rotting straw . . .'[3]

In one of numerous letters with which he bombarded Reich President Hindenburg in autumn 1933 on the 'violent activity and lawlessness (*Willkür*) in the German Reich ruled by you', his erstwhile comrade, now thorn in his flesh, Erich Ludendorff, reported 'unbelievable events' which were 'mounting up in horrifying fashion', and spoke of the final phase of Hindenburg's presidency as 'the blackest time in German history'. The letters were passed on to Hitler.[4] Appeals for discipline by Hitler were ignored. Even those by Röhm were not heeded.[5] Such appeals were in any case half-hearted and merely tactical. Behind the scenes, Hitler was quashing – often following requests from within the party leadership or from Reich Justice Minister Gürtner – case after case of maltreatment and torture of prisoners, many by SA men.[6]

As long as the terror was levelled in the main at Communists, Socialists and Jews, it was in any case not likely to be widely unpopular, and could be played down as 'excesses' of the 'national uprising'. But already by the summer, the number of incidents mounted in which overbearing and loutish behaviour by SA men caused widespread public offence even in pro-Nazi circles. By this time, complaints were pouring in from industry, commerce and local government offices about disturbances and intolerable actions by stormtroopers. The Foreign Office added its own protest at incidents where foreign diplomats had been insulted or even manhandled. The SA was threatening to become completely uncontrollable. Steps had to be taken.[7] Reich President Hindenburg, exercised about the upheavals in the Protestant Church, himself requested Hitler to restore order.[8]

The need for Hitler to act became especially urgent after Röhm, in a programmatic article in the *Nationalsozialistische Monatshefte* (National Socialist Monthly) in June 1933, had openly stated the SA's aim of continuing the 'German Revolution' in the teeth of attempts by conservatives, reactionaries, and opportunist fellow-travellers to undermine and tame it. 'The SA and SS will not allow the German Revolution to fall asleep or be betrayed half-way there by the non-fighters,' he railed. 'Whether they like it or not,' the article ended, 'we will carry on our struggle. If they finally grasp what it is about, with them! If they are not willing, without them! And if it has to be: against them!'[9]

Röhm was clearly signalling to the new rulers of Germany that for him the revolution was only just starting; and that he would demand a leading role for himself and the mighty organization he headed – by now some 4½ million strong.[10]

Forced now for the first time to choose between the demands of the party's paramilitary wing and the 'big battalions' pressing for order, Hitler summoned the Reich Governors to a meeting in the Reich Chancellery on 6 July. 'The revolution is not a permanent condition,' he announced; 'it must not turn into a lasting situation. It is necessary to divert the river of revolution that has broken free into the secure bed of evolution.'[11] Other Nazi leaders – Frick, Göring, Goebbels and Heß – took up the message in the weeks that followed.[12] There was an unmistakable change of course.

Röhm's ambitions were, however, undaunted. They amounted to little less than the creation of an 'SA state', with extensive powers in the police, in military matters, and in the civil administration. Little of this had been realized by the end of 1933. Göring had removed the SA from the role of auxiliary police in Prussia in the summer. By October, the SA had also been excluded from any control over concentration camps.[13] The army leadership had the sharpest of antennae towards Röhm's proclaimed intention of building up a huge people's militia alongside the Reichswehr. And the SA 'Special Commissioners' (*Sonderbeauftragte*) attached to government offices in the Länder, especially in Bavaria and Prussia, were indeed substantial irritation factors, but had advisory, not controlling, functions. Even so, there was enough for the growing number of powerful enemies of the SA to worry about. When, in December 1933, Röhm was given cabinet status as Reich Minister without Portfolio, it was mainly as a consolation for the major offices and powers which had not come his way. However, his own hints that this might be a step to an 'SA Ministry' and, possibly, in the end to his scarcely concealed hope of taking over the Defence Ministry, were hardly guaranteed to calm the nerves of the Reichswehr leadership.[14] Immediate steps were put in place to curtail cooperation with the SA and exclude it from influence in military matters.[15]

It was not just a matter of Röhm's own power ambitions. Within the gigantic army of Brownshirts, expectations of the wondrous shangri-la to follow the day when National Socialism took power had been hugely disappointed. Though they had poured out their bile on their political enemies, the offices, financial rewards, and power they had naïvely believed would flow their way remained elusive. Certainly, the top leaders of the SA fully exploited the new financial benefits which came the way of an organization now able to rely on extensive state funding.[16] There was no shortage of high living at this level. The ostentatious splendour of Röhm's own new villa in Munich's Prinzregentenplatz, complete with mahogany chairs from the château of Fontainebleau and sixteenth-century Florentine wall-mirrors, was only one indication of this.[17] But little filtered through to the base. Here, unemployment was higher than average. The reputation for poor work-discipline deterred many employers from taking on SA men, even now the National Socialists were in government.[18] The resentments against 'bourgeois' authorities or party opportunists seen to block chances of obtaining the posts or material benefits thought of right to be theirs were profound among the 'old fighters' in the SA. Talk of a 'second revolution', however little it was grounded in any clear programme of social change, was, therefore, bound to find strong resonance among rank-and-file stormtroopers.

Ernst Röhm had, then, no difficulty in expanding his popularity among SA men through his continued dark threats in early 1934 about further revolution which would accomplish what the 'national uprising' had failed to bring about. He remained publicly loyal to Hitler. Privately, he was highly critical of Hitler's policy towards the Reichswehr and his dependency on Blomberg and Reichenau. And he did nothing to deter the growth of a personality cult elevating his leadership of the SA.[19] At the Reich Party Rally of Victory in 1933, he had been the most prominent party leader after Hitler, clearly featuring as the Führer's right-hand man.[20] By early 1934, Hitler had been largely forced from the pages of the SA's newspaper, SA-Mann, by the expanding Röhm-cult.[21]

At least in public, the loyalty was reciprocated.[22] Hitler wavered, as he would continue to do during the first months of 1934, between Röhm's SA and the Reichswehr. He could not bring himself to discipline, let alone dismiss, Röhm. The political damage and loss of face and popularity involved made such a move risky. But the realities of power compelled him to side with the Reichswehr leadership.[23] This became fully clear only at the end of February. Before then, however much he had assuaged the Reichswehr leadership, he had never explicitly renounced the SA's claims in military matters.[24] But even thereafter, Hitler hesitated to take the action that this political choice demanded.[25] The consequence was that the crisis would gather throughout the spring and early summer.

By 2 February 1934, at a meeting of his Gauleiter, Hitler was again criticizing the SA in all but name. Only 'fools' (Narren) thought the revolution was not over; there were those in the Movement who only understood 'revolution' as meaning 'a permanent condition of chaos'.[26]

The previous day, Röhm had sent Blomberg a memorandum on relations between the army and the SA. What he appeared to be demanding – no copy of the actual memorandum has survived – was no less than the concession of national defence as the domain of the SA, and a reduction of the function of the armed forces to the provision of trained men for the SA.[27] So crass were the demands that it seems highly likely that Blomberg deliberately falsified or misconstrued them when addressing a meeting of army District Commanders on 2 February in Berlin. They were predictably horrified.[28] Now Hitler had to decide, stated Blomberg.[29] The army lobbied him. In a conscious attempt to win his support against the SA, Blomberg, without any pressure from the Nazi leadership, introduced the NSDAP's emblem into the army and accepted the 'Aryan Paragraph' for the officer corps, leading to the prompt dismissal of some seventy members of the armed forces.[30] Röhm, too, sought to win his support. But, faced with having to choose between the Reichswehr, with Hindenburg's backing, or his party army, Hitler could now only decide one way.

By 27 February the army leaders had worked out their 'guidelines for cooperation with the SA', which formed the basis for Hitler's speech the next day and had, therefore, certainly been agreed with him.[31] At the meeting in the Reichswehr Ministry on 28 February, attended by Reichswehr, SA, and SS leaders, Hitler rejected outright Röhm's plans for an SA-militia. The SA was to confine its activities to political, not military, matters.[32] Hitler indicated how he saw matters developing. The NSDAP had cleared away unemployment, he is reported as having stated, but within about eight years an economic blow-out (Durchschlag) was bound to take place unless living-space was created for the surplus population. It was typical Hitlerian rhetoric. Unemployment had fallen sharply but by this time had by no means been eliminated. And severe economic constraints were already making themselves acutely felt. But, as he invariably did, Hitler painted for his audience a black-and-white scenario: that of following his diagnosis – attainment of 'living-space' – or facing the consequences of certain economic collapse. He drew the military consequences. 'Short decisive blows against the West then against the East could therefore become necessary.' But a militia, such as Röhm was suggesting, was not suitable even for minimal national defence. He was determined to build up a well-trained 'people's army' (*Volksheer*) in the Reichswehr, equipped with the most modern weapons, which must be prepared for all eventualities on defence within five years and suitable for attack after eight years. 'In domestic politics, one had to be loyal, but in foreign policy one could break one's word,' he declared. He demanded of the SA that they obey his orders. For the transitional period before the planned Wehrmacht was set up, he approved Blomberg's suggestion to deploy the SA for tasks of border protection and pre-military training. But 'the Wehrmacht must be the sole bearer of weapons of the nation'.[33]

Röhm and Blomberg had to sign and shake hands on the 'agreement'. Hitler departed. Champagne followed. But the atmosphere was anything but cordial.[34] When the officers had left, Röhm was overheard to remark: 'What the ridiculous corporal declared doesn't apply to us. Hitler has no loyalty and has at least to be sent on leave. If not with, then we'll manage the thing without Hitler.' The person taking note of these treasonable remarks was SA-Obergruppenführer Viktor Lutze, who reported what had gone on to Hitler. 'We'll have to let the thing ripen' was all he gleaned as reply.[35] But the show of loyalty was noted. When he needed a new SA chief after the events of 30 June, Lutze was Hitler's man.

II

From the beginning of 1934, Hitler seems to have recognized that he would be faced with no choice but to cut down to size his over-mighty subject, Chief of Staff Ernst Röhm. How to tackle Röhm was, however, unclear. Hitler deferred the problem. He simply awaited developments.[36] The Reichswehr leadership, too, was biding its time, expecting a gradual escalation, but looking then to a final showdown.[37] Relations between the army and the SA continued to fester. But Hitler did, it seems, order the monitoring of SA activities. According to the later account of Gestapo chief Rudolf Diels, it was in January 1934 that Hitler requested him and Göring to collect material on the excesses of the SA.[38] From the end of February onwards, the Reichswehr leadership started assembling its own intelligence on SA activities, which was passed to Hitler.[39] Once Himmler and Heydrich had taken over the Prussian Gestapo in April, the build-up of a dossier on the SA was evidently intensified. Röhm's foreign contacts were noted, as well as those with figures at home known to be cool towards the regime, such as former Chancellor Schleicher.[40]

By this time, Röhm had incited an ensemble of powerful enemies, who would eventually coagulate into an unholy alliance against the SA. Göring was so keen to be rid of the SA's alternative power-base in Prussia – which he himself had done much to establish, starting when he made the SA auxiliary police in February 1933 – that he was even prepared by 20 April to concede control over the Prussian Gestapo to Heinrich Himmler, thus paving the way for the creation of a centralized police-state in the hands of the SS. Himmler himself, and even more so his cold and dangerous henchman Reinhard Heydrich, recognized that their ambitions to construct such an empire – the key edifice of power and control in the Third Reich – rested on the élite SS breaking with its superior body, the SA, and eliminating the power-base held by Röhm. In the party, the head of the organization, installed in April 1933 with the grand title of the Fuhrer's Deputy (for party affairs), Rudolf Heß, and the increasingly powerful figure behind the scenes, Martin Bormann, were more than aware of the contempt in which the Political Organization was held by Röhm's men and the threat of the SA actually replacing the party, or making it redundant.[41] For the army, as already noted, Röhm's aim to subordinate the Reichswehr to the interests of a people's militia was anathema. Intensified military exercises, expansive parades, and, not least, reports of extensive weapon collections in the hands of the SA, did little to calm the nerves.[42]

At the centre of this web of countervailing interests and intrigue, united only in the anxiety to be rid of the menace of the SA, Hitler's sharp instinct for the realities of power by now must have made it plain that he had to break with Röhm. How radical the break would be was at this stage unclear. In February, and again in April, he indicated to Anthony Eden, at that time Lord Privy Seal in the British government, that he would be prepared to reduce the SA by two-thirds and place the rest under international supervision to ensure their demilitarization. He told Eden that his common sense and political instinct would never allow him to sanction the creation of a second army in the state – 'never, never!' he repeated.[43] His remarks were a marker for the western powers both of an apparent accommodation in disarmament negotiations and of his gestating thoughts on the problem of the SA. There is no hint at this stage of a plot to kill Röhm, nor plans for a modern St Bartholomew's Night Massacre. These would be largely improvised only at the last moment.[44]

In the meantime, the problem of the SA was part of the first looming crisis of the regime's existence, as spring turned into summer in 1934. Hitler himself was well aware of the situation. The position of the German economy – chronically lacking raw materials, with falling exports, soaring imports, and a haemorrhage of hard currency fast approaching disaster level – had become highly precarious. The foreign press predicted Hitler's early downfall.[45] It was a matter of 'preventing a catastrophe', Hitler told a meeting of Reich Governors and other party high-ups on 22 March 1934. He went on to criticize the constant interference in the economy by party and SA activists. Continued boycotting of department stores could easily lead to a bank crisis, signalling the death of hopes of economic recovery, was his sombre assessment, based on the information he had been given in no uncertain terms by his economic advisers.[46]

At the level of the ordinary mass of the population, the excited and anticipatory mood of 'national renewal' that had swept the country during the breathless upheavals of 1933 had given way to widespread discontent and criticism as disillusionment and material disappointment took over. A nationwide propaganda campaign launched by Goebbels in May to combat the 'moaners' was a resounding failure. All across the country, there were reports of a deterioration in the mood of the people. Angered by the imposition of a maze of bureaucratic controls by the Reich Food Estate (Reichsnährstand) – the vast and unwieldy organization headed by agriculture minister Walther Darré and set up in September 1933 to direct every aspect of German farming – peasants vented their spleen on the corruption of a system in which only 'big-shots' profited. Industrial workers, cowed and intimidated, nevertheless revealed their feelings in elections for the newly established 'Councils of Trust' (Vertrauensräte) in April. The 'Councils of Trust' had been created in January 1934 in place of the former 'Works Councils' (Betriebsräte), purportedly to look after the interests of both employers and employees in the larger firms. Workers recognized them for the sham they were – largely vehicles for employer control. The results of the elections to the councils were so embarrassing to the regime that they were never published. The commercial middle class complained bitterly at poor economic prospects, currency and credit restrictions, raw material shortages, and the failure of the government to stimulate trade.[47] Also, for the millions still unemployed, the reality of the Third Reich bore little resemblance to its propaganda. Hitler himself was still massively popular. But criticism of corrupt and high-handed party functionaries was extensive. Not least, the arrogant, overbearing, and bullying behaviour of the SA – acceptable even to Nazi sympathizers only when directed at Communists, Socialists, Jews, or other disliked minorities – was for many the most intolerable daily manifestation of Nazi rule.

The wide-ranging public discontent amounted, of course, to nothing like rooted political opposition. As the exiled Social Democratic leadership acknowledged, much of it was little more than grumbling 'whose dissatis-faction has purely economic causes'. For most of the middle classes and peasants, Nazism, whatever its faults, was preferable to Bolshevism, which Hitler had successfully depicted as the only alternative. 'The anxiety about Bolshevism, about the chaos which in the opinion of the great mass in particular of the *Mittelstand* and the peasantry would follow on the fall of Hitler, is still the negative mass base of the regime,' adjudged the SPD's exiled analysts.[48] The 'dark side' of the regime, which had revealed itself only too clearly in the opening phase of Nazi rule, was seen by many in this light. It was bad; but Bolshevism would have been worse. There was also a good deal of feeling that those who had suffered most – Communists, Socialists and Jews – had deserved it. And that – sharing President Hinden-burg's views – much of what had happened, if at times regrettable, was inevitable amid such political upheaval, but would settle down. Whatever his minions might do, many thought, Hitler meant the best for Germany. Amid the continuing idealism and avid enthusiasm of millions of Hitler loyalists, it was certainly the case that National Socialism had lost ground in terms of public support by the spring of 1934. But this in itself, attributable only in part to the behaviour of the SA, did not suggest danger for the regime.

More threatening was the growing dismay among national-conservative élites about the Pandora's box they themselves had helped prise open. Some among them recognized the potential for exploiting the crisis to turn the party dictatorship they so detested into what they had always wanted: an authoritarian state without parties – and under their own control. The 'taming' of Hitler had failed disastrously in 1933. The antics of Röhm, and the wild talk of a 'second revolution', offered a second opportunity. 'We are partly responsible that this fellow has come to power,' commented Edgar Jung, an intellectual on the conservative Right and speech-writer for Papen, of Hitler. 'We must get rid of him again.'[49] Another member of Papen's circle, his press secretary Herbert von Bose, used his control over the

Vice-Chancellor's press agency to contact numerous generals known to be critical of the regime. His hope was to use the SA crisis to weaken Hitler. Crucially, given Hindenburg's frailty, it was urgently necessary to make plans for his replacement as Head of State. The restoration of the monarchy, perhaps with a Hohenzollern prince as regent in the first instance, was the hope of the conservatives. Hitler's chances of obtaining supreme power would thereby be blocked. However limited the realistic chances of success of this strategy were, the very substance of the National Socialist regime was at this time in question.[50]

In April it became known that Hindenburg was seriously ill.[51] Hitler and Blomberg had already been told that the end was not far off.[52] At the beginning of June, the Reich President retired to his estate at Neudeck in East Prussia. The most important prop of the conservatives was now far from the centre of the action. And the succession issue was imminent. Moreover, to remove the obstacle which the SA was providing to recommencing talks about rearmament with the western powers, Hitler had, at the end of May, ordered the SA to stop military exercises, and, in the last talks he had with Röhm, a few days later, had sent the stormtroopers on leave for a month.[53]

This defusing of the situation, together with Hindenburg's absence, made the situation more difficult, rather than easier, for the conservatives. But Bose was anxious not to let the initiative seep away. He knew that Jung had been working on and off since December on a speech for Papen which would attack the 'degeneration' (*Entartung*) of the new state. As it happened, Papen was due to deliver a speech on 17 June at the University of Marburg. The text prepared by Jung and completed eight days earlier was adopted for it. Papen's secretary was concerned at its tone. But Papen was given a copy only as he left for Marburg and was prevented from making any alterations.[54] Sensationally, he delivered his boldly challenging speech – a passionate warning against the dangers of a 'second revolution' and a heated broadside against the 'selfishness, lack of character, insincerity, lack of chivalry, and arrogance' featuring under the guise of the German revolution. He even criticized the creation of a 'false personality cult'. 'Great men are not made by propaganda, but grow out of their actions,' he declared. 'No nation can live in a continuous state of revolution,' he went on. 'Permanent dynamism permits no solid foundations to be laid. Germany cannot live in a continuous state of unrest, to which no one sees an end.'[55] The speech met with roars of applause within the hall. Outside, Goebbels moved swiftly to have it banned, though not before some extracts were printed in the *Frankfurter Zeitung*, one of Germany's most respected newspapers and still able to avoid the tightening Nazi straitjacket on the press. Copies of the speech were run off and circulated, both within Germany and to the foreign press.[56] Word of it quickly went round. Never again in the Third Reich was such striking criticism at the heart of the regime to come from such a prominent figure. But if Papen and his friends were hoping to prompt action by the army, supported by the President, to 'tame' Hitler, they were disappointed.[57] As it was, the Marburg speech served as the decisive trigger to the brutal action taken at the end of the month.

Hitler's own mood towards the 'reactionaries' was darkening visibly. Without specifying any names, his speech at Gera at the Party Rally of the Thuringian Gau on 17 June, the same day as Papen's speech, gave a plain indication of his fury at the activities of the Papen circle. He castigated them as 'dwarves', alluding, it seems, to Papen himself as a 'tiny worm'. Then came the threat: 'If they should at any time attempt, even in a small way, to move from their criticism to a new act of perjury (Meineidstat), they can be sure that what confronts them today is not the cowardly and corrupt bourgeoisie of 1918 but the fist of the entire people. It is the fist of the nation that is clenched and will smash down anyone who dares to undertake even the slightest attempt at sabotage.'[58] Such a mood prefigured the murder of some prominent members of the conservative 'reaction' on 30 June. In fact, in the immediate aftermath of the Papen speech, a strike against the 'reactionaries' seemed more likely than a showdown with the SA.[59]

At the imposition of the ban on publishing his speech, Papen went to see Hitler. He said Goebbels's action left him no alternative but to resign. He intended to inform the Reich President of this unless the ban were lifted and Hitler declared himself ready to follow the policies outlined in the speech. Hitler reacted cleverly – in wholly different manner from his tirades in the presence of his party members. He acknowledged that Goebbels was in the wrong in his action, and that he would order the ban to be lifted. He also attacked the insubordination of the SA and stated that they would have to be dealt with. He asked Papen, however, to delay his resignation until he could accompany him to visit the President for a joint interview to discuss the entire situation.[60] Papen conceded – and the moment was lost.

Hitler wasted no time. He arranged an audience alone with Hindenburg on 21 June, officially to discuss his meeting with Mussolini in Venice a few days earlier.[61] This, Hitler's first visit abroad (if we discount his time during the war spent in France and Belgium), had given the opportunity for an airing of the Austrian question. But Mussolini and Austria were not on Hitler's mind as he travelled to see the ailing Reich President.

On the way up the steps to Hindenburg's residence, Schloß Neudeck, he was met by Blomberg, who had been summoned by the President in the furore following Papen's speech. Blomberg told Hitler bluntly that it was urgently necessary to take measures necessary to ensure internal peace in Germany. If the Reich Government was incapable of relieving the current state of tension, the President would declare martial law and hand over control to the army.[62] The Reich President himself, according to Meissner's later account, told Hitler 'to bring the revolutionary trouble-makers finally to reason'.[63] Hitler realized that there could be no further prevarication. He had to act. There was no alternative but to placate the army – behind which stood the President. And that meant destroying the power of the SA without delay.

Any action had to be undertaken by 1 August, when the stormtroopers were due to return from leave. Probably the decision to purge the SA had already been taken by the date, four days after Hitler's audience with Hindenburg, when Heß ominously threatened, in a radio broadcast: 'Woe to anyone in breach of loyalty in the belief of serving the revolution through a revolt.'[64]

What Hitler had in mind at this stage is unclear. He seems to have spoken about deposing Röhm, or having him arrested.[65] By now, however, Heydrich's SD – the part of the labyrinthine SS organization responsible for internal surveillance – and the Gestapo were working overtime to concoct alarmist reports of an imminent SA putsch. SS and SD leaders were summoned to Berlin around 25 June to be instructed by Himmler and Heydrich about the measures to be taken in the event of an SA revolt expected any time.[66] For all their unruliness, the SA had never contemplated such a move. The leadership remained loyal to Hitler. But now, the readiness to believe that Röhm was planning a takeover was readily embraced by all the SA's powerful enemies. The Reichswehr, during May and June becoming increasingly suspicious about the ambitions of the SA leadership, made weapons and transport available to the SS (whose small size and – at this time – confinement to largely policing work posed no threat to the military). An SA putsch was now thought likely in summer or autumn. The entire Reichswehr leadership – most prominently Blomberg and Reichenau, but also Fritsch and Beck – were prepared for imminent action against Röhm.[67] The psychological state for a strike against the SA was rapidly forming. Alarm bells were set ringing loudly on 26 June through what seemed to be an order by Röhm for arming the SA in preparation for an attack on the Reichswehr. The 'order', in fact a near-certain fake (though by whom was never established), had mysteriously found its way into the office of the Abwehr chief, Captain Conrad Patzig. Lutze was present when Blomberg and Reichenau presented Hitler the following day with the 'evidence'. Hitler had already hinted to Blomberg two days earlier that he would summon SA leaders to a conference at Bad Wiessee on the Tegernsee, some fifty miles south-east of Munich, where Röhm was residing, and have them arrested. This decision seems to have been confirmed at the meeting with Blomberg and Reichenau on 27 June.[68] The same day, SS-Obergruppenführer Sepp Dietrich, commander of Hitler's house-guards, the Leibstandarte-SS Adolf Hitler, arranged with the Reichswehr to pick up the arms needed for a 'secret and very important commission of the Führer'.[69]

III

The timing of the 'action' seems to have been finally determined on the evening of 28 June, while Hitler, together with Göring and Lutze, was in Essen for the wedding of Gauleiter Terboven.[70] During the wedding reception, Hitler had received a message from Himmler, informing him that Oskar von Hindenburg had agreed to arrange for his father to receive Papen, probably on 30 June. The meeting had been initiated by Herbert von Bose and Fritz Günther von Tschirschky und Boegendorff, the personal secretary of the Vice-Chancellor. It marked a final attempt, after they had heard of the arrest of Edgar Jung by the Gestapo, to win the Reich President's approval for moves to constrain the power not only of Röhm and the SA, but of Hitler himself.[71] Hitler left the wedding reception straight away. As a non-drinker and non-smoker, content only when he was holding court and dominating proceedings, such festivities gave him little pleasure anyway (and his presence was presumably an inhibition as well as an honour to other guests). He raced back to his hotel. There, according to Lutze, he decided there was no time to lose: he had to strike.[72]

Röhm's adjutant was ordered by telephone to ensure that all SA leaders attended a meeting with Hitler in Bad Wiessee on the late morning of 30 June.[73] In the meantime, the army had been put on alert. Göring flew back to Berlin to take charge of matters there, ready at a word to move not only against the SA, but also the Papen group.[74] Hitler travelled to Bad Godesberg on the afternoon of 29 June, to be joined in the Rheinhotel Dreesen by Goebbels and Sepp Dietrich, flying in from Berlin. Goebbels had been impatient at Hitler's delay in dealing with the 'reaction'.[75] He flew to

Godesberg thinking the strike against Papen and his cronies was finally going to take place. Only on arrival did he learn that the main target was Röhm's SA. Hitler reported to him how serious the situation was. There was proof, he claimed (and evidently believed), that Röhm had conspired with the French ambassador François-Poncet, Schleicher and Strasser. So he was determined to act the very next day 'against Röhm and his rebels'. Blood would be shed. They should realize that people lose their heads through rebellion. While arrangements were made, total secrecy had to be maintained.[76]

Rumours of unrest in the SA were meanwhile being passed to Hitler, whose mood was becoming blacker by the minute. The telephone rang. The 'rebels', it was reported, were ready to strike in Berlin.[77] There was, in fact, no putsch attempt at all. But groups of SA men in different parts of Germany, aware of the stories circulating of an impending strike against the SA, or the deposition of Röhm, were going on the rampage. Sepp Dietrich was ordered to leave for Munich straight away. Soon after midnight, he phoned Hitler from Munich and was given further orders to pick up two companies of the Leibstandarte and be in Bad Wiessee by eleven in the morning.[78] Around 2a.m. Hitler left to fly to Munich, accompanied by his adjutants Brückner, Schaub and Schreck, along with Goebbels, Lutze and Press Chief Dietrich.[79] The first glimmers of dawn were breaking through as he arrived. He was met by Gauleiter Adolf Wagner and two Reichswehr officers, who told him that the Munich SA, shouting abuse at the Führer, had attempted an armed demonstration in the city. Though a serious disturbance, it was, in fact, merely the biggest of the protest actions of despairing stormtroopers, when as many as 3,000 armed SA men had rampaged through Munich in the early hours, denouncing the 'treachery' against the SA, shouting: 'The Führer is against us, the Reichswehr is against us; SA out on the streets.' However, Hitler had not heard of the Munich disturbances before he arrived there in the early hours of the morning. Now, in blind rage at what he interpreted as the betrayal by Röhm – 'the blackest day of my life', he was heard to say – he decided not to wait till the following morning, but to act immediately.[80]

He and his entourage raced to the Bavarian Ministry of the Interior. The local SA leaders Obergruppenführer Schneidhuber and Gruppenführer Schmid were peremptorily summoned. Hitler's fury was still rising as he awaited them. By now he had worked himself into a near-hysterical state of mind, reminiscent of the night of the Reichstag fire. Accepting no explanations, he ripped their rank badges from their shoulders, shouting, 'You are under arrest and will be shot.' Bewildered and frightened, they were taken off to Stadelheim prison.[81]

Hitler, without waiting for Dietrich's SS men to arrive, now demanded to be taken immediately to Bad Wiessee. It was just after 6.30a.m. as the three cars pulled up outside the Hotel Hanselbauer in the resort on the Tegernsee, where Röhm and other SA leaders were still sleeping off an evening's drinking. Hitler, followed by members of his entourage and a number of policemen, stormed up to Röhm's room and, pistol in hand, denounced him as a traitor (which the astonished Chief of Staff vehemently denied) and declared him under arrest. Edmund Heines, the Breslau SA leader, was found in a nearby room in bed with a young man – a scene that Goebbels's propaganda later made much of to heap moral opprobrium on the SA. Other arrests of Röhm's staff followed. Those taken in custody were held in the cellar of the hotel until a bus hurriedly chartered from a Bad Wiessee coach firm arrived to transport the SA leaders to Stadelheim prison in Munich. A potentially hazardous moment occurred while the prisoners were still being held in the cellar, as a lorry bringing more of Röhm's staff to the scheduled conference with Hitler arrived from Munich. Hitler stepped out and addressed the men, telling them that he had taken over the leadership of the SA himself, and ordered them to return to Munich. They obeyed without demur.[82]

Hitler and his entourage then travelled back themselves to the Brown House. At midday he spoke to party and SA leaders gathered in the 'Senators' Hall'. The atmosphere was murderous. Hitler was beside himself, in a frenzy of rage. One of those present later recalled spittle dribbling from Hitler's mouth as he began to speak. He spoke of the 'worst treachery in world history'. Röhm, he claimed, had received 12 million Marks in bribes from France to have him arrested and killed, to deliver Germany to its enemies. The SA chief and his co-conspirators, Hitler railed, would be punished as examples. He would have them all shot.[83] One after the other, the Nazi leaders demanded the extermination of the SA 'traitors'. Heß pleaded that the task of shooting Röhm fall to him.[84]

Back in his own room, Hitler gave the order for the immediate shooting of six of the SA men held in Stadelheim, marking crosses against their names in a list provided by the prison administration.[85] They were promptly taken out and shot by Dietrich's men. Not even a peremptory trial was held. The men were simply told before being shot: 'You have been condemned to death by the Führer! Heil Hitler!'[86]

Röhm's name was not among the initial six marked by Hitler for instant execution. One witness later claimed to have overheard Hitler saying that Röhm had been spared because of his many earlier services to the Movement.[87] A similar remark was noted by Alfred Rosenberg in his diary. 'Hitler did not want to have Röhm shot,' he wrote. 'He stood at one time at my side before the People's Court,' Hitler had said to the head of the Nazi publishing empire, Max Amann. (Amann's view was simply that 'the great swine had to go'. He told Heß he was ready to shoot Röhm himself. Heß retorted that, no, that was his duty, even if he himself should afterwards be shot for it.)[88]

The loss of face at having to murder his right-hand man on account of his alleged rebellion was most likely the chief reason for Hitler's reluctance to order Röhm's death. For the moment, at any rate, he hesitated about having Röhm killed. In Berlin, meanwhile, there was no hesitation. Immediately on return from Bad Wiessee, Goebbels had telephoned Göring with the password 'Kolibri' ('Humming Bird'), which set in motion the murder-squads in the capital city and the rest of the country.[89] As in Bavaria, a great deal was improvised. Göring later announced in a press conference that he had extended his commission to strike against 'these malcontents'.[90] He meant primarily the 'reactionaries' in the Papen group, and the former Chancellor Schleicher. Herbert von Bose was brutally shot down by a Gestapo hit-squad after the Vice-Chancellery had been stormed by SS men. Edgar Jung, in 'protective custody' since 25 June, was also murdered, found dead in a ditch near Oranienburg on 1 July. Papen's staff were arrested. The Vice-Chancellor himself, whose murder would have proved a diplomatic embarrassment, was placed under house-arrest. The killing was extended to others who had nothing to do with the leadership of the SA. The head of 'Catholic Action', Erich Klausener, who had at one time been head of the police department in the Prussian Ministry of the Interior, was also brutally shot down by an assassination squad of SS men, on Heydrich's orders. Old scores were settled. Gregor Strasser was taken to Gestapo headquarters and shot in one of the cells. General Schleicher and his wife were shot dead in their own home. Also among the victims was Major-General Bredow, one of Schleicher's right-hand men. In Munich, Hitler's old adversary Ritter von Kahr was dragged away by SS men and later found hacked to death near Dachau. The music critic Wilhelm Eduard Schmid was murdered by mistake; the SS men who killed him thought he was Dr Ludwig Schmitt, a one-time sympathizer of Otto Strasser. Among the twenty-two victims in and around Munich, mostly killed through 'local initiative', was one of Hitler's early supporters, Pater Bernhard Stempfle, who had helped with the editing of *Mein*

Kampf. No motive for his murder is known. It may also have been a case of mistaken identity. Nor in Silesia, where, under Heines, the terror of the SA had been a hallmark of political life, was the revenge-killing guided by any central directives.[91] The blood-lust had developed its own momentum. All in all, the 'action' was beginning to get out of hand.

Hitler arrived back in Berlin around ten o'clock on the evening of 30 June, tired, drawn and unshaven, to be met by Göring, Himmler and a guard of honour.[92] Later that evening, Göring recommended an end to the 'action'.[93] According to Göring's own comments in private to Papen, while in prison in Nuremberg after the war, Hitler only reluctantly agreed, insisting that there were still many who deserved to be shot.[94] Röhm, however, was still alive. Hitler hesitated until late the following morning about the fate of the former SA Chief of Staff. According to one piece of post-war testimony, there was talk of a show-trial, only for Hitler to dismiss the idea because of possible damaging revelations of Röhm's connections with the French ambassador, François-Poncet.[95] The story sounds dubious. Whatever the reasons for not having him dispatched immediately, Hitler was, it seems, put under pressure by Himmler and Göring to have Röhm liquidated. In the early afternoon of Sunday 1 July, during a garden party at the Reich Chancellery for cabinet members and their wives, Hitler finally agreed. Even now, however, he was keen that Röhm take his own life rather than be 'executed'. Theodor Eicke, Commandant of Dachau Concentration Camp, was ordered to go to Stadelheim and offer Röhm the chance to recognize the enormity of his actions by killing himself. If not, he was to be shot. Along with his deputy, SS-Sturmbannführer Michael Lippert, and a third SS man from the camp, Eicke drove to Stadelheim. Röhm was left with a pistol. He was also left the latest edition of the *Völkischer Beobachter*, a special edition containing the details of the 'Röhm Putsch'. It was hoped, presumably, that this would convince him that suicide was the only recourse left to him. But after ten minutes, no shot had been heard, and the pistol was untouched on the small table near the door of the cell, where it had been left. (Whether Röhm had used his last minutes alive to read the *Völkischer Beobachter* is not recorded.) The pistol was removed from the cell. Eicke and Lippert then returned to the cell, each with pistol drawn, signalled to Röhm, standing and bare-chested, and trying to speak, that they would wait no longer, took careful aim, and shot him dead.[96] Hitler's published announcement was terse: 'The former Chief of Staff Röhm was given the opportunity to draw the consequences of his treacherous behaviour. He did not do so and was thereupon shot.'[97]

On 2 July, Hitler formally announced the end of the 'cleansing action'.[98] On the same day, Göring ordered the police to burn all files connected with the affair.[99] Not all files, however, were destroyed. Enough survived to list the names of eighty-five known victims, only fifty of them SA men.[100] Some estimates, however, put the total number killed at between 150 and 200 persons.[101]

With the SA still in a state of shock and uncertainty, the purge of its mass membership began under the new leader, the Hitler loyalist Viktor Lutze. Within a year, the SA had been reduced in size by over 40 per cent. Many subordinate leaders were dismissed in disciplinary hearings. The structures built up by Röhm as the foundation of his power within the organization were meanwhile systematically dismantled. The SA was turned into little more than a military sports and training body.[102] For anyone still harbouring alternative ideas, the ruthlessness shown by Hitler had left its own unmistakable message.

IV

Outside Germany there was horror at the butchery, even more so at the gangster methods used by the state's leaders.[103] Within Germany, it was a different matter. Public expressions of gratitude to Hitler were not long in coming. Already on 1 July, Defence Minister Blomberg, in a statement to the armed forces, praised the 'soldierly determination and exemplary courage' shown by the Führer in attacking and crushing 'the traitors and mutineers'. The gratitude of the armed forces, he added, would be marked by 'devotion and loyalty'.[104] The following day, the Reich President sent Hitler a telegram expressing his own 'deep-felt gratitude' for the 'resolute intervention' and 'courageous personal involvement' which had 'rescued the German people from a serious danger'.[105] Much later, when they were both in prison in Nuremberg, Papen asked Göring whether the President had ever seen the congratulatory telegram sent in his name. Göring replied that Otto Meissner, Hindenburg's State Secretary, had asked him, half-jokingly, whether he had been 'satisfied with the text'.[106]

Hitler himself gave a lengthy account of the 'plot' by Röhm to a meeting of ministers on the morning of 3 July. Anticipating any allegations about the lawlessness of his actions, he likened his actions to those of the captain of a ship putting down a mutiny, where immediate action to smash a revolt was necessary, and a formal trial was impossible. Nor would there be a subsequent trial. Using language almost identical to that of his tirade in the Senators' Hall of the Brown House, he said he had made an example of the rebels not simply to quash the revolt, but to serve as a deterrent to any further conspirators against the regime, who would know they were risking their heads. 'The example he had given would be a healthy lesson for the entire future. He had stabilized the authority of the government for all time.' Even where guilt had not been fully proven, and though not all the shootings had been ordered by him, he took full responsibility, he went on, for the shootings which had saved the Reich. He asked the cabinet to accept the draft Law for the Emergency Defence of the State that he was laying before them. In a single, brief paragraph, the law read: 'The measures taken on 30 June and 1 and 2 July for the suppression of high treasonable and state treasonable attacks are, as emergency defence of the state, legal.' The Reich Minister of Justice, the conservative Franz Gürtner, declared that the draft did not create new law, but simply confirmed existing law. (According to the official communiqué, though not included in the cabinet minutes, Gürtner added that Hitler's actions had not merely to be seen as legal, but also as 'statesmanlike duty'.)[107] Reichswehr Minister Blomberg thanked the Chancellor in the name of the cabinet for his 'resolute and courageous action through which he had protected the German people from civil war. The Reich Chancellor had acted as statesman and soldier in a spirit which, among members of the Reich Government and the entire German people, called forth a pledge for attainment, loyalty, and devotion in this difficult hour.' With this statement of suppliance by the head of the armed forces, and the statement by the head of the judicial system accepting the legality of acts of brute violence, the law acknowledging Hitler's right to commit murder in the interest of the state was unanimously accepted. The law was signed by Hitler, Frick and Gürtner.[108]

The account to the cabinet was in essence the basis of the justification which Hitler offered in his lengthy speech to the Reichstag on 13 July. Why he delayed almost a fortnight before addressing the Reichstag is unclear. Mental and physical fatigue may have been one reason. He did not appear at a meeting of the Reichsleiter and Gauleiter in Flensburg on 4–5 July, which he might in the circumstances have been expected to address.[109] After returning on 4 July from an overnight stay in Neudeck, where he reported to Hindenburg, the only public duty he carried out was to receive the German ambassador to Ankara two days later.[110] Indicating a concern for overseas reactions, he granted on the same day, 6 July, an interview, for publication in the *New York Herald*, to Professor Alfred J. Pearson, a former American ambassador in Poland and Finland, currently head of a liberal arts college in the USA. Pearson was introduced by Schacht, who must have instigated the interview in an attempt to calm feelings abroad, especially in business circles.[111] Allowing the dust to settle, awaiting any further relevations of 'conspiracy' from the investigations still under way by the Gestapo,[112] and requiring the time to prepare a vital speech, one of the most difficult he had ever given, may have been further reasons why Hitler took so long before appearing before the Reichstag.[113]

Hitler's two-hour speech to the Reichstag on 13 July, if not one of his best rhetorical performances, was certainly one of the most remarkable, and most effective, that he was ever to deliver. The atmosphere was tense. Thirteen members of the Reichstag had been among those murdered; friends and former comrades-in-arms of the SA leaders were among those present. The presence of armed SS men flanking the rostrum and at various points of the hall was an indication of Hitler's wariness, even among the serried ranks of party members.[114] After he had offered a lengthy, fabricated account of the 'revolt' and the part allegedly played in the conspiracy by General Schleicher, Major-General Bredow and Gregor Strasser, he came to the most extraordinary sections of the speech. In these, the head of the German government openly accepted full responsibility for what amounted to mass murder. Hitler turned defence into attack. 'Mutinies are broken according to eternal, iron laws. If I am reproached with not turning to the law-courts for sentence, I can only say: in this hour, I was responsible for the fate of the German nation and thereby the supreme judge (*oberster Gerichtsherr*) of the German people . . . I gave the order to shoot those most guilty of this treason, and I further gave the order to burn out down to the raw flesh the ulcers of our internal well-poisoning and the poisoning from abroad.'[115] The cheering was tumultuous.[116] Not just among the Nazi Reichstag members, but in the country at large, Hitler's ruthless substitution of the rule of law by murder *raison d'état* was applauded. It matched exactly what Nazi parlance dubbed the 'healthy sentiments of the people'.

The public was ignorant of the plots, intrigues, and power-games taking place behind the scenes. What people saw for the most part was the welcome removal of a scourge. Once the SA had done its job in crushing the Left, the bullying and strutting arrogance, open acts of violence, daily disturbances, and constant unruliness of the stormtroopers were a massive affront to the sense of order, not just among the middle classes. Instead of being shocked by Hitler's resort to shooting without trial, most people – accepting, too, the official versions of the planned putsch – acclaimed the swift and resolute actions of their Leader. 'If only the Führer knew' was already a phrase on people's lips in this early phase of the Third Reich, excusing Hitler from knowledge of all that was felt to be negative. On this occasion, it seemed, he had learned of what was afoot, and had acted swiftly and resolutely, with utter ruthlessness, in the interests of the nation. As the Sopade, the SPD's organization in its Prague exile, perceptively remarked, not just the detestation of the despotic SA, but also the adaptation to violence which had systematically undermined a sense of legal norms since the start of the Third Reich had paved the way for 'strong sympathies for summary justice'.[117]

Already in the days immediately following the Night of the Long Knives (as the murderous 30 June 1934 came to be known), the authorities reported 'unreserved recognition for the energy, cleverness, and courage of the Führer'.[118] His standing had, it was claimed, risen even among those who had been previously unsympathetic to National Socialism. 'The Führer . . . is not only admired; he is deified,' ran a report from a small town in north-eastern Bavaria where the KPD had done well before 1933.[119] From all over Germany the picture was much the same.[120] Hitler's intervention was seen as a 'liberation from a strongly felt oppression'.[121] In this climate of opinion, Hitler's speech on 13 July struck all the right notes. The response to it was overwhelmingly positive.

There was great admiration for what was seen to be Hitler's protection of the 'little man' against the outrageous abuses of power of the overmighty SA leadership. Even more so, the emphasis that Hitler had placed in his speech on the immorality and corruption of the SA leaders left a big mark on public responses.[122] The twelve points laid down by Hitler in his order to the new Chief of Staff, Viktor Lutze, on 30 June had focused heavily on the need to eradicate homosexuality, debauchery, drunkenness and high living from the SA. Hitler had explicitly pointed to the misuse of large amounts of money for banquets and limousines.[123] The homosexuality of Röhm, Heines and others among the SA leaders, known to Hitler and other Nazi leaders for years, was highlighted as particularly shocking in Goebbels's propaganda. The Sopade commented shrewdly on the success of propaganda 'in diverting the attention of the great mass of the population from the political background to the action, and at the same time elevating Hitler's standing as the cleanser of the Movement'.[124] Above all, Hitler was seen as the restorer of order. That murder on the orders of the head of government was the basis of the 'restoration of order' passed people by, was ignored, or – most generally – met with their approval. There were wide expectations that Hitler would extend the purge to the rest of the party – an indication of the distance that had already developed between Hitler's own massive popularity and the sullied image of the party's 'little Hitlers', the power-crazed functionaries found in towns and villages throughout the land.[125]

There was no show of disapproval of Hitler's state murders from any quarter. Both Churches remained silent, even though the Catholic Action leader, Erich Klausener, had been among the victims.[126] Two generals had also been murdered. Though a few of their fellow officers momentarily thought there should be an investigation, most were too busy clinking their champagne glasses in celebration at the destruction of the SA. Blomberg forbade officers to attend Schleicher's funeral. Only one, General Hammerstein-Equord, disobeyed.[127] It could be overlooked. Hammerstein's antipathy to the Nazis had already led to his resigning his post as army commander (*Chef der Heeresleitung*) the previous February. He no longer mattered greatly. As for any sign that the legal profession might distance itself from acts of blatant illegality, the foremost legal theorist in the country, Carl Schmitt, published an article directly relating to Hitler's speech on 13 July. Its title was: 'The Führer Protects the Law'.[128]

The smashing of the SA removed the one organization that was seriously destabilizing the regime and directly threatening Hitler's own position. Thereafter the emasculated SA was no more than a loyalist section of the movement whose activism, when opportune, could be directed against the Jews (as in the November pogrom in 1938) or other helpless target-groups. Without the backing of the army, which had much to gain by the disempowering of the SA, Hitler's action would have been impossible. No longer would the SA pose a threat to the army or an obstacle to rearmament plans. The army leadership could celebrate the demise of their rival, and the fact that Hitler had backed their power in the state. 'The Reich Chancellor kept his word when he nipped in the bud Röhm's attempt to incorporate the SA in the Reichswehr,' wrote Reichenau a few weeks later. 'We love him because he has shown himself a true soldier.'[129] The army's triumph was, however, a hollow one. Its complicity in the events of 30 June 1934 bound it more closely to Hitler. But in so doing, it opened the door fully to the crucial extension of Hitler's power following Hindenburg's death. The generals might have thought Hitler was their man after 30 June. The reality was different. The next few years would show that the 'Röhm affair' was a vital stage on the way to the army becoming Hitler's tool, not his master.

The other major beneficiary was the SS. 'With regard to the great services of the SS, especially in connection with the events of the 30th of June',

Hitler removed its subordination to the SA. From 20 July 1934 onwards, it was responsible to him alone.[130] Instead of any dependence on the huge and unreliable SA, with its own power pretensions, Hitler had elevated the smaller, élite praetorian guard, its loyalty unquestioned, its leaders already in almost total command of the police. The most crucial ideological weapon in the armoury of Hitler's state was forged.

Not least, the crushing of the SA leadership showed what Hitler wanted it to show: that those opposing the regime had to reckon with losing their heads. All would-be opponents could now be absolutely clear that Hitler would stop at nothing to hold on to power, that he would not hesitate to use the utmost brutality to smash those in his way. But for all their repulsion at the public display of barbarism, observers abroad drew no lessons about Hitler's likely behaviour in matters of foreign policy. Most took the view that, brutal though it was, the purge of the SA was an internal affair – a type of political gangland bloodbath redolent of Al Capone's St Valentine's Day massacre. They still thought that in the business of diplomacy they could deal with Hitler as a responsible statesman. The next years would provide a bitter lesson that the Hitler conducting foreign affairs was the same one who had behaved with such savage and cynical brutality at home on 30 June 1934.

V

An early intimation that a head of government who had had his own immediate predecessor as Chancellor, General von Schleicher, murdered might also not shy away from involvement in violence abroad was provided by the assassination of the Austrian Chancellor Engelbert Dolfuss, in a failed putsch attempt undertaken by Austrian SS men on 25 July while Hitler was attending the Bayreuth Festival.

For months, Hitler had left Theo Habicht, a German member of the Reichstag whom he had appointed to head the Austrian wing of the NSDAP, on a long leash to put pressure on the Dollfuss government. Under Dollfuss, Austria was a repressive single-party dictatorship bearing some distinctly fascist traits. Bans on political parties were applied not just to socialists and liberals. The Austrian NSDAP had been banned since June 1933. From spring 1934, the terror campaign of the outlawed party had brought tough reaction from the government, leading to a further spiral of terrorist violence. The feeling among the underground, factionalized Austrian Nazis that they were being left in the lurch by Berlin was intensified by Hitler's meeting with Mussolini in Venice on 14–15 June. Mussolini had made it plain that Italy backed Dollfuss. Hitler had wanted elections, and National Socialists to be taken into the Austrian government. But he could not risk alienating Italy, and was prepared to let matters ride for the forseeable future. He gave an undertaking to respect Austrian independence. His underlings in Austria were less patient, and suspicious that Berlin was selling out their interests. The terror attacks, using bombs and grenades, increased. Hitler was told that the situation was highly volatile. Putsch plans were worked out among underground SS leaders and party functionaries.[131]

Hitler's own role, and the extent to which he had detailed information of the putsch plans, is less than wholly clear.[132] The initiative for the coup attempt clearly came from local Nazis. It seems that Hitler was aware of it, and gave his approval, but on the basis of misleading information from the Austrian Nazis. Hitler had rejected the idea of a putsch the previous autumn. In the immediate aftermath of the meeting with Mussolini, it was unlikely that he would readily back such a risky venture. However, it could not take place in clear breach of his wishes. Habicht misleadingly informed him, therefore, that officers of the Austrian army were planning a coup, and asked whether the National Socialists should not support the move to topple the Dollfuss government. Hitler agreed.[133] Whether it was a deliberate piece of deception on Habicht's part, or whether Hitler misconstrued what was said to him, is uncertain. However, that Hitler was aware of what was happening, but on the basis of a flawed understanding of what was to take place, is apparent from the post-war recollections of General Adam, at that time Army District Commander VII in Munich and formerly Chef des Truppenamts. At a meeting on the morning of 25 July, Hitler told Adam that on that very day the Austrian Federal Army would topple the government. When Adam seemed sceptical, Hitler insisted that the army would launch its strike, which would lead to the immediate return of those Nazis forced into exile. He wanted Adam to make preparations to send weapons for them into Austria. He promised to keep Adam informed about events in Vienna, and later that day rang to tell him that events were proceeding satisfactorily, and that Dollfuss was wounded.[134] In reality, there had been no putsch plans by the Austrian army. There had been only the hare-brained attempt at a coup by the Nazi activists. The putsch attempt – partly sabotaged even within the Nazi Movement by the SA – was rapidly put down.[135] Under Kurt Schuschnigg, successor to the murdered Dollfuss, the Austrian authoritarian regime, treading its tightrope between the predatory powers of Germany and Italy, continued in existence – for the present.

The international embarrassment for Hitler was enormous, the damage to relations with Italy considerable.[136] For a time, it even looked as if Italian intervention was likely.[137] Papen found Hitler in a near-hysterical state, denouncing the idiocy of the Austrian Nazis for landing him in such a mess.[138] Every attempt was made by the German government, however unconvincingly, to dissociate itself from the coup.[139] Habicht was dropped. The headquarters of the Austrian NSDAP in Munich were closed down. A new policy of restraint in Austria was imposed.[140] But at least one consequence of the ill-fated affair pleased Hitler. He found the answer to what to do with Papen – who had 'just been in our way since the Röhm business', as Göring reportedly put it.[141] He made him the new German ambassador in Vienna.[142]

VI

In Neudeck, meanwhile, Hindenburg was dying. His condition had been worsening during the previous weeks. Signing Papen's letters of appointment to Vienna was his last official act. At the end of July, the public was made aware of the grave condition of the Reich President.[143] On 1 August, Hitler flew to Neudeck. Hindenburg, mistaking him for the Kaiser, addressed him as 'Majesty'.[144] Hitler told the cabinet that evening that the doctors were giving Hindenburg less than twenty-four hours to live.[145] The following morning, the Reich President was dead.

So close to the goal of total power, Hitler had left nothing to chance. The Enabling Act had explicitly stipulated that the rights of the Reich President would be left untouched. But on 1 August, while Hindenburg was still alive, Hitler had all his ministers put their names to a law determining that, on Hindenburg's death, the office of the Reich President would be combined with that of the Reich Chancellor.[146] The reason subsequently given was that the title 'Reich President' was uniquely bound up with the 'greatness' of the deceased. Hitler wished from now on, in a ruling to apply 'for all time', to be addressed as 'Führer and Reich Chancellor'. The change in his powers was to be put to the German people for confirmation in a 'free plebiscite', scheduled for 19 August.[147]

Among the signatories to the 'Law on the Head of State of the German Reich' of 1 August 1934 had been Reichswehr Minister Blomberg. The law meant that, on Hindenburg's death, Hitler would automatically become Supreme Commander of the armed forces. The possibility of the army appealing over the head of the government to the Reich President as Supreme Commander thereby disappeared.[148] This caused no concern to the Reichswehr leadership. Blomberg and Reichenau were, in any case, determined to go further. They were keen to exploit the moment to bind Hitler, as they imagined, more closely to the armed forces. The fateful step they took, however, had precisely the opposite effect. As Blomberg later made clear, it was without any request by Hitler, and without consulting him, that he and Reichenau hastily devised the oath of unconditional loyalty to the person of the Führer, taken by every officer and soldier in the armed forces in ceremonies throughout the land on 2 August, almost before Hindenburg's corpse had gone cold.[149] It seems most likely that Blomberg discussed the oath with Hitler (who later offered his profuse thanks in public)[150] shortly before Hindenburg's death, probably on 1 August. The speed and coordination of the taking of the oath by all the troops throughout the entire country certainly needed preparation.[151] But, as Blomberg himself made clear, the initiative came from the Reichswehr leadership, not from Hitler. Reichenau had asked two members of his staff to prepare drafts, then rapidly dictated his own version. That Blomberg, as Reichswehr Minister, had no legal power to alter the oath, previously sworn to the Constitution and not to the person of the President, was simply ignored.[152]

Some traditionalists in the army, including the Chef der Heeresleitung Werner von Fritsch, saw the oath as reinstating the type of relationship that had existed under the Kaiser. But Blomberg and Reichenau thought in more modern, power-political terms. They hoped, through this personalized demonstration of loyalty, to cement a special relationship with Hitler which would separate him from the Nazi Party and consolidate the dominance of the army as the Third Reich's 'power-house'. 'We swore the oath on the flag to Hitler as Führer of the German people, not as head of the National Socialist Party,' was Blomberg's later comment.[153] Among the officers, the reaction to the oath was mixed. Some were sceptical or dubious. 'The darkest day of my life,' Beck was reported to have remarked.[154] 'A momentous oath. Pray God that both sides hold to it with the same loyalty for the good of Germany,' wrote Guderian.[155] But the majority spent little time reflecting on its implications.[156] The oath meant that the distinction between loyalty to the state and loyalty to Hitler had been eradicated. Opposition was made more difficult. For those later hesitant about joining the conspiracy against Hitler, the oath would also provide an excuse. Far from creating a dependence of Hitler on the army, the oath, stemming from ill-conceived ambitions of the Reichswehr leadership, marked the symbolic moment where the army chained itself to the Führer.[157]

'Today Hitler is the Whole of Germany,' ran a headline on 4 August.[158] The funeral of the Reich President, held with great pomp and circumstance at the Tannenberg Memorial in East Prussia, the scene of his great victory in the First World War, saw Hindenburg, who had represented the only countervailing source of loyalty, 'enter Valhalla', as Hitler put it.[159] Hindenburg had wanted to be buried at Neudeck. Ever alert to propaganda opportunities, Hitler insisted on his burial in the Tannenberg Memorial.[160] On 19 August, the silent coup of the first days of the month duly gained its ritual plebiscitary confirmation. According to the official figures, 89.9 per cent of the voters supported Hitler's constitutionally now unlimited powers as head of state, head of government, leader of the party, and Supreme Commander of the armed forces.[161] The result, disappointing though it was to the Nazi leadership,[162] and less impressive as a show of support than might perhaps have been imagined when all account is taken of the obvious pressures and manipulation, nevertheless reflected the fact that Hitler had the backing, much of it fervently enthusiastic, of the great majority of the German people.

In the few weeks embracing the Röhm affair and the death of Hindenburg, Hitler had removed all remaining threats to his position – with an ease which even in the spring and early summer of 1934 could have been barely imagined. He was now institutionally unchallengeable, backed by the 'big battalions', adored by much of the population. He had secured total power. The Führer state was established. Germany had bound itself to the dictatorship it had created.

After the crisis-ridden summer, Hitler was, by September, once again in his element on the huge propaganda stage of the Nuremberg Rally.[163] In contrast even to the previous year's Rally, this was consciously devised as a vehicle of the Führer cult. Hitler now towered above his Movement, which had assembled to pay him homage. The film which the talented and glamorous director Leni Riefenstahl made of the Rally subsequently played to packed houses throughout Germany, and made its own significant contribution to the glorification of Hitler. The title of the film, devised by Hitler himself, was *Triumph of the Will*.[164] In reality, his triumph owed only a little to will. It owed far more to those who, in the power-struggles of the summer, had much to gain – or thought they had – by placing the German state at Hitler's disposal.

13

WORKING TOWARDS THE FÜHRER

'It is the duty of every single person to attempt, in the spirit of the Führer, to work towards him.'   Werner Willikens, 21 February 1934

'The Führer had for outward appearances to ban individual actions against the Jews in consideration of foreign policy, but in reality was wholly in agreement that each individual should continue on his own initiative the fight against Jewry in the most rigorous and radical form.'
Reported opinion in Hessen, March 1936

'I go with the certainty of a sleepwalker along the path laid out for me by Providence.'   Hitler, 14 March 1936

Everyone with opportunity to observe it knows that the Führer can only with great difficulty order from above everything that he intends to carry out sooner or later. On the contrary, until now everyone has best worked in his place in the new Germany if, so to speak, he works towards the Führer.

This was the central idea of a speech made by Werner Willikens, State Secretary in the Prussian Agriculture Ministry, at a meeting of representatives from Länder agriculture ministries held in Berlin on 21 February 1934. Willikens continued:

Very often, and in many places, it has been the case that individuals, already in previous years, have waited for commands and orders. Unfortunately, that will probably also be so in future. Rather, however, it is the duty of every single person to attempt, in the spirit of the Führer, to work towards him. Anyone making mistakes will come to notice it soon enough. But the one who works correctly towards the Führer along his lines and towards his aim will in future as previously have the finest reward of one day suddenly attaining the legal confirmation of his work.[1]

These comments, made in a routine speech, hold a key to how the Third Reich operated. Between Hindenburg's death at the beginning of August 1934 and the Blomberg–Fritsch crisis in late January and early February 1938, the Führer state took shape. These were the 'normal' years of the Third Reich that lived in the memories of many contemporaries as the 'good' years (though they were scarcely that for the already growing numbers of victims of Nazism).[2] But they were also years in which the 'cumulative radicalization'[3] so characteristic of the Nazi regime began to gather pace. One feature of this process was the fragmentation of government as Hitler's form of personalized rule distorted the machinery of administration and called into being a panoply of overlapping and competing agencies dependent in differing ways upon the 'will of the Führer'. At the same time, the racial and expansionist goals at the heart of Hitler's own *Weltanschauung* began in these years gradually to come more sharply into focus, though by no means always as a direct consequence of Hitler's own actions. Not least, these were the years in which Hitler's prestige and power, institutionally unchallengeable after the summer of 1934, expanded to the point where it was absolute. This point was reached when the once mighty army officer corps surrendered what was left of its authority and independent power-base following a scandal relating to the private lives of the two most senior military leaders in the country in early 1938.[4]

These three tendencies – erosion of collective government, emergence of clearer ideological goals, and Führer absolutism – were closely interrelated. Hitler's personal actions, particularly in the realm of foreign policy, were certainly vital to the development. But the decisive component was that unwittingly singled out in his speech by Werner Willikens. Hitler's personalized form of rule invited radical initiatives from below and offered such initiatives backing, so long as they were in line with his broadly defined goals. This promoted ferocious competition at all levels of the regime, among competing agencies, and among individuals within those agencies. In the Darwinist jungle of the Third Reich, the way to power and advancement was through anticipating the 'Führer will', and, without waiting for directives, taking initiatives to promote what were presumed to be Hitler's aims and wishes. For party functionaries and ideologues and for SS 'technocrats of power', 'working towards the Führer' could have a literal meaning. But, metaphorically, ordinary citizens denouncing neighbours to the Gestapo, often turning personal animosity or resentment to their advantage through political slur, businessmen happy to exploit anti-Jewish legislation to rid themselves of competitors, and the many others whose daily forms of minor cooperation with the regime took place at the cost of others, were – whatever their motives – indirectly 'working towards the Führer'. They were as a consequence helping drive on an unstoppable radicalization which saw the gradual emergence in concrete shape of policy objectives embodied in the 'mission' of the Führer.

Through 'working towards the Führer', initiatives were taken, pressures created, legislation instigated – all in ways which fell into line with what were taken to be Hitler's aims, and without the dictator necessarily having to dictate. The result was continuing radicalization of policy in a direction which brought Hitler's own ideological imperatives more plainly into view as practicable policy options. The disintegration of the formal machinery of government and the accompanying ideological radicalization resulted then directly and inexorably from the specific form of personalized rule under Hitler. Conversely, both decisively shaped the process by which Hitler's personalized power was able to free itself from all institutional constraints and become absolute.

Within this process, Hitler's growing self-confidence – swollen with each international 'triumph' attained, as it appeared, through boldness in the face of the timidity of others, in reality achieved by pushing against a European state system which was as stable as a house of cards – intensified his already immense ego, magnified his megalomaniac tendencies, and underlined his contempt for more cautious spirits in the military leadership and Foreign Office. At the same time, every success accredited to Hitler increased his popular standing, undermined the hopes of opposition, and enhanced the readiness of any remaining doubters among the political élite to accept his outright supremacy without demur. And as the Führer cult moved towards its apogee, it became ever more clear that Hitler, too, had succumbed to it. The tense developments in foreign affairs culminating in the reoccupation of the Rhineland mark a crucial phase in this process. The successful outcome of the Rhineland crisis was Hitler's greatest triumph to date. By that point he had become more than ever a convinced believer in his own 'myth'.

I

Those close to Hitler later claimed that they detected a change in him after Hindenburg's death. According to Press Chief Otto Dietrich, the years 1935 and 1936, with Hitler 'now as absolute ruler on the lookout for new deeds', were 'the most significant' in his development 'from domestic reformer and social leader of the people to the later foreign-policy desperado and gambler in international politics'. 'In these years,' Dietrich went on, 'a certain change also made itself noticeable in Hitler's personal conduct and behaviour. He became increasingly unwilling to receive visitors on political matters if they had not been ordered by him to attend. Equally, he knew how to distance himself inwardly from his entourage. While, before the takeover of power, they had the possibility of putting forward their differing political opinion, he now as head of state and person of standing (*Respektsperson*) kept strictly out of all unrequested political discussion . . . Hitler began to hate objections to his views and doubts on their infallibility . . . He wanted to speak, but not to listen. He wanted to be the hammer, not the anvil.'[5]

Hitler's increasing withdrawal from domestic politics once the period of consolidation of power had come to an end in August 1934 was, as Dietrich's remarks suggest, not simply a matter of character and choice. It also directly mirrored his position as Leader, whose prestige and image could not allow him to be politically embarrassed or sullied by association with unpopular policy choices. Hitler represented, and as the regime's central integrating mechanism *had* to represent, the image of national unity. He could not be seen to be involved in internal, day-to-day political conflict. Beyond that, his growing aloofness reflected, too, the effective transformation of domestic politics into propaganda and indoctrination. Choice and debate about options – the essence of politics – had by now been removed from the public arena (even if, of course, bitter disputes and conflicts continued behind the scenes). 'Politics' within a 'coordinated' Germany now amounted to what Hitler had since the early 1920s regarded as its sole aim: the 'nationalization of the masses' in preparation for the great and inevitable struggle against external enemies. But this goal, the creation of a strong, united, and impreg- nable 'national community' (*Volksgemeinschaft*), was so all-embracing, so universal in its impact, that it amounted to little more than an extremely powerful emotional incitement to formulate policy initiatives in every sphere of the regime's activity, affecting all walks of life. Hitler – and the same would have been true of even a more administratively competent and efficient head of state – could not possibly have overseen, let alone directed, all such initiatives. What his form of leadership, linked to the broad 'directions for action'[6] which he embodied – national revival, 'removal' of Jews, racial 'improvement', and restoration of Germany's power and standing in the world – did, was to unleash an unending dynamic in all avenues of policy- making. As Willikens had remarked, the greatest chances of success (and best opportunities for personal aggrandizement) occurred where individuals could demonstrate how effectively they were 'working towards the Führer'. But since this frenzy of activity was uncoordinated – and could *not* be coordinated – because of Hitler's need to avoid being openly drawn into disputes, it inexorably led to endemic conflict (within the general understand- ing of following the 'Führer's will'). And this in turn merely reinforced the impossibility of Hitler's personal involvement in resolving the conflict. Hitler was, therefore, at one and the same time the absolutely indispensable fulcrum of the entire regime, and yet largely detached from any formal machinery of government. The result, inevitably, was a high level of governmental and administrative disorder.

Hitler's personal temperament, his unbureaucratic style of operating, his Darwinistic inclination to side with the stronger, and the aloofness necessitated by his role as Führer, all merged together to produce a most extraordinary phenomenon: a highly modern, advanced state without any central coordinating body and with a head of government largely disengaged from the machinery of government. However dominant, Benito Mussolini and Francisco Franco (dictator of Spain after 1939) continued to run affairs through their cabinets, even if these were largely consultative bodies. Josef Stalin retained his Politburo (despite having members of it shot on occasion). All three attempted to dominate and impose rigid control over the central machinery of government. But in Germany, cabinet meetings (which Hitler had never liked running) now lost significance. There were only twelve gatherings of ministers in 1935. By 1937, this had fallen to a mere six meetings. After 5 February 1938, the cabinet never met again. During the war, Hitler would even ban his ministers getting together occasionally over a glass of beer.[7] In the absence of cabinet discussions which might have determined priorities, a flood of legislation emanating independently from each ministry had to be formulated by a cumbersome and grossly inefficient process whereby drafts were circulated and recirculated among ministers until some agreement was reached. Only at that stage would Hitler, if he approved after its contents were briefly summarized for him, sign the bill (usually scarcely bothering to read it) and turn it into law. Hans Heinrich Lammers, the head of the Reich Chancellery, and sole link between the ministers and the Führer, naturally attained considerable influence over the way legislation (or other business of ministers) was presented to Hitler. Where Lammers decided that the Führer was too busy with other pressing matters of state, legislation that had taken months to prepare could simply be ignored or postponed, sometimes indefinitely. Alternatively, Hitler intervened, sometimes in minutiae, on the basis of some one-sided piece of information he had been fed. The result was an increasing arbitrariness as Hitler's highly personalized style of rule came into inevitable – and ultimately irreconcilable – conflict with bureaucracy's need for regulated norms and clearly defined procedures. Hitler's ingrained secretiveness, his preference for one-to-one meetings (which he could easily dominate) with his subordinates, and his strong favouritism among ministers and other leaders in party as well as state, were added ingredients that went to undermine formal patterns of government and administration.

Access to Hitler was naturally a key element in the continuing power-struggle within the regime. Ministers who had for some reason fallen out of favour could find it impossible to speak to Hitler. Agriculture Minister

Walther Darré, for instance, was in the later 1930s to attempt in vain for over two years to gain an audience with the Führer to discuss the country's seriously worsening agricultural problems. Though they could not hinder the access of 'court favourites' like Goebbels and the highly ambitious young architect Albert Speer – skilful in pandering to Hitler's obsession with building plans and a rapidly rising star in the Nazi firmament – Hitler's adjutants acquired a good deal of informal power through their control of the portals of the Führer.[8]

Fritz Wiedemann, during the First World War Hitler's immediate superior and in the mid-1930s one of his adjutants, later recalled the extraordinary style of his arbitrary and haphazard form of personal rule. In 1935, commented Wiedemann, Hitler still maintained a relatively orderly routine. Mornings, between about 10a.m. and lunch at 1 or 2p.m., were normally taken up with meetings with Lammers, State Secretary Meissner, Funk (from the Propaganda Ministry) and ministers or other significant figures who had pressing business to discuss. In the afternoons, Hitler held discussions with military or foreign-policy advisers, though he preferred to talk to Speer about building plans. Gradually, however, any formal routine crumbled. Hitler reverted to the type of dilettante lifestyle which, in essence, he had enjoyed as a youth in Linz and Vienna, and for which, as party leader, he had earned Gottfried Feder's reproof in the early 1920s. 'Later on,' recalled Wiedemann, 'Hitler appeared as a rule only just before lunch, quickly read the press summaries provided by Reich Press Chief Dr Dietrich, then went to eat. It became, therefore, ever more difficult for Lammers and Meissner to acquire decisions from Hitler which he alone as head of state could take.' When Hitler was at his residence on the Obersalzberg, it was even worse. 'There he invariably left his room only approaching 2p.m. Then it was lunch. The afternoon was mainly taken up with a walk, and in the evenings, straight after the evening meal, films were shown.'[9]

The walks were always downhill, with a car stationed at the bottom to ferry Hitler and his accompaniment back up again. Hitler's detestation of physical exercise and fear of embarrassment through lack of athleticism remained acute. The whole area was cordoned off during the afternoon walk, to keep away the crowds of sightseers eager for a glimpse of the Führer. Instead, the tradition set in of the visitors' 'march-past'. Up to 2,000 people of all ages and from all parts of Germany, whose devotion had persuaded them to follow the steep paths up to the Obersalzberg and often wait hours, marched, at a signal from one of the adjutants, in a silent column past Hitler. For Wiedemann, the adulation had quasi-religious overtones.[10]

Hitler rarely missed his evening film. The adjutants had to see to it that a fresh film was on offer each day – not always an easy task given the level of production of quality films. Hitler invariably preferred light entertainment to serious documentaries, and, according to Wiedemann, probably gleaned some of his strong prejudices about the culture of other nations from such films.[11]

In the Reich Chancellery, the company was almost exclusively male – the atmosphere part way between that of a men's club and an officers' mess (with a whiff of the gangsters' den thrown in). On the Obersalzberg – 'the mountain', as it came to be called – the presence of women (Eva Braun and wives or lady-friends of members of Hitler's entourage) helped to lighten the atmosphere, and political talk was banned as long as they were there. Hitler was courteous, even charming in a somewhat awkwardly stiff and formal fashion, to his guests, especially towards women. He was invariably correct and attentive in dealings with the secretaries, adjutants, and other attendants on his personal staff, who for the most part liked as well as respected him.[12] He could be kind and thoughtful, as well as generous, in his choice of birthday and Christmas presents for his entourage. Even so, whether at the Reich Chancellery or on the Obersalzberg, the constrictions and tedium of living in close proximity to Hitler were considerable. Genuine informality and relaxation were difficult when he was present. Wherever he was, he dominated. In conversation, he would brook no contradiction. Guests at meals were often nervous or hesitant lest a false word incur his displeasure. His adjutants were more concerned late at night lest a guest unwittingly lead on to one of Hitler's favourite topics – notably the First World War, or the navy – where he would launch into yet another endless monologue which they would be forced to sit through until the early hours.[13]

Hitler's unmethodical, even casual, approach to the flood of often serious matters of government brought to his attention was a guarantee of administrative disorder. 'He disliked reading files,' recalled Wiedemann. 'I got decisions out of him, even on very important matters, without him ever asking me for the relevant papers. He took the view that many things sorted themselves out if they were left alone.'[14]

Hitler's lethargy regarding paperwork knew one major exception. When it came to preparing his speeches, which he composed himself, he would withdraw into his room and could work deep into the night several evenings running, occupying three secretaries taking dictation straight into the typewriter before carefully correcting the drafts.[15] The public image was vital. He remained, above all, the propagandist *par excellence*.

Even had Hitler been far more conscientious and less idiosyncratic and haphazard in his style of leadership, he would have found the highly personalized direction of the complex and varied issues of a modern state beyond him. As it was, the doors were opened wide to mismanagement and corruption on a massive scale. Hitler coupled financial incompetence and disinterest with an entirely exploitative and cavalier usage of public funds. Posts were found for 'old fighters'. Vast amounts of money were poured into the construction of imposing representative buildings. Architects and builders were lavishly rewarded. For favoured building or artistic projects, money was no object.[16] Leading figures in the regime could draw upon enormous salaries, enjoy tax relief, and benefit further from gifts, donations and bribes to accommodate their extravagant tastes in palatial homes, fine trappings, works of art and other material luxuries – including, of course, the inevitable showy limousines. Labour Front boss Robert Ley, a former Rhineland Gauleiter with a doctorate in food chemistry, a notorious womanizer who acquired the well-earned nickname of 'Reich Drunkard' (*Reichstrunkenbold*), was one notable case – though he was merely part of the tip of a very large iceberg. His self-evident venality and luxury living were a blatant affront to many in the working class earning pitiful wages for backbreaking labour. But ordinary Germans knew nothing, for example, of his use of funds from the Bank of German Labour (Bank der deutschen Arbeit) to buy back at twice the purchase price the Berlin villa acquired by the commander of Hitler's bodyguard, Sepp Dietrich (who had soon tired of his luxury home in the capital and wanted to replace it with one in Munich), nor of the Bank's offer of what amounted to a handsome bribe to Hitler's adjutant Fritz Wiedemann.[17] Corruption was rife at all levels of the regime.[18] Hitler was happy to indulge the infinite craving for the material trappings of power and success of his underlings, aware that corruption on a massive scale ensured loyalty as the Third Reich developed into a modern variant of a feudal system resting on personal allegiance rewarded by private fiefdoms.[19] He himself, by now a millionaire on the proceeds of sales of *Mein Kampf*, led his publicly acclaimed spartan lifestyle (as regards his food and clothing) in a context of untold luxury. Alongside his magnificent apartments – his official one in Berlin and his private one in Munich – the initially somewhat modest alpine residence, Haus Wachenfeld on the Obersalzberg, was now converted at vast expense into the grandiose Berghof, suitable for state visits of foreign dignitaries.[20] His restless energy demanded that he and his sizeable entourage were almost constantly on the move within Germany. For that, a special train with eleven coaches containing sleeping compartments, a fleet of limousines, and three aeroplanes stood at his disposal.[21]

Even more serious than the way corrupt party despots profited from the bonanza of a seemingly unlimited free-for-all with public funds was the corruption of the political system itself. In the increasing absence of any formal procedures for arriving at political decisions, favoured party bosses with access to Hitler were often able, over lunch or at coffee, to put forward some initiative and manipulate a comment of approval to their own advantage.[22]

Hitler's impulsive verbal agreement to suggestions from subordinate leaders could prove embarrassing. When, in October 1934, Robert Ley obtained Hitler's signature on a decree which would have strengthened the hand of the Labour Front at the expense of employers and the state authorities, the Trustees of Labour, it led to difficulties. Neither the Ministry of Labour nor the Ministry of Economics had been properly consulted. The party's head, Rudolf Heß, personally at loggerheads with Ley (who in addition to being boss of the Labour Front had also been placed by Hitler in charge of the party's organizational matters, bringing him directly and repeatedly into conflict with Heß), also strongly protested. Unable to antagonize economics supremo Schacht and the industrial leadership, Hitler had to comply with the pressure. To preserve his prestige, the decree was not revoked, but simply ignored and fell into desuetude however much Ley tried to have recourse to it.[23]

A few months later, in early 1935, the reverse happened when Hitler bowed to party pressure having initially agreed to a proposal from a Reich government minister. Labour Minister Seldte had won Hitler's support for his plans to replace the regionally weighted wage structure for building workers by a unified structure across the Reich. This led to loud protests from the Gauleiter, the party's regional chieftains – Gauleiter Kaufmann of Hamburg was especially vociferous – about the impact of wage reductions in some areas on worker morale.[24] Hitler backed down. Again, for prestige purposes the earlier decision could not simply be rescinded as a mistake. Instead, Hitler ordered further deliberations over an indefinite period before the wage revision should be implemented. This meant the matter was shelved and forgotten.[25]

In the two examples just cited, specific policy initiatives which ran foul of the vested interests of powerful groups in the regime had to be jettisoned. Ley and Seldte found, on these occasions, that they ultimately turned out not to be 'working towards the Führer'. However, Hitler's sparse involvement in initiating domestic policy during the mid- and later 1930s and the disintegration of any centralized body for policy formulation meant that there was wide scope for those able to exert pressure for action in areas broadly echoing the aims of nationalization of the masses and exclusion of those deemed not to belong to the 'national community'. The pressure came above all from two sources: the party (both its central office and its provincial bosses, the Gauleiter) and the élite organization the SS (now merging into the police to become an ideologically driven state security force of immense power). Using Hitler's professed (and unlimited) goals of national rebirth and strength through racial purity to legitimate their demands and actions, they ensured that the dynamic unleashed by the takeover of power would not subside.

Once power had been attained in 1933, the NSDAP, its numbers now rapidly swelling through the intake of hundreds of thousands of opportunists, became in essence a loosely coordinated vehicle of propaganda and social control. Hitler had in any case, in destroying the organizational structure built up by Gregor Strasser, already determined in December 1932 that mobilization behind the 'National Socialist idea' embodied in his own person was the party's task.[26] After becoming Chancellor, he had taken little interest in the party as an institution. The weak and ineffectual, but devotedly loyal Rudolf Heß was in April made Hitler's deputy in charge of the party. Since Robert Ley, as we have noted, was left running the party's organizational matters, Heß's authority was from the outset far from complete.[27] Nor was Heß in a strong position in his dealings with the Gauleiter, most of whom could rely on their long-standing personal bonds with Hitler to uphold their power-base in the provinces. Neither a genuine hierarchical structure of command at the top of the party, nor a collective body for determining party policy, was ever instituted. The 'Reich Leadership' of the party remained a group of individuals who never met as a type of Politburo; Gauleiter conferences only took place at Hitler's own behest, to hear a speech from the Führer, not to discuss policy; while a party senate was never called into existence.[28] The party acquired, therefore, neither a coherent structure nor a systematic policy which it could enforce upon the state administration. Its essential nature – that of a 'Führer party' tied to emotively powerful but loosely defined general aims embodied in the person of the Führer and held together by the Führer cult – ruled out both. Even so, once Heß was given in 1934 what amounted to veto rights over draft legislation by government ministers and, the following year, over the appointment of higher civil servants, the party had indeed made significant inroads into the purely governmental arena.[29] The possibilities of intervention, however unsystematic, did now increase the party's influence, above all in what it saw as crucial ideological spheres. Race policy and the 'Church struggle' were among the most important of these.[30] In both areas, the party had no difficulty in mobilizing its activists, whose radicalism in turn forced the government into legislative action. In fact, the party leadership often found itself compelled to respond to pressures from below, stirred up by Gauleiter playing their own game, or emanating sometimes from radical activists at local level. Whatever the derivation, in this way the continuum of radicalization in issues associated with the Führer's aims was sustained.

By the mid-1930s, Hitler paid little attention to the workings of the party. 'His personal participation in the life of the party was limited from now on in essence to his appearance at the major representative occasions in Munich, Nuremberg etc., and to the speeches which he regularly held in November and February before his "old guard",' commented Otto Dietrich.[31] The dualism of party and state was never resolved – and was not resolvable. Hitler himself welcomed the overlaps in competence and lack of clarity. Sensitive as always to any organizational framework which might have constrained his own power, he undermined all attempts at 'Reich reform' by Frick, aimed at producing a more rational authoritarian state structure.[32]

Hitler's approach to the state, as to all power-relations, was purely exploitative and opportunistic. It was for him, as he had expressly stated in *Mein Kampf*, purely a means to an end – the vague notion of 'upholding and advancing a community of physically and mentally similar beings', the 'sustaining of those racial basic elements which, as bestowers of culture, create the beauty and dignity of a higher type of human being'.[33] It followed that he gave no consideration to forms and structures, only to effect. His crude notion was that if a specific sphere of policy could not be best served by a government ministry, weighed down by bureaucracy, then another organization, run as unbureaucratically as possible, should manage it. The new bodies were usually set up as directly responsible to Hitler himself, and straddled party and state without belonging to either. The Organisation Todt, the Hitler Youth, and, from 1936, the Four Year Plan, were such institutions. In reality, of course, this process merely erected new, competing, sometimes overlapping bureaucracies and led to unending demarcation disputes. These did not trouble Hitler. But their effect was at one and the same time to undermine still further any coherence of government and administration, and to promote the growing autonomy within the regime of Hitler's own position as Führer.

The most important, and ideologically radical, new plenipotentiary institution, directly dependent on Hitler, was the combined SS–police apparatus which had fully emerged by mid-1936. Already before the 'Röhm-Putsch', Himmler had extended his initial power-base in Bavaria to gain control over the police in one state after another, culminating in his nomination in April 1934 as 'Inspector of the Gestapo', accompanied by Reinhard Heydrich as head of the Office of the Prussian Secret State Police (Gestapa). After the SS had played such a key part in breaking the power of the SA leadership at the end of June, Himmler had been able to push home his advantage until Göring conceded full control over the security police in the largest of the states. Attempts by Reich Minister of the Interior Frick and Justice Minister Gürtner to curb autonomous police power, expanding through the unrestricted use of 'protective custody' (*Schutzhaft*) and control of the growing domain of the concentration camps, also ended in predictable failure. Where legal restrictions on the power of the police were mooted, Himmler could invariably reckon with Hitler's backing. When, in 1935, Gürtner complained about the number of deaths occurring in concentration camps and demanded the presence of lawyers in cases of 'protective custody', Himmler went to Hitler and won his support for a ban on consultation of lawyers and a block on any 'special measures' owing to 'the conscientious direction of the camps'.[34] Frick had no greater success with his protests at abuses of 'protective custody'.[35] Indeed, Himmler gained Hitler's authorization to expand the concentration camp system at a time, in summer 1935, when, with 3,500 internees, it was smaller than at any other period throughout the Third Reich and appeared to have exhausted its prime purpose. This was followed, in October 1935, by Hitler's backing for the Gestapo as the decisive agent in the 'struggle against the internal enemies of the nation'.[36]

Himmler's concessions in the Prussian Gestapo Law of 10 February 1936 were purely nominal. While one clause of the Law subordinated the Gestapo to the Ministry of the Interior, another emphasized that it was ultimately responsible to the Gestapa.[37] There was no doubt which would prevail in case of conflict. The next step was not long in coming. On 17 June, Hitler's decree created a unified Reich police under Himmler's command.[38] The most powerful agency of repression thus merged with the most dynamic ideological force in the Nazi Movement. Himmler's subordination to Frick through the office he had just taken up as Chief of the German Police existed only on paper. As head of the SS, Himmler was personally subordinate only to Hitler himself. With the politicization of conventional 'criminal' actions through the blending of the criminal and political police in the newly formed 'security police' a week later, the ideological power-house of the Third Reich and executive organ of the 'Führer will' had essentially taken shape.

The instrument had been forged which saw the realization of the Führer's *Weltanschauung* as its central aim. Himmler saw the prime task of the merged police and SS as 'the internal defence of the people' in 'one of the great struggles of human history' against 'the universally destructive force of Bolshevism'.[39] For Werner Best, Heydrich's deputy, the police were a 'fighting formation', existing to root out all symptoms of disease and germs of destruction that threatened the 'political health' of the nation.[40] No directions from Hitler were needed to encourage a police force starting from such premises to expand the target-groups of those dubbed 'enemies of the state' or 'harmful to the people'. The list could be extended almost at will. Alongside the prime racial victims, the Jews, and the foremost ideological and political enemies, Communists and Socialists, or the freemasons (a secret society held in deep suspicion for its alleged international power network and links with Jews engaged in world conspiracy), assiduous police careerists and SS ideologues blended their efforts to find new internal 'enemies' to combat. Most were weak, unpopular and marginalized social groups such as gypsies, homosexuals, beggars, 'antisocials', 'work-shy', and 'habitual criminals'.[41] In addition, the drive to eliminate any 'institutional space' turned persecution not only against those unprepared to yield to the total claim of the Nazi state – Jehovah's Witnesses or 'politically active' representatives of the main Christian denominations – but also against small Christian sects which bent over backwards to accommodate National Socialism (such as the Mormons, or the Seventh Day Adventists).[42]

Intensification of radicalism was built into the nature of such a police force which combined ruthlessness and efficiency of persecution with ideological purpose and dynamism. Directions and dictates from Hitler were not needed. The SS and police had individuals and departments more than capable of ensuring that the discrimination kept spiralling. The rise of Adolf Eichmann from an insignificant figure collecting information on Zionism, but located in what would rapidly emerge as a key department – the SD's 'Jewish Desk' in Berlin – to 'manager' of the 'Final Solution' showed how initiative and readiness to grasp opportunities not only brought rewards in power and aggrandizement to the individual concerned, but also pushed on the process of radicalization precisely in those areas most closely connected with Hitler's own ideological fixations.

In the mid-1930s this process was still in its early stages. But pressures for action from the party in ideological concerns regarded as central to National Socialism, and the instrumentalization of those concerns through the expanding repressive apparatus of the police, meant that there was no sagging ideological momentum once power had been consolidated, as was the case in Mussolini's Italy or Franco's Spain. And as initiatives formulated at different levels and by different agencies of the regime attempted to accommodate the ideological drive, the 'idea' of National Socialism, located in the person of the Führer, thus gradually became translated from utopian 'vision' into realizable policy objectives.

II

The beginnings of this process were also visible in Germany's foreign relations. Nothing did more to bolster Hitler's self-confidence than his successful coups in Europe's 'diplomatic revolution'.[43] Most spectacular were the reintroduction of conscription in March 1935 and the reoccupation of the Rhineland almost exactly a year later. The results abroad were to destroy the remnants of the post-war diplomatic settlement, upturn the European order, seal the fatal division and weakening of the western powers, and drastically to loosen the constraints on the build-up of German military might. At home, Hitler's immense popularity and acclaim attained untouched levels. The triumphs of boldness over caution, as it seemed, strengthened his hand over the more restrained and circumspect among the military and foreign-policy advisers. As Otto Dietrich detected, they also enhanced Hitler's belief in his own infallibility. Hitler's own greatest contribution to events with such momentous consequences lay in his gambling instinct, his use of bluff, and his sharp antennae for the weak spots of his opponents. He took the key decisions; he alone determined the timing. But little else was Hitler's own work. The broad aims of rearmament and revision of Versailles – though each notion hid a variety of interpretations – united policy-makers and power-groups, whatever the differences in emphasis, in the military and the foreign office.

Apart from the drama surrounding Germany's withdrawal from the League of Nations in October 1933, the first two years of Hitler's Chancellorship had been largely dominated by internal affairs. Given German defensive weakness (on both eastern and western borders) and diplomatic isolation, there was no alternative to wariness in foreign affairs in these early years.

The dangers of military intervention by either the Poles or the French were taken seriously. As Bernhard von Bülow, State Secretary in the Foreign Office, put it in his memorandum of 13 March 1933, Germany's 'dangerous weakness' compelled a policy of 'avoiding foreign-policy conflicts for as long as possible, until we are strong again'.[44] Rearmament in secret had to go along with public readiness to appear conciliatory. Repeated emphasis on the unfair treatment of Germany in the post-war settlement would continue to probe the obvious divisions between the French and British, arising from their differing views on the harshness of Versailles, their divergent foreign-policy interests (more obviously global in Britain's case), and the corresponding variation on the likely dangers of a resurgent Germany and the ways of containing rearmament and any revisionist claims.[45] Meanwhile, once Germany's diplomatic isolation was sealed by its withdrawal from the League of Nations, any opportunity of bilateral agreements in eastern Europe which would prevent German ambitions being contained by the multilateral pacts striven for by the French was to be seized.[46]

The first indicator of such a move was the non-aggression pact with Poland. Germany's departure from the League of Nations had intensified the mutual interest in an improved relationship. The pact benefited Germany in undermining French influence in eastern Europe (thereby removing the possibility of any combined Franco-Polish military action against Germany). For the Poles, it provided at least the temporary security felt necessary in the light of diminished protection afforded through the League of Nations, weakened by the German withdrawal.[47]

The first moves had come from the Poles. Bülow had recorded traditional Foreign Office animosity towards Poland when, in his March *tour d'horizon* of foreign-policy options, he had remarked that an understanding with the Poles was 'neither possible nor desired'.[48] Pilsudski's government had, however, put out feelers towards a better relationship the following month. It was, as Hitler realized, also in Germany's interests, whatever the official Foreign Office view, to lessen tension on its eastern borders. Diplomatic activity over the summer of 1933 succeeded in improving relations between Danzig (where National Socialists now dominated the government) and Poland.[49] Danzig had been a point of friction between Germany and Poland since the post-war peace settlement. Offering an outlet to the sea demanded by the new Polish state, and surrounded by territory taken from Germany and handed to Poland, Danzig's overwhelming German population had meant that the Versailles principles of territorial integrity and national self-determination could not be reconciled. The result was the compromise to make Danzig a 'free city', autonomous under League of Nations super-vision. The Poles had access to the sea, but no harbour of their own. The Germans had not ceded Danzig to Poland, but had not retained it for the Reich. No one was happy, least of all the people of Danzig. It was a solution unlikely to stand the test of time. But, for the moment, despite the almost inevitable upsurge of support in Danzig for a stridently nationalist govern-ment in the Reich, relations were improving between the Free City and the Polish government, prompted by the need for détente felt both in Berlin and in Warsaw.[50] Steps were also taken towards ending the long-standing trade war between Germany and Poland.[51] Hitler himself pressed for the trade agreement, which was being painstakingly worked out between the two countries, to be extended to a non-aggression treaty. From his point of view, treaties were matters of expediency. They were to be held to as long as they served their purpose.

He was prepared to appear generous in his dealings with the Poles. There was a new urgency in negotiations. Neurath and the Foreign Office, initially set for a different course, swiftly trimmed their sails to the new wind. 'As if by orders from the top, a change of front toward us is taking place all along the line. In Hitlerite spheres they talk about the new Polish-German friendship,' noted Józef Lipski, Polish minister to Berlin, on 3 December 1933.[52] In conditions of great secrecy, a ten-year non-aggression treaty was prepared and sprung on an astonished Europe on 26 January 1934.[53] This early shift in German foreign policy plainly bore Hitler's imprint. 'No parliamentary minister between 1920 and 1933 could have gone so far,' noted Ernst von Weizsäcker, at that time German ambassador in Bern.[54]

The rapprochement with Poland meant, inevitably, a new course towards the Soviet Union. Initially, little or nothing had altered the *modus vivendi* based on mutual advantage, which, despite deteriorating relations during the last years of the Weimar Republic, and despite ideological antipathy, had existed since the treaties of Rapallo in 1922 and Berlin in 1926. Soviet worries about the Hitler regime were soothed by the German ambassador Herbert von Dirksen, whose own expressed anxieties met with the reassur-ance of State Secretary Bülow: 'The National Socialists faced with responsi-bility are naturally different people and follow a policy other than that which they have previously proclaimed.' 'That's always been so and is the same with all parties,' he complacently added.[55] From summer onwards, however, contrary to the wishes of the Foreign Office and (despite mounting concern) of its Soviet equivalent though in line with the clamour of the Nazi

Movement, diplomatic relations worsened significantly. In autumn 1933, Hitler himself ruled out any repair of relations.[56] During 1934, despite the efforts of the German ambassador Rudolf Nadolny (who had replaced Dirksen in autumn the previous year) and Soviet overtures for better relations, the deterioration continued. Hitler himself blocked any improvement, leading to Nadolny's resignation.[57] The inevitable consequence was to push the Soviet Union closer to France, thus enlarging the spectre of encirclement on which Nazi propaganda so readily played.

In early 1935, the Soviet Union was still little more than a side issue in German foreign policy. Relations with the western powers were the chief concern. The divisions, weakness, and need to carry domestic opinion of the western democracies would soon play into Hitler's hands. But before taking any steps in foreign policy, or in addressing the increasingly pressing issue of the expansion of the armed forces, it was becoming imperative for Hitler to calm the internal tensions which had developed between the army and the Nazi Movement, overshadowing the last months of 1934 and threatening his relations with the military leadership. Underlying the tension were the promises Hitler had made to the SS at the time of the Röhm affair for the military arming of SS units – the origins of the later Waffen-SS – thus immediately breaking the promise he had made to the army that it alone would be the bearer of arms in the Reich.[58] The SS were then at the forefront of a wave of scarcely veiled attacks on the military leadership, also involving the SA and other sections of the Movement, which punctuated the autumn of 1934, doing little for the confidence of army leaders in Hitler or his party. Domestic unrest – continued criticism of local party leaders in the wake of intense disappointment at the failure to undertake a more drastic purge of the party following the murder of the SA leaders, and, not least, the damaging effects of the Church struggle on popular morale – also contributed. The military leadership plainly felt its position under threat by what it saw as the 'total claim' of the Nazi Movement.[59] For their part, Nazi activists were resentful of the power of what they took to be a bastion of reaction with protected status.

Hitler could afford, finally, to stand back no longer. He was compelled to intervene. At extraordinarily short notice – only one day – he summoned for 3 January 1935 a uniquely entitled meeting of the 'German Leadership' (*Deutsche Führerschaft*) in Berlin's State Opera House. Rudolf Heß took the chair. The Party Reichsleiter and Gauleiter were present. So were the top leaders of the armed forces. Hitler spoke for one and a half hours with the overriding object of restoring the faith of the military in the National

Socialist leadership. He stressed his will to make Germany a great power again, its defences secured through a strong Wehrmacht. This could only be attained through total unity. He referred again to the two pillars of the Wehrmacht and the army on which the National Socialist state rested. He demanded restoration of the mutual trust between the two. He assured the army that he was on their side. He would disbelieve any comments and tear up any reports from those in the Party claiming that army leaders were criticizing or opposing him, 'for my faith in the Wehrmacht is unshakable,' he declared. Weeping, he beseeched party leaders to see that only absolute loyalty and devotion to him in a united community would enable him to rebuild Germany. As in the Strasser crisis of 1932, the high-point of the theatricals was his threat to commit suicide if this unity were not forthcoming. The contrived drama of the speech did the trick. The applause was tumultu-ous. The army leaders were won over, impressed by what they saw as Hitler's moving declaration of loyalty to the armed forces. Göring ended the meeting, representing the unity of party, state and military leadership in his own person, with a vote of thanks to Hitler.[60] Once more, Hitler had succeeded in presenting himself as the indispensable unifier, reconciling through his 'mission' the conflicting interests of the differing sections of the 'power-cartel'.[61]

In the meantime, a rich propaganda gift was about to fall into Hitler's lap with the return of the Saar territory to Germany through the plebiscite of 13 January 1935. The Versailles Treaty had removed the Saarland from Germany, placing it under League of Nations control for fifteen years, and affording France the right to its resources. After fifteen years it was foreseen that the Saar inhabitants – roughly half a million voters – should decide whether they would prefer to return to Germany, become part of France, or retain the status quo. It was always likely that the majority of the largely German-speaking population, where resentment at the treatment meted out in 1919 still smouldered fiercely, would want to return to Germany. A good deal of work by the German government prepared the ground, and as the plebiscite day approached Goebbels unleashed a massive barrage of propaganda directed at the Saar inhabitants and raising consciousness of the issue at home.[62] Berlin could feel confident that the plebiscite would result in a vote to return the Saar to Germany. According to the French ambassador André François-Poncet, however, Hitler would not have been surprised if the French had attempted to forestall a German triumph by taking possession of the territory or by adjourning the date of the plebiscite.[63] Moreover, the Saar territory was overwhelmingly Catholic, with a large industrial working-class segment of the population – the two social groups which had proved least enthusiastic about Nazism within Germany itself.[64]

In the light of the ferocious repression of the Left and the threatening, if still largely sporadic, persecution of the Catholic Church that had followed the Nazi takeover in Germany, opponents of the Hitler regime in the Saar could still harbour illusions of a substantial anti-Nazi vote.[65] But the Catholic authorities put their weight behind a return to Germany. And many Saar Catholics already looked to Hitler as the leader who would rescue them from Bolshevism.[66] On the Left, the massive erosion of party loyalties had set in long before the plebiscite. For all their propaganda efforts, the message of the dwindling number of Social Democrat and Communist functionaries fell largely on stony ground. Nazi propaganda had little difficulty in trumpeting the alternative to a return to Germany: continued massive unemployment, economic exploitation by France, and lack of any political voice.[67] Some concerted intimidation, as in the Reich itself during the 'time of struggle', did the rest. For the vast majority – workers and Catholics, middle-class and better-off alike – there seemed no choice to speak of. The future lay with Hitler's Germany. Nationalist emotion and material self-interest went hand in hand.

When the votes were counted, just under 91 per cent of the Saar's electorate had freely chosen dictatorship.[68] At least two-thirds of the former supporters of both left-wing parties had supported the return to Germany.[69] Any lingering doubts about whether Hitler had the genuine backing of the German people were dispelled.

Hitler milked his triumph for all that it was worth. At the same time, he was careful to make dove-like noises for public consumption. 'Following the completion of your return,' he told the Saar people, the German Reich 'had no further territorial demands to make of France'.[70] And in an interview with the *Daily Mail* journalist Ward Price four days after the plebiscite, he intoned: 'Germany will of its own accord (*von sich aus*) never break the peace.'[71] On 1 March, the day of the formal incorporation of the Saar territory in the Reich, Hitler spoke in Saarbrücken. He was 'supremely happy' (*überglücklich*), he declared, to be able to take part 'in this day of happiness for the entire nation' and 'for the whole of Europe'. He hoped that as a consequence of the settlement of the Saar issue, 'relations between Germany and France had improved once and for all. Just as we want peace, so we must hope that our great neighbouring people is also willing and ready to seek this peace with us.'[72]

Hitler's true thoughts were different. The Saar triumph had strengthened his hand. He had to exploit the advantage. Western diplomats awaited his next move. They would not wait long.

Anxious to do nothing to jeopardize the Saar campaign, especial caution had been deployed in rearmament, either on Hitler's orders or those of the Foreign Office. It could, therefore, be expected that the demands of the armed forces leadership for accelerated rearmament, in which political and military considerations went hand in hand, would gain new impetus following the Saar triumph. The Saar was indirectly connected with the rearmament question in another way. The disarmament talks in Geneva – since Germany's withdrawal deprived of their substance – had been adjourned in November 1934 to await the outcome of the Saar plebiscite before attempting once more to propose internationally agreed limits on rearmament. This was of no interest to Hitler, concerned only with bilateral agreements.[73] But the prospect led to a memorandum from General Beck, written on 6 March, which gives clear insight into the army's views at the time.

The memorandum revolved around the notion of guaranteeing the 'security of our living-space' – a phrase indicating the widespread but varied usage of the term '*Lebensraum*'. Beck envisaged the possibility of attack from the Reich's neighbours – France, Czechoslovakia, Poland and Belgium – though he saw little danger of Soviet intervention. The likelihood in his view was of a limited central European war in which Britain would be merely a bystander. Germany's defence strength had to be measured in the context of the worst possible scenario. Beck looked to full equality for Germany in all questions of rearmament, and the removal of all restrictions – including those on the western borders of the Reich. The ending of the demilitarized zone in the Rhineland was a minimal demand. The army leadership had planned since December 1933, as a memorandum from Beck's office made clear, for a peacetime army of twenty-one divisions.[74] Beck now contemplated expansion in peacetime to twenty-three divisions, which could be rapidly increased to sixty-three divisions by 1939 – almost the size of the 1914 army – in the event of war. In an exchange of memoranda with army chief (Chef der Heeresleitung) Fritsch a few days later, it was plain that Beck saw the twenty-three divisions as a temporary arrangement for three or four years before further expansion to a peacetime army of thirty-six divisions. Fritsch, more anxious about the prospect of a preventive attack on Germany, argued that twenty-three divisions was too small a basis for the intended sixty-three-division war army, and advocated moving more swiftly to a thirty-six-division army. Fritsch too, however, was concerned that over-hasty expansion could produce foreign-policy tension, and perhaps even military danger – a view shared by Defence Minister Blomberg.[75]

Army leaders were thus divided about the tempo of expansion, but not about its necessity or the aim of an eventual thirty-six-division peacetime army, the size eventually determined by Hitler in March 1935. General conscription had already been foreseen in the programme of December 1933, put forward by Beck. It was an essential component of military planning, intended for introduction on 1 October 1934.[76] This date proved illusory. But military leaders still reckoned with the necessity of moving to a conscript army by summer 1935. Only the timing remained to be determined – on the basis of the foreign-policy situation.[77]

This had become strained again in early 1935. A joint British-French communiqué on 3 February had condemned unilateral rearmament, and advanced proposals for general restrictions of arms levels and an international defence-pact against aggression from the air.[78] After some delay, the German response on 15 February expressed the wish for clarificatory talks with the British government.[79] The British Foreign Secretary Sir John Simon and Lord Privy Seal Anthony Eden were accordingly invited for talks in Berlin on 7 March.[80] Three days before the planned visit, the publication of a British Government *White Book*, announcing increases in military expenditure as a result of the growing insecurity in Europe caused by German rearmament and the bellicose atmosphere being cultivated in the Reich, led to a furious outcry in the German press.[81] Hitler promptly developed a 'diplomatic' cold and sore throat, allegedly picked up during his trip to a rainy Saarbrücken at the start of the month, and postponed Simon's visit.[82] Rosenberg found him 'on the day of the outbreak of his hoarseness' in excellent mood, cheered by the cancellation. 'Again some time had been won,' Hitler commented. 'Those ruling England *must* get used to dealing with us only on an equal footing.' He would 'recover Germany's position centimetre for centimetre,' he added. 'After a year, nobody will dare any longer to attack us! These few years must do it. If we had begun rearmament only in 1936 it would have been too late.'[83]

Three days after the visit should have taken place, on 10 March, Göring announced the existence of a German air-force – an outright breach of the Versailles Treaty.[84] For effect, in comments to diplomats, he almost doubled the numbers of aircraft actually at Germany's disposal at the time.[85] Just prior to this, the French had renewed their military treaty of 1921 with Belgium.[86] And on 15 March the French National Assembly approved the lengthening of the period of military service from one to two years.[87] The moves of the arch-enemy, France, prompted Hitler's reaction. They provided the pretext.[88] Alert as ever to both the political and the propaganda advantages to be gained from the actions of his opponents, he decided to take the step now which in any case would soon have been forthcoming.

On 13 March, Lieutenant-Colonel Hoßbach, Hitler's Wehrmacht adjutant, was ordered to present himself the next morning in the Hotel Vier Jahreszeiten in Munich. When he arrived, Hitler was still in bed. Only shortly before midday was the military adjutant summoned to be told that the Führer had decided to reintroduce conscription in the immediate future – a move which would in the eyes of the entire world graphically demonstrate Germany's newly regained autonomy and cast aside the military restrictions of Versailles.[89] Hitler expounded his reasons for two hours. The advantageous foreign-policy situation, in which other European states were adjusting their military strength, and especially the measures being taken in France, were decisive. Hoßbach was then asked what size the new army should be. Astonishingly, Hitler did not consider directly consulting Fritsch or Beck on this vital topic. It was expected that Hoßbach would be familiar with the thinking of the military leadership. Subject to approval from War Minister Blomberg and Commander-in-Chief of the Army Fritsch, Hoßbach stipulated thirty-six divisions. This matched the final size of the peacetime army that the military leadership had envisaged *as a future goal.*[90] It implied an army of 550,000 men, five and a half times the size of the post-Versailles army, and a third larger than that envisaged by Beck in his memorandum written only nine days earlier. Hitler accepted Hoßbach's figures without demur. What had been meant by the army chiefs as a level to be attained only gradually was now determined as the immediate size.

The more spectacular the better, was always Hitler's maxim in a propaganda coup. Secrecy both to achieve the greatest surprise and avoid damaging leaks that could provoke dangerous repercussions was another. Hitler had taken his decision without consulting either his military leaders or relevant ministers.[91] It was the first time this had happened in a serious matter of foreign policy, and the first time that Hitler encountered opposition from the heads of the armed forces.[92] Only Hoßbach's pleading on 14 March had persuaded Hitler to inform Blomberg, Fritsch, and selected cabinet ministers of what he had in store two days later. He had initially been unwilling to disclose to them what he intended on the grounds that there might then be a risk to secrecy.[93] The War Minister and armed forces leadership were astonished and appalled that Hitler was prepared to take the step at such a sensitive juncture in foreign policy. It was not that they disagreed with the expansion of the armed forces, or its scale; merely that the timing and way it was done struck them as irresponsible and unnecessarily risky.[94] The Foreign Ministry was more sanguine about the risks involved, reckoning the danger of military intervention to be slight.[95] Britain's reaction would be decisive. And various indicators reaching Berlin pointed to the fact that the British were increasingly inclined to accept German rearmament.[96] While the military leadership recoiled, therefore, civilian members of the cabinet welcomed Hitler's move.[97]

The relative calm of the other members of the cabinet evidently helped to soothe Blomberg's nerves. Alongside the worries of foreign-policy repercussions had also to be weighed the advantages and opportunities that the move would afford the army. By the following day, the very day of the announcement, he had overcome his initial disapproval.[98] At the lunchtime cabinet meeting, the last before the announcement, he praised the Führer's 'great deed', led the other ministers in a three-fold 'Heil' to Hitler, and pledged his further loyalty.[99] Fritsch, too, had come round to giving his approval. His objections – remembered by Hitler years later – were by now confined to technical problems arising from the planned speed of rearmament.[100]

Later that afternoon, Saturday, 16 March, Hitler, with Neurath at his side, informed foreign ambassadors of his imminent action.[101] According to Hitler, the Italian ambassador, Vittorio Cerruti (replaced in the summer, at Hitler's request), went white with anger; the French, André François-Poncet, delivered an immediate verbal protest; the British ambassador, Sir Eric Phipps, merely inquired whether Germany's offers to Britain on relative sizes of air-forces and fleets still stood.[102] Then the dramatic news was announced. Hitler proclaimed the new Wehrmacht of thirty-six divisions, and the introduction of general military service. He justified the move through the steps taken by other states to rearm, spurning German offers for disarmament on an equal basis, and asserted that the government wished for nothing more than 'the power, for the Reich and thereby also for the whole of Europe, to be able to uphold peace'.[103]

Special editions of newspapers were rushed out, eulogizing 'the first great measure to liquidate Versailles', the erasing of the shame of defeat, and the restoration of Germany's military standing. Delirious crowds gathered outside the Reich Chancellery cheering Hitler.[104] 'Today's creation of a conscript army in open defiance of Versailles will greatly enhance his domestic position,' commented the American journalist William Shirer, who witnessed the scenes in Berlin, 'for there are few Germans, regardless of how much they hate the Nazis, who will not support it wholeheartedly. The great majority will like the way he has thumbed his nose at Versailles, which they all resented.'[105]

The following day, from now on renamed 'Heroes' Memorial Day', amid a sea of military uniforms and flags in the State Opera House in Berlin, the huge stage-curtain hung with an enormous silver and black iron cross, the sombre chords of Beethoven's 'Funeral March' (the second movement of the great Eroica symphony) sounding out, General Blomberg gave the address. 'The world has been made to realize that Germany did not die of its defeat in the World War,' he intoned. 'Germany will again take the place she deserves among the nations. We pledge ourselves to a Germany which will never surrender and never again sign a treaty which cannot be fulfilled.' Hitler looked on approvingly from the royal box.[106] A grandiose military display followed, the restored tradition of the German army as its centre-piece.[107] Hitler stood flanked on his right by a symbol of the old army, the aged Field Marshal August von Mackensen, who had commanded the German troops in Rumania during the First World War, with Blomberg, representing the new army, on his left.[108]

The German people were completely unprepared for what Hitler had done. Many reacted initially with shock, worried about the consequences abroad and the possibility even of a new war.[109] But the mood – at least of the vast majority – rapidly turned to euphoria when it was realized that the western powers would do nothing. It was felt that Germany had the right to *re*arm, since France had done nothing to *dis*arm. Hitler's prestige soared. People admired his nerve and boldness. He had put the French in their place, and achieved what 'the others' had failed to bring about in fourteen years.[110] 'Enthusiasm on 17 March enormous,' ran one report from oppositional sources sent from Bavaria to Sopade headquarters in Prague. 'The whole of Munich was on its feet. People can be compelled to sing, but not forced to sing with such enthusiasm. I witnessed the days of 1914 and can only say that the declaration of war did not make the same impact on me as Hitler's reception on 17 March ... The trust in the political talent and honest will of Hitler becomes greater all the time, as Hitler has again gained extraordinary ground among the people. He is loved by many.'[111]

Foreign governments were also taken by surprise by Hitler's move. French and Czech diplomacy went into overdrive. In each case, sluggish negotiations for treaties with Moscow were speeded up. In Italy, Mussolini made sabre-rattling noises against Germany, provoking for a time an atmosphere resembling that of 1915, and looked for closer alliance with France.[112] But Great

Britain held the key. And Britain's interests overseas in the Empire and in the troubled Far East, alongside a prevalent concern about the threat of Bolshevism, encouraged a more pro-German stance completely at odds with French diplomacy and to Hitler's direct advantage. Without consulting the French, the British government put out on 18 March a flat, formal protest at the German unilateral action, then, in the same protest note and to the astonishment of German diplomats, asked whether the Reich government was still interested in a meeting between Simon and Hitler.[113] The French ambassador, François-Poncet, had wanted the meeting abandoned, ambassadors to be recalled from Berlin, and the creation of a common defence-pact against Germany.[114] Instead, Britain was going its own way. The formal French and Italian protests, more sharply worded than the British, indicated to Berlin that Germany's isolation was breaking down.[115]

'I think we'll come through', Hitler had told Rosenberg, as the army leaders commissioned panicky war-games about the likely consequences of military intervention.[116] The response, at home and abroad, amounted, in Hitler's own eyes, to a triumph for boldness over timidity and a further indicator that he was unerringly right in his judgement.

Hitler was confident and self-assured when the postponed visit of Simon and Eden eventually took place in the Reich Chancellery, on 25 March. Paul Schmidt, meeting Hitler for the first time and acting as his interpreter, noted the cordial atmosphere at the beginning of the talks. He had expected the 'raging demagogue' he had heard on the radio, but was instead impressed by the skill and intelligence with which Hitler conducted the negotiations.[117] Anthony Eden noted a change in Hitler's demeanour since the first time he had met him, back in February 1934. 'Hitler was definitely more authoritative and less anxious to please than a year before,' he recalled. 'Another twelve months of a dictator's power and growing military force to back it had had its consequence.' He handled the talks 'without hesitation and without notes, as befitted the man who knew where he wanted to go'.[118] Hitler completely dominated the proceedings. In the first morning session of almost four hours, Simon and Eden could do no more than pose the occasional question during Hitler's monologues – translated by Schmidt at twenty-minute intervals – on the menace of Bolshevism. Only when Eden mentioned Lithuania as a member of a proposed 'Eastern Pact', intended to include Germany as another partner, did Hitler suddenly fall into a rage, his eyes blazing, his Rs rolling, his fists clenched. 'He suddenly seemed to have become another person,' noted Schmidt. 'We will under no circumstances take part in a pact with a state that is stamping on the German minority in

Memel,' he stormed, referring to the trial nearing its end of 128 Germans accused of treason.[119] Then, suddenly, the storm subsided as quickly as it had blown up. Hitler was once more the skilled negotiator, effectively countering all attempts to draw Germany into multilateral agreements. When Simon criticized the unilateral renunciation of treaty agreements on Germany's armaments level, Hitler asked ironically if Wellington had inquired of lawyers in the Foreign Office, as Blücher came to his assistance at Waterloo, whether Prussian army strength was in accord with treaty agreements. This struck Eden as a good parry – and the nearest Hitler came to humour.[120]

Alongside his repeated attacks on Soviet expansionist intentions, Hitler's main theme was equality of treatment for Germany in armaments levels. He insisted to Simon on parity in air-forces with Britain and France. Asked about the current strength of the German air-force, Hitler hesitated, then declared: 'We have already attained parity with Great Britain.'[121] Simon and Eden were sceptical, but said nothing. Nor did they when Hitler named a ratio of 35 per cent of English naval strength as the German demand, but their lack of immediate objection gave a hint to their hosts that they were not opposed. As he observed the patience with which the British ministers listened to Hitler's unyielding reassertions of German demands, Schmidt wondered whether his colleagues in the Foreign Office were not mistaken; perhaps Hitler was indeed able to achieve more with his method of the *fait accompli* than were conventional negotiating ploys. He reflected on his time as an interpreter at the disarmament talks: 'Two years ago in Geneva the heavens would have fallen in if German representatives had posed such demands as Hitler here advanced as if it were the most self-evident thing in the world.'[122]

Both sides had been keen to make a good impression. Hitler was, according to Schmidt, 'a charming host' at a reception in the Reich Chancellery at the end of the talks. Earlier in the day, at Hitler's first visit to a foreign embassy, the children of the British Ambassador, Sir Eric Phipps, had raised their arms in the 'German Greeting' when presented to the Chancellor.[123] Behind the official posturing, reactions differed. Hitler rejoiced in what he saw, with justification, as a diplomatic triumph.[124] The attitudes of the British ministers had darkened during the talks themselves as it became apparent that Hitler, despite his superficial cordiality, was in effect rejecting all their proposals. 'Results bad . . . whole tone and temper very different to a year ago,' noted Eden in his diary at the time, comparing the talks with his first discussion with Hitler in February 1934.[125] He formed the impression that

Hitler was shifty and devious, though skilful as well as tough in negoti-ations.[126] But the position adopted by the British government was a weak one. The British had shown themselves as pliant, willing to negotiate, insistent on upholding peace, but ready to make concessions at the expense of solidarity with the French. The German stance, on the other hand, had been unyielding, inflexible on all points of substance. The courting of the British appeared to be making headway. The post-war European settlement was visibly crumbling. All Hitler needed to do was to stand firm; all the signs were that the British would move to accommodate him. The seeds of appeasement had been sown.

Though British avowals of international solidarity continued, the much-trumpeted Stresa Front – the outcome of the meeting in Stresa of the leaders of Britain, France, and Italy on 11 April 1935, at which they pledged to uphold the 1925 Pact of Locarno guaranteeing the western borders of the Reich and to support Austria's integrity – existed on paper only.[127] Hitler appears to have been little worried by Stresa. 'Stresa wavers further. No danger,' Goebbels noted in his diary on 15 April, after talking to Hitler.[128] Two days later, the Propaganda Minister was a little less sanguine. The meeting of the League of Nations in Geneva leading to condemnation of the German introduction of conscription and French efforts to bring about a pact of mutual assistance with the Soviet Union (eventually concluded on 16 May) led Goebbels to remark that the military dangers ought not to be underrated. That meant, he added, that 'our only solution lies in power'. There was nothing for it but to carry on arming and put on a brave face. 'Let us get through this summer, O Lord,' he wrote.[129]

The isolation arising from Stresa, the League of Nations condemnation of Germany, and the French pact with the Soviet Union had to be broken. This was the backcloth to Hitler's second 'peace speech' – following that of 17 May 1933 – to the Reichstag on 21 May 1935. 'What else could I wish for other than calm and peace?' he rhetorically asked. 'Germany needs peace, and wants peace.'[130] He regretted the deterioration in relations with Italy, caused by conflict over Austria. 'Germany had neither the intention nor wish,' he asserted, 'to annex or incorporate Austria.'[131] This was a clear response to the signal sent by Mussolini through Stresa for Germany to keep its hands off its eastern neighbour.[132] Towards France, he was more hostile, if restrained. He attacked the treaty signed on 2 May between France and the Soviet Union, stated that Germany would only hold to the Locarno Pact as long as other signatories did the same, and hinted strongly that Germany's toleration of the demilitarized Rhineland might last only a little longer. The speech was, however, directed chiefly at Britain.[133] He was keen to appear reasonable and moderate while reiterating German demands for equal rights in armament. He dismissed any hint of a threat in the armaments programme. He wanted, he stated (as he had done privately to Simon and Eden), no more than parity in air weaponry and a limit of 35 per cent of British naval tonnage. He scorned press suggestions that this would lead to a demand for the possession of colonies. Nor had Germany any wish or capability for naval rivalry with Great Britain. 'The German Reich government recognizes of itself the overwhelming importance for existence (*Lebenswichtigkeit*) and thereby the justification of dominance at sea to protect the British Empire, just as, on the other hand, we are determined to do everything necessary in protection of our own continental existence and freedom.'[134] The framework of the desired alliance with Britain had been outlined.

The idea of a bilateral naval agreement between Britain and Germany, to regulate the relative size of the fleets, had first arisen in the British admiralty in early 1933.[135] The notion found support in Germany among some national-conservative politicians and naval officers before Hitler took it up in December 1933.[136] During the following year, he bowed to pressure from Admiral Raeder, head of the navy, for a rapid build-up of the fleet. Raeder's views of the navy's role went back to the traditions of Admiral Tirpitz's time under the Kaiser. Its keystone now was parity with France. But an arrangement with Britain about relative fleet sizes was envisaged merely as a temporary arrangement. At some future date an enlarged battle-fleet, imagined Raeder, might be needed to take on Britain itself.[137] Parity with France meant, in effect, a ratio of 1:3 with Britain (which was rounded up to 35 per cent). Ambitious expansionists on Raeder's staff wanted to push the demand up to 50 per cent, but Hitler – with a better sense of realism – insisted on the lower level. The Foreign Offices of both countries were critical of schemes for a naval accord. But the British Admiralty found the 35 per cent limit acceptable, as long as there was no weakening of the British position *vis à vis* the Japanese navy – seen as the greater threat. The British cabinet conceded. Despite the fact that Germany had been condemned for its breach of Versailles as recently as mid-April by the League of Nations, the British, following Hitler's 'peace speech' of 21 May, had taken up German feelers for the naval talks in London, first mooted on Simon's visit to Berlin in March.[138]

Leading the German delegation, when the talks began on 4 June, was Joachim von Ribbentrop. The linguistically able but boundlessly vain, arrogant and pompous former champagne salesman had joined the party only in 1932. But with the passion of the late convert he had from the start showed fanatical commitment and devotion to Hitler – reminding the interpreter Schmidt, who saw him frequently at close quarters, of the dog on the label of the gramophone company His Master's Voice.[139] In 1934, as newly appointed 'Commissioner for Disarmament Questions', he had been sent by Hitler as a type of roving envoy to Rome, London, and Paris to try to improve relations, though at the time he had achieved little.[140] Despite his lack of obvious success, Hitler, distrustful of the career diplomats at the Foreign Office, continued to favour him. On 1 June 1935 he was provided with the grand title of 'Ambassador Extraordinary and Plenipotentiary on Special Mission'.[141] His moment of triumph in London awaited.

The talks began in the imposing building of the Foreign Office in White-hall.[142] Ribbentrop imported a new style of diplomacy. Straight away, after the opening formalities led by Sir John Simon, he presented his ultimatum: acceptance of Germany's terms – the 35 per cent ratio – as a binding and lasting settlement; otherwise, it was pointless to continue the talks. This ratio, he stated, was 'not simply a demand to be put forward by the German side but a *final decision by the German Chancellor*'. Simon frostily remarked that 'the German delegation's demand was something which properly belonged not to the beginning but to the end of the negotiations'. He then left to attend another meeting.[143] So cool was the atmosphere following Ribbentrop's opening sally that the interpreter Schmidt was already contemplating what the weather would be like on the flight back to Berlin.[144] Undeterred, Ribbentrop requested the following morning an early reply on whether the British Government 'would clearly and formally recognize the Chancellor's decision on the 100:35 ratio'. If not, there might well be a delay before negotiations could resume.[145] Astonishingly, even to the German interpreter Schmidt, given Ribbentrop's crude diplomacy and the evident offence taken by the British Foreign Secretary, Sir John Simon opened the meeting in the British Admiralty on the evening of 6 June with the formal announcement to the German Delegation that the British Government intended to accept Hitler's proposal. The British delegates, meeting privately on the morning of the 5th, had told the cabinet that 'we may have cause to regret it if we fail to take this chance' and, after Hitler's withdrawal of his offer, Germany then built to a higher level than 35 per cent.[146]

The blackmail tactic had worked again. Schmidt had once more to revise his views of Nazi negotiating tactics. He concluded that the British must desperately have wanted an agreement with Germany to cave in so completely so quickly.[147] The Anglo-German Naval Agreement was finally concluded on 18 June. Germany could now construct a navy of 35 per cent of the British navy, and a submarine fleet the size of that of Britain. Ribbentrop had covered himself with glory. Hitler had gained a major diplomatic triumph – and experienced, he said, the happiest day of his life.[148] For the German people, Hitler seemed to be achieving the unimaginable. The world, meanwhile, looked on in astonishment. Great Britain, party to the condemnation of Germany for breach of treaties, had wholly undermined the Stresa Front, left its allies in the lurch, and assisted Hitler in tearing a further large strip off the Versailles Treaty.[149] Whether peace would be more secure as a result already gave grave cause for doubt.

Within little over three months, European diplomacy was plunged still further into turmoil. Mussolini's invasion of Abyssinia – an atavistic imperialist adventure designed to restore Italy's status as a world power and satisfy national pride and a dictator's ambitions – was launched on 3 October. It was no puny affair. Across wide tracts of eastern Africa, terror bombing of towns, destruction of villages, and poison gas attacks would all be put to use over the following months by a large army engaged in what Mussolini dubbed 'the greatest colonial war in all history'.[150] The invasion was unanimously condemned by the members of the League of Nations. But their slow and half-hearted application of economic sanctions – which left out the key commodity, oil – did little but show up once more the League's ineffectiveness.[151] Divisions were once more exposed between the two western democracies. France, through its foreign minister Pierre Laval, had, in fact, the previous January given the green light to Mussolini to invade Abyssinia.[152] The French had hoped by their compliance to keep Mussolini out of Hitler's orbit. Britain's line was different, as explained to Lammers by the German ambassador in London, Leopold von Hoesch, a week after the Italian invasion had begun. 'For England,' reported Hoesch, 'not imperialist aims but the establishment of "collective security" had priority at present. The view was generally adopted that some sort of adventure of Hitler would follow Mussolini's adventure in Abyssinia. The first priority in this regard was to prevent Europe being faced with surprises.'[153]

Mussolini's action had plunged the League into crisis once more. It had blasted apart the accord reached at Stresa. Europe was on the move. Hitler could await rich pickings.

III

While events on the diplomatic front were turning Hitler's way in the spring and summer of 1935, the new wave of anti-Jewish violence – after a relative lull since the later months of 1933 – that swept across the land between May and September spurred further radicalization in the area of his chief ideological obsession. Heavily preoccupied with foreign policy at this time, Hitler was only sporadically involved in the months before the hastily improvised promulgation of the notorious Nuremberg Laws at the Party Rally in September. 'With regard to the Jews, too,' Hitler commented at a much later date, 'I had for long to remain inactive.' His inactivity was tactical, not temperamental. 'There's no point in artificially creating additional difficulties,' he added. 'The more cleverly you proceed, the better.'[154] There was little need for him to be active. All he had to do was to provide backing for the party radicals – or, even less, do nothing to hinder their activism (until it eventually became counter-productive) – then to introduce the discriminatory legislation which the agitation had prompted. Knowing that actions to 'remove' the Jews were in line with Hitler's aims and met with his approval largely provided its own momentum.

Chiefly on account of foreign-policy sensitivities and economic precariousness, the regime had during 1934 reined in the violence against Jews which had characterized the early months of Nazi rule. Barbarity had merely subsided – and far from totally. Ferocious discrimination continued unabated. Intimidation was unrelenting. In some areas, like Streicher's Franconia, the economic boycott remained as fierce as ever and the poisonous atmosphere invited brutal actions. In one of the worst incidents encountered, in spring 1934, a local pogrom led by the SA and whipping up a mob of over 1,000 people had brought a vicious assault on thirty-five Jews. Two Jews were so terrified that they committed suicide.[155] Such a horrific explosion of violence was unusual at this time, even for Franconia. But it was the clearest indicator that any decline in the general scale of persecution was relative, less than universal, and likely to be temporary. Even so, the exodus of Jews fleeing from Germany slowed down markedly; some even came back, thinking the worst over.[156] Then, early in 1935 with the Saar plebiscite out of the way, the brakes on antisemitic action began to be loosened. Written and spoken propaganda stoked the fires of violence, inciting action from party formations – including units of the Hitler Youth, SA, SS, and the small traders' organization, NS-Hago – that scarcely needed encouragement.

The Franconian Gauleiter, Julius Streicher, the most rabid and primitive antisemite among the party leaders, was at the forefront. Other Gauleiter – Joseph Goebbels, Gauleiter of Berlin, Wilhelm Kube of the Kurmark, Jacob Sprenger of Hesse, and Josef Grohé of Cologne-Aachen – also distinguished themselves by their antisemitic tirades.[157] Party organs – particularly the newly-founded *Der Judenkenner* (The Jewish Expert) and Goebbels's *Der Angriff* (both of which aped much of *Der Stürmer*'s style) – stirred up heated feeling against Jews and pressed for immediate action to fulfil the party's programme.[158] Streicher's own quasi-pornographic newspaper, *Der Stürmer*, which had never ceased dispensing its poison despite frequent brushes even with Nazi authorities, now excelled itself in a new and intensified campaign of filth, centring upon endless stories of 'racial defilement'. The newspaper was displayed in the notorious '*Stürmer* Cases' in the streets and squares of cities, towns, and even villages in the backwaters. Posters advertising it could scarcely be missed. Sales quadrupled during 1935, chiefly on account of the support from local party organizations.[159]

The tone was changing at the very top. In March 1934, Heß had banned anti-Jewish propaganda by the NS-Hago, indicating that Hitler's authorization was needed for any boycott.[160] But at the end of April 1935, Wiedemann told Bormann that Hitler did not favour the prohibition, sought by some, of the anti-Jewish notice-boards – 'Jews Not Wanted Here' (or even more threatening versions) – on the roadside, at the entry to villages, and in public places.[161] The notice-boards as a result now spread rapidly. Radicals at the grass-roots gleaned the obvious message from the barrage of propaganda and the speeches of party notables that they were being given the green light to attack the Jews in any way they saw fit.

The party leaders were, in fact, reacting to and channelling pressures emanating from radicals at the grass-roots of the Movement. The continuing serious disaffection within the ranks of the SA, scarcely abated since the 'Röhm affair', was the underlying impetus to the new wave of violence directed at the Jews. Feeling cheated of the brave new world they thought was theirs, alienated and demoralized, the young toughs in the SA needed a new sense of purpose.[162] As internal SA reports indicated, they were also more than spoiling for a fight with their ideological enemies – Jews, Catholics, and capitalists. There was an expectation that, once the Saar plebiscite was out of the way, the true Nazi revolution – which the SA saw as derailed by conservatives – would regain its drive.[163] Against the bastions of economic power, the nihilistic fanaticism of SA and party radicals had little chance, and was kept closely in check. Against the Catholic Church, the most dominant remaining ideological barrier against Nazism in large tracts of the country, radicals could engage in a protracted war of attrition but faced the enormous resilience of a powerful establishment as well as widespread unpopularity at the grass-roots. But against the Jews, the prime ideological target, given a green light from above, they encountered no barrier and, in fact, every encouragement. The feeling among party activists, and especially stormtroopers, summarized in one Gestapo report in spring 1935, was that 'the Jewish problem' had to be 'set in motion by us from below', and 'that the government would then have to follow'.[164]

The instrumental value of the new wave of agitation and violence was made plain in reports from the Rhineland from Gauleiter Grohé of Cologne-Aachen, who thought in March and April 1935 that a new boycott and intensified attack on the Jews would help 'to raise the rather depressed mood among the lower-middle classes (*Mittelstand*)'.[165] Grohé, an ardent radical in the 'Jewish Question', went on to congratulate himself on the extent to which party activism had been revitalized and the morale of the lower-middle class reinvigorated by the new attacks on the Jews.[166] The new anti-Jewish wave was in the first instance, as such comments indicate, a release-valve allowing activists, frustrated and alienated by the evaporation of the revolutionary drive and purpose of the Movement, to let off steam at the expense of a disliked, unprotected, and brutally exposed minority.

Despite the aims of the Nazi programme, in the eyes of the Movement's radicals little had been done by early 1935 to eradicate the Jews from German society. There was a good deal of feeling among fanatical antisemites that the state bureaucracy had deflected the party's drive and not produced much by way of legislation to eliminate Jewish influence. The new wave of violence now led, therefore, to vociferous demands for the introduction of discriminatory legislation against the Jews which would go some way towards fulfilling the party's programme. The state bureaucracy also felt under pressure from actions of the Gestapo, demanding retrospective legal sanction for its own discriminatory measures, such as its ban, independently declared, in February 1935 on Jews raising the swastika flag.[167]

Attempts to mobilize the apathetic masses behind the violent antisemitic campaign of the party formations backfired. Beyond committed Nazis, the mood – to go from Gestapo and other internal reports as well as those from the exiled Social Democrats' (Sopade) underground network – was poor. The euphoria following national triumphs such as the return of the Saar and the reintroduction of military service was short-lived. The greyness of daily life returned all too soon for most ordinary citizens. Economic worries affecting different parts of the population, resentment among both Protestant and Catholic church-goers about the intensified attacks on the Churches, and antagonism towards local representatives of the party all contributed to the wide-ranging disaffection.[168] Instead of galvanizing the discontented, however, the antisemitic wave merely fuelled already prominent criticism of the party. There was little participation from those who did not belong to party formations. Many people ignored exhortations to boycott Jewish shops and stores. And the public displays of violence accompanying the 'boycott movement', as Jews were beaten up by Nazi thugs and their property vandalized, met with wide condemnation.[169] Not much of the criticism was on humanitarian grounds. Economic self-interest played a large part. So did worries that the violence might be extended to attacks on the Churches. The methods rather than the aims were attacked. There were few principled objections to discrimination against Jews. What concerned people above all were the hooliganism, mob violence, distasteful scenes, and disturbances of order.[170]

Accordingly, across the summer the violence became counter-productive, and the authorities felt compelled to take steps to condemn it and restore order. So heated was the mood in Munich, following riotous anti-Jewish 'demonstrations' in the city centre in the middle of May, that Adolf Wagner, Gauleiter of Munich-Upper Bavaria and Bavarian Minister of the Interior, went on the radio to denounce the 'terror groups' responsible. Wagner had, in fact, himself secretly instigated the action.[171] Unruly scenes on Berlin's Kurfürstendamm on 15 July 1935, when Jewish shops had been vandalized and Nazi thugs had beaten up Jews, scandalized onlookers and led immediately to the dismissal – already long desired by Goebbels and the Berlin party – of the Berlin Police Chief Magnus von Levetzow. The last straw had been when a group of Jews had protested in the darkness of a Berlin cinema against an antisemitic film. Goebbels immediately persuaded Hitler, who had just returned from a few days' holiday with the Propaganda Minister in Heiligendamm, a resort on the Baltic, to have Levetzow dismissed as police chief of the capital. He was replaced by Wolf Heinrich Graf von Helldorf, up to then police chief in Potsdam, of Saxon aristocratic descent, former head of the Berlin SA, with a reputation deeply sullied by scandal about his financial affairs and private life, but – compensating for everything – a radical antisemite who, the Propaganda Minister reckoned, would help him 'make Berlin clean again'.[172] Helldorf immediately had Jewish stores on the Kurfürstendamm closed. A week later, he banned 'individual actions' (Einzelaktionen) in the capital, blaming 'provocateurs' for the outrages.[173]

The terror on the streets had done its job for the time being. It had pushed the discrimination still further. The radicalization demanded action from above.

At last, Hitler, silent on the issue throughout the summer, was forced to take a stance. Schacht had warned him in a memorandum as early as 3 May of the economic damage being done by combating the Jews through illegal means.[174] Hitler had reacted at the time only by commenting that everything would turn out all right as matters developed. But now, on 8 August, he ordered a halt to all 'individual actions', which Heß relayed to the party the following day.[175] On 20 August, Minister of the Interior Frick took up Hitler's ban in threatening those continuing to perpetrate such acts with stiff punishment.[176] The stage had now been reached where the state authorities were engaged in the repression of party members seeking to implement what they knew Hitler wanted and what was a central tenet of party doctrine. It was little wonder that the police, increasingly compelled to intervene against party activists engaged in violent outrages against Jews, also wanted an end to the public disturbances.[177] Hitler stood aloof from the fray but uneasily positioned between the radicals and the conservatives. His instincts, as ever, were with the radicals, whose bitter disappointment at what they saw as a betrayal of Nazi principles was evident.[178] But political sense dictated that he should heed the conservatives. Led by Schacht, these wanted a regulation of antisemitic activity through legislation. This in any case fed into growing demands within the party for tough discriminatory measures, especially against 'racial defilement'. Out of the need to reconcile these conflicting positions, the Nuremberg Laws emerged.

Shrill demands for harsh legislation against the Jews had mounted sharply in spring and summer 1935. Reich Minister of the Interior Frick had appeared in April to offer the prospect of a new, discriminatory law on rights of state citizenship, but nothing had emerged to satisfy those who saw a central feature of the Party Programme still not implemented after two years of Nazi rule.[179] Party organs demanded in June that Jews be excluded from state citizenship and called for the death penalty for Jews renting property to 'Aryans', employing them as servants, serving them as doctors or lawyers, or engaging in 'racial defilement'.[180]

The issue of banning intermarriage and outlawing sexual relations between Jews and 'Aryans' had by this time gone to the top of the agenda of the demands of the radicals. Racial purity, they claimed, could only be attained through total physical apartheid. Even a single instance of sexual intercourse between a Jew and an 'Aryan', announced Streicher, was sufficient to prevent the woman from ever giving birth to a 'pure-blooded Aryan' child.[181] 'Defilement' of 'German' girls through predatory Jews, a constant allegation of the vicious *Stürmer* and its imitators, had by now become a central theme of the anti-Jewish agitation.

As early as 1930, Frick had introduced a draft bill 'for the Protection of the German Nation' in the Reichstag, threatening draconian punishment for engaging in sexual relations with Jews and 'coloured races'. After 1933, the idea had been taken up by National Socialist lawyers, but Reich Justice Minister Gürtner had rejected as late as June 1934 the practicality of legislation for 'racial protection'.[182] Even so, the judicial authorities could advance only tactical, not principled, arguments.

The clamour for legislation in 1935 could have come as little surprise. Nazi doctors joined in − the Reich Doctors' Leader Gerhard Wagner at their forefront. A meeting of physicians in Nuremberg had sent a telegram to Frick in December 1934 demanding 'the heaviest punishment' for any attempted sexual contact between a 'German woman' and a Jew. Only this way could German racial purity be maintained and 'further Jewish-racial poisoning and pollution of German blood prevented'.[183] Streicher spoke in May 1935 of a forthcoming ban on marriages between Jews and Germans. In early August, Goebbels proclaimed that such marriages would be prohibited. Meanwhile, activists were taking matters into their own hands. SA men demonstrated in front of the houses of newly-weds where one partner was Jewish.[184] Even without a law, officials at some registry offices were refusing to perform 'mixed marriages'.[185] Since they were not legally banned, others carried out the ceremony. Still others informed the Gestapo of an intended marriage. The Gestapo itself pressed the Justice Ministry for a speedy regulation of the confused situation. A further impulse arose from the new Defence Law of 21 May 1935, banning marriage with 'persons of non-Aryan origin' for members of the newly formed Wehrmacht. By July, bowing to pressure from within the Movement, Frick had decided to introduce legislation to ban 'mixed marriages'. Some form of draft bill had already been worked upon in the Justice Ministry. The delay in bringing forward legislation largely arose from the question of how to deal with the 'Mischlinge' − those of partial Jewish descent.[186]

Frick had told party members in early August that the 'Jewish Question' would be 'slowly but surely solved by legal means'.[187] On 18 August, in a speech in Königsberg, which, despite censorship in the official published version of those sections attacking the antisemitic violence, obtained wide circulation inside and outside Germany, Schacht had indicated that anti-Jewish legislation in accordance with the Party Programme was 'in preparation' and had to be regarded as a central aim of the government.[188]

Schacht summoned state and party leaders on 20 August to the Ministry of Economics to discuss the 'Jewish Question'. At a packed meeting, lasting almost two hours, Frick gave an account of work being undertaken in his ministry to prepare legislation in line with the Party Programme. Adolf Wagner, representing Heß, spoke of popular pressure for legislation and said that he too disapproved of the 'excesses' (which, in Munich, he had been instrumental in stimulating).[189] Nevertheless, the state had to take account of antisemitic public feeling by pursuing the exclusion of Jews from economic life through 'legal, if gradual, measures'. He demanded preliminary legal measures to quell the unrest: the exclusion of Jews in the placing of public contracts, and the prohibition of establishment of new Jewish businesses. Schacht said he agreed in principle with such measures.[190] Gürtner spoke of the need to combat the impression that the leadership was happy to turn a blind eye to breaches of the law since political considerations prevented it from the action it wanted to take. Johannes Popitz, the Prussian Finance Minister, pleaded for the government to set a specific limit to the treatment of Jews – it did not matter where, he stated – but then hold to it. Schacht himself fiercely attacked the party's violent methods as causing great harm to the economy and rearmament drive, concluding that it was vital to carry out the party's programme, but only through legislation. He agreed with Wagner's suggestion that such legislation should apply only to 'full Jews' (*Volljuden*) to avoid delay once more through the question of including Mischlinge. The meeting ended by agreeing that party and state should combine to bring suggestions to the Reich government 'about desirable measures'.[191]

An account of the meeting prepared for the State Secretary in the Foreign Ministry commented:

It emerged from the discussion that the Party's general programme in respect of the Jews was substantially adhered to but that the methods employed were subjected to criticism. The unbridled expansion of antisemitic activities in every conceivable sphere of life on the part of irresponsible organizations or private individuals should be stopped by legal measures. At the same time, the Jews should be subjected to special legislation in certain definite spheres, above all economic, but apart from this they should retain their freedom of movement.

An overall and uniform objective for Germany's policy towards the Jews did not emerge from the discussion. The arguments put forward by the Ministers responsible for the various Departments merely went to show that the Jewish question represented an obstacle to the performance of their political duties . . . In the main, the departmental representatives drew attention to the practical disadvantages for their departmental work, whilst the Party justified the necessity for radical action against the Jews with politico-emotional and abstract ideological considerations . . .[192]

For all the vehemence of his arguments, Schacht had not wanted to, or felt able to, challenge the principle of excluding the Jews. 'Herr Schacht did not draw the logical conclusion,' stated the Foreign Ministry's report, 'and demand a radical change in the Party's Jewish programme, nor even in the methods of applying it, for instance a ban on *Der Stürmer*. On the contrary, he kept up the fiction of abiding a hundred per cent by the Jewish programme.'[193] Schacht's meeting had clearly highlighted the differences between party and state, between radicals and pragmatists, between fanatics and conservatives. There was no fundamental disagreement about aims; merely about methods. However, the matter could not be allowed to drag on indefinitely. A resolution had to be found in the near future.

The minutes of the meeting were sent to Hitler, who also discussed the matter with Schacht on 9 September.[194] This was a day before Hitler left to join the hundreds of thousands of the party faithful assembled for the annual ritual in Nuremberg for the 'Reich Party Rally of Freedom' – 'the High Mass of our party', as Goebbels called it.[195] Eleven days before the Party Rally, the London weekly *Jewish Chronicle* reported on planned legislation 'to regulate the question of German citizenship, ban mixed marriages, and enact heavy penalties for "racial desecration"'. The new Citizenship Law, it went on, was to be officially proclaimed at the Nazi Congress in Nuremberg on 10 September.[196] This was reasoned speculation, not firm insider-knowledge. The Schacht meeting (where economic legislation had been the main demand) had demonstrated that, for all the talk of preparatory work, in mid-August, ten days before the appearance of the article in the *Jewish Chronicle*, there was still nothing available. The rapid drafting which was necessary during the Nuremberg Rally itself further indicated that the legislation was far from ready. For all its apparent prescience, the *Jewish Chronicle* had picked up the many hints at forthcoming legislation which had been made by Nazi leaders, and guessed that discriminatory laws would be announced at Nuremberg. It turned out to be a shrewd guess. But when Hitler left for Nuremberg, it was not with the intention of proclaiming the anti-Jewish 'citizenship' and 'blood' laws during the Party Rally. Once again, propaganda considerations played a significant part. And so did the lobbying at Nuremberg of one of the most fanatical proponents of a ban on sexual relations between Germans and Jews, Dr Gerhard Wagner, the Reich Doctors' Leader, who had been advocating a ban on marriages between 'Aryans' and Jews since 1933.[197]

Two days into the Party Rally, on 12 September, Wagner announced in a speech that within a short time a 'Law to Protect German Blood' would prevent the further 'bastardization' of the German people. A year later, Wagner claimed that he had no idea, when making his announcement, that the Führer would introduce the Nuremberg Laws within days. Probably Hitler had given Wagner no specific indication of when the 'Blood Law' would be promulgated. But since Wagner had unequivocally announced such a law as imminent, he must have been given an unambiguous sign by Hitler that action would follow in the immediate future.[198] At any rate, late the very next evening, 13 September, Dr Bernhard Lösener, in charge of preparation of legislation on the 'Jewish Question' in the Reich Ministry of the Interior, was, to his surprise, ordered to Nuremberg. He and a colleague, Ministerialrat Franz Albrecht Medicus, arrived in the morning of 14 September to be told by their superiors in the Interior Ministry, State Secretaries Hans Pfundtner and Wilhelm Stuckart, that Hitler had instructed them the previous day to prepare a law to regulate the problems of marriage between 'Aryans' and 'non-Aryans'. They had immediately begun work on a draft.[199] It seems likely that the urging of Wagner, in Hitler's company for hours at the crucial time and doubtless supported by other Nazi leaders, had been instrumental in the decision to bring in the long-desired law there and then. Wagner was the link between Hitler and those given the task of drafting the law, who were not altogether clear – since they had received no written instructions – on exactly what came from the Doctor's Leader and what came from Hitler himself.[200] But Hitler would not have acted on Wagner's prompting had he not seen the political and propaganda advantages in doing so.

From Hitler's point of view, such a move was most timely. To embellish the Party Rally – the first at which the new Wehrmacht was on show since the reintroduction of conscription – he had summoned the Reichstag to a symbolic meeting in the city where it had last met in 1543. It had been called to acclaim a law making the swastika banner the new Reich Flag – a move, replacing the traditional black-white-red horizontal stripes of the national flag of the Kaiser's era, of notable sensitivity in conservative and military circles.[201] The Diplomatic Corps was also to be present, apparently because Hitler had planned to exploit the mounting Abyssinian crisis – how the divided League of Nations, with Italian threats unmistakable, should respond to the likely assault (which in fact took place little over a fortnight later) on one of its members, Abyssinia, by another, Italy – to pose German revisionist demands. In the event, on 13 September Neurath had dissuaded him from this idea.[202] Hitler then needed something to 'fill out somewhat' the legislative programme for the Reichstag which, with only the Flag Law to promulgate, was looking rather thin.[203] Meeting Wagner's wishes – echoing those of many in the party – for a law against 'mixed' marriages of Germans and Jews, offered a satisfactory way round the problem.

The atmosphere was in any case ripe. The summer of intimidation and violence towards Jews had seen to that. The increasingly shrill demands for action in the 'Jewish Question' formed a menacing backcloth to the high-point of the party's year as hundreds of thousands of the faithful arrived in Nuremberg, its walls, towers, and houses bedecked by swastika banners, the air full of expectancy at the great spectacle to follow in what had been labelled the 'Reich Party Rally of Freedom'. As in the previous two years, the narrow streets of Nuremberg's beautiful old town were thronged with 'Party comrades', boys from the Hitler Youth, stormtroopers, and the black-uniformed élite corps of the SS. Hitler's reception had been, as always, that of a conquering hero when he arrived in the city. The Zeppelinfeld, to the south-east of the city, where Albert Speer's stadium, congress-hall, and parade-grounds, begun the previous year, and set to accommodate over 300,000 persons, were still being built, was a sea of swastika flags, lit at night with soaring searchlights. The scene captured Nazi aesthetics at their height.[204]

The tone of the Rally had been set by Hitler's opening proclamation, read out as usual by Adolf Wagner. Hitler threatened 'that the fight against the inner enemies of the nation' would 'never fail because of the formal state bureaucracy or its inadequacy'. What the state could not solve, would be solved through the party. And at the head of the list of internal enemies he mentioned stood 'Jewish Marxism'.[205] Exploiting attacks on National Socialism made at the Moscow conference of the Comintern in the summer, the shrill assault on 'Jewish Marxism' ran as a leitmotiv throughout the Rally.[206]

Preparations for the notorious laws which would determine the fate of thousands were little short of chaotic. Lösener and Medicus had arrived in Nuremberg on Saturday, 14 September. The Reichstag meeting was sched-uled for 8p.m. the following day.[207] There was little time for the already weary civil servants to draft the required legislation. Whatever the prior work on anti-Jewish legislation in the Ministries of the Interior and Justice had been, it had plainly not passed the initial stages. No definition of a Jew had been agreed upon. The party were pressing for inclusion of Mischlinge (those of mixed descent). But the complexities of this were considerable. The work went on at a furious pace. During the course of the day, Lösener was sent more than once to battle his way through the huge crowds to Frick, staying at a villa on the other side of the city and showing little interest in the matter. Hitler, at Wagner's insistence, rejected the first versions Frick brought to him as too mild.[208] Around midnight, Frick returned from Hitler with the order to prepare for him four versions of the Blood Law – varying in the severity of the penalties for offences against the law – and, in addition, to complete the legislative programme, to draft a Reich Citizenship Law.[209] Within half an hour, they had drawn up in the briefest of terms a law distinguishing state subjects from Reich citizens, which only those of German or related blood were eligible to become.[210] Though almost devoid of content, the law provided the framework for the mass of subsidiary decrees that in the following years were to push German Jews to the outer fringes of society, prisoners in their own land. At 2.30a.m. Frick returned with Hitler's approval.[211] The civil servants learnt only when the Reichstag assembled which of the four drafts of the 'Blood Law' Hitler had chosen. Possibly following the intervention of either Neurath or, more likely, Gürtner, he had chosen the mildest. However, he struck out with his own hand the restriction to 'full Jews', adding further to the confusion by ordering this restriction to be included in the version published by the German News Agency (Deutsches Nachrichtenbüro).[212] Marriage and extra-marital sexual relations between Jews and Germans were outlawed, and to be punished with stiff penalties. Jews were also barred from employing German women under the age of forty-five as servants.[213]

Hitler's speech – for him a remarkably short one – to the Reichstag on 15 September, recommending acceptance of the three laws (the Flag Law, the Citizenship Law, and the Blood Law), was the first time he had concentrated on the 'Jewish Question' in a major address since becoming Chancellor. Jews abroad, he declared, had been responsible for agitation and renewed boycotts against Germany. He blamed the 'Bolshevik revolutionary agitation' following the Comintern Congress in Moscow and the 'insulting of the German Flag' in New York (when dock workers had torn down the swastika banner from the steamer *Bremen*, giving rise to an international incident) on 'Jewish elements'.[214] The 'international unrest' had stirred Jews within Germany to 'provocative action' of an organized kind. If this were not to lead to uncontrollable 'defensive actions of the enraged population', there remained 'only the way of a legal regulation of the problem'. The German government was, therefore, Hitler went on, persuaded 'by the idea of being able, through a once and for all secular solution, of perhaps creating a basis on which the German people might possibly be able to find a tolerable relationship with the Jewish people'. From one whose first written political statement, in 1919, had specified that the final aim of government policy must be 'the removal of the Jews altogether',[215] and had made a political career out of his vitriolic hatred of the Jews, this was blatant deception, aimed at the outside world.[216] The threat, always near at hand for Hitler, followed immediately. Should the hope not be fulfilled, and international agitation continue, the situation would have to be re-examined. He sharpened the threat in a menacing remark in recommending the 'Blood Law'. This, he said, was 'the attempt at a legal regulation of a problem, which in the event of further failure would then have through law to be transferred to the final solution of the National Socialist Party'.[217]

This was a hint of Hitler's true feelings about radical measures on the 'Jewish Question'. But the reason – alongside propaganda advantages – why Hitler had been prepared to bow to the pressure to introduce the anti-Jewish legislation so hastily was apparent in further comments he made that evening. After Göring, as Reichstag President, had formally introduced the laws,[218] and they had received the unanimous vote of the delegates, Hitler returned to the podium. He appealed to the delegates to 'see to it that the nation itself does not depart from the rule of law', and 'that this law is ennobled by the most unprecedented discipline of the entire German people'.[219] In his fourth speech of the day, this time to party leaders, Hitler once more underlined the significance of the laws and renewed his command to the party to desist from 'every individual action against Jews'.[220] The Nuremberg Laws, it is plain, had been a compromise adopted by Hitler, counter to his instincts, to defuse the anti-Jewish agitation of the party, which over the summer had become unpopular not merely in wide sections of the population but, because of its harmful economic effects, among conservative sections of the leadership. The compromise did not please party radicals.[221] It was a compromise, even so, which placated those in the party who had been pressing for legislation, especially on 'racial defilement'. And in putting the brakes on agitation and open violence, it had nevertheless taken the discrimination on to new terrain. Disappointment among activists at the retreat from a direct assault on Jews was tempered by the recognition, as one report put it, 'that the Führer had for outward appearances to ban individual actions against the Jews in consideration of foreign policy, but in reality was wholly in agreement that each individual should continue on his own initiative the fight against Jewry in the most rigorous and radical form'.[222]

The dialectic of radicalization in the 'Jewish Question' in 1935 had been along the following lines: pressure from below; green light from above; further violence from below; brakes from above assuaging the radicals through discriminatory legislation. The process had ratcheted up the persecution several notches.

The Nuremberg Laws served their purpose in dampening the wild attacks on the Jews which had punctuated the summer.[223] Most ordinary Germans not among the ranks of the party fanatics had disapproved of the violence, but not of the aims of anti-Jewish policy – the exclusion of Jews from German society, and ultimately their removal from Germany itself. They mainly approved now of the legal framework to separate Jews and Germans as offering a permanent basis for discrimination without the unseemly violence.[224] Hitler had associated himself with the search for a 'legal' solution. His popularity was little affected.[225]

The thorny question of defining a Jew had still to be tackled. Since Hitler had ruled out the restriction of the 'Blood Law' to 'full Jews', civil servants in the Ministry of the Interior were left to struggle for weeks with party representatives in an attempt to reach agreement about the extent of partial 'Jewishness' needed to qualify under the law.[226] Drafts of the first implementation ordinances under the Reich Citizenship Law, legally defining a Jew, were formulated to try to comply with Hitler's presumed views.[227] But although Hitler intervened on occasion, even on points of minute detail, his sporadic involvement was insufficient to bring the tug-of-war between Heß's office and the Ministry of the Interior to a speedy end. The Ministry wanted to classify as 'Jews' only those with more than two 'non-Aryan' grandparents. The party – with Reich Doctors' Leader Wagner applying pressure – insisted on the inclusion of 'quarter-Jews'. Numerous meetings brought no result. Meanwhile, without awaiting a definition, some ministries were already imposing a variety of discriminatory measures on those of 'mixed' background, using different criteria.[228] A decision was urgently necessary. But Hitler would not come down on one side or the other. A decision was expected when he addressed a meeting of Gauleiter in Munich, to which Stuckart and Lösener were invited, on 24 September. However, Hitler contented himself with a discourse on the need to ensure the purity of German blood through the measures planned for implementation under the

Citizenship Law, then deviated into what Goebbels called a 'monumental foreign-policy preview'.[229] The definition of a Jew would, he said, have to be worked out between the party and the Ministry of the Interior.[230] The key question had been left unanswered. 'Jewish Question still not decided,' noted Goebbels on 1 October. 'We debate for a long time about it, but the Führer is still wavering.'[231]

By early November, with still no final resolution in sight, Schacht and the Reichsbank Directorate, claiming the uncertainty was damaging the economy and the foreign-exchange rate, joined in the pressure on Hitler to end the dispute. Hitler had no intention of being pinned down to accepting security of rights for Jews under the legislation, as the Reichsbank wanted. The prospect of open confrontation between party representatives and state ministers of the Interior, Economics, and Foreign Affairs, and likely defeat for the party, at a meeting scheduled for 5 November to reach a final decision, made Hitler call off the meeting at short notice.[232] He was looking for a compromise. 'Führer now wants a decision,' wrote Goebbels on 7 November. 'Compromise is in any case necessary and absolutely satisfactory solution impossible.'[233] A week later, the First Supplementary Decree to the Reich Citizenship Law finally ended the uncertainty. Wagner got his way on most points. But on the definition of a Jew, the Ministry of the Interior could point to some success. Three-quarter Jews were counted as Jewish. Half-Jews (with two Jewish and two 'Aryan' grandparents) were reckoned as Jewish only if practising the Jewish faith, married to a Jew, the child of a marriage with a Jewish partner, or the illegitimate child of a Jew and 'Aryan'.[234] 'A compromise, but the best possible one', was how Goebbels described the outcome. His distaste was evident. 'Quarter-Jews over to us. Half-Jews only in exceptional cases. In the name of God, so that we can have peace. Slickly and unobtrusively launch in the press. Not make too much noise about it.'[235] Whatever Goebbels's personal reservations, there was some sense in playing it down. For the definition of a Jew had ended with a contradiction, recognized by the Ministry of the Interior. For legislative purposes, it had been impossible to arrive at a biological definition of race dependent on blood types. So it had been necessary to resort to religious belief to determine who was racially a Jew. As a result, it was possible to imagine descendants of 'pure Aryan' parents converted to Judaism who would thereby be regarded as racial Jews.[236] It was absurd, but merely highlighted the absurdity of the entire exercise.

The approach of the Winter Olympics in Garmisch-Partenkirchen, then the summer games in Berlin, along with the sensitive foreign-policy situation, meant that the regime was anxious to avoid any repetition of the violence of the summer of 1935. For the next two years, though the wheel of discrimination carried on turning, the 'Jewish Question' was kept away from the forefront of politics. When Wilhelm Gustloff, the leading NSDAP representative (*Landesgruppenleiter*) in Switzerland, was assassinated by a young Jew in February 1936, the circumstances did not lend themselves to wild retaliation.[237] Frick, in collaboration with Heß, strictly banned 'individual actions'.[238] Hitler restrained his natural instinct, and confined himself to a relatively low-key generalized attack on Jewry at Gustloff's funeral.[239] Germany remained quiet. The absence of violence following Gustloff's murder is as clear a guide as the outrages in the anti-Jewish wave of 1935 to the fact that the regime could control, when it wanted to, the pressures for action within the ranks of the party radicals. In 1935 it had been useful to encourage and respond to such pressures. In 1936 it was opportune to keep them in check.

For Hitler, whatever the tactical considerations, the aim of destroying the Jews – his central political idea since 1919 – remained unaltered. He revealed his approach to a meeting of party District Leaders at the end of April 1937, in immediate juxtaposition to comments on the Jews: 'I don't straight away want violently to demand an opponent to fight. I don't say "fight" because I want to fight. Instead, I say: "I want to destroy you!" And now let skill help me to manoeuvre you so far into the corner that you can't strike any blow. And then you get the stab into the heart.'[240]

In practice, however, as had been the position during the summer of 1935 before the Nuremberg Rally, Hitler needed do little to push forward the radicalization of the 'Jewish Question'.[241] By now, even though still not centrally coordinated, the 'Jewish Question' pervaded all key areas of government; party pressure at headquarters and in the localities for new forms of discrimination was unceasing; civil servants complied with ever tighter constraints under the provisions of the 'Reich Citizenship Law'; the law-courts were engaged in the persecution of Jews under the provisions of the Nuremberg Laws; the police were looking for further ways to hasten the elimination of Jews and speed up their departure from Germany; and the general public, for the most part, passively accepted the discrimination where they did not directly encourage or participate in it. Antisemitism had come by now to suffuse all walks of life. 'The Nazis have indeed brought off a deepening of the gap between the people and the Jews,' ran a Sopade report from Berlin covering the month of January 1936. 'The feeling that the Jews are another race is today a general one.'[242]

IV

In one of the seventeen speeches he made at the 1935 Party Rally in Nuremberg, Hitler attempted – he was speaking after all to the party faithful – to
disclaim the evident wide disparity between his own massive popularity and
the poor image of the party. 'I must ... take a stance here against the
comment so often heard, especially among the bourgeoisie: "The Führer,
yes, – but the Party, that's a different matter!" To that, I give the answer:
"No, gentlemen! The Führer is the Party, and the Party is the Führer".'[243]
Since the mid-1920s the identity of Leader and Party had been a myth that
had served both well. It had given the party a cohesion and discipline
otherwise notably lacking. And it had established Hitler's supreme power-
base as the sole keeper of the party's Grail. But, however necessary Hitler's
attempts to uphold the myth were, the reality was that once in power the
popular images had inevitably diverged.

   Hitler, by late 1935, was already well on the way to establishing – backed
by the untiring efforts of the propaganda machine – his standing as a *national*
leader, transcending purely party interest. He stood for the successes, the
achievements of the regime. Within three years, his genius – so propaganda
proclaimed, and so the majority of the population believed – had
masterminded economic recovery, the removal of the scourge of unemployment, and (even by ordering the shooting of his own SA leaders) the
re-establishment of law and order. He had, it seemed, also single-handedly
broken the shackles of Versailles, restored military pride, and made Germany
once more a force to be reckoned with in international affairs – and all the
time skilfully avoiding conflict and upholding Germany's peaceful aims.
There was nothing specifically 'Nazi' about his 'achievements'. Any patriotic
German could find something to admire in them. His popularity soared
accordingly also among those who were otherwise critical of National
Socialism.

   With the party, it was a different matter. Where Hitler seemed to represent
national unity, the party functionaries were all too often seen as corrupt,
high-handed, and self-serving – sowing discord rather than embodying the
spirit of the 'national community'. The party could be, and often was,
blamed for all the continuing ills of daily life – for the gulf between
expectations and reality that had brought widespread disillusionment in the
wake of the initial exaggerated hopes of rapid material improvement in the
Third Reich.

Not least, the party's image had badly suffered through its attacks on the Christian Churches. As in the 'Jewish Question', much of the impetus came from the party's grass-roots and local or provincial leadership. The long-standing antagonisms built up in the 'time of struggle' before 1933 were not easy to contain now that the party held power.

The attack on the autonomy of the provincial Protestant Churches in Bavaria and Württemberg provided one notable flashpoint. The deposition in autumn 1934 by Reich Bishop Ludwig Müller (implemented, with strong-arm tactics, by his henchmen) of the popular Bishops Meiser and Wurm, who headed the resistance to incorporation of these independent churches in the 'coordinated' new creation of a 'Reich Church', had led to mass unrest among some of National Socialism's most loyal supporters.[244] The pious peasantry of Franconia, one of the NSDAP's bastions, bitterly blamed the party.[245] Hitler escaped the opprobrium. Personal loyalty to him was untouched. When he intervened in late October to reinstate Meiser and Wurm, it seemed yet another indication that he had been kept in the dark by his subordinates, intervening to restore justice once he realized what was taking place without his approval. His intervention had in fact been a capitulation to popular pressure, a necessary step to end the unrest and limit the damage being done. His emollient assurances to Meiser and Wurm contrasted with his angry denunciation of them, a few months earlier, as 'traitors to the people, enemies of the Fatherland, and the destroyers of Germany'.[246]

Among the Catholic population, too, the continued war of attrition against Church practices and institutions undermined the position – never as strong as in Protestant regions – of the NSDAP and its representatives in solidly Catholic areas. Hitler again escaped much of the blame. His popularity was certainly not left unscathed.[247] But it was easier (and less dangerous) to criticize the local party functionaries or the 'bogyman' usually singled out by Church leaders as the most pernicious anti-Christian radical, Alfred Rosenberg.[248] Concerned at the growth of unrest caused by the 'Church struggle', especially with vital issues in foreign policy still unsettled, Hitler told Goebbels in the summer of 1935 that he wanted 'peace with the Churches' – 'at least for a certain period of time'.[249] He took the 'question of Catholicism', noted Goebbels, 'very seriously'.[250] But, as with the 'Jewish Question', the radicals at the party's grass-roots, and in its leadership, were not so easily controlled. The 'Church struggle' in Catholic areas intensified. And by the winter of 1935–6, morale in such regions plummeted.[251]

The dismal mood in those parts of the country worst affected by the assault on the Churches was only part of a wider drop in the popularity of the regime in the winter of 1935–6. Hitler's personal standing was still largely untouched. But even the Führer was increasingly being drawn into the criticism. For a regime – and its Leader quite especially – which had built a doctrine on erasing the consequences of November 1918 and ensuring that no future people's rising could take place, the manifestations of unrest could not be ignored.[252]

Hitler was aware of the deterioration in the political situation within Germany, and of the material conditions underlying the worsening mood of the population. 'Führer gives an overview of the political situation. Sees a decline,' registered Goebbels in mid-August.[253] A summary of price and wage levels prepared for Hitler on 4 September 1935 showed almost half of the German work-force earning gross wages of 18 Reich Marks or less per week. This was substantially below the poverty line. The statistics went on to illustrate that a family of five – including three children of school age – existing on the low wage of even 25 Reich Marks a week earned by a typical urban worker and living on an exceedingly frugal diet could scarcely be expected to make ends meet. Wages, then, remained at the 1932 level – substantially lower than the last pre-Depression year of 1928 in the much-maligned Weimar Republic. Food-prices, on the other hand, had risen officially by 8 per cent since 1933. Overall living costs were higher by 5.4 per cent. Official rates did not, however, tell the whole tale. Increases of 33, 50, and even 150 per cent had been reported for some foodstuffs.[254] By late summer, the terms 'food crisis' (*Ernährungskrise*) and 'provisions crisis' (*Versorgungskrise*) were in common use.

Dwindling currency reserves and a chronic shortage of foreign exchange had already led in 1934 to Schacht being given near-dictatorial control over the economy. His 'New Plan' of September that year had imposed strict controls on allocation of foreign exchange for imports and aimed to reorientate Germany's foreign trade through bilateral agreements with countries in south-eastern Europe, essentially obtaining supplies of raw materials on credit set against subsequent exports of finished goods from Germany.[255] The problems, however, continued. The priority given to rearmament made them unavoidable. Noticeably rising armaments expenditure and expensive imports, given a refusal to entertain any consideration of currency devaluation, were creating inevitable difficulties. It was becoming impossible to provide both the imports of raw materials needed for the expanding armaments industry and the imports of foodstuffs required to keep down consumer prices. A bad harvest in 1934 and a combination of inefficiency, mismanagement and over-bureaucratization in Darré's Reich Food Estate further exacerbated the structural economic problem. The 'production battle' (*Erzeugungsschlacht*) trumpeted by Darré in November 1934 had, despite reducing imports, begun with some misplaced bureaucratic intervention by the Reich Food Estate. The result was a serious shortage of domestic fodder, falling livestock herds, and a vicious circle of food shortages. By the autumn of 1935, reserves of fats and eggs had been almost entirely used up.[256] But foreign exchange for imports could only be at the expense of industry – and primarily armaments manufacture.

All at once, it seemed, the food shops were empty. Queuing for food became part of a dismal daily routine in the big cities. Fats, butter, eggs, then meat became scarce and expensive. Farmers, with their usual public-spirited support for the 'national community', held back their produce to maximize profits. Standards of living, already depressed in the big cities, fell sharply. The industrial working class – the section of society treated with most suspicion and caution by the regime and worst hit by the 'food crisis' – was especially disaffected.

The Berlin police reported a serious deterioration in the mood of the population in autumn 1935 as a result of the fats and meats shortage, rising food-prices, and renewed growth in unemployment. There was great anger among those queuing for food. Butter sales had to be watched over by the police. There was ill-feeling towards hoarders. But most ill-feeling was directed at the government, which had proved incapable of controlling prices.[257] The situation was even worse in some other big cities. After all, the capital had been singled out for favourable treatment.[258] By January 1936, a further deterioration had set in. The mood among a 'shockingly high percentage of the population' in Berlin was said to be 'directly negative towards State and Movement'. Criticism was 'now moving into uncontrollable territory'. Income and food-prices stood in crass disproportion to each other. Rises in food-prices – 70 per cent in the case of frozen meat – were the main source of unrest. Reality stood in contradiction to official declarations about the situation. Food stalls in the markets of Moabit and Charlottenburg were hotbeds of discontent. Communist sentiments could be heard and were apparently falling increasingly on ready ears.[259] By March, the mood prompted 'great worry'. There was 'marked bitterness' in wide sections of the population. The 'Heil Hitler' greeting had largely vanished. There was a lot of talk of a second '30 June' (the Night of the Long Knives), bringing a military dictatorship and 'a fundamentally new and clean state leadership and administration under the dominant influence of the armed forces'. The food shortages had highlighted the enormous gulf between the poverty of the masses and the ostentatious wealth and blatant corruption of party bosses. Hitler himself came under fire for tolerating such a situation. 'Confidence of the population in the person of the Führer is also undergoing a crisis,' claimed the report of the Berlin police.[260]

'The mood in the people is not bad, but good. I know that better. It's made bad through such reports. I forbid such things in future,' raged Hitler, when his adjutant Fritz Wiedemann tried drawing the accounts of low morale to his attention.[261] But such an irrational response itself hinted that Hitler had a good impression of how the material shortages had affected the popularity of his regime. He was, in fact, fully in the picture of the seriousness of the situation.

He had been made well aware, as early as September 1934, of complaints from the poorer sections of society about the price of fat products. Darré was asked whether the complaints were justified and had to supply information on the price trends for milk and fats.[262] This was followed by a number of top-level discussions, involving the party's Gauleiter, with Hitler himself present on one occasion.[263] Two months later, Hitler ordered the appointment of Carl Goerdeler, Lord Mayor of Leipzig, as Reich Commissar for Price Surveillance. Hitler had, he told a meeting of ministers on 5 November 1934, 'given the working class his word that he would allow no price increases. Wage-earners would accuse him of breaking his word if he did not act against the rising prices. Revolutionary conditions among the people would be the further consequence. He would not, therefore, allow the shocking driving up of prices.'[264]

Goerdeler's position, however, had more to do with appearances than with any actual power to prevent the price-rises. By July 1935, Frick was sending copies of worrying reports from all parts of the country to the Reich Chancellery. He urgently requested that Hitler be made aware of the 'serious danger' they illustrated of the impact the rising prices was having on the working class.[265] The Trustees of Labour, meeting in Berlin on 27 August, painted the same picture.[266] Hitler demanded the statistical report on prices and income levels which we have already noted. The report, of 4 September, showed poor living-standards, falling real wages, and steep price increases in some necessities.[267] This was the dismal reality behind the 'fine façade of the Third Reich'.[268]

Hitler was told later in the month of the implications of the food shortage for the rearmament programme. The minimum from the critically depleted reserves of foreign exchange needed to import fats (especially cheap margarine) to overcome the shortages was estimated at 300,000 Reich Marks per day – and even this was well below what Darré was wanting. There was no doubt what this meant: 'All foreign exchange [expended] for fats provisions has as a consequence a drop in raw material imports and therefore increased unemployment. But even this must be accepted, for the provisioning of the population with fatstuffs must take precedence over all other needs.'[269] Rearmament had, for the time being, to take second place. By then, Schacht had already warned the Gauleiter, in Hitler's presence, that only 5 milliard Reich Marks were available for armaments, and that he would have to introduce cuts, 'otherwise the whole thing will collapse'.[270]

Price Commissar Goerdeler wanted more than a temporary reordering of the priority given to rearmament. In a devastating analysis of Germany's economic position, sent to Hitler towards the end of October 1935, he regarded 'the satisfactory provisioning of the population with fats, even in relation to armaments, as having political priority'. He favoured a return to a market economy, a renewed emphasis upon exports, and a corresponding reduction in the rearmament drive – in his view at the root of the economic problems. The only alternative, he apocalyptically proclaimed, was the return to a non-industrial economy with drastic reductions in the standard of living for every German. If things carried on as they were, only a hand-to-mouth existence would be possible after January 1936.[271] The prognosis was anathema to Hitler.[272] For Goerdeler, it marked the beginning of the path that led eventually into outright resistance.[273] His more immediate response, however, was to recommend the winding-up of the Reich Commissariat for Price Surveillance since, in his view, it served no useful purpose. On both occasions the suggestion was made, in November 1935 and again in February 1936, Hitler refused – plainly to retain appearances – to entertain the dissolution of the Price Commissariat 'until further notice'.[274]

Meanwhile, Hitler had intervened in October to ensure that Schacht made available an additional sum of 12.4 million Reich Marks in precious foreign exchange for the import of oil-seed for margarine production.[275] Göring – his first sally into the economic domain up to now rigidly in Schacht's hand – was deployed by Hitler to arbitrate between Schacht and Darré in the fight for foreign exchange.[276] He came down on the side of Darré – a decision that took Schacht and some business leaders by surprise. But for Hitler, the immediate prime need was to avoid the damaging psychological effects of the only alternative: food rationing. The press agency was confidentially informed in November of the Führer's decision 'that the card for fats should not be introduced and that instead sufficient currency for the import of foodstuffs should be made available by the Economics Minister'. Rearmament was affected. The War Ministry was prepared to forgo until spring some of its allocation of foreign exchange so that foodstuffs could be imported.[277] Popular unrest was directly impinging on the regime's absolute priority. Hitler had cause for concern.[278]

As the domestic problems deepened, however, the Abyssinian crisis, causing disarray in the League of Nations, presented Hitler with new opportunities to look to foreign-policy success. He was swiftly alert to the potential for breaking out of Germany's international isolation, driving a further deep wedge between the Stresa signatories, and attaining, perhaps, a further revision of Versailles. Given the domestic situation, a foreign-policy triumph would, moreover, be most welcome. Already in August, he had expressed eager anticipation of what he saw as a certain war about to take place in Abyssinia. He outlined in Goebbels's presence how he saw foreign-policy plans developing: 'with England, eternal alliance. Good relationship with Poland . . . Expansion to the east. The Baltic belongs to us . . . Conflicts Italy-Abyssinia-England, then Japan-Russia imminent.' Within a few years would arrive 'our great historic hour. We must be ready then.' 'Grandiose perspective,' added Goebbels. 'We're all deeply moved.'[279] Less than two months later, with the Italian war in Abyssinia now a reality, Goebbels recorded Hitler's view, expressed to ministers and army leaders, that 'everything is coming for us three years too soon'. He emphasized, however, the opportunity that Germany now faced: 'Rearm and get ready. Europe is on the move again. If we're clever, we'll be the winners.'[280]

But the rearmament drive was now seriously threatened by the food crisis. In spring 1936 Hitler again personally intervened, in the face of Schacht's bitter objections, to allocate Darré once more scarce foreign currency – 60 million Reich Marks on this occasion – for the import of seed-oil.[281] The armaments position was becoming desperate. Schacht had to explain to Blomberg in December that an increase in raw-material imports was out of the question. By early 1936, available supplies of raw materials for rearmament had shrunk to a precariously low level. Only one to two months' supplies were left. Schacht demanded a slow-down in the pace of rearmament.[282]

As Hitler entered his fourth year as Chancellor, the economic situation posed a real threat to rearmament plans. At the very time that international developments encouraged the most rapid expansion possible, the food crisis – and the social unrest it had stirred – was sharply applying the brakes to it. Other indicators were also discouraging. Fears of a new rise in unemployment seemed likely to be borne out. In January 1936 the Reich Labour Ministry was gloomily reporting unemployment still running at around 2.5 million, with, it seemed, little prospect of a further lasting reduction.[283] Any slow-down in rearmament, as Goerdeler and Schacht were advocating, would inevitably bring increased unemployment in its train. Politically, the problems of the winter had given new life to the underground KPD, while reports from within the NSDAP repeatedly emphasized the poor morale and low spirits of party members.[284] It was little wonder that Hitler and other Nazi leaders had been seriously concerned about the possible consequences of a lasting period of food shortages, rising prices, and social tension, both for domestic stability and for foreign-policy ambitions. Almost two years later, he would remark that a renewed food crisis, without adequate foreign exchange to master it, would amount to a 'waning point (*Schwächungsmoment*) of the regime'. He saw this as all the more reason to hasten expansion to gain 'living-space'.[285]

In early 1936, too, domestic as well as foreign-policy considerations almost certainly played a part in the timing of Hitler's next big gamble: to destroy what was left of the Versailles and Locarno treaties by reoccupying the demilitarized Rhineland.

Certainly, that was the view of Foreign Minister Neurath. Speaking to Ulrich von Hassell, German ambassador in Rome, who had been urgently summoned (for the second time within a few days) to Berlin on 18 February to discuss the Rhineland question, Neurath was of the opinion that 'for Hitler in the first instance domestic motives were decisive (*maßgebend*)'. Hitler, he went on, 'felt the deterioration of mood in favour of the regime and was looking for a new national slogan to fire the masses again'. The usual election, alongside a plebiscite, would be the way, the Foreign Minister presumed.[286] Hitler himself spoke openly of his domestic motives at a meeting with Hassell that evening, describing how he wanted to couch his appeal 'both abroad, as well as to his own nation'.[287] Weeks later, Hassell remained sure that domestic considerations had been dominant in Hitler's mind, and that the timing to coincide with 'Heroes' Memorial Day' on 8 March had been determined in order to maximize the propaganda effect.[288]

Hitler needed no convincing of the domestic advantages and propaganda capital to be gained from a dramatic national triumph. It would certainly offer an opportunity to deflect from the problems of the previous winter – the 'food crisis', the escalating 'Church struggle'. The sagging morale could be dispelled overnight, the regime's position strengthened at home as well as abroad, Hitler's own popularity still further enhanced. In the Rhineland

itself, where reports had been painting a dismal picture of especially unfavourable economic conditions, and where clashes between the party and the
Catholic Church were seriously undermining support for the regime – never
specially strong in this area – the abolition of the demilitarized zone through
unilateral German action was certain of a rapturous welcome.[289] A step
which could unquestionably – as the Foreign Ministry knew – have been
accomplished through patient diplomacy within a year or two was, then,
undertaken with all the risk and drama of a military coup at least in part
because of the notable propaganda gains Hitler saw to be made from a
sudden coup. As Neurath had foreseen, the elections and plebiscite immediately called for 29 March underlined the domestic considerations involved.
The masses could be reinvigorated, sagging morale among the party membership dispelled, activists again given activity.[290]

As on other occasions, domestic and foreign-policy considerations were
closely intertwined in Hitler's thinking. The domestic advantages would
not have weighed so heavily had not international circumstances, framed
by the Abyssinian crisis, opened up an opportunity to strike which Hitler
felt he could not miss.

V

Under the terms of the 1919 peace settlement, the German Reich had been
prohibited from erecting fortifications, stationing troops, or undertaking
any military preparations on the left bank of the Rhine and within a
50 kilometre strip on the right bank. The status of the demilitarized Rhineland
had subsequently been endorsed by the Locarno Pact of 1925, which Germany
had signed. Any unilateral alteration of that status by Germany would not
only amount to a devastating breach of the post-war settlement and reneging
on an international agreement; it would also threaten the very basis of
western security which that settlement had endeavoured to establish. From a
German nationalist perspective, however, the current status of the Rhineland
was intolerable.

The remilitarization of the Rhineland would have been on the agenda of
any German nationalist government. The army viewed it as essential for
the rearmament plans it had established in December 1933, and for western
defence.[291] The Foreign Ministry presumed the demilitarized status would
be ended by negotiation at some point. Diplomats were aware that it would
have been done away with when Germany reintroduced military service,

had not caution prevailed because of its anchorage in the Locarno Pact as well as the Versailles Treaty.[292] Hitler had talked confidentially of the abolition of the demilitarized zone as early as 1934. He spoke of it again, in broad terms, in summer 1935. By the end of the year, the French were reckoning that they would soon face a *fait accompli* in the Rhineland. Hitler referred in a meeting with the British Ambassador on 13 December to the need to end the demilitarized zone, saying he regretted not having taken the step along with the introduction of conscription the previous March. Around that time, Hitler discussed with his military advisers the problems that might arise from reoccupying the zone.[293] The opportunity was by then beginning to present itself. However likely the reoccupation would have been within the next year or two, the seizing of that opportunity, the timing and character of the coup, were Hitler's. They bore his hallmark at all points.

The opportunity was provided by Mussolini. As we have noted, his Abyssinian adventure, provoking the League of Nations' condemnation of an unprovoked attack on a member-state and the imposition of economic sanctions, broke the fragile Stresa Front. Italy, faced with a pessimistic military outlook, sanctions starting to bite, and looking for friends, turned away from France and Britain, towards Germany. The stumbling-block to good relations had since 1933 been the Austrian question. Since the Dollfuss assassination in mid-1934, the climate had been frosty. This now swiftly altered. Mussolini signalled in January 1936 that he had nothing against Austria in effect becoming a satellite of Germany.[294] The path to the 'Axis' immediately opened up. Later the same month he publicly claimed the French and British talk of possible joint military action against Italy in the Mediterranean – not that this was in reality ever likely – had destroyed the balance of Locarno, and could only lead to the collapse of the Locarno system. Hitler took note. Then, in an interview with Ambassador Hassell, Mussolini indicated that, for Italy, Stresa was 'finally dead', and that in the event of sharper sanctions, Italy would leave the League of Nations, thereby effectively killing the Locarno agreement. He acknowledged to Hassell that Italy would offer no support for France and Britain should Hitler decide to take action in response to the ratification of the Franco-Soviet mutual assistance pact, currently before the French Chamber of Deputies, and viewed by Berlin as a breach of Locarno.[295] The message was clear: from Italy's point of view, Germany could re-enter the Rhineland with impunity.

The Abyssinian crisis had also damaged Anglo-French relations, and driven the two democracies further apart. This was particularly the case after the storm of protest once news had leaked out in December 1935 of the proposed Hoare–Laval Plan (named after Sir Samuel Hoare and Pierre Laval, the British and French Foreign Ministers) – rewarding Italy's aggression (in a foretaste of what would happen in a different context at Munich in 1938) by offering it two-thirds of Abyssinian territory.[296] The French government realized that a move to remilitarize the Rhineland was inevitable. Most observers tipped autumn 1936, once the Olympics were out of the way. Few thought Hitler would take great risks over the Rhineland when conventional diplomacy would ultimately succeed. Ministers rejected independent military action against flagrant German violation. In any case, the French military leadership – grossly exaggerating German armed strength – had made it plain that they opposed military retaliation, and that the reaction to any *fait accompli* should be purely political.[297] The truth was: the French had no stomach for a fight over the Rhineland. And Hitler and the German Foreign Office sensed this.[298] Soundings had also led Hitler and Neurath to a strong presumption that Britain, too, would refrain from any military action in the event of a coup. They saw Britain as for the time being weakened militarily, preoccupied politically with domestic affairs and with the Abyssinian crisis, unwilling to regard the preservation of the demilitarization of the Rhineland as a vital British interest, and possessing some sympathy for German demands.[299] The chances of success in a swift move to remilitarize the Rhineland were, therefore, high; the likelihood of military retaliation by France or Britain relatively low. That was, of course, as long as the assessment in Berlin of the likely reactions of the European powers was correct. Nothing was certain. Not all Hitler's advisers favoured the risk he was increasingly prepared to take without delay. But Hitler had been proved right in his boldness when leaving the League of Nations in 1933 and reintroducing conscription in 1935. He had gained confidence. His role in the Rhineland crisis was still more assertive, less than ever ready to bow to the caution recommended by the military and diplomats.[300]

Rumours were rife in Berlin at the beginning of February that Hitler was planning to march troops into the Rhineland in the near future.[301] Nothing at that point had been decided. Hitler pondered the matter while he was in Garmisch-Partenkirchen for the opening of the Winter Olympics on 6 February.[302] He invited objections, particularly from the Foreign Office. During February, he discussed the pros and cons with Neurath, Blomberg, Fritsch, Ribbentrop, Göring, then with Hassell, the ambassador in Rome. A wider circle within the Foreign Office and military leadership were aware of the pending decision. Fritsch and Beck were opposed; Blomberg as usual went along with Hitler. Foreign Minister Neurath also had grave doubts.

He thought 'speeding up' the action was not worth the risk. Though it was not likely that Germany would face military retaliation, further international isolation would be the result. Hassell also argued that there was no hurry, since there would be future chances to abolish the demilitarized zone. Both were of the view that Hitler should at least await the ratification of the French–Soviet Pact by the Senate in Paris. This, as an alleged breach of Locarno, was to serve as the pretext. Hitler preferred to strike after ratification by the Chamber of Deputies, without waiting for the Senate.[303] Whatever the caution of the career diplomats, Hitler was, as always, egged on in the most unctuous fashion by the sycophantic Ribbentrop.[304]

Hitler told Hassell that the reoccupation of the Rhineland was 'from a military point of view an absolute necessity'. He had originally had 1937 in mind for such a step. But the favourable international constellation, the advantage of the French–Soviet Pact (given the anti-Soviet feeling in Britain and France) as the occasion, and the fact that the military strength of the other powers, especially of the Russians, was on the increase and would soon alter the military balance, were reasons for acting sooner, not later. He did not believe there would be military retaliation. At worst there might be economic sanctions.[305] At discussions on 19 February, Hassell argued that the change for the better in Italy's fortunes in Abyssinia and the dropping of oil sanctions had lessened the chances of Italian support. Hitler countered by stressing the disadvantages of delay. 'Attack in this case, too,' he characteristically argued – to 'lively assent from Ribbentrop' – 'was the better strategy.' He would use the Franco–Russian Pact as a pretext, and offer a seemingly generous package – continuation of the demilitarized zone on both sides, a three-power air pact, and non-aggression pact with France – to the western powers. There was little chance that it would prove acceptable. Hassell had even before this already formed the view that Hitler was 'more than 50 per cent determined' to act. The sceptical Fritsch also thought by the middle of the month that the decision had been taken. Neurath was by this time also resigned to the move, whatever his reservations.[306]

But Hitler continued to waver. His arguments had failed to convince the diplomats and military leaders. The sycophantic Ribbentrop was in favour, Blomberg nervously supportive. Otherwise, the advice he was receiving favoured caution, not boldness. This was the case as late as the end of February. However determined Hitler was on an early strike, the precise timing still had to be decided. On 27 February, remilitarizing the Rhineland was the topic at lunch. Göring and Goebbels had both joined Hitler. 'Still somewhat too early,' summed up Goebbels.[307] The following day, Hitler remained undecided. Goebbels advised him to wait till 'the Russian pact is perfect', meaning until it had been ratified by the French Senate.[308] Later that day, Goebbels accompanied Hitler to Munich, discussing the Rhineland question on the train. 'The Führer still wavering (*unschlüssig*),' noted Goebbels in his diary. He himself continued to argue for a delay until the Senate's ratification. There would be further talks next day before Hitler would decide.[309] At lunch on 29 February, he had yet to make up his mind.

But the following day, Sunday, 1 March, with Munich bathed in beautiful spring-like weather, Hitler turned up at the hotel where Goebbels was staying in a good mood. The decision had been taken. 'It's another critical moment, but now is the time for action,' wrote Goebbels. 'Fortune favours the brave! He who dares nothing wins nothing.'[310]

The next day, 2 March, Goebbels attended a meeting in the Reich Chancellery at 11a.m. The heads of the armed forces – Göring, Blomberg, Fritsch and Raeder – were there. So was Ribbentrop. Hitler told them he had made his decision. The Reichstag would be summoned for Saturday, 7 March. There the proclamation of the remilitarization of the Rhineland would be made. At the same time, he would offer Germany's re-entry into the League of Nations, an air pact, and a non-aggression treaty with France. The acute danger would thereby be reduced, Germany's isolation prevented, and sovereignty once and for all restored. The Reichstag would be dissolved and new elections announced, with foreign-policy slogans. Fritsch had to arrange for the troop transport during Friday night. 'Everything has to happen as quick as lightning.' Troop movements would be camouflaged by making them look like SA and Labour Front exercises. The military leaders had their doubts.[311] Members of the cabinet were informed individually only on the afternoon of the following day, Frick and Heß as late as the evening. By then, invitations to the Reichstag had already gone out – but, to keep up the deception, only to a beer evening.[312] By Wednesday Hitler was working on his Reichstag speech; Goebbels was already preparing the election campaign. Warning voices from the Foreign Ministry could still be registered on the Thursday. By Friday evening Hitler had completed his speech. The cabinet met to be informed for the first time collectively of what was planned. Goebbels announced that the Reichstag would meet at noon the next day.[313] The only item on the agenda was a government declaration.[314] Plans for the election campaign were finalized. Workers in the Propaganda Ministry were not permitted to leave the building overnight to prevent any leaks. 'Success lies in surprise,' noted Goebbels. 'Berlin trembles with tension,' he added next morning.[315]

The Reichstag, too, was tense as Hitler rose, amid enormous applause, to speak. The Kroll Opera, where the Reichstag still met, close to the ruins of the building that had burned down in 1933, was packed to the rafters. Hundreds of pressmen filled the galleries. Numerous diplomats were present – though the English and French ambassadors, guessing what was coming, had stayed away. On the platform, among the members of the cabinet, Blomberg was visibly white with nerves. None were visible in Göring, sitting behind Hitler and looking about to burst with pride. Goebbels read a typed copy of the speech as Hitler spoke. The deputies, all in Nazi uniform, still did not know what to expect.[316]

The speech was aimed not just at those present in the Kroll Opera, but at the millions of radio listeners. After a lengthy preamble denouncing Versailles, restating Germany's demands for equality and security, and declaring his peaceful aims, a screaming onslaught on Bolshevism brought wild applause. This took Hitler into his argument that the Soviet–French Pact had invalidated Locarno. He read out the memorandum which Neurath had given to the ambassadors of the Locarno signatories that morning, stating that the Locarno Treaty had lost its meaning. He paused for a brief moment, then continued: 'Germany regards itself, therefore, as for its part no longer bound by this dissolved pact . . . In the interest of the primitive rights of a people to the security of its borders and safeguarding of its defence capability, the German Reich government has therefore from today restored the full and unrestricted sovereignty of the Reich in the demilitarized zone of the Rhineland.'[317] At this, wrote William Shirer, witnessing the scene, the 600 Reichstag deputies, 'little men with big bodies and bulging necks and cropped hair and pouched bellies and brown uniforms and heavy boots, little men of clay in his fine hands, leap to their feet like automatons, their right arms upstretched in the Nazi salute, and scream "*Heil's*"'.[318] When the tumult eventually subsided, Hitler advanced his 'peace proposals' for Europe: a non-aggression pact with Belgium and France; demilitarization of *both* sides of their joint borders; an air-pact; non-aggression treaties, similar to that with Poland, with other eastern neighbours; and Germany's return to the League of Nations.[319] Some thought Hitler was offering too much.[320] They had no need to worry. As Hitler knew, there was not the slightest chance of his 'offer' proving acceptable. He moved to the climax. 'Men, deputies of the German Reichstag! In this historic hour when in the western provinces of the Reich German troops are at this moment moving into their future peace-time garrisons, we all unite in two sacred inner vows.' He was interrupted by a deafening tumult from the assembled deputies.

'They spring, yelling and crying, to their feet,' William Shirer recorded. 'The audience in the galleries does the same, all except a few diplomats and about fifty of us correspondents. Their hands are raised in slavish salute, their faces now contorted with hysteria, their mouths wide open, shouting, shouting, their eyes, burning with fanaticism, glued on the new god, the Messiah. The Messiah plays his role superbly.'[321] Patiently he waited for silence. Then he made the two vows: never to yield to force when the honour of the people was at stake; and to strive for better understanding with Germany's European neighbours. He repeated his promise of the previous year, that Germany had no territorial demands to make in Europe.[322] But outside Germany trust in Hitler's word was beginning to wear thin.[323]

Around 1p.m., just as Hitler was reaching the high-point of his peroration, German troops approached the Hohenzollern Bridge in Cologne.[324] Two plane-loads of journalists, hand-picked by Goebbels, were there to record the historic moment.[325] Word had quickly got round Cologne that morning. Thousands packed the banks of the Rhine and thronged the streets near the bridge. The soldiers received a delirious reception as they crossed. Women strewed the way with flowers. Catholic priests blessed them. Cardinal Schulte offered praise to Hitler for 'sending back our army'.[326] The 'Church struggle' was temporarily forgotten.

The force to be sent into the demilitarized zone numbered no more than 30,000 regulars, augmented by units of the Landespolizei. A mere 3,000 men were to penetrate deep into the zone. The remainder had taken up positions for the most part behind the eastern bank of the Rhine. The forward troops were to be prepared to withdraw within an hour in the event of likely military confrontation with the French.[327] There was no chance of this. As we have seen, it had been ruled out in advance by French military leaders. French intelligence – counting SA, SS, and other Nazi formations as soldiers – had come up with an extraordinary figure of 295,000 for the German military force in the Rhineland.[328] In reality, one French division would have sufficed to terminate Hitler's adventure. 'Had the French then marched into the Rhineland,' Hitler was reported to have commented more than once at a later date, 'we would have had to withdraw again with our tails between our legs (*mit Schimpf und Schande*). The military force at our disposal would not have sufficed even for limited resistance.' The forty-eight hours following the entry of the German troops into the Rhineland were, he claimed, the most tense of his life.[329] He was speaking, as usual, for effect. Hans Frank recorded similar comments. 'If the French had really been serious, it would have become the greatest political defeat for me,' he recalled

Hitler declaring.[330] But as the Dictator had correctly predicted, in fact, neither the French nor the British had the will for a fight. Already by the early evening of 7 March, it was plain that the coup had been a complete success. 'With the Führer,' noted Goebbels. 'Comments from abroad excellent. France wants to involve (*befassen*) the League of Nations. That's fine. So it [France] won't take action. That's the main thing. Nothing else matters . . . The reaction in the world was predicted. The Führer is immensely happy . . . The entry has gone according to plan . . . The Führer beams. England remains passive. France won't act alone. Italy is disappointed and America uninterested. We have sovereignty again over our own land.'[331]

The risk had, in fact, been only a moderate one. The western democracies had lacked both the will and the unity needed to make intervention likely. But the triumph for Hitler was priceless. Not only had he outwitted the major powers, which had again shown themselves incapable of adjusting to a style of power-politics that did not play by the rules of conventional diplomacy. He had scored a further victory over the conservative forces at home in the military and the Foreign Office. As in March 1935 the caution and timidity in the armed forces' leadership and among the career diplomats had proved misplaced. The Rhineland was the biggest reward yet for boldness. There had been no opposition from the military or Foreign Office. Remilitarization of the Rhineland was wanted by all. Objections had been no more than expressions of anxiety about timing and method. From Hitler's point of view, it was simply another case of 'cold feet'. His contempt for the 'professionals' in the army and Foreign Office deepened. His boundless egomania gained another massive boost.

This was not diminished by alarmist warnings of imminent danger of war from Leopold von Hoesch, German ambassador in London, a few days later, and Blomberg's loss of nerve.[332] By then, Hitler could afford to sweep aside such alarmism. Condemnation by the League of Nations on 19 March was also an irrelevance.[333] Locarno had been destroyed; Versailles was in tatters. The crisis was long past. 'Am I happy, my God am I happy that it has gone so smoothly!' Hitler remarked to Hans Frank as they sat in his special train, passing through the Ruhr, looking out on the furnaces of the steel mills lighting up the night sky, on the way back to Berlin from his triumphant visit to Cologne at the end of the month.[334]

VI

The popular euphoria at the news of the reoccupation of the Rhineland far outstripped even the feelings of national celebration in 1933 or 1935 following previous triumphs. People were beside themselves with delight. The initial widespread fear that Hitler's action would bring war was rapidly dissipated.[335] It was almost impossible not to be caught up in the infectious mood of joy. It extended far beyond firm Nazi supporters. Opposition groups were demoralized.[336] New admiration for Hitler, support for his defiance of the west, attack on Versailles, restoration of sovereignty over German territory, and promises of peace were – sometimes grudgingly – recorded by Sopade observers.[337] The Hamburg middle-class housewife Luise Solmitz, a conservative nationalist enthusiast dismayed in 1935 to find her husband, a former officer of part-Jewish descent, and their daughter rejected as German citizens under the Nuremberg Laws, did not conceal her praise for Hitler. 'I was totally overwhelmed by the events of this hour . . . overjoyed at the entry march of our soldiers, at the greatness of Hitler and the power of his speech, the force of this man.' A few years earlier, 'when demoralization (*Zersetzung*) ruled amongst us,' she wrote, 'we would not have dared contemplate such deeds. Again and again the Führer faces the world with a *fait accompli*. Along with the world, the individual holds his breath. Where is Hitler heading, what will be the end, the climax of this speech, what boldness, what surprise will there be? And then it comes, blow on blow, action as stated without fear of his own courage. That is so strengthening . . . That is the deep, unfathomable secret of the Führer's nature . . . And he is always lucky.'[338]

The 'election' campaign that followed the Rhineland spectacular – new elections had been set for 29 March – was no more than a triumphant procession for Hitler. Ecstatic, adoring crowds greeted him on his passage through Germany. Goebbels outdid himself in the saturation coverage of his propaganda – carried into the most outlying villages by armies of activists trumpeting the Führer's great deeds. 'The Dictator lets himself be bound by the people to the policy that he wanted,' summed up one Sopade agent.[339] The 'election' result – 98.9 per cent 'for the List and therefore for the Führer' – gave Hitler what he wanted: the overwhelming majority of the German people united behind him, massive popular support for his position at home and abroad.[340] Though the official figures owed something to electoral 'irregularities', and a good deal more to fear and intimidation, the overwhelming backing for Hitler – his enormous popularity now further bolstered by the Rhineland coup – could not be gainsaid.[341] The problems and concerns, the grumbles and complaints, of the long preceding autumn and winter had suddenly – if only fleetingly – evaporated.

The Rhineland triumph left a significant mark on Hitler. The change that Dietrich, Wiedemann and others saw in him dated from around this time. From now on he was more than ever a believer in his own infallibility. Pseudo-religious symbolism came to infuse his rhetoric. A few months later, at the Nuremberg 'Party Rally of Honour', messianic allusions from the New Testament would abound in his address to party functionaries: 'How deeply we feel once more in this hour the miracle that has brought us together! Once you heard the voice of a man, and it spoke to your hearts; it awakened you, and you followed that voice . . . Now that we meet here, we are all filled with the wonder of this gathering. Not every one of you can see me and I do not see each one of you. But I feel you, and you feel me! It is faith in our nation that has made us little people great . . . You come out of the little world of your daily struggle for life, and of your struggle for Germany and for our nation, to experience this feeling for once: Now we are together, we are with him and he is with us, and now we are Germany!'[342] Two days later, still in messianic mode, he saw a mystical fate uniting him and the German people: 'That you have found me . . . among so many millions is the miracle of our time! And that I have found you, that is Germany's fortune!'[343]

A sense of his own greatness had been instilled in Hitler by his admirers since the early 1920s. He had readily embraced the aura attached to him. It had offered insatiable nourishment for his already incipient all-consuming egomania. Since then, the internal, and above all the foreign-policy successes, since 1933, accredited by growing millions to the Führer's genius, had immensely magnified the tendency. Hitler swallowed the boundless adulation. He became the foremost believer in his own Führer cult. Hubris – that overweening arrogance which courts disaster – was inevitable. The point where nemesis takes over had been reached by 1936.

Germany had been conquered. It was not enough. Expansion beckoned. World peace would soon be threatened. Everything was coming about as he alone had foreseen it, thought Hitler. He had come to regard himself as ordained by Providence. 'I go with the certainty of a sleepwalker along the path laid out for me by Providence,' he told a huge gathering in Munich on 14 March.[344] His mastery over all other power-groups within the regime was by now well-nigh complete, his position unassailable, his popularity immense. Few at this point had the foresight to realize that the path laid out by Providence led into the abyss.

GLOSSARY OF ABBREVIATIONS

AdR	*Akten der Reichskanzlei*
ADGB	Allgemeiner Deutscher Gewerkschaftsbund (General German Trade Union Federation)
AG	Arbeitsgemeinschaft (Working Community)
AO	Auslandsorganisation (Foreign Organization of the Nazi Party)
BAK	Bundesarchiv Koblenz (German Federal Archives)
Bayern	*Bayern in der NS-Zeit*, ed. Martin Broszat *et al.*, 6 vols., Munich, 1977–83
BDC	Berlin Document Center
BDM	Bund Deutscher Mädel (League of German Girls; girls' organization within the Hitler Youth Movement)
BHStA	Bayerisches Hauptstaatsarchiv (Bavarian Main State Archive)
BVP	Bayerische Volkspartei (Bavarian People's Party)
DBFP	*Documents on British Foreign Policy, 1919–1939, 2nd Series, 1930–1937*, London, 1950–57
DAF	Deutsche Arbeitsfront (German Labour Front)
DAP	Deutsche Arbeiterpartei (German Workers' Party)
DBS	*Deutschland-Berichte der Sozialdemokratischen Partei Deutschlands, 1934–1940,* 7 vols., Frankfurt am Main, 1980
DDP	Deutsche Demokratische Partei (German Democratic Party)
DGFP	*Documents on German Foreign Policy, 1918–1945, Series C (1933–1937). The Third Reich: First Phase*, London, 1957–66
DNF	Deutschnationale Front (German National Front)

DNVP	Deutschnationale Volkspartei (German National People's Party)
Domarus	Max Domarus (ed.), *Hitler. Reden und Proklamationen 1932–1945*, 2 vols., in 4 parts, Wiesbaden, 1973
DRZW	*Das Deutsche Reich und der Zweite Weltkrieg*, 6 vols. so far published, ed. Militärgeschichtliches Forschungsamt, Stuttgart, 1979–
DSP	Deutschsozialistische Partei (German-Socialist Party)
DVFB	Deutschvölkische Freiheitsbewegung (German Folkish (= ethnic-nationalist) Freedom Movement)
DVFP	Deutschvölkische Freiheitspartei (German Folkish Freedom Party)
DVP	Deutsche Volkspartei (German People's Party)
Gestapo	Geheime Staatspolizei (Secret State Police)
GS	Gendarmerie-Station (police station)
GVG	Großdeutsche Volksgemeinschaft (Greater German National Community)
HA	NSDAP-Hauptarchiv (the Nazi Party's archive, microfilm collection: see *NSDAP-Hauptarchiv. Guide to the Hoover Institution Microfilm Collection*, compiled by Grete Heinz and Agnes F. Peterson, Stanford, 1964)
Hitler-Prozeß	*Der Hitler-Prozeß 1924. Wortlaut der Hauptverhandlung vor dem Volksgericht München I, Teil I*, ed. Lothar Gruchmann and Reinhard Weber, assisted by Otto Gritschneder, Munich, 1997
HJ	Hitlerjugend (Hitler Youth)
HMB	Halbmonatsbericht (Fortnightly Report)
IfZ	Institut für Zeitgeschichte, München (Institute of Contemporary History, Munich)
IML/ZPA	Institut für Marxismus-Leninismus, Zentrales Parteiarchiv (East Berlin, GDR)
IMT	*Trial of the Major War Criminals before the International Military Tribunal*, 42 vols., Nuremberg, 1947–9
JK	Eberhard Jäckel and Axel Kuhn (eds.), *Hitler. Sämtliche Aufzeichnungen 1905–1924*, Stuttgart, 1980

JMH	*Journal of Modern History*
KPD	Kommunistische Partei Deutschlands (Communist Party of Germany)
LB	Lagebericht (Situation Report)
MB	Monatsbericht (Monthly Report)
MF/OF	Mittelfranken/Oberfranken (Middle and Upper Franconia, administrative regions of Bavaria)
MK	Adolf Hitler, *Mein Kampf*, 876–880th reprint, Munich, 1943
MK Watt	Adolf Hitler, *Mein Kampf*, London, 1969, trans. by Ralph Manheim, with an introduction by D. C. Watt, paperback edition, London, 1973
Monologe	*Adolf Hitler: Monologe im Führerhauptquartier 1941–1944. Die Aufzeichnungen Heinrich Heims*, ed. Werner Jochmann, Hamburg, 1980
NA	National Archives, Washington
Nbg	Nürnberg (Nuremberg)
NCA	*Nazi Conspiracy and Aggression*, ed. Office of the United States Chief of Counsel for Prosecution of Axis Criminality, 9 vols. and 2 supplementary vols., Washington D.C., 1946–8
NB/OP	Niederbayern/Oberpfalz (Lower Bavaria/Upper Palatinate, administrative regions of Bavaria)
NSBO	Nationalsozialistische Betriebszellenorganisation (Nazi Factory Cell Organization)
NSDAP	Nationalsozialistische Deutsche Arbeiterpartei (Nazi Party)
NSDStB	Nationalsozialistischer Deutscher Studentenbund (National Socialist German Students' Federation)
NSFB	Nationalsozialistiche Freiheitsbewegung (National Socialist Freedom Movement)
NSFP	Nationalsozialistische Freiheitspartei (National Socialist Freedom Party)
NS-Hago	Nationalsozialistische Handwerks-, Handels-und Gewerbeorganisation (Nazi Craft, Commerce, and Trade Organization)

OB	Oberbayern (Upper Bavaria)
Pd Mü.	Polizeidirektion München (Munich Police Administration)
PRO	Public Record Office
RGBl	*Reichsgesetzblatt*
RGO	Revolutionäre Gewerkschafts-Opposition (Revolutionary Trade Union Opposition; Communist trades union organization)
RP	Regierungspräsident (Government President, head of state regional administration)
RSA	*Hitler. Reden, Schriften, Anordnungen: Februar 1925 bis Januar 1933*, ed. Institut für Zeitgeschichte, 5 vols. in 12 parts, Munich/London/New York/Paris, 1992–8
SA	Sturmabteilung (Storm Troop)
SD	Sicherheitsdienst (Security Service)
Sopade	Sozialdemokratische Partei Deutschlands (exiled SPD executive based in Prague (1933–8), then Paris (1938–40), and from 1940 onwards in London)
SS	Schutzstaffel (lit. Protection Squad)
SPD	Sozialdemokratische Partei Deutschlands (Social Democratic Party of Germany)
StA	Staatsarchiv (State Archive)
StdF	Stellvertreter des Führers (Führer's Deputy)
TBJG	*Die Tagebücher von Joseph Goebbels. Sämtliche Fragmente, Teil I, Aufzeichnungen 1924–1941*, 4 Bde., ed. Elke Fröhlich, Munich etc., 1987
Tb Reuth	*Joseph Goebbels. Tagebücher 1924–1945*, 5 Bde., ed. Ralf Georg Reuth, Munich/Zurich, 1992.
VB	*Völkischer Beobachter*
VfZ	*Vierteljahrshefte für Zeitgeschichte*
VVM	Vaterländische Vereine Münchens (Patriotic Associations of Munich)
VVVB	Vereinigte Vaterländische Verbände Bayerns (United Patriotic Associations of Bavaria)

NOTES

1. The title of the masterly analysis by Eric Hobsbawm, *Age of Extremes. The Short Twentieth Century, 1914–1991*, London, 1994.
2. An attempt to speculate counter-factually on how different world history would have been had Hitler been killed when the car in which he was travelling was struck by a large lorry in 1930 is offered by Henry A. Turner, *Geißel des Jahrhunderts. Hitler und seine Hinterlassenschaft*, Berlin, 1989. The accident is described in Otto Wagener, *Hitler aus nächster Nähe. Aufzeichnungen eines Vertrauten 1929–1932*, ed. Henry A. Turner, 2nd edn, Kiel, 1987, 155–6.
3. Karl Marx, *The Eighteenth Brumaire of Louis Bonaparte*, Moscow, 1954, 10.
4. A number of general analyses of the history of the Third Reich in recent years have made impressive advances in synthesizing and interpreting a vast outpouring of detailed research. These include: Hans-Ulrich Thamer, *Verführung und Gewalt. Deutschland 1933–1945*, Berlin, 1986; Norbert Frei, *National Socialist Rule in Germany: the Führer State 1933–1945*, Oxford/Cambridge Mass., 1993 (an extended version in English of the original German edition, *Der Führerstaat. Nationalsozialistische Herrschaft 1933 bis 1945*, Munich, 1987); Jost Dülffer, *Deutsche Geschichte 1933–1945. Führerglaube und Vernichtungskrieg*, Stuttgart/Berlin/Cologne, 1992 (Engl.: *Nazi Germany 1933–1945: Faith and Annihilation*, London, 1996); Karlheinz Weißmann, *Der Weg in den Abgrund 1933–1945*, Berlin, 1995; Klaus P. Fischer, *Nazi Germany: a New History*, London, 1995; and, a particularly valuable interpretative synthesis, Ludolf Herbst, *Das nationalsozialistische Deutschland 1933–1945*, Frankfurt am Main, 1996.
5. See the comment, still thought-provoking, of Wolfgang Sauer, 'National Socialism: Totalitarianism or Fascism?', *American Historical Review*, 73 (1967–8), 404–24; here 408: 'In Nazism, the historian faces a phenomenon that leaves him no way but rejection, whatever his individual position. There is literally no voice worth considering that disagrees on this matter . . . Does not such fundamental rejection imply a fundamental lack of understanding?'

6. This was the essential criticism of the incisive review of Joachim C. Fest, *Hitler. Eine Biographie*, Frankfurt am Main/Berlin/Vienna, 1973, by Hermann Graml, 'Probleme einer Hitler-Biographie. Kritische Bemerkungen zu Joachim C. Fest', *VfZ*, 22 (1974), 76–92. Graml regards (78, 84) the problems posed by the writing of a biography of Hitler – integrating a history of the individual into an analysis of his impact on German society – as 'insoluble'. A harsh judgement on biographies of Hitler in general, in a thoughtful and interesting approach to the social sources of Hitler's power, was also offered by Michael Kater, 'Hitler in a Social Context', *Central European History*, 14 (1981), 243–72, here esp. 243–6. A less pessimistic evaluation is provided by Gregor Schöllgen, 'Das Problem einer Hitler-Biographie. Überlegungen anhand neuerer Darstellungen des Falles Hitler', *Neue politische Literatur*, 23 (1978), 421–34, reprinted in Karl Dietrich Bracher, Manfred Funke, and Hans-Adolf Jacobsen (eds.), *Nationalsozialistische Diktatur 1933–1945. Eine Bilanz*, Bonn, 1983, 687–705.

7. Gerhard Schreiber, *Hitler. Interpretationen 1923–1983. Ergebnisse, Methoden und Probleme der Forschung*, Darmstadt, 1984, 13.

8. Guido Knopp, *Hitler. Eine Bilanz*, Berlin, 1995, 9.

9. The essential survey is that of Schreiber, *Hitler. Interpretationen*; a more recent critical and thoughtful assessment of the interpretations advanced by biographers of Hitler is provided by John Lukacs, *The Hitler of History*, New York, 1997. See also Ron Rosenbaum, 'Explaining Hitler', *New Yorker*, 1 May 1995, 50–70. For further evaluations of the differing approaches, see Klaus Hildebrand, *Das Dritte Reich*, Munich/Vienna, 1979, 132–46, and Ian Kershaw, *The Nazi Dictatorship. Problems and Perspectives of Interpretation,* 3rd edn, London, 1993, chs. 4–6. Earlier historiographical analyses and attempts to address the problem of the 'Hitler factor' were provided by: Klaus Hildebrand, 'Der "Fall" Hitler', *Neue politische Literatur*, 14 (1969), 375–86; Klaus Hildebrand, 'Hitlers Ort in der Geschichte des Preußisch-Deutschen Nationalstaates', *Historische Zeitschrift*, 217 (1973), 584–631; Wolf-Rüdiger Hartmann, 'Adolf Hitler: Möglichkeiten seiner Deutung', *Archiv für Sozialgeschichte*, 15 (1975), 521–35; Eberhard Jäckel, 'Rückblick auf die sogenannte Hitler-Welle', *Geschichte in Wissenschaft und Unterricht*, 28 (1977), 695–710; Andreas Hillgruber, 'Tendenzen, Ergebnisse und Perspektiven der gegenwärtigen Hitler-Forschung', *Historische Zeitschrift*, 226 (1978), 600–621; Wolfgang Michalka, 'Wege der Hitler-Forschung', *Quaderni di storia*, 8 (1978), 157–90, and 10 (1979), 125–51; John P. Fox, 'Adolf Hitler: the Continuing Debate', *International Affairs* (1979), 252–64; and William Carr, 'Historians and the Hitler Phenomenon', *German Life and Letters*, 34 (1981), 260–72.

10. Alan Bullock, *Hitler: a Study in Tyranny*, revised edn, Harmondsworth, 1962, 804. Bullock later completely revised his early views (see Rosenbaum, 67). The centrality of Hitler's ideology is fully incorporated into the analysis in Alan Bullock, *Hitler and Stalin. Parallel Lives*, London, 1991.

11. See, for example, the comment of Karl Dietrich Bracher, 'The Role of Hitler: Perspectives of Interpretation', in Walter Laqueur (ed.), *Fascism. A Reader's Guide,*

Harmondsworth, 1979, 193–212, here 201: 'It was indeed Hitler's *Weltanschauung* and nothing else that mattered in the end, as is seen from the terrible consequences of his racist anti-semitism in the planned murder of the Jews.' In the realm of foreign policy, the programmatic driving-force of Hitler's ideology is most strongly emphasized by Klaus Hildebrand, *Deutsche Außenpolitik 1933–1945. Kalkül oder Dogma?*, 4th edn, Stuttgart/Berlin/Cologne, 1980, 188–9. The internal coherence of Hitler's ideas was fully illustrated for the first time by Eberhard Jäckel, *Hitlers Weltanschauung. Entwurf einer Herrschaft*, Tübingen, 1969, extended and revised 4th edn, Stuttgart, 1991.

12. Cit. H. R. Trevor-Roper, *The Last Days of Hitler*, 3rd edn, London, 1962, 46.
13. This standard line of GDR historiography was nowhere more expressively captured than by Wolfgang Ruge, 'Monopolbourgeoisie, faschistischer Massenbasis und NS-Programmatik', in Dietrich Eichholtz and Kurt Gossweiler (eds.), *Faschismusforschung. Positionen, Probleme, Polemik*, Berlin (East), 1980, 125–55, who saw (141) *Mein Kampf* as having 'the role of a testimonial (*Empfehlungsschreiben*) to the great captains of industry (*Wirtschaftskapitäne*)', and spoke (144) of Hitler as the 'star agent' (*Staragenten*) of 'the most extreme monopolists (*Monopolherren*)' of big business. The full version of this interpretation is brought out in Wolfgang Ruge, *Das Ende von Weimar. Monopolkapital und Hitler*, Berlin (East), 1983, where Hitler is referred to (334, 336) as the 'compliant creature' (*willfährige Kreatur*) of the 'backers' (*Hintermänner*) from big business. Given such a premiss built into official state ideology, no biography of Hitler was possible in the GDR. Two historians who had produced the only general history of the Nazi Party to be published during the existence of the GDR (Kurt Pätzold and Manfred Weißbecker, *Geschichte der NSDAP*, Cologne, 1981; originally *Hakenkreuz und Totenkopf. Die Partei des Verbrechens*, Berlin (East), 1981) have subsequently brought out a personalized study of the German Dictator which had been impossible in their former State, expressly emphasizing (589) 'that the fascist Leader was no marionette' (Kurt Pätzold and Manfred Weißbecker, *Adolf Hitler. Eine politische Biographie*, Leipzig, 1995).
14. John Toland, *Adolf Hitler*, London, 1976, a work of 1,035 pages, begins with the comment (p.xiv): 'My book has no thesis.' Helmut Heiber, *Adolf Hitler. Eine Biographie*, Berlin, 1960, is far briefer but still a 'cradle-to-grave' description of Hitler's life which appears to lack a specific interpretative framework.
15. Joshua Rubenstein, *Hitler*, London, 1984, 87; Wulf Schwarzwäller, *The Unknown Hitler*, Bethesda, Maryland, 1989, 9. Guido Knopp's description (*Hitler, Eine Blianz*, 13) of Hitler as 'a sick swine' (*kranker Schweinehund*) might be seen to point in the same direction, though was actually framed within a multi-faceted attempt to grapple with the problem of understanding Hitler.
16. The descriptions are those, in turn, of Norman Rich, *Hitler's War Aims*, 2 vols., London, 1973–4, i.11, and Hans Mommsen, *Beamtentum im Dritten Reich*, Stuttgart, 1966, 98 n.26. The clash of these interpretations has been surveyed in Manfred Funke, *Starker oder schwacher Diktator? Hitlers Herrshaft und die Deutschen: Ein Essay*, Düsseldorf, 1989. See also Wolfgang Wippermann (ed.),

Kontroversen um Hitler, Frankfurt am Main, 1986, and Kershaw, *Nazi Dictatorship*, ch. 4.

17. Eberhard Jäckel has never deviated, in numerous publications, from the position that Hitler's rule was a 'monocracy', and 'sole rule' (*Alleinherrschaft*). See, for example, his *Hitler in History*, Hanover/London, 1984, 28–30; *Hitler's Herrschaft*, (1986) 2nd edn, Stuttgart, 1988, 59–65; and – strongly implied – *Das deutsche Jahrhundert. Eine historische Bilanz*, Stuttgart, 1996, 164. An emphatic argument against interpretations which diluted Hitler's 'monocracy' was advanced by Klaus Hildebrand, 'Monokratie oder Polykratie? Hitlers Herrschaft und das Dritte Reich', in Gerhard Hirschfeld and Lothar Kettenacker (eds.), *Der 'Führerstaat': Mythos und Realität. Studien zur Struktur und Politik des Dritten Reiches*, Stuttgart, 1981, 73–97.

18. Lines of interpretation which arise, most notably, from the numerous studies of Hans Mommsen and, to a lesser extent, of Martin Broszat. See especially Hans Mommsen, 'Hitlers Stellung im nationalsozialistischen Herrshaftssystem', in Hirschfeld and Kettenacker, 43–72, and his brief text *Adolf Hitler als 'Führer' der Nation*, Deutsches Institut für Fernstudien, Tübingen, 1984; also Martin Broszat, *Der Staat Hitlers*, Munich, 1969, and 'Soziale Motivation und Führer-Bindung des Nationalsozialismus', *VfZ*, 18 (1970), 392–409.

19. See Ernst Nolte's essays, 'Zwischen Geschichtslegende und Revisionismus?' and 'Vergangenheit, die nicht vergehen will', in *'Historikerstreit'. Die Dokumentation der Kontroverse um die Einzigartigkeit der nationalsozialistischen Judenverichtung*, Munich, 1987, 13–35, 39–47, and his *Der europäische Bürgerkrieg 1917–1945. Nationalsozialismus und Bolschewismus*, Berlin, 1987, esp. 501–2, 504, 506, 517.

20. Rainer Zitelmann, *Adolf Hitler. Eine politische Biographie*, Göttingen/Zurich, 1989, 9; and for the full unfolding of Hitler's statements over many years, on which the generalization rested, Rainer Zitelmann, *Hitler. Selbstverständnis eines Revolutionärs*, Hamburg/Leamington Spa/New York, 1987. See also the critical review by Reinhard Bollmus, 'Ein rationaler Diktator? Zu einer neuen Hitler-Biographie', *Die Zeit*, 22 September 1989, 45–6.

21. The thesis that Hitler's conscious intention was Germany's modernization was advanced in Rainer Zitelmann's essays, 'Nationalsozialismus und Moderne. Eine Zwischenbilanz', in Werner Süß (ed.), *Übergänge. Zeitgeschichte zwischen Utopie und Machbarkeit*, Berlin, 1990, 195–223, and 'Die totalitäre Seite der Moderne', in Michael Prinz and Rainer Zitelmann (eds.), *Nationalsozialismus und Modernisierung*, Darmstadt, 1991, 1–20.

22. Fest, *Hitler*, (paperback edn, 1976), 25.

23. The role of the individual – directed by the notion that 'men make history' – was a central feature of the German 'historicist' tradition which tended to idealize and heroize historical figures (notably Luther, Frederick the Great, and Bismarck) in its emphasis on the idea, intentions, and motives of great personalities as the framework of historical understanding. Even if 'greatness' could override conventional laws of morality, it was taken to embrace a certain – indefinable – nobility

of character. 'We cannot look, however imperfectly, on a great man,' wrote the British Germanophile biographer of Frederick the Great, Thomas Carlyle, himself much admired by Goebbels and Hitler, 'without gaining something by him. He is the living light-fountain, which it is good and pleasant to be near, . . . of native original insight, of manhood, and heroic nobleness.' (Cited, from Carlyle's 'Lecture One' 'On Heroes, Hero-Worship, and the Heroic in History', in Fritz Stern (ed.), *The Varieties of History. From Voltaire to the Present*, 2nd Macmillan edn, London, 1970, 101.) In the last weeks of the Third Reich, Goebbels spent time reading Carlyle's biography of Frederick the Great and recounted parts of it to Hitler who, the Propaganda Minister claimed, knew the book very well (*TBJG*, II.15, 384 (28 February 1945)).

24. See the 'aesthetic' more than moral doubts which Fest (*Hitler*, 19–20) emphasizes. Fest's answer to the question he himself raised (*Hitler*, 17): 'should he be called "great"?' is, accordingly, ambivalent. Elsewhere, however, he was less ambiguous. 'Any consideration of the personality and career of Adolf Hitler will for a long time to come be impossible without a feeling of moral outrage. Nevertheless he possesses historical greatness' (Joachim Fest, 'On Remembering Adolf Hitler', *Encounter*, 41 (October, 1973), 19–34, here 19). Fest's biography was written at a time when the biographical genre had fallen in Germany into disrepute, as part of the general rejection of the historicist tradition and its replacement by 'structural history' and 'historical social science' from the 1960s onwards. The introduction to his biography seems in part at least to have been a self-conscious defence against the contemporary scepticism. For the difficulties facing biography through the advance of 'structural history', see Imanuel Geiß, 'Die Rolle der Persönlichkeit in der Geschichte: Zwischen Überbewerten und Verdrängen', and Dieter Riesenberger, 'Biographie als historiographisches Problem', both in Michael Bosch (ed.), *Persönlichkeit und Struktur in der Geschichte*, Düsseldorf, 1977, 10–24, 25–39. Attempts to rehabilitate biography – though not of 'great' figures – as part of 'social' and 'mentality' history can be seen in Andreas Gestrich, Peter Knoch, and Helga Merkel, *Biographie – sozialgeschichtlich*, Göttingen, 1988.

25. Fest, 'On Remembering Adolf Hitler', 19, explained that what he saw as Hitler's 'greatness' lay chiefly in the fact that 'the things which happened in his time are inconceivable without him, in every respect and in every detail'.

26. Churchill's remark was his characterization of Russia in speaking of the uncertainties of Soviet actions in a broadcast he made on 1 October 1939 (Winston S. Churchill, *The Second World War, vol. 1: The Gathering Storm*, London, 1948, 403). I am grateful to Gitta Sereny for providing me with the reference.

27. Fest, *Hitler*, 697–741, devotes a chapter to a 'glance at an unperson' (*Blick auf eine Unperson*).

28. Cited in Dmitri Volkogonov, *Stalin: Triumph and Tragedy*, London, 1991, xxvi. This is a somewhat loose translation of the passage, defending the prowess and virtue of Alexander the Great, in Plutarch's *Moralia*, Loeb edn, vol. 4, London/Cambridge, Mass., 1936, 443f. I am grateful to Richard Winton for locating the text for me.

29. An insight offered in an extraordinarily perceptive early study by Sebastian Haffner, *Germany: Jekyll and Hyde*, London, 1940, 16. For an evaluation of this study, see Hans Mommsen, 'Ein schlecht getarnter Bandit. Sebastian Haffners historische Einschätzung Adolf Hitlers', *Frankfurter Allgemeine Zeitung*, 7 November 1997.

30. See Max Weber, *Wirtschaft und Gesellschaft*, 5th revised edn, Tübingen, 1972, 140ff. Hans-Ulrich Wehler, '30 January 1933 – Ein halbes Jahrhundert danach', *Aus Parlament und Zeitgeschichte*, 29 January 1983, 43–54, here 50, expressively recommended the application of Max Weber's concept of 'charismatic rule' as an interpretative model capable of overcoming some of the deep divides in approaching the historical problem of Hitler. See also Schreiber, *Hitler. Interpretationen*, 330.

31. See Franz Neumann, *Behemoth: the Structure and Practice of National Socialism*, London, 1942, 75.

32. Haffner, *Germany: Jekyll and Hyde*, 24. Sebastian Haffner's later work, *Anmerkungen zu Hitler*, Munich, 1978, remains, in its seven brilliant thematic essays, one of the most impressive studies of the Nazi dictator.

33. This stands in contrast to Alan Bullock's announced aim (13), at the beginning of his early and magisterial biography: 'My theme is not dictatorship, but the dictator, the personal power of one man.'

34. For the term and its implications, see Hans Mommsen, 'Cumulative Radicalisation and Progressive Self-Destruction as Structural Determinants of the Nazi Dictatorship', in Ian Kershaw and Moshe Lewin (eds.), *Stalinism and Nazism: Dictatorships in Comparison*, Cambridge, 1997, 75–87.

35. See note 1 to Chapter 13, below, for the reference to this document, which was published for the first time (in English translation) in Jeremy Noakes and Geoffrey Pridham (eds.), *Nazism 1919–1945. A Documentary Reader*, vol. 2, Exeter, 1984, 207.

36. While a tension in method between classical biography and social (or structural) history is undeniable, the irreconcilability is arguably fictive if 'power' is taken as the key focus of inquiry – particularly if the view of one prominent social historian is accepted that 'power, after all, is the key concept in the study of society' (Tony Judt, 'A Clown in Regal Purple: Social History and the Historians', *History Workshop Journal*, 7 (1979), 66–94, here 72).

37. Gerhard Schreiber ends his superb historiographical survey of differing interpretations of Hitler with a plea to seek, through a pluralism of methods, an understanding of the dictator and his regime – for which he sees the notion of 'charismatic rule' as offering a framework – anchored in a 'depiction of the National Socialist epoch' (Schreiber, *Hitler. Interpretationen*, 329–35). See also Gerhard Schreiber, 'Hitler und seine Zeit – Bilanzen, Thesen, Dokumente', in Wolfgang Michalka (ed.), *Die Deutsche Frage in der Weltpolitik*, Stuttgart, 1986, 137–64, here 162: 'What is still missing is an interpretation of Hitler and his era which integrates all essential components of the National Socialist system, acknowledging – and deploying where necessary – in unprejudiced fashion the given plurality of methodological approaches.'

38. For the phrase, see Mommsen, 'Hitlers Stellung', 70.

39. As Jürgen Kocka put it ('Struktur und Persönlichkeit als methodologisches Problem der Geschichtswissenschaft', in Bosch (ed.) *Persönlichkeit und Struktur*, 152–69, here 165); 'Every worthwhile explanation of National Socialism will have to deal with the person of Hitler, not reducible just to its structural conditions.

CHAPTER I: FANTASY AND FAILURE

1. August Kubizek, *Adolf Hitler. Mein Jugendfreund*, Graz (1953), 5th edn 1989, 50.
2. Hans-Jürgen Eitner, *'Der Führer'. Hitlers Persönlichkeit und Charakter*, Munich/ Vienna, 1981, 12.
3. Franz Jetzinger, *Hitlers Jugend*, Vienna, 1956, 16–18.
4. Bradley F. Smith, *Adolf Hitler. His Family, Childhood, and Youth*, Stanford, 1967, 19. Thomas Orr, 'Das war Hitler', *Revue*, Nr 37, Munich (13 September 1952), 4, states – though without a source – that Maria Anna (whom he misnames Anna Maria) brought 300 Gulden, the price of fifteen cows, into the marriage, contributed by her relatives and probably the reason why Hiedler was prepared to marry her at all. Thomas Orr was a pseudonym for a former employee of the NSDAP-Hauptarchiv (Werner Maser, *Adolf Hitler. Legende, Mythos, Wirklichkeit*, 3rd paperback edn, Munich, 1973, 541).
5. Smith, 19 n.7; Jetzinger, 19.
6. His initial opportunity came, it seems, through a recruitment drive to take on more lower civil servants from rural areas (Orr, *Revue*, Nr 37, 5).
7. Smith, 23; Jetzinger, 21, 44–6.
8. Smith, 20; Maser, *Hitler*, 43–4.
9. Smith, 30–31; Jetzinger, 21–2; Kubizek, 59.
10. Anton Joachimsthaler, *Korrektur einer Biographie*, Munich, 1989, 12–13.
11. Jetzinger, 16, 22.
12. Jetzinger, 22; Smith, 30.
13. Jetzinger, 22; Rudolf Koppensteiner (ed.), *Die Ahnentafel des Führers*, Leipzig, 1937, 39.
14. Maser, *Hitler*, 47; Jetzinger, 19–20.
15. See Jetzinger, 22–5, and Smith, 29, for the dubious character of the legitimation; see also Joachimsthaler, 12–13.
16. Maser, *Hitler*, 41–2; Smith, 48.
17. See Maser, *Hitler*, 34–5. Konrad Heiden, *Der Führer*, London (1944), 1967 edn, 38–9, had already noted this suggestion. Orr, *Revue*, Nr 37, 4, referred to village rumours that Nepomuk was the actual father.
18. Adolf Hitler, *Mein Kampf*, Munich, 1943 edn, 2: '*eines armen, kleinen Häuslers*'.
19. See Koppensteiner, 39–44. Jetzinger's claim (10–12) that the name 'Hitler' was of Czech origin has been shown to rest on flimsy grounds. 'Hüttler', meaning cottager or smallholder, was not an uncommon name in Austria. See Anton Adalbert Klein, 'Hitlers dunkler Punkt in Graz?', *Historisches Jahrbuch der Stadt Graz*, 3

(1970), 27–9; Orr, *Revue*, Nr 37, 6; and also Brigitte Hamann, *Hitlers Wien. Lehrjahre eines Diktators*, Munich, 1996, 64. Since the various forms of the name had evidently been for decades interchangeable, it is unclear why Maser, *Hitler*, 31, can be so adamant that Nepomuk (who himself had used more than one form) insisted at the legitimation upon 'Hitler' rather than 'Hiedler' as being closer to his own name of 'Hüttler'.

20. Koppensteiner, 46.

21. Joachimsthaler, 12–13.

22. Kubizek, 50.

23. Maser, *Hitler*, 12–15. One example of the sensationalism was an article published in the British *Daily Mirror* of 14 October 1933, purporting to show the 'Jewish grave of Hitler's grandfather' in a cemetery in Bucharest (IfZ, MA-731 (= NSDAP, Hauptarchiv, Reel 1)). The press interest in Hitler's alleged Jewish forebears had blown up in summer 1932, when the *Neue Zürcher Zeitung* had picked up on the name 'Salomon' that had appeared in the eighteenth century in the official genealogy approved by Hitler. In fact, the name 'Salomon' had been an error made by the Viennese genealogist Dr Karl Friedrich von Frank, which he hastily corrected. But the damage was done. See Hamann, 68–71.

24. Hans Frank, *Im Angesicht des Galgens*, Munich/Gräfelfing, 1953, 330–31.

25. Jetzinger's uncritical acceptance of Frank's recollection (see 28–32) was above all responsible for the spread of the story. One piece of his 'evidence', a picture of Hitler's father indicating his 'Jewish' looks, is self-evidently a portrait of someone other than Alois Hitler. See Jetzinger, picture opposite p. 16; Smith, pl. 5, following p. 24. For an early critical review of Jetzinger's book, and, particularly, a rejection, based on the findings of the Austrian scholar Dr Nikolaus Preradovic, of his claims that Hitler had a Jewish grandfather, see 'Hitler. Kein Ariernachweis', *Der Spiegel*, 12 June 1957, 54–9, esp. 57–8.

26. Klein, 10, 20–25.

27. Smith, 158–9.

28. Patrick Hitler, 'Mon oncle Adolf', *Paris soir* (5 August 1939), 4–5. The article amounted to no more than a largely worthless diatribe. See also Maser, *Hitler*, 18.

29. Robert G.L. Waite, *The Psychopathic God: Adolf Hitler*, New York, 1977, 129 n.; Maser, *Hitler*, 15 and n.

30. Smith, 158. Brigitte Hamann, also dismissive of the Frank story, speculates that his motive, as a long-standing Jew-hater himself, could have been to blame the Jews for producing an allegedly 'Jewish Hitler' (Hamann, 73–7, here 77).

31. It has been claimed that, as the motivation of his paranoid antisemitism, the more relevant question is not whether Hitler in fact had a Jewish grandfather, but whether he believed he was part Jewish (Waite, 126–31). The origins and sources of Hitler's hatred of the Jews are something to which we will return. But since there is no evidence to suggest that the idea that he was part-Jewish might have occurred to him before his political enemies started spreading the rumours in the 1920s, by which time his antisemitism was long-established, there is little to support the

speculation. Concern about whether he was part-Jewish would, of course, in any case have meant that Hitler was already antisemitic. See Rudolph Binion's review of Waite's book in *Journal of Psychohistory*, 5 (1977), 297.

32. According to Maser's account of the testimony of Adolf's remaining relatives in Spital long after the war, there was talk while Adolf was visiting Spital on leave from the army in 1917 of Nepomuk as his paternal grandfather (Maser, *Hitler*, 35). However, the testimony is worthless: Hitler never visited Spital in 1917. See Joachimsthaler, 171; and Rudolph Binion, 'Foam on the Hitler Wave', *JMH*, 46 (1974), 522–8, here 523.

33. Maser, *Hitler*, 35.

34. Smith, 39; Jetzinger, 39, 54.

35. Smith, 28, 35; Jetzinger, 50.

36. Pointed out by Rudolf Olden, *Hitler the Pawn*, London, 1936, 16.

37. Jetzinger, 48; Smith, 28; Orr, *Revue*, Nr 37, 5.

38. Jetzinger, 49; Smith, 28, 47; Orr, *Revue*, Nr 37, 5. According to Orr, Anna (whom he calls Anna Glasl-Hörer) was the adoptive daughter of a civil servant by the name of Hörer, who was a near neighbour of Alois in Braunau.

39. Jetzinger, 51; Smith, 29, 32–3; Orr, *Revue*, Nr 37, 6.

40. Smith, 32–3; Jetzinger, 52–3; Orr, *Revue*, Nr 37, 6, Nr 38, 2.

41. Jetzinger, 44; Smith, 35–7.

42. Jetzinger, 56–7; Smith, 40–41.

43. Maser, *Hitler*, 9.

44. Copy of birth-certificate in HA, Reel 1; IfZ, MA-731; Koppensteiner, 18.

45. *MK*, 1.

46. *MK*, 2; Smith, 53.

47. A point acknowledged by Waite, 145. See also Smith, 51 and n.5.

48. Smith, 46–9.

49. Following based upon Smith, 43–8; and Jetzinger, 58–63. Jetzinger's information on Hitler's father drew on an interview he conducted with one of Alois's former colleagues, Emanuel Lugert. This was also reproduced in Orr, *Revue*, Nr 39, 14, 35. The former cook in the Hitler household, Rosalia Hörl (*née* Schichtl), later told the NSDAP-Hauptarchiv that he was a 'good-natured (*gemütlicher*) but strict gentleman'. A colleague at the Customs Office in the early 1880s was less flattering, describing him as 'unsympathetic to all of us. He was very strict, exact, even pedantic at work and a very unapproachable person.' Both accounts in HA, Reel 1 (IfZ, MA-731).)

50. Smith, 51.

51. Smith, 45–8.

52. Smith, 43.

53. Kubizek, 46.

54. Eduard Bloch, 'My Patient, Hitler', *Collier's* (15 March 1941), 35.

55. For speculation on the psychological effect, see Alice Miller, *Am Anfang war Erziehung*, Frankfurt am Main, 1983, 213–15.

56. Smith, 41–3; Jetzinger, 62, 71–2; Kubizek, 38–45; Bloch, 36.

57. Bloch, 36.

58. *MK*, 16; and see Albert Zoller, *Hitler privat. Erlebnisbericht seiner Geheimsekretärin*, Düsseldorf, 1949, 46.

59. Waite, 141.

60. NA, NND/881077, Interview with Mrs Paula Wolf (i.e. Paula Hitler), Berchtesgaden, 5 June 1946 (transcript only in English). Hitler's half-sister Angela Hammitzsch (formerly Raubal) also spoke after the war of the regular beatings Adolf used to receive from his father. (Cit. in Christa Schroeder, *Er war mein Chef. Aus dem Nachlaß der Sekretärin von Adolf Hitler*, Munich/Vienna, 1985, 336 n.139.)

61. Schroeder, 63. Hitler described his father to Goebbels in 1932 as a 'tyrant in the home (*Haustyrann*)', while his mother was 'a source of goodness and love' (*TBJG*, I.2, 219 (9 August 1932)). See also *TBJG*, I.2, 727 (15 November 1936), where Hitler was reported to have spoken of his 'fanatical father'.

62. *MK*, 32–3. See also the commentaries on the passage by Helm Stierlin, *Adolf Hitler. Familienperspektiven*, Frankfurt am Main, 1976, 24–5; and Miller, 190–91. According to Hans Frank, Hitler told him of his shame as a boy at having to fetch his drunken father home from the pub at night (Frank, 331–2). However, Emanuel Lugert, who had worked with Alois Hitler for a time at Passau, told Jetzinger that Hitler's father had normally drunk at most four halves of beer a day, had never to his knowledge been drunk, and went home at the right time for his evening meal (Jetzinger, 61). The same witness apparently told Orr that Alois sometimes drank up to six halves of strong beer in an evening, but repeated that he had never seen him drunk (Orr, *Revue*, Nr 39, 35). Conceivably, Hitler's own aversion to alcohol had its roots in his father's drinking and behavioural habits.

63. Psychologists and 'psycho-historians' have seen Adolf's relationship to both parents, not just to his father, as disturbed in the extreme. Those who have looked to an underlying love–hate relationship with his mother include Waite, esp. 138–48; Miller, 212–28; Eitner, esp. 21–7; Stierlin, esp. ch.2 (who takes from family-therapy the notion that the child could identify itself in extreme fashion with the sense of being the 'delegate' of the unfulfilled dreams of the mother, in this case seeing the salvation of the mother in the quest to save Germany); Walter C. Langer, *The Mind of Adolf Hitler*, London, 1973, esp. 150–52; Rudolph Binion, *Hitler among the Germans*, New York, 1976 (who finds the key to Hitler's quest to kill the Jews in his subliminal reaction to the death of his mother at the hands of a Jewish doctor); Rudolph Binion, 'Hitler's Concept of "Lebensraum": the Psychological Basis', *History of Childhood Quarterly*, 1 (1973), 187–215 (with subsequent discussion of his hypotheses, 216–58), where Hitler's perceived mission to provide 'feeding-ground' for the 'motherland' is located in his need to save and avenge his mother, in the shape of Germany; Erich Fromm, *Anatomie der menschlichen Destruktivät*, Stuttgart, 1974, esp. 337–8; and Erik H. Erikson, 'The Legend of Hitler's Youth', in Robert Paul Wolff (ed.), *Political Man and Social Man*, New York, 1966, 370–96, here esp. 381–3. Surveys of psychological approaches to Hitler

are provided by William Carr, *Hitler: a Study in Personality and Politics*, London, 1978, esp. 149–55; Wolfgang Michalka, 'Hitler im Spiegel der Psycho-History', *Francia*, 8 (1980), 595–611; Schreiber, Hitler, 316–27; and, most extensively, Thomas Kornbichler, *Adolf-Hitler-Psychogramme*, Frankfurt am Main, 1994. For some of the difficulties in reaching any scientifically sound assessment of Hitler's later personality, see Desmond Henry and Dick Geary, 'Adolf Hitler: a re-assessment of his personality status', *Irish Journal of Psychological Medicine*, 10 (1993), 148–51.

64. Quotation from Waite, foreword to the 1992 edition, and see, especially, ch.3. The most critical review of Waite's book was that of another 'psycho-historian', Rudolph Binion, in *Journal of Psychohistory*, 5 (1977), 295–300. See also Binion's comment in his review article, 'Foam on the Hitler Wave', *JMH*, 46 (1974), 522–8, here 525: 'No hate was manifest in young Hitler as far as the direct evidence discloses.'

65. A point made by Smith, 8.

66. Smith, 55.

67. Max Domarus, *Hitler. Reden und Proklamationen 1932–1945*, Wiesbaden, 1973, 1935 (8 November 1942).

68. Smith, 56.

69. Smith, 58.

70. *MK*, 3.

71. *MK*, 3–4; Smith, 61; Jetzinger, 73.

72. Smith, 62.

73. See, e.g., *Tb* Reuth, iii.1254 (19 August 1938), where Hitler spoke of the happy days of his youth in Leonding and Lambach.

74. See Hermann Giesler, *Ein anderer Hitler*, Leoni am Starnberger See, 1977, 96, 99, 215–16, 479–80; Zoller, 57; Evan Burr Bukey, *Hitler's Hometown*, Bloomington/Indianapolis, 1986, esp. 196–201; and Hamann, 11–15. Hitler spoke during the war of turning Linz into a 'German Budapest', and was prepared to put 120 million Marks into his grandiose building schemes – 'money you can do something with', as Goebbels remarked. See, for example, *TBJG*, II.5, 367 (20 August 1942), 597 (29 September 1942), II.8, 265 (10 May 1943); *Monologe*, 284 (19–20 February 1942), 405 (25 June 1943).

75. *MK*, 3.

76. Jetzinger, 92.

77. Jetzinger, 92.

78. *MK*, 4. He still had the two-volume work – a 'treasure loyally guarded' – in 1912 in the Men's Home in Vienna (Hamann, 562).

79. *MK*, 173; Hugo Rabitsch, *Aus Adolf Hitlers Jugendzeit*, Munich, 1938, 12–13; Smith, 66.

80. Smith, 66–8; Waite, 11–12, 60. See Hamann, 544–8, for Hitler's enthusiasm after hearing Karl May speak – even on a pacifist theme – in Vienna in 1912.

81. Walter Görlitz, *Adolf Hitler*, Göttingen, 1960, 23.

82. *MK*, 6.

83. Smith, 64; Maser, *Hitler*, 62. Though it seems hard to believe, elderly inhabitants of Leonding in the 1950s claimed that Edmund's parents did not attend the boy's funeral. See Orr, *Revue*, Nr 40, 36; Waite, 169–70.

84. See Smith, 68–9.

85. *MK*, 5.

86. Kubizek, 57.

87. Jetzinger, 105–6; Smith, 76, 79.

88. Jetzinger, 105–6. For Huemer's subsequent relationship with Hitler, see Smith, 79 n.34. See also Rabitsch, 57–65 for Huemer's later visit to Hitler. For Hitler's schooling, see also Zoller, 47. Hitler later claimed the marks for his school-work dropped when he started to read Karl May (*Monologe*, 281 (17 February 1942)).

89. Jetzinger, 107, 109–11; Rabitsch, 72.

90. Kubizek, 61; *Monologe*, 185–8 (8–9 January 1942); Henry Picker, *Tischespräche im Hauptquartier*, Stuttgart, 1963, 273 (12 April 1942); Smith, 79; Eitner, 30–31; Maser, *Hitler*, 68–70; Zoller, 47–9.

91. *MK*, 12–13; Jetzinger, 110, 113 for German nationalism in Linz; see also Bukey, 7ff. Hamann, 23–7, describes the German nationalist political leanings in the school, as does Jetzinger, 99, 110, 113.

92. *MK*, 5–8.

93. Picker, 324 (10 May 1942).

94. *MK*, 6 (trans., *MK* Watt, 8).

95. *MK*, 7.

96. See Smith, 70–73, also for dismissal of the objections of Jetzinger, 98–9 to any substance in Hitler's depiction of a conflict with his father over a civil service career.

97. *MK*, 10. See Hamann, 23.

98. *MK*, 8–14; Smith, 81–5; Olden, 21; Hamann, 22–3.

99. *MK*, 15.

100. Jetzinger, 72–3. See also Olden, 21. The cause of the death was a haemorrhage of the lungs. He had suffered a prior haemorrhage the previous August (Jetzinger, 72).

101. Jetzinger, 122–9; Smith, 91, 97.

102. Kubizek's comment about Adolf's sobbing at the funeral (54) was only based on casual hearsay evidence and is not reliable.

103. Kubizek, 46, 61–2.

104. Jetzinger, 102; Smith, 92.

105. *TBJG*, I.3, 447 (3 June 38). In his recollections of his time in Steyr, he claimed to have disliked it as too Catholic-clerical and not nationalist enough compared with Linz (*Monologe*, 188 (8–9 January 1942)).

106. Smith, 95–6.

107. *MK*, 8.

108. This follows Heiden, *Der Führer*, 46, who lists the grades for both semesters of the school-year 1904–5, as given in the report issued on 16 September 1905

(including the re-sit in geometry), and Smith, who summarizes these results, 96. Maser, *Hitler*, 70, gives the results only in the report from 11 February, for the first semester, and has Hitler as 'unsatisfactory' in French (though this is not mentioned on Heiden's list). The results listed in Orr, *Revue*, Nr 42, 3, and repeated in Jetzinger, 103, as those of the report of 16 September 1905, correspond with those given by Heiden for the first semester and those provided by Maser (apart from the entry for French) for the report dated 11 February. See also Waite, 156.

109. According to stories he later told, Adolf mistakenly used one of his reports from Steyr as toilet paper after an evening with friends celebrating the end of term. (*Monologe*, 189–90 (8–9 January 1942); see Zoller, 49, for a different version in which he was sick over the report). Maser, *Hitler*, 70, presumes the report is that of February 1905, while Smith, 99, dates it to summer 1905. In the anecdote, Hitler claims that he slept out and was wakened by a milkwoman. This seems to rule out February. And in summer, Hitler only received his certificate following the re-sit examination in September, when there would have been no social gathering. Zoller's account is in at least one respect inaccurate, since Adolf allegedly had to show the report to his father, who by then was already dead. Whether Hitler's story had any substance to it at all must be regarded as doubtful.

110. Smith, 95–9; Jetzinger, 99–103.

111. Smith, 98.

112. Jetzinger, 148–51, denies an illness altogether, though his evidence is not strong. Smith, 97–8, provides some evidence for illness in summer 1905, though not for the autumn, accepts Adolf's pale and sickly appearance at this time, but rightly doubts that it was sufficient reason for ending his schooling.

113. *MK*, 16; Smith, 97–8. See also the picture of Hitler from this period, showing him as thin, weak and consumptive in appearance, in Smith, pl. 13.

114. *MK*, 16–17; see Jetzinger, 130.

115. Paula Hitler testimony, NA, NND-881077, 3; IfZ, MA-731 (=HA, Reel 1), 'Notizen für Kartei', 8 December 1938.

116. Kubizek, 63; IfZ, MA-731 (=HA, Reel 1), 'Adolf Hitler in Urfahr' (recollections in 1938–9 of the postmaster's widow who had lived in the same house as the Hitler family).

117. *MK*, 16.

118. Hamann, 80. Kubizek had already been approached by a representative of the NSDAP-Hauptarchiv at the end of 1938 with a view to writing up his memoirs of the youthful Hitler, foreseen as 'one of the most significant pieces of the central archive' in bringing out the 'inconceivable greatness of the Führer in his youth' (IfZ, MA-731 (= HA, Reel 1), 'Notizen für Kartei', 8 December 1938, and report on visit to Kubizek).

119. See Jetzinger, 117–22, 133–81; Smith, 101 n.30. Jetzinger had a personal animus against Kubizek, and his own – rival, though second-hand – account of Hitler's youth did most, deliberately, to discredit Kubizek. See Hamann, 83–6.

120. See Hamann, 77–86.

121. Kubizek, 17; Jetzinger, 140–41.
122. *MK*, 15; Paula Hitler testimony, NA, NND-881077, 3–4.
123. Kubizek, 22.
124. Kubizek, 18–25.
125. Kubizek, 22–3.
126. Kubizek, 17, 19, 112.
127. Kubizek, 75–86.
128. Smith, 103. Adolf was so stirred by a performance of Wagner's early opera, *Rienzi* (which glamorized the tale of a fourteenth-century Roman populist who in the opera purportedly attempted to unify Italy but was ultimately brought down by the people he had led) that he took Kubizek on a long nocturnal climb up the Freinberg, a mountain outside Linz, and lectured to him in a state of near ecstasy on the significance of what they had seen. Kubizek's account (111–18), is, however, highly fanciful, reading in mystical fashion back into the episode an early prophetic vision of Hitler's own future. Plainly, the strange evening had made a lasting impression on Kubizek. He reminded Hitler of it when they met at Bayreuth in 1939. On the spot, Hitler seized on the story to illustrate his early prophetic qualities to his hostess, Winifred Wagner, ending with the words: 'in that hour, it began' (Kubizek, 118). Kubizek, more impressed than ever, subsequently produced his post-war, highly imaginary depiction, with the melodramatically absurd claim at the forefront of his mind. This has not prevented the 'vision' on the Freinberg being taken seriously by some later writers. See e.g. Joachim Köhler, *Wagners Hitler. Der Prophet und sein Vollstrecker*, Munich, 1996, ch.2, esp. 34–5.
129. Köhler, *Wagners Hitler*, takes this on to a new plane, however, with his overdrawn claim that Hitler came to see it as his life's work to fulfil Wagner's visions and put his ideas into practice.
130. Kubizek, 83.
131. Kubizek, 18–19.
132. Kubizek, 97–110.
133. Kubizek, 64–74; see Jetzinger, 142–8; and Hamann, 41–2.
134. Kubizek, 106–9; see Jetzinger, 166–8.
135. According to Hitler himself, the trip lasted two weeks (*MK*, 18). Kubizek, 121–4, reckons it was around four weeks, and is followed by Smith, 104. Jetzinger, 151–5, concluded that Hitler's recollection was probably correct. The dating can only be determined by the postmarks (some indistinct) and dates (not always given) on the cards which Hitler sent to Kubizek. See Hamann, 42–4. The length of Hitler's visit is scarcely of prime historical importance.
136. Kubizek, 129; Hamann, 43–4.
137. Kubizek, 129.
138. Kubizek, 127–30. The objections came primarily from Leo Raubal, the husband of Adolf's half-sister, Angela. He tried to persuade Klara that it was about time that Adolf learnt something sensible. Adolf raged to Kubizek: 'This pharisee is ruining my home for me' (Kubizek, 128). Adolf won the battle. According to the

later testimony of a neighbour, he insisted so firmly on his intention of becoming an artist that he finally persuaded his mother to send him to the Academy in Vienna (IfZ, MA-731 (= HA, Reel 1), 'Adolf Hitler in Urfahr').

139. Gerhart Marckhgott, '"Von der Hohlheit des gemächlichen Lebens". Neues Material über die Familie Hitler in Linz', *Jahrbuch des Oberösterreichischen Museal-vereins*, 138/I (1993), 275–6. The entry by Aunt Johanna – twice-noted – in the family household-account book is undated, but from internal evidence can be seen to fall at the end of Adolf's time in Linz. Brigitte Hamann (196) suggests that it dates from August 1908, and that Adolf persuaded his aunt to loan him the money during a summer visit to the family home in the Waldviertel. Why, then, Aunt Johanna would have entered it in the family household-book which was kept in Urfahr is not apparent. It seems more likely, as Marckhgott infers, that the loan was made the previous year, in 1907, while Klara Hitler was still alive, and when Adolf needed to secure some funding before he left to take the admission examination for the Academy of Fine Arts in Vienna. As Marckhgott points out, the loan – amounting to about a fifth of Johanna Pölzl's entire savings – perhaps sparked the protest by Leo Raubal about Adolf being allowed to entertain studying art instead of earning his living. But once he had obtained funding, it was presumably more difficult for his mother to stand in his way of going to Vienna.

140. Binion, *Hitler among the Germans*, 138–43; Binion, 'Hitler's Concept of Lebensraum', 196–200; Bloch, 36; Jetzinger, 170–72; Smith, 105; Hamann, 46–8.

141. Hamann, 46–7.

142. Bloch, 36.

143. Bloch, 39.

144. Hamann, 47.

145. *MK*, 18.

146. Hamann, 51–2. Maser, *Hitler*, 75–7, 114, inverts the examinations procedures. Hamann, 51 (without source), refers to 112 candidates; Maser (75, 77, 114), with reference to information provided by the Academy itself, speaks of 113 candidates.

147. Maser, *Hitler*, 77. Among those who failed alongside Hitler was a subsequent rector of the Academy. See also Hamann, 52.

148. *MK*, 18–19 (trans., *MK* Watt, 18).

149. *MK*, 19 (trans., *MK* Watt, 18–19); and see Smith, 108–10. Orr, *Revue*, Nr 43, 40–41 (followed by Maser, *Hitler*, 78, and L.Sydney Jones, *Hitlers Weg begann in Wien*, Frankfurt am Main/Berlin, 1990, 64) has Hitler applying, after his rejection by the Academy of Fine Arts, for entry to the school of architecture, but the assertion is unsupported by any evidence. Even the most tentative inquiry would have revealed – as Hitler must surely have known – that he did not possess even the minimal qualifications for entry.

150. Kubizek, 133. Allegations that Hitler's antisemitism had its source in his rejection by Jewish examiners at the Academy are wide of the mark. Both Waite, 190, and Jones, 317, speak of four Jews among his examiners. In fact, none of the Academy's professors involved in rejecting Hitler was Jewish (Hamann, 53).

151. Hamann, 53; Binion, *Hitler among the Germans*, 139; IfZ, MA-731 (= HA, 1), 'Adolf Hitler in Urfahr.'

152. NA, NND-881077, 3; Bloch, 39. See also Kubizek, 138–41. Jetzinger's account, 176–81, claiming that Hitler did not return to Linz before his mother's death was at least in part aimed at discrediting Kubizek. However, both Paula Hitler and Dr Bloch independently confirm that Adolf was present while his mother was dying, thus lending support to Kubizek's account, despite its containing a number of factual inaccuracies. Smith, 110 and n.54, follows Jetzinger. See Waite, 180–83, and Hamann, 84–5.

153. Jetzinger, 179; Hamann, 54. According to two witnesses, Adolf sketched his mother on her deathbed (Bloch, 39; IfZ, MA-731 (= HA, Reel 1), 'Adolf Hitler in Urfahr').

154. Bloch, 39. Dr Bloch went on to mention Adolf's avowed lasting gratitude. Hitler subsequently sent Dr Bloch a number of picture-postcards and a present of a picture he had painted (Bloch, pt.II, *Colliers*, 22 March 1941, 69–70; Hamann, 56). After the Anschluß, Dr Bloch appealed to Hitler and was granted relatively favourable treatment. Even so, he lost his livelihood, was forced to emigrate to the USA, and died in straitened circumstances in New York in 1945 (Bloch, pt.II, 72–3; Hamann, 56–7).

155. *MK*, 16 (trans., *MK* Watt, 17).

156. Jetzinger, 181.

157. *MK*, 16–17 (trans., *MK* Watt, 17).

158. *MK*, 19–20 (trans., *MK* Watt, 19).

159. Jetzinger, 180; Hamann, 55; Marckhgott, 272.

160. Hamann, 58, 85.

161. E.g. Maser, *Hitler*, 81. See Hamann, 58.

162. Jetzinger, 180–82, 185–9; Smith, 111–12.

163. NA, NND-881077, 4; Jetzinger, 182, 186–7.

164. Jetzinger, 187.

165. Marckhgott, 271.

166. Kubizek, 146–55; Jetzinger, 189–92; Smith, 114–15.

167. IfZ, MA-731 (= HA, Reel 1), 'Adolf Hitler in Urfahr'.

CHAPTER 2: DROP-OUT

1. Above quotations from *MK*, 20–21 (trans., *MK* Watt, 20–21).

2. *MK*, chs.2–3, 18–137.

3. *MK*, 137.

4. The best account by far is that of Brigitte Hamann, *Hitlers Wien. Lehrjahre eines Diktators*, Munich, 1996.

5. See Hamann, 77–83, 264–75, for the credibility of these accounts.

6. Josef Greiner, *Das Ende des Hitler-Mythos*, Zürich/Leipzig/Vienna, 1947. Jetz-

inger, 225, 294; Waite, 427–32; Hamann, 275–80, are rightly dismissive, Smith, 165–6, less so.

7. See Carl E. Schorske, *Fin-de-Siècle Vienna. Politics and Culture*, New York, 1979, xviii, 3.

8. See William A. Jenks, *Vienna and the Young Hitler*, New York, 1960, 219.

9. See Schorske, 6, 12, 15, 19, 22.

10. Schorske, 129.

11. Hamann, chs.2–5, 9–10, provides an excellent description of the social and political fabric of the Vienna that Hitler experienced.

12. Jenks, 38–9.

13. Jenks, 39.

14. Jenks, 118.

15. See Jenks, 119–21.

16. See Peter Pulzer, *The Rise of Political Antisemitism in Germany and Austria*, rev. edn, London, 1988, esp. chs.14–15; Hamann, 470–71.

17. Schorske, pp. 146–80; Hamann, 486–8.

18. Jenks, 118.

19. *MK*, 135 (trans., *MK* Watt, 113).

20. See Hamann, 128–9; Joachimsthaler, 39–40.

21. Jenks, 53.

22. Jenks, 107.

23. Schorske, 130–31.

24. Hamann, 177–9.

25. Jenks, 54–5, 101.

26. *MK*, 80–101.

27. Jenks, 73–8.

28. Schorske, 129.

29. See, for Schönerer, Hamann, 337–64 (here esp. 362); and Andrew G. Whiteside, *The Socialism of Fools. Georg von Schönerer and Austrian Pan-Germanism*, Berkeley/Los Angeles, 1975.

30. Jenks, 106.

31. Schorske, 128.

32. Jenks, 91–6, 103–10.

33. *MK*, 106–30; and see Jenks, 110.

34. *MK* 106–10, 130–34. During reminiscences more than three decades later, Hitler was still singing the praises of Lueger (*Monologe*, 152–3, 17 December 1941). On Lueger, see esp. Hamann, 393–435, and John W. Boyer, *Political Radicalism in Late Imperial Vienna. Origins of the Christian Social Movement, 1848–1897*, Chicago, 1981, esp. ch.4.

35. *MK*, 108, 130.

36. Schorske, 139; Jenks, 88.

37. Cit. Hamann, 417; Schorske, 145.

38. Schorske, 145.

39. Jenks, 50.
40. Schorske, 140.
41. Hamann, 411.
42. Hamann, 413.
43. Hamann, 412.
44. Hamann, 412, and see 490.
45. *MK*, 132–3; and see Hamann, 431–2.
46. *MK*, 133–4.
47. *MK*, 108, 130.
48. Jenks, 168, 175.
49. Jenks, 158.
50. Jenks, 181–2.
51. Jenks, 178–9.
52. Jenks, 181.
53. Jenks, 168–9.
54. Jenks, 158.
55. Jenks, 179–80.
56. Jenks, 180.
57. Quotations from *MK*, 43–4 (trans., *MK* Watt, 38–9); and see Hamann, 254–7.
58. Marckhgott, 271.
59. Jetzinger, 206.
60. NA, NND-881077, 4, testimony of Paula Hitler (1946).
61. Marckhgott, 273, 275.
62. NA, NND-881077, 4; Jetzinger, 230–32, speculates that Adolf inherited a substantial legacy from Aunt Johanna in 1911. But she had loaned him 924 Kronen no later than 1908 (probably towards the end of 1907), a sum amounting to around a fifth of her savings, and probably constituting his share of the inheritance (Marckhgott, 275–6; Hamann, 196, 250). There is no hint from Hitler's lifestyle that he benefited from a significant inheritance in 1911.
63. Kubizek, 128, 148.
64. NA, NND-881077, 4.
65. Kubizek, 148–9.
66. Smith, 108, for the renting of the room in late September or early October 1907; he gives the date for the return to Vienna as 14–17 February 1908. The card to Kubizek is dated 18 February; Hitler was still in Urfahr on 14 February (Jetzinger, 187–8). Hamann (49) points out that Maria Zakreys was Czech and not Polish, as Kubizek (157) implied. She also corrects Kubizek's error (132, 156) that the address was Stumpergasse 29, not 31.
67. Kubizek, 152.
68. Kubizek, 153–4 (trans., August Kubizek, *Young Hitler*, London, 1973, 99).
69. Kubizek, 157–8.
70. Kubizek, 150, points out that Adolf was continuing more or less to lead the same sort of life in Vienna.

71. Kubizek, 159.

72. Kubizek, 159, 161.

73. Kubizek, 159–60.

74. Kubizek, 160.

75. Kubizek, 161–7; quotations 167 (trans., *Young Hitler*, 113).

76. Kubizek, 167 (trans., *Young Hitler*, 114).

77. Jetzinger, 187–8.

78. Kubizek, 163.

79. Kubizek, 165 (trans., *Young Hitler*, 111, where the words 'and cheated' – '*und betrogen*' – are omitted).

80. Kubizek, 182 (trans., *Young Hitler*, 129).

81. Kubizek, 163 (trans., *Young Hitler*, 109).

82. IfZ, F19/19 (copies of the correspondence). See Jones, 33–7; Smith, 113; Joachimsthaler, 35; Maser, *Hitler*, 81–4; Hamann, 59–62.

83. *Monologe*, 200. According to one story, Hitler tried several times to see Roller, but eventually gave up and tore up his letter of introduction (John Toland, *Adolf Hitler*, London, 1977, 31, 929 but on the basis of an interview carried out decades later, in 1971. See also Jones, 51).

84. Maser, *Hitler*, 84–5; Jones, 33, 121 (though on 311 n.65 he accepts the weakness of the evidence). And see Joachimsthaler, 35.

85. Despite Kubizek's propensity to fantasize parts of his memoirs (see Jetzinger, 117–21, 135ff.), the very singularity of the episodes he describes, when relating Hitler's 'projects', suggests they were beyond his own originality or fantasy, and the picture of Hitler which emerges has an authentic ring to it. See Hamann, 80–82. Hitler himself, in his wartime monologues, spoke of starting to write a play at the age of fifteen (*Monologe*, 187, 8–9 January 1942). The English translation, *Hitler's Table Talk*, *1941–1944*, London, 1953, 191, omits the relevant sentence.

86. Kubizek, 164–5.

87. Kubizek, 184–5.

88. Kubizek, 200–208, quotation, 208 (trans., *Young Hitler*, 153).

89. Kubizek, 179 (utopian plans); 172, 176–8 (housing in Vienna); 178–9 (new popular drink); 209–18 (travelling orchestra); 174, 197 (rebuilding of Linz).

90. Kubizek, 176–8. Jones, 62–3, 68–9, accepts Kubizek's story, though attributes Hitler's interest in the housing problem to his own conditions in the dismal room in Stumpergasse more than to any humanitarian sympathy with the underprivileged.

91. Kubizek, 211.

92. Jones, 52–8, 63–7. Hitler did later acquire some erotic paintings by Klimt's Munich counterpart Franz von Stuck, who was one of his favourite artists (Jones 57; Waite, 66–9).

93. For the ferocious opposition in Vienna to the work of Klimt and Kokoschka, see Schorske, chs.5, 7.

94. Kubizek, 186–7.

95. Kubizek, 173–4.

96. Kubizek, 173.

97. Kubizek, 188.

98. Kubizek, 153.

99. Kubizek, 188. Hitler had paid the relatively high subscription of 8.40 Kronen on 7 January 1908 to become a member of the Linzer Musealverein, giving him access to the Linz Landesmuseum and library. He resigned his membership on 4 March 1909 (Hamann, 57, 197).

100. Kubizek, 188, 191.

101. Kubizek, 189–90.

102. Jetzinger, 216.

103. Kubizek, 190; Jetzinger, 217. Hitler was later capable of conversing about the comparative merits of Kant, Schopenhauer and Nietzsche, though this is no proof that he had read their works (*TBJG*, II.7, 181, 21 January 1943). He had, in fact, been caught out 'lecturing' on Schopenhauer in the Men's Home in Vienna, conceded that he had only read 'some' of his work, and been admonished to 'speak about things that he understood' (Reinhold Hanisch, 'I Was Hitler's Buddy: III', *New Republic*, 19 April 1939, 297). According to Hans Frank, Hitler told him that he read Schopenhauer during the First World War and Nietzsche during his imprisonment in Landsberg in 1924 (Frank, 46).

104. In *MK*, 43, 56, 58, Hitler explicitly mentions the Social Democratic *Arbeiterzeitung*, the Liberal *Neue Freie Presse* and *Wiener Tagblatt*, and the Christian Socialist *Deutsches Volksblatt*. For his daily newspaper reading he probably turned first of all to the organ of the Schönerer movement, *Das Alldeutsche Tagblatt*, which was published a few doors down Stumpergasse from where he lived (Hamann, 50). He read these, and no doubt other newspapers as well as periodicals and political pamphlets, mainly in cafés (*MK*, 42–3, 65).

105. *MK*, 35–6. Maser, *Hitler*, 179–82 accepts that the sources on Hitler's reading in this early period are unreliable – which does not prevent him citing at length a passage from Greiner that is pure fantasy. See Binion's scathing comments on Maser's views of Hitler's alleged extensive reading in 'Foam on the Hitler Wave', *JMH*, 46 (1974), 522–4. Jones, 312 n.12, casts doubt upon Hitler's use of the Hofbibliothek.

106. NA, NND-881077, 4. An indication that the young Hitler had been something of a bookworm before he left Linz can be gleaned from the testimony of neighbours and relatives, though of course this was only gathered in 1938 (HA, Reel 1 (IfZ, MA-731), 'Adolf Hitler in Urfahr', and reported recollections of Johann Schmidt).

107. *MK*, 36–8 (trans., *MK* Watt, 33–4).

108. Maser, *Hitler*, 110; *Monologe*, 198; Jenks, 14; Zoller, 58.

109. Kubizek, 198.

110. Kubizek wrote (196) of 'the perfect interpretations of the musical dramas of Wagner by the Viennese Court Opera led by Gustav Mahler', and mentions (192) Hitler's admiration for Mahler, 'at that time the conductor' in the opera. Whether Hitler experienced Mahler conducting during his first two stays in Vienna cannot

be established, but he and Kubizek could not have seen Mahler together, since Mahler's last performance, before leaving to take up his appointment at the New York Metropolitan Opera, was on 15 October 1907, five months before Kubizek's arrival in Vienna (Jones, 40, 48; Maser, *Hitler*, 264; Hamann, 44, 94–5).

111. Kubizek, 196. Hitler's sister Paula claimed to remember him seeing *Götterdämmerung* thirteen times even while still in Linz (NA, NND-881077, 4). Hitler himself said he had seen *Tristan* (which he thought Wagner's greatest opera) 'thirty to forty times' during his years in Vienna (*Monologe*, 224, 294 (24–5 January 1942, 22–3 February 1942)).

112. Kubizek, 195.

113. Schorske, 163.

114. Jenks, 202; and see Hamann, 89–95.

115. Kubizek, 195 (trans., *Young Hitler*, 140).

116. *Monologe*, 234 (25–6 January 1942; trans., *Table Talk*, 251).

117. A point made by Joachim Fest, *Hitler. Eine Biographie*, Frankfurt am Main/ Berlin/Vienna, 1976 edn, 75.

118. Heiden, *Der Führer*, 52–3.

119. For an overdrawn depiction of Hitler as a self-styled Wagnerian hero, see Köhler, esp. ch.13; and also Waite, 99–113.

120. See Carr, 155; Waite, 184–6.

121. Without him, it has been rightly said, the reduction of politics in the Third Reich to drama and pageantry would be difficult to imagine (Fest, 74–7). It is nevertheless a gross oversimplification and distortion to reduce the Third Reich to the outcome of Hitler's alleged mission to fulfil Wagner's vision, as does Köhler, in *Wagners Hitler*.

122. Kubizek, 162, 238.

123. Kubizek, 163.

124. Kubizek, 162.

125. Kubizek, 193.

126. Kubizek, 230.

127. Hanisch, 297.

128. Hamann, 523–4.

129. Hanisch, 297–8.

130. See Hamann, 519–21.

131. Hanisch, 297.

132. Cited Waite, 51 ('*Eine Frau muß ein niedliches, molliges, Tschapperl sein: weich, süß und dumm*').

133. *MK*, 44 (trans., *MK* Watt, 39).

134. Kubizek, 231.

135. Maser, *Hitler*, 527–9.

136. Heiden, *Der Führer*, 63–4, makes this point.

137. The evidence that Hitler had only one testicle depends solely upon the Russian autopsy evidence (Lev Bezymenski, *The Death of Adolf Hitler*, London, 1968, 46,

49). This stands diametrically contradicted by several detailed medical examinations carried out at different times by his doctors, who were adamant that his sexual organs were quite normal. In a critical review in the *Sunday Times*, 29 September 1968, Hugh Trevor-Roper gave cogent reasons for scepticism about the general reliability of Bezymenski's report. Maser, *Hitler*, 527–9, summarizes the medical examinations of Hitler by his own doctors and raises the possibility that the body on which the Soviet autopsy was performed may not have been that of Hitler. Waite, 150–62, accepts the dubious evidence of monorchism and builds it into an elaborate explanation of Hitler's psychological abnormalities. Binion, in his biting review of Waite, *Journal of Psychohistory*, 5 (1977), 296–7, is more properly sceptical, coming down – as the weight and nature of the testimony surely demands – in favour of the several examinations of Hitler while he was alive, none of which indicated any genital abnormality.

138. Greiner, 54–67; Fest, 63, repeats the Greiner story and regards it as a plausible cause of Hitler's antisemitism. For reasons why Greiner's book should be totally discounted as worthwhile evidence, see Waite, 427–32.

139. See Schorske, chs.1, 5.

140. Jenks, 123–5; Jones, 72–9; Hamann, 519–22.

141. Jones, 73; Kubizek, 158–9.

142. Kubizek, 237.

143. Kubizek, 228–9.

144. Kubizek, 237.

145. Kubizek, 237.

146. Kubizek, 239. Later rumours that he had himself been infected with syphilis by a Jewish prostitute were without foundation. Medical tests in 1940 showed that Hitler had not suffered from syphilis. (See Maser, *Hitler*, 308, 377, 528).

147. Kubizek, 235–6.

148. *MK*, 63. Reliable figures on the extremely large numbers of prostitutes in Vienna at the time are unobtainable. That prostitution was run by Jews was a standard weapon of the antisemites' armoury. As always, it was a gross distortion. But to combat such allegations, the Jewish community itself supported and publicized attempts to break the criminal trade, in which some eastern Jews were involved, in importing young Jewish girls from poverty-stricken backgrounds in eastern Europe to Vienna's brothels. (See Hamann, 477–9, 521–2.)

149. Hitler's juvenile entry to the adult part of the Linz waxworks (see *Monologe*, 190) can doubtless be attributed to normal adolescent curiosity.

150. Kubizek, 233–5, 237; and see Waite, 241.

151. See Kubizek, 170–71, where it was said that he was 'almost pathologically sensitive about anything concerning the body', and 'disliked any physical contact with people' (trans., *Young Hitler*, 116–17).

152. See the references in ch.1, n.63.

153. Much goes back to NA, *The Hitler Source Book*, the OSS wartime compilation, and the book substantially based upon it, Walter C. Langer, *The Mind of Adolf*

Hitler, Pan Books edn, London, 1974, esp. 134, 165ff. The sensationalism of David Lewis, *The Secret Life of Adolf Hitler*, London, 1977, rests in good measure on the same material and adds little or nothing. Waite (237–43) infers that the perversion existed but accepts (239) that the 'shreds of evidence' are 'insufficient in themselves' to support such a conclusion. Based mainly on Langer and Waite, Jones, 91–4, 308, describes the same perversions (though they contribute nothing to his account of Hitler in the Vienna years). Hitler's erstwhile comrade, later bitter enemy, Otto Strasser was a source of some of the stories.

154. *MK*, 20.

155. *MK*, 17 (trans., *MK Watt*, 17).

156. Hamann, 58, 85; Maser, *Hitler*, 81; Smith, 108; Jetzinger, 172, 180–83. For further attempts to estimate Hitler's financial position at this time, see Smith, 112; Toland, 29, from NA, *The Hitler Source Book*, 925–6, interview with William Patrick Hitler; and Jones, 300–301 n.35. Hitler claimed in 1921 that he had had only 80 Kronen on him when he went to Vienna (Letter of 29 November 1921, in IfZ, MA-731 (= HA, Reel 1), reproduced in Joachimsthaler, 92.

157. Kubizek, 156 (trans., *Young Hitler*, 101).

158. Kubizek, 158.

159. Kubizek, 157, 160, 162, 170, 223, 247, 258 for descriptions of the room and surroundings.

160. Kubizek, 161.

161. Kubizek, 157, 161–2, 178, 273 (for eating and drinking habits).

162. Kubizek, 178. According to one account, he did smoke very occasionally when in the Men's Home (Honisch testimony in HA, Reel 1, File 17 (IfZ, MA-731), printed in Joachimsthaler, 58). Hitler himself much later claimed to have smoked, when down and out in Vienna, between twenty-four and forty cigarettes a day, before realizing how foolish this was when he had no money for food. It has the ring of a moralistic homily rather than a true story. (*Monologe*, 317, 11–12 March 1942).

163. Kubizek, 192.

164. Kubizek, 193.

165. Smith reckoned (119) that Hitler's monthly expenditure was in the region of 80–90 Kronen, meaning that his savings were falling by around 60 Kronen a month. The basis of his reckoning is not, however, given.

166. *Monologe*, 294 (22–3 February 1942).

167. Kubizek, 192–3.

168. Smith, 123.

169. Kubizek, 253–5.

170. Kubizek, 272–8.

171. Kubizek, 256–61.

172. Smith, 121. Two of his relatives told the NSDAP-Hauptarchiv in 1938 that they had last seen Hitler in the Waldviertel in 1907 (Binion, 'Foam', 523). The Kubizek postcards seem, however, to confirm that he paid a visit there in August 1908 (Kubizek, 260–61; Jetzinger, 204–6).

173. Kubizek, 261–2.

174. Jetzinger, 218; Smith, 122.

175. Heiden, 49.

176. Smith, 122. Hitler's shame at his failure was lasting. In 1912, according to the account of an anonymous co-resident of the Men's Home, he said that he had completed a few semesters at the Academy of Fine Arts but then had left because he had been too involved in student political organizations and because he did not have the means for further study (Anonymous, 'My Friend Hitler', 10 – see below, n.253, for full reference). If the account is accurate, then Hitler was already a practised liar.

177. See Smith, 8–9.

178. Kubizek, 246. See Jetzinger, 210–11 on the worker demonstration Kubizek allegedly witnessed with Hitler, and 210–14 on criticism of other parts of Kubizek's account of Hitler's political views at this time. The 'pacifism' might have been Kubizek's garbled version of Hitler's dislike of the Habsburg army and the annexation of Bosnia in 1908.

179. At the end of his lengthy contemptuous description in *Mein Kampf* (*MK*, 80–100), Hitler claimed (100) that he had attended the Vienna parliament for two years.

180. Kubizek, 249.

181. *MK*, 135 (trans., *MK* Watt, 113).

182. See *MK*, 14.

183. *MK*, ch.3.

184. *MK*, 59. In his letter to the anonymous 'Herr Doktor' of 29 November 1921 (IfZ, MA-731 (= HA Reel 1), repr. in Joachimsthaler, 92) Hitler wrote that he 'became an antisemite in scarcely a year' after arriving in Vienna. However, the letter contains numerous chronological inaccuracies. It would be unwise to accept the dating literally, as do Waite, 187 and Marlis Steinert, *Hitler*, Munich, 1994, 50. Smith, 148 is rightly sceptical that Hitler's 'conversion' took place in 1908, during the time he was mainly with Kubizek.

185. Kubizek, 251.

186. He was resident there from 18 November 1908 to 22 August 1909 (Smith, 122–3, 126).

187. Testimony of Marie Fellinger (*née* Rinke), IfZ, MA-731 (= HA, Reel 1), part of the recollections of Marie Fellinger and Maria Wohlrab (*née* Kubata) about Hitler in Vienna, collected for the party's archive on 11 June 1940. These relate to Hitler's frequenting of 'Kaffee Kubata', owned by Frau Wohlrab between 1912 and 1919, where Marie Fellinger had been an assistant. The café was in the vicinity of Felberstraße, but Hitler had long been departed from that area when Frau Wohlrab took over its running. She claimed to recall a lady-friend of Hitler – 'Dolferl' as she called him – by the name of Wetti or Pepi calling in the café to tell her that he was leaving for Germany and Hitler bidding her, Frau Wohlrab, a gracious farewell, saying he did not expect to return to Austria. It seems highly unlikely that Hitler would, in 1913, have been frequenting a little café in the south of the city when he

had for three years been living in Brigittenau, in the north. The whole tale sounds like a fabrication. Jones, 133, 271, 283, 344 n.92 accepts the story as valid (and turns Hitler's supposed lady friend into a man). See Joachimsthaler, 20, 161.

188. E.g. Smith, 148; implied in Jones, 135–8, and Fest, *Hitler*, 59–65; this timing is central to the argument of Wilfried Daim, *Der Mann, der Hitler die Ideen gab*, Vienna/Cologne/Graz, 1985.

189. The magazine claimed a circulation for itself of 100,000, and was apparently well known in student circles. However, it may be doubted that the circulation was anything so wide as Lanz claimed. (See Daim, 47, 127.)

190. Daim, 48; and see Hamann, 308–19.

191. Hamann, 293–308, here 293, 299, 303–5.

192. Hamann, 300–303.

193. Hamann, 309.

194. Daim, 48–207, describes at length Lanz and his extraordinary ideas. See also Nicholas Goodrick-Clarke, *The Occult Roots of Nazism*, Wellingborough, 1985, 90–105.

195. Daim, 25.

196. The title of Daim's book.

197. See e.g. Fest, 59–60; Steinert, 56, 109; Hamann, 317.

198. *MK*, 59–60 (trans., *MK* Watt, 52).

199. See Daim, 190–207, for illustration of the point in the dissection of Lanz's crackpot ideology. Issue Nr 25 of *Ostara* (July 1908) did have a section on 'the solution of the Jewish Question', within an essay on 'Aryanism and its Enemies', but was prepared even to state (7) that 'not all Jews are naturally hostile to aryanism' and that, consequently, 'not all Jews should be lumped into one pot'. Issue Nr 26, 'Introduction to Racial Knowledge', contains nothing specifically on the 'Jewish Question', and is largely devoted to evaluation of skull types, etc. I am grateful to Gerald Fleming for supplying me with these two issues of *Ostara*.

200. Daim, 25–6, 269–70 n.8.

201. A point made by Rudolph Binion, in the symposium following his paper, 'Hitler's Concept of Lebensraum', *History of Childhood Quarterly*, 1 (1973), 251. The suspicion must be that the obscure occultist Lanz was keen to establish his own place in history as 'the man who gave Hitler his ideas'. Compared with his apparently clear memory of the young Hitler, it is striking that Lanz could not remember the name of a journalist he also allegedly influenced, who was with Hitler in Landsberg after the putsch (Daim, 270 n.8). On the other hand, he claimed to have met Lenin, who had allegedly studied his ideas and approved of them (Daim, 110–11). Evidently, Lanz was keen to assert an influence for his ideas on important historical figures.

202. Daim, 36–7, 274–5 n.39.

203. Daim, 40, 275 n.42; Hamann, 318, for the absence of any provable ban on Lanz's works during the Third Reich.

204. As pointed out by George Mosse, *The Crisis of German Ideology*, London, 1966, 295.

205. Binion, 'Hitler's Concept of Lebensraum', symposium, 251.

206. See Hamann, 318–19.

207. Cit. Hamann, 318.

208. Address registration: IfZ, MA-731 (HA, Reel 1); Smith, 126; Hamann, 206.

209. Smith, 127; Hamann, 206. It was three months before he resurfaced in the police records. There is no first-hand account of his activities in this period.

210. Eberhard Jäckel and Axel Kuhn (eds.), *Hitler. Sämtliche Aufzeichnungen 1905–1924*, Stuttgart, 1980 (= JK), 55 (letter to the Magistrat der Stadt Linz of 21 January 1914). Hitler went on to claim that he had no income whatsoever when down and out. He was, in fact, still in receipt of his orphan's pension until 1911 (Jetzinger, 220).

211. Hitler later spoke of living on milk and dry bread in this period, and not having a warm meal 'for months' (*Monologe*, 317 (11–12 March 1942)).

212. Heiden, *Der Führer*, 50; Jetzinger, 219; Smith, 127.

213. Hanisch, 239.

214. Heiden, *Der Führer*, 50; Smith, 127 n.33; Joachimsthaler, 48–9, who also points out that Hitler by this time had no money to rent a furnished room; Hamann, 206–8, notes that the publicity given by the Nazis after the Anschluß to this one address at which Hitler was supposed to have lived in Vienna may well have been consciously intended to obscure any investigation of his time in the city.

215. Joachimsthaler, 49, 51 (Hanisch's testimony), for Hitler's appearance. For conditions in such hostels, and the life of down-and-outs in Vienna at that time, see Heiden, *Der Führer*, 60; Jenks, 31–9; Jones, 157–61; Hamann, 222–5. For Hitler, who had always been punctilious about personal hygiene and fearful of infection, the squalor must have been hard to take, and almost certainly contributed to his later cleanliness fetishism. In *Mein Kampf* he wrote: 'Even today it fills me with horror when I think of those wretched caverns, the lodging houses and tenements, sordid scenes of garbage, repulsive filth, and worse' (*MK*, 28 (trans., MK Watt, 26–7)).

216. See *MK*, 22.

217. Reinhold Hanisch, 'Meine Begegnung mit Hitler!', HA, Reel 3, File 64 (two-page account from 1933, reproduced in Joachimsthaler, 49–50); Reinhold Hanisch, 'I Was Hitler's Buddy', 3 parts, *New Republic*, 5, 12, 19 April 1939, 239–42, 270–72, 297–300. The lengthier version published only in English in *New Republic* appeared two years after Hanisch's death. The following passages are based on these descriptions, which, despite different length, correspond closely with each other. (See Smith, 161ff., and Hamann, 265–71, for Hanisch as a source and the context within which his accounts were written. Biographical details on Hanisch are provided by Joachimsthaler, 268 n.115. Hanisch was an important source for Heiden's early biography. See Heiden, *Der Führer*, 51ff.)

218. Joachimsthaler, 268. Hitler told the police in 1910 that he had met Hanisch in the Asyl in Meidling, and that he had only ever known him as Fritz Walter (Jetzinger, 224).

219. See Smith, 129 n.39 for acceptance of Hanisch's story of how he met Hitler, despite doubts raised by police records.

220. HA, Reel 3, File 64 (printed in Joachimsthaler, 49); Hanisch, 240; Heiden, *Der Führer*, 51. Hanisch found work again in domestic service on 21 December 1909 (Joachimsthaler, 268 n.115).

221. Hanisch, 240; Heiden, *Der Führer*, 51; and see Smith, 130–31 and n.41.

222. See Kubizek, 183–5.

223. According to Hanisch, he did contemplate digging ditches, but was dissuaded from the idea on the grounds that it was 'difficult to climb up' once started upon such a job (Hanisch, 240).

224. Joachimsthaler, 70.

225. *MK*, 40–42. In his 1921 account (IfZ, MA-731, repr. in Joachimsthaler, 92), Hitler claimed he was working as a labourer on a building site before he was eighteen years old. That was before he had even gone to live in Vienna.

226. Hanisch, 240.

227. See Hamann, 208–11. The suspicion voiced by Heiden, *Der Führer*, 60, that it might even have been 'copied . . . with small changes' from the autobiography of the first leader of the Nazi Party, Anton Drexler, *Mein politisches Erwachen*, Munich, 1919, seems baseless. None of Drexler's text bears close comparison.

228. Smith, 131–2; Jetzinger, 223; Hamann, 227. Hanisch's presumption (HA, 3/64; *New Republic*, 5 April 1939, 240) that Hitler had written to his sister and received the money from her was most probably incorrect.

229. Hanisch (HA, 3/64; *New Republic*, 5 April 1939, 240) stated that Hitler purchased the overcoat at Christmas 1909. In his account in the NSDAP-Hauptarchiv, he then inaccurately remarked that Hitler lived 'from now on' in the Men's Home in Meldemannstraße. In the later *New Republic* article, he more correctly states that Hitler subsequently moved to Meldemannstraße (where he lived from 9 February 1910) (Hamann, 227).

230. Hanisch, 242; Heiden, *Hitler*, 15; Heiden, *Der Führer*, 61; Smith, 136.

231. Hanisch, 241. Hanisch was registered on 11 February 1910 at an address in Herzstraße in the Favoriten district. He claimed (240) that he also moved into the Men's Home in Meldemannstraße. There is no record of him living in there at that time, though he certainly frequented it, and was indeed later resident, from November 1912 to March 1913, living under his pseudonym of Friedrich Walter (Joachimsthaler, 268 n.115; Hamann, 542).

232. Hanisch, HA, 3/64 and *New Republic*, 5 April 1939, 241; and Karl Honisch, 'Wie ich im Jahre 1913 Adolf Hitler kennen lernte', HA, Reel 1, File 17, printed, with some minor inaccuracies, in Joachimsthaler, 50–55; though this latter description relates to 1913, there is little doubt that it was the same in 1910. See also Smith, 132–3; Jenks, 26–8; Hamann, 229–34.

233. Hanisch, 272.

234. Hanisch, 241, 271–2. See Joachimsthaler, 67–9, 270 n.161; Smith, 137–8; Hamann, 499–500.

235. Hanisch, HA, 3/64, and *New Republic*, 5 April 1939, 240–41; Honisch, HA, 1/17; Smith, 135–6. Joachimsthaler, 58–76, deals with Hitler's pictures, and forgeries of them, including some by Hanisch (58–61). See also Hamann, 234–7.

236. Hanisch, HA, 3/64, and *New Republic*, 5 April 1939, 241–2. See also Smith, 137–40.

237. Hanisch, 297. And see Smith, 139.

238. Hanisch, HA, 3/64. For Karl Hermann Wolf, see Hamann, 375–93. About this time, too, according to Hanisch's account (also in *New Republic*, 5 April 1939, 242), Hitler was impressed by a silent film called *The Tunnel*, based on a novel by Bernhard Kellermann, in which the masses were stirred by a demagogue. Though he was said much later to have referred approvingly to the film (see Albert Speer, *Spandau. The Secret Diaries*, Fontana edn, London, 1977, 328), Hitler certainly did not see it during his time in Vienna. The film was only completed in 1915 (Hamann, 238, 605 n.20).

239. Hanisch, 241–2.

240. HA, 3/64; *New Republic*, 12 April 1939, 271; Smith, 136–7.

241. Hanisch, 241, 271–2, 297–8. See also Smith, 137, 139.

242. HA, 3/64; *New Republic*, 5 April 1939, 241; 19 April 1939, 298–9; Smith, 140.

243. Hanisch, 299.

244. Hanisch, 241.

245. See Joachimsthaler, 69; Smith, 138. Speculation – it can be no more – on a possible visit to the Waldviertel is made by Hamann, 245.

246. Smith, 137; this is one story that Hanisch and Greiner (39–42) have in common, and which has been taken to demonstrate that Greiner, for all his inaccuracies and fabrications, did indeed know Hitler in the Men's Home, and was almost certainly writing without any knowledge of Hanisch's account. (See Smith, 165–6.) Other anecdotes about Hitler in the Men's Home where Greiner overlaps with Hanisch – the poor state of Hitler's clothing, his support of the Schönerer movement, the disturbances caused by his verbal aggression towards Social Democracy – may also, therefore, be based on reality, unlike some of his wilder flights of fantasy. The most likely explanation is, however, that Greiner had come to know Hanisch, or at least to hear some of the stories he was putting round, in Vienna in the 1930s, and opportunistically embellished them for his own purposes.

247. Hanisch, 298–9; on Hanisch's later forgeries of Hitler paintings, Joachimsthaler, 59–61; Smith, 140; Heiden, 61–3; Hamann, 265–71.

248. Honisch, in HA, 17/1 (printed in Joachimsthaler, 54, 58).

249. When Hanisch had asked in 1909 about his future aims, Hitler had confessed that he did not know what they were (Hanisch, 240).

250. Honisch, HA, 17/1 (Joachimsthaler, 55).

251. See Christa Schroeder, *Er war mein Chef*, 134.

252. HA, 17/1 (Joachimsthaler, 55, 57–8); Smith, 141–2; Br.Anon. (Hamann, 541).

253. Anonymous, 'Muj Prítel Hitler' ('My Friend Hitler'), *Moravsky ilustrovany zpravodaj*, 40 (1935), 10–11 (in Czech). I am grateful to Neil Bermel for providing me with a translation.

254. Hanisch, 242, 272.

255. Smith, 141.

256. Jetzinger, 230–32; Smith, 143.

257. Jetzinger, 231.

258. Jetzinger, 226–7; Smith, 143.

259. Marckhgott, 273, 275–6; Hamann, 250–51.

260. Hamann, 251.

261. Smith, 9.

262. Smith, 140–41; Honisch, HA, 17/1 (Joachimsthaler, 54–5). Hitler was disparaging about his own paintings – though proud of his architectural drawings – when speaking to his photographer, Heinrich Hoffmann, in 1944, commenting that it was 'madness' to pay such high prices as they were fetching. He added that he had in Vienna around 1910 never received more than about (the equivalent of) 12 Reich Marks for a picture. He had painted, he said, only to earn a bare living and so that he 'could study'. He had not wanted to become an artist, he somewhat disingenuously claimed (omitting the fact that this had been a very real ambition in 1907–8) (Schroeder, 134).

263. Honisch, HA, 17/1 (Joachimsthaler, 54).

264. *MK*, 35 (trans., *MK* Watt, 32). And see Honisch, HA, 17/1 (Joachimsthaler, 54).

265. Above based on Honisch's testimony, in HA, 17/1 (Joachimsthaler, 54–7).

266. See *MK*, 117–21, for Hitler's attitude towards the Churches, and recognition of Schönerer's mistakes. For the lack of influence on Hitler of the National Socialist movement which had emerged in Bohemia in 1904, see Smith, 146–7.

267. *MK*, 40–42.

268. Greiner, 43–4.

269. Franz Stein, born in Vienna in 1869 in humble circumstances, was a fervent Schönerer admirer whose raucous agitation was directed at winning German-speaking workers in the industrialized region of northern Bohemia to a national, German, socialism. See Hamann, 354–75, here 367, and ch.9 for anti-Czech feeling. The growth of anti-Czech nationalist feelings among workers is dealt with by Andrew Whiteside, *Austrian National Socialism before 1918*, The Hague, 1962, ch.4.

270. See Heiden, *Der Führer*, 53.

271. *MK*, 30 (trans., *MK* Watt, 28).

272. *MK*, 22 (trans., *MK* Watt, 21).

273. *MK*, 40 (trans., *MK* Watt, 36).

274. See Kubizek, 30 (trousers under the bed to obtain correct creases); 156 (appearance when he meets Kubizek); 170 (anxious to keep clothes and underclothes spotlessly clean).

275. See Heiden, *Der Führer*, 60; the point is also made by Alan Bullock, *Hitler. A Study in Tyranny*, Harmondsworth, 1962 edn, 36.

276. *MK*, 22 (trans., *MK* Watt, 21–2).

277. *MK*, 24 (trans., *MK* Watt, 23).

278. *MK*, 43.

279. *MK*, 46 (trans., *MK* Watt, 41).

280. See Joachimsthaler, 45, and his comment: 'That Hitler already put forward in Vienna his political arguments of 1920/21 is not credible.'

281. *MK*, 55–9 (trans., *MK* Watt, 48–51). In his letter to the anonymous 'Herr Doktor' of 29 November 1921, Hitler wrote of his 'conversion': 'Coming from a family more attuned to more cosmopolitan (*weltbürgerlich*) views, I became an antisemite in scarcely a year through the school of hard reality' (IfZ, MA-731 (HA, Reel 1), repr. in Joachimsthaler, 92).

282. *MK*, 59 (trans., *MK* Watt, 52).

283. *MK*, 60 (trans., *MK* Watt, 52).

284. *MK*, 61.

285. *MK*, 64 (trans., *MK* Watt, 56).

286. *MK*, 65–6. Hitler singled out the names of four Jewish leaders of the working class: Viktor Adler, Friedrich Austerlitz, Wilhelm Ellenbogen, and Anton David. The first three were frequently linked together in the attacks of Viennese antisemites; the fourth played a leading role in worker demonstrations against inflation in 1911 (Hamann, 258–9).

287. *MK*, 66 (trans., *MK* Watt, 57).

288. *MK*, 69.

289. Kubizek, 94.

290. Kubizek, 62 (aversion to Jewish students in the Mensa); 249–50 (Jewish journalist).

291. Kubizek, 250–51. Kubizek's story was probably based on Hitler's own account in *Mein Kampf* (59). And see Jetzinger's criticism of Kubizek's account (214).

292. Hamann, 83.

293. See Hamann, 82–3.

294. Hamann, 22.

295. Hamann, 28–9. Hitler (*MK*, 55) claimed he was not antisemitic in Linz. Stronger emphasis is placed on antisemitism in Hitler's school in Linz, and on support in the school and town for the antisemitic programme of Schönerer, by Friedrich Heer, *Der Glaube des Adolf Hitler*, Munich/Eßlingen, 1968, 25, 72; Friedrich Heer, *Gottes erste Liebe*, Munich/Eßlingen, 1967, 355. But Bukey, 8–9, also implies that antisemitism in Linz, while widespread and pernicious, was far less significant than anti-Czech feeling.

296. Albert Speer, *Erinnerungen*, Frankfurt am Main/Berlin, 1969, 112; Hamann, 29–30. To Goebbels, too, Hitler spoke of Vienna as the place where he first became an antisemite (*Tb* Reuth, iii. 1334 (17 October 1939)).

297. See Hamann, 344–7, for Schönerer's racial antisemitism.

298. IfZ, MA-731 (HA, Reel 1), 'Notizen für Kartei' of 8 December 1938, refers to Bloch receiving two cards, one a nicely painted one with New Year greeting (presumably 1908), and 'cordial thanks' ('*herzlichem Dank*'). They were confiscated

by the Gestapo in March 1938. Bloch, 69–70, refers to the cards in his own account. See also Binion, *Hitler among the Germans*, 19.

299. *MK*, 59.

300. Daim, 25–6, 270.

301. *MK*, 59–60.

302. Hanisch, 271.

303. Hamann, 242.

304. Hanisch, 271–2, 299. And see Hamann, 242, 246–7, 498.

305. Smith, 149.

306. Anonymous, 'My Friend Hitler', 11.

307. Hanisch, 272.

308. Greiner, 75–82. Greiner (79) claimed Hitler brought his antisemitism with him from Linz.

309. Binion, *Hitler among the Germans*, 2, 19; Binion, 'Hitler's Concept of Lebensraum', 201–2.

310. See Binion, 'Hitler's Concept of Lebensraum', 189; Binion, *Hitler among the Germans*, 2. Joachimsthaler, 44, sees no significant hatred of the Jews in Hitler before as late as June 1919.

311. See *MK*, 71 for the implication that his unchanging political philosophy had been formed before entry into politics at the age of thirty.

312. Jones, 129. On the menacing anti-Jewish atmosphere in Vienna, see Hamann, 472–82.

313. Pulzer, 202.

314. Jenks, 127–33.

315. Hitler later claimed to have 'intensively studied' Theodor Fritsch's *Handbuch der Judenfrage* as a young man in Vienna (*Hitler. Reden, Schriften, Anordnungen. Februar 1925, bis Januar 1933*, Munich etc., 1992– (= RSA), IV/1, 133).

316. Carr, 123; Waite, 188.

317. Langer, 187. And see Carr, 121–2.

318. See Fest, *Hitler*, 65.

319. Hanisch, 272. Hitler referred in *Mein Kampf* (61) to 'the smell of these caftan-wearers'.

320. After the war, Hitler's sister, Paula, thought it 'possible that the hard years during his youth in Vienna caused his anti-Jewish attitude. He was starving severely in Vienna and he believed that his failure in painting was only due to the fact that trade in works of art was in Jewish hands.' This seems, however, merely a surmise on her part; there is no evidence that Hitler gave her such an explanation (NA, NND-881077).

321. Hanisch, 272.

322. Hanisch, 271–2.

323. Hamann, 246.

324. Smith, 149–50.

325. Honisch testimony, HA, 17/1 (Joachimsthaler, 54).

326. Anonymous, 'My Friend Hitler', 10.

327. Langer, 185–6, commented on the lack of explanation for Hitler's apparent reluctance for so long to leave Vienna (despite, as we have noted, his long-standing admiration for Germany and some reported talk of wanting to go to Munich). The wait for the inheritance provides the answer.

328. Hamann, 85, 568.

329. Jetzinger, 254.

330. Joachimsthaler, 25.

331. Smith, 150–51.

332. Jetzinger, 250.

333. Joachimsthaler, 15, 257–8. He established the fact, previously unknown, that Hitler's travelling companion was Häusler. See especially on Häusler, Hamann, 566–8.

334. *MK*, 137.

CHAPTER 3: ELATION AND EMBITTERMENT

1. The title of ch.4 of Ralf Dahrendorf, *Society and Democracy in Germany*, London, 1968.

2. The thesis of Germany's 'special path' (*Sonderweg*) to modernity found classical expression in Hans-Ulrich Wehler, *Das Deutsche Kaiserreich 1871–1918*, Göttingen, 1973. The clash of traditional and modern values and social structures as the framework for Hitler's rise was advanced by Ernst Bloch, 'Der Faschismus als Erscheinungsform der Ungleichzeitigkeit', in Ernst Nolte (ed.), *Theorien über den Faschismus*, 6th edn, Königstein/Ts., 1984, 182–204.

3. The possibilities are outlined most prominently in Manfred Rauh, *Die Parlamentarisierung des deutschen Reiches*, Düsseldorf, 1977, esp. here 13–14, 363–5; the openness of the future development of the Kaiserreich is emphasized by Thomas Nipperdey, *Deutsche Geschichte 1866–1918*, vol.ii, Munich, 1992, 755–7, 890–93. The rejection of the '*Sonderweg*' interpretation is most plainly evident in Nipperdey's comment (891), that 'the history of the Reich from 1871 to 1914 is a history of common European normality'.

4. The argument is most powerfully adduced by Hans-Ulrich Wehler, *Deutsche Gesellschaftsgeschichte 1849–1914*, Munich, 1995, esp. 460–86, 1279–95, restated briefly and pointedly in Hans-Ulrich Wehler, 'Wirtschaftliche Entwicklung, sozialer Wandel, politische Stagnation: Das Deutsche Kaiserreich am Vorabend des Ersten Weltkriegs', in Simone Lässig and Karl Heinrich Pohl (eds.), *Sachsen im Kaiserreich*, Dresden, 1997, 301–8.

5. Nipperdey's massive two-volume study of Imperial Germany ends with the comment: 'The basic colours of history are not black and white, their basic pattern not the contrast of a chess-board; the basic colour of history is grey, in endless variations' (Nipperdey, ii.905).

6. This was implicit in Gerhard Ritter's comment that it was 'almost unbearable' to think how 'the will of a single madman' had driven Germany into the Second World War (Gerhard Ritter, *Das deutsche Problem. Grundfragen deutschen Staatslebens gestern und heute*, Munich, 1962, 198). The use of the 'works accident' metaphor to describe Hitler as an unpredictable and sharp break in the continuity of German history is analysed by Jürgen Steinle, 'Hitler als "Betriebsunfall in der Geschichte" ', *Geschichte in Wissenschaft und Unterricht*, 45 (1994), 288–302. Eberhard Jäckel reverses the usual argument in insisting that Hitler was, indeed, the equivalent of a nuclear accident in society (Jäckel, *Das deutsche Jahrhundert*, ch.4, 153–82, and 'L'arrivée d'Hitler au pouvoir: un Tschernobyl de l'histoire', in Gilbert Krebs and Gérard Schneilin, *Weimar ou de la Démocratie en Allemagne*, Paris, 1994, 345–58). I had used precisely the same metaphor in *The Nazi Dictatorship. Problems and Perspectives of Interpretation*, 215–16, but emphasized – a point Jäckel included in his argument – that a nuclear accident did not occur without structural systemic causes as well as human errors and miscalculations.

7. See Geoff Eley, *Reshaping the German Right*, New Haven/London, 1980, ch.10.

8. The title of George Mosse's book, *The Nationalisation of the Masses*, New York, 1975.

9. Nipperdey, ii.265; see also Thomas Nipperdey, *Deutsche Geschichte 1866–1918*, vol.i, Munich, 1990, 599–600 for nationalist academics.

10. Cit. Pulzer, 242.

11. See Lothar Kettenacker, 'Der Mythos vom Reich', in K. H. Bohrer (ed.), *Mythos and Moderne*, Frankfurt am Main, 1983, 261–89.

12. Mosse, *Nationalisation*, 62–3 and pl. 9; Nipperdey, i.739, ii.599.

13. *MK*, 180. For the monuments, see Nipperdey, i.738–41, ii.261.

14. Mosse, 36–7; Nipperdey, ii.599.

15. Elisabeth Fehrenbach, 'Images of Kaiserdom: German attitudes to Kaiser Wilhelm II', in John C.G. Röhl and Nicolaus Sombart (eds.), *Kaiser Wilhelm II. New Interpretations*, Cambridge, 1982, 269–85, here 276.

16. Nipperdey, ii.289; Léon Poliakov, *The History of Anti-Semitism*, vol.iv, Oxford, 1985, 23–4, 31, 83ff.

17. See Fritz Stern, *The Politics of Cultural Despair*, Berkeley, 1961; George Mosse, *The Crisis of German Ideology*, pts. I–II; and – specifically for Paul de Lagarde's influence – Nipperdey, i.825–6.

18. Nipperdey, ii.256.

19. Pulzer, 231.

20. Pulzer, 236 (citing August Julius Langbehn).

21. See Nipperdey, ii.290.

22. Nipperdey, ii.299, 305; Mosse, *Crisis*, esp. 93–7, 112. Houston Stewart Chamberlain, born in England but an avid Germanophile, became a German citizen, married Richard Wagner's daughter, and developed his racist theories within the Wagner circle at Bayreuth. He saw history as racial struggle, with the German race representing good and the Jewish race evil. He was full of praise for Hitler, who visited

him shortly before his death in 1927. Theodor Fritsch was one of the most vitriolic early antisemitic writers and founder of the radical racist 'Hammerbund' to propagate his ideas, which linked racism to vehement opposition to urbanism and industrialization. He died, aged seventy-nine and much honoured by the Nazis, in 1933.

23. Jeremy Noakes, 'Nazism and Eugenics: the Background to the Nazi Sterilisation Law of 14 July 1933', in R.J. Bullen, H. Pogge von Strandmann and A.B. Polonsky (eds.), *Ideas into Politics*, London/Sydney, 1984, 79–80.

24. The title of the popular novel by Hans Grimm, *Volk ohne Raum*, Munich, 1926.

25. On the development of the dual forms of expansionist idea, see Woodruff D. Smith, *The Ideological Origins of Nazi Imperialism*, New York/Oxford, 1986.

26. Nipperdey, ii.601.

27. Eley, *Reshaping*, 218–23. Eley (230–31) notes that the Imperial League against Social Democracy put out close on 50 million pamphlets and leaflets between 1904 and 1914 attacking the Social Democrats.

28. Nipperdey, ii.601; Roger Chickering, *We Men Who Feel Most German. A Cultural Study of the Pan-German League, 1886–1914*, London, 1984, 191.

29. Nipperdey, ii.602–9; Chickering, esp. chs.4, 6; Eley, *Reshaping*, 337–43.

30. Nipperdey, ii.607–8.

31. Daniel Frymann (Heinrich Claß), *Wenn ich der Kaiser wär!*, 5th edn, Leipzig, 1914, 227.

32. See Axel Schildt, 'Radikale Antworten von rechts auf die Kulturkrise der Jahrhundertwende', *Jahrbuch für Antisemitismusforschung*, 4 (1995), 63–87.

33. See Geoff Eley, 'The German Right, 1860–1945: How it Changed', in his essay collection, *From Unification to Nazism*, London, 1986, 231–53, and his subsequent article along similar lines, 'Conservatives and radical nationalists in Germany: the production of fascist potentials, 1912–1928', in Martin Blinkhorn (ed.), *Fascists and Conservatives. The Radical Right and the Establishment in Twentieth-Century Europe*, London, 1990, 50–70.

34. Wilhelm II, born in Potsdam on 27 January 1859, became German Emperor and King of Prussia in 1888. His childish immaturity, extreme restlessness, imperious and explosive temperament, unbridled arrogance, intolerance of the slightest opposition, gross exaggeration of his own abilities, and obsessive hatreds – scarcely less violent than Hitler's – were unmistakable indicators of personality disturbances in the man who ruled Germany for thirty years. He was to die in exile at Doorn in Holland on 4 June 1941. See John C.G. Röhl, 'Kaiser Wilhelm II. Eine Charakterskizze', in his *Kaiser, Hof und Staat*, Munich, 1987, 17–34; and his major study, *Wilhelm II. Die Jugend des Kaisers 1859–1888*, Munich, 1993, where the birth trauma and withered left arm are strongly emphasized as contributory factors to the 'disturbed character-formation of the last German Emperor' (38).

35. *MK*, 138 and (139) 'I achieved the happiness of a truly inward contentment' (trans., *MK* Watt, 116–17).

36. *MK*, 138.

37. *MK*, 135–6 (trans., *MK* Watt, 113).

38. *MK*, 179 (trans., *MK* Watt, 150). In the *Reichshandbuch der deutschen Gesellschaft*, vol.1, Berlin, n.d. (1931?), 771, Hitler's entry – misleading both as to date and motive – stated: 'In spring 1912 he moved to Munich in order to have a greater, more promising, field for his political activity.' Also cited in Fest, i.91.

39. *MK*, 139 (trans., *MK* Watt, 117).

40. Cit. Max Spindler, *Handbuch der bayerischen Geschichte*, vol.iv, pt.2, Munich, 1975, 1195. Lovis Corinth (1858–1925), though he came from East Prussia, made his mark in Munich during the 1890s as part of a group of progressive Munich artists who formed the Münchner Sezession and was in his early period one of the leading exponents of Jugendstil. See Spindler, iv.1196. Also *Deutsche Biographische Enzyklopädie*, vol.2, Munich etc., 1995, 373. The artistic and literary scene in Munich at the turn of the century is fully described in the Introduction and ch.1 of David Clay Large, *Where Ghosts Walked. Munich's Road to the Third Reich*, New York, 1997.

41. *MK*, 139. Hitler claimed, too, that the Bavarian dialect had affinities for him – presumably a glamorized reference to the short time as a child that he had lived in Passau in Lower Bavaria (*MK*, 135, 138). His memories of Passau could not have been extensive. He had left around his sixth birthday, having lived there for only just over two and a half years (Jetzinger, 58, 64, 66; Smith, 53, 55).

42. *MK*, 139.

43. *Monologe*, 201 (15–16 January 1942).

44. Heinz A. Heinz, *Germany's Hitler*, London (1934), 2nd edn, 1938, 49. This account, written to portray Hitler, soon after his takeover of power, in the best possible light to an English readership, evidently draws in this passage on *Mein Kampf* (including giving the date of 1912 for the move to Munich). There is, however, no reason to doubt Hitler's admiration for the splendour of Munich's buildings.

45. *Monologe*, 400 (13 June 1943).

46. See, for the grandiose rebuilding plans for Munich, Hans-Peter Rasp, 'Bauten und Bauplanung für die "Hauptstadt der Bewegung"', in *München – 'Hauptstadt der Bewegung'*, ed. Münchner Stadtmuseum, Munich, 1993, 294–309.

47. *MK*, 136.

48. Heinz, 56 – the glowing account, given in the 1930s, of his landlady, Frau Popp (who repeated the incorrect date of 1912, as given in *Mein Kampf*, for his arrival). On his police registration form in Munich, Hitler described himself as a painter (*Kunstmaler*) (Joachimsthaler, 17, 32).

49. *JK*, 54, written as '*Architektur Maler*'; Werner Maser, *Hitlers Briefe und Notizen*, Düsseldorf, 1988, 40; Jetzinger, 262.

50. IfZ, MA-731 (= HA, Reel 1), repr. in Joachimsthaler, 91–2.

51. *Der Hitler-Prozeß 1924. Wortlaut der Hauptverhandlung vor dem Volksgericht München I, Teil 1*, ed. Lothar Gruchmann and Reinhard Weber, assisted by Otto Gritschneder, Munich, 1997, 19; *JK*, 1062. The wording given by Joachimsthaler, 31, based upon *Der Hitler-Prozeß vor dem Volksgericht in München*, Munich, 1924, deviates in places from the authentic text.

52. *Monologe*, 115 (29 October 1941). The translation in *Hitler's Table Talk*, 97–8 is incomplete and, as often, somewhat too loosely rendered.

53. Heinz, 49–50.

54. Orr, *Revue*, Nr 46 (1952), 3; Joachimsthaler, 16, 81; Hamann, 570–74. Häusler, unlike Hitler, returned to Vienna at the outbreak of the war (Joachimsthaler, 81). Curiously, in an application to rejoin the NSDAP in Austria on 1 May 1938, Häusler made no mention of his earlier connection with Hitler (BDC, Parteikorrespondenz, Rudolf Häusler, geb. 5 December 1893, Personal-Fragebogen, 1 May 1938).

55. Heinz, 50.

56. Joachimsthaler, 84–9.

57. Report of a discussion at the midday meal on 12 March 1944 on the Obersalzberg, HA, Reel 2, File 3, printed in Schroeder, 134 (see ch.2, n.262).

58. *JK*, 54; Schroeder, 134 (from HA Reel 2, File 3).

59. Heinz, 51.

60. Heinz, 50–52 (account of Frau Popp).

61. *MK*, 139.

62. *MK*, 169–70.

63. Heinz, 51.

64. Heiden, *Der Führer*, 65, remarks – though without references – on Hitler haranguing people in beerhalls, including the Schwemme of the Hofbräuhaus.

65. *MK*, 171 (trans., *MK* Watt, 142).

66. *MK*, 139–42.

67. Jetzinger, 254–7; Joachimsthaler, 25–6.

68. Jetzinger, 259–62.

69. Jetzinger, 262–4 (and part-reproduction between 272–3); Maser, *Hitlers Briefe*, 40–42; *JK*, 53–5. Jetzinger's criticism (265–72) of Hitler's letter is excessively pedantic.

70. Jetzinger, 258–65.

71. Joachimsthaler, 27–31.

72. Jetzinger, 284–92.

73. *MK*, 173 (trans., *MK* Watt, 145).

74. *MK*, 173–4, 177 (trans., *MK* Watt, 145–6, 148).

75. David Lloyd George, *War Memoirs*, vol.i, London, 1933, 52.

76. J.P. Stern, *Hitler: the Führer and the People*, London, 1975, 12.

77. Fritz Wiedemann, *Der Mann, der Feldherr werden wollte*, Velbert/Kettwig, 1964, 29.

78. Joachimsthaler, 159–60.

79. *MK*, 179 (trans., *MK* Watt, 150).

80. *Monologe*, 79 (13 October 1941).

81. *Monologe*, 46 (24–5 July 1941).

82. Heinrich Hoffmann, *Hitler Was My Friend*, London, 1955, 34.

83. Ernst Toller, *I Was a German*, London, 1934, 54.

84. Wolfgang J. Mommsen, *Der autoritäre Nationalstaat*, Frankfurt, 1990, 407. See

Richard Bessel, *Germany after the First World War*, Oxford, 1993, 2–4, for a balanced account of the varied mood and the differing motives for war enthusiasm.
85. Cit. Adrian Lyttelton (ed.), *Italian Fascisms from Pareto to Gentile*, London, 1973, 211.
86. Mommsen, *Der autoritäre Nationalstaat*, 407.
87. Werner Abelshauser, Anselm Faust and Dietmar Petzina (eds.), *Deutsche Sozialgeschichte 1914–1945. Ein historisches Lesebuch*, Munich, 1985, 215, cit. *Soziale Praxis*, 23 (1913–14), Sp. 1241–4.
88. One German soldier, in a letter to his father on 7 October 1915, wrote: 'What people call "patriotism" – I haven't got all that stuff (*den Klimbin*). Rather, pity, sympathy with the plight of the dear German people, the wish to understand its weaknesses and mistakes, and to help. So I don't want to flee from my people, also not in heart and mind. No, instead to place myself in the midst of the great misery and woe, to be a proper fighter for my people' (Philipp Witkop (ed.), *Kriegsbriefe gefallener Studenten*, Munich, 1928, 22).
89. *MK*, 177 (trans., *MK* Watt, 148).
90. Joachimsthaler, 101. The cited passage is not included in the English version of Hoffmann's memoirs – Heinrich Hoffmann, *Hitler Was My Friend*, London, 1955 – though the picture with Hitler ringed is printed opposite 16. The picture was publicized widely on the twentieth anniversary of the outbreak of the First World War (see *Daily Telegraph*, 3 August 1934). The picture without the famous ringing of Hitler is printed in Rudolf Herz, *Hoffmann und Hitler. Fotografie als Medium des Führer-Mythos*, Munich, 1994, 29. By 1943, Hoffmann enjoyed an annual income of over 3 million Marks, and his estate was worth over 6 million Marks (Herz, 37–8).
91. *MK*, 179.
92. Joachimsthaler, 102, 104.
93. Joachimsthaler, 108, attributes Hitler's acceptance in the Bavarian army to 'apparently the carelessness and lack of attention of some sergeant in the 2nd Infantry Regiment'.
94. Joachimsthaler, 103–8.
95. Joachimsthaler, 107. See Hitler's letter to the anonymous 'Herr Doktor' of 29 November 1921 (IfZ, MA-731 (= HA, Reel 1), reproduced in Joachimsthaler, 93).
96. Joachimsthaler, 106–7, 109–14, 116. Hitler was assigned to the First Company of the First Battalion of the Reserve Infantry Regiment 16 (List) in the Twelfth Infantry Brigade of the Sixth Bavarian Reserve Division (comprising in all around 17,000 men). The List Regiment was drawn mainly from Upper and Lower Bavaria. Difficulties in arming and uniforming the regiment meant that it only received spiked helmets in November 1914, and the full steel helmets in 1916 shortly before the Battle of the Somme.
97. *JK*, 59.
98. *JK*, 59 (postcard to Joseph Popp *en route* from Ulm to Antwerp); Joachimsthaler, 117.
99. *JK*, 60, 68.

100. Joachimsthaler, 120–21, 124.

101. *Monologe*, 71 (25–6 September 1941).

102. Joachimsthaler, 159–60.

103. Wiedemann, 26.

104. Joachimsthaler, 159–60.

105. Joachimsthaler, 126–7, 135, 277 n.339; Heinz, 65.

106. *MK*, 181–2; see Joachimsthaler, 129.

107. Examples cited in Joachimsthaler, 125, 128, 152–3, 155–6.

108. The regimental command post at Fromelles, from where military operations were directed, was about three kilometres behind the front. The regimental staff, forming the administrative support, were based an hour's walk away at Fournes. Hitler and the other dispatch runners worked in shifts of three days at Fromelles followed by three rest days at Fournes. (For Hitler's time there, see Joachimsthaler, 123, 126–7, 135–40.) Hitler claimed in 1944 that he had carried around with him throughout the entire First World War the five volumes of Schopenhauer's work (*Monologe*, 411 (19 May 1944)). Hans Frank remembered him saying much the same thing (Frank, 46).

109. Wiedemann, 24–5.

110. Balthasar Brandmayer, *Meldegänger Hitler 1914–18*, 2nd edn, Munich/Kolbermoor, 1933, 51–2. Brandmayer remained one of the few people allowed to address Hitler with the familiar '*Du*'. This did not prevent him receiving a warning in 1939, passed on by the Kanzlei des Führers, to avoid meddling in Party matters and 'sowing discontent among the people' through his complaints about the closure of a Catholic Kindergarten in his home town of Bruckmühl in Bavaria. Two years earlier, the Munich branch of the Reichsschrifttumskammer had sought permission to drop any reference to Hitler in the title of Brandmayer's book (BDC, Personal File of Balthasar Brandmayer, letters of Kanzlei des Führers, 18 October 1939, and Reichsschrifttumskammer München-Oberbayern, 12 November 1937).

111. *JK*, 68; Joachimsthaler, 130–31. The British journalist Ward Price much later recorded Hitler's characteristic embellishment of the story, claiming that he followed an inner voice as clear as a military command, telling him to leave the trench immediately (G. Ward Price, *I Know These Dictators*, London, 1937, 38).

112. *JK*, 60.

113. *JK*, 68.

114. *JK*, 61.

115. Wiedemann, 25–6; Brandmayer, 61, 68; Joachimsthaler, 140–44, 155–6. Two of those who knew Hitler during the war – Hans Mend and Korbinian Rutz – and subsequently published less than flattering recollections of him landed after 1933 in Dachau. See Joachimsthaler, 113, 143, 152–4, 271 n.193, 284 n.430. Rutz was dismissed from his teaching post after Hitler had been consulted but had declined to intervene on behalf of his former wartime comrade, declaring him to be 'inferior' (*minderwertig*) (BDC, Personal File, Korbinian Rutz, Hans-Heinrich Lammers to the Reich Governor of Bavaria, 17 March 1934).

116. Brandmayer, 105. For the suggestion that Hitler fathered a son, Jean-Marie Loret, during his time in the army, see Werner Maser, 'Adolf Hitler: Vater eines Sohnes', *Zeitgeschichte*, 5 (1977–8), 173–202. The extreme unlikeliness of this is emphasized by Joachimsthaler, 162–4. The alleged son, Jean-Marie Loret, went on to produce (in collaboration with René Mathot) his 'memoirs', *Ton père s'appelait Hitler*, Paris, 1981. They included (107–16) his mother's purported revelations of her relationship with Hitler and (127–49) an account of his own dealings with the German historian Werner Maser, on the trail of 'Hitler's son'. M. Loret had shown himself, in correspondence with Berlin museums in 1980, keen to establish the authenticity of a number of drawings which had been in his mother's possession as works of Hitler (IfZ, ZS 3133, Jean-Marie Loret).

117. Joachimsthaler, 144–6, 167. Max Amann and Fritz Wiedemann, who later made major careers for themselves in the Third Reich, of course did better than that. Amann's property in 1943 was worth more than 10 million Marks; though not in that league, Wiedemann was given a position as Hitler's adjutant, a six-seater Mercedes, and 'loans' and other gifts worth tens of thousands of Marks during the Third Reich (Joachimsthaler, 150).

118. Brandmayer, 72, 105; Joachimsthaler, 133, 156–8.

119. See Joachimsthaler, facing 128, 129, 161.

120. Brandmayer, 52–6.

121. Brandmayer, 43–4.

122. Brandmayer, 102.

123. *Monologe*, 219 (22–3 January 1942).

124. Hitler told Albert Speer in autumn 1943 that he would soon have only two friends, Fräulein Braun and his dog (Speer, 315). Around that time, Goebbels remarked in his diary: 'The Führer has his great happiness in his dog Blondi, who has become a true companion for him . . . It's good that the Führer has at least one living being who is constantly around him' (*TBJG*, 11.9, 477 (10 September 1943)).

125. *Monologe*, 219.

126. Heinrich Lugauer testimony in HA, Reel 2, Folder 47; extract printed in Joachimsthaler, 134.

127. Brandmayer, 66–8.

128. *JK*, 69; Maser, *Hitlers Briefe*, 100–101.

129. But see the comment of Ignaz Westenkirchner, one of Hitler's comrades, in the admittedly rosy-coloured Heinz, 66: 'For the most part he was always on about politics.'

130. *MK*, 182 (trans., *MK* Watt, 152), 192.

131. Joachimsthaler, 159. Ernst Schmidt, probably Hitler's closest comrade, also later remarked: 'He didn't try to bring any political influence to bear on me at that time' (Heinz, 98).

132. Toland, 66.

133. Brandmayer, 115. See also Westenkirchner's recollection in the 1930s: 'Two things seemed to get his goat – what the papers were saying at home about the war

and all, and the way the government, and particularly the Kaiser, were hampered by the Marxists and the Jews' (Heinz, 66). In a post-war interview, Westenkirchner reversed his position, denying that Hitler had spoken with any 'spitefulness' about the Jews (Toland, 66).

134. Brandmayer, 91–2.

135. *MK*, 209–12.

136. Joachimsthaler, 135.

137. *MK*, 209; Joachimsthaler, 164.

138. Hitler dated his wounding to 7 October (*MK*, 209). It seems more likely that it occurred two days earlier (see Joachimsthaler, 164–6, 286 n.487; also Brandmayer, 81, 89; Wiedemann, 28–9).

139. *MK*, 209–12. (Cited passages, 211, trans., *MK* Watt, 175); and see Joachimsthaler, 166. For the hatred of the Prussians in Bavaria, one of the foremost resentments of the civilian population, see Karl-Ludwig Ay, *Die Entstehung einer Revolution. Die Volksstimmung in Bayern während des Ersten Weltkrieges*, Berlin, 1968, 134–448.

140. Nipperdey, i.412; Werner Jochmann, 'Die Ausbreitung des Antisemitismus', in Werner Mosse (ed.), *Deutsches Judentum in Krieg und Revolution 1916–1923*, Tübingen, 1971, 425–7; Toland, 933; Wiedemann, 33.

141. Joachimsthaler, 174; Binion, *Hitler among the Germans*, 2; Toland, 66.

142. See above n.133.

143. See Ay, 32–3 for the growth of complaints in Bavaria about the Jews as alleged shirkers. How much, even at the beginning of the war, antisemitism had been part of Munich's popular culture is brought out by Robert Eben Sackett, 'Images of the Jew: Popular Joketelling in Munich on the Eve of World War I', *Theory and Society*, 16 (1987), 527–63, and his *Popular Entertainment, Class, and Politics in Munich, 1900–1923*, Cambridge, Mass., 1982. See also Large, *Where Ghosts Walked*, ch.1. For the spread and increasing ferocity of anti-Jewish feeling during the second half of the war, see, especially, Saul Friedländer, 'Die politischen Veränderungen der Kriegszeit und ihre Auswirkungen auf die Judenfrage', and Werner Jochmann, 'Die Ausbreitung des Antisemitismus', in Mosse, *Deutsches Judentum in Krieg und Revolution*, 27–65, 409–510.

144. *JK*, 78, 80; *MK*, 212.

145. Joachimsthaler, 169.

146. *MK*, 219–20; Joachimsthaler, 170.

147. Joachimsthaler, 170–71; *Monologe*, 100 (21–2 October 1941).

148. *JK*, 82. Joachimsthaler, 170–71, dispatches suggestions, which have found their way into the literature, that Hitler visited his relatives in Spital, or went to Dresden before going to Berlin.

149. Joachimsthaler, 172.

150. Wiedemann, 25–6. Wiedemann points out that he and Max Amann had unsuccessfully nominated Hitler on a previous occasion. Gutmann was generally unpopular with the men, and – whether simply because he was a Jew is uncertain

– detested by Hitler. See Brandmayer, 55; *Monologe*, 132 (10–11 November 1941); Toland, 932–3; Joachimsthaler, 173–4.

151. The figure fluctuated. Berlin newspapers wrote in 1933 of him capturing an officer and twenty soldiers (*Daily Telegraph*, 4 August 1933). The account by Westenkirchner in Heinz, 80–81, has twelve French soldiers captured by Hitler on 4 June 1918, but does not link this to the award of the Iron Cross. Toland, 69 (without source), speaks of Hitler delivering four prisoners to his commanding officer in June and being commended for it.

152. According to a letter from Eugen Tanhauser, Landrat in Schwabach, to the *Nürnberger Nachrichten*, of 4 August 1961, he had been told this by Gutmann himself, whom he had known for years and trusted implicitly (IfZ, ZS 1751, Eugen Tanhauser). This is cited by Joachimsthaler, 175–6, as the basis of his account, along with the post-war comments of Hitler's comrade, Johann Raab, and the remarks from 31 July 1918 on the nomination (from HA, Reel 2, File 47) of the Deputy Commander of the Regiment, Freiherr von Godin.

153. Joachimsthaler, 176. He did not travel to Spital, where his relatives lived, as stated by Maser, *Hitler*, 142, and Toland, 71.

154. *MK*, 220; Joachimsthaler, 176–7.

155. The testimony given to the NSDAP-Hauptarchiv (HA, Reel 2, Folder 47) of Johann Raab and Heinrich Lugauer, who were also blinded by the gas attack, is printed in Joachimsthaler, 177–8. Hitler said in his 1921 letter (see Joachimsthaler, 93) that he was 'at first totally blinded'; he used exactly the same words in his Munich trial in 1924 – *Hitler-Prozeß*, i.19. (The wording given by Joachimsthaler, 177, that he was for a time 'almost blind' is inaccurate.) His account in *Mein Kampf* suggests that he was partially blinded at first, stumbling back 'with burning eyes' before, a few hours later, the burning sensation had increased and 'it had grown dark around me' (*MK*, 220–21 (trans., *MK* Watt, 183).

156. Nipperdey, ii.861–2.

157. Adolf Hitler, *Mein Kampf. Bd.1, Eine Abrechnung*, Munich, 1925, 213 (trans., *MK* Watt, 183). In the single-volume 'Volksausgabe' (People's Edition) of *Mein Kampf*, the wording 'greatest villainy of the century' was changed to 'revolution' (*MK*, 221; Hermann Hammer, 'Die deutschen Ausgaben von Hitlers "Mein Kampf"', *VfZ*, 4 (1956), 161–78, here 173).

158. Nipperdey, ii.865–6.

159. Bessel, 46–7.

160. Bessel, 5–6, 10.

161. Toller, 100–101, and see also 95: 'There is only one way for us. We must revolt!'

162. See Bessel, 257.

163. Bessel, 258.

164. Nipperdey, ii.855.

165. Bessel, 33.

166. Ay, 101–2.

167. Nipperdey, i.412.

168. Poliakov, iv.148-9.

169. Nipperdey, ii.413.

170. Cit. Poliakov, iv.151.

171. Poliakov, iv.150, 152.

172. Poliakov, cit. iv.153.

173. *MK*, 218-19.

174. See Ay, 106-9 for the mood among Munich's soldiers in the last two war years.

175. *MK*, 213-14, 217.

176. Brandmayer, 92.

177. *MK*, 213-14, 218-19.

178. *MK*, 219.

179. *MK*, 219-20.

180. Brandmayer, 67.

181. *MK*, 222.

182. *MK*, 222-3.

183. *MK*, 223-5 (trans., *MK* Watt, 185-7).

184. Summarized in Binion, *Hitler among the Germans*, 136-8.

185. *JK*, 1064.

186. Cit. Binion, *Hitler among the Germans*, 137.

187. Binion, *Hitler among the Germans*, esp. 3-14; Toland (following Binion), 71, 934.

188. Binion, *Hitler among the Germans*, 14-35.

189. Ernst Günther Schenck, *Patient Hitler. Eine medizinische Biographie*, Düsseldorf, 1989, 298-9, 306-7. He refers to the comment of Dr Martin Dresse in 1952, after allegedly seeing the patient's record in Pasewalk, that Hitler was not blind, but suffered from severe 'burning eyes', a description which fits Hitler's own in *Mein Kampf*. Schenck is strongly critical, on the basis of medical knowledge, of Binion's interpretation, especially his views on Bloch and his treatment (Schenck, 515-33, esp. 523-9).

190. See Albrecht Tyrell, 'Wie er der "Führer" wurde', in Guido Knopp (ed.), *Hitler heute. Gespräche über ein deutsches Trauma*, Aschaffenburg, 1979, 20-48, here 25-6.

191. See Axel Kuhn, *Hitlers außenpolitisches Programm*, Stuttgart, 1971, esp. ch.5.

192. *MK*, 225; *JK*, 1064; *Hitler-Prozeß*, i.20.

193. Ernst Deuerlein, *Hitler. Eine politische Biographie*, Munich, 1969, 40.

194. The rapidity and success of the demobilization programme is emphasized by Richard Bessel, 'Unemployment and Demobilisation in Germany after the First World War', in Richard J. Evans and Dick Geary (eds.), *The German Unemployed*, London/Sydney, 1987, 23-43.

195. Joachimsthaler, 187, 203.

196. Joachimsthaler, 255.

CHAPTER 4: DISCOVERING A TALENT

1. Ernst Deuerlein, 'Hitlers Eintritt in die Politik und die Reichswehr', *VfZ*, 7 (1959), 177–227, here 200.

2. There is no evidence to support this story. Ernst Schmidt's account in Heinz, 92, simply echoes Hitler's in *MK*, 226. The 'Central Council' did not even exist any longer by that date. It had been dissolved on 13 April; and the Communist Executive Council, which replaced it, was by the last days of April in total disarray. (See Werner Maser, *Die Frühgeschichte der NSDAP. Hitlers Weg bis 1924*, Frankfurt am Main/Bonn, 1965, 131–2 (cit. information provided by Ernst Niekisch); Joachimsthaler, 212.) According to Ernst Schmidt (see Maser, *Frühgeschichte*, 132; Maser, *Hitler*, 159; Werner Maser, *Adolf Hitler. Das Ende der Führer-Legende*, Düsseldorf/Vienna, 1980, 263 n.), Hitler was briefly arrested by the 'white' troops of the Freikorps Epp, before being recognized and released. (See also Heinz, 95–6; Joachimsthaler, 218; and Heiden, *Hitler*, 54.) If the story is true, it suggests that they initially took him for a supporter of the 'Red Army'. In *Mein Kampf*, Hitler converted the tale into an attempt, which he fought off, at his arrest by soldiers of the 'Red Army'.

3. *MK*, 226–7 (trans., *MK* Watt, 188–9).

4. Eberhard Kolb, *Die Weimarer Republik*, 3rd edn, Munich, 1993, 4.

5. Ernst Toller, *I Was a German*, 133.

6. See Wolfgang J. Mommsen, 'Die deutsche Revolution 1918–1920', *Geschichte und Gesellschaft*, 4 (1978), 362–91. A different emphasis on the aims of the Councils is given by Reinhard Rürup, 'Demokratische Revolution und "dritter Weg"', *Geschichte und Gesellschaft*, 9 (1983), 278–301. Among the most important works dealing with the Councils are Eberhard Kolb, *Die Arbeiterräte in der deutschen Innenpolitik 1918–1919*, Düsseldorf, 1962; and Reinhard Rürup, *Probleme der Revolution in Deutschland 1918/19*, Wiesbaden, 1968.

7. Anthony Nicholls, 'The Bavarian Background to National Socialism', in Anthony Nicholls and Erich Matthias (eds.), *German Democracy and the Triumph of Hitler*, London, 1971, 105–6.

8. Most of the demonstrators, supporters of the Majority Social Democrats, had headed into the city centre, following a speech by their leader, Erhard Auer. The Independents, far smaller in number, had stayed behind to listen to Eisner, before heading for the barracks to win the support of the troops in the Munich garrison (Joachimsthaler, 180).

9. Abelshauser, Faust and Petzina (eds.), *Deutsche Sozialgeschichte 1914–1945*, 247.

10. *Monologe*, 64 (21 September 1941).

11. Hitler himself recognized this – though it was not convenient for him to admit until a much later date that he distinguished between the Social Democrats and more radical forces during the 1918 revolution (*Monologe*, 248 (1 February 1942)).

12. An immediate bloody reaction to the news of Eisner's assassination occurred

when a number of left-radical workers forced their way into the Bavarian Landtag, killing two members of the parliament and severely wounding through pistol shots the Bavarian Minister of the Interior and opponent of Eisner, Erhard Auer (Wilhelm Hoegner, *Die verratene Republik*, Munich, 1979, 87; Spindler, i.425–6). As conditions deteriorated, the Bavarian government and Landtag fled to Bamberg, leaving Munich to the radical forces which, on 7 April, proclaimed the Räterepublik.

13. Toller, 151.

14. Spindler, i.429; Gerhard Schmolze (ed.), *Revolution und Räterepublik in München 1918/19 in Augenzeugenberichten*, Düsseldorf, 1969, 263–71; Allan Mitchell, *Revolution in Bavaria 1918–1919. The Eisner Regime and the Soviet Republic*, Princeton, 1965, 299–311.

15. Heinrich August Winkler, *Weimar 1918–1933. Die Geschichte der ersten deutschen Demokratie*, Munich, 1993, 80. See also Joachimsthaler, 299 n.675; Schmolze, 298ff.; Mitchell, 317–19.

16. The above account draws on Spindler, i.430–34; Schmolze, 349–98; Mitchell, 329–31; Joachimsthaler, 219–20; Toller, 191ff.; and Ernst Deuerlein (ed.), *Der Aufstieg der NSDAP in Augenzeugenberichten*, Munich, 1974, 54–5. There are some discrepancies in the numbers given of those killed and injured.

17. Josef Karl (ed.), *Die Schreckensherrschaft in München und Spartakus im bayrischen Oberland 1919. Tagebuchblätter und Ereignisse aus der Zeit der 'bayrischen Räterepublik' und der Münchner Kommune im Frühjahr 1919*, Munich, n.d. (1919?), 45–8 (entry for 19 April 1919).

18. The title of Josef Karl's book.

19. *Münchner Neueste Nachrichten*, 3 May 1919.

20. See Hoegner, 87.

21. See Hoegner, 109ff. for the so-called 'Ordnungszelle Bayern'.

22. Joachimsthaler, 14, 184.

23. Joachimsthaler, 187, 189–90, where it is pointed out that the deputation to Traunstein followed a regimental order. But this does not rule out the likelihood that volunteers to serve at Traunstein were sought within the regiment.

24. Heinz, 89.

25. Cit. Joachimsthaler, 192.

26. Heinz, 90; Joachimsthaler, 193.

27. *MK*, 226; Joachimsthaler, 193–4.

28. See Bessel, *Germany after the First World War*, chs.2–7, and Bessel, 'Unemployment and Demobilisation'.

29. Joachimsthaler, 224.

30. Joachimsthaler, 198–9.

31. Heinz, 90.

32. Joachimsthaler, 195.

33. BHStA, Abt.IV, 2.I.R., Batl. Anordnungen, Bl.1504. The meeting which Hitler attended was to discuss 'the socialization in Bavaria and in Germany' and 'the existence of the councils' (Bl.1503). Hitler's involvement as a battalion representative

was brought to light by Joachimsthaler, 200–204, 211. See 188 for the establishment of battalion representatives in December 1918. Hitler's name appears in regimental records as 'Hittler', 'Hüttler', and 'Hietler', but from the 'Gesamtregister' of the 2nd Demobilization Company for this period it is plain that the same person is meant by the variable spellings (Joachimsthaler, 213, 217, 223, 296 n.641).

34. BHStA, Abt.IV, 2.I.R., Batl. Anordnungen, Bl.1505, 1516; Joachimsthaler, 212–13, 217.

35. Cit. Joachimsthaler, 201–2, 204.

36. See Joachimsthaler, 205–6, for references to comments in the *Berliner Tagblatt*, 20 October 1930 and *Westdeutsche Arbeiterzeitung*, 12 March 1932.

37. Toller, 256. Hitler, he said, had been silent during the revolution. Toller had not heard his name at that time.

38. Heiden, *Hitler*, 54; Joachimsthaler, 203. According to Deuerlein, *Hitler*, 41, the *Münchener Post* later reported that Hitler had thought about entering the SPD in the winter of 1918–19, but neither reference nor any supportive evidence for the assertion is provided. Hitler's cautious opportunism, and his reluctance in pre-war Vienna and Munich to commit himself to any political party or organization, pose grounds for scepticism about the rumours that he tried to join the Majority SPD in the revolutionary period.

39. *JK*, 448.

40. Joachimsthaler, 189.

41. Walter Görlitz and Herbert A. Quint, *Adolf Hitler. Eine Biographie*, Stuttgart, 1952, 120; Robert Wistrich, *Wer war wer im Dritten Reich*, Munich, 1983, 66. Esser had worked on the *Allgäuer Volkswacht*.

42. Albrecht Tyrell, *Vom 'Trommler' zum 'Führer'*, Munich, 1975, 23.

43. Brandmayer, 114–15.

44. This seems the implication of Joachimsthaler, 184–5, 200–206. Elsewhere, however, Joachimsthaler advances the more probable suggestion of a release of latent feelings of hatred through the events of 1918–19. See 179–80, 200, 234, 240.

45. See Rainer Zitelmann, *Hitler. Selbstverständnis eines Revolutionärs*, Hamburg/ Leamington Spa/New York, 1987, 22–6.

46. Heiden, *Hitler*, 35, repeated in Heiden, *Der Führer*, 75.

47. Joachimsthaler, 188, 197–8, 215; Maser, *Hitler*, 159; Maser, *Ende der Führer-Legende*, 263 n. (citing remarks made to him in the early 1950s by Otto Strasser and Hermann Esser); Eitner, 66.

48. Joachimsthaler, 189; Deuerlein, *Hitler*, 41 (without source).

49. Heiden, *Hitler*, 54.

50. Heinz, 92.

51. BHStA, Abt.IV, 2.I.R., Batl. Anordnungen, Bl.1516; Joachimsthaler, 213, 217.

52. Joachimsthaler, 201, 214, 221.

53. Maser, *Hitler*, 159.

54. BHStA, Abt.IV, 2.I.R., Batl. Anordnungen, Bl.1535; Regt. Anordnungen, Stadtkommandatur München, 'Auflösung der Garnison', 7 May 1919, Zusätze des

Regiments zur Stadtkommandaturverfügung, 9 May 1919; Joachimsthaler, 221, 223.

55. Joachimsthaler, 224.

56. Deuerlein, 'Hitlers Eintritt', 178.

57. See Oswald Spengler's description of the city centre in Deuerlein, *Aufstieg*, 83.

58. Deuerlein, 'Hitlers Eintritt', 178; Joachimsthaler, 224–8.

59. Over 500 officers and men attended the first three courses, according to a summary report compiled on 25 July 1919 by the course leader Karl Graf von Bothmer: BHStA, Abt.IV, Bd.307. The report, though with some omissions (including the reference to the numbers involved), is printed in Joachimsthaler, 235–40.

60. Helmuth Auerbach, 'Hitlers politische Lehrjahre und die Münchener Gesellschaft 1919–1923', *VfZ*, 25 (1977), 1–45, here 18.

61. Deuerlein, 'Hitlers Eintritt', 179; Joachimsthaler, 228, 304 n.744; Ernst Röhm, *Die Geschichte eines Hochverräters*, 2nd edn, Munich, 1930, 99–101.

62. Karl Mayr (= Anon.), 'I Was Hitler's Boss', *Current History*, Vol.1 No.3 (Nov. 1941), 193.

63. Deuerlein, 'Hitlers Eintritt', 179–80, 182 and n.19, 191–2; Joachimsthaler, 230–34, 242; *MK*, 228–9, 232–5; and see Albrecht Tyrell, 'Gottfried Feder and the NSDAP', in Peter Stachura (ed.), *The Shaping of the Nazi State*, London, 1978, 49–87, esp. 54–5.

64. Karl Alexander von Müller, *Mars und Venus. Erinnerungen 1914–1919*, Stuttgart, 1954, 338–9.

65. *MK*, 235; Joachimsthaler, 229–30, 250.

66. Deuerlein, 'Hitlers Eintritt', 179, 182–3, 194, 196; Joachimsthaler, 241. The instructors were provided with a mass of anti-Bolshevik pamphlets to assist them in their 'educational' task.

67. Deuerlein, 'Hitlers Eintritt', 197–200; Joachimsthaler, 247; *JK*, 87–8. He also lectured on capitalism.

68. *MK*, 235 (trans., *MK* Watt, 196). Hitler repeated the same stylized description of discovering that he could 'speak' in relation to his first notable success as a speaker for the DAP (*MK*, 390).

69. Deuerlein, 'Hitlers Eintritt', 200. The reports are contained in BHStA, Abt.IV, RW GrKdo 4, Nr 309.

70. For antisemitism in the army in early 1920, see Joachimsthaler, 248. The cited comments from reports on the popular mood are contained in BHStA, Abt.IV, RW GrKdo 4, Bd.204, 'Judenhetze'.

71. Deuerlein, 'Hitlers Eintritt', 199; Joachimsthaler, 247; *JK*, 88.

72. Deuerlein, 'Hitlers Eintritt', 184–5, 201–2; Joachimsthaler, 243–7. Mayr addressed Hitler as '*sehr verehrter Herr Hitler*', an unusually respectful form of address from a captain to a corporal.

73. *JK*, 88–90; Deuerlein, 'Hitlers Eintritt', 185, 202–5; Joachimsthaler, 243–9. Hitler's letter survives in typed copy, signed by him (BHStA, Abt.IV, RW GrKdo 4, Nr 314). Whether the original was handwritten or dictated is not known. Mayr

approved of Hitler's reply, apart from some reservations about his interpretation of the 'interest problem'.

74. Tyrell, *Trommler*, 25–6.

75. Deuerlein, 'Hitlers Eintritt', 186, 205.

76. Deuerlein, 'Hitlers Eintritt', 187. The V-Men wrote their reports under a code number. None from Hitler has survived, but numerous reports on early DAP meetings, including those addressed by Hitler, are in the files (BHStA, Abt.IV, RW GrKdo 4, Nr 287). Those concerning the DAP/NSDAP were printed by Deuerlein, 'Hitlers Eintritt', 205–27, and *JK*, 129–298.

77. Tyrell, *Trommler*, 195 n.77. On subsequent occasions, too, as Tyrell points out, he was accompanied by other military personnel and evidently did not go alone, as he implied in *Mein Kampf*, 236–7. The attendance list for 12 September 1919 contains thirty-nine names; Hitler gave a figure of between twenty and twenty-five as present.

78. *MK*, 237–8. See Tyrell, *Trommler*, 195 n.77, for a discussion of this first meeting on the basis of the early attendance lists. Baumann did not attend on 12 September according to those lists, though the dating was attached later and may be incorrect. The lists are part of the file on the early records of the DAP/NSDAP, 1919–1926, in the BDC, and in BAK, 26/80.

79. Cit. Georg Franz-Willing, *Die Hitlerbewegung. Der Ursprung 1919–1922*, Hamburg/Berlin, 1962, 66–7, reporting a comment to him by Michael Lotter, one of the original members of the DAP; see also Tyrell, *Trommler*, 196 n.99. Lotter's earlier version, from 1935, which he sent to the NSDAP-Hauptarchiv, runs along similar lines, though with slightly different wording (IfZ, Fa 88/Fasz.78, 'Vortrag des Gründungsmitglied der D.A.P. und 1. Schriftführer des politischen Arbeiterzirkels Michael Lotter am 19. Oktober 1935 vor der "Sterneckergruppe" im Leiberzimmer des "Sterneckers"' (also HA, 3/78), Fol.6). In this account, Lotter says Drexler requested Hitler to come back 'because we could use such people'. According to this account, Drexler went on to say: 'Now we have an Austrian. He's got such a gob' ('*Jetzt haben wir einen Österreicher, der hat eine solche Goschen*') (Lotter, Fol. 6; partly reproduced in Joachimsthaler, 251–2). Drexler himself, in a letter he composed but did not send to Hitler in 1940, spoke of pressing a copy of his pamphlet *Mein politisches Erwachen* into Hitler's hand, following his intervention in the discussion at the meeting 'attended by at least 80 persons', and urging him most strongly 'to join our party, because we needed to make use of such people' (*dringendst bat, sich doch unserer Partei anzuschließen, denn solche Leute könnten wir notwendig gebrauchen*) (BHStA, Abt.V, P3071, Slg. Personen, Anton Drexler, Abschrift, Drexler to Hitler, 'Ende Januar 1940', 1–2). Hitler's own version (*MK*, 238) says nothing about Drexler urging him to come back to and join the party.

80. Lotter gives the date of Hitler's entry to the party as 16 September 1919 (IfZ, Fa 88/Fasz.78, Lotter Vortrag, 19 October 1935, Fol. 6). Drexler claimed he asked Hitler to return in eight days, i.e. by 20 September. Hitler's own account suggests that something like a week and a half elapsed between his initial attendance at the

party meeting and going to the committee meeting, and that some further days followed thereafter before he finally made up his mind to join the party (*MK*, 239–44; Joachimsthaler, 251–2).

81. *MK*, 240. Max Amann spoke after the war in testimony to the denazification court of meeting Hitler in early 1920 and being told that Hitler was keen to establish his own party, to be called 'The Party of Social Revolutionaries' to win over the workers from Bolshevism (Joachimsthaler, 230–31, 252–3). That this was the case in spring 1920, after Hitler had launched the party programme of the DAP (now renamed NSDAP), can be dismissed. Probably Amann, speaking so many years later, was postdating Hitler's remarks (which he may well have taken from *Mein Kampf*). Hitler himself wrote of having such ideas in summer 1919, following the Munich course, which makes better chronological sense (*MK*, 227).

82. *MK*, 241 (trans., *MK* Watt, 201).

83. *MK*, 243 (trans., *MK* Watt, 202–3).

84. *MK*, 244. See Maser, *Hitler*, 173, 553 n.225. The precise date on which Hitler joined the party's steering committee cannot be determined (Tyrell, *Trommler*, 198 n.118).

85. BHStA, Abt.V, P3071, Slg. Personen, Anton Drexler, Abschrift, Drexler to Hitler, 'Ende Januar 1940', 2, partly printed in Deuerlein (ed.), *Aufstieg*, 97–8. And see the letter to the NSDAP Hauptarchiv of Michael Lotter, first secretary of the DAP, dated 17 October 1941, pointing out that – for 'image' reasons – the membership numbers began at number 501 and were then alphabetically assigned. Lotter confirmed that a membership card number 7 did not exist. He took it that the number 7 referred to Hitler's membership of the 'Politischer Arbeiterzirkel' (to which he himself belonged), but did not know who had given him the number 7 membership certificate (*Mitgliedschein*) (IfZ, Fa 88/Fasz.78, Fol.11–12 (and HA 3/78); Joachimsthaler, 252). Rudolf Schüssler recalled, so he wrote in 1941, Hitler receiving a small card in September 1919 registering him as the seventh member of the committee (*Arbeitsausschuß*), but distinguished this from his membership card no. 555 of the DAP (IfZ, MA-747, letter to NSDAP-Hauptarchiv, 20 November 1941). Schüssler had been in the same regiment as Hitler in the first half of 1919, and became the first 'business manager' (*Geschäftsführer*) of the infant DAP (Tyrell, *Trommler*, 28, 33; Joachimsthaler, 301 n.705).

86. Mayr, 195. Documents 62 and 64 in *JK*, 90–91, purporting to relate to Hitler's request of 19 October 1919 to join the DAP, after reporting on a meeting of the party on 3 October, are, according to information kindly provided by Prof. Eberhard Jäckel, to be regarded as forgeries.

87. Joachimsthaler, 255.

88. Joachimsthaler, 14.

CHAPTER 5: THE BEERHALL AGITATOR

1. *MK*, 388.
2. Tyrell, *Trommler*, 274 n.151.
3. Hoffmann, 46.
4. This strategic framework is broadly encapsulated in *MK*, 364–88; see also Tyrell, *Trommler*, 171; and Tyrell, 'Wie er der "Führer" wurde', 27–30.
5. Text of the letter in *JK*, 88–90.
6. For sharply differing views on this point, see the contributions by Klaus Hildebrand and Hans Mommsen on 'Nationalsozialismus oder Hitlerismus?', to Bosch (ed.), *Persönlichkeit und Struktur in der Geschichte*, 55–71.
7. Stern, *Hitler*, 12.
8. Tyrell, *Trommler*, 19–20.
9. Whiteside, esp. ch.5; and see Karl Dietrich Bracher, *The German Dictatorship*, Harmondsworth, 1973, 74–80.
10. *Hitler-Prozeß*, 19; *JK*, 1062; and see Tyrell, *Trommler*, 187–8 n.29.
11. *RSA*, II, 49, Dok.24 and n.2; Bracher, 80; the background is outlined in Bruce F. Pauley, *Hitler and the Forgotten Nazis. A History of Austrian National Socialism*, London/Basingstoke, 1981, ch.3.
12. See esp. Mosse, *Crisis of German Ideology*, pt.I; and George L. Mosse, *Germans and Jews*, London, 1971, Introduction.
13. See Kurt Sontheimer, *Antidemokratisches Denken in der Weimarer Republik*, 3rd edn, Munich, 1992, esp. ch.11; and Mosse, *Crisis of German Ideology*, ch.16.
14. See Sontheimer, 271–2.
15. Weimar coalition parties won only 44.6 per cent (205 seats out of 459) of the vote compared with over 78 per cent (331 seats out of 423) in the National Assembly elections of 1919 (Kolb, *Die Weimarer Republik*, 41).
16. *MK*, esp. 415–24; and see Martin Broszat, *Der Nationalsozialismus. Weltanschauung, Programm und Wirklichkeit*, Stuttgart, 1960, 29.
17. Broszat, *Nationalsozialismus*, 23.
18. Tyrell, *Trommler*, 191 n.53. A good description of the atmosphere in Munich at the time Hitler was stepping on to the political stage is provided by Large, *Where Ghosts Walked*, ch.4.
19. Helmuth Auerbach, 'Nationalsozialismus vor Hitler', in Wolfgang Benz, Hans Buchheim and Hans Mommsen (eds.), *Der Nationalsozialismus. Studien zur Ideologie und Herrschaft*, Frankfurt am Main, 1993, 13–28, here 26; Jeremy Noakes, *The Nazi Party in Lower Saxony, 1921–1933*, Oxford, 1971, 9. A comprehensive exploration of the organization is provided by Uwe Lohalm, *Völkischer Radikalismus. Die Geschichte des Deutschvölkischen Schutz-und Trutz-Bundes, 1919–1923*, Hamburg, 1970.
20. Noakes, *Nazi Party*, 9–10.
21. Lohalm, 89–90; Noakes, *Nazi Party*, 11.

22. Tyrell, *Trommler*, 20, 186 n.21; Lohalm, 283–302.

23. For the following see Tyrell, *Trommler*, 72–89; and Noakes, *Nazi Party*, 12–13.

24. Auerbach, 'Hitlers politische Lehrjahre', 6–8. Lehmann is one of the central subjects of the study of Gary D. Stark, *Entrepreneurs of Ideology. Neoconservative Publishers in Germany, 1890–1933*, Chapel Hill, 1981.

25. See Rudolf von Sebottendorff, *Bevor Hitler kam*, 2nd edn, Munich, 1934 (the account by the Society's leading figure); the scholarly analysis by Reginald H. Phelps, '"Before Hitler Came": Thule Society and Germanen Orden', *Journal of Modern History*, 35 (1963), 245–61; Goodrick-Clarke, 135–52; also Tyrell, *Trommler*, 22 and 188–9 n.38; Auerbach, 'Hitlers politische Lehrjahre', 8–9; and Noakes, *Nazi Party*, 13. The Thule Society took its name from that given by the ancient Greeks to the northernmost land they knew. The name had mystical significance for Nordic cultists.

26. A clear distinction between the Arbeiterzirkel (which Hitler attended for the first time on 16 November 1919) and the Arbeitsausschuß, the committee of the DAP, is difficult to draw. The former, controlled by Harrer and clearly bearing his imprint, remained reminiscent of the inner core of a secret society and seems to have been essentially a small debating club (Reginald H. Phelps, 'Hitler and the Deutsche Arbeiterpartei', in Henry A. Turner (ed.), *Nazism and the Third Reich*, New York, 1972, 5–19, here 11). The committee was officially responsible for party business matters, but in practice there was overlap in both personnel and matters under consideration (Tyrell, *Trommler*, 24–5, 190 n.48).

27. BHStA, Abt.V, Slg. Personen, Anton Drexler, 'Lebenslauf von Anton Drexler, 12.3.1935', 3 (partly printed in Deuerlein, *Aufstieg*, 59); Drexler's initial suggestion was 'Deutsche Sozialistische Arbeiterpartei', but Harrer objected to '*sozialistische*' and it was dropped (IfZ, Fa 88/Fasz.78, Fol.4 (Lotter Vortrag, 19 October 1935)). Harrer was not present at the foundation meeting of the DAP, and was possibly not enamoured by the creation of a 'party'. According to Sebottendorff, on 18 January 1919 he was named 1st Chairman and Drexler 2nd Chairman of the Deutscher Arbeiterverein, which was founded in the rooms of the Thule Society (Sebottendorff, 81; see also Tyrell, *Trommler*, 189 n.42).

28. BHStA, Abt.V, Slg. Personen, Anton Drexler, 'Lebenslauf von Anton Drexler, 12.3.1935', 3; Deuerlein, *Aufstieg*, 56–9; IfZ, Fa 88/Fasz. 78, Fol.4 (Lotter Vortrag, 19 October 1935); Phelps, 'Hitler', 8–9; Tyrell, *Trommler*, 22; Drexler states that there were around thirty present (not fifty, as given in Deuerlein, *Aufstieg*, 59). In his 1935 lecture, Lotter (Fol.4), probably from notes he made at the time, is more precise: 'There were 24 present, mainly railway workers' ('*Anwesend waren 24, überwiegend Eisenbahner*'). In his letter to the NSDAP Hauptarchiv six years later, on 17 October 1941 (Fol.10), Lotter refers to between twenty and thirty being present.

29. Phelps, 'Hitler', 10, where he gives the number of forty-two as attendance at the meeting on 12 September. Tyrell, *Trommler*, 195 n.77, refers to thirty-nine

signatures with four names of committee members added at the end. The manuscript of the attendance list (BDC, DAP/NSDAP File) actually contains thirty-eight signatures – one of those attending had taken up two spaces for his name and address – followed by three added names (including Harrer's) written in the same hand, presumably of well-known members attending but not signing themselves in.

30. *MK*, 388–9, 659–64, 669.

31. *MK*, 390–93; *JK*, 91. Hitler still spoke at this time in uniform. Part of his initial impact was unquestionably owing to the way he could portray himself as the spokesman for the ordinary soldier back from the war who could express, in their own earthy language, the sense of betrayal among his former comrades. One who heard him for the first time in the 'Deutsches Reich', Ulrich Graf, later became his chief bodyguard and leader of the Saalschutz, the protection squad which in 1921 turned into the SA. Graf was still bitterly angry at the events of the previous year – defeat, revolution, and especially the Soviet 'Councils Republic' in Munich. He was drawn to Hitler, according to his later (admittedly glorified) account, because he saw in him from the way he spoke and acted 'a soldier and comrade to be trusted' (IfZ, ZS F14, Ulrich Graf, 'Wie ich den Führer kennen lernte', 2).

32. *MK*, 400–406.

33. *MK*, 406 (trans., *MK* Watt, 336).

34. Phelps, 'Hitler', 7–8.

35. *MK*, 658–61.

36. As pointed out by Tyrell, *Trommler*, 10–11.

37. Tyrell, *Trommler*, 29–30, criticizing Franz-Willing, *Hitlerbewegung*, 68, 73, together with Maser, *Frühgeschichte*, 170; and Fest, *Hitler*, 175.

38. BHStA, Abt. V, Slg. Personen, Anton Drexler, typescript copy of Drexler's letter to Hitler (not sent), 'Ende Januar 1940', 7 (printed in Deuerlein, *Aufstieg*, 105).

39. Tyrell, *Trommler*, 30–31; Phelps, 'Hitler', 12; Maser, *Frühgeschichte*, 169.

40. *MK*, 390–91.

41. Reginald H. Phelps, 'Hitler als Parteiredner im Jahre 1920', *VfZ*, 11 (1963), 274–330, here 276.

42. Auerbach, 'Hitlers politische Lehrjahre', 10; see also Phelps, 'Hitler', 13.

43. *JK*, 101.

44. *MK*, 405; BHStA, Abt. V, Slg. Personen, Anton Drexler, typescript copy of Drexler's letter to Hitler (not sent), 'Ende Januar 1940', 7 (printed in Deuerlein, *Aufstieg*, 105); Phelps, 'Hitler', 13 (where reference is made to the fact that Dingfelder had given the speech five times before for the Heimatdienst).

45. Phelps, 'Hitler', 12–13.

46. Tyrell, *Trommler*, 76–83. There were also overlaps with the twelve-point *völkisch* programme that had been published in the *Münchener Beobachter* on 31 May 1919, which itself had possibly been intended as an initial statement of the DSP's aims (Auerbach, 'Hitlers politische Lehrjahre', 9–10 and n.34).

47. Printed in Deuerlein, *Aufstieg*, 108–12.

48. See Tyrell, *Trommler*, 84–5.

49. See Phelps, 'Hitler', 13.

50. *JK*, 447, 29 July 1921.

51. BHStA, Abt. V, Slg. Personen, Anton Drexler, typescript copy of Drexler's letter to Hitler (not sent), 'Ende Januar 1940', 1, 7 (trans., Phelps, 'Hitler', 13).

52. The police report, printed in Phelps, 'Hitler als Parteiredner', 292–6, speaks of over 2,000 persons present. Dingfelder later told the NSDAP-Hauptarchiv that 400 of them were 'Reds' (Phelps, 'Hitler', 14).

53. Phelps, 'Hitler als Parteiredner', 293–4.

54. Phelps, 'Hitler als Parteiredner', 294–6.

55. *MK*, 405 (trans., *MK* Watt, 336).

56. Phelps, 'Hitler', 15.

57. *VB*, Nr 17, 28 February 1920, 3, 'Aus der Bewegung' (trans., Phelps, 'Hitler', 14).

58. The new name appears to have come into use at the beginning of March, though, remarkably, there was no account of the change of name in the party's own archive. It may have been in the hope of forging closer links with the national socialist parties in Austria and Czechoslovakia (Phelps, 'Hitler', 13 and n.37). Police reports first added 'national socialist' to the party's name following a meeting (not addressed by Hitler) on 6 April 1920 (Phelps, 'Hitler als Parteiredner', 277).

59. *MK*, 544 (trans., *MK* Watt, 442).

60. *MK*, 538–51.

61. *MK*, 551–7. Hitler also designed the party insignia and, two years later, the SA standards. His banner design was based on that submitted by Friedrich Krohn, a Starnberg dentist and wealthy early supporter who left the party in 1921. Hitler gave Krohn only indirect credit, and not by name, in his account in *Mein Kampf* (556).

62. *MK*, 543.

63. *MK*, 549–51; and see Heinrich Bennecke, *Hitler und die SA*, Munich, 1962, 26–7. The name 'Gymnastics Section' (Turnabteilung) was used for the last time on 5 October 1921, and was thereafter replaced by 'Storm Section' (Sturmabteilung) (Tyrell, *Trommler*, 137, 266 n.25).

64. Though the meeting was no different in style to previous DAP meetings, announcing it for the first time in a newspaper alongside the usual invitations brought an attendance of over 100 persons. In *MK*, 390, Hitler gives the attendance as 111; the attendance list contains 131 names (Tyrell, *Trommler*, 27–8, 196–7, nn.100–101).

65. *MK*, 390 (trans., *MK* Watt, 323).

66. Oskar Maria Graf, *Gelächter von außen. Aus meinem Leben 1918–1933*, Munich, 1966, 114–15.

67. Frank, 38–42.

68. Tyrell, *Trommler*, 33; Phelps, 'Hitler als Parteiredner', 284, has slightly different figures.

69. *MK*, 561.

70. Phelps, 'Hitler als Parteiredner', 279–80; Tyrell, *Trommler*, 33.

71. Examples are given in *JK*, 126, 205–13, 271–6. Ulrich Graf, Hitler's bodyguard, was entrusted with the task of ensuring that the notes were correctly placed before the beginning of a speech. He confirmed that Hitler mainly improvised from them, claiming that he often scarcely glanced at them (IfZ, ZS F14, 4). Graf's account, written in August 1934, was, of course, attempting to highlight the extraordinary talent of the Führer at every opportunity. Comparison of the notes and the reports on the content of his speeches suggests that Hitler used his jottings more than Graf implies. Later, as Reich Chancellor, with the world's diplomats and press interpreting every word of what he said, the speeches had to be fully written out and carefully edited.

72. Meetings lasted generally between two and a half and three and three-quarter hours (Phelps, 'Hitler als Parteiredner', 275). Hitler mentioned in *Mein Kampf* that his first speech in the Circus Krone, on 3 February 1921, lasted about two and a half hours (*MK*, 561).

73. *MK*, 565.

74. The term 'November criminals' was, in fact, used by Hitler for the first time – to storms of applause that lasted for minutes – as late as September 1922 (*JK*, 692), and regularly (and unceasingly) only from December that year.

75. Phelps, 'Hitler als Parteiredner', 283–4.

76. *JK*, 126–7.

77. Phelps, 'Hitler als Parteiredner', 286.

78. E.g., *JK*, 179, 204, 281–2, 302, 312.

79. Carr, *Hitler*, 5.

80. In the *JK* collection of Hitler's speeches before the Putsch the word '*Lebensraum*' does not appear once. See also Karl Lange, 'Der Terminus 'Lebensraum' in Hitlers Mein Kampf', *VfZ*, 13 (1965), 426–37, for further insight into the development of the word '*Lebensraum*'.

81. *JK*, 213.

82. Phelps, 'Hitler als Parteiredner', 278, 288; *JK*, 126–7.

83. On other occasions he spoke more generally about 'nationally minded leadership personalities' or a 'government of power and authority', seeming to imply a collective rather than individual leadership. See Tyrell, *Trommler*, 60; Phelps, 'Hitler als Parteiredner', 299, 319, 321.

84. *JK*, 126–7 (27 April 1920), 140 (beginning of June 1920), 163 (21 July 1920).

85. Phelps, 'Hitler als Parteiredner', 288. For Hitler's sources, see Reginald H. Phelps, 'Hitlers "grundlegende" Rede über den Antisemitismus', *VfZ*, 16 (1968), 390–420, here 395–9.

86. See Phelps, 'Hitler als Parteiredner', 284.

87. *JK*, 200.

88. *JK*, 119–20.

89. *JK*, 119, 128, 184.

90. *JK*, 348.

91. *JK*, 115, 148, 215, 296.

92. *JK*, 201.

93. *JK*, 119.

94. One hostile commentator on a Hitler speech in late June 1920 even reported that he made 'demand upon demand for the murder of the Jews' ('*Aufforderung um Aufforderung zur Ermordung der Juden*'), *Der Kampf*, 28 June 1920 (*JK*, 152). An explicit call to murder can be found, however, in no other speech. It is fair to presume that it reflects the interpretation of the reporter rather than the precise word used by Hitler.

95. Cited in Alexander Bein, 'Der moderne Antisemitismus and seine Bedeutung für die Judenfrage', *VfZ*, 6 (1958), 340–60, here 359. See also Alexander Bein, ' "Der jüdische Parasit". Bemerkungen zur Semantik der Judenfrage', *VfZ*, 13 (1965), 121–49.

96. *JK*, 176–7.

97. Phelps, 'Hitler als Parteiredner', 286; and see, e.g., *JK*, 201.

98. See Phelps, 'Hitlers "grundlegende" Rede', 393–5, for the structure of his speech on antisemitism on 13 August 1920, and for audience reactions.

99. Phelps, 'Hitlers "grundlegende" Rede', 395. As Phelps notes (391), the full text (400–420; *JK*, 184–204) – unusually among early Hitler speeches – survives perhaps precisely because of its significance as a programmatic statement.

100. Deuerlein, 'Hitlers Eintritt', 215; *JK*, 231 n.7. Hitler recognized, in a letter of 3 July 1920, the difficulty of winning support from the industrial working class (*JK*, 155–6).

101. *MK*, 722 (trans., *MK* Watt, 620).

102. *JK*, 337 (speech of 6 March 1921); Phelps, 'Hitlers "grundlegende" Rede', 394, 398.

103. The view that Hitler's genocidal hatred of the Jews derived from his fear of Bolshevik terror, shored up by horror stories of barbarity during and after the Russian civil war, was famously advanced by Ernst Nolte in interpretations which were one of the triggers to the 'Historikerstreit' ('Historians' Dispute') of the late 1980s. See Ernst Nolte, 'Zwischen Geschichtslegende und Revisionismus', and 'Vergangenheit, die nicht vergehen will', in '*Historikerstreit*'. *Die Dokumentation der Kontroverse um die Einzigartigkeit der nationalsozialistischen Judenvernichtung*, 13–47, together with Nolte's book *Der europäische Bürgerkrieg 1917–1945*.

104. *JK*, 88–90.

105. *JK*, 126–7 (27 April 1920), 140 (beginning of June 1920), 163 (21 July 1920).

106. *JK*, 231.

107. Phelps, 'Hitlers "grundlegende" Rede', 398.

108. Nolte, *Bürgerkrieg*, 115, 564 n.24, pointed, for instance, to the publication in the *VB* of stories that during the Russian civil war the Cheka forced confessions out of prisoners by exposing their faces to hunger-crazed rats.

109. The swelling of KPD membership in Germany in autumn 1920 through the

influx of former adherents of the USPD's radical wing provided a further spur (Tyrell, *Trommler*, 49–50), but the focus on 'Jewish Bolshevism' was by then already well established. The onslaught on Jewish finance capital did not thereby abate. It became incorporated somewhat uneasily in the notion of international finance capital and the international element in Soviet Russia working together against Germany's national interests. (See *JK*, 337.)

110. Phelps, 'Hitlers "grundlegende" Rede', 398 and n.33. See *MK*, 337, for Hitler's acceptance of their authenticity.

111. Mayr, 195–6.

112. Phelps, 'Hitler', 11; *JK*, 106–11.

113. Dirk Stegmann, 'Zwischen Repression und Manipulation: Konservative Macht-eliten und Arbeiter- und Angestelltenbewegung 1910-1918. Ein Beitrag zur Vor-geschichte der DAP/NSDAP', *Archiv für Sozialgeschichte*, 12 (1972), 351–432, here 413. Mayr had already met Kapp personally on two occasions, once with Eckart and once alone, as the contact man of Generals Lüttwitz and von Oldershausen. Mayr was, according to Ernst Röhm, 'the most decisive promoter of the Kapp enterprise in Bavaria' (Röhm, *Die Geschichte eines Hochverräters*, 100–101).

114. Stegmann, 413–14. As Tyrell correctly remarked (*Trommler*, 296), this proves efforts to manipulate Hitler, not that Hitler was the tool of such external forces.

115. Röhm, 100–101, 107.

116. Tyrell, *Trommler*, 27–8, 61, 197 n.104; Auerbach, 'Hitlers politische Lehrjahre', 16, 18.

117. On Eckart, see Margarete Plewnia, *Auf dem Weg zu Hitler. Der völkische Publizist Dietrich Eckart*, Bremen, 1970; and Tyrell, *Trommler*, 190–91 n.49, 194 n.70. Tyrell is persuasive in his refutation of the view that Eckart's posthumous (1924) publication, *Der Bolschewismus von Moses bis Lenin. Zwiegespräch zwischen Adolf Hitler und mir*, Munich, 1924, was based on discussion with Hitler, as first claimed by Ernst Nolte, 'Eine frühe Quelle zu Hitlers Antisemitismus', *Historische Zeitschrift*, 192 (1961), 584–606, and Ernst Nolte, *Three Faces of Fascism*, Mentor edn, New York, 1969, 417–21. Eckart's financial support for Hitler is dealt with by Franz-Willing, *Hitlerbewegung*, 180ff. and Plewnia, 66–71.

118. Tyrell, *Trommler*, 23.

119. By 1923 Eckart was no longer in favour and in March was left greatly embittered by his dismissal as editor of the *Völkischer Beobachter*. He rarely saw Hitler thereafter, and took no part in the putsch. He became increasingly ill, and died towards the end of the year. The dedication of *Mein Kampf* to Eckart was pro forma – directed at the many who knew full well Hitler's early indebtedness to Eckart (Tyrell, *Trommler*, 194 n.70).

120. Franz-Willing, *Hitlerbewegung*, 179–80, 190.

121. Tyrell, *Trommler*, 110, 177. As Tyrell (*Trommler*, 110) points out, Grandel also brought the supporters from the Schutz- und Trutzbund that he had built up in Augsburg into the NSDAP after he himself had joined the party in August 1920.

122. BHStA, Abt.V, Slg. Personen, Anton Drexler, copy of Drexler's draft letter

to Hitler, end of January 1940, 3 (partly printed in Deuerlein, *Aufstieg*, 128–9). (See also Tyrell, *Trommler*, 175–7.)

123. *JK*, 277–8.

124. Tyrell, *Trommler*, 38, 42, 206 n.189.

125. Deuerlein, *Aufstieg*, 136.

126. Gustave Le Bon's study, published in France in 1895 and in English translation as *The Crowd* a year later, had appeared in a German edition, *Psychologie der Massen*, in 1908. A few days before Hitler joined the DAP, in September 1919, a lengthy article in the *VB* had drawn attention to a published lecture by a Dr J.R. Roßbach, a Munich nerve specialist, on 'The Soul of the Masses. Psychological Reflections on the Emergence of Popular Mass Movements' (*Die Massenseele. Psychologische Betrachtungen über die Entstehung von Volks-(Massen)- Bewegungen (Revolutionen)*). Roßbach made frequent use of quotations from Le Bon, and summarized his findings in pithy language. There are striking similarities between Roßbach's phraseology and that of Hitler in his comments on the psychology of the masses. Perhaps Hitler was drawn from Roßbach to read Le Bon's own work. But what does seem likely is that he read Roßbach and was influenced by him. (See Tyrell, *Trommler*, 54–6.)

127. Tyrell, *Trommler*, 42–64, for the above.

128. In April, the Reparations Commission reassessed the payments at 132,000 million Gold Marks (Kolb, *Weimarer Republik*, 44), which Hitler must have had in mind when he spoke in *Mein Kampf* of 'the insane sum of a hundred milliard [thousand million] gold marks' (*MK*, 558).

129. The Circus Krone's manager was said to have been a party member who charged a much reduced rent for the hire of the hall (Toland, 109, but without any supportive evidence).

130. *MK*, 558–62; *JK*, 311–12. In his own account, Hitler states that, following the Circus Krone triumph, he booked the hall for two more successful meetings in the coming two weeks. While the NSDAP did go on to use the hall increasingly for major rallies, the next meeting there did not take place until 6 March 1921, the one thereafter on 15 March. These were, however, the next two meetings after the one described by Hitler (*JK*, 335ff., 353ff.). The early meetings in the Circus Krone, and how nervous Hitler had felt about them, figured in his frequent reminiscences during the Second World War about the 'good old days' of the party's history. See, for example, his comments to Goebbels on the occasion of Heydrich's state funeral (*TBJG*, II,4, 492 (10 June 1942)).

131. *JK*, 312; Deuerlein, *Aufstieg*, 129–30.

132. *MK*, 562.

133. Based on *JK*, 279–538.

134. Ernst Hanfstaengl, *15 Jahre mit Hitler. Zwischen Weißem und Braunem Haus*, 2nd edn, Munich/Zurich, 1980, 52–3.

135. Tyrell, *Trommler*, 40–41.

136. Hoffmann, 50.

137. Auerbach, 'Hitlers politische Lehrjahre', 20–21.

138. Hanfstaengl, *15 Jahre*, 49.

139. Hanfstaengl, *15 Jahre*, 49–52.

140. Hanfstaengl, *15 Jahre*, 52.

141. Deuerlein, *Hitler*, 53.

142. Deuerlein, *Aufstieg*, 132–4.

143. Tyrell, *Trommler*, 208 n.215, cit. *VB*, 9 September 1920.

144. Tyrell, *Trommler*, 40 (reports of two visitors to Munich from the Deutschsoziali-stische Partei in February 1921); Deuerlein, *Aufstieg*, 139 (an extract from the anonymous pamphlet circulated by Hitler's enemies in the party in July 1921, entitled 'Adolf Hitler – Verräter').

145. *JK*, 529–30. He said nothing about fees received from the articles he wrote in 1921 in the *VB*, though he claimed in July 1921 that he lived from his earnings as a 'writer' (*Schriftsteller*) (*JK*, 448).

146. Tyrell, *Trommler*, 216 n.209, citing *Münchener Post*, 5 December 1921; Heiden, *Hitler*, 97.

147. Heiden, *Hitler*, 100.

148. Auerbach, 'Hitlers politische Lehrjahre', 22; Tyrell, *Trommler*, 267 n.54.

149. According to Heiden, *Hitler*, 116, though without supporting evidence, Hitler's lengthy absence in Berlin was spent at the Bechsteins while he was taking elocution lessons. Whether or not he was brushing up his diction at the same time, the real purpose of his visit was more important than elocution: trying – if without great success – to rustle up funds for the party newspaper, probably through contacts opened up to him by Max Maurenbrecher, the editor of the Pan-German newspaper *Deutsche Zeitung*, with a number of individuals connected with the Pan-Germans (Tyrell, *Trommler*, 117–18).

150. Tyrell, *Trommler*, 96.

151. Tyrell, *Trommler*, 103–4.

152. *JK*, 436 (Hitler's resignation letter of 14 July 1921).

153. Tyrell, *Trommler*, 99–100, 105.

154. Tyrell, *Trommler*, 101–3.

155. The above based on the findings of Tyrell, *Trommler*, 106–9, 122.

156. *JK*, 437; Tyrell, *Trommler*, 118–19.

157. Tyrell, *Trommler*, 110–16, 119–20.

158. *JK*, 437–8; Franz-Willing, *Hitlerbewegung*, 110.

159. Based on Tyrell, *Trommler*, 120–22.

160. *JK*, 438.

161. *JK*, 277. Dok. 198 (*JK*, 320), recording Hitler's resignation on 16 February 1921, must be regarded as a forgery.

162. Tyrell, *Trommler*, 123.

163. *JK*, 438.

164. Tyrell, *Trommler*, 126–8, 130. Hitler's ultimatum to the party committee of 26 July 1921, printed in *JK*, 445 (Dok.266), is a forgery.

165. *JK*, 446.
166. Deuerlein, *Aufstieg*, 138–41; *JK*, 446–7; Tyrell, *Trommler*, 128–30.
167. *JK*, 439–44; Tyrell, *Trommler*, 129 and 264 n.506.
168. See Tyrell, 130–50, for an examination of the new statutes.
169. *VB*, 11 August 1921, 3.
170. *VB*, 4 August 1921, 3.

CHAPTER 6: THE 'DRUMMER'

1. Rudolf Pechel, *Deutscher Widerstand*, Erlenbach/Zurich, 1947, 280.
2. Cit. Auerbach, 'Hitlers politische Lehrjahre', 29; Tyrell, *Trommler*, 117.
3. Bernd Weisbrod, 'Gewalt in der Politik. Zur politischen Kultur in Deutschland zwischen den beiden Weltkriegen', *Geschichte in Wissenschaft und Unterricht*, 43 (1992), 392–404, here esp. 392–5. See also George L. Mosse, *Fallen Soldiers*, New York/Oxford, 1990, ch.8; and Robert G.L. Waite, *Vanguard of Nazism. The Free Corps Movement in Postwar Germany 1918–1923*, Cambridge, Mass., 1952.
4. Weisbrod, 393; Peter Longerich, *Die braunen Bataillone. Geschichte der SA*, Munich, 1989, 12. Detailed accounts of the Einwohnerwehr are presented by Hans Fenske, *Konservativismus und Rechtsradikalismus in Bayern nach 1918*, Bad Homburg/Berlin/Zurich, 1969, ch.5, 76–112; Karl Schwend, *Bayern zwischen Monarchie und Diktatur*, Munich, 1954, 159–70; and, especially, David Clay Large, *The Politics of Law and Order: A History of the Bavarian Einwohnerwehr, 1918–1921*, Philadelphia, 1980.
5. See Fenske, 148–59; Hoegner, *Die verratene Republik*, 131; and Longerich, *Die braunen Bataillone*, 14, for 'Consul'. The figures for the numbers of political murders are taken from Ralf Dreier and Wolfgang Sellert (eds.), *Recht und Justiz im 'Dritten Reich'*, Frankfurt am Main, 1989, 328; most of the murders were leniently dealt with by the courts compared with the far fewer (twenty-two in all) committed by members of left-wing parties.
6. Deuerlein, *Aufstieg*, 143–4.
7. Deuerlein, *Aufstieg*, 142; Fenske, 89–108.
8. Georg Franz-Willing, *Ursprung der Hitlerbewegung, 1919–1922*, 2nd edn, Preußisch Oldendorf, 1974, 62–3 and n.15a.
9. Based on: Longerich, *Die braunen Bataillone*, 12–14, 23–4; Hoegner, 129–33; Harold J. Gordon, *Hitler and the Beer Hall Putsch*, Princeton, 1972, 88–92; Spindler, i.462–4; Fenske, 143–72; Large, *Where Ghosts Walked*, 142–6.
10. See Auerbach, 'Hitlers politische Lehrjahre', 35.
11. Longerich, *Die braunen Bataillone*, 22; Bennecke, 26, implies that the 'hall protection' began with the Hofbräuhaus meeting on 24 February 1920; Franz-Willing, *Ursprung*, 206, suggests that it went back even earlier, to the Eberlbräu meeting in October 1919. It is too early at these dates, however, to speak of anything more than the taking of obvious precautions at big meetings to have strong-arm

supporters at the ready to combat the expected violent disturbances from political opponents.

12. Longerich, *Die braunen Bataillone*, 23; Tyrell, *Trommler*, 137.

13. Tyrell, *Trommler*, 266 n.25; Longerich, *Die braunen Bataillone*, 25–6.

14. Franz-Willing, *Ursprung*, 205; see Auerbach, 'Hitlers politische Lehrjahre', 35 n.158; Longerich, *Die braunen Bataillone*, 23, 25.

15. See, esp., Klaus Theweleit, *Männerphantasien*, Rowohlt edn, 2 vols., Reinbek bei Hamburg, 1980.

16. Tyrell, *Trommler*, 28, 197 n.104.

17. Based on Röhm, *Die Geschichte eines Hochverräters*, esp. pt.II, chs.13–20, 75–145; and Longerich, *Die braunen Bataillone*, 15–22. See also the biographical sketch by Conan Fischer, 'Ernst Julius Röhm – Stabschef der SA und Außenseiter', in Ron Smelser and Rainer Zitelmann (eds.), *Die braune Elite*, Darmstadt, 1989, 212–22, and the character study by Joachim C. Fest in his *The Face of the Third Reich*, Pelican edn, Harmondsworth, 1972, 207–25.

18. Heiden, *Hitler*, 124.

19. The above relies mainly on Longerich, *Die braunen Bataillone*, 24–6; and Bennecke, 28–30. Hitler's proclamation of 3 August 1921, creating the party's own paramilitary organization, is printed in Deuerlein, *Aufstieg*, 144.

20. Cooperation with Ehrhardt came to an end with Klintzsch's resignation from the SA to return to his naval company on 11 May 1923 (Bennecke, 28–9).

21. See Heiden, *Hitler*, 121–2.

22. Auerbach, 'Hitlers politische Lehrjahre', 35 n.158.

23. Longerich, *Die braunen Bataillone*, 26–8.

24. Spindler, i.464; Franz-Willing, *Ursprung*, 244.

25. Dietmar Petzina, Werner Abelshauser and Anselm Faust (eds.), *Sozialgeschichtliches Arbeitsbuch, Band III. Materialen zur Statistik des Deutschen Reiches 1914–1945*, Munich, 1978, 83.

26. Deuerlein, *Aufstieg*, 145–6.

27. Heiden, *Hitler*, 125.

28. Deuerlein, *Aufstieg*, 150–51, 154; Heiden, *Hitler*, 125.

29. Deuerlein, *Aufstieg*, 147–9.

30. Deuerlein, *Aufstieg*, 147. The speaker at the SPD meeting, Erhard Auer, suffered an attempt on his life, which the Social Democrats suspected the Nazis of being involved in, on 25 October 1921 (Maser, *Frühgeschichte*, 301; see Hitler's comments in *MK*, 562–3).

31. Deuerlein, *Aufstieg*, 147.

32. *MK*, 563–7; and Heinz, 117–20, an eye-witness account of a Nazi supporter which also glorifies the brawl. Hitler's words to the SA before the meeting, and reports on the content of the speech, 'Who Are the Murderers?', are reproduced in *JK*, 513.

33. Hanfstaengel, *15 Jahre*, 59; and see Kurt G.W. Ludecke (= Lüdecke), *I Knew Hitler*, London, 1938, 123.

34. Spindler, i.466–8.

35. Franz-Willing, *Ursprung*, 247–9 (quotation, 248). In one incident, in September 1922, for which a National Socialist was arrested, hand-grenades made by a party comrade in Munich, a watch-maker by trade, were thrown at the Mannheim stock-exchange.

36. Deuerlein, *Aufstieg*, 153–4.

37. *JK*, 578–80.

38. *JK*, 625. Esser and Eckart made vague menacing noises about the party's possible retaliation should Hitler be expelled (Franz-Willing, *Ursprung*, 246–8).

39. *JK*, 679 and n.1.

40. Bennecke, 42; Auerbach, 'Hitlers politische Lehrjahre', 36. By the end of the year, the SA's numbers had risen to about 1,000 men, almost three-quarters of them based in Munich (Bennecke, 45).

41. *JK*, 687.

42. Ernst Deuerlein, *Der Hitler-Putsch. Bayerische Dokumente zum 8./9. November 1923*, Stuttgart, 1962, 42–4; Deuerlein, *Aufstieg*, 155–6; Auerbach, 'Hitlers politische Lehrjahre', 36 and n.160; Maser, *Frühgeschichte*, 353–4; Fenske, 182–4. Deuerlein, *Putsch*, 43, has the demonstration taking place on the Karolinenplatz; Fenske, 184, on the Königsplatz. Since the squares are almost adjacent to each other, it seems likely that the demonstration spilled over into both.

43. Lüdecke, 59–61 (where the events are misdated – and followed in this by Toland, 118 – to 20 September 1922). In a court case in 1925, in which Hitler alleged slander against Pittinger, he claimed that the latter had attempted the same thing in 1922 that had proved unsuccessful for him the following year (*RSA*, I, 10–14, here 11).

44. Wolfgang Benz (ed.), *Politik in Bayern. Berichte des württembergischen Gesandten Carl Moser von Filseck*, Stuttgart, 1971, 108; Deuerlein, *Putsch*, 44; Deuerlein, *Aufstieg*, 156.

45. Hitler's account is in *MK*, 614–18; Sonderarchiv Moscow, 1355-I-38, contains reports of the Vorstand of the Bezirksamt Coburg, on the disturbances to the Regierungspräsidium of Upper Franconia, 16 October 1922, and to the State Ministry of the Interior in Munich, 27 October 1922 (quotation from p. 5 of latter report); see also Franz-Willing, *Ursprung*, 249; Lüdecke, 85–92.

46. The reason was a rancorous split with Dickel over debts owed to the latter by the near-bankrupt Nuremberg branch of the Werkgemeinschaft. The NSDAP showed itself, with a grant to Streicher of 70,000 Marks, ready to pay off the debt and provide a loan to acquire the *Deutscher Volkswille* (Robin Lenman, 'Julius Streicher and the Origins of the NSDAP in Nuremberg', in Nicholls and Matthias, 129–59, here 135).

47. *Monologe*, 158, 293, 430–31 n.175–6.

48. Lenman, 129; Maser, *Frühgeschichte*, 355–6.

49. Auerbach, 'Hitlers politische Lehrjahre', 36 and n.162; Tyrell, *Trommler*, 33. For the social structure of the early party, see Michael Kater, 'Zur Soziographie der frühen NSDAP', *VfZ*, 19 (1971), 124–59.

50. *MK*, 375. Hitler was also effusive in private, even many years later, about Streicher's 'lasting service' to the party in subordinating himself and winning over Nuremberg. 'There would have been no National Socialist Nuremberg if Julius Streicher had not come,' he claimed (*Monologe*, 158 (28–9 December 1941)).

51. Lenman, 144–6, 149, 159.

52. Francis L. Carsten, *The Rise of Fascism*, London, 1967, 64–5.

53. Maser, *Frühgeschichte*, 356 and n.570, referring to oral testimony of Esser. *VB*, 8 November 1922, 2, has the illogical formulation: 'We, too, have Italy's Mussolini. He is called Adolf Hitler.' ('*Den Mussolini Italiens haben auch wir. Er heißt Adolf Hitler.*')

54. Günter Scholdt, *Autoren über Hitler. Deutschsprachige Schriftsteller 1919–1945 und ihr Bild vom 'Führer'*, Bonn, 1993, 34.

55. Scholdt, 35.

56. Cit. Sontheimer, 217. For a biographical sketch of Stapel, see Wolfgang Benz and Hermann Graml (eds.), *Biographisches Lexikon zur Weimarer Republik*, Munich, 1988, 325–6.

57. Sontheimer, 214–22, quotation 218.

58. See Tyrell, *Trommler*, 274 n.151.

59. Tyrell, *Trommler*, 161–2.

60. Tyrell, *Trommler*, 62.

61. Tyrell, *Trommler*, 274 n.152.

62. *JK*, 729.

63. Cornelia Berning, *Vom 'Abstammungsnachweis' zum 'Zuchtwart'. Vokabular des Nationalsozialismus*, Berlin, 1964, 82.

64. Maser, *Frühgeschichte*, 382; Georg Franz-Willing, *Krisenjahr der Hitlerbewegung 1923*, Preußisch Oldendorf, 1975, 73–4, 127–9 and 128 n.23. Letters poured in during 1923, from north as well as south Germany, seeing in Hitler the German 'redeemer'. Once Hitler had given up the ban on photographs of himself (see Hoffmann, 41–9), intended to add to the mystique about his person, the sale of portraits of him contributed to the spread of the cult. On Göring, see the character sketches in Fest, *The Face of the Third Reich*, 113–29; and Ron Smelser and Rainer Zitelmann (eds.), *Die braune Elite*, Darmstadt, 1989, 69–83. Göring succeeded Lieutenant Johann Klintzsch, formerly a member of the Ehrhardt Brigade, as leader of the SA in February 1923. Göring's standing as a war-hero, decorated with the highest award, the Pour le Mérite, could only benefit the SA, and was probably the reason for the change in leadership (see Bennecke, 54). According to Lüdecke, Hitler had remarked: 'Splendid, a war ace with the Pour le Mérite – imagine it! Excellent propaganda! Moreover, he has money and doesn't cost me a cent' (Lüdecke, 129).

65. Franz-Willing, *Krisenjahr*, 74 refers to Pittinger's contempt; as Heiden, *Der Führer*, 102, points out, for the Left Hitler was no more than 'the common demagogue'.

66. Hanfstaengel, *15 Jahre*, 109.

67. Oron James Hale, 'Gottfried Feder calls Hitler to Order: An Unpublished Letter on Nazi Party Affairs', *JMH*, 30 (1958), 358–62.

68. *JK*, 723–4 (8 November 1922).

69. *JK*, 729 (14 November 1922).

70. See Tyrell, *Trommler*, 60–62.

71. *JK*, 837 (26 February 1923).

72. *JK*, 916 (27 April 1923).

73. *JK*, 933 (1 June 1923).

74. *JK*, 923 (4 May 1923). The speech was given in the light of what Hitler saw as the 'capitulation' of Chancellor Cuno to the French through the policy of passive resistance in the Ruhr and the disaster of 'fulfilment policy'.

75. *JK*, 923–4.

76. *JK*, 946 (6 July 1923). See also 973 (14 August 1923), stressing the responsibility of the leader, who risked victory or defeat as in the army and could not pass the blame to parties. He returned to the theme of heroism, personality, and leadership in a speech on 12 September, though he spoke of leaders collectively (*JK*, 1012–13).

77. *JK*, 984 (21 August 1923).

78. A remark allegedly made to Hanfstaengl, if accurately recalled, in which Hitler commented 'I don't have the intention of playing the role of the drummer,' was made in the context of hints that he might become the tool of powerful conservative interests (Hanfstaengl, 47–8).

79. *JK*, 1027, cit. *Daily Mail*, 3 October 1923, under the heading 'A Visit to Hittler' (!).

80. Hitler appears to have compared himself with Mussolini in Lossow's presence (Georg Franz-Willing, *Putsch und Verbotszeit der Hitlerbewegung, November 1923–Februar 1925*, Preußisch Oldendorf, 1977, 56.

81. *JK*, 1034 (14 October 1923).

82. *JK*, 1043 (23 October 1923).

83. *JK*, 1034 (14 October 1923). At his trial, Hitler repeated that Kahr was 'no hero, no heroic figure' ('*kein Held, keine heldische Erscheinung*') (*JK*, 1212).

84. *JK*, 1032; Deuerlein, *Putsch*, 220.

85. As pointed out by Tyrell, *Trommler*, 162.

86. Tyrell, *Trommler*, 163.

87. *JK*, 1268.

88. See Tyrell, *Trommler*, 158–65.

89. *JK*, 939 (*Regensburger Neueste Nachrichten*, 26 June 1923).

90. Lüdecke, 17, 20. Hitler's speech (in *JK*, 679–81) was on 16 August, not 11 August, as Lüdecke (20) states. The general reliability of Lüdecke's memoirs – though there are numerous lapses as well as exaggerated claims – is upheld by Roland V. Layton, 'Kurt Ludecke [= Lüdecke] and I Knew Hitler: an Evaluation', *Central European History*, 12 (1979), 372–86.

91. Lüdecke, 22–3.

92. Lüdecke, 69–70, 83–4. His claim to have engineered the support of Ludendorff and Pöhner for Hitler was exaggerated in the attempt to bolster his own importance. Heß had established the first contact between Hitler and Ludendorff around May 1921 (Auerbach, 'Hitlers politische Lehrjahre', 30). Pöhner, through his close connection with Frick, needed no introduction to Hitler from Lüdecke and had been sympathetic to the NSDAP during his time as Police President of Munich before 1921.

93. Lüdecke, 71–4, 126–7.

94. Lüdecke, 108, and see also 103; Maser, *Frühgeschichte*, 402–3. Hitler was certainly underplaying Lüdecke's financial contribution when he claimed, in 1925, that the latter had given the Movement 7–8,000 Marks (*RSA*, I, 12).

95. Lüdecke, 101–6, 111–22; Franz-Willing, *Ursprung*, 286–7 and n.73.

96. Lüdecke, 156.

97. From Hanfstaengl's account, the meeting was on the day that Hitler had met in the morning the US Assistant Military Attaché Truman Smith, and took place in the Kindlkeller (Hanfstaengl, *15 Jahre*, 32–3, 35, 39). Hitler's discussion with Truman Smith was, however, on 20 November, in the afternoon, and Hitler next spoke publicly on 22 November in the Salvatorkeller (*JK*, 733–40). Hanfstaengl (35, 39) also mistakenly states that it was Hitler's first speech since serving a term of imprisonment for disturbance of the peace in the Ballerstedt incident. He held this speech on 28 July, after serving his sentence from 24 June to 27 July (*JK*, 656–71; Deuerlein, *Aufstieg*, 154).

98. Hanfstaengl, *15 Jahre*, 41 and see also 84–7.

99. The description of Hitler from Hanfstaengl, *15 Jahre*, 35, 44.

100. Hanfstaengl, *15 Jahre*, 71–4; visit to Berlin's museums.

101. Ernst 'Putzi' Hanfstaengl, 'I was Hitler's Closest Friend', *Cosmopolitan*, March 1943, 45.

102. Hanfstaengl, *15 Jahre*, 41.

103. Hanfstaengl, *Cosmopolitan*, 45.

104. Hanfstaengl, *15 Jahre*, 43–4.

105. Hanfstaengl, *15 Jahre*, 61.

106. Hanfstaengl, *15 Jahre*, 37, 61.

107. Hanfstaengl, *15 Jahre*, 55.

108. Lüdecke, 97.

109. See Hanfstaengl, *15 Jahre*, 47ff.

110. Lüdecke, 97; Auerbach, 'Hitlers politische Lehrjahre', 33–4.

111. Baldur von Schirach, *Ich glaubte an Hitler*, Hamburg, 1967, 66–7.

112. Hanfstaengl, *15 Jahre*, 48.

113. See the description in Karl-Alexander von Müller, *Im Wandel einer Welt, Erinnerungen 1919–1932*, Munich, 1966, 129.

114. Gerhard Roßbach, *Mein Weg durch die Zeit. Erinnerungen und Bekenntnisse*, Weilburg/Lahn, 1950, 215. In an interview in 1951, Roßbach described Hitler as 'a pitiful civilian with his tie out of place, who had nothing in his head but art, and

was always late', but was a 'brilliant speaker with suggestive effect'. (*'Erbärmlicher Zivilist mit schlecht sitzender Krawatte, der nichts wie Kunst im Kopf hatte, immer zu spät kam. Glänzender Redner von suggestiver Wirkung.'*) (IfZ, ZS 128, Gerhard Roßbach).

115. Hanfstaengl, *15 Jahre*, 48–9; Franz-Willing, *Ursprung*, 289–90; Auerbach, 'Hitlers politische Lehrjahre', 33–4 and n.150.

116. Friedelind Wagner, *The Royal Family of Bayreuth*, London, 1948, 8–9; interview with Friedelind Wagner in NA, *Hitler Source Book*, 933. On the same occasion, at the end of September 1923, Hitler had met Wagner's son-in-law, the now aged racist writer Houston Stewart Chamberlain, who subsequently wrote Hitler an effusive letter, saying that he had 'transformed the condition of his soul at one fell swoop', and 'that Germany should have brought forth a Hitler in the time of its greatest need' was proof of its continued vitality as a nation. (IfZ, MA-743 (= HA, 52/1210), letter of Chamberlain to Hitler, 7 October 1923. And see Auerbach, 34 and n.151.) Hitler still spoke fulsomely in the middle of the war of his admiration for the Wagner family, especially Winifred. He pointed out that he had never been introduced to the aged and blind widow of Richard Wagner, Cosima, although she lived for some time after he had first gone to Bayreuth (*TBJG*, II/4, 408 (30 May 1942)).

117. For funding and patrons, see Maser, *Frühgeschichte*, 396–412; Franz-Willing, *Ursprung*, 266–99; and Henry Ashby Turner, *German Big Business and the Rise of Hitler*, New York/Oxford, 1985, 59–60, who provides the most reliable assessment of the Nazis' sources of income at this time. Franz-Willing, 266–8, 280, 299 and Turner, 59–60, emphasize the contribution from ordinary members. For the continued reliance of the party on funding from its own members in the run-up to power, see Henry A. Turner and Horst Matzerath, 'Die Selbstfinanzierung der NSDAP 1930–32', *Geschichte und Gesellschaft*, 3 (1977), 59–92.

118. This is emphasized, for the period prior to the takeover of power, by Richard Bessel, 'The Rise of the NSDAP and the Myth of Nazi Propaganda', *Wiener Library Bulletin*, 33 (1980), 20–29, esp. 26–7.

119. Hanfstaengl, *15 Jahre*, 70, 76.

120. Lüdecke, 78–9.

121. Hanfstaengl, *15 Jahre*, 65.

122. Hanfstaengl, *15 Jahre*, 60. This format began, according to Hanfstaengl, on 29 August 1923. The *VB*, still in serious financial trouble in the second half of 1921, was able through financial assistance of Nazi patrons – Bechstein had supported it two or three times – to appear as a daily from 8 February 1922. (Hanfstaengl, *15 Jahre*, 60; Oron J. Hale, *The Captive Press in the Third Reich*, Princeton, 1964, 29–30; Franz-Willing, *Ursprung*, 277–8, 289).

123. See the biographical comments in Franz-Willing, *Ursprung*, 197.

124. Franz-Willing, *Ursprung*, 266 n.214, 281–8; and see Maser, *Frühgeschichte*, 397–412.

125. Turner, 50–55; Franz-Willing, *Ursprung*, 288. Turner, 54, points out that, other than a dubious passage in Thyssen's ghost-written memoirs, the evidence

points towards the donation being made to Ludendorff, and that Hitler most likely gained only the similar sort of portion that was given to others.

126. Franz-Willing, *Ursprung*, 291.

127. Deuerlein, *Putsch*, 63.

128. Deuerlein, *Putsch*, 62.

129. Franz-Willing, *Ursprung*, 296–7. On Gansser, see Turner, 49, 51–2, and 374–5 n.4.

130. Franz-Willing, *Ursprung*, 297.

131. Auerbach, 'Hitlers politische Lehrjahre', 31–2; Franz-Willing, *Ursprung*, 281.

132. *JK*, 725–6.

133. Lüdecke, 110.

134. Auerbach, 'Hitlers politische Lehrjahre', 36 n.162; Maser, *Frühgeschichte*, 376; Michael Kater, *The Nazi Party. A Social Profile of Members and Leaders, 1919–1945*, Oxford, 1983, 19–31, 243; and see Kater, 'Soziographie', 39.

135. See Hanfstaengl, *15 Jahre*, 85.

136. Franz-Willing, *Ursprung*, 357–8.

137. Winkler, *Weimar*, 194; Franz-Willing, *Krisenjahr*, 102.

138. Winkler, *Weimar*, 189; Hans Mommsen, *Die verspielte Freiheit. Der Weg der Republik von Weimar in den Untergang*, Frankfurt am Main/Berlin, 1989, 143. The execution of one saboteur, Albert Schlageter, on 26 May 1923, led to nationalist demonstrations of sympathy throughout Germany and was used by Nazi propaganda to create a martyr for the cause of the movement. See Franz-Willing, *Krisenjahr*, 102, 139–41. Hitler was at first uninterested in taking part. He was on holiday in Berchtesgaden with Eckart and Drexler, and had 'other worries' (Hanfstaengl, *15 Jahre*, 108). Hanfstaengl's suggestion (according to his own account) that great propaganda capital could be gained from it persuaded Hitler to become involved. Hitler's 'worries' in Berchtesgaden doubtless included the proceedings just begun against him for breach of the peace, which threatened to put him behind bars again for at least two months to complete the partly suspended sentence of January 1922.

139. Deuerlein, *Aufstieg*, 163–4.

140. *MK*, 768. His account of the Ruhr occupation is *MK*, 767–80.

141. See *JK*, 692, for the first usage, on 18 September 1922; also Maser, *Frühgeschichte*, 368 n.11.

142. *JK*, 783.

143. *JK*, 781–6.

144. Maser, *Frühgeschichte*, 368–9.

145. Deuerlein, *Aufstieg*, 164.

146. *JK*, 802–5.

147. *JK*, 805–26; Franz-Willing, *Ursprung*, 362–4; Maser, *Frühgeschichte*, 375.

148. Röhm, 2nd edn, 150–51. See also Franz-Willing, *Ursprung*, 361–2; Maser, *Frühgeschichte*, 375–6; and Hans Mommsen, 'Adolf Hitler und der 9. November 1923', in Johannes Willms (ed.), *Der 9. November. Fünf Essays zur deutschen Geschichte*, Munich, 1994, 33–48, here 40.

149. Wolfgang Horn, *Der Marsch zur Machtergreifung. Die NSDAP bis 1933*, Königstein/Ts./Düsseldorf, 1980, 102.

150. *JK*, 811.

151. See n.191 below.

152. Müller, *Wandel*, 144-8.

153. Maser, *Frühgeschichte*, 374, 376-7; Bennecke, 69.

154. Röhm, 2nd edn, 158-60; Maser, *Frühgeschichte*, 376-8; Franz-Willing, *Krisenjahr*, 36-76. Röhm's break with Pittinger's Bund Bayern und Reich at the end of January meant the split of the former VVVB into its 'white-blue' and nationalist components (Röhm, 2nd edn, 152-3; Franz-Willing, *Krisenjahr*, 37-9).

155. Auerbach, 'Hitlers politische Lehrjahre', 38; Franz-Willing, *Krisenjahr*, 42. 'Orgesch', named after its leader Georg Escherich, loosely linked together Einwohnerwehren within and outside Bavaria.

156. *JK*, 1109-11; Bennecke, 66-70; Franz-Willing, *Krisenjahr*, 55, 59-61; *Hitler-Prozeß*, LI. In his recollections of the year of the putsch, Theodor Endres, at the time Lieutenant-Colonel and 1. General Staff Officer under Lossow in Wehrkreiskommando VII, underlined the close connections between the Reichswehr in Bavaria and the Hitler Movement, which won notable support among the troops. Officers were willing to put in extra hours to train the nationalist paramilitaries (BHStA, Abt. IV, HS-925, Theodor Endres, 'Aufzeichnungen über den Hitlerputsch 1923', 10).

157. Franz-Willing, *Krisenjahr*, 43. Some 1,300 SA men took part on 25 March 1923 as a contingent of almost 3,000 paramilitaries in combined military exercises near Munich (Röhm, 2nd edn, 170; Bennecke, 57-8). The fact that Röhm had named Reichswehr officers as leaders of the exercise was publicized by the Social Democrats in the *Münchener Post* and led to a ban on members of the Reichswehr joining the patriotic organizations. Röhm had to resign the leadership of the Reichsflagge in Munich (Röhm, 2nd edn, 177; Franz-Willing, *Krisenjahr*, 75-6).

158. Franz-Willing, *Krisenjahr*, 43, 65.

159. Franz-Willing, *Krisenjahr*, 59.

160. Hitler's memorandum, which Röhm regarded as the Working Community's political programme, was dated 19 April 1923 (Röhm, 2nd edn, 175-7).

161. *JK*, 1136; Franz-Willing, *Krisenjahr*, 43; Feuchtwanger, 124.

162. Röhm, 2nd edn, 164-6.

163. Auerbach, 'Hitlers politische Lehrjahre', 30.

164. *JK*, 1111; Franz-Willing, *Krisenjahr*, 53-4; Maser, *Frühgeschichte*, 383.

165. *JK*, 1136; Franz-Willing, *Krisenjahr*, 55. The conflict between Seeckt and Lossow lasted until the autumn. At a meeting on 7 April in Berlin, Seeckt demanded that Lossow maintain independence of political parties and paramilitary organizations. Lossow had told Seeckt that he could not dispense with the 'patriotic associations' that controlled 51 per cent of the weapons in Bavaria (Franz-Willing, *Krisenjahr*, 68).

166. *JK*, 1111.

167. *JK*, 1110.

168. Deuerlein, *Putsch*, 56.

169. Cit. Franz-Willing, *Krisenjahr*, 76.

170. Gordon, 194, 196.

171. Deuerlein, *Putsch*, 56–7; Benz, *Politik in Bayern*, 125; Franz-Willing, *Krisenjahr*, 81.

172. Gordon, 196–7; Franz-Willing, *Krisenjahr*, 80.

173. Maser, *Frühgeschichte*, 393.

174. Gordon, 196–200; Deuerlein, *Putsch*, 56–60; Franz-Willing, *Krisenjahr*, 79–83; BHStA, Abt.IV, HS-925, Endres Aufzeichnungen, 19–23. See Deuerlein, *Aufstieg*, 170–73 for the police report of the demonstration on the Oberwiesenfeld; also Maser, *Frühgeschichte*, 394.

175. *JK*, 918.

176. Cit. Deuerlein, *Putsch*, 61. This was also the view of the acting United States Consul in Munich, Robert Murphy. He reported that people 'are wearied of Hitler's inflammatory agitation which yields no results and offers nothing constructive' (cit. Toland, 142).

177. Cit. Gordon, 194. A similar comment – 'the enemy stands on the right' – had been most famously made by Reich Chancellor Joseph Wirth in the Reichstag after Walther von Rathenau's murder in summer 1922 (Peter D. Stachura, *Political Leaders in Weimar Germany*, Hemel Hempstead, 1993, 187).

178. Other states had reacted more zealously to head off the evidently looming danger of a putsch attempt headed by Hitler's movement. The NSDAP had been banned since the previous autumn in Prussia and several other states (though not in Bavaria) for its blatant and continued agitation aimed at undermining the state in defiance of the Law for the Protection of the Republic, which had been promulgated following Rathenau's assassination in 1922 and aimed to combat the threat from the radical Right (Deuerlein, *Aufstieg*, 158, 166–70). Kahr remarked bitterly on 30 May 1924 that if the Bavarian government had wanted to bring it about, Hitler's ignoring of security restrictions on 1 May would, in the light of the depressed mood among his followers in the aftermath of the failure, have given the opportunity for the suppression of the NSDAP also in Bavaria. Then, he went on, the 'catastrophe of November 1923 and the still greater catastrophe of the Hitler trial would have been avoided'. This retrospective judgement was, however, quite different from Kahr's attitude towards the NSDAP during the previous year (Deuerlein, *Aufstieg*, 173).

179. See Maser, *Frühgeschichte*, 394–5.

180. Lothar Gruchmann, 'Hitlers Denkschrift an die bayerische Justiz vom 16. Mai 1923', *VfZ*, 39 (1991), 305–28; Maser, *Frühgeschichte*, 394; Franz-Willing, *Krisenjahr*, 86–9; *Hitler-Prozeß*, LIV. Had the prosecution been pursued, Hitler would with certainty have been put behind bars for at least the two months suspended from the sentence he had received in January 1922, but dependent on his good behaviour. This would have put him out of action in the late summer or autumn of 1923, and have ruled out his chances of taking a leading role in the Kampfbund.

The likelihood of a putsch taking place would, in such circumstances, have been significantly diminished. In fact, despite Hitler's blackmail, Gürtner could have pressed on with the case – had the political will been there – and had it heard in camera. He did not entertain this possibility because of the fear that Bavarian ministers would have been forced to appear as witnesses and thereby exposed to damaging cross-examination. More important than the blackmail attempt were ultimately the political motives related to the anti-Berlin aims of the leading forces in Bavaria (Gruchmann, 'Hitlers Denkschrift', 306–13).

181. See Franz-Willing, *Krisenjahr*, 159.

182. *JK*, 918–66; Milan Hauner, *Hitler. A Chronology of his Life and Time*, London, 1983, 40.

183. Franz-Willing, *Krisenjahr*, 110.

184. Deuerlein, *Aufstieg*, 177–9; Maser, *Frühgeschichte*, 414–16.

185. Maser, *Frühgeschichte*, 412–14.

186. Cit. Maser, *Frühgeschichte*, 421.

187. See Bennecke, 78, noting that the Munich regiment increased by around 400 to 1,560 men between the end of August and 6 November 1923.

188. Hanfstaengl, *15 Jahre*, 108. See also Auerbach, 'Hitler's politische Lehrjahre', 38–9; and Toland, 142–3.

189. See Franz-Willing, *Krisenjahr*, 117.

190. Deuerlein, *Aufstieg*, 181–3.

191. Deuerlein, *Aufstieg*, 182. The occasion was the first time that the Nazi greeting with raised right arm was in evidence in photographs. The form of greeting became uniformly deployed in the NSDAP for the party's rally in Nuremberg in 1927 (Gerhard Paul, *Aufstand der Bilder. Die NS-Propaganda vor 1933*, 2nd edn, Bonn, 1992, 175–6; *RSA*, III.3, 382–3 n.3).

192. Franz-Willing, *Krisenjahr*, 118; Maser, *Frühgeschichte*, 421.

193. Auerbach, 'Hitlers politische Lehrjahre', 39; Franz-Willing, *Krisenjahr*, 119–21; Maser, *Frühgeschichte*, 424.

194. Bennecke, 79; Longerich, *Die braunen Bataillone*, 39.

195. Longerich, *Die braunen Bataillone*, 39. Hitler's takeover of the leadership was the background to the splinter in the Reichsflagge, arising from the objections of its leader, Heiß (Horn, *Marsch*, 123–5).

196. Mommsen, 'Adolf Hitler und der 9. November 1923', 42.

197. Deuerlein, *Putsch*, 202–4 n.69.

198. See Deuerlein, *Aufstieg*, 188, for Hitler's reported comments at a meeting of Kampfbund leaders on 23 October 1923, summarized by a witness at his trial, on 4 March 1924: 'Independent action by the troops of the Kampfbund would be nonsense and was to be ruled out. The national uprising could only take place in the closest association with the Bavarian army and state police.' ('*Ein selbständiges Handeln seitens der Truppen des Kampfbundes sei ein Unding und sei ausgeschlossen. Die nationale Erhebung könne nur in engster Vereinigung mit der bayerischen Reichswehr und der Landespolizei erfolgen.*')

199. Deuerlein, *Aufstieg*, 176; Winkler, *Weimar*, 207; Franz-Willing, *Krisenjahr*, 158.

200. Winkler, *Weimar*, 225–6. The atmosphere in Hamburg is captured in the contemporary account, sympathetic to the insurgents, of Larissa Reissner, *Hamburg at the Barricades*, London, 1977.

201. Kolb, *Weimarer Republik*, 51–2; Winkler, *Weimar*, 213–16, 224–8; Mommsen, *Verspielte Freiheit*, 160–64; Peter Longerich, *Deutschland 1918–1933*, Hanover, 1995, 140–43. The radical Right had already made its own first amateurish attempt at a putsch by this time, with the action of volunteers of the 'Black Reichswehr' – secretly trained reserve formations of the army – on 1 October, led by Major Bruno Ernst Buchrucker, aimed at taking the fortresses of Küstrin and Spandau, near Berlin, as the signal for a general rising. The regular Reichswehr immediately intervened and the putsch fizzled out as quickly as it had started. (See Franz-Willing, *Krisenjahr*, 117, 300, 307–10.)

202. Winkler, 224–5; Kolb, *Weimarer Republik*, 51–2.

203. Deuerlein, *Putsch*, 70–71. He also hoped to put Kahr, whom he disliked and distrusted, in the firing line of responsibility for unpopular policies (Gordon, 217).

204. Deuerlein, *Putsch*, 72–3; Gordon, 220.

205. *JK*, 1017 (protest to Kahr); Deuerlein, *Putsch*, 74. One meeting of the Kampfbund, with Hitler as speaker, was held, despite the ban (*JK*, 1017–18).

206. Maser, *Frühgeschichte*, 417, 422–3, 425–6. Hitler's speeches between 29 September and the beerhall putsch on 8 November contain numerous criticisms of Kahr's inadequacies (*JK*, 1019–50).

207. Deuerlein, *Putsch*, 71–2, 164–5 (quotation, 165).

208. Gordon, 242.

209. Gordon, 241.

210. Deuerlein, *Putsch*, 162.

211. Deuerlein, *Putsch*, 164 (8 September 1923).

212. Deuerlein, *Aufstieg*, 185–6 for rumours circulating in mid-October in the left-wing press in Austria about a forthcoming putsch involving Hitler, Ludendorff and Kahr.

213. Cit. Gordon, 243.

214. Cit. Gordon, 244.

215. Cit. Gordon, 255.

216. Cit. Otto Gritschneder, *Bewährungsfrist für den Terroristen Adolf H. Der Hitler-Putsch und die bayerische Justiz*, Munich, 1990, 42. Not dissimilar retrospective sentiments were also recorded by Hanfstaengl, *15 Jahre*, 167.

217. Above based on Gordon, 246–9, 251–3, 256–7; and see Franz-Willing, *Putsch*, 57.

218. Deuerlein, *Putsch*, 258; *Hitler-Prozeß*, LXI and n.23. But see Gordon's qualifying comments, 253, on the reliability of the report.

219. See Gordon, 253–5.

220. Gordon, 255.

221. Deuerlein, *Aufstieg*, 189–90.

222. Franz-Willing, *Putsch*, 57–9, where the suggestion is raised that the action was agreed between Kahr and the Kampfbund, and that Kahr intended to proclaim Crown Prinz Rupprecht, who was present at the gathering, as King of Bavaria. It is difficult to see, however, why the nationalist Kampfbund, with no interest in the restoration of the Bavarian monarchy, would have agreed to such a move. And the orders to prepare for action were given, apparently, to the nationalist SA and Bund Oberland, but not to the 'white-blue' pro-monarchy paramilitary organizations.

223. See Hanfstaengl, *15 Jahre*, 126–7; Gordon, 259.

224. Deuerlein, *Aufstieg*, 190–91; Franz-Willing, *Putsch*, 59–60; Gordon, 248.

225. Deuerlein, *Aufstieg*, 191–2; Gordon, 255–6.

226. Franz-Willing, *Krisenjahr*, 386–7; see also Deuerlein, *Putsch*, 99. Rumours of an impending putsch were current in Munich at the beginning of November. According to one, the restoration of the monarchy was to be proclaimed on 9 November; in another, Captain Ehrhardt's organization intended to strike at Berlin on 15 November. In fact, 15 November was the date which Lossow had in mind for the Bavarian Reichswehr's march on Berlin (Hans Hubert Hofmann, *Der Hitlerputsch. Krisenjahre deutscher Geschichte 1920–1924*, Munich, 1961, 135, 141).

227. Franz-Willing, *Putsch*, 63–4, 68. Kahr, together with Seißer and Lossow, did have a meeting that day with Ludendorff, at which there were sharp differences of opinion (Franz-Willing, *Putsch*, 68).

228. Gordon, 259.

229. Gordon, 259–60; Franz-Willing, *Putsch*, 66.

230. Gordon, 260. It has been estimated that around 4,000 armed putschists would have confronted about 2,600 state police and army troops in Munich (Gordon, 273).

231. Hofmann, 146; Franz-Willing, *Putsch*, 66 (based on oral testimony from 1958). Gordon, 259 n.63, mentions that there may have been an alternative plan to move on 10 or 11 November, but does not amplify. Deuerlein, *Putsch*, 99; Deuerlein, *Aufstieg*, 192, refer to plans only for 8 November.

232. Franz-Willing, *Putsch*, 64, 67–9, accepts that such a proclamation to restore the monarchy was feared; Hofmann, 147, is sceptical, presuming they feared instead an independent strike by Kahr against Berlin. For Lossow's comment, see Deuerlein, *Putsch*, 99, 258.

233. Deuerlein, *Putsch*, 99; Hofmann, 147. According to Hanfstaengl, Hitler later acknowledged that Kahr's manoeuvrings had forced him to take immediate action 'to get the situation in hand again', and that he had in any case been compelled to act in order to fulfil the expectations that had been aroused among his supporters (Hanfstaengl, *15 Jahre*, 167–9).

234. *VB*, 10 November 1937, p. 2: '. . . *Unsere gegnerische Seite beabsichtigte, um den 12. November herum eine Revolution, und zwar eine bajuvarische, auszurufen . . . Da setzte ich den Entschluß, vier Tage zuvor loszuschlagen . . .*' Franz-Willing, *Putsch*, 64 n.166, has slightly different wording.

235. Graf testimony, IfZ, ZS-282/52, 60.

236. Hanfstaengl, *15 Jahre*, 129.

237. Franz-Willing, *Putsch*, 71, 73–4.

238. Franz-Willing, *Putsch*, 71, has Esser also left uninformed, but Maser, *Frühgeschichte*, 443–4, has him being told in mid-morning.

239. Franz-Willing, *Putsch*, 72–3.

240. Deuerlein, *Aufstieg*, 192–3; Müller, *Wandel*, 160–66; Gordon, 287–8; Franz-Willing, *Putsch*, 78–9.

241. *JK*, 1052. The police report has Hitler himself firing the shot. Müller's testimony at Hitler's trial (Deuerlein, *Aufstieg*, 193) mentioned two shots fired, the first by Hitler's guard, the second, minutes later, by Hitler himself. Probably Müller was mistaken. No one else recalled a second shot, or noted anyone other than Hitler firing the alleged first shot.

242. *JK*, 1052. Hanfstaengl, *15 Jahre*, 133, also has Hitler making this remark after his first entry to the hall. Müller (Deuerlein, *Aufstieg*, 194) has the remark made after Hitler's re-entry.

243. *JK*, 1052.

244. Hanfstaengl, *15 Jahre*, 134; Deuerlein, *Aufstieg*, 193–4.

245. *JK*, 1053.

246. *JK*, 1054–5. The police reporter evidently understood Ludendorff's designated position to be Reich President (*JK*, 1054), though it seems unlikely that Hitler used those words.

247. *JK*, 1054–5; Müller, *Wandel*, 162–3 (trans., Gordon, 288).

248. Müller, *Wandel*, 162 ('*ein rednerisches Meisterstück*'); also, Müller's trial testimony in Deuerlein, *Aufstieg*, 194 ('*rednerisch ein Meisterstück*').

249. Gordon, 288–9.

250. Deuerlein, *Aufstieg*, 195–6; Gordon, 288–9.

251. The above based on Gordon, 290–94.

252. Gordon, 289–90.

253. Deuerlein, *Aufstieg*, 196–7.

254. *JK*, 1056–7.

255. Maser, *Frühgeschichte*, 454. The proclamation appeared in the *Münchner Neueste Nachrichten*, which had rushed out its morning edition of 9 November with the banner headline 'Establishment of a National Directory' (*MNN*, 9 November 1923, reproduced in Hellmut Schöner (ed.), *Hitler-Putsch im Spiegel der Presse*, Munich, 1974, 34–7).

256. *JK*, 1058 (Dok.600); the authenticity of the accompanying Dok.599 (1057–8) is extremely doubtful. Hitler's authorization was dated 8 November. In his Nuremberg trial, Streicher stated that it was given after midnight, with the implication that Hitler was by then resigned to failure (see Maser, *Frühgeschichte*, 453). The date of 8 November suggests, however, that Hitler at the time of his authorization still believed in success.

257. Gordon, 316–20; Toland, 164,

258. Frank, 60; Gordon, 324–7.

259. Gordon, 327.

260. Graf testimony, IfZ, ZS-282/52, 63.

261. Gritschneder, *Bewährungsfrist*, 41.

262. Frank, 61.

263. Gritschneder, *Bewährungsfrist*, 21–2.

264. Maser, *Frühgeschichte*, 454; Franz-Willing, *Putsch*, 109. At some point on 8–9 November, an emissary did apparently visit the Crown Prince, though when precisely is unclear (Gordon, 445–6).

265. Frank, 60; Gordon, 330–32.

266. Gordon, 351–2. Hanfstaengl, *15 Jahre*, 141, and Frank, 60, mention the snowy and slushy conditions.

267. Gordon, 333; Hanfstaengl, *15 Jahre*, 141. The putschists were handed out 2 billion Marks each (Frank, 61).

268. Maser, *Frühgeschichte*, 457. According to Frau Ludendorff, the suggestion for the march came from the General (Margarethe Ludendorff, *My Married Life with Ludendorff*, London, n.d., c.1930, 251; see also Franz-Willing, *Putsch*, 110).

269. *JK*, 1117 (28 February 1924); Deuerlein, *Aufstieg*, 214.

270. Gordon, 350–52. Frau Ludendorff had the impression that the purpose of the march – or 'public procession' as she called it – was to test popular feeling in support of the overthrow of the Republic and the restoration of the monarchy (Margarethe Ludendorff, 251). Lieutenant-Colonel Endres thought the idea was to use the figure of Ludendorff to win over the Reichswehr to the putsch (BHStA, Abt.IV, HS-925, Endres Aufzeichnungen, 51).

271. See Deuerlein, *Aufstieg*, 199.

272. Gordon, 357–8; Deuerlein, *Aufstieg*, 197–8. In the view of one contemporary witness to the events, Lieutenant-Colonel Endres, however, the majority of the people of Munich were unenthusiastic (BHStA, Abt.IV, HS-925, Endres Aufzeichnungen, 52).

273. Frank, 61.

274. Frank, 61–2.

275. Deuerlein, *Aufstieg*, 197; Frank, 61–2.

276. Deuerlein, *Aufstieg*, 198–9 (Godin's account); Gordon, 360–65; Deuerlein, *Putsch*, 331; Maser, *Frühgeschichte*, 459–60 (hinting that the police opened fire first).

277. Deuerlein, *Aufstieg*, 200; Franz-Willing, *Putsch*, 116 n.182, 119; Gordon, 364. Two other putschists were killed in the Wehrkreiskommando, making up the sixteen dead in all who were, in the Third Reich, regarded as heroes of the Nazi Movement. The dead policemen have in the much more recent past been commemorated by a memorial near the Feldherrnhalle in Munich's Odeonsplatz.

278. Hanfstaengl, *15 Jahre*, 147; Gordon, 353 and n.124, 364 and n.152; Endres Aufzeichnungen, BHStA, Abt.IV, HS-925, 56 (where Endres, critical in every other respect of Hitler's action in the putsch, was certain that he had thrown himself to

the ground at the outbreak of gunfire, and thought this action 'absolutely right').

279. The initial diagnosis of the doctor in Landsberg, where Hitler was interned, that he had broken a bone in his upper arm, proved mistaken (Schenck, 299–300).

280. Gordon, 467.

281. Hanfstaengl, *15 Jahre*, 144–5; Maser, *Frühgeschichte*, 460; Gordon, 469–71. Ludendorff's wife had initially received the news that he, too, had been killed (Margarethe Ludendorff, 251–2).

282. Hanfstaengl, *15 Jahre*, 146–9; Toland, 174–6, based on Helene Hanfstaengl's unpublished notes.

283. Hanfstaengl, *15 Jahre*, 149.

284. Hanfstaengl, *15 Jahre*, 147.

285. Gordon, 465. According to Hanfstaengl, his wife Helene jerked the revolver from Hitler's hand as he threatened 'to end it all' (Hanfstaengl, *Cosmopolitan*, 45).

286. Gritschneder, *Bewährungsfrist*, 33–4, cit. the report of the Government President of Upper Bavaria on Hitler's arrest; Gordon, 465–6.

287. Deuerlein, *Aufstieg*, 201; and see Hanfstaengl, *15 Jahre*, 146; Gordon, 413–15, 442–3.

288. Deuerlein, *Aufstieg*, 202.

289. Cit. Deuerlein, *Aufstieg*, 202, from *Die Welt von gestern*, Stockholm, 1942, 441.

290. Auerbach, 'Hitlers politische Lehrjahre', 42. It attained twenty-three from 129 seats in the Bavarian Landtag (Deuerlein, *Aufstieg*, 231).

291. Dietrich Thränhardt, *Wahlen und politische Strukturen in Bayern 1848–1953*, Düsseldorf, 1973, 173; Meinrad Hagmann, *Der Weg ins Verhängnis*, Munich, 1946, 14*–20*.

292. Deuerlein, *Aufstieg*, 427.

293. Gordon, 495–503.

294. Gordon, 486–95; Seißer was subsequently restored to office, but was never again a powerful figure.

295. See Tyrell, *Trommler*, 166; and also Mommsen, 'Adolf Hitler und der 9. November 1923', 47.

296. Gritschneder, *Bewährungsfrist*, citing comments made to him in 1988 by the then ninety-eight-year-old Alois Maria Ott, former Anstalts-Psychologe at Landsberg.

297. Röhm, 2nd edn, 272; Deuerlein, *Aufstieg*, 203; Hanfstaengl, *15 Jahre*, 154; Heiden, *Hitler*, 175; Tyrell, *Trommler*, 277 n.178; *Hitler-Prozeß*, XXX–XXXI; and see Gordon, 477. Prison psychologist Ott also claimed to have calmed Hitler down in the course of several hours of discussion, and to have persuaded him to break off his hunger-strike (Gritschneder, *Bewährungsfrist*, 35).

298. Cit. Gritschneder, *Bewährungsfrist*, 37–42, from Ehard's private papers.

299. Cit. Gritschneder, *Bewährungsfrist*, 43.

300. Deuerlein, *Aufstieg*, 203; Gordon, 455, 476. Gritschneder, *Bewährungsfrist*, 49–52, clearly outlines the legal position: under Article 13 of the Law for the Protection of the Republic of 21 July 1922, the 'Staatsgerichtshof' (State Court)

placed under the aegis of the Reichsgericht (Reich Court) at Leipzig had competence to try cases of alleged high treason. However, the Bavarian government had refused to concede its judicial authority and had passed three days later a decree establishing People's Courts (*Volksgerichte*) for treason cases in Bavaria. Under the Reich Constitution of 1919, Reich law was superior to laws passed by individual states. Despite this, Bavaria refused to comply with the order of the Staatsgerichtshof in Leipzig, immediately following the putsch, to arrest Hitler, Göring and Ludendorff with a view to opening preliminary hearings against them. The only obvious way of overriding the Bavarian government in practice would have been through the use of force, which the Reich government was anxious to avoid. The complex and sensitive relations between the Reich and Bavaria at precisely this juncture, and the readiness of the Reich cabinet to concede – after pressure from the Bavarian Justice Minister Gürtner – that the trial should be held in Munich, are fully explored by Bernd Steger, 'Der Hitlerprozeß und Bayerns Verhältnis zum Reich 1923/24', *VfZ*, 25 (1977), 441–66, here esp. 442–9, 455.

301. Gordon, 476.

302. Hanfstaengl, *15 Jahre*, 156; and see Heiden, *Hitler*, 176–7.

303. Deuerlein, *Aufstieg*, 203–4.

304. Deuerlein, *Aufstieg*, 215; Gordon, 480.

305. Deuerlein, *Aufstieg*, 205–6, cit. Hans von Hülsen.

306. Deuerlein, *Aufstieg*, 215–16, 217–20.

307. Deuerlein, *Aufstieg*, 225.

308. *Monologe*, 260 (3–4 February 1942) and 453 n.168.

309. Deuerlein, *Aufstieg*, 227.

310. Deuerlein, *Aufstieg*, 227–8.

311. Gritschneder, *Bewährungsfrist*, 22, 48–54; and *Hitler-Prozeß*, esp. XXX–XXXVII.

312. Gritschneder, *Bewährungsfrist*, 58–60.

313. Laurence Rees, *The Nazis. A Warning from History*, London, 1997, 30. In this earlier trial, Judge Neithardt had sought an even more lenient punishment – a fine, instead of imprisonment – than the mild sentence actually imposed.

314. Deuerlein, *Aufstieg*, 234–6; Tyrell, *Trommler*, 277 n.180; Heiden, *Hitler*, 184–5; Hanfstaengl, *15 Jahre*, 156–7; Gritschneder, *Bewährungsfrist*, 98. And see Hermann Fobke's description of lazy days in Landsberg, in Werner Jochmann (ed.), *Nationalsozialismus und Revolution*, Frankfurt am Main, 1963, 91–2.

315. Deuerlein, *Aufstieg*, 232.

316. *MK*, 603–8, 619–20; Longerich, *Die braunen Bataillone*, 47.

317. See Tyrell, 'Wie er der "Führer" wurde', 34–5.

318. *JK*, 1188.

319. *JK*, 1210.

320. *JK*, 1212. 'There is a single person who seems fit to have the German army lower its weapons to him and to bring about in peacetime what we need.' ('*Es gibt einen einzigen, der in meinen Augen befähigt erscheint, daß das deutsche Heer die*

Waffen senkt vor ihm und daß im Frieden das erfolgt, was wir brauchen.')
321. Deuerlein, *Aufstieg*, 188 (23 October 1923).
322. *JK*, 1056–7.

CHAPTER 7: EMERGENCE OF THE LEADER

1. Georg Schott, *Das Volksbuch vom Hitler*, Munich, 1924, 18, 229.
2. *MK*, 362.
3. See Horn, *Marsch*, 174–5.
4. Horn, *Marsch*, 172 and n.56; Franz-Willing, *Putsch*, 193; David Jablonsky, *The Nazi Party in Dissolution. Hitler and the Verbotzeit 1923–25*, London, 1989, 43 and 189 n.99.
5. For biographical sketches, see Fest, *Face of the Third Reich*, 247–64; and Smelser/ Zitelmann, 223–35.
6. Alfred Rosenberg, *Letzte Aufzeichnungen. Ideale und Idole der nationalsozialistischen Revolution*, Göttingen, 1948, 107.
7. Bullock, *Hitler*, 122.
8. See Horn, *Marsch*, 172.
9. Jablonsky, 44.
10. Horn, *Marsch*, 173–5.
11. Jablonsky, 50.
12. Jablonsky, 46–7; Albrecht Tyrell, *Führer befiehl . . . Selbstzeugnisse aus der 'Kampfzeit' der NSDAP*, Düsseldorf, 1969, 68, 72–3; Franz-Willing, *Putsch*, 197.
13. Tyrell, *Führer*, 73.
14. Roland V. Layton, 'The *Völkischer Beobachter*, 1920–1933: The Nazi Party Newspaper in the Weimar Era', *Central European History*, 4 (1970), 353–82, here 359.
15. Tyrell, *Führer*, 68.
16. Jablonsky, 192 n.1.
17. Tyrell, *Führer*, 81–2.
18. Jablonsky, 10, 22, 179 n.16, 181–2 n.67.
19. Jablonsky, 58–63, 175.
20. Sonderarchiv Moscow, 1355/I/2, Fol. 75, Privatkanzlei Adolf Hitler, Rudolf Heß to Kurt Günther, 29 July 1925.
21. Tyrell, *Führer*, 76; Franz-Willing, *Putsch*, 231.
22. Lüdecke, 218; and see Jablonsky, 85.
23. Sonderarchiv Moscow, 1355/I/2, Fol.286. Rudolf Heß to Wilhelm Sievers, 11 May 1925.
24. Tyrell, *Führer*, 76.
25. Erich Matthias and Rudolf Morsey (eds.), *Das Ende der Parteien 1933*, Königstein, Ts/Düsseldorf, 1969, 782; Hagmann, 15*–16*. The Franconian heartlands of Nazism recorded even higher levels of support for the Völkischer Block: 24.5 per cent in Upper Franconia and 24.7 per cent in Middle Franconia (Hagmann, 18*).

26. Jablonsky, 85.

27. Jochmann (ed.), *Nationalsozialismus und Revolution*, 77, 114.

28. Jablonsky, 87–8.

29. Franz-Willing, *Putsch*, 252; Jablonsky, 89.

30. Tyrell, *Führer*, 77–8, cit. from *Der Pommersche Beobachter*, 11 June 1924; Franz-Willing, *Putsch*, 253.

31. Franz-Willing, *Putsch*, 256–7; Noakes, *Nazi Party*, 45.

32. Jablonsky, 93.

33. Jochmann, 77–8; Deuerlein, *Aufstieg*, 234; Jablonsky, 94–5; and see Hitler's letter of 23 June to Albert Stier, in Tyrell, *Führer*, 78.

34. Jochmann, 91; Jablonsky, 95.

35. Deuerlein, *Aufstieg*, 235–6; Jablonsky, 96. He had told Ludendorff of his decision to withdraw early in June but had been asked to delay a public announcement.

36. Jablonsky, 96.

37. Tyrell, *Führer*, 77–8.

38. Jochmann, 90. Hitler seems to have indicated his decision to Ludendorff at a meeting, also attended by Graefe, on 12 June, the day after the appearance of the newspaper statement in question (Jablonsky, 96 and 203 n.19).

39. See Lüdecke, 222, for such an interpretation.

40. Lüdecke, 222–4 (quotation, 224).

41. Jablonsky, 90–91, 99–101.

42. Tyrell, *Führer*, 79. The date is mistakenly given in the press statement as 15–17 July, not August.

43. Tyrell, *Führer*, 80; Jablonsky, 101–2.

44. Jochmann, 96–7.

45. Franz-Willing, *Putsch*, 261–5; Jablonsky, 103–7.

46. Jochmann, 120–21.

47. Jochmann, 122–4; Jablonsky, 111; Franz-Willing, *Putsch*, 266. Hitler, noted Fobke, was preoccupied with his book, of which he had high expectations. It was scheduled for mid-October. Hitler fully expected to be free on 1 October, though Fobke added that he could not see the reason for his optimism (Jochmann, 124).

48. Jochmann, 125–7 (quotation, 126).

49. Jablonsky, 118–23, 210 n.189, cit. *Völkischer Kurier*, Nr 165, 19 August 1924.

50. Jochmann, 130–37; Jablonsky, 124–5.

51. Jablonsky, 125–8.

52. Jochmann, 154, 165; Tyrell, *Trommler*, 167; Jablonsky, 135–9.

53. Tyrell, *Führer*, 86–7.

54. Jablonsky, 142–5.

55. Tyrell, *Führer*, 76; Deuerlein, *Aufstieg*, 241, 427; Hanfstaengl, *15 Jahre*, 163; Franz-Willing, *Putsch*, 276.

56. Deuerlein, *Aufstieg*, 241; Hanfstaengl, *15 Jahre*, 163; Jablonsky, 150.

57. Gritschneder, *Bewährungsfrist*, 97–8.

58. Deuerlein, *Aufstieg*, 238–9.

59. On 16 September, the Munich police had found incriminating files of members and correspondence in the house of Wilhelm Brückner, formerly the Munich SA leader, and Karl Osswald, a former leader of the Reichskriegsflagge (Jablonsky, 132).

60. Gritschneder, *Bewährungsfrist*, 101–2.

61. Gritschneder, *Bewährungsfrist*, 103–10.

62. In a report of 26 September, the day after this judgement, however, Prison Governor Leybold accepted the seriousness of the breach of trust in smuggling out a number of letters, though his criticism was aimed at Kriebel and Weber, not at Hitler (Gritschneder, *Bewährungsfrist*, 109–10).

63. Jablonsky, 132–3.

64. Gritschneder, *Bewährungsfrist*, 114–16.

65. Gritschneder, *Bewährungsfrist*, 116–18.

66. Hitler, Kriebel and Weber had attempted, in a declaration of 26 September, to distance themselves from Röhm's plans for the Frontbann and show their disapproval of his actions. Hitler emphasized that he had laid down his political leadership, and that his refusal to be involved in the defence organizations set up by Röhm followed as a matter of course (Gritschneder, *Bewährungsfrist*, 110–12; see also Jablonsky, 133, and Hanfstaengl, *15 Jahre*, 160–61).

67. Jablonsky, 150.

68. Deuerlein, *Aufstieg*, 239–40.

69. Jetzinger, 276–7; Donald Cameron Watt, 'Die bayerischen Bemühungen um Ausweisung Hitlers 1924', *VfZ*, 6 (1958), 270–80, here, 272; Jablonsky, 91 and 202 n.190; Deuerlein, *Aufstieg*, 239. The initial inquiry of the Bavarian police about deporting Hitler, in March 1924, had been prompted by concern that he would be acquitted at his trial, along with Ludendorff. The concern was also voiced by the Bavarian Minister President, Knilling.

70. Gritschneder, *Bewährungsfrist*, 101. As we have seen, the Munich Police Direction reinforced this opinion in its report of 23 September.

71. Watt, 'Die bayerischen Bemühungen', 273.

72. Jetzinger, 277.

73. Deuerlein, *Aufstieg*, 240. Hitler's war service, it was claimed, meant that he was no longer an Austrian citizen (Watt, 'Die bayerischen Bemühungen', 274).

74. Watt, 'Die bayerischen Bemühungen', 276–7; Jetzinger, 278.

75. Whether, as has often been accepted (see Bullock, 127; Toland, 203) Gürtner, influenced by the Austrian refusal to take him back, played a decisive role in having deportation proceedings against Hitler quashed remains, in the light of Watt's examination of the evidence, uncertain. See Watt, 'Die bayerischen Bemühungen', 270–71, 279.

76. Deuerlein, *Aufstieg*, 250–52; Jetzinger, 272, 279.

77. Jetzinger, 280.

78. Gritschneder, *Bewährungsfrist*, 119–30 (quotation, 130). Leybold had already further testified to Hitler's good conduct in a report of 13 November.

79. See Jablonsky, 150.

80. Gritschneder, *Bewährungsfrist*, 130.

81. *Monologe*, 259–60. For Müller, see *Monologe*, 146, and Heiden, *Hitler*, 199–200.

82. Gritschneder, *Bewährungsfrist*, 130.

83. *Monologe*, 259–60; Hoffmann, 60–61; Franz-Willing, *Putsch*, 278–9, cit. *Der Nationalsozialist* of 25 December 1924 and *Völkischer Kurier* of 23 December 1924.

84. *Monologe*, 261.

85. Frank, 46–7.

86. See Jochmann, 91–2, for Fobke's description of his normal day in Landsberg.

87. See *MK*, 36.

88. Frank, 47.

89. Frank, 45.

90. Eitner, 75. Eitner (75–82) was prepared to see the time in Landsberg as the major turning-point in Hitler's life, the 'Jordan experience' that convinced him of his messianic mission, that he was no longer Germany's 'John the Baptist', but its actual messiah.

91. Even allowing for Hitler's usual underlining of his own 'intuitive genius', his later comment, that it was during this time that a good deal of reflection made him for the first time grasp fully many things that he had earlier understood only by intuition, accords with this interpretation (*Monologe*, 262).

92. *Monologe*, 262.

93. Otto Strasser, *Hitler und ich*, Buenos Aires, n.d. (1941?), 56.

94. Franz-Willing, *Putsch*, 251; Jochmann, 92. Fobke speaks of one hour's 'lecture with the chief, or better, from the chief' ('*Vortrag beim Chef, besser vom Chef*'). According to one of his warders (who subsequently became an SS-Sturmführer), in an account published in 1933, Hitler read out chapters of his book on Saturday evenings (Otto Lurker, *Hitler hinter Festungsmauern*, Berlin, 1933, 56). See also Werner Maser, *Hitlers Mein Kampf*, Munich/Esslingen, 1966, 20–21 and Hammer, 'Die deutschen Ausgaben', 161–78, here 162.

95. Hinted at in Heiden, *Der Führer*, 226. Though plausible, there is no corroborative evidence for Heiden's inference (which did not appear in his 1936 biography of Hitler). Heiden, *Der Führer*, 226, also appears to be the source of the suggestion that Hitler had begun work in 1922 on a book entitled 'A Reckoning' (the title of the first volume of *Mein Kampf*), aimed at dealing with his enemies and rivals.

96. Hanfstaengl, *15 Jahre*, 172.

97. Heiden, *Hitler*, 206; Heiden, *Der Führer*, 226.

98. Franz-Willing, *Putsch*, 251.

99. Strongly hinted in Heiden, *Der Führer*, 226 (though without corroborative evidence).

100. Otto Strasser, *Hitler und ich*, 59; Frank, 45; Heiden, *Hitler*, 188–90; Hans Kallenbach, *Mit Adolf Hitler auf Festung Landsberg*, Munich, 1933, 56. See also Hammer, 'Die deutschen Ausgaben', 161–2; Lurker, 56; Maser, *Frühgeschichte*,

304 and n.325; Maser, *Adolf Hitler*, 192. Ilse Heß claimed after the war that her husband had not taken down the text in dictation, but that Hitler had typed it himself with two fingers on an old typewriter, and subsequently, after his release, dictated the second volume to a secretary (Maser, *Mein Kampf*, 20–21). Given Hitler's aversion to writing, and the availability of willing hands (including Heß's) in Landsberg, this seems highly unlikely.

101. Otto Strasser, *Hitler und ich*, Constance, 1948, 78.

102. Heiden, *Hitler*, 206; Hanfstaengl, *15 Jahre*, 172–3.

103. Hammer, 'Die deutschen Ausgaben', 163; Görlitz-Quint, 236–43. Ilse Heß claimed somewhat unpersuasively, after the war, that only she and her husband had been involved in what amounted to purely stylistic amendments to Hitler's text (Maser, *Mein Kampf*, 22–4).

104. Hanfstaengl, *15 Jahre*, 173–4.

105. Frank, 45–6. According to Frank, he said that had he guessed in 1924 that he would become Reich Chancellor, he would not have written the book.

106. Heiden, *Hitler*, 206; Maser, *Mein Kampf*, 24; Oron James Hale, 'Adolf Hitler: Taxpayer', *American Historical Review*, 60 (1955), 830–42, here 837.

107. Hammer, 'Die deutschen Ausgaben', 163; Maser, *Mein Kampf*, 26–7, 29; [No author given], 'The Story of Mein Kampf', *Wiener Library Bulletin*, 6 (1952), no.5–6, 31–2, here 31.

108. According to Otto Strasser, *Hitler und ich*, 60–61, the leading members of the party had privately to admit, during the Nuremberg Rally of 1927, that they had not read the book. See also Karl Lange, *Hitlers unbeachtete Maximen: 'Mein Kampf' und die Öffentlichkeit*, Stuttgart, 1968. Those well acquainted with Hitler from the earliest days of the party, such as Christian Weber, occasionally made fun of the contents of *Mein Kampf* (see Hanfstaengl, *15 Jahre*, 188).

109. Hitler's declared gross taxable income largely derived from the sales of *Mein Kampf*, was 19,843 RM in 1925, dipped to 11,494 RM by 1927, was 15,448 RM in 1929, rising sharply the following year to 48,472 RM, then soaring to 1,232,335 RM in 1933. Hitler was delinquent in paying his tax for 1933, but action by the revenue authorities was first delayed, then stopped when he was declared tax exempt. He paid no taxation, therefore, on the vast royalties earned on *Mein Kampf* during the Third Reich (Hale, 'Adolf Hitler: Taxpayer', 839–41).

110. The outstanding analysis is that of Eberhard Jäckel, *Hitlers Weltanschauung. Entwurf einer Herrschaft*, Tübingen, 1969; extended and revised 4th edn, Stuttgart, 1991.

111. See *MK*, 317–58.

112. *MK*, 372 (trans., *MK* Watt, 308).

113. *MK*, 358.

114. See *MK*, 742–3, 750–52. For the development of the '*Lebensraum*' idea from its early usage in a programmatic declaration by the Pan-Germans in 1894, see Lange, 'Der Terminus "Lebensraum"', 426–37, esp. 428ff.

115. See Martin Broszat, 'Soziale Motivation', 392–409, here esp. 403.

116. A point established, against the current interpretation at that time, as early as 1953 by Hugh Trevor-Roper, 'The Mind of Adolf Hitler', his introduction to *Hitler's Table Talk*, 1941–44, London, 1953, vii–xxxv. Trevor-Roper reinforced the argument in his article 'Hitlers Kriegsziele', *VfZ*, 8 (1960), 121–33. But it was only in the light of Jäckel's masterly analysis of *Mein Kampf*, in his book *Hitlers Weltanschauung*, in 1969 that Hitler's ideas became generally accepted as inherently cohesive as well as consistent.

117. Frank, 45. Subsequent editions of *Mein Kampf* down to 1939 nevertheless contained, in all, around 2,500 largely minor stylistic corrections (Hammer, 164; Maser, *Hitler*, 188).

118. See Jäckel, *Hitlers Weltanschauung*, esp. 152–8.

119. The linking role of the Deutschvölkischer Schutz- und Trutzbund in the continuity of extreme antisemitic ideas between the Pan-Germans and the Nazis is excellently brought out in Lohalm, *Völkischer Radikalismus*.

120. *JK*, 176–7.

121. *MK*, 372 (trans., *MK* Watt, 307).

122. *MK*, 772 (trans., *MK* Watt, 620).

123. As implied in the title of the important analysis of Nazi anti-Jewish policy by Karl A. Schleunes, *The Twisted Road to Auschwitz. Nazi Policy toward German Jews 1933–1939*, Urbana/Chicago/London, 1970.

124. *JK*, 646.

125. *JK*, 703–4.

126. *JK*, 1210.

127. *JK*, 1226.

128. *JK*, 1242 and n.2–3.

129. Wolfgang Horn, 'Ein unbekannter Aufsatz Hitlers aus dem Frühjahr 1924', *VfZ*, 16 (1968), 287, 288. For the conventionality of Hitler's Pan-German notion of foreign policy in the early 1920s, see Günter Schubert, *Anfänge nationalsozialistischer Außenpolitik*, Köln, 1963, esp. ch.1–2; Jäckel, *Hitlers Weltanschauung*, 31–8; and, in particular, Kuhn, *Hitlers außenpolitisches Programm*, 31–59, esp. 56.

130. Jäckel, *Hitlers Weltanschauung*, 33–4.

131. Horn, 'Ein unbekannter Aufsatz Hitlers', 283, 291; Jäckel, *Hitlers Weltanschauung*, 35–6; Geoffrey Stoakes, *Hitler and the Quest for World Dominion*, Leamington Spa, 1987, 137.

132. Horn, 'Ein unbekannter Aufsatz Hitlers', 284–91; Jäckel, *Hitlers Weltanschauung*, 35.

133. Horn, 'Ein unbekannter Aufsatz Hitlers', 285, 289–90; Stoakes, 122–35.

134. *JK*, 96; Jäckel, *Hitlers Weltanschauung*, 39.

135. *JK*, 427. See also Binion, *Hitler among the Germans*, 59. The May 1921 speech was shortly after Hitler's first visit to Ludendorff, who may have put the idea into his head (Auerbach, 'Hitlers politische Lehrjahre', 50 n.127). By the Treaty of Brest-Litovsk, Russia had withdrawn from the war at a cost of conceding vast tracts of territory to Germany.

136. *JK*, 505; Stoakes, 96.

137. See Stoakes, 120–21.

138. Stoakes, 118–20.

139. See Stoakes, 135, for Ludendorff's views, and the possibility of his influence on Hitler.

140. *JK*, 773 (trans., Stoakes, 137).

141. See Horn, 'Ein unbekannter Aufsatz Hitlers'; the text is printed in *JK*, 1216–27.

142. See Heiden, *Hitler*, 188.

143. Woodruff Smith, 110–11, 164.

144. See Woodruff Smith, esp. ch.6.

145. Woodruff Smith, 224–30. Despite a turgid style, the novel sold 265,000 copies between 1926 and 1933 (Lange, 'Der Terminus "Lebensraum"', 433).

146. Woodruff Smith, 223, 240; Lange, 'Der Terminus "Lebensraum"', 430–33. The part played by '*Lebensraum*' in Hitler's changing ideas on foreign policy at this time is brought out by Kuhn, ch.5, pt.3, 104–21, esp. 115–17.

147. Horn, 'Ein unbekannter Aufsatz Hitlers', 293 and n.67.

148. For Haushofer's denial at Nuremberg that Hitler had understood his works, see Lange, 'Der Terminus "Lebensraum"', 432 (where serious doubt is cast on that assertion).

149. Jäckel, *Hitlers Weltanschauung*, 37, points out that it is impossible to establish plainly the direct influence on the development of Hitler's ideas during the period in Landsberg. Maser, *Hitler*, 187, takes for granted, on the basis of comments in *Mein Kampf*, that Hitler knew the theories of Haushofer, Ratzel, and – though he did not read English – the Englishman Sir Halford Mackinder. Haushofer visited Heß in Landsberg. He later admitted that he had seen Hitler, though he denied seeing him alone (Toland, 199). His name does not appear in the list of Hitler's own visitors (Horn, 'Ein unbekannter Aufsatz Hitlers', 293, n.68).

150. See Jäckel, *Hitlers Weltanschauung*, 37; Kuhn, 104–21.

151. Jäckel, *Hitlers Weltanschauung*, 38–41.

152. *MK*, 741–3 (trans., slightly amended, *MK* Watt, 597–8). The first edition of *Mein Kampf* had 'Persian Empire' (*Perserreich*), not 'giant Empire' (*Riesenreich*) (Hammer, 175; Jäckel, *Hitlers Weltanschauung*, 45 n.32).

153. *Hitlers Zweites Buch. Ein Dokument aus dem Jahr 1928*, ed. Gerhard L. Weinberg, Stuttgart, 1961; republished under the title 'Außenpolitische Standortsbestimmung nach der Reichstagswahl Juni-Juli 1928', in *RSA*, IIA.

154. *Monologe*, 262.

155. *JK*, 1210; Tyrell, *Führer*, 64; Hanfstaengl, *15 Jahre*, 155.

156. Tyrell, *Trommler*, 166–7.

157. See Eitner, 75–84.

158. See Tyrell, *Trommler*, 167.

159. *MK*, 229–32 (quotations 231–2).

160. *MK*, 650–51 (trans., *MK* Watt, 528).

161. *MK*, 70.

162. Bullock's formulation (*Hitler*, 804) – 'an opportunist entirely without principle' in a system whose theme was 'domination, dressed up as the doctrine of race' – was guided by Hermann Rauschning, *Die Revolution des Nihilismus. Kulisse und Wirklichkeit im Dritten Reich*, Zürich/New York, 1938, esp. pt.I.

163. Tyrell, *Führer*, 85.

164. Jochmann, 134 (Fobke to Haase, 21 August 1924).

165. See Tyrell, *Trommler*, 174.

166. See Broszat, *Der Nationalsozialismus*, 21–2: *'The National Socialist ideology has correctly been spoken of as a mixed-brew, a conglomeration, a mush of ideas.'* (*'Man hat mit Recht von der Weltanschauung des Nationalsozialismus als von einem Mischkessel, einem Konglomerat, einem "Ideenbrei" gesprochen'*.)

167. See above, n.162.

CHAPTER 8: MASTERY OVER THE MOVEMENT

1. BAK, R43 I/2696, Fol.528. See also Thomas Childers (ed.), *The Formation of the Nazi Constituency, 1919–1933*, London/Sydney, 1986, 232.

2. See Jürgen Falter, Thomas Lindenberger and Siegfried Schumann (eds.), *Wahlen und Abstimmungen in der Weimarer Republik. Materialien zum Wahlverhalten*, Munich, 1986, 45.

3. See Detlev J. K. Peukert, *Die Weimarer Republik, Krisenjahre der Klassischen Moderne*, Frankfurt am Main, 1987, 125, 132ff., 141–2, 176; Petzina, Abelshauser and Faust (eds.), *Sozialgeschichtliches Arbeitsbuch, Band III*, 61, 98, 114–15, 125, 137. The extensive improvements in the framework of a welfare state are dealt with in Ludwig Preller, *Sozialpolitik in der Weimarer Republik*, Düsseldorf (1949), 1978.

4. See Peter Gay, *Weimar Culture*, London, 1969.

5. Peukert, *Die Weimarer Republik*, 175–6.

6. See Michael Kater, *Different Drummers. Jazz in the Culture of Nazi Germany*, New York/Oxford, 1992, 3–28, for the spread of jazz in the Weimar Republic.

7. BHStA, MA 102 137, RPvOB, HMB, 18 February 1928, S.1.

8. Tyrell, *Führer*, 382.

9. Tyrell, *Führer*, 352. The figures given by the party did not take account of those leaving, and are therefore too high.

10. A point made by Dietrich Orlow, *The History of the Nazi Party, vol. 1, 1919–33*, Newton Abbot, 1971, 76, of the 1926 party.

11. Tyrell, *Trommler*, 171.

12. Hanfstaengl, *15 Jahre*, 163; Lüdecke, 252.

13. Hanfstaengl had on a visit to Landsberg encouraged Hitler to take some physical exercise and play some sport to reduce the weight he was putting on. Hitler rejected the idea on the grounds that 'a leader cannot afford to be beaten by his followers – not even in gymnastic exercises or in games' (Hanfstaengl, *15 Jahre*, 157).

14. Hanfstaengl, *15 Jahre*, 164. On Hitler's later strict vegetarianism, and the varied explanations he and others gave for this, see Schenck, 27–42.

15. Hanfstaengl, *15 Jahre*, 166–7.

16. *Monologe*, 260–61, 453, n.170. Hitler had moaned to Hanfstaengl at Christmas that '*mein Rudi, mein Hesserl*' was still in prison (Hanfstaengl, *15 Jahre*, 165).

17. *Monologe*, 261 (where Hitler remarked that Held had been decent to him at their meeting and that he had later, therefore, 'done nothing to him'); Karl Schwend, *Bayern zwischen Monarchie und Diktatur*, Munich, 1954, 298; Hanfstaengl, *15 Jahre*, 169; Lüdecke, 255; Margarethe Ludendorff, 271–4.

18. Jochmann, *Nationalsozialismus und Revolution*, 193–4.

19. Schwend, 298. And see Jablonsky, 155 and 218–19 n.166–7.

20. Hanfstaengl, *15 Jahre*, 170. The ban automatically ceased with the lifting of the Bavarian state of emergency (Deuerlein, *Aufstieg*, 245).

21. Tyrell, *Führer*, 89–93, letter of the later Gauleiter of Pomerania (1927–31), Walther von Corswant-Cuntzow. See also Deuerlein, *Aufstieg*, 242–3, based on an account in the *Münchener Post*, 4 February 1925; and Jablonsky, 156. For Reventlow's public attack on Hitler soon after the '*Preußentagung*', see Horn, *Marsch*, 213.

22. Tyrell, *Führer*, 92.

23. Horn, *Marsch*, 216 and no.23.

24. Horn, *Marsch*, 212 n.6.

25. Jochmann, *Nationalsozialismus und Revolution*, 193–4. In a private letter in July 1925 dealing with Hitler's relationship with Ludendorff, Rudolf Heß wrote: 'Herr Hitler never authorized his Excellency Ludendorff to lead the National Socialist Movement. Herr Hitler repeatedly requested his Excellency to withdraw from the petty political dispute immediately after the trial. His Excellency L[udendorff] should retain his name for the nation and not enter it and use it up on behalf of a small party' (Sonderarchiv Moscow, 1355-I-2, Fol.75, Heß to Kurt Günther, 29 July 1925).

26. Tyrell, *Führer*, 93–4.

27. Horn, *Marsch*, 213 and n.13, 214 and n.14; Jablonsky, 158; Deuerlein, *Aufstieg*, 245. The DNVP immediately reformed itself as the DNVB (Deutschvölkische Freiheitsbewegung).

28. Tyrell, *Führer*, 104.

29. Tyrell, *Führer*, 71.

30. Hitler rejected the term '*völkisch*' as unclear. – RSA, I, 3. Despite his statement, some sympathizers of his Movement were still unclear about the attitude towards religion. On his behalf, Rudolf Heß answered a letter from a Fräulein Ilse Harff from Chemnitz on 22 May 1925 by stating that 'Herr Hitler has never opposed the Christian religion of any denomination, merely parties calling themselves Christian which misuse the Christian religion for political purposes' (Sonderarchiv Moscow, 1355/I/2, Fol.127).

31. *RSA*, I, 1–6.

32. Lüdecke, 248.

33. *RSA*, I, 9.

34. Longerich, *Die braunen Bataillone*, 51–2; Horn, *Marsch*, 226–7. Hitler waited more than a year before placing the reorganization of the SA in the hands of Franz Pfeffer von Salomon in autumn 1926.

35. *RSA*, I, 7–9.

36. Lüdecke, 256.

37. Heiden, *Hitler*, 198.

38. Jablonsky, 168, based on the police report of the meeting.

39. Rosenberg made plain in his memoirs that he stayed away from the meeting because of resentment which went back to the support Hitler had given during his internment to the clique around Esser and Streicher. He knew that Hitler planned a public display of mutual forgiveness for what had gone on, but wanted no part in the theatricals (Rosenberg, *Letzte Aufzeichnungen*, 114, 319–20).

40. Lüdecke, 257.

41. Lüdecke, 275.

42. Jablonsky, 168, 220 n.9. At the meeting in Munich in March to dissolve the Völkischer Block, Drexler is reported to have said that it was impossible to work alongside Esser. Nothing separated him from Hitler, but he could not continue with him as long as Esser was there (BHStA, Slg.Personen, Anton Drexler, Miesbacher Anzeiger, 19 May 1925).

43. Lüdecke, 255.

44. *RSA*, I, 14–28.

45. In his 'Call to Former Members' published the previous day, he had promised to account within a year for whether 'the party again became a movement or the movement became stifled as a party'. In either event, he accepted responsibility (*RSA*, I, 6).

46. BHStA, MA 101235/I, Pd. Mü., Nachrichtenblatt, 2 March 1925, S.16.

47. BHStA, MA 101235/I, Pd. Mü., Nachrichtenblatt, 2 March 1925, S.16; *RSA*, I, 28 n.9; Lüdecke, 258.

48. *RSA*, I, 446, 448.

49. *RSA*, I, 5, 28 n.9; Horn, *Marsch*, 216–17 and n.25–6.

50. According to Lüdecke, 253, Hitler fell into a rage about the inadequacies of generals as statesmen when the handling of Ludendorff was broached.

51. Horst Möller, *Weimar*, Munich, 1985, 54.

52. Ludwig Volk, *Der bayerische Episkopat und der Nationalsozialismus 1930–1934*, Mainz, 1965, 5, 7.

53. *RSA* I, 36.

54. Hanfstaengl, *15 Jahre*, 179–80; Horn, *Marsch*, 217.

55. See *RSA*, I, 38 n.2.

56. Lüdecke, 255.

57. Margarethe Ludendorff, 277–8.

58. Winkler, *Weimar*, 279; Horn, *Marsch*, 218 states that the choice for Jarres was

to prevent embarrassment for Ludendorff. This was surely, however, an excuse rather than a reason.

59. Julius Streicher stated in a speech on 27 March, two days before the election, that the meaning of the election was to show that Germany needed a man like Hitler at its head (cit. Horn, *Marsch*, 217 n.28).

60. Falter *et al.*, *Wahlen*, 76. The Communists also registered serious losses, as the radicalization of politics in the Weimar Republic was – temporarily as it turned out – reversed.

61. Hanfstaengl, *15 Jahre*, 180.

62. The Tannenbergbund was banned in 1933. For image reasons, however, the Ludendorffs were still allowed to publish. There was an official reconciliation of Hitler and Ludendorff in 1937, and at his death in December that year the General was accorded a state funeral. The *völkisch* religious movement he and his wife founded – the Deutsche Gotterkenntnis (German Knowledge of God) – was even granted formal status (Benz and Graml (eds.), *Biographisches Lexikon zur Weimarer Republik*, 212–13; Wistrich, *Wer war wer im Dritten Reich*, 180).

63. The death-throes of the DVFB were to last until 1933, but it was never again a force to be reckoned with (Horn, *Marsch*, 218 and n.32).

64. Horn, *Marsch*, 215–16; Nyomarkay, 72–3. On 8 March, the NSFB (Völkischer Block) was dissolved in Bavaria, and most members returned to the NSDAP. Four days later, the GVG dissolved itself with a unanimous pledge of support for Hitler and the NSDAP.

65. Tyrell, *Führer*, 107–8; Deuerlein, *Aufstieg*, 246–7; Horn, *Marsch*, 222 and n.43. Hitler was permitted during the period of the bans only to speak at private functions – such as the meeting of the Hamburger Nationalklub he addressed in February 1926 – and at closed party meetings (though in Bavaria even speaking at these was for some time prohibited).

66. Deuerlein, *Aufstieg*, 247; Reinhard Kühnl, 'Zur Programmatik der National-sozialistischen Linken. Das Strasser-Programm von 1925/26', *VfZ*, 14 (1966), 317–33, here 318.

67. Albert Krebs, *Tendenzen und Gestalten der NSDAP*, Stuttgart, 1959, 183, 185. Strasser's importance to the NSDAP is thoroughly examined by Peter D. Stachura, *Gregor Strasser and the Rise of Nazism*, London, 1983 and Udo Kissenkoetter, *Gregor Strasser und die NSDAP*, Stuttgart, 1978. Kissenkoetter provides a brief biographical sketch in Ronald Smelser and Rainer Zitelmann (eds.), *Die braune Elite*, Darmstadt, 1989, 273–85.

68. Nyomarkay, 72–3. In southern Germany, by contrast, the 222 local branches before the putsch (all but thirty-seven in Bavaria), compared with only 140 by late 1925.

69. Tyrell, *Führer*, 97–9.

70. See Jochmann, *Nationalsozialismus und Revolution*, 207; Tyrell, *Führer*, 113; Nyomarkay, 71–89; Jeremy Noakes, 'Conflict and Development in the NSDAP 1924–1927', *Journal of Contemporary History*, 1 (1966), 3–36.

71. Noakes, *Nazi Party*, 65.

72. Jochmann, *Nationalsozialismus und Revolution*, 207.

73. Jochmann, *Nationalsozialismus und Revolution*, 210–11; Noakes, *Nazi Party*, 84–5.

74. See Krebs, 187. Goebbels's radical, 'national' brand of 'socialism' is heavily emphasized by Ulrich Höver, *Joseph Goebbels – ein nationaler Sozialist*, Bonn/Berlin, 1992.

75. *TBJG*, I. i, 99 (27 March 1925). Three substantial biographies of Goebbels appeared during the 1990s: Ralf Georg Reuth, *Goebbels*, Munich, 1990; Höver (who, however, deals in detail only with the period before 1933); and David Irving, *Goebbels. Mastermind of the Third Reich*, London, 1996. Shorter character sketches are provided by Elke Fröhlich in Smelser-Zitelmann, *Die braune Elite*, 52–68, and Fest, *Face of the Third Reich*, 130–51.

76. Peter Hüttenberger, *Die Gauleiter. Studie zum Wandel des Machtgefüges in der NSDAP*, Stuttgart, 1969, 33, 223; Shelley Baranowski, *The Sanctity of Rural Life. Nobility, Protestantism, and Nazism in Weimar Prussia*, New York/Oxford, 1995, 136.

77. *TBJG*, I.1, 127 (11 September 1925).

78. For public consumption at least, Hitler did not distance himself from the idea at this time. Replying for Hitler on 4 June 1925 to a query from a party sympathizer, Heß was apologetic about the absence of trade unions attached to the Movement, which he blamed on lack of funding (Sonderarchiv Moscow, 1355–I–2, Fol.22, Heß to Alfred Barg, Kohlfurt-Dorf).

79. Noakes, *Nazi Party*, 85–6.

80. See Krebs, 119.

81. Krebs, 187.

82. This and the following paragraph are based on Jochmann, *Nationalsozialismus und Revolution*, 207–11. See also Noakes, *Nazi Party*, 71.

83. *TBJG*, I.1, 126 (11 September 1925). For Fobke's description of Strasser, see Jochmann, *Nationalsozialismus und Revolution*, 208.

84. Though the meeting had not attained all its goals, Goebbels noted his satisfaction: 'Everything then, just as we wanted' (*TBJG*, I.1, 126 (11 September 1925)).

85. The Göttingen group had regarded the Community as a vehicle for representing its views within the movement, for blocking electoral participation, and for purging the party of Esser and his clique (Jochmann, *Nationalsozialismus und Revolution*, 211).

86. Jochmann, *Nationalsozialismus und Revolution*, 212–13. The *Briefe* appeared for the first time on 1 October 1925. The statutes were approved at the second meeting of the Community, held at Hanover on 22 November 1925.

87. Tyrell, *Führer*, 116–17; Nyomarkay, 80–81; Kühnl, 321ff. Gregor Strasser recommended to Goebbels the exclusion of all personal factors in the case of Esser and Streicher. Both were in demand as speakers in northern Gaue.

88. Tyrell, *Führer*, 115–16; Nyomarkay, 80–81; Noakes, *Nazi Party*, 74.

89. Tyrell, *Führer*, 119; Noakes, 'Conflict', 23ff.; Orlow, i.67–8.

90. Noakes, *Nazi Party*, 74–5.

91. Jochmann, *Nationalsozialismus und Revolution*, 223.

92. Jochmann, *Nationalsozialismus und Revolution*, 220; *TBJG*, I.1, 157 (21 January 1926); Noakes, *Nazi Party*, 76; Tyrell, 'Gottfried Feder and the NSDAP', 48–87, here 69; Horn, *Marsch*, 237.

93. Jochmann, *Nationalsozialismus und Revolution*, 222. It is possible that there was direct criticism of Hitler. But the two witnesses, Otto Strasser, and Franz Pfeffer von Salomon – speaking many years after the events – cannot be relied upon. (See Noakes, *Nazi Party*, 76–8.)

94. Horn, *Marsch*, 237–8; Gerhard Schildt, 'Die Arbeitsgemeinschaft Nord-West. Untersuchungen zur Geschichte der NSDAP 1925/6', Diss.Phil., Freiburg, 1964, 148ff. Hitler had initiated the division of the Reich into *Gaue* following the refoundation of the party in 1925. There was a good deal of amalgamation and renaming of them in the late 1920s before the organizational structure of the party's regions settled down. (See Hüttenberger, *Gauleiter*, 221–4; and Wolfgang Benz, Hermann Graml and Herman Weiß (eds.), *Enzyklopädie des Nationalsozialismus*, Stuttgart, 1997, 478–9.) Hitler's chieftains in these areas were his vital props in extending and supporting his leadership in the provinces.

95. Jochmann, *Nationalsozialismus und Revolution*, 221. The plebiscite proposal was to fail, on 20 June, to acquire the necessary majority (*RSA*, 296 n.4, 451 n.26).

96. Jochmann, *Nationalsozialismus und Revolution*, 220; Tyrell, 'Feder', 69–70 and 85 n.105; *RSA*, 294 n.1.

97. Orlow, i.68–9; Nyomarkay, 83–4 and n.45.

98. Tyrell, 'Feder', 70.

99. *TBJG*, I.1, 161 (15 February 1926). Goebbels went on (161–2) to refer to a half hour's discussion after a speech of four hours. According to the police report, the speech lasted five hours (*RSA*, I, 294 n.1).

100. *VB* report in *RSA*, I, 294–6. See also HStA, MA 101235/II, Pd. Mü., LB, 8 March 1926, S.16.

101. The 'sic!' is in the original (*TBJG*, I.1, 161).

102. Though a member of the Working Community, Ley – described by Fobke in his report on the Community's first meeting as 'intellectually a nonentity' – had distinguished himself as an 'unconditional supporter of the person of Hitler' (Jochmann, *Nationalsozialismus und Revolution*, 209).

103. *TBJG*, I.1, 161–2. Goebbels was reported to have stated, following the Bamberg Meeting: 'Adolf Hitler betrayed socialism in 1923' (Tyrell, *Führer*, 128). On the Bamberg meeting (if inaccurate in detail) see also Krebs, 187–8.

104. Jochmann, *Nationalsozialismus und Revolution*, 225; Kühnl, 323.

105. Horn, *Marsch*, 243 and n.119; Noakes, *Nazi Party*, 83.

106. Orlow, i.72. He must have had reservations. When Goebbels was in Munich in April, he and Kaufmann were strongly criticized by Hitler for their part in the Working Community and the Gau Ruhr (*TBJG*, I.1, 172 (13 April 1926)).

107. Stachura, *Strasser*, 50.

108. Horn, *Marsch*, 243; Longerich, *Die braunen Bataillone*, 53.

109. See Horn, *Marsch*, 242 n.117; Orlow, i.72; Nyomarkay, 88. Goebbels had to respond publicly to 'Damascus' allegations (*TBJG*, I.1, 204 (25 August 1926)).

110. *TBJG*, I.1, 134–5 (14 October 1925).

111. *TBJG*, I.1, 141 (6 November 1925), 143 (23 November 1925).

112. Nyomarkay, 87.

113. *TBJG*, I.1, 167 (21 March 1926): 'Julius is at least honest,' he wrote. Strasser advised caution (Noakes, *Nazi Party*, 82).

114. *TBJG*, I.1, 169 (29 March 1926).

115. *TBJG*, I.1, 171 (13 April 1926)

116. Tyrell, *Führer*, 129; *TBJG*, I.1, 171–2 (13 April 1926). Goebbels gives no indication in his diary of the content of the speech. From Pfeffer's remarks to Kaufmann, that, having previously thought his and Goebbels's views on socialism went too far, he was almost persuaded to advocate socialism on the basis of the latter's speech, it can be presumed that Goebbels watered down his early views considerably for consumption for his Munich audience.

117. *TBJG*, I.1, 172–3 (13 April 1926).

118. *TBJG*, I.1, 175 (19 April 1926).

119. Horn, *Marsch*, 247. Martin Broszat, 'Die Anfänge der Berliner NSDAP, 1926/27', *VfZ*, 8 (1960), 88ff; Hüttenberger, *Gauleiter*, 39ff.

120. *TBJG*, I.1, 244 (13 July 1928).

121. Hanfstaengl, *15 Jahre*, 190.

122. Tyrell, *Führer*, 103.

123. *RSA*, I, 430; the police report spoke of around 2,500 members present (*RSA*, 430 n.18).

124. *RSA*, I, 431.

125. *RSA*, I, 437.

126. *RSA*, I, 430.

127. *RSA*, I, 461–5; Tyrell, *Führer*, 104, 136–41, 216; Horn, *Marsch*, 278–9; Orlow, i.72–3.

128. *RSA*, I, 461; and see Noakes, *Nazi Party*, 83 n.1.

129. *RSA*, II/1, 6–12 (quotations, 6, 7).

130. *RSA*, II/1, 15 n.1. The violence and thuggery of those attending led to a protest resolution of the Weimar town council and heated debate in the Thuringian Landtag. It also brought much welcome publicity for the NSDAP (*RSA*, II/1, 17 n.3).

131. It was subordinated, until 1934, to the SA. At the time of the Weimar Party Rally of 1926, it was no more than about 200 strong. (See Heinz Höhne, *The Order of the Death's Head*, London, 1969, 17–23.)

132. *RSA*, II/1, 16 and n.5.

133. Orlow, i.76; text of the speech, *RSA*, II/1, 17–25. Dinter had used his influence to obtain the National Theatre for the party congress (Tyrell, *Führer*, 149).

134. *TBJG*, I.1, 191 (6 July 1926).

135. Orlow, i.76. The party had an estimated 35,000 members at this time. Membership in many localities stagnated in 1926–7. (See Orlow, i.111.)

136. Orlow, i.75.

137. See Lüdecke, 250–52.

138. See Tyrell, *Führer*, 196.

139. See Krebs, 126–7 on Hitler's speech in Hamburg in early October 1927.

140. See Krebs, 128.

141. See Hanfstaengl, 183; Krebs, 134–5.

142. The following description draws in the main on Krebs, 126–35.

143. Krebs, 133.

144. Krebs, 132.

145. Krebs, 135.

146. Müller, *Wandel*, 301.

147. Krebs, 128–9.

148. Tyrell, *Führer*, 212, letter of Walter Buch, 1 October 1928. The document is a handwritten draft of a letter which may never have been sent.

149. Hanfstaengl, *15 Jahre*, 183. The 'coffee-house tirades' were, presumably, outbursts which Hanfstaengl frequently experienced during the regular gatherings of Hitler and his cronies in Munich's cafés.

150. Hanfstaengl, *15 Jahre*, 183–4. A similar incident had apparently caused trouble between Hermann Esser and his wife. According to Hanfstaengl, Hitler also found himself for a time *persona non grata* in the house of one of his Berlin benefactors, the later Minister for Post Wilhelm Ohnesorge, on account of pathetic professions to his daughter that though he could not marry he could not live without her. The reliability of the story might be justifiably doubted. Similarly, though Hitler greatly enjoyed the company of Winifred Wagner, the wife of the composer's son, Siegfried, there are no grounds to believe (as was hinted, for instance, by Heiden, *Hitler*, 349) that the relationship was other than platonic.

151. See the writer Hans Carossa's impressions in Deuerlein, *Hitler*, 86.

152. Müller, *Wandel*, 301.

153. Hanfstaengl, *15 Jahre*, 157.

154. Krebs, 126.

155. Lüdecke, 252; Hanfstaengl, *15 Jahre*, 163.

156. Krebs, 129; the Munich police noted in March 1925 that Hitler had bought the black Mercedes as a second car (BHStA, MA 101235/1, PD Mü., Nachrichtenblatt, 2 March 1925, S.17). The car cost a handsome 20,000 Reich Marks – more than Hitler's declared taxable income in the year 1925. He told the tax authorities that he had purchased the car through a bank loan (Hale, 'Adolf Hitler: Taxpayer', 831, 837).

157. See *Monologe*, 282–3, for Hitler's preference for Bavarian short trousers.

158. Heiden, *Hitler*, 184.

159. Hanfstaengl, *15 Jahre*, 185.

160. Müller, *Wandel*, 301.

161. See Krebs, 127–9, 132, 134 for the above.

162. Hanfstaengl, *15 Jahre*, 176.

163. Hitler was in Berchtesgaden from 18 July until the end of the month (*TBJG*, I.1, 194–8 (18 July – 1 August 1926)).

164. *Monologe*, 202–5. The first volume of *Mein Kampf*, originally intended for publication in March – the printers had pressed Hitler to no avail in February to let them have the final manuscript (Sonderarchiv Moscow, 1355–I–2, Fol.223) – was eventually published on 18 July 1925. Hitler's dictation must, therefore, have been of the second volume, work which he completed the following summer, not the first volume, as Toland, 211, thought. This is confirmed in a letter by Rudolf Heß on 11 August 1925 in which he states that Hitler 'is retreating for about 4 weeks to Berchtesgaden to write the second volume of his book' (Sonderarchiv Moscow, 1355–I–2, Fol.101). The second volume was published on 11 December 1926 (Maser, *Mein Kampf*, 272, 274).

165. *Monologe*, 206–7. In his related note, the editor, Werner Jochmann, 439 n.60, dates the renting to 1925, though without source, and in variation from Hitler's own dating in the text. Heiden, *Hitler*, 205 also dates it to 1925. Toland, 229, presumes the same date. Hitler himself seemed in no doubt, however, that the year was 1928. It is unlikely that, on a matter of such significance to him, his good factual memory was playing tricks on him. The businessman concerned was Kommerzienrat Winter from Buxtehude, near Hamburg. He had had Haus Wachenfeld built in 1916 (1917 according to Hitler, *Monologe*, 202) (Josef Weiß, *Obersalzberg. The History of a Mountain*, Berchtesgaden (n.d., 1955), 59, 67). The house was close to the Platterhof – the new name of what was formerly Pension Moritz. Hanfstaengl thought that the purchase was brought about with the financial help of the Bechsteins. But there is no evidence of this (Hanfstaengl, *15 Jahre*, 186).

166. Heiden, *Hitler*, 205: 'Seven Years on the Magic Mountain'. Gauleiter Giesler of Munich allegedly referred to the Obersalzberg as the 'Holy Mountain' (Weiß, 65).

167. For the Berghof, its prehistory, and its symbolism for Hitler's rule, see Ernst Hanisch, *Der Obersalzberg: das Kehlsteinhaus und Adolf Hitler*, Berchtesgaden, 1995.

168. Heiden, *Hitler*, 207–8.

169. *Monologe*, 206; *TBJG*, I.1, 195–7 (23–4 July 1926).

170. *TBJG*, I.1, 194–7 (18–26 July 1926), quotations, 196, 197.

171. This is presumably one of the two meetings Hitler addressed in Berchtesgaden on 9 and 13 October 1926 (*RSA*, II/1, 71). Mimi's mother had died on 11 September. Hitler and Mimi must have met around the end of September or beginning of October.

172. Günter Peis, 'Hitlers unbekannte Geliebte', *Der Stern*, 13 July 1959; see also Maser, *Hitler*, 312–13, 320–21; Ronald Hayman, *Hitler and Geli*, London, 1997, 93–6; Nerin E. Gun, *Eva Braun – Hitler. Leben und Schicksal*, Velbert/Kettwig, 1968, 62–4.

173. Knopp, 135, and see also 143–4. The source of Hitler's letter is not given.

174. *RSA*, I, 297 n.1–2 (text of the speech, 297–330). Hitler was allowed to speak, despite the still prevailing ban, because it was a closed society.

175. Falter *et al.*, *Wahlen*, 70; Edgar Feuchtwanger, *From Weimar to Hitler. Germany, 1918–33*, 2nd edn, London, 1995, 191.

176. *RSA*, I, 318.

177. Above quotations, *RSA*, I, 323.

178. *RSA*, I, 324.

179. *RSA*, I, 325.

180. *RSA*, I, 315.

181. *RSA*, I, 320.

182. *RSA*, I, 330.

183. See, for a few of many examples: *RSA*, I, 362 ('international Jewish stock-exchange and finance capital, supported by Marxist-democratic backers within'); *RSA*, I, 457 (mission to defend the German people against 'the Jewish international bloodsuckers'); *RSA*, I, 476 ('the profit landed in the pockets of the Jews'); *RSA*, II/1, 62 ('the possibility of a German resurrection only in the annihilation of Marxism', which could not be achieved without 'a solution of the race problem'); *RSA*, II/1, 105–6 (Hitler claiming to complete Christ's 'struggle against the Jew as the enemy of mankind'); *RSA*, II/1, 110 (the need for struggle against policies which 'hand over our people to the international stock-exchange and raise Jewish world capitalism to the unrestrained ruler of our Fatherland' and struggle against 'the Jewish plague of our press and newspaper poisoning'); *RSA*, II/1, 119 ('the international world-Jew is master in Germany').

184. E.g. *RSA*, II/2, 567, 742, 848, 858.

185. *RSA*, II/1, 158. See also *RSA*, I, 20.

186. He appears to have used the term '*Lebensraum*' on only one occasion, 30 March 1928 (*RSA*, II/2, 761).

187. *RSA*, I, 240–41.

188. *RSA*, I, 295.

189. *RSA*, II/I, 17–25, esp. 19–21.

190. *MK*, 726–58.

191. *RSA*, II/2, 552.

192. *RSA*, I, 137.

193. *RSA*, I, 25.

194. *RSA*, I, 100.

195. *RSA*, I, 102, II/1, 408.

196. E.g., *RSA*, I, 37, 472.

197. *RSA*, I, 426.

198. *TBJG*, I.1, 172 (13 April 1926), 196 (23 July 1926).

199. That Hitler held to a more or less coherent social revolutionary programme and consciously aimed to modernize German society has been consistently advanced by Rainer Zitelmann in his studies, notably: *Hitler. Selbstverständnis eines Revol-*

utionärs, Hamburg/Leamington Spa/New York, 1987; *Adolf Hitler*, Göttingen/ Zürich, 1989; and 'Die totalitäre Seite der Moderne', in Michael Prinz and Rainer Zitelmann (eds.), *Nationalsozialismus und Modernisierung*, Darmstadt, 1991, 1– 20, here esp. 12f.

200. *RSA*, I, 62.

201. *RSA*, II/2, 674.

202. Weinberg (ed.), *Hitlers Zweites Buch*. His dictation of the book can be dated to the last weeks of June and the first week of July 1928 (*RSA*, IIA, XIX). Gerhard Weinberg's introduction to the new edition of the work (*RSA*, IIA) – now given the descriptively accurate if less pithy designation 'Außenpolitische Standortsbestim- mung nach der Reichstagswahl' (Foreign Policy Position after the Reichstag Election) – authoritatively explains the background, timing, and content of the tract. See also *Hitlers Zweites Buch*, 7, 20; *RSA*, III/1, xi. For an analysis of the content, see Martin Broszat, 'Betrachtungen zu "Hitlers Zweitem Buch"', *Vfz*, 9 (1961), 417– 29.

203. *Hitlers Zweites Buch*, 21–6; *RSA*, IIA, 1–3.

204. *Hitlers Zweites Buch*, 21–2; *RSA*, I, 269–93; *MK*, 684–725 (with minor stylistic alterations).

205. *Hitlers Zweites Buch*, 23; *RSA*, IIA, XVI. The introduction in early 1928 of the Italian language for religious instruction in South Tyrol had prompted the revival of agitation.

206. *Hitlers Zweites Buch*, 36. Sales of *Mein Kampf* totalled only 3,015 in 1928, the worst sales figures since the publication of the first edition (*RSA*, IIA, XXI).

207. *RSA*, IIA, XXI–XXII.

208. *RSA*, IIA, 182–7.

209. *RSA*, IIA, XXIII. In contrast, see Toland's interpretation, which notably exaggerates the significance of the 'Second Book' as the point at which Hitler had 'seen the light' and 'finally come to the realization that his two most urgent convictions – danger from Jews and Germany's need for sufficient living space – were entwined' (Toland, 230–32).

210. Full recognition of this was late in coming, and only followed the publication in 1969 of Jäckel's study, *Hitlers Weltanschauung*. One of Hitler's early biographers, Alan Bullock, subsequently recognized that he had been mistaken, in the first edition of *Hitler. A Study in Tyranny*, in playing down the importance of Hitler's ideas (Ron Rosenbaum, 'Explaining Hitler', 50–70, here 67). Hitler's ideology figures prominently in Bullock's later work, *Hitler and Stalin. Parallel Lives*, London, 1991.

211. Tyrell, *Führer*, 107–8; Deuerlein, *Aufstieg*, 267–8. The ban had first been lifted in the small state of Oldenburg on 22 May 1926.

212. *RSA*, II/I, 165–79; Deuerlein, *Aufstieg*, 268–9.

213. Deuerlein, *Aufstieg*, 269–75.

214. *RSA*, II/1, 179–81.

215. Heiden, *Hitler*, 221.

216. *RSA*, II/1, 221 n.2.

217. *RSA*, II/1, 235, n.2.

218. BHStA, MA 102 137, RPvOB, HMB, 21 March 1927, S.3.

219. BHStA, MA 101 235/II, Pd. Mü., LB, 19 January 1928, S.11.

220. BHStA, MA 101 238/II, Pd. Nbg.-Fürth, LB, 22 November 1927. S.1, 4.

221. Tyrell, *Führer*, 108 (Prussia, 29 September 1928; Anhalt, November 1928).

222. Tyrell, *Führer*, 129–30, 163–4. The salute may, indeed, have been used sporadically (as Rudolf Heß claimed) as early as 1921, though he did not deny the likely influence from Fascist Italy. 'Heil' had long been used in the Schönerer Pan-German Movement and among Austrian as well as German youth groups as a mode of greeting before the turn of the century. (See Hamann, 347, 349; Klaus Vondung, *Magie und Manipulation. Ideologischer Kult und politische Religion des Nationalsozialismus*, Göttingen, 1971, 17; and also Hanfstaengl, *15 Jahre*, 181–2, for the Heil-Hitler greeting and the growing Führer cult in the party.)

223. Tyrell, *Führer*, 163–4.

224. See Theodore Abel, *Why Hitler came into Power*, Cambridge, Mass. (1938), 1986, 73, for Heß's eulogy of great leadership, claiming the need for a dictator, in a prize essay of 1921 written in a competition sponsored by a German-American on the 'cause of the suffering of the German people'.

225. Tyrell, *Führer*, 171.

226. Tyrell, *Führer*, 169.

227. Tyrell, *Führer*, 173.

228. Joseph Goebbels, *Die zweite Revolution. Briefe an Zeitgenossen*, Zwickau, n.d. (1926), 5 (trans., Ernest K. Bramsted, *Goebbels and National Socialist Propaganda 1925–1945*, Michigan, 1965, 199).

229. Abel, 70.

230. Abel, 152–3.

231. Peter Merkl, *Political Violence under the Swastika*, Princeton, 1975, 106.

232. Tyrell, *Führer*, 167; Hüttenberger, *Gauleiter*, 19, for Dincklage.

233. Tyrell, *Führer*, 186–8; and see Russel Lemmons, *Goebbels and Der Angriff*, Lexington, 1994, 23–4.

234. *RSA*, II/1, 309–11 (18 May 1927), and also 320–22 (25 May 1927); Orlow, i.106; Longerich, *Die braunen Bataillone*, 64.

235. See Tyrell, *Führer*, 147–8.

236. See Tyrell, *Führer*, 388 and illustration 5.

237. Tyrell, *Führer*, 145; Orlow, i.96–7 and n.86.

238. Albrecht Tyrell, *III. Reichsparteitag der NSDAP, 19.–21. August 1927*, Film-edition G122 des Instituts für den wissenschaftlichen Film, Ser.4 No.4/G122, Göttingen, 1976, esp. 20–1, 23–5, 42–5. The attendance was lower than had been hoped.

239. Tyrell, *Führer*, 149, 202–3. Dinter's book, *Die Sünden wider die Zeit (Sins against the Epoch)*, had appeared in several hundred thousand copies since its publication in 1917, and was a best-seller in nationalist-racist circles. Dinter published his exchange of letters with Hitler in his journal *Geistchristentum* (Spiritual Christianity).

240. Tyrell, *Führer*, 149, 208–10; Orlow, i.135–6, 143. Hitler had written in firm but conciliatory vein to Dinter in July, inviting him to discussions. Dinter had been summoned by telegram to the Party Leaders' Conference in September, but had failed to turn up.

241. Tyrell, *Führer*, 210–11.

242. Tyrell, *Führer*, 203–5.

243. Tyrell, *Führer*, 225–6.

244. See Tyrell, *Führer*, 170 (Heß to Hewel, 30 March 1927); and Krebs, 127 (Hamburg speech, October 1927).

245. Tyrell, *Führer*, 225. The total of 20,000 speeches given by only 300 or so party speakers during 1928 puts the number of Hitler speeches – though not of course their impact – into perspective (Tyrell, *Führer*, 224). Worries about his health may have been at least in part responsible for the decline in frequency of his speaking engagements. See David Irving, *The Secret Diaries of Hitler's Doctor*, paperback edn, London, 1990, 31–2, for Hitler's later comments about his violent stomach spasms in 1929.

246. Tyrell, *Führer*, 225, and 219–20 for the party's financial problems; see also Orlow, i.109–10.

247. Turner, *German Big Business*, 83–99; Orlow, i.110 n.137.

248. Orlow, i.109.

249. With typical exaggeration, Hitler told Goebbels nine years later that he had been so distressed at the party's financial state that he had thought of shooting himself. Then Kirdorf had come along with his contribution (*TBJG*, I.2, 727 (15 November 1936)). Turner, *German Big Business*, 91 regards the gift as 'improbable', though he refers (cf. 386 nn. 15, 17) only to the post-war memoirs of August Heinrichsbauer and Albert Speer's recollections of Hitler's comments, and not to Goebbels's diary entry. For the intermediacy of Elsa Bruckmann, see Deuerlein, *Aufstieg*, 285–6. Kirdorf asked Hitler to put down his views in a brochure to be distributed privately to industrialists (Adolf Hitler, *Der Weg zum Wiederaufstieg*, Munich, August 1927; reprinted in *RSA*, II/2, 501–9). Kirdorf, formerly a member of the DNVP, resigned his membership of the Nazi party in 1928, within a year of joining, because of the 'socialist' aims of the party, but was an honoured guest at the 1929 Party Rally and rejoined the NSDAP in 1934.

250. According to the party's own issue of membership cards, the number of members was 50,000 in December 1926 – still lower than before the putsch – 70,000 in November 1927, 80,000 on the eve of the 1928 election, and 100,000 by October 1928 (Tyrell, *Führer*, 352). These figures take no account of the considerable numbers leaving the party, nor of blocks of cards issued but not occupied. Real numbers were, therefore, substantially smaller. Local membership figures reveal stagnating membership (Orlow, i.110–11). See Deuerlein, *Aufstieg*, 291, for more exact figures for the distribution of membership cards by end of 1927 (72,590, marking a rise of 23,067 in the year).

251. Tyrell, *Führer*, 196.

252. Tyrell, *Führer*, 222.

253. Orlow, i.58–9. Philipp Bouhler became business manager (*Reichsgeschäfts-führer*) of the party after its refoundation in 1925 and rose rapidly through the ranks of the NSDAP, ultimately becoming Chef der Kanzlei des Führers and head of the 'Euthanasia Programme'. For a pen-portrait, see Wistrich, 29.

254. Stachura, *Strasser*, 62–5, 67ff.; Tyrell, *Führer*, 224.

255. Deuerlein, *Aufstieg*, 287.

256. Peter Stachura, 'Der kritische Wendepunkt? Die NSDAP und die Reichstags-wahlen vom 20. Mai 1928', *VfZ*, 26 (1978), 66–99, here 79–80.

257. Tyrell, *Führer*, 188.

258. Tyrell, *Führer*, 150.

259. See Bradley F. Smith, *Heinrich Himmler 1900–1926. Sein Weg in den deutschen Faschismus*, Munich, 1979; Peter Padfield, *Himmler. Reichsführer-SS*, London, 1990; character sketches of Himmler are provided by Fest, *Face of the Third Reich*, 171–90; and Josef Ackermann, in Smelser-Zitelmann, *Die braune Elite*, 115–33.

260. Tyrell, *Führer*, 224.

261. Deuerlein, *Aufstieg*, 292; Tyrell, *Führer*, 193.

262. Orlow, i.151 speaks of a 'new propaganda strategy, the rural-nationalist plan', to replace the failed 'urban plan'. (See also i.138.) Stachura, 'Wendepunkt?', 93 (discussion of the relevant literature, 66 n.2) also sees a fundamental shift, but as a consequence of the poor election results.

263. *Frankfurter Zeitung*, 26 January 1928, cit. in Philipp W. Fabry, *Mutmaßungen über Hitler. Urteile von Zeitgenossen*, Düsseldorf, 1979, 28.

264. See Deuerlein, *Aufstieg*, 249–50, cit. a *Weltbühne* comment of 17 March 1925, registering the 'death' of the *völkisch* movement.

265. See, for example, BHStA, MA 102 137, RPvOB, HMB, 19 May 1928, S.1: 'In broad circles there is indifference towards the electioneering of the party leaderships'. The Nazi campaign remained largely confined to towns and cities (Geoffrey Pridham, *Hitler's Rise to Power. The Nazi Movement in Bavaria, 1923–1933*, London, 1973, 80.) The turn-out was the lowest (75.6 per cent) of any Weimar Reichstag election (Falter *et al.*, *Wahlen*, 71).

266. See e.g. *RSA*, III/2, 202 for Hitler's criticism in April 1929 of the '20, 30 and more parties' and politicized economic interest groups, a reflection of the division in all areas.

267. Falter *et al.*, *Wahlen*, 44.

268. The Völkisch-Nationaler Block put up its own candidates in 1928 and, to the NSDAP's pleasure, gained only 0.9 per cent (266,430 votes) of the vote and not a single seat (Stachura, 'Wendepunkt?', 91).

269. Stachura, 'Wendepunkt?', 85–7. The party subsequently acknowledged publicly that 'the election results of the rural areas have proved that with a smaller expenditure of energy, money, and time, better results can be achieved than in the big cities' (*VB*, 31 May 1928, cit. in Noakes, *Nazi Party*, 123).

270. Noakes, *Nazi Party*, 121–3).

271. Falter *et al.*, *Wahlen*, 71; and Stachura, 'Wendepunkt?', 85-6, for derisory levels of support for the NSDAP in eastern regions. For the drop in votes for the DNVP, see also Baranowski, *Sanctity*, 127-8.

272. *TBJG*, I.1, 226 (22 May 1928), for Goebbels's appreciation of the importance of his immunity from prosecution. Hanfstaengl, *15 Jahre*, 192, recalled Göring's satisfaction at free first-class travel on the Reichsbahn and other material advantages from becoming a Reichstag deputy. According to Hanfstaengl, Göring had threatened Hitler with an ultimatum: he was to be put on the candidate's list, or he and Hitler would part as opponents. Hitler conceded.

273. Cit. Stachura, 'Wendepunkt?', 81, from *Der Angriff*, 30 May 1928.

274. Orlow, i.132.

275. Deuerlein, *Aufstieg*, 293; and see Stachura, 'Wendepunkt?', 91.

276. Orlow, i.137-8; *RSA*, III/1, 22, 35. For Hitler's passivity and near contemptuous indifference at the proceedings of the conference, condemning them to pointlessness since those attending looked all the time for decisions from Hitler that never came, see Krebs, 131-2 (misdated to October).

277. *RSA*, III/1, 56-62. For Gregor Strasser's organizational plan, see Stachura, 'Wendepunkt?', 94; Orlow, i.139-41.

278. Stachura, 'Wendepunkt?', 95.

279. *RSA*, II/2, 847.

280. *RSA*, III/1, XI; also *RSA*, IIA, XIV, XIX.

281. Tyrell, *Führer*, 289.

282. *RSA*, III/1, 3.

283. Wilhelm Hoegner, *Der schwierige Außenseiter. Erinnerungen eines Abgeordneten, Emigranten und Ministerpräsidenten*, Munich, 1959, 48; Stachura, 'Wendepunkt?', 90.

284. The ban was terminated on 28 September 1928 (*RSA*, III/1, 236 n.2). Hitler had spoken on 13 July to around 5,000 in Berlin, but at a closed party meeting. (*RSA*, III/1, 11-22; *TBJG*, I.1, 245 (14 July 1928)).

285. *RSA*, III/1, 236-40; *TBJG*, I.1, 291 (17 November 1928). Goebbels commented that the hall was closed by the police with 16,000 inside. The *VB*'s estimate (see *RSA*, III, 236 n.2) was 18,000.

286. *RSA*, III/1, 238-9.

287. *RSA*, III/1, 239.

288. See Sefton Delmer, *Trail Sinister*, London, 1961, 101-2.

289. Bernd Weisbrod, *Schwerindustrie in der Weimarer Republik*, Wuppertal, 1978, 415-56.

290. Deuerlein, *Aufstieg*, 297-8; Kolb, *Die Weimarer Republik*, 90. The annual average for 1929, at a little under 2 millions, was around half a million higher than the previous year. There was also a sharp rise in the numbers of workers on short-time (Petzina *et al.*, 119, 122).

291. Joseph P. Schumpeter, *Aufsätze zur Soziologie*, Tübingen, 1953, 225.

292. Deuerlein, *Aufstieg*, 296.

293. See Winkler, *Weimar*, ch.10; Peukert, *Die Weimarer Republik*, ch.7.

294. Ten per cent of the working-age population and 18 per cent of trade unionists were unemployed in 1926 (Petzina *et al.*, 119). For the extensive alienation of working-class youth, see Peter D. Stachura, *The Weimar Republic and the Younger Proletariat*, London, 1989. The particularly severe impact of unemployment on youth is dealt with by Dick Geary, 'Jugend, Arbeitslosigkeit und politischer Radikalismus am Ende der Weimarer Republik', *Gewerkschaftliche Monatshefte*, 4/5 (1983), 304–9.

295. See Larry Eugene Jones, 'The Dying Middle: Weimar Germany and the Fragmentation of Bourgeois Politics', *Central European History*, 5 (1969), 23–54; and his book, *German Liberalism and the Dissolution of the Weimar Party System, 1918–1933*, Chapel Hill, 1988.

296. See Heinrich August Winkler, 'Extremismus der Mitte? Sozialgeschichtliche Aspekte der nationalsozialistischen Machtergreifung', *VfZ*, 20 (1972), 175–91. Harold James, 'Economic Reasons for the Collapse of the Weimar Republic', in Ian Kershaw (ed.), *Weimar. Why did German Democracy Fail?*, London, 1990, 30–57, here 47, points out that in the 1928 election, a quarter of the total vote went to parties with an individual share of under 5 per cent.

297. James, 'Economic Reasons', 32–45. The underlying structural economic weaknesses of the Weimar Republic were most emphatically outlined by Knut Borchardt in his *Wachstum, Krisen, Handlungsspielräume der Wirtschaftspolitik*, Göttingen, 1982.

298. Deuerlein, *Aufstieg*, 297.

299. *RSA*, III, 245–53.

300. See Baldur von Schirach, 17–25, 58–61, 68; Fest, *The Face of the Third Reich*, 332–54; and Michael Wortmann's pen-portrait in Smelser-Zitelmann, *Die braune Elite*, 246–57. Figures for the Nazi successes in student union elections are given in Tyrell, *Führer*, 380–81.

301. Deuerlein, *Aufstieg*, 299–301; Hitler's own accounts, in articles published in the *VB*, are printed in *RSA*, III/2, 105–14. Orlow, i.154, referred to them as among 'the few humanly moving articles [Hitler] ever wrote'. The vivid, and rich, descriptive style is not, however, typically Hitlerian and suggests considerable editorial embellishment of the text. For 'Wöhrden's Night of Blood' (*Blutnacht von Wöhrden*), see also Gerhard Stoltenberg, *Politische Strömungen im schleswig-holsteinischen Landvolk 1918–1933*, Düsseldorf, 1962, 147; and Rudolf Heberle, *Landbevölkerung und Nationalsozialismus. Eine soziologische Untersuchung der politischen Willensbildung in Schleswig-Holstein 1918 bis 1932*, Stuttgart, 1963, 160.

302. For use of the term 'crisis before the crisis', see Dietmar Petzina, 'Was there a Crisis before the Crisis? The State of the German Economy in the 1920s', in Jürgen Baron von Kruedener (ed.), *Economic Crisis and Political Collapse. The Weimar Republic 1924–1933*, New York/Oxford/Munich, 1990, 1–19.

303. *RSA*, III/2, 202–13, 233–6, 238–9, 260–62.

304. *RSA*, III/2, 210.

305. *RSA*, III/2, 238.

306. Orlow, i.161–2; Stachura, *Strasser*, 69. Some support for the suggestion that Himmler was responsible for the tactic of 'speaker concentration' is offered by two letters from Gauleiter Kube to Himmler from 23 June and 4 November 1928 in BDC, Parteikanzlei, Correspondence, Heinrich Himmler.

307. See Ellsworth Faris, 'Takeoff Point for the National Socialist Party: The Landtag Election in Baden, 1929', *Central European History*, 8 (1975), 140–71, here 168. The penetration of social networks by the Nazis is emphasized by Rudy Koshar, *Social Life, Local Politics, and Nazism: Marburg, 1880–1935*, Chapel Hill, 1986; and, for Catholic districts in the Black Forest, by Oded Heilbronner, 'The Failure that Succeeded: Nazi Party Activity in a Catholic Region in Germany, 1929–32', *Journal of Contemporary History*, 27 (1992), 531–49; and 'Der verlassene Stammtisch. Vom Verfall der bürgerlichen Infrastruktur und dem Aufstieg der NSDAP am Beispiel der Region Schwarzwald', *Geschichte und Gesellschaft*, 19 (1993), 178–201.

308. Orlow, i.162.

309. See Faris, 168.

310. Falter *et al.*, *Wahlen*, 108.

311. Falter *et al.*, *Wahlen*, 98; Deuerlein, *Aufstieg*, 302.

312. *RSA*, III/2, 275–7, 277 n.3; Pridham, 85–6.

313. Falter *et al.*, *Wahlen*, 90; Faris, 144–6.

314. *RSA*, III/2, 291 n.10.

315. Winkler, *Weimar*, 346ff.

316. *RSA*, III/2, 290 n.1; Winkler, *Weimar*, 354. Hitler took the decision to join without consulting other leading figures in the party (Orlow, i.173).

317. *RSA*, III/2, 292 n.1.

318. Orlow, i.173. Goebbels claimed to be on the scent of a plot by Otto Strasser and his supporters against Hitler in early August 1929. Though this was a reflection of Goebbels's paranoia, Hitler's dealings with the 'reaction' had indeed sharpened the growing antagonism of the 'national revolutionary' grouping around Otto Strasser (*TBJG*, I.1, 405 (3 August 1929); *Tb* Reuth, i.393–4, note 54).

319. Winkler, *Weimar*, 354–6. Nine out of thirty-five electoral districts returned over a fifth of votes in favour of the plebiscite proposal.

320. The *VB*'s circulation was still only 18,400 (for a membership of around 150,000) (Tyrell, *Führer*, 223).

321. Albrecht Tyrell, *IV. Reichsparteitag der NSDAP, Nürnberg 1929*, Filmedition G140 des Instituts für den wissenschaftlichen Film, Ser.4, Nr.5/G140, Göttingen, 1978, 6–7; Orlow, i.173; *RSA*, III/2, 313–55, 357–61.

322. Otto Wagener, *Hitler aus nächster Nähe. Aufzeichnungen eines Vertrauten 1929–1932*, ed. Henry A. Turner, 2nd edn, Kiel, 1987, 16–17 (and 7–21 for a description of the Rally and the deep impression it made on Wagener). See also the description in *TBJG*, I.i, 403–6 (1–6 August 1929).

323. Tyrell, *Reichsparteitag 1929*, 6, 14.

324. Orlow, i.167, 169.

CHAPTER 9: BREAKTHROUGH

1. Abel, 126–7.
2. Abel, 126.
3. For the social structure of the party membership, see, among an extensive literature, Kater, *Nazi Party*, and Detlef Mühlberger, *Hitler's Followers. Studies in the Sociology of the Nazi Movement*, London, 1991 (containing, in ch.1, a detailed survey of the historiography).
4. Abel, 119.
5. See Juan J. Linz, 'Political Space and Fascism as a Late-Comer: Conditions Conducive to the Success or Failure of Fascism as a Mass Movement in Inter-War Europe', in Stein Ugelvik Larsen, Bernt Hagtvet and Jan Petter Myklebust (eds.), *Who Were the Fascists?*, Bergen/Oslo/Tromsø, 1980, 153–89.
6. Orlow, i.175 and n.166.
7. See, amid a vast literature, Harold James, *The German Slump. Politics and Economics, 1924–1936*, Oxford, 1986; and Dieter Petzina, 'Germany and the Great Depression', *Journal of Contemporary History*, 4 (1969), 59–74; Petzina *et al.*, 84, provide the bare statistical indices of the economic crisis and social misery. See also Peukert, *Die Weimarer Republik*, 245–6. Wilhelm Treue (ed.), *Deutschland in der Weltwirtschaftskrise in Augenzeugenberichten*, 2nd edn, Düsseldorf, 1967, esp. 245–53, provides some contemporary reflections of the social distress.
8. Deuerlein, *Aufstieg*, 305–6.
9. *RSA*, III/3, 63.
10. Tyrell, *Führer*, 383; Falter *et al.*, *Wahlen*, 90, 97, 107, 111; Martin Broszat, *Die Machtergreifung. Der Aufstieg der NSDAP und die Zerstörung der Weimarer Republik*, Munich, 1984, 103.
11. *RSA*, III/3, 59–60; Fritz Dickmann, 'Die Regierungsbildung in Thüringen als Modell der Machtergreifung', *VfZ*, 14 (1966), 454–64, here 461.
12. See Dickmann, 460–64.
13. *RSA*, III/3, 60.
14. *RSA*, III/3, 61–2. Günther was appointed to the Chair of Social Anthropology at Jena in 1930.
15. Broszat, *Die Machtergreifung*, 108. See Donald R. Tracy, 'The Development of the National Socialist Party in Thuringia 1924–30', *Central European History*, 8 (1975), 23–50, esp. 42–4, for Frick's period of office.
16. Tyrell, *Führer*, 352; *RSA*, III/3, 62 n.22. It has been estimated that real membership was probably some 10–15 per cent below the level given by the party. See ch.8, n. 250.
17. For the following account, see William Sheridan Allen, *The Nazi Seizure of Power*, revised edn, New York, 1984, here esp. 28–34.
18. Allen, 32.
19. Allen, 33.

20. Allen, 84. See Donald L. Niewyk, *The Jews in Weimar Germany*, Louisiana/ Manchester, 1980, ch.3, esp. 79–91, and Sarah Gordon, *Hitler, Germans, and the 'Jewish Question'*, Princeton, 1984, ch.2, esp. 88–90, for studies supporting this assertion.

21. Tyrell, *Führer*, 308.

22. See Allen, 32–3, and the works by Koshar and Heilbronner indicated in ch.8 n.307.

23. Rudolf Heberle, *From Democracy to Nazism. A Regional Case Study on Political Parties in Germany*, Baton Rouge, 1945, 109–11.

24. See Bessel, 'The Rise of the NSDAP', 20–29, esp. 26–7.

25. *RSA*, III/3, 63.

26. Tyrell, *Führer*, 327.

27. Wagener, 126–7.

28. Tyrell, 310, 327–8 (Hierl Denkschrift, 22 October 1929).

29. See Wagener, 127, reported comments of Gregor Strasser.

30. Winkler, *Weimar*, 366–71.

31. Broszat, *Die Machtergreifung*, 109–10; Winkler, *Weimar*, 367, 371.

32. Winkler, *Weimar*, 368–71.

33. Winkler, *Weimar*, 363.

34. *Quellen zur Geschichte des Parlamentarismus und der politischen Parteien*, ed. Karl Dietrich Bracher *et al.*, Bd.4/1, *Politik und Wirtschaft in der Krise 1930–1932. Quellen zur Ära Brüning*, Teil I, Bonn, 1980, 15–18, Doc. 7, here 15 (Aufzeichnung von Graf Westarp über eine Unterredung mit Reichspräsident v. Hindenburg, 15 January 1930); Broszat, *Die Machtergreifung*, 110–11.

35. Kolb, *Die Weimarer Republik*, 127–8; Winkler, *Weimar*, 378–81; Broszat, *Die Machtergreifung*, 111.

36. See Mommsen, *Die verspielte Freiheit*, 320.

37. Tyrell, *Führer*, 383. The election was held on 22 June 1930. The Nazis won fourteen of the ninety-six seats in the Saxon Landtag.

38. *TBJG*, I.1, 577–82 (18–29 July 1930).

39. Nyomarkay, 98 n.67; Tyrell, *Führer*, 312. With Gregor Strasser so heavily committed as Organization Leader of the NSDAP, Otto had become the effective head of the publishing house.

40. Tyrell, *Führer*, 312–13; Nyomarkay, 96–8.

41. *TBJG*, I.1, 492–3 (30–31 January 1930), 496–503 (6–22 February 1930). See also Lemmons, 44–7; Reuth, 163–5.

42. *TBJG*, I.1, 492 (31 January 1930).

43. See Reuth, 164–5 and *Tb* Reuth, ii.451 n.14 for the suggestion that this was possibly because of the prospect of spring elections, given the crisis of the government.

44. *TBJG*, I.1, 507 (2 March 1930). On the death of Wessel, see Thomas Oertel, *Horst Wessel. Untersuchung einer Legende*, Cologne, 1988, esp. 83–105. For Goebbels's irritation at Hitler's refusal to attend Horst Wessel's funeral, on 1 March, see *TBJG*, I.1, 507 (1–2 March 1930); see also Reuth, 161. Hitler was dissuaded by Göring, despite Goebbels's pleas, from attending the funeral because of the tension and threat of

violence (Hanfstaengl, *15 Jahre*, 204). Despite heavy police cordons, there were indeed disturbances between Communists and Nazis leading to a number of serious injuries (Oertel, 101–3; *TBJG*, I.1, 507–8 (1–2 March 1930)). The 'Horst-Wessel-Lied' became, under Goebbels's influence (though he privately thought little of its musical qualities) the party's own anthem and, especially after 1933, was frequently sung on major representative occasions after 'Deutschland, Deutschland über alles', the national anthem. Horst Wessel had provided only the text of the tune associated with him; the melody derived from an old army song (Oertel, 106–13).

45. *TBJG*, I.1, 507 (2 March 1930), 515 (16 March 1930).
46. *TBJG*, I.1, 515 (16 March 1930).
47. *TBJG*, I.1, 524 (5 April 1930).
48. *TBJG*, I.1, 528 (13 April 1930).
49. *TBJG*, I.1, 538 (28 April 1930); *RSA*, III/3, 168–9; Tyrell, *Führer*, 331–2.
50. *TBJG*, I.1, 538 (28 April 1930).
51. Strasser, *Hitler und ich*, 101.
52. Strasser, *Hitler und ich*, 105–6. The discussions are summarized by Patrick Moreau, *Nationalsozialismus von links*, Stuttgart, 1984, 30–35.
53. Strasser, *Hitler und ich*, 106.
54. Strasser, *Hitler und ich*, 104–7. An earlier version, which can be taken as authentic, since it was based on notes made at the time and was not disclaimed by the Nazis, was published by Strasser, in the form of a polemical pamphlet, immediately following the meeting: Otto Strasser, *Ministersessel oder Revolution?*, Berlin, 1930. See Moreau, 205, n.48. The pamphlet contained Otto Strasser's version of his dialogue with Hitler in May, which later served as the basis of his book *Hitler und ich*. Hitler's comments on socialism were similar to those he had made at the meeting of party leaders in Munich on 27 April (*RSA*, III/3, 168 n.4). At his meeting with Otto Strasser, there were also serious disagreements about foreign policy, on which Hitler upheld the notion of an alliance with Britain (Otto Strasser, *Hitler und ich*, 108–9; Nyomarkay, 99). See Gregor Strasser's comments – critical of his brother and of his 'one-sided' account of the meeting – in his letter to the Sudeten leader Rudolf Jung of 22 July 1930 (Tyrell, *Führer*, 332–3).
55. Strasser, *Hitler und ich*, 104. The diffuseness of the party's programme meant that total subordination to the Leader was the only device to prevent fragmentation. As Baldur von Schirach pointed out, with reference to this period, 'practically every leading National Socialist had his own National Socialism' (B. v. Schirach, 87).
56. Strasser, *Hitler und ich*, 107.
57. Strasser, *Hitler und ich*, 112–14.
58. *TBJG*, I.1, 550 (22 May 1930).
59. Tyrell, *Führer*, 333.
60. *TBJG*, I.1, 561 (14 June 1930).
61. *TBJG*, I.1, 568 (30 June 1930); Otto Strasser's published account was in his pamphlet, *Ministersessel oder Revolution?*
62. *TBJG*, I.1, 564 (23 June 1930).

63. *TBJG*, I.1, 565–6 (26 June 1930).

64. *TBJG*, I.1, 567 (29 June 1930). Goebbels wanted Hitler to attend a meeting of the membership of Gau Berlin at which he planned a showdown with his enemies. (See Reuth, 167–8; *Tb* Reuth, ii.493 n.54.)

65. *RSA*, III/3, 250 n.15.

66. *TBJG*, I.1, 568 (30 June 1930).

67. *RSA*, III/3, 249–50; *TBJG*, I.1, 568 (1 July 1930); *Tb* Reuth, ii.493 n.54.

68. *RSA*, III/3, 264 n.4; Moreau, 41, and 35–40 for the build-up to the expulsion.

69. *TBJG*, I.1, 569 (1 July 1930).

70. *TBJG*, I.1, 570 (3 July 1930).

71. *TBJG*, I.1, 572 (6 July 1930).

72. *TBJG*, I.1, 576 (16 July 1930), with reference to the suggestion – which in the event did not materialize into anything – that Gregor Strasser should become Minister for the Interior and for Labour in Saxony.

73. *TBJG*, I.1, 582 (29 July 1930). The former Barlow-Palais in Briennerstraße had been bought by the NSDAP on 26 May 1930 – the earlier headquarters in Schellingstraße had become far too cramped, given the party's expansion – and was soon known as the 'Brown House'. A special levy of at least 2 Marks per head for party members (though not SA and SS members) was imposed to help fund the purchase. (See *RSA*, III/3, 207–9, and 209 n.17.)

74. *TBJG*, I.1, 581 (28 July 1930).

75. *RSA*, III/3, 249 n.4.

76. Orlow, i.210–11; Tyrell, *Führer*, 312; Nyomarkay, 102.

77. *RSA*, III/3, 264; *TBJG*, I.1, 566 (26 June 1930).

78. Tyrell, *Führer*, 332–3. See *TBJG*, I.1, 571 (5 July 1930): '*Gregor ist voll Sauwut auf seinen Bruder*' ('Gregor is in a steaming rage at his brother').

79. See Benz/Graml, *Biographisches Lexikon*, 333, for a brief summary of Otto Strasser's subsequent political career.

80. Thomas Childers, *The Nazi Voter. The Social Foundations of Fascism in Germany, 1919–1933*, Chapel Hill/London, 1983, 138–9, 317 n.72, cit. *VB*, 20–21 July 1930; Orlow, i.183.

81. A brown uniform, based on the khaki shirts and trousers of the German colonial troops in East Africa before the war, had been worn by stormtroopers as early as 1921. It was officially adopted by the party in 1926, after which the term 'Brownshirts' was used to depict the NSDAP, especially by the opponents of the Nazis (Benz, Graml, and Weiß, *Enzyklopädie des Nationalsozialismus*, 403).

82. Wilfried Boehnke, *Die NSDAP im Ruhrgebiet, 1920–1933*, Bad Godesberg, 1974, 147, cit. *Dortmunder General-Anzeiger*, 5 May 1930.

83. Rainer Hambrecht, *Der Aufstieg der NSDAP in Mittel und Oberfranken (1925–1933)*, Nuremberg, 1976, 201.

84. Hambrecht, 186–7.

85. Childers, *Nazi Voter*, 139; *RSA*, III/3, 114 n.9, 322; Gerhard Paul, *Aufstand der Bilder. Die NS-Propaganda vor 1933*, Bonn, 1990, 125.

86. Orlow, i.183; *RSA*, III/3, VIII–X. The following analysis of the speeches is based on the texts of the twenty speeches held from 3 August to 13 September 1930 in *RSA*, III/3, 295–418.

87. *RSA* III/3, 408 n.2. According to the police report, which gave the estimated attendance, Hitler made a tired impression at first, and his audience showed signs of being bored, at least by the first part of his speech. Goebbels's record was quite different. 'For the first time in Berlin really big,' he wrote (*TBJG*, I.1, 601 (11 September 1930)). Hitler had to cancel a further speech the same evening through exhaustion.

88. *RSA*, III/3, 413 n.1.

89. See Thomas Childers, 'The Middle Classes and National Socialism', in David Blackbourn and Richard Evans (eds.), *The German Bourgeoisie*, London/New York, 1993, 328–40; and Thomas Childers, 'The Social Language of Politics in Germany. The Sociology of Political Discourse in the Weimar Republic', *American Historical Review*, 95 (1990), 331–58.

90. *RSA*, III/3, 368, for example. See also 391.

91. *RSA*, III/3, 317.

92. *RSA*, III/3, 411.

93. *RSA*, III/3, 355, for example. See also 337, where Hitler indicated that the only way out was through the re-establishment of foreign-political power.

94. *RSA*, III/3, 410.

95. Deuerlein, *Aufstieg*, 314. Carl von Ossietzky suffered imprisonment for his attacks on the Reichswehr even during the later years of the Weimar Republic. He was arrested by the Nazis at the end of February 1933 and spent over three and a half years in concentration camps. Following an international campaign, he was awarded at the end of 1936, while still in the hands of the Gestapo, the Nobel Peace Prize for 1935. He died in May 1938 of tuberculosis brought on by the conditions he endured in the concentration camps. (See Benz/Graml, *Biographisches Lexikon*, 244; Elke Suhr, *Carl von Ossietzky. Eine Biografie*, Cologne, 1988.)

96. See, for example, Martin Broszat, 'Zur Struktur der NS-Massenbewegung', *VfZ*, 31 (1983), 52–76, esp. 66–7; Michael H. Kater, 'Generationskonflikt als Entwicklungsfaktor in der NS-Bewegung vor 1933', *Geschichte und Gesellschaft*, 11 (1985), 217–43; Jürgen Reulecke, ' "Hat die Jugendbewegung den Nationalsozialismus vorbereitet?" Zum Umgang mit einer falschen Frage', in Wolfgang R. Krabbe (ed.), *Politische Jugend in der Weimarer Republik*, Bochum, 1993, 222–43; Ulrich Herbert, ' "Generation der Sachlichkeit". Die völkische Studentenbewegung der frühen zwanziger Jahre in Deutschland', in Frank Bajohr, Werner Johe and Uwe Lohalm (eds.), *Zivilisation und Barbarei*, Hamburg, 1991, 115–44.

97. See Karl Epting, *Generation der Mitte*, Bonn, 1953, 169. For the emphasis on the 'national community' (*Volksgemeinschaft*) in Nazi ideology, see Bernd Stöver, *Volksgemeinschaft im Dritten Reich*, Düsseldorf, 1993, ch.2.

98. Merkl, 12.

99. Merkl, 32–3, 453, 522–3.

100. The lack of ideological reflection among 'old fighters' of the NSDAP and among SA men is emphasized by Christoph Schmidt, 'Zu den Motiven "alter Kämpfer" in der NSDAP', in Detlev Peukert and Jürgen Reulecke (eds.), *Die Reihen fast geschlossen*, Wuppertal, 1981, 21–43, here 32–4; and Conan Fischer, *Stormtroopers. A Social, Economic, and Ideological Analysis 1925–35*, London, 1983, ch.6.

101. See Noakes, *Nazi Party*, 162–82; Orlow, i.193; Tyrell, *Führer*, 310.

102. Zdenek Zofka, *Die Ausbreitung des Nationalsozialismus auf dem Lande*, Munich, 1979, 89–90, 96, 105–16, 154, 341–50; Baranowski, *Sanctity*, 150ff. An over-emphasis on economic rationality as the determinant of Nazi support, as in William Brustein, *The Logic of Evil. The Social Origins of the Nazi Party 1925–1933*, New Haven/London, 1996, nevertheless produces a distorted perspective.

103. Falter *et al.*, *Wahlen*, 41, 44.

104. Falter *et al.*, *Wahlen*, 108.

105. *TBJG*, I.1, 522 (1 April 1930)

106. *TBJG*, I.1, 600 (9 September 1930)

107. *Monologe*, 170. In a speech on 20 August, he had mentioned the figure of 50 and 100 seats, but only to emphasize that no one could know how the election would turn out, and that the important thing was the continuation of the struggle as soon as it was over (*RSA*, III/3, 359). According to Hanfstaengl, Hitler was privately expecting between thirty and forty seats (Hanfstaengl, *15 Jahre*, 207).

108. *TBJG*, I.1, 603 (15–16 September 1930).

109. *TBJG*, I.1, 603 (16 September 1930); *Monologe*, 170.

110. Falter *et al.*, *Wahlen*, 44; Broszat, *Machtergreifung*, 112–13.

111. Jürgen W. Falter, *Hitlers Wähler*, Munich, 1991, 111, 365, and see the detailed analysis of Nazi voter support in ch.5.

112. Falter *et al.*, *Wahlen*, 44; Falter, *Hitlers Wähler*, 81–101, 365. See also Jürgen W. Falter, 'The National Socialist Mobilisation of New Voters', in Childers, *Formation*, 202–31.

113. Falter *et al.*, *Wahlen*, 71–2.

114. Falter, *Hitlers Wähler*, 287.

115. Falter, *Hitlers Wähler*, 143–6.

116. Winkler, *Weimar*, 389; Jürgen W. Falter, 'Unemployment and the Radicalisation of the German Electorate 1928–1933: An Aggregate Data Analysis with Special Emphasis on the Rise of National Socialism', in Peter D. Stachura (ed.), *Unemployment and the Great Depression in Weimar Germany*, London, 1986, 187–208.

117. Falter, *Hitlers Wähler* 287–9; Childers, *Nazi Voter*, esp. 268, where he describes the NSDAP as 'a unique phenomenon in German electoral politics, a catchall party of protest'.

118. See, esp., the studies of Mühlberger and Kater mentioned in n.3 to this chapter.

119. Mühlberger, 206–7.

120. Broszat, 'Struktur', 61.

121. Hambrecht, 307–8.

122. See the studies of Koshar, Heilbronner, and Zofka referred to in ch.8 n.307, and above n.102.

123. Deuerlein, *Aufstieg*, 318.

124. Scholdt, 488.

125. Weigand von Miltenberg (= Herbert Blank), *Adolf Hitler–Wilhelm III*, Berlin, 1931, 7; Fabry, 30; Schreiber, *Hitler. Interpretationen*, 44 n.64.

126. Miltenberg (= Blank), 7.

127. See Deuerlein, *Aufstieg*, 323; Heinrich August Winkler, *Der Weg in die Katastrophe. Arbeiter und Arbeiterbewegung in der Weimarer Republik 1930 bis 1933*, Berlin/Bonn, 1987, ch.2, pt.3, 207ff; Gerhard Schulz, *Von Brüning zu Hitler. Der Wandel des politischen Systems in Deutschland 1930–1933*, Berlin/New York, 1992, 202–7.

128. Cit. Winkler, *Der Weg in die Katastrophe*, 209.

129. Scholdt, 480–81.

130. Scholdt, 494.

131. Winkler, *Weimar*, 391: *TBJG*, I.1, 620 (19 October 1930).

132. Deuerlein, *Aufstieg*, 325; and see Fabry, 39–40.

133. *RSA*, III/3, 452/68, and 454 n.1; *RSA*, IV/1, 3–9.

134. *RSA*, III/3, 452 n.4; Deuerlein, *Aufstieg*, 322–3. The article appeared in the *Daily Mail* on 24 September 1930 and in German the following day in the *VB*.

135. *RSA*, III/3, 452 n.2, cit. *Daily Mail*, 27 September 1930.

136. E.g., *RSA*, III/3, 177 (2 May 1930), 320 (10 August 1930), 338 (15 August 1930), 359 (20 August 1930).

137. Reconstruction of his speech in *RSA*, III/3, 434–51; Peter Bucher, *Der Reichswehrprozeß. Der Hochverrat der Ulmer Reichswehroffiziere 1929–30*, Boppard am Rhein, 1967, 237–80; and see Deuerlein, *Aufstieg*, 328–36; Frank, 83–6. For personal details of those indicted, see *RSA*, III/3, 450 n.86.

138. *RSA*, III/3, 439.

139. *RSA*, III/3, 441.

140. *RSA*, III/3, 441.

141. *RSA*, III/3, 442.

142. *RSA*, III/3, 445. Hitler made plain that, for him, the state was merely a means to an end (Bucher, 275).

143. Bucher, 296–8.

144. Richard Scheringer, *Das große Los. Unter Soldaten, Bauern und Rebellen*, Hamburg, 1959, 236. Scheringer later became a Communist supporter.

145. *TBJG*, I.1, 608 (26 September 1930).

146. Hanfstaengl, *15 Jahre*, 213–16. In fact, during the Depression even luxury suites at the Kaiserhof dropped sharply in price. A surviving bill shows the cost of Hitler and his entourage for a stay of three days in 1931, including meals and service, at a modest 650.86 Reich Marks (Turner, *German Big Business*, 155).

147. Frank, 86.

148. Goebbels thought the Leipzig trial had won 'enormous sympathy' for the Nazis (*TBJG*, I.1, 609 (27 September 1930)). See also Reuth, 176.

149. Deuerlein, *Aufstieg*, 340–42; Heinrich Brüning, *Memoiren 1918–1934*, dtv edn, 2 vols., Munich, 1972, i.200ff.; Winkler, *Weimar*, 394.

150. Above from Brüning, i.203–7 (quotation, 207); see also Krebs, 140: Deuerlein, *Aufstieg*, 342; Winkler, *Weimar*, 393.

151. Brüning, i.207.

152. Krebs, 141.

153. *TBJG*, I.1, 614 (6 October 1930): '*Es bleibt bei unserer Opposition. Gottlob*' ('Our opposition remains, thank God').

154. *RSA*, III/3, 430.

155. Friedrich Franz von Unruh, *Der National-Sozialismus*, Frankfurt am Main, 1931, 17. See also Broszat, *Der Nationalsozialismus*, 43–4.

156. Bessel, 'Myth', 27.

157. Broszat, 'Struktur', 69–70.

158. On the high membership fluctuation within the NSDAP, see Hans Mommsen, 'National Socialism: Continuity and Change', in Walter Laqueur (ed.), *Fascism: A Reader's Guide*, Harmondsworth, 1979, 151–92, here 163; and Hans Mommsen, 'Die NSDAP als faschistische Partei', in Richard Saage (ed.), *Das Scheitern diktatorischer Legitimationsmuster und die Zukunftsfähigkeit der Demokratie*, Berlin, 1995, 257–71, here 265.

159. Deuerlein, *Aufstieg*, 319, cit. *Frankfurter Zeitung*, 15 September 1930.

160. Hanfstaengl, *15 Jahre*, 218.

161. Wagener, 24.

162. Wagener, 59, 73, 83–4.

163. Wagener, 128.

164. Tyrell, *Führer*, 348.

165. Wagener, 128. See former Leutnant Scheringer's recollection of a meeting with Hitler in 1930: 'Listening to him, I had the firm impression that the man believes what he says, as simple as the slogans are. He is suspended in his thinking three metres above the ground. He doesn't speak; he preaches ... He is incapable of a clear political analysis however powerful his talent as an agitator might be' (Scheringer, 242).

166. Wagener, 59.

167. Wagener, 84.

168. Wagener, 96.

169. Wagener, 98. According to Wagener, there were ten rooms, on two floors. Hanfstaengl, *15 Jahre*, 231, speaks of a 'nine-room apartment'. Schroeder, 153, like Wagener, spoke of a double-apartment. Lüdecke, 454, describes the 'luxurious, modern flat' as comprising 'eight or nine beautiful large rooms covering the entire second floor'.

170. Wagener, 98.

171. Hanfstaengl, *15 Jahre*, 223; *TBJG*, I.1, 578 (20 July 1930); Hoffmann, 49–50.

172. Hanfstaengl, *15 Jahre*, 182; Hoffmann, 70.

173. Wagener, 127.

174. Hitler's self-perceived infallibility left a striking impression on Albert Krebs in a speech Hitler made to party leaders in Munich (Krebs, 138–40). According to Krebs, the speech was made at the end of June 1930. This must be a mistake. Hitler held no speech in Munich in June 1930. Moreover, Krebs refers to a visit, before the speech, to the newly completed 'Brown House'. The contract for the purchase of what would become the party headquarters was signed on 26 May 1930. But major rebuilding to the former 'Barlow-Palais' took place before it was occupied by a number of central party offices on 1 January 1931 (*RSA*, III/3, 209 n.17; IV/1, 206–18).

175. Wagener, 127–8.

176. Wagener, 119–20.

177. Wagener, 128.

178. Frank, 93.

179. Frank, 91–2. Wagener, 107, refers to the ban on smoking in Hitler's room. From the date indicated, early summer 1930, this presumably refers to the party headquarters in Schellingstraße, before the move to the Brown House took place.

180. Hanfstaengl, *15 Jahre*, 223.

181. Frank, 93–4.

182. Wagener, 72.

183. See Wagener, 111–12 (Wagener's economic proposals).

184. See Tyrell, *Führer*, 311 for the suggestion that Hitler's self-belief was even now less pronounced than the image he presented to others – a possibility, but an unprovable assertion.

185. See the repeated references in Wagener, e.g., 43, 48, 56, 96–7, 111–12.

186. Wagener reported that Hitler stopped eating meat only after Geli Raubal's death (Wagener, 362). This contrasts with Hanfstaengl's less dramatic explanation, that Hitler gradually began to cut out meat (and alcohol) after putting on weight in Landsberg, until it turned into a dogma (Hanfstaengl, *15 Jahre*, 164). The health reasons adduced by Krebs would accord better with such an explanation, though it is possible that the trauma following his niece's death led to Hitler's final turn to complete vegetarianism.

187. Krebs, 136–7.

188. Wagener, 72; and see 127 for similar comments by Wagener and Gregor Strasser.

189. Wagener, 301.

190. Deuerlein, *Aufstieg*, 346; Longerich, *Die braunen Bataillone*, 108–9.

191. See OSAF-Stellvertreter Süd Schneidhuber's remarks in Longerich, *Die braunen Bataillone*, 106.

192. Longerich, *Die braunen Bataillone*, 102–4.

193. *TBJG*, I.1, 596–7 (1 September 1930).

194. Longerich, *Die braunen Bataillone*, 104; *RSA*, III/3, 377–81.

195. Tyrell, *Führer*, 338; Longerich, *Die braunen Bataillone*, 106.

196. Tyrell, *Führer*, 314; Wagener, 60–62. Hitler's personal aversion to smoking had, of course, no bearing on his party's readiness to benefit from its contact with cigarette firms.

197. Longerich, *Die braunen Bataillone*, 107.

198. *RSA*, IV/1, 183; Longerich, *Die braunen Bataillone*, 108–10.

199. Longerich, *Die braunen Bataillone*, 110–11.

200. *RSA*, IV/1, 200.

201. *RSA*, IV/1, 229–30. What the legal route to power would mean had again been explicitly stated, this time by Goebbels, in a speech to the Reichstag on 5 February: 'According to the constitution we are only bound to the legality of the way, not the legality of the goal. We want to take power legally. But what we once do with this power when we have it, that's our business' (Deuerlein, *Aufstieg*, 347). The 'Third Reich', which Hitler mentioned, today synonymous with the period of Nazi rule, derived originally from the apocalyptic notions of the twelfth-century mystic Joachim of Fiore, who had seen three ages – of the Father, the Son, and coming age of the Holy Spirit. The term had been made popular in more recent times by the book of that title published in 1923 by the neo-conservative Arthur Moeller van den Bruck, advocating a new state – the third great Reich to succeed those of the Holy Roman Empire and of Bismarck – to replace the detested Weimar democracy. Hitler famously declared in 1933 that 'the Third Reich' would last for 1,000 years. But already in 1939 the press was instructed to avoid usage of the term (Benz, Graml and Weiß, *Enzyklopädie des Nationalsozialismus*, 435).

202. In practice, Communists accounted for close on two-thirds of the arrests made under the decree (Winkler, *Weimar*, 401). For Hitler's response to the decree, see *RSA*, IV/1, 236–8. A uniform ban on the SA had already been attempted the previous year (Longerich, *Die braunen Bataillone*, 100).

203. *TBJG*, I.2, 41 (30 March 1931).

204. *RSA*, IV/1, 236–8.

205. *TBJG*, I.2, 42 (31 March 1931).

206. *TBJG*, I.2, 42–3 (2 April 1931); *Tb* Reuth, ii.575 n.25, cit. *Deutsche Allgemeine Zeitung*, 2 April 1931; *RSA*, IV/1, 248 n.2; Longerich, *Die braunen Bataillone*, 111.

207. *RSA*, IV/1, 246–8.

208. Longerich, *Die braunen Bataillone*, 111.

209. *RSA*, IV/1, 248–59.

210. *RSA*, IV/1, 251.

211. *RSA*, IV/1, 256.

212. *RSA*, IV/1, 258.

213. Longerich, *Die braunen Bataillone*, 111.

214. *RSA*, IV/1, 260.

215. *TBJG*, I.2, 44 (4 April 1931)

216. *RSA*, IV/1, 263–4; *TBJG*, I.2, 44 (4 April 1931).

217. Longerich, *Die braunen Bataillone*, 111.

218. The term 'politics of hooliganism' was coined with reference to the SA by Richard Bessel, *Political Violence and the Rise of Nazism. The Storm Troopers in Eastern Germany 1925–1934*, New Haven/London, 1984. 152.

219. Longerich, *Die braunen Bataillone*, 97–8; Broszat, 'Struktur', 61. And see Bessel, *Political Violence*, 33–45, for the social structure in eastern regions.

220. Hanfstaengl, *15 Jahre*, 243; Wagener, 98.

221. Hanfstaengl, *15 Jahre*, 183–4; Toland, 204, 236.

222. Heiden, *Hitler*, 347–9.

223. Hoffmann, 147–8.

224. Hoffmann, 161. For Hitler's first meeting with her, see Gun, *Eva Braun-Hitler*, 46. Gun suggests (55) that the relationship was a sexual one after the first months of 1932, but that Eva's infatuation for Hitler was not reciprocated. According to Fritz Wiedemann, Hitler casually commented – though conceivably for effect – around this time that being a bachelor had its uses, 'and as far as love goes, I keep a girl for myself in Munich' (*Und für die Liebe halte ich mir eben in München ein Mädchen*) (Gun, 57). On Eva Braun see also Henriette von Schirach, *Der Preis der Herrlichkeit. Erlebte Zeitgeschichte*, Munich/Berlin, 1975, 23–5.

225. Based on conversations with Anni Winter, housekeeper in Hitler's apartment, his later secretary, Christa Schroeder, was convinced that he had had no sexual relations with Geli (Schroeder, 153). She was, however, guessing – like everyone else.

226. Heiden, *Führer*, 304.

227. Strasser, *Hitler und ich*, 74–5, hinted strongly at perverted sexual practices inflicted by Hitler on his niece. In an interview for the American OSS on 13 May 1943 he was explicit (NA, *Hitler Source Book*, 918–19). See also Toland, 252; Hayman, 145; Lewis, *The Secret Life of Adolf Hitler*, 10, 136. This account (132–46) attributes sado-masochistic practices to Hitler, based on speculation and unreliable evidence, and concludes that the SS had Geli shot to prevent a scandal arising from her pregnancy by a Jewish student.

228. Heiden, *Hitler*, 352; Heiden, *Der Führer*, 304–6; Hanfstaengl, *15 Jahre*, 234–5. And see Hayman, 154.

229. Hoffmann, 148–9; B.v. Schirach, 106; Henriette von Schirach, 205. Hitler even took her in July 1930, along with Goebbels, to Oberammergau to see the Passion Play (*TBJG*, I.1, 578 (20 July 1930)).

230. Hanfstaengl, *15 Jahre*, 236.

231. Hoffmann, 151–2.

232. Hanfstaengl, *15 Jahre*, 232–3.

233. Hoffmann, 150; B.v. Schirach, 107.

234. Hanfstaengl, *15 Jahre*, 233. Hayman, 139–48, interprets the phrase to mean that Hitler demanded sexually perverted acts of his niece.

235. Hanfstaengl, *15 Jahre*, 242; Hoffmann, 151. Bridget Hitler, the first wife of Hitler's half-brother, Alois, related the story, allegedly told to her son, William Patrick, by Alois' second wife, Maimee (*The Memoirs of Bridget Hitler*, London,

1979, 70–77). These 'memoirs' (which include the tall story of Hitler's alleged stay in Liverpool in 1912) are notoriously unreliable. Lewis, 145, has a variant – based on an interview with a former SS officer in 1975 – of Geli discovering that she was bearing the child of a Jewish student in Munich and wanting to go to Vienna for an abortion. He takes this as the motive for the SS to kill Geli. According to Hans Frank's version, the relationship was with a young officer (Frank, 97).

236. Schroeder, 154, 296 n.34, 364–6 nn.280–82.

237. *RSA*, IV/2, 109 n.1, cit. MP, 22 September 1931; Hanfstaengl, *15 Jahre*, 239, 242.

238. In the *Münchener Post* article of 22 September 1931 (*RSA*, IV/2, 109 n.1).

239. Hayman, 164, 166.

240. *RSA*, IV/2, 109–10.

241. Hanfstaengl, *15 Jahre*, 238; Hoffmann, 152; B.v. Schirach, 108.

242. Hoffmann, 152–3, for a dramatized version; Hanfstaengl, *15 Jahre*, 238. See also, for Geli's relationship with Hitler, and on her suicide, with some inaccuracies, Gun, 17–28. The conflicting evidence is closely assessed by Hayman, 160–201, who strongly hints at Hitler's direct complicity in his niece's death. He refers to the speeding offence on 174.

243. Frank, 97; Hanfstaengl, *15 Jahre*, 239.

244. Hanfstaengl, *15 Jahre*, 239. Heiden, *Der Führer*, 307–8, speculated, on the basis of reported allegations by Geli's mother, Angela Raubal, exonerating Hitler from blame and claiming even that he had intended to marry Geli, that Himmler had been responsible.

245. A point made by Toland, 255. The police doctor certified that the cause of death was suicide, and that she had died during the evening of 18 September 1931 (Hayman, 164).

246. Hanfstaengl, *15 Jahre*, 239, 241; Wagener, 358–9; Hayman, 162–3.

247. The above based on Frank, 97–8; Hoffmann, 156–9 (a highly embellished account); Hanfstaengl, *15 Jahre*, 240; Heiden, *Der Führer*, 307.

248. Text of the speech in *RSA*, IV/2, 111–15. For Hitler's reception in Hamburg, Frank, 98.

249. *RSA*, IV/2, 111 n.1. Hitler did not appear in two parallel meetings addressed by leading Nazis. Illness was given as the reason.

250. See Hanfstaengl, *15 Jahre*, 242–3; Hoffmann, 159; also, implicitly, Wagener, 358; and H. v. Schirach, 205. Long after the war, Hitler's sister, Paula, suggested that everything might have been different had Hitler married Mimi Reiter (Peis, 'Die unbekannte Geliebte').

251. Hoffman, 155–6; Hanfstaengl, *15 Jahre*, 243–4. Hanfstaengl regarded it as a politically inspired, somewhat pathetic but unconvincing display of grief.

252. Falter *et al.*, *Wahlen*, 94. Tyrell, *Führer*, 383, has 25.9 per cent.

253. Falter *et al.*, *Wahlen*, 100; Deuerlein, *Aufstieg*, 352.

254. Falter *et al.*, *Wahlen*, 95.

255. Deuerlein, *Aufstieg*, 357; *RSA*, IV/2, 123–32.

256. Deuerlein, *Aufstieg*, 352–8; *RSA*, IV/2, 159–64; Turner, *German Big Business*, 189.

257. Turner, *German Big Business*, 167–71.

258. Turner, *German Big Business*, 144.

259. Turner, *German Big Business*, 144–5.

260. Hjalmar Schacht, *My First Seventy-Six Years*, London, 1955, 279.

261. Schacht, 279–80.

262. Turner, *German Big Business*, 145.

263. Cuno had been persuaded by some of his supporters – including the powerful Ruhr industrialist Paul Reusch – to consider making a political comeback and standing for the Reich Presidency. Retired Admiral Magnus Levetzow, one of those most keen to see Cuno stand, arranged for him to meet Hitler in Berlin in the hope of winning the backing of the NSDAP (Turner, *German Big Business*, 129).

264. Turner, *German Big Business*, 129–30.

265. Turner, *German Big Business*, 130–32.

266. Turner, *German Big Business*, 146, 150; Wagener, 368–74.

267. Turner, *German Big Business*, 142, 187.

268. Turner, *German Big Business*, 128, 181–2.

269. Turner, *German Big Business*, 191–203.

270. Otto Dietrich, *Mit Hitler an die Macht. Persönliche Erlebnisse mit meinem Führer*, 7th edn, Munich, 1934, 45–6; Turner, *German Big Business*, 171–2.

271. Henry Ashby Turner, 'Big Business and the Rise of Hitler', in Turner, *Nazism and Third Reich*, 93–7 (originally publ. in *American Historical Review*, 75 (1969), 56–70).

272. Turner, *German Big Business*, 204–19. Many leading industrialists were in any case conspicuous by their absence. Dietrich, *Mit Hitler*, 46–9, depicts Hitler winning the hearts and minds of his initially cool audience. In his post-war memoirs, Dietrich emphasized the limited financial contributions of big business to the Nazi Party before 1933 (Otto Dietrich, *Zwölf Jahre mit Hitler*, Cologne (n.d., 1955?), 185–6).

273. Turner, *German Big Business*, 208–10, 213–14; text of speech, *RSA*, IV/3, 74–110; and in Domarus, 68–90.

274. Turner, *German Big Business*, 217–19.

275. See the character sketch in Henry Ashby Turner, *Hitler's Thirty Days to Power: January 1933*, London, 1996, 39–41.

276. Turner, 'Big Business and the Rise of Hitler', 94, 97.

277. Turner, *German Big Business*, 111–24; Henry Ashby Turner and Horst Matzerath, 'Die Selbstfinanzierung der NSDAP 1930–32', 59–92.

278. Wagener, 221–2.

279. Turner, *German Big Business*, 148–52, 157; Wagener, 226–9.

280. Wagener, 227; Turner, *German Big Business*, 152.

281. See Turner, *German Big Business*, 47–60.

282. Above based on Turner, *German Big Business*, 153–6. Hitler's income tripled in 1930 to reported gross taxable receipts of 48,472 Reich Marks. This rose further

by 1932 to 64,639 Reich Marks (Hale, 'Adolf Hitler: Taxpayer', 837). See also, for Hitler's earnings around this time, Hanfstaengl, *15 Jahre*, 216; and B.v. Schirach, 112-13.

283. Franz von Papen, *Memoirs*, London, 1952, 142-3; Otto Meissner, *Staatssekretär unter Ebert – Hindenburg – Hitler*, Hamburg, 1950, 216.

284. *TBJG*, I.2, 106 (7 January 1932); Deuerlein, *Aufstieg*, 370-72; Papen, 146.

285. Deuerlein, *Aufstieg*, 372; Walther Hubatsch, *Hindenburg und der Staat*, Göttingen, 1966, 309-10.

286. The exchange was published by the Nazis in a brochure: *Hitlers Auseinandersetzung mit Brüning. Kampfschrift, Broschürenreihe der Reichspropagandaleitung der NSDAP*, Heft 5, Munich, 1932, 73-94. Hitler's open letter to Brüning, dated 15 January 1932, is reprinted in *RSA* IV/3, 34-44.

287. Meissner, 216-17.

288. *TBJG*, I.2, 120-21 (3 February 1932). See Fest, *Hitler*, 439-40.

289. *TBJG*, I.2, 130-31 (22 February 1932), 134 (27 February 1932).

290. Rudolf Morsey, 'Hitler als Braunschweigischer Regierungsrat', *VfZ*, 8 (1960), 419-48; Deuerlein, *Aufstieg*, 373-6.

291. See Papen, 147.

292. *RSA*, IV/3, 138-44 (quotation, 144); Domarus, 95; *TBJG*, I.2, 134 (27 February 1932).

293. Domarus, 96.

294. *TBJG*, I.2, 140-41 (13 March 1932).

295. Deuerlein, *Aufstieg*, 381; Falter *et al.*, *Wahlen*, 46.

296. *RSA*, V/1, 16-43; Domarus, 101-3.

297. Falter *et al.*, *Wahlen*, 46.

298. *TBJG*, I.2, 152-3 (8-11 April 1932).

299. Saxony, Baden, Hessen and Thuringia were the largest states, with a total population of just over 10 million, not voting on that day. Roughly another 2 million lived in the smaller states which were not holding Landtag elections on 24 April. The population of those states going to the polls that day numbered close on 50 million. Figures taken from Falter *et al.*, *Wahlen*, 90-113.

300. *RSA*, V/1, 59-97; Deuerlein, *Aufstieg*, 385-6; Domarus, 106-7.

301. *Miesbacher Anzeiger*, 19 April 1932.

302. Jochmann, *Nationalsozialismus und Revolution*, 404-5; Deuerlein, *Aufstieg*, 386-7; *RSA*, V/1, 97 and Doc.61 n.1-2 (and 92-6, Doc.60, for the speech).

303. Falter *et al.*, *Wahlen*, 89, 91, 94, 101; Deuerlein, *Aufstieg*, 387-8.

304. *TBJG*, I.2, 160 (23 April 1932).

305. Domarus, 105; Longerich, *Die braunen Bataillone*, 154.

306. Karl Dietrich Bracher, *Die Auflösung der Weimarer Republik. Eine Studie zum Problem des Machtverfalls in einer Demokratie*, Stuttgart/Düsseldorf, 1955, 481 and n.2; Longerich, *Die braunen Bataillone*, 153-4.

307. Ulrich Herbert, *Best. Biographische Studien über Radikalismus, Weltanschauung und Vernunft 1903-1989*, Bonn, 1996, 111-19.

308. Deuerlein, *Aufstieg*, 363.
309. Longerich, *Die braunen Bataillone*, 159 for membership growth in early 1932.
310. *TBJG*, I.2, 139 (11 March 1932).
311. Longerich, *Die braunen Bataillone*, 153.
312. *TBJG*, I.2, 150 (2 April 1932).
313. *TBJG*, I.2, 154 (11 April 1932). Goebbels had noted in his diary on 17 March that the Prussian Interior Minister Severing, following house-searches in Berlin, was apparently planning a ban on the SA (*TBJG*, I.2, 144).
314. Longerich, *Die braunen Bataillone*, 154.
315. *RSA*, V/1, 54–6; Domarus, 105–6. Hindenburg had wanted the ban extended to the Communists (Papen, 149).
316. Kolb, *Die Weimarer Republik*, 136–7.
317. *TBJG*, I.2, 162 (28 April 1932); Winkler, *Weimar*, 461–2. Schleicher had already had talks with Röhm and Graf Helldorf, the Berlin SA leader. See also Thilo Vogelsang, *Reichswehr, Staat und NSDAP*, Stuttgart, 1962, 188–9.
318. *TBJG*, I.2, 165 (8 May 1932).
319. Papen, 153; see Winkler, *Weimar*, 462–3.
320. *TBJG*, I.2, 166–7 (10–11 May 1932); Schulz, *Von Brüning zu Hitler*, 821.
321. *TBJG*, I.2, 168 (12 May 1932); see Winkler, *Weimar*, 465.
322. *TBJG*, I.2, 169 (13 May 1932).
323. Brüning, *Memoiren*, ii.632–8; Winkler, *Weimar*, 470–72.
324. Joseph Goebbels, *Vom Kaiserhof zur Reichskanzlei. Eine historische Darstellung in Tagebuchblättern (Vom 1. Januar 1932 bis zum 1. Mai 1933)*, 21st edn, Munich, 1937, 103–4 (30 May 1932); *TBJG*, I.2, 177.
325. Papen, 150–56.
326. Papen, 162.
327. Falter *et al.*, *Wahlen*, 98, 100.
328. Falter *et al.*, *Wahlen*, 95.
329. Papen, 163; Winkler, *Weimar*, 404.
330. See Goebbels, *Kaiserhof*, 111 (14 June 1932); *TBJG*, I.2, 185.
331. For evidence of the strong support offered to the NSDAP from the well-to-do middle classes, see the examination of votes cast at holiday resorts or on cruise liners in July 1932 in Richard F. Hamilton, *Who Voted for Hitler?*, Princeton, 1982, 220–28.
332. Deuerlein, *Aufstieg*, 392–3; Winkler, *Weimar*, 490–93. And see, for the local background to the violence in Altona, Anthony McElligott, ' ". . . und so kam es zu einer schweren Schlägerei". Straßenschlachten in Altona und Hamburg am Ende der Weimarer Republik', in Maike Bruns *et al.* (eds.), *'Hier war doch alles nicht so schlimm.' Wie die Nazis in Hamburg den Alltag eroberten*, Hamburg, 1984, 58–85.
333. Winkler, *Weimar*, 495–503; Broszat, *Machtergreifung*, 148–50.
334. *TBJG*, I.2, 155 (15 April 1932).
335. Childers, *Nazi Voter*, 203.

336. See Allen, 322, for the high percentage of Nazi meetings in the Lower Saxon town of Northeim that consisted of little beyond pageantry.

337. *RSA*, V/1, 216–19; Domarus, 115; Z.A.B. Zeman, *Nazi Propaganda*, 2nd edn, London/New York, 1973, 31.

338. Hamilton, 326.

339. *RSA*, V/1, 210–94; Deuerlein, *Aufstieg*, 394; Domarus, 114–20.

340. Hanfstaengl, *15 Jahre*, 267.

341. *RSA*, V/1, 216–19; Domarus, 115–17 (Adolf-Hitler-Schallplatte: 'Appell an die Nation').

342. Falter, *et al.*, *Wahlen*, 44. The turn-out, 84.1 per cent, was the largest for a Reichstag election during the period of the Weimar democracy.

343. *TBJG*, I.2, 211 (1 August 1932). The published 'Kaiserhof' version had a more optimistic tone: Goebbels, *Kaiserhof*, 135–6 (31 July 1932). The following day, in his unpublished diary entry for 2 August, Goebbels again expressed Hitler's agreement that the time for power had arrived. The only alternative was 'sharpest opposition'. There could be no more question of toleration of the Papen government (*TBJG*, I.2, 212–13).

344. *TBJG*, I.2, 214 (3 August 1932).

345. *TBJG*, I.2, 215 (5 August 1932).

346. *TBJG*, I.2, 217 (7 August 1932).

347. See Winkler, *Weimar*, 509.

348. Thilo Vogelsang, 'Zur Politik Schleichers gegenüber der NSDAP 1932', *VfZ*, 6 (1958), 86–118, here 89.

349. Hubatsch, *Hindenburg*, 335–8, Nr.87 (Meissner's minutes from 11 August 1932).

350. Winkler, *Weimar*, 509.

351. *TBJG*, I.2, 218 (9 August 1932).

352. Goebbels, *Kaiserhof*, 140 (8 August 1932); *TBJG*, I.2, 218.

353. Vogelsang, 'Zur Politik Schleichers', 93–8; Winkler, *Weimar*, 509–10.

354. *TBJG*, I.2, 221 (11 August 1932). For Gayl's speech, see Eberhard Kolb and Wolfram Pyta, 'Die Staatsnotstandsplanung unter Papen und Schleicher', in Heinrich August Winkler (ed.), *Die deutsche Staatskrise 1930–1933*, Munich, 1992, 155–81, here 160.

355. Goebbels, *Kaiserhof*, 142–4 (11–12 August 1932); *TBJG*, I.2, 222–3; see also Papen, 195.

356. Papen, 195–7; Goebbels, *Kaiserhof*, 144 (13 August 1932); *TBJG*, I.2, 224.

357. Goebbels, *Kaiserhof*, 144–5 (13 August 1932); *TBJG*, I.2, 224.

358. Hubatsch, 338–9, Nr.88; Deuerlein, *Aufstieg*, 397–8; Papen, 197. Hitler objected to Meissner's wording of the official communiqué and within hours dispatched his own version, put together, he said, together with Frick and Röhm immediately after they had returned from the meeting. This stressed Hitler's denial that he would demand all cabinet seats for his party, if he were given the leadership. It mainly, however, concentrated on the subsequent exchange in the corridor and on Hitler's

resentment that he had been called to the meeting when, in fact, the decision had already been taken in advance of it by Hindenburg. Unsurprisingly, neither Papen nor the Reich Chancellery were prepared to alter anything in the published communiqué (IfZ, Fa 296, Bl.165–71).

359. IfZ, Fa 296, Bl.169, 'Besprechung in der Reichskanzlei am 13.8.32', signed by Röhm, Frick and Hitler.

360. Goebbels, *Kaiserhof*, 145 (13 August 1932); *TBJG*, I.2, 225.

361. See Lüdecke, 351–2.

362. See Winkler, *Weimar*, 511–12.

CHAPTER 10: LEVERED INTO POWER

1. For the splits in élite strategies and aims during the final phase of the Weimar Republic, see the contributions by Henry Ashby Turner, Jürgen John and Wolfgang Zollitsch (together with the subsequent discussion) in Heinrich August Winkler (ed.), *Die deutsche Staatskrise 1930–1933*, Munich, 1992, 205–62.

2. A point emphasized by James, 'Economic Reasons for the Collapse of the Weimar Republic', in Kershaw (ed.), *Weimar: Why did German Democracy Fail?*, 30–57, here 55; see also the perceptive analysis by Gerald D. Feldmann, 'Der 30 Januar 1933 und die politische Kultur von Weimar', in Winkler, *Staatskrise*, 263–76. Eberhard Jäckel is adamant that Hitler's takeover of power did constitute a 'works accident', though on his own analysis (*Das deutsche Jahrhundert*, 126–58) of the behaviour of the national-conservative, pro-monarchist élites it was at the very least an accident waiting to happen.

3. Letter from Wilhelm Keppler to Kurt von Schröder, 26 December 1932, cit. in Vogelsang, 'Zur Politik Schleichers', 86.

4. Winkler, *Weimar*, 511; Schulz, *Von Brüning zu Hitler*, 964; Domarus, 123–4.

5. Vogelsang, 'Zur Politik Schleichers', 86–7.

6. Joachim von Ribbentrop, *The Ribbentrop Memoirs*, London, 1954, 21. This was the first time Ribbentrop had met Hitler, who told him he was prepared to work with other political forces but insisted upon the Chancellorship. Ribbentrop came away very impressed, convinced that only Hitler and his party could save Germany from Communism, and joined the NSDAP straight away.

7. Vogelsang, 'Zur Politik Schleichers', 87–8.

8. Vogelsang, 'Zur Politik Schleichers', 99–100 n.29; Werner Freiherr von Rheinbaben, *Viermal Deutschland. Aus dem Erleben eines Seemanns, Diplomaten, Politikers 1895–1954*, Berlin, 1954, 303–4.

9. See Domarus, 123 for such an inference.

10. Hanfstaengl, *15 Jahre*, 279. How accurate Hanfstaengl's recollection of Hitler's exact words was might justifiably be doubted. In his wartime interview for the American OSS, he had Hitler saying: 'We'll see. Perhaps it's better like this' ('*Wir werden ja sehen. Es ist vielleicht besser so*') (NA, *Hitler Source Book*, 911).

11. *RSA*, V/1, 304–9; Domarus, 125–9.

12. *RSA*, V/1, 316.

13. The following is based on Paul Kluke, 'Der Fall Potempa', *VfZ*, 5 (1957), 279–97 and Richard Bessel, 'The Potempa Murder', *Central European History*, 10 (1977), 241–54.

14. *RSA*, V/1, 317; Domarus, 130 (dated 23 August, when the telegram was published in the press).

15. Goebbels acknowledged that public opinion was against the party (*TBJG*, I/2, 230 (25 August 1932)).

16. *RSA*, V/1, 318–20 (quotation, 319); Domarus, 130; Kluke, 284–5.

17. Papen, 200. Hindenburg, on the other hand, claimed on 30 August at a meeting with Papen, Gayl and Schleicher in Neudeck that he was swayed only by legal, not political, considerations. Since the deed had been committed only an hour and a half after the decree came into effect, Hindenburg suggested that it could not be presumed that they had knowledge of it. This dubious argument was accepted by Papen and advanced as the reason for leniency (Winkler, *Weimar*, 514).

18. Kluke, 286.

19. Kluke, 281.

20. Kluke, 281–2, cit. *VB* (11 August 1932).

21. Kluke, 285, cit. *VB* (26 August 1932).

22. Vogelsang, 'Zur Politik Schleichers', 89, 110.

23. Brüning, ii.658; see Goebbels, *Kaiserhof*, 154–5, *TBJG* I.2, 235–6 (31 August 1932, 2 September 1932), where Hitler points for the first time to intrigues and opposition which he saw as emanating from Strasser and his 'clique'.

24. Goebbels, *Kaiserhof*, 160, *TBJG*, II.2, 239 (9 September 1932).

25. Brüning, ii.657–9.

26. Winkler, *Weimar*, 519–20; Papen, 215–16.

27. Vogelsang, 'Zur Politik Schleichers', 101.

28. Eberhard Kolb and Wolfram Pyta, 'Die Staatsnotstandsplanung unter den Regierungen Papen und Schleicher', in Winkler, *Staatskrise*, 155–81, here 161.

29. Winkler, *Weimar*, 518–19; Kolb and Pyta, 165–6. For wide-ranging hopes invested in a revised constitutional arrangement see Hans Mommsen, 'Regierung ohne Parteien. Konservative Pläne zum Verfassungsumbau am Ende der Weimarer Republik', in Winkler, *Staatskrise*, 1–18, here esp. 3–4.

30. Kolb and Pyta, 166.

31. Deuerlein, *Aufstieg*, 401; Papen, 207; Winkler, *Weimar*, 521; Mommsen, *Die verspielte Freiheit*, 474. Göring's extensive contacts with the national-conservative élite had been important to Hitler and promoted his own advancement within the Nazi Party (though he never became a 'party man' as such) and in the Reichstag, which he had joined as a Deputy in 1928.

32. Winkler, *Weimar*, 521.

33. Goebbels, *Kaiserhof*, 159–60 (8 September 1932, 10 September 1932), *TBJG*, I.2, 239–240.

34. Goebbels, *Kaiserhof*, 152 (28 August 1932), and also 153 (30 August 1932), *TBJG*, I.2, 233–4.

35. Goebbels, *Kaiserhof*, 159 (8 September 1932), *TBJG*, I.2, 238. Goebbels noted the demand for a Hitler Chancellorship again on 9 September. 'Only Strasser speaks against' (Goebbels, *Kaiserhof*, 160, *TBJG*, I.2, 239 (9 September 1932)).

36. Papen, 208.

37. Goebbels, *Kaiserhof*, 162 (12 September 1932), *TBJG*, I.2, 241; Papen, 208.

38. The above account is based on *Akten der Reichskanzlei. Das Kabinett von Papen*, ed. Karl-Heinz Minuth, Boppard am Rhein, 1989, ii.543–5; Papen, 208–9; Goebbels, *Kaiserhof*, 162–3 (12 September 1932), *TBJG*, I.2, 241–2; Lüdecke, 433–4; Winkler, *Weimar*, 522–4; Schulz, *Von Brüning zu Hitler*, 993–4; Bracher, *Auflösung*, 627–9; Mommsen, *Die verspielte Freiheit*, 475–6.

39. Goebbels, *Kaiserhof*, 163 (12 September 1932), *TBJG*, I.2, 242.

40. Mommsen, *Die verspielte Freiheit*, 476.

41. Kolb and Pyta, 166; Winkler, *Weimar*, 528.

42. Broadcasting was controlled by the government, which allowed little time for political broadcasts. The Nazis had had no access to the radio before the summer of 1932 (Zeman, 31).

43. Goebbels, *Kaiserhof*, 165 (16 September 1932), 167 (20 September 1932), for the quotation; *TBJG*, I.2, 243–4, 246–7. For extensive reports from regional and local party organizations of financial difficulties hampering the campaign, see Childers, 'Limits', 236–8.

44. Lüdecke, 438.

45. Domarus, 137. Goebbels, *Kaiserhof*, 176 (4 October 1932); *TBJG*, I.2, 254–5 (5 October 1932). See also Goebbels, *Kaiserhof*, 174 (2 October 1932), *TBJG*, I.2, 252 for Hitler's conveying of optimism to others, and Goebbels, *Kaiserhof*, 187 (28 October 1932), *TBJG*, I.2, 265 where Hitler was said to be 'very certain of victory'.

46. Lüdecke, 461–2, 469, 475–6.

47. Lüdecke, 476.

48. Lüdecke, 479. Above account based on Lüdecke, 475–9; Goebbels, *Kaiserhof*, 174 (2 October 1932), *TBJG*, I.2, 252.

49. Deuerlein, *Aufstieg*, 402–3 notes forty-nine speeches, but does not include Regensburg on 5 November; Domarus, 138–42 has forty-seven, including Regensburg, but omitting Gummersbach, Betzdorf-Walmenrot, and Limburg; Hauner, 85, lists forty-seven but omits Schweinfurt, Würzburg and Betzdorf-Walmenrot.

50. Maser, *Hitler*, 317 and n.

51. Gun, *Eva Braun-Hitler*, 55–7. Hoffman, 161–2, dates the incident to summer 1932. For other suicide attempts of women who knew Hitler, see Maser, *Hitler*, 313.

52. Domarus, 141.

53. *VB*, 14 October 1932, IfZ, MA-731, HA Reel 1 Folder 13.

54. *VB*, 14 October 1932, IfZ, MA-731, HA Reel 1 Folder 13.

55. IfZ, MA-731, NSDAP-HA, Reel 1 Folder 13, Pd Hof, 15 October 1932.

56. Domarus, 138.

57. Above quotations from IfZ, MA-1220, HA, Reel 1A Folder 13.

58. IfZ, MA-731, HA Reel 1 Folder 13.

59. See Childers, 'Limits', 236, 246–51.

60. Goebbels, *Kaiserhof*, 191 (2 November 1932), *TBJG*, I.2, 268. Goebbels may, like Hitler, have been deceived into over-optimism by the type of reception he had at his meetings. After a speech in Stettin on 31 October, he wrote in his diary: 'The mood is excellent everywhere. We are making mighty inroads.' His adjoining comment revealed, however, his concern: 'If it goes on like this, 6 November won't be all that bad.' And the next day he was already consoling himself for an impending defeat: 'It's not all that bad if we lose a few million votes' (Goebbels, *Kaiserhof*, 190 (31 October 1932, 1 November 1932), *TBJG*, I.2, 267).

61. IfZ, MA-731, HA Reel 1 Folder 13, Pd Nbg, 14 October 1932.

62. BHStA, MA 102144, RPvNB/OP, 19 October 1932.

63. Goebbels, *Kaiserhof*, 195 (5 November 1932), *TBJG*, I.2, 271. Even in early October, Gregor Strasser had predicted a loss of forty seats (Stachura, *Strasser*, 104).

64. Falter *et al.*, *Wahlen*, 41, 44.

65. Falter, *Hitlers Wähler*, 109.

66. Falter, 'National Socialist Mobilisation', 219.

67. Goebbels, *Kaiserhof*, 196 (6 November 1932), *TBJG*, I.2, 272.

68. See Goebbels, *Kaiserhof*, 192 (2 November 1932), *TBJG*, I.2, 269 where Goebbels had spoken of the lack of funding in the campaign as 'a chronic sickness'. On the very day before the election, he noted, it had been possible to drum up 10,000 Marks 'at the last minute', which were immediately thrown into the last efforts of propaganda (Goebbels, *Kaiserhof*, 195 (5 November 1932), *TBJG*, I.2, 271). The DNVP's propaganda had been better funded and, it was accepted, as a result quantitatively superior (Childers, 'Limits', 238).

69. Childers, 'Limits', 243–4; and see Goebbels, *Kaiserhof*, 196 (6 November 1932), *TBJG*, I.2, 272.

70. BHStA, MA 102151, RPvUF, 21 September 1932.

71. Goebbels, *Kaiserhof*, 196 (6 November 1932), *TBJG*, I.2, 272.

72. Childers, 'Limits', 238–42.

73. The strike, called by the Revolutionary Trade Union Opposition (Revolutionäre Gewerkschafts-Opposition (RGO)) – the factory-cell organization of the KPD – was in protest at wage reductions imposed on Berlin transport workers. Initially swingeing, these had been reduced to more modest levels, but were still sufficient to provoke the Communists into declaring a strike, opposed by the SPD-linked unions, but backed by the NSBO. The strike began on 3 November and was broken off by the strikers four days later. The underground was brought to a complete standstill; trams and buses attempting to leave the depots were in the main halted by pickets. There was a good deal of public disorder, including clashes between strikers and the police which ended with three dead and eight injured as police shot

into a crowd. See Winkler, *Weimar*, 533–5. Goebbels, overjoyed, described the mood as 'revolutionary' (Goebbels, *Kaiserhof*, 194 (4 November 1932), *TBJG*, I.2, 270). For the KPD, the strike probably played a part in the increased vote in the November election, and also shored up the already existent over-confidence in the party's ability to cope with a National Socialist government. (Christian Striefler, *Kampf um die Macht. Kommunisten und Nationalsozialisten am Ende der Weimarer Republik*, Berlin, 1993, 177–86).

74. Childers, 'Limits', 238.
75. Goebbels, *Kaiserhof*, 192 (2 November 1932), *TBJG*, I.2, 268–9.
76. Goebbels, *Kaiserhof*, 194 (4 November 1932), *TBJG*, I.2, 270.
77. Childers, 'Limits', 240.
78. Jochmann, *Nationalsozialismus und Revolution*, 416 (3 November 1932, 6 November 1932).
79. Jochmann, *Nationalsozialismus und Revolution*, 417 (7 November 1932, 9 November 1932).
80. Winkler, *Weimar*, 536–7.
81. *TBJG*, I.2, 274 (9 November 1932).
82. IMT, vol.35, 223–30, Docs. 633-D and 634-D; Domarus, 144–8; *AdR, Kabinett von Papen*, ii.952–60; Goebbels, *Kaiserhof*, 199 (9 November 1932), *TBJG*, I.2, 276; Papen, 212–13; Bracher, *Auflösung*, 659–60 and n.31; Winkler, *Weimar*, 543.
83. *AdR, Kabinett von Papen*, ii.951–2 (meeting of Papen and Schäffer, 16 November 1932). See also Winkler, *Weimar*, 541, 543.
84. Hubatsch, *Hindenburg*, 353.
85. Papen, 214; Winkler, *Weimar*, 543.
86. Printed in Eberhard Czichon, *Wer verhalf Hitler zur Macht? Zum Anteil der deutschen Industrie an der Zerstörung der Weimarer Republik*, Cologne (1967), 3rd edn, 1972, 69–71.
87. Based on Turner, *German Big Business*, 303–4; see also Winkler, *Weimar*, 540–41.
88. Lüdecke, 413.
89. Hubatsch, 350–52; Goebbels, *Kaiserhof*, 206 (20 November 1932), *TBJG*, I.2, 282.
90. Goebbels, *Kaiserhof*, 207 (20 November 1932), *TBJG*, I.2, 282.
91. Hubatsch, 350–52, here 352; Domarus, 149; Goebbels, *Kaiserhof*, 207–8 (20 November 1932, 21 November 1932), *TBJG*, I.2, 282–3.
92. Domarus, 150 (21 November 1932).
93. Hubatsch, 353–6; Domarus, 151: communiqué of the second discussion of Hindenburg and Hitler on the morning of 21 November 1932.
94. Hubatsch, 354–5; Domarus, 152 (21 November 1932); Goebbels, *Kaiserhof*, 208 (21 November 1932), *TBJG*, I.2, 283.
95. Hubatsch, 356–7; Domarus, 153–4 (22 November 1932); Goebbels, *Kaiserhof*, 208 (23 November 1932), *TBJG*, I.2, 283.
96. Goebbels, *Kaiserhof*, 209 (23 November 1932), *TBJG*, I.2, 284.

97. Hubatsch, 358–61; Domarus, 154–7 (23 November 1932).

98. Domarus, 157 n.274.

99. Hubatsch, 361–2; Domarus, 158 (24 November 1932).

100. Domarus, 159, Hitler's final letter on the matter, written on 24 November; Goebbels, *Kaiserhof*, 209–10 (24 November 1932), *TBJG*, I.2, 284.

101. Hubatsch, 365–6.

102. Vogelsang, 'Zur Politik Schleichers', 104–5; Goebbels, *Kaiserhof*, 209 (23 November 1932), *TBJG*, I.2, 284.

103. Stachura, *Strasser*, 107. Turner, *Hitler's Thirty Days to Power*, 25, states that Schleicher's hope was not to split the NSDAP but to win the backing of the whole party for such a strategy. He was sufficient of a realist, however, to recognize that, without Hitler's blessing, this was hardly likely.

104. *TBJG*, I.2, 288 (2 December 1932); Domarus, 161. Hitler, in Weimar on account of the Thuringian local elections (*Gemeindewahlen*), had declined to travel to Berlin to meet Schleicher.

105. Vogelsang, 'Zur Politik Schleichers', 105 and n.44.

106. Papen, 216–23; Vogelsang, 'Zur Politik Schleichers', 105–7, 110–11 and n.65; Winkler, *Weimar*, 547–50, 553–5; see also Kolb and Pyta, 170–77. Schleicher's expectations of support from the SPD would probably have proved illusory, though the party thought of him as a lesser evil than Papen or Hitler. He did, however, have good connections with the Reichsbanner. And the trade unions were inclined to give Schleicher a chance.

107. Peter D. Stachura, ' "Der Fall Strasser": Strasser, Hitler, and National Socialism, 1930–1932', in Stachura, *Shaping*, 88–130, here 88.

108. Hanfstaengl, *15 Jahre*, 281. The quoted comments of Spengler are a further illustration of the dangerous dismissal of Hitler by right-wing intellectuals. Spengler, made famous by his book on the decline of western civilization, became effectively the philosopher of the culturally pessimistic anti-democratic Right. His dislike of the vulgarity of the Nazis persisted, however, until his death in 1936.

109. Goebbels, *Kaiserhof*, 217–18 (6 December 1932), *TBJG*, I.2, 294.

110. Stachura, ' "Der Fall Strasser" ', 103, 108.

111. Turner, *German Big Business*, 311–12.

112. Stachura, ' "Der Fall Strasser" ', 90–91.

113. Stachura, ' "Der Fall Strasser" ', 94–95; Turner, *German Big Business*, 148–9.

114. Turner, *German Big Business*, 311–12.

115. Krebs, 191–2; Stachura, ' "Der Fall Strasser" ', 96–7. Hans Zehrer, a political journalist in his early thirties, had, together with a number of like-minded colleagues, used the periodical *Die Tat* since 1929 to expound his views of the cleansing nature of Weimar's crisis. He saw it as bringing about the end of capitalism and ushering in a new system of 'national socialism'. In this, he was close to the ideas of Gregor Strasser. The 'Tat Circle' developed links with General Schleicher in the summer of 1932. (Kurt Sontheimer, 'Der Tatkreis', *VfZ*, 7 (1959), 229–60; Benz-Graml, *Biographisches Lexikon*, 375–6; Winkler, *Weimar*, 525, 551; Mommsen, 'Regierung

ohne Parteien. Konservative Pläne zum Verfassungsumbau am Ende der Weimarer Republik', in Winkler, *Staatskrise*, 5–9, 15–17; Sontheimer, *Antidemokratisches Denken*, 205–6, 268–9).

116. For Strasser's inability to cope with probing questions on his economic ideas by the American journalist H. R. Knickerbocker, see Hanfstaengl, *15 Jahre*, 281–2.

117. Tyrell, *Führer*, 316.

118. In late August and September 1932, prompted by his good connections with Brüning, Strasser had pressed energetically for the NSDAP to come to terms with the Zentrum (Stachura, ' "Der Fall Strasser" ', 101). On 23 March 1932, he had written to Graf Reventlow insisting that the party must be ready to enter coalitions (even if that could not be broadcast too loudly). And earlier still, in a letter to Gauleiter Schlange of Brandenburg on 12 September 1931, he had suggested that the way to power was via a 'right-wing cabinet' (Tyrell, *Führer*, 316, 343–5).

119. Stachura, *Strasser*, 103.

120. Stachura, ' "Der Fall Strasser" ', 97–100.

121. Wagener, 477–80; Stachura, *Strasser*, 103–4.

122. Frank, 108.

123. Goebbels, *Kaiserhof*, 154 (31 August 1932), *TBJG*, I.2, 235.

124. Goebbels, *Kaiserhof*, 156 (3 September 1932), *TBJG*, I.2, 236.

125. Goebbels, *Kaiserhof*, 159–60 (8 and 9 September 1932), *TBJG*, I.2, 238–9.

126. Goebbels, *Kaiserhof*, 169–70 (25 September 1932), *TBJG*, I.2, 248.

127. Stachura, *Strasser*, 108.

128. Hanfstaengl, *15 Jahre*, 282.

129. Goebbels, *Kaiserhof*, 216 (5 December 1932), *TBJG*, I.2, 292–3; Stachura, *Strasser*, 108.

130. Stachura, *Strasser*, 108–12; Stachura, ' "Der Fall Strasser" ', 108–9.

131. Hinrich Lohse, 'Der Fall Strasser', unpubl. typescript, *c*.1960, Forschungsstelle für die Geschichte des Nationalsozialismus, Hamburg, sections 20–22.

132. Goebbels, *Kaiserhof*, 218 (8 December 1932), *TBJG*, I.2, 295.

133. Text of the letter in Stachura, ' "Der Fall Strasser" ', 113–15.

134. Lohse, section 23.

135. Lohse, sections 23–8. See Goebbels, *Kaiserhof*, 219 (8 December 1932), *TBJG*, I.2, 295.

136. *TBJG*, I.2 295 (unpublished entry, 9 December 1932); the published version (Goebbels, *Kaiserhof*, 220 (8 December 1932), *TBJG*, I.2, 296–7) adds 'with the pistol'.

137. Goebbels, *Kaiserhof*, 220 (8 December 1932), *TBJG*, I.2, 297–8.

138. Domarus, 166.

139. Lohse, section 30; Orlow, i.293–6.

140. Stachura, ' "Der Fall Strasser" ', 112.

141. Lohse, sections 30–33, Domarus, 165; Stachura, ' "Der Fall Strasser" ', 112; Orlow, i.293.

142. Domarus, 165; *TBJG*, I.2, 299 (10 December 1932, unpubl.).

143. *TBJG*, I.2, 299 (10 December 1932, unpubl.).

144. Domarus, 166–7; Orlow, i.293; see Goebbels, *Kaiserhof*, 226 (16 December 1932), *TBJG*, I.2, 309; Lohse, section 31.

145. Stachura, *Strasser*, 116, 118–19.

146. Lohse, section 33; *TBJG*, I.2, 340 (17 January 1933); Domarus, 180.

147. Goebbels, *Kaiserhof* 243, (16 January 1933), *TBJG*, I.2, 340–41. The unpublished diary entry is more prosaic: 'No more demand . . . He will end as nothing, as he deserves' (*TBJG*, I.2, 340–41, 17 January 1933).

148. BDC, Gregor Strasser, Parteikorrespondenz, Antragsschein zum Erwerb des Ehrenzeichens der alten Parteimitglieder der NSDAP, 29 January 1934; Besitzurkunde, 1 February 1934.

149. BDC, OPG-Akte Albert Pietzsch, Gregor Strasser to Rudolf Heß, 18 June 1934.

150. See Stachura, ' "Der Fall Strasser" ', 110.

151. See Stachura, ' "Der Fall Strasser" ', 113.

152. BAK, NS22/110, 'Denkschrift über die inneren Gründe für die Verfügungen zur Herstellung einer erhöhten Schlagkraft der Bewegung'; see Orlow, i.294–6. The directions for the reordering of the party's apparatus that followed the memorandum, drafted by Ley, put into operation the changes in the organizational structure which had been determined on 9 December (Orlow, i.293 and n.234, 294 and n.239). Goebbels showed a copy of the memorandum to Hitler at a crisis-point in the war, in January 1943, remarking in his diary that the memorandum contained 'such classical arguments' that it could still be used without any amendment. Hitler had completely forgotten about the document (*TBJG*, II.7, 177 (23 January 1943)).

153. All the above from BAK, NS 22/110.

154. See Orlow, i.296.

155. Abelshauser, Faust and Petzina (eds.), *Deutsche Sozialgeschichte 1914–1945*, 327–8; Petzina *et al.*, *Sozialgeschichtliches Arbeitsbuch III*, 61, 70, 84.

156. Deuerlein, *Aufstieg*, 411.

157. Abelshauser *et al.*, *Deutsche Sozialgeschichte*, 328.

158. See Allen, 136–7; Abelshauser *et al.*, *Deutsche Sozialgeschichte*, 343–4.

159. Siegfried Bahne, 'Die Kommunistische Partei Deutschlands', in Erich Matthias and Rudolf Morsey (eds.), *Das Ende der Parteien 1933*, Königstein/Ts., 1979, 655–739, here 662. For the radicalization of the unemployed, see Anthony McElligott, 'Mobilising the Unemployed: The KPD and the Unemployed Workers' Movement in Hamburg-Altona during the Weimar Republic', in Evans and Geary, *The German Unemployed*, 228–60; and Eva Rosenhaft, *Beating the Fascists? The German Communists and Political Violence, 1929–1933*, London, 1983.

160. See Fischer, *Stormtroopers*, esp. 45–8 and ch.8.

161. See Detlev Peukert, 'The Lost Generation: Youth Unemployment at the End of the Weimar Republic', in Evans and Geary, *The German Unemployed*, 172–93, here esp. 188–9; and Peter D. Stachura, 'The Social and Welfare Implications of

Youth Unemployment in Weimar Germany', in Stachura, *Unemployment*, 121–47, here 140.

162. Cornelia Rauh-Kühne, *Katholisches Milieu und Kleinstadtgesellschaft. Ettlingen 1918–1939*, Sigmaringen, 1991, 270.

163. A point emphasized by Dick Geary, 'Unemployment and Working-Class Solidarity: the German Experience 1929–33', in Evans and Geary, *The German Unemployed*, 261–80; see also the contribution to the same volume (194–227) by Eva Rosenhaft, 'The Unemployed in the Neighbourhood: Social Dislocation and Political Mobilisation in Germany, 1929–1933'.

164. Among many examples: BHStA, MA 102151, RPvUF, 5 January 1933; MA 102138, RPvOB, 5 December 1932.

165. See, e.g., BHStA, MA 102154, RPvMF, 19 October 1932.

166. BHStA, MA 102154, RPvOF/MF, 5 January 1933 (citing a report from the District Office (Bezirksamt) of Ansbach).

167. BHStA, MA 106672, RPvNB/OP, 19 January 1933.

168. BHStA, MA 106672, RPvNB/OP 3 February 1933.

169. BHStA, MA 102144, RPvNB/OP 6 December 1932.

170. BHStA, MA 106672, RPvNB/OP, 3 February 1933, 20 February 1933.

171. See the analysis of ideological preference, levels of disaffection, and dimensions of prejudice in Merkl, 450–527.

172. BHStA, MA 102155/3, RPvNB/OP 16 December 1932 (citing Bezirksamt Ebermannstadt).

173. Heinrich August Winkler, 'German Society, Hitler, and the Illusion of Restoration 1930–33', *Journal of Contemporary History*, 11 (1976), 10–11; Heinrich August Winkler, *Mittelstand, Demokratie und Nationalsozialismus*, Cologne, 1972, 166–79.

174. See Michael H. Kater, 'Physicians in Crisis at the End of the Weimar Republic', in Stachura, *Unemployment*, 49–77; also – a study which graphically brings out the impact of the Weimar years on medical practice in the Third Reich, and on the attractions for doctors of National Socialism – Michael H. Kater, *Doctors under Hitler*, Chapel Hill/London, 1989, here 12–15.

175. Based on: Peukert, 'The Lost Generation'; Elizabeth Harvey, 'Youth Unemployment and the State: Public Policies towards Unemployed Youth in Hamburg during the World Economic Crisis', in Evans and Geary, *The German Unemployed*, 142–71; Stachura, 'The Social and Welfare Implications of Youth Unemployment'; Elizabeth Harvey, *Youth and the Welfare State in Weimar Germany*, Oxford, 1993; Abelshauser *et al.*, *Deutsche Sozialgeschichte*, 332–4; Stachura, *The Weimar Republic and the Younger Proletariat*; Peter D. Stachura, *The German Youth Movement 1900–1945. An Interpretative and Documentary History*, London, 1981; Peter Loewenberg, 'The Psychohistorical Origins of the Nazi Youth Cohort', *American Historical Review*, 76 (1971), 1457–1502; Peter D. Stachura, *Nazi Youth in the Weimar Republic*, Santa Barbara/Oxford, 1975; and Kater, 'Generationskonflikt als Entwicklungsfaktor in der NS-Bewegung vor 1933', 217–43.

176. Karin Hausen, 'Unemployment Also Hits Women: the New and the Old Woman

on the Dark Side of the Golden Twenties in Germany', in Stachura, *Unemployment*, 78–120, here esp. 112; Helgard Kramer, 'Frankfurt's Working Women: Scapegoats or Winners of the Great Depression?', in Evans and Geary, *The German Unemployed*, 108–41, here esp. 134; Renate Bridenthal, 'Beyond Kinder, Küche, Kirche: Weimar Women at Work', *Central European History*, 6 (1973), 148–66; Tim Mason, 'Women in Germany, 1925–1940: Family, Welfare, and Work', *History Workshop Journal*, 1 (1976), 74–113; Richard J. Evans, 'German Women and the Triumph of Hitler', *Journal of Modern History*, 48 (1976, demand supplement), 1–53; Helen L. Boak, 'Women in Weimar Germany: the "Frauenfrage" and the Female Vote', in Richard Bessel and E. J. Feuchtwanger (eds.), *Social Change and Political Development in the Weimar Republic*, London, 1981, 155–73, here 165–8.

177. See Allen, 146.

178. See Allen, 147.

179. Statistics on the demographic and social structure of German Jewry are provided in Werner Mosse (ed.), *Entscheidungsjahr. Zur Judenfrage in der Endphase der Weimarer Republik*, Tübingen, 1965, 87–131 (94 for the proportion of Jews in the total population). See also Helmut Genschel, *Die Verdrängung der Juden aus der Wirtschaft im Dritten Reich*, Göttingen, 1966, 20–28.

180. Deuerlein, *Aufstieg*, 411. See also Tyrell, *Führer*, 352, where the membership numbers on 30 January 1933 were given as 1,435,530. Since the membership numbers were given out in continuous series and numbers of those leaving the party not renewed, the figures for members actually in the party were substantially lower.

181. Fischer, *Stormtroopers*, 6.

182. Fischer, *Stormtroopers*, ch.6 downplays the role of ideology at all in recruiting for the SA.

183. Cit. Niewyk, 82 and n.2.

184. Arnold Paucker, *Der jüdische Abwehrkampf gegen Antisemitismus und Nationalsozialismus in den letzten Jahren der Weimarer Republik*, Hamburg, 1968; Niewyk, 86ff.

185. Niewyk, 82–6.

186. See Peter Gay, 'In Deutschland zu Hause . . . Die Juden der Weimarer Zeit', in Arnold Paucker (ed.), *Die Juden im Nationalsozialistischen Deutschland 1933–1943*, Tübingen, 1986, 31–43.

187. Lion Feuchtwanger, *Die Geschwister Oppermann*, Fischer edn, Frankfurt, 1983, 116. The novel brings out brilliantly the anxieties, but also the complacency, in Jewish bourgeois society in the months immediately before Hitler's takeover of power. See, e.g., 15–16, 69, 119–32.

188. Richard J. Evans, 'Die Todesstrafe in der Weimarer Republik', in Bajohr *et al.*, *Zivilisation und Barbarei*, 156–61; and Richard J. Evans, *Rituals of Retribution: Capital Punishment in Germany, 1600–1987*, Oxford, 1996, ch.13, esp. 604–10.

189. Noakes, 'Nazism and Eugenics', 84–5.

190. The varied contemporary impressions of Hitler are excellently surveyed in Schreiber, Part I.

191. Turner, *German Big Business*, 314–15 and 460 n.2; Papen, 225–6. And see, for the Papen–Hitler meeting at Schröder's house, Turner, *Hitler's Thirty Days to Power*, 42–52.

192. *Geschichte der deutschen Arbeiterbewegung*, ed. Institut für Marxismus-Leninismus beim Zentralkomitee der SED, East Berlin, 1966, iv.604–7.

193. Turner, *German Big Business*, 315–17.

194. Turner, *German Big Business*, 311–12.

195. Turner, *German Big Business*, 321–2.

196. Winkler, *Weimar*, 570–72; Turner, *German Big Business*, 324.

197. Papen, 227–8.

198. See Winkler, *Weimar*, 568.

199. Domarus, 175; Papen, 227; Winkler, *Weimar*, 569; see Goebbels, *Kaiserhof*, 235 (5 January 1933), *TBJG*, I.2, 328 (6 January 1933, unpubl.).

200. *Geschichte der deutschen Arbeiterbewegung*, iv. 604–7; reprinted in Deuerlein, *Aufstieg*, 411–14, here 412.

201. Deuerlein, *Aufstieg*, 412.

202. *TBJG*, I.2, 332 (10 January 1933, unpubl.).

203. Papen, 228; Deuerlein, *Aufstieg*, 412–13; Winkler, *Weimar*, 568.

204. Meissner, *Staatssekretär*, 261–2; Turner, *Hitler's Thirty Days to Power*, 50–51.

205. Ribbentrop, 22 and n.1.

206. Falter *et al.*, *Wahlen*, 96.

207. Stories advanced at the time, and often repeated in later accounts, of subventions from big business to finance the Lippe campaign have been shown to be wide of the mark. The campaign had to pay for itself. Higher entrance fees than normal were charged for meetings addressed by Hitler and other celebrities. Funds raised were immediately poured back into the campaign. Financial embarrassment in settling the claims of creditors and in raising money to rent halls for speakers was on more than one occasion only narrowly avoided. See Turner, *German Big Business*, 318 and 463 n.25.

208. Winkler, *Weimar*, 573. A full analysis of the campaign is provided by Jutta Ciolek-Kümper, *Wahlkampf in Lippe*, Munich, 1976; for Nazi propaganda in Lippe, see also Paul, *Aufstand der Bilder*, 109–10.

209. Beginning on 4 and ending on 14 January 1933: Domarus, 175–80; Ciolek-Kümper, 318–64. Nazi gains at the election were over-average in places where Hitler spoke (Ciolek-Kümper, 264).

210. Falter *et al.*, *Wahlen*, 96; Deuerlein, *Aufstieg*, 415; Winkler, *Weimar*, 574. Despite the saturation propaganda, the Lippe election is a clear indicator of the limits of Nazi penetration in a pluralist system. Recent empirical findings have confirmed the view that propaganda success relied upon prior ideological leanings in those susceptible to it. (See Dieter Ohr, *Nationalsozialistische Propaganda und Weimarer Wahlen. Empirische Analysen zur Wirkung von NSDAP-Versammlungen*, Opladen, 1997.)

211. See Goebbels's diary entry (unpubl.), for 16 January 1933: 'Party again on the forward march. So, it has paid off' (*TBJG*, I.2, 339).

212. Schleicher had, by the time of his cabinet meeting on 16 January, still not completely given up hope of winning over Strasser, whose supporters had likewise not finally given up. Their efforts, and news of Strasser meeting President Hindenburg, sowed great distrust in the minds of Hitler and his entourage (Turner, *Hitler's Thirty Days to Power*, 60–61).

213. Papen, 234; Winkler, *Weimar*, 571–2, 578–80, 606–7; Turner, *German Big Business*, 324.

214. Winkler, *Weimar*, 574–5.

215. Ribbentrop, 22–3. After consultations with Hitler, he had tried to arrange the meeting on one of the previous two days, but the respective movements of Hitler and Papen had made this impossible. Papen stated in his memoirs that he did not meet Hitler between 4 and 22 January (Papen, 236). Frau Ribbentrop's dictated notes show that there were two meetings in the interim, on 10 and 18 January (Ribbentrop, 22–3).

216. Ribbentrop, 23; Papen, 235.

217. *TBJG*, I.2, 346 (22 January 1932, unpubl.). Goebbels does not appear to have been informed about the meeting until two days later, on 24 January (*TBJG*, I.2, 349 (25 January 1933, unpubl.)).

218. Domarus, 181–2; *TBJG*, I.2, 348 (23 January 1932, unpubl.). Goebbels attributed Hitler's poor form to the arrogance of Frau Wessel, Horst's mother, on the anniversary of her son's murder (*TBJG*, I.2, 347–8).

219. Papen, 235.

220. Hans Otto Meissner and Harry Wilde, *Die Machtergreifung*, Stuttgart, 1958, 148ff., esp. 162–3; Domarus, 183 (who states, mistakenly, that the demands were the same; moreover, the Göring ministry was left undetermined). See also Winkler, *Weimar*, 580.

221. *TBJG*, I.2, 349 (25 January 1933, unpubl.).

222. Ribbentrop, 23.

223. Winkler, *Weimar*, 580. Otto Meissner, *Staatssekretär*, 263, makes no mention of this conversation in his brief account of the meeting at Ribbentrop's house. The version of his son, Hans Otto Meissner, and Harry Wilde, noting Oskar von Hindenburg's seemingly grudging admission that Hitler's many concessions and solemn promises made it difficult to refuse him the Chancellorship, derived, however, from Otto Meissner's recollection (Meissner-Wilde, 163, 291 n.37).

224. *TBJG*, I.2, 349 (25 January 1933, unpubl.).

225. Papen, 236; Winkler, *Weimar*, 581. For reasons not entirely clear, Schleicher had not considered putting to Hindenburg the suggestion of his Defence Ministry staff, on the advice to legal theorists, that a loophole in the Weimar Constitution might allow the cabinet, even after defeat in a vote of confidence, to remain in office indefinitely as a caretaker government unless the other parties could agree on an alternative Chancellor and government (Turner, *Hitler's Thirty Days to Power*, 118–21, 124–5).

226. Ribbentrop, 23.

227. Winkler, *Weimar*, 581–3, 587–9.

228. *Akten der Reichskanzlei. Das Kabinett von Schleicher*, ed. Anton Golecki, Boppard am Rhein, 1986, 306–11, Nr.71–2; Papen, 237–8; Winkler, *Weimar*, 584–6.

229. *Schulthess' Europäischer Geschichtskalender 1933*, Bd. 74, Munich, 1934, 28–30; *AdR, Kabinett von Schleicher*, 316–19, Nr.77. And see Winkler, *Weimar*, 586.

230. Papen, 239. And see *AdR, Kabinett von Schleicher*, 318.

231. Ribbentrop, 25.

232. Winkler, *Weimar*, 584.

233. Ribbentrop, 24–5.

234. Papen, 239; Winkler, *Weimar*, 589. In a third meeting, Fritz Schäffer, the head of the BVP, probably speaking on behalf of the Zentrum as well as his own party, was prepared to support a parliamentary government under Hitler. But, as earlier, this proposal had no chance of meeting the approval of the Nazi leader.

235. Papen, 239.

236. Ribbentrop, 25; Papen, 241: Hitler was told on 29 January that the President would not appoint him Reich Commissar for Prussia.

237. *AdR, Kabinett von Schleicher*, 318; Papen, 240; Winkler, *Weimar*, 589.

238. Papen, 240; Winkler, *Weimar*, 590.

239. Papen, 241; Deuerlein, *Aufstieg*, 417; Winkler, *Weimar*, 590–91.

240. *TBJG*, I.2, 355 (30 January 1933, unpubl.); 357 (31 January 1933, unpubl.).

241. Papen, 241.

242. Hubatsch, 347 (18 November 1932).

243. Theodor Duesterberg, *Der Stahlhelm und Hitler*, Wolfenbüttel/Hanover, 1949, 38–9. Support from the Stahlhelm, the conservative veterans' organization, was still not guaranteed. While Seldte had been won over, Duesterberg remained irked by earlier Nazi insults about his 'non-Aryan' background. His backing for the cabinet was only assured on the morning of 30 January, when Hitler expressed his regrets for the attacks on Duesterberg by his party and, with tears in his eyes, gave the Stahlhelm deputy leader his word that he had not instigated them (Duesterberg, 40; Winkler, *Weimar*, 592). It did not take Hugenberg long to realize the error of his ways. The very day after Hitler's appointment to the Chancellorship, he was reported as saying: 'Yesterday, I did the most stupid thing of my life. I joined forces with the greatest demagogue in world history' (cit. in Gerhard Ritter, *Carl Goerdeler und die deutsche Widerstandsbewegung*, Stuttgart, 1956, 64. And see Larry Eugene Jones, ' "The Greatest Stupidity of My Life". Alfred Hugenberg and the Formation of the Hitler Cabinet, January 1933', *Journal of Contemporary History*, 27 (1992), 63–87).

244. Papen, 242.

245. Lutz Graf Schwerin von Krosigk, *Es geschah in Deutschland*, Tübingen/Stuttgart, 1951, 147. To the arch-conservative opponent of the Nazis, Ewald von Kleist-

Schmenzin, who would later pay for his principled opposition with his life, Papen asserted that within two months he would have Hitler pushed into a corner. Kleist-Schmenzin was duly scathing at such a presumption (Bodo Scheurig, *Ewald von Kleist-Schmenzin. Ein Konservativer gegen Hitler*, Frankfurt am Main, 1994, 121).

246. *TBJG*, I.2, 355 (30 January 1933, unpubl.).

247. Ribbentrop, 26; Winkler, *Weimar*, 590–91.

248. *TBJG*, I.2, 355–6 (30 January 1933, unpubl.). Hitler still vividly recalled Alvensleben's news in his story of the takeover of power, told on 21 May 1942 in his 'Special Train' *en route* to Berlin (Picker, 364).

249. Papen, 242–3; Duesterberg, 39; Winkler, *Weimar*, 591–2.

250. Papen, 243–4; Duesterberg, 40–41; Meissner, *Staatssekretär*, 269–70; Winkler, *Weimar*, 592.

251. *AdR, Kabinett von Schleicher*, 322–3; Meissner, *Staatssekretär*, 270. Remarkably, it was the first time that the Finance Minister, Schwerin von Krosigk, had seen Hitler. Half an hour before arriving in the Reich Chancellery, he had thought Papen, not Hitler, was to be sworn in as Chancellor (*AdR, Kabinett von Schleicher*, 321–3. Krosigk, *Es geschah in Deutschland*, 193; Turner, *Hitler's Thirty Days to Power*, 156–7).

252. Meissner, *Staatssekretär*, 270; Papen 244; Hans Otto Meissner, *30. Januar 1933. Hitlers Machtergreifung*, Munich 1979, 275–6 (Hindenburg's reply – see 388 n.31 – apparently based upon a verbal account by Otto Meissner); Winkler, *Weimar*, 593.

253. *TBJG* I.2, 357 (31 January 1933, unpubl.).

254. For an example of intellectual underestimation of National Socialism, see Thomas Mann's comments on 12 January 1933 in a letter to the Prussian Education Minister, Adolf Grimme: 'The social and democratic Germany, I am firmly convinced, can trust in the fact that the present constellation is a passing one and that, despite everything, the future is on its side. The raging of nationalist passions is nothing more than a late and final flickering of an already burnt-out fire, a dying flare mistaken for a new glow of life' (Deuerlein, *Aufstieg*, 414).

255. See, for the landed élites, Wolfgang Zollitsch, 'Adel und adlige Machteliten in der Endphase der Weimarer Republik. Standespolitik und agrarische Interessen', in Winkler, *Staatskrise*, 239–56; Horst Gies, 'NSDAP und landwirtschaftliche Organisationen in der Endphase der Weimarer Republik', *VfZ*, 15 (1967), 341–76; Dieter Gessner, *Agrarverbände in der Weimarer Republik*, Düsseldorf, 1976; Gustavo Corni and Horst Gies, *Brot, Butter, Kanonen: Die Ernährungswirtschaft in Deutschland unter der Diktatur Hitlers*, Berlin, 1997, Part I. For the military élite, the argument has been most cogently advanced by Michael Geyer in his study, *Aufrüstung oder Sicherheit. Die Reichswehr in der Krise der Machtpolitik 1924–1936*, Wiesbaden, 1980, his more general survey, *Deutsche Rüstungspolitik 1860–1980*, Frankfurt am Main, 1984, 188–39, and his essays, 'Etudes in Political History: Reichswehr, NSDAP, and the Seizure of Power', in Peter D. Stachura (ed.), *The*

Nazi Machtergreifung, London, 1983, 101–23, and 'Professionals and Junkers: German Rearmament and Politics in the Weimar Republic', in Bessel and Feuchtwanger, 77–133.

256. See Turner, *German Big Business*, 318–28, for the stance of big business in late January 1933; also, Reinhard Neebe, *Großindustrie, Staat und NSDAP 1930– 1933*, Göttingen, 1981.

257. An attempt to use the 'Bonapartist' model of Karl Marx and Friedrich Engels to explain how Hitler gained power is advanced by Eberhard Jäckel, 'Wie kam Hitler an die Macht?', in Karl Dietrich Erdmann and Hagen Schulze (eds.), *Weimar. Selbstpreisgabe einer Demokratie*, Düsseldorf, 1980, 305–21.

258. See, for instance, the recognition of this by Friedrich Meinecke, *Die deutsche Katastrophe*, 3rd edn, Wiesbaden, 1947, esp. 11–12, 39–40.

259. See Mosse, *Crisis*, esp. Part One, for a thorough exploration of the strands of this consciousness.

260. See, esp., the influential work of David Blackbourn and Geoff Eley, *The Peculiarities of German History*, Oxford, 1984, and the debate on the 'Sonderweg' question: *Deutscher Sonderweg – Mythos oder Realität, Kolloquien des Instituts für Zeitgeschichte*, Munich/Vienna, 1982. The complexity of the differing continuities in German history which made National Socialism and a Hitler dictatorship possible – but by no means inevitable – is emphasized in a sophisticated analysis by Thomas Nipperdey, '1933 und Kontinuität der deutschen Geschichte', *Historische Zeitschrift*, 227 (1978), 86–111.

261. See Lothar Kettenacker, 'Sozialpsychologische Aspekte der Führer-Herrschaft', in Gerhard Hirschfeld and Lothar Kettenacker (eds.), *Der 'Führerstaat': Mythos und Realität. Studien zur Struktur und Politik des Dritten Reiches*, Stuttgart, 1981, 98– 132.

262. *Regensburger Anzeiger*, 31 January 1933.

263. *Gutachen des Instituts für Zeitgeschichte*, vol.1, Munich, 1958, 367 (no reference given).

CHAPTER II: THE MAKING OF THE DICTATOR

1. Jochmann, *Nationalsozialismus und Revolution*, 421.

2. Julius Leber, *Ein Mann geht seinen Weg*, Berlin, 1952, 90.

3. Josef and Ruth Becker (eds.), *Hitlers Machtergreifung. Dokumente vom Machtantritt Hitlers 30. Januar 1933 bis zur Besiegelung des Einparteienstaates 14. Juli 1933*, 2nd edn, Munich, 1992, 45, cit. *Schwäbische Volkszeitung*, 7 February 1933.

4. Becker, *Hitlers Machtergreifung*, 32.

5. Becker, *Hitlers Machtergreifung*, 34–5.

6. John Conway, *The Nazi Persecution of the Churches 1933–45*, London, 1968, 9.

7. H. Rößler, 'Erinnerungen an den Kirchenkampf in Coburg', *Jahrbuch der Coburger Landesstiftung* (1975), 155–6.

8. Theophil Wurm, *Erinnerungen aus meinem Leben*, Stuttgart, 1953, 84.

9. Cit. in Klaus Scholder, *Die Kirchen und das Dritte Reich*, Frankfurt am Main/Berlin/Vienna, 1977, i.279–80.

10. *DBFP*, 2nd Ser., iv.401.

11. StA München, GS Ebersberg, 11 February 1933; see also BHStA, MA 106672, RPvNB/OP, 3 February 1933.

12. *Münchner Neueste Nachrichten*, 31 January 1933. The journalist was Erwein Freiherr von Aretin, a monarchist who was to be taken into 'protective custody' a few weeks later.

13. Hanfstaengl, *15 Jahre*, 288; *TBJG*, I.2, 357 (31 January 1933, unpubl.).

14. See Hoffmann, 69, for Hitler's praise and surprise at Goebbels's ability to stage it at such short notice.

15. *TBJG*, I.2, 358 (31 January 1933). The British Ambassador reported: 'During the demonstration Herr Göring, the President of the Reichstag, took possession of the microphone and after delivering a speech of the usual turgid kind handed the instrument to his followers. Berlin radio listeners were consequently deprived of their evening's entertainment and treated to an absurdly sentimental account of the torchlight procession and the final triumph of the National Socialist movement' (*DBFP*, 2nd Ser., iv.402).

16. *TBJG*, I.2, 358, 31 January 1933; *DBFP*, 2nd Ser., iv.402.

17. See Melita Maschmann, *Fazit. Mein Weg in der Hitler-Jugend*, 5th paperback edn, Munich, 1983, 7–9; André François-Poncet, *Souvenirs d'une ambassade à Berlin, Septembre 1931–Octobre 1938*, Paris, 1946, 70; Frank, 111; Harry Graf Kessler, *Tagebücher 1918–1937*, Frankfurt am Main, 1961, 704.

18. Maschmann, 8, 17–19.

19. Hans-Jochen Gamm, *Der Flüsterwitz im Dritten Reich*, Munich, 1963, 8. Sir Horace Rumbold remarked that the President normally retired at 7 p.m. but stood at his window until after midnight, saluting the cheering crowd (*DBFP*, 2nd Ser., iv.401). (Actually, as photos show, the President was seated, not standing. See the photo in Hans Otto Meissner, *30.Januar 1933. Hitlers Machtergreifung*, Munich, 1979, between 178 and 179.)

20. Papen, 264.

21. Papen, 264; *TBJG*, 358 (31 January 1933); Frank, 111.

22. Papen, 264.

23. Norbert Frei, ' "Machtergreifung". Anmerkungen zu einem historischen Begriff ', *VfZ*, 31 (1983), 136–45, here 139, 142.

24. *Monologe*, 155; Frei, ' "Machtergreifung" ', 136.

25. Frei, ' "Machtergreifung" ', esp. 141–2. '*Machtergreifung*' ('seizure of power') appears, from Frei's findings (143), to have been more a product of the historical writing of the 1950s than a term widely used during the Third Reich itself.

26. Papen, 264.

27. See Nipperdey, '1933 und Kontinuität der deutschen Geschichte', esp. 94–101. As Nipperdey points out (93), there were also important and long-standing counter-

continuities in German history – such as ideas of democracy and liberalism – that suffered an abrupt and lengthy break in 1933.

28. Nipperdey, '1933 und Kontinuität der deutschen Geschichte', 100–101.

29. See Richard Bessel, '1933: A Failed Counter-Revolution', in E. E. Riche (ed.), *Revolution and Counter Revolution*, Oxford, 1991, 109–227, esp. 120–21; and Martin Broszat *et al.* (eds.), *Deutschlands Weg in die Diktatur*, Berlin, 1983, 95 (comment of Richard Löwenthal). See also Horst Möller, 'Die nationalsozialistische Machtergreifung. Konterrevolution oder Revolution?', *VfZ*, 31 (1983), 25–51; Jeremy Noakes, 'Nazism and Revolution', in Noel O'Sullivan (ed.), *Revolutionary Theory and Political Reality*, London, 1983, 73–100; and for Hitler's views on revolution, Zitelmann, *Hitler. Selbstverständnis eines Revolutionärs*, 44–86.

30. *Akten der Reichskanzlei. Die Regierung Hitler. Teil I: 1933/34*, ed. Karl-Heinz Minuth, 2 vols., Boppard am Rhein, 1983, i.XVII.

31. Lutz Schwerin von Krosigk, *Staatsbankrott*, Göttingen, 1974, 185; Krosigk, *Es geschah*, 199; see also Papen, 260, and John L. Heinemann, *Hitler's First Foreign Minister*, Berkeley, 1979, 65.

32. *AdR, Reg. Hitler*, 1–4.

33. See Rudolf Morsey, 'Die deutsche Zentrumspartei' in Matthias and Morsey, *Ende der Parteien*, 281–453, here 340–43; and Rudolf Morsey, 'Hitlers Verhandlungen mit der Zentrumsführung am 31. Januar 1933', *VfZ*, 9 (1961), 182–94. See also Karl Dietrich Bracher, Gerhard Schulz and Wolfgang Sauer, *Die nationalsozialistische Machtergreifung* (1960), paperback edn, Frankfurt am Main/Berlin/Vienna, 3 vols., 1974, i. 85.

34. Bracher *et al.*, *Machtergreifung*, i.89.

35. Brüning, *Memoiren*, ii.684; *AdR, Reg. Hitler*, 2. Franz Gürtner was only confirmed in his office as Reich Justice Minister on 2 February. But his retention had already been agreed with the Reich President on 29 January. The delay was solely owing to Hitler's wish to use the occupancy of the Reich Ministry of Justice as a bargaining card in his negotiations with the Zentrum (Lothar Gruchmann, *Justiz im Dritten Reich 1933–1940. Anpassung und Unterwerfung in der Ära Gürtner*, 2nd edn, Munich, 1990, 9–10, 64).

36. *AdR, Reg. Hitler*, 5–7 and n.6; Becker, *Hitlers Machtergreifung*, 34–5.

37. Bracher *et al.*, *Machtergreifung*, i.85.

38. *AdR, Reg. Hitler*, 6. Another conservative, Hugenberg pressed to depose the 'so-called sovereignty government of Braun' in Prussia as soon as possible. State Secretary Meissner took this up and went on to propose the dissolution of the Prussian Landtag, if necessary by use of Article 48, since 'it is in any event necessary that the so-called sovereignty government of Braun soon disappears' (*AdR, Reg. Hitler*, 7–8 and n.10). (A decision of the Supreme Court – Staatsgerichtshof – of 25 October 1932 had upheld the removal of the Prussian government that had taken place on 20 July 1932, but ruled that the Prussian government still had the right to represent the Prussian state in dealings with the Reich and other states.)

39. Meissner, *Staatssekretär*, 225; Bracher *et al.*, *Machtergreifung*, i.86; Meissner and Wilde, *Machtergreifung*, 197–8.

40. A point made by Bracher *et al.*, *Machtergreifung*, i.86.

41. As regards economic recovery, Hitler's first move was to back the initiative to suspend compulsory farm sales, pointing to the necessity of satisfying the wishes of at least a part of the nation at first (*AdR, Reg. Hitler*, 7–8, 11).

42. *AdR, Reg. Hitler*, 9 and n.3.

43. *AdR, Reg. Hitler*, 29 and n.7, 30, 34–5 and n.7.

44. *AdR, Reg. Hitler*, 15.

45. Papen, 265.

46. Heinz Höhne, *Die Zeit der Illusionen. Hitler und die Anfänge des 3. Reiches 1933 bis 1936*, Düsseldorf/Vienna/New York, 1991, 13–14; see also Schacht, 300: 'I happened to be in the room with a mere handful of his entourage when he made his first speech to the German people over the radio . . . I had the impression that the burden of his new responsibilities weighed heavily upon him. At this moment he felt clearly what it meant to be transferred from the propaganda ranks of the Opposition to a post of Government responsibility.'

47. Papen, 265.

48. Domarus, 191–4.

49. Domarus, 193.

50. Thilo Vogelsang, 'Neue Dokumente zur Geschichte der Reichswehr 1930–1933', *VfZ*, 2 (1954), 434, n.127; Bracher *et al.*, *Machtergreifung*, i.88; Höhne, *Zeit der Illusionen*, 55. Earlier in the day, Blomberg had met District Commanders at the Reichswehr Ministry. Vogelsang links the Hammerstein invitation with this earlier meeting as an attempt to introduce Hitler to leading officers. He inclines to follow John W. Wheeler-Bennett, *The Nemesis of Power. The German Army in Politics*, London, 1953, 291, in seeing it as a response to Hitler's unannounced visits to a number of Berlin barracks on the morning of 31 January, which had caused a ripple of alarm as a reminder, it seemed, of the spirit of 1918. A different reason for Hammerstein's home as the venue and setting – a sixtieth birthday party for Neurath – is given by Wolfgang Sauer, Bracher *et al.*, *Machtergreifung*, iii.55, 387 n.107. The two reasons are, perhaps, complementary rather than contradictory.

51. Vogelsang, 'Neue Dokumente', 434–5 (notes of General Liebmann). According to the notes of Major von Mellenthin, also present at the meeting, Hitler's posed alternatives were markets or colonies, and he favoured the latter (cit. Höhne, *Zeit der Illusionen*, 55). It seems likely, however, that Mellenthin misinterpreted Hitler's reference to 'living-space' as meaning 'colonies'.

52. Bracher *et al.*, *Machtergreifung*, iii.75–6, 393 n.183–91; Höhne, *Zeit der Illusionen*, 56.

53. In a memorandum of 6 March 1926, Otto Stülpnagel, Abteilungschef in the Truppenamt, had spoken of the build-up of the armed forces as the basis of expansionism aimed at recovering Germany's territories lost in the Versailles Treaty, re-establishing its European supremacy (at the expense of France), and preparing

for ultimate global struggle for domination against the Anglo-Saxon powers (Klaus-Jürgen Müller, 'Deutsche Militär-Elite in der Vorgeschichte des Zweiten Weltkrieges', in Martin Broszat and Klaus Schwabe (eds.), *Deutsche Eliten und der Weg in den Zweiten Weltkrieg*, Munich, 1989, 226–90, here 246–7).

54. Vogelsang, 'Neue Dokumente', 432–4; Klaus-Jürgen Müller, *Armee und Drittes Reich 1933–1939. Darstellung und Dokumentation*, Paderborn, 1987, 158–9. The emotional and impressionable Blomberg had been completely won over to Hitler (Klaus-Jürgen Müller, *Das Heer und Hitler. Armee und nationalsozialistisches Regime 1933–1940*, (1969) 2nd edn, Stuttgart, 1988, 51).

55. Geyer, 'Reichswehr, NSDAP, and the Seizure of Power', 118.

56. Geyer, 'Reichswehr, NSDAP, and the Seizure of Power', 111; and Geyer, 'Professionals and Junkers', esp. 86–7, 116–23.

57. Klaus-Jürgen Müller, *Armee, Politik und Gesellschaft in Deutschland 1933–1945*, Paderborn, 1979, 11–33; Wilhelm Deist, *The Wehrmacht and German Rearmament*, London, 1981, ch.1; Geyer, 'Reichswehr, NSDAP, and the Seizure of Power', 101–23.

58. Müller, *Heer*, 53. Reichenau had first met Hitler, for a lengthy private talk, in spring 1932. The colonel had evidently seen in Hitler and his Movement the potential to instigate the revolutionary renewal that he himself was seeking. Hitler, for his part, had recognized Reichenau's instinctive backing for his radical approach. Aware of Reichenau's sympathies (and in reply to a request for clarification about his stance to the defence of East Prussia in the event of Polish aggression), Hitler had, in December 1932, overcome his normal aversion to letter-writing to compose a lengthy statement of the need for a 'deep process of regeneration', destruction of Marxism 'down to its complete extermination', and 'general psychological, ethical, and moral rearmament of the nation based on this new ideological unity' as the framework for national defence (Thilo Vogelsang, 'Hitlers Brief an Reichenau vom 4. Dezember 1932', *VfZ*, 7 (1959), 429–37, here esp. 437).

59. *DRZW*, i.404; Deist, *Wehrmacht*, 26.

60. Cit. Vogelsang, 'Hitlers Brief an Reichenau', 433; Bracher *et al.*, *Machtergreifung*, iii.68; Müller, *Armee*, 160; Müller, *Heer*, 61ff. for Blomberg's understanding of keeping the army out of politics.

61. Bracher *et al.*, *Machtergreifung*, iii.68. The officer was Oberstleutnant Ott.

62. *AdR, Reg. Hitler*, 50–51.

63. *AdR, Reg. Hitler*, 62–3; see *DRZW*, i.234.

64. See, for the above, *DRZW*, i.234–5, 404–5; Geyer, *Rüstungspolitik*, 140; Höhne, *Zeit der Illusionen*, 58.

65. *IMT*, xxxvi.586, Doc. 611–EC.

66. Deist, *Wehrmacht*, 24–6; Müller, *Heer*; Bracher *et al.*, *Machtergreifung*, iii.41ff; *DRZW*, i.403; Peter Hüttenberger, 'Nationalsozialistische Polykratie', *Geschichte und Gesellschaft*, 2 (1976), 417–42, here 423–5.

67. Müller, *Armee, Politik und Gesellschaft*, 44–5.

68. Dietmar Petzina, *Die deutsche Wirtschaft in der Zwischenkriegszeit*, Wiesbaden,

1977, 114—15; Dieter Petzina, 'Hauptprobleme der deutschen Wirtschaft 1932—1933', *VfZ*, 15 (1967), 18—55, here 41—3, 53—5; Gustavo Corni, *Hitler and the Peasants*, New York/Oxford/Munich, 1990, 41ff; Turner, *German Big Business*, 328.

69. For the meeting, see Turner, *German Big Business*, 328.

70. *IMT*, xxxv.42—7, Doc. 203—D.

71. *IMT*, xxv.48, Doc. 204—D.

72. *IMT*, xxxv.47—8, Doc. 203—D.

73. Turner, *German Big Business*, 330—31. At the cabinet meeting on 2 February, Frick had raised the question of subsidizing election propaganda of the government to the tune of a million Reich Marks. Objections were raised by Krosigk, the Finance Minister, and upheld by Hitler. At a subsequent cabinet meeting, on 21 February, it was, however, accepted that the Reichspost could be used to send out propaganda material (*AdR, Reg. Hitler*, 30—31, 102).

74. Turner, *German Big Business*, 332.

75. See Turner, *German Big Business*, 333—9.

76. Based on Turner, *German Big Business*, 71—83; Henry Ashby Turner, 'Hitlers Einstellung zu Wirtschaft und Gesellschaft vor 1933', *Geschichte und Gesellschaft*, 2 (1976), 89—117; Avraham Barkai, 'Sozialdarwinismus und Antiliberalismus in Hitlers Wirtschaftskonzept', *Geschichte und Gesellschaft*, 3 (1977), 406—17; James, *The German Slump*, 345—54; see also Avraham Barkai, *Das Wirtschaftssystem des Nationalsozialismus*, Fischer edn, Frankfurt am Main, 1988, ch.1, and Zitelmann, *Hitler. Selbstverständnis eines Revolutionärs*, ch.4, for Hitler's social and economic ideas.

77. James, *The German Slump*, 344.

78. Höhne, *Zeit der Illusionen*, 109—13, here 113.

79. Schacht, 317—19; Höhne, *Zeit der Illusionen*, 131—2; Richard J. Overy, *War and Economy in the Third Reich*, Oxford, 1994, 56. Following legislation brought in at the time of the currency stabilization in 1924, there were firm restrictions on the government's scope for printing money. The discount bills — greatly extended under Schacht — were a way of getting round such restrictions.

80. Richard J. Overy, *The Nazi Economic Recovery*, 2nd edn, Cambridge, 1996, 37.

81. Barkai, *Das Wirtschaftssystem des Nationalsozialismus*, 151; James, *The German Slump*, 344; Overy, *War and Economy*, 60.

82. Domarus, 208—9; Höhne, *Zeit der Illusionen*, 59.

83. Cit. Heidrun Edelmann, *Vom Luxusgut zum Gebrauchsgegenstand. Die Geschichte der Verbreitung von Personenkraftwagen in Deutschland*, Frankfurt am Main, 1989, 173.

84. *AdR, Reg. Hitler*, xliii; Edelmann, 173.

85. Edelmann, 189 n.141; Höhne, *Zeit der Illusionen* 62—3.

86. Hansjoachim Henning, 'Kraftfahrzeugindustrie und Autobahn in der Wirtschaftspolitik des Nationalsozialismus 1933 bis 1936', *Vierteljahrsschrift für Sozial- und Wirtschaftsgeschichte*, 65 (1978), 217—42, here, esp., 228.

87. *AdR, Reg. Hitler*, xliii. For Todt's contribution to motorway construction, see Franz W. Seidler, *Fritz Todt. Baumeister des Dritten Reiches*, Munich/Berlin, 1986, Part 3, here 97ff.

88. Kurt Kaftan, *Der Kampf um die Autobahnen*, Berlin, 1955, 81–3; and see Höhne, *Zeit der Illusionen*, 60, 62–3.

89. Höhne, *Zeit der Illusionen*, 59, 62. For Hitler's personal interest in cars, and his friendship with Jakob Werlin of Mercedes, see Overy, *War and Economy*, 72 n.17.

90. Höhne, *Zeit der Illusionen*, 60, cit. *VB*, 12–13 February 1933.

91. Hans Mommsen, *Das Volkswagenwerk und seine Arbeiter im Dritten Reich*, Düsseldorf, 1996, 56–60.

92. Henning, 226 n.37.

93. Henning, 221–7.

94. See Overy, *War and Economy*, 70–71.

95. *AdR, Reg. Hitler*, xliii.

96. *AdR, Reg. Hitler*, xliii–v. In fact, far more of the expenditure went on ordinary roads than motorways. (See Overy, *War and Economy*, 60, 85.)

97. Edelmann, 174–5. The motorways were at first not a major factor in the reduction of unemployment (Höhne, *Zeit der Illusionen*, 129–31).

98. Helmut Heiber, *Goebbels-Reden, Bd.1: 1932–1939*, Düsseldorf, 1971, 67–70 (with Heiber's editorial interpolations referring to the background acoustics in brackets); reprinted in Becker, *Hitlers Machtergreifung*, 57–60, here 58–9.

99. Domarus, 204–8.

100. *TBJG*, I.2, 371 (11 February 1933).

101. Erich Ebermayer, *Denn heute gehört uns Deutschland*, Hamburg/Vienna, 1959, 21.

102. Jochmann, *Nationalsozialismus und Revolution*, 424–5.

103. Becker, *Hitlers Machtergreifung*, 74–5; Martin Broszat, *Der Staat Hitlers. Grundlegung und Entwicklung seiner inneren Verfassung*, Munich, 1969, 93.

104. Broszat, *Der Staat Hitlers*, 90–95.

105. Papen, 260.

106. Domarus, 213; Broszat, *Der Staat Hitlers*, 95.

107. Domarus, 210–11; Broszat, *Der Staat Hitlers*, 98.

108. BHStA, MA 106672, RPvNB/OP, 20 February 1933.

109. Staatsarchiv München, LRA 76887, GS Anzing, 24 February 1933.

110. Broszat, *Der Staat Hitlers*, 99.

111. Hans Mommsen, 'Van der Lubbes Weg in den Reichstag – der Ablauf der Ereignisse', in Uwe Backes *et al.*, *Reichstagsbrand. Aufklärung einer historischen Legende*, Munich/Zurich, 1986, 33–57, here 33–42.

112. The question of who set the Reichstag ablaze has provoked the most rancorous of disputes. The Nazi version that it was a Communist plot was widely disbelieved at the time by critical observers and was not even convincing enough to secure the conviction of the leading Communists tried at the show trial at the supreme Reich Court in Leipzig in autumn 1933. The view that the Nazis, with most to gain, had

set fire to the Reichstag themselves was immediately given wide currency among diplomats and foreign journalists, and in liberal circles in Germany (see François-Poncet, 94–5). Nazi authorship, as put forward in Communist counter-propaganda, orchestrated by Willi Münzenberg, in *The Brown Book of the Hitler Terror and the Burning of the Reichstag*, Paris, 1933, carried the day for a long time. But the findings of Fritz Tobias in the 1960s, collected in his extensive evaluation and documentation (*Der Reichstagsbrand. Legende und Wirklichkeit*, Rastatt/Baden, 1962), supported by the scholarly analysis of Hans Mommsen ('Der Reichstagsbrand und seine politischen Folgen', *VfZ*, 12 (1964), 351–413), that Marinus van der Lubbe acted alone, are compelling and are now widely accepted, though not by Klaus P. Fischer, *Nazi Germany: A New History*, London, 1995, 272. The counter-claims of the Luxemburg Committee (see Walther Hofer *et al.* (eds.), *Der Reichstagsbrand. Eine wissenschaftliche Dokumentation*, 2 vols., Berlin, 1972, Munich, 1978), that the Nazis were indeed the perpetrators, are regarded by most experts as flawed. The consequences of the Reichstag fire were, of course, always more important than the identity of whoever instigated the blaze. But the question of authorship was nevertheless of significance, since it revolved around the question of whether the Nazis were following through carefully laid plans to institute totalitarian rule, or whether they were improvising reactions to events they had not expected. (See, for an assessment and re-evaluation of the debate, Backes *et al.*, *Reichstagsbrand*.)

113. Hanfstaengl, *15 Jahre*, 291–5.

114. Goebbels, *Kaiserhof*, 269–70 (27 February 1933), *TBJG*, I.2, 383.

115. Heiden, *Führer*, 434–7; Bracher *et al.*, *Machtergreifung*, i.123–4.

116. Mommsen, 'Van der Lubbes Weg', 44–7.

117. Mommsen 'Van der Lubbes Weg', 40–41.

118. Mommsen 'Der Reichstagsbrand', 382–3.

119. Mommsen 'Van der Lubbes Weg', 47–8; Mommsen, 'Der Reichstagsbrand', 384. Hitler appears at first, however, to have been less than wholly certain that it was the work of the Communists (Sefton Delmer, *Trail Sinister*, London, 1961, 187–9).

120. Rudolf Diels, *Lucifer ante Portas*, Stuttgart, 1950, 194; Mommsen, 'Der Reichstagsbrand', 116.

121. Delmer, *Trail*, 189; Mommsen, 'Der Reichstagsbrand', 384.

122. Diels, 194–5; Mommsen, 'Der Reichstagsbrand', 362, 385 and n.143. Göring's order to arrest all Social Democrat functionaries was omitted when the telex was transmitted.

123. *TBJG*, I.2, 383 (27 February 1933), gives the opposite impression, though this version of his diaries was the published account (Goebbels, *Kaiserhof*, 270).

124. Diels, 195; Mommsen, 'Der Reichstagsbrand', 362, 386.

125. *TBJG*, I.2, 383 (Goebbels, *Kaiserhof*, 270); Mommsen, 'Der Reichstagsbrand', 390.

126. Mommsen, 'Der Reichstagsbrand', 389–90.

127. Mommsen 'Van der Lubbes Weg', 51; *AdR, Reg. Hitler*, 130 and n.12: Frick

expressly stated that he had based the decree on Papen's decree for the 'Restoration of Public Security and Order in Greater Berlin and the Province of Brandenburg', of 20 July 1932.

128. Mommsen 'Van der Lubbes Weg', 51–3.

129. *AdR, Reg. Hitler*, 130–31.

130. *RGBl*, 1933. I. Nr.17, 83.

131. *AdR, Reg. Hitler*, 128.

132. See e.g. Kessler, *Tagebücher*, 710.

133. Hans-Norbert Burkert, Klaus Matußek and Wolfgang Wippermann, '*Machtergreifung' Berlin 1933*, Berlin, 1982, 65.

134. Hans Buchheim *et al.*, *Anatomie des SS-Staates*, 2 vols., Olten/Freiburg im Breisgau, 1965, ii.20.

135. *Miesbacher Anzeiger*, 2 March 1933.

136. *VB*, 2 March 1933; and see Bracher *et al.*, *Machtergreifung*, i.124–5, 515 n.17.

137. Jochmann, *Natonalsozialismus und Revolution*, 427–8.

138. Jochmann, *Nationalsozialismus und Revolution*, 427.

139. Jochmann, *Nationalsozialismus und Revolution*, 426.

140. Domarus, 216–17; Goebbels, *Kaiserhof*, 273–4 (4 March 1933), *TBJG*, I.2, 386.

141. Falter *et al.*, *Wahlen*, 44. (See the analysis in Bracher *et al.*, *Machtergreifung*, i.143–90.)

142. Goebbels, *Kaiserhof*, 275 (5 March 1933), *TBJG*, I.2, 387.

143. Martin H. Sommerfeld, *Ich war dabei. Die Verschwörung der Dämonen 1933–1939. Ein Augenzeugenbericht*, Darmstadt, 1949, 32.

144. Falter *et al.*, *Wahlen*, 44; Falter, *Hitlers Wähler*, 111–12.

145. Falter *et al.*, *Wahlen*, 74–5. And see Falter, *Hitlers Wähler*, 186–8. In Catholic rural districts of Bavaria, a double or even trebling of the Nazi vote was common (Hagmann, 12–27, and Thränhardt, 181–3).

146. Broszat, *Der Staat Hitlers*, 133–4. However, Hitler was not passive. The decision to extend the 'coordination' to Bavaria was taken in his presence on 8 March. Four days later he flew to Munich to discuss 'the most pressing Bavarian matters' with party leaders (Goebbels, *Kaiserhof*, 277 (8 March 1933), 280 (12 March 1933), *TBJG*, I.2, 389, 391).

147. Above based on Broszat, *Der Staat Hitlers*, 130–40; Bracher *et al.*, *Machtergreifung*, i.190–202.

148. *AdR, Reg. Hitler*, 188–92.

149. *AdR, Reg. Hitler*, 204–8; here 207.

150. Domarus, 219.

151. Domarus, 221.

152. *AdR, Reg. Hitler*, 190.

153. Martin Broszat, Elke Fröhlich and Falk Wiesemann (eds.), *Bayern in der NS-Zeit*, vol.1, Munich, 1977, 209 n.30, 240–41.

154. BHStA, MA 106682, RPvS, 6 April 1933; MA 106680, RPvUF, 20 April 1933. The extent to which, nevertheless, the police depended upon denunciations has been

emphasized – based on material drawn largely from Lower Franconia – by Robert Gellately, 'The Gestapo and German Society: Political Denunciation in the Gestapo Case Files', *Journal of Modern History*, 60 (1988), 654–94, and *The Gestapo and German Society. Enforcing Racial Policy 1933–1945*, Oxford, 1990, ch.5.

155. Becker, *Hitlers Machtergreifung*, 149–50.

156. Tony Barta, 'Living in Dachau, 1900–1950', unpublished paper, 14.

157. François-Poncet, 103–7; Ebermayer, 45–7; Bracher *et al.*, *Machtergreifung*, i.212; Höhne, *Zeit der Illusionen*, 74; Hans-Ulrich Thamer, *Verführung und Gewalt. Deutschland 1933–1945*, Berlin, 1986, 270–72; Klaus-Jürgen Müller, 'Der Tag von Potsdam und das Verhältnis der preußisch-deutschen Militär-Elite zum National-sozialismus', in Bernhard Kröner (ed.), *Potsdam – Stadt, Armee, Residenz*, Frankfurt am Main/Berlin, 1993, 435–49, here 435, 439, 448.

158. AdR, *Reg. Hitler*, 157–8.

159. Müller, 'Der Tag von Potsdam', 435.

160. Goebbels, *Kaiserhof*, 283–4 (16–19 March 1933), *TBJG*, I.2, 393–5. For Goebbels's own description of the day's events: *TBJG*, I.2, 395–6 (Goebbels, *Kaiserhof*, 285–6, 22 March 1933).

161. Müller, 'Der Tag von Potsdam', 435–8; Werner Freitag, 'Nationale Mythen und kirchliches Heil: Der "Tag von Potsdam"', *Westfälische Forschungen*, 41 (1991), 379–430, provides a good account of the ritualistic nature of the proceedings (esp. 389–404), and emphasizes their symbolic significance, in particular, for the Protestant Church through the express linkage of religious motifs and the glorifica-tion of the Prussian-German state (see esp. 427–30).

162. Domarus, 227–8.

163. Ebermayer, 46.

164. Müller, 'Der Tag von Potsdam', 438.

165. Domarus, 228.

166. Bracher *et al.*, *Machtergreifung*, i.213–15.

167. AdR, *Reg. Hitler*, 160.

168. AdR, *Reg. Hitler*, 213–14, 216.

169. AdR, *Reg. Hitler*, 239.

170. AdR, *Reg. Hitler*, 239–40.

171. Bracher *et al.*, *Machtergreifung*, i.221–4. See also, on the genesis of the Enabling Act, Hans Schneider, 'Das Ermächtigungsgesetz vom 24. März 1933. Bericht über das Zustandekommen und die Anwendung des Gesetzes', *VfZ*, 1 (1953), 197–221.

172. Domarus, 229–37; Rudolf Morsey (ed.), *Das 'Ermächtigungsgesetz' vom 24. März 1933*, Düsseldorf, 1992, 55–62; Bracher *et al.*, *Machtergreifung*, i.229–33.

173. Josef Becker, 'Zentrum und Ermächtigungsgesetz', *VfZ*, 9 (1961), 208–10; Morsey, 'Ermächtigungsgesetz', 63, 69–71.

174. Domarus, 239–41; Morsey, 'Ermächtigungsgesetz', 64–6.

175. Domarus, 242–6; Morsey, 'Ermächtigungsgesetz', 66–9. See Ebermayer, 48, for the impact Hitler's reply made on one critic: he thought Hitler had 'ripped poor Wels apart' (*Dann zerriß er den armen Wels förmlich in der Luft*).

176. Becker, *Hitlers Machtergreifung*, 176–7; Domarus, 246–7; Morsey, 'Ermächtigungsgesetz', 69–75; Bracher *et al.*, *Machtergreifung*, i.234–5.

177. *RGBl*, 1933, Teil I, Nr.25, S.141. Its duration was four years. But in 1937 it was renewed without discussion, as it was in 1939, and, finally – without limits on its duration – by Führer decree on 10 May 1943 (Broszat, *Der Staat Hitlers*, 117 and note).

178. *RGBl*, 1933, Teil I. Nr.33, S.173; Broszat, *Der Staat Hitlers*, 143.

179. AdR, *Reg. Hitler*, 273.

180. *RGBl*, 1933, Teil I. Nr.33, S.173; Broszat, *Der Staat Hitlers*, 143.

181. Broszat, *Der Staat Hitlers*, 144–50.

182. Peter Diehl-Thiele, *Partei und Staat im Dritten Reich. Untersuchungen zum Verhältnis von NSDAP und allgemeiner innerer Staatsverwaltung*, Munich, 1969, 61–9.

183. Broszat, *Der Staat Hitlers*, 150.

184. Broszat, *Der Staat Hitlers*, 153.

185. Broszat, *Der Staat Hitlers*, 145.

186. Alfred Kube, *Pour le mérite und Hakenkreuz. Hermann Göring im Dritten Reich*, Munich, 1986, 31–3; Höhne, *Zeit der Illusionen*, 96–7.

187. For the term, see Hans Mommsen, 'Kumulative Radikalisierung und Selbstzerstörung des Regimes', *Meyers Enzyklopädisches Lexikon, Bd.16*, Mannheim, 1976, 785–90.

188. Domarus 219; Broszat, *Der Staat Hitlers*, 249.

189. Höhne, *Zeit der Illusionen*, 84–5; for 'Einzelaktionen', see *Die Lage der Juden in Deutschland 1933. Das Schwarzbuch – Tatsachen und Dokumente*, ed. Comité des Délégations Juives, Paris, 1934, repr. Frankfurt am Main/Berlin/Vienna, 1983, 93ff.

190. *Die Lage der Juden*, 495–6.

191. Walter Tausk, *Breslauer Tagebuch 1933–1940*, East Berlin, 1975, 32–7.

192. *Die Lage der Juden*, 496.

193. See Höhne, *Zeit der Illusionen*, 76–9.

194. Hans Mommsen, 'Die Realisierung des Utopischen: Die "Endlösung der Judenfrage" im "Dritten Reich"', *Geschichte und Gesellschaft*, 9 (1983), 381–420, here 390. See also Genschel, 46–7; Höhne, *Zeit der Illusionen*, 86–7.

195. Höhne, *Zeit der Illusionen*, 87.

196. Goebbels, *Kaiserhof*, 288 (26 March 1933), *TBJG*, I.2, 398.

197. AdR, *Reg. Hitler*, 271 and n.3; Domarus, 248–51.

198. Höhne, *Zeit der Illusionen*, 87–8.

199. Jürgen Hagemann, *Die Presselenkung im Dritten Reich*, Bonn, 1970, 139 n.2; Uwe Dietrich Adam, *Judenpolitik im Dritten Reich*, Düsseldorf, 1972, 63 n.196.

200. AdR, *Reg. Hitler*, 277.

201. Höhne, *Zeit der Illusionen*, 91.

202. AdR, *Reg. Hitler*, 277.

203. Goebbels, *Kaiserhof*, 290 (31 March 1933), *TBJG*, 400; Höhne, *Zeit der Illusionen*, 91–2.

204. Schleunes, *The Twisted Road to Auschwitz*, 1970, 87.

205. Goebbels, *Kaiserhof*, 291–2 (1–2 April 1933), *TBJG*, 400–401; Höhne, *Zeit der Illusionen*, 92–3; *Die Lage der Juden*, 292–314; Rumbold report of 5 April 1933 in *DBFP*, V, No.22, 24–5, No.30, 38–44.

206. Tausk, 52; Schleunes, 88–9.

207. Tausk, 58; Allen, 219; Höhne, *Zeit der Illusionen*, 92–3.

208. Allen, 220–21. As Gay, 'In Deutschland zu Hause', 32–3, points out, however, many Jews continued to harbour the fateful illusion that the antisemitic whirlwind would blow itself out; that what was happening to them was something not typical of Germans, and would be eventually overcome by the strong civilizing traditions of the German culture which they shared with their non-Jewish neighbours.

209. Schleunes, 88.

210. Adam, 61 and n.190, 63–71; Schleunes, 101–3. And see Hans Mommsen, *Beamtentum im Dritten Reich*, Stuttgart, 1966, 48–53 for the background to the 'Aryan Paragraph' in the Civil Service Law of 7 April 1933.

211. Erich Matthias, 'Die Sozialdemokratische Partei Deutschlands', in Matthias and Morsey, *Das Ende der Parteien*, 101–278, here 177–8.

212. Matthias, 178–80.

213. Höhne, *Zeit der Illusionen*, 101–2, 105–7; Thamer, 284–6; Bracher *et al.*, *Machtergreifung*, i.254–9.

214. Domarus, 259–64.

215. Höhne, *Zeit der Illusionen*, 105.

216. On the formation of the Labour Front see Ronald Smelser, *Robert Ley: Hitler's Labor Front Leader*, Oxford/New York/Hamburg, 1988, ch.5.

217. Timothy W. Mason, *Arbeiterklasse und Volksgemeinschaft. Dokumente und Materialien zur deutschen Arbeiterpolitik 1936–1939*, Opladen, 1975, 78–81. The NSBO had effectively lost all influence by the turn of the year 1933–4, though was eventually extinguished only in mid-1934.

218. Domarus, 270–79.

219. Broszat, *Der Staat Hitlers*, 119–20; Thamer, 286–7.

220. Broszat, *Der Staat Hitlers*, 121–3; Höhne, *Zeit der Illusionen*, 114–15.

221. Hans Müller, *Katholische Kirche und Nationalsozialismus*, Munich, 1965, 88–9.

222. Broszat, *Der Staat Hitlers*, 123–6; Thamer, 289–90.

223. *RGBl*, 1933, Teil I, Nr.81, S.479; Broszat, *Der Staat Hitlers*, 126.

224. At the city level, the change of personnel at the top of local government was drastic: some three-fifths of Oberbürgermeister and Bürgermeister of towns and cities with more than 20,000 inhabitants had been dismissed by the end of 1933. The bigger the city, the greater was the turnover: in only four out of twenty-eight was the Oberbürgermeister not replaced by the end of 1933 (Horst Matzerath, *Nationalsozialismus und kommunale Selbstverwaltung*, Stuttgart, 1970, 79–80). See also Jeremy Noakes, 'Oberbürgermeister and Gauleiter. City Government between Party and State', and Horst Matzerath, 'Oberbürgermeister im Dritten Reich', both in Hirschfeld and Kettenacker, *Der 'Führerstaat'*, 194–227, 228–54.

225. See Zofka, 238–86 for examples.

226. Martin Broszat and Norbert Frei (eds.), *Das Dritte Reich im Überblick. Chronik, Ereignisse, Zusammenhänge*, Munich, 1989, 195, 212; Kater, *Nazi Party*, 262 (Figure 1).

227. Broszat *et al.*, *Bayern in der NS-Zeit*, i.494.

228. Cit. Thamer, 299.

229. E.g. see Allen, 222–32; Koshar, 253ff.

230. Allen, 222.

231. Thamer, 305. Hitler had promised a 'far-reaching moral renewal (*Sanierung*) of the public body', including education, theatre, film, literature, press, and radio (Domarus, 232 (23 March 1933)).

232. Paul Meier-Benneckenstein, *Dokumente der deutschen Politik, Bd.1*, 2nd edn, Berlin, 1937, 263–4; Heiber, *Goebbels-Reden*, i.90.

233. Thamer, 301.

234. See, from an extensive literature, the outstanding work of Michael H. Kater, *The Twisted Muse. Musicians and their Music in the Third Reich*, New York/Oxford, 1997.

235. J. M. Ritchie, *German Literature under National Socialism*, London/Canberra, 1983, 9–10. The regime remained cool towards Hauptmann, recognizing the superficiality of his commitment to National Socialism.

236. Cit. Thamer, 300–301.

237. Cit. Hans Mommsen, 'Der Mythos des nationalen Aufbruchs und die Haltung der deutschen Intellektuellen und funktionalen Eliten', in *1933 in Gesellschaft und Wissenschaft*, ed. Pressestelle der Universität Hamburg, Hamburg, 1983, 127–41, here 132.

238. Ritchie, 48–9.

239. Cit. Thamer, 301.

240. Cit. Mommsen, 'Mythos', 132.

241. Cit. Mommsen, 'Mythos', 129, 132.

242. Cit. Mommsen, 'Mythos', 131.

243. See the entries in Thomas Mann, *Diaries, 1918–1939*, paperback edn, London, 1984, 141–51 (1–13 April 1933).

244. Mann, *Diaries*, 150 (9 April 1933). And see Thamer, 302.

245. Cit. Mommsen, 'Mythos', 134.

246. See Mommsen, 'Mythos', 132–5.

247. Thamer, 303.

248. See Gerhard Sauder, *Die Bücherverbrennung*, Munich/Vienna, 1983.

249. Cit. Sauder, 181 (and see also 177).

250. Mommsen, 'Mythos', 128; Thamer, 304.

251. Cit. Thamer, 305.

252. Ian Kershaw, *The 'Hitler Myth'. Image and Reality in the Third Reich*, Oxford (1987), paperback edn., 1989, 53, 55.

253. Beatrice and Helmut Heiber (eds.), *Die Rückseite des Hakenkreuzes. Absonder-*

liches aus den Akten des Dritten Reiches, Munich, 1993, 119–20 and n.1, 181–3.

254. Rolf Steinberg, *Nazi-Kitsch*, Darmstadt, 1975.

255. Kershaw, *The 'Hitler Myth'*, 57–9.

256. BAK, R43II/1263, Fols. 93, 164.

257. Broszat, *Der Staat Hitlers*, 126–7.

258. Kershaw, *The 'Hitler Myth'*, 61, cit. *Schwäbisches Volksblatt*, 9 September 1933.

259. BHstA MA-106670, RPvOB, 19 August 1933; Heiber, *Rückseite*, 9.

260. Above from Hanfstaengl, *15 Jahre*, 309–17.

261. See Papen, 261.

262. *TBJG*, I.2, 410 (23 April 1933, unpubl.).

263. *RGBl*, 1933, Teil I, Nr.86, 529–31.

264. On Gütt, see Wistrich, *Wer war wer*, 106; Gisela Bock, *Zwangssterilisation im Nationalsozialismus. Studien zur Rassenpolitik und Frauenpolitik*, Opladen, 1986, 25.

265. *AdR, Reg. Hitler*, 664–5; Noakes, 'Nazism and Eugenics', 84–7.

266. Bock, 8, 238.

267. Lewy, 77; ch.3 deals with the background to the Concordat, and the important role played by Kaas. See also Conway, 24–8.

268. Conway, 41.

269. Lewy, 88–9.

270. Papen, 281; Lewy, 77–8.

271. Lewy, 72–7.

272. *AdR, Reg. Hitler*, 683; Lewy, 78. He had also not thought it possible, he said, that the Vatican would be so quickly ready to abandon the Christian trade unions and political parties.

273. Lewy, ch.4, esp. 99, 103–4. The text of the pastoral letter is printed in Müller, *Katholische Kirche*, 163–73.

274. Alfons Kupper (ed.), *Staatliche Akten über die Reichskonkordatsverhandlungen 1933*, Mainz, 1969, 293–4, Nr.117.

275. Conway, 33.

276. Kurt Meier, *Kreuz und Hakenkreuz. Die evangelische Kirche im Dritten Reich*, Munich, 1992, 42.

277. Bracher *et al.*, *Machtergreifung*, i.452; Domarus, 290–91.

278. Conway, 49.

279. Above from Conway, 34–55.

280. The term is the subtitle of the first volume of Gerhard L. Weinberg's authoritative study, *The Foreign Policy of Hitler's Germany. Diplomatic Revolution in Europe 1933–36*, Chicago/London, 1970.

281. Günter Wollstein, 'Eine Denkschrift des Staatssekretärs Bernhard von Bülow vom März 1933', *Militärgeschichtliche Mitteilungen*, 1 (1973), 77–94; *AdR, Reg. Hitler*, i.313–18; Bernd-Jürgen Wendt, *Großdeutschland. Außenpolitik und Kriegs-vorbereitung des Hitler-Regimes*, Munich, 1987, 72–9; Höhne, *Zeit der Illusionen*,

149. Bülow's memorandum provides the clearest indication of the thinking of the Foreign Ministry at the beginning of the Third Reich. The tone is one of the need for early caution and avoidance of external conflict, during which phase internal rebuilding as well as careful formation of bilateral alliances could pave the way for later revisionism and expansion. Drawing heavily upon the conception of an expansionist foreign policy developed in the Wilhelmine era, it demonstrates how extensive the platform was for close collaboration with Hitler even where, as in the case of Russia and Poland, the views were rapidly shown to differ sharply from his own notions. The structure of the Foreign Office, and how it altered under Hitler, was thoroughly explored in the extensive work of Hans-Adolf Jacobsen, *National-sozialistische Außenpolitik 1933–1938*, Frankfurt am Main, 1968.

282. Weinberg, i.161. Hitler had commented to Nadolny, soon after becoming Chancellor, that he knew nothing of foreign policy, that it would take him four years to make Germany National Socialist, and only after that would he be able to concern himself with foreign affairs. The Foreign Office, he remarked, was run according to traditional rules, and had to consider the wishes of the Reich President (Rudolf Nadolny, *Mein Beitrag. Erinnerungen eines Botschafters des Deutschen Reiches*, Cologne, 1985, 239).

283. Höhne, *Zeit der Illusionen*, 150, 152, 158.

284. Höhne, *Zeit der Illusionen*, 154–5, 161.

285. Weinberg, i.164. See also Gerhard Meinck, *Hitler und die deutsche Aufrüstung*, Wiesbaden, 1959, 22–6, 35–51.

286. Höhne, *Zeit der Illusionen*, 158, 166–8.

287. Höhne, *Zeit der Illusionen*, 158–9.

288. *AdR, Reg. Hitler*, 447–8.

289. Brüning, ii.706–7.

290. Morsey, 'Die Deutsche Zentrumspartei', 388.

291. Brüning, ii.707.

292. Wilhelm Hoegner, *Flucht vor Hitler*, Munich, 1977, 203.

293. Domarus, 273.

294. Domarus, 278; for the text of the speech, 270–79.

295. Höhne, *Zeit der Illusionen*, 161, 168, 169–70. Goebbels, visiting Geneva at the end of September, though full of contempt for what he saw, sounded like a peace-loving, amenable diplomat (Paul Schmidt, *Statist auf diplomatischer Bühne 1923–45, Erlebnisse des Chefdolmetschers im Auswärtigen Amt mit den Staatsmännern Europas*, Bonn, 1953, 283–6; *TBJG*, I.2, 465–6 (25 September 1933, 27 September 1933)). However, he appears to have favoured taking advantage of the impasse in negotiations to leave the talks (Weinberg, i.165 and refs. in n.28).

296. Weinberg, i.165 and n.29.

297. NCA, Supplement B, 1504; Bracher *et al.*, *Machtergreifung*, i.338.

298. Höhne, *Zeit der Illusionen*, 171; Weinberg, i.165 (with different emphasis); Papen, 297–8.

299. Höhne, *Zeit der Illusionen*, 172. Neurath, though strongly supportive of the

move, was in fact only informed once the decision had been taken. He was told by Bülow on the evening of 4 October that Hitler and Blomberg now intended to leave the League (Günter Wollstein, *Von Weimarer Revisionismus zu Hitler*, Bonn/Bad Godesberg, 1973, 201 and n.39–40).

300. *AdR, Reg. Hitler*, ii.903–7, here 904–5.

301. Weinberg, i.166. Formal notice of withdrawal from the League was only presented on 19 October (*DGFP*, C, II, 2 n.2).

302. Höhne, *Zeit der Illusionen*, 173, 178–9; Jost Dülffer, 'Zum "decision-making process" in der deutschen Außenpolitik 1933–1939', in Manfred Funke (ed.), *Hitler, Deutschland und die Mächte. Materialien zur Außenpolitik des Dritten Reichs*, 186–204, here 188–90.

303. Domarus, 308–14.

304. Domarus, 323–30.

305. Hans Baur, *Ich flog Mächtige der Erde*, Kempten (Allgäu), 1956, 108–10; Domarus, 325 and n.293.

306. Kershaw, *The 'Hitler Myth'*, 62.

307. Domarus, 331.

308. BAK, R18/5350, Fols. 95–104, 107–22, contains inquiries into complaints about irregularities in the election. See also *AdR, Reg. Hitler*, ii.939 n.1; and Bracher *et al.*, *Machtergreifung*, i.480–85.

309. If the point needed emphasis, the vote of 99.5 per cent in favour by the inmates of Dachau concentration camp underlined it (*Münchner Neueste Nachrichten*, 13 November 1933). In the circumstances, the levels of those refusing their support – greater in the election than the plebiscite – was sometimes remarkable (over 21 per cent in Hamburg and Berlin, over 15 per cent in Cologne-Aachen in the election) and corresponded broadly to the types of social structure and religious allegiance that had provided relative immunity to the Nazi breakthrough before 1933 (see Bracher *et al.*, *Machtergreifung*, i.486–97).

310. *AdR, Reg. Hitler*, ii.939 n.1.

311. *AdR, Reg. Hitler*, ii.939–41.

CHAPTER 12: SECURING TOTAL POWER

1. The term was coined by Richard Bessel, *Political Violence*, 152.

2. Longerich, *Die braunen Bataillone*, 165–76.

3. Diels, 254ff.

4. Sonderarchiv Moscow, 1235–VI–2, Fol.2–28, here 19–21.

5. Longerich, *Die braunen Bataillone*, 166, 198.

6. The file of Meissner's Präsidialkanzlei in Sonderarchiv Moscow, 1413–I–6, contains 460 folios relating to such cases between 1933 and 1935. The complicity of the judicial system, and of Gürtner personally, in the quashing of sentences against SA men convicted of acts of brutality is thoroughly explored by Gruchmann, *Justiz*, ch.4.

7. Longerich, *Die braunen Bataillone*, 177−9.

8. Heinz Höhne, *Mordsache Röhm. Hitlers Durchbruch zur Alleinherrschaft 1933−1934*, Reinbek bei Hamburg, 1934, 46, referring to remarks made by Hindenburg to Hitler on 29 June 1933. The comments were made in the context of the discord in the Protestant Church and did not mention the SA explicitly. Hindenburg's view on the 'excesses' was, however, that Hitler 'has the best will and is only working in with a pure heart in the interests of justice', while 'his subordinates unfortunately kick over the traces' − something which would be sorted out in time (Sonderarchiv Moscow, 1235−VI−2, Fol. 271, notes on a discussion of Hindenburg with Hugenberg, 17 May 1933).

9. *Nationalsozialistische Monatshefte*, 4 (1933), 251−4, passages quoted, 253−4.

10. Longerich, *Die braunen Bataillone*, 184. The figure was swollen by the paramilitary organizations incorporated in the SA, the most important of which was the Stahlhelm. Only around a third of the SA men were party members.

11. Domarus, 286.

12. Longerich, *Die braunen Bataillone*, 182−3; Höhne, *Mordsache Röhm*, 46−9.

13. Shlomo Aronson, *Reinhard Heydrich und die Frühgeschichte von Gestapo und SD*, Stuttgart, 1971, 71, 92.

14. Longerich, *Die braunen Bataillone*, 184−7.

15. Höhne, *Zeit der Illusionen*, 143−8.

16. Longerich, *Die braunen Bataillone*, 185, 188.

17. Höhne, *Mordsache Röhm*, 127−8.

18. Longerich, *Die braunen Bataillone*, 188−90. Unemployed workers had always, during the period of Nazism's surge to power and continuing throughout 1933 and 1934, constituted a substantial proportion of the SA's membership (Fischer, *Stormtroopers*, 45−8).

19. Longerich, *Die braunen Bataillone*, 200−205; Hermann Mau, 'Die "Zweite Revolution" − der 30. Juni 1934', *VfZ*, 1 (1953), 119−37, here esp. 124−7; Otto Gritschneder, '*Der Führer hat Sie zum Tode verurteilt . . .*'. Hitlers 'Röhm-Putsch'-Morde vor Gericht, Munich, 1993, 30, citing the testimony from 1953 of Paul Körner, formerly State Secretary in the Prussian Staatsministerium; Höhne, *Mordsache Röhm*, 218−19.

20. See Martin Loiperdinger and David Culbert, 'Leni Riefenstahl, the SA, and the Nazi Party Rally Films, Nuremberg 1933−1934: "Sieg des Glaubens" and "Triumph des Willens"', *Historical Journal of Film, Radio, and Television*, 8 (1988), 3−38, here esp. 12−13.

21. Longerich, *Die braunen Bataillone*, 201.

22. Domarus, 338, for a glowing expression of Hitler's thanks to Röhm on 31 December 1933 for his services to the Movement. Among the twelve such letters sent to Nazi leaders, only Röhm was addressed in the 'Du' form (Domarus, 338−42).

23. See Immo v. Fallois, *Kalkül und Illusion. Der Machtkampf zwischen Reichswehr und SA während der Röhm-Krise 1934*, Berlin, 1994, 101: the decision in principle for a Wehrmacht based on general conscription had already been taken. Hitler, in

his speech on 30 January 1934, praised the party and the armed forces, seen as two pillars of the state (Domarus, 355–6; and see Müller, *Heer*, 95).

24. Fallois, 105–6, 117.

25. Fallois, 123 and n.560.

26. Hans-Adolf Jacobsen and Werner Jochmann (eds.), *Ausgewählte Dokumente zur Geschichte des Nationalsozialismus*, 3 vols., Bielefeld, 1961, unpaginated, vol.I, C, 2 February 1934. Heß also gave a plain warning to the SA leadership around the same date in an article published in the *Völkischer Beobachter* and the *National-sozialistische Monatshefte* (Longerich, *Die braunen Bataillone*, 203).

27. Höhne, *Mordsache Röhm*, 200.

28. Höhne, *Zeit der Illusionen*, 181.

29. Fallois, 105, 117.

30. Bracher *et al.*, *Machtergreifung*, iii.336; Fallois, 106–8.

31. Fallois, 117–18.

32. Höhne, *Zeit der Illusionen*, 183.

33. Fallois, 118–19, cit. NL Weichs, BA/MA, Freiburg, N19/12, S.12.

34. Bracher *et al.*, *Machtergreifung*, iii.337; *Mordsache Röhm*, 205; Toland, 330 (based on Weich's testimony).

35. Höhne, *Mordsache Röhm*, 206.

36. Fallois, 123, 131 and n.602, but claiming Hitler was waiting for the right psychological moment; Zitelmann, *Selbstverständnis eines Revolutionärs*, 77, inter-prets Hitler's hesitancy to mean that he was incapable of coming to a decision in the conflict between the SA and the Reichswehr. Since he eventually did arrive at a decision – and one of the utmost ruthlessness – the former seems a more likely explanation.

37. Fallois, 125–6.

38. Diels, 379–82.

39. Fallois, 125, 131.

40. Longerich, *Die braunen Bataillone*, 205, 209; Bracher *et al.*, *Machtergreifung*, iii.343.

41. See Höhne, *Mordsache Röhm*, 218, 223–4.

42. Höhne, *Mordsache Röhm*, 210; Longerich, *Die braunen Bataillone*, 205; Fallois, 124. At the disarming of the SA following the Röhm crisis, the collection of arms found amounted to 177,000 rifles, 651 heavy and 1250 light machine-guns.

43. Anthony Eden, *The Eden Memoirs. Facing the Dictators*, London, 1962, 65.

44. See Höhne, *Mordsache Röhm*, 221–2; Longerich, *Die braunen Bataillone*, 213–14.

45. Kurt Gossweiler, *Die Röhm-Affäre. Hintergründe, Zusammenhänge, Aus-wirkungen*, Cologne, 1983, 76, cit. the headline of the *Evening Standard* (London), of 11 June 1934, that Hitler was on the verge of catastrophe, with the implication that the Reichswehr would step in should he fail.

46. AdR, *Reg. Hitler*, 1197–1200 (quoted words 1197); Norbert Frei, *Der Führerstaat. Nationalsozialistische Herrschaft 1933 bis 1945*, Munich, 1987, 13.

47. See Frei, *Führerstaat*, 14–15; Ian Kershaw, *Popular Opinion and Political Dissent in the Third Reich. Bavaria, 1933–1945*, Oxford, 1983, 46–7, 76, 120–21; Timothy W. Mason, *Sozialpolitik im Dritten Reich. Arbeiterklasse und Volksgemeinschaft*, Opladen, 1977, 192; Longerich, *Die braunen Bataillone*, 207.

48. *DBS*, i. 172 (26 June 1934).

49. Cit. Höhne, *Mordsache Röhm*, 232. Jung's fundamental resistance to Hitler from late 1933 onwards is emphasized in the memoirs of a former close acquaintance and sympathizer, Edmund Forschbach, *Edgar J. Jung. Ein konservativer Revolutionär, 30. Juni 1934*, Pfullingen, 1984. Fallois, 114 n.522, suggests, however, that Jung wanted only to modify, not replace, the regime. Even after Jung's arrest – ordered by Hitler (Hans-Günther Seraphim (ed.), *Das politische Tagebuch Alfred Rosenbergs 1934/35 und 1939/40*, Munich, 1964, 42–3) – following Papen's Marburg speech, the plan worked out by Bose and Tschirschky for Papen to put to Hindenburg still foresaw, as a continuation of the 'taming concept', the membership of Hitler and Göring in a Directory also including Fritsch, Papen, Brüning, and Goerdeler (Karl Martin Graß, *Edgar Jung, Papenkreis und Röhmkrise 1933–34*, Diss., Heidelberg, 1966, 264–6).

50. See Höhne, *Mordsache Röhm*, 233–4; Longerich, *Die braunen Bataillone*, 208. The Gestapo was well informed of their activities; and Blomberg and Reichenau in the Reichswehr leadership were aware of the advantages to the army that Hitler, removed from the clutches of the SA, would bring (Frei, *Führerstaat*, 23–5). See also the pessimistic evaluation of Fallois, 112–16, about the chances of an alternative to Hitler's regime, especially given the opportunities it provided for the rearmament plans of the army.

51. Heinrich Brüning, in a letter written after the war, said he had heard in April 1934 that Hindenburg was unlikely to live until August, and that three weeks afterwards he learnt of Hitler's plans to ensure that he would become head of state on the Reich President's death. Brüning received, too, he stated, information about a 'proscription list' containing the names of Schleicher, Strasser and others who were subsequently murdered, together with that of Papen (Heinrich Brüning, *Briefe und Gespräche 1934–1945*, ed. Claire Nix, Stuttgart, 1974, 26–7). Hindenburg's doctor, Ferdinand Sauerbruch, *Das war mein Leben*, Bad Wörishofen, 1951, 511, remarks simply that Hindenburg became ill in spring 1934. Meissner, *Staatssekretär*, 375, comments that the President became ill in spring with a bladder complaint. (See also Andreas Dorpalen, *Hindenburg and the Weimar Republic*, Princeton, 1964, 478.)

52. Wheeler-Bennett, *Nemesis*, 311–13, without giving any source, refers to a communiqué on Hindenburg's health on 27 April, over two weeks after Hitler and Blomberg had been informed that the President would not live much longer.

53. Höhne, *Mordsache Röhm*, 228–9; Höhne, *Zeit der Illusionen*, 207–8; Longerich *Die braunen Bataillone*, 120.

54. Graß, 227 and n.570; Forschbach, 115–16.

55. Jacobsen and Jochmann, *Ausgewählte Dokumente*, unpaginated, vol.I, CJ, 17 June 1934; Papen, 309.

56. Papen, 310–11.

57. Brüning commented, in a letter he wrote on 9 July to the former British Ambassador in Berlin, Sir Horace Rumbold, that to hold the speech without agreeing any subsequent action with the Reichswehr and Reich President was 'a huge mistake' (*ein riesiger Fehler*). Brüning added that he had heard from a reliable source that Papen had read the speech for the first time only two hours before speaking in Marburg. (See, on this point, Forschbach, 115–16.) After the war Brüning said he had himself received a copy of Edgar Jung's text in April or May, and strongly advised against putting it into Papen's hands (Brüning, *Briefe und Gespräche*, 25, 27).

58. Domarus, 390–91.

59. Fallois, 132.

60. Papen, 310–11.

61. Höhne, *Mordsache Röhm*, 237

62. Wheeler-Bennett, *Nemesis*, 319–20.

63. Meissner, *Staatssekretär*, 363.

64. Cit. Longerich, *Die braunen Bataillone*, 212.

65. Höhne, *Mordsache Röhm*, 239; Höhne, *Zeit der Illusionen*, 211.

66. Longerich, *Die braunen Bataillone*, 215.

67. Fallois, 126–30, 135–6, 138–9; Müller, *Heer*, 113–18.

68. Graß, 260–61; Höhne, *Mordsache Röhm*, 239–42.

69. Höhne, *Mordsache Röhm*, 242.

70. Domarus, 394, 399.

71. Graß, 264–8; Höhne, *Mordsache Röhm*, 247–51, 256.

72. Höhne, *Mordsache Röhm*, 256.

73. Graß, 263 and n.728; Höhne, *Mordsache Röhm*, 257.

74. Graß, 269; Longerich, *Die braunen Bataillone*, 216; Höhne, *Mordsache Röhm*, 256–7.

75. *TBJG*, I.2, 472–3 (29 June 1934).

76. *Tb* Reuth, ii.843 (1 July 1934); and see Reuth, *Goebbels*, 314.

77. *Tb* Reuth, ii.843 (1 July 1934).

78. Höhne, *Mordsache Röhm*, 265.

79. Domarus, 394–5; Longerich, *Die braunen Bataillone*, 216.

80. Domarus, 399; Höhne, *Mordsache Röhm*, 260–66 (quoted words, 266).

81. Höhne, *Mordsache Röhm*, 266–7; Gritschneder, 'Der Führer', 18.

82. Höhne, *Mordsache Röhm*, 267–8; Höhne, *Zeit der Illusionen*, 214; Domarus, 396, 399–400; Library of Congress: Adolf Hitler Collection, C–89, 9376–88A–B, Erich Kempka interview, 15 October 1971. Röhm was the only one of those arrested to be taken away in a car; the rest went in the chartered bus.

83. Höhne, *Mordsache Röhm*, 271, cit. Schreiben von Karl Schreyer an das Polizeipräsidium München, 27 May 1949, Prozeßakten Landgericht München I. See also IfZ, Fa 108, SA/OSAF, 1928–45, Bl.39, for the official report of the meeting by the Reichspressestelle der NSDAP.

84. Höhne, *Mordsache Röhm*, 273.

85. Domarus, 397; Gritschneder, '*Der Führer*', 21–8. Evidently in a calmer mood, Hitler went on to dictate a number of press communiqués and Lutze's letter of appointment as new SA Chief of Staff (Domarus, 397–402).

86. Gritschneder, '*Der Führer*', 24, 26.

87. Höhne, *Mordsache Röhm*, 274.

88. Seraphim, *Das politische Tagebuch Alfred Rosenbergs*, 46, (7 July 1934).

89. Domarus, 396; Höhne, *Mordsache Röhm*, 270–71.

90. Longerich, *Die braunen Bataillone*, 218.

91. For the above, see Papen, 315–18; Hans Bernd Gisevius, *Bis zum bittern Ende*, 2 vols., Zürich, 1946, i.225–81; Gritschneder, '*Der Führer*', 36–44, 135 (relating to Edgar Jung); Longerich, *Die braunen Bataillone*, 219; Höhne, *Mordsache Röhm*, 271, 281–2, 284–9. Klausener's name (along with those of Schleicher, Bredow, and Bose) had appeared on lists privately compiled – without any conspiratorial plans – by Edgar Jung of those who might belong to a future government (Höhne, *Mordsache Röhm*, 251–2).

92. Hans Bernd Gisevius, *Adolf Hitler. Versuch einer Deutung*, Munich, 1963, 291; Frei, *Führerstaat*, 32.

93. Gritschneder, '*Der Führer*', 30.

94. Papen, 320.

95. Gritschneder, '*Der Führer*', 32, based on Körner's testimony in 1953.

96. Gritschneder, '*Der Führer*', 32–6.

97. Domarus, 404.

98. Domarus, 405.

99. Gisevius, *Bis zum bittern Ende*, i.270.

100. Höhne, *Mordsache Röhm*, 296, 319–21; Longerich, *Die braunen Bataillone*, 219.

101. Bracher *et al.*, *Machtergreifung*, iii.359. Mau, 'Die "Zweite Revolution"', 134, guesses that the number of victims was at least twice, and perhaps three times, as many as the official figure given of seventy-seven. It was later officially announced that, on Göring's orders alone, as many as 1,124 persons had been taken into custody in connection with the 'Röhm revolt' (Domarus, 409).

102. Longerich, *Die braunen Bataillone*, 220–24.

103. On the reactions of the foreign press, see *AdR, Reg. Hitler*, 1376 n.3, citing Goebbels's radio comments on 10 July 1934, as reported in the *VB* the following day.

104. Domarus, 405.

105. Domarus, 405.

106. Papen, 320.

107. Domarus, 406. Gürtner's retrospective legalization of the murderous actions reflected the hopeless strategy followed by jurists in the Third Reich: seeking, so they imagined, to protect the principles of law against arbitrary and illegal force by declaring such force legal. See Gruchmann, *Justiz*, 448–55, for the mentality of

Gürtner which lay behind his framing of the law, and 433–84 for the reactions of the legal administration to the murders perpetrated in the 'Röhm affair'.

108. *AdR, Reg. Hitler*, ii.1354–8. According to the post-war testimony of Lammers, several cabinet ministers (including, he said, himself and Gürtner) preferred an amnesty for the actions rather than a declaration of their legality. But Hitler insisted on a law, and the rest of the cabinet came round to accepting this. Lammers said it amounted to one and the same thing in practice (Gritschneder, '*Der Führer*', 47–9).

109. Dietrich Orlow, *The History of the Nazi Party, vol.2, 1933–1945*, Newton Abbot, 1973, 114–15.

110. Domarus, 406.

111. *AdR, Reg. Hitler*, 1375–7. Pearson's question about whether the government would now swing to the Left or the Right – Hitler predictably answering that no other course than the one already charted would be followed – was presumably a somewhat clumsy attempt to allay fears that further turbulence, affecting the economy, might follow.

112. Papen, 321.

113. Domarus, 407, points out that the speech would have taken time to prepare. It is unlikely that the initial intention was not to give a public account, but to hush up the matter and simply let things die down. This would have flown in the face of all Hitler's propaganda instincts. Suggestions of inner uncertainty also seem wide of the mark (Fest, *Hitler*, ii.643–4). The justification, when it came, was framed consistently along the lines Hitler had taken both in public announcements and in his statements to party leaders in Munich and then to the cabinet in the immediate aftermath of the events. Nor was it the case, as has been claimed, that Hitler went on holiday with Goebbels and his family to Heiligendamm on the Baltic coast, then to Berchtesgaden, to recuperate (Höhne, *Mordsache Röhm*, 298–9; Orlow, ii.114; Frei, *Führerstaat*, 33). These accounts appear to draw on passages in Hanfstaengl, *15 Jahre*, 341ff., whose own account, however, makes it clear that he visited Hitler and Goebbels in Heiligendamm *after* Hitler's speech which he had heard on board ship while passing through the English Channel on his way back from a visit to America. The engagements Hitler held on 6 July left, in any case, only the period between 7 and 13 July available for any retreat – precisely the days when Hitler would have been involved in preparing his speech, not holidaying on the Baltic.

114. Domarus, 410; Gritschneder, '*Der Führer*', 52.

115. Domarus, 421.

116. Gritscheder, '*Der Führer*', 54.

117. *DBS*, i.250 (21 July 1934).

118. BHStA, MA 106670, RPvOB, 4 July 1934.

119. BHStA, MA 106675, Arbeitsamt Marktredwitz, 9 July 1934.

120. See the reports from the Prussian provinces in BAK, R43II/1263, Fols. 238–328.

121. BHStA, MA 106691, LB of RPvNB/OP, 8 August 1934.

122. BAK, R43II/1263, Fols. 238–328; *DBS*, i.198–201 (21 July 1934).

123. Domarus, 401–2. Almost a fifth of the SA leaders were eventually removed from office in a long-drawn-out purging process (Mathilde Jamin, 'Zur Rolle der SA im nationalsozialistischen Herrschaftssystem', in Hirschfeld and Kettenacker, *Der 'Führerstaat'*, 329–60, here 345.

124. *DBS*, i.249 (21 July 1934).

125. BAK, R43II/1263, Fols.235–7, letter of Göring to Heß, 31 August 1934. A copy of the letter was passed on to Hitler.

126. Gritschneder, '*Der Führer*', 71–2; Lewy, 169–70.

127. Höhne, *Mordsache Röhm*, 303–5; Müller, *Heer*, 125–33. When Hammerstein turned up at Lichterfelde Cemetery for the burial of his friend, it transpired that the bodies of Schleicher and his wife had been removed during the night.

128. Gritschneder, '*Der Führer*', 72–3.

129. Cit. Fallois, 9.

130. Mau, 'Die "Zweite Revolution"', 137.

131. Weinberg, i.87–101, esp. 99–101; Höhne, *Zeit der Illusionen*, 223–4; Bruce F. Pauley, *Hitler and the Forgotten Nazis*, chs.7–8.

132. Domarus, 426, has no doubt that Hitler gave Habicht, who would never have dared operate independently, the order. Weinberg, i.104, suggests that 'it may be assumed that the coup was launched with the knowledge and at least tacit approval of Hitler'. Pauley, 133–7, greatly modifies such views, reaching the conclusion that Hitler's responsibility lay in his reluctance to take any firm line on Austria, allowing policy to drift and be dominated by the local hot-head forces. Hermann Graml, *Europa zwischen den Kriegen*, Munich, 1969, 298, also suggests that misinterpretation by the Austrian Nazi leadership of Hitler's passivity, encouraged by the uncertain domestic situation following the Röhm affair, prompted the putsch attempt. Reinhard Spitzy, *So haben wir das Reich verspielt. Bekenntnisse eines Illegalen*, Munich (1986), 4th edn., 1994, 61–6, provides an account from an insider to the Austrian putsch plans, though without casting light on the question of Hitler's knowledge and approval.

133. Pauley, 134; Jens Petersen, *Hitler-Mussolini: Die Entstehung der Achse Berlin-Rom, 1933–1936*, Tübingen, 1973, 338; Höhne, *Zeit der Illusionen*, 224. See, however, Weinberg, i.104 n.89, suggesting that the reliability of Göring's testimony at Nuremberg (*IMT*, ix.294–5), on which this is based, may be questioned.

134. Anton Hoch and Hermann Weiß, 'Die Erinnerungen des Generalobersten Wilhelm Adam', in Wolfgang Benz (ed.), *Miscellanea. Festschrift für Helmut Krausnick*, Stuttgart, 1980, 32–62, here 47–8, 60 n.40.

135. Höhne, *Zeit der Illusionen*, 223.

136. Weinberg, i.105.

137. Hanfstaengl, *15 Jahre*, 353–4.

138. Papen, 339.

139. See Hanfstaengl, *15 Jahre*, 352 for Dietrich's press directions; Pauley, 134–6.

140. Domarus, 427; Weinberg, i.106.

141. Hanfstaengl, *15 Jahre*, 354. As a Catholic, experienced diplomat, and personal friend of the murdered Dollfuss, Papen evidently seemed to Hitler the right person to allay Austrian suspicions about German intentions and to pour oil on troubled water. According to his own version of events, Papen was able to extract conditions from Hitler for his appointment (Papen, 340–41; Pauley, 135).

142. Papen, 337ff; Domarus, 428; Weinberg, i.106.

143. Domarus, 429. Precisely when Hitler was told that the President's death was imminent is uncertain. Hanfstaengl's account has Hitler deciding to send Papen to Vienna in the immediate wake of a telephone call from Meissner with bad news of the President, then flying off to East Prussia to visit Hindenburg. The chronology is, however, conflated. Hitler's letter to Papen, requesting him to undertake the 'special mission' for a limited time as ambassador in Vienna, was dated 26 July. The public was informed of Hindenburg's condition on 31 July; Hitler, presumably, some time before that. Hitler's visit to Neudeck took place on 1 August (Hanfstaengl, *15 Jahre*, 354; Domarus, 429).

144. Sauerbruch, 520. Sauerbruch was Hindenburg's chief doctor during his last illness. See also Papen, 334, for Hitler's last visit to Hindenburg. Sauerbruch, 519 and, apparently following him, Meissner, *Staatssekretär*, 377, place Hitler's visit on 31 July. A notice in *VB*, 1 August 1934, makes it clear that Hitler flew to Neudeck that morning, returning within a few hours. He held a cabinet meeting that evening at 9.30 p.m. (*AdR, Reg. Hitler*, ii.1384). Hanfstaengl's story (*15 Jahre*, 355) that Hitler and his entourage spent the night in Neudeck – where Hitler allegedly refused to sleep in the same room used by Napoleon in a nearby Schloß – before returning to Bayreuth, where the news of Hindenburg's death was received, then returning immediately to Neudeck, appears to lack any foundation.

145. *AdR, Reg. Hitler*, ii.1384. Hindenburg died at 9.00 a.m. on 2 August.

146. *AdR, Reg. Hitler*, ii.1384; Domarus, 429; Gritschneder, 'Der Führer', 75–6; Müller, *Heer*, 133.

147. *AdR, Reg. Hitler*, ii.1387; Domarus, 431.

148. Müller, *Heer*, 134; Fallois, 161.

149. Müller, *Heer*, 135.

150. Domarus, 444. This was on 20 August, the day after the plebiscite. Hitler referred in his statement of thanks to the 'law of 3 August', though this was, of course, the law passed by the cabinet on the headship of state on 1 August – before, therefore, not after, Hindenburg's death.

151. Müller, *Heer*, 134; Papen, 335–6.

152. Müller, *Heer*, 134; Gritschneder, *'Der Führer'*, 76.

153. Cit. Müller, *Heer*, 135.

154. Cit. Müller, *Heer*, 136.

155. Cit. Müller, *Heer*, 137.

156. Müller, *Heer*, 138.

157. Müller, *Heer*, 139 and n.313–14.

158. *Münchner Neueste Nachrichten*, 4 August 1934.

159. Domarus, 438.

160. *AdR, Reg. Hitler*, ii.1385–6, 1388–9 and n.8; Meissner, *Staatssekretär*, 377–8.

161. *Statistisches Jahrbuch für das Deutsche Reich, 1935*, Berlin, 1935, 537. There were significant levels of no-votes – up to a third – in some working-class and Catholic areas.

162. *TBJG*, I.2, 475 (22 August 1934).

163. Domarus, 447–54.

164. Loiperdinger and Culbert, 17–18; David Welch, *Propaganda and the German Cinema, 1933–1945*, Oxford, 1983, 147–59. The account in Leni Riefenstahl, *A Memoir*, New York, 1993, 156–66, as Loiperdinger and Culbert (15–17) have pointed out, has to be treated with caution.

CHAPTER 13: WORKING TOWARDS THE FÜHRER

1. Niedersächsisches Staatsarchiv, Oldenburg, Best. 131 Nr.303, Fol. 131v.

2. See Ulrich Herbert, ' "Die guten und die schlechten Zeiten". Überlegungen zur diachronen Analyse lebensgeschichtlicher Interviews', in Lutz Niethammer (ed.), *'Die Jahre weiß man nicht, wo man sie heute hinsetzen soll'. Faschismuserfahrungen im Ruhrgebiet*, Berlin/Bonn, 1983, 67–96, here esp. 82, 88–93.

3. See, for the implications of the term, Mommsen, 'Kumulative Radikalisierung'; and Hans Mommsen, 'Cumulative Radicalisation and Progressive Self-Destruction as Structural Determinants of the Nazi Dictatorship', in Ian Kershaw and Moshe Lewin (eds.), *Stalinism and Nazism*, 75–87.

4. See Müller, *Armee, Politik und Gesellschaft*, 39–47.

5. Dietrich, *Zwölf Jahre*, 44–5.

6. Broszat, 'Soziale Motivation und Führer-Bindung', 403.

7. Lothar Gruchmann, 'Die "Reichsregierung" im Führerstaat. Stellung und Funktion des Kabinetts im nationalsozialistischen Herrschaftssystem', in Günther Doeker and Winfried Steffani (eds.), *Klassenjustiz und Pluralismus*, Hamburg, 1973, 192, 202.

8. See Wiedemann, 69, 71.

9. Wiedemann, 68–9.

10. Wiedemann, 80–82.

11. Wiedemann, 78. Once the Berghof had been completed, in 1936, with full projection facilities, it was frequently the case that two films would be shown each evening (BBC Archives, interview, 1997, with Hermann Döring, Manager (*Verwalter*) of the Berghof, transcript, Roll 243, 31).

12. Wiedemann, 79, 90–91. See Schroeder, 60, 81, 84, and the interviews conducted in 1971 (Library of Congress, Washington DC, Adolf Hitler Collection, C-63, 64, 9376 63–64, and C-86, 9376 85) with Gerda Dananowski and Traudl Junge for confirmation of this, mainly relating to later years. See also Gitta Sereny, *Albert Speer: his Battle with the Truth*, London, 1995, 113–14, for the comments of Maria

von Below, widow of Hitler's Luftwaffe adjutant (also referring to later years).

13. Wiedemann, 76, 78, 93; Percy Ernst Schramm, in the Introduction to Picker, 34; see also Spitzy, 126–7, 130 (though for a later period).

14. Wiedemann, 69.

15. Wiedemann, 85; Schroeder, 53, 78–82.

16. See, e.g., Friedelind Wagner, 93, 124–5, for Hitler's ambitions to be a patron of the arts in the grand style.

17. Wiedemann, 194ff.; Smelser, 166.

18. See Frank Bajohr, 'Gauleiter in Hamburg. Zur Person und Tätigkeit Karl Kaufmanns', *VfZ*, 43 (1995), 269–95, here 277–80, for specific examples of corruption in Hamburg which were characteristic for the local and regional level.

19. Robert Koehl, 'Feudal Aspects of National Socialism', *American Political Science Review*, 54 (1960), 921–33.

20. See Hanisch, 13ff; Geiß, 65–95.

21. Wiedemann, 72, 74–6, 94–6.

22. Wiedemann, 69–70.

23. The text of the decree is printed in Walther Hofer (ed.), *Der Nationalsozialismus. Dokumente 1933–1945*, Frankfurt am Main, 1957, 87.

24. See Bajohr, 286, for Kaufmann's attempts to uphold wage levels for workers in Hamburg.

25. BAK, R43II/541, Fols. 36–95; BAK, R43II/552, Fols.25–50; and see Mason, *Sozialpolitik*, 158–9.

26. BAK, NS22/110, Denkschrift, 15 December 1932; see Mommsen, 'Die NSDAP als faschistische Partei', 267–8.

27. Orlow, ii.67–70; Peter Longerich, *Hitlers Stellvertreter. Führung der Partei und Kontrolle des Staatsapparates durch den Stab Heß und die Partei-Kanzlei Bormann*, Munich/London/New York/Paris, 1992, 16 (and see Parts I–IV for the operations of the office of the Deputy Führer).

28. Orlow, ii.74–5; Mommsen, 'Die NSDAP als faschistische Partei', 262–3; and see Longerich, *Hitlers Stellvertreter*, 24, for emphasis on the improvised and unclear structure of the party at the top, under Heß.

29. Longerich, *Hitlers Stellvertreter*, 18–20, and Part II. As Longerich points out (257), from the state's point of view, the approval of the office of the StdF for civil service appointments was not recognized as legally binding, though in practice adhered to.

30. See Longerich, *Hitlers Stellvertreter*, ch.8, pts.2,4 210ff, 234ff.

31. Dietrich, *Zwölf Jahre*, 45.

32. See Diehl-Thiele, 69–73.

33. *MK*, 433–4.

34. *Anatomie*, ii.46. The conflict between the Gestapo and Reich Justice Ministry over the question of the representations of lawyers in cases of 'protective custody' stretched back to October 1934. Himmler had subsequently informed Gestapo offices in April 1935 that such representations were banned where political and

police interests might be endangered. Gürtner did not give up the attempt to preserve the rights of the legal profession, even after Hitler's intervention in the autumn. Himmler dragged the affair out, however, and the Reich Justice Minister made as good as no progress, whatever concessions he was prepared to make. Resting on Hitler's authority, the Gestapo was able to block all attempts to constrain the arbitrary use of its power. (See Gruchmann, *Justiz*, 564–73.) For his part, Gürtner was himself, however, woefully weak in upholding legal principles against political expediency. On 8 October 1935 he wrote to Hitler about the case of an SA man accused of the torture of six Communists in a Berlin 'SA-Home' in January 1934. 'Despite the seriousness of the maltreatment, which shows a certain sadism,' Gürtner wrote, he was prepared to recommend quashing the indictment (Sonderarchiv Moscow, 1413-I-6, Fol.36).

35. *Anatomie*, ii.39–40.

36. Johannes Tuchel, *Konzentrationslager*, Boppard am Rhein, 1991, 314–15. 'Kampf gegen die inneren Feinde der Nation' was a formulation used (Tuchel, 314) by Hitler at the Party Rally on 11 September 1935. See also Robert Gellately, 'Allwissend und allgegenwärtig? Entstehung, Funktion und Wandel des Gestapo-Mythos', in Gerhard Paul and Klaus-Michael Mallmann (eds.), *Die Gestapo: Mythos und Realität*, Darmstadt, 1995, 47–70, here 54–5.

37. *Anatomie*, i.50–54.

38. *RGBl*, 1936, Teil I, 487–8.

39. *Anatomie*, i.118.

40. *Anatomie*, ii.50–51. See also Herbert, *Best*, 163–8.

41. For the expansion of the Gestapo's spheres of activity, see Herbert, *Best*, 168–80. One example was the extension of persecution, not greatly in evidence before the publicity stirred up by the Röhm affair, to homosexuals. Lists of practising homosexuals were collected by a newly established department in the Gestapa in Berlin from October 1934 (Günter Grau (ed.), *Homosexualität in der NS-Zeit. Dokumente einer Diskriminierung und Verfolgung*, Frankfurt am Main, 1993, 74). Regional Gestapo offices joined suit in widening their persecution, coordinated from 1936 by the 'Reich Headquarters for the Combating of Homosexuality and Abortion' (Burkhard Jellonnek, 'Staatspolizeiliche Fahndungs- und Ermittlungsmethoden gegen Homosexuelle', in Paul and Mallmann, *Die Gestapo*, 343–56, here 348–9, 353. See also Burkhard Jellonnek's monograph, *Homosexuelle unter dem Haken-kreuz. Die Verfolgung von Homosexuellen im Dritten Reich*, Paderborn, 1990).

42. See Christine Elizabeth King, *The Nazi State and the New Religions: Five Case Studies in Non-Conformity*, New York/Toronto, 1982.

43. The subtitle of the first of Weinberg's two-volume analysis of German foreign policy between 1933 and 1939.

44. *AdR, Reg. Hitler*, i.313–18, here 318. See also Wollstein, 'Eine Denkschrift des Staatssekretärs Bernhard von Bülow vom März 1933', 87, 93; and Wendt, 75, 79.

45. See Weinberg, i.46, 166–70.

46. See Wendt, 85; Weinberg, i.171.

47. Weinberg, i.60–61, 69–73.

48. Cit. Wendt, 78.

49. Herbert S. Levine, *Hitler's Free City. A History of the Nazi Party in Danzig, 1925–39*, Chicago/London, 1973, 56–7.

50. See Levine, 9–17, 61–7.

51. Weinberg, i.63–8, 71.

52. Józef Lipski, *Diplomat in Berlin, 1933–1939*, New York/London, 1968, 105.

53. Weinberg, i.73.

54. Leonidas E. Hill (ed.), *Die Weizsäcker-Papiere 1933–1950*, Frankfurt am Main/Berlin/Vienna, 1974, 78.

55. Bayerische Staatsbibliothek, ANA-463, Sammlung Deuerlein, E200263-9, Dirksen to Bülow, 31 January 1933; Bülow to Dirksen, 6 February 1933, and E496961, Dirksen telegram to Neurath, 28 February 1933.

56. Weinberg, i.81.

57. Weinberg, i.180–83.

58. Müller, *Heer*, 147ff.

59. Müller, *Heer*, 155–7.

60. Domarus, 468 and n.8; Orlow, ii.138–9; Müller, *Heer*, 158–61.

61. For the term, see Hüttenberger, 'Nationalsozialistische Polykratie', 423ff., 432ff.

62. Patrik von zur Mühlen, *'Schlagt Hitler an der Saar!' Abstimmungskampf, Emigration und Widerstand im Saargebiet, 1933–1945*, Bonn, 1979, 230, refers to 1,500 meetings and rallies and over 80,000 posters as part of the campaign. For months before the plebiscite, special efforts had been made to organize broadcasting propaganda to the Saar, including distribution of cheap radios (the *Volksempfänger*) and transmission of a flow of programmes hammering home the message in different ways that the Saar was part of Germany (Zeman, 51–4).

63. François-Poncet, 221–2; Weinberg, i.173–4, 203.

64. See Gerhard Paul and Klaus-Michael Mahlmann, *Milieus und Widerstand. Eine Verhaltensgeschichte der Gesellschaft im Nationalsozialismus*, Bonn, 1995, 60–77, 203–23, 352–71. See also Gerhard Paul, *'Deutsche Mutter – heim zu Dir!' Warum es mißlang, Hitler an der Saar zu schlagen. Der Saarkampf 1933 bis 1935*, Cologne, 1984.

65. Höhne, *Zeit der Illusionen*, 284.

66. Paul and Mahlmann, *Milieus*, 66, 73–7.

67. Höhne, *Zeit der Illusionen*, 283.

68. *Schultheß' Europäischer Geschichtskalender*, Bd.76 (1936), Munich, 1936, 14 (90.76 per cent).

69. Paul and Mahlmann, *Milieus*, 222.

70. Domarus, 472.

71. Domarus, 476. Ward Price was convinced, so he wrote in the *Völkischer Beobachter* after the interview, of Hitler's 'love of peace' (cit. Domarus, 474 n.19). He still thought in 1937 that Hitler was sincere in his 'desire for peace' (G. Ward Price, *I Know these Dictators*, 143).

72. Domarus, 485.

73. *D R Z W*, i.415 and n.62, 416.

74. Klaus-Jürgen Müller, *General Ludwig Beck. Studien und Dokumente zur polit-isch-militärischen Vorstellungswelt und Tätigkeit des Generalstabschefs des deutschen Heeres 1933–1938*, Boppard am Rhein, 339–42; and Hans-Jürgen Rautenberg, 'Drei Dokumente zur Planung eines 300.000-Mann-Friedensheeres aus dem Dezember 1933', *Militärgeschichtliche Mitteilungen*, 22 (1977), 103–39.

75. *D R Z W*, i.403–10, 416; Müller, *Beck*, 192–4, 341; Müller, *Heer*, 208.

76. Müller, *Beck*, 189, 339–44.

77. Müller, *Beck*, 190.

78. François-Poncet, 224–5; Höhne, *Zeit der Illusionen*, 294–5; Domarus, 481; Müller, *Beck*, 195; Weinberg, i.205.

79. Domarus, 482.

80. Höhne, *Zeit der Illusionen*, 295.

81. Schmidt, 295–6; François-Poncet, 225; Höhne, *Zeit der Illusionen*, 297.

82. Domarus, 489.

83. Seraphim, *Das politische Tagebuch Rosenbergs*, 74–5. For the difficulties facing Hitler in the timing of announcing Germany's new military strength, see Höhne, *Zeit der Illusionen*, 295–6.

84. Domarus, 489; Müller, *Beck*, 195; François-Poncet, 226; Höhne, *Zeit der Illusionen*, 298. The secret decree on the air-force had been agreed in cabinet on 26 February – before the announcement of the visit by Simon and Eden – to take effect on 1 March, and be announced a few days later (Weinberg, i.205).

85. Höhne, *Zeit der Illusionen*, 298. Göring told the British Air Attaché that the Germans had 1,500 aircraft; in reality the number was 800. The British had reckoned with a Luftwaffe of 1,300 aircraft by October 1936.

86. Schmidt, 296.

87. Müller, *Beck*, 195; Höhne, *Zeit der Illusionen*, 287–8.

88. François-Poncet, 229.

89. Friedrich Hoßbach, *Zwischen Wehrmacht und Hitler 1934–1938*, Wolffenbüttel/Hanover, 1949, 94–5.

90. Hoßbach, 95.

91. Müller, *Heer*, 208; for the surprise of army leaders, see also Esmonde M. Robertson, *Hitler's Pre-War Policy and Military Plans, 1933–1939*, London, 1963, 56.

92. Müller, *Heer*, 209.

93. Hoßbach, 95–6.

94. Müller, *Heer*, 208–10; Müller, *Beck*, 196; Höhne, *Zeit der Illusionen*, 287–9, 298–9.

95. Müller, *Heer*, 208. Feeling in the Foreign Office was nevertheless that what was achieved by Hitler's action could have been brought about by negotiation (Schmidt, 296). Fritsch, too, was of the view that, though unavoidable, the announcement of general conscription could have been made 'with less drama' (cit. Müller, *Heer*, 209).

96. Höhne, *Zeit der Illusionen*, 303–4. And see Rosenberg's information from within the British Air Ministry, Seraphim, *Das politische Tagebuch Rosenbergs*, 75.

97. Hoßbach, 96.

98. Hoßbach, 96; Müller, *Heer*, 209.

99. Domarus, 491; Höhne, *Zeit der Illusionen*, 299.

100. Hoßbach, 96; Müller, *Heer*, 209; Höhne, *Zeit der Illusionen*, 299; Hitler, *Monologe*, 343 (16 August 1942).

101. François-Poncet, 228–9.

102. Seraphim, *Das politische Tagebuch Rosenbergs*, 77. See *DGFP*, C, III, 1005–6, No.532, 1015, No.538. The official record notes the French ambassador's protest, states that the Italian ambassador refrained from any comment, and indicates the British ambassador's inquiry about continuation of discussions raised in the Anglo-French communiqué of 3 February.

103. Domarus, 491–5, here 494.

104. François-Poncet, 230; William Shirer, *Berlin Diary, 1934–1941*, (1941) Sphere Book edn, London, 1970, 32.

105. Shirer, 33.

106. Shirer, 33–4.

107. Domarus, 491–5; Höhne, *Zeit der Illusionen*, 299.

108. François-Poncet, 230.

109. *DBS*, ii.275–82.

110. *DBS*, ii.277–9.

111. *DBS*, ii.279.

112. Jens Petersen, *Hitler-Mussolini*, 397–400.

113. Schmidt, 296; Höhne, *Zeit der Illusionen*, 304; Weinberg, i.206.

114. François-Poncet, 231.

115. Schmidt, 297.

116. Seraphim, *Das politische Tagebuch Rosenbergs*, 77; Höhne, *Zeit der Illusionen*, 302.

117. The following is based on Schmidt's account, 298–308.

118. Eden, *Facing the Dictators*, 133 (and, for Eden's impressions on first meeting Hitler on 20 February 1934, 61). See also Winston Churchill's published comment in 1935, 'Hitler and his Choice, 1935', reprinted in his *Great Contemporaries*, London, 1941, 223–31, here 230: 'Those who have met Herr Hitler face to face in public business or on social terms have found a highly competent, cool, well-informed functionary with an agreeable manner, a disarming smile, and few have been unaffected by a subtle personal magnetism.'

119. Schmidt, 301–2 (where he gives the figure of 126, not 128, *Memelländer*).

120. Eden, *Facing the Dictators*, 135.

121. Schmidt, 306.

122. Schmidt, 307. The official account of the talks is recorded in *DGFP*, C, III, 1043–80, No.555.

123. Schmidt, 306–8.

124. Friedelind Wagner, 128–9, recounted how her mother, Winifred Wagner, a guest at the banquet in honour of Simon and Eden, told of Hitler 'slapping his knees and clapping his hands like a schoolboy' in pleasure at his diplomatic success. For the suggestion that this meeting, nevertheless, brought the first sign of recognition on Hitlers part that British resistance to his desired alliance with Great Britain might be stronger than he had originally bargained for, see Josef Henke, *England in Hitler's politischem Kalkül 1935–1939*, Boppard am Rhein, 1973, 38–9. An indication of Hitler's new assertiveness, revealed at the discussions with his British guests, was the raising of demands for the return of colonies which he mistakenly regarded as an attempt to 'persuade' the British into friendly cooperation. (See Klaus Hildebrand, *Vom Reich zum Weltreich. Hitler, NSDAP und koloniale Frage 1919–1945*, Munich, 1969, 447ff.; Klaus Hildebrand, *The Foreign Policy of the Third Reich*, London, 1973, 36–7; Klaus Hildebrand, *Das vergangene Reich. Deutsche Außenpolitik von Bismarck bis Hitler 1871–1945*, Stuttgart, 1995, 598.)

125. Eden, *Facing the Dictators*, 136.

126. Eden, *Facing the Dictators*, 133–4, 139.

127. Weinberg, i.207; A. J. P. Taylor, *The Origins of the Second World War*, (1961) revised edn, Harmondsworth, 1964, 116–17.

128. *TBJG*, I.2, 485 (15 April 1935).

129. *TBJG*, I.2, 486 (17 April 1935).

130. Domarus, 506.

131. Domarus, 511.

132. After the Dollfuss affair of July 1934, and given the continued instability of the position of Austria, Mussolini was anxious to ward off any possible repeated German coup there, particularly since his own eyes were cast on Abyssinia, and he was aware of powerful opposition at home to his proposed adventure. Neurath was reportedly concerned – as the Italian leader no doubt intended him to be – about Mussolini's pro-western and anti-German position adopted at Stresa (William E. Dodd and Martha Dodd (eds.), *Ambassador Dodd's Diary, 1933–1938*, London, 1941, 236–45). See also Robert Mallett, *The Italian Navy and Fascist Expansionism, 1935–40*, London, 1998, 28–9.

133. Domarus, 505–14. For the reception in Germany, see Kershaw, *The 'Hitler Myth'*, 125–6. *The Times* described the speech as 'reasonable, straightforward, and comprehensive' (cit. Toland, 372).

134. Domarus, 512–13.

135. Jost Dülffer, *Weimar, Hitler und die Marine. Reichspolitik und Flottenbau 1920–1939*, Düsseldorf, 1973, 256–7.

136. Dülffer, *Weimar, Hitler und die Marine*, 266–7.

137. *DRZW*, i.455–8.

138. Dülffer, *Weimar, Hitler und die Marine*, 280, 291, 301, and see 319–20; Höhne, *Zeit der Illusionen*, 308–9; Weinberg, i.212.

139. Schmidt, 317. See Spitzy, 92–122, for a biting description of Ribbentrop's personality and style as German ambassador in London. The development of

Ribbentrop's foreign-policy ideas, with differing emphasis to those of Hitler but ultimately devoid of independent standing, is examined in Wolfgang Michalka, *Ribbentrop und die deutsche Weltpolitik 1933–1940. Außenpolitische Konzeptionen und Entscheidungsprozesse im Dritten Reich*, Munich, 1980.

140. Michael Bloch, *Ribbentrop*, paperback edn., London, 1994, 54–8. The continued efforts on Ribbentrop's part to cultivate good relations with 'fellow-travellers of the Right' in Britain and the mutual misunderstandings which ensued are detailed by G. T. Waddington, ' "An idyllic and unruffled atmosphere of complete Anglo-German misunderstanding": Aspects of the Operations of the Dienststelle Ribbentrop in Great Britain, 1934–1939', *History*, 82 (1997), 44–72.

141. Bloch, *Ribbentrop*, 69; Domarus, 515; *DGFP*, C, IV. 253, n.2.

142. For the talks, and their consequences, see esp. Dülffer, *Weimar, Hitler und die Marine*, 325–54.

143. *DGFP*, C, IV, 257.

144. Schmidt, 318.

145. *DGFP*, C, IV, 250.

146. *DGFP*, C, IV, 277–8; Bloch, *Ribbentrop*, 73.

147. Schmidt, 319.

148. Ribbentrop, 41. British sources in Berlin were nevertheless claiming by early 1936 that Hitler, disappointed that the Naval Treaty had not produced the desired close relations with Britain, regretted his haste in concluding it (Geoffrey T. Waddington, 'Hitler, Ribbentrop, die NSDAP und der Niedergang des Britischen Empire 1935–1938', *VfZ*, 40 (1992), 273–306, here 277).

149. Other powers, Sir John Simon had told the German delegation, were merely to be informed that the British Government 'had decided' to accept the German Reich Chancellor's proposal (*DGFP*, C, IV, 280).

150. Denis Mack Smith, *Mussolini*, London, 1983, 228–35, quotation 232.

151. See Taylor, 118–29, for the Abyssinian crisis and its impact. The feeble British response to Italian aggression underlined Hitler's growing feeling that Britain was weak and lacked the will to oppose his territorial ambitions in Europe. It played its part in persuading him that there was little prospect of Britain intervening should he act to remilitarize the Rhineland (Henke, 40–47).

152. See Donald Cameron Watt, 'The Secret Laval-Mussolini Agreement of 1935 on Ethiopia', in Esmonde M. Robertson (ed.), *The Origins of the Second World War*, London, 1971, 225–42.

153. Sonderarchiv Moscow, 1235-VI-2, Reichskanzlei, Lammers, Vermerk, 16 October 1935.

154. *Monologe*, 108 (25 October 1941).

155. See Kershaw, *Popular Opinion and Political Dissent*, 236–7.

156. Schleunes, 116.

157. Kurt Pätzold, *Faschismus, Rassenwahn, Judenverfolgung. Eine Studie zur politischen Strategie und Taktik des faschistischen deutschen Imperialismus 1933–1935*, Berlin (East), 1975, 194–5; Ian Kershaw, 'The Persecution of the Jews and

German Popular Opinion in the Third Reich', *Yearbook of the Leo Baeck Institute*, 26 (1981), 261–89, here 264–5; David Bankier, *The Germans and the Final Solution: Public Opinion under Nazism*, Oxford/Cambridge, Mass., 1992, 35; Saul Friedländer, *Nazi Germany and the Jews. The Years of Persecution, 1933–39*, London, 1997, 137ff.

158. Adam, 114–15, 119–20; Bankier, *The Germans and the Final Solution*, 35.

159. 'How Popular was Streicher?', (no author), *Wiener Library Bulletin*, 5/6 (1957), 48; Bankier, *The Germans and the Final Solution*, 35.

160. David Bankier, 'Hitler and the Policy-Making Process on the Jewish Question', *Holocaust and Genocide Studies*, 3 (1988), 1–20, here 9.

161. *Akten der Partei-Kanzlei*, 4 Bde., ed. Institut für Zeitgeschichte [Helmut Heiber (Bde.1–2) and Peter Longerich (Bde.3–4)], Munich etc., 1983–92, Teil I, Regesten, Bd. 1, 98, No.10807, Microfiche, 124 05038, Wiedemann to Bormann, 30 April 1935: 'I've told the Führer about the reservations over these signs on account of the Olympics. Nothing has changed in the Führer's decision that there is no objection to these signs' ('*Ich habe dem Führer von den Bedenken, die wegen der Olympiade in Bezug auf diese Schilder geltend gemacht wurden, erzählt. An der Entscheidung des Führers, daß gegen diese Schilder nichts einzuwenden ist, hat sich dadurch nichts geändert*)'. See also Bankier, 'Hitler and the Policy-Making Process on the Jewish Question', 9.

162. Bankier, *The Germans and the Final Solution*, 28–35.

163. Bankier, *The Germans and the Final Solution*, 33.

164. Otto Dov Kulka, 'Die Nürnberger Rassengesetze und die deutsche Bevölkerung im Lichte geheimer NS-Lage- und Stimmungsberichte', *VfZ*, 32 (1984), 582–624, here 609.

165. Cit. Marlis Steinert, *Hitlers Krieg und die Deutschen. Stimmung und Haltung der deutschen Bevölkerung im Zweiten Weltkrieg*, Düsseldorf, 1970, 57; Bankier, *The Germans and the Final Solution*, 38.

166. Bankier, *The Germans and the Final Solution*, 38.

167. Adam, 118 (where other examples are also given). See Hans Mommsen, 'Der nationalsozialistische Polizeistaat und die Judenverfolgung vor 1938', *VfZ*, 10 (1962), 73, 84, Dok. Nr.11, for the subsequent ban imposed in Bavaria by the Bavarian Political Police on 6 March 1935.

168. Bankier, *The Germans and the Final Solution*, 38–41; Kershaw, *Popular Opinion and Political Dissent*, 50, 127–30, 205–6; Kershaw, *The 'Hitler Myth'*, 101–2.

169. Bankier, *The Germans and the Final Solution*, 70–76; Kershaw, 'The Persecution of the Jews', 265–72.

170. Bankier, *The Germans and the Final Solution*, 74–5; Kershaw, 'The Persecution of the Jews', 268–70.

171. *Bayern*, i.430, 442–7; *Bayern* ii.293–4; Kershaw, *Popular Opinion and Political Dissent*, 234 n.28; Pätzold, *Faschismus, Rassenwahn, Judenverfolgung*, 216–21.

172. *TBJG*, I.2, 493–4 (15 July 1935); Adam, 120; Ted Harrison, ' "Alter Kämpfer" im Widerstand', *VfZ*, 45 (1997), 385–423, here 400–401; Reuth, *Goebbels*, 330–31; Irving, *Mastermind*, 206–7. See Helmut Genschel, *Die Verdrängung der Juden*, 109–10, for the spreading of the boycott to numerous other areas during the spring and summer.

173. Adam, 120.

174. Schacht, 347; Adam, 123; Genschel, 111. Economic concerns, alongside the need to avoid conflict with the police, had doubtless been behind the fruitless order by Heß to the party on 1 April 1935 to avoid 'terror actions against individual Jews'. A further order in June to maintain party discipline was equally ineffective (Longerich, *Hitlers Stellvertreter*, 212).

175. Longerich, *Hitlers Stellvertreter*, 212.

176. Adam, 121; see also Bankier, *The Germans and the Final Solution*, 37.

177. Lothar Gruchmann, ' "Blutschutzgesetz" und Justiz. Zu Entstehung und Auswirkung des Nürnberger Gesetzes vom 15. September 1935', *VfZ*, 3 (1983), 418–42, here 430; Mommsen 'Polizeistaat', 70–71.

178. Bankier, *The Germans and the Final Solution*, 36–7.

179. Adam, 115, 119.

180. Adam, 120.

181. 'Das Reichsministerium des Innern und die Judengesetzgebung. Aufzeichnungen von Dr. Bernhard Lösener', *VfZ*, 9 (1961), 262–311, here 277–8.

182. Gruchmann, ' "Blutschutzgesetz" und Justiz', 418–23.

183. Cit. Gruchmann, ' "Blutschutzgesetz" und Justiz', 425.

184. Bankier, *The Germans and the Final Solution*, 44.

185. Frick himself had on 26 July instructed registry offices to postpone such forthcoming marriages indefinitely (Adam, 122). An indefinite postponement was decreed in Württemberg in August (Bankier, *The Germans and the Final Solution*, 44).

186. Gruchmann, ' "Blutschutzgesetz" und Justiz', 426–30; Adam, 122; Jeremy Noakes, 'The Development of Nazi Policy towards the German-Jewish "Mischlinge" 1933–1945', *Yearbook of the Leo Baeck Institute*, 34 (1989), 291–354, here 307–8.

187. Adam, 122.

188. Kurt Pätzold (ed.), *Verfolgung, Vertreibung, Vernichtung. Dokumente des faschistischen Antisemitismus 1933 bis 1942*, Leipzig, 1983, 103; Adam, 123; Schacht, 349–52; Bankier, *The Germans and the Final Solution*, 44–5; *IMT*, xii, 638 (where Schacht claimed that the laws he expected were to give the Jews legal protection, in line with demands he claimed he had been making to Hitler).

189. *Bayern* i.430.

190. *DGFP*, C, IV, 569.

191. Kulka, 'Die Nürnberger Rassengesetze', 615–18; Adam, 123–4; Longerich, *Hitlers Stellvertreter*, 212–13; Schacht, 356, states that the meeting was packed to capacity, lasted nearly two hours, and that Frick protested at his 'over-trenchant method of speech'.

192. *DGFP*, C, IV, 570.

193. *DGFP*, C, IV, 570. In fact, during the Nuremberg Rally Hitler chastised Streicher – though in gentle fashion – for the mistakes of the *Stürmer*. Goebbels thought Streicher had taken note, but that it would make no difference. (*TBJG*, I.2, 513 (11 September 1935)).

194. Kulka, 'Die Nürnberger Rassengesetze', 618–19 and n.126; Adam, 124.

195. *TBJG*, I.2, 515 (17 September 1935).

196. Kulka, 'Die Nürnberger Rassengesetze', 620 n.128, citing the *Jewish Chronicle*, 30 August 1935. See also Bankier, *The Germans and the Final Solution*, 44.

197. Schleunes, 119.

198. Adam, 126 n.66.

199. IfZ, MA-1569/42, Frame 1081, Interrogation of Dr Bernhard Lösener for US War Crimes Trials at Nuremberg; 'Das Reichsministerium des Innern und die Judengesetzgebung', 273; Adam, 126–7. The comment indicates that little work had been done prior to this point on preparing legislation.

200. IfZ, MA-1569/42, Frames 1081–2, Lösener testimony: 'Das Reichsministerium des Innern und die Judengesetzgebung', 274.

201. Max Domarus, *Der Reichstag und die Macht*, Würzburg, 1968, 101–2; Bankier, *The Germans and the Final Solution*, 45.

202. Mommsen, 'Realisierung', 387 and n.20.

203. IfZ, MA-1569/42, Frame 1081, Lösener testimony; 'Das Reichsministerium des Innern und die Judengesetzgebung', 273; Domarus, *Der Reichstag und die Macht*, 102 n.21.

204. See Peter Reichel, *Der schöne Schein des Dritten Reiches. Faszination und Gewalt des Faschismus*, Frankfurt am Main, 1993, 116–38, esp. 126–31.

205. Domarus, 525.

206. Bankier, *The Germans and the Final Solution*, 45.

207. Domarus, 534.

208. IfZ, MA-1569/42, Frames 1081–2, Lösener testimony; 'Das Reichsministerium des Innern und die Judengesetzgebung', 274; Schleunes, 124; Adam, 127.

209. IfZ, MA-1569/42, Frame 1082, Lösener testimony; 'Das Reichsministerium des Innern und die Judengesetzgebung', 275.

210. The text of the law is published in Pätzold, *Verfolgung*, 114.

211. Adam, 128.

212. Gruchmann, '"Blutschutzgesetz" und Justiz', 431–2; Adam, 128 and n.74.

213. The text is published in Pätzold, *Verfolgung*, 113–14.

214. The incident took place on 26 July. Six dock workers involved were given mild sentences on 12 and 14 August, but five were ordered to be released on 7 September, when the magistrate, Louis Brodsky, delivered an attack on Nazism and described the *Bremen* as a 'pirate ship'. The incident, widely reported in the German press, soured German-American relations. 'The whole of Germany [is] enraged about the judgement in New York about the agitators who rioted around the "Bremen" and pulled down the swastika flag,' noted Louise Solmitz in her diary on 7 September 1935 (Forschungsstelle für die Geschichte des Nationalsozialismus, Hamburg, Louise

Solmitz, Tagebuch, Bd.I, 1932–1937, Fol. 248). Hitler's fury was said to have impulsively made him decide to proclaim the swastika banner as the new German Flag (Bankier, *The Germans and the Final Solution*, 45; Domarus, 534 and n.201).

215. *JK*, 89–90.

216. In an interview at the end of November for the American United Press, Hitler repeated his assertion that 'the necessity of combating Bolshevism is one of the main reasons for the Jewish legislation in Germany'. He claimed that the laws were there to protect the Jews, and that the decline in anti-Jewish agitation within Germany was proof of their success. The Reich government, he went on, had been led by the intention of 'preventing through legal measures the self-help of the people, which could unburden itself among other things in dangerous explosions . . .' (Domarus, 557–8).

217. Domarus, 536–7.

218. Domarus, 537–8. Goebbels, a radical on 'the Jewish Question', found Göring's speech 'almost unbearable'. Whether by accident or design, the broadcast of the speech was turned off (*TBJG*, I.2, 515 (17 September 1935)).

219. Domarus, 538.

220. Domarus, 538–9; and see Gruchmann, ' "Blutschutzgesetz" und Justiz', 432; *TBJG*, I.2, 515 (17 September 1935), where Goebbels mistakenly has the entry under 'Samstag', not 'Sonntag'. Hitler repeated his ban on all 'excesses' at a meeting of the Gauleiter on 17 September, though Goebbels was sceptical of its effect (*TBJG*, I.2, 516 (19 September 1935)).

221. A hint of Hitler's own ambivalence, and determination not to be pinned down by legalities, could be seen in his refusal to allow Frick to publish any commentary on the 'Jewish law' (*TBJG*, I.2, 517 (21 September 1935)).

222. ZStA, Potsdam, RMdI, 27079/71, Fol. 52, LB of RP in Kassel, 4 March 1936.

223. The violence had already been in decline during the weeks preceding the Rally (Adam, 124).

224. Kulka, 'Die Nürnberger Rassengesetze', 622–3; Bankier, *The Germans and the Final Solution*, 76–80.

225. Kershaw, *The 'Hitler Myth'*, 237.

226. Gruchmann, ' "Blutschutzgesetz" und Justiz', 433–4; Adam, 134; 'Das Reichsministerium des Innern und die Judengesetzgebung', 279–82; IfZ, MA-1569/42, Frames 1082–3, Lösener testimony. On the 'Mischling question', see especially Noakes, 'The Development of Nazi Policy towards the German-Jewish "Mischlinge" 1933–1945', 306–15.

227. Bankier, 'Hitler and the Policy-Making Process on the Jewish Question', 14.

228. Adam, 132–5.

229. *TBJG*, II.2, 518 (25 September 1935). Lösener ('Das Reichsministerium des Innern und die Judengesetzgebung', 281) mentions being summoned to a meeting of the party leadership in the Town Hall at Munich on 29 September. His memory must have been faulty, since, as Goebbels's diary entry makes clear, the meeting took place on 24 September.

230. 'Das Reichsministerium des Innern und die Judengesetzgebung', 281. According to confidential information passed to press representatives, Hitler had tended at the meeting to favour the position of the ministry officials (Mommsen, 'Realisierung', 387–8, n.20).

231. *TBJG*, I.2, 520 (1 October 1935).

232. Adam, 139–40.

233. *TBJG*, I.2, 537 (7 November 1935).

234. Adam, 140–41; Schleunes, 129; Friedländer, *Nazi Germany and the Jews*, 148–51 and (for consequences of the racial definition in a number of personal cases) 155–62; above all, Noakes, 'The Development of Nazi Policy towards the German-Jewish "Mischlinge" 1933–1945', 310–15, and Jeremy Noakes, 'Wohin gehören die "Juden-mischlinge"? Die Entstehung der ersten Durchführungsverordnungen zu den Nürn-berger Gesetzen', in Ursula Büttner (ed.), *Das Unrechtsregime. Verfolgung, Exil, Belasteter Neubeginn*, Hamburg, 1986, 69–90. Those not counting as Jews under this definition, but descended from one or two 'non-Aryan' grandparents, were labelled 'Mischlinge'. In practice, 'Mischlinge Grade I' (of two 'non-Aryan' grand-parents) came under the 'Blood Law' to be associated with 'full Jews' (see Adam, 143–4).

235. *TBJG*, I.2, 540 (15 November 1935).

236. Adam, 142–3 and 142 n.130.

237. Until Gustloff's death, the Auslandsorganisation (AO) of the NSDAP in Switzerland had a *Landesgruppenleiter* and constituency groups (*Ortsgruppen*) in various cities. Following the assassination of Gustloff, the Swiss government did not allow the filling of his post, but the duties of the *Landesgruppenleiter* were in practice taken over by the German embassy in Bern (Benz, Graml and Weiß, *Enzyklopädie*, 724).

238. *Bayern*, ii.297.

239. Domarus, 573–5.

240. Hildegard von Kotze and Helmut Krausnick (eds.), '*Es spricht der Führer*'. *7 exemplarische Hitler-Reden*, Gütersloh, 1966, 148.

241. For some cases of intervention by Hitler in 1936–7, see Bankier, 'Hitler and the Policy-Making Process on the Jewish Question', 15.

242. *DBS*, iii.27.

243. *Der Parteitag der Freiheit vom 10.–16. September 1935. Offizieller Bericht über den Verlauf des Reichsparteitages mit sämtlichen Kongreßreden*, Munich, 1935, 287; also in: *Parteitag der Freiheit. Reden des Führers und ausgewählte Kongreßreden am Reichsparteitag der NSDAP, 1935*, Munich, 1935, 134–5.

244. E. C. Helmreich, 'The Arrest and Freeing of the Protestant Bishops of Württem-berg and Bavaria, September–October 1934', *Central European History*, 2 (1969), 159–69; Paul Sauer, *Württemberg in der Zeit des Nationalsozialismus*, Ulm, 1975, 185–9; Kershaw, *Popular Opinion and Political Dissent*, 164–79.

245. Kershaw, *Popular Opinion and Political Dissent*, 170, 172, 178.

246. Cited in Conway, 76–7.

247. See Kershaw, *The 'Hitler Myth'*, 119.

248. Kershaw, *Popular Opinion and Political Dissent*, 205ff.

249. *TBJG*, I.2, 504 (19 August 1935). See also 505 (21 August 1935): 'Rosenberg, Himmler, and Darré must stop their cultist nonsense' ('*Rosenberg, Himmler und Darré müssen ihren kultischen Unfug abstellen*').

250. *TBJG*, I.2, 511 (6 September 1935): 'In the question of Catholicism, the Führer sees things as very serious.'

251. For the impact of the 'Church Struggle' on the attitudes of the Catholic population in Bavaria, see Kershaw, *Popular Opinion and Political Dissent*, ch.5.

252. For the '1918 syndrome' of Hitler and the Nazi leadership, see Mason, *Sozialpolitik*, ch.1.

253. *TBJG*, I.2, 504 (19 August 1935): '*Führer gibt Überblick politische Lage. Sieht Verfall.*'

254. BAK, R43II/318, Fols.205–13, 28, 61–2 (and also Fols.195–203, 214–15); R43II/318a, Fols.45–53. See also Mason, *Arbeiterklasse*, 72 and n.102.

255. *DRZW*, i.254–9. The extent to which Germany was successful in economically exploiting the Balkan countries has been disputed by Alan S. Milward, 'The Reichsmark Bloc and the International Economy', in Hirschfeld and Kettenacker, 377–413, drawing a rejoinder from Bernd-Jürgen Wendt, 'Südosteuropa in der nationalsozialistischen Großraumwirtschaft' in the same volume, 414–28.

256. John E. Farquharson, *The Plough and the Swastika. The NSDAP and Agriculture, 1928–1945*, London, 1976, 166–8.

257. BAK, R58/535, Fols.91–6, Stapo Berlin, October 1935.

258. *TBJG*, 522 (5 October 1935); see also BAK, R43II/863, Fols.69–83; R43II/318a, Fol.15.

259. BAK, R58/567, Fols.84–93, Stapo Berlin, January 1936. Police reports frequently pointed to a revival of the activities of the illegal KPD in the winter of 1935–6. It is doubtful whether much of the unrest was attributable to organized Communist agitation. Rather, underground opposition groups were easily able to exploit the prevailing poor mood (Detlev J. K. Peukert, *Die KPD im Widerstand. Verfolgung und Untergrundarbeit an Rhein und Ruhr 1933 bis 1945*, Wuppertal, 1980, 204–50). The renewed Communist activity predictably brought an intensified onslaught by the Gestapo, to the point where the KPD had to recognize that there was no longer the slightest prospect of mass action against the regime, and that this would only bring needless sacrifices. By spring 1936, the ferocity of Nazi repression drastically reduced KPD resistance groups in size and greatly limited the possibilities of contact between underground activists (Allan Merson, *Communist Resistance in Nazi Germany*, London, 1985, 186–7).

260. IML/ZPA, St.3/44/I, Fols.103–7, Stapo Berlin, 6 March 1936. See also *DBS*, ii.1013, 1251–5 (16 October 1935, 12 November 1935). There were increased numbers of strikes in 1935–6, and widespread reports of the revival of illegal opposition groups. The strikes were invariably on a small scale and lasted only a matter

of hours. Details of many such small strikes are contained in a 381-folio file, 'Streikbewegung', in IML/ZPA, St.3/463.

261. Wiedemann, 90.

262. BAK, R54II/193, Fol.157, Lammers to Darré, 30 September 1934. Complaints from different parts of Prussia, forwarded by Göring to the Reich Chancellery, are in the file.

263. BAK, R43II/193, Fols.122–245.

264. BAK, R43II/315a, Fol.31.

265. BAK, R43II/318, Fol.2; the reports are included in Fols.1–29.

266. BAK, R43II/318, Fols.62–4.

267. BAK, R43II/318, Fol.31, 205–13; R43II/318a, Fols.45–53.

268. The title of Reichel's study on the stage-management and aesthetics of coercion and force in Nazi imagery and propaganda: *Der schöne Schein des Dritten Reiches.*

269. BAK, R43II/318, Fols.219–22 'Vermerk' for Lammers, brought to Hitler's attention; (also Fols.205–13 and R43II/318a, Fols.45–53).

270. *TBJG*, I.2, 516 (19 September 1935).

271. BAK, R43II/318a, Fols.11–31. See also Ritter, 79. According to the later account of Alfred Sohn-Rethel, at the time aware of thinking in business circles, Goerdeler's memorandum encountered considerable support in some sections of industry and prompted a good deal of debate, with even some talk of a possible putsch (Alfred Sohn-Rethel, *Ökonomie und Klassenstruktur des deutschen Faschismus*, Frankfurt am Main, 1975, 177).

272. Similar ideas advanced by Goerdeler some months later, at the time of the introduction of the Four-Year Plan, were rejected out of hand by Göring in early September 1936 as 'completely unusable' ('*völlig unbrauchbar*') (Dieter Petzina, *Autarkiepolitik im Dritten Reich. Der nationalsozialistische Vierjahresplan*, Stuttgart, 1968, 47; and see Ritter, 80).

273. Ritter, 80. More critical and penetrating as an analysis of Goerdeler's actions in the early years of the regime, which gradually shaped his growing opposition to it, is Michael Krüger-Charlé, 'Carl Goerdelers Versuche der Durchsetzung einer alternativen Politik 1933 bis 1937', in Jürgen Schmädeke and Peter Steinbach (eds.), *Der Widerstand gegen den Nationalsozialismus. Die deutsche Gesellschaft und der Widerstand gegen Hitler*, Munich, 1986, 383–404.

274. BAK, R43II/318a, Fols.35, 66.

275. Petzina, *Autarkiepolitik*, 32–3; Farquharson, 168.

276. Petzina, *Autarkiepolitik*, 32–3.

277. BAK, ZSg. 101/28, Fol.331, 'Informationsbericht Nr.55', 7 November 1935.

278. Goebbels reflected the concern on a number of occasions in his diaries: *TBJG*, I.2, 501 (11 August 1935); 503–4 (19 August 1935); 505 (21 August 1935); 506–7 (25 August 1935); 507 (27 August 1935); 522 (5 October 1935).

279. *TBJG*, I.2, 504 (19 August 1935).

280. *TBJG*, I.2, 529 (19 October 1935).

281. Petzina, *Autarkiepolitik*, 33–4.

282. Petzina, *Autarkiepolitik*, 35.

283. BAK, R43II/533, Fols.91–6.

284. As we have noted, the savage repression of the Gestapo, able to infiltrate and smash KPD cells, meant that any new life in Communist illegal activity was rapidly extinguished. Material discontent rather than ideological commitment of the level needed to court exposure to the enormous personal risks involved had provided the background to the short-lived increased appeal of Communist verbal propaganda in urban working-class areas. For the adjustment of the KPD in western Germany to the far less favourable circumstances from 1936 onwards, see Peukert, *Die KPD im Widerstand*, 252ff. The poor morale of Nazi Party members in early 1936 is highlighted by Orlow, ii.170–75.

285. *IMT*, xxv, 402–13 (here 409), Doc. 386–PS.

286. Esmonde Robertson, 'Zur Wiederbesetzung des Rheinlandes 1936', *VfZ*, 10 (1962), 178–205, here 203. See Bankier, *The Germans and the Final Solution*, 50–55 for evidence of popular unrest to support the view that internal causes were decisive.

287. Robertson, 'Zur Wiederbesetzung des Rheinlandes 1936', 204.

288. Robertson, 'Zur Wiederbesetzung des Rheinlandes 1936', 204–5; Manfred Funke, '7. März 1936. Fallstudie zum außenpolitischen Führungsstil Hitlers', in Wolfgang Michalka (ed.), *Nationalsozialistische Außenpolitik*, Darmstadt, 1978, 277–324, here 279.

289. See BAK, R58/570, Fols. 104–8, report to Gestapo Cologne, 6 February 1936; and BAK, NS22/vorl.583, reports of Gauleiter Grohé of Cologne-Aachen, 8 June, 6 July, and 10 December 1935, for comments on the poor economic position of the demilitarized zone and the strength of the Catholic Church's position there. See also *TBJG*, I.2, 374 (19 February 1936).

290. The cancellation at the last minute of the Works Councils elections scheduled for April 1936 can probably be attributed to the assumption that the results would have been less favourable than those of the plebiscite (Mason, *Sozialpolitik*, 206). Labour Minister Seldte was told (after learning of the postponement in the evening papers) that Hitler wanted the elections postponed to prevent a large part of the population having to go to the polls again immediately after the Reichstag election (BAK, R43II/547b, Fols. 2, 19).

291. *DRZW*, i.424.

292. Robertson, 'Zur Wiederbesetzung des Rheinlandes 1936', 195; *DGFP*, C, IV, 1166.

293. Weinberg, i.240–42; James T. Emmerson, *The Rhineland Crisis, 7 March 1936. A Study in Multilateral Diplomacy*, London, 1977, 63.

294. Petersen, 466–71.

295. Robertson, 'Zur Wiederbesetzung des Rheinlandes 1936', 196–9; Funke, '7. März 1936', 298–9; Petersen, 468.

296. Höhne, *Zeit der Illusionen*, 320; Emmerson, 46; Taylor, 126–7.

297. Emmerson, 39–41, 47–8, 51–2; Weinberg, i.243.

298. Emmerson, 77; Funke, '7. März 1936', 287–9.

299. Emmerson, 57, 80; Funke, '7. März 1936', 283–6; Weinberg, i.244–5; *DRZW*, i.604.

300. See Dülffer, 'Zum "decision-making process"', 194–7.

301. Marquess of Londonderry (Charles S.H. Vane-Tempest-Stewart), *Ourselves and Germany*, London, 1938, 114.

302. Hoßbach, 97.

303. The Pact, signed on 2 May 1935, was submitted to the Chamber of Deputies on 11 February. The final vote in the Chamber took place on 27 February. The ratification bill was laid before the Senate on 3 March (*DGFP*, C, IV, 1142 n.4, 1145 n.).

304. Robertson, 'Zur Wiederbesetzung des Rheinlandes 1936', 192, 194–6, 203–4; Funke, '7. März 1936', 279–82; Höhne, *Zeit der Illusionen*, 323–4; *DGFP*, C, IV, 1164–6. The German Chargé d'Affaires in Paris, Dirk Forster, had also argued against unilateral action – meeting a sarcastic response from Hitler (Emmerson, 83–4 and 285 n.106).

305. Robertson, 'Zur Wiederbesetzung des Rheinlandes 1936', 192. For Hitler's later remarks that he had envisaged remilitarization in 1937, but that circumstances had favoured accomplishing it a year earlier, see Wolfgang Michalka (ed.), *Das Dritte Reich. Dokumente zur Innen- und Außenpolitik*, 2 vols. Munich, 1985, i.267–8 (Hitlers Geheimrede vor den Truppenkommandeurern, 10 February 1939).

306. Robertson, 'Zur Wiederbesetzung des Rheinlandes 1936', 194–6, 203–4; *DGFP*, C, IV, 1165.

307. *TBJG*, I.2, 575 (29 February 1936).

308. *TBJG*, I.2. 576 (29 February 1936).

309. *TBJG*, I.2, 576 (29 February 1936).

310. *TBJG*, I.2, 577 (2 March 1936).

311. *TBJG*, I.2, 578 (4 March 1936). See also NCA, v. 1102, Doc.3308-PS, testimony of Paul Schmidt; Hoßbach, 97; Emmerson, 98, for military anxieties.

312. *TBJG*, I.2, 579 (4 March 1936), 580 (6 March 1936). Goebbels instigated a rumour (580) that the Reichstag would meet again on 13 March.

313. *TBJG*, I.2, 579–81 (6–8 March 1936).

314. Domarus, 582.

315. *TBJG*, I.2, 581 (8 March 1936); Hoffmann, 83; and see Shirer, 46–7. The surprise element was maximized by staging the coup on a Saturday, when British and French cabinet members had dispersed for the weekend (Emmerson, 100). And see Shirer, 51.

316. Shirer, 48; *TBJG*, I.2, 581 (8 March 1936). For the text of the speech, Domarus, 583–97; and for the description of the atmosphere in the Reichstag, Shirer, 48–50; Dodd, 325.

317. Domarus, 594.

318. Shirer, 49.

319. Domarus, 595.

320. Robertson, 'Zur Wiederbesetzung des Rheinlandes 1936', 195, 205; and see Emmerson, 95.

321. Shirer, 49–50.

322. Domarus, 596.

323. Eden, *Facing the Dictators*, 343–5; Robertson, 'Zur Wiederbesetzung des Rheinlandes 1936', 205.

324. Emmerson, 102.

325. *TBJG*, I.2, 581 (8 March 1936); Höhne, *Zeit der Illusionen*, 325.

326. Shirer, 51, 54; Höhne, *Zeit der Illusionen*, 326. Bishop Galen of Münster and Bishop Sebastian of Speyer also voiced an unsolicited and effusive welcome for the remilitarization (Lewy, 202).

327. Höhne, *Zeit der Illusionen*, 325, Emmerson, 97–8; Hoßbach, 97. D. C. Watt, 'German Plans for the Reoccupation of the Rhineland. A Note', *JCH*, 1 (1966), 193–9, argues that German troops were under orders to resist, not withdraw, but accepts (199) that those units which actually crossed the Rhine were to withdraw to the defensive line Roer-Rhine-Black Forest. Any breach of German borders through enemy offensive action was to be resisted by armed force. (See also Max Braubach, *Der Einmarsch deutscher Truppen in die entmilitarisierte Zone am Rhein im März 1936*, Cologne/Opladen, 1956, 19.)

328. Emmerson, 106.

329. Schmidt, 327; see also Hoffmann, 84.

330. Frank, 211. This was the common view of western journalists in Berlin at the time (Shirer, 51–2).

331. *TBJG*, I.2, 581–2 (8 March 1936).

332. Emmerson, 162; Höhne, *Zeit der Illusionen*, 329–30; *TBJG*, I.2, 585–6 (15 March 1936); Hoßbach, 98.

333. Höhne, *Zeit der Illusionen*, 330.

334. Frank, 211–12; extracts from the text of Hitler's speech in Cologne are given in Domarus, 614–16.

335. *DBS*, iii.300ff.; 460ff.

336. *DBS*, iii.460.

337. See *DBS*, iii.303, 310, 468.

338. Forschungsstelle für die Geschichte des Nationalsozialismus, Hamburg, Louise Solmitz, Tagebuch, Bd.I, Fols. 282–3 (7 March 1936).

339. Archiv der sozialen Demokratie (Friedrich-Ebert-Stiftung), Bonn, ES/M33, Hans Dill to Otto Wels, 20 April 1936.

340. *Statistisches Jahrbuch für das Deutsche Reich*, ed. Statistisches Reichsamt, Berlin, 1936, 565. See *TBJG*, I.2, 594 (31 March 1936).

341. See Shirer, 55; and Theodor Eschenburg, 'Streiflichter zur Geschichte der Wahlen im Dritten Reich', *VfZ*, 3 (1955), 311–16, for polling irregularities.

342. Domarus, 641 (trans., Stern, *Hitler: the Führer and the People*, 90).

343. *Der Parteitag der Ehre vom 8. bis 14. September 1936*, Munich, 1936, 246–7; Domarus, 643.

344. Domarus, 606.

LIST OF WORKS CITED

Abel, Theodore, *Why Hitler Came into Power*, Cambridge, Mass. (1938), 1986.

Abelshauser, Werner, Petzina, Dietmar, and Faust, Anselm (eds.), *Deutsche Sozialgeschichte 1914–1945. Ein historisches Lesebuch*, Munich, 1985.

Adam, Uwe Dietrich, *Judenpolitik im Dritten Reich*, Düsseldorf, 1972.

Adolf Hitler: Monologe im Führerhauptquartier 1941–1944. Die Aufzeichnungen Heinrich Heims, ed. Werner Jochmann, Hamburg, 1980.

Akten der Partei-Kanzlei, 4 Bde., ed. Institut für Zeitgeschichte [Helmut Heiber (Bde. 1–2) and Peter Longerich (Bde. 3–4)], Munich etc., 1983–92.

Akten der Reichskanzlei. Das Kabinett von Papen, ed. Karl-Heinz Minuth, Boppard am Rheim, 1989.

Akten der Reichskanzlei. Das Kabinett von Schleicher, ed. Anton Golecki, Boppard am Rhein, 1986.

Akten der Reichskanzlei. Die Regierung Hitler. Teil I, 1933/34, ed. Karl-Heinz Minuth, 2 vols., Boppard am Rhein, 1983.

Allen, William Sheridan, *The Nazi Seizure of Power*, revised edn, New York, 1984.

Anonymous, 'Muj Prítel Hitler' (My Friend Hitler), *Moravsky ilustrovany zpravodaj*, 40(1935), 10–11 (in Czech).

——'How Popular was Streicher?', *Wiener Library Bulletin*, 5/6 (1957).

——'The Story of Mein Kampf', *Wiener Library Bulletin*, 6 (1952), no. 5–6, 31–2.

Aronson, Shlomo, *Reinhard Heydrich und die Frühgeschichte von Gestapo und SD*, Stuttgart, 1971.

Auerbach, Helmuth, 'Hitlers politische Lehrjahre und die Münchner Gesellschaft 1919–1923', *VfZ*, 25 (1977), 1–45.

——'Nationalsozialismus vor Hitler', in Wolfgang Benz, Hans Buchheim and Hans Mommsen (eds.), *Der Nationalsozialismus. Studien zur Ideologie und Herrschaft*, Frankfurt am Main, 1993, 13–28.

Ay, Karl-Ludwig, *Die Entstehung einer Revolution, Die Volksstimmung in Bayern während des Ersten Weltkrieges*, Berlin, 1968.

Bahne, Siegfried, 'Die Kommunistische Partei Deutschlands', in Erich Matthias and Rudolf Morsey (eds.), *Das Ende der Parteien 1933*, Königstein/Ts., 1979, 655–739.

Bajohr, Frank, 'Gauleiter in Hamburg. Zur Person und Tätigkeit Karl Kaufmanns', *VfZ*, 43 (1995), 269–95.

Bankier, David, 'Hitler and the Policy-Making Process on the Jewish Question', *Holocaust and Genocide Studies*, 3 (1988), 1–20.

——*The Germans and the Final Solution: Public Opinion under Nazism*, Oxford/ Cambridge, Mass., 1992.

Baranowski, Shelley, *The Sanctity of Rural Life. Nobility, Protestantism, and Nazism in Weimar Prussia*, New York/Oxford, 1995.

Barkai, Avraham, 'Sozialdarwinismus und Antiliberalismus in Hitlers Wirtschafts- konzept', *Geschichte und Gesellschaft*, 3 (1977), 406–17.

——*Das Wirtschaftssystem des Nationalsozialismus*, Fischer edn, Frankfurt am Main, 1988.

Barta, Tony, 'Living in Dachau, 1900–1950', unpublished paper.

Baur, Hans, *Ich flog Mächtige der Erde*, Kempten (Allgäu), 1956.

Bayern in der NS-Zeit, ed. Martin Broszat *et al.*, 6 vols., Munich, 1977–83.

Becker, Josef, 'Zentrum und Ermächtigungsgesetz', *VfZ*, 9 (1961), 195–210.

Becker, Josef and Ruth (eds.), *Hitlers Machtergreifung. Dokumente vom Machtan- tritt Hitlers 30. Januar 1933 bis zur Besiegelung des Einparteienstaates 14. Juli 1933*, 2nd edn, Munich, 1992.

Bein, Alexander, 'Der moderne Antisemitismus und seine Bedeutung für die Juden- frage', *VfZ*, 6 (1958), 340–60.

——' "Der jüdische Parasit". Bemerkungen zur Semantik der Judenfrage', *VfZ*, 13 (1965), 121–49.

Benz, Wolfgang (ed.), *Politik in Bayern. Berichte des württembergischen Gesandten Carl Moser von Filseck*, Stuttgart, 1971.

Benz, Wolfgang, and Graml, Hermann (eds.), *Biographisches Lexikon zur Weimarer Republik*, Munich, 1988.

Benz, Wolfgang, Graml, Hermann, and Weiß, Hermann (eds.), *Enzyklopädie des Nationalsozialismus*, Stuttgart, 1997.

Berning, Cornelia, *Vom 'Abstammungsnachweis' zum 'Zuchtwart'. Vokabular des Nationalsozialismus*, Berlin, 1964.

Bessel, Richard, 'The Potempa Murder', *Central European History*, 10 (1977), 241– 54.

——'The Rise of the NSDAP and the Myth of Nazi Propaganda', *Wiener Library Bulletin*, 33 (1980), 20–29.

——*Political Violence and the Rise of Nazism. The Storm Troopers in Eastern Germany 1925–1934*, New Haven/London, 1984.

——'Unemployment and Demobilisation in Germany after the First World War', in Richard J. Evans and Dick Geary (eds.), *The German Unemployed*, London/ Sydney, 1987, 23–43.

——'1933: A Failed Counter-Revolution', in E. E. Riche (ed.), *Revolution and Counter Revolution*, Oxford, 1991, 109–227.

——*Germany after the First World War*, Oxford, 1993.

Bezymenski, Lev, *The Death of Adolf Hitler*, London, 1968.

Binion, Rudolph, 'Hitler's Concept of "Lebensraum": the Psychological Basis', *History of Childhood Quarterly*, 1 (1973), 187–215 (with subsequent discussion of his hypotheses, 216–58).

——'Foam on the Hitler Wave', *JMH*, 46 (1974), 552–8.

——*Hitler among the Germans*, New York, 1976.

Blackbourn, David, and Eley, Geoff, *The Peculiarities of German History*, Oxford, 1984.

Bloch, Eduard, 'My Patient, Hitler', *Collier's*, 15 March 1941, 35–7; 22 March 1941, 69–73.

Bloch, Ernst, 'Der Faschismus als Erscheinungsform der Ungleichzeitigkeit', in Ernst Nolte (ed.), *Theorien über den Faschismus*, 6th edn, Königstein/Ts., 1984, 182–204.

Boak, Helen L., 'Women in Weimar Germany: the "Frauenfrage" and the Female Vote', in Richard Bessel and E. J. Feuchtwanger (eds.), *Social Change and Political Development in the Weimar Republic*, London, 1981, 155–73.

Bock, Gisela, *Zwangssterilisation im Nationalsozialismus. Studien zur Rassenpolitik und Frauenpolitik*, Opladen, 1986.

Boehnke, Wilfried, *Die NSDAP im Ruhrgebiet, 1920–1933*, Bad Godesberg, 1974.

Bollmus, Reinhard, 'Ein rationaler Diktator? Zu einer neuen Hitler-Biographie', *Die Zeit*, 22 September 1989, 45–6.

Borchardt, Knut, *Wachstum, Krisen, Handlungsspielräume der Wirtschaftspolitik*, Göttingen, 1982.

Boyer, John W., *Political Radicalism in Late Imperial Vienna. Origins of the Christian Social Movement, 1848–1897*, Chicago, 1981.

Bracher, Karl Dietrich, *Die Auflösung der Weimarer Republik. Eine Studie zum Problem des Machtverfalls in einer Demokratie*, Stuttgart/Düsseldorf, 1955.

——*The German Dictatorship*, Harmondsworth, 1973.

——'The Role of Hitler: Perspectives of Interpretation', in Walter Laqueur (ed.), *Fascism. A Reader's Guide*, Harmondsworth, 1979, 193–212.

Bracher, Karl Dietrich, Schulz, Gerhard, and Sauer, Wolfgang, *Die nationalsozialistische Machtergreifung*, (1960), paperback edn, 3 vols., Frankfurt am Main/Berlin/Vienna, 1974.

Bracher, Karl Dietrich et al. (ed.), *Quellen zur Geschichte des Parlamentarismus und der politischen Parteien, Bd. 4/1, Politik und Wirtschaft in der Krise 1930–1932. Quellen zur Ära Brüning, Teil I*, Bonn, 1980.

Brandmayer, Balthasar, *Meldegänger Hitler 1914–18*, Munich/Kolbermoor, 1933.

Braubach, Max, *Der Einmarsch deutscher Truppen in die entmilitarisierte Zone am Rhein im März 1936*, Cologne/Opladen, 1956.

Bridenthal, Renate, 'Beyond Kinder, Küche, Kirche: Weimar Women at Work', *Central European History*, 6 (1973), 148–66.

Broszat, Martin, 'Die Anfänge der Berliner NSDAP, 1926/27', *VfZ*, 8 (1960), 85–118.

——*Der Nationalsozialismus. Weltanschauung, Programm und Wirklichkeit*, Stuttgart, 1960.

——'Betrachtungen zu "Hitlers Zweitem Buch"', *VfZ*, 9 (1961), 417–30.

——*Der Staat Hitlers. Grundlegung und Entwicklung seiner inneren Verfassung*, Munich, 1969.

——'Soziale Motivation und Führer-Bindung im Nationalsozialismus', *VfZ*, 18 (1970), 392–409.

——'Zur Struktur der NS-Massenbewegung', *VfZ*, 31 (1983), 52–76.

——*Die Machtergreifung. Der Aufstieg der NSDAP und die Zerstörung der Weimarer Republik*, Munich, 1984.

Broszat, Martin, and Frei, Norbert (eds.), *Das Dritte Reich im Überblick. Chronik, Ereignisse, Zusammenhänge*, Munich, 1989.

Broszat, Martin, *et al.* (eds.), *Deutschlands Weg in die Diktatur*, Berlin, 1983.

Brüning, Heinrich, *Memoiren 1918–1934*, 2 vols., Munich, 1972.

——*Briefe und Gespräche 1934–1945*, ed. Claire Nix, Stuttgart, 1974.

Brustein, William, *The Logic of Evil. The Social Origins of the Nazi Party 1925–1933*, New Haven/London, 1996.

Bucher, Peter, *Der Reichswehrprozeß. Der Hochverrat der Ulmer Reichswehroffiziere 1929–30*, Boppard am Rhein, 1967.

Buchheim, Hans, *et al.*, *Anatomie des SS-Staates*, 2 vols., Olten/Freiburg im Breisgau, 1965.

Bukey, Evan Burr, *Hitler's Hometown*, Bloomington/Indianapolis, 1986.

Bullock, Alan, *Hitler. A Study in Tyranny*, rev. edn, Harmondsworth, 1962.

——*Hitler and Stalin. Parallel Lives*, London, 1991.

Burkert, Hans-Norbert, Matußek, Klaus, and Wippermann, Wolfgang, '*Machtergreifung', Berlin 1933*, Berlin, 1982.

Cameron Watt, Donald, 'Die bayerischen Bemühungen um Ausweisung Hitlers 1924', *VfZ*, 6 (1958), 270–80.

——'German Plans for the Reoccupation of the Rhineland. A Note', *JCH*, I (1966), 193–9.

——'The Secret Laval–Mussolini Agreement of 1935 on Ethiopia', in Esmonde M. Robertson, *The Origins of the Second World War*, London, 1971, 225–42.

Carlyle, Thomas, 'Lecture One' 'On Heroes, Hero-Worship, and the Heroic, in History', in Fritz Stern (ed.), *The Varieties of History. From Voltaire to the Present*, 2nd Macmillan edn, London, 1970, 90–107.

Carr, William, *Hitler: a Study in Personality and Politics*, London, 1978.

——'Historians and the Hitler Phenomenon', *German Life and Letters*, 34 (1981), 260–72.

Carsten, Francis L., *The Rise of Fascism*, London, 1967.

Chickering, Roger, *We Men Who Feel Most German. A Cultural Study of the Pan-German League, 1866–1914*, London, 1984.

Childers, Thomas, *The Nazi Voter. The Social Foundations of Fascism in Germany, 1919–1933*, Chapel Hill/London, 1983.

——'The Social Language of Politics in Germany. The Sociology of Political Discourse in the Weimar Republic', *American Historical Review*, 95 (1990), 331–58.

——'The Middle Classes and National Socialism', in David Blackbourn and Richard Evans (eds.), *The German Bourgeoisie*, London/New York, 1993, 328–40.

——(ed.), *The Formation of the Nazi Constituency, 1919–1933*, London/Sydney, 1986.

Churchill, Winston S., *Great Contemporaries*, London, 1941.

——*The Second World War, vol. 1: The Gathering Storm*, London, 1948.

Ciolek-Kümper, Jutta, *Wahlkampf in Lippe*, Munich, 1976.

Conway, John, *The Nazi Persecution of the Churches 1933–45*, London, 1968.

Corni, Gustavo, *Hitler and the Peasants*, New York/Oxford/Munich, 1990.

Corni, Gustavo, and Gies, Horst, *Brot, Butter, Kanonen: Die Ernährungswirtschaft in Deutschland unter der Diktatur Hitlers*, Berlin, 1997.

Czichon, Eberhard, *Wer verhalf Hitler zur Macht? Zum Anteil der deutschen Industrie an der Zerstörung der Weimarer Republik*, Cologne (1967), 3rd edn, 1972.

Dahrendorf, Ralf, *Society and Democracy in Germany*, London, 1968.

Daim, Wilfried, *Der Mann, der Hitler die Ideen gab*, Vienna/Cologne/Graz, 2nd edn, 1985.

Deist, Wilhelm, *The Wehrmacht and German Rearmament*, London, 1981.

Delmer, Sefton, *Trail Sinister*, London, 1961.

Deuerlein, Ernst, 'Hitlers Eintritt in die Politik und die Reichswehr', *VfZ*, 7 (1959), 177–227.

——*Hitler, Eine politische Biographie*, Munich, 1969.

——(ed.), *Der Hitler-Putsch. Bayerische Dokumente zum 8./9. November 1923*, Stuttgart, 1962.

——(ed.), *Der Aufstieg der NSDAP in Augenzeugenberichten*, Munich, 1974.

Das Deutsche Reich und der Zweite Weltkrieg, ed. Militärgeschichtliches Forschungsamt, 6 vols. so far published, Stuttgart, 1979–

Deutschland-Berichte der Sozialdemokratischen Partei Deutschlands, 1934–1940, 7 vols., Frankfurt am Main, 1980.

Dickmann, Fritz, 'Die Regierungsbildung in Thüringen als Modell der Machtergreifung', *VfZ*, 14 (1966), 454–64.

Diehl-Thiele, Peter, *Partei und Staat im Dritten Reich. Untersuchungen zum Verhältnis von NSDAP und allgemeiner innerer Staatsverwaltung*, Munich, 1969.

Diels, Rudolf, *Lucifer ante Portas*, Stuttgart, 1950.

Dietrich, Otto, *Mit Hitler in die Macht. Persönliche Erlebnisse mit meinem Führer*, 7th edn, Munich, 1934.

——*Zwölf Jahre mit Hitler*, Cologne (n.d., 1955?).

Documents on British Foreign Policy, 1919–1939, 2nd Series, 1930–1937, London, 1950–57.

Documents on German Foreign Policy, 1918–1945, Series C (1933–1937). The Third Reich: First Phase, London, 1957–66.

Dodd, William, E., and Dodd, Martha (eds.), *Ambassador Dodd's Diary, 1933–1938*, London, 1941.

Domarus, Max, *Der Reichstag und die Macht*, Würzburg, 1968.

——(ed.), *Hitler. Reden und Proklamationen 1932–1945*, 2 vols., in 4 parts, Wiesbaden, 1973.

Dorpalen, Andreas, *Hindenburg and the Weimar Republic*, Princeton, 1964.

Dreier, Ralf, and Sellert, Wolfgang (eds.), *Recht und Justiz im 'Dritten Reich'*, Frankfurt am Main, 1989.

Drexler, Anton, *Mein politisches Erwachen*, Munich, 1919.

Dülffer, Jost, *Weimar, Hitler und die Marine. Reichspolitik und Flottenbau 1920–1939*, Düsseldorf, 1973.

——'Zum "decision-making process" in der deutschen Außenpolitik 1933–1939', in Manfred Funke (ed.), *Hitler, Deutschland und die Mächte. Materalien zur Außenpolitik des Dritten Reichs*, Kronberg/Ts., 1978, 186–204.

——*Deutsche Geschichte 1933–1945, Führerglaube und Vernichtungskrieg*, Stuttgart/Berlin/Cologne, 1992.

Duesterberg, Theodor, *Der Stahlhelm und Hitler*, Wolfenbüttel/Hanover, 1949.

Ebermayer, Erich, *Denn heute gehört uns Deutschland*, Hamburg/Vienna, 1959.

Eckart, Dietrich, *Der Bolschewismus von Moses bis Lenin. Zwiegespräch zwischen Adolf Hitler und mir*, Munich, 1924.

Edelmann, Heidrun, *Vom Luxusgut zum Gebrauchsgegenstand. Die Geschichte der Verbreitung von Personenkraftwagen in Deutschland*, Frankfurt am Main, 1989.

Eden, Anthony, *The Eden Memoirs. Facing the Dictators*, London, 1962.

Eitner, Hans-Jürgen, *'Der Führer'. Hitlers Persönlichkeit und Charakter*, Munich/Vienna, 1981.

Eley, Geoff, *Reshaping the German Right*, New Haven/London, 1980.

——'The German Right, 1860–1945: How it changed', in Geoff Eley, *From Unification to Nazism*, London, 1986, 231–53.

——'Conservatives and radical nationalists in Germany: the production of fascist potentials, 1912–1928', in Martin Blinkhorn (ed.), *Fascists and Conservatives. The Radical Right and the Establishment in Twentieth-Century Europe*, London, 1990, 50–70.

Emmerson, James T., *The Rhineland Crisis, 7 March 1936. A Study in Multicultural Diplomacy*, London, 1977.

Epting, Karl, *Generation der Mitte*, Bonn, 1953.

Erikson, Erik H., 'The Legend of Hitler's Youth', in Robert Paul Wolff (ed.), *Political Man and Social Man*, New York, 1966, 370–96.

Eschenburg, Theodor, 'Streiflichter zur Geschichte der Wahlen im Dritten Reich', *VfZ*, 3 (1955), 311–16.

Evans, Richard, J., 'German Women and the Triumph of Hitler', *Journal of Modern History*, 48 (1976), 1–53 (Demand Supplement).

——'Die Todesstrafe in der Weimarer Republik', in Frank Bajohr, Werner Johe, and Uwe Lohalm (eds.), *Zivilisation und Barbarei*, Hamburg, 1991, 145–67.

——*Rituals of Retribution: Capital Punishment in Germany 1600–1987*, Oxford, 1996.

Fabry, Philipp W., *Mutmaßungen über Hitler. Urteile von Zeitgenossen*, Düsseldorf, 1979.

Fallois, Immo von, *Kalkül und Illusion. Der Machtkampf zwischen Reichswehr und SA während der Röhm-Krise 1934*, Berlin, 1994.

Falter, Jürgen W., 'The National Socialist Mobilisation of New Voters', in Thomas Childers (ed.), *The Formation of the Nazi Constituency, 1919–1933*, London/Sydney, 1986, 202–31.

——'Unemployment and the Radicalisation of the German Electorate 1928–1933: An Aggregate Data Analysis with Special Emphasis on the Rise of National Socialism', in Peter D. Stachura (ed.), *Unemployment and the Great Depression in Weimar Germany*, London, 1986, 187–208.

——*Hitler's Wähler*, Munich, 1991.

Falter, Jürgen, Lindenberger, Thomas, and Schumann, Siegfried (eds.), *Wahlen und Abstimmungen in der Weimarer Republik. Materialien zum Wahlverhalten 1919–1933*, Munich, 1986.

Faris, Ellsworth, 'Takeoff Point for the National Socialist Party: The Landtag Election in Baden, 1929', *Central European History*, 8 (1975), 140–71.

Farquharson, John E., *The Plough and the Swastika. The NSDAP and Agriculture, 1928–1945*, London, 1976.

Fehrenbach, Elisabeth, 'Images of Kaiserdom: German attitudes to Kaiser Wilhelm II', in John C. G. Röhl and Nicolaus Sombart (eds.), *Kaiser Wilhelm II. New Interpretations*, Cambridge, 1982, 269–85.

Feldman, Gerald D., 'Der 30. Januar 1933 und die politische Kultur von Weimar', in Heinrich August Winkler (ed.), *Die deutsche Staatskrise 1930–1933*, Munich, 1992, 263–76.

Fenske, Hans, *Konservativismus und Rechtsradikalismus in Bayern nach 1918*, Bad Homburg/Berlin/Zurich, 1969.

Fest, Joachim, *The Face of the Third Reich*, Pelican edn, Harmondsworth, 1972.

——'On Remembering Adolf Hitler', *Encounter*, 41 (October, 1973), 19–34.

——*Hitler, Eine Biographie*, Frankfurt am Main/Berlin/Vienna, 1976 edn.

Feuchtwanger, Edgar, *From Weimar to Hitler. Germany, 1918–33*, 2nd edn, London, 1995.

Feuchtwanger, Lion, *Die Geschwister Oppermann*, Fischer edn, Frankfurt, 1983.

Fischer, Conan, *Stormtroopers. A Social, Economic, and Ideological Analysis 1925–35*, London, 1983.

——'Ernst Julius Röhm – Stabschef der SA und Außenseiter', in Ron Smelser and Rainer Zitelmann (eds.), *Die braune Elite*, Darmstadt, 1989, 212–22.

Fischer, Klaus P., *Nazi Germany: A New History*, London, 1995.

Forschbach, Edmund, *Edgar J. Jung. Ein konservativer Revolutionär, 30. Juni 1934*, Pfullingen, 1984.

Fox, John P., 'Adolf Hitler: the Continuing Debate', *International Affairs* (1979), 252–64.

François-Poncet, André, *Souvenirs d'une ambassade à Berlin, Septembre 1931–Octobre 1938*, Paris, 1946.

Frank, Hans, *Im Angesicht des Galgens*, Munich/Gräfelfing, 1953.

Franz-Willing, Georg, *Die Hitlerbewegung. Der Ursprung 1919–1922*, Hamburg/Berlin, 1962.

——*Ursprung der Hitlerbewegung, 1919–1922*, 2nd edn, Preußisch Oldendorf, 1974.

——*Krisenjahr der Hitlerbewegung 1923*, Preußisch Oldendorf, 1975.

——*Putsch und Verbotszeit der Hitlerbewegung, November 1923–February 1925*, Preußisch Oldendorf, 1977.

Frei, Norbert, ' "Machtergreifung". Anmerkungen zu einem historischen Begriff', *VfZ*, 31 (1983), 136–45.

——*Der Führerstaat. Nationalsozialistische Herrschaft 1933 bis 1945*, Munich, 1987 (extended version in English, *National Socialist Rule in Germany: the Führer State 1933–1945*, Oxford/Cambridge, Mass., 1993).

Freitag, Werner, 'Nationale Mythen und kirchliches Heil: Der "Tag von Potsdam" ', *Westfälische Forschungen*, 41 (1991), 379–430.

Friedländer, Saul, 'Die politischen Veränderungen der Kriegszeit und ihre Auswirkungen auf die Judenfrage', in Werner Mosse (ed.), *Deutsches Judentum in Krieg und Revolution 1916–1923*, Tübingen, 1971, 27–65.

——*Nazi Germany and the Jews. The Years of Persecution, 1933–39*, London, 1997.

Fromm, Erich, *Anatomie der menschlichen Destruktivität*, Stuttgart, 1974.

Frymann, Daniel (Heinrich Class), *Wenn ich der Kaiser wär*, 5th edn, Leipzig, 1914.

Funke, Manfred, '7. März 1936. Fallstudie zum außenpolitischen Führungsstil Hitlers', in Wolfgang Michalka (ed.), *Nationalsozialistische Außenpolitik*, Darmstadt, 1978, 277–324.

——*Starker oder schwacher Diktator? Hitlers Herrschaft und die Deutschen: ein Essay*, Düsseldorf, 1989.

Gamm, Hans-Jochen, *Der Flüsterwitz im Dritten Reich*, Munich, 1963.

Gay, Peter, 'In Deutschland zu Hause . . . Die Juden der Weimarer Zeit', in Arnold Paucker (ed.), *Die Juden im Nationalsozialistischen Deutschland: 1933–1943*, Tübingen, 1986.

Geary, Dick, 'Jugend, Arbeitslosigkeit und politischer Radikalismus am Ende der Weimarer Republik', *Gewerkschaftliche Monatshefte*, 4/5 (1983), 304–9.

——'Unemployment and Working-Class Solidarity: the German Experience 1929–33', in Richard J. Evans and Dick Geary (eds.), *The German Unemployed*, London/Sydney, 1987, 261–80.

Geiß, Immanuel, 'Die Rolle der Persönlichkeit in der Geschichte: Zwischen

Überwerten und Verdrängen', in Michael Bosch (ed.), *Persönlichkeit und Struktur in der Geschichte*, Düsseldorf, 1977, 10–24.

Gellately, Robert, 'The Gestapo and German Society: Political Denunciation in Gestapo Case Files', *Journal of Modern History*, 60 (1988), 654–94.

——*The Gestapo and German Society. Enforcing Racial Policy 1933–1945*, Oxford, 1990.

——'Allwissend und allgegenwärtig? Entstehung, Funktion und Wandel des Gestapo-Mythos', in Gerhard Paul and Klaus-Michael Mallmann (eds.), *Die Gestapo: Mythos und Realität*, Darmstadt, 1995, 47–70.

Genschel, Helmut, *Die Verdrängung der Juden aus der Wirtschaft im Dritten Reich*, Göttingen, 1966.

Geschichte der deutschen Arbeiterbewegung, ed. Institut für Marxismus-Leninismus beim Zentralkomitee der SED, Berlin (East), 13 vols., 1966–9.

Gessner, Dieter, *Agrarverbände in der Weimarer Republik*, Düsseldorf, 1976.

Gestrich, Andreas, Knoch, Peter, and Merkel, Helga, *Biographie-sozialgeschichtlich*, Göttingen, 1988.

Geyer, Michael, *Aufrüstung oder Sicherheit. Die Reichswehr in der Krise der Machtpolitik 1924–1936*, Wiesbaden, 1980.

——'Professionals and Junkers: German Rearmament and Politics in the Weimar Republic', in Richard Bessel and E. J. Feuchtwanger (eds.), *Social Change and Political Development in the Weimar Republic*, London, 1981, 77–133.

——'Etudes in Political History: Reichswehr, NSDAP, and the Seizure of Power', in Peter D. Stachura (ed.), *The Nazi Machtergreifung*, London, 1983, 101–23.

——*Deutsche Rüstungspolitik 1860–1980*, Frankfurt am Main, 1984.

Giesler, Hermann, *Ein anderer Hitler*, Leoni am Starnberger See, 1977.

Gisevius, Hans Bernd, *Bis zum bittern Ende*, 2 vols., Zurich, 1946.

——*Adolf Hitler. Versuch einer Deutung*, Munich, 1963.

Goebbels, Joseph, *Die zweite Revolution. Briefe an Zeitgenossen*, Zwickau, n.d. (1926).

——*Vom Kaiserhof zur Reichskanzlei. Eine historische Darstellung in Tagebuchblättern (Vom 1. Januar 1932 bis zum 1. Mai 1933)*, 21st edn, Munich, 1937.

Görlitz, Walter, *Adolf Hitler*, Göttingen, 1960.

Görlitz, Walter, and Quint, Herbert A., *Adolf Hitler. Eine Biographie*, Stuttgart, 1952.

Goodrick-Clarke, Nicholas, *The Occult Roots of Nazism*, Wellingborough, 1985.

Gordon, Harold J., *Hitler and the Beer Hall Putsch*, Princeton, 1972.

Gordon, Sarah, *Hitler, Germans, and the 'Jewish Question'*, Princeton, 1984.

Gossweiler, Kurt, *Die Röhm-Affäre. Hintergründe, Zusammenhänge, Auswirkungen*, Cologne, 1983.

Graf, Oskar Maria, *Gelächter von außen. Aus meinem Leben 1918–1933*, Munich, 1966.

Graml, Hermann, *Europa zwischen den Kriegen*, Munich, 1969.

——'Probleme einer Hitler-Biographie. Kritische Bemerkungen zu Joachim C. Fest', *VfZ*, 22 (1974), 76–92.

Graß, Karl Martin, *Edgar Jung, Papenkreis und Röhmkrise 1933–34*, Diss., Heidelberg, 1966.

Grau, Günter (ed.), *Homosexualität in der NS-Zeit. Dokumente einer Diskriminierung und Verfolgung*, Frankfurt am Main, 1993.

Greiner, Josef, *Das Ende des Hitler-Mythos*, Zurich/Leipzig/Vienna, 1947.

Grimm, Hans, *Volk ohne Raum*, Munich, 1926.

Gritschneder, Otto, *Bewährungsfrist für den Terroristen Adolf H. Der Hitler-Putsch und die bayerische Justiz*, Munich, 1990.

——'*Der Führer hat Sie zum Tode verurteilt . . .'. Hitlers 'Röhm-Putsch'-Morde vor Gericht*, Munich, 1993.

Gruchmann, Lothar, 'Die "Reichsregierung" im Führerstaat. Stellung und Funktion des Kabinetts im nationalsozialistischen Herrschaftssystem', in Günther Doeker and Winfried Steffani (eds.), *Klassenjustiz und Pluralismus*, Hamburg, 1973.

——'"Blutschutzgesetz" und Justiz. Zu Entstehung und Auswirkung des Nürnberger Gesetzes vom 15. September 1935', *VfZ*, 3 (1983), 418–42.

——*Justiz im Dritten Reich 1933–1940. Anpassung und Unterwerfung in der Ära Gürtner*, 2nd edn, Munich, 1990.

Gun, Nerin E., *Eva Braun–Hitler. Leben und Schicksal*, Velbert/Kettwig, 1968.

Haffner, Sebastian, *Germany: Jekyll and Hyde*, London, 1940.

——*Anmerkungen zu Hitler*, Munich, 1978.

Hagemann, Jürgen, *Die Presselenkung im Dritten Reich*, Bonn, 1970.

Hale, Oron James, 'Adolf Hitler: Taxpayer', *American Historical Review*, 60 (1955), 830–42.

——'Gottfried Feder calls Hitler to Order: An Unpublished Letter on Nazi Party Affairs', *Journal of Modern History*, 30 (1958), 258–62.

——*The Captive Press in the Third Reich*, Princeton, 1964.

Hamann, Brigitte, *Hitlers Wien. Lehrjahre eines Diktators*, Munich, 1966.

Hambrecht, Rainer, *Der Aufstieg der NSDAP in Mittel- und Oberfranken (1925–1933)*, Nuremberg, 1976.

Hamilton, Richard F., *Who Voted for Hitler?*, Princeton, 1982.

Hammer, Hermann, 'Die deutschen Ausgaben von Hitlers "Mein Kampf"', *VfZ*, 4 (1956), 161–78.

Hanfstaengl, Ernst, 'I was Hitler's Closest Friend', *Cosmopolitan*, March 1943.

——*15 Jahre mit Hitler. Zwischen Weißem und Braunem Haus*, 2nd edn, Munich/Zurich, 1980.

Hanisch, Ernst, *Der Obersalzberg: das Kehlsteinhaus und Adolf Hitler*, Berchtesgaden, 1995.

Hanisch, Reinhold, 'I Was Hitler's Buddy', 3 parts, *New Republic*, 5, 12, 19 April 1939, 239–42, 270–272, 297–300.

Harrison, Ted, '"Alter Kämpfer" im Widerstand. Graf Helldorff, die NS-Bewegung und die Opposition gegen Hitler', *VfZ*, 45 (1997), 385–423.

Hartmann, Wolf-Rüdiger, 'Adolf Hitler: Möglichkeiten seiner Deutung', *Archiv für Sozialgeschichte*, 15 (1975), 521–35.

Harvey, Elizabeth, 'Youth Unemployment and the State: Public Policies towards Unemployed Youth in Hamburg during the World Economic Crisis', in Richard J. Evans and Dick Geary (eds.), *The German Unemployed*, London/Sydney, 1987, 142–71.

——*Youth and the Welfare State in Weimar Germany*, Oxford, 1993.

Hauner, Milan, *Hitler. A Chronology of his Life and Time*, London, 1983.

Hausen, Karin, 'Unemployment Also Hits Women: the New and the Old Woman on the Dark Side of the Golden Twenties in Germany', in Peter D. Stachura (ed.), *Unemployment and the Great Depression in Weimar Germany*, London, 1986, 78–120.

Heberle, Rudolf, *From Democracy to Nazism. A Regional Case Study on Political Parties in Germany*, Baton Rouge, 1945.

——*Landbevölkerung und Nationalsozialismus. Eine soziologische Untersuchung der politischen Willensbildung in Schleswig-Holstein 1918 bis 1932*, Stuttgart, 1963.

Heer, Friedrich, *Gottes erste Liebe*, Munich/Esslingen, 1967.

——*Der Glaube des Adolf Hitler*, Munich/Esslingen, 1968.

Heiber, Helmut, *Adolf Hitler. Eine Biographie*, Berlin, 1960.

——(ed.), *Die Rückseite des Hakenkreuzes. Absonderliches aus den Akten des Dritten Reiches*, Munich, 1993.

Heiden, Konrad, *Hitler: a Biography*, London, 1936.

——*Der Führer*, London (1944), 1967 edn.

Heilbronner, Oded, 'The Failure that Succeeded: Nazi Party Activity in a Catholic Region in Germany, 1929–32', *Journal of Contemporary History*, 27 (1992), 531–49.

——'Der verlassene Stammtisch. Vom Verfall der bürgerlichen Infrastruktur und dem Aufstieg der NSDAP am Beispiel der Region Schwarzwald', *Geschichte und Gesellschaft*, 19 (1993), 178–201.

Heinemann, John L., *Hitler's First Foreign Minister*, Berkeley, 1979.

Heinz, Heinz A., *Germany's Hitler*, London (1934), 2nd edn, 1938.

Helmreich, E. C., 'The Arrest and Freeing of the Protestant Bishops of Württemberg and Bavaria, September–October 1934', *Central European History*, 2 (1969), 159–69.

Henke, Josef, *England in Hitlers politischem Kalkül 1935–1939*, Boppard am Rhein, 1973.

Henning, Hansjoachim, 'Kraftfahrzeugindustrie und Autobahn in der Wirtschaftspolitik des Nationalsozialismus 1933 bis 1936', *Vierteljahresschrift für Sozial- und Wirtschaftsgeschichte*, 65 (1978), 217–42.

Henry, Desmond, and Geary, Dick, 'Adolf Hitler: a re-assessment of his personality status', *Irish Journal of Psychological Medicine*, 10 (1933), 148–51.

Herbert, Ulrich, '"Die guten und die schlechten Zeiten". Überlegungen zur diachronen Analyse lebensgeschichtlicher Interviews', in Lutz Niethammer (ed.), *'Die Jahre weiß man nicht, wo man die hinsetzen soll.' Faschismuserfahrungen im Ruhrgebiet*, Berlin/Bonn, 1983, 67–96.

——'"Generation der Sachlichkeit". Die völkische Studentenbewegung in den frühen zwanziger Jahren in Deutschland', in Frank Bajohr, Werner Johe, and Uwe Lohalm (eds.), *Zivilisation und Barbarei*, Hamburg, 1991, 115–44.

——*Best. Biographische Studien über Radikalismus, Weltanschauung und Vernunft 1903–1989*, Bonn, 1996.

Herbst, Ludolf, *Das nationalsozialistische Deutschland 1933–1945*, Frankfurt am Main, 1996.

Herz, Rudolf, *Hoffmann und Hitler, Fotografie als Medium des Führer-Mythos*, Munich, 1994.

Hildebrand, Klaus, 'Der "Fall" Hitler', *Neue politische Literatur*, 14 (1969), 375–86.

——*Vom Reich zur Weltmacht. Hitler, NSDAP und koloniale Frage 1919–1945*, Munich, 1969.

——*The Foreign Policy of the Third Reich*, London, 1973.

——'Hitlers Ort in der Geschichte des Preußisch-Deutschen Nationalstaates', *Historische Zeitschrift*, 217 (1973), 584–631.

——'Nationalsozialismus oder Hitlerismus?', in Michael Bosch (ed.), *Persönlichkeit und Struktur in der Geschichte*, Düsseldorf, 1977, 555–61.

——*Das Dritte Reich*, Munich/Vienna, 1979.

——*Deutsche Außenpolitik 1933–1945. Kalkül oder Dogma?*, 4th edn, Stuttgart/Berlin/Cologne, 1980.

——'Monokratie oder Polykratie? Hitlers Herrschaft und das Dritte Reich', in Gerhard Hirschfeld and Lothar Kettenacker (eds.), *Der 'Führerstaat': Mythos und Realität. Studien zur Struktur und Politik des Dritten Reiches*, Stuttgart, 1981, 73–97.

——*Das vergangene Reich. Deutsche Außenpolitik von Bismarck bis Hitler 1871–1945*, Stuttgart, 1995.

Hill, Leonidas E. (ed.), *Die Weizsäcker-Papier 1933–1950*, Frankfurt am Main/Berlin/Vienna, 1974.

Hillgruber, Andreas, 'Tendenzen, Ergebnisse und Perspektiven der gegenwärtigen Hitler-Forschung', *Historische Zeitschrift*, 226 (1978), 600–621.

Hitler, Adolf, *Mein Kampf*, 876–880th reprint, Munich, 1943.

——*Mein Kampf*, trans. Ralph Manheim, with an introduction by D. C. Watt, paperback edition, London, 1973.

'Hitler. Kein Ariernachweis', *Der Spiegel*, 12 June 1957, 54–9.

Hitler, Patrick, 'Mon oncle Adolf', *Paris soir* (5 August 1939), 4–5.

Der Hitler-Prozeß 1924. Wortlaut der Hauptverhandlung vor dem Volksgerichtshof München I, Teil I, ed. Lothar Gruchmann and Reinhard Weber, assisted by Otto Gritschneder, Munich, 1997.

Hitler. Reden, Schriften, Anordnungen: Februar 1925 bis Januar 1933, ed. Institut für

Zeitgeschichte, 5 vols. in 12 parts, Munich/London/New York/Paris, 1992–8.

Hitlers Auseinandersetzung mit Brüning. Kampfschrift, Broschürenreihe der Reichs-propagandaleitung der NSDAP, Heft 5, Munich, 1932.

Hitler's Table Talk, 1941–1944, introd. by H. R. Trevor-Roper, London, 1953.

Hobsbawm, Eric, *Age of Extremes. The Short Twentieth Century, 1914–1991*, London, 1994.

Hoch, Anton, and Weiß, Hermann, 'Die Erinnerungen des Generalobersten Wilhelm Adam', in Wolfgang Benz (ed.), *Miscellanea. Festschrift für Helmut Krausnick*, Stuttgart, 1980.

Hoegner, Wilhelm, *Der schwierige Außenseiter. Erinnerungen eines Abgeordneten, Emigranten und Ministerpräsidenten*, Munich, 1959.

——*Die verratene Republik*, Munich, 1979.

Hofer, Walther (ed.), *Der Nationalsozialismus. Dokumente 1933–1945*, Frankfurt am Main, 1957.

Hofer, Walther *et al.* (eds.), *Der Reichstagsbrand. Eine wissenschaftliche Dokument-ation*, 2 vols., Berlin, 1972, Munich, 1978.

Hoffmann, Heinrich, *Hitler Was My Friend*, London, 1955.

Hofmann, Hubert, *Der Hitlerputsch. Krisenjahre deutscher Geschichte 1920–1924*, Munich, 1961.

Höhne, Heinz, *The Order of the Death's Head*, London, 1969.

——*Mordsache Röhm. Hitlers Durchbruch zur Alleinherrschaft 1933–1934*, Rein-bek bei Hamburg, 1984.

——*Die Zeit der Illusionen, Hitler und die Anfänge des 3. Reiches 1933 bis 1936*, Düsseldorf/Vienna/New York, 1991.

Hoover Institution, *NSDAP-Hauptarchiv – the Nazi Party's archive, microfilm collection: Guide to the Hoover Institution Microfilm Collection*, compiled by Grete Heinz and Agnes F. Peterson, Stanford, 1964.

Horn, Wolfgang, 'Ein unbekannter Aufsatz Hitlers aus dem Frühjahr 1924', *VfZ*, 16 (1968), 280–94.

——*Der Marsch zur Machtergreifung. Die NSDAP bis 1933*, Königstein/Ts./Dussel-dorf, 1980.

Hoßbach, Friedrich, *Zwischen Wehrmacht und Hitler 1934–1938*, Wolffenbüttel/Hanover, 1949.

Höver, Ulrich, *Joseph Goebbels – ein nationaler Sozialist*, Bonn/Berlin, 1992.

Hubatsch, Walther, *Hindenburg und der Staat*, Göttingen, 1966.

Hüttenberger, Peter, *Die Gauleiter. Studie zum Wandel des Machtgefüges in der NSDAP*, Stuttgart, 1969.

——'Nationalsozialistische Polykratie', *Geschichte und Gesellschaft*, 2 (1976), 417–42.

Institut für Zeitgeschichte (ed.), *Deutscher Sonderweg – Mythos oder Realität, Kolloquien des Instituts für Zeitgeschichte*, Munich/ Vienna, 1982.

International Military Tribunal (ed.), *Trial of the Major War Criminals before the International Military Tribunal*, 42 vols., Nuremberg, 1947–9.

Irving, David, *The Secret Diaries of Hitler's Doctor*, paperback edn, London, 1990.

——*Goebbels. Mastermind of the Third Reich*, London, 1996.

Jablonsky, David, *The Nazi Party in Dissolution. Hitler and the Verbotszeit 1923–25*, London, 1989.

Jäckel, Eberhard, 'Rückblick auf die sogenannte Hitler-Welle', *Geschichte in Wissenschaft und Unterricht*, 28 (1977), 695–710.

——'Wie kam Hitler an die Macht?' in Karl Dietrich Erdmann and Hagen Schulze (eds.), *Weimar. Selbstpreisgabe einer Demokratie*, Düsseldorf, 1980, 305–21.

——*Hitler in History*, Hanover/London, 1984.

——*Hitlers Herrschaft*, (1986) 2nd edn, Stuttgart, 1988.

——*Hitlers Weltanschauung. Entwurf einer Herrschaft* (Tübingen, 1969), 4th edn, Stuttgart, 1991.

——'L'arrivée d'Hitler au pouvoir: un Tschernobyl de l'histoire', in Gilbert Krebs and Gérard Schneilin (eds.), *Weimar ou de la Démocratie en Allemagne*, Paris, 1994.

——*Das deutsche Jahrhundert. Eine historische Bilanz*, Stuttgart, 1996.

Jäckel, Eberhard, and Kuhn, Axel (eds.), *Hitler, Sämtliche Aufzeichnungen 1905–1924*, Stuttgart, 1980.

Jacobsen, Hans-Adolf, *Nationalsozialistische Außenpolitik 1933–1938*, Frankfurt am Main, 1968.

Jacobson, Hans-Adolf and Jochmann, Werner (eds.), *Ausgewählte Dokumente zur Geschichte des Nationalsozialismus*, 3 vols., Bielefeld, 1961.

James, Harold, *The German Slump. Politics and Economics, 1924–1936*, Oxford, 1986.

——'Economic Reasons for the Collapse of the Weimar Republic', in Ian Kershaw (ed.), *Weimar. Why Did German Democracy Fail?*, London, 1990, 30–57.

Jamin, Mathilde, 'Zur Rolle der SA im nationalsozialistischen Herrschaftssystem', in Gerhard Hirschfeld and Lothar Kettenacker (eds.), *Der 'Führerstaat': Mythos und Realität. Studien zur Struktur und Politik des Dritten Reiches*, Stuttgart, 1981, 329–60.

Jellonek, Burkhard, *Homoxuelle unter dem Hakenkreuz. Die Verfolgung von Homosexuellen im Dritten Reich*, Paderborn, 1990.

——'Staatspolizeiliche Fahndungs- und Ermittlungsmethoden gegen Homosexuelle', in Gerhard Paul and Klaus-Michael Mallmann (eds.), *Die Gestapo: Mythos und Realität*, Darmstadt, 1995, 343–56.

Jenks, William A., *Vienna and the Young Hitler*, New York, 1960.

Jetzinger, Franz, *Hitlers Jugend*, Vienna, 1956.

Joachimsthaler, Anton, *Korrektur einer Bibliographie. Adolf Hitler, 1908–1920*, Munich, 1989.

Jochmann, Werner, 'Die Ausbreitung des Antisemitismus', in Werner Mosse (ed.), *Deutsches Judentum in Krieg und Revolution 1916–1923*, Tübingen, 1971, 409–510.

——(ed.), *Nationalsozialismus und Revolution*, Frankfurt am Main, 1963.

Jones, Larry Eugene, 'The Dying Middle: Weimar Germany and the Fragmentation of Bourgeois Politics', *Central European History*, 5 (1969), 23–54.

——*German Liberalism and the Dissolution of the Weimar Party System, 1918–1933*, Chapel Hill, 1988.

——'"The Greatest Stupidity of My Life": Alfred Hugenberg and the Formation of the Hitler Cabinet, January 1933', *Journal of Contemporary History*, 27 (1992), 63–87.

Jones, L. Sydney, *Hitlers Weg begann in Wien*, Frankfurt am Main/Berlin, 1990.

Judt, Tony, 'A Clown in Regal Purple: Social History and the Historians', *History Workshop Journal*, 7 (1979), 66–94.

Kaftan, Kurt, *Der Kampf um die Autobahnen*, Berlin, 1955.

Karl, Josef (ed.), *Die Schreckensherrschaft in München und Spartakus im bayrischen Oberland 1919. Tagebuchblätter und Ereignisse aus der Zeit der 'bayrischen Räterepublik' und der Münchner Kommune im Frühjahr 1919*, Munich, n.d. (1919?).

Kater, Michael, 'Zur Soziographie der frühen NSDAP', *VfZ*, 19 (1971), 124–59.

——'Hitler in a Social Context', *Central European History*, 14 (1981), 243–72.

——*The Nazi Party. A Social Profile of Members and Leaders, 1919–1945*, Oxford, 1983.

——'Generationskonflikt als Entwicklungsfaktor in der NS-Bewegung vor 1933', *Geschichte und Gesellschaft*, 11 (1985), 217–43.

——'Physicians in Crisis at the End of the Weimar Republic', in Peter D. Stachura (ed.), *Unemployment and the Great Depression in Weimar Germany*, London, 1986, 49–77.

——*Doctors under Hitler*, Chapel Hill/London, 1989.

——*Different Drummers. Jazz in the Culture of Nazi Germany*, New York/Oxford, 1992.

——*The Twisted Muse. Musicians and their Music in the Third Reich*, New York/Oxford, 1997.

Kershaw, Ian, 'The Persecution of the Jews and German Popular Opinion in the Third Reich', *Yearbook of the Leo Baeck Institute*, 26 (1981), 261–89.

——*Popular Opinion and Political Dissent in the Third Reich. Bavaria, 1933–1945*, Munich, 1987.

——*The 'Hitler Myth'. Image and Reality in the Third Reich*, Oxford (1987), paperback edn, 1989.

——*The Nazi Dictatorship. Problems and Perspectives of Interpretation*, 3rd edn, London, 1993.

Kessler, Harry Graf, *Tagebücher 1918–1937*, Frankfurt am Main, 1961.

Kettenacker, Lothar, 'Sozialpsychologische Aspekte der Führer-Herrshaft', in Gerhard Hirschfeld and Lothar Kettenacker (eds.), *Der 'Führerstaat': Mythos und Realität. Studien zur Struktur und Politik des Dritten Reiches*, Stuttgart, 1981, 98–132.

——'Der Mythos vom Reich', in K. H. Bohrer (ed.), *Mythos und Moderne*, Frankfurt am Main, 1983, 261–89.

King, Christine Elizabeth, *The Nazi State and the New Religions: Five Cases in Non-Conformity*, New York/Toronto, 1982.

Kissenkoetter, Udo, *Gregor Strasser und die NSDAP*, Stuttgart, 1978.

Klein, Anton Adalbert, 'Hitlers dunkler Punkt in Graz?', *Historisches Jahrbuch der Stadt Graz*, 3 (1970), 7–30.

Kluke, Paul, 'Der Fall Potempa', *VfZ*, 5 (1957), 279–97.

Knopp, Guido, *Hitler. Eine Bilanz*, Berlin, 1995.

Koehl, Robert, 'Feudal Aspects of National Socialism', *American Political Science Review*, 54, 921–33.

Köhler, Joachim, *Wagners Hitler. Der Prophet und sein Vollstrecker*, Munich, 1996.

Kolb, Eberhard, *Die Arbeiterräte in der deutschen Innenpolitik 1918–1919*, Düsseldorf, 1962.

——*Die Weimarer Republik*, 3rd edn, Munich, 1993.

Kolb, Eberhard, and Pyta, Wolfram, 'Die Staatsnotstandsplanung unter den Regierungen Papen und Schleicher', in Heinrich August Winkler (ed.), *Die deutsche Staatskrise 1930–1933*, Munich, 1992, 155–81.

Koppensteiner, Rudolf (ed.), *Die Ahnentafel der Führers*, Leipzig, 1937.

Kornbichler, Thomas, *Adolf Hitler-Psychogramme*, Frankfurt am Main, 1994.

Koshar, Rudy, *Social Life, Local Politics, and Nazism: Marburg, 1880–1935*, Chapel Hill, 1986.

Kotze, Hildegard von, and Krausnick, Helmut (eds.), *'Es spricht der Führer'. 7 exemplarische Hitler-Reden*, Gütersloh, 1966.

Kramer, Helgard, 'Frankfurt's Working Women: Scapegoats or Winners of the Great Depression?', in Richard J. Evans and Dick Geary (eds.), *The German Unemployed*, London/Sydney, 108–41.

Krebs, Albert, *Tendenzen und Gestalten der NSDAP*, Stuttgart, 1959.

Krüger-Charlé, Michael, 'Carl Goerdelers Versuche der Durchsetzung einer alternativen Politik 1933 bis 1937', in Jürgen Schmädeke and Peter Steinbach (eds.), *Der Widerstand gegen den Nationalsozialismus. Die deutsche Gesellschaft und der Widerstand gegen Hitler*, Munich, 1986, 383–404.

Kube, Alfred, *Pour le mérite und Hakenkreuz. Hermann Göring im Dritten Reich*, Munich, 1986.

Kubizek, August, *Adolf Hitler. Mein Jugendfreund*, Graz (1953), 5th edn 1989 (trans., August Kubizek, *Young Hitler*, London, 1973).

Kuhn, Axel, *Hitlers außenpolitisches Programm*, Stuttgart, 1971.

Kühnl, Reinhard, 'Zur Programmatik der nationalsozialistischen Linken. Das Strasser-Programm von 1925/26', *VfZ*, 14 (1966), 317–33.

Kulka, Otto Dov, 'Die Nürnberge Rassengesetze und die deutsche Bevölkerung im Lichte geheimer NS-Lage-und Stimmungsberichte', *VfZ*, 32 (1984), 582–624.

Kupper, Alfons (ed.), *Staatliche Akten über die Reichskonkordatsverhandlungen 1933*, Mainz, 1969.

Die Lage der Juden in Deutschland 1933. Das Schwarzbuch – Tatsachen und

Dokumente, ed. Comité des Delegations Juives, Paris, 1934, repr. Frankfurt am Main/Berlin/Vienna, 1983.

Lange, Karl, 'Der Terminus "Lebensraum" in Hitler's Mein Kampf', *VfZ*, 13 (1965), 426–37.

——*Hitlers unbeachtete Maximen: 'Mein Kampf' und die Öffentlichkeit*, Stuttgart, 1968.

Langer, Walter C., *The Mind of Adolf Hitler*, London, 1973.

Large, David Clay, *The Politics of Law and Order: A History of the Bavarian Einwohnerwehr, 1918–1921*, Philadelphia, 1980.

——*Where Ghosts Walked. Munich's Road to the Third Reich*, New York, 1997.

Layton, Roland V., 'The *Völkischer Beobachter*, 1920–1933: The Nazi Party Newspaper in the Weimar Era', *Central European History*, 4 (1970), 353–82.

——'Kurt Ludecke [Lüdecke] and I Knew Hitler: an Evaluation', *Central European History*, 12 (1979), 372–86.

Lemmons, Russel, *Goebbels and Der Angriff*, Lexington, 1994.

Lenman, Robin, 'Julius Streicher and the Origins of the NSDAP in Nuremberg', in Anthony Nicholls and Erich Matthias (eds.), *German Democracy and the Triumph of Hitler*, London, 1971, 129–59.

Levine, Herbert S., *Hitler's Free City. A History of the Nazi Party in Danzig, 1925–39*, Chicago/London, 1973.

Lewis, David, *The Secret Life of Adolf Hitler*, London, 1974.

Linz, Juan J., 'Political Space and Fascism as a Late-Comer: Conditions Conducive to the Success or Failure of Fascism as a Mass Movement in Inter-War Europe', in Stein Ugelvik Larsen, Bernt Hagtvet, and Jan Petter Myklebus (eds.), *Who Were the Fascists?*, Bergen/Oslo/Tromsø, 1980, 153–89.

Lipski, Józef, *Diplomat in Berlin, 1933–1939*, New York/London, 1968.

Lloyd George, David, *War Memoirs*, vol. i, London, 1933.

Loewenberg, Peter, 'The Psychohistorical Origins of the Nazi Youth Cohort', *American Historical Review*, 76 (1971), 1457–1502.

Lohalm, Uwe, *Völkischer Radikalismus. Die Geschichte des Deutschvölkischen Schutz- und Trutz-Bundes, 1919–1923*, Hamburg, 1970.

Loiperdinger, Martin, and Culbert, David, 'Leni Riefenstahl, the SA, and the Nazi Party Rally Films, Nuremberg 1933–1934: "Sieg des Glaubens" and "Triumph des Willens"', *Historical Journal of Film, Radio, and Television*, 8 (1988), 3–38.

Londonderry, Marquess of (Charles S. H. Vane-Tempest-Stewart), *Ourselves and Germany*, London, 1938.

Longerich, Peter, *Die braunen Bataillone. Geschichte der SA*, Munich, 1989.

——*Hitlers Stellvertreter. Führung der Partei und Kontrolle des Staatsapparates durch den Stab Heß und die Partei-Kanzlei Bormann*, Munich/London/New York, 1992.

——*Deutschland 1918–1933*, Hanover, 1995.

Loret, Jean-Marie (in collaboration with René Mathot), *Ton pere s'appelait Hitler*, Paris, 1981.

Ludendorff, Margarethe, *My Married Life with Ludendorff*, London, n.d., c. 1930.

Lukacs, John, *The Hitler of History*, New York, 1997.

Lurker, Otto, *Hitler hinter Festungsmauern*, Berlin, 1933.

Lyttelton, Adrian (ed.), *Italian Fascisms from Pareto to Gentile*, London, 1973.

Mack Smith, Dennis, *Mussolini*, London, 1983.

Mallett, Robert, *The Italian Navy and Fascist Expansionism 1935–40*, London, 1998.

Mann, Thomas, *Diaries, 1918–1939*, paperback edn, London, 1984.

Marckhgott, Gerhart, '"Von der Hohlheit des gemächlichen Lebens". Neues Material über die Familie Hitler in Linz', *Jahrbuch des Oberösterreichischen Musealvereins*, 138/I (1993), 267–77.

Marx, Karl, *The Eighteenth Brumaire of Louis Bonaparte*, Moscow, 1954.

Maschmann, Melita, *Fazit. Mein Weg in der Hitler-Jugend*, 5th paperback edn, Munich, 1983.

Maser, Werner, *Die Frühgeschichte der NSDAP. Hitlers Weg bis 1924*, Frankfurt am Main/Bonn, 1965.

——*Hitlers Mein Kampf*, Munich/Esslingen, 1966.

——*Adolf Hitler, Legende, Mythos, Wirklichkeit*, 3rd paperback edn, Munich 1973.

——*Adolf Hitler. Das Ende der Führer-Legende*, Düsseldorf/Vienna, 1980.

——*Hitlers Briefe und Notizen*, Düsseldorf, 1988.

——'Adolf Hitler: Vater eines Sohnes', *Zeitgeschichte*, 5 (1997–8), 173–202.

Mason, Timothy W., *Arbeiterklasse und Volksgemeinschaft. Dokumente und Materialien zur deutschen Arbeiterpolitik 1936–1939*, Opladen, 1975.

——'Women in Germany, 1925–1940: Family, Welfare, and Work', *History Workshop Journal*, 1 (1976), 74–113.

——*Sozialpolitik im Dritten Reich. Arbeiterklasse und Volksgemeinschaft*, Opladen, 1977.

Matthias, Erich, 'Die Sozialdemokratische Partei Deutschlands', in Erich Matthias and Rudolf Morsey (eds.), *Das Ende der Parteien 1933*, Königstein/Ts., 1979, 101–278.

Matthias, Erich, and Morsey, Rudolf (eds.), *Das Ende der Parteien 1933*, Königstein/Ts./Düsseldorf, 1979.

Matzerath, Horst, *Nationalsozialismus und kommunale Selbstverwaltung*, Stuttgart, 1970.

——'Oberbürgermeister im Dritten Reich', in Gerhard Hirschfeld and Lothar Kettenacker (eds.), *Der 'Führerstaat': Mythos und Realität. Studien zur Struktur und Politik des Dritten Reiches*, Stuttgart, 1981, 228–54.

Mau, Hermann, 'Die "Zweite Revolution" – der 30. Juni 1934', *VfZ*, I (1953), 119–37.

Mayr, Karl (Anon.), 'I was Hitler's Boss', *Current History*, Vol. 1 No 3 (November 1941), 193–9.

McElligott, Anthony, '". . . und so kam es zu einer schweren Schlägerei". Straßenschlachten in Altona und Hamburg am Ende der Weimarer Republik', in Maike

Bruns *et al.* (eds.), *'Hier war doch alles nicht so schlimm'. Wie die Nazis in Hamburg den Alltag eroberten,* Hamburg, 1984, 58–85.

——'Mobilising the Unemployed: The KPD and the Unemployed Workers' Movement in Hamburg-Altona during the Weimar Republic', in Richard J. Evans and Dick Geary (eds.), *The German Unemployed,* London/Sydney, 1987, 228–60.

Meier, Kurt, *Kreuz und Hakenkreuz. Die evangelische Kirche im Dritten Reich,* Munich, 1992.

Meier-Benneckenstein, Paul, *Dokumente der deutschen Politik,* Bd. 1, 2nd edn, Berlin, 1937.

Meinck, Gerhard, *Hitler und die deutsche Aufrüstung,* Wiesbaden, 1959.

Meinecke, Friedrich, *Die deutsche Katastrophe,* 3rd edn, Wiesbaden, 1947.

Meissner, Otto, *Staatssekretär unter Ebert–Hindenburg–Hitler,* Hamburg, 1950.

Meissner, Hans Otto, *30. Januar 1933. Hitlers Machtergreifung,* Munich, 1979.

Meissner, Hans Otto, and Wilde, Harry, *Die Machtergreifung,* Stuttgart, 1958.

Merkl, Peter, *Political Violence under the Swastika,* Princeton, 1975.

Merson, Allan, *Communist Resistance in Nazi Germany,* London, 1985.

Michalka, Wolfgang, 'Hitler im Spiegel der Psycho-History', *Francia,* 8 (1980), 595–611.

——*Ribbentrop und die deutsche Weltpolitik 1933–1940. Außenpolitische Konzeption und Entscheidungsprozesse im Dritten Reich,* Munich, 1980.

——*Das Dritte Reich. Dokumente zur Innen- und Außenpolitik,* 2 vols., Munich, 1985.

——(ed.), 'Wege der Hitler-Forschung', *Quaderni di storia,* 8 (1978), 157–90.

Miller, Alice, *Am Angang war Erziehung,* Frankfurt am Main, 1983.

Miltenberg, Weigand von (Herbert Blank), *Adolf Hitler–Wilhelm III,* Berlin, 1931.

Milward, Alan S., 'The Reichsmark Bloc and the International Economy', in Gerhard Hirschfeld and Lothar Kettenacker (eds.), *Der 'Führerstaat': Mythos und Realität. Studien zur Struktur und Politik des Dritten Reiches,* Stuttgart, 1981, 377–413.

Mitchell, Allan, *Revolution in Bavaria 1918–1919. The Eisner Regime and the Soviet Republic,* Princeton, 1965.

Möller, Horst, 'Die nationalsozialistische Machtergreifung. Konterrevolution oder Revolution?, *VfZ,* 31 (1983), 25–51.

——*Weimar. Die unvollendete Demokratie,* Munich, 1985.

Mommsen, Hans, 'Der Reichstagsbrand und seine politischen Folgen', *VfZ,* 12 (1964), 351–413.

——*Beamtentum im Dritten Reich,* Stuttgart, 1966.

——'Kumulative Radikalisierung und Selbstzerstörung des Regimes', *Meyers Enzyklopädisches Lexikon,* Bd. 16, Mannheim, 1976.

——'Nationalsozialismus oder Hitlerismus?', in Michael Bosch (ed.), *Persönlichkeit oder Struktür in der Geschichte,* Düsseldorf, 1977, 62–7.

——'National Socialism: Continuity and Change', in Walter Laqueur (ed.), *Fascism: A Reader's Guide,* Harmondsworth, 1979, 151–92.

——'Hitlers Stellung im nationalsozialistichen Herrschaftssystem', in Gerhard

Hirschfeld and Lothar Kettenacker (eds.), *Der 'Führerstaat': Mythos und Realität. Studien zur Struktur und Politik des Dritten Reiches*, Stuttgart, 1981, 43–72.

——'Der Mythos des nationalen Aufbruchs und die Haltung der deutschen Intellektuellen und funktionalen Eliten', in *1933 in Gesellschaft und Wissenschaft*, ed. Pressestelle der Universität Hamburg, 1983, 127–41.

——'Die Realisierung des Utopischen: Die "Endlösung der Judenfrage" im "Dritten Reich"', *Geschichte und Gesellschaft*, 9 (1983), 381–420.

——*Adolf Hitler als 'Führer' der Nation*, Deutsches Institut für Fernstudien, Tübingen, 1984.

——'Van der Lubbes Weg in den Reichstag – der Ablauf der Ereignisse', in Uwe Backes *et al.*, *Reichstagsbrand. Aufklärung einer historischen Legende*, Munich/Zurich, 1986, 33–57.

——*Die verspielte Freiheit. Der Weg der Republik von Weimar in den Untergang*, Frankfurt am Main/Berlin, 1989.

——'Regierung ohne Parteien. Konservative Pläne zum Verfassungsumbau am Ende der Weimarer Republik', in Heinrich August Winkler (ed.), *Die deutsche Staatskrise 1930–1933*, Munich, 1992.

——'Adolf Hitler und der 9. November 1923', in Johannes Willms (ed.), *Der 9. November. Fünf Essays zur deutschen Geschichte*, Munich, 1994, 33–48.

——'Die NSDAP als faschistische Partei', in Richard Saage (ed.), *Das Scheitern diktatorischer Legitimationsmuster und die Zukunftsfähigkeit der Demokratie*, Berlin, 1995, 257–71.

——*Das Volkswagenwerk und seine Arbeiter im Dritten Reich*, Düsseldorf, 1996.

——'Cumulative Radicalisation and Progressive Self-Destruction as Structural Determinants of the Nazi Dictatorship', in Ian Kershaw and Moshe Lewin (eds.), *Stalinism and Nazism: Dictatorships in Comparison*, Cambridge, 1997, 75–87.

——'Ein schlecht getarnter Bandit. Sebastian Haffners historische Einschätzung Adolf Hitlers', *Frankfurter Allgemeine Zeitung*, 7 November 1997.

Mommsen, Wolfgang J., 'Die deutsche Revolution 1918–1920', *Geschichte und Gesellschaft*, 4 (1978), 362–91.

——*Der autoritäre Nationalstaat*, Frankfurt, 1990.

Moreau, Patrick, *Nationalsozialismus von links*, Stuttgart, 1984.

Morsey, Rudolf, 'Hitler als Braunschweiger Regierungsrat', *VfZ*, 8 (1960), 419–48.

——'Hitlers Verhandlungen mit der Zentrumsführung am 31. Januar 1933', *VfZ*, 9 (1961), 182–94.

——'Die deutsche Zentrumspartei', in Erich Matthias and Rudolf Morsey (eds.), *Das Ende der Parteien 1933*, Königstein/Ts., 1979, 281–453.

——(ed.), *Das 'Ermächtigungsgesetz' vom 24. März 1933*, Düsseldorf, 1992.

Mosse, George L., *The Crisis of German Ideology*, London, 1966.

——*Germans and Jews*, London, 1971.

——*The Nationalisation of the Masses*, New York, 1975.

——*Fallen Soldiers*, New York/Oxford, 1990.

Mosse, Werner (ed.), *Entscheidungsjahr. Zur Judenfrage in der Endphase der Weimarer Republik*, Tübingen, 1965.

Mühlberger, Detlef, *Hitler's Followers. Studies in the Sociology of the Nazi Movement*, London, 1991.

Mühlen, Patrik von zur, '*Schlagt Hitler an der Saar!' Abstimmungskampf, Emigranten und Widerstand im Saargebiet, 1933–1945*, Bonn, 1979.

Müller, Hans, *Katholische Kirche und Nationalsozialismus*, Munich, 1965.

Müller, Karl-Alexander von, *Mars und Venus. Erinnerungen 1914–1919*, Stuttgart, 1954.

——*Im Wandel einer Welt. Erinnerungen 1919–1932*, Munich, 1966.

Müller, Klaus-Jürgen, *General Ludwig Beck, Studien und Dokumente zur politisch-militärischen Vorstellungswelt und Tätigkeit des Generalstabschefs des deutschen Heeres 1933–1938*, Boppard am Rhein, 1980.

——*Armee und Drittes Reich 1933–1939. Darstellung und Dokumentation*, Paderborn, 1987.

——*Das Heer und Hitler. Armee und nationalsozialistisches Regime 1933–1940*, (1969) 2nd edn, Stuttgart, 1988.

——'Deutsche Militär-Elite in der Vorgeschichte des Zweiten Weltkrieges', in Martin Broszat and Klaus Schwabe (eds.), *Deutsche Eliten und der Weg in den Zweiten Weltkrieg*, Munich, 1989.

——'Der Tag von Potsdam und das Verhältnis der preußisch-deutschen Militär-Elite zum Nationalsozialismus', in Bernhard Kröner (ed.), *Potsdam – Stadt, Armee, Residenz*, Frankfurt am Main/Berlin, 1993, 435–49.

Münzenberg, Willi, *The Brown Book of the Hitler Terror and the Burning of the Reichstag*, Paris, 1933.

Nadolny, Rudolf, *Mein Beitrag. Erinnerungen eines Botschafters des Deutschen Reiches*, Cologne, 1985.

Nazi Conspiracy and Aggression, ed. Office of the United States Chief of Counsel for Prosecution of Axis Criminality, 9 vols. and 2 supplementary vols., Washington, DC. 1946–8.

Neumann, Franz, *Behemoth: the Structure and Practice of National Socialism*, London, 1942.

Nicholls, Anthony, 'The Bavarian Background to National Socialism', in Anthony Nicholls and Erich Matthias (eds.), *German Democracy and the Triumph of Hitler*, London, 1971, 99–128.

Niewyk, Donald L., *The Jews in Weimar Germany*, Louisiana/Manchester, 1980.

Nipperdey, Thomas, '1933 und Kontinuität der deutschen Geschichte', *Historische Zeitschrift*, 227 (1978), 86–111.

——*Deutsche Geschichte 1866–1918*, 2 vols., Munich, 1990–92.

Noakes, Jeremy, 'Conflict and Development in the NSDAP 1924–1927', *Journal of Contemporary History*, 1 (1966), 3–36.

——*The Nazi Party in Lower Saxony, 1921–1933*, Oxford, 1971.

——'Oberbürgermeister und Gauleiter im Dritten Reich', in Gerhard Hirschfeld and Lothar Kettenacker (eds.), *Der 'Führerstaat': Mythos und Realität. Studien zur Struktur und Politik des Dritten Reiches*, Stuttgart, 1981, 194–227.

——'Nazism and Revolution' in Noel O'Sullivan (ed.), *Revolutionary Theory and Political Reality*, London, 1983, 73–100.

——'Nazism and Eugenics: the Background to the Nazi Sterilisation Law of 14 July 1933', in R. J. Bullen, H. Pogge von Strandmann, and A. B. Polonsky (eds.), *Ideas into Politics*, London/Sydney, 1984, 75–94.

——'Wohin gehören die "Judenmischlinge"? Die Entstehung der ersten Durchführungsverordnungen zu den Nürnberger Gesetzen,' in Ursula Büttner (ed.), *Das Unrechtsregime. Verfolgung, Exil, Belasteter Neubeginn*, Hamburg, 1986, 69–90.

——'The Development of Nazi Policy towards the German-Jewish "Mischlinge" 1933–1945', *Yearbook of the Leo Baeck Institute*, 34 (1989), 291–354.

Noakes, Jeremy, and Pridham, Geoffrey (eds.), *Nazism 1919–1945: A Documentary Reader*, 4 vols., Exeter, 1983–98.

Nolte, Ernst, *Three Faces of Fascism*, Mentor edn, New York, 1969.

——*Der europäische Bürgerkrieg 1917–1945. Nationalsozialismus und Bolschewismus*, Berlin, 1987.

——'Zwischen Geschichtslegende und Revisionismus' and 'Vergangenheit, die nicht vergehen will', in *'Historikerstreit'. Die Dokumentation der Kontroverse um die Einzigartigkeit der nationalsozialistischen Judenvernichtung*, Munich, 1987, 13–47.

Oertel, Thomas, *Horst Wessel. Untersuchung einer Legende*, Cologne, 1980.

Ohr, Dieter, *Nationalsozialistische Propaganda und Weimarer Wahlen. Empirische Analysen zur Wirkung von NSDAP-Versammlungen*, Opladen, 1997.

Olden, Rudolf, *Hitler the Pawn*, London, 1936.

Orlow, Dietrich, *The History of the Nazi Party*, vol. 1, 1919–1933, Newton Abbot, 1971.

——*The History of the Nazi Party*, vol. 2, 1933–1945, Newton Abbot, 1973.

Orr, Thomas, 'Das war Hitler', *Revue*, Munich Series, Nr 37, 1952 – Nr 8, 1953.

Overy, Richard J., *War and Economy in the Third Reich*, Oxford, 1994.

——*The Nazi Economic Recovery*, 2nd edn, Cambridge, 1996.

Padfield, Peter, *Himmler. Reichsführer-SS*, London, 1990.

Der Parteitag der Ehre vom 8. bis 14. September 1936, Munich, 1936.

Der Parteitag der Freiheit. Reden des Führers und ausgewählte Kongreßreden am Reichsparteitag der NSDAP, 1935, Munich, 1935.

Der Parteitag der Freiheit vom 10.–16. September 1935. Offizieller Bericht über den Verlauf des Reichsparteitages mit sämtlichen Kongreßreden, Munich, 1935.

Pätzold, Kurt, *Faschismus, Rassenwahn, Judenverfolgung. Eine Studie zur politischen Strategie und Taktik des faschistischen deutschen Imperialismus 1933–1935*, Berlin (East), 1975.

——(ed.), *Verfolgung, Vertreibung, Vernichtung. Dokumente des faschistischen Antisemitismus 1933 bis 1942*, Leipzig, 1983.

Pätzold, Kurt, and Weißbecker, Manfred, *Geschichte der NSDAP*, Cologne, 1981.

——*Adolf Hitler, Eine politische Biographie*, Leipzig, 1995.

Paucker, Arnold, *Der jüdische Abwehrkampf gegen Antisemitismus und National-sozialismus in den letzten Jahren der Weimarer Republik*, Hamburg, 1968.

Paul, Gerhard, *'Deutsche Mutter – heim zu Dir!' Warum es mißlang, Hitler an der Saar zu schlagen. Der Saarkampf 1933 bis 1935*, Cologne, 1984.

——*Aufstand der Bilder. Die NS-Propaganda vor 1933*, 2nd edn, Bonn, 1992.

Paul, Gerhard, and Mahlmann, Klaus-Michael, *Milieus und Widerstand. Eine Verhaltensgeschichte der Gesellschaft im Nationalsozialismus*, Bonn, 1995.

Pauley, Bruce F., *Hitler and the Forgotten Nazis. A History of Austrian National Socialism*, London, 1981.

Pechel, Rudolf, *Deutscher Widerstand*, Erlenbach/Zurich, 1947.

Peis, Günter, 'Hitlers unbekannte Geliebte', *Der Stern*, 13 July 1959.

Petersen, Jens, *Hitler-Mussolini: Die Entstehung der Achse Berlin-Rom, 1933–1936*, Tübingen, 1973.

Petzina, Dietmar (Dieter), 'Hauptprobleme der deutschen Wirtschaft 1932–1933', *VfZ*, 15 (1967), 18–55.

——*Autarkiepolitik im Dritten Reich. Der nationalsozialistische Vierjahresplan*, Stuttgart, 1968.

——'Germany and the Great Depression', *Journal of Contemporary History*, 4 (1969), 59–74.

——*Die deutsche Wirtschaft in der Zwischenkriegszeit*, Wiesbaden, 1977.

——'Was there a Crisis before the Crisis? The State of the German Economy in the 1920s', in Jürgen Baron von Kruedener (ed.), *Economic Crisis and Political Collapse. The Weimar Republic 1924–1933*, New York/Oxford/Munich, 1990, 1–19.

Petzina, Dietmar, Abelshauser, Werner, and Faust, Anselm (eds.), *Sozialgeschicht-liches Arbeitsbuch, Band III. Materialen zur Statistik des Dritten Reiches 1914–1945*, Munich, 1978.

Peukert, Detlev J. K., *Die KPD im Widerstand. Verfolgung und Untergrundarbeit an Rhein und Ruhr 1933–1945*, Wuppertal, 1980.

——'The Lost Generation: Youth Unemployment at the End of the Weimar Repub-lic', in Richard J. Evans and Dick Geary (eds.), *The German Unemployed*, London/Sydney, 1987, 172–93.

——*Die Weimarer Republik. Krisenjahre der Klassischen Moderne*, Frankfurt am Main, 1987.

Phelps, Reginald H., '"Before Hitler Came": Thule Society and Germanen Orden', *Journal of Modern History*, 35 (1963), 245–61.

——'Hitler als Parteiredner im Jahre 1920', *VfZ*, 11 (1963), 274–330.

——'Hitlers "grundlegende" Rede über den Antisemitismus', *VfZ*, 16 (1968), 390–420.

——'Hitler and the Deutsche Arbeiterpartei', in Henry A. Turner (ed.), *Nazism and the Third Reich*, New York, 1972, 5–19.

Picker, Henry, *Tischgespräche im Hauptquartier 1941/42*, ed. Percy Ernst Schramm, Stuttgart, 1963.

Plewnia, Margarete, *Auf dem Weg zu Hitler. Der völkische Publizist Dietrich Eckart*, Bremen, 1970.

Poliakov, Léon, *The History of Anti-Semitism*, vol. iv., Oxford, 1985.

Preller, Ludwig, *Sozialpolitik in der Weimarer Republik*, Düsseldorf (1949), 1978.

Price, G. Ward, *I Know These Dictators*, London, 1937.

Pridham, Geoffrey, *Hitler's Rise to Power. The Nazi Movement in Bavaria, 1923–1933*, London, 1973.

Pulzer, Peter, *The Rise of Political Antisemitism in Germany and Austria*, rev. edn, London, 1988.

Rabitsch, Hugo, *Aus Adolf Hitlers Jugendzeit*, Munich, 1938.

Rasp, Hans-Peter, 'Bauten und Bauplanung für die "Haupstadt der Bewegung"', in *München – 'Hauptstadt der Bewegung'*, ed. Münchner Stadtmuseum, Munich, 1993.

Rauh, Manfred, *Die Parlamentarisierung des deutschen Reiches*, Düsseldorf, 1977.

Rauh-Kühne, Cornelia, *Katholisches Milieu und Kleinstadtgesellschaft. Ettlingen 1918–1939*, Sigmaringen, 1991.

Rauschning, Hermann, *Die Revolution des Nihilismus. Kulisse und Wirklichkeit im Dritten Reich*, Zurich/New York, 1938.

Rautenberg, Hans-Jürgen, 'Drei Dokumente zur Planung eines 300.000-Mann-Friedensheeres aus dem Dezember 1933', *Militärgeschichtliche Mitteilungen*, 22 (1977), 103–39.

Rees, Laurence, *The Nazis. A Warning from History*, London, 1997.

Reichel, Peter, *Der schöne Schein des Dritten Reiches. Faszination und Gewalt des Faschismus*, Frankfurt am Main, 1993.

'Das Reichministerium des Innern und die Judengesetzgebung. Aufzeichnungen von Dr. Bernhard Lösener', *VfZ*, 9 (1961), 262–311.

Reissner, Larissa, *Hamburg and the Barricades*, London, 1977.

Reulecke, Jürgen, '"Hat die Jugendbewegung den Nationalsozialismus vorbereitet?" Zum Umgang mit einer falschen Frage', in Wolfgang R. Krabbe (ed.), *Politische Jugend in der Weimarer Republik*, Bochum, 1993, 222–43.

Reuth, Ralf Georg, *Goebbels*, Munich, 1990.

——(ed.), *Joseph Goebbels, Tagebücher*, 5 vols., Munich, 1992.

Rheinbaben, Werner Freiherr von, *Viermal Deutschland. Aus dem Erleben eines Seemanns, Diplomaten, Politikers 1895–1954*, Berlin, 1954.

Ribbentrop, Joachim von, *The Ribbentrop Memoirs*, London, 1954.

Rich, Norman, *Hitler's War Aims*, 2 vols., London, 1973–4.

Riefenstahl, Leni, *A Memoir*, New York, 1993.

Riesenberger, Dieter, 'Biographie als historiographisches Problem', in Michael Bosch (ed.), *Persönlichkeit und Struktur in der Geschichte*, Düsseldorf, 1977, 25–39.

Ritchie, J. M., *German Literature under National Socialism*, London/Canberra, 1983.

Ritter, Gerhard, *Carl Goerdeler und die deutsche Widerstandsbewegung*, Stuttgart, 1956.

——*Das deutsche Problem. Grundfragen deutschen Staatslebens gestern und heute*, Munich, 1962.

Robertson, Esmonde M., 'Zur Wiederbesetzung des Rheinlandes 1936', *VfZ*, 10 (1962), 178–205.

——*Hitler's Pre-War Policy and Military Plans, 1933–1939*, London, 1963.

Röhl, John C. G., 'Kaiser Wilhelm II. eine Charakterskizze', in John C. G. Röhl, *Kaiser, Hof und Staat*, Munich, 1987, 17–34.

——*Wilhelm II. Die Jugend des Kaisers 1859–1888*, Munich, 1993.

Röhm, Ernst, *Die Geschichte eines Hochverräters*, 2nd edn, Munich, 1930.

Rosenbaum, Ron, 'Explaining Hitler', *New Yorker*, 1 May 1995, 50–70.

Rosenberg, Alfred, *Letzte Aufzeichnungen. Ideale und Idole der nationalsozialistischen Revolution*, Göttingen, 1948.

Rosenhaft, Eva, *Beating the Fascists? The German Communists and Political Violence, 1929–1933*, London, 1983.

——'The Unemployed in the Neighbourhood: Social Dislocation and Political Mobilisation in Germany, 1929–1933', in Richard J. Evans and Dick Geary (eds.), *The German Unemployed*, London/Sydney, 1987, 194–227.

Roßbach, Gerhard, *Mein Weg durch die Zeit. Erinnerungen und Bekenntnisse*, Weilburg/Lahn, 1950.

Rößler, H., 'Erinnerungen an den Kirchenkampf in Coburg', *Jahrbuch der Coburger Landesstiftung* (1975).

Rubenstein, Joshua, *Hitler*, London, 1984.

Ruge, Wolfgang, 'Monopolbourgeoisie, faschistische Massenbasis und NS-Programmatik', in Dietrich Eichholtz and Kurt Gossweiler (eds.), *Faschismusforschung. Positionen, Probleme, Polemik*, Berlin (East), 1980, 125–55.

——*Das Ende von Weimar. Monopolkapital und Hitler*, Berlin (East), 1983.

Rürup, Reinhard, *Probleme der Revolution in Deutschland 1918/19*, Wiesbaden, 1968.

——'Demokratische Revolution und "dritter Weg"', *Geschichte und Gesellschaft*, 9 (1983), 278–301.

Sackett, Robert Eben, *Popular Entertainment, Class and Politics in Munich, 1900–1923*, Cambridge, Mass., 1982.

——'Images of the Jew: Popular Joketelling in Munich on the Eve of World War I', *Theory and Society*, 16 (1987), 527–63.

Sauder, Gerhard, *Die Bücherverbrennung*, Munich/Vienna, 1983.

Sauer, Paul, *Württemberg in der Zeit des Nationalsozialismus*, Ulm, 1975.

Sauer, Wolfgang, 'National Socialism: Totalitarianism or Fascism?', *American Historical Review*, 73 (1967–8), 404–24.

Sauerbruch, Ferdinand, *Das war mein Leben*, Bad Wörishofen, 1951.

Schacht, Hjalmar, *My First Seventy-Six Years*, London, 1955.

Schenck, Ernst Gunther, *Patient Hitler. Eine medizinische Biographie*. Düsseldorf, 1989.

Scheringer, Richard, *Das große Los. Unter Soldaten, Bauern und Rebellen*, Hamburg, 1959.

Scheurig, Bodo, *Ewald von Kleist-Schmenzin. Ein Konservativer gegen Hitler*, Frankfurt am Main, 1994.

Schildt, Axel, 'Radikale Antworten von rechts auf die Kulturkrise der Jahrhundertwende', *Jahrbuch für Antisemitismusforschung*, 4 (1995), 63–87.

Schildt, Gerhard, *Die Arbeitsgemeinschaft Nord-West. Untersuchungen zur Geschichte der NSDAP 1925/6*, Diss.Phil., Freiburg, 1964.

Schirach, Baldur von, *Ich glaubte an Hitler*, Hamburg, 1967.

Schirach, Henriette von, *Der Preis der Herrlichkeit. Erlebte Zeitgeschichte*, Munich/Berlin, 1975.

Schleunes, Karl A., *The Twisted Road to Auschwitz. Nazi Policy towards German Jews 1933–1939*, Urbana/Chicago/London, 1970.

Schmidt, Christoph, 'Zu den Motiven "alter Kämpfer" in der NSDAP', in Detlev Peukert and Jürgen Reulecke (eds.), *Die Reihen fast geschlossen*, Wuppertal, 1981, 21–43.

Schmidt, Paul, *Statist auf diplomatischer Bühne 1923–45. Erlebnisse des Chefdolmetschers im Auswärtigen Amt mit den Staatsmännern Europas*, Bonn, 1953.

Schmolze, Gerhard (ed.), *Revolution und Räterepublik in München 1918/19 in Augenzeugenberichten*, Düsseldorf, 1969.

Schneider, Hans, 'Das Ermächtigungsgesetz vom 24. März 1933. Bericht über das Zustandekommen und die Anwendung des Gesetzes', *VfZ*, 1 (1953), 197–221.

Scholder, Klaus, *Die Kirchen und das Dritte Reich*, vol. 1, Frankfurt am Main/Berlin/Vienna, 1977.

Scholdt, Günter, *Autoren über Hitler. Deutschsprachige Schriftsteller 1919–1945 und ihr Bild vom 'Führer'*, Bonn, 1993.

Schöllgen, Gregor, 'Das Problem einer Hitler-Biographie. Überlegungen anhand neuerer Darstellungen des Falles Hitler', *Neue politische Literatur*, 23 (1978), 421–34; reprinted in Karl Dietrich Bracher, Manfred Funke, and Hans-Adolf Jacobsen (eds.), *Nationalsozialistische Diktatur 1933–1945. Eine Bilanz*, Bonn, 1983, 687–705.

Schöner, Hellmut (ed.), *Hitler-Putsch im Spiegel der Presse*, Munich, 1974.

Schorske, Carl E., *Fin-de-Siècle Vienna. Politics and Culture*, New York, 1979.

Schott, Georg, *Das Volksbuch vom Hitler*, Munich, 1924.

Schreiber, Gerhard, *Hitler, Interpretationen, 1923–1983. Ergebnisse, Methoden und Probleme der Forschung*, Darmstadt, 1984.

——'Hitler und seine Zeit – Bilanzen, Thesen, Dokumente', in Wolfgang Michalka (ed.), *Die deutsche Frage in der Weltpolitik*, Stuttgart, 1986, 137–64.

Schroeder, Christa, *Er war mein Chef. Aus dem Nachlaß der Sekretärin von Adolf Hitler*, Munich/Vienna, 1985.

Schubert, Günter, *Anfänge nationalsozialistischer Außenpolitik*, Cologne, 1963.

Schulthess' Europäischer Geschichtskalender, Bd. 74 (1933) and Bd. 76 (1936), Munich, 1934 and 1936.

Schulz, Gerhard, *Von Brüning zu Hitler. Der Wandel des politischen Systems in Deutschland 1930–1933*, Berlin/New York, 1992.

Schumpeter, Joseph P., *Aufsätze zur Soziologie*, Tübingen, 1953.

Schwarzwäller, Wulf, *The Unknown Hitler*, Bethesda, Maryland, 1989.

Schwend, Karl, *Bayern zwischen Monarchie und Diktatur*, Munich, 1954.

Schwerin von Krosigk, Lutz Graf, *Es geschah in Deutschland*, Tübingen/Stuttgart, 1951.

——*Staatsbankrott*, Göttingen, 1974.

Sebottendorff, Rudolf von, *Bevor Hitler kam*, 2nd edn, Munich, 1934.

Seidler, Franz W., *Fritz Todt. Baumeister des Dritten Reiches*, Munich/Berlin, 1986.

Seraphim, Hans-Günther (ed.), *Das politische Tagebuch Alfred Rosenbergs 1934/35 und 1939/40*, Munich, 1964.

Shirer, William, *Berlin Diary, 1934–1941*, (1941) Sphere Books edn, London, 1970.

Smelser, Ron, and Zitelmann, Rainer (eds.), *Die braune Elite*, Darmstadt, 1989.

Smelser, Ronald, *Robert Ley: Hitler's Labor Front Leader*, Oxford/New York/Hamburg, 1988.

Smith, Bradley F., *Adolf Hitler. His Family, Childhood, and Youth*, Stanford, 1967.

——*Heinrich Himmler 1900–1926. Sein Weg in den deutschen Faschismus*, Munich, 1979.

Smith, Woodruff D., *The Ideological Origins of Nazi Imperialism*, New York/Oxford, 1986.

Sohn-Rethel, Alfred, *Ökonomie und Klassenstruktur des deutschen Faschismus*, Frankfurt am Main, 1975.

Sommerfeld, Martin H., *Ich war dabei. Die Verschwörung der Dämonen 1933–1939. Ein Augenzeugenbericht*, Darmstadt, 1949.

Sontheimer, Kurt, 'Der Tatkreis', *VfZ*, 7 (1959), 229–60.

——*Antidemokratisches Denken in der Weimarer Republik*, 3rd edn, Munich, 1992.

Speer, Albert, *Erinnerungen*, Frankfurt am Main/Berlin, 1969.

——*Spandau. The Secret Diaries*, Fontana edn, London, 1977.

Spindler, Max, *Handbuch der bayerischen Geschichte*, vol. iv, p. 2, Munich, 1975.

Spitzy, Reinhard, *So haben wie das Reich verspielt. Bekenntnisse eines Illegalen*, Munich (1986), 4th edn, 1994.

Stachura, Peter D., *Nazi Youth in the Weimar Republic*, Santa Barbara/Oxford, 1975.

——'"Der Fall Strasser": Strasser, Hitler, and National Socialism, 1930–1932', in Peter Stachura (ed.), *The Shaping of the Nazi State*, London, 1978, 88–130.

——'Der kritische Wendepunkt? Die NSDAP und die Reichstagswahlen vom 20. Mai 1928', *VfZ*, 26 (1978), 66–99.

——*Gregor Strasser and the Rise of Nazism*, London, 1983.

——'The Social and Welfare Implications of Youth Unemployment in Weimar Germany', in Peter D. Stachura (ed.), *Unemployment and the Great Depression in Weimar Germany*, London, 1986, 121–47.

——*The Weimar Republic and the Younger Proletariat*, London, 1989.

——Political Leaders in Weimar Germany, Hemel Hempstead, 1993.

Stark, Gary D., Entrepreneurs of Ideology. Neoconservative Publishers in Germany, 1890–1933, Chapel Hill, 1981.

Statistisches Reichsamt (ed.), Statistisches Jahrbuch für das deutsche Reich, 1935, Berlin, 1935.

——Statistiches Jahrbuch für das deutsche Reich, 1936, Berlin, 1936.

Stegmann, Dirk, 'Zwischen Repression und Manipulation: Konservative Macht-eliten und Arbeiter – und Angestelltenbewegung 1910–1918. Ein Beitrag zur Vor-geschichte der DAP/NSDAP', Archiv für Sozialgeschichte, 12 (1972) 351–432.

Steinert, Marlis, Hitlers Krieg und die Deutschen. Stimmung und Haltung der deutschen Bevölkerung im Zweiten Weltkrieg, Düsseldorf, 1970.

——Hitler, Munich, 1994.

Steinle, Jürgen, 'Hitler als "Betriebsunfall in der Geschichte"', Geschichte in Wissen-schaft und Unterricht, 45 (1994), 288–302.

Stern, Fritz, The Politics of Cultural Despair, Berkeley, 1961.

Stern, J. P., Hitler: the Führer and the People, London, 1975.

Stierlin, Helm, Adolf Hitler. Familienperspektiven, Frankfurt am Main, 1976.

Stoakes, Geoffrey, Hitler and the Quest for World Domination, Leamington Spa, 1987.

Stöver, Bernd, Volksgemeinschaft im Dritten Reich, Düsseldorf, 1993.

Stoltenberg, Gerhard, Politische Strömungen im schleswig-holsteinischen Landvolk 1918–1933, Düsseldorf, 1962.

Strasser, Otto, Ministersessel oder Revolution?, Berlin, 1930.

——Hitler und ich, Buenos Aires, n.d. (1941?), and Constance, 1948.

Striefler, Christian, Kampf um die Macht. Kommunisten und Nationalsozialisten am Ende der Weimarer Republik, Berlin, 1993.

Suhr, Elke, Carl von Ossietzky. Eine Biografie, Cologne, 1988.

Die Tagebücher von Joseph Goebbels. Sämtliche Fragmente, Teil 1, Aufzeichnungen 1924–1941, ed. Elke Fröhlich, 4 Bde., Munich etc., 1987.

Tausk, Walter, Breslauer Tagebuch 1933–1940, Berlin (East), 1975.

Taylor, A. J. P., The Origins of the Second World War, (1961), revised edn, Harmondsworth, 1964.

Thamer, Hans-Ulrich, Verführung und Gewalt. Deutschland 1933–1945, Berlin, 1986.

Theweleit, Klaus, Männerphantasien, Rowohlt edn, 2 vols., Reinbek bei Hamburg, 1980.

Tobias, Fritz, Der Reichstagsbrand. Legende und Wirklichkeit, Rastatt/Baden, 1962.

Toland, John, Adolf Hitler, London, 1976.

Toller, Ernst, I Was a German, London, 1934.

Tracy, Donald R., 'The Development of the National Socialist Party in Thuringia 1924–30', Central European History, 8 (1975), 23–50.

Treue, Wilhelm (ed.), Deutschland in der Weltwirtschaftskrise in Augenzeugen-berichten, 2nd edn, Düsseldorf, 1967.

Trevor-Roper, Hugh, 'The Mind of Adolf Hitler', introduction to Hitler's Table Talk, 1941–44, London, 1953, vii–xxxv.

——'Hitlers Kriegsziele', VfZ, 8 (1960), 121–33.

——The Last Days of Hitler, 3rd edn, London, 1962.

Tuchel, Johannes, Konzentrationslager, Boppard am Rhein, 1991.

Turner, Henry Ashby, 'Big Business and the Rise of Hitler', in Henry A. Turner (ed.), Nazism and the Third Reich, New York, 1972, 89–108 (originally publ. in American Historical Review, 75 (1969), 56–70).

——'Hitlers Einstellung zu Wirtschaft und Gesellschaft vor 1933', Geschichte und Gesellschaft, 2 (1976), 89–117.

——German Big Business and the Rise of Hitler, New York/Oxford, 1985.

——Geißel des Jahrhunderts. Hitler und seine Hinterlassenschaft, Berlin, 1989.

——Hitler's Thirty Days to Power: January 1933, London, 1996.

Turner, Henry A., and Matzerath, Horst, 'Die Selbstfinanzierung der NSDAP 1930–1932', Geschichte und Gesellschaft, 3 (1977), 59–92.

Tyrell, Albrecht, Führer befiehl . . . Selbstzeugnisse aus der 'Kampfzeit' der NSDAP, Düsseldorf, 1969.

——Vom 'Trommler' zum 'Führer', Munich, 1975.

——'Gottfried Feder and the NSDAP', in Peter Stachura (ed.), The Shaping of the Nazi State, London, 1978, 49–87.

——'Wie er der "Führer" wurde', in Guido Knopp (ed.), Hitler heute. Gespräche über ein deutsches Trauma, Aschaffenburg, 1979, 20–48.

Unruh, Friedrich Franz von, Der National-Sozialismus, Frankfurt am Main, 1931.

Vogelsang, Thilo, 'Neue Dokumente zur Geschichte der Reichswehr 1930–1933', VfZ, 2 (1954), 397–436.

——'Zur Politik Schleichers gegenüber der NSDAP 1932', VfZ, 6 (1958), 86–118.

——'Hitlers Brief an Reichenau vom 4. December 1932', VfZ, 7 (1959), 429–37.

——Reichswehr, Staat und NSDAP, Stuttgart, 1962.

Volk, Ludwig, Der bayerische Episkopat und der Nationalsozialismus 1930–1934, Mainz, 1965.

Volkogonov, Dmitri, Stalin: Triumph and Tragedy, London, 1991.

Vondung, Klaus, Magie und Manipulation. Ideologischer Kult und politische Religion des Nationalsozialismus, Göttingen, 1971.

Waddington, Geoffrey T., 'Hitler, Ribbentrop, die NSDAP und der Niedergang des Britischen Empire 1935–1938', VfZ, 40 (1992), 273–306.

——' "An idyllic and unruffled atmosphere of complete Anglo-German misunderstanding": Aspects of the Operations of the Dienststelle Ribbentrop in Great Britain, 1934–1939', History, 82 (1997), 44–72.

Wagener, Otto, Hitler aus nächster Nähe. Aufzeichnungen eines Vertrauten 1929–1932, ed. Henry A. Turner, 2nd edn, Kiel, 1987.

Wagner, Friedelind, The Royal Family of Bayreuth, London, 1948.

Waite, Robert G. L., Vanguard of Nazism. The Free Corps Movement in Postwar Germany 1918–1923, Cambridge, Mass., 1952.

——*The Psychopathic God: Adolf Hitler*, New York, 1977.

Weber, Max, *Wirtschaft und Gesellschaft*, 5th revised edn, Tübingen, 1972.

Wehler, Hans-Ulrich, *Das Deutsche Kaiserreich 1871–1918*, Göttingen, 1973.

——'30. Januar 1933 – Ein halbes Jahrhundert danach', *Aus Parlament und Zeitgeschichte*, 29 January 1983, 43–54.

——*Deutsche Gesellschaftsgeschichte, Dritter Band, 1849–1914*, Munich, 1995.

——'Wirtschaftliche Entwicklung, sozialer Wandel, politische Stagnation: Das deutsche Kaiserreich am Vorabend des Ersten Weltkrieges', in Simone Lässig and Karl Heinrich Pohl (eds.), *Sachsen im Kaiserreich*, Dresden, 1997, 301–8.

Weinberg, Gerhard L., *The Foreign Policy of Hitler's Germany. Diplomatic Revolution in Europe 1933–36*, Chicago/London, 1970.

——(ed.), *Hitlers Zweites Buch. Ein Dokument aus dem Jahr 1928*, Stuttgart, 1961.

Weisbrod, Bernd, *Schwerindustrie in der Weimarer Republik*, Wuppertal, 1978.

——'Gewalt in der Politik. Zur politischen Kultur in Deutschland zwischen den beiden Weltkriegen', *Geschichte in Wissenschaft und Unterricht*, 43 (1992), 392–404.

Weiß, Josef, *Obersalzberg. The History of a Mountain*, Berchtesgaden (n.d., 1955).

Weißmann, Karlheinz, *Der Weg in den Abgrund 1933–1945*, Berlin, 1995.

Welch, David, *Propaganda and the German Cinema, 1933–1945*, Oxford, 1983.

Wendt, Bernd-Jürgen, 'Südosteuropa in der nationalsozialistischen Großraumwirtschaft', in Gerhard Hirschfeld and Lothar Kettenacker (eds.), *Der 'Führerstaat': Mythos und Realität. Studien zur Struktur und Politik des Dritten Reiches*, Stuttgart, 1981, 414–28.

——*Großdeutschland. Außenpolitik und Kriegsvorbereitung des Hitler-Regimes*, Munich, 1987.

Wheeler-Bennett, John W., *The Nemesis of Power, The German Army in Politics*, London, 1953.

Whiteside, Andrew G., *Austrian National Socialism before 1918*, The Hague, 1962.

——*The Socialism of Fools. Georg von Schönerer and Austrian Pan-Germanism*, Berkeley/Los Angeles, 1975.

Wiedemann, Fritz, *Der Mann, der Feldherr werden wollte*, Velbert/Kettwig, 1964.

Winkler, Heinrich August, 'Extremismus der Mitte? Sozialgeschichtliche Aspekte der nationalsozialistischen Machtergreifung', *VfZ*, 20 (1972), 175–91.

——*Mittelstand, Demokratie und Nationalsozialismus*, Cologne, 1972.

——'German Society, Hitler, and the Illusion of Restoration 1930–33', *Journal of Contemporary History*, 11 (1976), 1–16.

——*Der Weg in die Katastrophe. Arbeiter und Arbeiterbewegung in der Weimarer Republik 1930 bis 1933*, Berlin/Bonn, 1987.

——*Weimar 1918–1933. Die Geschichte der ersten deutschen Demokratie*, Munich, 1993.

Wippermann, Wolfgang (ed.), *Kontroversen um Hitler*, Frankfurt am Main, 1986.

Wistrich, Robert, *Wer war wer im Dritten Reich*, Munich, 1983.

Witkop, Philipp (ed.), *Kriegsbriefe gefallener Studenten*, Munich, 1928.

Wollstein, Günter, 'Eine Denkschrift des Staatssekretärs Bernhard von Bülow vom März 1933', *Militärgeschichtliche Mitteilungen*, 1 (1973), 77–94.

——*Vom Weimarer Revisionismus zu Hitler*, Bonn/Bad Godesberg, 1973.

Wurm, Theophil, *Erinnerungen aus meinem Leben*, Stuttgart, 1953.

Zitelmann, Rainer, *Hitler. Selbstverständnis eines Revolutionärs*, Hamburg/Leamington Spa/New York, 1987.

——*Adolf Hitler. Eine politische Biographie*, Göttingen/Zurich, 1989.

——'Nationalsozialismus und Moderne. Eine Zwischenbilanz', in Werner Süß (ed.), *Übergänge. Zeitgeschichte zwischen Utopie und Machbarkeit*, Berlin, 1990, 195–223.

——'Die totalitäre Seite der Moderne', in Michael Prinz and Rainer Zitelmann (eds.), *Nationalsozialismus und Modernisierung*, Darmstadt, 1991.

Zofka, Zdenek, *Die Ausbreitung des Nationalsozialismus auf dem Lande*, Munich, 1979.

Zoller, Albert, *Hitler privat. Erlebnisbericht seiner Geheimsekretärin*, Düsseldorf, 1949.

Zollitsch, Wolfgang, 'Adel und adlige Machteliten in der Endphase der Weimarer Republik. Standespolitik und agrarische Interessen', in Heinrich August Winkler (ed.), *Die deutsche Staatskrise 1930–1933*, Munich, 1992, 239–56.

INDEX

Representatives, 111; currency stabilization, 212; Defence Ministry, 323, 417, 420, 444, 502; development of German nationalism, 75–8; diplomatic relations with Russia, 290; divisions and tensions in post-war Germany, 98; economic crisis, 294, 305–6, 315, 317, 318, 355, 367, 404–5; economy of the mid-1920s, 258; emergency decrees, 324, 349, 355, 382, 383, 385; and the eugenics movement, 79; evocations of a heroic past, 17, 21; Executive Council, 639n.; expropriation of the princes, 274, 275; fear of racial degeneration, 79; foreign loans, 212, 307, 318; German-Austrian alliance, 85; H's desire to go to, 81; hyperinflation (1923), 175, 186, 200–201; imperialism, 76, 79, 80; inflation, 175, 178, 189; Law for the Protection of the Republic, 663n.; Ministry of the Interior, 420; munitions strike (1918), 101, 267–8; national rebirth, 132, 134, 180, 192, 260, 317, 332, 333, 336, 340, 481; national salvation, 250, 253, 331; national socialist parties, 161; 'national unity front', 191; naval mutiny, 102, 110; origins of sense of nationhood, 76; parliament, 74; party-political pluralism, 74, 75–6; 'passive resistance' against Ruhr occupation, 191, 192, 200, 202; plebiscites, 274, 310, 318; political culture, 75, 170, 181, 426, 434; political radicalization of German Society, 73, 80, 101; power, 74; presidential campaigns (1932), 359, 360; rapid spread of *völkisch* politics after the First World War, 80; the 'Red' government, 315, 316, 320; Reich Chancellor, 74; 'Reich myth',

77; Reichstag, 74, 76, 77, 89, 100, 180, 184, 227, 324–5, 328, 335, 361, 366, 367, 368, 379, 384–7, 393, 394, 417, 418, 421–2, 424, *see also under* Third Reich; Reichstag elections, 137, 212, 223, 225, 228, 229, 234, 239, 258–9, 268–9, 299, 302–3, 309, 321, 322, 324, 333–6, 356, 368, 369–70, 375, 386–91, 396, 416, 419; Reichstag fire, 456–9, 461, 492; reparations, 157, 191, 212, 257, 309–10, 330, 355, 367; as a republic, 102, 119, 128; resentment at supporting those seen as a burden on society, 79; restoration of borders of 1914, 246; Revolution of 1848, 73; Revolution of 1918, 97, 98, 101–4, 109–12, 119, 124, 150, 181, 191, 194, 205, 235, 268, 286, 304, 369, 481, 483, 489; rivalry with Britain, 78; 'search for strong man', 295; social and economic development (19th C), 74; Socialist Law, 76; Soldiers' Councils, 111; state of emergency, 202; Supreme Court (Staats-gerichtshof), 727n.; trans-formation of the officer corps, 446; Unification, 73, 76; a uniquely German social order, 135; Weimar culture, 258; Wilhelmine, 18, 75, 481, 739n.; Workers' Councils, 111; youth welfare system, 407–8; *see also* First World War; Third Reich
Gestapa *see* Office of the Prussian Secret State Police
Gestapo (Secret State Police), 561; anti-Jewish legislation, 564; arrests Edgar Jung, 512; attacks Communists, 762n., 764n.; confiscates H's postcards to Bloch, 626–7n.; H backs, 540; inquiries into H's family background, 9; and the SA purges, 519

death (1847), 3; and H's alleged
Jewish background, 8; marriage to
Johann Georg Hiedler, 3, 5, 6, 7
Hilferding, Rudolf, 336
Himmler, Heinrich, xxvii, 50, 414, 417,
500, 511, 512, 516, 706n.;
appearance, 301; appointed to lead
the SS, 301, 540; Bavarian Political
Police, 478, 485; and Brown House,
392; commander of the Munich
police, 462; and Dachau, 464; as
Deputy Reich Propaganda Leader,
301, 309; power-base in Bavaria,
540; private audiences with H, 485;
and the Prussian Gestapo, 506; and
Röhm's murder, 301
Hindemith, Paul, 258
Hindenburg, Field Marshal Paul von
Beneckendorff und von, 146, 323,
324, 357, 359, 361, 366, 367, 370,
379, 384, 385, 392, 405, 413, 421,
422, 424, 450, 461, 474, 501, 508,
510, 511, 512, 518; agrees to a Hitler
cabinet, 420; asks H to restore order
in the SA, 501; asks Papen to resume
office, 395; the choice of women,
409; death, 435, 436, 500, 521,
524–6, 529; dissolves military-like
organizations of the NSDAP, 365;
elected Reich President, 269; favours
Papen, 394, 396, 414, 419, 424, 500;
grants H the dissolution of the
Reichstag, 439; H is sworn in as
Chancellor, 423; H's contempt for,
393; as the link between the past and
the present, 465; and the Osthilfe
scandal, 416–17; presidential
elections (1932), 359, 361, 362, 363;
and the Protestant Church, 489;
refuses to appoint H to the
Chancellorship, 371, 373–4, 380,
381, 383, 393, 394–5, 415, 418–19;
and the SA purges, 517; seriously ill,

509; succession issue, 500; supreme
commander of the army, 500; view
of Nazis, 356; watches the torchlight
procession (1933), 434
Hindenburg, Oskar von, 417, 418, 422,
512
Hirschgarten, Munich, 197
Hitler, Adolf, admiration for Wagner,
21–2, 42–3, 55; adulation for, 131,
132, 181, 184, 223, 224, 251, 484,
486, 534, 591; aims to become an
architect, 24, 25, 82, 87, 127, 170;
aims to become an artist, 17–18, 22,
23, 26, 48, 170, 625n.; alleged Jewish
background, 7–9; alleged
monorchism, 45; and Angela
Raubal, 283, 284, 351–5, 703n.;
announces his decision to withdraw
from politics, 230–31, 232;
anti-parliamentarism, 33, 34, 228;
appearance, 16, 21, 23, 47, 52, 53,
56, 59, 86, 92, 148, 159, 187, 188,
189, 280, 281–2, 284, 337, 367, 609n;
appointed Chancellor, 423, 426, 431,
434, 436; attitude towards women,
44–7, 235, 281, 284, 343, 351–5;
autopsy, 45; avoidance of militiary
service, 68, 81, 82–3, 85–6; becomes
the leader of the radical Right, 259;
birth (20 April 1889), 10–11; his
cabinet, 420–21, 422; candidacy for
president, 361; character of his
power, xxvi–xxviii; chaste lifestyle,
44; and the Churches, 625n.; claim
to be Germany's coming 'great
leader', 65; cultural taste, 82; daily
routine as Chancellor, 485–6; death
of his father, 19; death of his
mother, 24, 26, 102, 103; decision to
parole H, 235–9; denounces Röhm
as a traitor, 514; diet, 47; dog-whips
given to H, 188; and dogs, 93;
drawing aptitude, 16, 19; as